A Companion to California

A COMPANION
TO
CALIFORNIA

by

James D. Hart

New York
Oxford University Press
1978

Copyright © 1978 by Oxford University Press, Inc.

Library of Congress Cataloging in Publication Data

Hart, James David, 1911–
    A companion to California.

    1. California—Dictionaries and encyclopedias.
I. Title.
F859.H33   979.4′003   76-57286
ISBN 0-19-502400-1

First printing August 1978
Second printing September 1978

Printed in the United States of America

For
Matthew, Alison, and Elizabeth

to help them appreciate their heritage
of five preceding generations in California

Preface

This work is intended as a useful companion for anybody interested in general or basic knowledge about any aspect of the most populous state in the Union. It is designed to be serviceable to a wide variety of readers and consultants, whose range might include residents and tourists, high-school and college students, as well as scholars seeking a ready reference. At present no single volume comprehends such a scope as this one and although it treats its subjects briefly, many an entry also includes data not found elsewhere in a single place. Reference to hundreds of books and articles would be required to provide the information that is here between two covers.

For proper perspective on California, the work includes matters of its Spanish colonial background and its Mexican history that pertain to the early years of the region now included in this state. During the era when the two Californias were closely allied, the book also treats subjects of major significance in the history of Baja California. After 1804 the work concentrates only on the region that was once Alta California. The contents that are concerned more exclusively with the area of present-day California treat its geology (including something of the continental shelf), geography, climatic conditions, and native flora and fauna. They deal also with the resources of the land, agricultural and mineral, as well as the resources related to water, ranging from offshore fisheries to projects for power and irrigation developed on the land.

Human history is represented by numerous but diverse entries related to Indian tribes and culture, to explorers, and to settlers and developers from the time of the Sacred Expedition (1769), which initiated California's substantial colonization, to our own day. History within the confines of the present state over the past two centuries is represented not only by brief articles on individuals but by a wide variety of entries treating all sorts of institutions, organizations, and settlements. Recent or immediately contemporary history is represented, but perhaps a little less fully, since an appropriate perspective is difficult to obtain.

The range of subjects is purposefully very wide, extending alphabetically from Abalone, a succulent local mollusk, to such contemporary crimes as those that go by the name of Zebra and Zodiac. The time span begins in prehistoric periods but, as revealed by the Chronological Index, the basic dates extend from 1510 to 1978. Always the intention is to provide information on matters about which many readers may know something and wish to know more or to provide brief authoritative statements for persons unacquainted with the subjects.

The entries inevitably relate to one another but the symbol ♦ for cross-reference is not used indiscriminately. The mere fact that an entry appears on a subject mentioned in another article is not sufficient justification for employing the symbol ♦. It is used only when the text to which it refers is considered to be specifically pertinent in presenting further information to the reader of the article in which the cross-reference occurs. A user of the book will soon become aware of the variety of materials he can find in it so that on his own he will presumably turn to other places to amplify the knowledge gained by the reading of an individual entry.

I have tried to take great precautions to make the book comprehensive, balanced, and accurate. Necessarily these precautions are limited by the time and energy at the disposal of one person during the period required for its writing: four years during which I held full-time academic and administrative positions on the faculty of a university and a fifth year of the same activities while working with the Press to enlarge or revise the basic text in its hands. There may be limitations because this is the work of a single individual rather than an edited compilation, but the fact that both the plan and the writing are the work of one person may also make for a carefully considered relationship among the entries and the achievement of appropriate balances among them.

Nevertheless, the length of any article should not be considered as a means of precisely marking the relative importance of its subject. Many considerations upset the use of exact standards of length so that regardless of the commonly recognized significance of a subject, the diffusion or the simplicity inherent in its explication may considerably affect both the detail and length of the entry on it. At all times consideration was given to the complete compass of the book so that it would not become too unwieldy for the traveler to take in his automobile or the casual reader to have on his desk or by his armchair.

The idea that I should write a book of this sort was suggested to me by my friend of forty years, the distinguished California historian and novelist, George R. Stewart, who deserves and receives the badge of distinction: ◆. For his suggestion I thank him, I think. Persons who assisted me on a variety of particulars as I was working on this book include Joseph M. Bransten, my brother-in-law, Peter D. Hart, my son, and Carol H. Field, my daughter. Friends also aided me because they took an interest in the undertaking. Above all I was helped, as always, by the sympathetic and affectionate support of my wife Ruth.

Several graduate students on the Berkeley campus aided me at different times but two were particularly good contributors in searching out basic data: Larry Gerber and Michael Griffith, the latter a valued assistant who stayed with the project from beginning to end. Three scholars of California history read through the entire eight volumes of my typescript to make suggestions and to point out

needed additions or emendations, and so I am particularly indebted to James T. Abajian, Ferol Egan, and James J. Rawls. After the manuscript was received by the Press, many good suggestions for further entries came from Sheldon Meyer and James Raimes, while Leona Capeless improved the work by sensitive editing.

An experience of more than forty years with another Companion has taught me that an encyclopedic volume of this sort cannot achieve its full potential upon first publication nor be judgmentally satisfactory to every user. But the work, if it is good, takes on a life of its own in progressive printings and subsequent editions during which it is constantly altered, augmented, and presumably improved. I hope this work is well begun. Surely I do not think of it as concluded. Readers, reviewers, and my own continuing interest should cause it to grow, change, and become better.

Berkeley, California
May 1978   JAMES D. HART

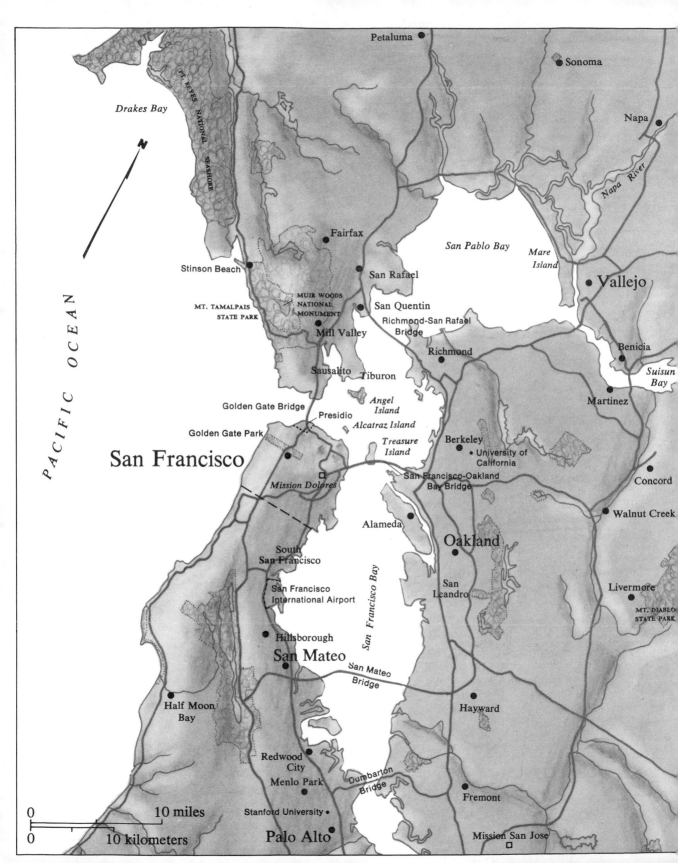

N

Fandango Pass

Honey Lake

LASSEN

SIERRA

Beckwourth Pass

Donner Lake

Lake Tahoe

Alturas

MODOC NATIONAL FOREST

MODOC

Susanville

PLUMAS

SIERRA

NEVADA

Truckee

PLACER

EL DORADO

ELDORADO NATIONAL FOREST

Downieville

TAHOE NATIONAL FOREST

Tule Lake

LASSEN NATIONAL FOREST

LASSEN VOLCANIC NATIONAL PARK

Lake Almanor

Quincy

PLUMAS NATIONAL FOREST

Nevada City

Grass Valley

Coloma

Lower Klamath Lake

LAVA BEDS NATIONAL MONUMENT

Auburn

Lassen Peak 10,457 ft.

Marysville

SUTTER

Chico

BUTTE

Oroville

YUBA

Yuba City

Feather River

Sacramento

▲ Mt. Shasta 14,162 ft.

SHASTA

Shasta Lake

River

SACRAMENTO

VALLEY

YOLO

Colusa

Sacrame

Shasta Dam

Whiskeytown Lake

Redding

Red Bluff

TEHAMA

Sacramento

GLENN

Willows

COLUSA

Yreka

SISKIYOU

Clair Engle Lake

Weaverville

TRINITY

SHASTA-TRINITY NATIONAL FOREST

MENDOCINO NATIONAL FOREST

Clear Lake

LAKE

Lakeport

Klamath River

Salmon River

HUMBOLDT

Mad River

Eel River

Russian River

DEL NORTE

SIX RIVERS NATIONAL FOREST

Willits

MENDOCINO

Ukiah

Boonville

JEDEDIAH SMITH REDWOODS STATE PARK

Crescent City

REDWOOD NATIONAL PARK

Eureka

Fort Bragg

Pt. Arena

ALPINE
ELDORADO NATIONAL FOREST
Bridgeport
Mono Lake
MONO
ANCIENT BRISTLECONE PINE FOREST
DEVIL'S POSTPILE NATIONAL MONUMENT
Bishop
Scotty's Castle
DEATH VALLEY NATIONAL MONUMENT
FUNERAL MOUNTAINS
AMARGOSA RANGE
DEATH VALLEY
Emigrant Gap
PANAMINT MOUNTAINS
TUOLUMNE
YOSEMITE NATIONAL PARK
SIERRA NEVADA
INYO NATIONAL FOREST
Independence
Lone Pine
INYO
Sonora
Tuolumne
Jamestown
KINGS CANYON NATIONAL PARK
Mt. Whitney 14,495 ft.
COSO RANGE
MARIPOSA
SEQUOIA NATIONAL PARK
River
MADERA
STANISLAUS
Merced River
Merced
Madera
River
San Joaquin
Fresno
Kings
SEQUOIA NATIONAL FOREST
Inyokern
SAN JOAQUIN VALLEY
Visalia
Tulare
TULARE
SIERRA NEVADA
FRESNO
MERCED
Hanford
COL. ALLENSWORTH STATE HISTORICAL PARK
Tehachapi Pass
KINGS
River
Bakersfield
KERN
Kern
TEHACHAPI MOUNTAINS
Hollister
San Juan Bautista
SAN BENITO
Coalinga
LOS ANGELES
Salinas
San Carlos Borromeo
SIERRA MADRE
Monterey
Carmel
Nuestra Senora de la Soledad
San Antonio de Padua
MONTEREY
TOPATOPA MOUNTAINS
NATIONAL FOREST
VENTURA
San Miguel Arcángel
Paso Robles
San Luis Obispo de Tolosa
SAN LUIS OBISPO
LOS PADRES
SANTA LUCIA RANGE
Big Sur
SANTA BARBARA
Ojai
San Buenaventura
San Simeon
Morro Bay
San Luis Obispo
Pismo Beach
SANTA INEZ MOUNTAINS
Santa Inés
La Purísima Concepción
Santa Barbara
Ventura
Oxnard
Port Hueneme
POINT SAL
Lompoc
Vandenberg AFB
PACIFIC OCEAN
SANTA BARBARA ISLANDS
Anacapa
Santa Cruz
Santa Rosa
San Miguel

Needles

Lake Havasu

Colorado

SAN BERNARDINO

Barstow

Apple Valley

Twentynine Palms

SAN BERNARDINO
NATIONAL FOREST

Big Bear Lake

RIVERSIDE

Joshua Tree
National Monument

Coachella

Blythe

River

**CHUCKWALLA
MOUNTAINS**

**CHOCOLATE
MOUNTAINS**

PICHACO STATE
REC. AREA

Salton Sea

**IMPERIAL
VALLEY**

IMPERIAL

San Bernardino
Redlands

Banning

Palm Springs

**SANTA ROSA
MOUNTAINS**

Mt. San Antonio
(Old Baldy)
(10,064 ft)

Imperial
El Centro

Calexico

San Gabriel

Riverside

Hemet

ANZA
BORREGO
DESERT
STATE
PARK

San Fernando Rey
de España
San Fernando
Pasadena
Glendale
Beverly Hills
Hollywood
Santa Monica
Venice
Malibu
Redondo Beach
San Pedro

ANGELES NATIONAL FOREST

San
Gabriel
San Gabriel
Arcángel
Pomona

Whittier

Los Angeles

Anaheim
Orange
ORANGE
Santa Ana

Long Beach

Dana Point
San Juan Capistrano
San Clemente

CLEVELAND
NATIONAL
FOREST

Mt. Palomar

Warner Sprs.

Ramona

SAN DIEGO

CUYAMACA RANCHO
STATE PARK

San Diego de Alcalá
Coronado
Chula Vista

San Luis Rey de Francia

La Jolla

San Diego

CABRILLO
NATIONAL
MONUMENT

CHANNEL ISLANDS
NATIONAL
MONUMENT

Santa Barbara

Santa Catalina

San Clemente

San Nicolas

CATALINA ISLANDS

County boundaries

Major highways

☐ Missions

50 miles

50 kilometers

0

0

N

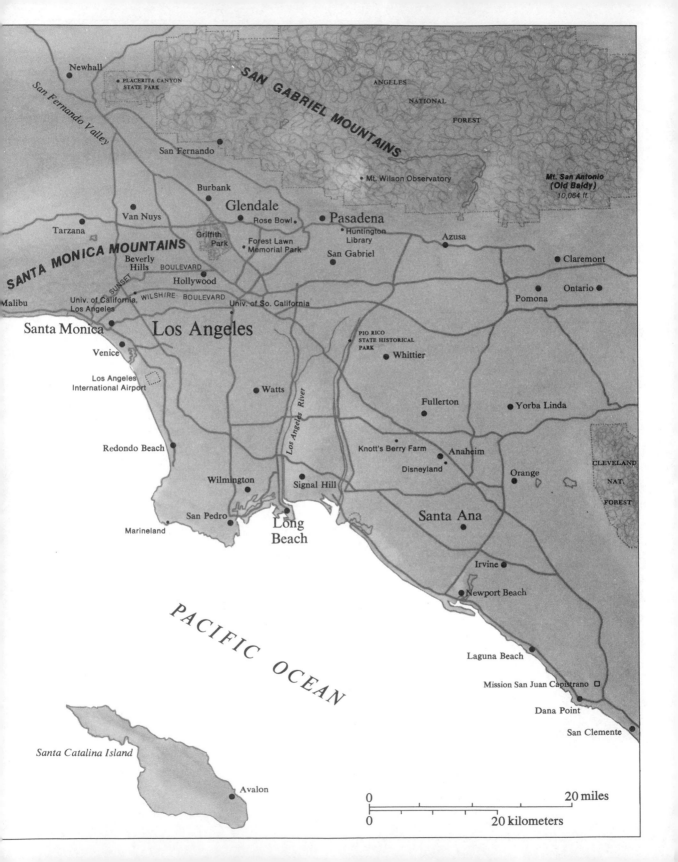

A Companion to California

A

Abalone, a rock-clinging mollusk with flattened shell lined with mother-of-pearl, found in abundance in three varieties along the California coast. Commercial abalone fishing, unique to California, is concentrated in the southern part of the state, while sport fishing is most common between San Diego and Santa Barbara and between Monterey and Fort Bragg. The meat is cut into steaks which must be pounded to be edible. The shells are now used for diverse curios, but Indians once used them for fishhooks, adornment, and currency. The Bohemians of early Carmel,♦ under George Sterling, enjoyed this local delicacy frequently and composed a kind of folk song, one of whose verses is: Oh! some folks boast of quail on toast, / Because they think it's tony; / But I'm content to owe my rent, / And live on abalone.

Abbey San Encino, see *Browne, Clyde.*

ABDUL-JABBAR, KAREEM, see *Alcindor, Lew.*

ABDUL-RAHMAN, MAHDI, see *Hazzard, Walt.*

ABRAMS, ALBERT (1863–1924), long a respected San Francisco physician and medical author who in his last years became notorious for his contention that every sickness has its own rate of electronic vibrations, to be measured only by an "oscilloclast," a sealed device he rented to patients at exorbitant prices. That and other practices caused him to be called a charlatan.

Academy Awards, prizes in the form of statuettes (called Oscars) given annually by the Academy of Motion Picture Arts and Sciences (est. 1927) in a number of categories: best directing, best writing, best music, best starring role, best supporting role, best film, etc. The first awards, made in 1929 for the 1927–28 season, went to Emil Jannings as best actor in *The Way of All Flesh* and *The Last Command;* to Janet Gaynor as best actress in *Seventh Heaven, Street Angel,* and *Sunrise;* and to *Wings* as best picture.

Academy of Pacific Coast History, private organization (1909–19) established to publish rare docu-

ments in The Bancroft Library.♦ Publications included a translation of the Diary of Pedro Font, the Papers of the San Francisco Vigilance Committee of 1851, and Patrick Breen's Diary.

Acagchemem, see *Boscana, Gerónimo.*

Achomawi, Indians who lived in the drainage area of the Pit River, from present Shasta County north to Goose Lake on the Oregon border. Their prehistoric number, including the Atsugewi, from whom they were culturally indistinguishable, was about 3,000; but by 1910 this was reduced to 1,250. They were friendly with the Wintun and fought occasionally with the Modoc and Klamath, but in peaceful periods served as intermediaries in trade between the Wintun and the Modoc and even the Paiute. They trapped deer in pits, thereby occasioning the name of the river on which they lived, although it is often misspelled Pitt.

Acorn, fruit or nut of the oak,♦ a tree of which many varieties flourish in California. Indians of many tribes gathered acorns, often stored them for future use, then husked them and made a flour by pulverizing them, usually with a stone mortar and pestle. After winnowing, the meal was leached numerous times with boiling water until the tannic acid was removed. Boiling the product created a kind of pudding, eaten by itself or with berries, meat, or fish.

A.C.T., acronym of American Conservatory Theater, founded by the drama director William Ball (1934–) in Pittsburgh (1965) and moved to San Francisco (Jan. 1967). It is a repertory theater known for its lively and innovative productions ranging from the classics of Shakespeare and Molière to works by new playwrights like Tom Stoppard, and also a conservatory or acting academy which trains talented persons from children to mature people.

ADAMS, ANSEL (1902–), San Francisco-born photographer, noted for his clear and sensitive pictures of Yosemite and other American wilderness areas. He has also been an active figure in movements for the preservation of the natural scene of

California and other regions. His photographs have been exhibited widely in major museums; he has collected original prints in six portfolios; and he has published some thirty books of his pictures, including *Born Free and Equal* (1944), depicting "loyal Japanese-Americans at Manzanar"; *Yosemite and the Sierra Nevada* (1947), related to the text of John Muir; *The Land of Little Rain* (1950), illustrating Mary Austin's text; *My Camera in the National Parks* (1950); and *Images, 1923–1974* (1974), with a foreword by Wallace Stegner.

ADAMS, HARRIET CHALMERS (1875–1937), born in Stockton of parents who went overland to California in 1842, was an intrepid traveler and with her husband, Franklin Pierce Adams, also of Stockton, visited every country which had ever been under the rule of Spain or Portugal, often to primitive areas never before seen by a white woman. She lectured widely on her travels and published frequently in the *National Geographic Magazine*.

ADAMS, JAMES CAPEN (1807?–60), Massachusetts-born frontiersman, the subject of *The Adventures of James Capen Adams, Mountaineer and Grizzly Bear Hunter . . .* (1860) by Theodore H. Hittell. He is said to have gone to California in the gold rush, and he later became a great hunter. He domesticated a grizzly bear, and other wild animals were exhibited by him in San Francisco and, under P. T. Barnum's auspices, in New York. Because of his exploits he was called "Old Grizzly Adams." Francis P. Farquhar has suggested that the hunter was really John Adams (1812–60), brother of James Capen.

Adams and Company, express firm founded (1839) to operate locally from Boston, became so successful that it was extended down the East Coast and into the South. A subsidiary not directly under management of the parent firm was opened in California (1850) to provide express service on the Pacific Coast, and banking facilities too, but it collapsed in the Panic of 1855, setting off runs on other banks and eventually leaving Wells, Fargo in control of local express and banking. The parent firm continued to be powerful in the East, but the western failure led Mart Taylor in his *Gold Digger's Song Book* (1856) to print: The Adams firm was good enough, / And flourished for a season. / They got the people's money, and / Pop went the weasel.

ADLER, KURT [HERBERT] (1905–), Viennese-born conductor, came to the U.S. (1938), became a citizen, joined the San Francisco Opera (1943), and was named its General Director (1957). During his directorship the season has been lengthened from five to eleven weeks, the annual budget has more than quadrupled, a Spring Opera Theater and a touring Western Opera Co. have been created, and notable operas (e.g. Britten's *A Midsummer Night's Dream*) and notable singers (e.g. Elisabeth Schwarzkopf) have been introduced to the U.S.

Admiral of the Californias, see *Atondo y Antillón, Ysidro.*

Admission Day, state holiday celebrating the entry of California into the U.S.—Sept. 9, 1850—as the 31st state.

Adobe, Spanish word for sun-baked bricks made of clay-like soil, water, and weeds, and for buildings made of such bricks. Missions, houses, and other structures built during the Spanish and Mexican periods were adobes, often whitewashed to give a striking appearance when combined with tiles and woodwork.

Aerospace industry, had its beginnings before World War I. The consistent climate, availability of local labor, and interest of local capital investors in experimental business encouraged Glenn Martin, Donald Douglas, Allan Loughead [Lockheed], and John K. Northrop to begin small production of airplanes in southern California. Military orders did not affect the business until after World War I, when two planes built for the army by Douglas were the first to make a round-the-world flight (1924).

This feat was overshadowed by that of another local manufacturer, T. Claude Ryan of San Diego, who built the *Spirit of St. Louis,* in which Lindbergh made his solo flight from New York to Paris (1927). The new firms continued to have some financial problems and to linger behind those of New York State in orders, but they also devised new ideas and achieved successes, e.g. those of Douglas and Lockheed, who developed an all-metal frame, a controlled pitch propeller, and a retractable landing gear. Despite the economic problems of the Depression, which led to financial failures, southern California firms survived and developed successful new models. Douglas created the DC-3, a major new passenger plane; Lockheed manufactured the Electra, a twin-engined all-metal transport plane, and Consolidated (located in San Diego in 1934) inaugurated its "flying boats" for commercial passengers and military alike.

4

By 1938 the Depression began to lift for the industry in California and elsewhere as military orders poured in from Europe and the U.S. on the eve of the impending war. In the period before the entry of the U.S. into the war at the end of 1941, large military purchases included Lockheed's P-38 fighter, Douglas' B-17 "Flying Fortress," Howard Hughes' experimental giant plywood plane, and other models from Consolidated Vultee (Convair) and Northrop Aircraft. These issued from huge new plants in Burbank, El Segundo, Ingleside, Long Beach, San Diego, Santa Monica, and other southern California communities to which industry had moved. The work force for the new plants increased from fewer than 20,000 employees in 1939 to some 243,000 in 1943. After World War II there was some decline in production, but it was not comparable to that which followed World War I. Although business fluctuated, with some downward cycles, it continued to expand greatly because of successive military needs during the Korean War, the Cold War, and the Vietnam War.

Increased commercial airplane travel also had a significant effect, as did new technological developments, including the jet-propelled airplane and the manufacture of helicopters which began with the Hiller Aircraft Co. in Menlo Park. The business is essentially concentrated in southern California, with Douglas remaining the world's largest manufacturer of commercial aircraft.

By the mid-1960s the aerospace industry employed almost 500,000 people in California, about one-third of all persons engaged in manufacturing. However, many of them were in the newly developing area of missile construction and electronic components. For the military there was the big new business of intercontinental ballistic missile development and manufacture, while other government agencies sponsored the aerodynamic research, engineering, and manufacturing, which helped to create the vast new program dedicated to exploration of outer space and other planets. (*See also individual entries.*)

Aetna Springs, site of hot mineral water springs discovered in the 1880s in foothills northeast of Calistoga (Napa County). It became a spa for vacationing health seekers. In 1976 the resort was bought by an organization supposedly affiliated with the Unification Church of Sun Myung Moon, Korean evangelist.

After Many a Summer Dies the Swan, satirical novel by Aldous Huxley.◆ This farcical but philosophical extravaganza deals with the life and the fear of death of an enormously wealthy southern Californian, said to be suggested by William Randolph Hearst.

Agricultural labor, initially consisted of Indians who, as neophytes (slavery was formally abolished by Mexico in 1829), cultivated orchards and gardens, raised grain, and herded livestock for the missions and also—in peonage or on salary— assisted on private *ranchos,* particularly during harvesting and branding seasons. Farm labor was scarce in the gold rush period as various kinds of agriculture increased, and soon there began in California a now long-established pattern of dependence on a minority, migratory labor force.

Unlike the small family farm of varied crops in the eastern or midwestern U.S. with its long-term hired hands, California agriculture was based on large ranches generally specializing in a seasonal crop that needed large supplies of temporary workers for planting or harvesting. After the Indians, the Chinese were the first ethnic group to be used, mainly for truck gardening,◆ becoming available upon the completion of the Central Pacific Railroad (1869). When the Exclusion Act (1882) ended Chinese immigration, Japanese were taken on, but they lost the favor of white employers by sometimes striking for better wages or conditions, or buying farms of their own. A "Gentlemen's Agreement" (1907) with Japan to restrict emigration also caused growers to turn elsewhere for labor.

For a time (1910–20) East Indians were much employed, though from about 1917 Mexico became the major source of the labor force as the U.S. raised immigration quotas, and Mexicans predominated until native whites took over during the Depression. Labor shortages during World War II caused the federal government to negotiate agreements for the importation of farm workers. They were superseded (1951–64) by a program to bring in *braceros.*◆ During the 1960s mechanized harvesting became common (e.g. 80% of the tomato crop was picked mechanically in 1968). Behind this lay a long history of abortive unionization. At the beginning of the 20th century the International Workers of the World, known as Wobblies, were active owing to conditions that brought about the Wheatland Riot, and they met with much opposition from ranchers, businessmen, press, and police. Intensified union activity occurred during the Depression as Okies from the Midwest and the Great Plains poured into the state in search of a living; large growers then created the counter-organization of Associated Farmers. This situation was dramatically presented in John Steinbeck's novels, *In Dubious Battle* (1936) and *The Grapes of Wrath* (1939). Reform movements died out during World War II, when Mexicans were again imported, and attempts at unionization did not do well until the 1960s. The greatest success was achieved by Cesar Chavez in his strikes against grape picking, begun in Delano (1965), and against lettuce harvesting in the 1970s. In 1975 a state law was passed giving farm workers the right for the first time to have secret ballot elections for the union of their choice, or for no union representation.

Agriculture, after some planting of seeds (corn, beans, pumpkins) by Mohave and Yuma Indians in the mud flooded from the lower Colorado River, was really begun by mission fathers, with their planting of wheat, barley, maize, beans, grapes, and many fruits and nuts. The fields and crops were tended by Indians who, previously, had only foraged the land. The Indians also herded the limited livestock of cattle, horses, mules, sheep, and swine. Presidios and pueblos did some farming, mainly for their own needs. After secularization (1833), cattle were raised on large *ranchos* for trade in hides and tallow but there was some farming: grapes began to be cultivated for wine by Jean Louis Vignes and others, and citrus fruit growing was started commercially by William Wolfskill.

Agriculture expanded enormously in response to the needs of gold rush pioneers. Thus cattle, improved and raised for beef, went from 262,000 head (1850) to 3,000,000 (1862), and sheep, unpopular with *rancheros,* numbered a million head by 1860, some having been driven across the continent. For a time apples far exceeded other fruits, but vineyards expanded and viticulture was improved greatly by Agostin Haraszthy and others. Cotton and tobacco were raised during the Civil War, when supplies of both crops were small.

The droughts of 1862 and 1865 killed many cattle, and the loss of open rangeland by the passage of fence laws helped to end the dominance of cattle raising, which by about 1870 was replaced by the growing of wheat. California became the nation's major wheat producer in the 1870s. Although cattle were fewer, emphasis was placed on improving herds for dairying and they were raised on farms instead of being allowed to roam the ranges. By 1900, milk cows comprised one-quarter of California cattle. Sheep, less hurt by the droughts of the 1860s, reached 7,000,000 head in 1874 but thereafter declined because of the costs of grazing and fencing lands. Wheat also declined in the 1890s when com-

petition came from the Mississippi Valley and Russia, but by then, with the introduction of irrigation, the San Joaquin Valley could grow more profitable crops.

After 1870 truck gardening increased greatly and citrus fruit growing simultaneously expanded with the introduction of the navel orange, the perfection of the Valencia orange and the Eureka lemon, and the development of heating and spraying. Raisins, whose commercial production began (1872) with six tons, increased to 47,000 tons in 1900. During this period the growing and sale of nuts also increased greatly. Apples, whose quality did not compare with those raised in eastern or northwestern climates, began to give way to orchards of peaches, plums, apricots, pears, melons, and berries, and by 1900 California produced 23% of the nation's canned fruits, including 95% of its apricots.

Grape vines, after the 1870s resistant to phylloxera, produced 19,000,000 gallons of wine in 1900, 80% of the nation's output. Production of vegetables increased greatly with improved transportation and the introduction of the refrigerator railroad car (1877); by 1890 the eastern U.S. began to get fresh California tomatoes and by 1910 lettuce became an important crop to send east. Beet-growing for sugar began in the 1870s, and by 1900 the state produced one-third of the national crop. Hops, first raised in 1865, went from a production of 625,000 pounds in 1870 to 10,125,000 pounds in 1900. Many new crops were grown commercially between 1900 and 1920.

Dates and olives were among them, the former raised in the new agricultural area of Coachella Valley. Avocado culture began shortly before World War I and became an important crop, while rice production at the same time increased from 1,800,000 bags in 1916 to 7,000,000 in 1946. During the 1920s cotton growing, particularly in the San Joaquin Valley, became a major business.

Water has been a major need and a major problem for California farming, presenting issues concerned with irrigation and supply throughout the state. Thus supplied, all parts of California (particularly its great Sacramento, San Joaquin, Imperial, and other valleys) still help to make agriculture the state's biggest business. Interconnected with canning and processing, transportation, and marketing, its economic importance remains immense. Farms have become larger and more specialized, and big producers (sometimes conglomerates of nonagricultural companies) own processing, packing, shipping, and marketing concerns as well as fields.

Agricultural labor has become unionized, and,

simultaneously, mechanization has increased tremendously in all aspects of agriculture. In 1970, some 36,800,000 acres were being farmed, making California the nation's major farming state, as it had been for 23 years. (*See also individual entries.*)

Agua Tibia Mountains, part of the Peninsular Range south of the Santa Ana Mts. and northwest of the Vallecito Mts., partly in the Cleveland National Forest of San Diego County.

AIMARD, GUSTAVE, pseudonym of Oliver Gloux (1818–83), popular French romancer of thrilling adventure tales who lived for ten years in Arkansas and other parts of the Old Southwest and later revisited the U.S. to gather more material for his fiction. Among his works set in California is *Le Roi des Placéres d'Or* (1869).

AIN, GREGORY (1908–   ), architect born in Pennsylvania and educated at UCLA and USC, has practiced in Los Angeles, first with Schindler and Neutra, since 1935 with his own office. His work, in a modernist idiom, consists mainly of residences, many in the International style.

Aircraft, achievements and innovations in California range from the first recorded flight of a heavier-than-air craft by John J. Montgomery♦ in 1883 to the first successful flight (three miles over a figure-eight course in Kern County) by a man-powered aircraft with pedals, accomplished by Dr. Paul MacCready of Pasadena in 1977. California is now widely recognized for its large and significant aerospace industry.♦

Aircraft industry, see *Aerospace industry.*

AITKEN, ROBERT INGERSOLL (1878–1949), San Francisco-born sculptor who created many local monuments, including the one in Union Square commemorating Admiral Dewey's victory at Manila Bay and a statue of Hall McAllister in front of City Hall.

Alameda, industrial and residential city in the county of the same name on the east shore of San Francisco Bay. Its name means "poplar grove." Founded (1853) on a flat peninsula formerly the property of the Peralta family,♦ it has been an island since 1902, when a canal was dug between the Oakland estuary and San Leandro Bay; city land has been extended by dredging and filling. On the north of the island is a U.S. Naval Air Station, and else-where are a shipbuilding plant, fishing harbor, and residences. A famous kitchen midden was excavated there. In 1970 it had a population of 70,968.

Alameda County, formed (1853) from parts of Contra Costa and Santa Clara counties, which lie on its north and south, respectively, has San Francisco Bay on its west and San Joaquin County on its east. The county extends from the southern terminus of San Francisco Bay north to Albany and 35 miles east over the Coast Range. Alvarado and San Leandro were the earliest county seats, but Oakland has been the seat since 1873.

The first whites to see this Costanoan Indian region were the explorers under Ortega (1769), Fages (1770), and Anza (1776). The initial settlement, Mission San José, was founded in 1797. Indian relics were long found in kitchen middens along the bay shore. The great early landholders were the Peralta family, on whose former properties were established the county's major cities, Alameda, Berkeley, Fremont, and Oakland, and the Castros, commemorated by Castro Valley.

Early foreign settlers were Robert Livermore and William Hayward, for whom two other major cities are named. The population grew rapidly in the 1870s after the Central Pacific transcontinental railroad (completed 1869) made Oakland its western terminus. In the decades that followed the county continued to develop because of various attractions, including the University of California, Berkeley, and the real estate activities of Borax Smith and others. Although the waterfront cities became, in part, residential suburbs of San Francisco, they also developed their own identities and businesses.

The county's economy is now partly agricultural, emphasizing wineries in Livermore Valley and the commercial growing of flowers and nursery stock elsewhere. It also has an increasingly important industrial base in Fremont and other cities, its major manufacturing being food processing and automobile assembly. In 1970 the population was 1,073,184; with an area of 469,376 acres, it had 1,463 persons per sq. mi. (*See also individual entries.*)

Alamo, see *Poplar.*

ALARCÓN, HERNANDO DE, see *Exploration.*

Alaska Commercial Company, San Francisco-based firm, founded in 1868 and granted a twenty-year monopoly (1870–90) by Congress for seal hunting in the Pribilof Islands. After the discovery of gold in the Yukon, the company entered into extensive trading activities. The firm was owned by the Sloss and Gerstle families of San Francisco and Capt. Niebaum.◆

Albacore, see *Tuna.*

ALBERT, FRANK (1920–　), Chicago-born football player, was quarterback of the Stanford University team (1939–41) and under Coach Clark Shaughnessy◆ used the then new T-formation effectively. He led Stanford to an undefeated season and a victory over Nebraska in the Rose Bowl (1940). He later played quarterback for the San Francisco Forty-Niners◆ (1946–52) and was that team's coach (1956–58).

Alcalde, leading civil officer of local government in a Spanish (and later Mexican) municipality. He was something of a combination of mayor and justice of the peace. The office originated in Spain and was established in California by the *Reglamento* (1779) of Gov. Felipe de Neve. Serving only in a sizable pueblo, by whose citizens he was annually elected, the *alcalde* (like the *regidores,* the other officers of the *ayuntamiento*) was subordinate to the governor's appointed military representative, the *comisionado.* The *alcalde* was not only president of the *ayuntamiento* but also a kind of police officer. Originally only Monterey, Los Angeles, San José, and Branciforte were pueblos qualified to have an *alcalde,* but in time many towns had such officers. In the early years of U.S. rule, before the adoption of the state Constitution, there were many American *alcaldes,* including Washington A. Bartlett, Walter Colton, Stephen J. Field, and Henry Delano Fitch. (*See also individual entries.*)

Alcatraz, name (meaning "pelican" in Spanish) given by Ayala (1775) to the San Francisco Bay island now called Yerba Buena but accidentally transferred on the map of F. W. Beechey (1826) to the island since known by that name. On it was built the first Pacific Coast lighthouse (1854), an army prison of the 1850s and 1886–1934, and a high-security federal penitentiary (1934–63). Among its famous prisoners was Robert Stroud,◆ the "Birdman of Alcatraz." After the prison was abandoned the island was for a time (1969–71) seized by Indians to attract attention to their mistreatment by the federal government. In 1972 it became part of the Golden Gate Recreational Area.

ALCINDOR, [FERDINAND] LEW[IS] (1947–　), New York City-born basketball player, was three times named All-American center during the years he played for UCLA, during which time the team, with a record of 88–2, was the first ever to win three consecutive NCAA championships. He led the team in scoring each year. While a student he converted to the Muslim religion and changed his name to Kareem Abdul-Jabbar. He played with the Milwaukee Bucks (1969–75) and the Los Angeles Lakers (1975–　). His career scoring average of 30.4 points per game and his .547 field goal shooting are the highest in NBA history. His height is officially listed as 7′2″, but he is often thought of as even taller. In 1977 he was injured in an altercation for which he was fined.

Alder, deciduous tree of the birch family which grows throughout California. The main varieties are *red alder,* found on the coast from Santa Barbara north, 25 to 90 feet tall, with a trunk about two and a half feet in diameter with a mottled white bark, and used for millwork and furniture; *white alder,* 30 to over 100 feet tall, with a smooth slender trunk of whitish or gray-brown bark; and *Sierra alder,* 6 to 25 feet tall with a gray bark, often planted to prevent soil erosion. As alders grow only by water sources, early travelers often gave the tree's name to geographic sites marked by streams and lakes, and the Spanish word *aliso* (also used for "sycamore") appears as Alisal in several places, e.g. Charles Lummis◆ called his house El Alisal and Jean Vignes◆ named his vineyard El Aliso. The *California sycamore,* or *plane tree,* also grows along creeks, as does the native *birch,* called the *red* or *water birch,* which ranges in height from a shrub to a 30-foot tree and grows along the eastern Sierra.

ALEMANY, JOSÉ SADOC (1814–88), Catalonian-born missionary of the Dominican order to the western U.S. who, upon the addition of California to the Union, was named bishop of Monterey (1850), and two years later the first archbishop of San Francisco. A gentle man, he fought hard for his church's financial security, first by gaining title to old mission lands and later by obtaining the long-unpaid interest on the Pious Fund◆ through international legal judgments. This money allowed him to develop Catholic educational and charitable organizations. He retired to Spain in 1884. A San Francisco boulevard is named for him.

Aleuts, natives of the Aleutian Islands (of the same racial stock as Eskimos), taken to California by the

Russian-American Co.♦ (1808 ff.) to hunt sea otters and seals from their *bidarkas* (skin-covered canoes). They hunted out of Fort Ross♦ and also on the Farallones and on the Santa Barbara and Catalina Islands, where it is said that they massacred the placid native Indians. Early 19th-century New England sea captains also picked up Aleut hunters in the spring and returned them in the fall after the otter-hunting season ended.

ALEXANDER, HENRY (1860–95), San Francisco-born artist, studied in Munich and painted interior scenes which are meticulously observed and very tightly rendered. The forms of furniture, decor, accoutrements, doors, and windows make shapes and patterns interesting in themselves. Alexander moved to New York (1887), where he died.

Alexander Valley, area northeast of Healdsburg in Sonoma County, named for its pioneer settler, Cyrus Alexander, a Pennsylvanian and a trapper and trader who went first to San Diego in 1833 and then to his valley. There, from Henry Delano Fitch,♦ he got property on which, in the 1840s, he founded the first tannery established by a U.S. citizen in California.

Alfalfa, a deep-rooted legume that can be cut without a need for subsequent reseeding, was first imported from Chile in the 1850s by David Quincy Adams, who grew it on his *rancho* beside Cache Creek in Yolo County. With irrigation several harvests can be realized annually, and a stand will last several years. It has therefore since 1900 become a major feed crop grown on a large scale throughout California (though now mainly in the San Joaquin♦ and Imperial♦ valleys) to provide forage or hay♦ for beef and dairy cattle, hogs, horses, sheep, and pountry. Henry Miller was once the largest alfalfa grower in the U.S.; he used his entire crop to feed his great cattle herds.

Alhambra, city in Los Angeles County, south of Pasadena, founded (1874) on property owned by Benjamin D. Wilson,♦ who named it and some streets from Washington Irving's book. Originally a farming community, it has long been a residential settlement, mainly of apartment buildings. The population in 1970 was 62,125.

Alien Land Law, act of the state legislature (1913), amended and extended by popular initiative (1920) and by the legislature (1923, 1927), aimed against Japanese farmers. It prohibited ownership of real estate by aliens ineligible for citizenship and by their corporations, except for those cases covered by international treaties. Prior federal law had made all Orientals ineligible for citizenship, but inasmuch as all Chinese had been barred from immigrating to California under the federal exclusion act of 1882, the California law was clearly aimed at the Japanese alone.

ALIOTO, JOSEPH L[AWRENCE] (1916–), San Francisco-born lawyer, elected mayor of his home city (1967–75), in which office he became a politically dynamic figure as the city's downtown area burgeoned with skyscrapers. He long engaged in protracted legal suits against *Look* magazine (1969 ff.) because of its contention that he once was associated with Mafia figures, and finally won his libel suit (1977).

Alisal, El, house built by Charles Lummis♦ on the Arroyo Seco♦ in Pasadena. He named it El Alisal (Spanish, meaning "sycamore tree") because its patio contains a large specimen. After his death (1928) the property became part of the Southwest Museum, of which he was a founder. It is now the headquarters of the Historical Society of Southern California.

All-American Canal, a major irrigation conduit to carry water from the Colorado River to the Imperial Valley,♦ bypassing a former route that had gone partly through Mexico. It was completed in 1943 and extended to the Coachella Valley♦ (1948). It also provides water for San Diego.

ALLEN, GEORGE (1922–), Detroit-born football coach, after graduation from the University of Michigan began the career that led him to coach the Los Angeles Rams (1966–70) in which he won divisional championships. He was famous as a stern taskmaster who concentrated only on winning football games.

Allen Press, private press noted for its fine typographic work produced entirely by hand. Founded in 1940 by Lewis and Dorothy Allen, it has used a number of slightly varying imprints and has occupied several locations in the San Francisco area.

ALLENSWORTH, ALLEN (1842–1914), born a Negro slave in Kentucky, went to California and developed (1908 ff.) in southwest Tulare County the farming town bearing his name, the state's only settlement founded and governed by blacks. He was in the army in the Civil War and became a chaplain (and lieutenant colonel) during the Spanish-American War. In 1971 the Department of Parks and Recreation began to restore the town to the appearance of its heyday (1908–18) as an Historic Park. A memorial was erected to him at the San Francisco Presidio (1975).

Alligator Farm, see *Buena Park*.

Almaden, see *New Almaden* and *Masson, Paul*.

Almanor, Lake, see *Plumas County*.

Almonds, see *Nuts*.

Almud, see *Fanega*.

Alpine County, formed (1864) from five adjacent counties, having earlier been considered part of the State of Nevada. Nevada and Mono County lie on its east, Tuolumne County on its south, Amador and Calaveras on its west, and El Dorado County on its north. It straddles the crest and eastern slopes of the Sierra Nevada, with its northern boundary about five miles south of Lake Tahoe and its eastern boundary that of the state itself. Tamarack, at the 8,000-foot level, has recorded the state's greatest seasonal snowfall (nearly 74 feet), its greatest monthly snowfall, and the greatest depth on the ground at one time (nearly 38 feet). Carson Pass♦ and Ebbetts Pass♦ are two major routes through the mountains. Part of Toiyabe National Forest♦ lies in the county. Silver mining was common from the 1850s to the 1870s. Markleeville, which in 1970 had a population of only 484, has been the seat of the county since 1875. With an area of 462,720 acres, the county had a population of 0.7 persons per sq. mi. in 1970.

ALSTON, WALT[ER EMMONS] (1911–), Ohio-born manager of the Dodgers baseball team, first in Brooklyn (1954–57), thereafter in Los Angeles, leading them to seven National League championships and four World Series victories. He retired in 1976.

Alta California, name applied to the upper portion of California, north of that part which the exploration of Kino proved to be a peninsula. Under the orders of José de Gálvez,♦ Portolá♦ and Serra♦ were sent to Alta California (1769) with colonists to establish the first settlements and missions. In 1804 California was divided into Antigua (Baja, or Lower) and Nueva (Alta, or Upper). Arrillaga♦ was the first governor charged only with the affairs of Alta California.

Alta California, The, San Francisco newspaper owned and edited by Edward C. Kemble♦ and Edward C. Gilbert♦ which was a successor to *The California Star & Californian.♦* Issued as a weekly from Jan. 4 to Dec. 10, 1849, it then appeared three times a week until it became the city's first daily (Jan. 22, 1850), remaining an important paper until it ceased publication in 1891. To it Mark Twain contributed his letters about his tour of the Holy Land (1867) on the *Quaker City,* later refashioned as *The Innocents Abroad.*

Altamont Festival, rock music concert held in an open field in a rural area of Alameda County near Livermore (Dec. 1969). The fanatically excited audience, which turned out by the thousands to hear the Rolling Stones and other popular groups, was supposed to be controlled by members of Hell's Angels, hired as guards by the promoters. Instead there was a wild melee, and a young man was stabbed to death in an encounter with a guard. The *Daily Californian,* in a review of a film of the event, called it "the end of a decade of dreams."

Altruria, Utopian colony established near Santa Rosa (1894–95) by a Christian socialist group that had been influenced by William Dean Howells' romance, *A Traveler from Altruria* (1894).

Alturas, seat and major city of Modoc County, located on the Pit River. Its name, adopted in 1876, means "heights." Population in 1970 was 2,799.

Alum Rock Park, natural area of 629 acres on the eastern side of San Jose, established as a park (1872) by the state legislature. A monolith powdered with potassium alum is found there, as are mineral springs.

ALVARADO, a leading early California family. Two of its founders, the brothers Bernardino and Juan Bautista, were with the Sacred Expedition♦ (1769) and married sisters of the Castro family.♦ The third, their younger relative, Francisco Xavier (1756–1831), also a soldier, married into the Amador family, and his daughters married Gabriel Moraga and Pío Pico. Juan Bautista's son, José Francisco, married Josefa Vallejo, the General's sister, and their son was Gov. Alvarado,♦ who again married into the Castro family. For a time San Jose was named Pueblo de Alvarado in his honor, and an Alameda County town was also named for him but it is now part of Union City.

ALVARADO, JUAN BAUTISTA (1800–82), 12th Mexican governor of California (1836–42), a native-born Californian who became president of the *diputación*◆ and thus in an influential position during the period of disturbance following the brief administrations of Govs. Victoria,◆ Figueroa,◆ Chico,◆ and two acting governors. Opposed to the way these governors looked to Mexico for decisions, Alvarado led the *Californios*◆ in company with riflemen under the U.S. frontiersman Isaac Graham◆ and the army under José Castro.◆ He was instrumental in getting the Mexican officials sent home and in having the *diputación* establish "a free and sovereign State" of California (1836) that was ·meant to last until the Mexicans returned to the principles of the Constitution of 1824 with its emphasis on federalism.

Alvarado was made provisional governor (1836) and his uncle, Mariano Vallejo, was made military commander. Monterey was kept as capital even though the Mexican congress had named Los Angeles capital (1835). Alvarado met opposition from the south, intensified when Mexico appointed another native Californian, Cárlos Carrillo, governor (1837), but in ensuing battles he prevailed. In 1839 he was officially appointed governor and began a turbulent term.

He quickly appointed a semi-independent prefect or subgovernor for the south, with his capital in Los Angeles. He also ensured his own security by deporting Graham and other American and English supporters before they might turn against him and seize power. However, his displeasure with the administration of the missions led him to appoint an Englishman, William Hartnell,◆ as their inspector (1839). When Hartnell disapproved of Vallejo's oversight of the San Rafael and Sonoma missions, Vallejo arrested Hartnell, and Alvarado fell out with his uncle, giving a large land grant and much power to John A. Sutter as a potential curb to Vallejo, who was the most important person in that part of California. This internecine fight led to governmental disorder, and both civil and military leaders were (not unwillingly) replaced by a new governor from Mexico, Micheltorena◆ (1842). However, Alvarado turned against him too, and by getting together with Castro in the north and the Picos in the south he managed to oust the new governor (1845). Then, without having lived on it, he sold to Larkin for Frémont the Mariposa land grant he had got from Micheltorena for $3,000, and retired for the rest of his life to a

great *rancho* in present Contra Costa County which belonged to his wife, Martina Castro.

ALVAREZ, LUIS W[ALTER] (1911–1978), San Francisco-born physicist, son of the prominent native San Francisco physician and columnist on medical matters, Walter C[lement] Alvarez (1884–   ). Luis was graduated from the University of California, Berkeley, and spent his entire academic career as a faculty member there but is internationally recognized for his research and was awarded a Nobel Prize in 1968.

ALVISO, a leading early California family whose founder, Domingo Alviso, was a soldier with the Anza expedition (1776). His daughter María Loreta (1770–1836) married Sgt. Luís María Peralta,◆ who became a major landowner of San Francisco's East Bay. A son, Juan Ignacio (1772–1848), also a sergeant, married Margarita Bernal and became a major *ranchero* in present Santa Clara County, where the town of Alviso, since absorbed into San Jose (1968), was named for him. His grandchildren married into the Alvarado, Livermore, Pacheco, and Soto families and were large landowners.

AMADOR, a leading early California family whose founder was Pedro Amador (1739–1824). He went to California with the Sacred Expedition.◆ He and his wife (a Noriega) had eleven children, some of whom married into the Alviso, Bernal, Berryessa, and Castro families. Amador County was named for one of them, Josef María (1794–1883), a rancher of the region.

Amador County, formed (1854) with Jackson as its county seat. El Dorado County lies on its north, Alpine on its east, Calaveras on its south, and Sacramento and San Joaquin counties on its west. Located on the west slope of the Sierra Nevada between the South Fork of the Cosumnes River◆ and the North Fork of the Mokelumne River,◆ it was once the home of the Maidu, and was probably first explored by John A. Sutter◆ (1846) and Charles M. Weber◆ (1848). It was the site of many mining camps of the gold rush era. Plymouth, Jackson, and Ione are its main towns. Lumbering, livestock, miscellaneous crops, sand and gravel, winter sports, and tourism are the bases of its economy. In 1970 it had a population of 11,821. With an area of 379,200 acres, it had 20 persons per sq. mi.

Amargosa, name, meaning "bitter" in Spanish, of a trans-Sierran mountain range east of Death Valley, which itself was once called Amargosa Valley because the Amargosa River runs through it to Badwater.

American Graffiti, film produced in 1973, set in Modesto, portrays teenage ways of life during the 1950s, showing the ambitions, resignation, eagerness, and sadness of an adolescent American generation living in a small town.

American party, see *Know-Nothing movement.*

American River, formed by three branches, all rising in the Sierra. The North Fork begins some 25 miles west of the northern tip of Lake Tahoe and flows 37 miles southwest to join the Middle Fork. The Middle Fork rises 11 miles west of the center of Lake Tahoe, flowing southwest to the junction and then into Folsom Lake. The South Fork, rising in two branches near the southern end of Lake Tahoe, joins the other forks at Folsom Lake. The united stream travels 21 miles southwest from Folsom Lake to the point where the American River joins the Sacramento River at the city of Sacramento. The river was named by John A. Sutter◆ for some local Canadian trappers called "Americanos" by the Indians. The major historical event which took place along its banks, also associated with Sutter, was the discovery of gold by Sutter's employee, James W. Marshall, while digging a tailrace for a lumber mill at Coloma on the South Fork, about 75 miles northeast of Sutter's Fort. The state's first power plant for long-distance transmission of electricity was built at Folsom (1895), and a later dam to control the river is a major part of the Central Valley Project.

American West, The, journal sponsored by the Western History Association◆ (1964–   ), initially a quarterly, later a bimonthly. It presents articles and many pictures on western historical subjects in an attractive format and a style designed for popular appeal.

Americans in the Spanish and Mexican periods of California, were originally attracted by possibilities for trade and acquiring furs and, later, hides, despite official prohibition against foreign visitors. Although John Green, an American, went to Monterey with Malaspina (1791), only to die there, the first real transgressors were Capt. William Shaler◆ and Mate Richard Cleveland, whose *Lelia Byrd* put into San Diego in the hope of getting otter skins, but had to fight their way out of the town and port (1803). The

first permanent U.S. settlers were Thomas Doak◆ and Daniel Call, who deserted their ships in 1816; followed by Joseph Chapman, who was captured from the crew of the privateer *Bouchard* (1818). Succeeding settlers were pioneers bent on business opportunities, like William G. Dana and H. D. Fitch in 1826. Abel Stearns in 1829, and Thomas O. Larkin in 1832. Larkin was the first and only U.S. consul to California, and the father of the first child of U.S. parents born in California (1834).

Soon the chance for trade in hides◆ and tallow from California cattle◆ brought to its ports vessels from Boston, like the one bearing Richard Henry Dana and established merchants like Alfred Robinson, each of whom was to give a New Englander's impression of the region during the 1830s in a book of his own. The period also saw the beginnings of U.S. infiltration of California by overland routes, initiated by mountain men attracted to the Far West by the search for beaver. The first was Jedediah Smith (1826). He was soon followed by James O. Pattie (1827); other trappers who made incursions into Mexican California included Kit Carson and Ewing Young (1829), J. J. Warner, William Wolfskill, and George Yount (1831), Joseph R. Walker and his companions Zenas Leonard and George Nidever (1833)—the first to enter California by crossing the central Sierra—and Isaac Graham (1834), who more than the others entered into the governmental and military fights of the *Californios.*

Different kinds of Americans and more substantial settlers arrived later in the persons of John Marsh (1836), a Harvard alumnus who settled down as both *ranchero* and doctor, and John A. Sutter,◆ the Swiss who was a U.S. citizen by adoption and envisioned California as the place for his personal barony. To his fortified settlement on the site of Sacramento the new decade soon brought parties of overland pioneers bent on permanent settlement, led by one in 1841 which included John Bidwell, John Bartleson, and Joseph Chiles. They were followed by many other travelers across the California Trail,◆ such as Elisha Stevens and Moses Schallenberger (1844), and the self-seeking Lansford Hastings, who championed the cut-off that proved disastrous for the Donner Party (1846).

Meanwhile, U.S. officials cast covetous eyes on California and made premature forays into it, such as the brief seizure of Monterey by Commodore Thomas ap Catesby Jones in 1842 and the unauthorized incursion by the governmental expedition of John Charles Frémont in 1845. All these stood behind the final attempt to wrest California from the Mexicans in the Bear Flag Revolt◆ (1846), itself quickly followed by the conquest achieved through the Mexican War.◆

Anacapa Island, see *Santa Barbara Islands.*

Anaheim, city in Orange County founded (1857) by German settlers as a vineyard and agricultural community. It also was the site of an experimental colony of Polish settlers, including Sienckiewicz◆ and Modjeska.◆ It now has aerospace and other industries, but is best known for Disneyland◆ and other tourist attractions, including the stadium for its baseball team, the California Angels.◆ In 1970 it had a population of 166,701.

Anchovy, herring-like fish, usually smaller than seven inches and weighing less than two ounces, of whose several local varieties only the *northern* is commercially important. Schools by the millions run off the entire California coast and over 100,000 tons are caught annually for fishmeal and oil; livestock, poultry, and pet food; and a smaller number as live bait for commercial and sport fishermen.

ANDERSON, PETER (1818?–79), went to San Francisco (1854) from his native Philadelphia and became a leading spokesman for other blacks. He published *Pacific Appeal* (1862–79), which emphasized civil rights but was also for a time essentially an organ of Freemasonry.

Anderson Valley, most northerly part of the Sacramento Valley, extending from Red Bluff to Redding in Tehama and Shasta counties, is about 30 miles long and 30 miles wide. A cattle-ranching area with some orchards and lumber mills, it is known locally as the Redding District. Another Anderson Valley, located in an isolated part of Mendocino County near Ukiah, incorporates Boonville (where Boontling◆ is spoken) and has long been a lumbering, sheep-raising, and apple-growing area.

Angeles National Forest, a reserve of 643,656 acres on the northern border of Los Angeles, for which it is a major recreational area. Under the name San Gabriel Timberland Reserve, it was the first National Forest in the state (1892). Very mountainous, it includes the San Gabriels, Old Baldy, Mt. Wilson, and a large reservoir, Castaic Lake. (*See also individual entries.*)

Angel Island, largest island in San Francisco Bay, named by Ayala◆ (1775) Isla de Los Angeles and anglicized by Beechey◆ in 1826. From 1850 to 1853

the state anchored ships' hulks off the island and incarcerated prisoners in them. The island has recently become part of the Golden Gate National Recreational Area.

Angels, California, baseball team in the Western Division of the American League. Known as the Los Angeles Angels when the team became part of the American League (1961), it initially played in Wrigley Field of downtown Los Angeles and in the Dodgers' stadium at Chavez Ravine. It had some stars (outfielder Leon Wagner, who briefly led the league in home runs and runs batted in, and pitcher Dean Chance) but never did better than finish in third place (1962). In 1965 the team became the California Angels and the next year moved to its new stadium in Anaheim. In 1969 it became part of the Western Division of the American League. Although there were some distinctions (e.g. in 1973 pitcher Nolan Ryan struck out 383 batters, setting a new major league record, and in 1974 he equaled Sandy Koufax's record as the greatest no-hit pitcher in history), the team has not fared well in its division.

Angels Camp, gold rush mining town in southwestern Calaveras County, founded (1848) by George Angel, a member of Stevenson's Regiment.◆ After the placers along Angels Creek were exhausted, the deep mining of lodes was very successful. Bret Harte set several stories in the town and its vicinity, and Mark Twain's "Jumping Frog" is set there. Since the late 1930s it has been the scene of an annual Jumping Frog Jubilee and contest.

Angel's Flight, tiny, open-car cable railway constructed in 1901 to climb the eastern slope of Bunker Hill, a onetime elegant residential area of Los Angeles situated near its present Civic Center.

Angle of Repose, novel by Wallace Stegner,◆ adapted as an opera by Andrew Imbrie and Oakley Hall. The plot is in large part a fictive treatment of the life of Mary Hallock Foote.◆

Anián, Strait of, legendary body of water thought by the Spanish to connect the Pacific and Atlantic oceans. Called by the English the Northwest Passage, this fabled route to the Pacific Northwest coast was sought by explorers from Cabrillo to Malaspina.

Annals of San Francisco, narrative history from earliest explorations to 1855, the date of publication, presents a month-by-month account from 1846 along with diverse essays and biographies of leading citizens. Written by Frank Soulé,♦ Frank Gihon, and James Nisbet, local journalists, it draws heavily on newspapers of that period and is thus a primary source.

Antelope, prong-horned, native hoofed animals, not of the true African or Asian antelope family. They are fawn colored, with two horns and a white patch on the rump. The male weighs over 100 pounds (the doe about 90), and they run at a speed of about 50 miles an hour. They once ranged over the Central Valley, some of the deserts, and many parts of the U.S. outside the state, but overhunting (the meat was cheaper than beef in San Francisco) reduced their number to about 2,500, which now range over Lassen, Modoc, Shasta, and Siskiyou counties and are protected from all but occasional special hunting.

Antelope Valley, located in north central Los Angeles County, west of the Mojave Desert and north of Palmdale♦ and Lancaster,♦ was long an alfalfa, truck farming, and poultry raising area but has become an urban center with aerospace industry. It also contains a large poppy preserve, where the state's official flower grows wild in great abundance. The valley was first seen by whites when Pedro Fages traveled through it while pursuing deserters from the army (1772). Another Antelope Valley is in northeastern Kern County.

ANTONINUS, BROTHER, see *Everson, William.*

ANZA, JUAN BAUTISTA DE (1735–*c*.88), born in Mexico of Spanish parents, became captain of the presidio at Tubac (1760), south of present Tucson, Arizona, and was permitted by Viceroy Bucareli to develop his plan for opening a land route from northern Sonora to San Gabriel. With 34 men, including Father Garcés,♦ he made the difficult journey across the Colorado Desert (Jan. 8–March 22, 1774) to the California missions, and from there to Monterey and back again to Tubac. In September of the next year he traveled a route farther to the south, through Nogales and Tubac to Tucson and into California (at present Calexico), when Bucareli sent him at the head of a party of 240 people, including women and children with cattle and substantial supplies, to establish a presidio and mission at San Francisco. The 1,500-mile journey, begun Sept. 29, 1775, was brought to conclusion when his second in command, Lt. José Moraga,♦

founded the presidio on July 27, 1776, after Anza had returned to Mexico. Anza was later governor of New Mexico (1777–88).

Anza-Borrego Desert, largest State Park (470,000 acres), established (1933) as a desert recreational area southwest of Coachella on the edge of the Colorado Desert, in San Diego County. It was named for the Spanish military leader who crossed the area (1774) and for the bighorn sheep (*borrego*) which ranged there.

ANZAR, JOSÉ ANTONIO (*c*.1792–1874), Mexican-born Franciscan missionary, went to California (1831) and remained there until 1854. During the last eleven years of his stay, he was President-General♦ of the northern missions and presided at San Juan Bautista.

Apparel Industry, began in California during the gold rush when tough work clothes were needed by miners. The most famous and longest-lived of the early firms was that which manufactured Levi's,♦ copper-riveted blue denim trousers. As the state's population grew and became more sophisticated and diversified, so did the industry. In the latter part of the 19th century electric-powered cutting and sewing machinery were introduced to supply ready-made clothes to the new department stores that were beginning to replace the retail dry goods establishments which had catered to home dressmakers.

Until the 1920s San Francisco remained the manufacturing center of what had begun to be a national business. Los Angeles at that time became a production center and a source of informal and often unusual styles suited both to its sunny climate and emphasis on recreation and to its less established and less conventional residents. Colorful, innovative, and sporty styles were well publicized by the motion picture industry; the very name California, or, specifically Hollywood and Los Angeles, added a touch of glamour to the clothes.

The firms were generally smaller than their East Coast counterparts and also more flexible. While some emphasized play clothes, others featured high style in keeping with the movie stars, whose studios had their own well-known designers like Edith Head.♦ The region also attracted creators of exotic apparel, like Rudi Gernreich,♦ who designed revealing swimwear. However, San Francisco was the home base of the biggest apparel firm, Levi Strauss, whose Levi's led in creating the worldwide fashion of wearing blue denim. By

1970 the statewide business of apparel manufacture was a major industry, as large in dollar value as that of paper production.

Appeal, Courts of, see *Courts of Appeal.*

Apple Valley, Mojave Desert resort area located southeast of Victorville in San Bernardino County. A Roy Rogers Museum is located there.

Applegate Cut-off, trail through the northeast corner of California, developed (1846) by Jesse and Lindsley Applegate, Oregon pioneers, to guide settlers from Fort Hall, Idaho, to Oregon. It was later used by Peter Lassen, Peter Burnett, and forty-niners from Oregon.

Apples, important fruit crop, first grown at the missions but not raised in quantity until after the gold rush, and always restricted by competition from other states. Santa Clara County was the major orchard center until 1910, but the Pajaro Valley near Watsonville and Gold Ridge near Petaluma are now prime areas, with Sebastopol an important processing and shipping site. In 1970 the crop was grown on some 22,000 acres and was worth about $16,800,000.

Apricots, fruit first grown at the missions by the founding fathers but in improved varieties during the gold rush. Only 81,000 trees had been set out by 1859, and there was no great increase until shipment could be made by transcontinental rail and until the dried fruit became popular in the 1880s. There were 3,150,000 pounds of dried fruit produced in 1886; by 1914 this increased to 40,000,000 pounds. Canning became important after 1900, rising from 532,000 cases in 1904 to 3,000,000 by 1935. California grows more apricots than the rest of the U.S.; the major orchard area is in Santa Clara County, followed by San Benito, Stanislaus, and Contra Costra counties. In 1970 the crop was grown on 34,500 acres and was worth $18,360,000.

Arcadia, city in Los Angeles County, southeast of Pasadena, known as the site of the County Arboretum (127 acres) on which is located the adobe of Hugo Reid.♦ Santa Anita Park♦ is also in the city. All are part of the former estate of E. J. [''Lucky''] Baldwin. In 1970 the city had a population of 42,868.

Arcata, city on Arcata Bay in Humboldt County, given its present name (1860), of unknown Indian meaning, when the original name of Uniontown

was confused with that of another settlement in El Dorado County. It is known as a lumber center, a place where Bret Harte's journalistic career began, the site of a community redwood forest, and home of Humboldt State University. An Azalea State Reserve is located nearby. The city was thoroughly documented in photographs by Augustus W. Ericson.♦ In 1970 the population was 8,985.

ARCE, Francisco (1819–78), taken as a boy from Baja California to Monterey (1833), where he became active in military and civil affairs. As a lieutenant under Vallejo he was driving horses from Sonoma to reinforce Castro's militia when he was intercepted by Ezekiel Merritt♦ (June 10, 1846) on the ranch of Martin Murphy, Jr., in present Sacramento County,♦ in the first action of the Bear Flag Revolt. At the end of the war, as Castro's secretary, he fled with his commander to Mexico.

Architecture, began with the primitive dwellings of the Yurok Indians, conical cabins of redwood planks built over a circular cellar, but is more commonly considered to have had its start with Spanish settlers. Their dwellings and other buildings were one-story, flat-roofed structures of adobe, except for the elaborate and tasteful missions first built toward the end of the 18th century to supplant the initial, unpretentious thatch-covered shelters created during Serra's day.

Franciscan fathers emulated Mexican models or drew upon other sophisticated sources (such as copying a drawing of Vitruvius for the façade of the mission at Santa Barbara) in the design of their churches and related buildings. Actual construction and decoration were often executed by the neophyte Indians, to whom were imparted the needed skills. Pueblo, presidio, and private buildings remained simple through the Mexican era down to the eve of American occupation, which saw the beginnings of the Monterey Colonial style in the house of Thomas Larkin. That two-story house with its surrounding veranda adapted New England styles (and possibly French colonial ones encountered when Larkin lived in the South) to the local Latin heritage. With American supremacy, lumber mills came into being and allowed the use of clapboard and shingles as well as other forms of wooden building, which varied from the Greek Revival style of Walter Colton's Colton Hall in Monterey (1847–49) to the flamboyant frame structures in the new cities and some larger mining towns—some of them in San Francisco being converted from deserted ships, others made with pre-fabricated elements shipped from the East Coast, such as peaked roofs, window frames and shutters, Gothic decorations, and turned wooden balustrades.

The early flush days of the gold rush were marked by jerry-built structures and by the frequent fires that destroyed them; as a result later commercial buildings were often made of brick or stone and incorporated iron doors and shutters. Domestic architecture continued to employ wood for the most part and shaped it in diverse, luxuriant styles, including the Italianate, which featured a Corinthian-columned front entry porch, on either side of which was a tall window (frequently an angled bay), elaborate pseudo-classical pediments, and a flat, heavily bracketed roof. The initial Italianate form was later further embellished by such high Victorian styles as the Mansard roof, the stylized patterns of the Stick style with elaborate sculptural decorations made of wood, and the related Eastlake style of decorated wooden features, partly derived from English furniture design. These were later replaced by the asymmetrical Queen Anne style, which featured high gable roofs and a florid tower. Such modes and combinations of them were particularly striking in San Francisco, whose views encouraged bay windows, and ranged from row houses to elaborate mansions of the nouveaux riches on Nob Hill or down the Peninsula at such estates as those of William Ralston or James C. Flood. But the San Francisco style could be seen also in such commercial buildings as the Palace Hotel and the Baldwin Hotel, and it flourished farther afield too in the Carson House at Eureka.

In reaction to these ornate houses produced by builders, at the end of the century professional architects began to design buildings that used native materials or local traditions in ways they felt suited the region. Attempts were made at a Mission Revival style, but more successful was a regional version of the shingle style as employed in the homes built by diverse and influential architects including Willis Polk, A. Page Brown (influenced by Joseph Worcester), Ernest Coxhead, Greene and Greene, A. C. Schweinfurth, and Bernard Maybeck. These architects were by no means limited to a single style, and over the years their creativity was displayed in forms as diverse as Polk's glass-fronted office building and Maybeck's own variety of redwood bungalows to the romantic Hellenism of his Palace of Fine Arts, in San Francisco.

Other architects of the early 20th century brought formal elegance to California design as the Beaux-Arts traditions were employed by Albert Pissis, Walter Bliss and William Faville, John Bakewell and Arthur Brown, and Lewis Hobart. After the San Francisco earthquake and fire of 1906 the city was offered, and declined, a plan by Daniel Burnham to rebuild in the style of Hausmann's Paris, but across the Bay the University of California followed a French master plan of dignified formality with great white granite buildings by John Galen Howard arranged on a central axis.

Meanwhile still other architects were more experimental. Julia Morgan, who had studied at the Beaux-Arts and worked for both Maybeck and Howard, developed her own idioms, most dramatically presented at William Randolph Hearst's castle at San Simeon, and Louis Mullgardt employed some similar forms. John Hudson Thomas of Berkeley built homes in his native city reflecting the influence of Maybeck and, in addition, the principles of the Secessionist architects of Austria, but such an advanced international style was more commonly found in the less tradition-bound southern California, where it was employed with great distinction by Rudolph Schindler and Richard Neutra.

The more experimental atmosphere of Los Angeles and its environs was also particularly hospitable to Frank Lloyd Wright and his son Lloyd Wright. That region's eclecticism and experimentalism were also evident in the houses of Irving Gill, which combined a forthright modern simplicity with a modified Mission tradition. But the area also espoused a pseudo-Spanish style, fostered by the design of San Diego's Exposition of 1915–16 and the opportunity to rebuild Santa Barbara after its earthquake of 1925. Foremost among its practitioners was George Washington Smith.

Northern California revived its so-called Bay Area style beginning in the 1930s under the aegis of William Wurster and Gardner Dailey, the former also initiating a revival of Monterey Colonial forms. They worked closely with Thomas Church, Garrett Eckbo, and Lawrence Halprin as landscape designers. The architects' use of wood in vernacular ways and the landscapers' informal ordering of the surrounding terrain were also to be seen in the work of younger architects, such as Joseph Esherick.

Other architects prominent in recent years are indicative of the eclecticism of their art in California, for they include persons so diverse as Paul Revere Williams, known for his stylish structures for film stars; William Pereira, creator of imposing buildings including Ahmanson Center at USC and the Transamerica Pyramid in San Francisco; and Charles W. Moore, who employs a simple wood-sheathed style. (*See also individual entries.*)

Archives, see *State Archives* and *California Archives.*

Archy Lee Case, see *Lee, Archy.*

Arden-Arcade, suburb of Sacramento which after World War II grew rapidly and became one of the state's fifty largest cities. In 1970 it had a population of 82,492.

ARELLANO, MANUEL RAMIREZ (1742–*c*.1800), Mexican-born soldier on the Sacred Expedition♦ (1769) who took his wife, a de Haro, with him. He became an *alcalde* of Los Angeles (1797) and his children, who changed their name to Arellanes, were prominent in that pueblo and in Santa Barbara. A daughter married Ignacio Martinez, *comandante* of the San Francisco Presidio.

Arena, Point, cape on the ocean shoreline of mid-Humboldt County, first named Cabo de Fortunas by Bartolomé Ferrelo (1543), then called Punta Delgada♦ by Bodéga y Cuadro (1775), and finally known as Barra de Arena (''sand bar'').

Argonaut, The, San Francisco weekly founded (1877) by Frank Pixley♦ and Fred M. Somers, who derived the name from a Bret Harte story. A lively journal of sharp comment on current events, it supported Stanford and the railroad, was anti-Catholic, opposed immigrants, and attacked the Workingmen's party. Ambrose Bierce was briefly (1877–79) a columnist, and later literary contributors included Ina Coolbrith, Gertrude Atherton, and Charles Warren Stoddard. In addition to satirical commentary, some translations from the French, and ''selections'' from other journals, it concentrated on social news and the arts. Pixley left (1893) and the journal was edited by Jerome Hart (1891–1907), who was part owner, but after his day it dwindled in importance, although it lasted until 1958.

Argonauts, name given during the gold rush to pioneers whose hardships in reaching California were thus popularly related to those of the mythological heroes who, with Jason, recovered the Golden Fleece.

ARGÜELLO, CONCEPCIÓN, see *Argüello, José,* and *Rezanov, Nikolai.*

ARGÜELLO, JOSÉ DARÍO (1754–1827?), Spanish governor of Alta California (1814–15), served in campaigns against the Sonora Indians before going to Alta California on the last expedition of Rivera y Moncada.

Appointed *comisionado* at Los Angeles (1781), he married Ignacia Moraga, niece of José Joaquin Moraga,♦ founder of San Francisco, thereby establishing a distinguished family of *Californios*. He was next appointed *comandante* of the presidios at San Francisco (1787–91, 1796–1806) and Monterey (1791–96), and he left his son, Luís Antonio, in charge when he became *comandante* of Santa Barbara (1806–14). During that period Rezanov♦ ingratiated himself with the family and became engaged to Don José's daughter Concepción (1791–1857). Upon the death of Gov. Arrillaga, Argüello served as governor for a year, continuing to live in and hold his Santa Barbara post. After this term he was appointed governor of Baja California (1815–22) without pay and he died impoverished in Guadalajara. Point Arguello♦ is named for him.

ARGÜELLO, LUÍS ANTONIO (1784–1830), 2nd Mexican governor of Alta California (1822–25) and the first native-born Californian to hold that office, entered the military in San Francisco as a cadet (1799). As a young captain (1817) he succeeded his father, José Darío Argüello, as *comandante* of San Francisco, remaining in that post until he became governor. He presided during the transition from the Iturbide empire of Mexico to the new Mexican republic, of which California became a territory. He was in office when the brief revolt of the mission Indians of Santa Barbara was quelled (1825). Argüello had a more liberal attitude than his predecessors toward foreign trade. He even participated in it, using government money to buy a Boston-owned ship which he sent to China with a cargo of otter skins obtained from the Russians at Fort Ross and Bodega Bay. He also allowed William A. Gale to open the first American business house in Monterey, and William E. P. Hartnell to open the first British house in 1825. When Echeandía replaced him as governor, Argüello returned to his post in San Francisco, only to be removed (1829) after complaints that he was profiting from Russian otter-hunting in San Francisco Bay. His sister, Concepción, had years before been engaged to Rezanov♦ and his brother Santiago married into the Ortega family and became a prominent landowner and military leader.

Argus Range, see *Coso Range.*

Arlington Hotel, popular resort hotel of Santa Barbara built by W. W. Hollister.♦ The original 90-room structure helped make the city a vacation center (1876–1909). A rebuilt Arlington was destroyed by the earthquake of 1925.

Armenians in California, settlement began when two brothers named Seropian settled in Fresno, which they found similar in soil and climate to their homeland. Large-scale immigration began in the 1890s and continued into the second decade of the next century, with settlement concentrated in the San Joaquin Valley around Fresno. Most men entered farming, raising crops like those known in their own land: figs, raisins, pistachio nuts, and melons. Armenians first shipped California figs east (1894) and they were also active in dried and fancy fruit-packing and distribution and, for a time, in viticulture. A winery was established in Yettem, Tulare County, an exclusively Armenian community (the name means "Garden of Eden"), which flourished from 1901 to 1936 and was later known as Calgro. Armenians have also been prominent as Oriental rug dealers, as lawyers, and in other businesses. At least one, George Mardikian (1903–77), was well known as a restaurateur. Major figures in the arts include sculptor Haig Patigian,♦ writer William Saroyan,♦ and motion picture director Reuben Mamoulian. The San Francisco lawyer specializing in civil rights cases, Charles R. Garry, an Armenian, was originally named Garabedian.

ARMONA, MATÍAS DE (*fl.* 1769–70), nominally served as governor of California when Portolá was on the Sacred Expedition, his term technically extending from June 12, 1769, to Nov. 9, 1770. He visited Loreto during this time but never went to Alta California.

ARMSTRONG, HENRY (1912–), Mississippi-born boxing champion (originally named Henry Jackson), moved to Los Angeles (1931). He is the only man ever to have held three different world boxing championships at the same time: featherweight (1937–38), welterweight (1938–40), and lightweight (1938–39). His boxing record was 144 wins, 22 losses, and 9 no decision. He later became a lay Baptist preacher to fellow blacks.

Army Museum, see *Fort Mason.*

Arrastre, a rotary contrivance of abrasive stones moved over a track by a mule plodding in a circle, developed by Spanish Americans and used to grind gold-bearing quartz.

ARRILLAGA, JOSÉ JOAQUIN DE (*c.* 1750–1814), twice governor of the Californias (1792–94 and 1800–1806), was also the first governor to be charged with the administration of Alta California only (1804–14). He went with the army from Spain to Mexico (1777) and, after campaigning for six years against the Seri and Pima Indians, was appointed *comandante* of the presidio at Loreto as a captain (1783).

When he was named governor he went north to Monterey (1793) and requested support from the other presidios to defend Alta California, overseeing the building of fortifications on the site of the present Fort Point in San Francisco.

After he was succeeded by Borica, Arrillaga returned to his post at Loreto and was also concerned with the founding of missions in the interior of Baja California to link the Californias more securely to Sonora. In 1800 he became civil governor *ad interim* when Borica was taken ill. Then a royal order designating Arrillaga as Borica's successor (1804) also separated the Californias, making him the first governor of Alta California. However, he was allowed to remain as head of both regions until Felipe de Goyoechea♦ was appointed governor of Baja California (1806).

During his second term Arrillaga discouraged the Russian attempt to establish commercial relations with the Spanish settlements around San Francisco, although he approved of the engagement of Rezanov to Concepción Argüello. He put down uprisings of Indians at the poorly supported missions of San Gabriel and San José. Arrillaga died in office; his was the longest governorship of the Spanish period.

Arroba, a Spanish measure of weight equal to 25.37 pounds; a liquid measure equal to 4.26 gallons.

Arrowhead Springs, resort in the San Bernardino National Forest over which towers Arrowhead Peak (5,174 feet), adjacent to man-made Arrowhead Lake (1901), once called Little Bear Lake because of the nearby reservoir, Big Bear Lake.♦

Arroyo Seco, river flowing from the San Gabriel Mts. through the western part of Pasadena before emptying into the Los Angeles River. On its generally dry course in Pasadena, Charles Fletcher Lummis built his home, El Alisal,♦ and Clyde Brown his stone Abbey San Encino.♦ With other writers and artists, they formed a coterie under which an arts and crafts movement flourished at the end of the 19th century and in the opening decades of the 20th.

Art galleries, see *Museums*.

Artichoke, thistle-like plant with a partially edible flowerhead. This popular vegetable was introduced to California by Italians, and although the French also grew them in Louisiana, California has long been the major U.S. producer, mainly from the Castroville area of the Salinas Valley.

Art in California, may be said to have begun with the pictographs made by Indians, but its beginnings would more commonly be identified with the decorations of the missions, including the reredos in San Juan Bautista painted by an American, Thomas Doak, in 1818. The first European views of California were drawn by an artist who accompanied the expedition of Malaspina (1791); and others soon followed, such as those of John Sykes, who was with Vancouver (1792–94), Ludovic Choris, and Georg Heinrich von Langsdorff, who were with Rezanov (1806), and R. B. Beechey, who paid visits in 1826–28.

Art by longer-term residents essentially began when numerous people from diverse lands were attracted to California in the gold rush and were moved to document the novel scenes of new settlements and of mining methods. Among them were J. D. Borthwick, Albertus Browere, Alexander Edouart, Edward Jump, and Augusto Ferran, who came from Scotland, New York, England, France, and Spain, respectively. Many artists of the mid- to late-19th century were captivated by the region's grand and exotic scenery and concentrated on landscapes, such as Thomas Ayres, the first to sketch Yosemite; Frederick Butman, who often painted Mt. Shasta; Ransom Holdredge, who also depicted Indian life in the wilderness; John Ross Key, who presented quieter rural scenes; Jules Tavernier, who painted both natural and urban views; and Raymond Yelland, known for his poetic presentations of the land.

Several German artists, trained in their native land, were particularly admired for their canvases of the California scene, among them Hermann Herzog, Edouard Hildebrandt, and Frederick

Schaefer. But greatest of them all were the romantic and dramatic painter, Albert Bierstadt, who focused on wild and spacious scenes, and Charles C. Nahl, the more gifted of two brothers, who specialized in large, highly colored storytelling genre scenes. Two British artists were also among the most esteemed depicters of California nature: Thomas Hill, an Englishman, who concentrated on views of Yosemite, and William Keith, a Scotsman, who presented a great variety of forest and other mountainous settings. A local artist who was trained in Germany and returned to paint genre scenes that had no reference to California was the immensely popular Toby Rosenthal.

By contrast, an English artist, James Walker, went to California to live and to depict its Mexican ways of life, which were fast disappearing. Virgil Williams was an influential figure, not so much for his paintings as for his directorship of the San Francisco Art Institute, where his students included the successful Christian Jorgensen. An even more influential instructor was Arthur Mathews, who, with his wife Lucia, not only established a style of decorative romantic Hellenism in symbolic portrayals of the California scene but as director of the California School of Design had an effect upon such important latter-day painters as Francis McComas, Xavier Martinez, and Gottardo Piazzoni.

Other esteemed artists at the turn of the century included Charles Rollo Peters, known for his nocturnes of early California buildings, Thaddeus Welch, popular for his quiet, bucolic scenes, and Giuseppe Cadenasso, a landscape painter. In the early years of the 20th century Joseph Raphael and Theodore Wores showed the effect of Impressionism in their landscapes, and Maynard Dixon's paintings and murals of western scenes used flat colors in a style approaching the abstract.

Two popular etchers, Armin Hansen and J. E. Borein, whose subjects were waterfronts and cowboys, respectively, worked in traditional styles. Later, European visitors like Léger and Hans Hoffman and visiting teachers like Mark Rothko, Clyfford Still, and Theodoros Stamos had an effect on younger local artists, and both abstract expressionism and hard-edged abstraction were among the popular idioms.

But the Californians found their own way as David Park, Elmer Bischoff, and Richard Diebenkorn turned to figurative painting. Others, including Sam Francis and Robert Motherwell, had their own modes of abstraction or pure painting, and still others, like Edward Ruscha and Wayne

Thiebaud, interpreted the local scene in terms of Pop Art. (*See also individual entries.*)

Asbestos, mined sporadically since 1882, long had a limited Pacific Coast market and could not compete with the product of Quebec mines until the 1960s, when it became an important mineral product of the state. Mined mainly in Amador, Calaveras, Fresno, and Napa counties, it is spun into a yarn and woven into heat-resistant fibers used for such purposes as brake linings and insulation. One of the world's largest deposits lies some twenty miles northwest of Coalinga.

ASCENSCIÓN, ANTONIO DE (1573?–1636), Spanish-born friar and geographer, accompanied Vizcaíno♦ (1602–3) to Alta California. After hope for immediate colonization there was abandoned, he encouraged settlement of Baja California.

Ash, tree of which four varieties are found in the state. *Oregon ash,* 30 to 80 feet tall with a trunk up to 3 feet in diameter, grows throughout the Coast Range and the Sierra Nevada up to a 5,500-foot elevation and is the only variety used for timber. *Arizona ash,* 15 to 30 feet tall, grows in southeastern California. *Leather-leaf ash,* about the same height, grows in other southern areas of the state. *Dwarf ash,* 15 to 20 feet, grows in the Providence Mts. of San Bernardino County. Fresno, the Spanish word for "ash," indicates that *Oregon ash* flourished there. The Luiseño Indians made bows of ash.

Asian Art Museum, one of the Fine Arts Museums of San Francisco, housed in its own wing of the de Young Museum.♦

Asilomar, conference center located at Pacific Grove. Established by the YWCA (1913), its 60 acres became a State Park (1956). The center is operated by the city primarily for meetings with international, religious, or civic concerns.

Asistencia, outlying branch of a mission but without a resident priest. The five establishments created by the Spanish served the missions of San Luis Obispo, San Luis Rey, San Diego, Los Angeles, and San Francisco.

Asparagus, vegetable grown commercially in California since the 1870s and, after the 1890s, mainly in the Sacramento–San Joaquin River Delta Lands.♦ Approximately half the California produc-

tion comes from that area, and the state leads the nation in the crop, most of it green, but some still white, the favored variety until the 1930s. Canneries own most of the 42,900 acres on which the 1970 crop, valued at $26,221,000, was grown.

Aspen, species of poplar, growing in California as a slender tree 10 to 60 feet high with a trunk 3 to 6 inches in diameter with a greenish-white bark that turns nearly black on older trees. Its heart-shaped leaves, which dance in the breeze, cause it to be called the *quaking* or *quivering aspen*. It grows in swampy meadows and on Sierra slopes from 5,000- to 10,000-foot elevations. It can be used for making veneer, boxes, and matches, but provides an insignificant part of the state's timber crop.

Asphalt, a bituminous substance found in various coastal deposits from Santa Clara County to Orange County and in Kern County, thus giving rise to place-names incorporating the words Asphalt, Pitch, and Tar, as well as La Brea and Pismo. The last two words are Spanish and Indian terms for the substance, which was the state's earliest known form of oil.♦ Crespí commented upon its use by Indians at Carpenteria.♦

ASPINWALL, WILLIAM HENRY (1807–75), New York City trader with Mexico and Latin America, who with other financiers founded the Pacific Mail Steamship Co.♦ (1848) which profited enormously from the gold rush. He, his brother Lloyd, and others then built a railway across the Isthmus of Panama (1850–55), giving them a monopoly on a rapid shipping route from New York to San Francisco until the completion of the transcontinental railroad (1869). The Panama railway's western terminus town was named for him. A wealthy New York entrepreneur, he did not live in the Pacific areas from which his fortune derived.

Assembly, lower house of the state's bicameral legislature, composed of 80 members elected for two-year terms. The assemblymen's districts are all nearly equal in population. At each session the Assembly elects a Speaker to preside over it and to appoint all committees and chairmen. Also elected is the Speaker pro Tempore who usually actually presides over the Assembly. Each of the two major parties also elects its own floor leader as majority and minority leader.

Associated Farmers, statewide organization of large growers founded (1934) to combat strikes of farm laborers, to lobby for antipicketing ordinances, to shift unemployment relief administration from the state to the county level, and to oppose the Cannery and Agricultural Workers Industrial Union, charged with being a Communist-led group. Their power and influence dwindled after an investigation by a committee of the U.S. Senate under Robert La Follette, and as economic prosperity returned in the 1940s.

ASTAIRE, FRED (1899–), Nebraska-born actor and dancer who, after a successful musical comedy career with his sister Adele, went to Hollywood (1933) where he was a star in sophisticated, witty roles that featured his remarkable and seemingly effortless dancing. Ginger Rogers was his partner in eight films (1933–49), whose urbane and high-spirited stories were marked by lively choreography. After embarking on his film career he made his home in Beverly Hills.

Asti, see *Italian-Swiss Colony.*

Atchison, Topeka, & Santa Fe Railroad, see *Santa Fe Railroad.*

Athabascan, Indians who inhabited the most northwestern part of California. They fell into four major linguistic groups: Tolowa, Hupa, Mattole, and Wailaki. The Tolowa and Hupa on the north (each having fewer than 1,000 members in prehistoric times) culturally resembled their neighbors, the Yuroks.♦ The more southerly Athabascan tribes (Mattole and Wailaki) were more numerous and more independent, and warred with the Yuki.♦

Athenaeum, San Francisco, library association and debating society (1853–58) of blacks, located in a building owned by Mifflin W. Gibbs♦ and other founders, among whom was William Henry Newby (1828–59). He modeled the association on Franklin's old Library Co., which he had known in Philadelphia. In 1854 the Athenaeum owned 800 volumes.

ATHERTON, FAXON DEAN (1815–77), Massachusetts-born merchant. After a very successful career as a trader in Valparaiso (1833–60), where he had married into an aristocratic Chilean family, he moved to California (1860), although he had already visited it (1836–38) on a voyage about which he wrote a diary (published 1964). Of his life in California during his last seventeen years he left no record, but he lived as a country squire on a great estate in the part of Menlo Park♦ renamed Atherton for him. His son George married Gertrude Atherton.

ATHERTON, GERTRUDE [FRANKLIN HORN] (1857–1948), reared in San Francisco and its peninsula by her divorced mother and her grandfather, a great-grandnephew of Benjamin Franklin, and at a finishing school in Kentucky, from which she returned to find her mother contemplating a third marriage: to George Atherton—son of a wealthy merchant and aristocratic Chilean mother—with whom Gertrude eloped (1876). She was freed of this marriage and her imperious mother-in-law when her husband died at sea (1887), his body returned to her preserved in a barrel of rum, as she recalled in her *Adventures of a Novelist* (1932).

Her diverse experiences and associations served her in the dramatic fiction she began to write as a liberated lady. An early sensation was *A Daughter of the Vine* (1899), based on the lurid lives of George and Nelly Gordon.♦ Other fiction about her native state from Spanish times to the 20th century included *The Californians* (1898, rev. 1935), a Jamesian contrast of cultures; *Before the Gringo Came* (1894), stories revised as *The Splendid Idle Forties* (1902); *Rezanov* (1906); *The Sisters-in-Law* (1921); *Sleeping Fires* (1922); and *Horn of Life* (1942).

Her prolific output of fiction, generally exciting but carelessly written, also includes *The Conqueror* (1902), a life of Alexander Hamilton; *Julia France and Her Times* (1912), about women's rights; *The Immortal Marriage* (1927) and *The Jealous Gods* (1928), treatments of classical Greece; and *Black Oxen* (1923), *The Crystal Cup* (1925), and *The Sophisticates* (1931), sensational scenes of international sophistication emphasizing sexual rejuvenation of older women. She also wrote *Golden Gate Country* (1945) and *My San Francisco* (1946.)

Athletics, see *Sports.*

Athletics, Oakland, baseball team in the Western Division of the American League, moved to California from Kansas City by the team's president, Charles O. Finley♦ (1968). From 1971 to 1975 they won five consecutive division titles, and they won the World Series (1972, 73, 74) as well. Their stars have included young left-handed pitcher Vida Blue;♦ Jim ("Catfish") Hunter,♦ another great pitcher; shortstop Bert Campaneris, who stole 52 bases in 1972; right fielder Reggie Jackson,♦ recipient of the Most Valuable Player award (1973); and Gene Tenace, who tied a World Series record by hitting 4 home runs (1972). Finley's constant squabbling with his players over financial and contractual issues essentially broke up the team (1975–76). Finley's failure to be released from his Coliseum lease abrogated his sale (1977) of the team's franchise to a Denver financier.

ATKINS, MARY (1819–82), Ohio-born educator. After graduation from Oberlin College, she went to California (1855), where she became proprietor and principal of a Young Ladies' Seminary at Benicia. In 1866 she sold it to Cyrus and Susan Mills, who moved their Mills Seminary to Oakland, where it was the forerunner of Mills College.♦ Mary Atkins then bought back the Benicia establishment (1879) and was its principal for the rest of her life.

ATONDO Y ANTILLÓN, YSIDRO (1639–post-89), Spanish soldier, later a naval officer, was appointed Governor of Sinaloa (1676). He was next given the title of Admiral of the Californias (1679) and put in command of an expedition of colonists for Baja California. They sailed to La Paz (1679) in a company whose most distinguished member was Kino.♦ The next year Atondo crossed the Baja California peninsula to the Pacific. He was then ordered home and the colonization plan was suspended.

Atsugewi, see *Achomawi.*

Attorney General, the state's chief law officer, is elected at the same time and for the same term as the governor. He supervises all district attorneys, sheriffs, and police departments of the state.

Auburn, county seat of Placer County, named (1849) for a city in New York State, was a rich and active gold rush town, of which remnants may be seen today. It was also a major road center. Its population in 1970 was 6,570.

Audiencia, in the colonial era was Mexico's supreme court, whose *presidente* and four justices served as the chief administrative authority in the absence of the viceroy. In California a comparable judicial body held similar executive power.

AUDUBON, JOHN WOODHOUSE (1812–62), son of the great painter, went to California (1849–50) to fulfill his father's plans to depict the birds of California as well as to visit the mines. He made drawings of both subjects, but nearly all of them have been lost. A selection was published in 1957, subsequent to a fragment, *Illustrated Notes of an Expedition* (1852), and *Western Journal* (1906), about his trip via Mexico and brief residence in California.

Auerhahn Press, private press (1958–64) of San Francisco, run by David Haslewood and Andrew Hoyem, which published the works of young local writers in fine format. Their authors included William Everson, Philip Lamantia, and Michael McClure. The press was named "after a large game bird that lives in the Black Forest."

AUSTIN, MARY [HUNTER] (1868–1934), went from her native Illinois to homestead with her family on the desert near the San Joaquin Valley and there, while teaching school, wed Stafford Austin, the manager of an Owens Valley irrigation project. During her brief and unhappy marriage she began to write sensitive sketches of the region for the *Overland Monthly,* collected in *The Land of Little Rain*♦ (1903), following them with stories of the Paiutes, *The Basket Woman* (1904); a romantic novel of Mexican California, *Isidro* (1905); and a poetic account of sheepherding in the land of little rain, *The Flock* (1906). These works established her as a literary figure, and she moved with other local bohemians as a founder of the artists' colony at Carmel.

After 1912 she lived as much in New York as in Carmel, and her writings had wider settings and broader subjects. She published essays on women and on socialism, and thesis novels on contemporary issues, such as *A Woman of Genius* (1912), and *No. 26 Jayne Street* (1920). But she also continued her concern with Californian issues in *The Ford* (1917), a realistic novel treating conflict between real estate interests and social reformers, and *California, the Land of the Sun* (1914).

Her mystical and religious views appeared in her tales of Christ, *The Green Bough* (1913) and *The Man Jesus* (1915), and also in her exaltation of primitive values in the romance *Outland* (1919). Her continuing concern with the Indians manifested itself in *The Arrow Maker* (1911), a poetic drama; *The American Rhythm* (1923), studies of their songs, accompanied by her own poems in the same vein; and *Children Sing in the Far West* (1928), a similar collection created with children she taught.

Her dedication to Indian culture led her to settle in Santa Fe (1924), but she returned to her California experiences in the recollections of her own rebellion, her search for mystical selfhood, and her love of the land, recounted in the autobiographical *Earth Horizon* (1932).

Australians in California, an association begun when three Australian whaling vessels captured the Spanish ship *El Plumier* off the California coast (1800). Settlement did not really become significant until the gold rush, when many Australians went to San Francisco and the mines, some of them becoming the notorious Sydney Ducks♦ who attacked Chileans and other Spanish-speaking peoples and created a crime wave that led to the creation of the first Vigilance Committee. A respectable immigrant, Edward Hammond Hargreaves, noticed the resemblance of the Mother Lode to his native terrain and returned to Australia to search for and discover gold there (1851). Another significant relationship was established in 1885 when Alfred Deakin, prime minister of Victoria, visited the Mojave Desert area and enlisted George Chaffey♦ with his irrigation techniques to aid him in the Australian wastelands. An earlier agricultural relationship was the wholesale importation into California of Australia's eucalyptus.♦

Austrians in California, first arrived during the gold rush but there were only 87 recorded in the state in 1850. That number increased to more than 1,000 by 1870 and nearly 2,000 by 1880, during a decade when some of them began to make wine, leading to the place-name Austrian Gulch in Santa Clara County. In the 20th century, when immigration increased, Austrians made significant cultural contributions, some as motion picture directors (Max Reinhardt, Erich von Stroheim, Josef von Sternberg, Otto Preminger, Billy Wilder); as stars (Paul Muni and Hedy Lamarr); as architects (Richard Neutra and R. M. Schindler); as professors (Robert Lowie); as musicians (Ernestine Schumann-Heink, Arnold Schoenberg, and Kurt Adler); and as authors (Franz Werfel).

Automobile, see *Car culture.*

Automobile Association of California, see *California State Automobile Association.*

Automobile Club of Southern California, founded in Los Angeles (1900), a year before five autos were featured in the Tournament of Roses Parade, it had fewer than 15 members when it affiliated with the Automobile Association of America (1903). Its activities included work for improved roads and for direction signs (which bore the club symbol of a bell within a wheel) and it offered maps, tour books, and insurance. By 1908 it had 1,000 members, increased to more than 30,000 by 1920. Meanwhile it founded branch offices, organized safety patrols for schoolchildren, and sponsored vehicle laws. For a time it sanctioned track and open road races, which were not countenanced by the AAA, thereby breaking that affiliation until after World War II. Over the years the club added numerous services and programs, and its journal, *Touring Topics* (founded 1909), was retitled *Westways* (1933) in accord with its development into a regional monthly of general interest, with frequent contributions from Lawrence Clark Powell, W. W. Robinson, Phil Townsend Hanna, and other notables. By 1975 the club had nearly 2,000,000 members.

Automobile racing, begun in California in the first decade of the 20th century, although the first nationally recognized race was not run until 1913, when the Vanderbilt Cup (initiated in New York, 1904) was staged in San Francisco. Another Vanderbilt Cup contest was held (1915) in conjunction with the Panama-Pacific Exposition. Prior to World War I, races were held in Santa Monica and between Los Angeles and Phoenix, but after the war road races grew uncommon and wooden tracks were built in Los Angeles and Culver City. In the 1920s hot-rod racing (to cover one-quarter mile from a standing start) was held at Muroc Lake, later the site of other sports car racing. Major racing courses have been established at Riverside, Ontario, Laguna Seca, and Monterey for stock car, midget, and Grand Prix racing. Many champions have lived in the state, including Earl Cooper (national champion, 1913, 15, 17), Dan Gurney (winner, Le Mans 24-hour race, 1967), Phil Hill (world champion, 1961), Parnelli Jones (winner, Indianapolis 500, 1963), Bill Vukovich (winner, Indianapolis 500, 1953–54), and Roger Ward (winner, Indianapolis 500, 1959 and 62).

AUTRY, [ORVON] GENE (1907–), Texas-born motion picture actor, starred in 82 Western films and became known as the Singing Cowboy. He also wrote more than 250 songs and had a television series. His financial success led to ownership of television and radio stations in the state and, at one time, of the Mark Hopkins Hotel in San Francisco. He is a major stockholder of the California Angels.

AVERY, Benjamin Parke (1828–75), went from New York City to California (1849) and there became state printer and editor of the *San Francisco Bulletin* and of the *Overland Monthly* (1874) before being appointed U.S. Minister to China, where he died.

Aviation, see *Marriott, Frederick; Montgomery, John J.; Aerospace industry;* and *Aircraft.*

Avocado, pulpy fruit of the laurel family, indigenous to tropical and subtropical America, first grown on a large scale in California at the beginning of the 20th century. Frederick O. Popenoe (1863–1934) and Charles Parkinson Taft (1856–1934) were among those responsible for introducing the fruit, which was then often called alligator pear because of the texture and color of its skin. In 1924 an Avocado Marketing Exchange (soon called Calavo Growers of California) was organized as a growers' cooperative. Before long it was marketing half of the California crop. Sensitive to cold, avocados are grown chiefly along the southern California coast, but they survive as far north as the Sacramento Valley. By 1967 California had come to produce 90% of the crop grown in the U.S.

Awani, see *Yosemite Valley.*

Axe, Stanford, see *Big Game.*

AYALA, Juan Manuel de (*fl.* 1775), Spanish navigator in command of the *San Carlos.* It sailed from San Blas (March 1775) to Monterey and then to San Francisco Bay as part of Viceroy Bucareli's project of exploration to precede the land party under Anza♦ to found a settlement there. Ayala and his pilot, José de Cañizares,♦ explored San Francisco Bay (Aug. 5–Sept. 17) and returned to San Blas in November with a favorable report on its harborage and its first map. They also named its main features.

AYRES, Thomas A. (*c.* 1816–58), artist who went to California (1849), sketched the diggings, made the earliest known views of Yosemite (1855), and drew pictures of southern California (1858). His work is mostly in black chalk on marbleized paper.

Ayuntamiento, board of municipal officers created as a colonial measure by the *Reglamento* (1779) of Gov. Felipe de Neve.♦ It initially included the *alcalde*♦ and two *regidores*♦ appointed by the governor, but was later expanded to twelve elected members. Their jurisdiction, restricted to the pueblo, dealt with such matters as schools, prisons, hospitals, sanitation, and streets. It was subordinate to the *comisionado,* the governor's military representative.

Azalea, flowering shrub of North America and Asia, whose native California variety grows along stream borders and at the edge of woodlands and meadows in the Sierra and Coast Range. Though admired for its varicolored flowers and spicy odor, it is disliked by sheepmen because the plant is poisonous to their flocks. An Azalea State Reserve is located just outside Arcata.

Azusa, Los Angeles County city north of Claremont and east of downtown Los Angeles at the foot of the San Gabriel Mts., developed (1887) as a citrus center. The name is probably a corruption of an Indian word, perhaps for "skunk." The population in 1970 was 25,217.

B

BACON, FRANK (1864–1922), born in Marysville, popular stock company actor in California who became famous with the play *Lightnin',* written with Winchell Smith (1918). Its homespun character was so well enacted by Bacon that it ran 153 weeks in New York.

Bad and the Beautiful, The, motion picture (1953) about a film producer advancing the careers of a writer, a director, and an actress, who in time he turns against, though they still later help him to make a comeback. It is a study of megalomania and ruthlessness in Hollywood.

Badger, large member of the weasel family, found in unforested areas throughout the state except the extreme northwestern corner. It burrows in the ground, feeding mostly on squirrels and other small rodents. The Spanish name for badger, *tejón,* is preserved in several place-names.

BAEGERT, JAKOB (1717–72), German-born Jesuit missionary to Baja California (1751–68), about which he wrote *Nachrichten von der Amerikanischen Halbinsel Californien* (1772).

BAER, MAX[IMILIAN ADELBERT] (1909–59), Nebraska-born boxer, reared in Livermore, then resident in Sacramento. He won the world's heavyweight championship from Primo Carnera (1934) and lost it to James Braddock (1935). He was later known as a clowning actor and entertainer. An actor in *The Beverly Hillbillies* and other Hollywood productions also bore the name Max Baer.

BAEZ, JOAN (1941–), New York-born singer of folk songs in concert halls, coffeehouses, and in public halls for the benefit of antimilitary movements and other liberal or civil liberties causes to which she is dedicated. She is also known for refusing to pay income taxes that support war activities, for her trip to North Vietnam during the U.S. war against that country (1975), and as the founder of an Institute for the Study of Nonviolence, located at Palo Alto, where she lives. She has also organized an annual folk festival at Big Sur.

Baja California, name applied to the lower portion of California, from Tijuana to Cape San Lucas, discovered by Fortún Jiménez on a naval expedition sent by Cortés (1533). The expedition of Ulloa♦ (1539–40), also dispatched by Cortés, proved the area to be a peninsula, not an island, a discovery confirmed by the land explorations of Kino.♦ In 1804 California was divided into Baja (Antigua) and Alta (Nueva) and separately administered. After the Mexican War, Baja California remained part of Mexico while Alta California was ceded to the U.S.

BAKER, DOROTHY (1907–68), Montana-born novelist. After attendance at Whittier College and graduation from UCLA, she lived in Porterville with her husband, Howard Baker (1905–), a literary critic, novelist, and rancher. He wrote *Orange Valley* (1931), about his home area; her novels include *Young Man with a Horn* (1938), inspired by the music of Bix Beiderbecke.

BAKER, EDWARD DICKINSON (1811–61), English-born political figure who defeated Abraham Lincoln for Congress in 1844 and served in the Mexican War before moving (1852) from Illinois to California, where he became a prominent lawyer and well-known public speaker. His best-known orations were one against the vigilantes of 1856 in defense of his client Charles Cora,♦ accused of murdering Gen. William D. Richardson, and another, his funeral elegy (1859) over Sen. David Broderick, lauding him as a martyred opponent of slavery. Presumably he also helped to swing California behind Lincoln. He moved to Oregon in 1860 and in that year was elected as a Republican to the U.S. Senate. A colonel leading a Union regiment, he was killed early in the Civil War. Fort Baker, overlooking the Golden Gate, was named for him.

BAKER, GEORGE HOLBROOK (1827–1906), Massachusetts-born artist, went to California in the gold rush and there created lithographs of local events and scenes.

Bakersfield, seat of Kern County, is its major city. Named for a founder, Col. Thomas Baker, who tried to develop a navigable waterway from former Kern

Lake to San Francisco Bay, the site's history dates back to the explorations of Garcés (1776) and other travelers through the Tehachapi Mts. The settlement of the 1870s mushroomed with the discovery of gold (1885) in Kern River Canyon and through the succeeding and more significant nearby discoveries of oil (1860s–90s). It has long been the market and shipping center both for the region's diverse crops and for its oil products. Although seriously damaged by an earthquake (1952), it grew considerably in the following decades. Major sights are the County Museum and a reconstructed Pioneer Village. Natives of the city include Clair Engle and Lawrence Tibbett. In 1970 the population was 69,515.

BAKEWELL, John Jr. (1872–1963), Kansas-born architect, educated at the University of California and the École des Beaux-Arts. In partnership with Arthur Brown♦ in San Francisco he built its City Hall and Temple Emanu-El.

Bakke Case, suit brought by Allan Bakke, a white applicant to the medical school of the University of California, Davis, who claimed that it had discriminated against him when he was rejected (1973 and 1974) although his grades were better than those of some applicants from racial minorities for whom 16% of the total admissions were reserved. The state and U.S. supreme courts upheld Bakke (1976, 1978), but the latter's ruling against a quota also held that race and ethnic origin may be elements of admission policies.

Balboa Park, also known as Exposition Park, recreational and cultural center of San Diego, whose 1,400 acres were early set aside (1868) for a park but first were improved by Kate Sessions♦ in the 1890s. It was the site of the Panama-California Exposition (1915–16) and the California Pacific International Exposition (1935–36). In it are located the city's museums♦ and zoo.♦

BALDWIN, Elias Jackson ["Lucky"] (1828–1909), on arrival in San Francisco (1853) entered the hotel business (in which he had previously engaged in Indiana) and also made a fortune in bricks and real estate. He won his nickname by getting key holdings in the Comstock mines and selling out at the peak. After selling his Ophir stock to William Ralston at $1,800 a share (1872), for which two years earlier he had paid $2 a share, Baldwin built the lavish San Francisco hotel and theater bearing his name (both burned down in 1898) and a Lake Tahoe resort at Tallac.♦ He also developed the Santa Anita

Rancho in the San Gabriel Valley, with large vineyards and the largest racing stable in the U.S. In later years he lost much of his fortune and was involved in sensational marital and extramarital lawsuits.

BALE, Edward Turner (1811–49), English surgeon, arrived in Monterey on a British ship and remained there several years practicing medicine and as surgeon to the army of *Californios*. In 1843 he moved to his rancho in present Napa County with his wife, Carolina Soberanes, a niece of Gen. Vallejo, and there built the flour mill near St. Helena that is still a landmark.

Ballet, see *Dance*.

Bally, see *Yolla Bolley*.

BANCROFT, Hubert Howe (1832–1918), born in Ohio, went to California (1852) to try his hand at mining and to sell books, which he had done in Buffalo, N.Y. In 1855 he went east and returned with books and stationery to open a San Francisco store (1856) that within two years began to grow into a publishing firm issuing, among other items, law books and legal stationery, texts and maps for schools, and music, and also printing colored labels for cans as well as controlling a large staff of salesmen of subscription books.

As an outgrowth of his publication of a Pacific Coast handbook in 1859 be began a collection of regional writings pertinent to the projected issuance of an encyclopedia of the Pacific Coast. This was the beginning of his astounding book collection. Within a decade he had 16,000 volumes, some collected on trips east and to Europe, encompassing in area not only the Pacific Coast but British Columbia and Alaska to the north, the Rocky Mts. to the east, and Mexico and Central America to the south, and extending in time through Spanish control in the New World and native Indian cultures from all these regions.

His collection was initially created as a resource for a huge history of all those regions, times, and cultures, with California as a central subject. But the aggregation grew larger and larger, providing more material than one man could read or digest, as he assembled not only books and pamphlets but manuscripts, maps, and periodicals; transcriptions of manuscripts made by his corps of copyists from originals in private hands; and governmental and church archives. He even created his own texts by having some of his staff interview pioneers whose recollections might otherwise not have been preserved.

As he continued to acquire materials he also planned a vast cooperative history based on the works in his private library. He utilized the services of staff to create a card catalog for a subject index and then of a corps of assistants to prepare the texts, many of which he hardly altered before issuing them over his own name. Among his major assistants were Henry L. Oak♦ and Frances Fuller Victor.♦

From what he called his "history factory" there came, first, five volumes on *The Native Races* (1874–75) and then three volumes of the *History of Central America* and six more on a *History of Mexico,* followed by two on the *Northern Mexican States and Texas,* and one treating Arizona and New Mexico. All of them preceded his central topic: a seven-volume *History of California* (1886–90), followed by nine more volumes on other parts of western North America, U.S. and British.

In addition to these works, which were vigorously sold by his subscription agents, he himself wrote some more informal works: *California Pastoral* (1888) and *California Inter Pocula* (1888), on the Spanish and Mexican eras and on the gold rush periods, respectively, and two autobiographical books, *Literary Industries* (1890) and *Retrospection, Political and Personal* (1910).

His reputation suffered because some of his writers complained that they were not properly recognized, some historians particularly criticized his adulatory works, such as *Chronicles of the Builders* (7 vols., 1891–92), and some buyers objected to the high-pressure techniques of his salesmen. As a result there was even skepticism about The Bancroft Library,♦ which he sold to the University of California (1905) for $250,000 while making a gift of $100,000 toward the purchase.

Bancroft Library, The, formed by Hubert Howe Bancroft,♦ sold by him to the University of California (1905), and thereafter located at Berkeley. It is an outstanding collection of books, journals, manuscripts, maps, and pictures concentrating on Bancroft's original fields of collecting: the western part of North America, with emphasis on California, Mexico, and Central America. It has been greatly augmented and by 1970 contained about 250,000 printed works, 26,000,000 manuscripts, some 1,000,000 pictures—of which the most significant were in the Honeyman Collection of drawings and paintings of early California—and much microfilm. In 1969 it became the major library of rare materials on its campus, including many Mark Twain manuscripts and diverse rare books in all fields. Its directors include Professors H. E. Bolton♦ and G. P. Hammond.♦

BANDINI, JUAN (1800–59), went from his native Peru to California (*c.* 1822) with his father, José Bandini (1771–1841), a Spanish-born sea captain. In California he became a *ranchero* and a social and political leader in San Diego and Los Angeles. He was a member of the *diputación* (1827–28), a *sub-comisario* of revenues at San Diego (1828–32), *suplente* congressman (1831–32), and a holder of other minor political posts. At various times he opposed Govs. Victoria, Zamorano, and Alvarado. He supported the U.S., supplied Stockton's battalion, and became *alcalde* of San Diego (1848). Dana depicted him symbolically but somewhat unfairly as a representative of the graceful, elegant, and impoverished grandees of California. He did lose his properties after U.S. occupation, even though he had three American sons-in-law, including Abel Stearns♦ and Cave J. Couts.♦

Banking, as a business came into being during the gold rush, although hide and tallow traders, mission prefects, government accountants, and, later, American quartermasters had carried on that activity in a limited, simple way. Then firms which held gold for miners, such as merchants with safes, express and stage company agents, and saloonkeepers began to develop some banking business. Eastern banking firms soon opened branches in California, but Robert A. Parker of Dupont St. in San Francisco may have been the first (1848) real local banker, soon followed by James King of William, Henry N. Naglee, and others.

Abundance of gold and the general American distrust of bankers led to a state prohibition (1850) against local issuance of paper currency, but by 1855 there were nineteen banks in San Francisco, all affected or ruined that year by runs demanding specie. A major firm to fail was Adams & Co.,♦ and a local survivor was Wells, Fargo,♦ the express company. Thereafter banking was better regulated, and nationally established banks, clearing houses, and other, sounder kinds of structures arose from the 1860s to 1900.

The first bank in southern California was founded in Los Angeles by Alvinza Hayward♦ and J. G. Downey.♦ The state's first nationally chartered bank (1870) was San Francisco's First National Gold Bank, opened by the father of James Phelan♦ and by James Moffitt.

In the last three decades of the 19th century the

number of savings banks increased from 12 to 104 and commercial banks from 3 to 189. However, heavy speculation, a severe decline in the value of mining stocks, and a general depression in 1875 led that year to the failure of the Bank of California and, with the death of its president, William Ralston,♦ set off a panic and the failure of other banks, e.g. that of William Workman♦ in Los Angeles. As a result a three-man State Banking Commission, appointed by the governor to regulate state-chartered institutions, was created, but it became a tool of the Southern Pacific Railroad, which was then in a position to oversee the funding of its opponents. Foreign chartered banks and private banks were not affected until 1887 and 1905, respectively.

Despite legislation, the state's banks were hard hit by the Panic of 1893, but economic impetus through expanded trade and the Klondike gold strike had a good effect, and the opening decade of the 20th century saw resources more than doubled. Nevertheless, national financial problems led to bank failures throughout the nation, and the state required more control of its banks through an act (1909) which established far greater scrutiny of banking practices. It also permitted branch banking.

A. P. Giannini♦ was a major leader in branch banking, expanding his Bank of Italy (later named the Bank of America) throughout the state. Older established institutions moved more slowly: Wells Fargo in San Francisco, whose ownership had passed from the Fair and Flood families to that of I. W. Hellman, remained separate from the Merchants and Farmers Bank of Los Angeles, although it was controlled by another branch of the Hellman♦ family. Similarly, the bank established by the Crocker family long remained only a San Francisco institution. More regulation occurred after the creation of the Federal Reserve System, which also simplified national money management, assisting the smooth operation of banks during the expansionist and speculative period of the 1920s and the Depression of the 1930s.

The great influx of population to California after World War II brought about unparalleled economic growth and expansion of banking as well as mergers into a few very large banks during the 1950s. Several of them—Bank of California, Crocker, United California, and Wells Fargo—joined to create a great credit card system, Master Charge, in response to the charge card developed in the late 1950s by the nation's largest bank, the California-based Bank of America. That move was indicative of the tendency of many individual banks to merge into a few large systems. By the mid-1970s there were more branches and offices of banks in California than in any other state.

Bank of America, see *Giannini, A. P.*

BANNING, PHINEAS (1830–85), went to the Los Angeles area (1851) from his native Delaware and soon concentrated on developing a port for the land-locked city. This he achieved at San Pedro♦ and at Wilmington (named after his home town), to which he organized stagecoach and railroad lines from the interior city. He married a niece of W. W. Hollister. His development of transportation, aided by his brother Albert, is memorialized in the town of Banning (Riverside County), an orchard center which holds an annual Stagecoach Days Festival.

BARBADOES, FREDERICK G. (d. 1899), born in Boston of an old free black family, went to San Francisco in the early 1850s, and both there and in the Mother Lode region was a leading advocate of civil rights. He left California (1868) and became a doorkeeper and messenger in the U.S. Senate.

Barbary Coast, name popularly used from the 1860s to the era of the great earthquake and fire of 1906 for that portion of San Francisco known for its bordellos, bars, gambling houses, dancehalls, and general depravity. It was probably so called by a sailor who thought its denizens resembled the pirates of the North African coast of that name. Originally bounded, roughly, by the waterfront on the east, Clay and Commercial streets on the south, Chinatown of present Grant Ave. on the west, and Broadway and its Telegraph Hill area on the north, later it referred only to Pacific St. (later Ave.) between Kearny and Montgomery streets. Reform movements after 1906, particularly a decade later, closed the area, but part of it, under the name of North Beach,♦ has become the section for the city's most lurid nightclub entertainment.

BARD, THOMAS ROBERT (1841–1915), born in Pennsylvania, moved to present Ventura County (1864), and there became one of the first persons to drill successfully for oil.♦ He was also a founder of the town of Hueneme. He united with others to create the Union Oil Co. (1890). A Republican, he was elected to the U.S. Senate (1899–1905) as a conservative opponent of the Southern Pacific Railroad machine.

Bard Valley, in the extreme southeastern part of Imperial County, the corner of the state adjoining

Arizona, was the site of a Spanish mission and the Gila River Trail♦ for emigrants. The Fort Yuma Indian Reservation (est. 1884) is located in the valley, which produces the same crops as Imperial Valley. It was named for Sen. Thomas R. Bard,♦ who sponsored its irrigation district.

Barley, grain grown extensively in the state since the early days of large-scale wheat ranching (*c.* 1870). Originally used mainly as feed for draft horses, in more recent times it has been raised for local livestock, but significant quantities from the western Sacramento Valley, the Tulelake area (Siskiyou County), and the northwestern San Joaquin Valley are used by brewers. About half of the crop is grown around Fresno, but Monterey County, the Delta, and Imperial Valley are also important. California is the third largest producer in the U.S. (1970). In 1970 there were 1,188,000 acres planted, and the crop was worth $69,807,000.

BARNES, Stanley (1900–), football player reared in San Diego, the star tackle of the Wonder Teams♦ (1920–21) of the University of California, Berkeley. He was later a U.S. Assistant Attorney General and U.S. Circuit Court Judge, resident in Los Angeles.

Barnsdall Park, an art and cultural center on a hill of olive trees in Hollywood, whose main building, Hollyhock House, was designed by Frank Lloyd Wright♦ for Aline Barnsdall, who donated it to the city (1927). Hollywood refurbished the building in the 1970s.

Barracuda, subtropical predatory fish found off the coast south of Point Concepcion in rather shallow water. It is fished both commercially and for sport.

BARRI, Felipe de (*fl.* 1770–75), governor of the Californias (1771–74) who, when the capital was in Loreto, never visited Alta California where Fages♦ acted as *gobernante* ("commanding officer") although Fages was essentially only the lieutenant governor. Barri's administration was mainly concerned with the rivalry between the missionaries, led by Serra, and the military, led by Fages, for the dominance of Alta California. Although Viceroy Bucareli sided with Fages, he relieved Barri of office, just as Fages too was given another post.

Barrio, Spanish word for a "city ward" or "district." In recent years it has been applied to urban

areas considered to be Spanish-speaking ghettos.

BARRY, Rick (Richard Francis Barry) (1944–), New Jersey-born basketball player. After graduation from the University of Miami, where he was twice selected as an All-American player, he joined the San Francisco Warriors (1965). He later played for the Oakland Oaks and other teams before joining the Golden State Warriors (1972), in the succeeding years leading them in scoring and to a National Basketball Association championship. A forward, he is one of the most versatile players in basketball history and was voted to the NBA All-Star team in each of his first five years in the league. In 1978 he joined the Houston Rockets.

Barstow, city in northwestern San Bernardino County, at the foot of the Calico Mts. When gold and silver were discovered in the mountains (1890s), Barstow became a supply center. It was also a desert junction for overland and Death Valley expeditions. Originally called Fishpond, then Waterman Junction (in honor of the governor, who had a nearby silver mine), it gots its present name when it received its main business as a division point for the Santa Fe Railroad (1886), whose president, William Barstow Strong, had already had his surname used for another settlement. In 1970 the population was 17,442.

BART, acronym of Bay Area Rapid Transit, a high-speed transportation system of the San Francisco Bay region. A nine-county planning commission's recommendations (1951) led the legislature to create a five-county rapid transit district, eventually reduced to San Francisco, Alameda, and Contra Costa counties. Financed by a $792,000,000 bond issue (1962), construction of the 75-mile system was begun, with part of its track elevated, part underground, and its Bay crossing by tunnel. Federal funding of $200,000,000 and a state sales tax in the affected counties augmented the construction funds. The first part of the system opened in 1972; somewhat later it added service from Daly City to San Francisco and under the Bay with termini at Richmond, Concord, and Fremont, and expansion to all nine Bay Area counties is still being considered.

BARTER, Richard (*fl.* 1849–59), British-born highwayman, went to California during the gold rush and prospected at Rattlesnake Bar (Placer County). From there he derived his nickname, Rattlesnake Dick, when he turned to robbery, for which he was finally shot to death. He is one of the seven bandits described in Joseph Henry Jackson's *Bad Company* (1949).

Bartleson-Bidwell Party, first group of settlers to cross the Sierra (probably through Ebbetts Pass) to California (1841). The party of 69 persons left Westport, Mo. (May 19, 1841), guided by the old trapper Thomas Fitzpatrick and the Northwest missionary Father Pierre-Jean de Smet (who left them at Fort Hall), and reached the ranch of John Marsh on Nov. 4, having abandoned wagons in the mountains. John Bidwell♦ became the actual leader en route. The party also included Josiah Belden,♦ Joseph Chiles,♦ Nicholas Dawson,♦ Pierson B. Redding, R. H. Thomes,♦ and Charles M. Weber.♦

BARTLETT, WASHINGTON (1824–87), a native of Georgia, went to California (1849) from Florida and continued work as a printer, issuing Wierzbicki's *California As It Is and As It May Be* (1849), the first English-language book printed in California. Active in the Democratic party and the Vigilance Committee of 1856, he was mayor of San Francisco (1882–86) and governor of California from inauguration on Jan. 8 to his death on Sept. 12, 1887. He and Washington Allon Bartlett were distant relatives.

BARTLETT, WASHINGTON ALLON (1820?–71), born in Maine, went to California with the navy aboard the *Portsmouth* and was appointed first American *alcalde* of San Francisco (1846) because of his command of Spanish. He renamed the city, which had been called Yerba Buena, San Francisco (Jan. 30, 1847) to forestall Vallejo's plan to create a city of Francisca on the Carquinez strait, and he had San Francisco surveyed by Jasper O'Farrell.♦ His later naval service took him elsewhere and he retired in New York.

BARTLETT, WILLIAM C[HAUNCEY] (1818–1907), after a career as a lawyer in Ohio and as an itinerant preacher in California (1860–65), became a journalist on the San Francisco *Bulletin* (1866–93) and a coeditor with Bret Harte of the *Overland Monthly* (1868–71), later joining the Forest Service. His essays, *A Breeze from the Woods* (1880), quietly witty and philosophic ruminations, elicited caustic comments from Ambrose Bierce.

Baseball, teams were probably first formally organized in San Francisco in 1859 as the Eagles and the Pacifics. In the next decade other teams came into being (e.g. the Wide Awakes of Oakland) and still more clubs were organized in the 1870s (e.g., the San

Francisco Baseball Club). A California League♦ was active from the 1880s, including teams from San Francisco, Oakland, Sacramento, San Jose, Los Angeles, Stockton, Fresno, Santa Cruz, Alameda, and other major cities. It evolved into the Pacific Coast League (1903), with selected clubs from California (Los Angeles, Oakland, Sacramento, and San Francisco) and Portland and Seattle from the Pacific Northwest. The league was altered and enlarged over the years, coming to include Fresno, Vernon, San Diego, Venice, Hollywood, Salt Lake, Tacoma, and Vancouver at various times. The most notable California teams were the Seals of San Francisco, Oaks of Oakland, Solons of Sacramento, Stars of Hollywood, and Angels of Los Angeles. In 1958, major league baseball came to the state with the supplanting of the old San Francisco and Los Angeles teams by the Giants♦ and the Dodgers,♦ followed by the Angels♦ in Anaheim, the Athletics♦ in Oakland, and the Padres♦ in San Diego. A minor California League was continued in other cities.

Basketball, game devised by James Naismith at the International YMCA Training School in Springfield, Mass. (1891), where one of the players, W. O. Black, learned it and then introduced the sport at Stanford University (1893) as part of its physical education program. There he also organized the state's first college team. However, the sport did not quickly become important or common. The first University of California team, at Berkeley, was composed of women students who lost their first game (1892) to Miss Anna Head's neighboring school for girls.

Eventually the sport became a major one with its own playing pavilions and competition in National Collegiate Athletic Association and Pacific Coast Conference championships. In time California college teams won more NCAA basketball titles than teams from any other state. In the 1930s Hank Luisetti of Stanford popularized the one-hand shot; in the 1960s and 70s the UCLA teams of John Wooden dominated the sport, winning ten NCAA championships in twelve years. California's greatest college stars have included Lew Alcindor, Gail Goodrich, Walt Hazzard, Hank Luisetti, Bill Russell, Bill Sharman, and Bill Walton.

Major league professional basketball came to California (1960) when the Minneapolis Lakers of the National Basketball Association moved to Los Angeles. They were followed (1962) by the Philadelphia Warriors, who were first a San Francisco team and then became the Golden State Warriors of Oakland. Less successful were the Rockets of San Diego

(1967–71) in the years before they moved to Houston. Besides the Western Division (later the Pacific Division) of the National Basketball Association, the state has had a short-lived American Basketball League (1961–62) for Los Angeles, Long Beach, and Oakland teams, and the American Basketball Association (1967–76), whose teams have included the Oakland Oaks (1967–69), the Anaheim Amigos, the Los Angeles Stars, and the San Diego Conquistadors. Major players on the state's professional teams have included Rick Barry, Elgin Baylor, Wilt Chamberlain, Gail Goodrich, and Jerry West. (*See also individual entries.*)

Basques in California, originally migrated to coastal areas of California during the era of Spanish dominion. Some were of the highest class, including three governors—Arrillaga, Borica, and de Solá—while others continued their Old World activity of sheepherding. After American occupation many more Basques came from South America, to which they had migrated earlier. Gradually the Basques moved into the state's interior, particularly to the northeastern area around Alturas, where they engaged in two other traditional occupations, mining and fishing, and to Kern County. Basques from the French part of the Pyrenees migrated later, a large number at the end of World War II, and they have settled mainly in San Francisco, Bakersfield, Fresno, and La Puente, east of Los Angeles. Their ethnic restaurants with family-style service survive in several cities and an annual Basque Woolgrowers Picnic is held in Bakersfield on the last Sunday in June.

BASS, CHARLOTTA A. (1874–1969), black civil rights leader. She went from Rhode Island to Los Angeles, where she published and edited the *California Eagle* (1912–51), about which she wrote in *Forty Years* (1960). She was the vice presidential candidate of the Progressive party (1952).

Bass, a spiny-finned fish of many varieties, some living in the ocean, some in fresh water. The only natives are sea bass: *black sea* (or *jewfish* or *giant sea*) *bass,* weighing 200 to 300 pounds, up to 7 feet long, most common around Point Concepcion but found from Baja California to the Farallones and fished commercially with a high catch of 716,000 pounds in 1937; *rock bass,* found along the entire coast, fished commercially with a high catch of 852,000 pounds in 1916; and *kelp bass,* found from San Francisco to the Mexican border but common only below Point Concepcion. *Striped bass,* imported from New Jersey (1879), averaged an annual commercial

catch of 658,000 pounds in the decade before 1935, the year when fishing was restricted to sportsmen; it is found in the Sacramento–San Joaquin Delta, San Francisco Bay, and the adjacent ocean. So-called *black, blue,* and *white sea bass* are actually rockfish or croakers. Three species of freshwater bass—*smallmouth, largemouth,* and *spotted*—were introduced to California, in the 1870s, in 1874, and in 1933, respectively, the *smallmouth* thriving in the Russian River, tributaries of the Sacramento and San Joaquin, and in the Colorado; the *largemouth* in lakes, rivers, ponds, and sloughs throughout the state; and the *spotted* in the Cosumnes River.

Batea, see *Placer mining.*

BATES, BLANCHE (1873–1941), Oregon-born actress who was reared in San Francisco, where she established a successful stage career. She continued it in New York, where she created lead roles in *Madame Butterfly* and *The Girl of the Golden West* by Belasco.♦ She was married to George Creel.♦

Battle of Mussel Slough, see *Mussel Slough.*

Bay, see *Laurel.*

Bay Area, name loosely applied to the general region of San Francisco Bay,♦ including San Francisco, Alameda, Marin, and San Mateo counties, and the nearby portions of Napa, Sonoma, Solano, Contra Costa, and Santa Clara counties. Besides the central Bay it also includes Tomales, Drake's, San Pablo, Richardson, and Suisun bays.

Bay Bridge, see *San Francisco–Oakland Bay Bridge.*

BAYLOR, ELGIN (1934–), basketball player. After graduation from Seattle University as an All-American star and two years with the Minneapolis Lakers he moved with them to Los Angeles (1960), playing with them until retirement because of an injury (1971). As an offensive forward his career average scoring was 27.4 points a game, rising once to 71 points (1960).

BCDC, see *San Francisco Bay Conservation and Development Commission.*

Beach Boys, The, rock singing group of the Los Angeles area whose members include the brothers Brian, Carl, and Dennis Wilson, Mike Love, and Alan Jardine, all but the last born in southern California. Their first record, *Surfin'* (1961), was followed by others with surfing and automobile themes whose lyrics were in accord with the group's striped shirt clothing and general All-American-Boy appearance. Later songs, such as *Good Vibrations,* are more sophisticated.

Beaches, found along much of the length of 1,264 miles of coastal shore, but the cool climate, frequently difficult access, rocky shores, cold water, and common undertow discourage much beach life and water sports in the northern part of the state. The Mendocino coast is an increasingly popular weekend and summer home area, but recreation on beaches is not common that far north.

To the south and in more protected areas, such as Inverness and Stinson Beach, beach life flourishes on good days, as it does on some of the coast of San Mateo and Santa Cruz counties. Monterey Bay is a good beach area but except for Morro Bay and Pismo Beach there is little other beach use between San Francisco and Santa Barbara. From there south through San Diego, beaches are an important part of the geographic and cultural scene.

During the successive real estate booms of southern California, beginning in the 1880s, developers created seaside resorts, ranging from the elegant hostelries of Santa Barbara, such as the Arlington, and of Coronado, to the baroque fantasies of Venice. Most of these places attracted older people, many of whom had retired from business in colder climates and inland terrain.

By the 1920s the motion picture colony of Los Angeles and other newly wealthy people began to build elaborate beachside houses and to create beach clubs on the sand just south of Malibu, which was itself heavily developed a decade later when the Rindge estate was opened to traffic and subdivision. After World War II the increased population of the state included more people who went frequently to the shore for recreation at the augmented sites placed under the custody of the Division of Beaches and Parks. Many of them were young people who found a beach life congenial to their hedonistic enjoyment of the outdoors and their scorn of conventional social distinctions associated with an urban setting.

By the 1960s some youthful enthusiasts had made something of a cult of surfing, a sport introduced to California from Hawaii in 1907 but not popularized until much later. Their way of life was celebrated in the rock music of the Beach Boys and a number of films, beginning with *Beach Party* (1963), that featured their activities, which came to include riding in

dune buggies and outings and parties. At about the same time some of these young people began to stake out certain areas as so-called free beaches, where nudism could be practiced. Despite much controversy some of these have tacitly or explicitly been accepted for their special sort of sunning, playing of frisbee or volley ball, and swimming without clothing.

Still other beaches, mainly in southern California, have become specialized locations for men devoted to calisthenic development of their bodies, and are known as muscle beaches. Plainer, more conventional citizens of more mature years continue to enjoy the beaches in the established ways: fishing for sport from piers and the shore; indulging in such activities as digging clams, mainly at Pismo Beach; and, at the right season, hunting for grunion. Use of the beaches has been threatened by developments ranging from private subdivision to offshore oil drilling, the cause of the disastrous oil spill of 1969. For these reasons the state's voters in 1972 approved a Coastal Preservation Act to ensure the conservation of a major natural resource.

Beach Party films, genre of motion pictures begun (1963) with the one whose title was given to numerous others produced by several companies. They all featured teenage romances on southern California beaches, untroubled by parents, schools, and most of the realities of life.

BEALE, EDWARD FITZGERALD (1822–93), went to California (1846) as a young naval officer aboard the frigate *Congress* under Commodore Stockton. He was immediately detached to serve with the land forces under Stephen W. Kearny, after whose defeat near San Pasqual♦ Beale and Kit Carson sneaked through enemy lines to carry the news to Stockton that led to the sending of a relief force. During and after the war Beale made six overland voyages to carry dispatches to and from Washington, that of 1848 bearing news and samples of the gold discovery. From 1853 to 1856 Beale was both brigadier general of the state militia and U.S. Superintendent for Indian Affairs in California, a post he handled with humanity, creating five small reservations, each for about 2,500 Indians. He also made governmental surveys for a railway between Missouri and California (1853) and for a wagon road from New Mexico to the California border (1857). For the latter project he imported camels♦ for transport over the 1,200-mile route to Fort Tejón, near which he settled on a large ranch. During Lincoln's administration he served as Surveyor General of California and Nevada.

Beale Air Force Base, strategic air command installation established (1948) on the site of an army training camp (est. 1942) near Marysville and named for Gen. Edward F. Beale. A 10-story radar station is to be completed in 1979.

BEAN, WALTON E. (1914–78), historian of California, was professor at the University of California, Berkeley. His books include *Boss Ruef's San Francisco* (1952) and *California, an Interpretive History* (1968).

Beans, major vegetable crop, grown mainly in the Sacramento Valley in the 19th century. Large producing areas have since included the San Joaquin Valley, Orange County, and the Salinas Valley. After the 1920s the Oxnard Plain was the center for lima beans, of which the state is the major national producer. The total bean crop in 1970 was grown on 174,000 acres and was worth $29,326,000.

Bear, two varieties are native to California. The largest, the *grizzly,* distinguished by size, weight, humped shoulder area, and brown fur, was once found in many parts of the state, though not in the high mountains, and was exterminated (the last recorded killing was in 1922) because its ferocity was a threat to explorers, trappers, miners, and the expanding white population. The largest creature of California, it was feared and honored by Indians, most of whom abstained from eating bear meat and who had shamans called bear doctors. In contrast, the Spanish often lassoed bears and staged bear-and-bull fights in plazas or special arenas. Americans commonly hunted the bears. The most famous hunter and tamer of grizzlies was James Capen Adams,♦ and the most famous specimen caught alive was Monarch, displayed by the S.F. *Examiner.*♦ Americans early took the animal as an important symbol, initially for the Bear Flag Revolt, later for the state seal and flag;♦ and Bret Harte also used it symbolically on the cover of the *Overland Monthly.*♦

The *black bear* (basically vegetarian), found mostly in the Sierra Nevada from Siskiyou to Kern County, weighs from 150 to 400 pounds, is over 5 feet long, and has fur of varying color, which causes it to be also called the *brown, cinnamon, yellow,* and *sun bear.* The state university's symbolic mascot, a *golden bear,* however, is generally referred to as a *grizzly.* The *black bear* is actively hunted by sportsmen, who shoot hundreds annually. The frequency of both varieties is indicated by the existence of some 500 place-names incorporating "bear" found throughout the state except in the desert.

Bear Flag Republic, see *Bear Flag Revolt.*

Bear Flag Revolt, as a result of diverse confusing acts in which Frémont was a precipitating force, established a so-called Republic of California for a month (June 10–July 9, 1846) prior to the U.S. conquest of the region as part of the Mexican War. When Frémont returned from Oregon (May 30, 1846), and after Lt. Archibald Gillespie allegedly handed him secret official dispatches as well as bellicose letters from Frémont's father-in-law, Sen. Benton, he championed the cause of American settlers in northern California who feared that Col. José Castro♦ would soon expel them.

On June 10 the Americans, led by Ezekiel Merritt♦ began the revolt by seizing Francisco Arce,♦ near Sonoma, with horses on their way to Castro's militia in Monterey. Then on the 14th, with Frémont's concurrence, Merritt, William B. Ide,♦ Robert Semple,♦ and others captured Col. Mariano G. Vallejo,♦ his brother Salvador, and his brother-in-law Jacob Leese♦ while taking Sonoma, which Castro attempted—and failed—to recapture in the Battle of Olompali.♦ Another incident led to the shooting of the sons of Francisco de Haro.♦

The twenty-four Americans then proclaimed an independent Republic with Ide as president. For their nation William C. Todd,♦ using unbleached cotton, designed a flag with a brownish star toward the upper left corner, a brown grizzly bear facing it (both drawn with blackberry juice), and below them the words CALIFORNIA REPUBLIC in black, with a red stripe (made of a piece of flannel) at the bottom. The banner was modified (1911) when the state's legislature adopted it as the official state flag.♦ In the brief period of its original use, the flag flew over Sonoma, to which Frémont had come from New Helvetia to aid the Americans and where he held his command.

Upon learning on July 9 that the U.S. and Mexico were at war and that Commodore Sloat had occupied Monterey (July 7), Frémont and his California Battalion♦ enlisted under Sloat's command and their Republic of California ceased to exist. The battalion's projected conquest of California was then completed as part of the Mexican War.♦

Bear River, begins at man-made Lake Spaulding north of Emigrant Gap in the Sierra, flows southwest into Camp Far West Reservoir, and then farther southwest to join the Feather River about 13 miles south of Yuba City. The name derives from an incident in which a member of Josiah Gregg's exploring party (1850) was mauled by a grizzly. There are six other rivers with the same name in the state. The next largest rises 30 miles southwest of Lake Tahoe in Amador County and flows 16 miles southwest into the North Fork of the Mokelumne River.

BEASLEY, DELILAH LEONTIUM (1866?–1934), went to Oakland (1909) from her native Ohio and became a journalist, women's rights leader, and author of a history of her people, *The Negro Trail Blazers of California* (1919).

Beat movement, bohemian artists' rebellious opposition to the established patterns of society, came into being in San Francisco and New York City about 1956. The word "Beat" was taken to express both exhaustion or weariness with the conventional world and a sense of beatification. The followers of the movement were assumed to achieve a kind of blissful illumination, aided by drink and drugs, upon dissociating themselves from the crass and commercial corruption of the Establishment whose manners and mores they excoriated. In its most seriously expressive manifestation it was largely a literary movement marked by emphasis on selfhood, personal association, and mysticism, which were expounded in a style employing now "hip" language, now Buddhist terminology. Less creative followers, hangers-on at coffeehouses who affected the dress and lifestyle of more serious leaders, were satirically called "Beatniks" by Herb Caen. The major literary figures associated to a greater or lesser degree with the so-called San Francisco Renaissance♦ included poets Allen Ginsberg,♦ Gregory Corso, and their local publisher, Lawrence Ferlinghetti,♦ and the novelist Jack Kerouac.♦ Older writers of the region who were related to the movement included Henry Miller♦ and Kenneth Rexroth.♦

Beaver, largest of U.S. rodents, with a 30-inch-long body and a 16-inch flat, powerful tail and webbed feet, weighs upwards of 40 pounds, with a golden brown fur that accounts for the name of the most common California species, *golden beaver.* An amphibious animal, it is found mainly along the San Joaquin and Sacramento rivers and their tributaries from sea level to 300 feet, although specimens have been seen up to a 1,000-foot elevation. It builds stick and mud dams, creating ponds where it may have a safe house and a route to transport willow saplings and larger bark for food and building. These dams in irrigation ditches, rivers, and sloughs are about 30 inches high and 50 feet long and have caused the beaver to be hunted because of the harm it does to fence posts, fruit trees, and drainage canals, with consequent flooding of agricultural land. From the earliest days of American exploration the beaver has been trapped for its pelt. In the West trapping began with such pioneers as Jedediah Smith, Pattie, Yount, and Wolfskill, although for a time in the 20th century they were entirely protected. Variant species include the *Shasta beaver,* in the drainages of the Pit and Klamath rivers, and the *Sonora beaver,* along the lower Colorado River.

BEBAN, GARY (1946–), football player born in Redwood City, was a star quarterback of UCLA (1964–67), who as a sophomore led his team to a Rose Bowl victory over Michigan State (1966). He was named an All-American quarterback (1966–67) and awarded the Heisman Trophy as the outstanding college football player of the year (1967).

BECHDOLDT, FREDERICK [RITCHIE] (1874–1950), Pennsylvania-born writer, after graduation from the University of Washington and a brief experience of the Klondike gold rush, settled in California as a newspaperman. He wrote cowboy stories (e.g. *When the West Was Young,* 1922), collaborated with James Hopper on *9009* (1908), a novel of prison life, and was a member of the Carmel Bohemian colony.

BECHTEL, STEPHEN D[AVISON] (1900–), Indiana-born engineer and constructor. After education at the University of California he entered the general construction business with his father (1919), becoming president of W. A. Bechtel Co. in 1936. He was one of the builders of Hoover Dam and a major builder of ships during World War II. His large-scale construction activities extend worldwide.

BECKET, WELTON [DAVID] (1902–69), Los Angeles architect whose firm designed the Music Center and Memorial Sports Arena of that city, created a master plan for UCLA, and was a pioneer in the design of large shopping centers.

BECKWOURTH, JAMES P[IERSON] (1798–c. 1867), Virginia-born hunter, adventurer, and mountain man in the Rocky Mts. who was part of the Ashley-Henry fur-trapping and trading expedition up the

Missouri River (1823), probably serving as a horse wrangler. Later he lived easily among the Crow and other Indian tribes in part because as a mulatto he did not appear entirely alien. In 1844 he was in California and fought against Micheltorena's forces. Returning late in the gold rush in 1851, he discovered the northern Sierra Nevada pass (in easternmost Plumas County) named for him. Over it that year he took young Ina Coolbrith on his saddle as he guided her family party to safety. His experiences were told "from his own dictation" by T. D. Bonner in a book entitled *Life and Adventures* (1856).

Bee newspapers, chain of journals consisting of the Sacramento *Bee* (1857–), Modesto *Bee* (1884–), and Fresno *Bee* (1922–). The Sacramento paper was founded by James McClatchey (1824–83), who had been on the *New-York Tribune* staff before going to California (1849). He immediately took an independent, reform-minded stand with an exposé of the handling of government tax funds. He championed squatters' rights in the gold country, called for regulation of hydraulic mining, and opposed private ownership of Yosemite lands. After his death his sons, C. K.♦ and Valentine Stuart, bought the one-third interest of John F. Sheehan and made the original paper and its two affiliates leading voices in the Central Valley. As editor (1883–1936), C. K. was liberal and progressive, supporting Hiram Johnson for governor (1910) and F. D. Roosevelt for President (1932). Although he called for suppression of the I.W.W. after the Wheatland Riot,♦ he condemned employers for creating conditions that encouraged the union's growth. The Sacramento *Bee* received a Pulitzer Prize (1935) for exposés of political corruption in Nevada, and all three journals continue to be highly regarded for their fine standards. The newspapers early added a radio broadcasting chain which includes a station in Reno. After C. K.'s death his daughter Eleanor succeeded him as owner and publisher, and his grandson and namesake is editor of the Sacramento *Bee*.

BEECHEY, Frederick William (1796–1856), commander of the British exploring vessel *Blossom,* who visited San Francisco Bay in 1826 and 1827–28. His important chart of the Bay named Blossom Rock and, accidentally but permanently, reversed Ayala's names for Alcatraz and Yerba Buena islands. He described California in his *Narrative of a Voyage to the Pacific* (2 vols., 1831). His brother, Richard Brydges Beechey (1809–95), a midshipman on the *Blossom,* painted fine watercolors of the region.

Beekeeping, see *Honey*.

Beer, see *Breweries*.

Behavioral Sciences, Center for Advanced Study in, see *Center for Advanced Study in the Behavioral Sciences*.

Bel Air, see *Beverly Hills*.

BELASCO, David (1853–1931), San Francisco-born actor, dramatist, and producer, began his career in his twenties by acting in Virginia City, managing the theater of Tom Maguire♦ and Lucky Baldwin's Academy of Music in San Francisco, tinkering with plays to suit stars, and making a character of himself by wearing a clerical collar in honor of the Catholic priests who gave him his early education. In New York he became famous for developing David Warfield♦ and other actors, for creating realistic stage settings, and for writing popular plays, including *Hearts of Oak* (1879) with James A. Herne; *Lord Chumley* (1888) with Henry C. DeMille; *The Heart of Maryland* (1895); *Madame Butterfly* (1900) with James A. Long; and *The Girl of the Golden West*♦ (1905), the last two adapted by Puccini for operas, but with stage roles originally created by Blanche Bates.♦

BELCHER, Edward (1799–1877), British naval officer, first visited California on the expedition of Capt. F. W. Beechey♦ (1826), returning (1836–37, 1839) in command of a surveying expedition which also studied local flora and fauna. Accounts based on the 1839 voyage include his own *Narrative of a Voyage Round the World* (2 vols., 1843).

BELDEN, Josiah (1815–92), Connecticut-born, went to California with the Bartleson and Bidwell Party, the first to travel overland (1841). In Monterey he was named *alcalde* during the brief time that Commodore Thomas ap Catesby Jones occupied the town (1842). He later became a naturalized Mexican but after American occupation was elected the first mayor of San Jose (1850).

Belgians in California, date back to Victor Janssens of the Híjar♦ and Padres colony; more arrived during the gold rush, although in small numbers, possibly through a Belgian branch of a French mining expeditionary company. Few made permanent settlement, and immigration in subsequent periods was small. Impressions of the gold rush occur in the paintings of Theodore T'Scharner (1826–1900), a visitor (1850–53); the popular novel *Het Goudland* (1862, translated as *The Boys of the Sierra,* 1883) by Hendrick Conscience, who never visited California; and *Vie et Aventures d'un Enfant de l'Ardenne,* by J. N. Perlot, who spent some years in the mines.

BELL, HORACE (1830–1918), went from his native Indiana to California in the gold rush, moved to Los Angeles (1852), drifted into the filibustering adventures of William Walker, and became a Union scout or ranger in the Civil War before returning to Los Angeles in 1866. There he became a lawyer and for a time was the vigorous editor of a prickly paper properly named *Porcupine.* He is best remembered for his salty memoir, *Reminiscences of a Ranger* (1881). *On the Old West Coast* (1930) is a posthumous collection.

BELL, JAMES MADISON (1826–1902), Ohio-born advocate of civil rights for his fellow blacks and a friend and abettor of the abolitionist leader John Brown. While resident in San Francisco (1860–65) he wrote "The Progress of Liberty" (1866), a poem celebrating the Emancipation Proclamation.

BELL, PHILIP ALEXANDER (1809–89), went from his native New York to San Francisco to continue his journalistic work for the civil rights of his fellow blacks. In San Francisco he founded and edited *Pacific Appeal* (1862–64) and the *Elevator* (1865–89), which were merged after his death to become the *Pacific Coast Appeal and San Francisco Elevator.*

Bellflower, suburb of Los Angeles southeast of the city, founded (1906) in a dairy and orchard area and named for the kind of apples grown there. It has developed into a residential and metropolitan region, among the fifty most populous in the state. In 1970 it had 51,454 people.

Belvedere, small island off Tiburon in Richardson Bay, long the site of fine summer homes. It was augmented by land fill that created the Belvedere Lagoon (1920–40) and became a year-round residential area.

BENDER, ALBERT M[AURICE] (1866–1941), Irish-born philanthropist and patron of the arts in San Francisco to which he went (1883) and where he carried on an insurance business. He aided artists, authors, photographers (he sponsored Ansel Adams' first prints), musicians, and fine printers, contributed to all the rare book libraries of the area,

and was a founder of The Book Club of California. Stanford University and Mills College have rare book rooms named for him.

Benicia, city on the north shore of Carquinez Strait, founded (1847) by Robert Semple and Thomas Larkin on land deeded to them by Gen. Vallejo. First named Francisca for the General's wife, it was soon given her second name because the rival Yerba Buena had meanwhile assumed the name San Francisco. It did not develop into the great port that was hoped for but did become a major stopping place on the way to the mines and was briefly the state's capital (1853–54). Its arsenal (1851) made it an important army ordnance base, and it became a significant coaling and repair base for Sacramento River boats. Benicia was also the site of the state's first Protestant church and its first Masonic Hall, of the forerunner of Mills College, of the cemetery where Doña María Concepción Argüello was buried, of the first bouts of the prizefighter John C. Heenan, and of some of Jack London's exploits as an oyster pirate. Its port, industries, oil refinery, and tourist trade support the present population, 8,783 in 1970.

Benicia Boy, The, see *Heenan, John.*

BENJAMIN, ROBERT CHARLES O'HARA (1855–1900), native of the British West Indies who became a leading black attorney and author in San Francisco. He later practiced in Los Angeles, where he was also a newspaper editor. His writings include *Don't* (1891), an etiquette book for girls; *Life of Toussaint L'Ouverture* (1888); and *Africa, the Hope of the Negro.* He moved to Kentucky, where he was murdered.

BENNY, JACK (1894–1974), Illinois-born comedian, after a career in vaudeville, radio, and motion pictures, became an established television entertainer, resident in California for more than 40 years. His comedy was constructed to display his persona as a niggardly, pusillanimous, and put-upon character, always living through situations which depended upon his carefully timed slow responses to verbal insults.

BENTON, JOSEPH AUGUSTINE (1815–92), descendant of John Eliot, the 17th-century "Apostle to the Indians" of New England, and a Yale alumnus, went to California in 1849. There he founded the First Congregational Church. He became a leading California preacher, a hymnologist, and a missionary to outlying regions. He was also a founder of the

College of California (forerunner of the state university), and a professor at the Pacific Theological Seminary, now the Pacific School of Religion.

BERGERON, VICTOR (1903–), California-born restaurateur who expanded his first place, Hinky Dink's, founded in Oakland (1934), into Trader Vic's (1938), the original of a chain of restaurants in major cities of the U.S. and overseas. They emphasize his own variations of South Pacific cuisine elegantly served in an appropriate ambience.

BERINGER, FREDERICK (1840–1901), and JACOB L. (1845–1915), German-born vintners who emigrated to the U.S. and near St. Helena founded their winery (1876), naming it Los Hermanos (The Brothers). Their descendants incorporated the winery as Beringer Brothers (1914) and continued to run it as a family enterprise until it was sold to a large non-California corporation (1971).

BERKELEY, BUSBY [WILLIAM BERKELEY ENOS], (1895–1976), Los Angeles-born choreographer of spectacular Hollywood song-and-dance films of the 1930s which ingeniously presented chorus girls going through routines in lavish, many-tiered, or multi-faceted settings. He photographed them from a great variety of camera angles and at sufficient distances to create large, divergent, kaleidoscopic patterns.

Berkeley, city in Alameda County. It was founded (1866) on part of the former *rancho* of José Domingo Peralta as the site for the new University of California.◆ The name was selected because Irish Bishop George Berkeley wrote, "Westward the course of empire takes its way," when he contemplated founding a college in the western hemisphere. Although best known for the University, the city has other educational institutions, such as the Pacific School of Religion.◆ It supports a good deal of light industry on the flatlands along the San Francisco Bay shore.

Above the residential districts that climb up the steep hills lies a chain of regional parks stretching over 8200 acres, the one directly behind the city being named for Charles Lee Tilden,◆ who was instrumental in bringing them into being. On the lower levels of the city where shops and small factories are located there are no clear demarcation lines between Oakland on Berkeley's south and Albany on its north.

But the city has a definite character of its own,

even though it has grown greatly since World War II and most of it was newly built after the disastrous fire of Sept. 1923 that swept over the entire northeast residential region. In large part this character derives from the city's major economic and cultural force, the University.

The University, physically at the city's center with its large campus, handsomely landscaped by Thomas D. Church, lying athwart major east-west and north-south axes, is central to the community and divides it into more or less separate regions. Directly outside Sather Gate on its south is Telegraph Ave., site of shops catering to students' changing cultural interests, home of "street people" with their own lifestyles, and location in the 1960s of demonstrations and riots that began with the Free Speech Movement (1964) and culminated (1969) in an attack on the so-called People's Park, a large empty lot that was reserved for a future University housing project.

During that era Berkeley was the soil more than the seed for new radical behavior, sexual experimentation, drug culture, mysticism and meditation, and the most revolutionary of all groups, the Symbionese Liberation Army.◆ The hill area, which remained relatively untouched by those movements, is the site of homes of faculty members and other established persons, many of whom commute to work in San Francisco or Oakland. On the flatlands to the west lie less elegant residential areas and commercial sections, terminating at the bayside's Yacht Harbor and Aquatic Park and a large addition of filled land in the Bay itself.

Natives of Berkeley include Elmer Bischoff, Hazel Hotchkiss, Billy Martin, and John Hudson Thomas. Distinguished residents of the past have included Charles Keeler, a poet; Bernard Maybeck, Julia Morgan, and William Wurster, architects whose work is particularly prized in the city; Stitt Wilson, its one-time Socialist mayor; August Vollmer, a developer of a distinguished police department; Chester Rowell, a newspaper editor; and many professors, including several Nobel Prize winners.

The University itself is often referred to simply as Berkeley, but it has cast distinction on the city's name too, in that one of the trans-uranium elements discovered at the Lawrence Laboratory was named "Berkelium."

The population of the city in 1970 was 116,716. With about one-quarter of its residents black, the city early instituted a voluntary and successful scheme of busing children to achieve integration in its public schools.

Berkeley Barb (1965–), anti-Establishment, counterculture weekly appealing to radical New Left and avant-garde views, student protest, bohemianism, sexual freedom, drug culture, and general opposition to accepted U.S. patterns. Its publisher, Max Scherr, had a dispute with his staff (called The Red Mountain Tribe) that led to his selling the journal (1969) and their issuing an opposition paper, *The Berkeley Tribe,* with similar writers and policy and explicitly erotic advertisements, but it did not last, and Scherr regained his journal (1970) without competition.

BERNAL, name of a prominent early California family whose founder was Juan Francisco Bernal (1737?–1802), a soldier with Anza.♦ Family holdings included a *rancho* of 4,400 acres south of San Francisco, partly included in the modern Bernal Heights. Other family members settled in Livermore Valley and around San Jose in the Santa Clara Valley, where they held very large *ranchos.* They married into the Moraga, Peralta, and Soberanes families.

BERNARD Duhaut-Cilly, August, see *Duhaut-Cilly, Auguste Bernard.*

Berries, found wild in many varieties and many areas of California and served as part of the diet of Indians. They were first cultivated by the mission fathers, who raised *raspberries* and *strawberries.* After the gold rush commercial growers added *blackberries.* A major California contribution to berry culture came in 1882 when James H. Logan, a lawyer of Santa Cruz, created the *loganberry* by crossing the *Pacific Slope wild blackberry* and the *raspberry,* marketing it in the next decade. Later Luther Burbank developed other variants. The *Olallieberry,* a cross of two kinds of *blackberry,* was created in Oregon (1950) but is widely grown in California from Mendocino and Sonoma counties south along the coast and in the Central Valley. The large commercial growth of *strawberries* occurred when the so-called *banner* was first commercially grown for plants in Shasta County and for fruit in the Pajaro Valley (1904). About half of the state's crop now comes from the Watsonville area, and the Sacramento, Fresno, and Santa Clara Valley regions are also important. The many hybridized types developed from the *banner* include the popular *Shasta* and *Lassen.* Before America entered World War II about 5,000 acres were planted with *strawberries,* but the acreage dropped to 1,000 upon internment of the Japanese, who were then the major field laborers. Fresh-freezing

techniques developed in the 1950s helped increase growing acreage to 22,000 by 1956. In 1970 California produced about 40% of the nation's crop. California also raises most of the *boysenberries* in the U.S. *Blueberries,* grown along the coast north of San Francisco to Oregon, have become a major fruit since commercial growing began in the 1930s.

BERRYESSA, prominent early California family whose founder, Nicolas Antonio (1761–1804), went north with Anza♦ (1776). He married a member of the Peralta family and settled in San Jose. Of their eleven children, María Gabriella married Francisco María Castro, a member of another prominent family. The Berryessas acquired—and lost—large landholdings in the present counties of Santa Clara, Napa, Alameda, and Sonoma. The family is commemorated by the place-names for a valley and an artificial lake in Napa County and a creek in Alameda County. Some members of the family spelled their name Berryesa or Berreyesa.

Bethany Bible College, coeducational religious institution founded (1919) by the Assemblies of God, located in the Santa Cruz Mts.

BETZ, Pauline (1919–), tennis player from Los Angeles who was four times the U.S. women's singles champion (1942–44, 1946) and once the British champion (1946).

Beverly Hillbillies, The, television comedy series (1962–71) about a family of uncouth Ozark mountaineers who make a fortune from discovery of oil on their land and move to Los Angeles where they have fantastic adventures.

Beverly Hills, independent municipality some dozen miles west of downtown Los Angeles but entirely surrounded by that city. Established (1906) by a real estate subdivider from Beverly Farms, Mass., it became a sequestered resort when its lavish Beverly Hills Hotel was built (1912), and even as late as 1920 it had only 674 residents. With the growth of the motion picture industry the town's broad tree-lined streets and spacious hilltop sites, lying at the foot of the Santa Monica Mts., became the accepted location for film stars' mansions, and the hotel became, as it has remained, a chic rendezvous as well as a hostelry convenient to the studios and expanded city. The town's public gardens and the sweeping front lawns of the stylish homes give its residential area a special elegance. This atmosphere carries over to the shopping district, which is studded with boutiques for luxury goods, attractive restaurants, art galleries, large, exclusive stores, and fine hotels. Nearby lies Bel Air, a more secluded area for estates, and not far from it is the Los Angeles campus of the University of California and its town of Westwood. The population of Beverly Hills in 1970 was 33,416.

BIDWELL, JOHN (1819–1900), New York-born resident of Missouri, where he heard from one of the Rubidoux brothers of the attractions of California. Accordingly, he organized the first overland party (1841), nominally captained by John Bartleson,◆ and including Josiah Belden, Joseph Chiles, and Nicholas Dawson, but with Bidwell in command. After a terrible trek of 24 weeks during which they had to eat their mules, they arrived in November at the ranch of John Marsh. Bidwell worked for John A. Sutter for several years, was naturalized as a Mexican citizen, received a large land grant, and, with Sutter, defended Micheltorena in the revolt of 1844. In 1846 he drew up the resolution of independence from Mexico and became a lieutenant in Frémont's California Battalion. He discovered gold on the Feather River, but in 1849 his interests turned to agriculture. He acquired the 22,000-acre ranch in Chico◆ and cultivated it for the rest of his life. Though appointed a general of the state militia by Gov. Stanford, his career was more political than martial. He became a Congressman (1865–67), ran unsuccessfully three times for the governorship on Republican, Independent, and Prohibition tickets, and was the Prohibition party's nominee for President (1892). *A Journey to California in 1841* (1843?) was reprinted in his *Addresses, Reminiscences, Etc.* (1907) with other accounts of his historic trek. The site of his discovery of gold became Bidwell's Bar, the mining town which was buried under water when Oroville Dam was built. He is memorialized in other sites, including the State Park in Butte County—located on land given by his wife, Annie—a lake in Lassen County, and a peak and a fort in Modoc County.

BIERCE, AMBROSE [GWINETT] (1842–1914?), born in Ohio, reared in Indiana, at 18 enlisted in the Union Army, and, though once wounded, fought through the whole Civil War, after which he was sent to San Francisco on an army assignment. There began his literary career as a writer for *The Golden Era,* the *News Letter,* and the *Overland Monthly.* During his residence in England and France (1872–75) he wrote for *Fun* and *Figaro,* edited two issues of *The Lantern,* a journal sub-

sidized by the exiled Empress Eugénie, and published, under the pseudonym Dod Grile, three books collecting vitriolic sketches and witticisms, *The Fiend's Delight* (1873), *Nuggets and Dust Panned Out in California* (1873), and *Cobwebs from an Empty Skull* (1874).

On returning to San Francisco he became an Associate Editor of *The Argonaut* and Editor of the *Wasp,* for which he wrote a satirical column, "Prattle," continued in the San Francisco *Examiner,* he having become a Hearst staff writer in 1887. His trenchant commentary on local affairs and satirical wit in prose and verse made him a local literary dictator and the head of a coterie which included George Sterling and Herman Schefauer. His own literary works were greatly admired too. First among them was *Tales of Soldiers and Civilians* (1892; entitled *In the Midst of Life* in England), horror stories, somewhat in the vein of Poe, marked by sardonic humor, morbidity, and irony, realistic treatment of intense emotional states, and ingenuity in surprise endings.

Other works included *The Monk and the Hangman's Daughter* (1892), an adaptation with a collaborator of a German gothic romance; *Black Beetles in Amber* (1892), satirical verses, frequently attacking prominent local people; and *Can Such Things Be?* (1893), another collection of stories, marked by the same characteristics that distinguished the earlier tales and like them treating battlefield situations in the Civil War and episodes on the California frontier, bearing such titles as "My Favorite Murder," "The Realm of the Unreal," and "Bodies of the Dead."

In 1896 Hearst sent Bierce to Washington to write against Collis Huntington's Funding Bill for the Central and Southern Pacific Railroads and, although he returned to San Francisco, after 1900 his permanent residence was Washington. During his later years he issued more books, including *Fantastic Fables* (1899), an Aesop-like collection on contemporary politics and social and economic situations; *Shapes of Clay* (1903), a collection of poems; *The Cynic's Word Book* (1906; retitled *The Devil's Dictionary,* 1911), a collection of bitter, pessimistic, ironic definitions of words (e.g. "Edible, *adj.* Good to eat, and wholesome to digest, as a worm to a toad, a toad to a snake, a snake to a pig, a pig to a man, and a man to a worm"); *The Shadow on the Dial* (1909), essays expressing disillusionment with the modern world; and *Write It Right* (1909), a lively treatment of literary expression in keeping with the reputation he enjoyed as a great stylist.

In his last years he busied himself editing his old newspaper contributions and his books into a great twelve-volume *Collected Works* (1909–12). Thoroughly misanthropic, after a tour of Civil War battlefields, he went, he said, to seek "the good, kind darkness," disappearing over the border into war-torn Mexico and probably finding his sought-after death on a Mexican battlefield.

BIERSTADT, ALBERT (1830–1902), German-born landscape painter, brought to the U.S. as a child and reared here. He returned to his native Düsseldorf to study painting. He came back to the U.S. (1857), and the next year joined an overland military surveying expedition which took him to the Far West and provided inspiration for his grandiloquent canvases of the Rocky Mts. and other vast subjects painted in the next few years. In 1863 he made his first visit to California; he also had a studio in San Francisco during the early 1870s. Thus he knew the region which provided him with settings for large landscapes, many of them depicting Yosemite, Lake Tahoe, the Sierra Nevada, great redwood forests, and even "The Settlement of California by Junipero Serra," commissioned for the Capitol in Washington, D.C.

Big Basin, the first State Park of redwoods (est. 1902), located northwest of Santa Cruz. A. P. Hill♦ was instrumental in its establishment.

Big Bear Lake, seven-mile-long reservoir in the San Bernardino National Forest, a popular resort area. Its name derives from the nearby natural Bear Lake (since disappeared) which Benjamin D. Wilson discovered (1845) while on a search for marauding Indians. Gold was found there in 1860.

Big Four, The, name popularly given to Charles Crocker,♦ Mark Hopkins,♦ Collis P. Huntington,♦ and Leland Stanford,♦ the heads of the Central Pacific Railroad,♦ and later of the Southern Pacific Railroad,♦ who referred to themselves simply as "the associates." Their manager, David D. Colton,♦ liked to speak of "we five," but newspapers satirically referred to "the Big Four and a Half."

Big Game, popular name given to the annual football game between Stanford University and the University of California, Berkeley. The first game was played in San Francisco (1892), but since 1904 the site has been Stanford and Berkeley in alternate years. Because of numerous injuries in the rough play, American football was abandoned (1906–15)

and rugby was substituted until revised rules made the American style acceptable again. The symbolic Axe of Stanford is awarded to the winner for the year. Perhaps the most sensational competitors were California's "Wonder Teams."♦

Big Knife, The, play by Clifford Odets,♦ produced (1949) and filmed with his script (1955). It is about an actor who wants to break away from Hollywood to be an artist again but is blackmailed into signing a long-term film contract because he had let another person take the blame for an auto accident he had caused in which a child had been killed.

Big Oak Flat, town in Tuolumne County, founded by James Savage♦ (1850), explorer of nearby Yosemite Valley. It was first named Savage Diggings but renamed for a large tree in the center of town that was undermined by gold seekers.

Big Pine, town south of Bishop in Inyo County, near which is located the 28,000-acre Bristlecone Pine Forest of ancient, twisted trees, part of Inyo National Forest.

Big Sleep, The, detective novel by Raymond Chandler,♦ published in 1939, presented for the first time his tough, cynical detective hero, Philip Marlowe. The complicated and violent case on which Marlowe works is set in Los Angeles. The film version (1946), with additional dialogue by William Faulkner, starred Humphrey Bogart and Lauren Bacall.

Big Sur, coastal region 25 miles south of Carmel, named for *El Rio Grande del Sur* ("The Big River of the South"), was once a *rancho* granted to Juan B. Alvarado (1834). Noted for its spectacular scenic setting, it is an area of great cliffs plunging to the ocean and, behind them, of rugged mountains in the Los Padres National Forest with steep canyons in which grow the southernmost of the redwoods. Besides having a State Park, the area has a rustic settlement for the bohemian and artistic colony that grew up there after Carmel became too developed as a conventional community. More recently it too has become a site for restaurants and lodging places. Robinson Jeffers wrote about the region, the author Henry Miller long lived there, Jack Kerouac wrote *Big Sur,* a novel about a Beat leader settling there, Joan Baez has organized an annual folk festival, "Celebration at Big Sur," and the psychological Esalen Institute♦ has its headquarters there. Some 100,000 acres of the Ventana National

Forest near Big Sur were burned in a forest fire (1977).

BIGGERS, EARL DERR (1884–1933), Ohio-born novelist whose early works combined mystery and romance in a very successful blend for his first work, *Seven Keys to Baldpate* (1913), which was popular not only as a book but as a long-run Broadway play when adapted by George M. Cohan. After 1923 he lived in Pasadena where he created the six novels by which he is probably best remembered, all featuring Charlie Chan, a quiet, shrewd, amiable Chinese-American detective from Hawaii, who expressed himself in pseudo-Oriental aphorisms.

BIGLER, JOHN (1805–71), 3rd governor of the state (1852–56), who went (1849) from his native Pennsylvania, where he had been a printer and lawyer, to Sacramento, where his wife was the first American woman. Bigler was immediately elected to the Assembly and as a popular Democrat soon was elected governor, but his failure to cope with financial problems kept him from being elected to a third term. President Buchanan later appointed him Minister to Chile. Admiring Democrats named (1854) in his honor the lake now known as Tahoe, but in part because of his secessionist views the Indian name came into use during the Civil War, even though the legislature did not make the change official until 1945.

BILLINGS, FREDERICK (1823–90), a lawyer, went to San Francisco (1849) from his native Vermont and established there a partnership with Henry W. Halleck♦ and Archibald Peachy which became the state's leading law firm. After service as California's Attorney General, he returned to Vermont (1864). He was also the builder and president of the Northern Pacific Railroad, and Billings, Montana, located on the railroad line, is named for him.

BILLINGS, WARREN K., see *Mooney, Tom.*

BILLINGTON, RAY ALLEN (1903–), Michigan-born historian of the Far West. After an academic career at Northwestern University, he became a senior research associate at the Huntington Library (1963). His books include *Westward Expansion* (1949), *The Far Western Frontier* (1956), and *Frederick Jackson Turner* (1973).

BIRCH, JOHN, see *John Birch Society.*

Birch, see *Alder.*

BIRD, ROSE [ELIZABETH] (1936–), Arizona-born lawyer who, after receiving her law degree from the University of California, Berkeley, served in the public defender's office of Santa Clara County. Gov. Edmund G. Brown, Jr., appointed her Secretary of Agriculture and Services (1975) and then Chief Justice of the state's Supreme Court.

Birdman of Alcatraz, see *Stroud, Robert.*

Birds, The, film directed and produced by Alfred Hitchcock. Set at Bodega Bay, it presents a spoiled San Francisco society girl and other people terrorized by inexplicable attacks of flocks of birds.

BISCHOFF, ELMER (1916–), Berkeley-born painter who studied art at the University of California, Berkeley, where he later became a member of the faculty after having taught at the California School of Fine Arts. Since the 1950s his paintings have depicted representational figures in atmospheric spaces.

BIXBY, prominent southern California family, whose first members to leave their native Maine were brothers, Llewellyn and Amasa (1851) and Jotham (1852), all in their twenties. Llewellyn returned east and with his cousins Benjamin Flint and Dr. Thomas Flint drove nearly 2,000 sheep from Illinois to San Gabriel, while Jotham, after mining and farming in the Mother Lode area, joined Llewellyn, the Flints, and W. W. Hollister♦ in sheep ranching in Monterey County. Llewellyn and Jotham were joined (1871) by another cousin, John Bixby, and the three men married three Hathaway sisters from Maine; when Llewellyn's wife died, he married a fourth Hathaway, her youngest sister.

The Bixbys acquired extensive ranch lands in Monterey, Los Angeles, San Luis Obispo, and Orange counties, in part with I. W. Hellman,♦ and even in the early 20th century they were the largest landholders in the Los Angeles area. To their basic sheep ranching they added horses and cattle, and the family's fortune was further enhanced by the discovery of oil on their properties, particularly at Signal Hill,♦ and by the increased value of their real estate.

Numerous descendants of the Bixbys still reside in southern California and are still involved in ranching and land development. Two of their ancestral dwellings, the adobe ranch houses of Los

Alamitos and Los Cerritos in Long Beach, are historic sites open to the public.

Family background and early California history have been recorded in *Adobe Days* (1925) by Sarah Bixby Smith (1871–1935), Llewellyn's daughter, and by her cousin, Susanna Bryant Dakin (1905–66), the author of biographies of Hugo Reid (1939) and William Hartnell (1949) and works on other early California subjects.

BLACK, WINIFRED SWEET (1863–1936), born in Wisconsin, in 1890 went to San Francisco and got a job with the *Examiner,* beginning a career as a reporter, mainly for William Randolph Hearst, under the pseudonym of Annie Laurie. Her work was marked by sentimental stories and sensational exposés.

Black Bart, alias of Charles E. Bolton, originally Charles Boles (1830?–88?), a legendary figure who 28 times robbed Wells, Fargo stagecoaches (1875–83). Disguised by a flour-sack mask and armed with a shotgun, he always commanded the driver to "Throw down the box." He sometimes left poems for his victims signed "Black Bart P08" such as: I've labored long and hard for bread / For honor and for riches / But on my corns too long you've trod, / You fine-haired sons of bitches.

Apprehended, he served a five-year sentence in San Quentin, then disappeared.

Black Butte Reservoir, spanning the boundary of Tehama and Glenn counties, formed (1963) by a dam built by the army engineers. Another Black Butte lies southwest of Mt. Shasta.

Black Panther party, militant organization of blacks founded in Oakland (1966) by Bobby Seale♦ and Huey Newton,♦ called Chairman and Minister of Defense, respectively. They were influenced by the writings of Malcolm X, Frantz Fanon, Mao, Che Guevara, and Marxism in general. Their ten-point program called for black people to determine their own destiny; "an end to robbery by the white man"; an end to "police brutality"; freedom for jailed blacks; trials of blacks only by other blacks; exemption from military service; and better food, housing, and education. To help realize those goals they wore uniforms and carried rifles and legal texts as they trailed police. The party attracted many adherents, including Eldridge Cleaver♦ as Minister of Information. A fracas (1967) in which an Oakland police officer was killed and Newton wounded led to the latter being jailed and a "Free Huey" cam-

paign which ended when his manslaughter conviction was reversed. He later fled to Cuba (1974–77) when accused of murder in another shooting. The Panthers made a coalition with the Peace and Freedom party to gain their ends politically, but Cleaver, their candidate for President of the U.S., was jailed and then escaped to become an expatriate (1968–75). He dropped out of the Panthers, who became less militant as the group undertook such programs as feeding schoolchildren. Some of its objectives were realized when it entered upon active aid to the Democratic party in Oakland.

Black Point, name of two sites on San Francisco Bay: Fort Mason♦ and the mouth of the Petaluma River (Marin County), presumably named for James Black, a Scottish sailor who arrived in 1832. At the former site Frémont had a home from which he was dispossessed by federal order when the land was wanted for a military reservation.

Blacks in California, probably first arrived with Spanish exploring parties. Persons of mixed blood (mulattoes), free and slave, are mentioned in founding records of missions and pueblos. Almost half the founding adults of Los Angeles were all or partly black, and it is claimed that if children are counted, the majority of the pueblo's founders were black.

The earliest black settlers from the U.S. included John Gibson, a sailor who came to Monterey in 1796, and one Bob, who jumped ship (1816) with Thomas Doak. During the Spanish period some Mexicans of black ancestry achieved distinction, notably Francisco Reyes, *alcalde* of Los Angeles in 1794. In the late Mexican period some persons of black heritage also occupied important positions, including a rich San Francisco civic leader, W. A. Leidesdorff; frontiersman James Beckwourth; and the last governor of the regime, Pío Pico.

Blacks were also involved in early U.S. migration and in battles that led to the U.S. conquest. The early years of American government were marked by political struggles over slavery and the possible exclusion of free Negroes. Even though the state Constitution prohibited slavery, only white males were allowed to vote. A feud between two early U.S. Senators, Gwin and Broderick, was based partly on opposing views of slavery held by Democrats from northern and from southern states.

The gold rush attracted some free blacks to the mines, recalled in the place-name Negro Bar (present-day Folsom), and many southern slave-holders brought their Negroes to work for them in the mines or elsewhere, causing great opposition by whites. A few Negroes who were successful miners bought their freedom in California, and so did others who prospered elsewhere, like Biddy Mason. Nevertheless, blacks who arrived before statehood were subject to the Fugitive Slave Law and, like Archy Lee, were always in danger of being returned to their home states and to slavery.

The population of blacks grew from about 1,000 to 2,200 in the first two years of the 1850s, the decade during which they established their first churches (Sacramento, 1850; San Francisco, 1852; Grass Valley and Marysville, 1854; Oakland, 1858), held a state Convention of Colored Citizens (Sacramento, 1855), founded a newspaper (the weekly *Mirror of the Times,* 1856–58), and formed the Athenaeum, a San Francisco library and debating society. Meanwhile some blacks rose from menial positions to help establish themselves in better situations and to help others of their people to do likewise.

Among those who early occupied places of consequence were James Madison Bell and Philip Bell, Barney Fletcher, Mifflin Gibbs, George Monroe, Mammy Pleasant, William Robinson, Jeremiah Sanderson, and Darius Stokes. But blacks continued to suffer from degrading prejudice and hostility: for example, they were prohibited from giving testimony in a court of law, from owning land, and from attending any but segregated public schools. Therefore in 1858 some 250 blacks, led by the Rev. J. J. Moore, Mifflin Gibbs, and John W. Townsend, moved to Victoria, B.C. Eventually most of them returned, and after the Civil War and after the 13th Amendment to the U.S. Constitution was ratified, their lot improved, despite continuing Jim Crow practices.

In the postwar years a more militant journal, *The Elevator,* was issued and the artist Grafton Brown was recognized for his talents. At the opening of the 20th century there were about 11,000 Negroes in California. Then the population began to expand tremendously, to 21,645 in 1910 and 38,763 in 1920, more blacks settling in the Los Angeles area than elsewhere. During that period they developed a community of their own under the leadership of Allen Allensworth.

By 1940 the number of blacks had reached 124,306, which was still less than 2% of the entire state population, but with the outbreak of World War II, the black population increased dramatically, in large part because huge numbers of laborers were needed for the new shipyards, steelmills, aircraft plants, and other industries.

By 1950 blacks numbered 462,172, about 4.4% of the state's population, and by 1970 the figure was 1,400,143, or 7% of all the people in California, with the percentage much higher in parts of Los Angeles County, San Francisco, Oakland, and Richmond.

This led both to militant white opposition and to legislative response such as the Rumford Act, but when it was voted out of being by a new referendum, temporarily considered legal, the bitter frustration of discrimination and problems of unemployment led to many violent outbursts like that in Watts (1965).

To combat what they found to be an oppressive social system some blacks formed radical organizations like the Black Panthers and looked to militant leaders like Bobby Seale, Eldridge Cleaver, Angela Davis, and Huey Newton. Others worked within a society that had already brought honorable distinction to such California figures as Ralph Bunche, Walter Gordon, and Jackie Robinson, and even some militant leaders adopted more conventional programs.

By the 1960s and 70s blacks came to hold important legislative posts: U.S. Congressmen, among them Augustus F. Hawkins, Ronald V. Dellums, and Yvonne Braithwaite Burke, and several representatives in the state Assembly and Senate. Mayors included Thomas Bradley, who administered the state's most populous city. The first black elected to a statewide office was Wilson Riles, Superintendent of Public Instruction, soon followed by Mervyn M. Dymally, elected Lieutenant Governor (1974). *(See also individual entries.)*

BLANCO, Antonio de Fierro, see *Nordhoff, Walter.*

BLAND, Henry Meade (1863–1931), native California poet who succeeded Ina Coolbrith♦ as the state's Poet Laureate♦ (1929). After graduate study at the University of the Pacific and Stanford, he taught English at San Jose State Teachers College (1899–1931), the forerunner of California State University, San Jose. His verse, which bears the characteristic of his surname, was published in *Sierran Pan and Other Poems* (1924) and other volumes.

BLANDA, George (1927–   ), Pennsylvania-born professional football player who after 1949 was quarterback for the Oakland Raiders (1967–69, 1970–76). He played more seasons and more games and scored more points as a place kicker than anyone else in football history, despite his age.

BLINN, HOLBROOK (1872–1928), began his acting career as a child in his native San Francisco, graduating to characters like Wing Shee in *The Cat and the Cherub* by Chester Bailey Fernald♦ and the dashingly romantic protagonist of *The Bad Man.*

BLISS, WALTER D[ANFORTH] (1873–1956), San Francisco-born architect. After serving with McKim, Mead & White in New York, he opened his San Francisco office with William B. Faville (1866–1946), also a Californian, with whom he had worked in New York. Their buildings included the St. Francis Hotel, the Bank of California, and the mansion of the Flood family on Broadway (now Convent of the Sacred Heart). Bliss alone was responsible for the I. W. Hellman mansion at Lake Tahoe.

BLOCH, ERNEST (1880–1959), Swiss-born musical composer, first came to the U.S. (1916) as a conductor. After naturalization (1924) he became director of the San Francisco Conservatory (1925–30) and professor of music at the University of California, Berkeley (1940–52). His large body of various works include an opera, *Macbeth* (1909); string quartets; concertos; a liturgical *Sacred Service* (1933) commissioned for a San Francisco synagogue and, like the earlier *Schelomo,* a rhapsody, and the symphonic poem, *Israel* (both 1916), suggestive of his Jewish heritage.

Bloody Thursday, see *General Strike of San Francisco.*

BLUE, VIDA [ROCHELLE] (1949–), Louisiana-born pitcher for the Oakland Athletics, with whom he signed in 1968. His first year with the A's (1969) was unpromising, but he did well in 1970 and in 1971 became a superstar. That year the left-handed black pitcher led his league in strikeouts (240), completed games (19), and shutouts (8). His sale to the New York Yankees (1976) was blocked by the Commissioner of baseball and thereby became a subject of litigation.

Blue jay, bird of the crow-raven-magpie family found throughout the state. The most common type is the *California jay,* whose colors are gray-blue, dark blue, and some white and brown-gray. Other varieties are the *Oregon jay,* which inhabits the northernmost part of the state; the *stellar jay,* conspicuously crested with rich blue plumage, found from the Oregon border down to middle California; the *woodhouse jay,* less vividly colored than the *California jay,* which lives in the desert mountains of eastern California; and the *Santa Cruz jay,* bigger than the *California jay* and with a larger bill and richer colors, found only on Santa Cruz Island. Jays eat acorns, chestnuts, grasshoppers, and other insects, and rob eggs from other birds' nests. In *A Tramp Abroad* Mark Twain tells the story of Jim Baker, a California miner who could understand the raucous chatter of jays and thereby learned of one bemused bird which kept dropping acorns through a knothole in the roof of a log cabin in a vain attempt to fill the "hole" it had discovered.

Blythe, see *Palo Verde Valley.*

Boar, wild animal first introduced into the state in Monterey County (*c.* 1925), now found not only in the mountains north of Santa Barbara and east of Big Sur but also in the Santa Barbara Islands and Catalina Islands, to which they were also brought for game hunting.

Board of Equalization, State, body created by the Constitutional Convention of 1878 to equalize tax valuations among the counties and to assess all railroads operated in more than one county. At first it had a member from each county; now it consists of four members elected from different districts and the state controller. It is charged with maintaining uniform property tax assessments throughout all counties, establishing criteria for distributing school aid, and administering state sales, use, cigarette, beer, wine, liquor, gasoline, and BART taxes, thus overseeing 70% of the state's revenue. It is also the appeals board for business and franchise tax issues. It is elected at the same time as a governor and also for four years.

Bobcat, see *Wildcat.*

BODDY, MANCHESTER, see *Los Angeles Daily News.*

Bodega Bay, shallow inlet on Point Reyes,♦ sometimes thought to have been the place where Francis Drake anchored. It and Tomales Bay just to the south were named and probably discovered by Lt. Francisco de la Bodéga y Cuadro from the schooner *Sonora* (Oct. 3, 1775), dispatched for maritime discovery under Capt. Heceta♦ by Viceroy Bucareli as an adjunct to the sea voyage of Ayala and the land expedition of Anza. As part of the Russian

American Co.'s program, Ivan Kuskov founded a settlement there (1809) to grow wheat and to hunt sea otter, naming it Romanzov after a Russian imperial chancellor. In 1835, to stem Russian expansion, Vallejo gave three American sailors some land on the Russians' border. The Russian possession was sold to John A. Sutter (1841), and later Gov. Micheltorena granted over 35,000 acres to Stephen Smith, an American who created his Rancho Bodega that included some former Russian property. Still later the port became a busy place for shipment of locally grown potatoes. Oysters are now raised at Tomales Bay, and the nearby countryside supports dairies. Inverness, on Tomales Bay, is a small secluded resort town. The University of California has a Marine Biology Laboratory at Bodega Bay. Nearby is the excavated but abandoned site of a projected nuclear power generating station.

Bodie, Mono County gold mining town named after the discoverer of the ore, William S. (or Waterman S.) Bodey (1859), with a changed spelling. During its boom days to 1870 and again from 1876 to 1880 its population mushroomed to over 10,000 and it was known as a wide-open town. It later became a ghost town, but its buildings and atmosphere have been preserved in the State Historic Park (est. 1964).

BOGART, HUMPHREY (1900–57), New York-born Hollywood film star, best known for his roles as a tough man with a good heart in adaptations of Dashiell Hammett's *The Maltese Falcon* (1941), Raymond Chandler's *The Big Sleep* (1946), and C. S. Forester's *The African Queen* (1951). His role of the hard-boiled detective Sam Spade in *The Maltese Falcon* was set against a San Francisco background, and his depiction of Philip Marlowe, a similar detective hero in *The Big Sleep,* was set in Los Angeles.

Bohemian Club, men's club in San Francisco, founded (1872) by working newspapermen, has as its purpose the promotion of good fellowship among persons concerned with the arts. Since 1878 the club has had a midsummer encampment (after 1900 in its own grove of redwoods, presently covering 2,700 acres on the Russian River) in which are presented an annual Cremation of Care dramatized ceremony, a Low Jinks or musical comedy, and a High Jinks or pageant-like Grove Play, all written and produced by members. Entertainments are offered weekly during the winter in the city

clubhouse, which includes among other amenities a fine library containing the works of the many writers, mainly Californians, who have been and are among its present distinguished membership of about 2,000. The Bohemian's friendly counterpart, the Family Club,♦ was founded (1900) by dissident members.

BOLAÑOS, FRANCISCO DE, see *Exploration*.

Bolinas, seashore town on the base of Point Reyes opposite Stinson Beach in Marin County. Once a dairy area, it is now a quiet summer home and recreational region. Drake's Bay lies northwest of Bolinas Bay. Some historians believe Drake careened his ship in Bodega Bay.

BOLTON, HERBERT E[UGENE] (1870–1953), studied in the state university of his native Wisconsin under Frederick Jackson Turner, the theorist of frontier development, then at the University of Pennsylvania before entering upon his own academic career. He is best known for his professorship of history at the University of California, Berkeley (1911–40), where he was also director of The Bancroft Library. He was distinguished for his dynamic lectures to large classes of undergraduates and for his guidance of great numbers of graduate students in his field, the history of the Spanish-American frontier. To this area of scholarship he contributed many books, including *The Spanish Borderlands* (1921); *Outpost of Empire* (1931), treating Anza's California expedition; *New Spain and the Anglo-American West* (1933); and *Rim of Christendom* (1936), a biography of Father Kino.

Bonanza Kings, name given to James G. Fair,♦ James C. Flood,♦ John Mackay,♦ and William S. O'Brien,♦ sometimes also called the Silver Kings, who in 1871 created the Consolidated Virginia Silver Mine from a number of small claims of the Comstock Lode near Virginia City, Nevada. In a single month in 1876, $6,000,000 worth of ore was mined. The fortunes thus obtained flowed to San Francisco, where the mine owners lived. There they founded the Nevada Bank (1875), later merged (1905) with the Wells Fargo Bank.

BOND, CARRIE JACOBS (1862–1946), Wisconsin-born composer of sentimental songs, including the tremendously popular "A Perfect Day" (1910), inspired by a sunset near her Riverside home and moonlight on the Mojave Desert, and written the year she moved to California.

Bonita, see *Tuna.*

BONNEVILLE, BENJAMIN LOUIS EULALIE DE (1796–1878), French-born U.S. Army officer, was given a leave (1832–34) to head a party of 110 trappers into the Far West to see how the land lay. He was the first to take wagons through the South Pass of the Rockies, and he sent a detachment under Joseph Walker,♦ including Zenas Leonard,♦ which was the first to make a westward crossing of the Sierra Nevada. That crossing and life at the California missions were described by Leonard, and in Washington Irving's *Adventures of Captain Bonneville, U.S.A.* (1837).

Book Club of California, The, bibliophile society, located in San Francisco, was founded in 1912 to foster fine printing, the graphic arts, and publications about California and the West. It issues three volumes a year, handsomely printed by major presses of the state, often featuring rare texts, scholarly introductions, and beautiful illustrations. It also issues a quarterly *News-Letter* and a keepsake to its 900 members.

Book publishing, began in California when its first printer, Agustin Zamorano, in 1834 issued the *Reglamento Provincial,* or rules of government, that comprised the first of his six books. With the establishment of American rule, booklets such as *The Laws of the Town of San Francisco* (1847), *Translation and Digest . . . of Mexican Laws* (1849), and *Constitution of the State of California* (1849) were published by newspaper presses before a State Printer began to function (1850).

The earliest real book publication, one that was nongovernmental, was the printing by Washington Bartlett of Felix Wierzbicki's *California As It Is and As It May Be* (1849). During the gold rush, city directories began to be issued for the more stable communities, followed by an occasional work on mining or geology (e.g. a *Report* by J. B. Trask, 1853, and *The Miner's Own Book,* 1858), some recollections or instant history, and useful compendia like *Put's Golden Songster* (1858).

California got a real publishing house when Anton Roman♦ in 1860 began to issue well-made volumes of local interest, including Bret Harte's anthology of poetry, *Outcroppings,* James M. Hutchings' *Scenes of Wonder and Curiosity in California,* and Charles Warren Stoddard's *Poems.* Roman was soon challenged by an even more substantial publisher, Hubert Howe Bancroft,♦ whose firm lasted far longer and issued a more extensive series of works, including the histories written and compiled by the owner.

A competitor of both men was Edward Bosqui,♦ whose volumes were marked by fine design and good typography, the beginning of a tradition that has remained strong in San Francisco, where the three men carried on their businesses. Along side of the last two in the final decade of the century came William Doxey,♦ an Englishman whose interest was not in local writers or regional history but in fin de siècle British authors, such as W. S. Blunt, Rudyard Kipling, and Andrew Lang.

In the opening decades of the 20th century two other San Francisco retail booksellers also undertook significant publishing. Alexander M. Robertson was the publisher of George Sterling and of a volume of essays by Ambrose Bierce among other local literati, while Paul Elder♦ engaged John Henry Nash for his Tomoyé Press, thereby firmly establishing the city's fusion of Californiana and fine printing. That combination was given a tremendous lift by the founding of The Book Club of California (1912), which has had a schedule of several elegant volumes issued annually, although it has only infrequently printed the writings of contemporary authors.

In this century leading rare book dealers of San Francisco and Los Angeles have also issued books, usually limited editions treating some aspect of California. Most of them have come from the long succession of fine printers of the state, including John Henry Nash, Taylor and Taylor, the Grabhorn Press, Ward Ritchie, the Plantin Press, Adrian Wilson, and Andrew Hoyem. Plainer but substantial presswork has marked the long-established program of the Arthur H. Clark Co. of Glendale to print scholarly studies of western history.

This has been true also of the books of the California Historical Society and of the presses of Stanford University and the University of California. Elegant and attractive books have come from Lane Publishing Co. in the vein of its journal, *Sunset,* to present regional subjects, generally related to contemporary suburban living and local travel. Somewhat similar in appearance but grander in conception are numerous books issued by the Sierra Club and American West, dwelling on conservation or the natural scene and on California history, respectively, all marked by handsome and glossy colored pictures.

Not interested in such elegant presentation are the publishers who have flourished for some time disseminating radical or cult beliefs and the small presses that print avant garde poetry and other literature. They came into greater prominence during the Beat movement, which needed to communicate the ideas and the expressions of counterculture writers. Of them the most significant has been the City Lights Publishing Co.♦ of Lawrence Ferlinghetti, famous for issuing Allen Ginsberg's *Howl* (1956) and successfully defending it against a charge of obscenity. Another established firm representative of a youthful culture opposed to conventional bourgeois standards is the Straight Arrow Books of the journal *Rolling Stone,* and the *Whole Earth Catalogue* was a similar success in counterculture publishing. Such works are, however, found in regular bookstores along with the local history, biography, and fiction printed by a major newspaper's Chronicle Books and the full list of titles issued by publishers of works for children. So the book publishing of California has developed into a various and lively undertaking, mainly but not entirely restricted to local authors and subjects and of interest to booksellers and readers far beyond the state.

The vitality of California's literary activity has led major New York and Boston publishers to have editorial representatives and even branches in the state to stay close to the active scene as well as to keep in touch with the burgeoning market for school texts.

Boontling, name given by its speakers to a special jargon cultivated in the upper Anderson Valley♦ of Mendocino County, particularly between 1880 and 1920 but still surviving today. *Boont* derives from Boonville, the valley's largest town (1970 population, 500), *ling* abbreviates "lingo." The speech has many clipped forms, some 3,000 specialized names, over 1,000 unique words and phrases, and a syntax characterized by ellipsis. A book on the subject by Charles C. Adams (1971) presents as an example the phrase "Kimmies [men] japin' [driving] broadies [cows] to the airtight [sawmill]!" in which the first word derives from Scotch, the second is extended from a reference to a local stage driver nicknamed J. P., the third is intended to describe broad-horn cattle, and the fourth is based on a local anecdote.

BOOTH, NEWTON (1825–92), 11th governor of the state (1871–75), was born in Indiana and, after graduation from the university later named De-Pauw, practiced law there. In 1850 he went to Sacramento to continue law practice, to enter the grocery business, and to contribute influential writing to the *Sacramento Union.* Known as a strong supporter of Grant, he was also an opponent of subsidies for the railroad. He resigned the governorship upon election to the U. S. Senate, and during his single term in that office secured passage of a bill to settle land titles in his state.

Borax, white crystalline substance used in various kinds of manufacturing, particularly of glass and ceramics, in agriculture, and for diverse other purposes, was first discovered in the U.S. in California (1856) and there first produced (1864) in Lake County. A more important discovery was made by Francis M. Smith♦ in Nevada and by others in Death Valley which he developed. From the latter site the ore was hauled (*c.*1885–1907) in 16-foot-long wagons by 20-mule teams (actually two horses at the wagon and 18 mules ahead) to Mojave, the Southern Pacific railhead 165 miles distant. By that means some 2,500,000 pounds of borax were hauled annually. The borax properties, first owned by William T. Coleman,♦ were bought by Smith (1890), who created the Pacific Coast Borax Co., which merged (1896) with a British chemical firm. Major mining operations are now carried on in the briny wells of Searles Lake, San Bernardino County,♦ and in an open pit at Boron, Kern County. In the first year of production (1864) about twelve tons were mined in California; a century later about 1,000,000 tons are extracted annually. The major producer, U.S. Borax Co., uses text about and pictures of the 20-mule teams as a trademark and once sponsored a popular television series, starring Ronald Reagan, of romantic stories dramatizing the mines and the teams.

BOREIN, JOHN EDWARD (1873–1945), cowboy artist, born in San Leandro. After working on ranches he became a resident of Santa Barbara, and there became noted for his etchings of California cowboys and ranch life. He also made pen and ink sketches and oil paintings. He was the initiator of the Rancheros Visitadores.♦

BORG, CARL OSCAR (1879–1947), Swedish-born artist. He went to Los Angeles (1904) where he became a protégé of Phoebe Apperson Hearst. She commissioned him to photograph and paint the Indians of the Southwest for the University of California.

BORGLUM, [JOHN] GUTZON [DE LA MOTHE] (1867–1941), Idaho-born artist who went to

Los Angeles (1884) and studied in San Francisco with Keith and Virgil Williams. He turned from painting to sculpture, made busts of Jessie Frémont and the founder of Throop Institute, and then moved to New York and began a career of creating colossal statues. The Presidents at Mt. Rushmore, S.D., are his most famous sculptures.

BORICA, DIEGO DE (1742–1800), Spanish governor of the Californias (1794–1800) who had previously served as the inspector of presidios in Chihuahua. As governor he continued Arrillaga's program of improving fortifications and further to secure Alta California he created Branciforte,◆ the third pueblo established by a Spanish governor, and, with Lasuén, founded five other missions (1797–98). Not only did he have good relations with the missionaries, but he improved the lot of neophyte Indians, teaching them trades and farming. He abolished the decree under which they suffered capital punishment for any crime. An enlightened governor, he also attempted to establish compulsory primary education (1795). Even though it meant a reduction of his power he worked to separate the Californias, and he drew the boundary line later settled upon.

Borrego Valley, located in the north-central area of the Anza-Borrego State Park,◆ which surrounds it. On the route of Anza's trail (1774), its name is Spanish for sheep. It is an agricultural area in which cotton, vegetables, table grapes, and livestock feed are raised. A monument to Pegleg Smith◆ memorializes his legendary gold mine.

BORTHWICK, J[OHN] D[AVID] (*fl.*1825–70), Scottish artist resident in New York before his trip via Panama to California during the gold rush. The result of his residence in San Francisco and the mining country was *Three Years in California* (Edinburgh, 1857), a lively text with his own fine illustrations.

BOSCANA, GERÓNIMO (1775–1831), Majorcan-born Franciscan missionary, sent to California in 1806. He became the Padre of Mission San Juan Capistrano (1814–26), where he wrote a "Relacion Histórica . . . ," an account of the origin, customs, and traditions of the Acagchemem Indians of his mission. The work was translated by Alfred Robinson◆ and, when first published (1846) as a supplement to his *Life in California,* Robinson entitled it Chinigchinich,◆ the name of the Indian prophet or god often cited in Boscana's account, also

called Chingichnich. Boscana died at Mission San Gabriel, where he was buried.

BOSQUI, EDWARD (1832–1917), born in Montreal where as a young man he was a bookseller before going to San Francisco (1850). There he worked in banking and real estate and managed the Mariposa Grant properties of Frémont before establishing himself as a printer, lithographer, bookbinder, and publisher. In the 1860s, 70s, and even later, he was the city's and the state's best publisher, distinguished for his choice of texts, good typography, fine design, and handsome illustrations. His publications include volumes of poems by Stoddard and Ridge; *Grapes and Grapevines of California* (1877); *Illustrations of West American Oaks* (1889); and his limited edition of *Memoirs* (1904). He was a founder of the San Francisco Art Association, the Bohemian Club, and the California Academy of Sciences, a noted bibliophile, and a collector of local art.

BOTTA, PAUL EMILE, see *Duhaut-Cilly, Auguste Bernard.*

BOUCHARD, HIPPOLYTE DE (*c.*1785–1843), French-born privateer, engaged in the cause of Mexican independence for which he attacked the outlying royalist possession of California. Under the flag of independent Buenos Aires he sailed two black-painted vessels into Monterey Bay, seized and ransacked the town (Nov. 20–27, 1818), caused Gov. de Solá to flee, then sailed south to pillage the Ortega *rancho* at Refugio and to loot San Juan Capistrano (Dec. 14–15). Joseph Chapman, a U.S. crewman of his, was captured in Monterey and settled there permanently.

BOUCHARD, JAMES [CHRYSOSTOM] (1823–89), Delaware Indian born in present Kansas and named Watomika. He was sent to school in St. Louis and there converted to Catholicism. Trained as a Jesuit priest, he was sent to San Francisco in 1861. He remained there the rest of his life as a preacher. He was very popular with many Catholics but not with Archbishop Alemany, who considered Bouchard disturbing to the city's normal parochial life. He was a flamboyant and evangelical figure who battled with Protestant clergy and also supported the anti-Chinese views of Denis Kearney. His missionary preaching took him throughout California and to Utah, Oregon, Vancouver, and elsewhere in the Far West.

Boulder Dam, see *Water.*

BOURN, WILLIAM (1857–1936), inherited a gold rush mining fortune and in time became president of the San Francisco Gas Co. and of Spring Valley Water Co.,♦ as well as the founder of the Napa Valley vineyard and winery that later became the property of the Christian Brothers. Willis Polk designed a city house for him as well as a country estate in Woodside, Filoli (1916), later owned by the daughter of William Matson, Mrs. William P. Roth.

BOW, CLARA (1905–65), Brooklyn-born Hollywood film star famed for brash, pert, sexy roles. The most famous of which, in Elinor Glyn's *It* (1927), led to her being called the It Girl. She lived in the Hollywood area during her motion picture career in the late 1920s, retired to her husband's Nevada ranch for many years, and returned to Los Angeles toward the end of her life.

BOWERS, J. MILTON (1843–1904), Baltimore-born physician who moved to San Francisco, where he became the center of one of the city's most famous crimes when his third wife, like his first two, died suddenly (1885) and he was convicted of poisoning her. While Bowers was awaiting execution or retrial on appeal, his brother-in-law was found dead, an ostensible suicide, with a note admitting he was his sister's murderer. Although Bowers' case was dismissed, he was thought responsible for his brother-in-law's death too. Bowers' second wife, Teresa (1857?–81), had attained some notoriety when her book, *The Dance of Life* (1877), praising the waltz, was answered by an anonymous parody, *The Dance of Death* (1877), in which W. H. Rulofson and Ambrose Bierce blasted ballroom dancing.

Box, see *Maple.*

Boxing, the sport of fist-fighting has undergone great variation in rules and style since it first became popular in the state during the gold rush era. The first state claimant to a national championship was John C. Morrisey (1852), who was defeated (1859) by John Heenan,♦ the Benicia Boy. Heenan then became an international contestant by fighting the English champion, Tom Sayres, in Hampshire (1860). A later noted prizefighter from the state was Joseph Choynski,♦ who as an amateur and later as a professional had bouts with the popular San Francisco favorite, James J. Corbett.♦ In the year that gloved pugilism replaced bare-knuckled contests (1892), Corbett knocked out John L. Sullivan, winning the world's heavyweight championship. Corbett, a native Californian, lost the title in 1897, but two years later it was won by a longtime California resident, James J. Jeffries,♦ who held it until 1905. Even after he retired, boxing remained popular in the state and eight world championship bouts were held there between 1901 and 1907. California has always been enthusiastic about boxing and has also continued to develop its own champions. Among them have been Henry Armstrong,♦ who held three different world titles simultaneously; Max Baer,♦ briefly the world's heavyweight champion; George Foreman,♦ another heavyweight champion; and Archie Moore,♦ long the world's light-heavyweight champion.

Braceros, Mexican laborers brought to the U.S. under Public Law 78 of the U.S. Congress (1951). The law required farm owners to certify that they could find no domestic workers to harvest crops and also required governmental determination that U.S. wage standards would not be impaired. These migratory workers (their Spanish name means "strong-armed ones") were the principal source of agricultural labor♦ in the state until union protests ended the program (1964). These legal entrants should be distinguished from "wetbacks."♦

BRADBURY, RAY [DOUGLAS] (1920–), Illinois-born author of science fiction, long resident in Los Angeles. He graduated from pulp magazines to serious writing about 1945. His many works include *The Martian Chronicles* (1950) and *The Illustrated Man* (1951), novels with social and religious themes; *The Golden Apples of the Sun* (1953), satirical sketches; *Fahrenheit 451* (1953), depicting a totalitarian state's control of people, ideas, and books; and *A Medicine for Melancholy* (1959), humorous and fantastic tales. He has written many other novels and stories and some plays and motion picture scripts.

BRADLEY, THOMAS (1917–), born in Texas, was brought to Los Angeles aged seven and there made the career that has led him to be a leading black citizen. From the police force (1940–61) he went on to election to the City Council (1961–73), and after a bitter campaign for mayor (1969) he was elected with a great plurality (1973), even though only about 16% of the city's population is black.

Branciforte, pueblo established (1797) by Gov. Borica◆ on the site of present Santa Cruz. It honored the Marqués de Branciforte, then viceroy of New Spain, who conceived of the so-called villa as a settlement of retired soldiers and their families to provide cheap colonization and a ready military reserve against threats from foreign powers. When Mexican soldiers shunned the ill-funded project, Spanish authorities dispatched to it some men convicted of minor crimes. Begun with 40 persons, the settlement's largest population was 101 in 1802, when a new viceroy suspended further support, and it dwindled to 53 by 1815. The present county of Santa Cruz temporarily took this name (Feb. 18–April 5, 1850).

BRAND, Max, pseudonym of Frederick Faust.◆

BRANDEGEE, Mary Katharine Layne (1844–1920), botanist born in Tennessee but reared near Folsom. She received an M.D. from the University of California (1878) and became curator of the California Academy of Sciences for two decades, beginning in 1883. She and her husband, Townsend Stith Brandegee, spent their honeymoon on a botanizing walk from San Diego to San Francisco and later worked together editing and contributing to a botanical journal, *Zoe* (1890–1908), and administering the herbarium of the University of California, Berkeley (1906 ff.).

BRANDO, Marlon [Jr.] (1924–   ), Nebraska-born actor who after success on Broadway, began his film career in Hollywood (1950) and achieved great popularity with the motion picture version (1951) of the part he had created on stage in *A Streetcar Named Desire* and in Budd Schulberg's *On the Waterfront* (1954), for which he won an Academy Award. His talent as an actor was unevenly displayed in many later pictures, but he was very successful in *The Wild One* (1953) and *The Godfather* (1971).

BRANNAN, Samuel (1819–89), lived in his native Maine as a boy, then went to Ohio where he became a journeyman printer, a trade that took him through most of the U.S. He became interested in the Mormon faith, to which he was converted in 1842, the year he moved to New York, where he published a religious paper. In 1845 he was chosen leader of a contingent of 238 Mormons, including 100 children, to found a colony outside the U.S. Their chartered ship *Brooklyn* took them and their equipment, including a printing press, to Yerba

Buena on July 31, 1846, to find, to their disappointment, that California had been seized by the U.S. A dynamic opportunist, Brannan established California's first flour mill and began (Jan. 9, 1847) San Francisco's first newspaper, *The California Star.*◆ Use of Mormon funds for his own purposes led to his trial before California's first jury (a hung one) for embezzlement. He brought news of the discovery of gold to San Francisco, having, it is said, previously stocked his store at Sutter's Fort with necessities for miners. He became rich through real estate deals and other business investments, established himself as a leader, organizing the Society of California Pioneers, and became president of the 1851 Vigilance Committee. A heavy drinker, he lost his money and spent his last years, poor and forgotten, in Escondido, San Diego County.

BRAUTIGAN, Richard (1935–   ), author associated with the San Francisco Beat movement, whose whimsical, amusing, and atmospheric sketches have been collected in short books called "novels," including *A Confederate General from Big Sur* (1964), *Trout Fishing in America* (1967), and *The Abortion* (1970). He has also gathered brief poems in *The Pill versus the Springhill Mine Disaster* (1968), *Rommel Drives on Deep into Egypt* (1970), and other works.

BREEN, Patrick (*c.*1805–68), born in Ireland, went to Canada and Iowa before making his way west with the Donner Party◆ (1846), whose dreadful experiences he recorded in a diary he kept at Donner Lake. In 1848 he became the first non-Spanish-speaking resident of San Juan Bautista.◆

BREWER, William Henry (1828–1910), New York-born scientist who, after graduation from Yale and further study in Europe, was appointed Principal Assistant to Josiah Dwight Whitney◆ for his geological survey of California (1860–64). In that work Brewer was assisted by Clarence King, and both were major contributors to the *Geological Survey of California* (1865). Brewer's letters to his brother made a sequential journal and were edited as such by Francis P. Farquhar and published as *Up and Down California* (1930). The work shows him to have been an interesting and vivid observer of many aspects of California far beyond the geological, botanical, and geographical subjects in which he professionally specialized. Associates named Mt. Brewer (which he was the first to ascend, July 1864) in Kings Canyon

National Park for him. He was a professor of agriculture at Yale from 1864 to 1903.

Breweries, established during the gold rush, the first regular business was probably William Bull's Empire Brewery (1849) of San Francisco. Although one William McGlove may have made beer in California in 1837, the little that was drunk here before the Mexican War was imported. J. J. Hartmann, in San Jose, established the state's first steam-beer brewery, employing a process in which fermentation (with a pressure akin to steam) is continued in the barrel for a long time. He thus introduced the beverage long associated with San Francisco because Frank Norris emphasized its popularity in his novel *McTeague.*

German immigrants of the 1850s established many breweries which within a decade could depend on locally grown hops♦ and barley.♦ Annual beer production grew from 300,000 barrels in 1880 to 750,000 in 1900. During that period production was improved, particularly through the scientific control based on Pasteur's experiments with fermentation in France (1876). Other important developments of the period included the nation-wide switch in taste from top-fermented stout to bottom-fermented lager. The late 19th century also was a period in which many independent breweries were consolidated and British syndicates bought quite a few of them.

Breweries went out of business during Prohibition (1920–33) but came back quickly after Repeal. Annual state output increased from 2,500,000 barrels in 1937 to 6,500,000 in 1955 to 9,900,000 in 1968, making California the fifth among beer-brewing states (1968). During that period national brewers opened their own plants in California and numerous local independent breweries disappeared. The era also was marked by a switch from draught to packaged products and the growth of canned beer at the expense of the conventional bottled beer.

BREWERTON, GEORGE DOUGLAS (1827–1901), son of a superintendent of West Point, went to California with Stevenson's Regiment♦ (1847). After service there he was sent east via the Old Spanish Trail with Kit Carson to bear news about the gold rush (1848). He later wrote books about his experiences and painted Western scenes.

Bridgeport, Sierra town, seat of Mono County since 1864, smallest community in California to have such a distinction. Population in 1970 was 458.

BRIDGES, HARRY (1901–   ), born in Australia and named Alfred Renton Bridges. After completing secondary education (1917) and clerking in a stationery store he was inspired by Jack London's fiction to ship on sailing vessels, first arriving at San Francisco aboard a barkentine (1920). After rigging work in Mexican oil fields, further sailing, and picket duty during a New Orleans maritime strike, he settled in San Francisco where, as the militant union leader of the International Longshoremens Association,♦ he led a strike against Pacific Coast shipowners which became a general strike (1934) with San Francisco under martial law. Federal trials were later held to try to oust him as an illegal immigrant. He remained as the West Coast dock leader of another long strike in 1971–72 on behalf of his longshoremen.♦

Bristlecone Pine Forest, preserve of 28,000 acres, part of Inyo National Forest,♦ contains the type of pine♦ that is the longest-living species of tree. One example is known to be over 4,600 years old.

British in California, the first foreigners after Cabrillo to visit the region, arrived in June 1579 when Francis Drake♦ repaired his ship in a harbor and claimed the land for Queen Elizabeth. Other English voyagers did not put in again until the 18th and 19th centuries, long after Spanish dominion had been established. They included the naval missions of George Vancouver (1792), Frederick Beechey (1826, 1827–28), and Edward Belcher (1836–37, 1839) and the horticultural expedition of David Douglas (1823 ff.).

Their visits were followed by those of mariners engaged in whaling and the hide and tallow business and other trade, some of whom became settlers, like John Gilroy♦ (1814), a Scot who jumped ship; William A. Richardson (1822), the first British inhabitant of San Francisco; W. E. P. Hartnell (1822), a dealer in mission produce; Robert Livermore (1822), another sailor who jumped ship; and Hugo Reid, a Scot who came from Mexico to settle in Los Angeles.

Meanwhile, trappers of the Hudson's Bay Co., mostly Canadians,♦ began to infiltrate the valleys annually, beginning in 1826. Sir George Simpson, the company's head, visited California (1841), claimed it had 100 British subjects, and hoped for its alliance with England. Naturally enough, President Polk and other Americans feared British interest, which ranged from a scheme for colonization by the Irish♦ to the writing of a book about California (1839) by Alexander Forbes and the establishment of his relative J. A. Forbes as vice-consul at Monterey (1834–51).

British capital investments in various ventures, including those of independent ranchers like John Forster (1814), William Workman (1841), and William B. Foxen, and the running of the New Almaden mine, were disturbing, although the *rancheros* turned out to be supporters of the Americans. After U.S. occupation, emigrants from the British Isles, including Cornish♦ and Welsh,♦ experienced in mining, were the major settlers in California. Some of the visitors wrote books about their experiences, including J. D. Borthwick and Frederick Marryat.

As California became a thoroughly settled land, the British continued to strengthen their affiliations and to immigrate in significant numbers. They enriched all sorts of economic, cultural, intellectual, and artistic activities in California. Many prominent British authors have resided in the state and written about it, including Robert Louis Stevenson, Aldous Huxley, and Christopher Isherwood, while still more have made briefer visits to lecture, teach, or work in film studios.

Britton and Rey, firm of lithographers in San Francisco (1852–92), the oldest west of the Rocky Mts., also engaged in printing, engraving, and decoration on tin. The senior partner, Joseph Britton (1820–1901), was a Yorkshireman who went to California in 1849. His brother-in-law, Jacques Joseph Rey (1820–92), an Alsatian, joined him in other businesses, including some financing of the dirigible of Frederick Marriott. Britton was also active as a Supervisor in San Francisco on the People's party ticket and as a financier of Hallidie's first cable car line.

Broccoli, vegetable grown more in California than elsewhere in the U.S. The Oxnard Plain is a major center for the crop, which in 1970 was produced on 33,900 acres and was worth $24,328,000.

BRODERICK, DAVID C[OLBRETH] (1820–59), born in Ireland, went to San Francisco (1849) after a career as a New York saloonkeeper and Tammany Hall politician. In San Francisco he grew rich by private coining of slugs with stated face values far above their gold content and by dealing in waterfront real estate. He gathered around himself such political henchmen as Edward McGowan♦ and James P. Casey♦ and soon became a leading Democrat intent upon membership in the U.S. Senate. He reached his goal (1857) by vote of the state legislature, in which he had served. He vehemently opposed the senior Senator, William M. Gwin,♦ a southern supporter of slavery who controlled federal patronage in the state. Broderick's failure to get power from Gwin and President Buchanan turned him violently against both men. His denunciation of Gwin's champion, California Chief Justice David S. Terry, led to his being challenged to a pistol duel. They fought near Lake Merced (San Francisco County) and Terry mortally wounded Broderick. He was eulogized in a funeral oration by Col. Edward D. Baker,♦ who depicted him as a martyr "opposed to the extension of slavery and a corrupt administration."

BRODIE, JOHN [RILEY] (1935–), San Francisco-born football player. After playing quarterback at Stanford (1953–56) and being named All-American, he played for the San Francisco Forty-Niners (1957–73) and was cited as Most Valuable Player in his league. He later became a sports broadcaster.

BROOKES, SAMUEL MARSDEN (1816–92), English-born artist, reared in the U.S. He moved to California (1862), where he became well known as a meticulously realistic painter of still-life canvases of fish, birds, fruit, flowers, and other genre subjects. He was a founder of the organization which became the San Francisco Art Institute.

BROOKS, NOAH (1830–1903), Maine-born journalist and author. He went to California with an ox team (1859), the basis of his fictive *The Boy Emigrants* (1876). Until he returned east (1862) he was editor of a Marysville newspaper and contributor to the *Overland Monthly*. He went again to California (1866–71) and edited the *Alta California* and was a coeditor of the *Overland Monthly*.

BROUGHTON, JAMES (1913–), California-born poet, a graduate of Stanford University and active in San Francisco's Beat movement. His books include *The Playground* (1949), *Musical Chairs* (1950), and *An Almanac for Amorists* (1955). He has also produced experimental motion pictures and plays.

BROWER, DAVID [ROSS] (1912–), California-born conservationist. A longtime Executive Director of the Sierra Club (1952–69). He was ousted on charges that he had led the club into issues foreign to its region and its immediate concerns and that he was an extremist. He then founded and became President of Friends of the Earth♦ (1969). He has edited numerous handsome books about the natural scene and wilderness areas, mainly of the Far West.

BROWERE, ALBERTUS DEL ORIENT (1814–87), artist, mainly of landscapes, who left New York (1852) to paint life in the California mines and remained four years. He went back to California (1858–61) for further painting.

BROWN, A. PAGE (1859–96), New York-born architect who worked with McKim, Mead & White before he went to San Francisco (1889), where he designed the California pavilion in Mission Revival style for the Columbian Exposition in Chicago (1893). For his adopted city he built several distinguished structures, including the Ferry Building (1898). Bernard Maybeck and Willis Polk were collaborators in his office, the former being partly responsible for the design of the Church of the New Jerusalem (Swedenborgian).

BROWN, ARTHUR, JR. (1874–1957), Oakland-born architect educated at the University of California, Berkeley (for which he was later the supervising architect), and L'École des Beaux-Arts. Working with John Bakewell, Jr.,♦ he built the present San Francisco City Hall and, independently, Coit Tower (1934). He was not related to A. Page Brown, another distinguished San Francisco architect.

BROWN, CHARLOTTE AMANDA BLAKE (1846–1904), born in Philadelphia, moved to California with her husband when in her twenties and began a career as physician and surgeon for women and children which led to the founding of Children's Hospital in San Francisco with her own children, also doctors, Adelaide (1868–1940) and Philip King (1869–1940).

BROWN, EDMUND G[ERALD] (1905–), 32nd governor of the state (1959–67). After graduating from high school in San Francisco and receiving a law degree from the San Francisco College of Law, he ran for the Assembly as a Republican, switching in 1934 to the Democratic party. After serving as District Attorney of San Francisco (1944–50), he was elected the state's Attorney General (1950–59) and worked well with Gov. Earl Warren. His own governorship was marked by what he called "responsible liberalism" with broad-gauged programs for using the state's water resources, plans

for developing beaches and parks, welfare and fair employment practices plans, governmental re-organization, and a master plan for higher education. In 1962 he defeated Richard M. Nixon and won a second term. He tried for a third term, previously only achieved by Warren, and was defeated by Ronald Reagan, who was in turn succeeded by Brown's son, Edmund G. Brown, Jr.♦ The senior Brown was generally known as Pat.

BROWN, EDMUND G[ERALD], JR. (1938–), 34th governor of the state (1975–), was born in San Francisco, a fourth-generation Californian. After study for the priesthood at a seminary and of religion at the University of Santa Clara and graduation from the University of California, Berkeley, with a major in the classics, he received a law degree from Yale. In 1970 he was elected Secretary of State as a Democrat in a predominantly Republican election year. After little more than a year as governor he ran for the Democratic nomination for the presidency.

He is known for his independent lifestyle: he has never married, lives simply in a small rented apartment, refuses to follow many conventional procedures (his state speeches generally last less than ten minutes), would rather ask questions than provide answers, and is interested in various aspects of alternative culture such as Zen Buddhism.

BROWN, GRAFTON TYLER (1841–1918), Pennsylvania-born black artist, resident in San Francisco (1861–*c*.85), where he was a student of and later a lithographer for Charles C. Kuchel, for whom he depicted a view of San Francisco. He established his own lithographic firm (1867–*c*.1872) in San Francisco before traveling elsewhere in the West as an artist and then moving to Wyoming.

BROWN, JOHN (1800?–59), familiarly known as Juan Flaco (Lean John) Brown, a onetime fur trapper who aided the American conquest of California by summoning reinforcements for the American detachment in Los Angeles under Capt. Gillespie when it was besieged by the troops of Capt. Flores. In Sept. 1846 he concealed in his long hair a message Gillespie wrote on cigarette paper and rode through enemy country to Monterey and then to San Francisco (about 500 miles on horseback and 27 on foot in five days) to seek aid from Commodore Stockton. The troops, sent under Capt. Mervine, were embroiled in new battles of the Mexican War in California.♦

BROWN, JUAN FLACO, see *Brown, John*.

BROWNE, CLYDE (1872–1942), was taken to California from his native Ohio as an infant. After working for newspapers he created his own print-shop in his stone Abbey San Encino, which he built by hand in the Arroyo Seco♦ area of Pasadena (1909–25). Influenced by William Morris, he printed his own verse, *Cloisters of California* (1917), and a lush prose description, *Abbey Fantasy* (1929). He did printing for Occidental College and for a time rented one of his studios to Lawrence Clark Powell and Ward Ritchie, who carried on the arts and crafts interests Browne fostered.

BROWNE, J[OHN] ROSS (1821–75), born in Ireland, was brought to Kentucky age 11, and as a young man became a shorthand reporter for the U.S. Senate. His love of travel soon took him to a wide range of places and occupations, out of which came his diverse writings.

His first major voyage, aboard a whaler in the Indian Ocean, resulted in *Etchings of a Whaling Cruise* (1846), influenced by *Two Years Before the Mast*. He next got an appointment in the Revenue Service, which took him to California on a voyage around the Horn and in time provided part of the material for *Crusoe's Island . . . with Sketches of Adventures in California and Washoe* (1864).

After three months in California (1849) he found his post gone but got another for himself as the official reporter of the Constitutional Convention that led to California's statehood. He next made a Mediterranean tour, reported in *Yusef* (1853), a volume of his text and witty drawings, anticipating Clemens' *Innocents Abroad* in its amused depiction of Americans and the foreign lands to which they traveled.

Granted a government appointment to inspect federal custom houses, Browne returned to California (1854) and the next year moved his family to Oakland into a house later enlarged to become known as the exotic edifice, Pagoda Hill. In succeeding years he held other governmental posts, including an appointment to study Indian affairs, which led to reports (including "Indian Reservations" printed in *Harper's,* 1861) that exposed corruption and mismanagement and also revealed the complex causes of Indian wars in Oregon. The work also resulted in a book for the general public, *Adventures in the Apache Country, a Tour through Arizona and Sonora with Notes on the Silver Regions of Nevada* (1869).

Another federal appointment, as commissioner of mines and mining, which led to further reports, was followed by his final governmental post as minister to China (1868). *A Dangerous Journey* (1950) and *A Peep at Washoe* (1968) were reprinted from *Crusoe's Island. Muleback to the Convention* (1950) gathered some early California letters, and *The Land of Thor* (1867) treated a second European journey.

BRUBECK, DAVE (DAVID WARREN BRUBECK) (1920–   ), pianist and composer born in Concord, who studied with Milhaud and Schoenberg before turning to jazz. In 1951 he and Paul Desmond, an alto saxophone player from San Francisco, formed a quartet in that city, and it helped bring national attention to the so-called West Coast Jazz.♦ He has composed cantatas, a symphony, and many jazz works.

BRUFF, J[OSEPH] GOLDSBOROUGH (1804–89), author of an unusually full, precise, and carefully documented gold rush journal. It is illustrative of his maturity, his precision as a West Point graduate, and his skill as an artist and observer cultivated as a draftsman in the U.S. Bureau of Topographical Engineers. His intention to write a thorough guide to the Overland Trail was never realized, but the lengthy account of his journey from Washington, D.C., into California via the Lassen Trail and his residence north of the mining country (April 1849–July 1851) was finally edited and published as *Gold Rush* (1944).

BRUGUIÈRE, FRANCIS (1880–1945), member of a socially prominent San Francisco family who was influenced by Stieglitz to become a photographer. His soft-focus poetic pictures of his native city appeared in *San Francisco* (1918).

BRUNDAGE, AVERY (1887–1975), Michigan-born engineering company executive and amateur sportsman, long resident in Santa Barbara. He was president of the Comité Internationale Olympique (1952–72). His great collection of Oriental art was given to the de Young Museum♦ in San Francisco (1960), and a wing built for it became the foundation of the city's Asian Art Museum.

Brussels sprouts, vegetable grown mainly in Santa Cruz and San Mateo counties but also in the Salinas Valley. California produces 90% of the nation's crop and 70% of its harvest is frozen for the market.

BRYANT, EDWIN (1805–69), born in Massachusetts and reared in Kentucky, where he was a journalist on various newspapers before going to California (1846). He soon enlisted American residents for Frémont in the war, was appointed lieutenant, and after the war was made *alcalde* of San Francisco. He returned home in 1847, and those two overland voyages provided background for his *What I Saw in California* (1848), a prime document of the gold rush because as a trained newspaperman his observations on the trail and his knowledge of California made his work superior to other writings. He led an expedition west (1849), then sold real estate in San Francisco until 1853, when he returned to Kentucky. He went back to California only in the year of his death.

Bryant, Sturgis & Company, see *Hide trade.*

BUCARELI Y URSÚA, ANTONIO MARÍA (1717–79), Spanish army officer and viceroy of New Spain (1771–79) who sponsored the two expeditions of Anza♦ that established a land route from Sonora to California to colonize it. He also sponsored the maritime explorations of Ayala,♦ Heceta,♦ and Bodéga y Cuadro and improved the schedule of supply ships to California. His *Reglamento* (1773) was the basic constitution of California throughout the Spanish era, although it was amplified by Felipe de Neve♦ (1779).

Buckeye, tree that grows 10 to 30 feet tall with a broad rounded crown, found throughout the Coast Range and the foothills of the Sierra Nevada, generally near water. The tree was so common that over 50 place-names incorporate its name, although the town in Shasta County was named by Ohio settlers for their home state. Yokuts, Salinans, and other Indians ate the tree's fruit, although the seeds are poisonous.

BUCKLEY, CHRISTOPHER (1845–1922), Irish-born political boss of San Francisco, where he ran a successful saloon. Despite having lost his eyesight in the 1870s, Buckley, through patronage and bribery, controlled the local Democratic party. He generally cooperated with the Central Pacific Railroad, but when he switched to aid Republican Leland Stanford in his campaign for the Senate against Huntington's official choice, Aaron Sargent, Buckley's fortunes turned (1890), and the next year he left the state to avoid indictment.

BUDD, JAMES HERBERT (1851–1908), 19th governor of California (1895–99). Born in Wisconsin and reared in California, he was the first governor to be graduated from the state university (1873). He had a term in Congress and an active legal practice in Stockton, and was the successful Democratic candidate for governor after Republican problems resulting from the Panic of 1893. He aided higher education and created a Bureau of Highways.

BUDGE, [JAMES] DON[ALD] (1916–), Oakland-born tennis champion who in 1937 and again in 1938 won the U.S. singles, doubles, and mixed doubles championships and the same three English titles at Wimbledon. He was the first tennis player to achieve that record. In 1938 he won the French and Australian championships, thereby becoming the first person to win the "Grand Slam" of all four major national championships. He turned professional after 1938 and became the leading player in that class for some years. He is often considered to have had the best backhand stroke of any player in the history of tennis.

Buena Park, Orange County city, most widely known for its tourist attractions, including Knott's Berry Farm,♦ Movieland Wax Museum, Japanese Village and Deer Park, California Alligator Farm, Movieworld Cars of the Stars, and Enchanted Village of wild animals.

Buenaventura River, legendary river whose name was variously spelled, long thought to flow from Salt Lake or the Rocky Mts. through California into the Pacific, perhaps at San Francisco Bay. Sacramento River and San Joaquin River were at times thought to be part of it and Pit River was once considered a northern branch. It was sought or ostensibly seen by Escalante (1776), Jedediah Smith (1827), John Work (1832), and even Frémont, the last on the expedition that named the Great Basin and proved the river did not exist.

Buena Vista County, a projected but never organized county intended to be created (1855) from northern Tulare County. Visalia was originally named Buena Vista.

BUFANO, BENIAMINO (1890?–1970), Italian-born sculptor, reared in New York, continued his career in San Francisco, which was his home for over fifty years except for a lengthy stay in Paris and travel around the world. His pacifist views in World War I (which led him to cut off his trigger finger—and allegedly mail it to President Wilson) and his attachment to the beliefs of Saint Francis, as well as the views of Sun Yat-sen♦ and Gandhi (each of whom he met in China and India), are often evident in his sculpture of animals, of the persons who influenced him, and of figures symbolizing Peace. His work is generally very simple in style, monumental in scale, and striking in its use of stainless steel and mosaic insets.

BUFFUM, EDWARD GOULD (1820–67), went to California with Stevenson's Regiment♦ and upon deactivation joined the gold rush (Oct. 1849), about which, having been a New York journalist, he wrote a vivid account, *Six Months in the Gold Mines: From a Journal of Three Years in Upper and Lower California, 1847–1849* (1850). He was later an editor of the *Alta California* and returned east to work on the New York *Herald*.

Bull-and-bear fight, see *Bear.*

Bulletin, see *San Francisco Bulletin.*

BUNCHE, RALPH J[OHNSON] (1904–71), born in Detroit and reared in Los Angeles, where he received his A.B. from UCLA. After receiving his Ph.D. from Harvard, and further research, he became a professor of government at Howard University (1928–41). He then entered government service. He was principal secretary of the U.N. Palestine Commission and for his work won a Nobel Peace Prize (1950), the first U.S. black so honored. He was later under secretary of the U.N.

BUNDY, MAY SUTTON (1887–1975), tennis player resident in Pasadena who at sixteen was the youngest person to win the national women's singles championship. In 1905 she became the first American singles champion at Wimbledon, a title she won again in 1907.

Bungalow, a domestic architectural style developed early in the 20th century for a one-story or a story-and-a-half house. It featured a large porch across the front, often a patio on one side or at the rear, and a generally informal atmosphere, with an interior plan that was simple and open. Distantly derived, as is its name, from the Bengali cottages of India, the style achieved distinction in the redwood versions created by the Greene brothers and Maybeck, but it became a sterile form when hundreds of stucco examples were constructed along city streets by ordinary builders.

Bunker Hill, see *Angel's Flight.*

BUNN, JOHN (1898–), Ohio-born basketball coach. While at Stanford University (1930–38) he had Hank Luisetti♦ on his victorious teams and altered the game by helping to get rid of the center jump required to put the ball back in play after each score.

BUNNELL, LAFAYETTE HOUGHTON (1824–1903), a leader of the Mariposa Battalion♦ with James D. Savage♦ and therefore one of the white discoverers and namers of Yosemite Valley (1851). He was a surgeon in the Civil War and wrote *Discovery of the Yosemite* (1880).

BURBANK, LUTHER (1849–1926), born and reared on a Massachusetts farm, was influenced by Darwin's writings. His life work was the breeding of plants and cultivating of new species. In 1875 he followed his three brothers to California, his total capital being ten of his Burbank potatoes, and lived in Santa Rosa for the rest of his life. There he expanded his experiments in hybridizing and producing variants of fruits, flowers, and vegetables, including over forty new plums and prunes, ten or more new berries, diverse lilies, roses, and poppies, and new tomatoes, corn, and peas. The results were described in *New Creations* (1893–1901), a series of catalogues, and several books which made him an almost mythic figure, a kind of beneficent wizard of the plant world.

Burbank, a city northeast of Hollywood in Los Angeles County, and a motion picture and television production center. It also has aircraft plants and residences. Founded in 1887 and named for a subdivider, a Los Angeles dentist, in 1970 it had a population of 88,871.

BURGESS, GELETT [FRANK] (1866–1951), Boston-born humorist. After studying engineering at the Massachusetts Institute of Technology he went to San Francisco to work as a draftsman for the Southern Pacific and as an instructor of topographical drawing at the University of California. From there he drifted into the bohemian life of San Francisco. As a member of Les Jeunes he edited *The Lark*♦ (1895–97), a little magazine joyous and whimsical in tone. To it he contributed the quatrain that made him famous: I never saw a Purple Cow / I never hope to see one / But I can tell you anyhow / I'd rather see than be one!

Other contributions included his drawings of boneless, quasi-human creatures called Goops, who writhed about in what he called "a co-tangent harmonious loop." From *The Lark* he moved to *The Wave*♦ to take over the editing and writing Frank Norris had previously done. He then went to New York, and later to London, but he always remembered San Francisco with pleasure. Of the slap and rattle of its cable cars he wrote a rollicking "Ballad of the Hyde Street Grip" (1901), and its craze for spiritualism is depicted in his local color novel *The Heart Line* (1907).

As a journalist and professional author he wrote a great many other works, including a popular illustrated series of works for juveniles about a new species of Goops reincarnated as balloon-headed naughty children. The first was *Goops and How To Be Them* (1900). Other writings included detective stories, light verse and light romance, and amusing essays such as *Are You a Bromide?* (1906), which contributed a new word—"bromide," meaning platitudinous and boring—to the language, for which he had already coined "blurb," an effusive advertisement. *Bayside Bohemia* (1954) and *Behind the Scenes* (1968) are collections of writings related to his early journalism in San Francisco.

BURGESS, GEORGE HENRY (1830–1905), English-born artist who went to San Francisco in 1849. He made the Bay Area his home thereafter, except for visits to England and elsewhere. He was a founder of the San Francisco Art Institute. His best-known canvas is the very large *San Francisco in 1849,* painted in the 1880s and made into a popular lithograph in the following decade.

Burlingame, elegant suburban residential community south of San Francisco in San Mateo County. It was named (1868) by William C. Ralston for his friend Anson C. Burlingame, then U.S. Minister to China. The great estates include New Place, built as the home of W. H. Crocker (1910–11) but since 1954 the clubhouse of the exclusive Burlingame Country Club, the first country club in California (est. 1893). Redistricting has placed the edifice in Hillsborough.♦ Population in 1970 was 27,320.

BURNETT, PETER HARDEMAN (1807–95), 1st governor of the state of California (Dec. 20, 1849–Jan. 9, 1851). A native of Tennessee who practiced law in Missouri, he went to Oregon in 1843, where he played a prominent part in organizing the territorial government. In 1848 he left for California with the first company of gold seekers but soon quit the mines to serve for six months as the agent of Sutter's son, handling the family's complicated business affairs. Although appointed a superior court judge by the military governor, Gen. Riley, Burnett opposed the principle of military government, urged formation of a state government prior to admission into the Union, and promoted a Constitutional Convention. Under the new Constitution he was elected governor and immediately took office in the temporary capital of San Jose, although California was not admitted until Sept. 1850. Tiring of the post, in Jan. 1851 he resumed law practice in San Francisco and in 1857 was appointed a justice of the state Supreme Court but resigned in 1858. From 1863 to 1880 he was president of the Pacific Bank in San Francisco and retired with a fortune. His writings include *The Path Which Led a Protestant Lawyer to the Catholic Church* (1860), *Recollections and Opinions of an Old Pioneer* (1880), and *Reasons Why We Should Believe in God, Love God, and Obey God* (1884).

BURNHAM, DANIEL HUDSON (1846–1912), Chicago architect and city planner known for his general plan for the Columbian Exposition at Chicago (1893) and for some of that city's major downtown buildings, was invited by Mayor James D. Phelan of San Francisco to provide that city with a plan. Beginning in 1904 and aided by Willis Polk in 1905, he proposed a civic center (like the Place de la Concorde) at Market and Van Ness, with eight broad boulevards radiating from it, lesser streets to follow contours of hills which would be crowned by neoclassical parks, and a subway. The desire for rapid rebuilding after the earthquake and fire of 1906 and concentration on the prosecution of Mayor Schmitz for graft drained off the enthusiasm for the plan beyond the building of a modified version of the civic center.

Burns Committee, see *Tenney, Jack.*

BURROUGHS, EDGAR RICE (1875–1950), Chicago-born author of popular adventure fiction, notably a series of novels begun with *Tarzan of the Apes* (1914), about Tarzan, the son of a British nobleman, reared by apes after having been deserted as an infant in an African jungle. After 1919 Burroughs lived just north of Los Angeles on an estate he called Tarzana, from which the adjacent town later derived its name. He was also known as an early writer of science fiction. His Tarzan novels have frequently been adapted for motion pictures, notably those starring Johnny Weissmuller.♦

Busch Gardens, tourist attraction near Van Nuys on the gardened estate associated with a brewery. It features a tropical setting, a large aviary, amphitheaters, and brewery tours.

BUSH, Norton (1834–94), New York-born landscape painter who, beginning in the 1850s, was mainly a resident of San Francisco and Sacramento, and was known for his depictions of local scenes and of Central and South America, made during his travels.

BUTMAN, Frederick A. (1820–71), went from Maine to San Francisco (1857) and remained there most of the rest of his life, painting dramatic landscapes, often of Mt. Shasta and similar scenes.

Butte County, one of the state's original 27 counties (1850). Glenn and Colusa counties lie on the west, Tehama County on the north, Plumas County on the east, and Sutter and Yuba counties on the south. The Sacramento River forms the western boundary. Since 1856 Oroville◆ has been the county seat. The largest city, Chico,◆ was founded by John Bidwell,◆ founder also of the first county seat, Bidwell Bar, which, like many mining camps, grew up along the Feather River◆ during the gold rush. The building of the Oroville Dam on the Feather River during the 1960s created Lake Oroville and inundated some of those mountain camps. Thermalito Dam and its bay lie nearby. Paradise, once a center of apple-growing, has become a large residential community in this county of small urban settlements. The economy is based on the raising of rice, almonds, fruit, and olives, as well as livestock farming, lumbering, food processing, and production of natural gas. In 1970 the population was 101,969. With an area of 1,067,584 acres, it had 61.1 persons per sq. mi.

BUTTERFIELD, John (1801–69), rose from stagecoach driving in western New York to establish the American Express Co. and a great stagecoach line (begun in 1858) to cross 2,800 miles of the continent from St. Louis to California, traveling via Arkansas, El Paso, Tucson, and Yuma to Los Angeles and San Francisco. The semiweekly run of his Overland Mail Co. covered the route in 28 days or less. Objections by northern Congressmen to the company's federal subsidy for travel through the South, and Confederate depredations, caused the line to be shifted in 1861 to the central route of the Oregon Trail. Part of the contract was assumed by Ben Holladay◆ (1862) and then by Wells, Fargo,◆ which later ran the stages (1866–69).

Butterflies, in California there are 236 distinct species. These can be grouped into 10 families: *brush-footed; hair-streaks, coppers,* and *blues; metal-marks; milkweeds, ringlets, satyrs* and allies; *skippers; snouts; swallowtails* and allies; *whites* and *sulphurs;* and *yucca borers.* (1) *Brush-footed* include the largest number of characteristic California varieties; among the members of this family the most common are: *gulf frittilary, chalcedon checker-spot, field crescent, satyr* (an *angle wing*), *California tortoise-shell, West Coast lady,* and *Lorquin's admiral.* (2) *Hair-streaks* are medium sized and obscurely colored, but the related *coppers* have rich metallic hues. The related *blues,* though not very common, are found more frequently than in any other state. (3) *Metal-marks* are small, and the California varieties are not unusually colorful as are the species found in the tropics. (4) *Milkweeds* are medium sized with subdued colors in bold patterns. The state has two varieties: the *striated* and the *monarch,* the latter well known for its annual winter migration to the "Butterfly Trees" of Pacific Grove.◆ (5) *Ringlets* are medium sized and dull colored, the most common being the *California ringlet.* (6) *Skippers,* of which the most common are the *woodland* and *western checkered,* lack much color, and (7) *snouts,* with unusually formed mouthparts, are rare in the state. (8) *Swallowtails* include the largest butterflies in California, but the colors are not gaudy, being mainly black and yellow with bits of blue and red. Of the *swallowtails* the most common are the *anise* and *western tiger.* (9) *Whites* and *sulphurs* are mostly medium sized, generally colored orange, yellow, or white with superimposed black markings. Both subtropical and boreal varieties flourish in the state, and the *common white* and *cabbage* are destructive to produce. The *dog-face* of this species was named the state insect (1973). (10) *Yucca borers,* resembling the *snout,* may be closely related to day moths. *Mariposa,* Spanish for "butterfly," was used as a name for several sites within the present county of that name because the expedition of Gabriel Moraga (1806) encountered so many butterflies there.

Buttes, see *Sierra Buttes* and *Sutter Buttes.*

C

CA, official abbreviation for the state, authorized by the Post Office Department (1963) at the time it introduced the ZIP Code.

Cable car, form of transportation invented (1871 ff.) by Andrew S. Hallidie♦ to traverse and climb the steep hills of San Francisco. The basic mechanism is a motorized endless cable sunk in a slot below and between the car tracks so that it can be gripped and released by a device operated by the car's motorman. The first car to be drawn uphill by that means ran on Clay St. from Kearny St. to Leavenworth St. (Aug. 1, 1873) and won an immediate and great success for its company. The cable car permitted easy access to parts of the city previously difficult to reach: for example, Nob Hill♦ soon had its own line, allowing development of the summit as a particularly stylish new residential area. Numerous other tracks were soon built, on some of which ran not only a cable-gripping lead car but a "dummy" car or two that it towed. Although cable cars might long since have been rendered obsolete by other forms of transportation, San Francisco still retains some because the mode of travel and the Victorian design arouse popular sentiment among residents and they serve as a quaint and exciting attraction for tourists.

CABRILLO, JUAN RODRÍGUEZ (d. 1543), Portuguese-born sailor who, having participated in Cortés' conquest of Mexico, was ordered by Viceroy Antonio de Mendoza to try to discover the Strait of Anián (the Northwest Passage). In June 1542 he sailed north with his two little ships, *San Salvador* and *Victoria*, voyaging from Navidad, on the west coast of Mexico, to a landing at San Diego on Sept. 28, thus becoming the first European discoverer of California. He went on to visit Catalina Island, the sites of San Pedro and Santa Monica, and the Santa Barbara Channel Islands. On the island now called San Miguel he fell and broke his arm but soon resumed his voyage north to a point near later Fort Ross. Heavy seas and winter weather made Cabrillo turn his ship back to San Miguel where, on Jan. 3, 1543, he died, probably from an infection in his injured arm. He was buried on the island his sailors named for him which Vizcaíno renamed San Miguel. The grave has never been lo-

cated, but an incised rock thought to be his tombstone was found on neighboring Santa Rosa Island. Cabrillo's pilot, Bartolomé Ferrelo (or Ferrer), carried out his captain's dying wish to explore northward, and he sailed to the present Oregon-California border before being forced to return to Navidad (April 14, 1543) in starving and sickly condition. The probable site of Cabrillo's first landing in California was made a national monument (1913). The coastline honors him with a Point Cabrillo in Mendocino County and a Cabrillo Point in Monterey County.

Cache Creek, stream in Yolo County,♦ named by Hudson's Bay Co. trappers because they hid their traps on its banks. Nowadays it helps to irrigate a major agricultural area.

Cachuma, Lake, like the creek and mountain of the same Indian name, is located in the Santa Ynez Mts., northwest of San Marcos Pass. It is a manmade reservoir (created 1953) of the Santa Ynez River.

Cactus, succulent plant which stores water in stems and leaves and produces spines, flowers, and branches from areoles, found in numerous varieties in California. The first scientific study was made by Thomas Nuttall♦ (1834).

More than half the state's cacti species belong to the genus *Opuntia,* of which there are two major subgenera. Examples of the first subgenus, the *Cylindropuntia,* or *cholla,* distinguished by cylindrical stems, are found in nine varieties. They are *pencil cactus,* low and bushy with solitary spines, colored flowers, and fruit like sand burrs, found in the southern Mojave, Colorado, and Borrego deserts; the *jumping cholla* or *teddy bear cactus,* a three- to four-foot tree with dense, spiny branches and silvery bristles, found in the southern Mojave and Colorado deserts; the *silver* or *golden cholla,* three to four feet with a trunk crowned by cylindrical branches with silver or golden spines and flowers, the most widely distributed cholla in the state, found on deserts, mesas, and foothills from sea level to 6,000 feet; *buckhorn cholla,* similar to the silver but bushier; *devil's cactus,* with short stems forming broad mats and yellow flowers and

59

fruit; *coast cholla,* two to three feet tall with fruits growing serially on one another, found near the ocean south from Ventura County and on the Channel Islands; *snake cholla,* named for its spreading branches, found only at Point Loma and near Chula Vista and San Ysidro; *valley cholla,* four to six feet tall with a few canelike branches and inconspicuous flowers and spines, flourishing in interior valleys south and west of southern California deserts; and *dwarf cholla,* small, with large purple flowers, found in eastern Mono County and the White Mts.

The other subgenus, the *Platyopuntia,* or prickly pear, has stems that are flattened pads. There are fourteen varieties: *beaver tail cactus,* descriptively named, has rose- to orchid-colored flowers, and is found throughout the Mojave, Borrego, and Colorado deserts; *old man prickly pear* or *grizzly bear cactus,* similar, but with gray, white, or blackish spines and yellow flowers, found in much of the Mojave Desert and the Santa Rosa and White mountains; *golden prickly pear* or *pancake pear,* with a trunk six feet or higher, with yellow spines and flowers and red or purplish fruit, grows in eastern San Bernardino County; *Banning prickly pear,* is short, erect, with long pads and white and yellow spines, found on the edging slopes of deserts, in Riverside County, and in the Peninsular and Transverse ranges; *Pierce's prostrate prickly pear,* has creeping clumps that root and yellow flowers and lives in the same mountains; *Mojave Desert prickly pear,* grows low with yellow-brown spines and yellow flowers, is seen along the Nevada boundary and in the Providence Mts.; *salmon-flowered prickly pear,* low growing but wide spreading, grows in southern California's interior valleys; *Colville's prickly pear,* similar in appearance and location but has lemon flowers touched with red; *western prickly pear,* reaches six feet in large bushes with long leaves, yellow to cream flowers, and large reddish fruit, grows in Orange County to the San Gabriel Mts.; *short coastal prickly pear,* with oblong pads and white spines, the major *Platyopuntia* along the southern coast; *tall coast prickly pear,* reaches up to six feet, has nearly circular pads and translucent yellow spines, and grows in the same region; *Indian fig,* which is almost spineless and ranges from a shrub to a tree, was brought from Mexico by the mission padres and is now found west of the mountains of the state; *mission cactus,* also brought by the padres, is treelike and its reddish, spineless fruit is the most edible variety, now grows from Santa Barbara to San Diego; and *pigmy tuna,* a low, spreading pear which grows in Siskiyou County and other cold climates.

There are sixteen other varieties, nine of the most common being desert cacti: *hedgehog* or *strawberry cactus,* spiny, with brilliant magenta to purplish flowers; *mound* or *Mojave hedgehog cactus,* whose appearance and locale are described by its name; *desert barrel cactus,* varies in appearance but is generally heavy and less than three feet tall; *pygmy barrel cactus,* less than ten inches tall with colorful flowers, is found in the northeastern Mojave Desert; *desert pincushion cactus,* also very small with white spines and colorful flowers; *foxtail cactus,* somewhat larger but otherwise similar to the desert pincushion; *nigger heads,* multiheaded cacti with wooly fruit and yellow flowers; *long-spined fishhook cactus,* grows to a foot high with magenta flowers and smooth red fruit; and *cork-seeded fishhook,* with large flowers.

Two other common cacti, not growing in deserts, are *coastal fishhook* or *nipple cactus* and *coast barrel cactus,* both found in San Diego County. Five less common cacti are *giant cactus,* or *saguaro,* known for its huge fleshy stem that reaches sixty feet, which grows along the Colorado River and in the Whipple Mts.; *velvet cactus,* with spiny red globular fruit, found near the San Diego coast; and *Boyce Thompson hedgehog cactus, Arizona pincushion,* and *desert fishhook cactus,* all found just west of the state line. Some fruits are edible, and Indians sometimes also ate the stalks, leaves, or seeds of cacti, which have also been employed medicinally. Legends also tell of emigrants saved from death by drinking barrel cactus juice. The prevalence and importance of cacti are indicated by the many place-names referring to them, such as Cholla (San Diego County).

CADENASSO, Giuseppe (1858–1918), Italian-born painter known for his California landscapes, was long a teacher of art at Mills College.

CADMAN, Charles Wakefield (1881–1946), Pennsylvania-born composer, went to California (1911) and took up residence in La Mesa (San Diego County). His works include the operas *Shenewis* (1918) and *A Witch of Salem* (1927), numerous cantatas, and a popular song, "From the Land of the Sky Blue Water," for which he used an Indian melody.

Cady Mountains, range in north-central San Bernardino County.

CAEN, Herb[ert] (1916–   ), born in Sacramento but often considered the quintessential San Franciscan because of his lively commentary on the daily doings of the city in a column for the *Chronicle* (1938–50, 1958–   ) and the *Examiner* (1950–58). In it he also evokes the history and atmosphere of the city, to which he is deeply devoted. His many books include *Baghdad-by-the-Bay* (1949), *Don't Call It Frisco* (1953), *Only in San Francisco* (1960), and *One Man's San Francisco* (1976).

CAGE, John [Milton, Jr.] (1912–   ), Los Angeles-born composer, studied at Pomona College and with Henry Cowell and Arnold Schoenberg, and for a time taught at Mills College. His compositions incorporate natural sounds and sometimes are created by chance relationships. His works include *Sonatas and Interludes* (1946–48), *Water Music* (1952), and *Variations* (1958–65). He also performs his own works in piano concerts that smack of happenings. He has composed music for dances choreographed and performed by Merce Cunningham, and has written books including *Silence* (1961) and *A Year from Monday* (1967).

CAGNEY, James (1904–   ), New York-born film star of Hollywood who played roles as a bright, nervously vital, and tough-acting young man in such diverse films as *Public Enemy* (1931); *Yankee Doodle Dandy* (1943), in which he portrayed George M. Cohan; and *Mister Roberts* (1955). He lived in the Los Angeles area over 40 years.

Cahuenga Pass, located near the present intersection of the Ventura and Hollywood freeways in Los Angeles, got its name from a Shoshonean word. Portolá traversed the pass in exploring the San Fernando Valley and it is famous as the site of one battle (1831) in which Gov. Manuel Victoria♦ was defeated and of another (1845) in which Alvarado and Castro overthrew Gov. Micheltorena.♦ Nearby, Andrés Pico♦ and Frémont♦ signed the Cahuenga Capitulation Treaty (Jan. 13, 1847), which ended the war between Mexican and American forces in California.

Cahuilla, Indians resident between the San Bernardino and San Jacinto mountains in present Riverside County, where they now have a reservation. Prehistorically they numbered about 2,500 but the 1910 census counted only 750. The aridity of their land made them rely on the mesquite tree and the roots of various desert plants for food. They believed all food had once been human and able to speak. They did not know the Chinigchinich♦ religion, but they consumed toloache or jimson weed

like the Miwok and like them considered each person to belong to a moiety or category that had special animal-like attributes and believed that one might not marry a person of one's own moiety. In the 20th century the Cahuilla have grown in population as well as tremendously in wealth. A U.S. Supreme Court ruling (1944) determined that as a result of a federal government grant (1870) of odd-numbered sections of desert land to the Southern Pacific and even-numbered sections to the Cahuilla, each Indian should receive the rental from $350,000 worth of land and a share of the 30,000 acres of tribal land.

CAIN, James M[allahan] (1892–1977), novelist and newspaperman of Maryland, from the 1930s on occasionally resident in California, where he wrote for films. Some of his fiction is set in California, notably *The Postman Always Rings Twice* (1934), a work in the vein of tough detective fiction♦ about a young drifter who comes to a lonely gas station, falls in love with the wife of the Greek owner, and murders him; and *Mildred Pierce* (1941), about a woman in Glendale who makes a business success and has an affair with her daughter's boy friend. Both were made into successful films, the latter starring Joan Crawford in an Academy Award winning role. Another successful film adaptation was from his novelette, *Double Indemnity* (1943). His *Past All Dishonor* (1946) is an historical novel set in Virginia City, Nevada.

Cajón Pass, located in the mountains 20 miles north of San Bernardino at an elevation of 4,301 feet, derives its name from the Spanish word for "box." The pass was traveled by Pedro Fages (1772) and Padre Garcés (1776) and later by Jedediah Smith (1827); William Wolfskill established its trail for pack trains from New Mexico to California (1831).

Calafia, see *Sergas de Esplandián, Las.*

Calaveras, Spanish word for "skulls," often used in naming places where Indian remains were found. The most famous example is the discovery by John Marsh♦ in 1836 or 1837 of skeletons on the banks of the river to which he gave that name. The river rises in the Sierra Nevada about 37 miles south of Lake Tahoe and flows about 70 miles southwest to join the San Joaquin River at Stockton. Ironically, in 1866 Josiah Dwight Whitney♦ delivered a paper before the California Academy of Sciences contending that a newly found modern relic, the "Calaveras Skull," discovered in a mining shaft of the region, was a remnant of prehistoric man. Bret Harte satirized that view in two poems, "To the Pliocene Skull" and "The Society upon the Stanislaus," the former including the lines: Which my name is Bowers, and my crust was busted / Falling down a shaft in Calaveras County; / But I'd take it kindly if you'd send the pieces / Home to old Missouri.

The county, which takes its name from the river, is one of the original 27 (1850) and was a major part of the Mother Lode region. Bounded by the Mokelumne River on the north (from Amador County) and by the Stanislaus River on the south (from Tuolumne County), it has Stanislaus County on the west and Alpine County on the east. The county includes Angels Camp and Mokelumne Hill and is often distinguished as the site of some of Bret Harte's stories, but it figures most prominently in literature in Mark Twain's "The Celebrated Jumping Frog of Calaveras County," set in Angels Camp. The county is also the site of the Calaveras Grove of Big Trees, the first-discovered Sequoias (1854). The Melones Water Project♦ lies on the county's Stanislaus River border. The county is also known for livestock and poultry raising and for asbestos and cement mining, the latter near the county seat of San Andreas.♦ In 1970 the county population was 13,585. With an area of 660,352 acres, that gave it 13.2 persons per sq. mi.

CALDER, ALEXANDER STIRLING (1870–1945), Philadelphia sculptor, because of his health moved to Los Angeles (1906–10), where he created panels for the entrance to Throop Polytechnic Institute in Pasadena. He returned (1915) to oversee all sculpture for the Panama-Pacific International Exposition. With Maybeck, Porter Garnett, and Bruce Porter he wrote the book *Art in California* (1916). His son, Alexander Calder, later the noted maker of mobiles, was with him along with the rest of his family.

Calexico, international border town on the southern edge of Imperial County with Mexicali♦ as its Mexican counterpart across the line that is only a street. Once the site of Salvation Camp, founded by Cave J. Couts as a refugee center for forty-niners taking a southern route to the gold mines, the town itself was founded (1908) on land owned by George Chaffey for his irrigation project. The All-American Canal now runs near it. In 1970 its population was 10,625.

Calico Mountains, range in San Bernardino County, just north of Daggett in the Mojave Desert; they de-

rive their name from the term miners applied to the multicolored rock formations, which range from yellow-white to red. A ghost town, Calico—restored by the owner of Knott's Berry Farm—was a lively silver mining center in the 1880s. There are also Calico Peaks in Death Valley.

Caliente Range, mountains lying between the Cuyama River and the Carrizo Plain♦ along the southeastern border of San Luis Obispo County.

California Academy of Sciences, privately funded San Francisco institution, oldest of its kind in the western U.S., was founded in 1853. Located in Golden Gate Park since 1916, its buildings include a planetarium and museums and it runs the adjacent city-supported Steinhart Aquarium. The Academy sponsors scientific expeditions and related research and publications, concentrating on California, North America, the Pacific basin, and Africa.

California admission to the Union, see *Admission Day*.

California Angels, see *Angels, California*.

California Aqueduct, part of the California Water Plan, a joint state and federal undertaking begun in the 1960s. The Aqueduct carries water♦ from the Sacramento-San Joaquin Delta through a huge pumping plant at Tracy in order to send it down the west side of the San Joaquin Valley to irrigate farmlands and dry areas farther south. It terminates in the artificial Lake Perris of northwestern Riverside County.

California Archives, huge aggregation of proclamations, decrees, records, reports, laws, dispatches, letters, journals, diaries, and other documents covering the period from 1768, gathered into 289 volumes averaging 700 pages each, assembled in Monterey (1847 ff.) by Henry W. Halleck as secretary of state under the military governors Mason and Riley. They were moved to San Francisco (1858), partly copied by H. H. Bancroft, and used by other historians before most of them were destroyed in the fire following the San Francisco earthquake (1906). They are not to be confused with the State Archives♦ in Sacramento.

California as a "free and sovereign State," see *Alvarado, Juan B.*

California as a name, see *Sergas de Esplandían, Las*.

California as an island, see *Islands of California.*

California As It Is . . . , see *Wierzbicki, Felix.*

California Battalion, Frémont's contingent of some 230 American settlers who served in the Bear Flag Revolt and who, on July 23, 1846, were enlisted by Commodore Stockton as a Navy Battalion of Mounted Riflemen. With further volunteers the battalion served under Frémont♦ throughout the campaign against the *Californios* until mustered out in April 1847. Its equivocal relation to the forces of Gen. Kearny♦ played a large part in Frémont's subsequent court-martial.

California Club, oldest men's social club in Los Angeles, founded (1887) mainly by professional men, including B. C. Truman, I. W. Hellman, Gaylord Wilshire, J. J. Mellus, and J. deBarth Shorb. Since 1930 it has been housed in a handsome seven-story downtown building.

California College of Arts and Crafts, founded in Berkeley (1907) by the German-born furniture designer Frederick H. Meyer, with Xavier Martinez, Perham Nahl, and Percy West as faculty. It early moved to nearby Oakland and has branched out into general education. In 1970 it had a student body of more than 1,300 men and women.

California Conservation Corps, government program (est. 1976) designed for 1,000 youths (aged 18–20) to undertake a year of public service environmental work at minimum wages while resident in camps located throughout the state.

California Current, ocean current that begins near Taiwan, moves along the coast of Japan (where it is called the Japan or Kuroshio Current, or sometimes the Black Stream because of its deep blue color), and then crosses the Pacific to southern Alaska. As the California Current it then sweeps south along the coast to about 10 degrees above the Equator before flowing westward back across the Pacific as the North Equatorial Current. The strong southerly flow along the California coast impeded sailing ships headed north and therefore long helped to discourage exploration and colonization, although it assisted the Manila galleons on their sailing route across the Pacific. The cool water of the current, when met by warm air from the Central Valley, causes coastal fog.♦

California Democratic Council, unofficial party association founded (1953) to link local clubs into a dynamic statewide political organization. It is generally known by its initials, CDC.

California dimensions and distances, the state ranks third in area after Alaska and Texas, encompassing 158,693 sq. mi., of which 156,537 are land and 2,156 are inland water. It extends from *c.*32° to 42° north and from 114° to 124° west. It is about 780 miles long and about 825 miles from its northwest corner to the southeast corner. Its maximum width is about 350 miles; at minimum it narrows to about 150 miles. There are 1,264 miles of coastal shore and 291 additional miles of shoreline around the state's offshore islands. It extends into the Pacific's Continental Shelf♦ for 3.45 statute miles. The geographic center lies in Madera County, 35 miles northeast of its county seat. Elevations range from 14,495 feet at the summit of Mt. Whitney to 282 feet below sea level at Bad Water, Death Valley, both of which are in Inyo County.

California Farm Bureau Federation, an organization (est. 1919) made up of local bureaus which cooperates with the University of California in teaching farmers better techniques and managerial practices. It has also been involved with lobbying for licensing of seed dealers, state beef inspection, and similar matters, as well as in providing research and marketing information. Early members were mostly prosperous farmers, generally from southern California, and during the Depression the Bureau cooperated with the Associated Farmers♦ in opposing unionization of agricultural workers.

California Fruit Growers Exchange, cooperative association founded (1905) as an outgrowth of two other marketing groups, the earliest established in 1893, followed by the Southern California Fruit Growers Association (1895). It improved orange growing by controlling pests and encouraging the Valencia species; standardizing the cleaning and packing of fruit; creating the trade name Sunkist; employing widespread publicity; establishing uniform techniques of grading, marketing, and pricing; and lobbying. It came to control over 70% of the state's citrus crop and made itself the world's leading association of its type. C. C. Teague♦ was its president (1930–50). In 1952 the name was changed to Sunkist Growers, Inc.

California Golden Seals, ice hockey team (1970–76), founded (1967) as the Oakland Seals in the expansion that created a Western Division of the National Hockey League. Owned by Charles O. Finley (1972–74), the team then played in the Alameda County Coliseum. It moved to Cleveland in 1976, and was renamed the Barons.

California, Gulf of, arm of the Pacific Ocean, about 700 miles long from the southern tip of Baja California to the point where waters of the Colorado River flow into it. Long considered to be a strait that separated the mainland of Mexico from an island of California, early explorers included Cortés, Alarcón, and Ulloa,♦ the last-named determining that Baja California was a peninsula. In the 17th century it was the site of much fishing for pearls. Ugarte built the first ship (1719) to explore the gulf, which at its widest is 100 miles across. It is also called the Sea of Cortés or Cortez (as in a book by John Steinbeck about a marine expedition there) and Vermilion Sea.

"California, Here I Come," popular song whose words and music were written by Al Jolson, B. G. Sylva, and Joseph Meyer. Sung by Jolson in the revue *Bombo* (1921), it was later featured in three of his films (1939, 46, 49).

California Historical Society, founded (1871) at Santa Clara College, reorganized (1886) to read and issue papers, and again in 1922 as an organization for the collection and dissemination of knowledge about California through publication of a *Quarterly,* monthly notes, occasional books, and meetings. It has some 6,800 members (1976), a headquarters in San Francisco that has a library and art gallery, and a smaller headquarters in San Marino at El Molino Viejo.♦

California Institute of Technology, private university located at Pasadena, founded (1891) as Throop Polytechnic Institute,♦ which name it changed to its present one in 1920. It operates the observatory at Mt. Palomar,♦ and it has been instrumental in developing jet propulsion for missiles and moon landings. Distinguished faculty members have included Robert A. Millikan (Nobel Prize, 1923). It is also noted for instruction in the humanities, using the nearby resource of the Huntington Library. In 1970 it had a faculty of about 450 and fewer than 1,500 students.

California Institute of the Arts, private educational institution created (1961) by incorporating the

Chouinard Art Institute, a school of art and design founded in Los Angeles (1921) by Nelbert Chouinard, and the Los Angeles Conservatory of Music (est. 1883). Walt Disney left a large endowment to the school and his family has made sizable contributions also, the two totaling some $30,000,000, so that the Institute was able to move to fine new quarters on its own campus (1971) in Valencia in the San Fernando Valley.

California League, organization of baseball teams♦ begun in the 1880s that evolved into the Pacific Coast League♦ (1903). An "outlaw" California State League continued (1903–10) until it was recognized and developed into a Class A minor league.

California Maritime Academy, state-supported private institution located on the north shore of Carquinez Strait, offering undergraduate instruction in nautical science and marine engineering. Founded in 1929, in the 1970s it began to accept a few women. Its total enrollment is over 200 and it is headed by a USMS admiral.

California Museum of Science and Industry, a major exhibition hall located in Exposition Park, Los Angeles, which provides an audio-visual understanding of scientific, industrial, agricultural, and human physiological subjects, largely through devices operated by the visitors.

California official symbols, see *State symbols.*

California Palace of the Legion of Honor, art museum founded by Adolph and Alma de Bretteville Spreckels (1924) located at Land's End in a neoclassical building based on the one in Paris for which it is named. The collection is known for its sculptures by Rodin, French paintings, and Achenbach Foundation for Graphic Arts. In 1972 it was merged with the de Young Museum to form the Fine Arts Museums of San Francisco.

California Republican Assembly, unofficial party association founded (1934) to fuse local groups into a dynamic statewide political organization. It is best known by its initials, CRA.

California School of Fine Arts, see *San Francisco Art Institute.*

California Stage Company, founded (1854) by two New Englanders under the age of 25, James E.

Birch, a whip (driver) who had established the state's first stage line, from Coloma to Sacramento (1849), and Frank Stevens, a tavernkeeper. Their firm, with headquarters in Sacramento, was capitalized at $1,000,000, owned 750 horses, and operated 450 miles of regular route service. It consolidated five-sixths of the state's stagecoach lines. In 1855 service was extended beyond the mining country and San Francisco through lines from Oakland to San Jose and from San Francisco to Monterey. A year later it operated 1,500 miles of line, half the state's total, and in that year, when Birch sought to enter a nationwide stage business, James Haworth took over the presidency. By 1858 the company operated 28 daily stage lines with 1,000 horses and 134 Concord stages and wagons over nearly 2,000 miles of routes. In 1860 it began to carry U.S. mail from Sacramento to Portland and was the second largest stage company in the U.S. Soon thereafter it began to dispose of lines south of Sacramento, operating from Sacramento, Folsom, and Marysville north into Oregon. It remained the dominant power in northern California transportation until the 1870s, when railroads made stagecoaches obsolete.

California Star, The, weekly newspaper founded by Samuel Brannan,♦ the first to be published in San Francisco, began regular publication on Jan. 9, 1847. It was a lively journal, attacking Colton and Semple, publishers of the rival *Californian,* and *Alcalde* Bartlett for changing the name Yerba Buena to San Francisco. C. E. Pickett was a contributor and E. C. Kemble became editor (1847) and owner (Sept. 1848), buying the opposition paper to create *The California Star & Californian* (Nov. 1848), which in turn was taken over by the *Alta California* (Jan. 1849).

California State Automobile Association, founded (1907) as an outgrowth of the Automobile Club of California (1901) and as an affiliate of the Automobile Association of America. Its purposes included the improvement of driving and road conditions, the creation of a better image of motoring and motorists, and the fostering of favorable legislation. By 1912 it had 1,600 members and had led campaigns for improved road surfaces and highway signs. It went on to provide touring information and maps; insurance; a magazine, *California Motorist* (1917), later *Motorland;* emergency road service (1922); a list of selected hotels; bail bond service; and association with affiliated clubs beyond the state. By 1959 it had more than 500,000 members and in 1977 it was approaching 2,000,000 members.

The other major organization serving similar purposes is the Automobile Club of Southern California.♦

California State Library, see *State Library*.

California State Universities, see *State Universities and Colleges.*

California Tomorrow, nonprofit foundation (est. 1965), concerned with regional planning and the state's natural environment. It issues a quarterly, *Cry California.*

California Trail, name commonly given to the overland route to California following the pathway of earlier emigration to Oregon as far as Fort Hall. Never a single trail, it was a broad route over which people, livestock, and covered wagons moved, converging closely only as required by river and mountain crossings. It began at Westport, Independence, Fort Leavenworth, and St. Joseph at the Missouri River and moved across the northeast corner of Kansas to strike the North Platte River at Fort Kearny, following its south bank to Fort Laramie, then crossing the river to South Pass. Proceeding southwest to Fort Bridger in present Wyoming, it then turned north toward or to Fort Hall on the Snake River in present Idaho.

Near there the routes separated, one going north to Oregon, the other going southwest to the headwaters of the Humboldt River in the northeast of present Nevada. Thence it generally proceeded across the Humboldt and Carson sinks to reach the Sierra Nevada, which was crossed north or south of Lake Tahoe by various routes: Carson Pass, Donner Pass, Emigrant Gap, Henness Pass, and Beckwourth Pass. The entire route covered about 2,000 miles and took about five months to travel between spring and autumn before snowfall.

The general Oregon Trail branch to California was pioneered by Bartleson and Bidwell♦ as the first emigrant party (1841), one of whose members, Joseph Chiles,♦ led a party west in 1842. Another major crossing was that of Elisha Stevens♦ and Moses Schallenberger♦ (1844), the former being the first to take wagons over the Sierra (via Donner Pass♦ which the party discovered) and the latter being the first emigrant to winter in those mountains. In succeeding years the covered wagon♦ became the standard transportation for large parties. In 1845 a horseback party led by Lansford Hastings♦ tried—and flamboyantly advised—an alternate route which, in 1846, was disastrously followed by the Donner Party.♦

Emigration increased after California became part of the U.S. and swelled enormously after the gold discovery. In 1849 travelers jostled one another on the trail, and George R. Stewart has estimated that "if all the wagons of '49 had been organized into a single close-spaced train, they would have extended for some sixty miles." Perhaps 21,500 people and 6,200 wagons were en route. In 1850 about 45,000 people took to the trail.

By the beginning of the next decade the stagecoaches of Butterfield♦ and the pony express♦ were covering the route. But during the 1850s the trail through the steep Sierra Nevada mountains was an arduous route, particularly after the hard transcontinental crossing, whether one selected Beckwourth Pass in the north; Donner,♦ Carson, and Ebbets♦ passes; or Emigrant Gap.♦

California Water Plan, see *California Aqueduct* and *Water.*

Californian, first newspaper published within the area of the present state. Founded by Walter Colton♦ and Robert Semple,♦ a onetime editor and a former printer, respectively, it was established, according to Semple, at the end of the Bear Flag Revolt "to conciliate the Natives and unite the foreigners residing in California." Aided initially by the American military forces and using the former press and type of Zamorano,♦ the weekly began publication Aug. 15, 1846. Written in English with some Spanish texts of official documents prepared by W. E. P. Hartnell, it contained war news and general information. For a time Colton issued it alone, then Semple became the publisher and moved the paper from Monterey to San Francisco (May 1847), but soon others took over. Subscribers gave it up during the gold rush, and the final issue appeared Nov. 11, 1848, when it was merged with *The California Star.*♦

Californian, The, (1864–66), weekly San Francisco journal, founded by Charles Henry Webb,♦ its editor and a steady contributor of humorous pieces. Its major and consistent contributor was Mark Twain, who wrote burlesques and sketches for it. Bret Harte was a steady contributor of parodies, and other writers included Ambrose Bierce, Ina Coolbrith, Henry George, Prentice Mulford, and Charles Warren Stoddard. Its tone of witty satire of the gold rush pioneer period and the California scene in general was adulterated by frequent reprinting of ordinary fiction from England and France.

Californian, The (1880–83), journal founded by Anton Roman,♦ subtitled *A Western Monthly Magazine.* Contributors included Ambrose Bierce and Joaquin Miller. It was merged with the revived *Overland Monthly* (1883).

Californios, persons of Spanish or Mexican heritage whose place of birth or residence was California, as distinct from residents who went to California from the U.S. or elsewhere. The term has been used particularly in relation to the period from *c.*1830 through the U.S. conquest in 1846.

Californios, Los, San Francisco-based organization concerned with "the heritage of early Spanish Californians in Alta California." It is open to descendants of Spanish-speaking persons who arrived in California before Feb. 2, 1848, and to historians and educational institutions.

Californium, transuranium element artificially produced in the cyclotron at the University of California, Berkeley, by Glenn T. Seaborg and his team (1950) and named by them in honor of the state and its university.

Calistoga, residential and summer resort town of Napa County, founded (1859) by Samuel Brannan,♦ who created its name by combining, perhaps inadvertently, the names of California and Saratoga, a famous New York State spa. In one of his cottages Robert Louis and Fanny Stevenson spent the first part of their honeymoon (1880). The heyday of the elaborate resort with its medicinal hot springs was during the 1860s and 70s.

Call, see *San Francisco Call.*

CalTrans, name given to the Department of Transportation created (1973) by the state legislature to plan a coordinated and balanced system employing mass transportation, highways, aviation, and maritime and railroad facilities and services.

Camels, imported by Edward F. Beale♦ in his capacity as a government agent, came from a herd used in Texas (1856) and directly from Tunis. Most of the animals were single-humped dromedaries but some were the slower moving two-humped bactrians. For the federal government expedition he commanded (1857), Beale used both kinds to aid freighting along the 1,200-mile route to be surveyed for a wagon road between Fort Defiance, N.M., and the Colorado River border of California. After being tried for that purpose the camels were swum across the river and kept at Fort Tejón♦ (1857–61). For a time some were used for transport between Los Angeles and its Wilmington harbor, but since other army officers found them less desirable than Beale did they were taken to Benicia Arsenal and auctioned (1863) to private individuals. Thereafter some of the animals were used for a while to carry freight in Nevada during its mining boom days. An unrelated later use of camels occurs annually during the Date Festival at Indio, where camel races are featured.

CAMERON, DONALDINA (1869–1968), born in New Zealand, reared in San Francisco and the San Joaquin Valley, devoted her life to rescuing and aiding immigrant Chinese girls sold into slavery as prostitutes. She established a Presbyterian mission for them in San Francisco's Chinatown.

CAMINETTI, ANTHONY (1854–1923), began his political career as district attorney (1879) of his home county, Amador; as its state senator (1886, 1906–13) he was known as an opponent of the railroad's political power, a champion of organized labor, but an antagonist of Chinese, Japanese, and radicals. He was also a U.S. congressman (1890–94).

Camino Reál, El, literally, ''the royal highway'' or ''the king's highway,'' was a term for ''public road'' when employed initially in California in the 18th century to describe the route through Baja California and up through Alta California linking the missions and presidios. It began with Portolá's Sacred Expedition of 1769 to locate the ports of San Diego and Monterey and to found churches and military posts en route. The trail north from San Diego went through the sites of the missions San Luis Rey, San Juan Capistrano, and San Gabriel, west to Los Angeles, north through Ventura, Santa Barbara, and San Luis Obispo, over to Morro Bay, through the Salinas Valley inland from Monterey, and up to Mission Dolores, San Francisco. In large part modern Highway 101 follows the route, which is often marked by standards bearing a facsimile of a mission bell, recalling the original reason for establishing the road.

CAMP, CHARLES L[EWIS] (1893–1975), professor of paleontology at his alma mater, the University of California, Berkeley, was known not only for his studies of fossils in Nevada and elsewhere but for his accounts of western history, including *George*

C. Yount and His Chronicles of the West (1966), *James Clyman* (1928, rev. 1960), and his substantial amplification of the bibliography *The Plains and the Rockies* by Henry R. Wagner (1953).

Camp Curry, Yosemite Valley tent village and hotel resort founded (1899) by David and Jennie Curry. It continued in family ownership until 1973 and was later known as Curry Village.

Camp Pendleton, U.S. Marine Corps training area, established (1942) on the vast, old Rancho Santa Margarita y Las Flores of the Pico and Forster families, with an 18-mile ocean frontage between San Clemente and Oceanside, San Diego County. It served as a receiving center for refugees from Vietnam (1975).

Camp Roberts, military post near San Miguel, established as part of Fort Ord,♦ later put under the control of the California National Guard.

Campanario, see *Missions.*

Camping, as a recreation for urban dwellers dates back to the earliest tourist interest in California's scenic highlights.♦ Relatively accessible areas, such as the Santa Cruz Mts., were initially the most popular locations, although Yosemite was the goal of a hardy band of travelers led by James M. Hutchings (1855), soon followed by other visitors to the valley, the Mariposa and Calaveras groves of big trees, and other parts of the Sierra. Those expeditions were popularized by such writings as Thomas Starr King's account of a vacation trip (1860) and Charles Nordhoff's appeal to health seekers (1872). They were also aided by the opening of more stage routes, followed in time by access via the Southern Pacific Railroad, which in the 1890s offered special rates to campers.

At the same time, John Muir was preaching the gospel of wilderness to invigorate and inspire people, and in 1892 he was a founding father of the Sierra Club,♦ which sponsored hiking and camping trips. For somewhat more sedentary outings, the tent resort of Camp Curry was established in Yosemite in 1899. Residents of Los Angeles and other southern California cities found that the nearby San Gabriel Mts. afforded excellent opportunities for excursions on foot or horseback.

Improvements in automobiles, better roads, and labor practices allowing greater leisure all made for a substantially wider and more enthusiastic interest in spending time in wilderness surroundings. The great growth of national and state parks and forests in the 20th century not only provided magnificent settings that could be readily reached but equipped them with good campgrounds that came to be numbered by the thousands. During the Great Depression such facilities and their surrounding trails were improved by the Civilian Conservation Corps, to the delight of many people but to the despair of the Wilderness Society (est. 1935) and the sympathetic *Nature Magazine,* which declared that the problems of wilderness were being treated in "much the same way the Turks set about solving the Armenian problem—by annihilation."

The fear thus expressed became more evident as automobiles packed with camping gear gave way to trailers which in turn were superseded by recreational vehicles called campers, sometimes of monstrous scale. Many people, seeking to avoid these intruders, who brought the accoutrements of the city into the forest, took to backpacking, a popular new form of recreation in the 1970s which allowed vacationers to penetrate the newly established Wilderness Areas using lightweight equipment and supplies.

Canadians in California, first arrived as trappers working for the Hudson's Bay Company.◆ The earliest was Peter Skene Ogden, who trapped along the Shasta River (1826) and later made his way down to the Colorado River and the Gulf of California (1829–30). He was followed by Alexander McLeod (1828), the Irish-born John Work who trapped along the Pit, Bear, and Sacramento rivers (1832–33), and Michael La Framboise (1833). From division headquarters at Fort Vancouver (Oregon), expeditions were sent annually to San Francisco Bay and the nearby valleys until a trading post was opened at Yerba Buena (1841) under William Glenn Rae, son-in-law of John McLaughlin, the Company's leading factor. This was closed when Rae killed himself (1845).

The gold rush attracted many Canadians but their numbers were not generally recognized because the French-Canadians were often considered to be French, and the English-speaking ones were not distinguished from other persons using the language. Thus the American River was named by Sutter for some Canadians whom the local Indians called *Americanos.* However, a Canadian Creek (Trinity County) and other geographic features commemorate Canadian settlements, but of course in California a place-name incorporating "Canada" is usually derived from the Spanish word for valley, *cañada.*

The many prominent Canadians who have contributed to California life include W. H. Rulofson, a pioneer photographer; Anthony Chabot, a developer of water systems; Lyman Ryce, who introduced Canadian white leghorns to Petaluma when he established it as a poultry center; George Chaffey, who devised the irrigation that turned the Colorado Desert into Imperial Valley; Phimester Proctor, a sculptor and mountaineer; Edward Bosqui, a fine publisher; John Henry Nash, the distinguished typographer; and J. Stitt Wilson, a socialist mayor of Berkeley.

The Canadian population of California has grown from 854 (1850) to 10,660 (1870) to 29,818 (1900) to 153,725 to become the second largest (after Mexican) foreign-born element in the state.

Candlestick Park, stadium with a capacity of 58,000 opened in 1960 in the southeasternmost part of San Francisco at Candlestick Point. It was created for the Giants,◆ the city's National League baseball club, but was expanded to serve as the home football field of the Forty-Niners. The damp, foggy, and very windy location, particularly unpleasant in summer, has been much criticized, and attendance has not been good. The point was named for a pinnacle rock long gone from the bayside site.

CAÑIZARES, JOSÉ DE (*fl.* 1769–90), Spanish navigator who came overland to California with Rivera y Moncada on the Sacred Expedition (1769) and remained at San Diego. He served as the pilot to Ayala◆ in the explorations that made the first entry into and first chart of San Francisco Bay (1775). After returning to San Blas he came back to the Bay and again mapped it (1776). Later, at least until 1790, he was a captain of California transports.

Cannery, The, a complex of specialty shops, restaurants, and art galleries housed in a large brick building with arcades and terraces refurbished in the 1960s from its original use as a sardine cannery site. It is located between Fisherman's Wharf and Ghirardelli Square in San Francisco.

Cannery Row, name given to part of Ocean View Ave., Monterey, because at one time there were some 30 sardine canneries along it. On it were also located the marine laboratory of Edward Ricketts,◆ small restaurants, and a brothel or two, all romanticized by John Steinbeck in his novel, *Cannery Row* (1945). It later became a tourist area of gift shops, bars, and nice restaurants, its canneries deserted since the disappearance of the sardine.◆

Canning, see *Food processing.*

Cape Horn, name given to a sheer, thousand-foot-high granite cliff the Central Pacific Railroad♦ had to round in building its line. The imposing obstacle, just beyond Colfax (Placer County), had a narrow ledge chipped along it by Chinese workers who were lowered to the site by ropes.

Cape Mendocino, see *Mendocino.*

Capital, first transferred from Loreto, Baja California, to Alta California (1777) with Monterey named as the seat. Under the governorship of Pío Pico (1845–46) the capital and assembly were transferred to Los Angeles and the customs and treasury left in Monterey. The Constitutional Convention meeting at Monterey (1849) selected San Jose as the first capital of the new state. The session there (Dec. 1849–Oct. 1850) was known as the Legislature of 1,000 Drinks.♦ In June 1851 the capital moved to Vallejo but tried San Jose once more as well as Sacramento and Vallejo again before moving to Benicia (1853) and finally settling permanently in Sacramento (1854).

Cappy Ricks, see *Kyne, Peter B.*

CAPRA, Frank (1897–   ), Sicilian-born director and producer of motion pictures, reared in California, after attending the California Institute of Technology began his career in Hollywood in 1921. He was particularly successful during the Depression with films that included comedy and fantasy and helped to popularize Jean Harlow, Clark Gable, James Stewart, and Gary Cooper. During World War II Capra produced documentaries for the War Department.

Captain Jack, see *Modoc.*

Car culture, term applied to ways of life dependent on the use of the automobile. Although the auto has had a major impact upon all of 20th-century U.S., it has been even more significant in California than elsewhere. In part this is owing to the climate, which allows year-round easy pleasure driving, in part because more Californians are newcomers without rooted associations in a neighborhood and are therefore inclined to travel around quite freely, often to tourist attractions, in part because autos and the state's population (particularly in southern California) developed simultaneously, and, early on, in part because petroleum products were so readily available that, for example, young Earl Gilmore in 1909 sold gasoline from his father's oil wells at ten cents a gallon to motorists along the newly developed Wilshire Boulevard.

Indeed, Los Angeles became the prime example of a city created during the age of the automobile and specifically developed for cars. The Automobile Club of Southern California♦ and the California State Automobile Association,♦ founded in 1900 and 1901, respectively, were responsible for better driving and road conditions. By 1925 Los Angeles had one automobile for every three persons, over twice the average for the nation. Concomitantly, the city developed the first modern supermarket and was a pioneer in the creation of drive-in restaurants.

In time the term "drive-in" became commonplace, as all kinds of activities, including banks and motion picture theaters, catered to persons who did not want to step out of their automobiles. In 1925 the owner of a hostelry in San Luis Obispo created the concept of a motel and coined the word for it. During that era the automobile became a status symbol, as film stars drove about or were chauffeured in especially exotic or expensive machines, while Hollywood also aggrandized the appeal of cars by featuring them in all sorts of situations, including exciting chases.

Automobile racing♦ also became a popular recreation and spectator sport. Automobiles became objects of such esteem beyond their usefulness for transportation that in the 1930s a motion picture star, James Melton, created a great collection of old-time cars, and in that decade California possessed one of the three Horseless Carriage Clubs in the nation. These antique vehicles, along with the most luxurious modern custom-designed models, began to be displayed in special rallies called *concours d'élégance.* In time, permanent museums were also established for them, notably one in Buena Park called the Movieworld Cars of the Stars.

The fascination that autos exerted and the dependence upon them made a new big business of dealerships for popular models and thereby created a whole new group of California millionaires. It also turned San Francisco's Van Ness Avenue from the city's most elegant residential street into an automobile row with tawdry lots of second-hand cars interspersed among magnificent showrooms, including one designed by Bernard Maybeck in 1928 with great Corinthian columns and a coffered ceiling.

As highways♦ improved and freeways♦ were

developed, the ubiquitous private auto, bigger and bigger trucks, and large passenger buses crowded them more and more, creating at peak hours the very traffic problems they were intended to obviate. In 1950 over 3,000,000 automobiles were registered in the state; two decades later that figure had grown to 10,000,000, representing 10% of all personal vehicles in the nation. Only New York, Pennsylvania, and Texas had greater numbers of cars registered than did Los Angeles County. As the so-called hippie style of living developed, it took over the auto for its own purposes, popularizing newly developed car models called vans, in which their owners for some periods of time found privacy surrounded by curtains, carpets, large beds, and stereo sound systems. The exteriors, the only areas visible to passersby, were often colorfully painted to alter in overwhelming ways the uniform designs of the manufacturers. Other young people, who remodeled conventional cars into hot rods of diverse sorts, often found their recreation or release simply by driving the freeways, or as their spokesmen, The Beach Boys, declared, ''Honking down the gosh darn highway.''

More specialized examples of creative and playful use of cars brought into being ''dune buggies,''◆ designed for cavorting on beaches and deserts. Meanwhile, older and more sedate but not always more sedentary people made California a leading market for the newly conceived and ever more luxurious mobile homes and for the development of trailer parks. Despite growing smog and other pollution, the opposition of groups concerned with conservation, and the deepening energy crisis which made petroleum expensive, California continues to consume more gasoline than any other state in the Union, much of it for private vehicles, and the automobile remains a major element in its society.

Carlsbad, city in San Diego County, named (1886) because its mineral waters resembled those of the Czechoslovakian spa. It is a beach resort also known for its commercial growing of poinsettias and other flowers.

CARMANY, John H[enry] (1840–1910), Pennsylvania-born publisher, went to California (1858) to mine but soon became a printer. In 1869 he bought the *Overland Monthly*◆ from Anton Roman and tried to retain Bret Harte as editor, but after Harte resigned it began to slip financially, so Carmany sold it in 1875.

Carmel (or Carmel-by-the-Sea), a town deriving its name from that given its bay and river (1602–3) by Vizcaíno because his expedition was accompanied by three Carmelite friars. In 1771 Serra and Crespí moved Mission San Carlos from neighboring Monterey to the Rio del Carmelo site, which caused it to be known as the Carmel Mission,◆ although its name was not changed. At the end of the 19th century David Starr Jordan and Gertrude Atherton visited the area and praised it, but not until about 1904 did it begin to become a colony for authors, artists, and university professors. Under the influence of Mary Austin and George Sterling it became a bucolic bohemian village which attracted other artistic residents including Arnold Genthe, James Hopper, Nora May French, and Xavier Martinez. Less intimately identified visitors included Jack London, Herman Scheffauer, and Charles Warren Stoddard. Writers associated with it somewhat later included Lincoln Steffens, Upton Sinclair, Sinclair Lewis, William Rose Benét, and Harry Leon Wilson; then in 1914 Robinson Jeffers moved there and made its region the setting for much of his poetry. Later it developed into a large residential area—preserving some of its traditions in a rather self-conscious way—and into a popular tourist attraction for weekend visitors. Among its special appeals since the late 1930s has been an annual midsummer Bach Festival, held outdoors over a period of several days, at which the music not only of Bach but of other classical composers is played. The population in 1970 was 4,525.

Carmichael, residential suburb northwest of Sacramento, named (1910) by the owner of the land for himself. It is the site of the new Governor's Mansion, built but not completed in the 1970s during Reagan's administration. The Mansion has not been used by his successor, Edmund G. Brown, Jr.

Carpenteria, oceanside residential and resort community of Santa Barbara County, sighted by Cabrillo (1542) and named (1769) by Father Crespí ''carpenter shop'' because he found Indians building a canoe there and caulking it with local asphalt. Population in 1970 was 6,982.

CARPENTIER, Horace W[alpole] (1824–1918), after graduation from Columbia University's Law School in his native New York went to California (1850). He and some associates moved onto East Bay land belonging to the Peralta family, and he was instrumental in having it incorporated as the city of Oakland (1852) without the owner's knowledge or permission. Carpentier had himself made mayor and, by ordinance, guaranteed that in return for building a public schoolhouse and some small wharves (costing about $20,000) he would receive title to all the city's waterfront and the exclusive right to build wharves, piers, and docks, and to collect all fees. He turned the land over to the Central Pacific Railroad Co., of which he was a stockholder. Lawsuits, compromises, and countersuits continued until the port finally came into the city's hands in 1910, with leases still granted to Carpentier's assigns. He himself, long since called "General" for service in the state militia, moved back to New York.

Carquinez Strait, narrow body of water linking San Pablo Bay and Suisun Bay. Adjacent to it are the towns of Crockett,♦ Port Costa,♦ and Benicia,♦ and the shipyard of Mare Island.♦ The strait is spanned by twin automobile bridges, built in 1927 and 1958.

CARRILLO, prominent family whose first California member, José Raimundo Carrillo, came from Loreto with Portolá (1769) and served in the army at Santa Barbara for twelve years. His daughter María Antonia married José de la Guerra.♦ One of his sons, Cárlos Antonio (1783–1852), owner of Rancho Sespe,♦ was appointed governor of California (1837–38) but was unsuccessful in his fight against Alvarado♦ to exercise his office. Another son, José Antonio (1796–1862), was an *alcalde* of Los Angeles who joined Cárlos in a revolt against Gov. Victoria (1831).

During the Mexican War José defeated American troops in their battle to seize Los Angeles but soon capitulated and signed the Cahuenga Treaty. Cárlos married María Josefa Castro, and José in succession married two sisters of Pío Pico. Cárlos' son Juan José was the first mayor of Santa Monica, and three of his daughters married U.S. citizens, one of them being William G. Dana.♦ Juan José's son Leo (1880–1961) was a motion picture star whose roles as a partner of the Cisco Kid glorified the romantic tradition of Spanish California.

Another branch of the family stems from Joaquin Carrillo, who came from Loreto to San Diego after 1800. He was the father of five sons and seven daughters who made important marriages. They include Josefa (1810–93), who wed Henry D. Fitch;♦ Francisca Benicia (1815–91), after whom the town of Benicia is named, who wed Gen. Mariano Vallejo,♦ and had two daughters who

married two sons of Agoston Haraszthy; María de la Luz (1813–90), who wed José Manuel Vallejo; Felicidad (1833–56), who wed Victor Castro; and Ramona (1811–85), who wed Romualdo Pacheco and was the mother of the younger Romualdo Pacheco (1831–99), governor of California (1875).

Carrizo Plain, lying between the Panza Range of Los Padres National Forest and the Temblor Range on the San Andreas fault line in eastern San Luis Obispo County, is an isolated basin used for sheep and cattle grazing. The name, meaning "common reed grass," was used by the Spanish for places in Imperial, Riverside, and San Diego counties. Among its variant spellings is *Carrisa.*

Carrots, major vegetable crop, more being grown in California than in any other state. Produced mainly in the Imperial and Salinas valleys, the crop in 1970 was grown on 23,900 acres and was worth $26,741,000.

CARSON, Kit (Christopher Carson) (1809–68), born in Kentucky, reared in Missouri, ran away (1826) to join an expedition to Santa Fe, becoming a guide along its Trail, then joined a party of trappers (1829) led by Ewing Young that made its way to California, where he remained until 1831. During the next eight years he became a leading mountain man, known for his daring exploits and Indian fighting. A chance meeting with Frémont led to his being made a guide on Frémont's first three expeditions.

The Sierra pass named for him was discovered by him and Frémont on the second expedition (1843–44). The *Reports* of those expeditions brought him great fame. During the third he became involved with Frémont's activities relating to the conquest of California, including the deaths of the young sons of Francisco De Haro.♦ He was en route to Washington with Stockton's dispatch to say that all was well when he met Gen. Kearny in New Mexico and was requested to return with the small army force that was soon involved in the Battle of San Pasqual.♦ When the American cavalry was trapped by Pico, Carson crawled through the enemy lines to seek help from San Diego. As a hero of the war he was appointed a lieutenant by President Polk but anti-Frémont forces in the Senate disapproved of his commission.

He returned to California (1853) driving 6,500 sheep which he sold on arrival. The rest of his career was spent first as an Indian agent in Taos and then as a commander in Indian warfare during the Civil War, for which he was made a brigadier general. In time he became a popular heroic figure in many dime novels, and, although illiterate, he dictated a work that was later published as *Kit Carson's Own Story of His Life* (1926).

CARVALHO, SOLOMON NUNES (1815–97), born in South Carolina of a Sephardic Jewish family, accompanied Frémont as a photographer on the expedition of 1853 seeking a route for a transcontinental rail line. In Los Angeles and San Francisco (1854–55) he made daguerreotypes and painted portraits, but the rest of his life was spent elsewhere.

Casa de Adobe, La, a reproduction of an early California home with a patio of native shrubs; it is furnished with genuine antiques. A part of the Southwest Museum,♦ this popular tourist site is located on North Figueroa St. in Los Angeles.

Cascade Range, mountains lying mostly north of California and running up into British Columbia. The California section extends from the Oregon border down to about the North Fork of Feather River between Susanville and Chico. That area includes many extinct volcanos rising to 8,000 feet. The major one, Mt. Shasta, rises beyond that to 14,162 feet. There is also a live volcano, Lassen Peak (10,457 feet).

CASEY, JAMES P. (d. 1856), political supporter of David C. Broderick,♦ castigated by James King of William♦ as a ballot-box stuffer and former Sing Sing prisoner. When King refused to retract, Casey killed him, leading to the creation of the Vigilance Committee♦ of 1856 and Casey's hanging.

CASPER, BILLY (WILLIAM EARL CASPER) (1931–), San Diego-born professional golfer. His tournament victories include the U.S. Open (1959, 1966) and the Masters (1970) and by 1974 he had earned almost $1,500,000. He is particularly known for his putting.

CASSERLY, EUGENE (1820–83), born in Ireland, was brought to the U.S. (1822), and grew up in New York City, where he became a lawyer and newspaper contributor before settling in San Francisco (1850). He published journals, was elected State Printer (1851), practiced law, and was elected to the U.S. Senate (1869), where he served until he resigned (1873) and returned to legal practice in San Francisco.

Castaic Lake, reservoir in Angeles National Forest,♦ bearing the Chumash name of an Indian *ranchería* once established in the area. A nearby town, valley, and creek bear the same name.

Castilleja, flowering plant of the figwort family found in seventeen species in California. The best known is the *Indian paintbrush,* whose red flowers are seen in early summer on hillsides throughout much of the state. The plant name has been used for such diverse purposes as the title of a girls' finishing school in Palo Alto and a lake in Sequoia National Park.

Castle Air Force Base, a strategic air force training installation founded at the outset of World War II. It is located near Merced.

Castle Crags, geologically ancient granitic spires rising some 4,000 feet from the upper Sacramento River canyon, located six miles south of Dunsmuir on the northwestern border of Shasta County. They were the site of a battle between whites and Modocs (1855) in which Joaquin Miller claimed to have participated. The area is now a State Park.

CASTRO, prominent California family of several branches. One traces back to Joaquin Ysidro Castro (1732–1801), who was a soldier under Anza (1776). He and his wife had nine children who married into the Bandini, Bernal, Berryessa, Cota, Pacheco, Soberanes, and other prominent families and came to have large landholdings from San Francisco Bay down the coast to Santa Barbara. One of the family's few alliances with Americans was the marriage of María Lugardo Castro to Thomas Doak.♦ Joaquin Ysidro's son was Francisco María (1773–1831), who settled on his vast Rancho San Pablo (Contra Costa County). Francisco María's daughter, Maria Martina (1814–75), married Gov. Juan Bautista Alvarado. Castro Valley (Alameda County) was named for another grandchild, Guillermo (b. 1810). Another branch descends from Macario Castro (1753–1809), who arrived in 1784. He was the father of twelve children. One of his grandsons was Juan B[autista] (1835–1915), who laid out the town of Castroville (Monterey County) in 1864 and was active in Democratic party politics.

CASTRO, JOSÉ (*c.* 1810–60), 8th Mexican governor of California (Sept. 1835–Jan. 1836) and again Nov. 5–Dec. 7, 1836, started his career as secretary of the *ayuntamiento* of Monterey (1828). From then almost until his death in a brawl in Baja California, where he was military commander (1856–60), he was active in major military and political events of Alta California. He was arrested by rebels (1829) and again by the government (1830) for making insulting remarks about Mexico in his opposition to its Gov. Gutierrez.♦ He took part in the struggle against Mariano Chico♦ (1836) and was Alvarado's military chief in defeating Pío Pico♦ (1838) and overthrowing Gov. Micheltorena♦ (1845). After the expulsion of Micheltorena and while Pico was governor (1845–46) with his capital in Los Angeles, Col. Castro was California's military commander, headquartered in Monterey. He and Pico became embroiled in disputes about the funding of the political and military branches of government and the location of the capital, which made it easier for Frémont to force Castro's retreat to Mexico (1846). Castro returned in 1848 as a private citizen to ranch near Monterey, departing in 1853 to take an official post in Baja California.

CATALÁ, Magín Matías (1761–1830), Spanish-born Franciscan missionary stationed at Santa Clara (1794–1830), where he personally baptized 3,067 of the 5,471 Indians introduced to the faith during his era. He came to be known as the Holy Man of Santa Clara, and a petition for his beatification was first submitted in 1882.

Catalina Islands, four islands southeast of the Santa Barbara Islands,♦ from 27 to 76 miles off the coast from Santa Monica to La Jolla. From north to south they are Santa Barbara, the smallest (two miles long, one mile wide), part of the federally owned Channel Islands National Monument;♦ San Nicolás, the farthest offshore, from which George Nidever♦ transferred to the mainland all Indian residents (1835) except one mother who became separated from the group while searching for her son and, upon being deserted by chance, lived there alone until 1853; Santa Catalina,♦ the largest, the closest to shore, and the only one developed as a tourist resort; and San Clemente, a U.S. naval training ground, about 22 miles long. The islands were discovered by Cabrillo♦ (1542) but named by Vizcaíno (1602).

Catastrophes, see *Disasters.*

Cattle, were first brought to California by Portolá and Anza, but the raising of cattle in California dates back to the beginnings of the missions, which had their own herds. It was soon extended to the private land grants made by the Spanish govern-

ment. Numbering twenty in 1800, these were greatly increased after the Mexican Revolution (1822) and the secularization of the missions (1833) when the *ranchos* flourished. The *rancheros* ate beef but sold the hides, which they simply staked out to dry in the sun, and the tallow, rendered in kettles and stored in whole hide bags called *botas.* The trade in hides and tallow,♦ the former called "California banknotes," was controlled by U.S. firms, which sent their ships from Boston (as described by Richard Henry Dana in *Two Years Before the Mast*♦), and by agents who resided in California ports, like Alfred Robinson♦ and Abel Stearns.♦

The cattle which grazed freely over vast ranges were rounded up at annual rodeos,♦ a time of branding and festivities. There may have been about 400,000 head in 1846 worth about $4 each, then valued at $500 in Sacramento at the end of 1849, and later reduced to about $50. Herds of stock better than the Mexican "black cattle" were driven across the continent, until there were about 3,000,000 head in 1862. By that time the California *rancheros* had been bankrupted by poor business dealings, loss of land titles, and new taxes.

During the 1850s cattlemen were so much in control of the state's lands that a law required the farmer to fence his fields if he wished to keep out livestock. Increasing population and many federal grants to homesteaders and to railroads changed the situation, so that by 1872, when there were only 630,000 cattle in the state, the cattlemen were required to erect fences or be responsible for damage to farmlands. In the mid-1880s feeding on lots or irrigated pasturelands began to replace running on ranges, although vast landholdings, like those of Henry Miller♦ of Miller and Lux, continued. The Hereford, introduced to the state in that decade, was common by the 1920s, and by the 1960s Black Angus were also common. The dairy business grew, disease was controlled, and stock continued to increase. By the late 1960s cattle-raising was the state's most important agricultural business.

CAUGHEY, John Walton (1902–   ), Kansas-born historian of California, was a professor of history at UCLA (1930–70) after doing graduate study at Berkeley. His books include *California* (1940), *Hubert Howe Bancroft* (1946), and *Gold Is the Cornerstone* (1948).

Cauliflower, grown mainly in Monterey County, after decline of demand for the crop since the 1940s and growing urbanization caused production in the San Jose and Los Angeles areas to dwindle. In 1970 the crop was grown on 17,700 acres and was worth $16,211,000. California leads the nation in growing the vegetable.

Caxton, see *Rhodes, W. H.*

CDC, see *California Democratic Council.*

Ceanothus, wild lilac of the buckthorn family, whose more than forty native species range from creeping shrubs to small trees. Their flowers vary from deep blue to lavender, white, and pink, blossoming in small clusters or in large flowers at branch ends. They flourish throughout the state from the Sierra to the coast, providing food and cover for some wildlife.

Cedar, native coniferous evergreen found in three varieties in California. The *giant* (also called *canoe*) grows in coastal valleys of the northwest, reaching a height of 200 feet. Its trunk can reach 16 feet in diameter at the base and has cinnamon-colored bark which splits easily and is therefore much used for shingles. It also provides lumber for house and ship building, crates, millwork, and fence posts. The *Port Orford,* found in the same area, grows 80 to 175 feet tall and has a trunk of smooth reddish bark up to 6 feet. Its wood serves for construction, flooring, furniture, boats, and mothproof boxes and closets. The *incense,* found in the Coastal ranges and the Sierra, is between 50 and 125 feet high and has a cinnamon-brown bark that comes off in long strips. As the name indicates, the foliage is fragrant. Its timber is used for purposes as various as making pencils, shingles, roofing materials, and railroad ties. Despite such variety, all cedars account for only a negligible part of the state's timber crop. *Red cedar* is actually a juniper.

"Celebrated Jumping Frog of Calaveras County, The," sketch by Samuel Clemens, printed under his pseudonym Mark Twain, was his most important work written in California and the first to gain him wide fame. Initially submitted for an anthology being prepared by Artemus Ward, it arrived too late for that use and was printed instead in the New York *Saturday Press* (Nov. 18, 1865) and reprinted as the title piece of Mark Twain's first book (1867). The source was an old folk tale of which a version had been printed in the Sonora *Herald* in 1853, but the Mark Twain version

is more elaborate and ingenious, placing within a pseudo-realistic frame the account of the jumping frog Dan'l Webster, pet of the gambler Jim Smiley, which is defeated in a jumping contest when a stranger slyly fills its gullet with quail shot. Mark Twain later wrote a "Private History of the 'Jumping Frog' Story," including a retranslation into English of a French version. The story is nominally set in Angels Camp, which, since the 1930s, has been the site of an annual jumping frog competition.

Celery, once grown mainly in the Sacramento–San Joaquin Delta, since the 1950s has been raised mostly in the Salinas Valley, which has a longer growing season. Ventura, Orange, and San Diego counties are also major producing centers. The crop, in which the state leads the nation, in 1970 was grown on 16,500 acres and was worth $50,634,000.

Cement, limestone compound that is found naturally and can be made from calcium carbonate, silica, and alumina. While California has only one major natural deposit (in Orange County), it has ample and widely distributed resources for making it. The first cement mill was established at Benicia (1868) and the first high-grade (Portland) cement was made at Santa Cruz (c.1877), but significant production began in the 20th century. Most production is near major metropolitan areas in northern and southern California, with plants also located in Calaveras and El Dorado counties. Limestone deposits are common, the largest being in the Mojave Desert, the northern Transverse Mts., and the eastern Peninsular Range. The Cowell♦ family and Henry Kaiser♦ were major developers of cement in California.

Center for Advanced Study in the Behavioral Sciences, an independent postdoctoral research institution founded in 1952 and located behind the Stanford University campus. Approximately fifty fellows are invited annually to pursue their own research. Most of the distinguished scholars are in fields of the social and behavioral sciences, but a few are in the humanities and natural sciences.

Center for the Study of Democratic Institutions, located in Santa Barbara, founded (1954) by Robert M. Hutchins (1899–1977), onetime president of the University of Chicago, and financed by the Fund for the Republic. Through conferences, discussions, and publications it works for international understanding and peace, the preservation of civil liberties, the improvement of the natural environment, and social responsibility. Financial difficulties caused a severe curtailment of the program, some of which went to the University of Chicago (1975).

Central Avenue, a Los Angeles street running north-south from Wilshire Boulevard to Victoria St. in Willow Brook, was the black community's main thoroughfare from 1910 to the 1940s and described as "the Lenox Avenue of the Far West." During the 30s and 40s it was known for night clubs where musicians developed their styles of jazz.◆

Central Pacific Railroad, western part of a transcontinental railroad, was conceived by Theodore D. Judah,◆ its chief engineer, and founded as a corporation (1861) with financing from Crocker,◆ Hopkins,◆ Huntington,◆ and Stanford,◆ the Big Four. After Judah selected a Dutch Flat and Donner Pass crossing of the Sierra he was instrumental in obtaining congressional funding of twenty alternate sections (sq. mi.) of land in checkerboard pattern and a bonus ranging from $16,000 to $48,000 per mile of track built. The higher bonus for mountainous land was extended by the claim that the rise of the Sierra began only six miles east of Sacramento. State subsidies and some county funds were also obtained. Construction by the Big Four's own Contract and Finance Co. also yielded large profits despite the great expenses occasioned by the need to hire up to 15,000 Chinese,◆ (even though at low pay), by difficult grades, by the urge to move fast, and by winter weather. Construction eastward from Sacramento began on Jan. 8, 1863, and the last spike◆ was driven at Promontory Point, Utah, on May 10, 1869, on the meeting with the rails of the westward-building Union Pacific Railroad.◆ The Big Four in 1868 gained greater control of California transportation by acquiring the Southern Pacific,◆ the company that in turn absorbed the parent firm in 1899 after transcontinental rail competition and declining traffic from Nevada's silver mines had hurt the Central Pacific.

Central Valley, sometimes called the Great Central Valley or Great Valley and named Valle Grande by the Spanish, runs some 450 miles from about Redding in the north to a point below Bakersfield in the south, being bounded by the Klamath Mts. and the southern Cascades on the north and by the Tehachapi Mts., Transverse Ranges, and the southern Coast Range on the south. Its eastern boundary consists of the Cascade and Sierra

Nevada ranges; its western boundary—about 50 miles away—is the Coast Range. It is commonly divided into Anderson Valley◆ and the Sacramento Valley◆ in the north with the Delta Lands◆ linking it to the San Joaquin Valley◆ on the south, the whole extending over an area of 25,000 sq. mi. It is a prime region for livestock and agriculture; its field crops include cotton, fruits, grains, nuts, rice, sugar beets, and vegetables grown on the great flatlands watered by the Sacramento, the San Joaquin, and other rivers that flow into them.

Central Valley Project, federal program for the supply of water,◆ initially conceived by Robert B. Marshall in 1919 but undertaken in 1935 under the auspices of the U.S. Bureau of Reclamation. Commonly known as CVP, it moves surplus water from northern California 400 miles south to provide irrigation of farmlands, to impede flooding, to improve the lower Sacramento River for navigation, to create hydroelectric power, to restrain salt water entry into the Delta, and to provide increased aquatic recreational areas. The first stage, completed in 1955, constructed the Shasta◆ and Keswick◆ dams on the Sacramento River, the Folsom Dam◆ on the American River, and the Friant Dam◆ on the San Joaquin River. The impounded water is moved in several directions: via the Delta Cross Canal into the Contra Costa Canal◆ for use along Suisun Bay and the Carquinez Strait; via the Tehama-Colusa Canal down the west side of the Sacramento Valley; and via the Delta Cross Canal into the Delta-Mendota Canal◆ for use in the San Joaquin Valley, which is also furnished water by the Friant-Kern◆ and Madera◆ canals. The valley's Westlands receive water from the San Luis Canal.

Century City, urban development of Los Angeles, situated on the site of an old *rancho* that became the home of the 20th Century-Fox motion picture studio. Located in western Los Angeles just off Santa Monica Boulevard, it was created (1961 ff.) by Alcoa (accounting for the heavy structural use of aluminum) as an enclave of a high-rise hotel, commercial structures, and shopping centers linked by great pedestrian malls. The master plan was developed by Welton Beckett.

CEPEDA, ORLANDO [MANUEL] (1937–), Puerto Rico-born first baseman for the San Francisco Giants (1958–66) who later played for St. Louis (1966–68), Atlanta (1969–72), Oakland (1972), and Boston (1973).

CERMEÑO, Sebastían Rodríguez (*fl.* 1595), Portuguese-born navigator who was given command of the Manila galleon♦ of 1595 on the condition that he explore the California coast for a good port. His very bad western crossing of the Pacific led his nearly mutinous officers to urge that he avoid the northern coast and sail directly for Acapulco, but on Nov. 6 he took his heavily laden *San Agustín* into what he called the Bay of San Francisco, which is today called Drake's Bay. He found no evidence that the English had been there sixteen years earlier. On Nov. 30 his ship was driven ashore and wrecked by a storm, but he got his crew aboard the open launch *San Buenaventura,* which had been used for coastal exploration, and sailed south, continuing his explorations, including the sighting of the entrance to Monterey Bay. They finally reached their home port of Navidad on Jan. 7, 1596, with an exhausted crew. Despite the remarkable voyage back and his discoveries, Cermeño was disgraced for losing his cargo and his galleon.

CHABOT, Anthony (1814–88), Canadian-born businessman who went to California (1849) to become a miner and to pioneer in hydraulic techniques. That led him to found a water system for San Francisco (1856), a forerunner of Spring Valley Water Co. In the East Bay after 1866 he became the sole owner of Oakland's water system and a developer of other systems for San Jose and Vallejo. His resultant wealth allowed him to become Oakland's chief philanthropist, and a donor of Chabot Observatory, among other benefactions. A reservoir lake of the East Bay Municipal Utility District near Vallejo is named for him, as are a park and its lake in the East Bay Regional Park District.

CHAFFEE, George, see *Chaffey, George.*

CHAFFEY, George (1848–1932), Canadian-born engineer. He went to California (1880) where, with his brother William, he laid out—and named for his native province—the town of Ontario (1882) and its neighbor Etiwanda in San Bernardino County as model communities. The towns were to have an agricultural economy based on a mutually owned irrigation system and hydroelectric power. He also founded an agricultural college. After work in Australia (1886–97), where he and his brother irrigated once barren lands and developed communities, he returned to California and became the engineer for Charles Rockwood♦ in the irrigation project to turn part of the Colorado Desert into rich agricultural and residential lands to be known as Imperial Valley.♦ To that end he built a canal (opened 1901), largely through Mexican territory, to carry Colorado River water into the area. When it failed to bring in enough water during dry years, Rockwood created a bypass that had the disastrous effect of flooding the area, which became the Salton Sea.♦ A great feud arose between Rockwood and Chaffey, resulting in the ouster of Chaffey from the project. His surname is sometimes spelled Chaffee.

CHAMBERLAIN, Owen (1920–), professor of physics at the University of California, Berkeley. He shared the Nobel Prize (1959) with fellow faculty member Emilio Segrè (1905–) for high energy physics and the joint discovery of antiprotons.

CHAMBERLAIN, Wilt[on norman] (1936–), basketball player. After graduation from the University of Kansas, where he was an All-American star, and play with the Harlem Globetrotters, he moved with the Philadelphia Warriors to San Francisco (1962–65). He joined the Los Angeles Lakers (1968–73) and led them through 33 winning games to the NBA championship (1971–72), and then became coach of the San Diego Conquistadors in the ABA. Known as Wilt the Stilt (he is 7′ 1⅛″), his records as a center include 100 points scored in a game, 50.4 points averaged per game, and 4,029 points scored in a season (1961–62).

CHAMISSO, Adelbert von (1781–1838), German naturalist of French descent, went to California (1816) with the first expedition of Kotzebue,♦ to whose *Entdeckungs Reise* (1821) he contributed. Chamisso's own account appeared as "Reise um die Welt" in his collected works (1836), which also presented his lyric poems and his symbolic, fictional story (which has almost passed into folk legend) about Peter Schlemihl, who sold his own shadow. Chamisso is also remembered for having named California's state flower, the golden poppy (*Eschscholtzia Californica*) in honor of the surgeon on the Kotzebue expedition, Johann Friedrich Eschscholtz.

CHANCE, Frank [Leroy] (1877–1924), Fresno-born baseball player (first base) and manager. While playing with the Chicago Cubs (1898–1912) he was part of the famous double-play combination (Tinker to Evers to Chance), and he also managed the team (1905–12), leading it to four National

League championships and two World Series wins (1907, 1908). He later managed the Yankees (1913–14) and the Boston Red Sox (1923).

CHANDLER, HARRY (1864–1944), New Hampshire-born journalist, succeeded his father-in-law, Harrison Gray Otis,♦ as publisher (1917–41) of the *Los Angeles Times.*♦ He was succeeded (1941–60) by his son Norman (1899–1973), whose wife, Dorothy B[uffum] Chandler, has been a leader in cultural activities in Los Angeles, particularly its Music Center,♦ whose main building is named for her. Their son, Otis Chandler (1927–), became the publisher of the *Times* in 1960. Harry Chandler furthered the family fortunes as a major landholder of southern California, and his newspaper's campaign for William Mulholland's plan to bring Owens Valley water to Los Angeles enhanced the value of his real estate interests.

CHANDLER, RAYMOND (1888–1959), born in Chicago, reared in England, and moved to southern California in 1912. Chandler was in the oil business until he began to write mystery stories (1932) during the Depression with such success that he became a full-fledged author of hardboiled detective fiction featuring his hero, the tough sleuth, Philip Marlowe,♦ corrupt politicians, and police, set in Los Angeles, mainly. His best-known works are *The Big Sleep* (1939); *Farewell, My Lovely* (1940); *The Lady in the Lake* (1943); and *The Long Goodbye* (1954). All were made into films.

CHANEY, LON (1883–1930), Colorado-born Hollywood film star, known for his elaborate and frightening makeup for character parts in such films as *The Hunchback of Notre Dame* (1923) and *The Phantom of the Opera* (1925). The leading authority on screen makeup during his lifetime, he was a well-known resident of Hollywood from 1912 to his death.

Channel Islands National Monument, federally owned ecological preserve consisting of Anacapa Island of the Santa Barbara Islands♦ and Santa Barbara Island of the Catalina Islands.♦

Chaparral, dense thickets of shrubs and dwarf trees covering foothills and mountains, derive their name from the Spanish word for a place where the evergreen oak *(chaparro)* grows.

Chapel, see *Presidio.*

CHAPLIN, CHARLIE (CHARLES SPENCER CHAPLIN) (1889–1977), after a vaudeville career in his native England came to the U.S. (1910). He began his motion picture career (1914) which made him a leading star of Hollywood from the beginning by his brilliant pantomime of the humorous and wistful character of a little tramp. After many short films he portrayed that appealing figure in such features as *The Kid* (1921), *The Gold Rush* (1925), and *City Lights* (1931). To produce those films he established his own motion picture studio (1919), United Artists, with D. W. Griffith, Douglas Fairbanks, and Mary Pickford. The Congressional Committee on Un-American Activities, which indicted the Hollywood Ten, castigated him for ostensible communist sympathies and moral turpitude and he then elected to move to Switzerland. However, he never gave up his British citizenship and was knighted in 1975. He returned to Hollywood briefly (1972) for a very warm welcome.

CHAPMAN, CAROLINE (1818?–76), London-born actress who, after a career on her family's Mississippi River showboat, went to San Francisco (1852) and there and in mining camps was popular in roles ranging from the tragic heroine opposite Junius B. Booth to a burlesque of Lola Montez.

CHAPMAN, JOSEPH, see *Bouchard, H., Shipbuilding, Santa Inés,* and *Vineyards.*

CHAPMAN, WILLIAM S. (1827–1906), land speculator who went to California from Minnesota in the early 1860s and began a career of buying undeveloped land from federal and state offices, developing it, and selling it at large profits. In that undertaking he sometimes worked with the "Grain King," Isaac Friedlander,♦ growing wheat on a large scale, producing alfalfa as a feed crop for beef, and developing the San Joaquin and Kings River Canal and Irrigation Co., a construction program which anticipated some of the later Central Valley Project.♦ To encourage land use he also fostered innovative farming techniques and model farming communities. After coming to control more than 1,000,000 acres, he overextended himself and lost most of his holdings to Henry Miller,♦ Charles Lux,♦ and others.

Chapman College, private, coeducational liberal arts college affiliated with the Disciples of Christ. Founded in 1861 at Woodland as Hesperian College, after several changes of name it took its present one (1934) from a large donor, although it did not move to its campus in Orange until 1954. Until 1975 it chartered a large liner on which faculty and students pursued studies during a semester-long world cruise.

Chargers, San Diego, professional football team, originally (1960–61) the Los Angeles Chargers, since 1959 has been part of the American Football League, whose championship it won (1964), as well as being divisional title holder several times. Until 1966 it was owned by Conrad Hilton's son, Barron Hilton, a hotel executive in Beverly Hills. The name "Chargers" was a play on words, because Hilton also owned a large credit card firm.

CHASE J[OSEPH] SMEATON (1864–1923), emigrated from England (1890) to California, serving there as a social worker and as a boys' tutor. Fascinated by the natural scene of his adopted land, he traveled over it widely on horseback, his longest trip taking him from Los Angeles to the Oregon border (1911). Out of such treks came his accounts: *Yosemite Trails* (1911), *California Coast Trails* (1913), and *California Desert Trails* (1913), which were sensitive to the scenery, the simple country people, particularly Mexicans, and the flora which he knew almost as well as a professional botanist.

CHAVEZ, CESAR [ESTRADA] (1927–   ), Arizona-born labor organizer, reared in a large family of itinerant workers, he attended over thirty schools before he had to drop out of the seventh grade to work. After navy service he became active in union organizations and in 1962 launched his own National Farm Workers Union while also working at manual labor jobs in Delano. His union made coalitions with civil rights groups, liberal clergy, and the striking Filipino grape pickers who were members of the AFL-CIO Agricultural Workers Organizing Committee. In 1965 he began to support them against the grape growers of the San Joaquin, Imperial, and Coachella valleys, and in 1966 merged his followers with the larger union to form the United Farm Workers Organizing Committee. The long strike, or *huelga,* he led was marked by an almost religious fervor as he dramatized the workers' plight by a 300-mile march from Delano to Sacramento, by a 25-day fast, and by an emphasis on nonviolent resistance until he got great public support for his boycott of table grapes and won recognition by the growers and better working conditions. He later led a comparable strike of lettuce pickers. Both as a striking union and as a kind of social movement, Chavez and his follow-

ers have had a great impact upon the public in their protests against long-standing grievances of workers in agricultural labor.♦ Chavez himself became sufficiently symbolic to have his cause espoused by Robert Kennedy in the presidential primary of 1968 and to be selected by Gov. "Jerry" Brown as the only man to nominate him for President at the 1976 Democratic National Convention. He achieved a major agreement with the long-time rival Teamsters Union (1977), which granted his union the exclusive right to represent field workers, while cannery and other nonfield laborers would fall under Teamster jurisdiction.

Chavez Ravine, site just north of downtown Los Angeles, named for an early owner, Julian Chavez. The land was used as a potter's field in pueblo days and during the 1850 and 1880 smallpox epidemics it served as the county infirmary farm. Portions of it were incorporated into Elysian Park in the 1880s. After lengthy negotiations some 300 acres were sold to Walter O'Malley, owner of the Dodgers baseball team, which played its first game in its new stadium there in 1962.

Cheese, began to be made commercially during the gold rush as a product of dairying♦ introduced by Americans. Dairymen first located along the coast because grass was available there more of the year and because their products could be readily transported by water to San Francisco Bay communities. One of the big dairymen of early days, Edgar W. Steele, located first at Point Reyes, later on the San Mateo County coast, made a 3,850-pound cheese to exhibit at a Mechanics Institute fair and to sell for the Sanitary Commission.♦ The introduction of railroads, irrigation, and alfalfa all allowed the cheese industry to shift from the coast to the San Joaquin Valley by the 1890s. Nevertheless, some important cheese making continues elsewhere (e.g. in Marin and Sonoma counties), and it was near Monterey that David Jacks♦ in 1892 introduced the only native California cheese—Monterey Jack—and manufactured it on a factory scale rising to 9,796,000 pounds in 1918. Dairymen, some of foreign heritage, have popularized numerous foreign types, particularly French and Italian, while cottage cheese and processed cheeses have become popular American contributions. In 1974 cheese production amounted to 66,426,000 pounds.

Chemehuevi, Indians of Shoshonean stock who were actually southern Paiutes living west of the Colorado River. Their home was in the Kingston Range south of Death Valley until pressure from the Yuman tribes drove them to settle on the boundary of the present Imperial and Riverside counties, the eastern half of the Mojave Desert. In prehistory there were 500 to 800 Chemehuevi, but by 1910 there were only 260 left in California according to the census. They exhibited greater cultural affinity with the Shoshonean of the Great Basin than with their California neighbors. Mountains and a valley in San Bernardino County bear their name.

CHENEY, JOHN VANCE (1848–1922), moved from his native New York State to California (1876) and there became known as a poet of collections of conventional lyrics such as *Thistle-Drift* (1887) and *Wood Blooms* (1888). He also wrote essays collected in *The Golden Guess* (1892) and *That Dome in the Air* (1895). He was a friend of Edwin Markham (to whose "The Man with the Hoe" he wrote a verse reply), Joaquin Miller, and John Muir. He was librarian of the San Francisco Public Library (1887–94) and moved to Chicago to head the Newberry Library (1894–1909), returning to live in retirement in San Diego.

Cherries, fruit crop first grown at the missions but not raised in quantity until after the gold rush. Leading orchard areas are in the Santa Clara Valley and near Stockton. The crop in 1970 was grown on 11,200 acres and was worth about $12,090,000.

CHESSMAN, CARYL (CAROL WHITTIER CHESSMAN) (1921–60), reared in Los Angeles where he began to accumulate the lengthy police record that culminated in an arrest for kidnapping (1948), for which he was condemned to death. He became a *cause célèbre* for opponents of capital punishment because of his many successful appeals to postpone execution and because of his widely read *Cell 2455, Death Row* (1954), but he was nevertheless finally executed.

CHEW, NG POON (1866–1931), came to San Francisco (1881) from his native Canton and was converted to Christianity. He graduated from the San Francisco Theological Seminary (1892) and became a Presbyterian minister in that city. He founded a weekly Chinese newspaper in Los Angeles (1898) and a daily in San Francisco (1900), the first in the U.S. The papers worked for better relations between his native and his adopted peoples and their cultures.

Chicanos, see *Mexicans.*

Chickens, see *Poultry*.

CHICO, MARIANO (1796–1850), 10th Mexican governor of California (May 1–July 30, 1836), was a colonel in Mexico and member of Congress from Guanajato before he became *jefe politico* of California. He quickly alienated Californians by his petulant insistence on centralist government—that is, dependence on Mexico in all matters—and by his unpleasant personal behavior. After only three months in office he sailed for Mexico, ostensibly, Bancroft says, "in quest of aid by which to restore order." He never returned but he did hold other offices, as governor of Agua Caliente (1844) and *comandante general* of Guanajato (1846).

Chico, city in Butte County, founded on ranchland bought by John Bidwell♦ (1849), on which he established his home, farms, and experimental orchard of fruit and olive trees. The name (Spanish, "little") was originally given to the nearby creek. The city is now the home of a campus of the California State University. It also contains a 2,400-acre park, as an urban preserve surpassed only by Griffith Park of Los Angeles.

Chileans in California, came early and easily because Valparaiso was a regular port of call for ships that rounded Cape Horn. Chilean pre-gold-rush trade was considerably expanded in 1848–49 as thousands of Chileans flocked to San Francisco and mining areas; names like Chileno Creek and Chili Gulch became common, while their development of a mining technique was called a Chili wheel.♦ At Chili Gulch (Calaveras County) the Chileans, under the leadership of a Dr. Concha, imported Chinese coolies for a sort of slave labor, and because they were thus able to take over an inordinately large number of mining claims the Americans attacked them (successfully) in the local so-called Chilean War. Like other Latins, they were the subject of discrimination, as described by one immigrant, Vicente Pérez Rosales (1807–86), later a distinguished man of letters, whose *California Adventure* (1947) is a translated extract from *Recuerdos del Posado*. The *barrio* (district) called Little Chile at the foot of Telegraph Hill was the scene of lawless attacks by the Hounds and the Sydney Ducks♦ (1849). Among the English and American merchants of Valparaiso who migrated to California and established themselves there were Faxon Atherton and James Lick. Jasper O'Farrell, an Irish engineer, also went to California from Chile.

CHILES, JOSEPH B[ALLINGER] (1810–85), born in Kentucky, went with the Bartleson-Bidwell♦ Party (1841) overland to California. There Vallejo promised him a mill site and Chiles went east again to buy equipment, returning in 1843 with Joseph Walker.♦ From his Napa Valley *rancho* he supplied Frémont in the Bear Flag Revolt. Chiles aided Frémont later by testifying at his court-martial and by making another transcontinental trip west as escort to Frémont's children (1848).

Chili, see *Peppers.*

Chili wheel, a refinement of an *arrastre,*♦ in which heavy stone wheels rotating around a central pivot were used to crush gold-bearing quartz. Sometimes called a Chili mill.

Chilula, Indians who shared linguistic and cultural affinities with the Hupa,♦ with whom they were allied against the coastal Yurok. They lived around the drainage of Redwood Creek from near the inland edge of the redwood stand to a few miles above Minor Creek in what is now Humboldt County. At one time they numbered 500 to 600, but because of battles with placer miners they were extinct by 1910.

Chimariko, Indians remotely related to the Hokan family,♦ held a territory covering a 20-mile area along the Trinity River from its South Fork to French Creek (Humboldt County). As a result of their chronic hostilities with the miners of the area, their population of 250 in 1849 had been reduced to extinction by the time of the 1910 census. Although they had conflicts with the Hupa and were friendly with the Wintun, their culture, like that of most of the small and poor northwestern California tribes, imitated that of the Hupa and the Yurok.

China Lake Ordnance Station, see *Kern County.*

Chinatown, name used for the settlements of Chinese♦ in American cities. California has notable examples in San Francisco, Los Angeles, Sacramento, and Stockton; the district in San Francisco is said to be the largest Chinese settlement outside the Orient. Long a quasi-autonomous area, and much of it a slum-like ghetto of overcrowded tenements, it was also fascinating for its exotic architecture, markets, shops, and restaurants, native theater, newspaper, and, for a long time, special telephone exchange, and traditions of joss houses (temples), opium dens, and subterranean tunnels. Tourists like to browse through Chinatown's curio shops, sam-

ple its food, and visit the small factories where fortune cookies♦ are baked. To a lesser degree the special institutions found in San Francisco were evident in other Chinese quarters elsewhere in the state. The governing body for San Francisco and for all Chinese in California was long the Six Companies.♦ More sinister figures, like "Little Pete,"♦ also had great power from time to time. In the 1970s a vendetta between youthful gangs led to individual and mass murders. Occidental views of the San Francisco area are numerous, including two issued in 1908 which depict it in pre-earthquake and fire days: Arnold Genthe's *Pictures of Old Chinatown* and Will Irwin's text, *Old Chinatown.* Many films have been set there, all of them melodramatic, as is Roman Polanski's *Chinatown* (1974), about the comparable community in Los Angeles.

Chinese in California, became a significant part of the population (following two early immigrants—servants—of 1848) when a depression in Kwangtung Province and news of the gold discovery in California caused many to leave Canton for the "Golden Mountain" (America). Travel was easy, for passage costs were repaid by the garnisheeing of future California earnings, but for that reason most of the 25,000 who arrived by 1852 were in virtual bondage to their employers.

Although the Chinese met antipathy from white laborers, they still flocked into the country, working in San Francisco, in the mines (where they were heavily taxed), in laundries, as domestics, in cigar factories, and—after Charles Crocker's experiment (1865) with a 50-man all-Chinese crew—on the Central Pacific Railroad, which came to employ 10,000 of them as laborers. They were excellent workers, and cheap, although they once struck (1867) for a 12-hour day and $40 a month (a $10 increase).

The treaty negotiated with China (1868) by Ambassador Burlingame increased emigration to 16,000 annually, but with the completion of the railroad (1869) many Chinese turned to other jobs. They supplied an overwhelming part of the state's agricultural labor, dominated mining and heavy construction, and were major workers in fisheries, canneries, and lumber mills. By 1872 they held half the factory jobs in San Francisco, and by 1875 the population in Chinatown there was *c.*47,000.

Chinese competition with white labor, and the willingness of the Chinese to work hard for lower wages, lead to great opposition: white workers attempted to burn the San Francisco docks of the Pacific Mail Steamship Co. (1877)—said to be the major importer of "coolies"—and the agitation headed by Denis Kearney♦ in the 1870s resulted in such actions as a riot in San Francisco in which twenty-one Chinese were killed and much property in Chinatown was destroyed. There was also mob pillaging in Los Angeles, and fifteen or more Chinese men were hanged there (1871).

For a long time (1854–72) the state's supreme court ruled that Chinese could not testify against whites. Legal discrimination also went on at the federal level: the Exclusion Acts of 1882, 1892, and 1902 prohibited further immigration of Orientals, although one notable refugee was Sun Yat-sen.♦ The Chinese themselves sometimes engaged in tong wars between gangs from different parts of their homeland or emigrants who represented conflicting fraternal organizations, but the Six Companies♦ generally were able to keep the peace, despite occasional corrupt highbinders such as the notorious "Little Pete."♦ The most prominent convert to Christianity and advocate of better relations between Chinese and Americans was Ng Poon Chew.♦

Although there are still Chinatowns in San Francisco, Los Angeles, and elsewhere, as well as the separate community of Locke,♦ Chinese people have long been integrated throughout the state.

Chinigchinich, Indian prophet or god (also spelled Chungichnish and Chingichnich), treated in an historical account of California Indians by Padre Boscana.♦ Ritual of the god's worship included the toloache cult,♦ in which young boys consumed the narcotic jimson weed♦ and experienced visions of animals while priests addressed them on proper behavior and threatened them with punishments by animals who were the messengers of Chinigchinich.

Chino, community in southwestern San Bernardino County near Ontario. It grew up on the *rancho* of the Lugos developed by Isaac Williams.♦ It is in an orchard and sugar-beet growing area and is well known for its state prison for young people and first offenders.

Chinquapin, evergreen flowering shrub of the beech family, found in two species in California: *golden* and *bush* or *Sierra.* The *golden,* three to fifteen feet tall, with leaves golden underneath, is found in coastal mountains from San Luis Obispo County north to the Oregon border and, occasionally, on the western slope of the Sierra. The *bush,* or *Sierra,* is spreading and round-crowned, only one to eight feet tall, its flowers having an unpleasant odor. It grows on dry mountain ridges and rocky areas of forests

north from the San Jacinto Mts. to the Oregon border, a particularly great stand being found in Yosemite. Chinquapin is also the name of an evergreen oak.

Chipmunk, small member of the squirrel family, distinguished by four light stripes, separated by dark bands, which run down the back, by stripes on either side of the head, and by hairy rather than bushy tails. Although these rodents bear the same name as the species in the eastern U.S., they differ from them. Indeed, there are 11 varieties within California, the best known being the *lodgepole,* found in the Sierra from Mt. Lassen south and in the mountains of southern California. All chipmunks feed on seeds, fruit, nuts, berries, and fungus. They served as a food for Salinan Indians and, probably, other tribes.

Chivs, nickname for members of the so-called Chivalry wing of the Democratic party who supported southern views of slavery in the Civil War years. Their state leader was Sen. William M. Gwin.♦

Chocolate Mountains, southeastern boundary of the Colorado Desert in Imperial County.

Cholame Hills, range in eastern Monterey and San Luis Obispo counties, south of the Gabilan Range and west of the San Joaquin Valley.

Cholla, see *Cactus.*

CHORIS, Ludovik [or Louis] (1795–1828), Russian-born artist aboard the *Rurik* of the Kotzebue♦ expedition (1815–16), whose sketches of California served as the basis for lithographs in his *Voyage Pittoresque autour du Monde* (1822).

Chouinard Art Institute, see *California Institute of the Arts.*

Chowchilla, place-name derived from names of neighboring Yokuts and Miwok tribes, applied first to the river that flows along the border of Merced and Madera counties and since then to the town, reservoir, and canal in Madera County. The mountains of this name are in Mariposa County, where a battle against the Chowchilla Indians (1851) was led by James D. Savage. The town achieved national notoriety (1976) when a busload of its schoolchildren was kidnapped. The children were rescued, and their kidnappers have been sentenced to life imprisonment.

CHOYNSKI, JOE [JOSEPH] (1868–1943), San Francisco-born heavyweight prizefighter, son of Polish-born San Francisco antiquarian bookdealer, journalist, and muckraking publisher of *Public Opinion,* Isidor Nathan Choynski (1836–99). A boyish feud between J. J. Corbett and Choynski led to amateur fights continued in three professional bouts (1889) as part of a career that included a draw (1897) with world heavyweight champion J. J. Jeffries.◆

Christensen brothers, see *San Francisco Ballet.*

Christian Brothers, a Catholic teaching order which has administered St. Vincent's School for Boys (1855 ff.) near San Rafael and St. Mary's College◆ (1868 ff.). To finance its activities the Brothers sold wine made in Martinez (1881–1930), a business greatly expanded after its entry into the making of brandy and the purchase (1950) of the large winery in Saint Helena, formerly the home of Cresta Blanca and originally built by William Bourn (1889).

CHRISTIE, WALTER (1868–1958), track coach at the University of California, Berkeley (1900–31), whose teams won the ICAA (1920–23).

Christmasberry, see *Toyon.*

Chromite, mineral whose ore is a principal source of chromium, which is itself used to strengthen steel alloys and improve their resistance to corrosion, as well as being employed in plating and, by the chemical industry, as a basis for dyes. Until 1940 California was a major source but the various known mine deposits are small. They are mainly located in the Klamath Mts., the northern Sierra Nevada, and the southern Coast Range.

Chronicle, see *San Francisco Chronicle.*

Chuckwalla Mountains, in the desert area of southeastern Riverside County, with Chuckwalla Valley on the north and the Chocolate Mts. to the south. The name is that of a lizard.

Chula Vista, city south of San Diego, founded (1888) as a real estate development, was for some time an agricultural region known for its flowers. It has become not only a large residential area but a center for aircraft parts production and other industry. Its population grew from 42,034 in 1960 to 67,901 in 1970.

Chumash, Indians of the Penutian◆ language family whose territory extended from Malibu Canyon west to Point Concepcion and from there north to Estero Bay. They were respected by the Spanish above other Indians because of their technical skill and economic development. They had partitioned rooms in their houses, used beds, fashioned a primitive spear thrower, and were expert potters and basket makers. Their most distinctive achievement was a canoe or *tomol(o)* built of lashed planks caulked with asphalt, a major improvement on the dugout and the reed float common among most California Indians. The Chumash numbered 8,000 to 10,000 in precontact times but were extinct by 1910. Their religion seems to have been a variety of that devoted to Chinigchinich.◆ The Chumash who lived on the Santa Barbara Islands were the first California Indians to be seen by whites when Cabrillo landed there (1542). In 1824 those attached to the Santa Barbara Mission led a revolt, put down with the aid of Father Sarría.

CHURCH, THOMAS D. (1902–   ), landscape architect known for his designs of gardens suited to their sites, their houses, and their owners. His work and his ideas are depicted in his *Gardens Are for People* (1955) and *Your Private World* (1969).

Cinnabar, see *Mercury* and *New Almaden.*

Citrus fruit growing, began when oranges and lemons were planted in Baja California (*c.*1739) and at the Alta California missions (1769), although the fruit was pulpy and thick-skinned and the oranges were sour. The padres planted the first sizable grove (*c.*400 trees on six acres) at Mission San Gabriel (1804) but secularization (1835) ended such farming. Jean Louis Vignes probably set out the first private grove of orange trees in Los Angeles (1834) but William Wolfskill, the onetime fur trapper, became the first commercial grower of the area (1841).

The gold rush created an increased market for oranges and expansion of orchards followed, though slowly. When Wolfskill reported an annual profit of $1,000 an acre during the early 1870s, more farmers began to develop orange groves. That was also the decade of improved fruit. The Rev. F. I. C. Schneider, a Presbyterian missionary in Bahia, Brazil, in 1873 shipped navel orange plants to the U.S. Department of Agriculture in Washington, which distributed samples to growers. The earliest cultivators were Luther and Eliza Tibbetts, who planted a grove near present Riverside. In 1876 A. B. Chapman of San Gabriel began to cultivate the Valencia, an orange which matures during summer and fall, whereas the navel ripens in winter, thus providing oranges the year round.

In the same period there was introduced from Sicily the relatively thornless Eureka lemon and from Spain the Lisbon lemon with a winter crop distributed over the whole tree. The decades of the 1870s and 80s also provided new incentives for citrus growing because new markets were created by the completion of the Southern Pacific's San Joaquin Valley line (1877), its route to New Orleans (1881), and the Santa Fe's competitive line (1885) in California. Ventilated boxcars and other shipping improvements were also introduced at the time. A frenzy of planting orange trees accordingly overtook southern California. Meanwhile grapefruit was introduced from Florida in the 1880s.

During the 1890s scale was eliminated, spraying and fumigation techniques were developed, and heaters (later replaced by wind machines) were introduced. In 1907 the University of California established its Citrus Experiment Station, the forerunner of its Riverside campus. Cooperative marketing also aided farmers, who created a California Fruit Growers Exchange♦ (1905) which developed the brand name Sunkist and therefore later changed the Exchange name to Sunkist Growers Inc. (1952). By the 1960s California was the major producer of the nation's oranges, the grower of 84% of its lemons, third in grapefruit crops, and a major source of the country's limes and tangerines.

City, The, sobriquet of San Francisco, popularized from the 1850s through 1910, when it was by far the largest, most populous, and most substantial urban settlement in the state, but in common use later in the 20th century as well.

City Lights, a paperback bookstore of North Beach in San Francisco, served both as a gathering place for writers during the San Francisco Renaissance♦ and as a publishing house for such Beat authors as its owner, Lawrence Ferlinghetti,♦ and Allen Ginsberg.♦

Civil War, The (1861–65), affected California, even though probably less than 7% of the population had gone there from the area of the Confederacy and all the state's Negroes were legally free. Nevertheless, there was a deep split between the Democrats who followed Sen. Gwin, the supporter of slavery, and the adherents of Sen. Broderick, the former Tammany Hall politician who championed the Union. Some clandestinely organized Southerners dreamed of seizing Fort Point♦ or other strategic sites and

some of California's gold, but their schemes amounted to no more than did the abortive plan of Asbury Harpending,♦ who thought to use an armed schooner for intercepting passenger ships to be pressed into Confederate service. Confederate champions included Charles E. Pickett,♦ Lovick P. Hall,♦ and John R. Ridge.♦ Strong leaders of Union sympathies included Col. Edward D. Baker, Thomas Starr King, and Leland Stanford, and to aid its causes they arranged various programs, chief of which was fund-raising for the Sanitary Commission.♦ There was no conscription in the state, but a California battalion served with the Massachusetts cavalry in Virginia and a California column was sent to New Mexico to prevent a Confederate invasion. However, most volunteers served in the West on such duties as guarding overland mail. The state's gold and some of its produce (e.g. wool and wheat) were important to the Union economy. Many West Point officers on both sides had earlier served in California, among them Grant, Sherman, and Albert S. Johnston.

Clamor Público, El, weekly Los Angeles newspaper (1855–59), the city's first Spanish-language journal. Published and edited by Francisco P. Ramirez, it was the voice of the Latin American community of southern California.

Clampus Vitus, E, see *E Clampus Vitus.*

Clams, bivalve mollusks, whose best-known California species is the *Pismo clam,* which prefers flat sandy beaches along open shorelines, like the one for which it is named, but can be found also in water ten to twenty feet deep, in many places south from Half Moon Bay to Mexico. For 25 years, beginning in 1916, over 100,000 pounds of Pismo clams were taken annually, the biggest harvest being 666,000 pounds in 1918. The largest specimen was eight inches wide and weighed four pounds. In 1947, after the annual haul fell below 100,000 pounds, commercial digging was prohibited. Other clams of the state include the *Washington* and *gaper clams,* usually found together, whose recorded high take was 42,000 pounds (1935); the *bean clam,* found on many ocean beaches, whose small size makes them desirable for chowders, leading to commercial gathering that yielded 100,000 pounds in 1916 but has steadily declined to less than 3,000 pounds; the *softshell clam,* not native but accidentally introduced and once (1917–36) yielding an annual haul of 100,000 pounds; the *jackknife clam,* found on southern California beaches and estuaries, which is inedible and is used only for bait; and the *razor clam,* found on the surf line of flat northern California beaches, which has little commercial importance although it is extensively taken by sportsmen. *Cockles* are found in bays or protected shoreline areas and once had a great commercial importance, the harvest reaching a high of 153,000 pounds in 1932. Since the late 1940s dredging, pollution, and overdigging have reduced the harvest of all clams to a minor take; by the mid-1960s only *Washington, gaper,* and *Pismo clams* were important to sportsmen and no clams are now commercially important. Costanoan and Wintun Indians ate clams, and probably other California tribes did too; they also used clamshells to make strings of beads employed as money.

CLAPP, Louise Amelia Knapp Smith (1819–1906), was reared in her native New Jersey and in Amherst, Mass., before marriage to Dr. Fayette Clapp (she often spelled his name Clappe) and their move soon thereafter (1849) to California. There they lived in rough mining camps (Rich Bar and Indian Bar on a fork of the Feather River), where he had his practice. That life provided material for the 23 extended letters the self-styled "frail, home-loving little thistle" wrote to her sister Molly (1851–52). Although perhaps not originally intended for publication, the letters are a carefully, indeed, self-consciously composed commentary upon a masculine society in which "Dame Shirley" wittily and sometimes sentimentally displayed her compassion for the Mexicans, her realistic observation of coarse and barbarous ways of life, and her feeling for a beautiful natural setting. She had previously contributed rather conventional literary poetry and sketches to a journal, and Ferdinand Ewer was happy to publish her letters in his *Pioneer* (1854–55). They were well received, and Bret Harte is even considered to have been indebted to her view of mining town life, but they were not published in book form as *The Shirley Letters* until 1922, and then in a limited edition. Ever independent, she established herself as a San Francisco public school teacher (Charles Warren Stoddard was one of her pupils) in 1854, divorced her husband (1857), and then in 1878 returned to the East.

CLARE, Ada, pseudonym of Jane McElheney (c. 1836–74), popular as a New York actress, sensational as its "Queen of Bohemia," and notorious for her romances. She visited California (1864–65) where she enacted Camille, wrote for the *Golden Era,* and was friendly with the writers of the time.

Claremont, city in eastern Los Angeles County, at the foot of the San Gabriel Mts., laid out by a real estate subsidiary of the Santa Fe Railroad (1887) and incorporated twenty years later. The residential community is known for its Claremont Colleges,♦ the Padua Hills Theatre,♦ Southern California School of Theology, and Webb School, a boys' preparatory school founded in 1922. In 1970 it had a population of 23,464.

Claremont Colleges, associated colleges located adjacent to one another in Claremont at the base of the San Gabriel Mts. in southeast Los Angeles County. This confederation is composed of Pomona College (est. 1887), a coeducational liberal arts college with about 1,300 students; Claremont Graduate School (est. 1925), a coordinating body, whose 1,200 students are taught by its own faculty and those of associated institutions; Scripps College (est. 1926), a liberal arts college with about 500 women, concentrating on the humanities; Claremont Men's College (est. 1946), a liberal arts college with about 800 men, emphasizing economics and political science; Harvey Mudd College (est. 1955), a coeducational college offering the B.S. to about 400 students, featuring engineering and the physical sciences; and Pitzer College (est. 1963), a coeducational liberal arts college, with about 800 students, specializing in social and behavioral sciences. Each institution has its own campus, faculty, student body, board of trustees, and endowment but they share a library, some special facilities such as an infirmary, a theater arts center, and a science center. Students at one college may take courses at another. The complex also includes an affiliated School of Theology and special institutes.

CLARK, Galen (1814–1910), discoverer of the Mariposa Grove♦ and first settler of Wawona♦ (1857), at the age of 90 published his first book, *Indians of Yosemite,* followed by *Big Trees of California* (1907), and *The Yosemite Valley* (1910).

CLARK, Walter Van Tilburg (1909–71), born in Maine, was reared in Reno, where his father was president of the University of Nevada. After education there, he taught English and creative writing for a long time at San Francisco State College before returning (1962) to the University of Nevada as a writer in residence. His own fiction includes *The Ox-Bow Incident* (1940), a taut novel about a lynching in Nevada's cattle country; *The City of Trembling Leaves* (1945), about the adolescence of a sensitive boy in Reno; *The Track of the Cat* (1949), a symbolical depiction of a hunt for a panther in the Sierra; and *The Watchful Gods* (1950), short stories.

CLARK, WILLIAM ANDREWS, see *Clark Library*.

Clark Library (William Andrews Clark, Jr., Memorial Library), created by an ardent bibliophile of Los Angeles, heir to a copper fortune and son of a U.S. Senator from Montana, bequeathed to UCLA on his death in 1934. Housed on his former estate in downtown Los Angeles, it is particularly distinguished for its collections of Dryden, English drama to 1700, early 18th-century English literature, Oscar Wilde, and fine printing.

CLAVIGERO, FRANCISCO JAVIER (1731–87), Mexican-born Jesuit father and historian, whose works include *Storia del California,* written in Italian after he, like all other Jesuits, was exiled from Mexico (1768). Posthumously published (1789) in Venice, one of the cities in which he had lived, this descriptive and historical study of Baja California was translated into English in 1937.

Clear Lake, largest body of natural fresh water (19.5 miles long) entirely within the state, once the home of Pomos, whose legendry tells of a rock-throwing battle between two ancient chiefs that formed boulder-strewn Mt. Konocti, which looms above East Lake and Lower Lake, twin tails of the main body of water. Called Laguna Grande by the Spanish, the lake was later known to trappers, such as Ewing Young and James Clyman. It has long made Lake County a popular resort area. Another Clear Lake is in northwest Modoc County.

CLEAVER, ELDRIDGE (1935–), revolutionary black leader, born in Watts, got his education in prisons where he had been an inmate since youth for crimes beginning with bicycle theft and marijuana peddling and rising to rape, which he interpreted as an "insurrectionary act" to defy and defile "the white man's law." During a sentence for assault with intent to kill he familiarized himself with the works of Paine, Voltaire, Bakunin, and Marx to become an "extreme iconoclast" and a leader of the Black Panthers.♦ In 1966 he was paroled from a nine-year sentence and became a staff writer for *Ramparts.*♦ He later reworked his articles (apparently with the aid of his wife, Kathleen) as *Soul on Ice* (1968). When his release was overruled by a court decision (1968), Cleaver was in the midst of a campaign for the Presidency of the U.S. on the Peace and Freedom party♦ ticket. He broke with the

Panthers because they took a more moderate stance and he wanted increased militancy. Then, declaring that he could not suffer another prison sentence, he fled to Algeria (1968), but finally returned to the U.S. and surrendered (1975). Thereafter, while free on bail, he espoused a revivalist Christian religious cause.

CLELAND, ROBERT GLASS (1885–1957), professor of history at his alma mater, Occidental College, whose works include *From Wilderness to Empire, a History of California, 1542–1900* (1944), *California in Our Time* (1947), *The Place Called Sespe* (1953), and *The Irvine Ranch of Orange County, 1850–1950* (1962).

CLEMENS, SAMUEL L[ANGHORNE] (1835–1910), went to the Far West (1861) after spending his youth in his native Missouri. In his early years he did some journalistic writing and was a steamboat pilot on the Mississippi River. During the Civil War Clemens served briefly in a volunteer company, but when his older brother Orion was appointed secretary to the territorial governor of Nevada, Samuel quit the Confederate Army and the two young Clemens men traveled for 20 days by stagecoach to Carson City (1861). Once arrived in Washoe, Samuel nominally served as the unpaid secretary to his brother, the official secretary, but soon drifted off into prospecting and mining for silver during the great mining boom days.

Unlucky in his prospecting, he began to contribute some sketches (signed "Josh") to the *Territorial Enterprise* of Virginia City, much as he had submitted pieces to local newspapers in Missouri and Iowa when he had lived there. They were liked so much that when Dan De Quille♦ was about to leave his regular job on the paper, its editor, Joseph T. Goodman,♦ hired Clemens as a replacement (Aug. 1862). For the next two years he not only reported real doings around the Comstock Lode♦ in a lively style but created many fantastic tales of frontier humor which, for the first time, he signed with his pseudonym, Mark Twain.♦

His hoaxes, burlesques, and straight-faced wild exaggerations included an account of a 300-year-old petrified man. His reputation having spread to San Francisco, he went there (May 1864) and became a part of its literary life, associating with Bret Harte, C. H. Webb, Prentice Mulford, and Charles Warren Stoddard. He became a regular contributor of sketches to the *Golden Era*♦ and, later, the *Californian,*♦ as well as a reporter for the *Call* and a San Francisco correspondent for the *Territorial Enter-*

prise. He also visited the gold mining country (1864–65), then in its autumn days, and for five months stayed in the cabin of Jim Gillis at Jackass Hill, Tuolumne County,♦ where he apparently heard a version of the Jumping Frog story♦ which was to bring him his first large eastern audience.

In March 1866 he sailed to Hawaii to write sketches of that island kingdom for the Sacramento *Weekly Union*. The success of his Jumping Frog tale, published in book form in 1867, turned him toward the East for future writing and lecturing. An offer from the *Alta California* to write another series of sketches about travels beyond the U.S., this time about a voyage in the summer of 1867 on a tour ship to the Holy Land, resulted in his leaving the Far West forever in June 1868.

But the region's influence upon Clemens was lasting, and he evoked the sense of the place and the period he had known in his third book, *Roughing It* (1872), a humorous yet symbolically significant depiction of the ways in which he himself had been converted from a greenhorn into a knowledgeable westerner.

Clementine, see "Oh, My Darling Clementine."

CLEVELAND, RICHARD J., see *Shaler, William.*

Cleveland National Forest, a reserve of 815,000 acres in San Diego, Riverside, and Orange counties. It was named for President Cleveland shortly after his death (1908) by his successor, Theodore Roosevelt. It includes Mt. Palomar and the Agua Tibia Mts.

Cliff House, roadside restaurant in the westernmost part of San Francisco, overlooking the Pacific Ocean and nearby Seal Rocks. The original structure (1863–94) burned, and its owner, Adolph Sutro,♦ replaced it with a kind of elaborate Victorian chateau which also burned (1907). The smaller, simpler building which replaced it (1908) continues to be a popular place for Sunday lunch. In 1977 it and the surrounding land became part of the Golden Gate National Recreational Area.

Climate, one of California's major features, often popularly thought of as "Mediterranean" (i.e. rain only in winter, general sun and warmth), actually varies from semitropical to alpine, depending upon oceanic and continental pressure areas and the state's widely varied topography. The climate may thus be roughly divided into five types: Coastal or Marine, Valley, Foothill, Mountain, and Desert.

Coastal climate is most widely known because it prevails in the most populous areas, but it varies greatly, not only up and down the Pacific shore but even within the limited range around its two major cities. The San Francisco area has two mountain chains running north-south and the Bay basin between them. The farther to the east a location is from the ocean, the drier it is, but gaps—most significantly the Golden Gate—modify the pattern by letting ocean air go inland easily. But basically the East Bay is warmer and drier than San Francisco.

Sunny weather increases and rain decreases on the Peninsula south from San Francisco to San Jose, while on the north, in Marin and adjacent counties, there are wide ranges in annual precipitation. Beginning the Bay Area's annual weather cycle in spring, a high pressure area forms over the Pacific (Pacific High) while the Central Valley starts to warm and its hot air creates a low pressure area. Air moving from high to low pressure areas brings west winds that absorb ocean moisture with resultant fogs♦ over the Bay region. These are augmented during the summer when the Pacific High comes closer to San Francisco and causes greater winds, while the fogs continue.

In fall the Pacific High moves south and the Central Valley loses heat so winds die down and fogs abate as warmer temperatures occur. In winter, land temperatures drop below those of the ocean, so inland tule fogs♦ occur in interior valleys. In this season too transoceanic storms can reach the Bay Area as the Pacific High is still south and cannot block them. The coastal climate of southern California varies by becoming sunnier, warmer, and drier the farther one travels from the ocean. Nevertheless, throughout the area summer is marked by warm days and little rainfall because large placid air pools at sea absorb storms originating at higher latitudes and form inversion layers of warm air. In winter these pools shrink and let storms through. The area has also been plagued by drought, by smog♦ trapped in a low inversion layer of warm air, and by Santa Ana winds♦ (the fall season's warm dry winds).

Valley climate, characteristic of the Sacramento and San Joaquin valleys, is marked by high temperature and low humidity in the summer and by low temperature and high humidity in the winter, when tule fog occasionally covers the Central Valley. Mean temperature variations between the extreme months run from thirty to thirty-five degrees.

Foothill climate occurs in areas between 1,000 and 3,000 feet in elevation, such as the rises to the Sierra Nevada. Its temperature is similar to that of the valley but it is relatively free of fog and is also without snow. Precipitation rises rapidly with increased elevation.

Mountain climate, found in the Sierra Nevada and other ranges north and south, is marked by fairly warm summers and fairly cold winters with precipitation increasing up to 6,000 feet, then decreasing. The northwest, both mountains and coast, get the state's heaviest rains. However, mountains are the sole California region with heavy snow.♦

Desert climate, found in the Mojave and Colorado deserts, features great daily as well as annual variations in temperature and very light rainfall,♦ although even the driest area receives some precipitation. At lower elevations summers are very hot and dry and winters are merely warm and sunny by day; at higher elevations summer days are also warm but winter nights often have subzero temperatures.

Diverse as these climates are, they have in their several ways been a major force in the development of the state. For example, because the state is the only one marked by winter rain and summer drought it has been able to create an almost complete monopoly of much agriculture.♦ The many days of sun and lack of rain, particularly in southern California, have not only attracted innumerable inhabitants and thereby created real estate booms but they have been primary reasons for the location of certain industries in California, such as motion picture production.

Despite the general reputation for an equable climate, variations are great. The state's record high temperature was 134 degrees at Greenland Ranch, Death Valley (July 10, 1913), and the record low was −45 degrees at Boca, Nevada County (Jan. 20, 1937). The heaviest daily rainfall was 16.71 inches at Squirrel Inn, San Bernardino County (1916), and the heaviest annual rainfall was 153.54 inches at Monumental, Del Norte County (1909); Bagdad, San Bernardino County, recorded no rain for two years (Oct. 3, 1912–Nov. 8, 1914).

Climbing, see *Mountaineering.*

Clipper ships, probably deriving their name from the word "clip" (to move swiftly), were speedy vessels, long and narrow with an enormous sail area, designed to bring tea from China to the U.S. before its flavor was lost. After service in the China trade in the 1840s they became a popular means of bringing goods and passengers to California around the Horn during the gold rush, sometimes continuing on to China before returning to the eastern U.S. The *Flying Cloud* (built in Boston, 1851) established a westbound record of 89 days (New York to San Francisco, 1851), but many voyages were made in 100 days or less.

Clover, legume plant cultivated for forage, known in many species, almost all imported from Europe. Its seed is an important California crop, the *red clover* yielding over 350,000 pounds annually in the 1970s. The *ladino* seed crop comes mainly from the Orland area of Glenn County. It furnished 80 to 90% of the nation's supply in 1971, when it amounted to nearly 5,000,000 pounds.

CLYMAN, James (1792–1881), Virginia-born frontiersman, a member of Ashley's second expedition up the Missouri (1823) and then a mountain man before going to Oregon (1844). In 1845 he led a party to California, ranged widely from Monterey to Napa to Sacramento, and offered to join forces with Frémont on a return trip to the U.S. (1846). However, he returned alone. He went back to California (1848) to mine gold, settling in Sonoma and Napa for the rest of his life. His diaries and other homespun narratives were collected by Charles L. Camp (1928; rev., 1960).

Coachella Valley, in Riverside County, extending from San Gorgonio Pass to the north end of the Salton Sea, is bounded on the east by the Little San Bernardino Mts. and on the west by the Santa Rosa and San Jacinto mountains. Irrigation at the opening of the 20th century from wells and, later, via the All-American Canal♦ from the Colorado River has made it a major agricultural area for dates, grapefruit, cotton, alfalfa, and vegetables. Palm Springs and Indio are major cities. The name, which has been variously spelled, derives from a Shoshonean tribal name.

Coal, mined in California as early as 1855, has never been consequential because only subbituminous and low-grade lignite are found there. Major production was by Welsh miners on the northeast slope of Mt. Diablo during the 1860s. Other mining sites were at Ione, Corral Hollow near Livermore, Stone Canyon near Coalinga, and Alberhill near Elsinore (Riverside County).

Coalinga, city in southwestern Fresno County, and birthplace of Cornelius Warmerdam.♦ Originally the town was known as Coaling Station when the Southern Pacific built a branch line to tap its lignite deposits (1888), but later it was given the more euphonious variant by a railway official. About twenty miles to the northwest lies one of the world's largest asbestos deposits. In 1970 Coalinga had a population of 6,161.

Coastal Zone Conservation Commission, body (est. 1972) to control development on the state's 1,264 miles of coastal shoreline. Initially it cooperated with six regional commissions but a state law (1976) made it a permanent body which may overrule the zoning laws of local governments.

Coastline, see *Beaches* and *California dimensions*.

Coast Range, chain of mountains whose northern part extends from the Oregon border to Marin County, the Pacific Ocean and the Central Valley marking the western and eastern boundaries. The elevations range from 2,000 to 7,000 feet. The central part of the range extends from San Francisco Bay to the Santa Ynez Valley. Included are Mt. Diablo, Mt. Hamilton, and the Santa Cruz, Gabilan, and Santa Lucia ranges, terminating at the convergence of the Tehachapi Mts. and Transverse Ranges. The southern part of the range is less rugged than the northern but has a higher peak, Mt. Pinos (8,826 feet), near its lower terminus.

Cockles, see *Clams*.

Cod, name applied in California to *rockfish* and *sablefish,* which are not true cod, are found off the entire coast but mostly north of Point Concepcion. The *sablefish* or *black cod* weighs 40 to 50 pounds. The annual catch is about 3,000,000 pounds, most of which is smoked, but the liver is used for Vitamin A. *Rockfish* or *rock cod* are found in some 50 varieties all along the coast but are fished mainly off Eureka, Monterey, and Santa Barbara. The annual catch is about 10,000,000 pounds, most of it sold as fillets. *Lingcod,* not a true cod either, once common in California waters, does not now yield a large catch.

Coffee, popular as a drink during the gold rush when imported beans were first locally roasted commercially in 1850. The high cost of this green coffee led to attempts to cultivate trees in Fresno County and the Sierra foothills during the 1870s, but they were a complete failure. However, importing businesses were established by San Francisco families, including the Folgers, the Hills Brothers, the Brandensteins of M.J.B., and the Schillings. Hills Brothers, which had packed butter in vacuum cans for shipment to Alaska during the Yukon gold rush, was the first U.S. firm to pack coffee in vacuum cans (1900).

Coffee has been a major import of San Francisco and roasting and packing have long been significant local businesses.

COGSWELL, HENRY DANIEL (1819–1900), Connecticut-born dentist and philanthropist in San Francisco whose local benefactions include Cogswell Polytechnic College, the first engineering institute founded (1887) west of St. Louis. A teetotaler, he also presented to his adopted city several cast-iron statues of himself proffering a glass of water, ever filled by a pipe concealed within the sculpture. One of these was destroyed by Gelett Burgess and other members of Les Jeunes♦ (1894), leading to Burgess' dismissal from the University of California staff.

COIT, DANIEL WADSWORTH (1787–1876), Connecticut-born banker in Mexico City who went to California during the gold rush (1849) and remained there for three years. An accomplished amateur artist, he made fine sketches which were published with some letters in *An Artist in El Dorado* (1937). More letters, edited by George P. Hammond, appeared as *Digging Gold Without a Shovel* (1967).

COIT, LILLIE HITCHCOCK (ELIZA WYCHIE HITCH-COCK COIT) (1843–1929), taken to San Francisco (1851) from New York State and reared there in the best social circles, early became known for her unusual behavior, particularly as an enthusiastic fire buff (she was made an honorary member of Knickerbocker Number Five Fire Company). In keeping with her mother's North Carolina heritage, she was a southern sympathizer in the Civil War, spending it in the Confederacy and in Paris, where she was presented to Napoleon III. Briefly married to a mining engineer, Howard Coit, her real love was San Francisco, and she left her adopted city $100,000 to erect Coit Tower (1933), on the site of Telegraph Hill's signal station, as a memorial to San Francisco's volunteer firemen.

Coit Tower, edifice on the summit of Telegraph Hill (itself 274 ft. high) in San Francisco, erected (1933) as a memorial to the city's volunteer firemen. Lillie Hitchcock Coit bequeathed $100,000 to pay for its construction. The 210-foot-tall cylindrical tower was designed by Arthur Brown, Jr., and its interior is decorated with murals of local subjects by local artists.

COLE, CORNELIUS (1822–1924), after graduation from Wesleyan College (Conn.), practiced law in his native New York State until going to California in the gold rush. He continued his practice in Sacramento (1852) and published the city's *Times* with James McClatchey. An organizer of the Republican party and a supporter of the Union, he served in Congress (1863–65) and the Senate (1867–73) but became unpopular because of his support of the Big Four. He continued to be active, and at age 98 campaigned for the Republican party.

COLEMAN, WILLIAM T[ELL] (1824–93), born in Kentucky, went to California (1849) where he was a successful merchant in mining towns and in San Francisco. He became a leader of the Vigilance Committee♦ of 1851, a member of its residual Committee of Thirteen, and also a leader of the second Vigilance Committee (1856) created following the murder of James King of William. After several years in New York he returned and became the organizer of a 6,000-member Committee of Public Safety (1877) which worked against the activities of Denis Kearney and his followers, using a "pick handle brigade" to quash the anti-Chinese riots. He was an early developer of borax♦ in the Calico and Funeral mountains (whence the name "colemanite") and of sugar refining in the state. He lost his fortune in 1888.

Coliseum, Los Angeles Memorial, see *Los Angeles Memorial Sports Arena.*

College of Arts and Crafts, see *California College of Arts and Crafts.*

College of the Pacific, see *University of the Pacific.*

COLLINS, HENRY M. (1819–74), Pittsburgh-born black civil rights advocate, went to San Francisco (1852), where he became a financial, religious, and cultural leader of his race.

Coloma, see *Marshall, James W.*

Color, term coined by miners during the gold rush to indicate the discernment of the metal as distinct from "dust" (particles), and a "nugget" (a piece weighing an ounce or more).

Colorado, Territory of, see *Cow counties* and *Southern California.*

Colorado Desert, area of 4,000 sq. mi. in southeastern California including Coachella Valley♦ and Imperial Valley♦ with the Salton Sea♦ between them. It is bounded by the Peninsular Ranges on the west,

the Little San Bernardino Mts. of the Mojave Desert and the Chocolate Mts. on the east, and the Mexican border on the south. Water♦ for irrigation has made it an important farming region, and although its urban settlements of Brawley and El Centro are small, it has developed a large winter resort area at Palm Springs and elsewhere.

Colorado River, rises at the Continental Divide and flows about 1,400 miles through Colorado, Utah, Arizona, and then on the California-Arizona border to empty into the Gulf of California. Among the early trailblazers on the California border were Alarcón, Díaz, Anza, Font, Garcés, and Rivera y Moncada, the last two being killed there in the Yuma Massacre. U.S. trappers who later explored the area included Jedediah Smith and James O. Pattie. Beginning with George Chaffey and Charles Rockwood, in the 20th century the river has been a major source of water♦ for California irrigation and flood control programs through a lengthy aqueduct system including the All-American Canal to Imperial and Coachella valleys, and the Colorado River Aqueduct, whose major reservoirs are Lake Havasu in San Bernardino County and Lake Mathews in Riverside County.

Colt Press, see *Grabhorn Press.*

COLTON, DAVID D[OUTY] (1832–78), junior partner of the Big Four.♦ Born in Maine and reared in Illinois, where he attended Knox College, he went to California (1850) to take part in the gold rush to Siskiyou County, but made his first fortune in the Amador gold mine. He became a leader in Democratic party politics. Later association with Charles Crocker (in coal mine ownership) and with Collis Huntington led to his relationship with Stanford and Hopkins too, becoming the junior member of what newspapers called "The Big Four and a Half." In that capacity he managed some finances as well as political and legislative relations, becoming president of the Western Development Co. and a vice president of the Southern Pacific. With part of his fortune he built an impressive mansion on Nob Hill. Disputes between his senior partners and his widow over matters of his estate led to her release of Collis Huntington's letters describing attempts to influence elections and to bribe Congressmen. Ironically, Huntington acquired the Colton mansion for his San Francisco home.

COLTON, WALTER (1797–1851), born in Vermont and educated at Yale, went to California (1846) as chaplain aboard the USS *Congress*. He was named an admiralty judge and *alcalde* of Monterey by Commodore Stockton. A former editor of journals in Washington, D.C., and Philadelphia, after the conquest he founded and edited *The Californian*◆ (1846–47), the region's first newspaper, an undertaking he carried on with Robert Semple.◆ He sponsored a schoolhouse in his Colton Hall, the two-story columned edifice he built in Monterey (1847–49). The hall was also the site of the Constitutional Convention (1849). His recollections appeared as *Three Years in California* (1850).

Colton Hall, see *Colton, Walter*.

Columbia, mining town in Tuolumne County, so named (1850) because it was called the gem of the southern Mother Lode. The initial strike was made on March 27, 1850, and some $87,000,000 was extracted from the area over the next three decades. It was a metropolis of mushroom towns whose population is said to have been anywhere from 5,000 to 15,000 at the height of the boom. A State Historic Park now preserves about twelve square blocks of restored or reconstructed buildings, including a Wells, Fargo office, a Masonic Temple, saloons and stores, churches, a firehouse, hotels, a schoolhouse, and a newspaper office on both sides of tree-lined streets that preserve the flavor of gold rush days.

Colusa, seat of Colusa County, founded (1850) on the Sacramento River by a brother of Robert Semple on land bought from John Bidwell and given the Indian name of a local *rancho*. It is a residential community with food-processing plants and light industry, having a population in 1970 of 3,842.

Colusa County, one of the original 27 counties formed in 1850, is bordered by Lake County on the west, Glenn on the north, Butte and Sutter on the east, and Yolo on the south. Until 1854 it was called Colusi, a closer approximation to Korusi, the Indian tribe from which the name derives. Monroeville, now in Glenn County, was the county seat until the town of Colusa◆ on the Sacramento River took over (1854). Bidwell was the first known white explorer of the area (1843–44); he traversed it while mapping a land grant for the children of Thomas Larkin. It is a farming area, the main crop being rice, but sugar beets and livestock raising are also important. The population in 1970 was 12,430. With an area of 737,024 acres, it had 10.8 persons per sq. mi.

Comisionado, see *Ayuntamiento*.

Committee of Public Safety, see *Coleman, William T.*

Committees of Vigilance, see *Vigilance Committees*.

Commonwealth Club, The, San Francisco organization founded (1903) to "investigate and discuss problems affecting the welfare of the Commonwealth [of California] and to aid in their solution. . . ." Open to persons interested in these purposes on nominations of members, it has a large attendance at its frequent lectures on public issues and serves as an important platform for policy statements by major public figures. Its many activities include numerous sections for fuller consideration of contemporary issues and the annual award of medals for books by local authors. It had some 14,000 members in 1970.

Community colleges, formerly known as junior colleges, provide two years of higher education to all graduates of the state's high schools. In addition to a basic college curriculum they offer technical and vocational courses in both daytime and evening classes. They also have a large adult education program. They are administered by a board of governors but do not have the identity of a system like that of the state universities and colleges or the University of California, the other two parts of California's tripartite scheme of higher education. They retain close association with their communities through local boards and local financing. In 1970 there were 99 community colleges, an outgrowth of the first one, founded at Fresno (1910).

Compromise of 1850, term applied to measures passed by both houses of Congress to settle disputes following the Mexican War on achieving an equitable balance of power between slavery and anti-slavery factions in the representation of newly acquired territories. Among other things it called for admission of California as a free state and more stringent fugitive slave laws to apply there as well as elsewhere.

Compton, city south of Los Angeles, on the site of the Rancho San Pedro of the Domínguez family, was named (1869) for Griffith D. Compton, founder of a Methodist temperance college there. It became a farming center and later, in the post-World War II era, developed rapidly as a residential and manufacturing community, becoming one of the fifty largest cities of the state. Its population, like that of nearby Watts, is predominantly black. In 1970, 78,611 persons lived in Compton.

Comstock Lode, mines of silver and gold quartz located in Virginia City, Nevada, less than two miles long and only a few hundred feet wide at most. Discovered in 1859 and named for Henry Comstock, an early developer, the mines created what was called the Big Bonanza, yielding about $400,000,000 before the ore dwindled out about 1880. To provide ventilation, drainage, and transportation to the deep and cramped mine shafts, Adolph Sutro♦ constructed the Sutro Tunnel (1869–79), a remarkable feat of engineering. The mines attracted many San Franciscans, some of whom made great fortunes which they spent in their home city as well as in the eastern U.S. and Europe. Among those who became outstandingly rich were "Lucky" Baldwin, George Hearst, William Ralston, and William Sharon; but topping them all were the so-called Silver Kings: James G. Fair, James C. Flood, John W. Mackay, and William S. O'Brien. Virginia City attracted visitors from all over the world, including journalists like Horace Greeley, but it had its own writers who grew famous there, often as contributors to the local newspaper, *The Territorial Enterprise,* and these included Mark Twain, William T. Goodman, and Dan De Quille, the author of an informal account, *The History of the Big Bonanza* (1877). (*See also individual entries.*)

Concepcion, Point, see *Point Concepcion.*

Concord coach, stagecoach originally built by Abbott, Downing & Co. of Concord, N.H., and introduced to California (1850) to become the conventional vehicle of the California Stage Co.♦ and overland stagecoach♦ lines. It accommodated up to ten passengers inside, with others on top alongside the driver (or "whip"), who handled the reins for six horses. In time Phineas Banning♦ manufactured the coaches locally.

Condor, native vulture with black plumage, naked orange head and neck, and a 10-foot wingspread. David Douglas first identified it as a separate species. Condors are noted for their gliding flight as they circle over the dead meat on which they scavenge. Only about 60 survive (1974); thousands were poisoned or shot by farmers. Their habitat is the central Coast Range from Monterey County to northern Los Angeles County, and sanctuaries exist in the San Rafael Wild Area♦ behind Santa Barbara and in the Sespe area behind Fillmore in Ventura County.

Congressional districts, determined by population so as to give equal representation in the House of Representatives of the U.S. Congress, have increased as California's population has grown. In 1960 the state had 38 districts, while in 1970 it had 43. They vary in geographic scale from the First, which represents Del Norte, Siskiyou, Modoc, Humboldt, Trinity, Shasta, Lassen, Tehama, Plumas, Glenn, Butte, Yuba, Sierra, Nevada, and Placer counties, to the fifteen which represent Los Angeles County alone.

CONNELL, EVAN S., JR. (1924–), Kansas-born author, long resident in the San Francisco Bay area. His novels of character, including *Mrs. Bridge* (1959), an ironic portrait of a frustrated society woman, and *The Patriot* (1960), about a young man in World War II naval air service, are not related to California as are his stories in *The Anatomy Lesson* (1957). His poems include *Notes from a Bottle Found on the Beach at Carmel* (1963) and *Points for a Compass Rose* (1973).

CONNESS, JOHN (1821–1909), Irish-born, came to the U.S. (1833) and went to California (1849), where he was a miner and member of the state assembly before being elected to the U. S. Senate (1863–69) on the Union party ticket. After his term he moved to Boston. Conness Peak (12,565 feet) in Tuolumne County was named for him (1863) because of his work to establish the California geological survey.

CONNOLLY, MAUREEN [CATHERINE] (1934–69), San Diego-born tennis star who won the U.S. women's singles championship at age 16 and held it for two more years (1951–53). She also won the comparable English championships (1952–54) and those of France and Australia (1953), becoming the first woman to win the Grand Slam of all major singles titles in one year. She broke a leg while horseback riding and had to retire from competition.

Conquest of California, see *Mexican War.*

CONSAG, FERNANDO, see *Islands of California.*

Conservation, the preservation, and careful treatment, of natural resources has essentially been a 20th-century concern because in the 19th century the natural bounty of the state was considered, if at all, as inexhaustible and its protection of trivial importance compared to its productive utilization. Thus hydraulic mining♦ washed away mountain sides and let the debris of rocks and silt clog rivers and ruin fertile land, while avaricious lumbermen logged off great stands of ancient redwoods and left in their place a denuded wilderness open to erosion.

Nevertheless, a few sites were so obviously worthy of preservation that they received affectionate attention even in the early days of large-scale spoliation. So Yosemite Valley and the Mariposa Grove were put under the care of federal and state authorities during Lincoln's administration. One of the great spokesmen for the Valley's protection was John Muir, who inspired many followers as he preached the gospel of preserving God's mountain scenes for their beauty, a view called aesthetic conservationism. For that purpose he founded the Sierra Club♦ (1892), a society whose activities still keep it in the forefront of concern with natural resources although, like most modern organizations, it has come to accept a more utilitarian idea of conservation.

The cleavage between the two views was early and dramatically illustrated in the long battle over Hetch Hetchy♦ (1905 ff.) between Muir, who wanted to keep the beautiful but remote valley near Yosemite untouched, and those who saw it as the ideal site for a reservoir to supply needed water from the Tuolumne River to San Francisco and thus make a good use of natural resources. Muir's ideas continued to have a significant impact, however, even after his lifetime, as evidenced by the 5 National Parks♦ created between 1890 and 1968, the 18 National Forests♦ established since 1892, the National Monuments♦ (including Muir Woods), and the comparable State Parks♦ and Forests♦ and smaller Recreational Areas which have been founded throughout California.

As the enormously increased population of the state caused greatly augmented problems of pollution♦ in the 20th century, conservation programs have also been increased by the federal government, the state, and private organizations, although their establishment has always met with opposition from powers dedicated to "progress." The conflicts have been particularly severe since the post-World War II era attracted so many new residents and industries to California.

Among the state's four major administrative departments is its Resources Agency, whose component elements include ones specifically concerned with conservation, fish and game, parks and recreation, and water resources. There are also a San Francisco Bay Conservation and Development Commission, a Tahoe Regional Planning Agency, authorized by Congress as a Nevada-California organization to combat sewage damage to the mountain lake, a California Coastal Zone Conservation Commission, an Air Resources Board to cope with ever-increasing smog,♦ and other regulatory bodies which attempt to preserve the seriously threatened quality of life in California. In the sense that irrigation makes arid areas fruitfully productive, the diverse and large-scale schemes of the state and the federal government for the beneficial employment of water♦ are also part of over-all conservation measures.

Numerous private organizations have also had a significant direct effect upon conservation programs and have served as important contributory factors to the creation of more forceful governmental bodies. Among the early ones have been not only the Sierra Club but also the Save-the-Redwoods League (est. 1918), which over the years has helped to fund the purchase of more than 135,000 acres of State Parks with their great groves of trees. Others include the Save San Francisco Bay Association, created in 1962 to work against more fill and for regional legislation, California Tomorrow, a foundation established in 1965 to foster planning and to preserve a good natural environment, and Friends of the Earth, a politically oriented conservationist organization founded in 1969 to take more aggressive stands than the other societies did.

Constitution, initially created by a convention of 48 delegates (including seven native Californians and eight foreign-born) called by Gov. Bennet Riley from the 10 districts into which he had divided California for representation. They met at Colton Hall, Monterey (Sept.–Nov. 1849). Robert Semple was president, J. Ross Browne reporter, and William Hartnell translator of the document, written in English and Spanish, which provided that future major legislation also be in both languages. The delegates decided not to create an interim territorial government, and, in addition to writing the state Constitution (modeled on those of New York and Iowa), they established the state's boundaries, chose the site of its capital, and designed its Great Seal. The Constitution was ratified by popular vote on Nov. 13, 1849, and the same day officials were elected to office (including Gov. Peter Burnett) so that California began to act as a state before its official admission to statehood♦ (Sept. 9, 1850). A second convention of 152 delegates met in Sacramento (1878–79) to formulate a new Constitution which included an extended Bill of Rights, restrictions on legislative power, the dropping of Spanish as a second legal language, and many miscellaneous provisions. Since 1879 many emendations and additions have been made by amendments (direct legislation by initiative and referendum was added in 1911), for revisions no longer require the calling of a convention. Thus the California Constitution is an unusually long and amorphous document.

Continental shelf, that part of the ocean lying between the low-water line and the sharp inclination of the ocean bottom that marks the edge of the continental slope, having a depth of about 600 feet. The continental shelf off California is generally less than 10 miles wide north of Point Concepcion, although it is about 30 miles wide off San Francisco. South of Point Concepcion it extends out as far as 160 miles. The entire shelf covers over 27,000 sq. mi. The U.S. Supreme Court ruled (1965) that the boundary of the State of California extends 3.45 statute miles from the low-tide line of the mainland and a like distance around each of its ocean islands, adding up to about 5,000 sq. mi. altogether.

Contra Costa, literally the "coast opposite," refers to the eastern shore of the Bay opposite present San Francisco. It was discovered in Nov. 1769 by Juan Ortega♦ while reconnoitering on behalf of Portolá.

Contra Costa Canal, aqueduct to bring fresh Sacramento River and San Joaquin River water 58 miles from the Delta to the Suisun Bay and Carquinez Strait area as part of the Central Valley Project.♦

Contra Costa County, one of the original 27 counties (1850) from which Alameda County was separated (1853). Martinez♦ has always been the county seat. San Joaquin County lies on its east, and Alameda County is on the south and some of the west. The other borders are formed by the San Francisco, San Pablo, and Suisun bays and a spit of Sacramento County on the north. The major landmark is Mt. Diablo.♦

A home of the Bolbones Indians, the early white explorers of the area included Fages (1772), Anza (1776), and Durán (1817). Among early settlers were the Castro family,♦ whose *rancho* included the sites of Richmond,♦ the largest city, El Cerrito, and San Pablo; and John Marsh,♦ the Harvard graduate who built his home near the base of Mt. Diablo (1837). Coal, although of poor quality, was discovered in the area during the 1850s and caused the rise of Pittsburg♦ as a port of shipment,

although it was later known for its steel mill. Other shipping towns on the Carquinez Strait♦ include Port Costa, once a major port for wheat, and Crockett, the site of a major sugar refinery, while farther east on Suisun Bay lies Port Chicago,♦ and still beyond it, at the confluence of the Sacramento and San Joaquin rivers, is Antioch. On the Bay, Point Richmond and Point San Pablo, flanking the Richmond–San Rafael Bridge, are ports for nearby oil refineries.

Regional parks—Wildcat Canyon and Charles Lee Tilden behind Richmond and Berkeley; Las Trampas, where Eugene O'Neill once lived; Briones, near the reservoir of that name; and Mt. Diablo—preserve open spaces, but onetime ranch lands in the county's interior have given way more and more to residential subdivisions and brought growing numbers of families to Orinda, Lafayette, Walnut Creek, Concord, Danville, Moraga (the site of Saint Mary's College), and other former farming communities.

Nevertheless, dairying, poultry raising, the growing of fruit, nut and field crops, and large-scale nurseries are major forces in the economy, along with petroleum refining, natural gas production, and varied manufacturing industries. The population in 1970 was 555,805. With an area of 468,864 acres, it then had 756.1 persons per sq. mi.

Controller, elected at the same time and for the same term as the governor, is the state's chief financial officer. He is responsible for control of all revenues and expenditures of the state, oversees all state inheritance tax referees, and is chairman of the Franchise Tax Board,♦ which collects personal income taxes in the state, and a member of the State Board of Equalization.♦

COOGAN, JACKIE (1914–), Los Angeles-born child star in Hollywood films who first appeared as an appealing wide-eyed waif in Charlie Chaplin's *The Kid* (1921).

COOK, S[HERBURNE] F[RIEND] (1896–1974), professor of physiology and anatomy at the University of California, Berkeley (1928–64), known for his dating of fossil remains and his studies of the aboriginal population of California and Mexico. His major work is *The Conflict between the California Indian and White Civilization* (4 vols., 1943).

COOKE, JACK KENT, see *Forum, The*.

COOKE, PHILIP ST. GEORGE (1809–95), served as a lieutenant-colonel under Kearny in the conquest of New Mexico and California during the Mexican War. The troops he led from Santa Fe to San Diego (1846–47) included the specially enlisted Mormon Battalion.♦ After service in the Union Army during the Civil War Cooke published *The Conquest of New Mexico and California* (1878) which was based on his diaries.

COOLBRITH, INA (1841–1928), christened Josephine Donna Coolbrith, at Nauvoo, Ill., the Mormon capital where she was born, was a niece of the church founder Joseph Smith. Her mother went to California with a second husband (1851), and young Ina claimed she was taken across the Sierra on the saddle of James P. Beckwourth.♦ She lived in mining towns and Los Angeles, where she wed at 17 and was divorced three years later. She moved to San Francisco, and there she became known as a poet, was friendly with Bret Harte, Charles Warren Stoddard, Joaquin Miller, Mark Twain, and Ambrose Bierce. She supported herself by working for the Oakland Public Library, where she befriended and guided the young Jack London and Isadora Duncan, and later for the library of the Bohemian Club, which made her an honorary member. Her personal lyric poems were collected in *A Perfect Day* (1881), *The Singer of the Sea* (1894), and *Songs of the Golden Gate* (1895). In 1915 she organized a World Congress of Authors for the Panama-Pacific Exposition and in recognition was named by the legislature as the state's first poet laureate. She also had named for her an 8,000-foot peak in Sierra County near Beckwourth Pass, where she first entered California.

COOLIDGE, DANE (1873–1940), Massachusetts-born writer about the West, brought to Los Angeles (1877), where he was reared. After graduation from Stanford and work gathering zoological specimens for the university and other institutions, he began the literary career that resulted in more than 40 popular cowboy and other kinds of Western novels. His books include *Hidden Water* (1910), *The Law West of the Pecos* (1924), *Gun Smoke* (1928), *Snake-Bit Jones* (1936), set in Death Valley, and *Gringo Gold* (1939), about Joaquin Murieta. He also wrote nonfictional works about cowboys, including *Old California Cowboys* (1939), and produced an archive of photographs of them. With his wife, Mary Roberts Coolidge, he wrote *The Navajo Indians* (1930) and *The Last of the Seris* (1939), about a Baja California tribe.

COOPER, ELIAS SAMUEL (1822–62), San Francisco surgeon and founder of California's first medical school, affiliated with the College of the Pacific. Most of its staff joined Dr. Hugh H. Toland♦ when he founded his Toland Medical College (1864) but a dispute with Cooper's nephew, Dr. Levi Cooper Lane, led to the resignation of most of the remaining members (1870). They joined the Cooper Medical College (1882) which, with the large Lane Medical Library, became part of Stanford University (1908).

COOPER, GARY (1901–61), Montana-born film star in Hollywood, began his career in the screen version of Harold Bell Wright's *The Winning of Barbara Worth* (1926). Thereafter he played many other cowboy roles, including *High Noon* (1952), but in all kinds of parts he always portrayed an honest, simple, manly, back-country sort of American. He maintained a home in the Los Angeles area for the last 35 years of his life.

COOPER, JOHN ROGERS (1792–1872), English-born merchant of Mexican California, reared in Massachusetts, was the half-brother of Thomas O. Larkin by his mother's second marriage. He settled in Monterey (1826), became a Catholic convert and Mexican citizen, and married Gen. Vallejo's sister. As a shipmaster, trader, and rancher he was an important figure in the California of his day. He was also known as Juan Bautista Ruggiero Cooper and simply as Captain Cooper.

COOPER, SARAH BROWN INGERSOLL (1835–96), went to San Francisco (1869) where she was influenced by Kate Douglas Wiggin♦ but directed her own kindergarten work toward slum children in the Barbary Coast and elsewhere. She went on to found 40 allied kindergartens for all kinds of children, and in San Francisco she organized a major national Woman's Congress meeting (1891).

Cooperative communities, see *Fountain Grove, Harris, Thomas Lake; Holy City; Kaweah; Llano del Rio; Point Loma;* and *Sienkiewicz, Henryk.*

Coordinating Council for Higher Education, established in 1960, consisted of three members from each of the four elements of higher education in the state: the University of California, state colleges and universities, junior colleges, private colleges and universities, and six representatives of the general public. It reviewed budgets, oversaw functional differentiations among the state-supported institutions, and developed plans for the expansion of the state's higher education.◆ In 1974 its functions were taken over by a similar Postsecondary Education Commission, whose 23 members include more representatives of the general public.

Copley Press, a chain of newspapers incorporated (1928) by Ira Clifton Copley (1864–1947), an Illinois public utilities magnate and Congressman whose parents had moved to San Diego in the 1880s. In 1928 he bought the *San Diego Union*◆ and the *Tribune* from the Spreckels family and from Frederic Kellogg acquired smaller dailies in Alhambra, Burbank, Culver City, Glendale, Monrovia, Redondo Beach, San Pedro, and Venice. They were all strongly Republican, although the *Tribune* was more independent—it attempted to appeal to labor. Of Copley's two adopted sons, James [Strohn] Copley (1916–73) became the publisher and finally bought out the other son, William Nelson Copley, and ran the papers from his San Diego home. He established the Copley News Service (1955), a major national agency, bought the *Sacramento Union*◆ (1966), and owned 15 daily papers and 32 weeklies, all strongly Republican, at the time of his death. His wife, Helen Kinney Hunt, once his secretary, succeeded him as head of the Copley empire.

Coppa's, Italian restaurant in San Francisco, a bohemian rendezvous for George Sterling, Gelett Burgess, Xavier Martinez, and others, flourished from 1903 until the earthquake of 1906, although the owner, Giuseppe (Papa) Coppa (1860–1948), ran other restaurants at other sites into the late 1930s.

Copper, first mined in the Mother Lode country during the 1860s, a major site being located in southwestern Calaveras County, where the town of Copperopolis grew up. Other veins or deposits in igneous or metamorphic rocks were found to the north; they were mined mainly in Shasta and Plumas counties and elsewhere in the Sierra Nevada foothills. Those regions were fairly well exhausted by about 1948 and since then copper has been obtained as a by-product of tungsten mining in Inyo County.

CORA, CHARLES (d. 1856), San Francisco gambler who brought his mistress, a notorious madam, to sit in a theater box with Gen. William H. Richardson, a U.S. Marshal, and his wife. Richardson, angered by what he considered to be an insult, next day accosted Cora with a drawn pistol and Cora

shot him dead. Cora's lawyers, Edward D. Baker◆ and James A. McDougall,◆ argued that Cora had been defending himself, and the case ended in a hung jury. Nevertheless, the Vigilance Committee,◆ created in part because of the sensational murders committed by Cora and James Casey,◆ took the two men from the county jail, tried them before a Vigilance tribunal at their committee's headquarters, Fort Gunnybags, and hanged them together there.

CORBETT, JAMES J [OHN] (1866–1933), San Francisco-born heavyweight boxing champion of the U.S. defeated John L. Sullivan (1892) and was himself defeated by Bob Fitzsimmons (1897). Known as "Gentleman Jim" because he had been in banking (as a clerk) before his professional career, because he was a member of the Olympic Club, and because his boxing style was also in accord with his sobriquet, he was a popular figure in his home city. He fought three successful bouts against Joe Choynski◆ before he was champion and two unsuccessful ones against J. J. Jeffries◆ after he was no longer champion.

CORBUS, BILL (WILLIAM CORBUS) (1911–), San Francisco-born football player, was the star guard of Stanford University's team (1931–33) and captain of the 1933 team of Vow Boys.◆

CORLE, EDWIN (1906–56), New Jersey-born author of books about the southwest of California, Arizona, and New Mexico, whose novels include *Fig Tree John* (1935); *People of the Earth* (1937); and *Listen, Bright Angel* (1946). *Mojave* (1934) is a collection of stories with desert settings, and his nonfiction includes *Desert Country* (1941) and *The Valley of Death* (1962).

Corn, a major field crop since the beginning of the century. The leading area both for grain and for silage remains the Sacramento-San Joaquin Delta. In 1970 216,000 acres of grain worth $33,455 were harvested, and the same year corn for silage was grown on 113,000 acres. Sweet corn, once a significant crop in the Santa Clara Valley, is now grown mainly in the south of the San Joaquin Valley and in the Coachella Valley.

Cornishmen, went to California during the gold rush either directly from the lead and tin mines of their native Cornwall or after having worked in the lead region of Wisconsin and Illinois. They made Grass Valley and Nevada City into "Cornish capitals" and provided sophisticated technological information in the mines there. They also opposed less skilled Irish and Chinese workers and cruder mining methods. They continued to emigrate in great numbers during the 1870s and 80s and then became active in the silver mines of Nevada and replaced Mexicans in the quicksilver mines of New Almaden. Cornishmen were called "Cousin Jack" (and Cornish women "Cousin Jennie") because intermarriage in their native land was supposedly so common that every Cornishman was said to be related to every other one.

CORONA, JUAN (1934–), Mexican-born rancher of Solano County, convicted (1972) of the murders of 25 migrant farmworkers in his orchards and condemned to consecutive life sentences for each slaying. He was granted a new trial (1978).

CORONADO, FRANCISCO VÁSQUEZ DE, see *Exploration.*

Coronado, peninsula located in San Diego Bay, deriving its name from the farther offshore and more southerly Coronado Islands of Mexico which were themselves named by Vizcaíno (1602) for the saints' day celebrating four Romans "crowned" as Christian martyrs. The area near San Diego was developed as a resort with the construction (1888) of the elaborate white wooden Hotel del Coronado, bought by John D. Spreckels in 1903. It still stands as the last of the great Victorian spas of California. The peninsula is also the site of a navy amphibious training school. In 1970 the population was 20,910.

CORONEL, IGNACIO (1796–1862), went from Mexico (where he had been a soldier) to California with the Hijar and Padrés colonists (1834) and founded the first school of consequence in Los Angeles (c. 1838). His son, Antonio Franco (1817–94), went with him from Mexico City and in Los Angeles became a justice of the peace and inspector of missions. He fought against the U.S. (1846–47) but later was a staunch citizen, a mayor of Los Angeles (1853), and treasurer of the state. He provided Helen Hunt Jackson with information for *Ramona,* was a founder of the Historical Society of Southern California, and gave to his city memorabilia and relics of early days, now called the Coronel Collection of the Los Angeles County Museum. Antonio's cousin was Agustin Olvera,♦ for whom a well-known Los Angeles street is named.

CORTÉS, HERNANDO (1485–1547), Spanish conquistador, the conqueror of Mexico (1519–21), in

1533 sent a naval expedition north under Diego Becerra which led to the discovery of Baja California (then thought to be an island) by Fortún Jiménez, the pilot who had mutinied and killed the commander and who was himself killed by Indians at La Paz. Cortés visited the site (1535) and named the area Santa Cruz. In 1539–40 he dispatched Ulloa♦ northward on a voyage that reached the head of the Sea of Cortés, later called the Gulf of California,♦ and discovered that Santa Cruz (Baja California) was a peninsula, not an island. After the expedition returned, Cortés went back to Spain, where he remained the rest of his life.

Cortés, Sea of, see *California, Gulf of.*

COSGRAVE, JOHN O'HARA, see *Wave, The.*

Coso County, a projected county (1864) to be created from territory in Mono and Tulare counties but never officially organized. Two years later Inyo County was formed on the same territory.

Coso Range, mountains in Inyo County (once to have been called Coso County) to the south of Owens Lake, adjoining the Argus Range farther southeast. There are also a peak (8,160 ft.) and hot springs of this name, derived from the Koso Indians.♦ The area was the site of active gold mining from the 1850s through the 1870s.

Costa Mesa, a residential and industrial city in Orange County, founded (1915) as a real estate subdivision with a pseudo-Spanish descriptive name meaning "Coast Tableland." It contains an *estancia* of Mission San Juan Capistrano and the Briggs Cunningham Automotive Museum. In 1970 it had a population of 72,660.

Costanoan, Indians of the Penutian♦ language family who lived on the San Francisco peninsula, the east shore of the Bay, and as far south as Big Sur and Soledad. Seven missions were established in their territory. According to the 1910 census their prehistoric population of 7,000 had been reduced to extinction. They were exposed to the Kuksu cult which originated with the Wintun.♦ Their housing and rafts were made of tules and their food included acorns, salmon, and oysters. The tribal name derives from a Spanish word for "coastal dweller."

COSTANSÓ, MIGUEL (*fl.* 1770), military engineer and cartographer aboard the *San Carlos* on the

Sacred Expedition under the command of Portolá (1769–1770). He wrote an account of the expedition itself, the terrain, the natives (including something of their language), and the flora and fauna of California. This was published as *Diario histórico de los viages de mar, y tierra hechos al norte de la California....* It appeared in Madrid and perhaps Mexico (1770), and in London in 1790 as *An Historical Journal of the Expeditions, by Sea and Land, to the North of California....* He also wrote a more personal diary, first published in 1911.

Cosumnes River, named for an Indian tribe that lived along its banks, rises in El Dorado County, flows from the Sierra into the Mokelumne River south of the city of Sacramento, and through the Central Valley into the Delta.

COTA, prominent early California family whose oldest branch was founded by Roque Jacinto de Cota (1724–98), who was settled in San Gabriel by 1778. His numerous descendants and collateral relatives include residents of Santa Barbara, San Fernando, and Los Angeles. Among the last was Guillermo Cota, several times *alcalde* of Los Angeles.

Cotton, first imported from Mexico and grown by padres at missions in Baja and Alta California, but those small ventures ended with secularization (1833) and serious large-scale cultivation came only with the Civil War when the state government gave prizes for first crops. About 2,000 acres are said to have been planted in cotton by 1863, but competition from more profitable crops soon ended the cultivation. Reintroduced on an extensive scale in 1909, cotton growing became far larger in the 1920s. It was centered in the San Joaquin Valley, well suited because of its medium sandy loam soil, rain-free seven-month growing season, use of irrigation, and freedom from pests. The discovery of the Acala strain, excellent for that soil and climate, boosted production, which grew considerably in the 1930s. After World War II crops boomed, increasing over 100% from 1947 through 1948. It has been concentrated in the San Joaquin, Imperial, and Coachella valleys. By 1970 cotton was the leading cash crop of California, and the state was the third largest producer after Texas and Mississippi. Cotton manufacturing has never been successful in the state because labor costs have always been too high to compete with southern or foreign mills.

Cottonwood, see *Poplar.*

COULTER, WILLIAM A. (1849–1937), Irish-born artist who went to California as a sailor (1880) and in time became an illustrator for the San Francisco *Call.* He gained fame for his precise, accurate, but romantically conceived paintings of sailing ships.

Counterculture, see *Beat movement, Hippie movement,* and *Rock music.*

Counties (58):

	Pop. 1970	Sq. Mi.	Date Est.	County Seat
Alameda	1,073,184	733	1853	Oakland
Alpine	484	727	1864	Markleeville
Amador	11,821	583	1854	Jackson
Butte	101,969	1,645	1854	Oroville
Calaveras	13,585	1,024	1850	San Andreas
Colusa	12,430	1,152	1850	Colusa
Contra Costa	558,389	735	1850	Martinez
Del Norte	14,580	1,007	1857	Crescent City
El Dorado	43,833	1,715	1850	Placerville
Fresno	313,053	5,966	1850	Fresno
Glenn	17,521	1,314	1891	Willows
Humboldt	99,692	3,586	1853	Eureka
Imperial	74,492	4,241	1907	El Centro
Inyo	15,571	10,130	1866	Independence
Kern	329,162	8,152	1866	Bakersfield
Kings	64,610	1,396	1893	Hanford
Lake	19,548	1,261	1861	Lakeport

Counties (58) (Continued):

	Pop. 1970	Sq. Mi.	Date Est.	County Seat
Lassen	14,960	4,561	1864	Susanville
Los Angeles	7,032,075	4,069	1850	Los Angeles
Madera	41,519	2,145	1893	Madera
Marin	206,038	520	1850	San Rafael
Mariposa	6,015	1,453	1850	Mariposa
Mendocino	51,101	3,511	1850	Ukiah
Merced	104,629	1,958	1855	Merced
Modoc	7,469	4,097	1874	Alturas
Mono	4,016	3,027	1861	Bridgeport
Monterey	250,071	3,324	1850	Salinas
Napa	79,140	787	1850	Napa
Nevada	26,346	973	1851	Nevada City
Orange	1,420,386	782	1889	Santa Ana
Placer	77,306	1,431	1851	Auburn
Plumas	11,707	2,566	1854	Quincy
Riverside	459,074	7,176	1893	Riverside
Sacramento	631,498	975	1850	Sacramento
San Benito	18,226	1,396	1874	Hollister
San Bernardino	684,072	20,117	1853	San Bernardino
San Diego	1,357,854	4,261	1850	San Diego
San Francisco	715,674	45	1850	San Francisco
San Joaquin	290,208	1,412	1850	Stockton
San Luis Obispo	105,690	3,183	1850	San Luis Obispo
San Mateo	556,234	447	1856	Redwood City
Santa Barbara	264,324	2,737	1850	Santa Barbara
Santa Clara	1,064,714	1,300	1850	San Jose
Santa Cruz	123,790	440	1850	Santa Cruz
Shasta	77,640	3,788	1850	Redding
Sierra	2,365	968	1852	Downieville
Siskiyou	33,225	6,262	1852	Yreka
Solano	169,941	823	1850	Fairfield
Sonoma	204,885	1,604	1850	Santa Rosa
Stanislaus	194,506	1,511	1854	Modesto
Sutter	41,935	603	1850	Yuba City
Tehama	29,517	2,982	1856	Red Bluff
Trinity	7,615	3,173	1850	Weaverville
Tulare	188,322	4,812	1852	Visalia
Tuolumne	22,169	2,252	1850	Sonora
Ventura	376,430	1,863	1872	Ventura
Yolo	91,788	1,028	1850	Woodland
Yuba	44,736	639	1850	Marysville

(See entries under separate county names; see also **Coso, Nataqua,** *and* **Pautah.***)*

Courts of Appeal, major appellate courts directly below the Supreme Court, their cases being primarily appeals from the decisions of the 58 Superior Courts and also from Municipal and Justice Courts. There are five Courts of Appeal in Los Angeles, four in San Francisco, two in San Diego–San Bernardino, one in Sacramento, and one in Fresno.

Each court has three to five judges who are appointed by a governor, confirmed by the Commission on Judicial Appointments, and approved in a district election.

Cousin Jack, see *Cornishmen.*

COUTS, CAVE J[OHNSON] (1821–74), Tennessee-born graduate of West Point who, after service in the Mexican War, was sent to San Diego (1848), whose pueblo lands he surveyed and mapped. He also established a refugee camp at present Calexico♦ for forty-niners stranded on the way to the gold fields. He married a daughter of Don Juan Bandini (1851), resigned from the army, and presided, although tempestuously, over Rancho Guajome (near present Oceanside), a gift from his brother-in-law Abel Stearns.

COUTTS, PETER, name employed by Jean-Baptiste Paulin Caperon (1822–89), a liberal republican French banker who opposed Napoleon III and for that reason and for his health's sake left France to settle on a 1,242-acre farm in Mayfield (1874–80). There he built an elaborate house, a brick tower that was part library and part water tank, and irrigation tunnels. The property was later part of Stanford University, whose students told, and believed, all kinds of romantic stories about the "mysterious Frenchman."

Covered wagon, vehicle used to carry goods and people across the continent in the westward movement that grew to a climax during the gold rush to California for a decade after 1849. The vehicle originated in colonial Pennsylvania as a Conestoga wagon, marked by a raised bed at either end to prevent the spilling of contents, but the transcontinental 19th-century version was smaller, had an ordinary wagon-box and a curved canvas cover with neither front nor rear overhang. It was called a prairie schooner because from a distance it resembled a ship at sea.

Covina, city west of Glendora in the east-central San Gabriel Valley, grew up in the 1880s as a settlement among citrus groves. In the period after World War II it and neighboring West Covina, with freeway access, expanded enormously and became huge housing areas. Two musicians are associated with Covina: Roy Harris,♦ the composer, who was reared there, and Ellen Beach Yaw (1868–1947), a soprano opera star sometimes called "Lark Ellen," who retired there.

Cow counties, pejorative name given in the gold rush and succeeding era to counties not involved in mining. The reference was generally to southern California: Los Angeles, San Bernardino, San Diego, San Luis Obispo, Santa Barbara, and Tulare counties. Since they were heavily taxed but poorly represented in the legislature they seriously considered secession. Andrés Pico projected (1859) a separate Territory of Colorado for the six counties.

Cow Hollow, name given to a San Francisco area between the Presidio and Van Ness Ave. and Vallejo and Greenwich streets. Once noted for its dairies (*c.* 1860–80), it is now a fashionable shopping and residential district.

Cow Palace, name given to the huge arena on the outskirts of San Francisco constructed in 1936. It has served not only for livestock expositions but for other events, including the Republican party's national convention of 1964 which nominated Barry Goldwater.

COWAN, ROBERT ERNEST (1862–1942), Canadian-born bibliophile and bibliographer. He came to the U.S. (1870), attended the University of California (1882–84), opened a bookstore in San Francisco, and created a great collection of Californiana. In 1914 The Book Club of California published his first work, his *Bibliography of California,* listing 1,000 items. William Andrews Clark♦ made Cowan his librarian (1919–33), in which capacity he prepared bibliographies of Clark's collection of various English authors' works. With his son Robert Grannis Cowan he greatly enlarged his *Bibliography of California* (3 vols., 1933).

COWELL, HENRY (1820–1903), Massachusetts-born businessman who with his brother John developed limestone deposits and operated lime kilns on his large Santa Cruz ranch. His fortune eventually created a charitable trust that has made large gifts (mainly for health) to northern California colleges and universities, while the ranch has become the Santa Cruz campus of the University of California. His son memorialized him by giving the state a 1,600-acre park of redwoods bearing his name. The pianist-composer Henry Cowell was a descendant.

COWELL, HENRY [DIXON] (1897–1965), California-born pianist and composer and member of the prominent pioneer Cowell family of Santa Cruz. His avant-garde piano compositions include works to be played with the arm and fist and directly on the strings. His compositions include a *Concerto* (1932), written for the mechanical Rhythmicon, which he invented to create cross-rhythms, and five *Hymns and Fuguing Tunes* (1941–45), marked by their counterpoint.

COX, PALMER (1840–1924), Canadian-born author and illustrator, resident in California (1863–75), where he contributed to the *Golden Era* and *Alta California*. He wrote *Squibs of California* (1875) but was only successful later with his series of *Brownies* book (1887 ff.), which present amusing pixies in verse and pictures.

COXHEAD, ERNEST (1863–1933), British-born architect who with his brother Almeric went to Los Angeles (1888) where they designed churches and residences, and then moved to San Francisco (*c.*1890). Maybeck worked with them for a time, and they helped to develop the regional simple shingle home style.

Coyote, predatory animal (sometimes called a prairie wolf outside the state), with light gray or tawny fur, weighing about eighteen to thirty pounds. Stigmatized as a killer of livestock and poultry, it can be hunted at any time of year, but it actually feeds mostly on rabbits, squirrels, rodents, reptiles, eggs, insects, and fruit. Found throughout most of the state, it is celebrated in many place-names, the earliest of which was given by Anza (1776) to a creek in Santa Clara County. The name it bears is derived from *coyotl,* an Aztec word for the animal. It figures in California Indian legendry, e.g. the Costanoans conceived the coyote to be the creator of humans.

CRA, see *California Republican Assembly.*

Crab, the crustacean known as the *Dungeness* or *market crab* is found north of Morro Bay in ocean waters less than 75 fathoms deep, mainly from San Francisco to Bodega Bay and from Eureka to Crescent City. Commercial fishing, largely by Italians, is mainly by traps during the season which extends from mid-November to May. Regulations limit the catch to males at least six and a quarter inches wide, therefore three and a half to four years old. In the 1960s the north coast catch averaged 7,400,000 annually and that of the central coast 3,100,000, but it has dwindled since then.

CRABTREE, LOTTA (1847–1924), taken to Grass Valley in 1852 by her English parents and tutored there by Lola Montez, she began her theatrical career as a child singer, dancer, and mimic in the mining country. Her success became national as she matured and appeared both in adaptations of Dickens' fiction and in plays specially written for her and produced by her own touring company.

The most highly paid American actress of her day, she delighted audiences with her high spirits, childish appearance, and youthful parts until her retirement in 1891. Her $4,000,000 fortune went to charity, the best-known object being "Lotta's Fountain," a cast-iron column on San Francisco's Market St., presented in 1875.

CRANSTON, ALAN (1914–   ), born in Palo Alto, after graduation from Stanford and work in a real estate business and activity in Democratic politics, was elected controller of the state (1959–67) then U.S. Senator (1969).

CRAWFORD, JOAN (1908–77), Texas-born film star in Hollywood for almost 50 years, during which she changed her image from a brash flapper (*Our Dancing Daughters,* 1925) to a mature, sophisticated woman (*The Last of Mrs. Cheyney,* 1937) to a serious dramatic actress (*Whatever Happened to Baby Jane?* 1962). She won an Academy Award (1945) for her role in *Mildred Pierce,* adapted from the novel by James M. Cain.♦

Crayfish, small fresh-water crustacean similar to the lobster, found in streams and ponds. Called *crawfish* and used as bait, they are also admired as a gourmet delicacy and easily caught as sport but are not common enough for commercial fishing.

CREEL, GEORGE (1876–1953), Missouri-born journalist, appointed (1917) by President Wilson to head the wartime U.S. Commission on Public Information, for which he developed effective techniques later employed in mass advertising. After moving to San Francisco (1926) he was active in Democratic party affairs, ran unsuccessfully against Upton Sinclair for the gubernatorial nomination (1934), and was a civic and cultural leader in northern California. His wife was Blanche Bates.♦

CREMONY, JOHN C[AREY] (1815–79), San Francisco newspaperman from the late 1850s and afterwards a contributor to the *Overland Monthly.* He was known at the Bohemian Club, of which he was a founder, as a raconteur and teller of tall tales. His own life as an adventurer was his best subject, including his service as an officer in the Mexican War and the Civil War, and his surveying of the U.S.–Mexican boundary, the latter work leading to experiences he recounted in *Life among the Apaches* (1868).

Crescent City, county seat of Del Norte County,♦ founded (1853) during the gold rush and named for its bay, a lumber shipping area. A tidal wave destroyed a large downtown area (1964), which was replaced by a mall. In 1970 the population was 2,586.

CRESPÍ, JUAN (1721–82), Majorca-born missionary who went to the Franciscan's College of San Fernando in Mexico with his teacher, Junípero Serra, and with him and Palóu went to Baja California (1767) and then on the Sacred Expedition of 1769 to Alta California. Having gone to San Diego with Rivera y Moncada he continued north with Portolá, seeking the port of Monterey and becoming a discoverer of San Francisco Bay, which he later explored with Fages. He accompanied the Pérez expedition to Alaska (1774) but most of his later life was spent with Serra at Mission Carmel, where he died. His diaries of his various expeditions were translated and edited by Herbert E. Bolton in *Juan Crespí* (1927).

Crew, a sport of rowing in racing shells, dates back to 1811 in an organized competition in New York and to the first Harvard-Yale regatta in 1852, but it was not introduced to California until 1886, when the San Diego Rowing Club was organized. The first intercollegiate team was that of the University of California (1893), soon followed by one at Stanford. In 1903 the Pacific Coast Regatta was inaugurated with those two teams and that of the University of Washington. The University of California became a significant force in the sport when it brought Ky Ebright♦ to the Berkeley campus from the University of Washington (1924). During his career, which ended in 1959, the University of California won six Intercollegiate Rowing Association championships (1928, 32, 34–35, 39, 49) and represented the U.S. in the Olympic Games (1928, 32, 48), winning the gold medal for eight-oar rowing each time. The San Diego club and the Long Beach Rowing Association have also won championships, as did the University of California again during the 1960s.

CREWS, LAURA HOPE (1879–1942), San Francisco-born actress, played her first role at the age of four with her mother, an established local actress. The two played in stock companies of San Francisco and New York after Miss Crews finished high school. As a comedienne she acted in plays of Shakespeare with John Drew and Sir Herbert Beerbohm Tree, but her most famous role was that of the possessive mother in *The Silver Cord* (1926) by Sidney Howard. She repeated the role in a film

during her successful motion picture career in the 1930s.

Criminal Syndicalism Act, statute of the state legislature of 1919 declaring illegal "any doctrine or precept advocating . . . unlawful acts of violence . . . as a means of accomplishing a change in industrial ownership or control, or effecting any political change." Among the hundreds of persons prosecuted under the law the most prominent was Anita Whitney.♦ It was invoked as late as the 1930s to prosecute "radicals" and had a devastating effect upon labor unions when employed, for example, against the Cannery and Agricultural Workers Industrial Union, whose leaders were convicted under the act (1934). It was finally ruled unconstitutional by a U.S. Appeals Court (1968).

CROCKER, CHARLES (1822–88), born in Troy, N.Y., after mining iron in Indiana went to California (1850) to mine gold. Unsuccessful at that, he went into storekeeping in Sacramento, where he became acquainted with three other merchants, Mark Hopkins, Collis Huntington, and Leland Stanford, and with them became one of the Big Four♦ who built the Central Pacific Railroad.♦ While Hopkins, Huntington, and Stanford administered other parts of the great enterprise, Crocker, a huge man weighing over 250 pounds, stayed on the line supervising the actual construction of the track, bellowing like a bull (as he said) to drive on the foremen and the Chinese♦ whom he had brought from the Orient to do the hard labor. He not only pushed the rails through sheer granite cliffs but built miles-long protective snowsheds♦ above them. After construction was completed Crocker invested in large land holdings and related irrigation projects, was president of the Southern Pacific Railroad,♦ and developed the Del Monte Hotel♦ and other properties. His son, William H. Crocker (1861–1937), married a member of the wealthy pioneer Stockton family of Simon Willard Sperry,♦ so his descendants, like those of Charles Crocker's brother, Edwin Bryant Crocker, founder of the Crocker Art Gallery,♦ have continued to be prominent socially and financially in San Francisco and elsewhere and are associated with the bank bearing the family name.

Crocker Art Gallery, The, created in Sacramento by Edwin Bryant Crocker (1818–75), brother of Charles Crocker,♦ briefly a State Supreme Court Justice (appointed by Gov. Stanford), and long chief legal counsel of the Central Pacific Railroad. As a result of a grand tour of Europe (1870) he and his wife acquired a large, miscellaneous collection of works of art, including a number of notable drawings by old masters. His handsome Victorian home and the collection now form a municipal museum.

Crockett, city on Carquinez Strait in Contra Costa County, the site of a major sugar refinery, was named (1881) for a State Supreme Court Justice.

CROMWELL, DEAN [BARTLETT] (1879–1962), after graduation from Occidental College (1902), where he was a star athlete, became football and track coach at the University of Southern California (1909) and then coached track alone (1919–48). His teams won twelve NCAA championships, including nine in a row (1935–43), and his athletes won 33 individual NCAA titles and 39 individual AAU championships. He was also head coach of the U.S. Olympic track team (1948).

CRONIN, JOE (JOSEPH EDWARD CRONIN) (1906–), San Francisco-born baseball player and manager, was a shortstop with the Washington Senators (1928–34) and Boston Red Sox (1935–45), also serving as manager of the Boston team until 1947. He was elected to the Baseball Hall of Fame and was president of the American League (1959–73).

CROSBY, BING (HARRY LILLIS CROSBY) (1904–77), Washington-born singer, entertainer, and film actor, long resident in California. He began his career as a sophisticated, romantic singer who crooned popular songs with jazz dance bands in 1925 and had great popularity in that career. In the 1930s he became a motion picture star and public idol. His films were mostly musical comedies (*Pennies from Heaven,* 1938) but he also had numerous successes co-starring with Bob Hope in comedies including song and dance routines (*The Road to Singapore,* 1939) and later enacted more serious roles, such as that of a warm-hearted priest (*Going My Way,* 1944, Academy Award). His enthusiasm for golf led him to sponsor a "Crosby Clambake" tournament (1937) at Rancho Santa Fe, followed (1946) by an annual tournament for men, professional and amateur, bearing his name and played at Pebble Beach.

CROSETTI, FRANK (PETER JOSEPH CROSETTI) (1910–), San Francisco-born shortstop for the New

York Yankees (1932–48) and later a coach of the team, appearing in one guise or another in its uniform at 22 World Series.

Cross-filing, procedure of direct primary election in which a candidate (without party identification) may be listed on the ballot of political parties other than his own. First introduced in Berkeley (1909), the legislature approved it (1913) for state elections after sponsorship by the Progressives as part of their opposition to established political machines and as a means of letting all voters choose the candidates they most favored regardless of their party affiliation. It was rescinded (1959) when it was considered confusing to voters because many newly enfranchised Democrats in ignorance helped re-elect Republicans who were listed first on their ballots and identified only as "Incumbent."

Crossing of the Fathers, see *Escalante, Silvestre.*

Crystal Springs Lakes, see *Spring Valley Water Company.*

Cucamonga, small city in southwest San Bernardino County, its Shoshonean place-name ("sandy place"), like that of the nearby canyon, peak, and park, derives from the exploring expedition of Moraga (1819). The town grew up around an early commercial vineyard (1839 ff.) and the region is still a major one for wineries and olive growing. Nearby to the south lies Guasti, the town named for Secondo Guasti, whose Italian Vineyard Co. was founded there at the opening of the 20th century.

Cuesta Pass, route through the Santa Lucia Mts. just north of San Luis Obispo, traveled by Portolá, Anza, and Frémont. It was on El Camino Reál and the railroad also passed through it, as does the modern highway. It is located in the northernmost part of Los Padres National Forest.

Cults, have flourished in California, particularly in the southern part of the state, perhaps to a large degree because its pleasant climate has already attracted somewhat rootless people searching for an easier life than they had previously known. Lacking established associations, these people also quested for new kinds of communities. Moreover, since many went to California for health, they were more receptive to faith healing and other occult schemes for improving their well-being. William Money◆ (c. 1840 ff.) antedated the eccentric reformers for which California later became famous, but he also anticipated them in opposing established religion and proposing a new faith.

Later and more persuasive were the French who founded the colony of Icaria Speranza; the theosophists; Mrs. Tingley, the Purple Mother of Point Loma; and Krishnamurti in Ojai; a Rosicrucian sect with an Egyptian temple in San Jose; the "Theo-Socialist" colony of Thomas Lake Harris; Fountain Grove, near Santa Rosa; and the poor, freakish Holy City near Los Gatos.

Not isolated in their own special communities and more widely accepted were Aimee Semple McPherson with her Angelus Temple and its "Foursquare Gospel," and Mankind United and the Mighty I Am, the former flourishing particularly in the lush days of the 1920s and the latter among the many popular movements during the deepening days of the Depression.

California had also long provided a happy home for political and social reformers from the fanciful to the more pragmatic and less extreme like J. Stitt Wilson, elected mayor of Berkeley (1911) as a Socialist, and Job Harriman, also a Socialist, who very nearly became mayor of Los Angeles the same year. Harriman went on to found the Socialist community of Llano del Rio, no more successful than the earlier Marxist colony in Tulare County, the Kaweah Cooperative Commonwealth.

However, although such special Utopian communities flourished no better than the one founded by some Polish émigrés at Anaheim, including Sienkiewicz and Modjeska, the people of California have often been attracted by a tincture of Utopia in their politics. This was particularly true during the days of the Depression when the Townsend Plan, to provide pensions for older people, and its more fanciful successor, Ham 'n Eggs, built up vast followings that also subscribed to the EPIC principles of Upton Sinclair and nearly won the gubernatorial election of 1934 for him.

All of these kinds of cultism and others continue to flourish in California, which has more recently been a center for the anticonventional cultures of the Beat movement and the Hippie movement, seeking a freer emotional life through Zen Buddhism, rock music, drugs, and communes. *(See also individual entries.)*

Cultural Heritage Board, Los Angeles city agency established (1962) with power to name historic or cultural monuments on selected city or privately owned property and to delay demolition of such landmarks.

Culver City, residential and manufacturing community located about ten miles west of downtown Los Angeles, is the site of many former film studios, some of which remain. It was named (1914) for its real estate subdivider. The population in 1970 was over 34,000.

CUMMINS, ELLA STERLING, see *Mighels, Ella Sterling.*

CUNEO, RINALDO (1877–1939), San Francisco-born artist, known for his paintings of its waterfront, where he worked for a tugboat firm.

CUNNINGHAM, IMOGEN (1883–1976), photographer born in Portland, Wash., and reared in Seattle, whose life after 1917 was spent in the San Francisco Bay area. Her career began at the opening of the century with soft-focus pictures of people, plants, and objects, but over the years, initially under the influence of Edward Weston, she began to emphasize sharp and detailed depiction. A collection of her photographs (the first taken in 1910) was published in 1974.

CUNNINGHAM, KATE RICHARDS O'HARE (1877–1948), Kansas-born reformer, a member of the Socialist party, widely known as a speaker, whose opposition to World War I led her to be imprisoned (1919–20) and to become a champion of prison reform. She married Charles C. Cunningham, a San Francisco lawyer (1928), and thereafter lived in California, where she was prominent in Upton Sinclair's EPIC campaign and, under Gov. Olson, an official in the state prison system.

Cunningham Automotive Museum, see *Costa Mesa.*

Cupeño, Indians who lived in two villages: Kupa (whence their name derives) and Wilabal, both located at the headwaters of the San Luis Rey River (San Diego County). Their preconquest population of 500 had been reduced to 200 by 1910. They belonged to the Luiseño-Cahuilla group and practiced all the major ceremonies common to most southern California tribes, including the initiation of adolescent girls, the anniversary mourning ceremony, and the tolache cult.◆ The Garrá Revolt◆ against Americans in 1851 was led by their chief.

Cupertino, city in Santa Clara County on the site of land settled by Elisha Stevens in the 1840s. It long remained farming and vineyard land with large residences, but as San Jose grew in the 1960s it boomed as a suburb and acquired an electronics and aerospace industry. Its population in 1970 was 18,216.

Curry, see *Camp Curry.*

CURTIS, EDWARD (1868–1952), Wisconsin-born photographer, made his home in southern California from the 1920s on. Even then he was famous for his great portraits of Indians of many regions. His works, backed by J. P. Morgan, finally amounted to 20 volumes, including documentary pictures of Hupa, Yurok, and Karok Indians of California.

Cuyama Valley, lies between the Sierra Madre Mts. and the Caliente Range near the northwest boundary of Santa Barbara County. The name, a Chumash word, probably meaning "clams," was first applied to the valley's river, which now forms the border between San Luis Obispo and Santa Barbara counties. Long a dry farming area known only for hay and alfalfa, when wells were sunk vegetables could be grown and cattle grazed in the valley. Since 1948 oil drilling has ended the valley's isolation.

Cuyamaca Rancho State Park, lying between the Anza-Borrego State Park on its east and the Cleve-land National Forest on its west, is a rugged mountainous region which also was the site of gold mining in the 1870s that created the town of Julian just to the north. The place-name is Diegueño and means "rainy region."

CVP, see *Central Valley Project.*

Cypress, evergreen coniferous trees and shrubs related to the pine. The best-known California variety is the Monterey, native only to the county of that name. Fifteen to 80 feet tall, gnarled and hung with lichen, its conical crown is irregularly flattened when exposed to ocean winds. Its isolated locations and exotic, Oriental shapes occasioned legends that it was planted by Buddhist monks or other explorers who came to California before the Spanish. Other cypress varieties include the *McNab,* a bushy tree 5 to 25 feet tall with a smooth light gray bark, found in the Sierra foothills and northern coastal ranges; the *Gowen,* a small tree with brown bark growing to 20 feet, found at elevations under 1,000 feet from Mendocino to the Mexican border; the *Piute,* native only to Kern and Tulare counties; the *Modoc,* a shrub with red-brown bark growing to 10 feet; and the *Sargent,* with gray-brown fibrous bark, reaching a maximum of 15 feet. The trees are not commercially important.

D

DAGGETT, ROLLIN [MALLORY] (1831–1909), walked from Ohio to California (1850) and in San Francisco founded the *Golden Era*♦ (1852), the state's first literary weekly. A decade later he moved to Virginia City, Nevada, and there established the *Territorial Enterprise*. A later political career made him a Congressman and Minister to Hawaii (1882–85).

DAHLGREN, CHARLES CHRISTIAN (1841–1920), and his brother, MARIUS (1844–1920), Danish-born artists, went to California in the 1870s, where they lived in the Bay Area and painted scenes of local life and landscapes.

DAILEY, GARDNER [ACTON] (1895–1967), Minnesota-born architect, reared in California, where he attended both Stanford and the University of California, Berkeley. He was first noted for his simple but elegantly designed residences and later for public buildings, incuding Hertz Hall and Tolman Hall on the Berkeley campus and BART headquarters in Oakland.

Daily Evening Bulletin, see *San Francisco Bulletin.*

Dairying, essentially began with Americans, since little milk, cream, butter, or cheese♦ was wanted or produced by the Spanish or Mexicans in California (they raised cattle essentially for meat, hides, and tallow). The Americans early began to import dairy stock, so that by 1860 there were about 100,000 milch cows in the state. Butter was initially the most important product (about 6,000,000 pounds were produced in 1867), but beginning in 1860 the demand for milk grew steadily until it became the dominant one. Dairying has long been widespread throughout the state but it is particularly important in Los Angeles, Merced, San Bernardino, San Joaquin, San Luis Obispo, Stanislaus, and Tulare counties.

DAKIN, SUSANNA BRYANT, see *Bixby.*

DALLMAR, HOWARD (1923–   ), began his career in basketball as a star guard at Stanford University (1942–43), continued it as a successful professional player, later head coach at the University of Pennsylvania, and climaxed it by coaching the teams of his alma mater (1954–75).

Daly City, located just south of San Francisco, came into being when many San Franciscans fled to John Daly's dairy ranch after the earthquake and fire of 1906. A residential community, it mushroomed after World War II to become one of the state's fifty most populous communities. In 1970 the population was 66,922.

Dame Shirley, see *Clapp, Louise.*

DANA, RICHARD HENRY, JR. (1815–82), scion of a cultivated, patrician family of Cambridge, Mass., where he was reared in keeping with the best New England traditions. During his sophomore year at Harvard a case of measles left his eyesight so weak that to regain it he had to live an outdoor life free of studies. Accordingly he shipped as a common sailor aboard a brig to California (1834). He came to know the various ports from which his ship gathered hides and in which it carried on trade or got supplies during the sixteen months (Jan. 1835–May 1836) that he was on the Pacific Coast. His health restored, he returned to Boston and completed his undergraduate studies and legal training at Harvard. His shipboard vow "to redress the grievances and sufferings of that class of beings with whom my lot had so long been cast," was initially fulfilled by an article, "Cruelty to Seamen," written for the *American Jurist* (1839). In 1840, the year he was admitted to the bar, he presented a more thorough description of a sailor's life in *Two Years Before the Mast,*♦ the popular and distinguished account of his time at sea and residence in California. That work was followed by *The Seaman's Friend* (1841), a manual to let sailors know their legal rights and obligations. For more than thirty years thereafter his experiences were little related to the sea or to California, although he enjoyed nautical outings, of which the most extended resulted in a lesser book, *To Cuba and Back* (1859), and although he made a nostalgic visit to his old California haunts (1859) on a voyage around the world. But for the rest he devoted himself to a legal career including defense of fugitive slaves and to a minor political career that did not reach the diplomatic heights to which he aspired. Late in life he declared sadly: "My life has been a failure compared with what I might and ought to have done" and "My great success—my book—was a boy's work done before I came to the Bar."

DANA, WILLIAM GOODWIN (1797–1858), member of the prominent Massachusetts family, went to California as master of a trading vessel (1825). There he was converted to Catholicism, naturalized, and married to a Carrillo. He became a *ranchero* at Nipomo, north of Santa Barbara. Because of family estrangement, his distant younger relative Richard Henry Dana seems never to have met him. He was also a cousin of William Heath Davis.

Dana, Mount, see *Mount Dana.*

Dana Point, headland between Laguna Beach and San Clemente, named for the exploit of Richard Henry Dana, who swung over a cliff on halyards and dislodged some cowhides fellow sailors had tried to throw to the beach below for transporting to their ship. It is now a residential and resort area with a huge yacht harbor.

Dance, as a social entertainment flourished during the Mexican period of California, and accounts of festive events highlighted by lively fandangos are common. The grace and skill of local dancers, both male and female, are the subject of comments by U.S. visitors, notably in Dana's account of the de la Guerra–Robinson wedding celebration. American settlers brought their own folk dances with them but sometimes had occasion to employ the Spanish term for their performance, as in the naming of Fandango Pass.♦

Other tunes and steps were introduced by migrants from various European regions so that cosmopolitan versions of the dance flourished during the gold rush despite the few women settlers. Formal exhibitions by professional dancers were produced in the theaters of San Francisco and mining towns, and one finds records as early as 1849 and 1850 of dances being staged, although originally they were only a part of performances which included acrobatics or other vaudeville entertainment.

The first ballet was produced in San Francisco by a touring Spanish troupe in 1851 but the first real terpsichorean star associated with California

was the notorious Lola Montez,♦ whose "spider dance" was a sensation on the San Francisco stage (1853) and in theaters of the Mother Lode country. Within a year the Monplaisir Troupe arrived as a corps de ballet from France to offer "La Fille Mal Gardée" and other established full-length performances, and by 1858 a member of a touring company from Philadelphia remained in San Francisco to open a dancing school. Another academy for instruction was opened the same year in Sacramento by one Madame Celeste, who as early as 1852 was said to have had a great success as La Sylphide.

Meanwhile, less elegant forms of dancing flourished: in the 1860s rival companies presented "The Black Crook," stigmatized by some moralistic writers for its featuring of long-legged girls in flesh colored tights, and the can-can from Offenbach's operetta was another sensation. After the completion of the transcontinental railway in 1869, touring companies of diverse sorts brought many forms of dance to San Francisco and other cities for brief appearances that were evidently sufficiently stimulating to warrant the creation in 1879 of a local ballet company as part of San Francisco's Tivoli Opera productions.

Ballroom dancing attracted a good deal of attention when the wife of J. Milton Bowers♦ wrote *The Dance of Life* (1877) to praise it, and Ambrose Bierce replied in the satirical and anonymous *Dance of Death.* More sensational forms of dancing were featured on the little stages of the Barbary Coast♦ or on its dance floors by the patrons. At the same time, toward the end of the century, new aesthetic conceptions of dancing fused a kind of art nouveau with versions of Greek classicism in the appearances that Loie Fuller made on California stages and the instruction and recitals offered by Isadora Duncan,♦ a local performer from the Bay Area.

In the 20th century most of the great dancers, classical and modern, American and foreign, have visited San Francisco and Los Angeles. Hollywood has attracted many dancers for appearances in films, sometimes designed by choreographers permanently identified with the industry. Among the popular persons associated with the motion pictures are Fred Astaire,♦ Busby Berkeley,♦ Gene Kelly,♦ and Ginger Rogers,♦ while those who have had briefer but highly successful affiliation with films include Agnes deMille, George Balanchine, Margot Fonteyn, Moira Shearer, and Ulanova.

The San Francisco Opera Co., permanently established in 1923, soon created a ballet said to be the oldest continuously performing company in the U.S.; since 1937 it has been known as the independent San Francisco Ballet.♦ More recently Los Angeles has also founded a ballet company for performances in its Music Center. Dance of a very different kind also has its own California associations with rock music,♦ which has flourished in the state.

Danes in California, first arrived with a few pioneers in the early 1840s, of whom the most notable was Peter Lassen.♦ Peter Sherreback (Scherrebach) went to San Francisco (1840) where, after aiding Sutter in support of Micheltorena, he became a public official. Later Danes included the Dahlgren brothers,♦ who were painters, and a group who established an agricultural colony near Fresno (1878). With the 1890s a larger influx began, which included a group of faculty members for a college in Des Moines who established (1911) the community of Solvang ("sunny meadow" in Danish) that has capitalized on its heritage as a tourist attraction.

Daring Young Man on the Flying Trapeze, The, first book by William Saroyan,♦ a collection of his earliest short stories.

Dates, some date palms were planted by the mission fathers in the 18th century but they bore little or no fruit. The first successful cultivation was private, in San Diego and elsewhere in southern California. Substantial commercial growing began in the Coachella Valley (1902) and the Imperial Valley. Offshoots of trees from the Middle East and Algeria flourished under scientific methods, including the eradication of scale, making large-sized orchards profitable despite competition from foreign imports. Display and advertising at the Panama-Pacific International Exposition helped popularize dates, although by 1925 California produced only 1,000,000 pounds for U.S. consumption as against an importation of 66,000,000 pounds. Cooperative marketing programs later aided growers, as did the disappearance of foreign dates during World War II. In 1970, 32,800,000 lbs. were produced in Riverside and Imperial counties. Indio, which calls itself the U.S. date capital, holds an annual Date Festival.

DAVIDSON, GEORGE (1825–1911), English-born, Philadelphia-reared scientist and a major member of the U.S. Coast Survey (1845–95), headed the survey of the California coast (1850–57) resulting in the *Directory of the Pacific Coast* (1858), later entitled *Coast Pilot.* A similar Alaskan survey resulted in the *Coast Pilot of Alaska* (1869). His work in applied astronomy to establish coastal longitudes led to his founding California's first observatory and his guidance of James Lick♦ to choose Mt. Hamilton for his telescope site. He was president of the California Academy of Sciences, a professor of geodesy and astronomy, and later a Regent of the University of California. Mt. Davidson in San Francisco County was named for him.

DAVIES, MARION (1905–61), stage name of Marion Douras, Brooklyn-born Ziegfeld Follies girl who became a motion picture star. Her career was widely publicized by William Randolph Hearst,♦ who loved her and installed her as the mistress of his great San Simeon estate. About their relationship and her film roles as a comedienne she dictated a series of tapes. They were published as *The Times We Had* (1975).

DAVIS, AL[LEN] (1929–), after serving as a football coach at the University of Southern California (1957–60) and of the Los Angeles Chargers, became head coach, general manager, and, later, partner of the Oakland Raiders (1963–), which he helped make into a leading professional football team. Its success in winning division and league titles is largely the result of his judgment of talent among associates and players.

DAVIS, ANGELA [YVONNE] (1944–), native of Alabama, having spent a year at the Sorbonne, received her A.B. from Brandeis. After study in Frankfurt she completed almost all work for a Ph.D. in philosophy at UCLA under the direction of Professor Herbert Marcuse. Appointed an acting assistant professor there (1969), she was not reappointed when the Regents learned of her membership in the Communist party and her talks supporting its views. She was the subject of further notoriety during a long trial (1972) in which she was acquitted of complicity in the attempt of black convicts to escape from the Marin County Courthouse during which event four persons, including a judge, were killed by weapons she had legally bought at an earlier date.

DAVIS, ANTHONY (1952–), University of Southern California football player (1972–74), as a sophomore fullback he scored six touchdowns against Notre Dame, helped his team win in the Rose Bowl over Ohio State, and was awarded the Voit Trophy as the outstanding player on the

West Coast. All told, in his college career he scored 50 touchdowns, six on kickoff returns. He also played outfield on USC's championship baseball teams (1973–74).

DAVIS, BETTE (1908–   ), Massachusetts-born actress, first on Broadway and after 1931 in Hollywood. She achieved stardom early as a serious actress in greatly varied roles which she enacted in a highly professional but markedly dramatic style. They include leads in *Of Human Bondage* (1934), *The Little Foxes* (1941), and *Whatever Happened to Baby Jane?* (1962). She won Academy Awards for *Dangerous* (1935) and *Jezebel* (1938). After 1930 she made her home mostly in southern California.

DAVIS, WILLIAM HEATH (1822–1909), born in Hawaii, son of a Boston shipmaster and Polynesian mother, was taken to California on trading expeditions in his youth. On his third trip (1838) he remained to enter the employ of his uncle, Nathan Spear,♦ branching out to open markets at *ranchos* and becoming a wealthy merchant and shipowner. It was he who guided Sutter to the site of Sacramento (1839). His wedding to the heiress of the Estudillo family (1847) made him a great landowner in the present San Leandro area, and in San Francisco he built the first brick building of more than one story, which he rented to the U.S. government as a customs house for $36,000 a year. A partner's misjudgments and the 1851 San Francisco fire cost him most of his fortune and sent him back to ranching on Estudillo lands. He collected reminiscent articles into a valuable source book, *Sixty Years in California* (1889), later enlarged to *Seventy-Five Years in California* (1929).

Davis, city in Yolo County on the outskirts of Sacramento, named for Jerome C. Davis, a large landholder and rancher of the 1850s. In 1907 the University of California began to develop an agricultural school there which grew into a branch of Berkeley's College of Agriculture (1922), then into a separate campus, and finally into a general campus (1959) with its own graduate studies in law, engineering, medicine, and other fields (1961). The campus (over 1,000 acres) now dominates the town, which, with the University development, grew enormously, from a population of 8,910 in 1960 to 23,488 in 1970.

DAWSON, NICHOLAS (1819–1903), went to California (1841) with the Bartleson-Bidwell Party,♦

then went east via Sonora in 1849. His memoirs appeared as *California in '41, Texas in '51* (1901).

Day of the Locust, The, novel by Nathanael West,♦ published in 1939 and produced as a film in 1975. It is a grotesque, surrealistic satire of pathological misfits on the fringe of Hollywood, exposing the anxiety and lunacy of people pursuing false values in a meretricious world.

DEAKIN, EDWARD (1838–1923), English-born artist, moved to San Francisco (1870), then Berkeley (1890), and thereafter painted the missions, mountain landscapes, and the Berkeley scene.

DEAN, JAMES (1931–55), after studying drama at UCLA and having a Broadway career, became a popular Hollywood star and an idol of adolescents such as the one he played in the symbolically titled *Rebel Without a Cause* (1955), made just before he was killed in a racing-car accident. The picture was set in southern California, and his own lifestyle presaged a restless mood that only became dominant in the next decade. A memorial sculpture was erected (1977) at the site of his fatal accident, Cholane (San Luis Obispo County).

DEAN, [HAROLD] MALLETTE (1908–75), Washington-born artist, known for the wood engravings and decorative initials that illustrated books by the Grabhorn Press, the Allen Press, and those of his own typography.

Death Valley, extending 140 miles through eastern California (Inyo County) and southwestern Nevada, about four to sixteen miles wide between the Panamint Range and the Amargosa Range, is one of the world's hottest and driest places, and contains Badwater, 282 feet below sea level, the lowest spot in the U.S. Known to the Panamint Indians, whites discovered it when W. L. Manly♦ and the Jayhawker Party of Galesburg, Ill., entered it (Dec. 1849) as a shortcut to the gold mines, and they named it. Small gold and silver strikes have been made, creating boom towns, but the major mining has been of borax,♦ discovered in 1880 and developed by F. M. Smith, whose 20-mule teams which hauled out the mineral became a noted trademark. Among the colorful residents was Death Valley Scotty.♦ In the 20th century the desert began to be appreciated for beauty and quiet, and some spots like Furnace Creek became resorts, even offering entertainment such as the ballet at the nearby Amargosa Opera House. The valley itself was made a National Monument (1933).

Death Valley Days, 30-minute weekly television program (1952–72), presented stories of pioneer Nevada and California in the last half of the nineteenth century. It helped make Ronald Reagan widely admired and assisted him toward later political success.

Death Valley Scotty, sobriquet of Walter Perry Scott (1872?–1953), ostensibly the owner of a secret Death Valley mine, the source of funds for his Castle, a great house in Death Valley, and such exploits as chartering a train (1905) to take him from Los Angeles to Chicago in 45 hours. He actually got his money from a Chicago millionaire who was amused by his style.

DEDEAUX, ROD (RAOUL DEDEAUX) (1915–   ), New Orleans-born baseball coach of his alma mater, the University of Southern California (1942–   ), whose teams have won more games and more NCAA championships (10) than those of any other college coach in history.

Deep Springs College, private two-year college for men, founded in 1917 and located on an Inyo County desert cattle ranch (southeast of Bishop) to which the students (only about twenty in all) contribute twenty hours of work a week. The college has high intellectual standards and emphasizes independent study.

Deer, found throughout California, exist there in six species. The *Rocky Mountain mule deer,* though the most common, are found only in the northeast. Weighing between 100 and 300 pounds, the buck in winter is gray-brown, with a large white rump patch circling its white tail tipped with black, but in summer is reddish brown. The *California mule deer,* with similar coloring, are found from Ventura to Salinas counties and from Kern to Yuba counties. The *Inyo mule deer,* in size between the previous two although colored like them but with a white stripe on each side of the stomach, inhabit the eastern Sierra and the Inyo and White mountains and wander into eastern San Diego County. The *southern mule deer,* very dark in color and with a black line down the back, live only in southern California. *Burro mule deer* resemble *Rocky Mountain deer* but are lighter colored; they inhabit Imperial, Riverside, and San Bernardino counties. *Columbia blacktailed deer* are found along the coast as far south as Santa Barbara County and in the oak woodlands, Sierra foothills, and large mountains east and north of the San Francisco Bay. Deer provided food and

clothing for Indians and have been hunted by whites since the time of the first explorers. Early commentators wrote of quantities of deer on the hillsides of San Francisco Bay and all other parts of California. Over 150 place-names incorporating the word "deer" indicate how often the animal was met. There are estimated to be over 1,000,000 in the state now (1970s), although they are widely hunted during regulated seasons.

DE FOREST, LEE (1873–1961), Iowa-born inventor who, after receiving a B.S. and Ph.D. from Yale, began to build improved apparatus for radio telegraphy. This led to his invention of the triode (1906), the prototype of all electronic amplifiers, and the device needed for transcontinental telephoning. He soon after moved to Palo Alto to work for the Federal Telegraph Co. Further inventions, including those related to sound motion pictures, led to his being granted over 300 patents.

DE HARO, FRANCISCO (1803–48), went to California with Luís Argüello (1821), led a punitive expedition against Indians in revolt (1824), and was *comandante* of the San Francisco presidio and first *alcalde* (1835, 38–39) of Yerba Buena, ordering the survey by Vioget♦ (1839) in that capacity. His young twin sons Francisco, Jr., and Ramón (1830–46), with their uncle, José de los Reyes Berryessa, were shot to death by Kit Carson and other followers of Frémont while approaching the San Rafael shore in a rowboat (June 28, 1846) because they were thought, incorrectly, to be carrying messages to Castro's army. The event became a rousing symbol for *Californios,* illustrating American brutality during the Bear Flag Revolt.

DE LA GUERRA, a leading early Santa Barbara family whose founder was José Antonio Julián de la Guerra y Noriego (1779–1858), of an old Spanish family from Santander, who went with the army to Mexico and then to California (1801), where he wed (1804) María Antoniá Carrillo, of another leading California family. Their several children included Anita (1820–55), who wed Alfred Robinson;♦ María Teresa, who wed William Hartnell;♦ and Pablo (1819–74), who had a great *rancho,* El Nicasio, in present Marin County but kept his Santa Barbara associations as a state senator from that city.

DELANO, ALONZO (1802?–74), born in upstate New York, went to Illinois and from there in 1849 to California to take part in the gold rush. His account of his overland voyage, *Across the Plains and*

Among the Diggings (1854), although having a diary structure, is far more spacious in tone and style than other works of the kind and displays the sentiment and humor for which he later became noted. After experience in mining, Delano became the Wells Fargo agent in Grass Valley and then a private banker, but he drifted into writing and was a major contributor to journals of the time. His good-natured, humorous sketches in which he presented himself as a long-nosed Old Block, depicted in illustrations by his collaborator Charles Nahl,♦ were collected in *Pen-Knife Sketches, or Chips of the Old Block* (1853) and *Old Block's Sketch Book* (1856). He also wrote a topical play, *A Live Woman in the Mines* (1857). His reputation almost a century later warranted the collection of seven sketches, including one on George Derby♦ in *A Sojourn with Royalty* (1936) and the publication of 36 letters to newspapers on his trip to California and residence in the Feather River mines, *Alonzo Delano's California Correspondence* (1952).

Delano, city in north central Kern County, was created when the Southern Pacific railway reached that point (1873) and named it for the then Secretary of the Interior. It has long been a center for the agriculture of its part of the San Joaquin Valley and became headquarters for the union of Cesar Chavez. It is also the home of the Voice of America short-wave radio station.

Delgada, Point, name ("narrow" in Spanish) applied by Lt. Bodéga y Cuadro to Point Arena (Mendocino County), given its present name by Vancouver (1792). The name was thereafter variously applied until the expedition of Wilkes♦ fixed it on the cape in southernmost Humboldt County.

DELLENBAUGH, Frederick S. (1853–1935), New York artist who served with J. W. Powell on his exploring expeditions of the Green and Colorado rivers (1871), of which he wrote *A Canyon Voyage* (1908). He later followed the trails of Frémont and other explorers, an experience which led to his book *Frémont and '49* (1914).

Del Mar, residential and resort community on the oceanside north of San Diego. It is the site of the annual County Fair and of a Turf Club for horse racing.♦ Nearby lies Torrey Pines State Park.♦

Del Monte Hotel, elegant resort hotel near Monterey, established (1880) by Charles Crocker and served by the Southern Pacific Railroad. Set in a park of 126 acres, the three-story "Swiss Gothic" edifice could house 750 guests, "millionaires of the Big Bonanza" resident in a "flaunting caravanserai," according to Robert Louis Stevenson. Destroyed by fire in 1887, it was quickly rebuilt in the same style; burned down once again in 1924, it was reconstructed in Spanish-California style and remained a great resort until commandeered by the navy in World War II, remaining thereafter a naval installation. A luxurious lodge under the same ownership is located at nearby Pebble Beach.♦

Del Norte County, created (1857) from a part of Klamath County, has as its western and northern boundaries the ocean and the state of Oregon. Siskiyou County lies on the east and Humboldt County on the south. Crescent City♦ has always been the county seat and is by far the largest community in the county. Requa, another important town, is at the mouth of the Klamath River. Peter Ogden of the Hudson's Bay Co. and Jedediah Smith were the first white explorers (1826, 1827) of the land, which was inhabited by Tolowa and Yurok Indians. It remained wilderness until the gold rush brought placer miners, succeeded by men using the more elaborate hydraulic mining, but no large or lasting settlements were created. Most of the county, except for the area toward the coast, lies in the Six Rivers National Forest, whose mountains include the Four Brothers, rising to 5,310 feet. Near the coast lie the Del Norte Coast and the Jedediah Smith state parks of redwoods, the latter a memorial to the pioneer also remembered in the Smith River and the town of that name. The Trees of Mystery,♦ north of the town of Klamath, is a tourist attraction. Logging, lumber products, livestock ranching, and the cultivation of Easter lilies (near Smith River) are the county's major businesses. The county had a population of 14,580 in 1970; with an area of 644,352 acres, it had 14.5 persons per sq. mi.

Delta Lands, at the confluence of the Sacramento♦ and San Joaquin rivers,♦ east of Suisun Bay.♦ The triangular points of the Delta are located at Sacramento, the apex, and Antioch and Stockton, at each end of the base. It is laced with waterways, marshes, tule swamps, and moisture-laden peat, and has always needed levees and dikes to control the water. It is the state's major area for producing asparagus (stalks grown under peat also provide most of the U.S. canned white asparagus), tomatoes, pears, field corn, sugar beets, and alfalfa. It is also a popular fishing, hunting, and boating region. From there the California Aqueduct♦ carries water down the west side of the San Joaquin Valley to drier areas in southern California.

Delta-Mendota Canal, part of the Central Valley Project,♦ begins in the Delta at the Tracy Pumping Plant, where water from the Sacramento River is raised 196 feet so that it can flow by gravity down the west side of the Central Valley to the south for 117 miles into the Mendota Pool near Fresno. It thus irrigates the western portion of the valley by replacing San Joaquin River water, now diverted by the Friant Canal for use on the east side.

DE MILLE, CECIL B[LOUNT] (1881–1959), pioneer motion picture director and producer whose first spectacular film, *Carmen* (1915), was followed by decades of grandiose, lavish epics, often of biblical, historical, or fabulous subjects, such as *The Ten Commandments* (1923), *The Crusades, The Plainsman* (1937), and a new, even more elaborate version of *The Ten Commandments* (1956). For almost a half-century he was associated with Hollywood and its films (his first feature-length picture was *The Squaw Man,* 1913) and he has been called "the quintessential Hollywood showman," as was recognized by his selection to enact the veteran director in *Sunset Boulevard* (1950), the film starring Gloria Swanson, whose career he had launched thirty years earlier.

Democratic Institutions, Center for the Study of, see *Center for the Study of Democratic Institutions.*

DE NEVE, FELIPE, see *Neve, Felipe de.*

DENNY, GIDEON JACQUES (1830–86), first went to California in the gold rush (1849), then returned to San Francisco (1862) as a painter to work with Samuel Marsden Brookes. He became best known for his marine scenes.

DENVER, JAMES WILLIAM (1817–92), born in Virginia, reared in Ohio, where he was admitted to the bar, after service in the Mexican War went to California (1850). While a state Senator he defended Gov. Bigler from verbal attacks by Edward C. Gilbert♦ which led to a duel in which Gilbert was killed. Denver was an anti-Broderick Democrat in Congress (1855–57), then moved to Kansas, whose Territorial Governor he became (1857–58). Kansas then included the present capital of Colorado, which was named for him. Still later he was Commissioner of Indian Affairs and a Civil War general.

DE QUILLE, DAN, pseudonym of William Wright (1829–98), who left his native Ohio for farming in Iowa and then went to California and Nevada (1857) to prospect for gold and silver. Unsuccessful in mining, he drifted into newspaper work and became the city editor of the *Territorial Enterprise* (1861) during the years when its influence extended far beyond Virginia City, Nevada. There he became a great friend of Mark Twain, who later urged him to write *The Big Bonanza* for Clemens' publishing company (1876) and thus preserve the history and legendry of the Comstock Lode.♦ De Quille continued to live in Virginia City until it, the mines, and he were all ghosts of their former selves.

DERBY, GEORGE HORATIO (1823–61), Massachusetts-born army officer who established a reputation as a wit and practical joker even while at West Point. After service in the Mexican War he was assigned to California (1852–56) as a lieutenant charged with making explorations and reports on the gold mining country, the San Joaquin Valley, and the Colorado River area. He was also stationed at San Diego (1853), where he assumed unofficial responsibility for editing the San Diego *Herald* during the temporary absence of his friend, the editor J. J. Ames. In the few issues under his editorship he changed its party alliance from Democratic to Whig and made the weekly into a comic journal by such devices as using its supply of the usual country newspaper stock cuts to create humorous pictorial effects, once lining up ten pictures of sailing ships (meant to announce departures of vessels) in naval formation under the caption, "Battle of Lake Erie." His own humorous sketches next appeared in the San Francisco monthly *The Pioneer,* and from those contributions Ames prepared a book, *Phoenixiana; or Sketches and Burlesques♦* (1855). After Derby's army career took him east he continued to write similar pieces, posthumously gathered in *Squibob Papers♦* (1865). Although often called a western humorist, the urbanity of his wit is more in the vein of Washington Irving, but Derby was more boisterous in tone, as suited a man who at least experienced the frontier spirit. His burlesques and other comic writings and clever drawings appeared under one or the other of two pseudonyms: John Phoenix or Squibob.

Descanso Gardens, tourist attraction located in La Cañada, northwest of Pasadena, containing over 100,000 camellias, 6,000 roses, and diverse other flowers and trees. The name is Spanish for "repose."

Desert, lands that occupy about one-third of California, all lying east of the Sierra Nevada and the Transverse and Peninsular mountains. They are part of the far larger Intermontane Region stretching from the Rocky Mts. to the Sierra and the Cascade ranges. There are four major intermontane regions in California: the *Colorado Desert,*♦ the *Mojave Desert,*♦ the *Trans-Sierra Desert,* and the *Northeast Desert.*

The *Colorado* is a low desert area of about 4,000 sq. mi. in the southeastern part of the state. It contains agricultural centers in the Imperial Valley♦ and the Coachella Valley,♦ on its south and north, respectively, and it also has the Salton Sea♦ and the Anza-Borrego Desert,♦ the latter a State Park. The Colorado is also a resort area, most notably at Palm Springs.♦ Since Spanish times it has served as a transportation corridor.

The *Mojave* is a high desert area and is sometimes simply called the High Desert. An area of basins and eroded mountains, it occupies about one-sixth of California. Long established as a transportation route, it has also been a center for mining, with borax still obtained there, and has supported agriculture in Antelope Valley and other places where water is available. Mostly within San Bernardino County, it also contains resort areas such as Twentynine Palms and the Joshua Tree National Monument.♦

The *Trans-Sierra* is a desert area of 3,000 sq. mi. that stretches north from Inyo County into a land of sparsely vegetated mountains and basins. It includes Owens Valley,♦ lovingly described by Mary Austin in *The Land of Little Rain,* and Death Valley,♦ the latter lying between the Panamint and Amargosa mountain ranges. It supports some ranching and mining and has military testing grounds as well.

The *Northeast,* a triangular area occupying Modoc and Lassen counties, is most marked by its lava lands and only about one-tenth of it can be cultivated. Ranching is the chief economic activity.

The several desert areas are notable for their unusual flora, including cacti, and for their own fauna, including gila monsters and desert iguanas, but they have had their character changed by the introduction of water♦ in modern times.

Desert Tortoise, see *Tortoise.*

DE SOLÁ, PABLO VICENTE, see *Solá, Pablo de.*

Desolation Valley, a preserved primitive area of 41,380 acres at the headwaters of Rubicon River (El Dorado County). Its alpine lakes and granite crags were formed by glaciers. It is now heavily forested.

Detective fiction, literary genre that has had some early notable practitioners resident in or associated with California, including Earl Derr Biggers and Willard Huntington Wright. Many detective stories set in California employ a tough point of view, sardonic and often elliptical dialogue, sharply focused description, and unexpected violence.

Dashiell Hammett♦ was a pioneer of this vein with *The Maltese Falcon* (1930) set in San Francisco and featuring his private detective Sam Spade, whose style was perfectly captured in the film version (1941) featuring Humphrey Bogart. Perhaps the best-known practitioner of the so-called tough school was Raymond Chandler,♦ who set *The Big Sleep* (1939), *Farewell, My Lovely* (1940), and five succeeding novels, all made into successful films, in southern California, where his detective hero, Philip Marlowe, found the Establishment conspiring to pervert justice in a region whose glamour was contrasted sharply with its tawdriness. Another writer in this general idiom was James M. Cain,♦ whose *The Postman Always Rings Twice* (1934) and *Double Indemnity* (1936) were very successful as books and as motion pictures. John Gregory Dunne♦ is a more recent author of a vivid police novel set in Los Angeles.

Other extremely popular regional writers of detective fiction did not belong to the "tough" school. The vast outpouring of novels by Erle Stanley Gardner♦ was written in a straightforward conventional style to tell the adventures of his lawyer-sleuth, Perry Mason, who was a featured figure in radio and television as well as on the screen. Similarly, Ross MacDonald♦ played down violence and emphasized family and generational relations and conflicts in a southern California setting.

In addition to the television shows deriving from published fiction, several programs originated for the medium concentrated on detection or police work in California, including *Dragnet* and *77 Sunset Strip,* set in Los Angeles and Hollywood, respectively, and *Ironside* and *Streets of San Francisco,* presenting rather straightforward police drama in San Francisco.

Devil's Postpile, National Monument of about 800 acres established (1911) in the Sierra Nevada, famous for its columns of solidified lava standing 40 to 60 feet high. It is surrounded by Inyo National Forest.

DE YOUNG, CHARLES (1845–80), born in Louisiana, and his brother, M[ICHAEL] H[ARRY] (1849–1925), born in St. Louis, were taken to San Francisco (1854) by their parents. In 1865 Charles founded the *Daily Dramatic Chronicle* to report theatrical news and with his brother soon made it a general newspaper renamed the *Daily Morning Chronicle* (1868). They used the paper to further their political interests and Charles tried to merge his supporters with the Workingmen's party of Denis Kearney♦ to form a New Constitution party. A rebuff led to a feud in which Charles shot and wounded Kearney's mayoral candidate, Isaac Kalloch,♦ whose son in turn killed de Young. The *Chronicle* continued to be edited in flamboyant style by M. H., which led to his being shot and wounded by Adolph Spreckels♦ (1884) in retaliation for allegations against the family sugar business. M. H. went on to become a leader in local Republican party affairs and in civic activities. He was instrumental in creating the Midwinter Fair of 1894 and using its profits to establish a permanent art museum, to which he gave a new building (1916) named in his honor. To the de Young Museum was added (1960) a wing to house the Asian Art Museum (based on the Avery Brundage Collection). In 1972 the de Young was merged with the Legion of Honor Museum, which had been founded by Adolph Spreckels, to form the Fine Arts Museums of San Francisco. The de Young family is allied by marriages to the Tobin family.♦

Diablo, see *Mount Diablo.*

Diablo Range, chain of the Coast Range extending from Mt. Diablo south through Alameda, Santa Clara (where Mt. Hamilton is a high point), and San Benito counties. Pacheco Pass is the major eastern entry point through Merced County.♦ Diablo Range extends south to Priest Valley and New Idria. South of the Diablo Range is the Temblor Range.♦

Diamond Hoax, see *Harpending, Asbury.*

Dianetics, cult founded in the early 1950s by L[afayette] Ron Hubbard, a writer of science fiction, who established a foundation in New Jersey with an important branch in Los Angeles. At both locations and elsewhere, emotionally disturbed people, called "pre-clears," pay for courses of instruction from persons who are called "dianetic clears." These therapists use the school's own version of psychoanalysis and instruction to rid the "pre-clears" of their injurious "engrams" so as to render them physically and psychically whole.

Diatomite, sedimentary rock composed of chalky algae fossils which is used in insulation, ceramics, and filtering materials. The state produces about 80% of U.S. diatomite, major deposits being mined near Lompoc and the not-distant Bradley and Monterey; southern Napa and Sonoma counties and Palos Verde in Riverside County are also sources.

DÍAZ, MELCHIOR, see *Exploration.*

DICKSON, EDWARD A[UGUSTUS] (1879–1956), Wisconsin-born newspaper owner and editor, reared in Sacramento. After graduation from the University of California, Berkeley, he became a reporter for the *Sacramento Union* and then, under Edwin Earl, associate editor of the *Los Angeles Evening Express,* of which he later became owner. In time he owned fifteen newspapers. He was a leader of the Lincoln-Roosevelt League♦ and later was an advocate of U.S. participation in the League of Nations. From 1913 until his death he was a Regent of the University of California, for the last eight years Chairman of the Board, and consistently a champion of the development of UCLA.

DIDION, JOAN (1934–), author of *Run River* (1963), an evocative novel of changed ways of life in her native Sacramento Valley; *Slouching Toward Bethlehem* (1968), essays; *Play It as It Lays* (1970), a novel about a woman's intense experiences lived out in southern California; and *A Book of Common Prayer* (1977), a novel presenting a California woman's shattering life at home and in Central America. She has also written film scripts, including a version of *A Star Is Born* (in which Barbra Streisand starred), in collaboration with her husband, John Gregory Dunne.♦

DIEBENKORN, RICHARD (1922–), Portland-born painter, after studying at Stanford and the University of California taught at the California School of Fine Arts (1947–50). His early paintings, often on large square canvases, were vivid, expressionist, nonobjective works; later he turned to figurative paintings, generally of solitary persons in a colorful, patterned setting.

Diegueño, Indians of the Hokan♦ family, who lived in the present San Diego County between the San Dieguito River and the present border with Mexico. Along with the Kamia, a neighboring tribe of similar culture, they numbered about 3000 in prehistoric times. In the 1910 census they had been reduced to 700 to 800. Although their name derives from their location in the area under the influence of the San Diego Mission, the Dieguño resisted conversion to Christianity and had numerous conflicts with the missionaries. Their native religion was heavily influenced by the Chinigchinich religion, which originated among the Gabrieleño.◆ The Diegueño were the only California tribe to have a system of color-direction symbolism; in it white indicated east; green and blue, south; black, west; and red, north.

Diggers, opprobrious term applied by American trappers and later by forty-niners to Shoshone Indians (and by extension to other tribes) because they used sticks to dig roots for food. They were considered to be at a contemptible cultural level because they did not practice agriculture. Paradoxically, the miners themselves were frequently called diggers.

Diggers, The, group of Hippies led by Emmett Grogan known for their gratis distribution in the Haight-Ashbury district of San Francisco (and New York, too) of food and clothing that Grogan claimed had been stolen. They also provided free housing and were even said to have furnished free drugs between 1966 and 1970, when they disappeared.

Diggings, The, popular name applied to the Mother Lode region and related mining areas during the gold rush.

DI GIORGIO, Joseph, see *Food processing.*

DILLON, Richard [Hugh] (1924–), born in Sausalito, after education at the University of California, Berkeley, became head of the Sutro Library◆ (1953–). His numerous books about the West include *Embarcadero* (1959), *The Hatchet Men* (1962), *J. Ross Browne* (1965), and *Burnt-Out Fires* (1973).

DiMAGGIO, Joe (Joseph Paul DiMaggio) (1914–), born in Martinez, began his baseball career (1932) with the Seals (S.F.) and went on to stardom as a batter and center fielder with the Yankees (N.Y.). He was married to Marilyn Monroe. His brothers Vince[nt Paul] (1912–) and Dom[inic Paul] (1917–) were also noted players, the former for various eastern teams, the latter for the Boston Red Sox. Joe DiMaggio holds the record (1941) for hitting safely in consecutive games (56).

Dipsea race, footrace held annually (since 1905) on a 6.8-mile course from Mill Valley over a ridge of Mt. Tamalpais to Stinson Beach, where contestants take a "dip in the sea." Initiated by the Olympic Club, it was canceled for a few years in the 1930s and is now sponsored by the Junior Chamber of Commerce of Mill Valley.

Diputación, local legislature created under the first Mexican constitution (1836). The members were elected but they served more as advisers to the governor than as independent legislators.

Disasters, have occurred in California and are associated with it because of their scope (e.g. the Salton Sea flooding, the Owens Valley debacle upon the breaking of the St. Francis Dam, the great oil spill off Santa Barbara), but they are not peculiar to it. However, certain kinds of disasters are more clearly endemic to the terrain or the climate of the state. Most notably these include the faults that cause earthquakes◆ which have spasmodically rocked parts of the land from prehistoric times down to the present and, it is assumed, will continue into the future. Because the great wooded areas of the state are located in regions with limited summer rainfall, forest fires◆ are annual disasters. On the other hand, fires that destroy groundcover in mountainous areas often leave the terrain open to landslides when the rains come. Devastating examples include the disaster at La Crescenta (1934), at the foot of the San Gabriel Mts. behind Los Angeles, and frequent if lesser floods in the region behind Beverly Hills and Bel Air. Inundations caused by the upper Sacramento River and the Russian River have been almost annual, with some historically great floods, such as that of 1850 at the City of Sacramento. Occasional very light rainfall in the northern and central parts of the state and very light winter snow packs in the Sierra have created severe droughts. The worst of these winters occurred in 1924; other years of low water crises were 1928, 1931, 1948, 1976, and 1977. They have resulted in severe crop losses, drastic cuts in utility services to preserve energy, the enactment of an emergency daylight saving law, and such panaceas as the seeding of clouds by aircraft and the use of the secret chemical contrivances of Charles M. Hatfield.◆

Diseño, topographic sketch of rather primitive design presented to a Mexican governor of California to define the boundaries of a *rancho*◆ that an individual had requested as a grant.

DISNEY, Walt[er Elias] (1901–66), Chicago-born creator of animated cartoon films, went to Hollywood (1923), where he slowly achieved success that became phenomenal (1928) upon the creation of a talking film of his cartoon character Mickey Mouse. The tremendous popularity of his films, noted for their whimsically humorous presentation of animals and for their technical ingenuity, led to the establishment of his own studio (1940) with hundreds of employees. In time he developed full-length films featuring imaginative renderings of human characters, as in *Snow White and the Seven Dwarfs* (1938) and *Pinocchio* (1940), as well as colorful nature films presenting real animals in their natural habitats. He also developed Disneyland♦ (1955), a tourist's amusement area near Anaheim (Orange County) which is a tremendously popular attraction for children and adults. Disney bequeathed a large part of his great fortune to endow the California Institute of the Arts.

Disneyland, amusement park near Anaheim (Orange County) created by Walt Disney♦ and opened in 1955 on 160 acres, later enlarged to 185 acres. It was an immediate success, attracting over 1,000,000 visitors in the first six months, and has been widely imitated in California and elsewhere. Divided into four sections—Fantasyland, Frontierland, Adventureland, and Tomorrowland—it provides for children and adults a scaled-down facsimile of an idyllic U.S. small town's main street in the 1890s, a storybook castle, and other settings created like motion picture sets through which one many wander or which may be seen from a monorail train. Its technologically sophisticated rides and ingenious exhibits include a Mississippi river steamboat, a jungle filled with crocodiles and orchids, and a simulated rocket voyage to the moon.

Districts, governmental divisions established by state, county, or special regional administrative entities to provide specific services not limited to the conventional jurisdictions. Thus there is a Bay Area Rapid Transit District, BART,♦ as well as a Metropolitan Water District of Southern California.♦ There are also numerous districts for an extremely wide variety of other services, e.g. state school districts, irrigation districts, municipal utility districts, county air pollution districts, highway districts, and library districts.

DIXON, [LAFAYETTE] MAYNARD (1875–1946), California-born artist who after 1906 progressed from magazine illustrations, often in the vein of Frederic Remington, to paintings and murals of western

scenes, often of the Southwest, marked by flat colors and strong patterns.

DOAK, THOMAS (*c.*1787–1847), Boston sailor who went to California on the *Albatross* (1816) and deserted ship to become the first U.S. citizen to settle permanently in California. Baptized as Felipe Santiago in Monterey (1816), he married a Castro heiress. His name is sometimes misspelled Duke. A black shipmate named Bob also stayed ashore; he was baptized Juan Cristóbal. Doak painted the reredos in Mission San Juan Bautista (1818).

DOBIE, CHARLES CALDWELL (1881–1943), San Francisco writer who celebrated his native city in several novels and collections of stories, including *San Francisco Tales* (1935) and, in nonfiction, *San Francisco: A Pageant* (1933).

Dodge Ridge, see *Tuolumne County.*

Dodgers, Los Angeles, baseball team in the Western Division of the National League, brought to California from Brooklyn by the team's president, Walter O'Malley,♦ at the end of the 1957 season. The team played in the Los Angeles Coliseum until its own stadium, seating 56,000 persons, was completed in Chavez Ravine♦ (1962), the year it attracted 2,755,184 spectators, by far the largest number to attend one team's games up to that time. The Dodgers won the World Series against the Chicago White Sox in 1959, against the New York Yankees in 1963, and against the Minnesota Twins in 1965. Its stars included the pitchers Don Drysdale♦ and Sandy Koufax♦ and the shortstop Maury Wills.♦ In 1966 the Dodgers won the National League pennant from their traditional rivals, the S.F. Giants, but lost the World Series to the Baltimore Orioles. The next seven years were difficult for the team after the loss of Koufax and Wills and other players, although Don Drysdale set a major league record by pitching 58⅔ scoreless innings and six consecutive shutouts. With new players the Dodgers again became powerful and won the league pennant but lost the World Series to the Oakland Athletics in 1974. They also won the pennant in 1977 but lost the Series to the New York Yankees.

Dogwood, flowering shrub found in the Sierra and the north central part of the Coast Range. The *mountain dogwood,* found in mountains below 6,000 feet throughout the state, grows to 50 feet and bears white flowers and red fruit.

DOHENY, Edward L[aurence] (1856–1935), Wisconsin-born prospector whose discovery of oil near Los Angeles (1892) started the city's first boom and began his career as a wealthy oil producer. During Harding's administration he received drilling rights on 32,000 acres of government land in Elk Hills♦ without competitive bidding. A Senate investigation (1923) disclosed his loan of $100,000 to Secretary of Interior Fall and led to Fall's conviction for accepting a bribe and Doheny's acquittal for offering one. His wife, Carrie Estelle (1875–1958), gave her fine rare book collection to St. John's Seminary in Camarillo, made many other benefactions, mainly to Catholic institutions, and became a papal countess.

DOLBEER, John (1827–1902), New Hampshire-born businessman, went to California (1850) and entered the lumber industry in Humboldt County. He revolutionized logging practices by inventing a portable steam engine used in the forest to hoist logs rapidly to supply timber with a speed comparable to that of the saws in the mills and thus keep production flowing swiftly and evenly. The invention (1882) was called a "donkey engine." It made a fortune for its creator.

DOLLAR, Robert (1844–1932), born in Scotland, was reared in Canada, where he worked his way up in the lumber business and entered into shipping to export his products. His operations extended to northern California (1880) and by 1901 he established in San Francisco the Dollar Steamship Co. It became a worldwide freight shipping and passenger service, known for its transpacific liners bearing the names of U.S. Presidents. He built the largest ships constructed in the U.S. and became the nation's largest shipowner. His powerful individualism made him an enemy of unions, and during the longshoreman's strike in San Francisco (1916) his inflammatory talk came close to creating a latter-day vigilance committee. He wrote *Memoirs* (1918) and was a model for the Cappy Ricks stories by Peter B. Kyne.♦

Dolores, Mission, see *San Francisco de Asís.*

DOMÍNGUEZ, prominent early California family whose ancestor, Juan José (1736–1809), first came to Alta California as a soldier on the Sacred Expedition. His mother was a Sepúlveda. He came to own Rancho San Pedro (1784), which extended from present Wilmington halfway to Los Angeles. Other cities now located on it include Compton, Domin-guez, Gardena, and Redondo Beach, but the family retained much of its land into the 20th century.

Dominican College, Catholic liberal arts institution located in San Rafael, Marin County, since 1889. It traces its heritage to the settlement of Dominican sisters in California (1851) at Monterey, where Concepción Argüello♦ became the first native-born novice. She moved with the convent to Benicia (1854). The convent became a woman's college (1950) and began to admit men in 1971. It had about 700 students in 1970.

Don, Spanish title, probably derived from *dominus,* the Latin for "lord," was loosely applied during the period of Mexican rule to any gentleman in California, particularly a *ranchero* or landowner. Foreigners, including those from the U.S. like William G. Dana and Abel Stearns, were given the title with a Spanish Christian name when baptized prior to becoming Mexican citizens empowered to hold lands in California.

DONAHUE, Peter (1822–85), Irish immigrant from Scotland, went to California (1849) and continued a business learned in the East by opening in San Francisco the state's first iron works and machine shop, expanded into the Union Iron Works (1851). He built mining machinery and constructed the first government steamer on the Pacific Coast (1860), the first printing press, and the first locomotive made in California. The foundry remained important in shipbuilding♦ after Irving M. Scott became its head (1865). Meanwhile Donahue entered other businesses, establishing the first gas company for street lighting in San Francisco (1852), a forerunner of the Pacific Gas and Electric Co., and founding the city's first streetcar line, as well as several railroad lines. He is memorialized by a town that was a railroad terminus in Sonoma County named for him and by the Mechanics Fountain in San Francisco, sculpted by Douglas Tilden.

Donner Party, group numbering 87 men, women, and children in twenty wagons, whose leaders included the brothers George and Jacob Donner of Illinois, en route to California in 1846. At the Continental Divide in July they were persuaded by an open letter from Lansford Hastings♦ to try a new route south of the Great Salt Lake. It led them over difficult mountain passes and dry desert (at one period they made only 36 miles in 21 days) in which they lost oxen and had to jettison wagons. In early November the travelers were caught by heavy snows and, being blocked at the Sierra pass later named for them, they were forced to settle at the nearby lake where Moses Schallenberger♦ had wintered two years earlier and which is now also named for them. A leader, James Reed, who made his way to Sutter's Fort, was blocked by snow from returning with provisions until March 1. Over the ensuing weeks all those trapped at the lake began to starve and many died. Finally the survivors were reduced to eating the flesh of their dead. Three relief parties arrived (Feb. 18, March 1, later March), but some members died as they were being led out and those who had to be left behind continued to suffer, starve, and die. At that time one member, Louis Keseberg, may have murdered George Donner's wife to steal her money and to eat her body. All told, thirty-four died in the Sierra, five having died earlier, and one dying upon arrival in the Sacramento Valley. The last of the forty-seven survivors got out late in April 1847. One survivor, Patrick Breen, kept a diary, a prime source which has been edited by George R. Stewart and also used by him in his account of the Donner Party, *Ordeal by Hunger* (1936).

Donner Pass, Sierra pass west of Truckee, named for the Donner Party,♦ which was blocked there in the late fall of 1846 and forced to spend the winter at the nearby lake, also later named for them. The first use of the pass by white men was by the Elisha Stevens Party♦ during the winter of 1844–45, some of whom, under Moses Schallenberger,♦ camped for the winter at the lake to guard against Indian raids on the covered wagons which could not be got across the mountains because they were blocked by snow. The route was little used during the gold rush but was selected by Theodore Judah for the Central Pacific Railroad and was later also chosen for the main transcontinental highway.

DONOHOE, JOSEPH A. (1826–95), Irish-born banker in San Francisco, briefly associated with Ralston (1861–64). Later the head of a private bank, he was also a founding investor in other local businesses, including a gas light company and a hotel. His son married into the family of John Parrott.

Dons, Los Angeles, professional football team (est. 1946), a member of the All-American Football Conference while it lasted (until 1949).

DORGAN, THOMAS ALOYSIUS (1877–1929), San Francisco-born cartoonist for the Hearst papers, known as Tad because of his initials. An artist who depicted prizefights, a satirical caricaturist, and a comic strip creator, he was also known for his verbal innovations, including "twenty-three skidoo," "Yes, we have no bananas," and "The first hundred years are the hardest."

DORR, EBENEZER, JR. (1762–1847), Boston sea captain in the China trade who put his ship *Otter* into Monterey for provisions (1796), making it the first U.S. vessel to anchor in a California port. His voyage is described in *Mémoires du Capitaine Péron* (Paris, 1824).

DORSEY, SUSAN ALMIRA [MILLER] (1857–1946), after graduation from Vassar went to Los Angeles (1880s) with her husband, the Rev. Patrick William Dorsey, and when he deserted her (1894) she became a teacher in Los Angeles High School. She rose to become the city's superintendent of schools (1920–29), and a city school was named for her during her lifetime.

DOUGLAS, DAVID (1798?–1834), Scottish botanist, sent by the Royal Horticultural Society to the U.S. (1823, 24–27), where he spent much time on the West Coast. He went from there to Hudson's Bay, returning (1829) to live almost three years in California. His best-known discovery is the fir♦ named for him. He also described the California condor. He introduced to Europe over 50 trees and shrubs and over 100 flowers from the Pacific Coast, including the California poppy.

DOUGLAS, DONALD [WILLS] (1892–), after being the first graduate of Massachusetts Institute of Technology in aeronautical engineering (1914), joined the company of Glenn Martin♦ in building planes in Los Angeles. In 1920 he founded his own firm with a factory in an old motion picture studio where he produced a plane a week, mainly for the military. The first round-the-world flight was made by two of his planes (1924), and soon he was making economically successful passenger planes. His firm, Douglas Aircraft, was famous for its Flying Fortress (B-17) of World War II. The company later built DC-8 jet airliners and contributed to the making of ballistic missiles.

DOUGLAS, HELEN GAHAGAN (1900–), stage and screen actress, married to actor Melvyn Douglas, also had a political career as a Democrat, including serving in Congress (1945–51). She was defeated for the U.S. Senate (1951) by Richard M. Nixon in a campaign in which he dwelt on the communist threat to the U.S. and accused her of being "soft" on communism.

Douglas fir, see *Douglas, David,* and *Fir.*

Dove, see *Mourning Dove* and *Pigeon.*

DOWNEY, JOHN GATELY (1826–94), 7th governor of the state (1860–62), went to California without money from his native Ireland but made a fortune in his Los Angeles drugstore, the only one between San Diego and San Francisco, and in ranching and real estate operations near the town he named for himself. He later became a banker, first with Alvinza Hayward, then with I. W. Hellman. As acting lieutenant governor he succeeded to the governorship upon the retirement of Latham. He was a strong Union supporter in the Civil War.

DOWNEY, SHERIDAN (1884–1961), Wyoming-born lawyer and political leader in California, to which he moved in 1912. He was a Democratic supporter of the New Deal, Upton Sinclair, Dr. Townsend, and the Ham 'n Eggs movement.♦ With such backing he was twice elected to the U.S. Senate (1939–50), from which he resigned because of illness.

Downey, a residential city with aerospace industry southeast of Los Angeles. It was subdivided from a *rancho* by Gov. John G. Downey, who named it after himself (1865). In 1970 the population was 88,445.

Downieville, seat of Sierra County located on a fork of the Yuba River, sometimes called the Downie River. It was first settled by a group of prospectors, black and white, led by "Major" William Downie, a Scotsman (1849) who later published his recollections. Successful gold mining led to the creation of the town, which had a population of 5,000 the next year. It became notorious as the site of a kangaroo court trial and the hanging (July 5, 1851) of Juanita, a Sonoran♦ woman who had stabbed to death a drunken American when he tried to break into her house in the aftermath of celebrating Independence Day. The community is now attractive, but almost a ghost town.

DOXEY, WILLIAM (1845–1916), English-born bookseller and publisher, resident in San Francisco (1878–1900) where he was the sponsor of *The Lark*♦ and of a series of Lark Classics, little books by Rudyard Kipling, Andrew Lang, W. S. Blunt, and others, well printed by Charles Murdock. His

shop not only had fine books by Robert Louis Stevenson and others he admired but was a gathering place for the city's fin de siècle authors and artists.

DOYLE, ALEXANDER PATRICK (1857–1912), Catholic missionary, born in San Francisco, after graduation from St. Mary's College and theological training became the first native Californian to be ordained a priest. He labored as a missionary throughout the U.S. and edited *Temperance Truth* (1892–1903), *The Catholic World* (1893–1904), and *The Missionary* (1896–1912).

DOYLE, JOHN THOMAS (1819–1906), New York-born lawyer, went to California (1852) and there became the attorney for Bishop Alemany♦ in the Pious Fund♦ litigation. He wrote a history of the subject and was the founding president of the California Historical Society.

Dragnet, television series of 30-minute programs (1951–59, 1967–70) based on actual case histories of the Los Angeles police. It featured the assignments of Sergeant Joe Friday, played by Jack Webb, who was also the program's producer and director. At the end of each sequence the decision of the resultant trial was announced.

DRAKE, FRANCIS (1540?–96), English navigator, had sailed as a privateer attacking Spanish vessels in the West Indies before setting off from Plymouth (Dec. 1577) to circumnavigate the globe with five ships. The voyage took him through the Strait of Magellan in his only remaining vessel, *Pelican,* there renamed *Golden Hind.* As he had in the Atlantic, Drake plundered Spanish treasure ships in the Pacific, but when prevented by unfavorable winds from sailing to the Moluccas and when he did not find the fabled Northwest Passage (or Strait of Anián), he came down from the Pacific Northwest coast and in June of 1579 put into "a convenient and fit harborough" according to *The World Encompassed by Sir Francis Drake* (1628), a work attributed to Francis Fletcher, the chaplain on his ship, and there Drake beached his vessel for repairs. That landing site in California has never been determined, but the various places claimed for it include Bodega Bay, Bolinas Bay, Drake's Bay, Point Reyes, and the Marin shore of San Francisco Bay. In the last area, near San Quentin, there was found in 1936 a plate of brass, now in The Bancroft Library, whose authenticity is much questioned, although it closely fits the description in *The World*

Encompassed of the metal document nailed to a stout post by Drake to proclaim that he took possession of the land for Queen Elizabeth of England and that he named it Nova Albion. After remaining for 36 days, during which he established good relations with the "king," or Hioh, of the Indians and was himself crowned by that monarch, presumably a Miwok, he sailed westward on his voyage round the world. The incursion caused the Spanish to think more seriously about reconaissance of the region and eventual settlement. After his return to England Drake was knighted by Queen Elizabeth.

Drake's Bay, Pacific Ocean bay northwest of Bolinas in Marin County whose westernmost boundary is Point Reyes. An estuary off it is named Drake's Estero. The bay was named San Francisco by Cermeño (1595) and first given its present name on a map in 1625. It is considered by many scholars to be the site where Drake repaired his ship.

Drought, see *Disasters.*

DRURY, MORLEY (1903–   ), Canadian-born football player, was the star running back of the University of Southern California team (1925–27).

DRYSDALE, DON[ALD SCOTT] (1936–   ), born in Van Nuys, became a pitcher for the Brooklyn Dodgers (1956), and moved with his team to Los Angeles after the next year's season. In 1968 he set a major league record by pitching 58⅔ scoreless innings and 6 consecutive shutouts, and the next year he held the club's record for most games won (209), most strikeouts (2,486), and most shutouts (49). He also became a wealthy racehorse breeder and owner. He injured his shoulder in a fall and retired in 1969.

Duarte, suburban community of Los Angeles County, lying between Azusa and Monrovia, derives its name from the original *ranchero* of the region, Andrés Duarte. Once known for citrus groves, it has become a residential settlement. The City of Hope National Medical Center is located there.

Duck, wild waterfowl of which many varieties are found in California during the winter. Only four are native: the *mallard, teal,* and *wood,* river or freshwater birds, and the *red-head,* a sea bird. The thirteen most common winter residents which do not generally breed in the state are the *American golden-eye,* the *baldpate* (or *widgeon*), the *buffle-*

head, the *canvas-back,* two *mergansers* (the *American* and the *red-breasted*), the *pintail,* the *ruddy,* two *scaups* (the *greater* and *lesser*), two *scoters* (the *surf* and the *white-winged*), and the *shoveler.* First hunted by Maidu and other Indians, they have always been sought by whites for their meat. Despite the early regulations (first state law, 1852), they were overhunted and greatly reduced in number. At the end of the 1960s about 10,000,000 were thought to winter in California, but at the same time over 150,000 hunting licenses were issued annually.

Duel, combat sanctioned by aristocratic tradition, declared illegal by the democratically oriented Constitution enacted in 1849. Nevertheless, duels were fought surreptitiously in California, generally by men from the southern states. The most famous were those between (state) Senator James W. Denver and Edward C. Gilbert (1852) and between California Chief Justice David S. Terry and U.S. Senator David Broderick (1859).

DUFLOT DE MOFRAS, EUGÈNE, see *Mofras, Eugène Duflot de.*

DUHAUT-CILLY, AUGUSTE BERNARD (1790–1849), captain in French merchant marine who commanded *Le Héros,* as described in his *Voyage autour du monde* (2 vols., 1834). The book treats vividly his visits to California (1827–28). Paul Emile Botta (1802–70), the Italian doctor who accompanied him as naturalist, described the Indians and fauna encountered in California and translated his book into Italian (1841). A variety of gopher he described was named the *Botta gopher.*

DUMAS, ALEXANDRE (1802–70), French author of romances who set two of his many works in California, although he never visited it. They are *A Gil Blas in California* (1852, trans. 1933) and *Journal of Mme. Giovanni* (1856, trans. 1944).

DUMAS, CHARLES (1937–   ), Los Angeles-born high jumper, became the first person to jump higher than seven feet (7'½"). He also won the Olympic Games championship in the same year (1956).

Dumbarton Bridge, first span for autos built across San Francisco Bay (1927) close to a train bridge (1911). It crosses the southern Bay tip from Newark (Alameda County) to a point south of Redwood City (San Mateo County).

DUNCAN, ISADORA (1878–1927), reared by her divorced mother in San Francisco in an extremely permissive, agnostic, antipuritan, and poetic style, by the age of 10 she was already teaching dancing. When only 18 she became a dancer and actress in Augustin Daly's New York company, then moved to London and soon to Athens, where she created her Temple of the Dance for free, interpretive performances. There and elsewhere in Europe she established her own romantically Hellenistic style, rejected conventions of ballet movement, and looked to Whitman's poetry as guidance for her freedom of movement and ideas. Married late to a young Russian poet, she previously had had three children by different fathers, the first by the stage designer, Gordon Craig. She told of her experiences and views in *My Life* (1927). Raymond Duncan♦ was her brother.

DUNCAN, RAYMOND (1874–1966), like his sister Isadora was devoted to classical dance and also to his own interpretation of Greek culture. This he taught in the Akademia he established in Paris, where he was an expatriate for over fifty years.

DUNCAN, ROBERT (1919–   ), poet born in Oakland and resident in the East Bay, where he attended the University of California and edited the *Berkeley Miscellany* (1948–49). He is a major figure in the Projectivist school of poetry, influenced by Ezra Pound. His many books include *Heavenly City, Earthly City* (1947), *Medieval Scenes* (1950), *Roots and Branches* (1964), and *Bending the Bow* (1969). He has also written plays: *Medea at Kolchis* (1965) and *Adam's Way* (1966).

Dune buggies, vehicles for recreation, created from stripped-down cars to which are added minimal plastic bodies and large tires. Used for sport driving on beaches, they became popular in California during the 1960s after Bruce Meyers, a commercial artist of Costa Mesa, began to market a reasonably priced kit to create these specialized automobiles. They are used for outings, informal rallies, and even races between rival clubs.

Dungeness crab, see *Crab*.

DUNNE, JOHN GREGORY (1932–   ), Connecticut-born writer resident in southern California since 1964. His books include three works of nonfiction about phenomena of the western scene: *Delano* (1967), treating the movement of Cesar Chavez; *The Studio* (1969), about the film industry; and *Vegas* (1974), about Nevada's gambling city; as well as *True Confessions* (1977), a tough police novel set

in Los Angeles. With his wife, Joan Didion,k he has written film scripts.

DUNNEL, JOHN HENRY (1813–1904), Massachusetts-born artist, went to California in the gold rush (1849–51), returned (1857–60) and drew some pictures of the mining country.

DUPLEX, EDWARD PARKER (1830?–1900), went to California in the early 1850s from Connecticut, where his family were prominent free blacks. Settling in Marysville, he was active in civil rights affairs and was elected mayor of Wheatland (1888). He was thus the first black mayor on the Pacific Coast, although he had in a sense been preceded by Francisco Reyes, who was *alcalde* of Los Angeles (1794).

DU PONT, SAMUEL FRANCIS (1803–65), naval officer and member of the distinguished Delaware family, served as commander under Stockton during the Mexican War. He took Frémont's forces to San Diego aboard the *Cyane* and later captured La Paz, Guaymas, and Mazatlan. A San Francisco street was named Dupont for him. A portion of it became a Chinatown route and was later notorious for its brothels, so merchants had its northern section renamed Grant, after the President. The southern part later took that name too.

DURÁN, NARCISCO (1776–1846), Franciscan missionary from Catalonia, went from Mexico to California (1806) and became president of the missions (1825–27, 1831–38), after 1833 heading only those from San Diego to Soledad, the northern missions being put under separate jurisdiction. He was an able administrator and a firm opponent both of secularization and of foreigners, arresting Jedediah Smith♦ (1827) for fear that he would cause neophytes to desert the missions. In 1817 he explored the Sacramento River to the Feather River. An accomplished musician, he devised a scheme to teach Indians to read music and organized a 30-piece orchestra for those at Mission San José. One of his prize pupils was Estanislao,♦ until he defected back to his own culture.

DURANT, HENRY (1802–75), Congregational clergyman and later headmaster of a boy's academy in his native Massachusetts before going to Oakland (1853), where he opened the Contra Costa Academy, a private school for boys. In 1855 it was chartered as the College of California, a nondenominational institution of higher learning that was disincorporated (1867) so that it might be merged to form the basis for the new University of California (est. 1868). Durant was the University's first president (1870–72) and then mayor of Oakland.

Dust, see *Color*.

Dutch in California, may date back to the pirates who raided Spanish ships in the Pacific during the 17th century, some of whom may have put into Baja California. Much later trade between the East Indies and San Francisco in Dutch ships came into being during the 19th century, but there was little settlement from the Netherlands. The many gold rush place-names like Dutch Flat refer almost entirely to Germans, not Hollanders. However, some were from Holland, like John Henry Schnell, who, paradoxically, helped found the Wakamatsu Colony♦ (1869) of Japanese, while others later established the Queen Wilhelmina Kolonie (1891) for fruit farming near Hanford. Eminent early settlers include James de Fremery, a pioneer of Oakland, and the Magnin family; later ones include Dirk Van Erp and A. C. Vroman.

Dutch Flat, gold rush mining town of Placer County, settled (1851) by Germans, from whose presence comes its name. It was later a stagecoach stop en route to Washoe and on the line for transcontinental track selected by Theodore Judah.

DWINELLE, JOHN WHIPPLE (1816–81), went to Los Angeles (1849) from Rochester, N.Y., where he had been city attorney, and three years later moved to Oakland, becoming its mayor, while continuing his legal practice, which involved Spanish and Mexican land grant cases and the rights of Negro children to attend public schools. In the state legislature he wrote the bill (1868) creating the University of California, which has a Berkeley building named for him. His writings include *The Colonial History of the City of San Francisco* (1863).

DYE, JOB [FRANCIS] (1895–83), Kentucky-born mountain man and trapper, went from New Mexico to California with Ewing Young♦ on his second trip (1832). He trapped otter, worked on Capt. John R. Cooper's *rancho,* ran a store and distillery in Santa Cruz, and became a *ranchero* in present Tehama County. During the conquest of California he carried dispatches for Sloat and after it he made money as a trader and merchant during the gold rush. His "Recollections of a Pioneer of California" was first printed in a Santa Cruz newspaper (1869).

E

E Clampus Vitus, Ancient Order of, an organization founded in Sierra City (1857) as a burlesque of fraternal societies. Its head is the "Noble Grand Humbug." Its members are "Clampers," and they are called to their "Hall of Comparative Ovations" by the braying of the "Hewgag." Although it was a hoaxing society, it also engaged in some charitable activities in the various mining towns where local chapters were organized. Revived in 1931 by Carl I. Wheat and other members of the California Historical Society, the society Redivivus exists for fun, for the revival of gold rush lore, and for the placing of plaques at historical sites.

Eagle Lake, large lake northwest of Susanville in Lassen County. It is on the eastern edge of Lassen National Forest.

Eagles, two varieties are native to California. The *golden eagle,* which lives in mountainous areas throughout the state, is up to 40 inches long and has a wing span up to 7 feet. It has dark brown plumage except for golden feathers high on its neck and blackish feathers with gray bars on its tail. It feeds on small game, such as rabbits, young foxes, coyotes, and snakes. The *bald eagle,* the kind depicted as the national emblem, lives in the Santa Barbara Mts. and some coastal sites. It is about the same size as the *golden* but is sooty brown with white on head and tail. It is a scavenger, but also hunts gophers and rabbits. The birds were once common enough to give their names to ten Eagle Peaks, ten Eagle Rocks, and many similar place-names throughout the state.

EAMES, CHARLES (1907–), St. Louis-born designer, long resident in Venice, Calif., where he and his wife create furniture and toys in a modern idiom, and where he bases his headquarters for his architectural work and the making of experimental motion pictures.

EARL, EDWIN T. (1856–1919), born in Inyo County, at the age of 17 entered the fruit shipping business for which he invented (1890) the first successful combination ventilator-refrigerator rail-road car to transport fresh fruit to the East Coast. His success led to the Earl Fruit Co., for many years the state's largest fruit-packing and -shipping firm. In 1900 he sold his interest for about $2,000,000 and bought the *Los Angeles Evening Express,* made Edward A. Dickson♦ editor, then established the *Los Angeles Tribune*♦ (1911) which emphasized opposition to Harrison Gray Otis' *Times.* Earl was a political reformer who supported Hiram Johnson and the Progressive party. He and his brother Guy also organized the company that became the Great Western Power Co. (1902), bringing hydroelectric power from Feather River to Oakland.

EARL, GUY, see *Earl, Edwin.*

Earthquakes, sudden shifts of earth some 10 to 30 miles deep along lines of weakness—faults—with violent releases of strains that occasion shock waves. The faults are not single breaks in the earth, but broad zones. Many scarps—steep cliffs or ridges—have resulted, of which the most striking is the east face of the Sierra Nevada, formed over several million years.

Of the hundreds of California faults, the major ones, north to south, are the San Andreas Fault♦ and Hayward Fault, a branch of the former extending from Hollister through the city of its name; Sierra Nevada Fault, of the Owens Valley quake (1872), largest in all California history; White Wolf Fault, of the Bakersfield quake (1952), the worst in over a half-century of the state's history; Garlock Fault, along the Tehachapi, the dominant east-west fault; Santa Ynez Fault, of the Santa Barbara earthquake (1925); Newport-Inglewood Fault, a recently discovered fault, of the Long Beach quake (1933); Elsinore Fault, which lies along the terrain to the northeast and southeast of San Diego; San Jacinto Fault, essentially a southern extension of the San Andreas zone and parallel to its southern part; and Imperial Fault, the southernmost branch of the San Andreas Fault, extending over the Mexican border.

Earthquakes have been known throughout California's history and occurred long before they were recorded. Costanoan and other Indians told legends about them and Portolá experienced one in 1769. In recent years they have been measured on the Richter Scale, devised by Charles F[rancis] Richter (1900–   ), a professor and seismologist at the California Institute of Technology. In that scale each number expresses a 10-fold increase in magnitude and a 60-fold increase in energy for each of its digits from 1 to 8.9, the figure for the largest earthquake known.

Richter readings of major California quakes include Tejon Pass, *c.*7.75 (1857); Hayward, *c.*7 (1868); Owens Valley, *c.*8.3 (1872); San Francisco, 8.3 (1906); Santa Barbara, 6.3 (1925); Long Beach, 6.3 (1933); Tehachapi and Bakersfield, 7.7 (1952); San Fernando, 6.6 (1971). The most famous is the 1906 San Francisco earthquake.◆

East Bay, name applied to bay shore area of Alameda and Contra Costa counties from a location south of Alameda to one north of Richmond. The East Bay Regional Parks,◆ on and behind the hilltops from San Leandro to El Cerrito, were established (1934) by the state legislature, but their more than 27,000 acres are kept up by adjacent Alameda County cities.

East Bay Regional Parks, park district created (1934) on the watershed land of the East Bay Municipal Utility District's hilly preserves. It was accomplished by means of a legislative permit and the votes of citizens of Alameda, Albany, Berkeley, Emeryville, Oakland, Piedmont, and San Leandro. The Parks began the purchase of land (1936) under the aegis of Charles Lee Tilden.◆ In the 1960s and 70s other parts of Alameda and Contra Costa counties joined the system until it came to include over 27,000 acres. The Utility District (est. 1923) obtains its water from the Mokelumne River,◆ using Pardee and Camanche reservoirs in the river area and Lafayette and Chabot reservoirs in the East Bay for storage purposes.

EASTMAN, BEN[JAMIN BANGS] (1911–   ), California-born track star, as a Stanford student set world records for running 440 yards (in 46.4 seconds) and 880 yards (in 1:50.9). Two years later he also held world records for 600 yards, 500 meters, and 800 meters.

East of Eden, novel by John Steinbeck,◆ published in 1952. Set in part in the Salinas Valley, it traces a New England family's heritage in California and uses the story of Cain and Abel to show that although God exiled Cain to the land east of Eden,

He said to him, "if thou doest well . . . thou mayest rule over sin." The film version (1955) provided James Dean with his first starring role.

East-West Game, annual postseason football game, played (1925–74) in San Francisco (except for 1942 in New Orleans) and since 1975 at Stanford between two teams of collegiate players selected by coaches among outstanding athletes in the western and eastern U.S., respectively. The proceeds of this charity game go to the organizers, the Masonic Order of Shriners. An earlier East-West football game was played Christmas Day 1894 between Stanford University and the University of Chicago.

EATON, FREDERICK B. (1855–1934), civic leader of his native city, Los Angeles, who helped to create its parks system, particularly Pershing Square, and to found Los Angeles' electric railway. Having served as City Engineer, he conceived of Owens River as the best source for needed water supply, a program he fostered during his term as mayor. William Mulholland,◆ his friend and successor as City Engineer, carried out his plans for constructing an aqueduct, but they fell out over the purchase of land by Eaton for a reservoir. In later years Eaton suffered from economic difficulties and disaffection.

Ebbetts Pass, route across the Sierra to Angels Camp (8,730-ft. summit) from the Oregon Trail,◆ used during the gold rush. It was named for John Ebbetts, a New Yorker who crossed it in 1851 and died in 1854, although the first over it may have been the Bartleson-Bidwell Party◆ (1841).

Ebony Showcase Theatre, repertory theater founded (1950) in Los Angeles to give black actors the opportunity to play roles in popular Broadway shows originally restricted to whites and thus broaden their professional experiences. The organization also has a program to train black youths in drama.

EBRIGHT, KY [CARROLL] (1893–   ), coach of the crew of the University of California, Berkeley (1924–59). Under his tutelage crews from Berkeley three times won championships at Olympic Games (1928, 1932, 1948), earning gold medals for 27 Berkeley competitors.

ECHEANDÍA, JOSÉ MARÍA (*fl.* 1825–55), had been a lieutenant-colonel of engineers in Mexico before he became the first governor of California to be appointed under the republican constitution of Mexico (1824). He arrived in 1825 intent on secularizing the missions, but found the undertaking difficult. His administration was further troubled by a revolt (1829) led by his financial commissioner, José María Herrera, and Joaquín Solís♦ on behalf of the soldiers of Monterey, who had not been paid for a long time. Echeandía put down the uprising, but in time he planned to resign; instead he was replaced (1831) by Manuel Victoria, against whom he successfully led a revolt before the year was out. The *Diputación* appointed Pío Pico governor for three weeks thereafter. Then a permanent governor was appointed: Echeandía returned to power as the interim chief officer for the south of California (1831–33), while Zamorano held the same post for the north (1832–33). After Echeandía vacated his office he returned to Mexico.

ECKBO, GARRETT (1910–), after study at the University of California, Berkeley, and Harvard, became a leading landscape architect of the Bay Area in the 1950s. His projects have varied from large-scale housing communities to private country estates and have included the small city park in San Francisco atop a garage which features Bufano's statue of Sun Yat-sen.

EDOUART, ALEXANDER (1818–92), English-born artist who went to California in 1852. He lived in San Francisco, Mendocino, and Los Angeles, where he painted landscapes and historic scenes. He was also known as a photographer.

EDSON, KATHERINE PHILLIPS (1870–1933), social reformer and feminist, went from her native Midwest to Antelope Valley (1890), and there and in neighboring Los Angeles, to which she moved (1900), she became a leading campaigner for woman suffrage. Under Gov. Hiram Johnson she worked to better wages and hours for women and entered state government, becoming (1927) chief of the Division of Industrial Welfare. She was also a prominent industrial mediator and a leader in the League of Women Voters.

Education, introduced by the Franciscan missionaries beginning in 1769 to convert and train Indians, was not extended to the children of Spanish or Mexican settlers until Gov. Borica introduced compulsory primary education (1795) in the pueblos, but after his administration the little schools dwindled away. Govs. Figueroa and Alvarado reinstituted educational requirements of a minimal sort for young children, but most *gente de razon* looked to private tutoring at home.

The first school for American settlers was

created at Mission Santa Clara (1846) and was secular in nature, as was the one founded at Monterey (1847). San Francisco had the first public school established by city ordinance (1850), but Chinese, Negro, and Indian children were not admitted, and from 1866 to 1890 many segregated schools existed. The state Constitution (1849) required a school in every school district to be open at least three months a year. The next decade schools were extended and improved under better legislation and the distinguished Superintendent John Swett.♦ Nevertheless, despite the opening of a public high school in San Francisco in 1856, for a long time the state legislature did not assist secondary schools.

During the 20th century the state developed a distinguished school system under a Superintendent of Public Instruction,♦ state certification of teachers, training in teachers' colleges, and student admission standards set by the University of California. These received strong community support.

Higher education began in 1851 with the founding of the California Wesleyan College (now University of the Pacific) and the forerunner of Santa Clara University; the first women's college foreshadowed in the seminary (1852) that became Mills College; and the roots of the University of California, found in the College of California (1855), itself the outgrowth of a Congregational academy (1853). An Agricultural, Mining and Mechanical Arts College chartered by the legislature (1866) and funded by 150,000 acres of land obtained through the Morrill Land Grant Act was the other forerunner of the University of California (est. 1868).

The first state normal school was founded at San Francisco (1862), followed by others at San Jose (1870) and Los Angeles (1881), the last named becoming the southern branch of the University of California (1919), the other two and many later ones becoming first teachers' colleges (1921), then state colleges (1935), and, still more recently, state universities (1972). Community colleges, for a long time known as junior colleges, offering the first two years of college instruction and more vocational teaching, ensure that any high school graduate may go on to some institution of higher education. The first of these was founded in 1910 and numerous others have been established since throughout the state under the administration of district boards of trustees.

In 1960 a Master Plan for Higher Education assigned functions to each element of the state's tri-partite system of higher education. The state universities and colleges under an over-all Chancellor and a governor-appointed Board of Trustees were given responsibility for four-year undergraduate instruction and the M.A. and the opportunity to award a doctoral degree in certain fields with the University of California, but that institution alone was charged with undergraduate teaching and given sole jurisdiction over graduate instruction in the professions, made the only public education authority to award the doctorate, and named the primary state-supported academic agency for research.

The activities of the three elements of public higher education and those of private education in the state were related by the creation (1960) of a Coordinating Council for Higher Education,♦ replaced (1974) by a 23-member Postsecondary Education Commission, which includes representatives of the public as well as of private institutions. Among those institutions, in addition to ones founded earlier, are Stanford University,♦ the Claremont Colleges,♦ and Occidental College.♦

Eel River, formed by three forks rising in the Coast Range. The Middle Fork rises about 50 miles south and 50 miles east of Eureka, flowing south and west to join the South Fork, which begins some 15 miles above Clear Lake and flows north to the modern reservoir of Lake Pillsbury, while the North Fork rises some 35 miles below Eureka and curves south and east to join the others, all emptying into the Pacific. The Eel, which is subject to floods, has the largest runoff of any river originating in the Coast Range. It was so named by Josiah Gregg♦ because he obtained eels from Indians along the banks. It was there that he died.

Eggs, see *Poultry* and *Farallones.*

Ejido, tract of public land belonging to a pueblo and intended for the use of its residents.

El Alisal, see *Alisal, El.*

El Camino Reál, see *Camino Reál, El.*

El Centro, major trade center of the Imperial Valley and county seat of Imperial County. It was named and laid out (1905) by W. F. Holt, and is known as the "largest city below sea level in the Western Hemisphere." In 1970 it had a population of 19,272.

ELDER, [DAVID] PAUL (1872–1948), bookseller of San Francisco whose shop, designed by Maybeck, featured local arts and crafts. He was also the proprietor of the Tomoyé Press, for which John Henry Nash printed books (1901–11), including

some of Nash's own essays and works by other writers of the region. Morgan Shepard (1865–1947) was a partner until 1903.

Elderberry, deciduous, flat-topped tree or shrub of the genus *Sambucus*, also known as elder, found in the Sierra Nevada and the Coast Range down to Los Angeles. It ranges in height from a bush to a tree of about 30 feet, and has white or pink flowers and purple-black berries. They are used for wine, jelly, and medicinal purposes. Cahuilla Indians are known to have eaten the fruit.

El Dorado, name meaning "the gilded one," that is, gilded man, refers to the mythic Indian chief of Bogotá, Colombia, who was said to have been anointed and covered with gold during religious rites. That chief and his land were sought by Spanish conquistadors and associated with any gold-producing land. Naturally, it was applied to California during the gold rush, so that in 1848 Preuss inscribed the text "El Dorado or Gold Region" on a map of the area. The name was given to one of the original counties of the new state (1850), and in the same year Bayard Taylor entitled his book about the state *Eldorado.* El Dorado National Forest, on the western Sierra Nevada in Amador, El Dorado, and Placer counties, includes the south end of Lake Tahoe.

El Dorado County, one of the original 27 counties (1850), has Placer County on the north, the state of Nevada on the east, Alpine and Amador counties on the south, and Sacramento and Placer counties on the west. The first county seat was Coloma,♦ but since 1857 it has been Placerville.♦ Following Marshall's discovery of gold at Sutter's mill at Coloma, there was a gigantic rush of men to the area along the American River♦ and the Cosumnes River,♦ which form the county's northern and southern boundaries, where innumerable jerry-built mining camps and towns came and went, and cropped up in the mountains between them as well. Among these temporary settlements were Murderer's Bar, Spanish Hill, Mud Springs (later El Dorado), and Loafer's Hollow. The only sizable and permanent communities were Placerville and Georgetown.♦ Ghost towns are among the attractions that now make the county a tourist area, but many summer visitors also go there because of the recreational and vacation resorts at Fallen Leaf Lake♦ and the southern part of Lake Tahoe, which lies within the county. Also within it is part of the Carson Range, and Luther Pass (7,735-ft. elevation), which leads to Alpine County, and part of the El Dorado National Forest. The forest also covers parts of Amador and Placer counties. The county's economy is based mainly on tourism, fruit orchards, and lumber mills. The population in 1970 was 43,833. With an area of 1,104,576 acres, it had 25.4 persons per sq. mi.

ELDREDGE, ZOETH SKINNER (1846–1918), San Francisco historian, author of *The March of Portolá* (1909), a history of early San Francisco (2 vols., 1913), and editor of a five-volume *History of California* (1915) which appeared under his name. Together with George Davidson, he campaigned (*c.*1905) to change numerous California place-names to their actual or ostensible Spanish originals.

Electricity, generated by several different kinds of agencies: private utility firms, such as Pacific Gas and Electric Co.,♦ Southern California Edison Co.,♦ Southern California Gas Co.,♦ and the former Great Western Power Co.;♦ municipal, state, and regional agencies, such as the Department of Water and Power of the city of Los Angeles; and the U.S. Bureau of Reclamation. They generate electricity by several means: hydroelectric power,♦ fossil fuel (gas and oil) plants for steam-generated electricity, nuclear energy,♦ geothermal energy,♦ and natural gas.♦

Electronics, major area of technological research and manufacturing, within California developed primarily on the San Francisco peninsula, where it forms what has been called "the densest concentration of innovative industry that exists anywhere in the world." Some firms in this field date back to the beginning of the 20th century; they were organized in part to supply wireless equipment to ships that came into San Francisco Bay. The predecessor of the Federal Telegraph Corp. (formed 1909) first built wireless stations and then manufactured radio wave generators. Two Federal employees founded Magnavox Corp. (1917) in Oakland to manufacture coils used in their invention of the loudspeaker. Another Federal alumnus was Charles Litton, whose work with vacuum tubes developed into Litton Industries.

The first two decades of the century were also marked by the beginnings of electronic experimentation in the Bay Area. A striking example was the development by Lee De Forest of the triode, or vacuum tube, as a sound amplifier. Between World War I and World War II more inventors founded

their own firms. The Remler Co. (1918) built amateur radio kits and transmitters, Heintz and Kaufman (1924) made shortwave aircraft radios, Eitel McCullogh (1934) manufactured transmitting tubes, Kaar Engineering (1936) built two-way radio telephones, Fisher Research Laboratories (1936) constructed marine radios and other electronic products, and Hewlett-Packard, founded (1938) by William R. Hewlett♦ and David Packard,♦ built electronic measuring instruments. All of these firms, located between San Francisco and San Jose, grew in response to World War II needs and demands for consumer goods by an increased postwar population.

Hewlitt-Packard and some companies founded later clustered around Stanford University in part because Frederick Terman,♦ its dean of engineering and, later, provost and vice president, had once taught some of these inventors and developers and encouraged them and others to relate research to manufacturing and business. He also sponsored Stanford Industrial Park, over 8,000 acres of University land where plants could be located on rental property close to classrooms and University laboratories. Some significant electronics research was developed a little farther away—Philo T. Farnsworth♦ worked on television in San Francisco—but more and more during the 1930s and 40s the Palo Alto area became the major center. There the Sigurd and Russell Varian brothers and William Hansen invented the klystron tube, a basis of radar and microwave (1937), and their company developed into Varian Associates (1948); Alexander M. Poniatoff founded Ampex (1944) to manufacture parts for radar and eventually to build tape recording equipment; William B. Shockley,♦ the co-inventor of the transistor, set up a corporation (1956), and some of his assistants split off to create Fairchild Semiconductor (1957).

Terman also recruited chemists for the University's faculty, and a number, among them Alejandro Zaffaroni and Carl Djerassi, went on to found or to join businesses, some of which relate to electronics. National firms have also established facilities near San Francisco, thus putting Admiral, General Electric, IBM, Lockheed, and others into the region.

"Elephant, To See the," slang expression popular during the 1840s and 1850s that came to be applied to gold rush experiences. It then came to mean to have gone to the mining country with the hope of having an experience as exotic as seeing an elephant—then a rare creature even in a circus—

but to have come away disappointed upon finding that, like other exhibits of showmanship, it was not so wonderful as advertised.

Elevator, The, militant black weekly newspaper, founded and edited (1865–89) by Philip A. Bell.◆ In 1904 it merged with the *Pacific Coast Appeal,* the outgrowth of another journal founded by Bell. Under the latter title it continued publication for at least two more decades.

Elk, members of the deer family, also called wapiti. They are of three varieties: the *Roosevelt elk,* about 8 feet long and 4 to 6 feet tall, found in Humboldt and Del Norte counties; the *tule elk,* a smaller and paler kind found in some parts of Inyo, Kern, Colusa, and Yolo counties; and the *Rocky Mountain elk,* introduced into the state (1916) and now found in the Santa Lucia, Tehachapi, and Cascade ranges. Once heavily hunted for sport, food, and such products as leather and teeth, elk are now entirely protected. Only about 2,000 *Roosevelt,* 400 *tule,* and 700 *Rocky Mountain* are thought to be alive, although until the 1850s great herds roamed the state. A State Reserve for *tule elk* covers almost 1,000 acres in Kern County, north of Taft.

Elk Hills Petroleum Reserve, U.S. Navy oil reserve near Taft (Kern County). E. L. Doheny and other oil producers in 1923 persuaded U.S. Secretary of Interior Fall to lease them the land gratis so that they might pump out the oil and store it in tanks for ready use, reserving a certain percentage for their own purposes. The bargain involved payment of $100,000 to Fall, who was convicted of accepting a bribe. Doheny was acquitted of giving one: he claimed the payment was just a friendly loan. Another result of the scandal was the return of the lands to the U.S. Navy.

ELKUS, ALBERT [ISRAEL] (1884--1962), Sacramento-born pianist and musical conductor, a member of the de Young family, was best known as a professor at Dominican College, Mills College, and the University of California, Berkeley (1931–51).

El Monte, city of Los Angeles County, southeast of Pasadena, is named for a thicket of willows once located there. The site was considered the terminus of the Santa Fe Trail. It is now a residential suburb, with light industry, which had an enormous increase of population in the 1960s. In 1970 it had 69,892 residents.

El Paso Mountains, range in Kern County, north of the Mojave Desert.

El Segundo, industrial and residential community near Santa Monica Bay, just south of the Los Angeles International Airport, was named (1911) "the second" in Spanish for Standard Oil's second refinery in the state, located there. It is a major port for petroleum products.

Elsinore, name given in the 1880s to a lake, mountain, valley, and town on the edge of Cleveland National Forest in southwestern Riverside County, and to a nearby earthquake fault. *Hamlet* is presumably the source in all instances. Both Anza and, much later, the Butterfield stages passed through this area, which is now something of a vacation region. Coal has been mined at nearby Alberhill.

Elsinore Fault, see *Earthquakes.*

Elysian Park, downtown Los Angeles recreational area, established in the 1880s. The ancient Indian village of Yang-na was located on the site. In 1962, on the adjacent Chavez Ravine, the Dodgers opened their baseball stadium.

Embarcadero, Spanish for "wharf" or "harbor," is the name of several districts in California, most notably the northeastern waterfront of San Francisco. Long dominated by the Ferry Building,◆ it has in recent years been marred by an elevated freeway but at the same time enhanced by a variety of redevelopment projects. First came the Golden Gateway, designed by the firm of William Wurster and others, for high-rise apartments, adjacent two-story private houses in rows atop large garages, office towers, and large open spaces, including a block-square park. A later development includes three great high-rise buildings comprising Embarcadero Center, one of them for the firm of Levi Strauss, and all having shopping malls; all of them, like the dramatic Hyatt Regency Hotel were designed by John Portman of Georgia. Between them and the Bay is a small park with a great modern fountain whose concrete forms echo the adjacent freeway.

Emerald Bay, large cove—with an uninhabited island—on the southwest side of Lake Tahoe,◆ set aside as a State Park.

Emigrant Gap, mountain notch on the route from Donner Lake to Sacramento, the steep descent marking the point between the Sierra and the gold-bearing foothills. The old Emigrant Trail pass, over which covered wagons were lowered by block and tackle, became a Central Pacific Railroad station.

Emigrant Trail, name applied to routes into California during the 1840s and 50s. One major route given the name was that pioneered by Pedro Fages (1782) on a variant of the trail of Anza from present Arizona to California via passes within present Riverside County. A northern route given the name was the last leg of the California Trail at the crossing of the Sierra into California, commonly via Donner Pass♦ and Emigrant Gap.♦

Emperor Norton, see *Norton, Joshua A.*

Encomienda, originally a grant from the Spanish crown giving manorial rights over lands seized from the Moors to knights who had helped wrest those lands for Spain. Soldiers who came to the New World were given not land but a grant of Indian labor bestowed in return for the grantee's (*encomendero*'s) aid to and conversion of the Indians.

ENGELHARDT, ZEPHYRIN (1851–1934), German-born priest, educated in the U.S. and ordained at St. Louis (1878), was sent to California (1885) as a missionary to the Pomo Indians, of whose language he compiled a vocabulary. His interest in his own order led him to obtain a handpress on which he printed his historical studies, *The Franciscans in California* (1897) and *The Franciscans in Arizona* (1899). His major work, *Missions and Missionaries of California* (4 vols., 1908–15), was beyond the scale of his amateur printing and is considered an important primary source, though marked by special pleading.

ENGLE, CLAIR (1911–65), born in Bakersfield, became district attorney of Tehama County before being elected to Congress as a Democrat (1943–59) and then to the U.S. Senate (1958–65). A large man-made lake in northwest Trinity County was named for him.

English in California, see *British in California.*

EPIC, acronym for "End Poverty in California," the slogan and program of Upton Sinclair♦ during his campaign for the governorship in 1934.

Equalization, See *Board of Equalization.*

ERICSON, AUGUSTUS WILLIAM (1848–1927), Swedish-born photographer of his home town, Arcata, and of people and places in Humboldt County and of California down to Monterey from the 1880s to his death. A collection of his work was published in 1975.

Esalen Institute, educational organization (est. 1962) near Big Sur, derived its name from that of former Indian inhabitants. Combining humanistic psychology of the Occident and philosophy of the Orient, it aimed at expanding individual sensitivity through psychedelic perception, meditation, and intense sensory experience. Its program, expanded to a San Francisco branch, included workshops and seminars. Its following waned in the 1970s.

ESCALANTE, SILVESTRE VÉLEZ DE (*fl.*1776), Franciscan priest dispatched (July 1776) with his colleague, Francisco Dominguez, by the Mexican government to open a route between Santa Fe and Monterey. They followed a trappers' trail northwest, then pioneered their own route on what came to be called the Old Spanish Trail,♦ reaching the Colorado River on the present Utah-Arizona boundary. This "Crossing of the Fathers" was ended when cold weather in October forced them to turn back.

ESCHSCHOLTZ, JOHANN FRIEDERICH, see *Chamisso, Adelbert.*

ESHERICK, JOSEPH (1914–), Philadelphia-born architect, moved to San Francisco in the late 1930s and, after work with Gardner Dailey, began his own practice. He became a professor at the University of California, Berkeley, in the 1960s and was among the builders of the rural residential community of wooden houses with shed roofs at Sea Ranch on the Mendocino coast. His other works include Adlai Stevenson College at the University of California, Santa Cruz, and The Cannery in San Francisco.

ESPINOSA, prominent early California family whose forebear was José Joaquin Espinosa, a soldier on the Sacred Expedition. He was married to a member of the Lugo family, like himself, from Sinaloa.

Esplandián, see *Sergas de Esplandián, Las.*

Esselen (or Esalen), Indians of the Hokan family resident in the hinterland Carmel River and Big

Sur country down to Point Lopez. They numbered only 500 to 1,000 in prehistoric times. Their name survives in the Esalen Institute♦ of Big Sur.

Estancia, ranch for livestock operated by the missions some distance from their main establishments. Some of them included chapels. There were eleven *estancias* founded between 1785 and 1840.

Estanislao, see *Stanislaus.*

Estero Bay, large lagoon on the central coastline of San Luis Obispo County whose interior portion is Morro Bay. The name (English, "estuary") dates to the expedition of Costansó (1769).

ESTUDILLO, prominent early California family whose founder, José Maria Estudillo, arrived (1806) as a soldier. His sons, born at the Monterey presidio, were José Joaquin (1800–52), *alcalde* of San Francisco (1836), on whose *rancho* south of Oakland the town of San Leandro was laid out (1854) by his son-in-law, William Heath Davis; and José Antonio (1805–52), a *ranchero* and official in present Riverside and San Diego counties. Marcelina Estudillo married William A. Gale.♦

Ethnic groups, contributed to the culture of California from the earliest times of European settlement, since the region was colonized by persons of diverse racial backgrounds. Thus, the 44 original settlers of Los Angeles (1781) included many Mexicans from Sinaloa who were black or Indian or of mixed background. However, despite limited colonization by Russians in the north and the settlement of a few British in the 1820s and some French in the 1830s, along with occasional Belgians, Danes, Irish, and other Europeans, the culture of the Spanish and Mexicans clearly dominated California.

Americans became more and more frequent settlers and increasingly influential during the first half of the 19th century as they pioneered in business and ranching and married into the families of established *Californios.* The discovery of gold quickly sent venturesome people from relatively accessible regions, such as Sonorans and Chileans, and they were soon followed by great numbers from European nations which had been little represented, including Germans, Poles, Irish, Welsh, Italians, and Portuguese; Scandinavians, including Finns, Norwegians, and Swedes; and some Swiss—whose previous, very early settler was the most important northern European of all, John Sutter.

From across the Pacific came Australians, who were notorious for their Sidney Ducks, and Chinese, most of whom were brought under a system of virtual bondage to their importing employers. They all contributed to the cultural diversity of the mining towns and camps, as evidenced by such place-names as Sonora Bar, Chili Camp, Dutch Flat, Irishtown, Italian Gulch, Portuguese Flat, Norwegian Mine, Swiss Bar, and Chinee Camp. They also made San Francisco a remarkably cosmopolitan city, known for its French restaurants, German and Italian opera, Chinatown, and much other ethnic variety. They were sustained by patriotic groups who had their own social clubs, celebrated their own national holidays, and often even created their own institutions, ranging from banks to hospitals bearing names of different nationalities.

However, the diversity of ethnic groups also led to racial conflict, generally involving Americans, but sometimes inspired by other peoples, as when the Irish, led by Denis Kearney, trumpeted "The Chinese must go!" in the bitter competition for jobs during the 1870s. As the white population grew, it overwhelmed the native Indians, who were reduced by more than two-thirds between 1846 and 1870 as a result of massacres and attacks by whites and susceptibility to alien diseases. In the latter part of the 19th century most ethnic groups, other than Indians, slowly but surely became absorbed into a common American culture, although some, like the Portuguese and Norwegians, tended to isolate themselves by pursuing traditional Old World occupations, such as fishing.

Occasionally, the continuance of an ethnic culture and its practice in an essentially separate community, like that of the Chinese in Chinatown, reflected the limited desire for integration by both the smaller and the larger society. Such separatism occurred too among settlers from lands which had not previously been the source of much immigration. The Japanese, who only began to arrive in large numbers after 1890, were the most striking example, but it was evident also among Greeks, as well as Danes and Armenians, who founded their own colonies in Solvang and Fresno, respectively. In the 20th century still other ethnic groups began to go to California in large numbers because of improved economic opportunities.

After the first decade, Mexicans moved north as agricultural workers and in time established their own sense of identity through their Chicano culture. Many Filipinos were attracted after the Immigration Act of 1924 excluded Japanese. Blacks, although present in noteworthy numbers earlier in the 20th century, did not become a truly significant element until shipyards and other defense industries recruited them to fill jobs during World War II. Although numerically far less consequential, other ethnic groups went to California during and after the war. Among them were Russians, Basques from the French Pyrenees, Austrians, Hungarians following their revolution of 1956, and fairly substantial numbers of Poles and Swedes from other parts of the U.S. Second or continuing waves of other ethnic groups also went to California, and its population grew greatly during the 1950s and 60s.

The civil rights movements which concentrated on the needs and demands of blacks during those decades not only had the effect of improving their situation and leading the way for them to achieve important positions in government, business, and professions, but it occasioned other ethnic groups to oppose discrimination while at the same time working for the preservation of their own cultures and the recognition of their significance and dignity. (*See also individual entries.*)

Eucalyptus, the blue gum tree native to Australia, is the most common in California of some 300 species known in its original home. Its introduction to California, where it has naturalized itself with great success, is often attributed to William Taylor,◆ a missionary who sent seeds to his wife (1863), but William C. Walker's Golden Gate Nursery (San Francisco) advertised seedlings in 1856 and other nurserymen soon followed. William Wolfskill is said to have been the first southern Californian to cultivate the trees in the 1860s. Later great stands were planted commercially for hardwood and oil, but proved of unsuitable, inferior quality, and extensive planting generally ended by the 1880s. Nevertheless they have become a characteristic feature of large parts of the California landscape. Stands of trees in the Oakland and Berkeley hills were killed by frost (1972–73), and, because they were a fire hazard, they had to be logged with federal and state funds.

Eureka, city on Arcata and Humboldt bays in Humboldt County and its county seat, founded (1850) as a port and shipping center, first for the Klamath mines, since then for lumber. It remains the major port between San Francisco and the Columbia River. An outpost in Wiyot Indian territory, Fort Humboldt was built there (1853) as a garrison, and its officers included (1854) young Capt. Ulysses S. Grant. There was a dreadful massacre of Indian women and children (1860) when the men were away hunting and fishing, an outrage condemned by Bret Harte, then a newspaperman at Arcata. Similar xenophobia led to the ousting of the city's Chinese in 1885. The modern city recalls better parts of its past by preserving the great mansion of William Carson, a Victorian lumber baron of the 1880s, which is a monument of jigsaw Gothic architecture. The city also includes Sequoia Park, a large grove of redwood trees. In 1970 the city had a population of 24,337.

EVANS, ALBERT S. (1831–72), New Hampshire-born journalist on the *Alta California* staff and correspondent for the *New-York Tribune* and the Chicago *Tribune,* was the subject of satirical attack by rival newspaperman Mark Twain, who referred to him only by his pseudonym, Fitz Smythe. Evans wrote attractive sketches of the local scene and life in *A la California* (1873) and a book about a visit to Mexico, *Our Sister Republic* (1870).

EVANS, LEE (1948–   ), track star, born in Fresno, established the world's record for 400 meters (43.8 sec.) in the 1968 Olympic Games, at which he also helped set the 1,600-meter relay record. Like his teammate Tommie Smith,◆ he gave a Black Power salute on the official victory platform at the Games, but unlike Smith, he was not disciplined for the act.

EVERSON, WILLIAM (1912–   ), began his poetic career as a student at Fresno State College upon discovering Robinson Jeffers' writings. Everson's early poems (1934–40) were later collected in *Single Source* (1966). During World War II he was a conscientious objector and while at a camp in Waldport, Oregon, he founded the Untide Press to print poetry, a forerunner of the far more distinguished typography he achieved on a handpress directly after the war. His *War Elegies* (1943) and *The Waldport Poems* (1944) were followed by more mature works, still showing an appreciation of Jeffers and using a regional imagery, but marked by an intense Christian character and passionate exaltation. In 1951 he joined the Dominican order as a lay brother, employing the name Brother Antoninus. His poems of those years were collected in *The Residual Years* (1948), *A Privacy of Speech* (1949), *Triptych for the Living* (1951), *The Crooked Lines of God* (1959), and *The Hazards of Holiness* (1962), among other volumes. His twentieth book, but first sustained prose work, was *Robinson Jeffers: Fragments of an Older Fury*

(1968). In 1971 he left the Dominican order and entered upon a university teaching career while still continuing to write poetry of power and distinction. His prose includes *Archetype West* (1976), a personal view of the Pacific Coast as a literary region.

EWER, FERDINAND C[ARTWRIGHT] (1826–83), after attending Harvard, went to California (1849), where he became a journalist, first as editor of the *Pacific News,* later as editor (1854–55) of the *Pioneer,*♦ the state's first literary monthly, in which he published works by Dame Shirley, J. S. Hittell, and Frank Soulé. In 1857 he became an Episcopalian minister and after leaving San Francisco for New York (1860) was known for his opposition to extremes of Protestantism and for his desire to unite Roman, Greek, and Anglo-Catholicism, expressed in *Sermons on the Failure of Protestantism and on Catholicity* (1869).

Examiner, see *Los Angeles Examiner* and *San Francisco Examiner.*

Exeter, farming community in Tulare County, a center for packing and shipping oranges, grapes, and dried fruit. It was the site of a riotous attack by whites on Filipino laborers in 1929. The name was given by pioneers from the area around Exeter, England.

Exploration of California by Europeans, begun with the discovery of Baja California by Fortún Jiménez of the expedition of Cortés (1533) and his dispatch of Ulloa (1539–40) on a voyage to the head of the Sea of Cortés which proved that land to be a peninsula, not an island, even though the island legend lasted a long time, like that which associated the region with the mythical California of *Las Sergas de Esplandián.* Further exploration was carried out by Hernando de Alarcón, who sailed up the Colorado River (1540), perhaps to Alta California; Melchior Díaz, whose quest of the Seven Cities of Cíbola under Coronado took him up that river and probably on to Alta California (1540); and Francisco de Bolaños, who, on the same search, voyaged around both sides of the peninsula (1541).

The first known European discoverer of Alta California was Juan Rodríguez Cabrillo, whose vessels took him to the Santa Barbara Islands, where he died (1543). The next European landing

in Alta California was that of Francis Drake (1579), who claimed it for Queen Elizabeth. Spanish knowledge of the region was extended by navigators of the Manila galleons, including Pedro de Unamuno, who put into land (1587), and Sebastián Cermeño, who made several landings (1595).

More formal exploration, particularly of Monterey, was made by Sebastián Vizcaíno (1602–03). Explorations by land, as the initial stage of the settlement of Alta California, took a long time, though missions were founded in Pimería Alta by Father Kino beginning in 1687 and in Baja California by Father Salvatierra (1690) and Father Ugarte. The exploration and settlement of Alta California was begun by the Sacred Expedition of Portolá and Serra (1769) from Baja California and Anza's opening of a land route from Sonora to Monterey (1774) and to San Francisco (1776).

The interior valleys and mountains of California remained almost unknown despite limited exploration by Gov. Fages and more by one of Anza's soldiers, Gabriel Moraga, who also opened trade with the Russians, themselves explorers and then settlers along the northern coast, near Fort Ross (1808–12). The knowledge of the eastern land approaches to California, the Sierra, and Yosemite came from trappers and adventuresome U.S. mountain men like James O. Pattie, Jedediah Smith, and Joseph R. Walker, the formal explorer Frémont, and early emigrants like the Bartleson-Bidwell Party (1841). Both naval and overland routes were also explored by Charles Wilkes (1841). (*See also individual entries.*)

Exploratorium, privately directed and funded science museum housed in the Palace of Fine Arts,♦ San Francisco. Opened (1969), under the direction of Frank Oppenheimer, brother of J. Robert Oppenheimer, it features lively exhibits on basic scientific principles and offers classes for adults and children.

Exposition Park, Los Angeles recreational area (114 acres) southwest of City Hall, until 1910 the site of agricultural fairs. It includes a Museum of Science and Industry, a Museum of Natural History, and the Memorial Coliseum (95,000 seats) in which the Olympic Games of 1932 were held. The University of Southern California adjoins the Park.

Expositions, frequently held in California in the form of local fairs or the annual State Fair♦ founded in 1854, have included San Francisco's California

Midwinter Exposition♦ (1894) in Golden Gate Park, which achieved international recognition, as did the Panama-Pacific Exposition (1915) in San Francisco, the Panama California Exposition in San Diego (1915–16), the California Pacific Interna-tional Exposition, also in San Diego (1935), and the Golden Gate International Exposition on Treasure Island in San Francisco Bay (1939).

Express companies, see *Overland stages.*

FACTOR, MAX (1877–1938), born in Poland, went to America (1904), and four years later settled in Los Angeles. There he created makeup for the earliest film stars. From his successful service for actresses he went on to establish a leading business in the manufacture and sale of cosmetics.

FAGES, PEDRO (1730–94), left his native Catalonia for Mexico (1767) as an infantry lieutenant and in 1769 was made military head of the seagoing part of the Sacred Expedition from Baja California to Alta California under the leadership of Portolá.◆ Later that year he was with Portolá's party which discovered San Francisco Bay. Fages became governor when Portolá left (1770), and even after Barri set up government in Baja California (1771) he continued as *gobernante,* or commanding officer, in Alta California, although he could otherwise be considered Barri's lieutenant governor.

Fages led expeditions through the Salinas and Santa Clara valleys to the east side of San Francisco Bay. His contention that he did not have enough soldiers to protect the additional missions Serra proposed to establish led to such a severe rift between the two leaders that Serra traveled to Mexico City (1773) to plead his cause and to ask for Fages' removal. In 1774 Fages was ordered to new posts, including service in the wars against the Apache, but in 1782 he was reappointed governor of California and arrived there the next year.

This time he was accompanied by his wife, Doña Eulalia, a lively young aristocrat who could not bear the crudity of their capital, Monterey, nor the poverty of the Indians. For a time she made her husband's life miserable as she sought to have him give up his post or be removed from it, creating a scandal by her demand for a divorce, based in part on a charge that he had had relations with an Indian girl. But in time she settled down and bore Fages two California-born children.

He finally gave up the governorship in 1791 to spend his last years in Mexico. His manuscript, "A Historical, Political and Natural Description of California" (1775), was translated by Herbert I. Priestley and published in 1937.

FAIR, JAMES G[RAHAM] (1831–94), was brought from his native Ireland to the U.S. (1843) and joined the gold rush in 1849. Placer mining and an understanding of quartz mining made him a well-to-do mine- and mill-owner before he became a superintendent of Nevada mines and then, in association with Flood, Mackay, and O'Brien, one of the enormously wealthy developers of the Comstock Lode. Like other bonanza millionaires, he persuaded the Nevada legislature to elect him to the U.S. Senate (1881–87). He was a colorful figure in San Francisco, where he owned extensive property. Though he and his wife were divorced and his daughters reared by his ex-wife, nevertheless they made great marriages, one to W. K. Vanderbilt, Jr., brother of the Duchess of Marlborough. Another daughter, Mrs. Herman Oelrichs, built the Fairmont Hotel (opened 1907) in his honor. He had planned to build a mansion on the site.

FAIRBANKS, DOUGLAS, stage name of Douglas Elton Ulman (1883–1939), popular star of silent films, long married to Mary Pickford◆ with whom he established their home, Pickfair, the most prestigious and one of the grandest mansions of the film colony in Beverly Hills. With her and with Charlie Chaplin and D. W. Griffith he founded the independent studio, United Artists. His many swashbuckling roles included *The Mark of Zorro* (1921), adapted from a romance set in Spanish California by Johnston McCulley; *The Three Musketeers* (1921); and *The Thief of Bagdad* (1924). DOUGLAS, JR. (1909–), his son, played in similar motion pictures beginning in 1920. He retired after World War II naval service, moved to England, and there was knighted.

Fairfax, suburban residential community in Marin County with nearby camping areas, named for Charles, Lord Fairfax, who went to California in the gold rush and settled in an elaborate home with his bride on the site of the present town (1856).

Fairfield, seat of Solano County, replacing Benicia (1858). It is also the business community for nearby Travis Air Force Base. The population in 1970 was 44,146.

Fairmont Hotel, located on the Nob Hill site in San Francisco that James G. Fair◆ had selected for the mansion he did not live to build. His daughter, Mrs. Herman Oelrichs, constructed in his honor the grand neoclassical edifice, which on the eve of its opening was gutted by the fire following the earthquake of 1906. It was opened a year later. A 29-story tower added in 1961 has been described as a "contemporary-anywhere hotel."

Fallen Leaf Lake, located just southwest of Lake Tahoe in El Dorado County, presumably named by Whitney's survey (1860) for its appearance from surrounding peaks. It is a summer resort area.

Family Club, men's social club of San Francisco, founded (1900) by Hearst newspapermen who resigned from the Bohemian Club♦ when it canceled its subscription to the *Examiner* as a protest against the publication of a poem by Ambrose Bierce that seemed to call for the assassination of President McKinley. Like the larger Bohemian Club, the Family (as members call it) emphasizes music, drama, and other arts and has a summer encampment grounds on the Peninsula near Woodside. The antipathy between the two clubs has long since disappeared and now they not only share many members but provide special entertainments for one another.

Fandango Pass, route (6,250 ft. elevation) through the Warner Mts. of northeast Modoc County, allowing travel between Nevada and Oregon through the corner of California. Its name, like that of the neighboring valley, creek, and mountain, is said to come from some forty-niners whose camp there was so cold one night that they had to dance to keep warm.

Fanega, a Spanish measure of grain and seed equal to 1.58 U.S. bushels; also, a Mexican land measure equal to 8.81 acres. A *fanega* contained 12 *almuds.*

FANTE, JOHN (1909–), Colorado-born author, long resident in California, where his novels of Italian life, *Wait Until Spring, Bandini* (1938) and *The Brotherhood of the Grape* (1977), are set. His other works include *Ask the Dust* (1939); *Full of Life* (1952); *Bravo Burro* (1969); and a collection of stories, *Dago Red* (1940); as well as the scripts for many motion pictures.

Farallones, The, Spanish term for "small rocky islands," used as the name of the 7 Farallon Islands about 30 miles off San Francisco Bay. Drake called

them Islands of Saint James when he landed there (1579), and Vizcaíno named them Los Frayles (The Friars) but referred to them as being "farallones." In the early 19th century Russians established a station there from which they hunted and nearly exterminated seal♦ that flourished in the nearby waters. William A. Gale was an early hunter from the U.S. In the 1850s Americans collected gull and murre eggs by the tens of thousands to sell in San Francisco. A lighthouse was installed in 1855. In 1909 the islands were made a bird sanctuary, and since 1856 they have been a part of the city and county of San Francisco.

FARLEY, JAMES THOMPSON (1829–86), Virginia-born figure in Democratic party politics of California, to which he moved in 1850. There he was a lawyer, Speaker of the state Assembly, state Senator, and U.S. Senator (1879–85).

Farm Bureau Federation, see *California Farm Bureau Federation.*

Farm labor, see *Agricultural labor.*

FARNHAM, ELIZA W[OOD BURHANS] (1815–64), married to Thomas Jefferson Farnham.♦ Their life in Illinois provided background for her *Life in Prairie Land* (1846), but instead of accompanying him on his travels west she became interested in feminism and prison reform, serving as matron of women at Sing Sing (N.Y.). After his death she sailed to San Francisco (1849) to settle his estate, chaperoning a few proper, unmarried women to help bring the decorum of feminine values to California during the gold rush. Of the voyage and her experiences in California to 1856, where she married again and divorced, she wrote in *California, In-doors and Out* (1856). The rest of her life was spent in the East working on women's causes and social reforms.

FARNHAM, THOMAS JEFFERSON (1804–48), moved from Illinois to Oregon (1839), which he petitioned the U.S. to protect and which he described, with other regions, in his *Travels in the Great Western Prairies . . .* (1841). After a period in the eastern U.S. he went to San Francisco (1846?) to practice law and wrote a sensational account in *Life and Adventures in California* (1846). His wife was Eliza W. B. Farmham.♦

FARNSWORTH, PHILO T[AYLOR] (1906–71), went to San Francisco (1925) from his native Utah to extend his career as a scientific inventor. There he developed his techniques of electronic projection of pictures, the forerunner of modern television, achieving the first transmission in 1927. Russell Varian contributed aid on the lighting of the screen. In the 1930s Farnsworth moved his laboratory and manufacturing plant out of California.

FARQUHAR, FRANCIS P[ELOUBET] (1887–1974), Massachusetts-born writer about California and its mountains after he moved to the Bay Area (1910). His works include an edition of the journal of William H. Brewer (1930) and a *History of the Sierra Nevada* (1965).

FARR, ALBERT (1871–1945), Nebraska-born architect, practiced in San Francisco from the 1890s, specializing in residences, many in Tudor style. His most famous building was Jack London's Wolf House, burned down on the eve of its completion.

Father-President, see *President-General.*

Fault lines, see *Earthquakes.*

FAUST, FREDERICK [SCHILLER] (1892–1944), popular writer, born in Seattle, and reared in California. After attending the University of California he became a professional writer of adventure stories. He achieved tremendous success, turning out fiction at such a pace that in his relatively short career he wrote some 30,000,000 words and often had several stories in the same issue of a journal as well as several books printed in one year. His annual output was sometimes the equivalent of 25 novels. For that reason he used 19 pseudonyms, the best known being Max Brand, under which he published his popular cowboy novel *Destry Rides Again* (1930) and a series about Dr. Kildare. These were among his many works to be dramatized for radio, television, and motion pictures, but he was prouder of his romantic poetry, such as *Dionysus in Hades* (1931).

FAVILLE, WILLIAM B., see *Bliss, Walter.*

FEARS, TOM (1923–   ), Los Angeles-born football player, a star end on the UCLA team (1946–47), who was selected as an All-American. He later played for the Los Angeles Rams (1948–56), finishing his career with 400 receptions and 5,000 yards gained. He became the first coach of the California Sun of the World Football League (1974).

Feather River, rising at the base of Mt. Lassen and along the Sierra, has three forks—North, Middle, and South—that meet near Oroville. At Marysville the river is joined by the Yuba and, farther south, by the Bear. The Feather River empties into the Sacramento just north of the meeting point of Sutter, Yolo, and Sacramento counties. It was said to have been named (1817) El Rio de las Plumas by Luís Argüello for the bird feathers (perhaps only pollen) he saw on the water. Sutter later claimed he gave the name and that he chose it because of the local Indians' great use of feathers. Frémont camped on the river just before setting out on the Bear Flag Revolt, and the river became famous during the gold rush as the site of many mining camps, including Rich Bar, remembered because of Dame Shirley, and Bidwell Bar. It was later the site of much hydraulic mining which clogged the river bed and caused floods. The first wagon route through the region was blazed by J. B. Beckwourth and is named for him. Power developments on the river created Lake Almanor♦ for the Great Western Electric Power Co.♦ and were expanded after 1960 with the construction of Oroville Dam (tallest in the U.S.) as part of the California Water Plan.

FÉLIX, prominent early California family whose founder, José Vicente Félix, was with Anza's expedition (1774). He brought along his wife and seven children. She died en route giving birth to the youngest. He was a founder of the Los Angeles pueblo and owned a *rancho* in its area. The name is also spelled Feliz, as in the boulevard near Griffith Park (L.A.), the site of their property.

FELTON, CHARLES NORTON (1828–1914), moved to California (1849) from his native Buffalo (N.Y.), was elected as a Republican to Congress (1885–89), and appointed to fill the U.S. Senate vacancy (1891–93) left by the death of George Hearst. With Lloyd Tevis, he was one of the early developers of oil♦ in the state. A town in Santa Cruz County and a redwood grove in Humboldt County were named in Felton's honor.

FERGUSON, ALEXANDER (1821?–*c*.80), Virginia-born, after his arrival in California in the 1850s became a leader of the black community. As a captain of the first known black military group of the West (organized in San Francisco, 1863), he visited President Lincoln (1864), and was also briefly an editor of the *Elevator,* founded by P. A. Bell.♦

FERGUSSON, HARVEY (1890–1973), New Mexico-born author, most of whose fiction is set there, but who was in later life long a resident of Berkeley. He is best known for his trilogy of novels about the Southwest: *Blood of the Conquerors* (1921), *Wolf Song* (1927), and *In Those Days* (1929). *Home in the West* (1945) is autobiographical.

FERLINGHETTI, LAWRENCE (1920–), New York-born publisher and poet, after education at the University of North Carolina (A.B.), Columbia (M.A.), and the Sorbonne (Doctorat) and navy service in World War II, he went to San Francisco. There he was a leader of the Beat movement♦ and his City Lights bookshop, said to be the first all-paperback store in the U.S., provided a cultural center for the San Francisco Renaissance,♦ some of whose major writings were printed by its affiliated publishing house. He issued *Howl,* by Allen Ginsberg,♦ causing him to be tried for and acquitted of publishing an obscene work. His own poetry includes *Pictures of the Gone World* (1955), *A Coney Island of the Mind* (1958), and *Starting from San Francisco* (1961), poems; *Her* (1960), a novel; and *Routines* (1964), short plays.

Fermin, Cape, the westernmost part of the entry to San Pedro Bay (L.A. County), was named by Vancouver (1792) to honor Fermin Lasuén, the padre who was then President-General♦ of the missions.

FERNALD, CHESTER B[AILEY] (1869–1938), Boston-born author who lived in California (1889–98), later was an expatriate in England, and wrote short stories about San Francisco's Chinatown, collected in *The Cat and the Cherub* (1896), and sea tales, collected in *Under the Jack-Staff* (1903).

Fernandeño, see *Gabrileño* and *San Fernando College.*

FERNÁNDEZ DE SAN VICENTE, AGUSTÍN (*fl.* 1822–23), canon of the cathedral of Durango, Mexico, selected by Iturbide,♦ in his capacity as Emperor Agustín I, to be his commissioner to the Californias. Fernández went to Monterey in Sept. 1822 and spent the rest of the year in Alta California overseeing the government and the missions. He also arranged that Gov. de Sola's successor be the Mexican-born Luís Argüello rather than a Spaniard.

FERRAN, AUGUSTO (1813–79), Spanish artist, went to California in the gold rush. He painted vivid depictions of California life and landscapes, and collaborated with J. Baturone on a set of colored lithographs of *Tipos Californianos* (Havana, 1849).

FERRARO, JOHN (1924–), football player born in Cudahy (L.A. County) who played tackle for the University of Southern California, competing in three Rose Bowl games and three times being named an All-American (1944, 46, 47).

FERRELO, BARTOLOMÉ, see *Cabrillo, Juan Rodriguez.*

FERRER, BARTOLOMÉ, see *Cabrillo, Juan Rodriguez.*

Ferries, first employed in the state to transport passengers and supplies during the gold rush. Early commercial lines included one across the Colorado River (1850–77) linking overland trails and San Diego, flatboats run by Robert Semple♦ (1848) between Benicia and Martinez, and the first San Francisco–Oakland vessel (1850). One line, the Contra Costa Steam Navigation Co., plied the Bay for over a century (1852–1957), but the major ferry service (1865 ff.) was a subsidiary of the Central Pacific Railroad (for most of its life known as the Southern Pacific), which connected San Francisco with the eastern transcontinental train terminal on the Oakland shore. In 1903 that line instituted an auto ferry. Its main competitor was the Key Route system (1903–40) of Francis Marion Smith,♦ whose bright orange boats ran from San Francisco to the long key pier of the east shore and transported passengers with greater speed via his connecting interurban train lines, both stimulants to his real estate business. When the Western Pacific completed its transcontinental rail line (1909) it ran boats until 1933, and they, along with almost 30 other lines, eventually carried about 51,000,000 passengers annually.

The only major collision (1901), in a fog off Alcatraz, did not result in any deaths, but inspired the opening of Jack London's *Sea Wolf.* The largest ferries (over 400 feet long) were those of the S. P., which carried entire passenger trains on runs between Benicia and Port Costa, thus cutting the distance between Oakland and Sacramento by more than 50 miles. The longest Bay ferry route covered the 30 miles between South Vallejo and San Francisco in an hour and forty-five minutes. When the Santa Fe Railroad completed its terminus in Richmond it ran ferries to San Francisco (1901–33), and other lines made a run between Richmond and San Rafael (1915–57) until a bridge between those points was opened.

Similarly, the opening of the San Francisco–Oakland Bay Bridge and the Golden Gate Bridge (1936–37) ended ferry service on the Bay until the introduction in the 1970s of smaller boats (including gas turbine ones) which run between San Francisco and Marin County. Introduced late and lasting longer (1886–1969) was the trans-Bay service of the southern part of the state which ran between San Diego and Coronado, long dominated by the Spreckels family.

Ferry Building, edifice on the Embarcadero♦ at the foot of Market St. in San Francisco, a landmark for its long arcaded front and its 235-foot-high clock tower modeled on the Giralda of Seville. Built of gray sandstone from Colusa by A. Page Brown (1898), it withstood the earthquake of 1906 and long served as the major entry point to the city for visitors, including arrivals by overland train to Oakland. With the opening of the Bay Bridge its importance declined and it was used for other purposes. An automobile freeway cutting midway up and directly in front of its façade diminished its symbolic status.

FEUCHTWANGER, LION (1884–1958), prominent German author of historical novels, because of his Jewish heritage left his native country for France (1933), where he was arrested after its occupation. He escaped (1940) to the U.S. and lived in Pacific Palisades from 1941 until his death. There he wrote *Proud Destiny* (1947), about Franklin; *This Is the Hour* (1951), about Goya; and *'Tis Folly To Be Wise* (1953), about Rousseau.

FIELD, CHARLES K[ELLOGG] (1873–1948), born in Vermont, was educated at Stanford, where he wrote *Four-Leaved Clover* (1896) and, with Will Irwin, *Stanford Stories* (1900). He was editor of *Sunset* (1911–25) and, later, a popular radio personality. He wrote several Grove Plays for the Bohemian Club.♦

FIELD, SARA BARD (1883–1974), feminist leader in civil liberties and other liberal activities in the San Francisco Bay area; wife of Charles Erskine Scott Wood;♦ and author of poems published in *The Pale Woman* (1927), *Barabbas* (1932), and *Darkling Plain* (1936).

FIELD, STEPHEN J[OHNSON] (1816–99), born in Connecticut of a distinguished old family, graduated

from Williams College, and studied law prior to moving to California (1849), where he practiced law and served as *alcalde* of Marysville and in the state legislature before becoming Chief Justice of the state Supreme Court. This period is treated in *Reminiscences of Early Days in California* (1881), a dictation made into a book by T. H. Hittell. Appointed to the U.S. Supreme Court by Lincoln, he served the longest term in the Court's history (1863–97), and was famous as a strict constructionist. He decided against anti-Chinese statutes. Another unpopular decision was his finding of fraudulence in the will of U.S. Sen. Sharon submitted by Sarah Althea Hill and holding her in contempt of court along with her attorney (later husband), David Terry,♦ Field's onetime colleague on the California bench. When the two met by chance, Terry slapped Field and threatened to shoot him. Accordingly Field's U.S.-appointed bodyguard, David Neagle, shot Terry dead (1889). Neagle, who was defended by William F. Herrin,♦ was found blameless by the U.S. Supreme Court.

Field crops, see *Alfalfa, Barley, Beans, Corn, Cotton, Hay, Hops, Oats, Potatoes, Rice, Sorghum,* and *Wheat.*

FIELDS, W[ILLIAM] C[LAUDE] (1897–1946), Philadelphia-born Hollywood film star, known for his comic character portrayals of a heavy-drinking antagonist of all conventional virtues and bourgeois behavior. His Hollywood career, begun under the direction of D. W. Griffith (1925), extended over two decades.

Figs, first grown at the missions and then in larger orchards in the 1850s with the introduction of new varieties, were not commercially significant until the 20th century. *Smyrna* and *Kadota* types were imported (1880 and 1890), and the former flourished only when George C. Roeding♦ imported the fig wasp for pollination (1899). California grows most of the nation's figs, and its crop is second only to Italy's. Most of the trees are in the San Joaquin Valley around Fresno, and in 1970 the production from 16,600 acres was worth $5,016,000.

FIGUEROA, JOSÉ (1792–18435), after serving as *comandante general* of Sonora and Sinaloa was appointed *comandante general* and *jefe politico,* or governor, of California (1832) to fill the post vacated by the ousting of Manuel Victoria.♦ He arrived in Jan. 1833 and soon became concerned with the Mexican Congress' order to secularize the missions and also with the related plans of José María Padrés and José María Híjar♦ to import Mexicans under their command as colonists for the mission lands they tried to obtain.

Padrés, a friend of Mexico's acting President Farías, got Híjar named not only chief of colonization but governor of California, but the latter appointment was withdrawn by a new shift of Mexican power to Santa Anna, who sent a special courier in a record-breaking overland trip to tell Figueroa to continue in office. Nevertheless, Padrés and Híjar and their 250 followers apparently plotted to establish colonies on mission lands but were prevented from doing so by Figueroa, who required them to settle either as a group in the northern frontier area of Sonoma, Solano, and Petaluma, partly as a buffer against the Russians, or as individuals in established communities. Continued friction led to his having Padrés and Híjar deported.

On Aug. 4, 1834, Figueroa issued his own proclamation for procedures of secularization,♦ calling for 10 missions to be secularized that year, 6 the next, and the remaining 5 in 1836, with half the property to go to the Indians, toward whom he had always been sympathetic, perhaps because he himself had much Indian blood. Next Figueroa issued an elaborate 180-page *Manifiesto a la república Mexicana* (1835; English text, 1855) from the press of Zamorano, telling the history of his relations with Padrés and Híjar and their proposed colonies and justifying his own actions. Thereafter he worked to establish a garrison and town in the Sonoma Valley to forestall Russian advances. His relatively short term of office was ended by sudden death, but Bancroft considered him to be "the best Mexican governor ever sent to rule California."

Filipinos in California, were attracted in large numbers when the Immigration Act of 1924 excluded Japanese. By 1930 some 35,000 Filipinos were providing cheap agricultural labor in the Central Valley, most being single young men brought from Hawaii for the purpose. In time they came to provide 80% of the asparagus harvesters, but they also entered into hotel and restaurant work. Displaced white laborers attacked them in violent riots at Exeter (1929), Watsonville (1930), in the Salinas lettuce fields (1934), and elsewhere. Many Filipinos left when a bill was passed (1935) granting them free transportation home on the pledge that they would not return. A smaller work force continued as migratory agricultural labor,

as domestics, in restaurants, and in laundries. With the ending of national quotas for immigrants (1965) many Filipinos came to the U.S. again: there were 138,859 in California in 1970.

Fillmore Auditorium, rock music concert hall, established (1966) in an old skating rink of uptown San Francisco, was noted for introducing and popularizing The Jefferson Airplane,♦ The Grateful Dead,♦ and other groups. The producer, Bill Graham,♦ opened a similar hall in New York and, after moving the San Francisco one to a new location (1968), called it Fillmore West. He closed his enterprises in 1971, but a film of major band performances during the last week was released as *Fillmore* (1972). The Auditorium also introduced a new style of poster which in color and design was a kind of psychedelic version of art nouveau.

Fine Arts Museums of San Francisco, see *de Young* and *California Palace of the Legion of Honor*.

FINLEY, CHARLIE O. (CHARLES OSCAR FINLEY) (1918–   ), owner of the Oakland Athletics baseball team, was born in Alabama and lives in Chicago, but since 1968, when he moved his Kansas City Athletics to Oakland, has strongly influenced California sports. His colorful and controversial innovations and activities have led him to be called the P. T. Barnum of baseball. He is also notorious for disputes with his players, the most sensational being the ones in which he lost Catfish Hunter♦ and attempted to sell Vida Blue and other team members. This behavior essentially broke up the team (1975–76) because of financial and contractual disputes. He has also had twelve managers in fifteen years. But he has been successful, the A's becoming winners of three World Series championships in a row (1972–74). Finley also owned the California Golden Seals hockey team (1972–74).

Finns in California, arrived initially as sailors, mainly on English or Russian vessels, during the gold rush. Like other people, most went to the gold mines. Although latecomers were mostly lumbermen, some engaged in seafaring, carpentry, and egg production, settling mainly in San Francisco, Eureka, Fort Bragg, and the northern California coast or in Los Angeles County. The best-known Finn was Capt. Gustave Niebaum, a partner in the seal hunting business of the Alaska Commercial Co.♦ who later retired to found (1868) a successful winery at Inglenook. Immigration from Finland was slight after 1920, and population increase was due mainly to migration from the north central U.S. into the Los Angeles area.

Fir, coniferous tree whose major varieties are *white fir,* found chiefly on the west side of the Sierra Nevada and the Cascades and in southern California at elevations of 3,000 to 10,000 feet, much desired as a Christmas tree, and sometimes growing 200 feet tall; *California red fir,* found at 5,000- to 9,000-feet elevations, also prized as a Christmas tree; *Santa Lucia fir,* found at heights from 2,000 to 4,500 feet in Monterey County and southward on the ocean side of the Santa Lucia Mts.; and *Douglas fir,* named for David Douglas,♦ the early 19th-century Scottish botanist and traveler, sometimes called *Oregon pine,* for it is not a true fir and is found both in California and to the north at elevations from 3,000 to 6,000 feet. After World War II, *Douglas fir* became the major source of California lumber production, used for rough construction and for plywood. It remains the most common Christmas tree derived from the state's forests and forestry.♦

Fish, see *Anchovy, Barracuda, Bass, Cod, Grunion, Halibut, Mackerel, Marlin, Perch, Salmon, Sanddab, Sardines, Shad, Shark, Sole, Steelhead, Swordfish, Trout,* and *Tuna.*

Fisherman's Wharf, port for the small commercial fishing boats, originally sailing vessels, established by Italians, mainly Genoese and Sicilians, in San Francisco during the latter part of the 19th century. Although the catch of crab,♦ shrimp,♦ and fish♦ is sold on the wharfside even today, the area has developed into a tourist center in which the fishing boats, now under power, and still run by Italians, seem no more important than the restaurants and souvenir shops which overcrowd the area.

Fishing, commercial, begun with whaling, in the gold rush era also included some catching and canning of salmon. In the 1870s, partly because of the population influx from Italy, Greece, China, and Portugal, significant expansion of commercial fishing occurred. By the opening of the 20th century the most important catches were salmon, oysters, crabs, and cod, but by 1910 tuna dominated the business and in 1920 sardines began to be the biggest catch, with Monterey then added to San Francisco and Sacramento as a major port. Anchovies, usually reduced to industrial oil or fish meal and also used as a dietary supplement for livestock and poultry, became the next most im-

portant catch. Bass, mackerel, shark, squid, shrimp, and abalone were significant too. Other ports developed in the 20th century include San Pedro, Terminal Island, San Diego, Crescent City, Eureka, and Fort Bragg. Commercial fishing is regulated by the state Department of Fish and Game, founded in 1951 as an outgrowth of licensing and other law enforcement dating back to the 1850s. *(See also individual entries.)*

Fishing, sport, an activity not much pursued by the Spanish or Mexicans, has been popular since gold rush days. With 1,264 miles of coastal shoreline, a good part of which is readily accessible for surf casting, ocean fishing from the shore is a favorite pursuit. The most common, simple form, and one that does not require a license, is to try to hook bass, cod, halibut, mackerel, and other species from public piers. An even simpler form of "fishing" is the quest for grunion♦ on southern California beaches during those seasons when they come ashore to spawn. Far more venturesome is sailing offshore to seek barracuda, tuna, and salmon, the last also sought in rivers during their first year. Fishing in lakes, both natural and man-made and stocked, brings in various fish, including freshwater bass, but the most sought after variety, found in the more mountainous area, is trout.♦ The rivers that flow into the ocean and the Delta are fished for salmon, steelhead, striped bass, and shad. The major stream fishing is for trout of diverse sorts and by various means, ranging from dry fly fishing by sophisticated sportsmen to baiting of hooks with worms and salmon eggs. In 1970 some 2,200,000 fishing licenses were sold in the state.

FITCH, GEORGE K[ENYON] (1826–1906), journalist who went to California (1849), where, with F. C. Ewer,♦ he founded the *Sacramento Transcript* (1850), and the *Placer Times and Transcript* (1851–52). In San Francisco he published the daily *Alta California*♦ (1855–56) and the *Daily Evening Bulletin*♦ (1859–95).

FITCH, HENRY DELANO (1799–1849), born in Massachusetts, went to California (1826) as a ship's master, and settled in San Diego. There, after his naturalization and baptism, he was to marry Josefa, the daughter of the prominent Joaquin Carrillo,♦ but the wedding ceremony (April 1829) was stopped by her Uncle Domingo, an aide to Gov. Echeandía, perhaps because the governor had been an unsuccessful suitor. Aided by the bride's cousin, Pío

Pico, the couple fled and were married (July 1829) in Valparaiso. They returned to San Diego (1830), Fitch was acquitted of forcibly abducting Josefa, and he became a leading figure in local politics and a successful merchant there. He later became a *ranchero* near Healdsburg—where a mountain was named for him—a resident in Sonoma near his brother-in-law, Vallejo, and a San Francisco property owner.

FITCH, THOMAS (1838–1923), born in New York City, went to California (1860), where he became a dynamic lawyer, journalist, and politician. Generally known as "Colonel Tom," he was first a San Francisco newspaperman and an assemblyman, then an editor and district attorney in Virginia City, Nevada, during its Comstock Lode days. There he was elected to Congress (1869–71). Still later he was a member of the Arizona assembly (1879), and he finally settled in Los Angeles (1909) as a real estate promoter. With his wife, Anna M[ariska] Fitch, he wrote *Better Days; or, A Millionaire of Tomorrow* (1891), a fictional fantasy of social reform in which the world's leaders hold a peace meeting at Coronado; she herself wrote a romantic novel, *The Loves of Paul Fenix* (1893).

FITZGERALD, F. SCOTT, see *Last Tycoon, The*.

FLACO, JUAN, see *Brown, John*.

Flag, State, modified from the one designed (1846) by William C. Todd for the Bear Flag Revolt,◆ it has a large brown grizzly bear in its center and a small red star above the bear's head. Below the green ground on which the bear walks are the words CALIFORNIA REPUBLIC in black, with a red stripe at the bottom. It was adopted as the official flag by the legislature in 1911.

Flags of California, prior to the flag accepted by the state legislature in 1911, eleven other flags are said to have been flown over parts of California. They were the standards of the Spanish Empire; England (Cross of St. George); the Spanish national ensign; Russia (Cross of St. Andrew); the Russian-American Co.; Buenos Aires, raised by Bouchard;◆ the Mexican Empire of Iturbide;◆ the Mexican republic; U.S. Topographical Engineers, of which Frémont was a captain; the California Republic of the Bear Flag Revolt; and the U.S. national flag.

FLAVIN, MARTIN (1883–1967), San Francisco-born dramatist and novelist whose successful Broadway plays included *The Criminal Code* (1929). His novel *Journey in the Dark* (1943), about a businessman who achieves wealth but not maturity, won a Pulitzer Prize.

FLEISHHACKER, prominent San Francisco family, founded by Aaron Fleishhacker (1820–98). Born in Germany, he went to California (1853), where he was a merchant in mining towns before moving to San Francisco. There he established a successful wholesale paper and box business and was prominent in the community, becoming a member of the second Vigilance Committee. His sons Herbert (1872–1957) and Mortimer (1866–1953) became bankers in San Francisco and executives of the Great Western Electric Power Co.◆

FLEMING, PEGGY [GALE] (1948–   ), ice skating star, born in San Jose and reared in Pasadena. She was U.S. figure skating champion (1964–68), world skating champion (1964–68), and Olympic gold medal winner (1968). She was noted for her grace and ballet-like style and later had a career as an entertainer.

FLETCHER, BARNEY (1820?–84), born a slave in Maryland, went to Sacramento in the gold rush and there founded the first African Methodist Episcopal church on the Pacific Coast (1850). He remained a prominent clergyman and a leader in civil rights affairs in San Francisco and elsewhere.

FLINT, FRANK PUTNAM (1862–1929), born in Massachusetts, reared in California, where he became a leading Los Angeles lawyer. A Republican, he was elected to the U.S. Senate (1905–11). Flintridge in Los Angeles County was named for him.

FLINT, THOMAS, see *Bixby*.

FLOOD, JAMES C[LAIR] (1826–89), born in New York of Irish immigrant parents, went to California in 1849, and in San Francisco opened a saloon with William S. O'Brien.◆ There the two men picked up mining tips and thus graduated to the stock brokerage business. They controlled Nevada mines at the time of the Big Bonanza, and formed the Consolidated Virginia mine of the Comstock Lode.◆ Four years after quitting saloonkeeping they had an income of more than $500,000 a month. Flood soon built a great estate in Atherton and a substantial sandstone mansion atop Nob Hill which, with modifications by Willis Polk (1911), became the home of the Pacific Union Club. With his partners, Flood established the Nevada Bank (1875), merged after his death with the Wells Fargo Bank.

Floods, see *Disasters.*

FLORES, JOSÉ MARÍA (*fl.* 1842–46), Mexican Army captain who went to Alta California as secretary of Micheltorena♦ (1842) and was sent back to Mexico (1844) as the governor's representative to seek aid in coping with California's anti-centralist rebels. Later José Castro used him to attempt negotiations with Stockton (Aug. 1846) and during the war he was appointed commanding general and governor (Oct. 31, 1846–Jan. 11, 1847) by the *Californios* in their fight against the military command of Los Angeles under Lieut. Archibald H. Gillespie.♦ Flores' forces controlled the area from Santa Barbara to San Diego until Stockton and Kearny seized Los Angeles (Jan. 10, 1847). Flores then fled to Sonora before the surrender to Frémont. Flores later served in the Mexican Army and became its commanding general of the military colonies of the west.

FLORES, JUAN (1836?–57), leader of southern California bandit gang who was seized and publicly hanged in Los Angeles by a vigilante association. The peak in Orange County where he was captured is named for him.

Flour, originally milled in small quantities by the padres, e.g. at Mission San Gabriel (1816), or for neighborhood needs, e.g. by Nathan Spear at Yerba Buena (1839–40)), it was also imported into California, even from places as distant as Chile. By the time of the gold rush larger-scale mills clustered near the bigger cities because of the demand and because wheat could be easily shipped. The earliest major miller was Simon Willard Sperry♦ of Stockton. As the production of wheat♦ increased, so did the flour mills. They were required not only for local use but also for extensive export, because the hard, dry, white California product shipped particularly well. By 1870 the state had 115 mills. In the 1880s the wheat trade and flour business concentrated warehousing, loading, and shipping at Carquinez Strait, and part of Crockett was then known as Wheatport. An oversupply of wheat caused a market collapse in the 1890s, and exports declined from 1,305,000 barrels of flour in

1884–85 to 288,000 barrels in 1910–11. Meanwhile more modern and efficient milling grew up in the Midwest, the new home of wheat raising.

Flower, State, see *State symbols.*

Flower children, see *Hippie movement.*

Flower Drum Song, musical drama (1958) by Richard Rogers and Oscar Hammerstein based on a novel of the same name by Chin-yang Li, deals with the romantic problems of a Chinese American in San Francisco whose father attempts to arrange his marriage with a girl known to him only by a photo. The work was adapted as a film (1961).

Flower growing, commerical, see *Nurseries, horticultural.*

Fog, a thick mist which is a major factor in the climate♦ of California in two areas: the central coast and the Central Valley. Fog occurs along the entire coast, particularly in late spring and early summer, from early evening to midmorning, but is most common north of Point Arguello♦ with Point Reyes♦ the foggiest spot and, indeed, the coolest place in the continental U.S. during midsummer. The ocean waters along the central and north coast are cool because of the California Current♦ and the steady northwest winds that bring subsurface water to the top, and fog occurs when the warm inland air passes over those cool waters and absorbs their moisture. Fog abates in fall, when the Central Valley loses heat. Fog signals are in operation only an average of 261 hours a year at Point Loma, south of San Diego, but increase to 424 hours at Los Angeles harbor, to 906 at San Luis Obispo, and to 1,316 at Point Reyes. The sun shines only 69% of the possible daylight hours in San Francisco, while at the peak of nearby Mt. Tamalpais, above the fog line, it shines 92% of the same hours. Fog in the Central Valley has a different meteorological origin, for it generally occurs when high humidity exists with relatively stable air—usually after a heavy rain—or when moist marine air is trapped by a stagnant high pressure system. Those conditions occur mostly in winter (December and January in particular) and create very dense condensation at ground level. It is called a tule fog because it is met most frequently in the marshy areas of the Valley (tule is the name given to marsh vegetation). Since 1943 the state has been plagued by smog,♦ a combination of smoke and fog occurring most commonly in Los Angeles and other heavily populated areas.

FOLSOM, JOSEPH L[IBBY] (1817–55), West Point graduate who went to San Francisco as a captain and quartermaster in Stevenson's Regiment♦ (1847). He remained and became a rich landowner by buying the properties left at his death by William Leidesdorff,♦ including a *rancho* in present Sacramento County on which the town of Folsom is now located.

Folsom, town founded (1855) on the American River *rancho* owned by Joseph L. Folsom. It was created by Theodore Judah as the eastern terminus of the state's first rail line, the Sacramento Valley Railroad, from which the Central Pacific was extended eastward. It is also the site of a state penitentiary (opened 1880) and of Folsom Dam, whose water is used to irrigate the San Joaquin Valley and to hold back salt water intrusion into the Delta.

Folsom Dam, part of the Central Valley Project,♦ creates Folsom Lake on the American River in Sacramento County. Completed in 1955, it stands 340 feet high and serves to regulate water into the Delta, provide power, control floods, and aid irrigation. About seven miles below the dam is Nimbus Dam, which reregulates the water flow. Associated with the dams are fish hatcheries to replace spawning grounds they cut off. An earlier (1895) Folsom Dam provided the state's first long-distance transmission of electricity.

FOLTZ, CLARA SHORTRIDGE (1849–1934), went to San Jose (1872) where as a young widowed mother of five children she decided to support her family as a lawyer. Upon finding the state bar limited to "white male" citizens, she and Laura Gordon♦ lobbied for a change in the law and were admitted to the state bar (1879), having previously forced the state-funded Hastings College♦ to accept women. In addition to having a successful legal career in San Francisco, San Diego, and Los Angeles, she was a leading suffragette, worked for penal reform and the establishment of public defenders, edited a daily newspaper and magazine, and was a force in Republican party politics, considerably aiding her brother, Samuel Shortridge, U.S. Senator (1921–33).

FONT, PEDRO (d. 1781), Franciscan missionary, born in Catalonia, went to Mexico and then was sent from Sonora to serve as chaplain and cartographer on the second expedition of Anza♦ (1776), which went north to San Francisco. There Font mapped the Bay, sketched some of its islands, took the elevation of the Farallones, and—based on the records

of Crespí and on his own observation—selected the site for the San Francisco presidio. His precise, day-by-day account of the expedition was first translated from the manuscript of his *Short Diary* (1913). The expanded *Complete Diary,* which he wrote out in 1777, was published in 1930.

FONTANA, MARK J. (1849–1922), Italian-born businessman who went to California (1867) where he entered the produce trade. To merchandise the state's produce he formed a syndicate, the California Fruit Canners Association (1899), and then established the California Packing Corp. (1916), which under its trade name, Del Monte, became the largest seller of canned fruit in the U.S. and a leader in food processing.♦

Fontana, San Bernardino County town given its present name (1913) either because of the Spanish word for "fountain" or from some family. It is best known as the site of the state's major steel making.♦

Food processing, an outgrowth of the state's agriculture, began in the post-gold-rush era with the first cannery for fruits and vegetables established (1858) in San Francisco by Francis Cutting, who began shipping fruit east (1862). Although expanded to include salmon by 1864, crude machinery, uncertain procedures, and high freight charges kept the industry small so that the pack of all produce was only 61,000 cases in 1875. Soon thereafter fruit and vegetable processing grew greatly, attaining a pack of 539,000 cases by 1881 and rising to 1,495,000 cases in 1890.

Diversification also increased: commercial packing of asparagus was introduced in 1892 and olive canning and pickling were begun in the 1890s. A San Francisco firm, Hills Bros., originated vacuum packing of foodstuffs, using it first for canned butter (1899), then for coffee and tea (1900). The technique of canning sardines about 1900 led to the creation of Cannery Row♦ at Monterey. Tuna was first canned in 1903 and it soon became a huge business.

Techniques improved at the turn of the century with such inventions as the unwelded sanitary can, and business expanded greatly. Peaches became the largest product in fruit canning, in 1902 accounting for 900,000 of the 2,410,000 cases of fruit packed in the state, by then the major supplier of the world.

Early in the 20th century large corporations were formed to merge all agricultural business, from growing through processing, shipping, and marketing. Thus Mark J. Fontana,♦ an Italian immigrant, founded the California Fruit Canners Association

(1899) and went on to merge four large packing concerns into the California Packing Corp. (1916), which thereafter sold its produce under the trade name Del Monte. By 1965 Del Monte was doing an annual business of $400,000,000.

Similarly, Joseph DiGiorgio, another Italian immigrant, expanded his farming business in the San Joaquin Valley by purchasing the state's largest fruit packing firm, owned by Edwin T. Earl,♦ and by canning, shipping, and marketing under an older and once independent trademark, S&W Fine Foods. Such large-scale enterprises processed food for canning, as dried fruits, and in beverages ranging from orange juice to wine; and, after World War II, they developed a vast frozen food business.

The value of manufactured food and related products grew from nearly $295,000,000 in 1939 to over $4,000,000,000 by 1972.

Football, the game was introduced as English-style soccer in intramural sports at the University of California (1877), but was soon replaced by rugby in a game (1882) against Bay Area residents, including English settlers. American-style football, with 11 men on a side, was initiated by Oscar W. Howard (1886), coaching the University of California team in the game he had played at Harvard. The University of Southern California picked up the game in 1888, but the first intercollegiate contest was between the University of California and St. Vincent's College (now Loyola) in 1889.

American football was abandoned by California and Stanford (1905) after it had become too rough, but the return to soccer did not last and with rule changes the American game was picked up by those teams in 1915 and 1919, respectively. They joined Pacific Northwest institutions to form a Pacific Coast Conference (1920), which was expanded to include other major California universities and colleges until it was replaced (1959) by a new organization intended to avoid professionalism and excesses of competition.

Only when Andy Smith created the Wonder Teams♦ of the University of California in the 1920s did college football in California equal that in other parts of the U.S., as made evident in the Rose Bowl games,♦ begun in 1916. The succeeding popularity and achievements of the game may be measured by the fact that between 1925 and 1975 California has been the home of more All-American players than any other state. Professional football came into being for one year only with the Los Angeles Buccaneers and the Los Angeles Wildcats (1926), not followed until 1937, when another abortive attempt was made to introduce professional play to Los Angeles.

The first major league team went to the state when the Rams♦ moved from Cleveland to Los Angeles (1946). In that year, too, an All-America Football Conference created the Forty-Niners♦ in San Francisco and the Dons♦ in Los Angeles. In 1960 a new league was established, with the Raiders♦ in Oakland and the Chargers♦ in Los Angeles (San Diego after 1961) included.

FOOTE, MARY HALLOCK (1847–1938), New York-born novelist, married a civil engineer (1876) who took her west (1876). In Colorado she wrote *The Led-Horse Claim* (1883), about the local silver boom, and obtained background for *Coeur d'Alene* (1894), another romance. Her last 30 years were spent in Grass Valley, and the state is a setting for *The Prodigal* (1901), *A Picked Company* (1912), *The Valley Road* (1915), and other novels. Her life suggested the plot of *Angle of Repose*♦ by Wallace Stegner.

FORBES, ALEXANDER (*c.* 1778–1864), while a British merchant at Tepic, Mexico, where he was later vice-consul (1847–49), wrote *California: A History of Upper and Lower California* (1839), the first English book wholly devoted to California. Although he had not seen Upper California and drew upon old Spanish sources, Forbes also gathered data on then current conditions. His proposal that British investors write off their bond holdings in exchange for vast tracts of land led Americans to feel they should hurry their own acquisition of California. He is not to be confused with James Alexander Forbes (1804–81), British vice-consul at Monterey (1843–51), who was his nephew. They met when the elder Forbes first visited Alta California (1847) to oversee the mercury mine at New Almaden,♦ operated by his firm, Barron, Forbes & Co.

FORBES, KATHRYN, see *Norwegians in California.*

FORD, HENRY CHAPMAN (1828–94), New York-born artist who moved to Santa Barbara (1875), from which he traveled to make etchings of the missions, a valuable record of their appearance at that time.

FORD, JOHN (1895–1973), a leading film director of Hollywood whose career there began in 1913 and continued for nearly sixty years. His earliest films included an adaptation of Bret Harte's *The Out-*

casts of *Poker Flat* (1919) and *The Prince of Avenue A* (1920), starring the prizefighter, James J. Corbett. Among his major achievements were an adaptation of Liam O'Flaherty's *The Informer* (1935), pertinent to his family's Irish background, and various interpretations of American ways of life, including John Steinbeck's *The Grapes of Wrath* (1940) and many western stories.

Foreign Miners' License Tax, an act passed by the state legislature (1850) requiring miners who were not U.S. citizens to pay $20 monthly to work their claims. It was preceded by informal mining-camp codes, enforced by vigilance committees, which often wholly excluded foreigners from certain areas. An uprising of Mexicans occurred at Sonora (1850), abetted by so many Frenchmen that it was also called a French Revolution. It ended with the expulsion of many foreigners. In 1851 the original tax was repealed but a more moderate one was soon enacted. The original law was aimed mainly at Mexicans (both native-born and immigrants from Sonora), Chileans, and other Spanish-speaking persons; the second one was directed specifically against the Chinese.

FOREMAN, GEORGE (1949–), Texas-born boxing champion, resident of California after 1966. He won the Olympic Games heavyweight championship (1968) and held the professional heavyweight championship of the world (1973–74).

Forest fires, major hazards of the state because the long dry season comes to a climax in the fall and because the southern part of the state is subject to the intensely hot Santa Ana winds.♦ Except for the fire following the San Francisco earthquake of 1906 the most severe fires of the state have been in its forests and its brush-covered hills. Some of the worst in modern times have been the Matilija Canyon fire (Sept. 1932), which ravaged nearly 220,000 acres of Ventura and Santa Barbara counties; the Griffith Park fire in Los Angeles (1933), in which 29 firemen died; the Haystack fire (Sept. 1955), which destroyed over 63,500 acres of timber in Siskiyou County; the Weferling Fire (July 1960), which ravaged 50,000 acres of watershed of the Nacimiento Reservoir in Monterey County; the Hanly and Coyote fires (Sept. 1964), which simultaneously devastated over 50,000 acres of Napa and Sonoma counties and almost 65,000 acres of the Santa Ynez Mts., threatening the city of Santa Barbara; the Santa Monica Mts. fire (Nov. 1961), which swept into Bel Air; two fires of Sept. 1970, the Laguna in

San Diego County, which burned over 175,000 acres, and the Clampert-Guiberson-Wright blaze, which swept through more than 147,000 acres of Los Angeles and Ventura counties; and the fire of some 100,000 acres in the Ventura National Wilderness near Big Sur (1977). The California Division of Forestry and the U.S. Forest Service are the main agencies concerned with preventing and controlling fires. Their equipment includes helicopters and converted military airplanes, often called borate bombers.

FORESTIERE, BALDESARE, see *Fresno.*

Forest Lawn Memorial Park, cemetery of several hundred acres located in Glendale. Conceived (1917) by Hubert C. Eaton, a banker, upon his acquisition of the original old graveyard on which he had foreclosed, it is intended to be elegantly reverential but not depressing. Burial plots are inconspicuous because markers must be laid flat, but other adornment is ostentatiously evident in the landscaped grounds whose various subdivisions bear such names as Slumberland, Vale of Memory, and Whispering Pines. The elaborate art includes reproductions of all Michelangelo's major works, a stained-glass version of da Vinci's painting of the Last Supper, a painting of the crucifixion (44 feet high by 195 feet long), facsimiles of Ghiberti's Baptistry doors in Florence, and a sculptured Duck Baby, called the Spirit of Forest Lawn. Buildings on the grounds include a vast mausoleum; an 87-foot-high Tower of Legends; the Little Church of the Flowers, a copy of the 14th-century English church about which Gray wrote his famous elegy; the Wee Kirk o' the Heather, a reproduction of the church where Annie Laurie worshipped and itself very popular for weddings; and the actual old Roman temple of Santa Sabina, now housing the remains of Edgar L. Doheny. Other famous Californians interred there include Carrie Jacobs Bond, Will Rogers, and Aimee Semple McPherson. A subsidiary cemetery in Hollywood emphasizes colonial American themes. *The Loved One,* a satirical novel by Evelyn Waugh, is said to have been suggested by Forest Lawn and cemeteries that imitated it.

Forests and forestry, important concerns of California since about 17,000,000 of the state's 100,000,000 acres are timber forests of fir,♦ redwood,♦ Douglas fir,♦ and pine.♦ The main forest belt starts north of San Francisco, continues along the Coast Range into Oregon, east across northern California, and then south along the Sierra to

Bakersfield, with smaller stands in the Santa Cruz Mts., the Santa Lucia Mts., and in ranges north and east of Los Angeles, San Bernardino, and San Diego.

Spanish and Mexican settlers made little use of wood, so lumbering began with Americans: J. B. R. Cooper (Larkin's half-brother) built a water-powered sawmill on the Russian River (1834), Isaac Graham established a power sawmill in the Santa Cruz Mts. (1842), Capt. Stephen Smith created a steam-driven sawmill near Bodega Bay (1844), and John A. Sutter and James Marshall built a mill on the American River (1848) in whose tailrace gold was discovered. The gold rush led to a need for wood for sluices, flumes, and dams, for timbering for tunnels and fences, and for construction of jerry-built towns, so sawmills soon arose in Mendocino, Humboldt, and Santa Cruz counties and in the Sierra.

By 1870 the best and most accessible pine and redwood had been logged from almost 100,000 acres, less than 1% of the state's forests. From 1870 to 1890 less accessible pine stands of the Sierra were cut in the present Plumas National Forest region for timber and for turpentine. The use of flumes— V-shaped troughs holding flowing water—made possible the transport of lumber from the Sierra to Sacramento Valley lumber companies.

From the 1890s to the mid-1930s forest exploitation worsened, as clear cutting without reforestation was common and steam donkey engines and logging railroads caused considerable damage to forests. Concern about depletion and destructive practices led to the creation of a state Board of Forestry (1885) and a State Forester (1905). Forest protection duties were still left largely to the counties under state supervision, and the first forest rangers (1919) were funded by counties.

In the 1930s the federal Civilian Conservation Corps and state labor camps considerably improved fire protection and forest conservation, including protection of timber and watershed land against disease and insects. The 20th century has also seen greatly enhanced protection achieved through the 17 National Forests,♦ which contain about half of the state's commercial forest lands, the National Parks,♦ which protect great groves, the State Forests,♦ which practice conservation and do research, and the State Parks.♦ Private organizations, particularly the Save-the-Redwoods League♦ and the Sierra Club,♦ have also been instrumental in the preservation of the forests.

Meanwhile lumber production has also increased tremendously so that the state is the third largest producer (after Oregon and Washington), having cut fewer than 2,000,000 board feet in 1940 but increasing that to over 5,000,000 in the 1960s, most of it sawn lumber but substantial amounts also for plywood, while residues are used to create pulp for paper. Recognition that old growth was very limited, as well as ecological awareness, have led to more selective cutting and more careful practices in industrial forestry.

FORSTER, JOHN (1814–82), went to San Diego (1833) from his native England as a sailor, later settled down, married the sister of Pío Pico (1837), and acquired vast landholdings, making his headquarters at San Juan Capistrano, whose secularized mission he bought. Some of his property eventually became Camp Pendleton.

Fort Baker, former military post, named for Col. Edward D. Baker,♦ adjacent to Fort Barry (named for a Mexican War and Civil War general) and Fort Cronkhite (named for a World War I general), overlooks the Golden Gate from Marin County. Another Fort Baker was created in Humboldt County during Indian warfare (1862–63).

Fort Barry, see *Fort Baker.*

Fort Bragg, lumbering town in Mendocino County, founded (1885) and taking the name of a military post established on this site (1855) which honored an army officer who was a hero in the Mexican War. It is a terminus of the famous Skunk Railroad.♦ In 1970 its population was 4,455.

Fort Cronkhite, see *Fort Baker.*

Fort Defiance, see *Sagebrush War.*

Fort Gunnybags, name given to the Sacramento St. headquarters of the second Vigilance Committee♦ (1856), founded in San Francisco under William T. Coleman after the murders of James King of William by James Casey and of Gen. W. H. Richardson by Charles Cora. The two culprits were tried and hanged at the Fort.

Fort Irwin, an Army Corps of Engineers base used by the state's National Guard, is located near Barstow.

Fort MacArthur, U.S. Army air defense post in San Diego, founded (1914) and named for Gen. Arthur MacArthur.

Fort Mason, former U.S. Army port in San Francisco, named Black Point when Frémont lived there (1860–61) but renamed (1882) for Col. R. B. Mason♦ because he executed the order to dispossess "squatters," including Frémont, from the military land. In 1973 it became part of the Golden Gate Recreational Area and was demilitarized. It contains an Army Museum displaying materials related to the U.S. Army in California from the time of the Mexican War to the present, and other former military facilities are used for civic, educational, and recreational purposes.

Fort Miley, military reservation of 50 acres near Land's End, San Francisco. It was named for an army officer who died in the Spanish-American War.

Fort Ord, U.S. Army infantry training center, said to be the largest military reservation in the U.S. Located northeast of Monterey, its subposts are the presidio there and Hunter Liggett Military Reservation, near King City. Founded as a Camp in honor of Gen. E. O. C. Ord,♦ it became a Fort in 1940.

Fort Point, San Francisco's most northern promontory into the Bay over which the Golden Gate Bridge approach now runs, was selected by Anza (1776) as a fortification site. In 1794 the Castillo de San Joaquin was built but it fell to ruin by 1835. The U.S. Army constructed a modern military building (1857) with 149 guns to guard the Bay entrance, modeling it on Fort Sumter, Charleston, S.C., but it was declared obsolete in 1905 and has since become an Historic Monument.

Fort Ross, center of settlements of Russians in California,♦ was founded (1812) by their governor, Ivan Alexander Kuskov, who in 1808, two years after Rezanov's visit, was sent by the Russian-American Co. to explore the coast and in 1811 returned to settle it. In addition to carrying on trade, the original 95 Russians, aided by 80 Aleuts, hunted sea otters and obviously thought about establishing a Russian state, to the dismay of Spain, Mexico, and the U.S., whose Monroe Doctrine was issued in 1823. Behind its palisade and blockhouses the Fort's buildings included the governor's residence and a chapel with a Russian-style dome and bells cast in St. Petersburg, and outside were some 50 other structures, including a boathouse and barn for 200 cows. After the sea otters began to be hunted out of existence the Russians withdrew their colonists (1839) and sold the property to Sutter (1841). The

Fort, poetically named for the motherland (Rossiya), was bought (1906) by the *San Francisco Examiner* and presented to the state. All its original buildings were destroyed or damaged by earthquake or fire, but they have been carefully reconstructed, properly furnished, and are now part of a State Historical Monument.

Fort Tejón, founded (1854) on the recommendation of Gen. Edward F. Beale,♦ Commissioner of Indian Affairs for California and Nevada, this military post 36 miles south of present Bakersfield for ten years oversaw nearby Sebastian Indian Reservation, controlled Tejón Pass♦ in the Tehachapi Mt. range, guarded miners, and explored and patrolled the isolated region. Camels♦ were used there from 1857 to 1861. Native flora and fauna were collected and described by Janos Xantus.♦ The Overland Mail Co. and the stagecoach line of John Butterfield♦ had a station there. After the Civil War the army gave up the post, which became part of Gen. Beale's own ranch. In 1939 it became a State Historic Park.

Fortune cookie, pseudo-Chinese pastry, said to have been created in California (*c.* 1920) and now mainly made in family bakeries of San Francisco's Chinatown: some 200,000 cookies are thought to be turned out there daily for local consumption and for export as far off as Japan and Taiwan. A strip of paper on which is printed a message (usually predicting good events) is laid on the baked disk of wheat flour that is then folded by hand before cooling. It is served with dessert.

Forty-niners, gold seekers who went to California during the year after the discovery of gold by James Marshall♦ (Jan. 1848). A massive local rush occurred in 1848, augmented that year by emigration from Oregon, the Sandwich Islands, Mexico, and even South America, but the great influx from the U.S. and other parts of the world was initiated by the message of President Polk to Congress (Dec. 5, 1848) confirming the rich discoveries. Ships from all over the world arrived in San Francisco where sailors deserted and crews and passengers rushed to the gold fields. The forty-niners from the U.S. used three major routes: a combination of sea and land travel down the Atlantic, across the Isthmus of Panama or Nicaragua, often by rail, and up the Pacific; by ship around Cape Horn; and across the plains, Rockies, and Sierra mainly by the California Trail♦ and also by southwestern routes, often using covered wagons. The earliest arrivals by the first route came in late February, the ocean voyagers came in summer, and the overland caravans reached the Mother Lode♦ area in late summer or early fall. Innumerable diaries, letters, and journals of the early migrants have been published; those who wrote specifically of 1849 included Alonzo Delano,♦ J. Goldsborough Bruff,♦ and Sarah Royce.♦ Men descended from persons who arrived in California before 1850 are eligible for membership in the Society of Pioneers.♦

Forty-Niners, San Francisco, professional football team, established 1946, until 1949 a member of the All-American Football Conference, thereafter of the National Football League, whose Western Division championship they won (1970–72). Stars of early teams include Frankie Albert, John Brodie, Leo Nomelini, and Joe Perry. The home field was Kezar Stadium from founding until 1971 when the team moved to Candlestick Point.

Forum, The, circular arena in a Roman style with huge columns in Inglewood, it is the 17,000-seat home ground for the Los Angeles professional basketball team, the Lakers, and its professional ice hockey team, the Kings. It was built (1967) with private financing by Jack Kent Cooke (1912–), the Canadian-born owner of the teams, purchased by him in 1965 and 1967, respectively.

FOSS, CLARK (1820–85), proprietor and driver (1863–85) of a stagecoach line in Napa and Sonoma counties to The Geysers,♦ a popular spa. His hair-raising driving over mountain roads was as memorable a part of one's vacation as the baths in the mineral springs.

FOSTER, STEPHEN CLARK (1820–98), born in Maine, alumnus of Yale, after becoming a trader in Sonora and northern Mexico, joined the Mormon Battalion♦ as an interpreter and with it went to California (1847). He was *alcalde* (1848–49) of Los Angeles and later its mayor (1854–56) and served in the Constitutional Convention (1849). He married into the Lugo family.

Fountain Grove, see *Harris, Thomas Lake.*

FOURGEAUD, VICTOR (1815–75), South Carolina-born doctor, trained in France, who went from Missouri to San Francisco (1847) to practice medicine. His article in Brannan's *California Star* (April 1, 1848) was among the first to announce the discovery of gold. He himself tried mining, made a fortune as a merchant, and served in the legislature.

After a return visit to Paris he brought a cure for diphtheria to California.

FOX, WILLIAM (1879–1952), Hungarian-born film producer whose name originally was Friedman, after success with nickelodeon theaters in New York moved to Hollywood. There he was a major producer of the 1920s, an early developer of talking pictures, the creator of a chain of lavish theaters, and, briefly, the owner of Metro-Goldwyn-Mayer. A federal antitrust suit and overextended finances undid him and he went into bankruptcy (1936) and to prison for trying to bribe a judge (1942). His defenders included Upton Sinclair, who wrote a book on his behalf.

Fox, predatory carnivorous member of the dog family smaller than the wolf (which is very rare in California), whose diverse varieties are classified as *red fox, kit fox, gray fox,* and *island fox.* The *red fox* is the largest (3 feet or longer) and is found on Mt. Lassen, Mt. Shasta, and the Sierra above the 7,000-foot level. The *kit fox,* a little over 1½ feet long, is found mainly in the San Joaquin Valley and the southeastern desert areas. The *gray fox* is medium size, found in the lower mountains and foothills west of the Sierra, and is very scarce in the southeast. The foxes of the Santa Barbara Islands are similar but smaller. All varieties feed on poultry, rabbits, rodents, and young deer, and all are trapped for their pelts.

Foxen Canyon, see *San Marcos Pass.*

Franchise Tax Board, chaired by the controller of the state, is the agency responsible for collecting personal income taxes. Other major taxes are administered by the State Board of Equalization, of which the controller is also a member.

FRANCIS, SAM (1923–), San Mateo-born painter, studied art at the University of California, Berkeley, and the California School of Fine Arts, where he was influenced by David Park. His own canvases of abstract forms, generally large, give the sense of richly colorful cloud formations in illuminated spaces.

Franciscans, religious order founded by St. Francis of Assisi, became the first missionaries in the New World when representatives accompanied Columbus' second voyage (1493). Early established in Mexico, they came to Baja California as missionaries under Junípero Serra (1769) when the

Jesuits were expelled from the peninsula, and they remained until 1773 when they were replaced by the Dominicans. In 1769 under Serra they were the religious element of the Sacred Expedition♦ of Gálvez to Alta California, where they established the missions.♦ They had been trained at the College of San Fernando♦ in Mexico. They were sometimes called Grey Friars because of the color of their habit, altered by Pope Leo XIII (1897) to the present brown. Father Engelhardt♦ was the 20th-century historian of the order in California.

FRANKENSTEIN, ALFRED (1906–), Chicago-born critic, reviewer of music (1934–65) and of art (1934–) for the *San Francisco Chronicle,* also a longtime lecturer on art at Mills College and the University of California, Berkeley. His books include *After the Hunt* (1953, 69), on Harnett and other American *trompe l'oeil* painters.

Free Speech Movement, activist student movement on the Berkeley campus of the University of California, also known by its initials, occurred during the fall of 1964. It arose from a standing interpretation of the state Constitution by University administrators, who held that for the University to be free of political or sectarian influence it could not permit students to advocate political or social action on the campus. The immediate cause was an administrative decision (Sept. 1964) that students could not solicit funds for social and political activities on a strip of land at the edge of the campus which once had been considered city property and a no-man's-land in regard to that ruling. When students contended their constitutional rights to free speech had been abridged they took to bellicose demonstrations and sit-ins that culminated the night of Dec. 2–3 with the occupation of Sproul Hall. Over 750 students and nonstudents were herded out of the building in the state's greatest mass arrest. Some measure of peace returned to the campus in December when the Academic Senate voted to have speech on campus circumscribed only by rules for time, place, and manner, rather than subject matter. The impact of the FSM was nationwide and also continued to drive for other reforms within the University of California which in turn led to changes in the University's regulations and administration.

Freeways, see *Highways.*

FRÉMONT, JESSIE BENTON (1824–1902), daughter of Sen. Thomas Hart Benton of Missouri, the champion of westward expansion, through whom she met the explorer Lt. John Charles Frémont.♦ She eloped with Frémont when she was 16 and he 27 and aided him in his fight against what they considered to be conservative governmental restraints and helped him write his romantic reports on his exploring expeditions. She also wrote *The Story of the Guard* (1863), an autobiographical defense of her husband's actions during the Civil War; *A Year of American Travel* (1878), about her voyage to California (1848) and residence there; and *Far-West Sketches* (1890).

FRÉMONT, JOHN CHARLES (1813–90), had been for five years an officer in the Topographical Corps of the U.S. Army and had led an expedition along the Oregon Trail to the Rockies (1842) before he set off (1843) on the government expedition that took him to California. He and his 40 men, including Kit Carson♦ and Charles Preuss,♦ were ordered by Congress (prompted by his father-in-law, Sen. Benton of Missouri) to the Oregon country so that their findings could supplement those of the naval expedition of Charles Wilkes.

Having achieved that purpose Frémont decided, in keeping with his romantic spirit of derring-do and Benton's expansionist ideas, to make a foray into Mexican California. From Oregon he went to Nevada, where he named the Great Basin, Pyramid Lake, and Carson River. Then, despite heavy snow, he crossed the Sierra (Feb. 1844), visited Sutter at his fort, and observed the weakness of the Mexicans in California before moving south through California to strike the Spanish Trail and take a route that, with the guidance of Joseph Walker,♦ led him to Bent's Fort and home.

With the aid of his wife Jessie♦ he told of his adventures in the *Report of the Exploring Expedition to Oregon and North California* (1845), a Senate-sponsored document which, despite all its data on geology and flora and its tables of latitudes and longitudes, reads almost as excitingly as Washington Irving's account of the adventures of Capt. Bonneville. The warm response to it (10,000 copies were printed) and the general sense of manifest destiny which anticipated a war with Mexico made Frémont a natural leader for another expedition proposed by Sen. Benton.

This one, on which he led 60 armed men, including Carson, Walker, and Edward Kern, was to survey the central Rockies, the area of Salt Lake, and part of the Sierra. He approached Nevada (1845) by what was later called Hasting's Cut-Off, named the Humboldt River, and again decided on his own to make a winter crossing to Sutter's Fort.

Next, contending he needed supplies, he spent time in and near Monterey (Jan.–March 1846), conferring with Larkin.

Ordered out by the Mexicans, he was momentarily defiant: he made camp and raised the U.S. flag at Gabilan (now Fremont) Peak, but he soon went to Klamath Lake (Oregon). There, on May 8, Lt. A. H. Gillespie♦ met him and, according to some reports, gave him a secret message and bellicose words from Benton, which inspired his subsequent actions. He went to Sutter's Fort, stirred the American settlers of the area, and was a leading force in the Bear Flag Revolt,♦ abetting the capture of Sonoma and planning further conquest. This was interrupted by the actual outbreak of the Mexican War.♦

Commodore Stockton commissioned Frémont a major in command of a Battalion of Mounted Riflemen, mainly composed of Frémont's former California Battalion,♦ and sent him to take San Diego, then go north to recruit forces, and back again to Santa Barbara, suppressing revolts and evading ambush. The success of U.S. forces put Frémont in a position to accept the surrender of Andres Pico♦ at Cahuenga.

After being named California's military governor by Stockton, Frémont refused to obey Gen. Kearny, unaware that the General had conflicting orders from Washington to organize a government. As a result, Frémont's governorship (Jan. 19–March 1,1847) was ended and he was charged with mutiny. A court-martial in Washington found him guilty, and even though he was pardoned by President Polk, Frémont resigned from the army.

The public adored his defiant style, which was later to make him a national political figure. Meanwhile he wrote a *Geographical Memoir upon Upper California* (1848), briefly describing his expedition of 1845–46. Then he entered upon a private expedition (1848–49) to find a route for a railroad to California. This took him back to California shortly after the discovery of gold, in whose wealth he shared when a rich vein was discovered on the Mariposa Grant♦ which Larkin had bought for him earlier at Frémont's request.

Frémont became a wealthy man and he was also named to the U.S. Senate for the new state's first short term (Sept. 1850–March 1851). Later he traveled in Europe, made another expedition for a railroad route, and, as a continuing popular figure, ran for the presidency (1856) on the ticket of the new antislavery Republican party. After his defeat he returned to develop his Mariposa Grant.

He was commissioned a major general by Lincoln at the outbreak of the Civil War and put in command of the Department of the West with headquarters in St. Louis, but his unilateral, high-handed act of confiscating the property and freeing the slaves of Missourians in rebellion led Lincoln to reassign him to the battlefields of Virginia, where Stonewall Jackson defeated him.

Frémont's neglect of the Mariposa property caused him to lose both it and his wealth. Although he again lived for a time in California toward the end of his life, most of his remaining years were spent elsewhere, as territorial governor of Arizona (1878–83) and as a promoter of western railroad projects.

Fremont, city in Alameda County between Oakland and San Jose, created (1956) by merging five farming settlements: Niles, Centerville, Irvington, Mission San Jose, and Warm Springs. Long an isolated farming region, it mushroomed quickly to become a major residential center and the site of light industry and a huge auto assembly plant. The population in 1960 was 43,790 and in 1970 was 100,869.

FRENCH, NORA MAY (1881–1907), poet born in New York State, lived all but her first six years in California. There she was a member of the bohemian group at Carmel, where she took her own life. Her lyric *Poems* was published in 1910.

French bread, see *Sourdough.*

French in California, the first explorers to visit California after Drake, their association with the region began with the exploring party of La Pérouse♦ (1786) and was continued with other commercial or exploratory visits, including those of Duhaut-Cilly♦ (1827), Capt. Cyrille Pierre Laplace (1837, 1839) and Eugène Duflot de Mofras♦ (1841–42), and the very different kind of visit of the privateer Bouchard♦ (1818). A French consulate was established at Monterey (c.1843–56) as a few Frenchmen settled in California (e.g. J. L. Vignes♦ in southern California [1831] and J. J. Vioget in Yerba Buena [1839]) and became orchardists, merchants, and workmen. More numerous but transient were the French-Canadian trappers of the Hudson's Bay Co., who wintered in the Sierra. The gold rush attracted over 4,100 Frenchmen by 1851, and by 1853 the *Echo du Pacifique,* a San Francisco journal (est. 1850), claimed 32,000 Frenchmen resident in California. Certainly the region was of great interest to the French, as indicated by Daumier's many caricatures on the subject for a Parisian journal and by Dumas' romantic novels set there. Nevertheless, the numerous immigrants met antipathy as they crowded into the mines (note the many place-names like French Gulf), and when they were subjected to the Foreign Miners' Tax (also aimed at Chinese, Chileans, and Mexicans) they refused to pay, siding with the Mexicans in a so-called French Revolution (Sonora, 1850). Many Frenchmen, like F. L. Pioche,♦ settled in San Francisco. There they established a hospital. They also enhanced the quality of the city's life as importers of fine merchandise, as hotel and restaurant keepers, and as journalists. For example, Raphael Weill and Emile Verdier established the city's fine department stores—the White House and City of Paris. Meanwhile, other Frenchmen cultivated vineyards for fine wines, like Vignes, his nephews Pierre and Jean Louis Sansevain, Charles LeFranc, and Paul Masson. French Basques later were active in ranching and sheep raising. The French population has continued to be a substantial element in California, reaching about 20,000 in 1920, while the number of those of French descent is far greater.

Fresno, seat of the county of the same name, is the market and shipping center of the San Joaquin Valley. Its history is without Spanish or Mexican roots and is all post-gold-rush, beginning with agricultural development in the 1860s and burgeoning with the coming of the Central Pacific Railroad (1872) which laid out the town and gave it the county's name. Early growers include Agoston Haraszthy,♦ developer of the region's wine grapes; M. Theo Kearney,♦ creator of the raisin industry; and Frank Roeding and his son George Christian Roeding,♦ who introduced the Smyrna fig. These remain major crops of the area to which have been added cotton, vegetables, fruits and nuts, and field and seed crops, while poultry and livestock and wine making are other bases of the economy, along with increasing industrialization. Over the years farm work has attracted many foreigners, among them Armenians, Orientals, and Mexicans. The city's sights include Kearney's mansion, Roeding Park, and a vast catacomb of underground rooms and gardens created by a simple Sicilian, Baldesare Forestiere (1879–1954), a subterranean counterpart of Simon Rodia, who built his towers in Watts. Another feature was added to the city (1965) with the construction of a major pedestrian mall enhanced by monumental sculptures. Fresno's Junior College, opened in 1910, is the oldest in the

state and one of the first in the nation. William Saroyan is a famous member of the local Armenian colony, and other natives of the city include athletes Frank Chance, Lee Evans, Sammy Lee, and Tom Seaver. In 1970 the city's population was 165,972.

Fresno County, formed (1856) from parts of Mariposa, Merced, and Tulare counties, got its name from the Spanish word for the ash tree which flourishes along the San Joaquin and Kings rivers. The county extends from the coast ranges to the peaks of the Sierra across the San Joaquin Valley. It is bounded by Merced and Madera counties on the north, the latter line formed by the San Joaquin River; Mono and Inyo counties on the east; Tulare and Kings counties on the south; and San Benito and Monterey counties on the west. Since 1874 the county seat has been Fresno, the largest city in the county and all of the San Joaquin Valley. The eastern area of the county includes the mountainous Sierra Nevada's Kings Canyon National Park as well as the Sierra National Forest, Huntington Lake, the John Muir Wilderness, and the northern part of Sequoia National Forest. The county began to be populated during the gold rush into the mountains, but valley settlements by cattle ranchers and farmers soon followed. The one large urban center is the county seat; other, smaller ones are Coalinga, Clovis, and Sanger. Lemoore Naval Air Station spans Kings and Fresno county lines. For many years Fresno has been the state's major agricultural county, producing grapes, cotton, alfalfa, fruit (particularly cantaloupes, plums, and peaches), lima beans, and tomatoes in great quantities, as well as seed and field crops and poultry. The dollar value of its farm products is annually the greatest of any county in the U.S. It is also important in food processing and as an oil producer. In 1970 the population was 413,053. With an area of 3,819,456 acres, it had 69.2 persons per sq. mi. (*See also individual entries.*)

Fresno River, originates about 45 miles northeast of Madera and runs northwest from that city for 25 miles to its junction with the San Joaquin River. Its name, like that of the county in which it was originally located, is Spanish for "ash," a tree found along its banks. The eastern Fresno was the site of mining camps during the gold rush, and an Indian reservation was established along the river in the early 1850s.

Friant-Kern Canal, part of the Central Valley Project,♦ begins below the Friant Dam on the San

Joaquin River and its Millerton Lake,♦ about 20 miles northeast of Fresno. The canal extends 152 miles south along the dry eastern side of the San Joaquin Valley to a point just below Bakersfield. Opened in the 1950s, its name derives from that of Thomas Friant, a lumberman of the area, and Kern County. The Madera Canal♦ begins at the same point and carries water northwest.

FRIEDLANDER, ISAAC (1833?–78), German-born financier who was reared in South Carolina, went to San Francisco (1849) and soon made a fortune milling flour and speculating in it. He became known as the "Grain King" because he owned vast farming lands, sometimes with William S. Chapman,♦ and because he cornered the state's shipping to carry wheat to England, Europe, and the Orient during the 1870s. He was an imposing figure, standing 6 feet 7 inches and weighing 300 pounds. When he overextended his speculation he went bankrupt.

Friends of the Earth, conservationist organization, founded in 1969 under the leadership of David Brower♦ after his aggressive programs caused his ouster from the Sierra Club. Unlike the society he had previously led, the new one is dedicated to legal and political action to preserve the wilderness and to restore purity to the environment.

Frisco, nickname for San Francisco, common in the late 19th century when it was popularized also as a reference to the St. Louis and San Francisco Railroad. Natives of the city frown upon it as a vulgarism (see Herb Caen, *Don't Call It Frisco,* 1953), as do most people now, so that it has become uncommon.

Frog, tail-less amphibian found in many species throughout the state, is related to the toad♦ and eats the same food but sometimes also eats birds, mice, turtles, and snakes. The *red-legged frog* lives in the Coast Range, Transverse Mts., and western slopes of the Sierra Nevada and Cascades, the last area also the home of the frog of that name. The *mountain yellow-legged frog* lives in many of the same areas and other regions of northern California. The *leopard frog* lives by the Colorado River, near Lake Tahoe, and in parts of the San Joaquin and Imperial valleys. The *bullfrog,* introduced to the state (1922) from Louisiana, lives throughout the state except for the desert and high mountains. Commercially caught for food and for biology instruction and experiments, it has begun to disappear, perhaps in part the result of pesticides,

so that it is illegal to hunt them in some areas. It is also the frog used in the modern Jumping Frog Jubilee of Angels Camp. Other species include the *Pacific* and *California treefrogs,* found throughout the state; the *spotted frog,* found in Modoc County; and the *tailed frog,* named for its tail-like reproductive organ.

Fruit growing, an important part of the state's agriculture, began with the padres at the missions who introduced the major berries, deciduous trees (apples, cherries, figs, pears, peaches, plums), and citrus still grown in California, though their varieties, of grape, for instance, were poor. Their orchards were abandoned on secularization (1833), although some were absorbed into *ranchos.*

More extensive farming began with Americans after the gold rush. The major deciduous crop was apples and by 1872 over 2,000,000 trees were planted, mostly in the north central valleys. Cherries, peaches, and pears were also grown early in large orchards, mainly in the Napa, Feather River, and Santa Clara valleys, respectively, the last two crops having approximately 1,000,000 and 350,000 trees by 1860. Plums and the newly introduced nectarines had a limited demand.

Citrus fruits expanded greatly with the introduction of new types in the 1870s. Grapes also increased tremendously, from 1,000,000 vines in 1855 to 26,500,000 in 1870, and after the successful grafting of European cuttings on phylloxera-free native stock the plantings were expanded further to 130,000,000 vines in the late 1880s, and raisins became a large commercial product.

Expansion of other fruit crops was very great too in the last part of the century, as eastern markets became available through transcontinental railroads and improved shipping conditions. Thus, for example, farmers planted between 3,000,000 and 4,000,000 peach trees in the 1880s and 90s. New techniques of food processing and canning also made for greater growing and for new products, such as dried fruits, as well as for new crops, such as dates.

During the 20th century, particularly since World War II, fruit-growing regions have changed considerably as their former orchard lands have been squeezed by suburban expansion. Thus citrus growing has moved from the Los Angeles area to the San Joaquin Valley, and the deciduous fruit trees of Santa Clara Valley have been crowded out, in part into the Sacramento Valley.

This century has also seen the development of new orchard areas: melons are grown in the Imperial Valley and grapefruit, dates, and grapes in the Coachella Valley. Acreage devoted in 1970 to growing major deciduous fruits (apples, apricots, cherries, nectarines, peaches, pears, plums, prunes) amounted to more than 316,000 acres, and that devoted in 1970 to growing major citrus fruits (grapefruit, lemons, oranges, tangerines) amounted to more than 218,000 acres. (*See also individual entries.*)

Fruit packing and canning, see *Food processing.*

FSM, see *Free Speech Movement.*

Fullerton, city in northern Orange County, founded in 1887 and named for the Santa Fe representative who arranged to route the railroad through the site. It has grown rapidly in recent years as an industrial center, the home of Hughes Aircraft, among other plants, but it is also a residential settlement (Norton Simon is among the inhabitants) and a California State University campus is located there. In 1970 the population was 85,826.

Funeral Mountains, name sometimes applied to the Black Mts. or to the Amargosa Range in Death Valley because their fringes of black basalt look like mourning crepe.

FUNSTON, FREDERICK (1865–1917), son of a Kansas Congressman, became a soldier with the Cuban insurrectionists (1895) and later with the U.S. Army in the Spanish-American War, capturing Aguinaldo, the Philippine rebel, before being put in command of the military department of California. In that capacity he took charge of assuring order in San Francisco after its earthquake and fire (1906). He is memorialized by an avenue bearing his name in the city, and at one time a Fort Funston stood near Lake Merced.

Fur trapping, initiated by the Spanish in the 1780s, when they encouraged Indians to snare sea otter, whose skins were then obtained by barter for sale or trade in China. Larger enterprise was begun by the Russians,♦ who began hunting otter (1808) and established as an outpost of their Fort Ross a station for obtaining seal.♦ Americans in association with the Russians and independent hunters like George Nidever♦ also sought various fur-bearing sea mammals, while other U.S. frontiersmen, like Ewing Young,♦ George Yount,♦ and William Wolfskill♦ also trapped beaver♦ and otter♦ in rivers. Explorations such as those of James Pattie♦ and Jedediah Smith♦ were encouraged by the business of fur trapping and trading. The same purposes brought Peter Ogden♦ and other Canadians♦ of the Hudson's Bay Co. south to California to range around its rivers for beaver. Sutter also undertook extensive trapping in the early 1840s. Interrupted by the gold rush and adversely affected by the great influx of population into once remote regions and by the concomitant extension of agriculture, particularly around the Sacramento and San Joaquin rivers, trapping fell off in the latter part of the 19th century, when some fur animals had been almost exterminated by excessive hunting. The state began regulatory laws in 1911 with protection of beaver, extended (1913) to sea otter, and in 1917 to many other animals. Under licensing and seasonal restrictions, trapping has been continued as a sport and as a business, although domestic rearing of fur animals has also contributed substantially to the obtaining of furs.

FURUSETH, ANDREW (1854–1938), Norwegian-born labor leader who, after sailing in the merchant marine of many nations (1873–91), settled in California and devoted his life to improving the sailors' lot. He was president of the International Seamans Union (1908–38), for which he accepted only the pay of an able-bodied seaman. A bust by Jo Davidson on the San Francisco waterfront commemorates this passionately dedicated man.

G

Gabilan Range, mountains south of the Santa Cruz Range, extending behind and south of the area from Salinas to King City, forming the boundary between Monterey and San Benito counties. Gabilan means "hawk" in Spanish. To the north lies Fremont (or Gabilan or Hawk) Peak; to the south is the Pinnacles National Monument (est. 1908), an ancient volcanic area of crags and spires behind Soledad.

GABLE, CLARK (1901–60), Ohio-born film star of Hollywood from the 1930s until well into the 1950s, admired for his ruggedly masculine manner and appearance and, often, easy comic style. His popular films included *It Happened One Night* (1934), *Gone With the Wind* (1939), and *Across the Wide Missouri* (1951). He won only one Academy Award (for his film of 1934) but from then on was known as the King of Hollywood.

Gabrieleño, Indians of Shoshonean stock whose Spanish name derives from the fact that they were neophytes of Mission San Gabriel. They shared some lands with the Fernandeños (whose name came from Mission San Fernando), for their area of residence was not only the mainland of present Los Angeles County but the islands of San Clemente and Santa Catalina. The Gabrieleño are thought to have been the originators of the toloache♦ or jimson weed cult, which with them, as with the neighboring Juaneño,♦ was associated with the Chinigchinich religion.♦ Their aboriginal population was about 1,000, but they were nearly extinct in 1910 according to the census of that date. A Gabrieleño neophyte woman became the wife of Hugo Reid, a major landholder and trader of southern California.

Gachupin, Mexican term for men born in Spain, used pejoratively, to suggest smug superiority.

GAGE, HENRY TIFFT (1852–1924), 20th governor of the state (1899–1903), born in New York State, went to California (1874), where he practiced law and was active in Republican politics. He was later Minister to Portugal (1909–11).

GAINES, ERNEST J. (1933–), black author resident in San Francisco who returns annually to the boyhood home on a Louisiana plantation which has formed a major setting for fictional treatment of his people. His novels include *Catherine Carmier* (1964), *Of Love and Dust* (1967), and *Miss Jane Pittman* (1971), and some of his stories have been collected in *Bloodline* (1968).

GALE, WILLIAM A[LDEN] (1790?–1841), Boston trader in California, first for seal furs from the Farallones (1810), then in the hide business (1822–35) and as an agent of Bryant, Sturgis Co. His wife, an Estudillo, was the first Californian to visit Boston.

GALLO, ERNEST (1910–) and JULIO (1911–), brothers and partners in wine making, born in Modesto, began by working in a small vineyard there owned by their father. After the repeal of Prohibition (1933) they entered business, with Julio heading their manufacturing and Ernest their marketing. In 1940 they acquired bottlers in Los Angeles and New Orleans and began national distribution. In the 1950s they had great success with low-priced products and in the 1960s with so-called "pop" wines, but in the 1970s they began to emphasize more expensive varieties. In 1975 about 28% of all wine sold in the U.S. came from their large, automated wineries.

GÁLVEZ, JOSÉ DE (1720–87), practiced law and held minor diplomatic posts before his appointment (1765) by Charles III as *visitador-general* of New Spain. As a special deputy of the king for specific investigations, he was ordered to increase revenues and to replace the then suspect Jesuits by Franciscans and members of other orders. To further his major assignment he established the port of San Blas from which he personally oversaw the departure of the Sacred Expedition♦ (1769), which he planned, with his appointee Portolá,♦ to establish missions and otherwise colonize and develop Alta California as a source of revenue for Spain. He also proposed that California be joined with Nuevo Viscaya, Sinaloa, and Sonora as a commandancy general separate from the Mexican viceroyalty. His appointment as *visitador-general* ended in 1771, and he later became Minister of the

Indies. Gálvez possessed great energy and ability as an administrator but he was also Machiavellian and so unstable as to be insane at times. Married to a Frenchwoman, he usually spelled his Christian name in the French style as Josèphe.

GARBO, GRETA (1906–   ), Swedish-born film star whose aristocratic and magnetic beauty and reserved manner made her a new kind of figure in Hollywood. There she made such great successes as *Flesh and the Devil* (1927), *Anna Christie* (1930), and *Anna Karenina* (1935), but she never became part of the southern California scene and withdrew from it entirely in the 1940s.

GARCÉS, FRANCISCO TOMÁS HERMENEGILDO (1738–81), Franciscan father who went to San Xavier del Bac (Ariz.) in 1768, from there exploring the Gila Valley, the trans-Colorado wilderness, and Baja California deserts, thus opening the Sonora-California Trail. His successes inspired Anza's expedition to California, which Garcés followed by opening the Mojave Trail to San Gabriel (1776), whence he went to the Santa Clara and Tulare valleys and the Tehachapi Pass. Despite earlier good relations with the Yuma, he was killed by them.

GARCÍA DIEGO Y MORENO, FRANCISCO (1785–1846), Mexican-born Franciscan missionary who went to California (1831) to become President-General◆ of the missions from Soledad to Sonoma (1831–35) and the first bishop of the two Californias (1840). He established his residence at Santa Barbara.

Garden Grove, city in northwestern Orange County, was a farming settlement among citrus groves until the period after World War II, when it boomed fantastically and developed mile after mile of tract housing. In 1970 it had a population of 121,357.

Gardens, see *Horticulture.*

GARDNER, ERLE STANLEY (1889–1970), Massachusetts-born author who was admitted to the California bar (1911) and from a successful career in criminal law moved to the writing of tremendously popular detective fiction. His central figure in a long series of novels was Perry Mason,◆ a lawyer who served as a sleuth. His first works were *The Case of the Velvet Claws* (1933) and *The Case of the Sulky Girl* (1933). He was so prolific that he also wrote under pseudonyms. Over 30 years his books had sold more than 135,000,000 copies in the U.S.

GARLAND, JUDY (1922–69), Minnesota-born film star who graduated from child performances in vaudeville to juvenile stardom in motion pictures as singer, dancer, and actress. Essentially, she grew up in a film studio, where she not only acted but went to school. Her greatest role was as the heroine of *The Wizard of Oz* (1939) in which she displayed an indomitable enthusiasm. After numerous musical comedies and premature retirement she returned to appear in more mature films such as *A Star Is Born* (1954) and *I Could Go on Singing* (1963).

GARLAND, WILLIAM MAY (1866–1948), went to Los Angeles (1890) from his native Maine and not only had success in the real estate business but developed into a leading booster of his adopted city. He was twice president of the California Chamber of Commerce and was instrumental in bringing the Olympic Games to Los Angeles (1932).

Garlic, commercially raised in California since at least the end of the 19th century, the crop of the herb, grown mainly in the Santa Clara and San Benito valleys, and more recently in the San Joaquin Valley, now accounts for most of the U.S. supply. In 1970 it was raised on 5,600 acres and was worth $6,844,000, but acreage and crop yield have increased very sharply during the 1970s.

Garlock Fault, see *Earthquakes.*

GARNETT, PORTER (1871–1951), San Francisco-born man of arts. During his youth a member of Les Jeunes◆ and a contributor to *The Lark,* he became known as a calligrapher and woodcarver, a producer of Bohemian Club plays, and the author of one, *The Green Knight.* He established (1922) the Laboratory Press at the Carnegie Institute of Technology, Pittsburgh, where he taught fine printing and set standards for distinguished typography even beyond those of his own press.

Garrá Revolt, occurred near Warner's Ranch◆ in 1851 when Antonio Garrá, chief of the Cupeño Indians,◆ baptized at Mission San Luis Rey, attempted to create a great union of tribes for an uprising that would drive the Americans out of southern California. He gained recruits who plundered *ranchos* and killed several Americans but he himself was captured by the chief of the Cahuillas, who would not join his uprising. For the revolt he and some other Indians were executed, as was William Marshall (1827–51), a New England seaman resident in the region, whose association with Garrá led him to be found guilty of high treason.

GARRETT, MIKE (MICHAEL LOCKETT GARRETT) (1944–   ), football player born in East Los Angeles, played halfback for the University of Southern California (1963–65), and became the first person from the state to win the Heisman Trophy as outstanding college player of the year (1965). He later played with the Kansas City Chiefs (1966–70) and the San Diego Chargers (1970–73).

Gaviota Pass, located in the mountains 30 miles northwest of Santa Barbara at an elevation of 918 feet, derives its name from a seagull (*gaviota*) killed there by the forces of Portolá (1769). Mexican forces were expected to ambush Frémont there (Dec. 25, 1846) during his advance on Santa Barbara, but he avoided them by using San Marcos Pass.♦

GAYLEY, CHARLES MILLS (1858–1932), professor of English at the University of California, Berkeley (1889–1923), known for his popular course on Great Books and as a faculty leader. He was also the author of a popular book on classical mythology.

GEARY, JOHN WHITE (1819–73), after leading his Pennsylvania infantry company to capture Chapultepec in the Mexican War was named by President Polk to be San Francisco's first postmaster and mail agent for the Pacific Coast (1849). Soon replaced, he was elected the city's last *alcalde* (1849) and then its first mayor (1850–52). After he left California in 1852 he became governor of the Kansas Territory, a Civil War officer, and governor of Pennsylvania. He is memorialized by the name of a San Francisco boulevard that passes Union Square, which property he had given to the city.

GEIGER, MAYNARD J[OSEPH] (1901–77), Franciscan priest, born in Pennsylvania and reared in California, which is the main subject of his historical studies. His works include *The Life and Times of Fray Junípero Serra* (1959), *Mission Santa Barbara* (1965), *Franciscan Missionaries in Hispanic California* (1969), and an annotated translation of Palóu's life of Serra (1965). In 1937 he was appointed archivist of Mission Santa Barbara.

General Strike of San Francisco, occurred (July 16–19, 1934) as an outgrowth of the International Longshoremen's Association strike for control of hiring halls and better pay and hours which had closed most Pacific ports except Los Angeles. The attempt of San Francisco employers to open local docks led to a battle between strikers and police on "Bloody Thursday" (July 5), which left two dead and many injured. Harry Bridges,♦ head of the city's division of the ILA, got the general support of other unions, although electricity and food remained available. The four-day strike ended with agreement on arbitration in which the ILA got most of the demands it had made on behalf of its longshoremen.♦

Gente de razón, Spanish term for colonials who were not Indians. These civilized or "rational" persons included *mestizos* and mulattoes who were not fully Indian.

GENTHE, ARNOLD (1869–1942), German-born photographer who went to San Francisco (1895), where his sensitive pictures captured the look and spirit of the pre-1906 city and many of its most interesting residents. Some of these were published in *Pictures of Old Chinatown* (1908). With their perceptive vision, frequent use of backlighting, and other experimental techniques, they were esteemed as much for their aesthetic qualities as for their documentary sense, even when made under pressure, as was a remarkable series showing the fire advancing through San Francisco after the earthquake of April 18, 1906. After 1911 Genthe's life and craft were focused on other places, but he left a fine memoir of his life in California in *As I Remember* (1936).

Geographic dimensions of the land, see *California dimensions.*

Geology of California, marked by distinct natural provinces of geographic regions, each characterized by similar land forms, has a complex and diverse history stretching back many hundreds of millions of years through the nineteen periods, or epochs, that form four geologic eras: *Precambrian* (2,700 million to 600 million years old), *Paleozoic* (600 million to 225 million years old), *Mesozoic* (225 million to 70 million years old), and *Cenozoic* (the last 70 million years).

California is generally considered to have 11 geomorphic provinces: (1) COAST RANGE,♦ of some 400 miles, whose mountains are made of rocks from the *Mesozoic* and *Cenozoic* eras. (2) KLAMATH MTS.,♦ in the state's northwest, and as a continuation of the Sierra Nevada, are composed of rugged *Paleozoic* and *Mesozoic* rocks. (3) SOUTHERN CASCADE MTS.,♦ were created during the *Miocene* and *Pliocene* epochs (25 million to 3 million years of the *Cenozoic* era), while the volcanic formation of Mt. Shasta and Lassen Peak is of the *Pleistocene* period (less than 3 million years old), although beneath the range lie granitic and metamorphic rocks like those of the Sierra Nevada and Klamath Mts. (4) MODOC PLATEAU,♦ is composed of a volcanic rock of approximately the same type and age as that of the Cascade Mts., with which it is sometimes considered to be allied as a single natural province. (5) SIERRA NEVADA,♦ a great westward-tilting granite block that forms the largest and highest single mountain range of the state, was lifted to its present altitude and forms by earth movements near the end of the *Pliocene* period of the *Cenozoic* era (11 million to 3 million years old). (6) CENTRAL VALLEY,♦ extending some 400 miles north and south and averaging 50 miles in width, is a structural trough filled with gravel, sand, silt, and clay produced by the erosion of the Sierra Nevada, and is underlaid by rocks of the *Mesozoic* and *Cenozoic* eras. (7) GREAT BASIN,♦ northwest-trending mountains with fault blocks made of *Precambrian* and *Cenozoic* rocks, includes the White, Inyo, Panamint, Black, Amargosa, and Funeral mountains, as well as the intervening alluvial-filled valleys, such as Owens, Death, and Panamint. (8) TRANSVERSE RANGES,♦ west-to-east oriented mountains stretching some 300 miles from the Channel Islands through the Santa Ynez, Santa Monica, San Gabriel, and San Bernardino mountains to within 60 miles of the Colorado River, are made of rock ranging from *Precambrian* to very late and intense folding and faulting of the *Cenozoic* era. (9) MOJAVE DESERT,♦ sometimes considered to be part of the natural province of the Great Basin, but more often considered to be independent because of its separation by the Garlock Fault, consists of isolated northwest-trending mountains of the *Precambrian* to *Cenozoic* eras and broad valleys. (10) SALTON TROUGH,♦ a desert area which is a northwest extension of the Gulf of California region, was created when the peninsula of Baja California pulled away from the Mexican mainland, probably during the *Miocene* era. (11) PENINSULAR RANGES,♦ trending northwest for some 140 miles plus an added 750 miles in Baja California, include the offshore islands from San Nicolas to San Clemente as well as the Santa Ana, San Jacinto, and Santa Rosa mountains, with the Los Angeles Basin as one of their valleys, were formed over long periods of time from the *Paleozoic* era through the *Jurassic* and *Cretaceous* portions of the *Mesozoic* era (180 million to 70 million years old) to the *Cenozoic* era.

Looking at the state's land chronologically rather than by geomorphic regions, one begins with the earliest geologic era, the *Precambrian* era, when only southern California was part of the North American continental platform that was followed by the seven epochs of the *Paleozoic* era, when most of California still lay under the Pacific Ocean. *Precambrian* rocks are found in the Transverse Ranges, along the San Andreas Fault, and in Death, Panamint, and Mojave valleys.

Paleozoic rocks are found in the Great Basin, the Sierra Nevada, and the Klamath Mts.

During the succeeding era, the *Mesozoic,* and particularly during the *Jurassic* and *Cretaceous* periods, the last two of its three divisions in time, the beginnings of the Klamath Mts., the Sierra Nevada, Yosemite Valley, and the Transverse and Peninsular ranges were formed, along with their minerals.♦ That was also the time of the creation of the Central Valley.

In the succeeding *Cenozoic* era, the most recent in geologic time, extensive volcanic activity occurred in the Cascade and northern Sierra Nevada ranges during and after its *Miocene* period (25 million to 11 million years old) and the mountain chains continued to be built to their present altitudes. At the same time lava flows created the Modoc Plateau, while the Cascade Range began to be formed, as were the later aspects of the Central Valley. In that epoch the Coast Range and its systems of faults (the source of earthquakes♦) also came into being, while the San Francisco Bay landscape took on its present appearance, with the Sacramento and San Joaquin rivers making their ways to the ocean.

During the *Cenozoic*'s *Pleistocene* epoch (3 million years and less old), Ice Age glaciers came down the valleys, and Yosemite assumed its present form. That was also the period of the great land mammals whose fossils have been found in the La Brea tar pits. The Mojave Desert and Great Basin probably were uplifted areas by the beginning of the *Cenozoic* era, with Death Valley formed by the time of the *Pleistocene* period.

In the most recent of the seven periods of the *Cenozoic* era, the *Quaternary* (the last 10 million years), the building of mountains and of faults has continued, for, as the state's Division of Mines and Geology declared in its report of 1966 on mineral resources, "California is still an uneasy land."

GEORGE, HENRY (1839–97), left his middle-class Philadelphia home (1855) to sail as a foremast boy to Calcutta, where he was first struck by the contrast between poverty and wealth that animated his later socioeconomic theories. In 1857 his search for work took him to California. There, with interruptions for other travels, he struggled against want for a decade, working as a printer, miner, author, and newspaperman, observing the underpopulated land come under the control of land-hungry speculators and a wealthy monopoly.

His first article (*Overland Monthly*, Oct. 1868) argued that the railroads would bring wealth to a few and poverty to many. That view was strengthened in 1870 when as editor of the *Transcript* of Oakland he learned of the enormous increase in the cost of neighboring agricultural land, partly occasioned by railroad building, and he argued that with population growth, "land grows in value, and the men who work it must pay more for the privilege"; indeed, too much went to the land speculators, like the railroad, who had gained the land as subsidy. Contending that agriculture was the noblest labor because it produced food, he said it was treated most meanly, farmers being forced to make extortionate payment to land speculators for their unearned increment. Therefore in 1871 he urged in a pamphlet, *Our Land and Land Policy*, that land speculation and private rent be done away with by a program to "charge the expenses of government upon our land" through the creation of what he came to call a single tax upon land equal to its rental value.

This theory was elaborated in *Progress and Poverty* (1879) which, often with illustrative stories, vividly argued that the labor force must be freed of the incubus of rent for, although land is necessary to labor, every increase in production only causes private landowners to increase their rents, the price that labor is forced to pay for use of its own powers. That contention, coming at a time of labor unrest and depression, was enormously popular. The book, first privately printed in San Francisco, was reissued (1880) by a New York publisher and became a national best-seller.

George continued to develop his doctrine in other books and in his own weekly journal after moving to New York (1880), where he was nearly elected mayor (1886). He preached his thesis in the U.S. and abroad with a religious fervor.

George Air Force Base, a tactical air fighter command located near Victorville, San Bernardino County.

Georgetown, town in the middle of El Dorado County gold mines, a major trading and residential center of the 1850s and 60s. Edwin Markham taught school there and in Coloma.

Geothermal energy, derived from the earth's natural heat by tapping underground deposits of steam or scalding water used, respectively, to drive a generator and thus be converted into electricity or to boil a liquid that will power a turbine. The first active commercial geothermal plant in the U.S. was located at The Geysers♦ in Sonoma County. It has been used since 1922 for power generation, but only extensively since 1960. It is a so-called "dry" field, in that it is free of brine and minerals which can clog pipes or corrode machinery and is therefore easier to employ than the resources around the Salton Sea, in the Imperial Valley, at Mono Lake, and near Mt. Lassen, all under investigation but all having problems caused by minerals and brine. Nevertheless, a power plant was constructed (1975) at Niland in the Imperial Valley.

Germans in California, came first on exploring and trading expeditions like those involving Langsdorff♦ (1806) and Kotzebue♦ and Chamisso♦ (1816), the last being the first to describe and name the native poppy. Early permanent settlers included the German Swiss John Sutter, who arrived in 1838, Jacob Leese, who built San Francisco's first substantial house (1836), Edward Vischer, who sketched the missions in the 1840s, and Charles Weber, founder of Stockton.

The gold rush attracted many Germans, accounting for place-names like Dutch Flat ("Deutsch" was pronounced Dutch). Some immigrants came for a time, like the novelist Gerstäcker, and Schliemann, the excavator of Troy, but those who stayed grew in number from about 3,000 in 1850 to about 30,000 in 1870. Some helped establish the wine business, like Charles Krug and the Wente brothers, and in 1857 Charles Kohler, John Frohling, and others organized the Los Angeles Vineyard Society with a cooperative vineyard at the German settlement of Anaheim.

Germans went into many other businesses: sugar refining (Claus Spreckels), publishing (Anton Roman), and clock making (Hermann Wenzel). Some immigrants operated breweries and beer gardens and many entered the grocery business. In the last enterprise, as in many other wholesale and retail merchandising ventures and in banking, a major power was the substantial Jewish community from Germany that settled in San Francisco, leading mining towns and supply centers, and Los Angeles. They included Levi Strauss, Adolph Sutro, Harris Newmark, I. W. Hellman, Raphael Weill, and the Weinstock and Lubin families, one of whose descendants, Simon Lubin, is an example of the group's diverse contributions to the social and cultural life of their adopted home.

An unusual enterprise was the Alaska Commercial Co., run by members of the Sloss and Gerstle families, leaders of San Francisco financial and social life. Simpler German settlers of the period are depicted in Norris' *McTeague*.♦ Germans who made major contributions to the arts included C. C. and H. W. A. Nahl; the landscape painter E. Hildebrandt, who visited San Francisco in 1864; the Düsseldorf-trained artists Albert Bierstadt♦ and Toby Rosenthal;♦ the creator of lithographic views, the Swiss Charles Kuchel (his grandnephew became a U.S. Senator); and Emil Dresel. A later contributor to San Francisco's cultural life was the symphony conductor Alfred Hertz.

In the 20th century many German-born producers, actors, and directors like Carl Laemmle, Emil Jannings, Marlene Dietrich, and Joseph von Sternberg enhanced the motion picture business and the cultural atmosphere of Los Angeles, which was also enriched by refugees from the Nazi regime, some remaining the rest of their lives, like the conductor Bruno Walter and the author Lion Feuchtwanger; the latter and Thomas Mann were resident in Pacific Palisades, a colony of cultivated German exiles.

GERNREICH, Rudi (1922–), Vienna-born designer who went to Los Angeles (1938) where, after study at its City College and its Art Center, he became a designer of women's knitwear, and was particularly famous for his exotic and daring swimming apparel.

GERSTÄCKER, Friedrich (1816–72), came from his native Germany to the U.S. (1837), where he traveled widely, particularly on the old Southwest frontier in Arkansas, about which he wrote in letters that when published upon a return to Germany led him to professional authorship. Having translated (1849) the ostensibly autobiographical *Four Months Among the Gold Fields* by Vizetelly,♦ he himself went to California (1849–50), of which he wrote in his *Reisen,* translated as *Narrative of a Journey Around the World* (1853), later excerpted in *California Gold Mines* (1946). He then wrote many popular stories and sketches, some collected in *Californische Skizzen* (1856),

translated as *Scenes of Life in California* (1942). Some, like *Steel Arm; or, The Robbers and Regulators of California* (1862) and its sequel, *Big Goliath; or, The Terror of the Mines,* and the juvenile, *The Young Gold-Digger* (1860), are not much different from dime novels. He also wrote a longer melodramatic novel, *Gold* (1858).

GETTY, J[ean] Paul (1892–1976), born in Minneapolis, long resident in California, attended UCLA and the University of California, Berkeley, graduated from Oxford, much later settling in England. The principal owner of the Getty Oil Co., he was considered one of the world's richest men. He wrote a history of his firm, an autobiography, and other books. He also formed a notable collection of works of art including Greek and Roman antiquities, paintings, sculpture, and furniture, housed in a museum near Pacific Palisades modeled on a villa at Herculaneum, and to it he bequeathed the largest part of his fortune.

Geysers, The, mineral hot springs and steam jets in the northwest corner of Sonoma County. The area, sacred to the local Indians, was discovered by an American in 1847 and ever since has been a tourist attraction. The Devil's Grist Mill and other fancifully named volcanic vents spew steam 100 or more feet high. The nearby resort town of Geyserville was founded in 1851. From the 1860s through the 80s a hotel, The Geysers, was a popular spa visited for thermal cures. Since 1960 the geysers themselves have served as a source of geothermal power♦ by the Pacific Gas and Electric Co., which by 1976 had a power plant with a generating capacity of 502,000 kilowatts.

GHIRARDELLI, Domingo (1817–94), Italian-born confectioner who went to California (1849) from Peru but after being unsuccessful at mining established a firm that began to manufacture chocolate (1856), a business carried on by successive generations in San Francisco. An old plant on the north bayside was transformed in the mid-1960s into an attractive shopping and exhibition area under the name Ghirardelli Square, even though it was no longer a family property, having been bought and developed by William M. Roth, a grandson of William Matson.♦

Ghost Dance, see *Paiute.*

GIANNINI, A[madeo] P[eter] (1870–1949), born in San Jose of Italian immigrant parents, began his remarkable business career at 12 as a clerk in the family produce firm. Two years after becoming a director of a savings and loan society catering to San Francisco's Italian community, he opened his own Bank of Italy in the city (1904). His bank prospered and acquired its first branch in San Jose (1909) and soon had others, including two in Los Angeles (1913), thereby pioneering in statewide branch banking despite opposition from independent bankers and the Federal Reserve Board. By 1918 he had 24 branches and his bank's assets were fourth largest in the state.

In 1919 he founded Bancitaly Corp., a holding company for banks not formally part of the Bank of Italy, including (1928) a Bank of America located in New York City that had been founded in 1812. Bancitaly Corp. was succeeded by Transamerica Corp. (1928), which not only assumed control of the Bank of Italy stock but became the world's largest holding company. In 1930 Giannini merged the Bank of Italy, the Bank of America in New York, and another Bank of America he had formed (1928) in California for some Los Angeles banks he had acquired into a new Bank of America National Trust and Savings Association.

Having retired from the presidency of Transamerica before the Depression, Giannini was infuriated when his successor during bad economic times retrenched by selling some banks, and by means of a successful proxy fight he ousted the new management and at 62 assumed the leadership of both the bank and the holding company he had founded. He served also as a Regent of the University of California, to whose Berkeley campus he gave a building and a foundation for agricultural economics.

He was succeeded by his son, Lawrence Mario Giannini (1894–1952). Under later presidents the bank greatly extended overseas business and international branches in which the founder had also been much interested. At the end of 1974 the Bank had assets of $60.4 billion and employed 62,000 people in 90 countries. Its size and power also made it the target of dissidents who attacked its offices, most notably by burning down the branch at Isla Vista, near the campus of the University of California, Santa Barbara (1970). In Giannini's last years his Transamerica Corp. was under federal attack for violating the Clayton Anti-Trust Act and in 1952 the corporation sold its remaining stock in the Bank and severed its corporate relations.

Long after its separation from the Bank and from the business of banking, the Transamerica Corp. headquarters in San Francisco became a landmark by its construction (1972) on the site of the old Montgomery Block of a slender 48-story pyramid designed by William Pereira.

Giants, San Francisco, baseball team in the Western Division of the National League, taken to California from New York by the team's president, Horace Stoneham,♦ at the end of the 1957 season. Originally settled in the old stadium of the Seals, the team got its own Candlestick Park♦ stadium (1960), soon found to be unsatisfactory because of its cold winds and fog. The stars included Orlando Cepeda,♦ Juan Marichal,♦ Willie Mays,♦ and Willy McCovey.♦ They helped win the National League pennant (1962), but they lost the World Series to the Yankees. For several years (1965–69) the team finished in second place, but in 1971 it was first in its division.

GIBBS, MIFFLIN WISTAR (1823–1915), black civil rights leader, born in Pennsylvania, resident in San Francisco (1850?–58), where he helped to organize the San Francisco Athenaeum.♦ Later he was elected a city judge in Little Rock, Ark. (1873), the first black jurist in the nation, and was also U.S. Consul in Madagascar. He entitled his autobiography *Shadow and Light* (1902).

Gila monster, see *Lizard.*

Gila River Trail, route pioneered by James Pattie and Ewing Young and used by Gen. Kearny's army, Col. Cooke's Mormon Battalion, and some forty-niners, was the stage route of John Butterfield and later travelers from the Southwest. The entry into California was generally made from the area of Yuma, Ariz., on the Gila River, through Bard Valley.♦

GILBERT, EDWARD C. (1819–52), went from New York with Stevenson's Regiment♦ (1846) and soon became a partner of Edward C. Kemble in owning and editing the *Alta California.*♦ He was a U.S. Congressman (1850–51), but his political attacks upon Gov. Bigler led to a dispute with State Sen. James W. Denver,♦ whom he challenged to a duel in which he was shot to death.

GILL, IRVING (1870–1936), went to San Diego (1893) from Chicago (where he had worked in Louis Sullivan's architectural firm) and, affected by the missions, developed for homes and public buildings a modified modern mission style using stucco and tile with arched windows and arcades. Eclectic and experimental, he also built homes in redwood shingle style and later adapted elements of modern technology into the basic, unornamented, forthright design of his houses, which featured ingenious labor-saving devices.

GILLESPIE, ARCHIBALD HAMILTON (1812?–73), lieutenant in the U.S. Marines sent by President Polk and Secretary of State Buchanan (1846) as a secret agent in the guise of a merchant to cooperate with Larkin in persuading Californians to join the U.S. and, according to some reports, with a secret message to Frémont that encouraged him to join the Bear Flag Revolt. In the Mexican War,♦ Stockton appointed him a captain in Frémont's California Battalion of Mounted Riflemen in command of the Los Angeles garrison. Under José Flores, Angelenos revolted against his arbitrary and harsh regulations, forcing Gillespie to surrender the pueblo. After he sent Juan Flaco Brown♦ to ask Stockton for reinforcements led by Mervine, battles followed in which Los Angeles was regained more than three months later by other troops. The rest of Gillespie's life was spent outside the public sphere.

GILLETT, JAMES NORRIS (1860–1937), 22nd governor of the state (1907–11), went to California in 1884 from his native Wisconsin, practiced law, was a Congressman, was active as a Republican, and helped create the state highway system.

GILLIAM, HAROLD [THOMPSON] (1918–   ), feature writer for the *San Francisco Chronicle* on environmental subjects and conservation whose own books include *San Francisco Bay* (1957); *The Natural World of San Francisco* (1967); *Between the Devil and the Deep Blue Bay* (1969), on the struggle to preserve San Francisco Bay; and *For Better or Worse: The Ecology of an Urban Area* (1972).

GILLIS, JAMES, see *Clemens, Samuel L.*

GILLIS, JAMES L[OUIS] (1857–1917), State Librarian (1899–1917) distinguished for developing the county library system and for creating the first union catalog in the U.S. (1909), which listed books in all county and many city libraries of the state. His daughter, Mabel R[ay] Gillis (1882–1961), was also a State Librarian (1930–51), the first woman to hold that post, and was noted for expanding reference materials and services related to California history.

GILLMAN, SID[NEY] (1911–   ), Minneapolis-born football coach, was coach for the Los Angeles Rams (1955–59) and the Chargers of Los Angeles and, later, of San Diego (1960–69, 1971). His teams won five Western Division championships and one American Football League championship.

GILMAN, CHARLOTTE PERKINS, see *Perkins, Charlotte.*

GILMAN, DANIEL COIT (1831–1908), after service at Yale as librarian and a founder and professor of geography in its Sheffield Scientific School, was appointed the first president of the University of California (1872–75). He resigned to become the first president of The Johns Hopkins University (1876–1901).

GILROY, JOHN (1796–1869), name adopted by John Cameron (whose mother was a Gilroy), a Scot who jumped ship at Monterey (1814) and is said to have been the first white non-Hispanic settler in California. Soon baptized and changing his given name to Juan Bautista, he wed the granddaughter of José F. Ortega and, as a naturalized Mexican (1833), became part owner of an Ortega property, Rancho San Ysidro, near present Gilroy. He died impoverished.

Gilroy, small city in the lower Santa Clara Valley, a center for neighboring orchardists and farmers, which has food-processing plants. It was founded in 1870 and named for John Gilroy, who had died the year before. Each summer a major rodeo attracts tourists. In 1970 it had a population of 12,665.

GINSBERG, ALLEN (1926–   ), New Jersey-born poet, long identified with the Beat movement♦ of San Francisco, where he has intermittently spent some time. His best-known poem, *Howl,*♦ was published (1956) by the small San Francisco firm, City Lights, whose owner, Lawrence Ferlinghetti,♦ was put on trial for issuing an allegedly obscene poem. This passionate, frank, Whitman-like mystical view of modern corruption was recognized as an important poetic statement and its publisher was acquitted. Despite a worldwide reputation, Ginsberg has continued to have City Lights issue many of his other writings, including *Kaddish and Other Poems* (1961) and *Reality Sandwiches* (1963). His affiliation with the San Francisco Renaissance is treated in *Journals* (1977).

Girl of the Golden West, The, play by David Belasco,♦ produced in 1905 and adapted by Puccini as an Italian opera in 1910. It depicts the love of "The Girl," a saloonkeeper and schoolmistress of a mining town, for an outlaw whom she conceals in her cabin and whom she saves from jail, first by cheating the sheriff in a poker game whose stakes are "The Girl" or her lover, and then, after the lover is captured, by convincing the miners to let him go away with her.

GLEASON, RALPH J[OSEPH] (1917–75), New York-born music critic and longtime columnist for the *San Francisco Chronicle* on jazz and popular modern♦ music. He was a cofounder of *Rolling Stone*♦ and the author of several books, including *The San Francisco Scene* (1968), dealing with rock music, a subject he was one of the first to treat critically as a serious art form.

Glendale, city in Los Angeles County, located on the Rancho San Rafael granted to José María Verdugo (1784), founder of a family prominent in the region and remembered in various place-names. The town came into being in the 1880s after rail connections were made between Los Angeles and the San Fernando Valley. Its settlers were for the most part conservative orchardists, and the settlement grew with successive land booms. Light industry has long since replaced agriculture, and the residential community of many elderly, well-to-do persons is known for its symphony orchestra and other cultural activities. Forest Lawn Memorial Park♦ is located there.

Glendora, residential community northeast of Los Angeles at the foot of the San Gabriel Mts., founded on the old Rancho Azusa. The coming of the Santa Fe (1887) and the interurban Pacific Electric (1907) tracks created land booms. The economy was based on citrus and other fruit growing and packing, aided by irrigation. The city was named by its founder, a Chicago manufacturer, George Whitcomb, by combining "glen" and part of his wife's name, Ledora.

Glen Ellen, see *Sonoma Valley.*

GLENN, HUGH JAMES (1824–82), Missouri dentist who went to California (1849) to mine gold but in the 1860s began wheat ranching, at which he was so successful that he became the state's largest grower, known as the "Wheat King" for his production (1880) of more than a half million bushels on his 55,000 acres in that part of Colusa County which was split off (1891) and named Glenn County in his memory.

Glenn County, incorporated (1891) from part of Colusa County, was named for Dr. Hugh J. Glenn,♦ the "Wheat King." Tehama County lies on its north; Butte County on the east, the Sacramento River forming that boundary; Colusa and Lake counties on the south; and Lake and Mendocino counties on the west. Some of Mendocino National Forest lies in the western part of the county. Once predominantly a wheat raising area, nowadays rice is the major crop, while most of the Ladino clover seed grown in the U.S. comes from the area of Orland, also the site of the first federal irrigation project. Livestock ranching and dairying are other major sources of the economy, as is natural gas production. Willows♦ has always been the county seat. In 1970 the county population was 17,521. With an area of 844,288 acres, that gave it 13.3 persons per sq. mi.

Gliding, recreational sport, pioneered by John J. Montgomery♦ (1883), was first popularized during the late 1920s as enthusiasts made gradual descents to earth in motorless planes. Soaring is a variation in which rising air masses are used to allow a glider to gain altitude for a cross-country flight. The Mojave Desert and Torrey Pines both afford fine updrafts for the purpose. Another variation, popularized in the 1970s, is hang gliding, in which the person gliding uses only a wing engineered by a Stanford graduate, Francis Rogallo, to sustain the flight that begins with a leap from a height. The first national hang gliding competition took place near Sylmar in 1973.

Goat Island, see *Yerba Buena.*

Goats, not native to California, were introduced and raised both by Spanish missionaries and Russian settlers. Nathan Spear raised goats on the San Francisco Bay's Yerba Buena Island, long called Goat Island because of the hundreds of animals there during the gold rush period. However, goats did not become important as producers of milk, and the Angora species, introduced during the gold rush, has not been the basis of a big mohair business. Goat Mts. and similar names in the state were probably occasioned by the presence of antelope or mountain sheep, identified as goats at a distance.

GODDARD, GEORGE HENRY (1817–1906), English-born civil engineer and artist, after education at Oxford went to California during the gold rush (1850) and later undertook governmental surveys, created a precise and detailed map of the state (1857), and made many drawings and lithographs of California.

GOLD, HERBERT (1924–), Ohio-born novelist, after education at Columbia University and residence in France and on the East Coast, settled in San Francisco. His fiction, often quasi-autobiographical in that it treats experiences of adolescence and a background of Jewish life, includes *Birth of a Hero* (1951); *The Prospect before Us* (1954); *The Man Who Was Not with It* (1956); *Therefore Be Bold* (1960); *Salt* (1963); *Fathers* (1967); *The Great American Jackpot* (1970), concerned with the San Francisco hippie scene; and *Waiting for Cordelia* (1977), about San Francisco prostitutes organizing a union. His nonfiction includes *The Age of Happy Problems* (1962), essays; and *My Last Two Thousand Years* (1972), an autobiography. He has also published volumes of collected stories.

Gold mining, dates back almost to the earliest European settlement of California, when some of the metal was collected on the lower Colorado River (1775–80) in the Picacho area. More placer deposits were discovered during the early 19th century in the San Gabriel Mts. and near San Diego, but commercially significant mining was first undertaken in 1842 at Placerita Canyon.♦

Mining by large numbers of people began very quickly after the discovery (Jan. 24, 1848) by James W. Marshall of nuggets in the tailrace of the sawmill being built for Sutter♦ at Coloma on the South Fork of the American River.♦ The revelation of that find started the great gold rush,♦ which led thousands upon thousands of people to the rivers and creeks of the Mother Lode region,♦ up into the Trinity, Klamath, and Salmon rivers area, and out to other likely places.

The first and most common form of retrieval was that in which gold was extracted from a river bed by panning, a simple system soon replaced by the use of a rocker, itself further developed into a long tom and a sluice box, all refinements of placer mining.♦ Miners followed color♦ to get from the dirt gold dust and nuggets (such nuggets could weigh more than 100 ounces each) by sifting the heavier metal from the surrounding lighter debris. In the early years those primitive methods sufficed to get at the gold in river beds, particularly when their channels were made available by dams, canals, and flumes that diverted the water elsewhere.

After 1856 recovery from streams began to diminish, and by 1859 white miners had abandoned most of the original American River area to the Chinese, who took over more and more rivers within a few years. By that time quartz mining♦ was developed, and miners followed subterranean veins which could range from thin filaments near the surface to thick deposits going down thousands of feet through the rock.

In the 1850s only about 1% of the gold came from quartz mines; in the 1870s it rose to 30%. Even at its simplest the process required some elaborate techniques, such as the use of a stamp mill or a rotary contrivance called an arrastre♦ to crush the rock and extract its gold. Tunneling to follow the drift of the veins that flowed through fissures in the rocks was also an elaborate process requiring many workers and some initial capital.

A simpler substitute was the locally devised hydraulic mining,♦ in which powerful jets of water from high-pressure hoses were played on hillsides, exposing their inner veins and washing the gold out of them. That technique was eventually prohibited (1884) because it clogged rivers and polluted the downstream soil which was needed for farming.

Still another late system employed dredges on the rivers: they gathered low-grade ores by using endless bucket lines which scooped out the beds and recovered tailings (residue) not garnered by earlier and simpler means such as panning. Gold has been discovered at one time or another in 52 of the present 58 counties of the state, although the great sources have been limited to the Mother Lode region, the state's northwestern mountains and rivers, Bodie, the Rand District, and southern California areas down to its very southeasternmost boundary.

No contemporary records were kept of the amount of gold mined annually during the gold rush and subsequent years, but estimates for salient dates are: *1848,* $245,301; *1849,* $10,151,360; *1850,* $41,273,106; *1851,* $75,938,232; *1852,* $81,294,700; *1853,* $67,613,487; *1855,* $55,485,395; *1860,* $44,095,163; *1865,* $17,930,858.

Gold Rush, term commonly used for the great migration to California and its attendant circumstances after the discovery of the Wimmer Nugget♦ (Jan. 24, 1848) by James W. Marshall♦ in the tailrace of the sawmill on the South Fork of the American River,♦ whose construction he was supervising for the owner, Sutter,♦ at the site of the present town of Coloma.

The news soon leaked out, but large numbers did not rush to the site and nearby likely places until after Samuel Brannan dramatically displayed gold dust from the American River in San Francisco on May 12. Then Californians of all sorts and from all places began to converge on the so-called diggings, soon followed by persons who could get there relatively easily from Oregon and Utah, from Hawaii, and from Sonora and other parts of Mexico as well as from Chile and other coastal areas of South America. The immigrants of 1848 were enormously swelled by forty-niners♦ after President Polk made an official announcement of the discovery (Dec. 5, 1848) and displayed 230 ounces of California gold.

American immigrants followed three major routes in reaching California: by sea and land travel down the Atlantic to cross the Isthmus of Panama or Nicaragua and then go up the Pacific by vessel; by a journey of several months during spring and summer across the midwestern plains, then through the Rocky Mts. and across the Sierra, on foot, horseback, and by covered wagon, along the California Trail,♦ or by southwestern routes such as the Santa Fe Trail♦ and the Old Spanish Trail♦ or through Mexico; or by ship around Cape Horn. Travelers by the Isthmus arrived as early as February; some ocean voyagers docked in San Francisco during the summer; and the larger contingents of overland voyagers came later still but, necessarily, before winter snow blocked the mountain routes.

Most of them were young white males, although some women and children came too, and southerners sometimes brought slaves to assist in the digging. In time people representing the widest diversity of ethnic groups♦ made their way to California's mines. Virtually all of them headed for the so-called Mother Lode♦ region, extending roughly from Mariposa in present Merced County to Georgetown on the north in present El Dorado County, or to the mining area farther northwest in the region of the Trinity, Klamath, and Salmon rivers. Other likely places were tried too in the quest for the best sites in the land of El Dorado as techniques of gold mining were developed.

The quest for rich spots along river beds led to the rapid creation of mining camps with colorful names like Fiddletown, French Camp, Greenhorn Bar, Humbug Hill, Sixbit Gulch, and Whiskey Flat. Many disappeared quickly as their placer mines gave out, others became mining towns with stone and brick buildings, like Columbia, and with opera houses where Lotta Crabtree and Lola Montez appeared. Some miners made fortunes, others were disappointed "to see the elephant,"♦ as they made

clear in the letter sheets♦ they sent home to describe their experiences. Still others moved into the big supply centers that with great speed became cities, particularly San Francisco; Sacramento, the port on the Sacramento River; Stockton, the port on the San Joaquin River; and Marysville, strategically located on the confluence of the Feather and Yuba rivers. The mining area itself grew from a population of about 6,000 at the end of 1848 to perhaps 100,000 in the peak year of 1852, after which it declined sharply in people and production.

While it lasted, the gold rush was a fascinating topic for books by cultivated residents of the camps and towns, among them J. D. Borthwick,♦ Alonzo Delano,♦ and Dame Shirley,♦ and a great subject for visiting journalists like Bayard Taylor.♦ After the rush dwindled away in the 1860s, it and the life of its deserted camps became an appealing literary subject both for nostalgia and for romance, particularly capitalized upon in the stories that Bret Harte began to write in 1869; and even a latecomer like Samuel Clemens could find folk humor out of which he created his "Celebrated Jumping Frog of Calaveras County."

Gold spike, used in the ceremony on May 10, 1869, at Promontory Point, Utah, to mark the meeting of the rails of the Central Pacific♦ and the Union Pacific♦ railroads. In the ceremony Leland Stanford of the Central Pacific and T. C. Durant, vice president of the Union Pacific, dropped four spikes, two of gold, one of Nevada silver, and one of Arizona iron, silver, and gold into holes of a laurel wood tie; then both executives tried and failed to hit the spikes with a sledge wired to telegraph the blow. They may next have tapped the spikes with a silver-coated sledge. Workers then removed the ceremonial objects and drove regular spikes into a standard tie. A famous fictionized painting of the ceremony was made by Thomas Hill.♦

GOLDBERG, RUBE (REUBEN LUCIUS GOLDBERG) (1883–1970), San Francisco-born and educated (University of California B.S. in engineering, 1904) cartoonist. In addition to creating characters such as Boob McNutt and Mike and Ike—They Look Alike, he depicted fantastic devices that in complicated fashion solved simple needs, and they became so popular that his name became associated with the idea of curious contrivances. He also won a Pulitzer Prize (1948) for a serious cartoon on the threat of the atom bomb.

Golden Era (1852–93), literary weekly founded and edited (to 1860) by Rollin M. Daggett♦ and J. Macdonough Ford to give a view of the life and culture of California in literary contributions and informal columns as well as summaries of news. Early contributors included William H. Rhodes ("Caxton"), Alonzo Delano ("Old Block"), Stephen Massett ("Jeems Pipes"), and John R. Ridge ("Yellow Bird"). Sold in 1860 to Joseph E. Lawrence and James Brooks, its policies were continued but it was enlarged to an eight-page, six-column newspaper format and it attracted many young contributors. These included Bret Harte (who there printed his first important story, "M'liss"), Mark Twain, C. W. Stoddard, Prentice Mulford, Fitz Hugh Ludlow, Joaquin Miller, J. S. Hittell, and Charles Henry Webb, as well as much criticism of drama and many columns of reprinted materials, including serialized sensation novels. After Lawrence quit (1866) the paper was less impressive. In 1882 it moved to San Diego and had a succession of editors, including Harr Wagner.♦ It had always depended on women, such as Frances Fuller Victor, to do much basic writing, but in later years it put even more emphasis on female journalists.

Golden Gate, name given to the entrance to San Francisco Bay by Frémont in 1846, as explained in his *Geographical Memoir* (1848): "Called *Chrysopylae* (Golden gate) on the map, on the same principle that the harbor of *Byzantium* (Constantinople afterwards) was called *Chrysoceras* (golden horn). The form of the harbor, and its advantages for commerce . . . suggested the name to the Greek founders of Byzantium. The form of the entrance into the bay of San Francisco, and its advantages for commerce, (Asiatic inclusive,) suggest the name which is given to this entrance." Unless Drake sailed into San Francisco Bay, as some persons contend, Pedro Fages may have been the first European to see the entrance (1770).

Golden Gate Bridge, steel suspension bridge for vehicles and pedestrians extending from Fort Point♦ in San Francisco to the Marin County shore over the mile-wide Bay. The central span is 4,200 feet long and its 746-feet-high towers are the largest ever built; clearance for a vessel is 220 feet. Erected under the direction and plans of Joseph B. Strauss,♦ it was opened in 1937. Unfortunately, the great orange span has been the scene of a steady succession of suicides.

Golden Gate International Exposition, celebrated the recent openings of the two bridges over San Francisco Bay. From Feb. 19 to Oct. 29, 1939, over 10,000,000 people visited the exposition located on Treasure Island, a man-made island created in the Bay adjacent to Yerba Buena Island. The theme was symbolized by Ralph Stackpole's huge statue of Pacifica. A reorganized exposition was opened on the site (May 25–Sept. 29, 1940).

Golden Gate National Recreational Area, federal park of 34,000,000 acres in San Francisco and Marin counties, established in 1972. Incorporating previous city, state, and National Parks and beaches as well as formerly privately owned land, on the southern side of the Bay and Golden Gate it includes Alcatraz and stretches from Aquatic Park through parts of the Presidio, past Seal Rocks, and down the Pacific shoreline to San Mateo County. On the northern side of the Bay it includes Angel Island, and extends from the Golden Gate Bridge through the western side of Marin County through Muir Woods and Mt. Tamalpais up for 23 miles to the town of Olema.

Golden Gate Park, San Francisco public landscaped area of 1,017 acres purchased by the city in 1868. A plan for the sand dunes on the site was made by the first superintendent (1871–87), William Hammond Hall,♦ but the landscaping, done in a natural English garden style, was the work of his assistant, then second superintendent (1887–1943), John McLaren,♦ a Scot properly called the "Father of Golden Gate Park." In addition to its meadows, playfields, gardens, lakes, and waterfalls, the Park contains a great Victorian conservatory, a gift of James Lick and Charles Crocker; a concourse with a bandstand; the California Academy of Sciences, including a planetarium and the Steinhart Aquarium; the Japanese Tea Garden, developed for the California Midwinter International Exposition (1894) located there; the M. H. de Young Memorial Museum, also an outgrowth of the Midwinter Exposition, now containing European and American works of art and the Avery Brundage Collection in the Asian Art Museum; Kezar Stadium, used mainly for professional football; a polo field; and much statuary.

Golden Gate University, San Francisco institution, founded (1881) by the YMCA as an evening high school. In 1901 it added a college level and in 1928 it became Golden Gate College. A private, coeducational school, it emphasizes law, business, and public administration for its 5,000 students, nearly all employed, who at odd hours attend classes taught by part-time instructors in a downtown office building.

Golden Gateway, area of downtown San Francisco, exceeding 45 acres, once occupied by wholesale produce firms. It is on the fringe of the financial district, near the waterfront, and was redeveloped in the 1960s for apartment and office buildings, townhouses, shops, and landscaped areas.

Golden Hind, see *Drake, Francis.*

Golden Seals, see *California Golden Seals.*

Golden State, sobriquet for California, coined early because of the gold discovery and the Golden Gate.

Golden State Warriors, National Basketball Association team, known as the San Francisco Warriors (1962–71) after moving from Philadelphia. Its home site is Oakland. It won divisional championships (1964, 1967, 1975), in the last year winning the NBA title. Star players have included Rick Barry, Wilt Chamberlain, and Nate Thurmond.

GOLDWYN, SAMUEL (1882–1974), Polish-born motion picture producer who came to the U.S. (1906) and in time changed his surname, which had been Goldfish. With his brother-in-law, Jesse Lasky,◆ he moved from glove manufacturing into film production (1910), taking Cecil B. De Mille as a third partner and later merging (1916) with a company owned by Adolph Zukor. The firm became Metro-Goldwyn-Mayer (1924), but the next year Goldwyn withdrew to become an independent producer associated with other companies. For at least thirty years he was known for developing major stars, for engaging important authors (e.g. Lillian Hellman and Robert Sherwood) to write or adapt screenplays, and for assembling and dominating diverse talented contributors to his films. He was also known for mixed metaphors, grammatical blunders, and malapropisms (many probably coined by press agents or gossips), such as: "Include me out" and "An oral agreement isn't worth the paper it's written on."

Goleta, suburb of Santa Barbara, just to its west on the ocean front. A University of California campus is located there. The name may derive from an American schooner (Spanish "goleta") long stranded in its estuary. A Japanese submarine shelled an oil field near there (Feb. 23, 1942).

Golf, popular sport introduced to the state with the building of its first course at Riverside (1891), only three years after the first one in the nation had been opened in New York State. Others quickly followed in southern California at Catalina (1892); Pasadena (1894); Redlands, Santa Barbara, and Santa Monica (1896); and Coronado, Hemet, Los Angeles, and San Diego (1897).

The Southern California Golf Association was created (1899) and its first annual amateur championship competition was held at the Los Angeles Country Club (1900). The first such statewide tournament was held in 1908.

The first important professional tournaments began in the 1920s in Los Angeles (its annual Los Angeles Open dates from 1906), Sacramento, and San Diego. The first U.S. Amateur championship held in California took place at the Del Monte Golf and Country Club (1929) and the first U.S. Open to be held in the state took place at the Riviera Country Club of Los Angeles (1948). Since then California has become known for important amateur and professional tournaments of its own, including the Bing Crosby, on the Monterey Peninsula, and the Palm Springs, sponsored by Bob Hope.

The first national champions from the state were George Von Elm, who won the U.S. Amateur in 1926; and Olin Dutra, who won the U.S. Open in 1934. Other outstanding golfers from California include Lawson Little (U.S. Amateur champion 1934–35, U.S. Open champion 1940), Billy Casper (U.S. Open champion 1959, 1966), Gene Littler (U.S. Amateur champion 1953, U.S. Open champion 1961), Ken Venturi (U.S. Open champion 1964), and Mickey Wright (U.S. Open women's champion 1958–59, 1961, 1964). (*See also individual entries.*)

GOMEZ, LEFTY (VERNON LOUIS GOMEZ) (1908–), baseball player born in Rodeo, was a pitcher for the N.Y. Yankees (1930–42) and the Washington Senators (1943). He led the American League in strikeouts for three years, and played in seven World Series, where he had six wins and no losses. He was elected to the Baseball Hall of Fame (1972).

GONZALES, PANCHO (RICHARD ALONZO GONZALES) (1928–), Los Angeles-born tennis star, as an amateur won the U.S. men's singles championship (1948, 1949) and that of England (1949) before turning professional. From 1954 to 1961 he was the top-ranking professional, particularly known for his great serves and smashes in a well-balanced game. At Wimbledon (1969) he won a match that lasted five hours and twenty minutes.

GONZÁLEZ RUBIO, JOSÉ MARÍA DE JESÚS (1804–75), Mexican-born Franciscan missionary to California (1833) who became President-General♦ of the northern missions, Soledad to Sonoma (1835–43).

GOODMAN, JOSEPH T[HOMPSON] (1838–1917), went from his native New York State to California in the gold rush and there worked as a typesetter on the *Golden Era.* In 1861 he went to Virginia City, Nevada, where he became co-owner of the *Territorial Enterprise,* employing Mark Twain, who became a lifelong friend. He later traveled in Mexico and Central America, becoming an authority on Mayan glyphs, about which he wrote a book.

GOODRICH, GAIL (1943–   ), Los Angeles-born basketball player, graduated from UCLA (1965), where as a guard he was the leading scorer for the championship teams of John Wooden.♦ After 1965 he was with the Los Angeles Lakers, except for 1968–70, when he played for the Phoenix Suns, and continued his record scoring, averaging nearly 20 points a game. He now plays for New Orleans.

Goops, see *Burgess, Gelett.*

Goose, wild bird not native to the state, but perhaps 1,000,000 geese of different varieties winter there annually. Most come from central Canada. The major varieties are the *lesser snow goose,* found mostly in the Central Valley and the western Santa Barbara Islands; the *Ross snow goose,* wintering in the Central Valley and around Los Angeles; the *white-fronted goose* (and the variant *tule*), found in the Sacramento and San Joaquin valleys; the *Canada goose,* quite common in interior areas; the similar *lesser Canada goose* and *cackling goose;* the *Great Basin Canada goose,* found at mountain lakes; and the *black brant goose,* which keeps to the coast, particularly at Humboldt and Tomales bays. The Maidu Indians ate geese and white residents killed the birds in great numbers until hunting laws and federal and state♦ reserves were instituted.

Gopher, burrowing, fur-bearing rodent of which four species flourish in almost all parts of California except the southwestern desert region. In the most populated areas (e.g. Fresno County foothills), as many as 30 may be found per acre. The most common variety is the *Botta pocket gopher,* named for the naturalist who visited California with Duhaut-Cilly. Gophers served as food for Indians.

Gordo Basin, underwater ocean plain extending from a deep-sea area off Cape Mendocino north nearly to the Canadian border. Bearing the Spanish

name for "big", the Basin is about 150 miles wide. Lying between the Pacific Plate and the North American Plate, it is subject to frequent earthquakes.

GORDON, GEORGE (1818–69), English-born financier (originally named George Cummings), who went to San Francisco (1849) and there built an elegant house (1854) on the oval of South Park,♦ the fashionable neighborhood he designed. He also acquired a ranch and country house (1863) which, after Gordon's death, Leland Stanford bought for his home (later the site of Stanford University). Gordon founded the first sugar refinery in California (1856). His tragic relations with his dipsomaniac wife, Nelly, were fictionized by Gertrude Atherton in "The Randolphs of the Redwoods" (1883), revised as *A Daughter of the Vine* (1899).

GORDON, LAURA DE FORCE (1838–1907), born in Pennsylvania, went to California (1870) with her husband, Dr. Gordon, and there became an important advocate of women's rights. Resident in Lodi, she traveled widely as a speaker, was a journalist in Stockton and Oakland, and with Clara Foltz♦ brought successful suit for women to be admitted to the state-funded Hastings College of the Law. The two women were also simultaneously admitted to the California bar (1879).

GORDON, WALTER [ARTHUR] (1894–1976), Georgia-born jurist, educated at the University of California (A.B., 1918; J.D., 1922), became governor of the Virgin Islands (1955–58), the first black person to hold that post, and its district court judge (1958–76).

GORDON, WILLIAM (1801–76), Ohio-born pioneer of present New Mexico, where he married a Mexican woman and with her traveled to California in the party of William Workman♦ (1841). There he became the first white settler of present Yolo County, living on a large ranch on Cache Creek♦ until he moved (1866) to Lake County.

Governor, chief executive of the state, elected to a four-year term (until 1862, a two-year term) and eligible for unlimited reelection. Any citizen of the U.S. over age 25 and resident in California for five years immediately preceding the election may run for the office. Within the state his powers and responsibilities are like those of the President of the U.S. He makes all nonelective or non-Civil Service appointments to departments, agencies, commissions, the Board of Regents of the University of California, etc. He prepares the budget, which he submits to the legislature, and to it he also sends messages and proposals for laws. He has a veto power like that of the President, and he may delete items in budgets. He appoints state, county, and municipal judges and has powers to pardon or grant clemency to convicted persons. He serves as president of the Board of Regents and of the Board of Trustees of State Universities and Colleges. He is the commander in chief of the National Guard and other armed services.

Governors of California

Spanish Governors

1. Gaspar de Portolá (*comandante;* Matías de Armona, gov.)	1769–1770
2. Pedro Fages (de facto as *comandante-militar,* Alta Calif.)	1770–1774
[Felipe de Barri (gov. of Los Californios from Loreto)	1771–1774]
3. Fernando Rivera y Moncada (de facto as *comandante-militar,* Alta Calif.)	1774–1777
4. Felipe de Neve (gov. of Los Californios from Loreto 1775–77, from Monterey)	1777–1782
5. Pedro Fages	1782–1791
6. José Antonio Roméu	1791–1792
7. José Joaquín de Arrillaga	1792–1794
8. Diego de Borica	1794–1800
9. José Joaquín de Arrillaga (after 1804, all governors for Alta Calif. only)	1800–1814
10. José Darío de Argüello	1814–1815
11. Pablo Vicente de Solá	1815–April 11, 1822

Mexican Governors

1. Pablo Vicente de Solá	April 11–Nov. 22, 1822
2. Luís Antonio de Argüello	1822–1825
3. José María de Echeandía	1825–1831
4. Manuel Victoria	Jan. 31–Dec. 6, 1831
5. Pío Pico	Jan. 27–Feb. 18, 1832
6a. Agustin V. Zamorano (north)	1832–1833
6b. José María de Echeandía (south)	1832–1833
7. José Figueroa	1833–1835
8. José Castro	Oct. 8, 1835–Jan. 2, 1836
9. Nicolas Gutiérrez	Jan. 2–May 1, 1836
10. Mariano Chico	May 1–July 30, 1836
11. Nicolas Gutiérrez	July 30–Nov. 5, 1836
12. Juan Bautista Alvarado (José Castro, Nov. 5–Dec. 7, 1836)	1836–1842
13. Manuel Micheltorena	1842–1845
14. Pío Pico	1845–1846
15. José María Flores	Oct. 31, 1846–Jan. 11, 1847
16. Andrés Pico	Jan. 11–13, 1847

American Military Governors

1. John Drake Sloat	July 7–29, 1846
2. Robert Field Stockton	July 29, 1846–Jan. 19, 1847
3. John Charles Frémont	Jan. 19–March 1, 1847
4. Stephen Watts Kearny	March 1–May 31, 1847
5. Richard Barnes Mason	May 31, 1847–Feb. 28, 1849
6. Persifor F. Smith	Feb. 28–April 12, 1849
7. Bennet Riley	April 12–Dec. 20, 1849

California State Governors

1. Peter H. Burnett	Dec. 20, 1849–Jan. 9, 1851
2. John McDougal	Jan. 9, 1851–Jan. 8, 1852

3. John Bigler	1852–1856
4. John Neely Johnson	1856–1858
5. John B. Weller	1858–1860
6. Milton S. Latham	Jan. 9–14, 1860
7. John G. Downey	1860–1862
8. Leland Stanford	1862–1863
9. Frederick F. Low	1863–1867
10. Henry H. Haight	1867–1871
11. Newton Booth	1871–1875
12. Romualdo Pacheco	Feb. 27–Dec. 9, 1875
13. William Irwin	1875–1880
14. George C. Perkins	1880–1883
15. George Stoneman	1883–1887
16. Washington Bartlett	Jan. 8–Sept. 12, 1887
17. Robert W. Waterman	1887–1891
18. Henry H. Markham	1891–1895
19. James H. Budd	1895–1899
20. Henry T. Gage	1899–1903
21. George C. Pardee	1903–1907
22. James N. Gillett	1907–1911
23. Hiram W. Johnson	1911–1917
24. William D. Stephens	1917–1923
25. William Friend Richardson	1923–1927
26. Clement C. Young	1927–1931
27. James Rolph, Jr.	1931–1934
28. Frank F. Merriam	1934–1939
29. Culbert L. Olson	1939–1943
30. Earl Warren	1943–1953
31. Goodwin J. Knight	1953–1959
32. Edmund G. Brown, Sr.	1959–1967
33. Ronald Reagan	1967–1975
34. Edmund G. Brown, Jr.	1975–

GOYCOECHEA, Felipe de (1747–1814), Mexican-born army officer, served as *comandante* of the presidio at Santa Barbara (1784–1802). After Arrillaga became the first person to be appointed governor of the separate province of Alta California (1804), Goycoechea was made governor of Baja California (1806–14). Although impeached (1811) for official misconduct, he was not convicted.

Grabhorn Press, The, fine printing firm, founded in San Francisco (1920) by the brothers Edwin (1889–1968) and Robert (1900–73) Grabhorn of Indiana. It became internationally distinguished for striking design, fine craftsmanship, and publication of rare early western Americana, particularly Californiana, often from Edwin Grabhorn's large book collection. The Press *Bibliography* appeared in two folio volumes (1940, 1957). The brothers separated (1965) when the firm was discontinued shortly before the death of Edwin. Robert, in association with Andrew Hoyem,♦ formed the comparable Grabhorn-Hoyem

Press (1966–73). Robert's wife, Jane (1911–73), was a witty author and, as proprietor of the Colt Press, a printer in her own right.

Grace Cathedral, located on the Nob Hill, San Francisco, site of the mansion of Charles Crocker,♦ whose family donated the land to be used for the seat of the Episcopal bishop of California. The initial architect was Lewis Hobart and the cornerstone was laid in 1910. The gothic structure of brushed concrete has a nave 300 feet long and 87 feet high. The east front has doors that are casts of those created by Ghiberti for the Baptistry in Florence.

Graduate Theological Union, consortium of schools and seminaries in Berkeley, formed in 1962 to offer cooperative graduate programs of studies leading to higher degrees. It includes the Pacific School of Religion♦ and the San Francisco Theological Seminary,♦ and in addition to offering Roman Catholic,

Protestant, and Jewish studies, it has a Center for Urban-Black Studies, an Office of Women's Affairs, and a Center for Ethics and Social Policy. In 1977 it had 135 full-time faculty members and 1,100 resident students.

GRAHAM, BARBARA (1923–55), had a criminal record from age 14 of theft, prostitution, and perjury before she and two male companions murdered a southern California widow during a robbery (1953). She was executed at San Quentin. The film, *I Want To Live!*♦ (1955) was based on her experiences.

GRAHAM, BILL (1931–), German-born impresario of rock music (original name, Wolfgang Grajonca), best known for his Fillmore Auditorium.♦

GRAHAM, ISAAC (1800–63), Kentucky-born mountain man who went to California (1834) and for a time had a distillery near Monterey. He and a group of his followers aided the attempt of Juan Bautista Alvarado♦ to establish a free state (1836), then tried to overthrow Gov. Alvarado (1840), by whom Graham was exiled to Baja California. In 1845 he first supported Gov. Micheltorena, then aided Alvarado's revolt against him. On his Santa Cruz *rancho,* he later ran a sawmill and did tanning. H. H. Bancroft called him "a loud-mouthed, unprincipled, profligate, and reckless man."

GRAHAM, MARGARET COLLIER (1850–1910), Iowa-born resident of southern California after 1876, who wrote low-key local-color stories collected in *Stories of the Foot-hills* (1895), and essays, often feminist, for *Land of Sunshine,* collected posthumously in *Do They Really Respect Us?* (1912).

GRANT, CARY (1904–), English-born film actor, began his career in Hollywood in 1932 and has been a U.S. citizen since 1942, continuing to make his home in the Los Angeles area. Known for his urbane style and pleasant good looks, his dramatic talent has been displayed mainly in comic roles acted with a casual flair.

GRANT, ULYSSES S[IMPSON] (1822–85), 18th President of the U.S., after graduation from West Point and service in the Mexican War and elsewhere, was sent to Benicia, then as a captain to Fort Humboldt (1853–54), a frontier outpost against Indians. His boredom led him to drink, and a reprimand from his commanding officer led him to resign from the army (1854). After his presidency Grant visited San Francisco (1879) as part of a world tour, and there he was

lavishly entertained by Flood and Sharon. A giant redwood standing in Kings Canyon National Park was named for him.

Grapefruit, see *Citrus, Coachella Valley,* and *California Fruit Growers Exchange.*

Grapes, first grown in California by the mission fathers who cultivated in their vineyards♦ a hardy variety known as the mission grape, to make wine not only for sacramental use but for drinking as they had been accustomed to at home. They also grew table grapes and dried them to make raisins. Commercial grape production and better-quality grapes were introduced by Jean Louis Vignes♦ (*c.* 1831), a vintner of Bordeaux, whose grape growing and wine making in Los Angeles were followed by those of William Wolfskill.

During the gold rush the cultivation of grapes and making of wine moved to the valleys near San Francisco. The major figure and the founder of modern California wine making was Agoston Haraszthy,♦ who in the 1850s developed a large vineyard in Sonoma Valley on which he grew tokay and zinfandel, from his native Hungary, and other varieties of fine grapes. These were augmented by vast quantities of cuttings he imported (1861) from Europe, where the state legislature sent him as a commissioner to find means to extend and improve the new industry.

In the 1870s and 80s the roots of many grape vines in France were destroyed by the phylloxera, a plant louse, which paradoxically had beneficial results too, for it eliminated many poor vines imported from Europe, ended the mission grape, drove out hasty speculators, and forced growers to concentrate on improved and immune American stock and the best use of European vines. From that time on the making of wine♦ increased and improved.

Meanwhile growing grapes for table use continued, and commercial raisin production began in 1873. The hot rainless summer weather of the San Joaquin Valley made it a center of raisin making, which requires four times the amount of fresh grapes that will finally be yielded in the dried product. The muscat and the Thompson (or seedless) were the major varieties cultivated for curing, but some grapes were imported from Chile, where labor costs were lower. Of the cooperative associations for marketing, the most successful was founded in 1913 and used the trademark "Sun-Maid."

By 1923 California produced 90% of the raisins in the U.S. and 60% of those throughout the world. It is the largest producer of grapes in the nation. In

1970 raisin grapes were valued at nearly $135,000,000, wine grapes at $61,000,000, and table grapes at nearly $32,000,000. Grape picking labor, long mainly Mexican, was finally unionized by Cesar Chavez♦ in the 1960s.

Grapes of Wrath, The, novel by John Steinbeck,♦ published in 1939 and awarded a Pulitzer Prize. A full-bodied saga, the story presents the Joad family, dispossessed Oklahoma farmers on their way to California in a dilapidated car in quest of a land of plenty. They meet nothing but hardship and adversity, and in California itself they discover that the land is controlled by almost feudally organized big ranchers who try to get migratory labor at the lowest possible wages. But they also find good among the simple, downtrodden poor, and the patient, strong mother of the family concludes, "We ain' gonna die out. People is goin' on—changin' a little, maybe, but goin' right on." Darryl Zanuck produced and John Ford directed a notable film adaptation (1940).

Grapevine Canyon, deep gap in the Tehachapi Mts.♦ in Kern County, first explored by Fages (1772). This winding pass north of Tejon Pass became the terminus of the Ridge Route for early automobile travel between Los Angeles and Bakersfield.

Grass Valley, mining town of Nevada County, whose adjacent quartz mines are said to have yielded $5,000,000 annually during the peak years (1850–57). Mines continued in production for more than a century, and the town preserves much of its past charm. Lola Montez and Lotta Crabtree lived there, Josiah Royce was born there, and Mary Hallock Foote lived there in the 20th century.

Grateful Dead, The, rock music band, founded in San Francisco (1965) as The Warlocks by Jerry Garcia, a native Californian, as were all but one of the other five members. By 1966 they had their present name, were playing all over California, and provided music for Ken Kesey's "Trips Festivals," creating an appropriate environment for "consciousness expanding" drug experience. As part of the life of the Haight-Ashbury district of San Francisco, and through their numerous free concerts for causes in Golden Gate Park they came to be described as "not so much a band as a social institution." They played both hard, driving rock music and extended improvisations fostering a sense of community between band and audience at psychedelic clubs such as the Avalon Ballroom and the Fillmore Auditorium. In the 1970s they have explored more native American musical forms—folk, country, and blues in particular.

GRAUMAN, Sid[ney] (1879–1950), motion picture theater owner, born "South of the Slot"♦ in San Francisco, originated the idea of the spectacular "premiere" at his lavish and fantastically designed Egyptian Theatre in Hollywood (opened 1922). A few blocks away he open the even more opulent Grauman's Chinese Theatre (1927), famous for its entry court in whose concrete slabs are the handprints, congratulatory messages, and other memorabilia of movie stars. In the 1970s its initial name was changed to Mann's.

Gravel, see *Sand and gravel.*

GRAY, [Henry] Percy (1869–1952), San Francisco-born artist and newspaper illustrator, known mainly for his landscapes of the San Francisco Peninsula and Monterey, Marin, and Sonoma counties.

Graylodge Wildlife Area, reserved region of 7,500 acres in Butte County, west of Gridley and north of the Sutter Buttes.

GRAYSON, Andrew Jackson (1819–69), native of Louisiana who went to California (1846) with his family and served as an officer under Frémont. Without formal training, he began in 1854 to paint the birds of this region, becoming the Audubon of California. In 1860 he went to Mexico, where he continued his ornithological studies until he died.

GRAYSON, Robert H. (1914–   ), Oregon-born football player, was star fullback of the Stanford University teams (1933–35) known as the Vow Boys♦ which went to the Rose Bowl each of his years.

Great America, see *Santa Clara.*

Great Basin, name for the desert-like plains that extend into southeastern California from parts of Utah and most of Nevada. The name was created by Frémont in his *Report* of 1845. He explored the region between 1843 and 1853.

Great Central Valley, see *Central Valley.*

Great Diamond Hoax, see *Harpending, Asbury.*

Great Seal, see *State symbols.*

Great Western Power Company, public utility whose corporate name was slightly changed over the years, organized (1902) by Edwin T. Earl, his brother Guy, and others under the ownership of a New Jersey holding company. It developed the Big Bend plant on the Feather River (1908), the largest hydroelectric power transmitter west of the Mississippi. In 1911 the company purchased City Electric Co. (est. 1907) from Mortimer and Herbert Fleishhacker, who became president (1912–24) and vice president, respectively. It expanded capacity by building a dam at Lake Almanor (1914, enlarged, 1927) and extended its interests by gaining control (1924) of the San Joaquin Light and Power Co. of William G. Kerchoff.♦ In 1930 it in turn was absorbed by Pacific Gas and Electric Co.

Greed, motion picture adaptation of Frank Norris' novel, *McTeague,*♦ directed by Erich von Stroheim (1923). The very detailed film version originally took ten hours to screen but on orders of Irving Thalberg was cut to two and a half hours. Even in this abbreviated version it is esteemed as one of the great early productions of Hollywood, noted for its realistic settings, effective characterizations, fidelity to the novel, and symbolic interpretation.

Greeks in California, did not become a significant part of the population until the opening of the 20th century. The first Greek Orthodox Church was founded in San Francisco in 1904. Since then Greek communities have established churches in Los Angeles and many other cities and have erected an imposing cathedral in Oakland (1961). Settlements grew up in Bakersfield, Fresno, and other farming communities, for Greeks have tried small ranching and early attempted tobacco growing. However, more have settled in cities, where their businesses have included produce markets and small restaurants. Many have also become ocean fishermen. Outstanding Greeks in the state have included Spyros Skouras, the motion picture producer; Mayor George Christopher of San Francisco; and State Senator Nicholas C. Petris of Alameda County.

GREELEY, Horace (1811–72), editor of the *New-York Tribune* (1841–72), in which he published influential editorials, including one to support the homestead law popularizing J. L. B. Soule's famous phrase, "Go West, Young Man." He himself made a trip to California with Hank Monk, the stagecoach driver, as recounted in a lively passage of *Roughing It* by Mark Twain and in more sober style by Greeley in *An Overland Journey from New York to San Francisco in the Summer of 1859* (1860).

GREEN, John, see *Malaspina, Alejandro.*

GREENE, Charles Sumner (1868–1957) and Henry Mather Greene (1870–1954), Ohio-born brothers, trained as architects at the Massachusetts Institute of Technology, went to Pasadena in 1893. There they built redwood shingled bungalows showing an Oriental influence and some art-nouveau character, their second stories often marked by sleeping porches under broad eaves with strong, sculpturesque woodwork. Sometimes their houses were built around patios, but always they were possessed of fine detailing, subtle wrought iron decor, original stained glass, and the architects' own designs in furnishings.

GREGG, Josiah (1806–50), Tennessee-born trader who conducted commercial caravans between Independence, Mo., and Santa Fe, N.M. (1831–40), and wrote the popular *Commerce of the Prairies* (2 vols., 1844). After governmental service in Mexico during the Mexican War he went to California, which he described in his *Diary and Letters* (1944). There he led an exploring party which surveyed the Mad River,♦ named for an incident concerning him; the Bear; and the Eel. He died of a fall while exploring the Eel.

GREY, Zane (1872–1939), Ohio-born popular writer of cowboy stories, resident in California after 1906. His melodramatic fiction, a kind of modern dime novel, presenting life as a fight between evil villains and self-reliant frontier heroes, sold over 13,000,000 copies in his lifetime and has continued to be popular. His best-known works include *Riders of the Purple Sage* (1912) and its sequel, *The Rainbow Trail* (1915), set in the Southwest. He also wrote books about his fishing experiences.

GRIFFITH, D[avid] W[ark] (1875–1948), leading early motion picture director and producer (1908 ff.) who made the first important long film, *The Birth of a Nation* (1914), a spectacle based on Thomas Dixon's novel *The Clansman* which, as the son of a Confederate general, Griffith liked as an interpretation of the Civil War. In it and elsewhere he introduced such techniques as the long shot, crosscutting, the fade in and fade out, soft focus, high- and low-angle shots, and the moving camera. In

1910 he made his first film in Hollywood, with which his career, extending to 1931, was thereafter mainly identified. During that time he discovered numerous stars, including Mary Pickford and Douglas Fairbanks. With them and Charlie Chaplin he founded an independent studio, United Artists (1919), where he made *Broken Blossoms* (1919), a tragic tale of London's Limehouse or Chinatown area, and *Orphans of the Storm* (1922), a drama of the French Revolution featuring his discoveries, the Gish sisters. Other important films include *Intolerance* (1916), four interrelated stories illustrating the abstract theme of the title, and *Hearts of the World* (1918), a story of a German-occupied French village, with some realistic film made in the war zone.

Griffith Park, Los Angeles city park named for its donor (1896), Griffith J. Griffith, located on 3,761 acres of the eastern part of the Santa Monica Mts.◆ It is the largest urban park in the state and contains a zoo, a 4,000-seat Greek theater, a planetarium, and an observatory.

Grizzly, see *Bear*.

Grouse, game bird, three varieties of which are found in the state. *Sierra* (or *blue*) *grouse* is the commonest, found in the Sierra Nevada south to Mt. Whitney and in the Coast Range south to Lake County, distinguished by its large size, bluish color, and nearly square-ended tail; *Oregon ruffed grouse,* native to the northwest part of the state south to Humboldt Bay and east to the Siskiyou Mts., is slightly smaller, reddish-brown in color, with ruffs of dark feathers on its neck and a black band on its tail. The *Columbian sharp-tailed grouse,* also called the *sage grouse* and the *sage hen,* is found east of the Sierra, particularly in the northeast of the state, is medium sized, has a pointed tail, and pale colors above and white below. The *Sierra grouse* was once shot commercially as a market bird. The commonness of grouse is indicated by some geographic features incorporating its name.

Grunion, small and slender smelt that spawn on the sandy beaches of southern California during the high tides of March through June. The female fish rides to shore on a high wave, for about 30 seconds digs her tail into the sand, and deposits eggs before returning to the ocean on the next wave. On the nights of high tide people enjoy gathering these fish by hand during their momentary time on the beach and cooking them immediately over bonfires. The eggs remain in the sand for two weeks until the next high tide, when the hatched grunion are washed into the ocean.

GRUNSKY, CARL EWALD (1855–1934), Stockton-born engineer, after receiving a civil engineering degree from Stuttgart developed major water supply and irrigation projects for California, both in his private practice and for a time in the State Engineer's office. As the first City Engineer of San Francisco he was instrumental in developing the system based on Hetch Hetchy.◆ He wrote reminiscences, posthumously published as *Stockton Boyhood* (1959).

Guadalupe Hidalgo, Treaty of, concluded the Mexican War. It was negotiated in the little town whose name it bears. Representatives of Mexico and the American envoy, Nicholas P. Trist, signed it there on Feb. 2, 1848. It set the Rio Grande as the new boundary of the U.S., which was granted territory comprising the present states of California, Nevada, Utah, New Mexico, Arizona, and parts of Wyoming and Colorado. The U.S. paid $15,000,000 to Mexico and up to $3,250,000 for claims of its citizens.

Gualala Point, ocean headland in northernmost Sonoma County near the river of the same name. The town of Gualala lies just across the border, in Mendocino County. The name is variously thought to derive from a Pomo word or from a Spanish rendition of the mythological Teutonic hall of Valhalla. It is a fishing and lumbering center.

Guasti, see *Cucamonga*.

GUDDE, ERWIN G. (1889–1969), German-born professor of German at the University of California, Berkeley (1923–56), and scholar of western American history, author of *California Place Names* (1949), the standard geographical dictionary of the state.

GUERRA, DE LA, see *de la Guerra*.

GUINN, JAMES M. (1834–1918), Ohio-born historian of California, to which he moved in the 1860s and where he was an administrator of Los Angeles public schools. He was a founder of the Historical Society of Southern California, to whose publications he contributed profusely. Other works include a *History of California . . .* (1907), which emphasizes southern California.

Gulf of California, see *California, Gulf of*.

Gull, aquatic bird, many varieties of which are found in the state. The most common seagull and the only one to breed there is the *western gull,* with a body over two feet long, found along the shore of the entire Pacific Coast. The *California gull,* a little smaller, is an inland bird which visits the coast during the winter, and is best known as the species that saved the crops of early Mormons because it fed on Utah's destructive insects. Its largest rookery in California is at Mono Lake. Other species of gulls, all of which live along the ocean, include the *glaucous-winged gull,* a common bird the size of the *western gull,* which winters as far south as Baja California; the *herring gull,* slightly smaller, a winter visitor to California's river mouths and harbors; the *Heermann gull,* somewhat smaller, common along the coast but migrates particularly from the north to California during winter; the *Bonaparte gull,* just over a foot long, which rarely winters north of Monterey; the *short-billed gull,* which winters only in well-sheltered bays; and the *ring-billed gull,* common along the shore from Tomales Bay south. *Gaviota,* the Spanish word for "gull," has been incorporated in several place-names of Santa Barbara County.

GUNTER, ARCHIBALD CLAVERING (1847–1907), English-born author who was reared in San Francisco. After graduation from the state university and work as a stockbroker, he moved to New York (1879). There he wrote popular plays and even more successful light novels, of which the first, *Mr. Barnes of New York* (1887), was typical in its tale of a dynamic young American besting English and European prejudice and old-fashioned beliefs.

GUTIÉRREZ, NICOLAS (*fl.* 1833–36), twice governor of Alta California (Jan. 2–May 1 and July 30–Dec. 7, 1836), went to California as an army captain with newly appointed Governor José Figueroa (1833) and was promoted to lieutenant colonel the same year. He became commanding general of the army in Alta California before serving as interim governor from the death of Figueroa until the arrival of the new appointee of the central government, Mariano Chico.◆ Under Chico, Gutiérrez served as commanding general of the south. After Chico's expulsion by anticentralist factions, Gutiérrez became governor again until he too was expelled by anticentralist rebels led by Juan Bautista Alvarado, who succeeded him as governor.

GWIN, WILLIAM M[CKENDREE] (1805–85), Tennessee-born political leader who, after a medical education at Transylvania University, practice of medicine and of law, and election to Congress from Mississippi, settled in San Francisco (1849). He was a member of the Constitutional Convention in Monterey, the beginning of the political career in California on which he was intent. Elected by the legislature as the new state's first U.S. Senator (1850–55, 1857–61), he was a Chivalry ("Chiv") Democrat who supported slavery. He had a great political feud with David Broderick,◆ who opposed him on issues and in a party fight for power and patronage. Gwin got the Mare Island Navy Yard and a San Francisco branch of the Mint for California and worked hard for a transcontinental railroad. After his term of office, rumors about his disloyalty to the U.S. on the outbreak of the Civil War led to his arrest. Soon freed, he later went to Paris (1863), where he interested Napoleon III in a plan to create colonies in Mexico for southern settlers, but Maximilian opposed the project. Gwin's later career was obscure.

Gypsum, hydrated calcium sulfate, quarried as a mineral, used in portland cement, as plaster in wallboard, and as a soil conditioner. It is found in greater quantities in California than elsewhere in the U.S., the major part coming from the Imperial Valley and San Diego County. It is also produced in many other areas, the first having been Point Sal (1880).

H

Hacienda, Spanish word for "landed property," commonly used in Mexico but rarely in California, where the usual term was *"rancho,"*♦ indicating a farm on which one raised livestock rather than an estate on which one grew crops.

HACK, STAN[LEY CAMFIELD] (1909–), Sacramento-born baseball player who was third baseman for Sacramento (1931) and the Chicago Cubs (1932–47), twice leading the National League in hits. He was manager of the Cubs (1954–56) and the St. Louis Cardinals (1958).

HADLEY, HENRY [KIMBALL] (1871–1937), Massachusetts-born composer and conductor who left Seattle's symphony to lead the San Francisco Symphony Orchestra (1911–15). After he went to New York he was succeeded by Alfred Hertz. Hadley was also known for his melodic compositions, including the symphonic "Four Seasons" and four operas.

HAGER, JOHN S[HARPENSTEIN] (1818–90), New Jersey-born lawyer and graduate of Princeton who practiced law in his native state until he moved to San Francisco (1849). There he was a state Senator and judge until appointed to the unfinished U.S. Senate term (1873–75) of Eugene Casserly.♦

HAGGIN, JAMES BEN ALI (1821–1914), member of a prominent Kentucky family whose maternal grandfather was a Turkish physician, went to Sacramento (1850). There he continued his practice of law, first with Milton Latham,♦ then with his fellow Kentuckian and brother-in-law Lloyd Tevis♦ and Latham. Haggin and Tevis moved their office to San Francisco (1853) and became involved in major businesses, including association with George Hearst in mining, large holdings in the Anaconda Copper Co., and ownership of vast ranch lands in the Central Valley for wheat, hops, and other produce. The latter property, which eventually passed to Kern County Land Co., involved Haggin and Tevis in a protracted but finally successful battle against Miller and Lux over riparian control and irrigation rights. In Lexington, Ky., on one of his several estates, Haggin established a major horse breeding and rac-

ing stable. Haggin Art Galleries in Stockton is a museum founded (1931) by his granddaughter and featuring the collection of 19th-century paintings owned by her father, Louis Terah Haggin, the son of James Ben Ali Haggin.

HAHN, WILLIAM (*c.*1840–91), German-born artist of the Düsseldorf school, lived mainly in San Francisco and northern California from 1872 to 1881, and there painted large, detailed canvases of city and country life.

HAIGHT, HENRY HUNTLY (1825–78), 10th governor of the state (1867–71), born in New York, after graduation from Yale moved to St. Louis, where he practiced law until he went to California (1850). He continued his practice in San Francisco, for a time in partnership with future U.S. Senator James A. McDougall. Haight was active in politics, and although he shifted between the two major parties, he was elected governor as a Democrat. He opposed continued immigration of Chinese and suffrage for blacks and advocated free trade and an eight-hour day. The University of California was established during his administration, and he was later a member of its Board of Regents. A San Francisco street is named for him and its intersection with Ashbury St. became the local center for hippies in the 1960s.

Haight-Ashbury, two streets in San Francisco near Golden Gate Park whose intersection, once a middle-class shopping and residential district, became the focal point for the local hippie movement♦ in the 1960s. No longer thought of as an address, the location became the symbolic center for new communal ways of life that attracted adolescents from all parts of the U.S. in search of a youthful utopia to be achieved through drugs, Oriental religions, defiance of convention and tradition, enjoyment of rock music and psychedelic art, and the free sharing of sex and love. After 1967 the district quickly deteriorated into a teen-age slum with serious crimes, often fomented by drug vendors, and harassment by attacking motorcycle gangs, but it was later rehabilitated.

HALE, GEORGE ELLERY (1868–1938), professor of astronomy at the University of Chicago before becoming Director of the Mt. Wilson Observatory♦ (1904–23) and a planner of the Mt. Palomar Observatory.

Half Dome, monolithic flat-faced granite headwall rising 8,927 feet above Yosemite Valley. Indians called it Tissack, supposedly the name of a woman changed into a half mountain, some gold rush prospectors (1849) called it Rock of Ages, and the Mariposa Battalion♦ coined the present name.

Half Moon Bay, inlet and community on the ocean border of San Francisco Peninsula. Located on an old *rancho,* it was once called Spanish Town. A dairying, fishing, and truck farm area, a residential community has also grown up around this, the only protected harbor between San Francisco and Santa Cruz.

Halibut, flatfish of the flounder family, found generally from Tomales Bay south and, even more commonly, from Morro Bay south, in sandy-bottomed waters shallower than 120 feet. Prehistoric Indians ate them, for remains have been found in ancient middens. The fish are now caught both for sport and commerce.

HALL, LOVICK P[IERCE] (1813–post-80), Mississippi-born newspaperman who, after a journalistic career in Oregon, went to California, where he edited several small-town newspapers, including the *Equal Rights Expositor* (1862–63) of Visalia, a hotbed of Confederate sympathizers, to champion slavery and secession. His press was wrecked by soldiers from a nearby army post.

HALL, OAKLEY (1920–), San Diego-born novelist who attended the University of California, Berkeley, and served with the marines in World War II. His fiction includes *Corpus of Joe Bailey* (1953) and its sequel, *Report from Beau Harbor* (1971), wry presentations of California ways of life; *Warlock* (1958), set in a Southwest frontier mining town of the 1880s; *The Downhill Racers* (1963), about people dedicated to skiing; and *The Adelita* (1975), about an American caught up in the Mexican Revolution. With Andrew Imbrie he adapted Wallace Stegner's *Angle of Repose* as an opera (1976). Hall also teaches creative writing at the University of California, Irvine, and in a school at his home in Squaw Valley.

HALL, WILLIAM HAMMOND (1846–1934), Maryland-born engineer, reared in California. He made the first topographic survey of the present Golden Gate Park (1870) and as the city's Superintendent of Parks began the reclamation of land from sand dunes for that park. He became the first State Engineer of California (1878–89).

HALL, WILLIAM HENRY (1823?–1902?), went from his native Washington, D.C., to San Francisco (1849) to becme a leader in the black community and a founder of the San Francisco Athenaeum.♦

HALLECK, HENRY W[AGER] (1816–72), New York-born army officer sent to California (1847), where he served as Secretary of State under military Govs. Mason and Riley, in which capacity he compiled the California Archives.♦ His *Report on Land Titles in California* (1850) contended that most Mexican claims were imperfect and he thus encouraged U.S. squatters. His views were disputed by William Carey Jones.♦ Halleck was influential in the Constitutional Convention (1849). As a civilian lawyer in partnership with Frederick Billings♦ and Archibald Peachy he established the new state's major legal firm in San Francisco, growing rich out of land grant cases. With his wealth he bought property and built the Montgomery Block (1853) in San Francisco, the largest office building on the Pacific Coast. After the Civil War, during which he served as Lincoln's Chief of Staff, he became the army general commanding the Department of the Pacific (1865–69) from San Francisco.

HALLIDIE, ANDREW SMITH (1836–1900), English-born inventor and engineer, taken to California (1852) where in time he built bridges, produced the coast's first wire cable, and created a means of transporting freight across mountainous terrain on an endless moving cable. That contrivance led to his more important invention of the mechanism for the cable car♦ (1871) to travel San Francisco's steep hills. The first car to employ this scheme commercially made its initial trip in 1873; it began the transportation system for which San Francisco is famous and for which, a century later, Hallidie was honored by having a Market St. plaza named for him. He also created an aerial tramway to his mountain home in Portola Valley. As a Regent of the University of California he was memorialized by a building named in his honor (1918) when the University had Willis Polk construct a downtown San Francisco edifice as an investment. It has since become notable as an early example of a glass curtain wall with fine decorative iron work.

Hall of Science, permanent display of exhibits concerning physical science in Griffith Park, Los Angeles.

HALPRIN, LAWRENCE (1916–   ), New York City-born landscape architect and planner, moved to San Francisco, where he was first associated (1946–49) with Thomas D. Church.♦ His own works in that city include the design related to the buildings that William Wurster remodeled as Ghirardelli Square and the reconstruction of Market St. He also designed Sea Ranch, Mendocino County, and landscaped the BART system. His wife, Ann (1920–   ), was the founder and is the choreographer of Dancers' Workshop in San Francisco.

HAMILTON, BONES (ROBERT ANTHONY HAMILTON) (1912–   ), Pennsylvania-born football player, a halfback on the Vow Boys♦ football teams of Stanford (1932–35), which competed in three consecutive Rose Bowl games. He was noted as a great blocker.

HAMILTON, BRUTUS (1901–71), succeeded Walter Christie♦ as coach of track and field sports at the University of California, Berkeley (1933–65), and was its athletic director (1947–56).

Hamilton Air Force Base, major defense command base and flight center for Pacific bases, located near San Rafael, founded in 1930, and deactivated in 1975. It was named for a pilot killed in World War I.

HAMMETT, DASHIELL (1894–1961), born in Connecticut, went to San Francisco as a Pinkerton detective agent and soon drew upon the city's atmosphere and his business background for the novels he began to write at the end of the 1920s. Cool, tough, and hard-boiled in attitude, his works allied Hemingway's mood with the subject of detective fiction, giving that genre a new tone and style which affected Raymond Chandler and other writers. His major works include *Red Harvest* (1929); *The Maltese Falcon* (1930), in which he created his new style of detective, Sam Spade;♦ and *The Thin Man* (1932). *The Maltese Falcon* was considered a classic of its kind, both as a novel and in several film versions, notably that directed by John Huston (1941), with Humphrey Bogart in the role of the unconventional detective. *The Thin Man* was the source of a series of light-hearted motion pictures beginning in 1934. Hammett himself moved to southern California in the 1930s to write film scripts. Although not one of the Hollywood Ten, he

too refused to testify about so-called un-American activities and was sent to prison. His friend Lillian Hellman wrote about the era and his stand in *Scoundrel Time* (1976).

HAMMOND, GEORGE P[ETER] (1896–   ), scholar of western U.S. and Latin American history who was brought to California (1909) from Minnesota and North Dakota. He was a professor at the universities of Arizona, Southern California, and New Mexico (1935–46) before he went to the faculty of his alma mater, the University of California, Berkeley, and assumed the directorship of The Bancroft Library (1946–65). His many publications include an edition of *The Larkin Papers* (10 vols., 1951–64), the correspondence of Thomas O. Larkin.

Ham 'n Eggs, a pension plan formulated as a substitute for the proposed Townsend Plan♦ (1933 ff.), was based on the idea of paying "Thirty Dollars Every Thursday" to pensioners of California, who could thus afford to eat ham and eggs. The plan, sponsored by two advertising agents, Willis and Lawrence Allen, was politically significant as a proposition voted on during the election of 1938. Although supported by Sheridan Downey, who was elected to the U.S. Senate, it was defeated.

HAMPTON, LIONEL [LEO] (1914–   ), Alabama-born orchestra leader, moved to southern California (1927), and after studying at the University of Southern California, played in Los Angeles and with Benny Goodman's Quartet. He then organized his own jazz band in which he plays the vibraphone dynamically.

HANCOCK, G[EORGE] ALLAN (1876–1965), Los Angeles financier whose father, Henry Hancock, moved from Maine to California (1849) and bought Rancho La Brea (the site of Hollywood and the Wilshire district of Los Angeles), which established the family fortune later made in real estate and oil. The Allan Hancock Foundation for Marine Research, part of the University of Southern California, was founded (1905) and mainly funded by the younger Hancock. He was also a donor of Hancock Park, the site of the La Brea Pits,♦ once owned by him.

Hanford, seat of Kings County, named (1877) by the Central Pacific (forerunner of Southern Pacific) for James Hanford, its treasurer. The Mussel Slough♦ shoot-out occurred six miles northwest of the city. It is now a center for trade, food processing, and oil refining. The population in 1970 was 15,179.

Hangtown, name informally applied to Placerville♦ after three gold thieves were summarily hanged there (1848), although that was never its proper title. The name is also celebrated in Hangtown Fry, a dish of scrambled eggs, fried oysters, and bacon whose origin is variously said to be a lucky miner's idea of a luxurious treat or a condemned convict's request for a last meal whose ingredients could not be speedily procured.

HANSEN, ARMIN [CARL] (1886–1957), San Francisco-born artist, an early member of the art colony in Monterey, well known for his paintings and Whistler-like etchings of marine scenes and fishermen.

Happy Valley, name given during the gold rush to a region of San Francisco roughly bounded by present Mission and Market streets and First and Second streets. It was sheltered from winds by neighboring sand dunes. A settlement of about 1,000 tents grew up there (1849–50) around the springs of the area.

HARASZTHY, AGOSTON (*c.*1812–69), pioneer, migrated (1840) from his native Hungary, where he had served as private secretary to the viceroy. He settled first in Wisconsin, where he founded and developed the settlement that has become Sauk City and planted the state's first hop yard. In search of a better climate he and his family went to San Diego in 1849. There he was elected county sheriff and a member of the state legislature in 1852. Moving to San Francisco, he held posts with the Mint until forced to resign on charges of embezzlement later found to be false. In 1858, in Sonoma County, he developed the state's first large vineyard, importing tokay and zinfandel vines from his native land. He returned to Europe in 1861 as a commissioner appointed by the legislature to discover the best means to improve the cultivation of vineyards in California. His report was published as *Grape Culture, Wines and Wine-Making; with Notes upon Agriculture and Horticulture* (1862). His own 300 acres of vines and 5,000 acres of farmland just east of Sonoma were lost by business reverses (1866). Ever an adventurer, he moved to Nicaragua and soon acquired 100,000 acres of land and a license to manufacture sugar. His death by drowning put an end to that venture. Two of his sons, Attilla and Arpad, married daughters of Gen. Vallejo.

HARBISON, JOHN S., see *Honey.*

HARLOW, JEAN (1911–37), born in Kansas City, catapulted to stardom in Hollywood when still in her teens. During the few years before her death in her midtwenties she symbolized one aspect of Hollywood as the platinum blonde inheritor of Clara Bow's crown as the brash, tantalizing, sexy playgirl. Her popular films included Howard Hughes' *Hell's Angels* (1930) and *Hold Your Man* (1933), in which she starred with Clark Gable.

HARPENDING, ASBURY (1839–1923), Kentucky-born adventurer who, after participating in William Walker's filibustering expedition to Nicaragua, went to California in 1856. During the Civil War he devised various plots to aid the Confederacy, for one of which he was convicted of treason but jailed only briefly. Having made a fortune in gold mining, he next engaged in real estate promotions, aided by the banker William Ralston. In 1871 he was persuaded that a mining field in which Ralston became interested was a rich source of diamonds and other jewels. The field, which had actually been salted by two men named Philip Arnold and John Slack, was located in a remote part of Wyoming Territory. It was investigated by Harpending in 1872, and his enthusiastic reports as well as those of other seemingly knowledgeable experts led to the formation in San Francisco of a company whose officers included Ralston, Gen. George B. McClellan, and David D. Colton. The firm collapsed in 1873 when Clarence King proved the mining field to be a fraud. The affair soon came to be known as the Great Diamond Hoax, the title later used by Harpending for a reminiscent book (1913).

HARRADEN, BEATRICE (1864–1936), English author and feminist, resident for some time near San Diego, where she had gone to recover from illness. This served as background for her *Hilda Strafford: A California Story* (1897), a novel about an English bride's unhappy life on an isolated lemon ranch. With Dr. William A. Edwards she wrote *Two Health Seekers in Southern California* (1896).

HARRIMAN, EDWARD HENRY (1848–1909), New York railroad executive who became head of the Union Pacific system (1897) and controlled it thereafter. He made its line from New York to Portland, Oregon, a major transcontinental route, augmented when the Union Pacific bought (1901) the late Collis P. Huntington's stock in the Southern Pacific and took over its old Central Pacific line, the initial transcontinental railroad. After Harriman's death the affiliation was broken up because it was found in violation of the Sherman Anti-Trust Act, but during his last years he had continued to buy the stock of other lines, notably the Northern Pacific. Another of his associations with California occurred during the flooding of the Colorado River that created the Salton Sea,♦ when he led the Southern Pacific's ultimately successful attempts to stop the deluge by gaining control of the California Development Co. (1905), which had unintentionally caused the inundation and was unable to arrest it.

HARRIMAN, JOB (1841–1925), moved to California (1886) from his native Indiana, becoming a leading labor union lawyer and the successor to Gaylord Wilshire as the state's major Socialist, running for governor on the party's ticket (1898) and for Vice President with Debs (1900). He might have become mayor of Los Angeles (1911) had he not proclaimed the innocence of his clients, the McNamara Brothers,♦ a few days before the election and before their admission of guilt. In 1913 he came within 800 votes of being elected mayor. He then quit politics to run the communal Llano del Rio.♦

HARRIS, [ELSWORTH LE]ROY (1898–), Nebraska-born composer who was brought to California at age 5 and reared in Covina. His compositions, which began to be performed in 1925, include *Symphony 1933* (1934), *When Johnny Comes Marching Home* (1934), *Folksong Symphony* (1940), and many works of chamber music. After a long teaching career out of the state, he became a faculty member of UCLA in 1961.

HARRIS, THOMAS LAKE (1823–1906), English-born Utopian who was reared as a Calvinist in Utica, N.Y., and became a believer in spiritualism and Swedenborgianism. He created his own cult of direct communion with God and Christ's Second Coming, to be announced through himself as "pivotal man." To provide a home for his cult he established a colony named Fountain Grove near Santa Rosa (1875–92). There he raised grapes, made wine, and autocratically committed his community to what he called "Theo-Socialism." After his death the winery was carried on for many years by one of his disciples.

HART, JEROME A[LFRED] (1854–1937), native Californian who served on the staffs of the *Sacramento Union* and *Alta California* before becoming associate editor (1880–91) and editor of the *Argonaut* (1891–1907). In addition to the novels *A Vigi-*

lante Girl (1910) and *The Golconda Bonanza* (1923), he wrote a reminiscence of San Francisco bohemian and social life, *In Our Second Century* (1931), and travel books.

HART, WILLIAM S[URREY] (1862?–1946), popular stage actor who reached even greater success after 1914 when he entered motion pictures and played the part of the strong, silent cowboy, a role later glamourized by Tom Mix. His ranch in Newhall, located in a county park named for him, is now a museum of his career and of western art.

HARTE, [FRANCIS] BRET[T] (1836–1902), born in Albany, N.Y., quit school at 13 to help support his family, and in 1854 went via Nicaragua to California, where his widowed mother had married an Oakland man soon to be the city's mayor. Harte supported himself by working for an apothecary, teaching, serving for a while as some sort of expressman (not on a Wells, Fargo stagecoach, as legend later had it), visiting the southern mines, writing prose and poetry, and by newspaper work, including an attack on whites who had massacred Indians (1860) near Union (now Arcata), where he lived for a time.

In 1860 he settled in San Francisco, working for the *Golden Era*,♦ first as a typesetter, then as an author. His contributions included the first version of *M'liss*.♦ Work in the Mint, almost a sinecure, gave him enough money to marry, to continue a rather unremunerative literary career, and to move in the city's cultural circles. His status was marked by his becoming a contributor to the *Atlantic Monthly* (1863) with an amusing Irving-like tale of Spanish California, "Legend of Monte del Diablo." It was one of his many contributions to the *Californian*,♦ occasionally edited by him, from which his witty parodies, *Condensed Novels and Other Papers* (1867), were later drawn. He also assembled an anthology of local verse, *Outcroppings* (1865); and a collection of his own poems, *The Lost Galleon* (1867).

In 1868 Anton Roman♦ named him the editor of the new *Overland Monthly*♦ and his talents flowered. In its second issue (Aug.) he printed "The Luck of Roaring Camp,"♦ the first of his local-color stories of life in the mines; followed by the equally appealing "The Outcasts of Poker Flat"♦ (Jan. 1869); and then by the comic ballad, "Plain Language from Truthful James"♦ (Sept. 1870), often called "The Heathen Chinee." His writings became tremendously popular in the East, which found his quaintly whimsical and humorous depictions of moral contrasts to be just the sort of view of the California frontier that suited its sentiments about a new land. His prose was collected in *The Luck of Roaring Camp and Other Sketches* (1870), and as an enormously popular author he went east to contribute twelve pieces to the *Atlantic* for $10,000.

He was never to return to California, the site of his first success and ever afterwards the setting of his fiction and poetry. During the long years after he left the West he wrote a great number of poems, stories, and plays, many so repetitive that he became little better than an accomplished hack writer, although he did essay a longer work than was usual for him in the novel *Gabriel Conroy* (1876) and did introduce a fine new, rather Dickensian character, Colonel Starbottle. To support himself he also accepted consulates in Prussia (1878) and Glasgow (1880–85) and finally became an expatriate in London, where his presentations of California life continued to be more popular than they were in the U.S.

HARTMANN, [CARL] SADAKICHI (1867?–1944), born in Japan of a Japanese mother and German father, brought to the U.S. and naturalized (1894), he spent the rest of his life, first on the East Coast, later around Hollywood, as a minor author of poems, plays, and art criticism and as a cult figure of bohemian groups.

HARTNELL, WILLIAM EDWARD PETTY (1798–1854), born in England, went to California (1822) as a hide trader. He became a merchant in mission produce, was naturalized (1830), married into the de la Guerra family,♦ was a large *ranchero* near Monterey, served as agent for the Russians (1833–36), and acted as Alvarado's collector of customs and *visitador-general* of missions (1839–40). He later supported the Americans in the Mexican War and was appointed appraiser of customs by Stockton. He also founded a school for his own children (he had 25) and other youngsters; and a junior college in Salinas (est. 1920) is named after him.

Harvey Mudd College, see *Claremont Colleges.*

Hashimura Togo, character in humorous sketches by Wallace Irwin.♦

HASKELL, BURNETTE G. (1857–1907), born in Sierra County, after attending the University of California and admission to the bar (1879), became the editor of *Truth,* a radical journal of his International Workingmens Association, a union with

secret membership. The paper's motto was "*Truth is five cents a copy and dynamite is forty cents a pound.*" Later he founded Kaweah♦ (1885), an idealistic cooperative community situated in present Sequoia National Park, but it was a failure, partly because Haskell was as cantankerous as he was ingenuous, but mainly because of opposition from the world he wanted to change.

HASTINGS, LANSFORD W[ARREN] (1819–70), Ohio-born lawyer who led an overland expedition to Oregon (1842) and then the next year to California, hoping to see it, as was Texas, freed of Mexican control and under an American leader, himself. To gain supporters and settlers he went east, made enthusiastic speeches, and published an *Emigrants' Guide* (1845) to deflect emigration from Oregon by proposing a route to California of which he had heard from Frémont but had not seen. It was the Hastings' Cut-off—southwest from Fort Bridger to the south side of Salt Lake, to Pilot Knob, then below the Ruby Mts. and thence to the Humboldt River near present Elko. He did not attempt the route when he returned (1845), leading Robert Semple and others, but it was that dreadful desert cut-off that slowed the Donner Party and led to its sufferings after its belated arrival in the Sierra. Hastings' other schemes included promoting the town of Sutterville and serving as an agent for Mormon business. He was also a judge and a delegate to the Constitutional Convention of 1849. He later lived in Mexico, Arizona (which he hoped to seize for the Confederacy), and Brazil.

Hastings College of the Law, located in San Francisco, was founded (1878) by Serranus Clinton Hastings, California's first chief justice, and named for him. It was the first law school of the University of California, to which it remains affiliated, in that its dean is a member of the Berkeley faculty and its faculty grants diplomas issued by the University's president, even though the college has its own board of directors, headed by the state's chief justice. For its first year it was restricted to men; then Clara Foltz♦ and Laura Gordon♦ successfully sued to open it to women too.

Hastings' Cut-off, see *Hastings, Lansford W.*

HATFIELD, CHARLES M. (*fl.* 1915), creator of a device of so-called evaporating tanks filled with his secret chemical formula which was supposed to induce rain in dry regions. He began his career in

1902, but became famous in 1915–16. That winter the city government of San Diego, his home town, promised him $10,000 if he could get its Morena Reservoir filled. Within weeks storms filled the reservoir, caused it to overflow, washed out a dam below it, and flooded part of the city. The city council refused payment on the ground that he had gone beyond his contract, and Hatfield was unsuccessful in his suit for his fee. Nevertheless, the incident brought him later contracts from Texas, Canada, and Honduras.

HAUN, HENRY PETER (1815–60), Kentucky-born lawyer who moved to California (1849), where he practiced in Marysville. A prominent Democrat, he was appointed to the U.S. Senate (Nov. 1859–March 1860) to fill the vacancy left by the death of David Broderick.◆

HAUT-CILLY, AUGUSTE BERNARD DU, see *Duhaut-Cilly, Auguste Bernard.*

Havasu, Lake, artificial lake 45 miles long, created (1938) in the Colorado River by Parker Dam. The California part, extending to the Arizona border, is in San Bernardino County. It lies between the Chemehuevi and Whipple mountains, southeast of Needles. In the Mohave Indian language the name means "blue." The lake and its State Park form a resort and sport region, made famous by the reconstruction, over a desert channel, of the old London Bridge, moved stone by stone from its original Thames River site to Arizona.

Hawaiians in California, came originally during the Mexican era. They included not only the natives, called Kanakas, who were employed aboard merchant vessels or in the hide houses ashore, as described in *Two Years Before the Mast,* but New England-born traders and merchants resident in the Islands and their descendants, like William Heath Davis.◆ The Russian-American Co. also hired about 1,000 Kanakas for fur hunting and trapping, and Sutter employed some of them too. Many more came in the gold rush, accounting for about a dozen place-names in the northern counties that incorporated the word Kanaka. However, the population in California has always been relatively small. There were 319 native-born in the 1850 census, 840 in 1900, and 1,990 in 1920. Hawaiian contributions to California life include the sport of surfing.◆ Over the years Californians have significantly affected Hawaiian life, particularly through investments of financiers, including Claus Spreckels and William Matson.

HAWKS, HOWARD [WINCHESTER] (1896–1977), Indiana-born motion picture director who began his Hollywood career in 1922. Among his notable films are ones dealing with professional automobile racing and with aviation in World War I, both of which he experienced, as well as comedies and an adaptation of Raymond Chandler's *The Big Sleep* (1946). During Hollywood's heyday he was as glamorous a figure of its society as the film stars he directed.

Hay, a California crop since mission days at the opening of the 19th century. Production in 1970, grown on 1,907,000 acres, was worth $229,333,000. Alfalfa◆ accounted for over half the acreage and almost five-sixths of the crop, the remainder being grain and other cultivated hay. Virtually all parts of the state produce hay, but the major harvest comes from the Central Valley, northeastern California, Monterey County, and, in southern California, from San Bernardino and Riverside counties. In 1970 there were also 92,000 acres of wild hay harvested.

HAYAKAWA, S[AMUEL] I[CHIYE] (1906–), Canadian-born educator, a professor of English at San Francisco State College, specializing in semantics. He became president of the college (1968–73) and was responsible for quelling the dissident demonstrations that occurred during the 1960s. In 1976 he entered politics for the first time and ran successfully for a seat in the U.S. Senate.

HAYES, BENJAMIN (1815–77), moved to California (1850) from his native Baltimore and settled in Los Angeles, where he became a prominent lawyer, jurist, and state legislator. He was also a local historian and one of the three authors of *Historical Sketch of Los Angeles County* (1876), generally called the Centennial History. He also kept diaries from which *Pioneer Notes* was collected (1929) and compiled numerous scrapbooks of local information now possessed by The Bancroft Library.

HAYNES, JOHN R[ANDOLPH] (1853–1937), born in Pennsylvania, after receiving an M.D. and a Ph.D. in philosophy from its state university moved to Los Angeles (1887). There he became a very successful doctor and made a fortune in real estate but found time to be a leader in political reform, opposing the power of the Southern Pacific, and for a brief time headed a Christian Socialist Club. He also led a Direct Legislation League in his city and was instrumental in getting voters to approve a new charter (1903) that made Los Angeles the first city in the world to adopt the initiative, referendum, and recall. Recall was first used (1904) by the Good Government League to remove a councilman who had awarded printing contracts to the *Los Angeles Times* despite lower bids. Haynes next led a successful fight to have the city employ a direct primary and have election of councilmen at large (1909). He also helped secure state adoption of the initiative, referendum, and recall. He worked too for municipal and state ownership of water and power facilities, serving on city and regional boards created for them, as well as on diverse other commissions and as Regent of the University of California (1922–37). He established a foundation in his and his wife's name to aid study of his areas of interest in Los Angeles.

HAYWARD, ALVINZA (1822–1904), went to California from his native Vermont (1850) during the gold rush to become a miner in Amador County. Persisting with a claim that others had given up on, he struck gold at 400 feet. He continued his Hayward Mine at Crown Point down to 1,350 feet, extracting over $25,000,000 worth of ore. In 1867 he made it the state's first incorporated mine, with stock sold to the public, and it also made Hayward reputedly the richest man in California. With John G. Downey♦ he founded Hayward & Co., the first bank in southern California (1868). He built a great country estate, with racing stables and a deer park, in San Mateo.

Hayward, city in Alameda County, founded (1854) by Guillermo Castro on his *rancho,* which lay on a road to the gold mines. Named for a local hotel proprietor, it developed into a farming center. However, it lies on a major fault, and was hard hit by a severe earthquake (1868). After World War II it became a residential and industrial city served by BART, and the site of a California State University. In 1970 the population was 93,058.

Hayward Fault, see *Earthquakes.*

HAZZARD, WALT[ER] (1942–), Philadelphia-born basketball player who was a guard on the team of UCLA, from which he graduated (1964), helping in his last year to lead the team to a 30-0 record. He later played for the Los Angeles Lakers (1964–67), the Golden State Warriors (1972–73), and Seattle, Atlanta, and Buffalo teams. He converted to the Muslim religion in the early 1970s, changing his name to Mahdi Abdul-Rahman.

HEAD, EDITH (1907–), Los Angeles-born costume designer who, after graduation from the University of California and further study at Stanford and art schools, became a widely publicized designer of clothes worn by motion picture stars in their films.

Healdsburg, town on the Russian River in Sonoma County, named (1857) for a pioneer trader. It is now a center for grape growing, lumbering, shipment of hops and fruits, and site of the world's largest geothermal generating plant for the nearby Geysers.♦ Residents have included Clark Foss, Ellen Gould White, and Ralph Rose. In 1970 the population was 2,438.

HEARST, GEORGE (1820–91), born in Missouri, walked across the continent (1850) to prospect in California without much success. He began to strike it rich in Nevada mines in 1859. His mining interests came to include the fabulously wealthy Ophir in Nevada, Homestake in South Dakota, Anaconda in Montana, and San Luis in Mexico. His business associates included James Ben Ali Haggin♦ and Lloyd Tevis.♦ After an unsuccessful campaign for the Senate against Leland Stanford, Hearst was appointed a U.S. Senator upon the death of John Miller (1886) and was elected by the Democratic legislature of California to a full term beginning in 1887. His wife, Phoebe Apperson Hearst,♦ was known for her cultural interests and charities; he for his casual and lavish style of life. Their only child was William Randolph Hearst.

HEARST, PATRICIA, see *Symbionese Liberation Army.*

HEARST, PHOEBE APPERSON (1842–1919), reared in Missouri like George Hearst,♦ whom she wed in 1862. She went with him to California, where his great wealth let her live and entertain lavishly and where she also became a very generous charitable benefactor and supporter of education, including kindergartens and the state university. Her numerous benefactions included underwriting the architectural competition for a Berkeley campus plan; the construction of its mining building, named for her late husband; the financing of archaeological expeditions in Egypt, Italy, and Mexico for the University; and the subsidization of a department of anthropology. She lived part of the time on an elaborate estate in Pleasanton,♦ in a mansion built by A. C. Schweinfurth and Julia Morgan. William Randolph Hearst was her only child.

HEARST, WILLIAM RANDOLPH (1863–1951), only child of Phoebe Apperson and George Hearst, after a brief period at Harvard returned to San Francisco to take over the *Examiner* (1887), which his father had used to advance a political career. Although California was one home for him, he moved to New York City, which he served as a Congressman (1903–7) and where he was an unsuccessful candidate for mayor and governor. His newspaper career, begun in San Francisco, became national with a great chain of dailies and with many syndicated features, including the development of comic strips. The chain was noted for its flamboyant style of journalism, including advocacy of war with Spain (1897–98) and extreme nationalism and patriotism. His publishing interests were expanded internationally to include magazines and he became the owner of motion picture companies and radio stations, as well as much real estate, all the while also managing the mines on which his father's fortune had been based. He was known for his lavish living, his grandly acquisitive style of purchasing objects of art, including whole castles and monastaries exported to the U.S., and the grandeur of his so-called ranch, the estate at San Simeon,♦ constructed for him by Julia Morgan.♦ His fabulous ways of life inspired Orson Welles' interpretive film, *Citizen Kane* (1941).

Heathen Chinee, The, see *Plain Language from Truthful James.*

HECETA, BRUNO (*fl.* 1775), Spanish captain and the commander of the *Santiago,* who was sent on an exploring expedition along the California coast and northwest of it by Viceroy Bucareli as an adjunct to the land voyage of Anza and subsequent to the explorations by sea of Juan Pérez.♦ Heceta, accompanied by his lieutenant, Juan Francisco de la Bodéga y Cuadro, discovered and named Trinidad Bay. Heceta continued north to discover the Columbia River and to reach Nootka on Vancouver Island; his lieutenant returned south independently and discovered Bodega Bay.♦

Hecker Pass, gap through the Santa Cruz Mts. between Gilroy and Watsonville, named for Henry Hecker, a Santa Clara County supervisor, who was instrumental in creating the highway which traverses the pass, connecting Yosemite and the ocean (1928).

HEENAN, JOHN C[ARMEL] (*fl.* 1835–60), New York-born prizefighter who went to California in the gold rush, and while a machinist at Benicia be-

came known as a boxer, nicknamed The Benicia Boy. He became the unofficial American heavyweight champion and fought his British counterpart, Tom Sayres, in England (1860) to a draw in a sensational bout that lasted two hours and twenty minutes. He was at one time married to Adah Menken.♦

HEILMAN, HARRY [EDWARD] (1894–1951), San Francisco-born baseball player. As an outfielder for the Detroit Tigers (1914–29) he and Ty Cobb made one of baseball's great outfield combinations. He led the American League four times in hitting and was elected to baseball's Hall of Fame (1952).

HELLMAN, prominent California family, founded by Isaiah M. Hellman (1831–90) and his brother Samuel, who left their native Bavaria to go to California (1852). They settled in Los Angeles, to which in 1854 they brought their cousin Isaiah W. Hellman (1842–1900). From successful retail merchandising I. W. Hellman moved to banking (first with William Workman and F. P. F. Temple) and made a fortune through real estate investments, mainly in Los Angeles, that later included oil interests with the Bixby family♦ on Signal Hill.♦ He moved to San Francisco (1890) to become president of the Nevada Bank founded by the Silver Kings, which in 1905 became the Wells Fargo Bank. His relatives included Harris Newmark, and his family continued to be socially, financially, and culturally prominent in the state.

Hell's Angels, association of motorcyclists, founded (1950) in San Bernardino, but a decade later, in its heyday, centered in Oakland with a warehouseman, Ralph "Sonny" Barger, as the leader, and with chapters in other cities and a membership that fluctuated between 85 and 200. They and other somewhat less notorious clubs flourished more in California than elsewhere because good climate the year round let them travel the highways whenever they pleased. The members reveled in looks and behavior of a repugnantly savage style. Some of their outrageous actions, intended to shock and frighten outsiders, were exaggerated by the press, but they did behave like outlaws. They menaced bourgeois society and even more violently opposed whatever they considered to be communistic. The outings, called "runs," of these black-jacketed hoodlums led them to swoop down in gangs on out-of-the-way communities where they enjoyed holiday orgies. In Dec. 1969 the promoters of the Altamont Festival♦ of rock music hired a number of them as guards, but in a wild melee one member of the audience was stabbed to death. That event and date marked the beginning of the end of the Angels, who were further demoralized by Barger's imprisonment (1973–77) for illegal possession of a weapon and narcotics.

HELPER, HINTON R[OWAN] (1829–1909), North Carolina author of popular tracts who went to California during the gold rush and after a residence of three years wrote *Land of Gold: Reality versus Fiction* (1855), a bitter attack on the region, its settlers, and their mores. He was later famous for his *The Impending Crisis of the South* (1857), proposing abolition of slavery, but only to improve the economic status of whites.

Hemet, small city in the San Jacinto Basin,♦ west of San Bernardino National Forest in Riverside County, founded in 1898. Nearby are many petroglyphs and other Indian relics, and it is the site of an annual pageant about Ramona.♦ It is a farming region with retirement homes, and has grown rapidly since World War II. In 1970 it had a population of 12,252.

Hemlock, coniferous evergreen tree of the pine family, is found in two varieties in California. The *western* (or *coast*) *hemlock* grows in the coastal fog belt from Oregon to Marin County and rises 90 to 180 feet, with a narrow, sometimes pyramidal crown. Its lumber is used for building, boxes, and furniture. The *mountain* or *black hemlock* (also called Williamson spruce) grows 20 to 90 feet high in elevations from 6,000 to 11,000 feet in the Sierra.

HENEY, FRANCIS JOSEPH (1859–1937), known as a rough-and-ready trial lawyer in Tucson until he returned to San Francisco (1895), where he had been reared, to continue his career with prosecution of a U.S. Senator from Oregon and a U.S. attorney. Then, as assistant district attorney of San Francisco directly after the earthquake and fire, he exposed criminal behavior in its city government, securing the conviction of Mayor Schmitz♦ and prosecuting Abe Ruef.♦ When he was shot by an ex-convict he had to give the Ruef case over to Hiram Johnson, who thereafter rose to fame and had the political career which had seemed to be in Heney's future.

Henness Pass, route through the Sierra Nevada leading to the Yuba River. Opened in 1852, it later became a wagon road. It is in present Nevada County.

Henry E. Huntington Library and Art Gallery, located in San Marino, was founded (1919) by the financier for whom it is named. It is based on his great collections. By gift and bequest he endowed the research institution with $10,500,000 and placed it under the administration of five self-perpetuating trustees. The major element is a library made up of libraries already distinguished when they came into Huntington's possession, for just as he made large-scale purchases in business, so also did he spend fortunes on his hobby.

The first of his great acquisitions was made in 1911: it cost $1,000,000 and brought him over 2,000 volumes including 12 folios and 37 quartos of Shakespeare and the manuscript of Franklin's autobiography. Year after year Huntington augmented his holdings by such acquisitions as a collection of books by England's first printer, William Caxton, from the ancestral library of the Duke of Devonshire; a large assemblage of manuscripts by Washington and Lincoln; and the library of Bridgewater House, formed between the 16th and 19th centuries but including earlier treasures, such as the Ellesmere manuscript of Chaucer's writings.

At the same time he assembled a major art collection, concentrating on 18th-century England, the most publicized painting of which is Gainsborough's "Blue Boy," purchased for $620,000 in 1922. Since Huntington's death the collections have been greatly augmented in established fields that include Californiana, American history, incunabula (over 5,400 examples), and British history. The collections of fine and decorative arts have also been greatly increased, and the surrounding property contains 200 acres of botanical gardens specializing in camellias, cacti and succulents, and Japanese landscaping. The institution, open to the public, attracts scholars from all over the world and has a distinguished research staff.

Hermosa Beach, city on the South Bay oceanfront of Los Angeles between Manhattan Beach and Redondo Beach, founded as a residential subdivision (1901). Its name means "beautiful" in Spanish.

HERNE, JAMES A. (1839–1901), New York-born actor and playwright who first achieved success in San Francisco during the 1870s as a protégé of Tom Maguire,♦ director of the Baldwin Theatre and friend of David Belasco.♦ Herne wrote his first hit, *Hearts of Oak* (1879), a simple and realistic drama, with Belasco. The rest of Herne's career on Broadway was even more successful.

HERRERA, José María, see *Solís, Joaquín.*

HERRIN, William Franklin (1854–1927), Oregon-born lawyer who settled in San Francisco, where he early gained a national reputation by successfully defending David Neagle against a murder charge for his killing of onetime Chief Justice David Terry♦ on the ground that as a federal officer Neagle was not subject to California law. Because of Herrin's abilities he became chief counsel for the estate of William Sharon,♦ intimately related to the Neagle case. He also became chief counsel for Miller and Lux and the Spring Valley Water Co. From 1893 to 1910 he served Huntington as the chief counsel for the Southern Pacific, in which capacity he became a major boss of state government and Republican party affairs, developing a surreptitious and corrupt but vastly powerful political machine. He later became vice president of the Southern Pacific and president of the Pacific Electric Railway.

HERTZ, Alfred (1872–1942), German-born musical conductor, maestro of the San Francisco Symphony (1915–30), known for his interpretations of Wagner. He bequeathed funds to the University of California, Berkeley, for its Hertz Hall for concerts.

HERWIG, Robert J. (1914–74), football player born in Woodford who was the star center on the University of California, Berkeley, teams (1935–37). His last year included an undefeated season and a victory over Alabama in the Rose Bowl.

HERZOG, Hermann (1832–1932), German-born artist who visited California in the 1870s and there painted many perceptive, pleasant landscapes, particularly of southern California.

Hesperian (1858–63), journal of literature and art for women, initially a semimonthly, from 1859 on a monthly. It aimed to bring culture to ladies by discussing literary classics; by providing information about niceties of housekeeping; and through the printing of colored fashion plates, its main attraction. Contributors included "Caxton" (W. H. Rhodes), J. S. Hittell, Frank Soulé, and "Yellow Bird" (John Rollin Ridge). Continued (1863–64) as *Pacific Monthly*, it attempted to appeal to men also and ran a series of recollections by such pioneers as Larkin and Lassen.

Hetch Hetchy, valley in the northwest part of Yosemite National Park, bearing an Indian name for its food crop of grass seed or acorns, watered by the Tuolumne River. To supplement the Spring Valley water supply for San Francisco, City Engineer C. E. Grunsky♦ persuaded Mayor Phelan to request the federal government's permission to dam the river and flood the valley (1905). The proposal was opposed by conservationists led by John Muir as well as by Modesto farmers who feared the loss of their irrigation water. President Roosevelt endorsed the reservoir (1906), but President Taft's Secretary of Interior Ballinger withdrew approval (1910). Finally President Wilson and his Secretary of Interior Franklin Lane♦ gave permission to proceed, and the water system, designed by M. M. O'Shaughnessy,♦ was in full operation by 1934. The dam, completed in 1923, was heightened in 1938. Despite the Raker Act (1913) of Congress prohibiting private firms from distributing its power, San Francisco voters granted that right to the Pacific Gas and Electric Co. (1925).

HEWLETT, William R. (1913–), born in Michigan, graduated from Stanford (1934), where he also took a degree in electrical engineering, and as a student of Frederick Terman was encouraged to apply his knowledge and his inventive ability to found, with David Packard,♦ the firm of Hewlett-Packard (1938), a leading developer and manufacturer in the field of electronics♦ located at Stanford Industrial Park. Hewlett has used his fortune to establish a large charitable foundation (1976).

HEZETA, Bruno de, see *Heceta, Bruno.*

Hide trade of Mexican era, begun after the government allowed foreign vessels to enter its ports (1821). The trade was initiated (1822) with English ships, whose representative was William Hartnell, although the Massachusetts firm of Bryant, Sturgis & Co. sent its first frigate around the Horn to Monterey that year with William A. Gale as its agent.

Not until 1828, when the rival English firm was dissolved, did the New Englanders come to monopolize the business of selling or swapping manufactured goods to the missions, pueblos, and *ranchos,* from which were obtained hides, tallow, and cowhorns. Before Bryant, Sturgis got out of the business (1842), it had collected some 500,000 hides, many made into shoes and boots by New England manufacturers and brought back to California to be sold at handsome profits.

The classic account of the trade from a sailor's point of view is Richard Henry Dana's *Two Years*

Before the Mast. Others who participated on one level or another of the New England business, and generally left some record of it in a published book or later issued diary or letters, include Faxon Dean Atherton, William Sturgis Hinckley, W. D. M. Howard, Thomas O. Larkin, Henry Mellus, Alfred Robinson, Abel Stearns, William Henry Thomes, and Alpheus B. Thompson.

Other traders also carried on business with Hawaii, and still others had a triangular business— sending manufactured goods to California, getting sea otter pelts from there, and trading them in China for Oriental goods which were transported back to Boston. But the basic hide business was generally a limited trade between Boston and California ports.

It was disrupted as the old *rancheros* were driven out by the American conquest in the Mexican War and it ended when all commercial activity in California was concentrated on the gold rush. Later a large and different kind of business in raising cattle developed under the Americans. *(See also individual entries.)*

High Desert, see *Desert.*

High Sierra Wilderness Area, largest primitive preserve in California (615 sq. mi.), established (1931) within the Kings Canyon and Sequoia national parks. In the Sierra Nevada♦ it extends from Tioga Pass to Walker Pass. W. R. Burnett's novel, *High Sierra* (1940), about a gangster who robs a California resort hotel and escapes into the mountains, was adapted by him and John Huston into a successful film (1941) featuring Humphrey Bogart.

Higher education, see *Education.*

"Hights, The," see *Miller, Joaquin.*

Highway Patrol, motorized state police system organized in 1929 to patrol the state's roads and enforce its speed and safety regulations and the code of the Dept. of Motor Vehicles, which tests and licenses drivers and registers their vehicles.

Highways, dating back to the earliest days of the automobile (a State Bureau of Highways for wagons was founded *c.*1895), their financing began in 1909 through bond issues but has long been largely funded by taxes on vehicles, gasoline, and tires. By the 1920s paved roads and numbered routes had come into being. For the 14,800,000 vehicles registered in the state (1972) and the numerous autos and trucks from out of state, California has 166,000 miles of highways, county roads, and city streets.

Of the federally financed national system of Interstate and Defense Highways created by Congress (1956), 2,288 miles are to be in California and about 70% had been completed by 1973. Highways of this system are marked by shields with the national colors and even numbers (in single or double digits) for east-west routes and odd ones for north-south routes. The first of the state's numerous superhighways with overpasses and other elaborate construction to eliminate crossroads was the Pasadena Freeway, completed in 1940. One freeway stopped in midconstruction was that along the Embarcadero of San Francisco. In 1971, of the 14,581 miles of state highways, 4,647 were freeways, with another 735 miles budgeted or under construction.

The state's major highways are: *1*, a coastal road from Eureka to San Juan Capistrano; *5*, from the Oregon border, past Yreka, along the western side of the Central Valley, and through Los Angeles and San Diego to the Mexican border; *10*, from Santa Monica, past Riverside, through Indio and Blythe to Arizona; *15*, from San Diego through San Bernardino and Barstow to Las Vegas, Nev.; *49*, from Yuba Pass and Downieville through the gold rush country of Grass Valley, Auburn, Placerville, Mokelumne Hill, and Sonora to Mariposa; *80*, from San Francisco through Sacramento to the Nevada border and on beyond Reno as a major transcontinental route; *99*, from a junction with *5* at Red Bluff through the Central Valley cities of Chico, Sacramento, Modesto, Merced, Fresno, and Bakersfield, near which it rejoins *5*; *101*, from the Oregon border along the coast via Eureka, as the Redwood Highway through Ukiah, across the Golden Gate Bridge into San Francisco, past San Jose to follow an approximation of the old Camino Reál through Salinas, San Luis Obispo, and Santa Barbara to Los Ángeles; *395*, from Carson City, Nev., skirting Yosemite National Park to Bishop and Lone Pine south nearly to San Bernardino.

HÍJAR, JOSÉ MARÍA, (*fl.* 1834–45), wealthy Mexican from Jalisco who with José María Padrés, an army officer from Puebla, organized a *Compania Cosmopolitan,* better known as a company bearing their surnames, to import Mexicans to colonize secularized mission lands in Alta California. Padrés had been an inspector of troops and customs in Alta California (1830–31) and there had tried to secularize the missions until ousted to Mexico by Gov. Manuel Victoria. In Mexico he was close to Acting President Farías, whom he persuaded to appoint Híjar not only chief of the colonization plan but governor of Alta California. The latter appointment was canceled by Santa Anna, the new President, before it could take effect, for he sent a fast courier to instruct Figueroa♦ to remain in office. When Híjar and Padrés arrived (1834) with their 250 followers (including Ignacio Coronel, José Noé, and Agustín Olvera), Figueroa kept them away from the as-yet-unsecularized mission lands and, for safety's sake, limited them to settlement as individuals in established pueblos or as group colonists in the Sonoma-Solano-Petaluma area on the northern frontier, where they could also act as a buffer against the Russians at Fort Ross. Further friction with Figueroa led him to deport them to Mexico (May 1834), charged with conspiracy against the established government. Padrés had no further association with California, but Híjar was sent back in 1845 as a government commissioner to prepare resistance against threatened U.S. intervention. He died in Los Angeles soon after his arrival.

HILDEBRANDT, Edouard (1817–68), German painter, studied in France under Isabey, visited and painted in California in the 1860s.

HILGARD, Eugene W[oldemar] (1833–1916), professor of agriculture at the University of California, Berkeley (1874–1904), noted for study of the relation of soils to climate and vegetation. He founded the Botanical Garden of the campus.

HILL, A[ndrew] P[utnam] (1854–1922), Indiana-born photographer and painter resident in San Jose, who became leader of an early conservation movement to preserve the coastal redwoods. He founded a Sempervirens Club (1900) which was instrumental in creating the first State Park at Big Basin. His club was reactivated (1968) as the Sempervirens Fund to acquire more forest land in the area.

HILL, Morgan, see *Morgan Hill.*

HILL, Sarah Althea (1832–1937), mistress of William Sharon, a wealthy Nevada and San Francisco banker, who sued him (1883) for support under the terms of a "marriage contract." One court granted her a divorce and alimony of $2,500

monthly, while another overturned the ruling and called the contract a forgery, but the state Supreme Court upheld the divorce ruling. After Sharon's death (1885) she continued suit against his estate, using the document said to have been forged by Mammy Pleasant. A federal suit over its validity went against her, as did a review by U.S. Supreme Court Justice Stephen Field and two other Justices. Meanwhile she had married her attorney, David S. Terry, and when they met Field by accident at a railway restaurant in Lathrop (near Stockton) during a train stop, Terry slapped and threatened Field, whose bodyguard, David Neagle, then shot Terry dead. She continued her suits unsuccessfully, lost her money and her mind, and was committed to a state insane asylum (1892), where she lived for 45 years. Her brother was Morgan Hill, for whom the community of Morgan Hill was named. *(See also individual entries.)*

HILL, Thomas (1829–1908), English-born artist who was reared in the U.S., went to San Francisco (1861), and, except for absences in Paris and Massachusetts (1866–71), lived the rest of his life in California, where he painted many romantic canvases, most of them large, often landscapes of Yosemite which he turned out for tourists at his Wawona studio. Perhaps his best-known work is "Driving the Last Spike," commissioned but refused as unhistorical by Leland Stanford because of such poetic license as the inclusion of Theodore Judah, who had died six years before the incident depicted took place.

Hillsborough, elegant residential community south of San Francisco and adjacent to Burlingame,♦ founded in 1910 by Henry T. Scott. The smallest lots are one-half acre and large estates are common. Among the great ones built earlier in the century were those of the Crocker, Newhall, and Tobin families. In 1970 the population was 8,753.

HINCKLEY, William S[turgis] (1807–46), Boston-born ship captain in the hide trade who settled in California (1832) and became a businessman with Jacob Leese and Nathan Spear. An early resident of Yerba Buena, he was *alcalde* (1844) and captain of the port (1846). He married a daughter of Ignacio Martínez, commander of the presidio, and thus became a brother-in-law of William A. Richardson.

Hippie movement, an attitude of mind and a way of life of young people arising during the 1960s in opposition to the prevailing American Establishment. The youths who developed this counterculture dropped out of colleges and universities and any other organizations they considered to be materialistic, lacking individualism, or unduly rational.

Gathering together their own "families" and communes, they established new centers, of which the largest was in the Haight-Ashbury♦ district of San Francisco, where they plucked blossoms from the nearby Golden Gate Park and accepted the designation "flower children" enjoying a "summer of love." A few of them created their own version of a social agency, The Diggers.♦ Other centers were in Berkeley and on Sunset Strip and Fairfax Ave., in Los Angeles and Hollywood.

But the temper, remotely akin to the Beat movement♦ of an earlier generation, was not confined to a particular locale: the young people cultivated a free emotional life; sought nirvana through drugs, Zen Buddhism, and other Oriental faiths; enjoyed rock music and psychedelic art; and cut loose from the conventional society which they found decadent and immoral, marked by corrupt government and the horrors of the Vietnamese war.

The movement subsided somewhat in the 1970s for a variety of reasons, including degradation of the communal centers either into commercial districts, or, far worse, into squalid slums; the spawning of crime to satisfy the need for drugs; the growth of violence from such opponents as motorcycle gangs and by such wild extremists as Charles Manson;♦ and simply by the recognition that their new way of life and desire for peace and love had not solved problems of individual identity or created a better society. Nevertheless, the movement did not die out, and it clearly did affect the views, morality, manners, and style of Americans at large, far removed from the world of the hippie or opposed to it as they might have considered themselves to have been.

HIRSCH, ELROY (1923–   ), Wisconsin-born football player known as "Crazylegs Hirsch," after starring as a halfback at Wisconsin and Michigan universities played end for the Los Angeles Rams (1949–57) and later was general manager of the team.

Historical Society of Southern California, founded at Los Angeles (1883) "to preserve and protect the archives and historic sights of the Southwest, with particular accent on Southern California." It issued an "Annual Publication" (1888–1935)

and then a *Quarterly* (1935–   ). Its headquarters is El Alisal,♦ Charles Lummis' former home.

Historic buildings, necessarily more commonly found in the older and more heavily settled areas of the state, but are by no means restricted to such regions, and historic significance is not always correlated with age. Thus, the missions (all 21 of which have been reconstructed) are frequently located in places with little other settlement; and such modern edifices as houses designed by Frank Lloyd Wright or the Transamerica Pyramid in San Francisco can be considered historic too. Surviving historic buildings so defined (other than missions) are listed here first as found in large and old communities, next in a rough overview of the state geographically from north to south. (Each structure is given greater attention in an entry of its own or of its architect or other association or under its city, county, or region.)

San Francisco: Downtown and adjacent areas include the Ferry Building; the Palace, St. Francis, and Fairmont hotels; Hallidie Building, headquarters of the Bank of California and of the Hibernia Bank; the Old Mint; Jackson Square; a Frank Lloyd Wright-designed store in Maiden Lane; Old St. Mary's Church and Grace Cathedral; the Pacific Union Club; Coit Tower; City Hall and other Civic Center buildings; and the octagon house headquarters of the D.A.R. The residential areas include the Palace of Fine Arts; Ghirardelli Square; Officers Club (Presidio); Church of the New Jerusalem (Swedenborgian); Temple Emanu-El; McLaren Lodge; Japanese Tea Garden and Conservatory in Golden Gate Park; houses by Coxhead, Bruce Porter, and Maybeck on the Pacific Ave. Presidio Wall; and many other fine old residences—e.g., the Spreckels mansion on Washington St.

Los Angeles and environs: The Old Plaza and its church; Olvera St. and its buildings; Pico House; Casa de Adobe; Los Angeles Public Library; City Hall; Baker Building; Wilshire Boulevard Temple; Angelus Temple (pulpit of Aimee Semple McPherson); Farmers Market; Grauman's Chinese Theatre; Simon Rodia's towers in Watts; several houses designed by Frank Lloyd Wright; some early 19th-century residences, including the Banning mansion in Wilmington and the Bixby ranch house in Long Beach; El Alisal, which once belonged to C. F. Lummis; Southwest Museum; buildings on college campuses, particularly UCLA and USC; Huntington Library and Art Gallery; Gamble House in Pasadena, built by the Greene brothers; Lucky Baldwin's Queen Anne cottage in Arcadia; and the adjacent adobe of Hugo Reid.

San Diego: Balboa Park and its former Exposition buildings, Old Town restored buildings, and Coronado Hotel. *Monterey:* Custom House; Larkin House; Royal Presidio Chapel; Colton Hall, California's first theater; Gov. Alvarado House; Vásquez House; R. L. Stevenson House; House of Four Winds; Cooper-Molera House; Boronda adobe, and, nearby, Richardson adobe; and the Vallejos' Glass House. *Sacramento:* Sutter's Fort, State Capitol, Old Governor's Mansion, Crocker Art Gallery, Stanford-Lathrop Mansion, Railroad Museum, and restored area of the old city.

Other areas, from north to south: *Humboldt County:* Fort Humboldt, Carson House in Eureka. *Trinity County:* Joss House and other gold rush remnants in Weaverville. *Shasta County:* Old jail (and museum) and other gold rush structures in the city of Shasta. *Lassen County:* Fort Defiance in Susanville. *Mendocino County:* Many New England-style houses of the 1860s and a Masonic temple topped by a fine woodcarving in Mendocino City. *Tehama County:* William B. Ide's adobe near Red Bluff. *Butte County:* Bidwell mansion in Chico and the Chinese Temple in Oroville. *Sierra, Yuba, Nevada, Placer, El Dorado, Amador, Alpine, Calaveras, Tuolumne, and Stanislaus counties:* Remnants of gold rush in small settlements and some larger towns, e.g. Marysville, Grass Valley, Coloma, Placerville, Auburn, and Dutch Flat; the State Historic Park at Columbia, and Mark Twain's Cabin nearby. *Sonoma County:* Fort Ross; Jack London's ranch at Glen Ellen; Sonoma Plaza and Gen. Vallejo's home; Vallejo's adobe on Rancho Petaluma; Asti, Fountain Grove, and other wineries; and Burbank's home and gardens in Santa Rosa. *Napa County:* Bale's Mill; the Schramsberg, Krug, Beringer, and other wineries. *Yolo County:* The Opera House and Gable mansion in Woodland. *Marin County:* Fine 19th-century houses in Sausalito, San Rafael, Ross, and elsewhere. *Solano County:* The Arsenal (1859), the Capitol Building (1853), and other structures of Benicia, once the state capital. *Contra Costa County:* John Marsh House; the estate of Eugene O'Neill, Tao House, near Mt. Diablo; John Muir home, near Martinez. *Alameda County:* Cameron-Stanford, de Fremery, Moss, and Pardee homes and Bret Harte Boardwalk in Oakland; Mills Hall at Mills College; John Galen Howard buildings at the University of California; and wineries in Livermore area. *San Joaquin County:* Old buildings of Stockton and its Haggin Art Galleries and county

Pioneer Museum. *San Mateo County:* Ralston mansion, now College of Notre Dame. *Santa Cruz County:* Castro adobe near Watsonville; Wurster's Gregory farmhouse in Scotts Valley. *Santa Clara County:* Stanford University's original quadrangles; *hacienda* and other old buildings at New Almaden; James Lick mansion at Agnew; Peralta adobe in San Jose; Winchester House; Almadén and Paul Masson wineries. *Mariposa County:* Wawona Hotel and the adjacent Pioneer Yosemite History Center; old mining towns. *Mono County:* Bodie, a well-preserved mining town. *San Benito County:* Buildings on the Plaza of San Juan Bautista. *Fresno County:* M. Theo Kearney House; Forestiere's underground gardens. *Inyo County:* Mary Austin's home in Independence; Death Valley Scotty's Castle. *San Luis Obispo County:* Hearst Castle at San Simeon; Ah Louis and Sinsheimer stores in San Luis Obispo. *Kern County:* Fort Tejón; Glennville Adobe; Pioneer Village in Bakersfield. *Santa Barbara County:* de la Guerra House; Carrillo adobe; Trussel-Winchester adobe; and other old structures in Santa Barbara. *Ventura County:* Olivas adobe and County Court House in Ventura; Stagecoach Inn in Newbury Park; Doheny Library at Camarillo; arcaded street of Ojai. *San Bernardino County:* Yorba-Slaughter adobe and Yucaipa adobe in San Bernardino Cucamonga Winery. *Orange County:* Mother Colony House of Anaheim; Modjeska's home; Serrano and Sepulveda adobes; and old houses moved to Knott's Berry Farm. *Riverside County:* Mission Inn. *Imperial County:* Picacho ghost town.

HITCHCOCK, ALFRED [JOSEPH] (1899–), English-born motion picture director who, after success in his homeland, continued his career in Hollywood (1940 ff.). There he has become the recognized master of mystery films, sometimes stylized, symbolic, and psychological, sometimes lively melodramas featuring thrilling chases. He has also produced television series and written books of horror and suspense stories. Although his films generally have exotic foreign settings, *The Birds* (1963), presenting an attack of flocks of birds on humans, was laid in California on the Mendocino coast, and *Shadow of a Doubt* (1943) features the small-town atmosphere of Santa Rosa.

HITTELL, CHARLES J[ACOB] (1861–1938), son of Theodore Hittell, studied under Virgil Williams and in Europe and became a painter of western scenes and an illustrator of books by Mary Austin and others. He chose to be called Carlos rather than Charles.

HITTELL, JOHN S[HERTZER] (1825–1901), went to California (1849) to mine gold but soon made use of the studious inclination which had won him a degree from Ohio's Miami University (1843). He became a major writer for the *Alta California*♦ (1852–80). He wrote guidebooks and statistical works for H. H. Bancroft's publishing firm, but his most important books include *The Resources of California* (1863), *A History of the City of San Francisco, and Incidentally of the State of California* (1878), and *The Commerce and Industries of the Pacific Coast* (1882). His wide-ranging interests led him to write an unorthodox book on the papacy, a defense of phrenology, a proposed revision of the U.S. Constitution, and a work championing the cause of José Limantour.♦ He was the brother of T. H. Hittell.

HITTELL, THEODORE HENRY (1830–1917), after graduation from Yale (1849) and law practice in Ohio, followed his brother John to California (1855), where he worked for James King of William and succeeded him as editor of the San Francisco *Bulletin.* Although he later practiced law and became an authority on land titles, he is remembered not only for his legal works but for his other books, including a biography of James Capen Adams;♦ the *Reminiscences of Early Days* of Stephen J. Field,♦ of which Hittell was the actual author; and a four-volume *History of California* (1885–97).

HOBART, LEWIS P. (1873–1954), Missouri-born architect, educated at the University of California and the Beaux-Arts in Paris, opened his San Francisco office in 1906. His buildings include Grace Cathedral; Bohemian Club; Steinhart Aquarium; Del Monte Lodge; and the new section of the Del Monte Hotel, now the U.S. Naval Post Graduate School at Monterey.

Hockey, see *Ice Hockey.*

HOFFER, ERIC (1902–   ), New York-born longshoreman on the San Francisco waterfront, as a self-taught author became a homespun aphoristic philosopher. He wrote *The True Believer* (1951), *The Ordeal of Change* (1963), and other books.

HOFMANN, HANS (1880–1966), German-born painter, famous for his vivid, abstract canvases displaying planes of color. He first visited the U.S.

(1930, 1931) to teach at the University of California, Berkeley, and the Chouinard Art Institute, settled permanently (1932), and became a citizen (1941). Although his career as artist and teacher was continued elsewhere, he always remembered that the Berkeley campus had introduced him to the U.S., and he gave it a major collection of his paintings and a fund to establish a special exhibit gallery in its Museum of Art.

Hogs, see *Swine.*

HOHFELD, WESLEY NEWCOMB (1879–1918), Oakland-born legal scholar, on the faculties of Stanford (1905–14) and Yale (1914–18), known for his *Fundamental Legal Conceptions* (1919), which set forth the "Hohfeld system" of precise legal terminology.

Hokan, Indian family whose groups resided in isolated pockets throughout the state. The Shasta, Atsugewi, Achomawi, Karok, Yana, and Chimariko formed a contiguous group in the north; the Esselen, Salinan, and Chumash occupied a coastal area in the center of the state; and the Yuman tribes lived in the extreme south. The Pomo and Washo, also Hokan, were cut off from contact with the other tribes.

HOLDREDGE, RANSOM G[ILLET] (1836–99), New York-born painter who moved to San Francisco (1864), where he became known for his accomplished landscapes of Yosemite, the Sierra, and the Bay Area. He also often depicted Indian life.

HOLLADAY, BEN[JAMIN] (1819–87), in 1862 bought the firm begun by John Butterfield♦ to create the Central Overland California and Pike's Peak Express Co. that carried mail and passengers from Missouri to Virginia City (and by the Pioneer Stage Co. on to San Francisco) via a central transcontinental route. Its Concord stagecoaches, drawn by four or six horses, made a trip in 20 days during the Civil War years. He sold out to Wells, Fargo (1866), but continued in the transportation business, sailing steamships from Sitka to Oregon, California, and Mexico, and running his Oregon Central Railroad.

HOLLISTER, prominent family of Santa Barbara County to which they came from Missouri and Ohio. The first California generation included W[ILLIAM] W[ELLS] Hollister (1818–86), who was born in Ohio and attended Kenyon College and had been a farmer in his native state before he took 200 to 300 head of cattle to California (1852). He sold them, returned home, and in 1853 drove some 5,000 sheep from St. Louis to San Diego County. En route he met the party of Thomas and Benjamin Flint and Llewellyn Bixby,♦ who were also driving sheep westward, but Hollister is said to have entered California a day earlier than they did. He became associated (1855–61) with the Bixby and Flint families as a rancher. Later, with a brother of his and with Albert and Thomas Diblee, he held over 200,000 acres of land, from Rancho San Justo in Monterey County (where the town of Hollister was named for him) to Santa Barbara. There he raised sheep, grew fruit, had other ranching interests, and developed a vacation center on Santa Barbara's beach with his Arlington Hotel.♦ One of his brothers was Joseph Hubbard Hollister (1820–73), who accompanied him on his great sheep drive. One of Joseph Hubbard Hollister's daughters, Nellie, married Phineas Banning. Another brother of W. W. Hollister was Albert G. Hollister (1811–91), a relative latecomer to California (1870), who joined him in settling on part of the former land grant of Nicholas Den, Los Dos Pueblos Rancho. W. W. also had a sister, Mary, who married Ariel Flint, member of another great ranching family allied to the Bixbys.

Hollister, town in northern San Benito County, founded (1868) and named for Col. William W. Hollister,♦ owner of the ranch on which it was established and first man to drive sheep♦ across the country to California. It remains a ranching center and is the county seat. Frank Norris gathered background for *The Octopus* in the area. Hollister is the site of an invasion (1947) by hordes of motorcyclists, which incident inspired the film *The Wild One* (1953), featuring Marlon Brando. It is also famous as the center of numerous small and not-so-small earthquakes: the San Andreas, Calaveras, Hayward, and Tres Pinos faults meet there. Appropriately enough, Don Tocher, a leading seismologist, was born in Hollister (1926). Nearby is the town of Paicines, long known for its quicksilver mining. Hollister's population in 1970 was 7,663.

Hollywood, district of Los Angeles, about eight miles northwest of the city's downtown area, in the foothills of the Santa Monica Mts., there called the Hollywood Hills. Begun as a real estate development (1887), it was briefly (1903–10) a small independent city. Not until 1911 did the first studio

for motion pictures♦ move into what was then a quiet, conservative community of about 4,000 people. It was soon followed by others until in the 1920s the radically changed settlement (population 50,000) became synonymous with the entire film industry and its flamboyant, glamorous stars; newly rich, autocratic producers; and ostentatious or scandalous ways of life. Hollywood Boulevard, a major east-west artery, became the equivalent of New York's Broadway and attracted tourists as well as aspiring actors and actresses.

In keeping with the prevailing dramatic atmosphere of Hollywood, its architecture included such bizarre edifices as the Chinese and Egyptian theaters of Sid Grauman,♦ which featured lavish premieres, and a popular restaurant shaped and colored like a brown derby. Looking down from the hills is a huge sign (the white sheetmetal letters are 50 feet high and 30 feet wide) reading HOLLYWOOD. Erected in 1923, until 1949 the full text was "Hollywoodland," advertising a real estate development.

The stars themselves mainly moved to estates in Beverly Hills,♦ which lies nearby on the west, and between the two communities arose a section of Sunset Boulevard♦ (called "the Strip") on which elegant shops and restaurants flourished. The studios located in the area engaged many talented and cultivated foreigners who introduced cosmopolitan culture; Hollywood also attracted America's leading figures in the worlds of theater, literature, and music for its one great industry. It fostered American arts in other ways too, such as through a center in Barnsdall Park,♦ once a private home designed by Frank Lloyd Wright. Not far away are the Hollywood Bowl,♦ Griffith Park,♦ and Century City.♦ Nearby too are the Hollywood Hills portion of Forest Lawn,♦ a burial ground which features colonial Americana, and the Hollywood Cemetery, where Rudolph Valentino and other notable figures of the region's past are interred.

Many motion picture studios were located elsewhere in the Los Angeles area after the early days of Hollywood's settlement, and both the entire industry and its unofficial capital were hard hit by the advent of television. Nevertheless, Hollywood continued to be an important place for its radio broadcasting and its recording businesses and as the West Coast center for the newest form of entertainment, with many of its former motion picture lots used to make films especially for television.

Its palmiest days over, Hollywood still conveys associations of perfervid glamour, which have been celebrated in motion pictures about its own legendry, ranging in time from *Merton of the Movies* (1924), based on the novel by Harry Leon Wilson, through *Sunset Boulevard* (1950), to the various versions of the perennial favorite, *A Star Is Born.*♦ Although often treated as a curious culture to be studied by anthropologists (e.g. Hortense Powdermaker's *Hollywood: The Dream Factory,* 1950) or as a subject for fiction (e.g. Fitzgerald's *The Last Tycoon,*♦ Schulberg's *What Makes Sammy Run?,* and Waugh's *The Loved One*♦), Hollywood is a very real place. In 1970 it had a population of about 194,000.

Hollywood Bowl, natural amphitheater of 50 acres, owned by Los Angeles County. Established (1922) as a concert area, its acoustics were improved by shells designed by Lloyd Wright (1924, 1928). The Bowl seats 20,000 persons and has standing room for another 10,000. Famous for its "Symphonies under the Stars," it is also the site of an annual Easter Sunrise Service.

Hollywood Hotel, title of a radio program featuring interviews by Louella Parsons,♦ drew its name from a famous early-day hostelry of the film capital. It was also the title of a musical film (1937) directed by Busby Berkeley, featuring the gossip columnist and her radio program, and telling a conventional story about a young singer who makes good in the motion pictures.

Hollywood Park, track for thoroughbred horse-racing, located in Inglewood, known as the "track of lakes and flowers" because of its beautiful landscaping. The ten-acre area, opened in 1938, is owned by the Hollywood Turf Club. The track's great races include Hollywood Gold Cup, California Stakes and Century Handicap for three-year-olds and up, and Vanity Handicap and Hollywood Oaks for fillies and mares of those ages.

Hollywood Ten, name given to ten persons in the film world (including Alvah Bessie, Ring Lardner, Jr., John Howard Lawson, Albert Maltz, and Dalton Trumbo) who refused to testify before the Congressional Committee on Un-American Activities (1947). They were indicted and some were imprisoned for contempt of Congress, while all were publicly blacklisted by the film world of Hollywood.

HOLT, Benjamin (1849–1920), established a wagon-parts business with his brothers in their

native New Hampshire, continuing it in California, to which he moved (1883). There he invented and manufactured improved farm machinery, including a steam-powered harvester (*c.*1885) and a steam and gasoline tractor whose wheels moved inside endless track belts on either side of the machine (1904–8). This so-called caterpillar not only made possible the harvesting of wheat on rough and soft terrain in California but was adapted by the British army in World War I to create the first original tanks used in combat. Later it was basic to development of the bulldozer and the snowmobile.

Holy City, see *Los Gatos.*

Honey, created commercially by the introduction of honey bees to the state (1853), followed by their more extensive importation from Italy (1859–69) by John S. Harbison, the author of *The Bee-Keeper's Directory* (San Francisco, 1861), who cultivated them on large sage and buckwheat ranches in San Diego County. From there he shipped large quantities of honey east (100 tons in 1876) at a time when few eastern apiarists produced as much as a ton a year. California now supplies most of the U.S. honey, totaling about 25,000,000 tons annually.

Honey Lake, dry basin retaining some shallow water in a southeastern Lassen County valley. One of its early explorers, J. G. Bruff, named it for George Derby, but its established name came from aphis deposits on wild oats. It was part of the region that Isaac Roop♦ tried to establish as the separate territory of Nataqua♦ and was the scene of the Sagebrush War.♦

Hoopa Valley Reservation, see *Humboldt County, Hupa,* and *Indian reservations and rancherías.*

HOOVER, Herbert [Clark] (1874–1964), born in Iowa, moved to California as a young man, earning his way through Stanford University, where he studied engineering and graduated with its first class (1895). He had a successful career as a mining engineer and an expert on mineral matters in foreign countries until World War I, when he began his life of public service. Initially he aided the many Americans stranded in Europe; then he headed an organization which provided food and clothing to Belgian and French civilians.

When the U.S. entered the war he became the nation's Food Administrator, and when peace was achieved he coordinated relief activities for devastated European countries, including the famine-stricken USSR. After serving as Secretary of Commerce under Harding and Coolidge (1921–28) and successfully introducing engineering methods to cope with economic issues, he became the Republican candidate for the presidency.

He was the first Californian to be elected President of the U.S. (1928–32). Within a year the stock market collapse began the Great Depression. It proved his undoing as President. He took only limited governmental action to stimulate the economy, and he came to be seen as an unsympathetic leader when he called in the army to oust unemployed ex-servicemen who marched on Washington to fulminate for an immediate payment of a bonus. The resulting disfavor with his policies and personality lost Hoover election to a second term.

Not until the late 1940s, when he headed a commission to propose better organization of the executive branch of the federal government, did he return to favor. Hoover expanded his economic theory of "rugged individualism" and his trust in private endeavor in *American Individualism* (1922).

His scholarly knowledge of mining occasioned the translation, with his wife, of a 16th-century treatise written in Latin, *De re metallica* (1912). The sense of history there displayed was developed far more fully in various other writings and in his *Memoirs* (3 vols., 1951–52), and most strikingly in his remarkable collection of pertinent manuscripts, documents, and diverse printed materials used as the basis for establishing at his alma mater a great library of primary resources for research, the Hoover Institution on War, Revolution and Peace.◆

A major building of the Institution is named for his wife, Lou Henry Hoover (1874–1944), also born in Iowa, whom he met when they were students at Stanford. She participated actively in all his interests and in the design of their home on the Stanford campus. That home was bequeathed to the University, and it serves as the official residence of the president.

Hoover Dam, see *Water.*

Hoover Institution on War, Revolution and Peace, library and research organization founded by Herbert Hoover (1919) at Stanford University. Its collections concentrate on late 19th- and early 20th-century political, social, and economic change throughout the world.

HOPE, Bob (1904–   ), English-born film, radio, and television comedian, began his motion picture career in 1938. He co-starred often with Bing Crosby and like him has come to be considered one of the pillars of the industry. He is both a highly professional performer and an effective spokesman for the world of entertainment. He has often toured the world for personal appearances before U.S. troops abroad and has also contributed his time and his wit to many charity performances in the U.S. In 1960 he established a golf tournament in Palm Springs.◆

HOPKINS, Mark (1813–78), began his business career as a country storekeeper in his native upstate New York, but, after being attracted to California during the gold rush, continued it in a Sacramento hardware store with Collis P. Huntington. With Huntington he became an investor in the Sacramento-financed Central Pacific Railroad. As a major investor and its treasurer, he became one of the Big Four,◆ but he was the oldest, the most modest, and the first to die. His young widow, a cousin, completed the ostentatious mansion they had planned on Nob Hill and had it furnished by Edwin T. Searles, a decorator, who became her second husband. After her death the mansion became the first home of the forerunner of the San Francisco Art Institute and, still later, the grounds of a hotel named for the original owner who never lived on the site: the Mark Hopkins.

Hopkins Marine Laboratory, research facility of Stanford University, founded 1892, and located at Pacific Grove.◆ It is primarily devoted to coastal marine biology. Timothy Hopkins, the adopted son of Mark Hopkins, endowed it.

HOPPER, Hedda (1890–1966), gossip columnist who wrote about the personal lives of film celebrities, was also a Hollywood celebrity who affected the wearing of bizarre hats (hence the title of her book, *From Under My Hat,* 1952) and had a career as a minor comic actress (she portrayed herself in *Sunset Boulevard,* 1950).

HOPPER, James M[arie] (1876–1956), French-born American writer reared in California, was generally known as Jimmy Hopper and as a founder of Carmel's bohemian colony. A journalist for magazines and newspapers, he was a popular story writer too. His Kiplingesque tales set in the Philippines, such as *Caybigan* (1906), used a background garnered there as a school teacher, while his athletic prowess and other collegiate experiences at the University of California provided material for *Coming Back with the Spitball* (1914) and other tales. He collaborated with Frederick Bechdolt♦ on *9009* (1908), a novel about American prison life.

Hops, conelike flowers of the tall vine of the mulberry family used by breweries.♦ Hops were first raised in California in 1865. The state's low rainfall was particularly good for the crop, and production expanded constantly from 625,000 pounds in 1870 to 10,125,000 pounds in 1900. In the 20th century production did not increase because the rich bottom lands needed for the crops could more profitably be used for other foods. Sacramento, Sonoma, and Mendocino counties have been the leading areas for growing hops, in which California still ranks high. The poor working conditions of the migratory laborers used as pickers led to the Wheatland Riot♦ of 1913.

Horned toad, see *Lizard.*

Hornitos, gold rush mining town in western Mariposa County, populated mainly by Mexicans and said to have been so named because their tombs looked like bake ovens *(hornitos).* A founder of the Ghirardelli♦ family ran a general merchandise store there.

HORRELL, BABE (EDWIN G. HORRELL) (1902–), Missouri-born football player, reared in Pasadena, who was a star center of the Wonder Teams♦ of the University of California, Berkeley (1922–24). He coached football at the University of California, Los Angeles (1937–44).

Horse racing, a sport popular in Mexican California as an informal competition of the sort viewed on the Santa Barbara beach and described by Richard Henry Dana in *Two Years Before the Mast.*

The first formal track with established U.S. rules was the Pioneer Course, opened in San Francisco (1850). Others soon followed, and by 1894 there were 40 tracks in the state. A governing board to regulate racing had been projected as early as the 1870s by Gov. Leland Stanford. He and other millionaires also created private tracks for their own stock, including his at Palo Alto, Ben Ali Haggin's near Sacramento, Alvinza Hayward's at San Mateo, and Lucky Baldwin's at Santa Anita Rancho.

The first modern commercial track was Tanforan, north of San Mateo, built in the 1920s; in 1942 its stalls were used as a Relocation Center to house Japanese internees. With the legalization of parimutuel betting (1933) racing became a big business.

Santa Anita Park♦ was opened the following year, soon followed by the Del Mar Turf Club track and Hollywood Park♦ (1938). In the north of the state, near San Francisco, Bay Meadows and Golden Gate Fields were built later. In addition to thoroughbred racing, harness and quarter-horse racing are popular.

The two most successful U.S. jockeys are both associated with California: Johnny Longden♦ and Willie Shoemaker.♦ Seabiscuit, Swaps, and Round Table were great winners identified with the state's horse raising.

Horse raising, became common during California's *rancho* era of the 1830s and 1840s, and visitors like Richard Henry Dana constantly observed that Californians were not only great horsemen but would rarely go even the shortest distance except on horseback. The *gente de razón* prided themselves on fine saddles and bridles for their stock (mainly mustangs), on their equestrian skill, and on the festivities of their rodeos. Partly because of this heritage and partly because of the great ranches, Californians have continued to cultivate their horses and horseback riding, have enjoyed the prowess displayed at rodeos,♦ and have created a club known as the Rancheros Visitadores♦ for those purposes. Famous California horses include Lou Dillion, bred in the state, and the world's champion trotter (1903); Seabiscuit, foaled in California, owned by Charles Howard, a San Franciscan, as a racehorse was at one time the turf's greatest money winner (1940); Chief of Longview, prizewinning five-gaited stallion show horse of the 1930s, owned by Mrs. W. P. Roth, daughter of William Matson; Swaps, foaled near Ontario, Cal. (1952), was named (race) horse of the year (1956); and Round Table, brought from Kentucky and Oklahoma to California for a racing career that led him to be named horse of the year (1958), when he was temporarily the top money winner of U.S. racing history.

Horticulture, began in California with the growing of fruits, vegetables, plants, and flowers by the padres at the missions, but lay Spanish and Mexican settlers had only small and simple gardens, in part because of a lack of water.

Only with the gold rush did extensive horticulture begin with such foreign nurserymen as Louis Pellier and his brothers, who developed plum trees in the Santa Clara Valley (1856 ff.) for so-called French prunes. Other commercial nurseries♦ were established in the 1850s for more fruit and plants, while the early growing of grapes by Joseph Chapman and Louis Vignes was much extended commercially by the establishment of a vineyard in Sonoma County by Agoston Haraszthy♦ (1852).

Before long the newly rich capitalists, like D. O. Mills and William Ralston, had lavish gardens created for their estates on the San Francisco Peninsula. A little later Leland Stanford established a vineyard in Tehama County and a farm in Santa Clara County, the latter to become the home of Stanford University. Landscaped and beautifully planted areas were created for the public too, first in such a commercial venture as Woodward's Gardens♦ (1866), later in civic enterprises, of which the most notable was Golden Gate Park♦ (1871 ff.).

California's climate was also responsible for extensive horticultural experimentation, particularly winter cultivation. The importation of eucalyptus trees was widespread beginning in the 1860s and citrus fruit growing,♦ first commercially attempted in the 1840s, became a major business of southern California in the 1870s and thereafter, often for settlers newly arrived from the East. Both climate and an exotic appeal also helped to popularize the domesticating of cactus♦ and of other succulents. Even more appealing was the cultivation of roses for winter bloom, ranging from those grown in the little gardens which became commonplace for urban homes to those cultivated by women's clubs, in specialized public parks, and publicized by the creation of Pasadena's Tournament of Roses,♦ held each New Year's day beginning in 1890.

Toward the turn of the 19th century California became increasingly famous for the development of new species or ones not previously grown there. Most famous of the experimentalists was Luther Burbank of Santa Rosa, while James H. Logan of Santa Cruz created the berry named for him, and the seedless grape was for a time known by the name of its developer as the Thompson grape. George Roeding, for the first time, cultivated figs in California, and other growers refined the so-called alligator pear into the avocado.

A Nurserymen's Association was established in 1915, and during that same period two related businesses came into being—growing flowers for cutting on large acreage and growing fields of flowers for seed, as was done by John Bodger at Santa Paula, by Theodosia Burr Shepherd at Ventura, and by Ferry Morse Co. at Lompoc. In time the state provided most of the nation's cut flowers and flower seeds. Great horticultural nurseries also developed, such as Dr. Francesco Franceschi's in Santa Barbara and Kate Olivia Sessions' in San Diego. The latter was the forerunner of Balboa Park.

With increased costs of land and labor and the changed tempo of modern life, the great gardens that characterized earlier estates became less common, though some continued to thrive, like that of Filoli, on the San Francisco Peninsula, which was first the home of William Bourn, then of the daughter of William Matson. Some were retained but opened to the public, like the botanical gardens associated with the Henry E. Huntington Library, famous for their camellias and cacti. Others became entirely public facilities, like the Los Angeles State and County Arboretum at Arcadia, located on the former estate of Lucky Baldwin; the Santa Barbara Botanic Garden (begun in 1926); Balboa Park in San Diego; the two botanic gardens of the University of California, the one at Berkeley begun by Eugene Hilgard and formally established in 1891, the other at Los Angeles, created in 1929; and the Rancho Santa Ana Botanic Garden, affiliated with Claremont Colleges.

Public education in the field included a Department of Horticultural Science at the University of California, Riverside. While an occasional private individual created a notable garden, as Baldesare Forestiere did at Fresno, horticulture and landscape design were clearly recognized professional fields only in the 20th century. Among the great figures in those areas was John McLaren, while others included Thomas D. Church, Garret Eckbo, and Lawrence Halprin, whose projects ranged from domestic gardens to large-scale housing projects, and the landscaping of large public edifices and the land alongside freeways.

HOTCHKISS, Hazel (1890–1974), Berkeley-born tennis champion who won the U.S. women's singles, doubles, and mixed doubles championships (1909, 10, 11). She married George Wightman (1911), and they donated the trophy for English and American women's singles that bears their surname.

Hotels, essentially came into being with the great influx during the gold rush, although at least one in San Francisco (Vioget House) dated from 1846. Some early hotels had exotic structures; one was in the hull of the *Niantic,* a converted ship. By 1850 San Francisco had 28 places that called themselves hotels, one of them the original St. Francis, which was created from several houses, and as a social gathering place foreshadowed its later namesake on Union Square. In 1852 the What Cheer House offered even more amenities, but to men only.

At the mines themselves ramshackle places of the sort Dame Shirley remarked upon were replaced by substantial buildings, some of which have lasted to this day and serve their original purpose (as in Volcano and Murphys). San Francisco got its first great luxury hotel in 1862 with the opening of the Lick House, whose dining room had a ceiling 48 feet high and walls with murals painted by Thomas Hill. The smaller and quieter city of Los Angeles did not get a hotel of any size until Pico House was opened in 1870, and it was a rather simple place. But in the 1870s San Francisco got two huge and elegant establishments, the one named for its owner, E. J. "Lucky" Baldwin, the other the great Palace Hotel, built by William Ralston. The Palace, whose post-earthquake and fire successor is still on the same Market St. site, retains an impressive Palm Court.

Toward the end of the century fine hotels were available not only in the major cities of the state but in smaller communities, to which the new railroad lines brought many travelers for business or pleasure. The Southern Pacific itself created California's most lavish and stylish resort, Del Monte Hotel (1880), but other elegant vacation spots were built, such as the one at Coronado, the Arlington in Santa Barbara, the Raymond in Pasadena, and the Mission Inn in Riverside. In addition, many persons attracted to California's favorable climate for their health sought out a spa, and they patronized many resorts that had mineral waters, including Aetna Springs, Calistoga, The Geysers, Napa Soda Springs, Paso Robles, and Tassajara Hot Springs.

Scenic wonders also appealed to many tourists, and hotels like that at Wawona (1875) and the simpler Camp Curry (1899) in Yosemite were built to accommodate them. In the 20th century new, large luxury hotels were built in San Francisco and the rapidly growing Los Angeles. In the northern city several of these multistoried edifices were built on Nob Hill and employed the names of the nabobs who once owned their sites for residences: Mark Hopkins, Fairmont (for James G. Fair), Huntington, and Stanford.

Urban luxury hotels erected in the Los Angeles area sought a different ambience: the Ambassador on Wilshire Boulevard, the Beverly Hills in the community of that name, the Huntington in Pasadena, and the Bel Air all are rambling, low-lying structures which give easy access to great gardens containing swimming pools, tennis courts, and other amenities previously associated with country resorts. But new hotels were also built at established resorts, like the Biltmore in Santa Barbara, and new vacation areas were developed, like Palm Springs, which offered a warm place for a winter holiday in the once-scorned desert.

The tremendous growth of tourism to the state and the ease of intrastate travel by auto and plane, particularly after World War II, led to a great increase in new kinds of hotels, many of them standardized chain operations geared to accommodating travelers who were unaccustomed to the services—and expenses—of bellboys, headwaiters and waitresses in formal dining rooms, or central garages with mechanics in attendance. So cheaper motels began to rise in the cities and along the highways and near the freeways leading to them. They also were built at airports to accommodate travelers making quick overnight stops and to cater to conferences of businessmen and other persons who found them convenient central meeting places.

But there also were exotic variations on these standard operations. Motels on the highways or outskirts of cities vied with one another to offer more appealing swimming pools or more fanciful restaurants and decor. These were outdone by the most exotic of all, the Madonna Inn near San Luis Obispo, aptly described as "very uniquely decorated."

Similarly, the proliferation of city hotels led some national chains to construct great structures that would provide exciting designs in contrast to the plainness of home. For example, John Portman created for San Francisco's Hyatt Regency and Los Angeles' Bonaventure massive atrium lobbies rising many stories through strangely shaped and attractively gardened walls, affording dramatic views from the floor or from rides in their glass-capsuled elevators. Thus hotels were transformed from simple accommodations away from home to surroundings suggestive of new and liberating experiences. (*See also individual entries.*)

Hounds, The, name given to a San Francisco group who called themselves Regulators and who were mainly veterans of Stevenson's Regiment,♦ discharged after the Mexican War. Ostensibly volunteers devoted to maintaining law and order in the city, they harassed Spanish Americans and tried to hound them out of town. Their brutality culminated in a murderous, looting raid upon the city's tent community of Little Chile (July 15, 1849), which incident aroused Samuel Brannan and others to form a Law and Order party and, eventually, the Vigilance Committee♦ (1851). The Hounds were abetted by the Sydney Ducks (Australian escaped or ex-convicts), who also set many fires and looted the burned buildings to equip their "Sydney Town."

HOUSER, Bud (Clarence Houser) (1904?–), shot put and discus star as a Santa Barbara high school student and at USC before setting records in the Olympic Games (1924), in which he excelled for discus in 1928. He established a discus world record of 155′ 2¾″ (1926).

HOWARD, JOHN GALEN (1864–1931), Massachusetts-born architect who went to Berkeley (1901) to oversee the campus plan of the University of California sponsored by Phoebe Apperson Hearst. He remained on the faculty until 1925, founding the school of architecture and designing major edifices including the Greek Theatre, the Campanile, Sather Gate, and Hearst Mining Building. He employed a neoclassical Beaux-Arts style for those buildings, though his own Berkeley home was in the simple local redwood shingle style. In San Francisco he was an architect of the Civic Auditorium and, with Frederick Law Olmsted, Jr., designed St. Francis Wood.

HOWARD, SIDNEY [COE] (1891–1939), born in Oakland, began his career as a dramatist while at the University of California, continued it in George P. Baker's 47 Workshop at Harvard, and after ambulance and air force service in World War I became a professional dramatist. He began with rather remote materials, such as *Swords* (1921), the romantic blank verse tragedy set in medieval times, and adaptations from foreign dramas, such as *Casanova* (1923), but went on to realistic studies of contemporary life, among them *The Silver Cord* (1926), about a mother's pathological love for her sons. Many of his plays were set elsewhere, like *Ned McCobb's Daughter* (1926), laid in New England, to which he had moved, but he won a Pulitzer Prize for a play with a California background, *They Knew What They Wanted* (1924), about the uneasy marriage of an aging Italian wine grower in the Napa Valley and a San Francisco waitress. Other works included a dramatization of Sinclair Lewis' *Dodsworth* and film adaptations of *Gone With the Wind* and a Faulkner novel.

HOWARD, W[ILLIAM] D[AVIS] M[ERRY] (1819–56), Boston-born merchant who went to California (1839), dealt in the hide trade, and grew rich selling general merchandise with Henry Mellus.♦ Their firm was located in the former Hudson's Bay Co. headquarters in San Francisco. Because he was a generous benefactor of the city, Howard St. was named for him. He also owned property in other cities and a *rancho* in San Mateo.

Howl, title poem of a collection by Allen Ginsberg,♦ issued in San Francisco by Lawrence Ferlinghetti in 1956. The powerful apocalyptic statement about the physical and psychic destruction of his generation of Americans by their nation's values had a Whitman-like style and what Ginsberg called a "Hebraic-Melvillian bardic breath." The publisher was arrested, and acquitted, for issuing the allegedly obscene poem.

HOYEM, ANDREW, see *Auerhahn Press* and *Grabhorn Press.*

HUDSON, GRACE CARPENTER (1865–1937), California-born artist known for her paintings of Indians, particularly of Pomo children.

Hudson's Bay Company, fur trapping and trading organization, established (1821) as an outgrowth of a 17th-century enterprise. It had its West Coast headquarters at Vancouver. An employee, Peter Skene Ogden, was the first Canadian♦ to explore the trapping possibilities of California (1826), but the company's first actual trapping expedition was led by Alexander McLeod (1828), for whom the (misspelled) McCloud River was named. He returned the next year and penetrated as far south as Stockton,♦ but lost his equipment in bad winter weather. Ogden also returned (1829–30) and went as far south as the present Needles before returning to trap in the Sacramento Valley. An expedition under John Work♦ (1832–33) and another under Michel La Framboise (1833) were followed by annual parties also traveling the Siskiyou and the Trinity trails to hunt along central California streams. The association with California was sufficient to lead Sir James Douglas to come by ship to Yerba Buena (1841), where he undertook some trade and negotiated with Gov. Alvarado for the establishment of a mercantile outpost there in that year. It was run by William Glenn Rae, the son-in-law of John McLoughlin, the company's chief factor in Canada, but after Rae committed suicide (1845) it was closed by Sir George Simpson.

Hueneme, see *Port Hueneme.*

HUGHES, HOWARD [ROBARD] (1905–76), born in Houston, Tex., educated there at Rice, then at California Institute of Technology, began his business career at age 19, when he inherited the Hughes Tool Co., a producer of oil-drilling bits. Profits from that company funded other ventures, including a $12,000,000 investment in TWA, which Hughes parlayed into $560,000,000. He was a sensational but not financially successful producer of motion pictures (including *Hell's Angels*) and a flamboyant aviator who set the world's land speed record (352 m.p.h., 1935) and the transcontinental record (7 hrs., 28 min., 1937), and designed, built, and flew the world's largest plane (1947). His business interests expanded to his Hughes Aircraft Company, manufacturers, his Hughes Air Corp., airlines, and vast real estate holdings in the Los Angeles area and in Nevada, where he purchased five major hotel-casino combinations in Las Vegas. As his businesses grew larger he withdrew from public life until, finally, he became a recluse, resident in barricaded quarters of one of his hotels or in sequestered areas in foreign lands. He refused even to venture out to testify in huge lawsuits related to his TWA investments or to deny a spurious biography concocted by an imaginative writer, Clifford Irving, who was jailed as a result of the hoax.

HUGHES, RUPERT (1872–1956), Missouri-born author, long resident in Los Angeles, about which he wrote *City of Angels* (1941), was best known for biographical fiction, popular plays and novels, and a biography of George Washington (3 vols., 1926–30). He was an uncle of Howard Hughes.

Humboldt County, incorporated in 1853, was formed in part from Trinity County and augmented (1875) from part of onetime Klamath County. Del Norte and Siskiyou counties lie on the north; Siskiyou and Trinity counties, separated in part by the Salmon Mts., on the east; Mendocino County on the south; and the Pacific Ocean on the west.

Cape Mendocino is the westernmost point of the mainland U.S. outside Alaska. The county has three major bays: Trinidad,♦ Arcata, and Humboldt. Part of the Six Rivers National Forest lies on the county's east side and includes Tish-Tang-A-Tang Ridge.♦ The Prairie Creek Redwoods State Park and the Lady Bird Johnson Grove, in the north, and Humboldt Redwoods State Park and King Range National Conservation Area, in the south, are also in the county.

Union (present Arcata) was the county seat until it was shifted to Eureka♦ (1856). In the 1850s and 60s, when gold mining flourished along the Klamath♦ and Trinity♦ rivers, there were many battles with the Hupa, Wiyot, Yurok, and other Indians, leading to the establishment of Fort Humboldt, where Capt. Ulysses S. Grant was stationed (1854). Despite the existence of the military outpost, citizens conducted a massacre of Indians (1860) that was vigorously condemned by Bret Harte, then on a newspaper at nearby Arcata.♦

Now the state's largest reservation—Hoopa Valley—is located in the county and the two major rivers flow through the nearly 93,000 acres set aside for the Klamath and other Indians. Lumbering along the Eel River, e.g. at Scotia♦ and elsewhere, as well as wood products are the county's major economic bases, but livestock ranching and dairying are also important. The county population in 1970 was 99,692. With an area of 2,295,232 acres, it had 27.8 persons per sq. mi.

Hungarians in California, first emigrated in small numbers during the gold rush. The most distinguished were Agoston Haraszthy,♦ who arrived in 1849 and was the most successful of his countrymen as a vintner, and János Xántus, a naturalist who arrived in 1851, studied the region around Fort Tejón, and wrote two books about California and the U.S. (Pest, 1858, 1860). Xántus believed that by 1859 there were 30 Hungarians in San Francisco. By 1890 there were 369 in California, and by 1920 there were 5,252. The revolution of 1956 caused many Hungarians to flee to California among other places, so that by 1970 there were 58,097 in the state. Among prominent Hungarians settled in California was the film magnate Adolph Zukor.

HUNT, ROCKWELL D. (1868–1966), native-born California historian and professor of government on the faculty of the University of Southern California (1908–45) and the University of the Pacific (1945–52) as director of its California History Foundation. He was the author of many works on the state's history, including a biography of John Bidwell (1942).

HUNTER, CATFISH (JAMES AUGUSTUS HUNTER) (1946–), North Carolina-born baseball player who entered professional play (1964) as a pitcher with the Kansas City Athletics and moved with the team to Oakland (1968). In that year he pitched a perfect no-hit, no-run game against the Minnesota Twins. He also helped lead Oakland to four straight Western Division championships (1971–74) and to three consecutive World Series victories (1972–74). A contract dispute with Athletics owner Charles Finley led to Hunter's becoming a free agent subject to the greatest bidding war in baseball history. It was concluded by his signing (1974) with the New York Yankees for what was reputed to be the highest salary ever paid a baseball player.

Hunter Liggett Military Reservation, a subpost of Fort Ord,♦ located southwest of King City. Hunter, an army training and testing center of some 175,000 acres, was bought (1940) from the San Simeon estate of William Randolph Hearst. The Reservation surrounds Mission San Antonio de Padua, near Jolon. It is named for a World War I general who had held a command in San Francisco at the end of his life.

Hunters Point, spit of land in southeast San Francisco projecting into the Bay, named for a forty-niner, Robert E. Hunter, who planned to create a city on the site. In 1868 William C. Ralston built the first of several drydocks located there, all succeeded (1941) by a huge U.S. Navy shipyard. It flourished during World War II and afterward, attracting many thousands of workers, most of them black, who lived in the adjacent housing on the tidelands. As jobs became scarce in the 1960s, the workers fell into financial difficulties and the housing area became a slum. The shipyard was closed in 1974.

Hunting, a major means of obtaining food and clothing for Indians, was also of great importance to early explorers and settlers. During the gold rush the shooting of wild game such as deer, ducks, geese, and quail became an important commercial activity in cities and smaller settlements. Market hunting continued well into the 20th century, though it was more and more regulated. Before the turn of the century hunting for sport also became common. Big game included bear, deer, and elk; birds included ducks, geese, mourning doves, and quail. To rid the area of destructive animals there was also hunting of beaver, coyotes, mountain lions, and rabbits. Hunting for sport has long been licensed and at the opening of the 1970s almost 700,000 licenses were sold annually. According to rules established by the State Department of Fish and Game, most game animals are protected by seasonal prohibition or other means, and some, such as condors, eagles, foxes, otters, porpoises, and whales, may not be hunted at all. Prior to those regulations some species, such as the grizzly bear, were exterminated.

HUNTINGTON, COLLIS P[OTTER] (1821–1900), began work in his native Connecticut at age 14 as a peddler and later was a storekeeper in upstate New York. He went from there to California with a stock of goods (1849). He and Mark Hopkins soon set up a store in Sacramento for miners' supplies, and there he learned from Theodore Judah♦ of his plan to build a transcontinental railroad across the Sierra via Dutch Flat.

Huntington, Hopkins, Leland Stanford, and

Charles Crocker, the Sacramento men who became the Big Four,♦ determined to finance a survey and to help get government grants. When Judah died (1863) the associates took over the Central Pacific Railroad♦ completely, with Stanford as president and handler of political matters in California, Crocker in charge of construction, and Huntington in charge of all eastern business arrangements and matters related to federal financing.

They all made vast fortunes through construction (completed 1869) and went on to make more through subsequent building of a railroad line from San Francisco through the San Joaquin Valley to San Diego and east through El Paso to New Orleans by their Southern Pacific Railroad.♦ That move gave them the control of transportation into and within the state and caused their latest company (which absorbed the Central Pacific, 1884) to be stigmatized as "The Octopus."

Huntington continued to be the eastern financial head of the lines and their high-level lobbyist in Washington, and his secret machinations were later revealed when the widow of David Colton♦ released his letters to her husband describing his bribery of public officials and means of influencing elections. The correspondence made it clear that Huntington was a tough, shrewd, cynical big businessman who used power ruthlessly for his own ends and to make money for his enterprises.

Those enterprises were later extended to the Chesapeake and Ohio Railroad, of which he became president, to various steamship lines, to San Francisco's Market Street Railway, and to other transportation firms in addition to the Southern Pacific, of which he became president (1890) after a falling out with Stanford over business policy. After his death his second wife, Arabella, married his nephew, business associate, and follower, Henry E. Huntington.♦

HUNTINGTON, HENRY E[DWARDS] (1850–1927), nephew of Collis P. Huntington,♦ like his uncle, began a great business career by working as a youth in a small upstate New York store. Later he supervised construction and became an officer of various of his uncle's railroads, moving to San Francisco (1892) to become a vice president of the Southern Pacific Railroad.

Upon his uncle's death (1900) he inherited a large fortune but sold his controlling interest in the Southern Pacific to E. H. Harriman and invested in the urban transportation of Los Angeles, to which he moved. Not only did he create the great Pacific Electric Railway Co.♦ but he became a big developer of electric power systems and such a tremendous investor in real estate that he became the largest single landowner in southern California.

The Huntington fortune was kept in the family by his marriages, first (1873–1906) to Mary Alice Prentice, the sister of his uncle's adopted daughter, and, after their divorce, to his uncle's wealthy widow, Arabella Duval Huntington (1913). On a great estate in San Marino, adjacent to Pasadena, he built an elegant mansion surrounded by elaborate botanical gardens. There he housed the tremendous rare book and art collections to which he devoted the last years of his life. In 1919 he deeded the estate, library, art gallery, and gardens to create the Henry E. Huntington Library and Art Gallery.♦

Huntington Beach, oceanside city of Orange County, is a residential and resort community which also produces large quantities of oil. In 1970 it had a population of 115,960.

Huntington Lake, reservoir in the Sierra National Forest (Fresno County), created by the Pacific Light and Power Co. (1912) and named for the company's president, Henry E. Huntington.

Huntington Library, see *Henry E. Huntington Library and Art Gallery.*

Hupa, Indians of the Athabascan family who lived in the drainage area of the Trinity River. Their pre-contact population of about 1,000 was reduced to 600 by 1910. They traded skins and inland foods to the Yurok for canoes and seafood. They performed a series of complex religious dances to celebrate major events of the year, such as the corn harvest and the catching of the first salmon. This practice they shared with the Yurok, as they did the belief that shamanistic ability worked through the use of pains which were physical objects like obsidian stones rather than working through the control of guardian spirits. They owned land in common but, again like the Yurok, placed emphasis on the holding of private property, like rare furs or obsidian knives, and on exclusive fishing rights. Their Hoopa Valley Indian Reservation in Humboldt County is now the largest (93,000 acres) in the state.

HUTCHINGS, JAMES M[ASON] (1818–1902), English-born author and editor who went to California (1849) and after trying his hand at mining concocted "The Miner's Ten Commandments," a highly successful letter sheet♦ whose sales furnished him capital to found *Hutchings' California Magazine.*♦ He

later wrote *Scenes of Wonder and Curiosity in California* (1870) and *In the Heart of the Sierras* (1886). In the 1860s he and his wife built a home in Yosemite and settled there.

Hutchings' California Magazine (1856–61), local literary and pictorial journal, founded by James M. Hutchings,♦ an Englishman who went to California in 1849. After some time in the mines he made more money by writing "The Miner's Ten Commandments" (the first commandment is "Thou shalt have no other claim than one") and issuing it as a single-page letter sheet on souvenir stationery. With that financial and literary background he began his journal, which eventually reached a circulation of 8,000. Less literary than its competitor, *The Pioneer,* it printed articles on unusual local subjects such as Snowshoe Thompson♦ and the use of camels♦ in the Far West. It was heavily illustrated—C. C. Nahl was among its artists—and particular stress was laid on California's mountain scenery. Yosemite was often featured, for Hutchings was one of its earliest settlers and opened the first hotel in the valley. Beginning in 1858 the title was *Hutchings' Illustrated California Magazine,* but in 1861 it was merged with the *California Mountaineer* to become the *California Magazine and Mountaineer.*

HUTCHINS, ROBERT M., see *Center for the Study of Democratic Institutions.*

HUXLEY, ALDOUS (1894–1963), English man of letters, novelist, and essayist who went to Los Angeles (1937) and made it his home for the rest of his life. His witty, ironic, and intellectual fiction of the 1920s, like *Antic Hay* (1923) and *Point Counter Point* (1928), culminating in the satirical novel of an anti-Utopian future, *Brave New World* (1932), was followed by works written in the U.S. in a different vein. Like his onetime friend Christopher Isherwood,♦ he was attracted to Oriental religion and occult studies. He also experimented with the mental release offered by nonhabituating narcotics like mescalin and peyote, a subject treated in *The Doors of Perception* (1954) and *Heaven and Hell* (1956). Those newer interests are evident in his later novels, including *Eyeless in Gaza* (1936), celebrating mysticism; *After Many a Summer Dies the Swan* (1939), satirizing a California tycoon's quest for an elizir to stave off death; and *Time Must Have a Stop* (1944), which deals with related themes.

Hyampon Trail, see *Mad River.*

HYERS, ANNA (1855?–192?) and her sister EMMA LOUISE (1857?–*c*. 1901), were black opera stars resident in Sacramento and nationally recognized as prodigies from 1867 to the 1890s.

HYDE, GEORGE (1819–90), Philadelphia-born lawyer who went to California (1845) as secretary to Commodore Stockton. He worked in Yerba Buena as a lawyer concerned with land grant cases and was the town's *alcalde* (1847–48). A San Francisco street was named for him, and he may have been responsible for the selection by Jasper O'Farrell◆ of two Philadelphia street names: Market and Sansome.

Hydraulic mining, the use of a high-powered stream of water from a large hose to wash away hillsides to get the gold buried within them. The scheme was essentially devised in 1853 by Edward E. Matteson of Connecticut and represented a major contribution of the California gold rush to mining techniques. It was developed after placer mining◆ had exhausted much of the gold readily obtained from riverbeds. While "hydraulicking" yielded much gold, it devastated the landscape and clogged streams. It was prohibited in 1884 because of the pollution◆ it caused.

Hydroelectric power, first developed in California by George Chaffey◆ in conjunction with his Etiwanda Irrigation System at Ontario (1822 ff.), which pro-

vided water power for street lights in Riverside and Colton. A similar use of an irrigation project made power available in Pomona (1893). The state's first long-distance hydroelectric power transmission (22 miles) was between the Folsom plant, on the American River, and Sacramento (1895). Other sites for hydroelectric power were developed by the Pacific Gas and Electric Co.,◆ (a consolidation of smaller companies, 1905) in the southern Cascade mountains and on the Pit and McCloud rivers in the north and on Kings River in the south.

The latter region had Southern California Edison Co.◆ as its major public utility to develop power in the Sierra Nevada between Yosemite and Kings Canyon. The Los Angeles Municipal Power Co. generated power from the Owens Valley. The San Francisco Public Utilities Commission developed facilities on the Tuolumne River, while the East Bay Municipal Utility District built plants on the Mokelumne River system. Hydroelectric sites in the eastern Sierra have been developed by the Los Angeles Dept. of Water and Power, the Sierra Pacific Electric Co., and the California Electric Power Co. Hoover Dam, when completed in 1936, had the world's largest turbines and generators, but even more elaborate systems for utilizing water◆ in the state have been developed since that time. By 1970 hydroelectric plants supplied nearly 29% of the state's electricity.

I

I Am, Mighty, see *Mighty I Am.*

"I Left My Heart in San Francisco," popular song with lyrics by Douglas Cross (1921–75) and music by George Cory, both natives of the Bay Area. Written in 1953, it was published in 1961 and proclaimed the city's official song in 1969.

"I Love You, California," since 1951 the official state song and therefore one of the legislated state symbols.◆ Published in 1913, the lyrics are by F. B. Silverwood and the music by A. F. Frankenstein.

I Remember Mama, see *Norwegians in California.*

I Want To Live! motion picture (1958) based on the life and death of Barbara Graham,◆ depicting in morbid detail the effect of the two last-minute stays of execution on the day she finally died.

Icaria Speranza, Utopian colony of French settlers, located near Cloverdale (1881–86), based on the principles set forth by the French Communist Étienne Cabet (1788–1856) in his romance *Voyage . . . en Icarie* (1840). Partly an outgrowth of earlier Icarian colonies in the Midwest, the settlement emphasized family life but in other ways was a cooperative community.

Ice Hockey, sport introduced late to California from the East Coast, the initial association for amateurs, the California Hockey League, being founded in 1928. The next to be established, the Pacific Coast League (1944), turned professional in 1948 and changed its name to the Western Hockey League in 1952. Its teams include the Los Angeles Monarchs, the San Francisco Seals (to 1976), and the San Diego Skyhawks (later the Gulls). The National Hockey League was expanded in 1967 to incorporate a Western Division including the Golden Seals of Oakland and the Los Angeles Kings, whose home is the Forum.◆ The World Hockey Association includes the San Diego Mariners among its fourteen teams.

IDE, William B[rown] (1796–1852), native of Massachusetts, went to California from New Hamp-

shire (1845) and settled in present Tehama County, where his adobe is part of a State Historic Park near Red Bluff. He became a leader of the Bear Flag Revolt◆ and as a result was named the one and only President of the independent Republic of California. He was soon embittered by Frémont's assumption of leadership. Later he became a surveyor, miner, and judge.

Ignacio, see *Pacheco.*

Illustrated Daily News, see *Los Angeles Daily News.*

IMBRIE, Andrew W[elsh] (1921–   ), composer born in New York City, a resident of Berkeley since 1947, when he joined the faculty of the University of California. His compositions include string quartets, trios, sonatas, songs, and orchestral and choral works, as well as the opera *Angle of Repose* (1976), based on the novel by Wallace Stegner, with libretto by Oakley Hall.

Imperial Beach, south of San Diego, the site of a major U.S. Navy helicopter base.

Imperial County, incorporated (1907) from part of San Diego County, now on its western border. Riverside County is on the north, the state of Arizona on the east, and Mexico on the south. Inhabited originally by the Yuma Indians, the area's first white visitors may have been Alarcón and Melchior Díaz, whose exploration (1540) probably led them across the Colorado River.◆ Later came Kino and Garcés, and then Anza (1774), accompanied by Garcés and Fray Juan Díaz. The trails they blazed were deserted after the Yuma Massacre (1781).

Nevertheless, those routes were followed again by trappers and traders and were used by Gen. Kearny in his march to San Pasqual (1846). The route was also followed by the Overland Mail Co. of John Butterfield.◆ Gold attracted prospectors to the Picacho area, 25 miles north of Yuma, in the 1860s and then southwest to Tumco from 1884 to 1914, but permanent settlement waited until the desert could be made to bloom by diversion of Colorado River water to the Imperial Valley,◆ in keeping with plans conceived by O. M. Wozencraft,

C. R. Rockwood, and George Chaffey. Although an overflow created the Salton Sea♦ (1905–7), water has otherwise brought great prosperity to the area.

This southeastern corner of the state, with its long hot growing season, is a major area for pasturing and raising cattle and producing sugar beets, alfalfa, cotton, barley, sorghum, lettuce, cantaloupes, and other fruits and vegetables. The cities of Brawley, El Centro (the county seat), and Calexico (the American border town whose Mexican counterpart is Mexicali) are small, and the population of the entire county in 1970 was 74,492. With an area of 2,713,920 acres, it had 17.6 persons per sq. mi.

Imperial Fault, see *Earthquakes.*

Imperial Valley, the southern part of the Colorado Desert, a flat valley extending from the Salton Sea on the north to the Mexican border on the south, and from the Coast Range near San Diego on the west to the Colorado River basin on the east. The 8,000-sq. mi. desert valley of rich alluvial soil is now a major farming region.

Father Garcés brought Anza through the area but his attempt to found missions was ended by Yuma Indian attacks (1781). During the 19th century it was seldom visited, although the Butterfield stage lines and, later, the Southern Pacific tracks traversed it, and cattlemen grazed herds there when the Colorado River overflowed the area.

Development occurred (1900 ff.) when the engineers Charles Rockwood♦ and George Chaffey♦ irrigated the once barren desert, renamed it the Imperial Valley, and set up a real estate and colonizing firm. Chaffey's canal (opened 1901) ran 70 miles from the Colorado Valley, mostly through Mexican territory, entering the state at the border towns, which he named Mexicali and Calexico.

The successful farming begun by 2,000 settlers in 1902 was nearly ended forever when Rockwood, as successor to Chaffey, built a bypass canal whose intake broke, pouring river waters into the valley to turn dry land into the Salton Sea♦ in an inundation that lasted from 1905 to 1907. In the latter year Imperial County was separated from San Diego County because it had unique problems. Valley settlers, seeking freedom from dependence on an expensive Mexican canal which flooded without control, finally acquired an improved source of water with the building of the Hoover Dam complex, part of which was the All-American Canal.♦ The congressional bill, proposed in 1904, was finally passed in 1928; the dam was completed in 1936, and the canal was first used in 1940.

Agriculture has since thrived, and in 1970 the major products, in order of importance, were livestock; lettuce, fruits, and vegetables; livestock feed (such as alfalfa); cotton; and sugar beets. Food is processed and packed and gypsum is quarried in the valley. Seasonal workers are used on the farms. Until 1964 many of them were *braceros,* but since then much of the planting and harvesting has been mechanized. Earlier there were severe strikes, the worst in 1934. The major cities are El Centro,♦ Brawley,♦ and Calexico.♦

INCE, THOMAS [HARPER] (1882–1924), Rhode Island-born motion picture director, moved his firm to Los Angeles (1911) and came to be considered second only to D. W. Griffith in his productions. These included *The Battle of Gettysburg* (1913) and *Civilization* (1916), grandly epic in style; the first version of Eugene O'Neill's *Anna Christie* (1923); and many films featuring his stars William S. Hart, Charles Ray, and Billie Burke. His sudden death, due to thrombosis, aboard William Randolph Hearst's yacht led to wild stories of poisoning.

Independence, seat of Inyo County, named for an army camp established there July 4, 1862. When Mary Austin was a resident of Independence she wrote about the adjacent Owens Valley, and the town itself contains an Eastern California museum with valley memorabilia. Manzanar, a Japanese Relocation Center, is six miles south. In 1970 the population of Independence was 1,990.

Indian paintbrush, see *Castilleja.*

Indian reservations and *rancherías*, created because from the time of white settlement Indians have been dispossessed of their lands and attempts have been made to keep them in restricted areas. During the era of the missions they were often settled on *rancherías,* outlying places of residence. Remnants of some of these exist in the late 20th century, particularly in Riverside County, where outside Banning there is the Morongo settlement of more than 32,000 acres and at Palm Springs the Agua Caliente settlement of more than 25,000 acres. In San Diego County there are numerous smaller reserves, such as that of Pala. Other areas were set aside by various U.S. acts to be administered by the Bureau of Indian Affairs for the use of remnants of neighboring tribes. Agreements were frequently altered or abrogated entirely, but as late as 1971 there were still 540 areas under such jurisdiction, of which the largest was the Hoopa Valley Reservation in Humboldt County, totaling nearly 93,000 acres. At that date about 6,000 of California's native Indians lived on *rancherías* and reservations.

Indians, residents of California for at least 7,000 and perhaps for 30,000 years. Prehistoric remains include not only bones and burial sites but shell mounds and petroglyphs. The Indians themselves were encountered by all the early European explorers, who made comments of varying accuracy and detail upon their ways of life, including those upon the Chumash discovered (1542) by Cabrillo on offshore islands, and upon the "king" (presumably a Miwok) who greeted and crowned Drake (1579).

In the 16th century the California Indians were divided into about 105 separate nations or tribes whose more than 100 different dialects derived from five language stocks. All told, the Indians may have numbered some 300,000 at the time they first met white settlers (1769) concerned with founding missions for their conversion to Christianity. That number amounted to about 13% of all North American Indians. About 56,000 were converted to Christianity, most being Chumash, Costanoan, Esselen, Gabrieleño, Juaneño, Maidu (among those scornfully called "Diggers" by whites), Miwok, Salinan, and Yokut.

Tribes that lived in the north and were therefore little affected by the southerly based missions included the Modoc, Pomo, and Wintun—who practiced the Kuksu cult—and the Hupa, Yana, Yuki, and Yurok. The farthest ranging tribe was the Mohave, whose trade took them from their Colorado River home to coastal mission settlements. An early sympathetic account of mission Indians was written by Father Boscana, who described the cult of Chinigchinich and its related cult of toloache. Despite this understanding interpretation, these Indians too had enough bad treatment to lead to revolts (e.g. at San Diego, 1775, and at Santa Barbara and *rancherías* of neighboring settlements, 1825)—although they were not comparable in intensity to the Yuma massacre (1775).

Mistreatment, armed attack, and disease reduced the total Indian population to about 150,000 by the time the missions were secularized in 1834. Fifteen years later their lot grew much worse, as far more of California was inhabited by whites attracted by the gold rush. Indian lands were commonly appropriated by whites, and even the reservations to which the Indians were remanded were often reappropriated for gold mining or other uses. The homeless

Indians were not only dispossessed but subjected to starvation, kidnapping for enslavement, legalized long-term indentured service, and casual killings or organized massacres. Despite occasional sympathetic and helpful treatment like that of J. Ross Browne, by 1870 the Indian population was reduced to about 58,000. The enmity between white and Indian not only continued but led to some uprisings (e.g. Pauma Massacre, 1846, and Garra Revolt, 1851) and reached the level of full-fledged military campaigns, of which the most dreadful was the Modoc War of 1872–73.

The brutal behavior of whites toward Indians was documented by Helen Hunt Jackson in *A Century of Dishonor* (1881). Serious anthropological study by a few persons, such as Stephen Powers, began even earlier and was continued by the Sequoya League, founded (1901) by Charles Lummis, which provided land and financial aid to some Indians. However, by 1913 the Indian population was reduced to about 17,000 and the threat presented by these poor remnants was so dissipated that they were generally ignored as unattractive indigents, although upon occasion sentimentalists began to think of the Indians' forefathers as romantic noble savages. Far rarer was serious and understanding study of Indian cultures, the most dramatic example being that which the anthropologist Alfred Kroeber devoted to Ishi, the last of the Yahi.

Most California Indians did not even have many reservations, like tribes in other parts of the U.S., for the 7,000,000 acres promised by treaties in the 1850s to 1880s were never ratified. Some compensation, such as that to the Cahuilla, and the U.S. award of some $29,000,000 in 1965 for expropriated lands, was eventually paid to a few tribes. Despite all these difficulties, in the 20th century Indians have become the fastest-growing minority group in the state. Counted at 23,450 in the 1928 census, they were considered to number 91,000 in 1970, partly owing to extrastate migration as well as to increased birthrate. Substantially less than 10% live on reservations. They have also become better organized and more politically conscious, achieving much attention and some effectiveness by such actions as the seizure of Alcatraz (1969–71). (*See also individual entries.*)

Indio, city in central Riverside County, begun (1876) as a construction camp for the Southern Pacific. Its name (Spanish for "Indian") indicates the town's early population. It is now a resort, travel, and trade center, known as the capital for the production of dates.♦ In 1970 the population was 14,459.

In Dubious Battle, novel by John Steinbeck♦ published in 1936. The first of his novels to treat the migratory farm laborer, the story depicts a strike of migrant fruit pickers and the ensuing battle involving vigilante orchard owners and Communist organizers.

Industrial Workers of the World, see *I.W.W.*

Inglewood, city southwest of Los Angeles, named (1887) after the home town of its Canadian founder, Daniel Freeman, when he began his real estate development on the Rancho Aguaje de la Centinela, whose adobe (1822) has been preserved. The city is now known not only for its aircraft industry but for a sports center, Hollywood Park,♦ and The Forum.♦ In 1970 the city's population was 89,985.

Initiative, governmental procedure allowing a specified number of voters to propose a statute, constitutional amendment, or ordinance for popular vote, introduced to California by Dr. John R. Haynes.♦ The first city in the world to incorporate the process in its charter was Los Angeles (1903). A comparable procedure was enacted for the state (1911) by its Senate. It required that a statute, amendment, or ordinance be placed on the next election ballot if demanded through a petition signed by 8% of the total number who had voted in the previous gubernatorial election.

Inland Valleys, name given to the area of the Pomona and San Bernardino valleys and Riverside Basin, surrounding the cities of those names.

International Longshoremen's Association, union originally affiliated with the American Federation of Labor, first had a San Francisco local in 1898. There it became involved in major strikes (1916 and 1919), the last one ending in a disastrous defeat for the union that caused it to be overshadowed by a company-dominated organization, Longshoremen's Association of San Francisco, until 1933. Then, under the National Industrial Recovery Act's guarantee of collective organization and bargaining, it regained strength on the waterfront. Under Harry Bridges♦ its 1934 dock strike soon went beyond the area of longshoremen♦ to burgeon into a violent general strike. After another strike (1936–37), Bridges led his union into the CIO as the International Longshoremen's and Warehousemen's Union. Subsequently, the original ILA of the AFL has had little force in California.

Intrastate migration, see *Migration.*

Inverness, summer resort town and beach area on the west side of Tomales Bay, so named (*c.*1889) by a Scot who saw the resemblance of the long inlet to his native firth. Many professors from Berkeley and other campuses have long had second homes in this secluded setting.

Inyo County, incorporated (1866) from territory in Mono and Tulare counties that had been intended in 1864 to create a Coso County. Mono County is on the north, Fresno and Tulare on the west, Kern and San Bernardino on the south, and the state of Nevada on the east. Lying between the Sierra Nevada range and the Nevada state boundary, the county includes the highest and the lowest points in the coterminous U.S., Mt. Whitney♦ and Death Valley,♦ which is indicative of the range of temperature in the county. Inyo National Forest, located partly in the county, includes in the White Mountain Range a bristlecone pine tree aged 4,600 years, the oldest living object in the U.S., and the Devil's Postpile♦ lies nearby. The first whites to traverse the area, originally inhabited by Mono and Koso Indians, were Joseph Walker,♦ Joseph Chiles,♦ Kit Carson,♦ Richard Owens♦ (a lieutenant with Frémont♦ for whom many sites are named), and, later, Frémont himself. The Old Spanish Trail♦ was opened by William Wolfskill. Silver mines created a rush in the 1870s, followed by gold and copper finds. Boron and tungsten are also mined there, but cattle raising and alfalfa growing are now more important. The only sizable towns are Independence (the county seat)—where Mary Austin lived and wrote of Owens Valley and Inyo desert country in *Land of Little Rain*—Bishop, and Lone Pine. In 1970 the population of the county was 15,571. With an area of 6,483,136 acres, it had 1.5 persons per sq. mi.

Irish in California, first arrived during the Spanish and Mexican periods in various ways and capacities. For example, John Read arrived as a sailor (1826), remained to be naturalized, married a Spanish widow, and became a *ranchero* in Marin County; James Richard Berry, an Irish gentleman who had traveled in Spain and its colonies, arrived in 1836 and soon also had a grant of land in Marin; Timothy Murphy ("Don Timoteo") took charge of the secularized Mission San Rafael; and Jasper O'Farrell, a civil engineer, migrated from Chile (1843) and was appointed Surveyor-General of Alta California. An Irish priest, Eugene McNamara, obtained a vast land grant from Gov. Pico (1846) on which he planned to settle 10,000 of his countrymen, but the title was not confirmed by the U.S. Other Irishmen went overland, like the mountain man Thomas Fitzpatrick, a guide for Frémont and Kearny; Martin Murphy, who, with Elisha Stevens, took the first wagons over the Sierra Nevada (1844); and Patrick Breen, a member of the Donner Party. J. Ross Browne, born in Ireland but reared in the U.S., went first to California in 1849 but returned later to hold important governmental posts which led to his literary career.

A great influx of Irish occurred in the early 1850s, impelled by the gold rush and the effect of the potato blight in their homeland. Some prospered in the mines, others elsewhere, like Martin Murphy's son, a pioneer of Santa Clara County and mayor of San Jose, and John G. Downey, a southern California rancher and real estate developer who was the state's 7th governor. In the post-gold-rush era many Irish settlers or their descendants had a significant impact on the state. These included Denis Kearney,♦ the rabble-rousing labor leader; the "Silver Kings" of the Comstock mines: James G. Fair,♦ James C. Flood,♦ John W. Mackay,♦ and William G. O'Brien;♦ the noted lawyer for Catholic affairs, John Thomas Doyle;♦ the scion of a banking family, James Phelan,♦ who became a reform mayor of San Francisco and U.S. Senator; the Tobin family;♦ Frank Roney,♦ long the dominating force of San Francisco's labor movement in the 1880s; and C. K. McClatchey,♦ the newspaper publisher. During the 1870s persons of Irish descent accounted for almost 30% of the state's population. The ratio declined considerably in the later 19th and 20th centuries. During that period the Irish became so integrated into all aspects of California life that they are not often thought of as a separate ethnic group.

Iron, initially mined in Sierra County during the gold rush, was not a significant mineral because of the lack of coke and the cheapness of iron brought to California as ship ballast. Steelmaking♦ was begun in San Francisco with the founding (1849) of the Union Iron Works, and blast furnaces, foundries, and rolling mills were attempted elsewhere, sometimes near mining camps. But imported iron remained the major source. Only upon the completion of the Kaiser steel plant (1948) at Fontana did iron mining and the production of pig iron begin on a large scale. Most of the state's iron deposits are in the Mojave Desert area at Eagle Mountain in Riverside County (Kaiser's major supply) and in San Bernardino County. Annual production in the 1970s was about 4,400,000 long tons of 60% iron ore —about 3% of the U.S. total.

Ironside, hour-long television crime drama (1967–75) presenting mysteries solved by the observant and perceptive Robert T. Ironside (played by Raymond Burr), former chief of San Francisco police, who has been paralyzed by a criminal's bullet.

Irrigation, a major state need, practiced by the Spanish and Mexicans in small-scale diversion of streams through *zanjas* (open ditches) to mission orchards and gardens and to pueblos. It became a subject of great importance with the development of large farms in the post-gold-rush era. The state's adherence to the English common law of riparian rights, which gave water to owners of riverbank land and denied it to others, precipitated a major suit (1886) in which Miller and Lux, streamland owners, prohibited Haggin and Tevis from diverting Kern River water to their lands. A compromise was effected by the Wright Act♦ (1887), continuing landowners' riparian rights but allowing condemnation suits to form public irrigation districts. That spurred the development of canals and reservoirs; the opening of new areas for farming, orchards, and vineyards; and the creation of irrigation centers for citrus groves like Ontario, Pomona, and Riverside. The greatest development occurred under the aegis of George Chaffey,♦ a Canadian-born engineer who substantially altered both rural and urban lands by such means as the mutual irrigation company (in which a land purchaser also had to buy stock in a company to provide irrigation to his property) and by large-scale underground piped irrigation like that by which he transformed the Colorado Desert into Imperial Valley.♦ Later, even far larger-scale transfers of water♦ extend beyond agricultural irrigation into supply for industrial and domestic electric power, for flood control, and for the creation of substantial recreation areas. Thus, although the Central Valley contains one-sixth of all the irrigated land in the U.S., the state's Central Valley Project♦ is but a preface to the vast California Water Plan♦ which will shift the state's most vital natural resource for a diversity of uses far beyond irrigation alone.

Irvine Ranch, originally the *ranchos* Lomas and Santiago de Santa Ana and San Joaquin of the Sepúlveda♦ and Yorba♦ families. Containing 93,000 acres covering almost one-fifth of Orange County, it extends from the mountains to the sea. Obtained in the 1870s by a Scotch-Irish settler, James Irvine (1827–86), who had made a fortune in merchandising during the gold rush, it was at first a sheep ranch owned in partnership with the Bixby♦ family. Irvine bought out his partners, diversified his ranching, and sold some land to create the cities of Santa Ana and Tustin, but held most of it intact. It was finally broken up by his heirs when a campus of the University of California was established on part of it (1965) and a community was planned in relation to the campus. The city of Irvine was incorporated in 1971 and has rapidly added population, both residential and in the industrial park that borders the San Diego Freeway.

IRWIN, WALLACE [ADMAH] (1875–1959), born in New York, reared in Colorado, attended Stanford University (1896–99), after which he began his journalistic career in San Francisco. His early writing emphasized light verse, including *The Love Sonnets of a Hoodlum* (1902), *The Rubáiyát of Omar Khayyám, Jr.* (1902), *Nautical Lays of a Landsman* (1904), and *Random Rhymes and Odd Numbers* (1906). After moving to New York to continue his journalistic career, he became widely known for his letters from Hashimura Togo, ostensibly the work of a Japanese making amusing and telling comments on American society and politics. These were collected in *Letters of a Japanese Schoolboy* (1909), *Mr. Togo, Maid of All Work* (1913), and *More Letters of a Japanese Schoolboy* (1923). Irwin later wrote stories and some novels, including *Seed of the Sun* (1921), depicting the strife between white and Japanese farmers in California, which showed his hardened view of the Japanese; and *The Days of Her Life* (1931), set against a background of earlier California. His brother was Will Irwin.

IRWIN, WILLIAM (1827–86), 13th governor of the state (1875–80), went from his native Ohio to Oregon and then in 1854 to California, where he published the *Yreka Union.* His political career as a conservative Democrat began in 1861 when he was elected assemblyman.

IRWIN, WILL[IAM HENRY] (1873–1948), like his brother Wallace, was born in New York State and reared on a Colorado ranch before attending Stanford University, from which he was graduated in 1899. His brief San Francisco journalistic career as editor of *The Wave* and as a newspaper reporter was followed after 1904 with more important work on New York newspapers and magazines. His many books include *Old Chinatown* (1908); *A Reporter in Armageddon* (1918), on his experiences as a World War I correspondent; *The Next War: An Appeal to Commonsense* (1921); *How Red Is America?* (1927); and *Propaganda and the News; or, What Makes You Think So?* (1936). He collaborated with

Sidney Howard on *Lute Song* (1930), recalling his earlier interest in Chinatown.

Isabella, Lake, see *Kern River* and *Kern County.*

ISHERWOOD, CHRISTOPHER (1904–), English author, studied at Cambridge, collaborated with W. H. Auden on plays and an account of their voyage to China. He had lived in Berlin for four years and written about it in *Goodbye to Berlin* (1939)—sketches later dramatized by John van Druten as *I Am a Camera* (1951)—before moving to California in 1939. He settled near Los Angeles and was naturalized in 1946. His frankly autobiographical fiction written and set there includes *Down There on a Visit* (1962), about a quest for selfhood, and *A Single Man* (1964), about the lonely life of a middle-aged professor after the death of the man he loves. He wrote of his parents' lives in *Kathleen and Frank* (1971) and of his own in *Christopher and His Kind* (1976).

ISHI (1860?–1916), last survivor of the Yahi,♦ a tribe which had been hunted out of existence by whites, was discovered (1911) in a slaughterhouse near Oroville where he had gone to seek food. Fortunately, Professors Thomas T. Waterman and Alfred L. Kroeber♦ gave him a home in the University of California's Museum of Anthropology in San Francisco, for, as Mrs. Kroeber, his biographer, said, "Ishi was the last wild Indian in North America, a man of Stone Age culture subjected for the first time when he was past middle age to twentieth-century culture." He adapted to that culture remarkably well, and learned about 500 English words as well as teaching the anthropologists about his people's way of life, before he died of tuberculosis after catching his first cold.

Isidro, see *Austin, Mary.*

Islands of California, most significant are the Farallones,♦ the four Catalina Islands♦ (Santa Barbara, San Nicolás, Santa Catalina, and San Clemente—in the Pacific off the coast from Santa Monica to La Jolla), and the four Santa Barbara Islands♦ (San Miguel, Santa Rosa, Santa Cruz, and Anacapa—off the coast from Point Concepcion to Port Hueneme). There are also small islands—Alcatraz, Angel, Brooks, Treasure, and Yerba Buena—in San Francisco Bay; Mare in San Pablo Bay; and Brown, Chipps, Roe, Ryer, and Seal in Suisun Bay. Furthermore, there are islands in natural and manmade lakes, e.g. in Emerald Bay♦ of Lake Tahoe, Clear Lake,♦ Lake Berryessa,♦ and Mono Lake.♦

California itself was long considered to be an island, as was first contended in the fictional *Las Sergas de Esplandián*♦ (1510). Explorers and cartographers agreed with that view, although the voyage of Ulloa♦ in the Gulf of California (1539) proved otherwise. Antonio de la Ascensión, a friar on Vizcaíno's expedition (1602–03), in a personal account picked up by another Franciscan, Juan Torquemada, in his *Monarquía Indiana* (1613), again contended that California was indeed an island. Then Juan de Iturbe, ship commander for the Cardona family's pearl fishing monopoly in Baja California, declared that he had sailed up the gulf (1615) far enough to prove it to be a strait and thus that California was really an island. Those views reestablished the theory of an insular California for more than a century despite the proof to the contrary advanced by Kino♦ (1702). A voyage by Padre Fernando Consag up the east coast to the Colorado River mouth (1746) finally ended forever the island myth.

Italians in California, date to the very beginnings, when Father Salvatierra♦ founded the first permanent settlement, a Jesuit mission, in Baja California (1697). A century later Malaspina,♦ the navigator, led a Spanish expedition (1791), which spent twelve days at Monterey. Later explorers included Paolo Emilio Botta, the doctor and naturalist aboard the vessel commanded by Duhaut-Cilly (1827–28).

Settlement began during the gold rush, but many Italians soon forsook mining for agriculture, especially in southern California, although enough stayed in the Mother Lode country to create a camp known as Italian Bar. But the major place of settlement was San Francisco, where residents early built the community that became North Beach♦ and founded a newspaper, *La Voce del Popolo* (1859). Numbered among its early settlers were Domingo Ghirardelli; Count Leonetto Cipriani, who began the Belmont villa, which William Ralston developed into his country mansion; Father Anthony Maraschi, who founded St. Ignatius College (1855), forerunner of the University of San Francisco; and another Jesuit father, John Nobili, who established Santa Clara College (1851).

The major influx came in the 1880s, primarily from Genoa, Turin, Lombardy, and the Piedmont, although many fishermen were Sicilians. Andrea Sbarbaro, a banker from Genoa, and Pietro C. Rossi, a chemist, established the successful Italian-Swiss Colony♦ (1881) at Asti. In nearby Napa Valley wineries were established by the Martini, Mondavi, Petri, and other Italian families, while Secondo

Guasti pioneered viticulture in the rather arid Cucamonga, near San Bernardino. Other Italians developed other agricultural activities—Camilio Pregno grew tomatoes, Cristofero Colombo Brevidero raised lilacs; while a few like Mark J. Fontana and Joseph DiGiorgio expanded their farming into packing and shipping so as to become leaders of the state's food processing♦ industry.

Major figures in other fields include J. Sartori, a Los Angeles banker; A. P. Giannini,♦ who moved beyond his family produce business to create the world's largest bank; Angelo Rossi and Joseph Alioto, two mayors of San Francisco; Joe DiMaggio and Henry Luisetti, great athletes in baseball and basketball, respectively; opera impresario Gaetano Merola; and folk artist Simon Rodia. As early as 1920, Italians were second only to Mexicans in the foreign-born population of the state.

Italian-Swiss Colony, an agricultural society originally limited to 100 stock-owning members. It was organized (1881) by Andrea Sbarbaro with Pietro C. Rossi, a chemist, the chief adviser on winemaking, in which the members engaged on their 1,500-acre tract along the Russian River. The wines produced at the colony's settlement of Asti became famous, and the enterprise was a great commercial success. It was absorbed in 1953 by Louis A. Petri♦ and then by a large eastern corporation.

ITURBIDE, AGUSTIN (1783–1824), Mexican-born army officer who in 1821 was a leader in unifying Mexico and in achieving its independence from the Spanish throne. In May 1822 the Mexican Congress proclaimed him Emperor Agustín I and thus he became the first and only Emperor of Alta California. In that capacity he sent Agustín Fernandez de San Vicente♦ to the Californias as his commissioner. Iturbide's tyrannical behavior led to opposition and his forced abdication in March 1823. After exile in Italy he returned to Mexico, where he was executed. Later he came to be considered Mexico's liberator.

I.W.W., common name for the Industrial Workers of the World, a labor organization (est. Chicago, 1905). Led by Eugene Debs, "Big Bill" Haywood, and other socialists, its program called for unionization of skilled and unskilled labor on industry lines (rather than the AFL's craft unionism), for sabotage when needed, and for the eventual overthrow of capitalism. Its heyday was from about 1910 to 1920. In California it led fights for freedom of speech, attempted to unionize farm workers at Fresno (1910) and elsewhere, and played an important part in the Wheatland Riot♦ (1913) and a strike on the San Pedro waterfront (1923). Persons hurt by some association with the I.W.W. included Anita Whitney,♦ a member of the Communist party who endorsed the organization, and Tom Mooney. Harri-

son Gray Otis♦ excoriated the members as "Wobblies," a name that stuck, and other opponents said the initials stood for "I Won't Work." The union was weakened during World War I when many members were jailed on various charges and others deserted it for the Communist party. It finally dwindled away.

J

JACKS, DAVID (1823–1909), Scottish-born, settled in Monterey (1850) where he bought up great holdings of real estate, including the sites of Pacific Grove and Del Monte. He was very unpopular, as Robert Louis Stevenson observed, because of his grasping, tight-fisted practices. He also controlled the market of California's only native cheese,♦ first made (1892) about 20 miles south of Monterey, and still known as Monterey Jack or Jack cheese. He was a benefactor of the University of the Pacific and the Pacific Grove settlement. A peak between Monterey and Carmel was named for him.

JACKSON, GEORGE, see *San Quentin* and *Soledad Brothers.*

JACKSON, HELEN [MARIA FISKE] HUNT (1830–85), reared in her native Amherst, Mass., was the same age as her friend Emily Dickinson, who was part-model for the heroine of her anonymous novel *Mercy Philbrick's Choice* (1876). She published other literary works, including *Verses* (1870), under her initials "H.H.," after the death of her first husband, Major E. B. Hunt. After her marriage to William S. Jackson of Colorado (1875), she heard western Indians tell of the mistreatment of their tribes by whites, and found a new subject. Those tales led her to undertake research that resulted in *A Century of Dishonor* (1881), a documented attack on the government's treatment of America's Indians. The book in turn brought her a commission from the U.S. Dept. of Interior to work with Abbott Kinney on the needs of California's so-called Mission Indians. The report (1883) was not acted upon, so, using atmosphere gained in visiting California, she wrote a romantic view of the Indians in *Ramona*♦ (1884), a novel meant to be comparable to her friend Mrs. Stowe's *Uncle Tom's Cabin.* That final work was tremendously popular, but she was disappointed that it was not esteemed as a brief for the Indians. Instead, readers enjoyed its sentimental plot concerning the old Spanish aristocracy of California and the Indians whom they ostensibly aided as it compared the honor of the Spanish with the vulgarity and meanness of the Yankee usurpers.

JACKSON, JOSEPH HENRY (1894–1955), literary critic, was the editor of *Sunset* (1926–28) and book reviewer for the *San Francisco Chronicle* (1930–55). He also presented his "Bookman's Guide" over a Pacific Coast radio network from 1924 to 1943. His many books about California include *Anybody's Gold* (1941), *Bad Company* (1949), and *The Western Gate* (1952). His own encouragement of young local writers was continued after his death by the establishment of the Joseph Henry Jackson Award, an annual grant-in-aid.

JACKSON, REGGIE (REGINALD MARTINEZ JACKSON) (1946–   ), Pennsylvania-born baseball player, after attending Arizona State University and playing with the Athletics of Kansas City, was with the team in Oakland (1968). As a star outfielder he was named the Most Valuable Player in the American League (1973). In 1976 he was traded to Baltimore, and in 1977 to the New York Yankees. On their World-Series winning team he became the first man since Babe Ruth to hit three home runs in a Series game, set other records, and was voted the Most Valuable Player in the Series.

Jackson, seat of Amador County, located in its southwestern area, is a former gold rush mining town named for "Col." Alden M. Jackson, a New England lawyer known for settling disputes out of court. Nearby diggings were rich (the deep Argonaut and Kennedy mines are said to have yielded over $25,000,000 and $45,000,000, respectively), but the settlement itself was important as a central crossroads of the Mother Lode region. In 1970 its population was under 2,000.

Jackson Square, a downtown San Francisco area, not actually a square, but an area of old brick buildings (some of them once warehouses) which survived the earthquake of 1906. Though gutted by its fire, they were much later remodeled as sites for elegant decorators' shops, fine restaurants, and even offices, all decorated in the style of the original period of construction: 1850s to 70s.

JACOBS, HELEN [HULL] (1908–   ), Arizona-born tennis player, reared in Berkeley. She was the first person to win the U.S. women's singles four times in a row (1932–35). She also won the U.S. women's doubles (1932, 34, 35) and the Wimbledon singles (1936). Her great competitor was Helen Wills.◆

Jacumba Mountains, range at the extreme southern end of the Anza-Borrego Desert State Park in San Diego County.

JAMES, GEORGE WHARTON (1858–1923), born in England, went to Nevada as a young Methodist circuit-riding minister and later to a pastorate in Long Beach. Ousted from the church after a scandalous divorce, he became a popular public lecturer on social issues, on his own philosophy (a sentimentalized idealism), and on the western scene. He placed particular stress on the beauties of the desert, which he helped to popularize by declaring that it was a region to inspire one to higher and nobler things. His writings include *In and Out of California's Missions* (1905), *Through Ramona's Country* (1908), *In and Around the Grand Canyon* (1900), and *The Wonders of the Colorado Desert* (1906).

Jamestown, gold rush settlement of Tuolumne County just southwest of Sonora, named for an early settler and *alcalde,* Col. George F. James, a lawyer also commemorated at James Bar on the Amador-Calaveras border. It is generally called Jimtown, as in the stories of Prentice Mulford, who taught school there.

Japanese Current, see *California Current.*

Japanese in California, with rare exceptions, came long after the gold rush, because until 1866 it was illegal for a subject to leave Japan. Soon thereafter a small number of persons came with their labor contracted ahead of time, and the Wakamatsu Colony◆ (1869) tried unsuccessfully to grow tea and silk. A few other Japanese came from Hawaii, but all told there were only 86 Japanese in California by 1880. Only when restrictions were lifted (1891) did the influx exceed 1,000 a year.

Prior to 1900 most immigrants were young, single, adult males who worked in agriculture or took up residence in a few centers—San Francisco, Sacramento, San Jose, Fresno, Los Angeles—to work as domestics, gardeners, and small businessmen catering to their own communities. Even those few met opposition. In part this was a carryover from the anti-Chinese bias common in the state, so that for a time Chinese and Japanese children in San Francisco were accepted only in a segregated Oriental public school (1906). The Japanese were also disliked because, through diligence and ingenuity,

some had come to cultivate crops more successfully than the Americans. Thus George Shima was called the "potato king" because he was the state's largest producer, on his Delta land.

The international restrictive policy of a "Gentleman's Agreement" (1907) whereby Japan would grant passports only to nonlaborers or the relatives of U.S. residents in return for American curbing of prejudicial acts—followed by the state's Alien Land Law◆ (1913) and statutory exclusion by a federal immigration act (1924–52)—kept the number of Japanese down, so the state never had as many as 100,000. The long-standing antipathy flared into hysterical opposition after Japan's bombing of Pearl Harbor (Dec. 7, 1941), two Japanese submarine attacks on ships off the California coast, and the shelling of an oil tank on the shore in Santa Barbara County.

As a result all Japanese in the state, the great majority being Nisei (American born U.S. citizens), were forced into relocation centers◆ for almost three years. Meanwhile, a combat regiment composed entirely of Nisei took part in the invasion of Italy, and its bravery and outstanding performance led it to became the most decorated regiment in U.S. Army history. When the internees were permitted to leave, almost half returned to their home towns, although a population shift led about four times as many to settle in the Los Angeles–Long Beach area as in the San Francisco Bay region.

Among the many distinguished Japanese associated with California are poet Yone Noguchi,◆ educator and U.S. Senator S. I. Hayakawa,◆ motion picture star Sesue Hayakawa,◆ author Sadakichi Hartmann,◆ sculptor Ruth Asawa,◆ and orchestra leader Seiji Ozawa.◆

Japanese relocation centers, established during the period of hysteria after the Japanese bombing of Pearl Harbor (Dec. 7, 1941). Fears, wholly unfounded, of sabotage and espionage by persons of Japanese descent resident in the U.S. led President Roosevelt to order (Feb. 19, 1942) that the Secretary of War or any designated military commander might bar any person from sensitive regions.

Under that order Lt. Gen. John L. De Witt, commander of the Western Defense Command, removed from their normal places of residence and business some 93,000 Japanese in California, 14,000 in Washington State, and 4,000 in Oregon, of whom more than 71,000 were Nisei, i.e. American born and thus U.S. citizens. After assembly at such places as the Santa Anita and Tanforan racetracks, they were shunted to makeshift camps, which included two in California, at Manzanar in Owens Valley and at Tule Lake in the lava beds near the Oregon border. Those bleak barracks settlements, guarded by soldiers and surrounded by barbed wire, were run by the civilian War Relocation Authority.

The U.S. Supreme Court upheld the removal and the use of the so-called relocation centers on the ground that in time of war military judgments must supersede civilian rights. Incarceration continued until Dec. 1944, when the War Department rescinded its exclusion orders and permitted the internees to go where they would and try to pick up the pieces of their shattered lives.

Japanese Tea Garden, three-acre landscaped area of Golden Gate Park created as the Japanese Village of the Midwinter Exposition (1894) in San Francisco. It is known for its authentic tea house in a setting of pools, streams, Oriental trees and shrubs, and a sand-and-stone garden.

Jarvis-Gann, popular name of an initiative amendment to the Constitution passed as state Proposition 13 in the election of June 1978. Sponsored by Howard Jarvis and Paul Gann, the complex measure limits the amount of property taxes that local governments may collect to one percent of assessed value in 1975-76 unless the property has since been improved or resold, and requires a two-thirds vote of the legislature to raise other taxes.

Jazz, came early to California from its birthplaces and home areas of New Orleans, New York City's Harlem, Chicago, and Kansas City, since black residents of San Francisco are known for their performances of ragtime in the 1890s. After the turn of the century and during the first decade of the 20th, San Francisco's Barbary Coast became notorious for, among other reasons, its loose dance-halls and their syncopated music, celebrated by lyrics proclaiming "They've got a dance out there, they call the grizzly bear," which described the fast steps of a hugging couple.

From that setting jazz quickly spread to more respectable places and simultaneously attracted outstanding musicians from other parts of the country: Jelly Roll Morton lived in California during the decade before American entry into World War I; Kid Ory,♦ the trombonist, made recordings in San Francisco and stayed in the area between 1919 and 1925; and King Oliver, the pioneer cornetist, brought his band to the Bay Area in 1921. Meanwhile, Oakland-born Art Hickman (1886–1930) created the most famous white band in the West and

at his base of the St. Francis Hotel helped to pioneer and establish the instrumentation, voicing, and style of early dance bands, based on what he had learned in the Barbary Coast.

In Los Angeles jazz was established in night clubs and hotels for both entertainment and dancing by the mid-1920s. Late in the decade Les Hite led a successful band, including Lionel Hampton♦ and Lawrence Brown, the trombonist, later a mainstay of Duke Ellington's band. Louis Armstrong, a sensation at the Cotton Club, recorded with Hite's band and took some of its members east to join his permanent band. The California Ramblers was another popular band of the period. Benny Goodman's swing band made an immediate success at the Palomar Ballroom (1935), launching the swing and big band era, and a year later he got Hampton to join the Goodman Quartet within his larger band.

Other black jazz musicians who developed their styles on Central Ave. of Los Angeles in the 1930s and 1940s included saxophonists Dexter Gordon and Wardell Gray, reed players Eric Dolphy and Buddy Collette, trumpet player Art Farmer, and bassist Charlie Mingus. Disc jockeys helped develop jazz, as did "Jazz at the Philharmonic"♦ (Auditorium) concerts sponsored by Norman Granz that featured, among others, trumpeter Dizzy [John Birks] Gillespie and alto saxophonist Charlie Parker, known for their bop quintet.

Stan Kenton,♦ who had his first band at Balboa Beach (1934), by the mid-1940s led a progressive jazz group later involved in symphony orchestra presentations and in atonality. His impact also came through his musicians, including bassist Howard Rumsey, who at the Lighthouse in Hermosa Beach played a subtle, low-key jazz, often featuring unusual instruments, which contributed strongly to the "cool" West Coast Jazz.♦ Related to this group was baritone saxophonist Gerry Mulligan,♦ whose pianoless quartet (1952 ff.) featured trumpeter Chet Baker and drummer Chico Hamilton in contrapuntal arrangements.

In San Francisco the quartet (1951 ff.) of Dave Brubeck♦ also featured close harmonic interplay, principally with alto saxophonist Paul Desmond, and had the greatest success of any California group. The Beat movement of the 1950s was much affected by the rhythms and ambience of West Coast Jazz. A parallel movement in traditional jazz began in the 1940s with the return of Kid Ory and his group to San Francisco, while California-born Lu Watters formed a white traditional group, the Yerba Buena Jazz Band,♦ featuring Turk [Melvin E.] Murphy and ragtime pianist Wally

Rose, playing in the New Orleans style of the Creole Jazz Band and of Jelly Roll Morton. The Monterey Jazz Festival♦ became a major force too, especially in 1971 when Charlie Mingus' band performed.

The spirit of the Jazz Age was early embraced by Hollywood, and the first sound film with spoken dialogue was *The Jazz Singer* (1927) featuring Al Jolson. The great popularity of jazz led to a cycle of musical films beginning with *42nd Street* (1933), as well as to major film careers for singers, so that Bing Crosby, a vocalist of the local Rhythm Boys, became a major Hollywood star in the 1930s, as did Tommy Dorsey's vocalist, Frank Sinatra, in the 1940s.

Jeems Pipes, see *Massett, Stephen C.*

JEFFERS, [JOHN] ROBINSON (1887–1962), born in Pittsburgh, traveled widely in Europe until his family settled in Pasadena (1903) and he entered Occidental College, from which he graduated two years later (1905). He next studied medicine at USC and forestry at the University of Washington, two subjects which affected the imagery of his poetry, particularly after his first rather conventional volumes of verse, *Flagons and Apples* (1912) and *Californians* (1916).

By his move to Carmel♦ in 1916 with his wife Una and his building there a house and studio tower of native stone (1919), he found his own way and discovered a meaningful setting for his poetry in the surrounding region, where, he wrote, "for the first time in my life I could see people living—amid magnificent unspoiled scenery—essentially as they did in the Idyls or the Sagas, or in Homer's Ithaca. Here life was purged of its ephemeral accretions. Men were plowing the headland, hovered by white sea-gulls, as they have done for thousands of years."

His work came to fruition in *Tamar and Other Poems* (1924), which included the title narrative, relating a biblical story to modern life and a California setting; "The Tower Beyond Tragedy," his version of the tale of Orestes and Electra, in which Orestes finds salvation from the madness of self-centered humanity by "falling in love outward" with his natural surroundings; and "Shine Perishing Republic," advising his young twin sons to "be in nothing so moderate as in love of man. . . . When the cities lie at the monster's feet there are left the mountains." These works, as well as lyrics celebrating the spare beauty of his coast and a poem relating his writing to the work of a stone cutter, were augmented by "Roan Stallion," a poem that gave the title to a new collection (1925) and allegorically presented a half-breed woman named California who mystically and passionately loves a stallion which she gets to kill her sordid husband but which, "moved by some obscure human fidelity," she then shoots.

The beliefs, symbols, and images, long unrhymed lines, and allegorical narratives and intense lyrics that characterized his early works were also present in his later writings, including *The Women at Point Sur* (1927), *Cawdor and Other Poems* (1928), *Dear Judas and Other Poems* (1929), *Thurso's Landing, and Other Poems* (1932), *Give Your Heart to the Hawks, and Other Poems* (1933), *Solstice, and Other Poems* (1935), and *Such Counsels You Gave to Me, and Other Poems* (1937). He also wrote an adaptation of Euripides' *Medea* (1946), which was successfully staged.

His later poetry, in *Be Angry at the Sun* (1941) and more strikingly in *The Double Axe* (1948), written after the start of World War II, grew more vitriolic about society, the product of "the animals Christ was rumored to have died for"; although he found a value in war since it helped to kill civilization and lead individuals to "the primal and the latter silences."

Jefferson Airplane, The, rock music band of San Francisco, organized (1965) by Marty Balin, who grew up in the state. Their music—featuring what Ralph Gleason called the San Francisco Sound—and their lyrics—expressing the social attitudes of contemporary counterculture youth—became enormously popular. Their second album, *Surrealistic Pillow* (1967), was particularly admired and influential. By the 1970s the original group split into two factions: The Jefferson Starship and Hot Tuna.

JEFFRIES, JAMES J. (1875–1953), Ohio-born boxing champion, was taken to Los Angeles at age 7. From 1893 to 1905 he fought 25 times, always successfully, holding the world's heavyweight championship from 1899 until his retirement (1905). Among his major title-holding bouts was one in San Francisco against Corbett♦ (1903). He was persuaded to come out of retirement as the "great white hope" to challenge the black champion Jack Johnson on July 4, 1910, in Reno, and he was knocked out, the only defeat in his career. He then returned to his stock ranch in Burbank. Jeffries was known for introducing a defensive crouching posture in place of the upright stance previously employed.

JENSEN, JACKIE [EUGENE] (1927–), San Francisco-born football and baseball player, was a star fullback on the University of California, Berkeley, teams (1946–48), including an undefeated last season and competition in the Rose Bowl. He became a professional baseball player with the Oakland Oaks (1949) and went on to play with the New York Yankees, Washington Senators, and Boston Red Sox. He became the baseball coach of his alma mater (1973–77).

JEPSON, WILLIS LINN (1867–1946), California-born botanist who spent his entire career as student and professor at the University of California, Berkeley. His monographic *Flora of California* (1909–43), *Silva of California* (1910), and *Manual of the Flowering Plants of California* (1923–25) established him as one of the nation's leading regional botanists.

JEUNES, LES, *fin-de-siècle* group of aesthetes associated with *The Lark,*♦ led by Gelett Burgess but including also Ernest Peixotto,♦ Willis Polk,♦ Bruce Porter,♦ and, rather remotely, Frank Norris.

JEWETT, WILLIAM SMITH (1812–73), the first established professional artist in the state, went from his New York home to live in California (1849–69) and paint numerous commissioned portraits as well as landscapes.

JIMÉNEZ, FORTÚN, see *Cortés, Hernando.*

JIMENO, JOSÉ JOAQUIN (1804–56), Mexican-born missionary in California beginning in 1827. In 1838 he became president of the missions from San Miguel to San Diego, and remained so until the end of the mission era.

Jimson weed, coarse annual with white or purple flowers, ill-smelling foliage, and spiny fruit. It yields a drug, used medically, which can be poisonous, which was employed as a potent narcotic in the toloache cult of Chinigchinich.♦

Jimtown, see *Jamestown.*

John Barleycorn, fictionized tract against alcohol by Jack London, based upon his own experiences. Serialized in *The Saturday Evening Post,* it was also issued as a book in 1913.

John Birch Society, semisecret, ultraconservative anti-Communist organization (est. 1958) in New England by a retired candy manufacturer, Robert Welch, and named for an American intelligence officer considered to be a martyr because he was killed in China (1945) by Communists. Although a nationwide right-wing society, its greatest following was in southern California, prompting Thomas M. Storke to investigate and expose it in his *Santa Barbara News-Press* (1961), for which he received a Pulitzer Prize. Its call for the impeachment of Chief Justice Earl Warren and other extreme stands brought opposition from less militant conservatives, although two southern California Congressmen openly identified themselves as Birch Society members.

JOHNSON, GEORGE PERRY (1885–), Colorado-born journalist and film producer, associated (1916–23) with the Lincoln Motion Picture Co. in Los Angeles "to produce and distribute photoplays of and by Negroes." He later gathered a significant collection of materials on blacks in films.

JOHNSON, HIRAM W[ARREN] (1866–1945), began his legal career in his native Sacramento but later moved to San Francisco and there became prominent as the prosecuting attorney who succeeded Heney♦ and secured the conviction of Abe Ruef♦ and others in the city's graft trials. Selected as a reform candidate on the Republican ticket, he was elected governor in a campaign attacking the Southern Pacific's political power. As governor (1911–17) he worked for the initiative, referendum, and recall, cross filing, an extended civil service, workman's compensation, water conservation, and other political and social reforms. He ran for Vice President under Theodore Roosevelt on the Progressive (Bull Moose) ticket (1912), carrying the state by 174 votes over the nationally victorious Woodrow Wilson. In 1916 he was elected to the Senate as a Progressive Republican with a 300,000-vote plurality, while the Republican presidential contender, Charles Evans Hughes, who had slighted Johnson in his local campaigning, lost the state to Wilson by 4,000 votes and thereby lost the national election. Johnson served in the Senate from 1917 until his death, first as a Progressive and after 1920 as a Republican. A great orator who had the bearing of an old-time high-minded public servant, he was re-elected four times; but he grew more and more conservative and crusty. He led the fight for immigration legislation that long barred more Japanese from the U.S. and kept those resident from having full rights. He was an entrenched isolationist, first strongly opposing the League of Nations, later fighting F. D. Roosevelt's foreign policy, and finally voting against U.S. participation in the United Nations.

JOHNSON, JOHN NEELY (*c.*1828–72), 4th governor of the state (1856–58). He left his native Indiana in 1849 and, after practicing law in Sacramento, was elected governor on the Know-Nothing ticket. Unable to solve the state's financial problems, he was also unsuccessful in his attempt to suppress the Vigilance Committee of 1856. He moved to Nevada (1860), where he was appointed to its Supreme Court.

JOHNSON, RAFER [LEWIS] (1934–   ), Texas-born track star, reared in California. As a freshman at UCLA (1955) he set a world's record in the decathalon, finished second in that event in the Olympic Games (1956), beat his leading rival in a Russian-American meet (1958), again won first place in the Olympic Games (1960), and that year won the Sullivan Award as outstanding U.S. amateur athlete. He also played basketball at UCLA and in his senior year was elected student body president, then an unusual recognition for a black student.

JOLSON, AL (1880?–1950), Russian-born entertainer, reared in the U.S., became a popular entertainer who first sang his best-known song, "Mammy," in San Francisco (1909). After a Broadway career he was identified with Hollywood when his *The Jazz Singer* (1927) became the first successful musical sound film and made him world famous for his sentimental portrayals of a Jewish entertainer rendering Negro songs in blackface. He was co-author of "California, Here I Come."◆

Jonathan Club, men's social club in Los Angeles, founded (1895) by supporters of President McKinley. They addressed one another as Brother Jonathan, the name George Washington called Jonathan Trumbull. It first concentrated on political concerns, but became a social organization emphasizing theatrical and other cultural activities.

JONES, HOWARD [HARDING] (1885–1941), Ohio-born football coach at his alma mater (Yale) and elsewhere, until he went to the University of Southern California (1925–41), where in 16 years he won 121 games, lost 38, tied 13, and five times took his team, always successfully, to the Rose Bowl.

JONES, IDWAL (1887–1964), Welsh-born author, reared in Pennsylvania and New York, moved to California (1911) where he engaged in diverse activities. He was a journalist for Hearst papers, first in San Francisco, later in Los Angeles. His books include *The Splendid Shilling* (1926), a novel set in Wales; *China Boy* (1936), stories about the lives of Chinese in California; *The Vineyard* (1942), a novel set in the Napa Valley; *Vines in the Sun* (1949), a nonfictional work about California wines; *Vermillion* (1947), a novel about a California family, centered on a fictive counterpart of the New Almaden mine; and *Ark of Empire* (1951), an historic account of H. W. Halleck's Montgomery Block in San Francisco, once a building for lawyers and bankers, later used for artists' studios.

JONES, THOMAS AP CATESBY (1790–1859), Virginia-born naval officer, was in command of the Pacific Squadron in 1842 when he received a false report at Callao that the U.S. and Mexico were at war and that California was to be ceded by Mexico to the British to save it from the U.S. He sailed from Peru to Monterey, whose surrender he demanded (Oct. 19) and received (Oct. 20), whereupon he installed Josiah Belden as *alcalde* until examination of local records convinced Jones of his error. He lowered the stars and stripes (Oct. 21), went to Los Angeles to apologize to Gov. Micheltorena, and sailed away. The U.S. apologized to Mexico and the navy briefly relieved Jones of his command, but he continued as a commodore and was later reinstated in his Pacific command.

JONES, WILLIAM CAREY (1814–67), son-in-law of Sen. Thomas Hart Benton of Missouri, was sent to California by the Secretary of the Interior as an attorney to investigate the legitimacy of Mexican land grant claims. He upheld the majority of them, including those of his wife's brother-in-law Frémont, which Henry W. Halleck◆ did not, but Congress ignored Jones' recommendations. He settled in San Francisco, and his son of the same name (1854–1923) was a pioneer professor of law at the University of California.

JORDAN, DAVID STARR (1851–1931), New York-born educator, graduated from Cornell. After teaching natural science and gaining an M.D., he became president of Indiana University (1885–91) from whence he was called to become the first president of Stanford University (1891–1913) and its first chancellor (1913–16). He was reputed to be the world's leading ichthyologist, but his general scientific knowledge and his interests were very broad. Furthermore, he was an outstanding teacher, a distinguished administrator, and a leading pacifist. His writings include an autobiography, *The Days of a Man* (2 vols., 1922).

JÖRGENSEN, CHRISTIAN A. (1860–1935), Norwegian-born artist, taken to California as a child, studied under Virgil Williams and in Europe, and married a member of the Ghirardelli family. He is known for his paintings of missions and California landscapes.

Joshua tree, a native giant yucca, more a plant than a tree, is found widely throughout Utah, Nevada, Arizona, and parts of southern California. It was named by Mormon pioneers from the text of the Book of Joshua: "Thou shalt follow the way pointed for thee by the trees." This member of the lily family is just a stalk in its early years, then puts out spearlike limbs whose leaves die back when the limbs bear creamy waxen flowers in the spring. The plant reaches heights up to 50 feet and presumably lives several hundred years. Joshua Tree National Monument (est. 1936), east of Palm Springs, is an area (870 sq. mi.) noted for its fantastically twisted specimens.

JOULLIN, AMEDEE (1862–1917), San Francisco-born painter of French descent who studied at home under Tavernier and in Paris under Bouguereau. He was known for his canvases of Chinatown and of southwestern Indians.

Journalism, see *Magazines* and *Newspapers.*

Juaneño, Indians of Shoshonean stock who derived their name from Mission San Juan Capistrano. They adopted the toloache or jimson-weed cult of the Chinigchinich♦ religion from the neighboring Gabrieleño but added the use of a wankech (a ceremonial chamber), which contained an inner and an outer section as well as an altar. According to the 1910 census, the prehistoric population of 1,000 was reduced to extinction.

Juan Flaco, see *Brown, James.*

Juanita, see *Sonorans.*

JUDAH, THEODORE D[EHONE] (1826–63), after graduation from Rensselaer Polytechnic Institute and engineering work on eastern railways, was called to California (1854) to build a railway from Sacramento to Folsom, the first in the state. In 1857 he published an influential pamphlet on a transcontinental railroad, and in 1861 he got the Big Four♦ to join him in creating the Central Pacific Railroad Co.♦ He proposed the Dutch Flat crossing of the Sierra and the general route, for which he got financial support from Congress. Friction with his partners led to an agreement that they could buy him out for $100,000 or he could purchase their shares for the same amount to each. Sailing east to secure financing for this purpose from Vanderbilts or other financiers, he contracted typhoid fever while crossing the Isthmus and died soon after.

JUDD, WINNIE RUTH (1905–   ), known as the "trunk murderess" because in 1931, during a separation from her husband, a physician, she murdered the two women with whom she had temporarily lived, dismembered their bodies, and shipped them in trunks to Los Angeles, where she planned to claim the remains and bury them. Sentenced to hang, on the eve of her execution she was declared insane and sentenced to life imprisonment. During 40 years in a mental hospital she escaped 7 times, once for 7 years (1962–69), before she was paroled in 1971.

Judiciary, see *Supreme Court, Courts of Appeal, Superior Courts, Municipal Courts,* and *Justice Courts.*

JULIAN, C[OURTNEY] C. (1885–1934), oil speculator in the Los Angeles area, created a Julian Petroleum Co. whose stock he marketed by flamboyant, breezy ads and promises of exorbitant dividends far beyond the earnings of his leased wells (1922–25). He was driven out of his company by government regulations and pressure from established oil firms and local newspapers. His successors indulged in even wilder speculation, fed by counterfeit stock and bribery of civic officials, until the company collapsed (1927) with a loss of $150,000,000 to 40,000 shareholders. Julian himself got into other questionable businesses, fled from a mail fraud charge to Shanghai, and there killed himself.

Julian, gold rush town of the 1870s in the mountains just north of Cuyamaca Rancho State Park♦ in San Diego County. Julian was the surname of a miner.

JUMP, EDWARD (1832?–83), French-born caricaturist, resident in California (*c.*1852–68), where he depicted local San Francisco characters, scenes, and situations in amusing drawings and lithographs.

"Jumping Frog," see *Celebrated Jumping Frog of Calaveras County, The*.

Juncos, birds of the finch family, formerly called snowbirds, about five or six inches long, colored buff, slate-black, and white. The *Thurber* or *Sierra junco* inhabits the south coastal ranges, the Sierra, and deserts; the *Point Pinos junco* is found from San Mateo County to Point Sur; and the *Oregon junco* is seen in its winter and early summer migrations. They all feed on wild seeds and insects.

Junior colleges, see *Community colleges*.

Juniper, coniferous aromatic evergreen, found in three varieties in California. *Western juniper,* or *Sierra juniper* (also called red cedar), is a gnarled, thick-trunked tree, generally 10 to 25 feet tall, which grows in rocky mountainous sites. Its wood is used for fence posts and for pencils. The most sensational example, both largest and oldest, is a tree near Dardanelle (Tuolumne County), 85 feet tall and several thousand years old, called the *Bennet juniper* after its discoverer (1932). The *California juniper* is a bushy shrub, 2 to 15 feet tall, which grows on dry slopes and plains below 5,000 feet. The *desert juniper* is a somewhat similar bush but no higher than 10 feet.

Justice Courts, established in judicial districts with less than the 40,000 population required for a Municipal Court, their jurisdiction is limited to misdemeanors. Each is presided over by a judge elected to a six-year term.

K

KAEL, PAULINE (1919–), film critic, born in Petaluma. After attending the University of California, Berkeley, she began a writing career that led to her reviewing for *The New Yorker* (1968 ff.). Collections of her reviews appear in *I Lost It at the Movies* (1965), *Kiss Kiss Bang Bang* (1968), *Going Steady* (1970), and *Deeper into Movies* (1973).

KAER, MORTON [ARMOR] (1902–), Nebraska-born football player, a star halfback for the University of Southern California (1923–26). He was selected as All-American and later was an outstanding high school coach at Weed.

KAHN, JULIUS (1861–1924), born in Germany, went to California as a child. After a career as an actor he became a lawyer and then was a Republican party leader and long-time member of Congress (1899–1903, 1905–24). He was succeeded (1925–37) by his wife, Florence Prag Kahn (1866–1948).

KAISER, HENRY J. (1882–1967), New York-born son of German immigrants, founded the firm bearing his name (1914), which constructed highways in the Pacific Northwest. Moving his headquarters to Oakland (1921), he undertook even larger projects: highways and bridges in Cuba, Hoover and Bonneville dams, and S.F. Bay Bridge piers. He also founded corporations concerned with manufacturing steel, cement, aluminum, chemicals, and, for a time after World War II, automobiles bearing his name. During the war he was the nation's largest shipbuidler, employing some 200,000 persons and launching a quarter of the U.S. cargo vessels. In 1959 he was succeeded by his son Edgar (1908–).

KALLOCH, ISAAC S[MITH] (1831–87), flamboyant Baptist pastor of Boston, tried but not convicted of adultery, then moved to Kansas where he indulged in land speculation, shady railroad ventures, and political maneuvers before moving to San Francisco (1875) because "there are more wicked people of both sexes in that city . . . and I feel called by God to convert them." He became pastor of Metropolitan Temple, the city's largest church, and the candidate of the Workingmen's party♦ for mayor. His campaign attacked not only Chinese labor and the Big Four but also Charles de Young, whose *Chronicle* opposed him. In cold blood de Young shot Kalloch at his church but he survived to become mayor (1879–81), and his son, Isaac Martin Kalloch, in turn shot and killed de Young (1880). The father weathered impeachment attempts and the son was acquitted of murder, then both moved to Washington Territory (1883) to become lawyers there.

Kamia, see *Diegueño.*

Karok, see *Yurok.*

Kawaiisu, Indians of the Tehachapi Mts. who lived in present Kern County. Their precontact population of 500 had been reduced to 150 by the time of the 1910 census. They absorbed more elements of California Indian culture than the Chemehuevi, of whom they were an offshoot. They practiced the toloache cult♦ but, unlike the neighboring Yokuts and Luiseño, they gave the drug to girls as well as boys.

Kaweah Co-operative Commonwealth, Marxist colony located in eastern Tulare County on the banks of the Kaweah River. During its lifetime (1885–92) it attracted about 400 people. The colony was bitterly opposed by neighbors and by the federal government, in part because it was alleged to have plans to log all the great redwoods on adjacent territory—now the Sequoia National Park—to which it laid claim. It was founded by Burnette G. Haskell.♦

Kaweah Delta, agricultural region of the San Joaquin Valley southeast of Fresno. This Tulare County area is a major producer of oranges, plums, and peaches. Visalia and Tulare are its chief marketing cities.

Kaweah River, rises in four locations in or near Sequoia National Park,♦ the several forks meeting at Terminus Lake and traveling 15 miles southwest to dissipate into a delta near Visalia. The river is named for a Yokut tribe once resident on its north side and was first explored by whites in 1815. A socialist utopian colony, Kaweah Cooperative Commonwealth,♦ was founded on its banks.

KEARNEY, DENIS (1847–1907), born in Ireland, went to sea as a cabin boy at age 11. Wholly without formal education, he rose to be a first mate on American ships before settling in San Francisco (1868) where he built up a draying business, became a citizen (1876), read widely in Spencer and other social writers, and entered into political and labor agitation. He became president of the Workingmen's party of California♦ (1877) and led its campaigns against major capitalists of the area, the established political parties, and Chinese workers who took jobs at lower pay than white workers during this period of economic depression. He harangued crowds on San Francisco's empty sand lots with flamboyant speeches, invariably concluding: "The Chinese must go!" and once (Oct. 29, 1877) gathered a menacing following on Nob Hill that seemed to threaten violence to the surrounding houses of multimillionaires. In retaliation, a Committee of Public Safety was organized by William T. Coleman♦ to quash the threat. Acquitted of violating a hastily enacted "gag law," Kearney's political party went on to some temporary success and helped prepare the way for the federal law (1882) banning Chinese immigration. He himself returned to his business and disappeared from public life in 1880.

KEARNEY, M[ARTIN] THEO[DORE] (1838?–1906), English-born land developer in the Fresno area who was one of the nonresident purchasers involved in the Mussel Slough♦ affair (1880). He later organized an association of raisin growers which made him both rich and known for his ruthless methods. He died before constructing the elegant mansion modeled on Chenonceaux planned for his Fresno estate and before establishing his projected Kearney Agricultural College, but the home he built for a superintendent is now a landmark and local sight.

KEARNY, STEPHEN WATTS (1794–1848), began his army career as an infantry lieutenant in the War of 1812, and after 1819 served on the western frontier, rising in rank to general, and to command of the Army of the West in 1846. After seizing Santa Fé he served as military governor of New Mexico and then left with 300 dragoons for California. Incorrectly informed by Kit Carson that California was in American hands and that the *Californios* would not fight, Kearny sent 200 men back to Santa Fé and, despite the exhaustion of his remaining forces upon arrival at the coast, he immediately attacked at San Pasqual.♦ In that unsuccessful engagement many of his men were killed and wounded. The succeeding battles were won only because he got relief forces from Commodore Stockton. Within five weeks the *Californios* surrendered to Frémont and soon Kearny and Stockton quarreled over who was commander in chief and over Frémont's assumption of the civil governorship by Stockton's appointment. Stockton left for Mexico, the government in Washington upheld Kearny, and Frémont was deposed and later arrested and court-martialed. Kearny became civil governor of Vera Cruz and Mexico City but soon was back in St. Louis with a tropical disease of which he died. A street in San Francisco was named in his honor.

Kearsarge Peak, located just north of Independence (Inyo County), took its name from a mining district so called in honor of the Union battleship that sank the Confederate raider *Alabama* (1864). Nearby Kearsarge Pass lies on the southeastern Fresno border in Sequoia National Park.

KEATON, BUSTER (JOSEPH FRANCIS KEATON) (1895–1966), Kansas-born vaudeville comedian who became one of the earliest and greatest Hollywood actors of the silent screen. He also directed his own films. He passed beyond slapstick comedy to create his own persona of a frozen-faced, dramatically understated individual coping with and finally triumphing over unbelievably difficult situations.

KEELER, CHARLES A[UGUSTUS] (1871–1937), Milwaukee-born poet, went to live in Berkeley (1893) and gathered his verse in several volumes, including *The Siege of the Golden City* (1896) and *Sequoia Sonnets* (1919), as well as writing ornithological studies of American birds. His idea of the good life in the Bay region was set forth in *San Francisco and Thereabouts* (1902) and in his aesthetic treatise, *The Simple Home* (1904).

KEELER, RALPH OLMSTEAD (1840–73), Ohio-born journalist, whose *Vagabond Adventures* (1870) describe his life on a Mississippi River showboat, as a Heidelberg student tramping through Europe, and as a columnist and story writer for the *Golden*

Era (1864–66) during a period when he also taught in a San Francisco private school. *Gloverson and His Silent Partners* (1869) is a novel set in San Francisco.

KEITH, WILLIAM (1839–1911), Scottish-born painter, went to California (1859). His paintings of local landscapes sold well enough to allow him to go to Düsseldorf (1869–71) for study, supplemented by a trip to Munich and Spain (1893), but the rest of his life was spent in San Francisco and Berkeley. He frequently went on outings throughout the state with John Muir and John Burroughs, making observations for his paintings. His canvases concentrated on mountains, redwoods, oaks, and local scenes. In his day he was esteemed as the leading depicter of California's natural setting.

KELHAM, GEORGE W. (1871–1936), architect who went to San Francisco to supervise a New York firm's construction of the new Palace Hotel♦ and remained in the city, where he designed the Public Library, the Standard Oil and Shell Oil buildings, and the Russ Building.

KELLEY, HALL JACKSON (1790–1874), New Hampshire-born fanatical propagandist for American settlement of the West, particularly Oregon. He made his way there via Mexico and California (1834). From Gov. Figueroa he got permission to survey, map, and perhaps eventually settle some interior valley areas. He began and ended his project by traveling with Ewing Young and others up the Central Valley from San Jose to Oregon, making a map and later writing a memoir printed as part of a U.S. congressional report (1839).

Kelley's Army, force of about 1,500 unemployed migratory farm laborers and unskilled workers recruited by "General" Charles T. Kelley during a depression in 1914 and as an aftermath of the Wheatland Riot.♦ Twenty years earlier Kelley had earned his title by leading a California detachment (which included Jack London) of Coxey's Army that had marched on Washington, D.C., to present a "petition in boots" to Congress. Similarly, in 1914 Kelley's followers had marched on Sacramento to demand legislative aid and were met by a brigade of some 800 deputized citizens armed with pick handles. The "army" was driven from the capitol grounds and the city.

Kelp, see *Seaweed*.

KEMBLE, EDWARD CLEVELAND (1828–86), went from New York to California with Brannan's Mormon emigrants (1846), having worked with him on his New York newspaper, even though he was not a member of Brannan's faith. In San Francisco he edited Brannan's *California Star*,♦ which he bought and merged with *The Californian*,♦ succeeding it in 1849 with the *Alta California*,♦ jointly owned and edited with Edward C. Gilbert.♦ Kemble was later identified with other newspapers in Sacramento, San Francisco, and New York, and he wrote a good deal about his adopted state, including "A History of California Newspapers, 1846–1858" (1858) and shorter pieces collected later in *A Kemble Reader* (1963).

KEMBLE, JOHN HASKELL (1912–), historian of California and maritime matters. Born in Iowa, reared and educated in California, he is a professor of history at Pomona College (1936–). His books include *San Francisco Bay* (1957) and editions of the journals of William H. Meyers.

KENDALL, W A. (d. 1876), Massachusetts-born poet. After teaching school in Petaluma he contributed poetry to the *Golden Era* and other journals. He was temporarily known for his lush love lyrics but had no financial success and had to seek aid from Mark Twain and Bret Harte. He committed suicide.

KENNEDY, KATE (1827–90), Irish-born teacher and reformer, went with her family to San Francisco in the 1850s. There she became a principal in the public schools and successfully fought for equal pay for women. She also successfully sued the Board of Education in a case that established teacher tenure in the state (1890). A San Francisco public school is named for her. Her niece, Katherine Delmar Burke, founded what was long the city's leading private school for girls.

KENNEDY, LAWTON (1902–), native Californian, entered on a career of fine printing as a young man in Oakland and San Francisco. After doing presswork for Nash, Grabhorn, and other distinguished typographers, he established his own firm (1933) from which he has issued a substantial body of well-designed and well-made books under his own imprint as well as for the Book Club of California and other patrons.

KENT, WILLIAM (1864–1928), after graduation from Yale and work in the family's Chicago grain commission business, returned to the family home in Marin County (1907). He was a Progressive Republican, serving in Congress (1911–17) where he worked for social and ecological causes. As a conservationist he presented to the U.S. two pieces of family property: Mt. Tamalpais♦ and the nearby redwood grove that he asked to have named for John Muir.♦ However, he opposed Muir in supporting the use of Hetch Hetchy for water supply.

KENTON, Stan[ley Newcomb] (1912–), Kansas-born jazz orchestra leader, reared near Los Angeles, became famous with his Balboa Beach Band (1941), particularly through his theme song, "Artistry in Rhythm" (1943). A leader of progressive jazz, he is known for his atonality, for his symphonic arrangements, and for his accompanists and arrangers.

KERCHOFF, William George (1856–1929), Indiana-born industrialist of southern California, to which he moved in 1878. He developed a large lumber business, pioneered the use of hydroelectric power from the San Gabriel River to Los Angeles, and brought to that city its first natural gas (from Taft, 1913). He was also a well-known conservationist of Yosemite Valley.

KERN, Edward M[eyer] (1823–63), Philadelphia-born artist, served on Frémont's expedition of 1845–46 as a topographer and acted as an officer in the Bear Flag Revolt. Under Frémont's orders he seized and occupied Sutter's Fort and temporarily held Vallejo and Leese. He also helped in the relief of the Donner Party and led a force against Indians in the Sacramento Valley. Frémont gave Kern's name to a river in which he almost drowned (1845), and from Kern River have come Kern County and other place-names. He later accompanied Frémont on his 4th expedition (winter, 1848–49) searching for an all-year transcontinental railroad route.

Kern County, incorporated (1866) from parts of Los Angeles and Tulare counties to its south and north, its seat has been Bakersfield♦ since 1874. Other bounding counties are Ventura on the south, Kings on the north, San Luis Obispo on the west, and San Bernardino on the east.

Major routes that cross it include Walker Pass, used for an east-west trail by Joseph R. Walker♦ (1834) and again by Chiles (1843) and Frémont (1845), the last-named accompanied by Edward Kern,♦ for whom he named the river; Tejon Pass,♦

used by Fages (1772) in traveling north across the Tehachapi Mts.;♦ and Tehachapi Pass,♦ into the Sierra Nevada and down to the Mojave Desert through the Mojave Range, which forms the southern boundary of the San Joaquin Valley where the Sierra Nevada and Coast Range come to their ends on the east and west, respectively. The names and routes of these passes have been changed over the years. The Butterfield stages traveled from Los Angeles to Stockton with a station at old Fort Tejón,♦ founded as a military post by Edward Beale.

The Kern River,♦ from which the county takes its name, was the scene of a gold rush in 1855 to the area near the present artificial Lake Isabella (created 1953) where many jerry-built towns flourished until the 1880s, among them the onetime county seat Havilah (1866–74), named by Asbury Harpending for a biblical land of gold. Another mining rush (1895) occurred in the El Paso and Rand mountains along the eastern border with San Bernardino County, having Randsburg as its center.

Since the 1870s the main city has been Bakersfield. Prosperity first came to it with the building of the Southern Pacific Railroad in that decade, for this permitted the development of agriculture and livestock ranching (Miller and Lux had the major landholdings), which continue to the present, with great field crops, fruit and grape orchards, vegetable farms, alfalfa and cotton fields, and flower nurseries, as well as cattle, poultry, and sheep ranches. However, modern prosperity also depends heavily on the oil fields of Taft,♦ Maricopa, and those near Bakersfield, which—like the asphalt mined near McKittrick and borax at Boron—were known early but not exploited until 1899 and the years thereafter. A major oil field is the naval reserve at Elk Hills.♦

Muroc, a 65-mile-square dry lake bed, is the site of Edwards Air Force Base, and north of it is China Lake Ordnance Test Station (partly in San Bernardino County) for rocket firing. The county population in 1970 was 329,271. With an area of 5,217,472 acres, it had 40.3 persons per sq. mi.

Kern River, rises in the Sierra Nevada, drains the west slope of Mt. Whitney, flowing down close to Bakersfield. It originally drained into the San Joaquin River and out to the ocean through San Francisco Bay, but since 1953 water from its North and South forks is impounded by Isabella Dam near Bakersfield. It was named by Frémont for Edward Kern♦ (1845), although the first white man to see it was Father Garces.

KEROUAC, JACK (1922–69), born in Massachusetts, studied at Columbia, roamed about and worked at odd jobs before becoming associated with the Beat movement,♦ which brought him to San Francisco. His novel *On the Road* (1957), drawing upon this background of movement, feeling for jazz, and search for experience through drugs, wine, and sex, was widely read and very influential upon young readers. *The Subterraneans* (1958), treating the romance between a Beat writer and a black girl in San Francisco, is another fictive expression of the same quest. *The Dharma Bums* (1958) is a more philosophic novel, seeking truth through Zen Buddhism. *Big Sur* (1962), a sequel to *On the Road,* depicts the breakdown of a Beat leader retreating to a more isolated region.

KERR, CLARK (1911–), Pennsylvania-born industrial relations economist, joined the faculty of the University of California, Berkeley (1945), and became the first chancellor of that campus in 1952. After a brilliant administration in that capacity he was made president of the University (1958), developing new campuses at Irvine, Santa Cruz, and San Diego and augmenting established ones, as well as being the primary architect of the Master Plan for Higher Education in the state. As a development of the turmoil begun by the Free Speech Movement,♦ he was removed from the presidency (1967). In succeeding years he headed a comprehensive study of higher education in the U.S. for the Carnegie Foundation. His writings include *The Uses of the University* (1963), based on lectures delivered at Harvard, in which he described the modern institution as a "multiversity" obligated to diverse constituencies and purposes.

KESEY, KEN (1935–), born in Colorado, reared in Oregon. After graduation from the University of Oregon and studies in creative writing at Stanford, he worked for a time as a ward attendant in a mental hospital, which provided the background for *One Flew Over the Cuckoo's Nest* (1962), his comic, macabre novel suggesting the breakdown of modern society. *Sometimes a Great Notion* (1964) is a novel about a wealthy logging family. His adoption of a loose lifestyle, touring the country with a busload of so-called Merry Madcaps using drugs, took him away from writing and led to troubles with the law. During this period The Grateful Dead♦ band affiliated themselves with him. These adventures were the subject of a book by Tom Wolfe.♦

Keswick Dam, an element of the Central Valley Project,♦ on the Sacramento River, regulates the flow of water released nine miles north by Shasta Dam and Shasta Lake.♦ It also has a fish elevator for trout and salmon.

Kettleman Hills, part of the southern Coast Range which adjoins the Tulare Lake basin (Kings County) and is about 20 miles long and 5 miles wide. They are named (with a misspelling) after Dave Kettelman, a local cattleman. After the water supply dried up, the region went into a decline and settlements, such as that of the Kaweah Co-operative Commonwealth,♦ were unsuccessful. It has long been a U.S. Navy oil reserve after wells were brought in (1928) on land that once was leased at 2.5 cents an acre. In the first three years 14,000,000 barrels of oil, 300,000,000 gallons of gasoline, and 280,000,000 cubic feet of gas were extracted.

KEY, JOHN ROSS (1832–1920), grandson of Francis Scott Key, was a landscape artist and illustrator who visited California, probably in the 1870s, and depicted some of its scenery. His views of California were often reproduced as popular chromolithographs.

Key Route, interurban transportation system of electric trains throughout the East Bay that came to be connected by ferries♦ to San Francisco. Tracing its origin to the Oakland Consolidated Street Railway between Oakland and Berkeley, founded in 1891, the system really came into being in 1893 when Francis M. ("Borax") Smith♦ and Frank C. Havens bought this line, another extending to San Leandro and Hayward, and other independent lines and consolidated them. By 1901 they controlled some 75 miles of track, and the next year extended across the Bay with the creation of a San Francisco, Oakland and San Jose Railway Co.

In 1903 they added ferries, whose trestles and piers in relation to the rail lines gave their system the appearance of a key, a symbol thereafter used as firm name and trademark. The transportation system fed the properties of Smith's and Havens' Realty Syndicate as well as their elegant resort, the Claremont Hotel, a huge edifice dominating the hills behind Berkeley. After Havens sold his interest in the business (1910), Smith extended his dominion further by attempting to control water, light, and electric power throughout the area from Contra Costa County even down so far as Gilroy. This overexpansion led to a financial collapse in

1912, causing the Key Route to be placed in receivership (1914–23).

A reorganized Key System Transit Co. was established (1923) and run with success but the ferries were discontinued (1940) after the line's trains were able to cross the newly opened San Francisco-Oakland Bay Bridge. However, competition from private automobiles and from buses (a mode of transportation into which the Key System had ventured as early as 1921 in the area of Mills College) in time led to the ending of streetcar service. The last East Bay streetcar ended its run in 1948. The remaining properties and lines of the Key System were purchased by the AC [Alameda-Contra Costa] Transit District, which was established as a public utility by popular vote in 1959.

Kezar Stadium, athletic facility in Golden Gate Park, constructed (1925) and enlarged (1928) to seat about 60,000. It was used (until 1971) by the Forty-Niners, the city's professional football team. It was the site (1925–74) of the East-West Game, played on New Year's Day, and is used by several high school teams. The stadium was named for Mary Kezar (d. 1922), who bequeathed $100,000 to the city for a playground, which a judge ruled could include a football field.

KIENTEPOOS, see *Modoc.*

KIMBALL, CHARLES P. (1821–94), moved from his native Maine to San Francisco (1849) and soon established an aggressive book-selling and publishing business aptly named the Noisy Carrier Book and Stationery Co. He published his own verse (1868) but is best remembered for issuing San Francisco's first city directory (1850).

Kindergarten, see *Emma Marwedel, Phoebe Hearst,* and *Kate Wiggin.*

KING, BILLIE JEAN [MOFFITT] (1943–   ), tennis star, born in Long Beach, held the women's singles championships of England (1966–68, 1972–73, 75) and of the U.S. (1967, 71, 72), as well as those of Australia, Italy, and France, along with numerous doubles titles before turning professional. In the last capacity she was known for her straight set defeat of Bobby Riggs♦ (1973) in a contest as much concerned with women's liberation as with tennis.

KING, CLARENCE (1842–1901), born at Newport, R.I., after graduation from Yale made a horseback trip across the U.S. (1863), stopping for some time

to work in the Comstock Lode♦ before proceeding to San Francisco. On the last leg of his journey, he met William H. Brewer♦ who hired him to work on the geological survey of California which Brewer was conducting under Josiah Dwight Whitney. King remained with it for three years, his work being mainly exploratory. During the winter of 1865–66 he also served as a scientific assistant to Gen. McDowell's exploration of desert areas in southern California. Late in 1866 he returned to the East but until 1877 he headed a corps of geologists on a congressionally funded survey of eastern Colorado to the California border along the 40th parallel, resulting in a seven-volume *Report* (1870–80). In 1873 he exposed the Great Diamond Hoax that had fooled Asbury Harpending.♦ He headed the U.S. Geological Survey (1878–81) and then became a private mining engineer. In 1887 he secretly married a black woman by whom he had five children, but the strain of living a double life and financial reverses led to a breakdown that caused him to be committed to a mental hospital (1884). In addition to his scientific writings, King is remembered for his sketches collected as *Mountaineering in the Sierra Nevada*♦ (1872), which possess the scientific precision, sensitive and witty observation, and attractive style that delighted his latter-day friends, such as Henry Adams, John Hay, and John LaFarge, who left records of his charm as a person and conversationalist.

KING, THOMAS STARR (1824–64), born in New York, became a popular Unitarian minister in Boston (1846–60) but accepted a call to the Unitarian parish of San Francisco (1860), feeling he was wrong "in huddling so closely around the cosy stove of civilization in this blessed Boston." During the four years before his premature death from diphtheria he was as popular as both preacher and person in his new city as he had been in his old. His eloquent talks for the Sanitary Commission♦ tremendously aided support of the Union Army and helped influence California to the Union side. The admiration of nature displayed in the East in his book *The White Hills* (1860) was equally well exhibited in his letters about the western landscape sent to the Boston *Transcript* and collected in *A Vacation Among the Sierras* (1962). Some of his sermons were also collected posthumously in *Christianity and Humanity* (1877). A mountain, lake, and meadow in Yosemite National Park are named for him; he is one of California's two representatives in the national Statuary Hall;♦ and a bronze statue of him by Daniel Chester French stands in Golden Gate Park.

KING OF WILLIAM, JAMES (1822–56), prior to coming to California (1848) from his native Georgetown, D.C., had added "of William" (his father's name) to distinguish himself from others named James King. He was known by this style in the mines and as a San Francisco banker. He made a fortune and after he lost it because of a dishonest employee, he began to publish a newspaper, the *Bulletin*♦ (1855), in which he excoriated politicians, lawyers, and judges as well as institutions whose actions he found responsible for local corruption. His vigorous muckraking led him to call a county supervisor, James P. Casey,♦ crooked and to reveal that Casey was an ex-convict. When the infuriated Casey could not get a retraction, he openly shot down King of William on the street. King of William, who had been on the executive committee of the first Vigilance Committee♦ (1851), was by death responsible for bringing a second such committee into being. It tried Casey and executed him at the very hour King of William was being buried. His brother, Thomas Sim King (1823–1911), succeeded him as editor of the *Bulletin* (1856–59), which he made a strong supporter of the Vigilance Committee and opponent of Sen. David C. Broderick.

King City, market center of the southern Salinas Valley, located in southeastern Monterey County. It was named for C. H. King, on whose ranch the town was laid out when the Southern Pacific Railroad reached the site on the Salinas River. Population in 1970 was 3,717.

Kings Canyon National Park, located in Fresno and Tulare counties on the western side of the Sierra, just north of Sequoia National Park. Its name is derived from the river that Spanish explorers in 1805 called the Rio de los Santos Reyes ("River of the Holy Kings"). Made a National Park in 1940, it contains great groves of redwoods, including the General Grant (267 feet tall).

Kings County, incorporated (1893) from part of Tulare County (on the east) to which about 100 sq. mi. of Fresno County (on the north and west) were added (1908). Monterey County bounds it on the west and Kern County on the south. Hanford♦ is the county seat. The name comes from that of the river (originally Rio de los Santos Reyes) in honor of the Wise Men on whose feast day explorers first saw the river (1805). Its waters and those of the Kaweah and Tule rivers once flooded Tulare Lake, now drained for irrigation ditches. Located in the southern part of the San Joaquin Valley, the county is known for its field crops, fruit and nut orchards, stock raising, dairying, and poultry. Oil and natural gas are derived from Kettleman Hills.♦ Near Hanford occurred the battle of Mussel Slough♦ (1880), the conflict between wheat ranchers and railroad interests celebrated in Frank Norris' *The Octopus*. In 1970 the population of the county was 66,717; with an area of 893,504 acres, it had 47.7 persons per sq. mi.

Kings River, rises in three forks in the Sierra Nevada, flows southwest for 125 miles, marks the border between Fresno and Kings counties, and emptied into Tulare Lake (Kings County) but since 1954 into the reservoir created by Pine Flat Dam. It is part of the Central Valley Project that links it with the San Joaquin River. Its Middle and South forks created the gorges of Kings Canyon. It was named (1805) Rio de los Santos Reyes by the explorer Gabriel Moraga.

KINNEY, ABBOTT (1850–1920), heir to a cigarette fortune, arrived in southern California (1873) from his native Midwest via travels in Africa and Asia, and settled near Pasadena, where he became the champion of many causes. He created two local public libraries, founded an agricultural journal, *Los Angeles Saturday Post* (1900–1906), served as a U.S. congressional commissioner with Helen Hunt Jackson♦ to investigate the conditions of southern California Indians, was a pioneer planter of eucalyptus trees, worked for the adoption of the Australian ballot in California, propagandized for national parks and forest reserves, and wrote many pamphlets, including *Tasks by Twilight* (1893), a treatise on sexual relations. On 160 acres of tidal flats which he owned, located 25 miles from Los Angeles, he created and named the city of Venice, whose canals he planned, whose gondolas and gondoliers he imported, and whose pseudo-Renaissance houses he built as part of an unsuccessful development to combine real estate sales with chautauqua culture—including a production of *Camille,* with Sarah Bernhardt, enacted at the end of his ocean pier.

KINO, EUSEBIO FRANCISCO (1645–1711), born in Italy (where the family name was spelled Chino), educated in Germany, at age 20 became a Jesuit missionary in the service of Spain. In 1681 he was sent to Mexico to do missionary work and in 1683 he went by sea to Baja California as part of an unsuccessful colonizing venture (1683–85) in which he was the religious superior and the royal cosmographer of an expedition commanded by Don Ysidro Atondo y Antillón.◆ His experiences were recorded in a diary that tells of dedication to the Indians and his keen desire to bring them to Christianity. Kino's more lasting accomplishments occurred between 1687 and his death when he made many intrepid trail-blazing expeditions into Pimería Alta, the region of the Pima Indians covering present northern Sonora (Mexico) and present southern Arizona, but extending even to the confluence of the Gila and Colorado rivers on the present border of California. In Pimerí Alta he explored and mapped the land, founded many missions, converted Indians, established agriculture, and introduced cattle raising. In several expeditions (1699–1702) he found evidence from shells and plants to indicate that Baja California could be reached by land and that therefore it was a peninsula, not an island as was commonly contended. He envisioned it as part of an overland supply route to future missions that he wished to see established in both Baja and Alta California. His extensive *Favores celestiales* is a reminiscent account, both personal and general, with a typically modest and religious title, translated by his biographer Herbert E. Bolton◆ as *Kino's Historical Memoir of Pimería Alta* (2 vols., 1919).

KIP, WILLIAM INGRAHAM (1811–93), New York-born and Yale-educated clergyman, the first Episcopal bishop of California, arrived in San Francisco in 1854. Over the years he was responsible for the dioceses of San Francisco, Los Angeles, and Sacramento.

KIPLING, RUDYARD (1865–1936), British poet, novelist, and short story writer, born in India but educated in England. He visited San Francisco (1889) en route from India and wrote colorful articles about the city for the *Civil and Military Gazette* of Lahore and the *Pioneer* of Allahabad. He declared: "San Francisco is a mad city—inhabited by perfectly insane people whose women are of a remarkable beauty."

Kitchen middens, see *Shell mounds.*

Klamath County, founded (1851), it extended from the mouth of the Mad River to the Coast Range summit and north to 42 degrees latitude, then west

to the ocean and south along its shoreline. Its name came from that of a tribe allied to the Modoc. It is the only disestablished California county. Its county seats were Trinidad, Crescent City (1853 to its ceding to Del Norte County, 1857), and Orleans Bar. A small population and low assessed values made county government too burdensome, so the people voted (1874) to petition the legislature to divide it between Siskiyou and Humboldt counties, an act finally completed in 1876.

Klamath Mountains, extend from southern Oregon for about 130 miles in northwest California between the Coast and the Cascade ranges. They reach 8,000-foot elevations and include the Siskiyou, Salmon, Marble, Scott Bar, and Trinity mountains, the latter including the Trinity Alps, high glaciated peaks. The Klamath River rises in Klamath Lake, Oregon, flows into California near Yreka, through the Mountains and into the Pacific 13 miles south of Crescent City. It carries more water than any other California river except the Sacramento and has flooded several times. Along its rugged banks many towns grew up, like Scott Bar and Happy Camp, during the gold rush of the 1850s, and along it and the Trinity, which flows into it, hydraulic mining was later common. The name is derived from that of a Chinook tribe allied to the Modoc and was first used by Peter Ogden (1826); two years later Jedediah Smith explored it and for a time the lower Klamath was called Smith River. Much of the area is included in the Klamath National Forest, which covers nearly 1,700,000 acres.

KLEMPERER, OTTO (1885–1973), German-born conductor of the Berlin State Opera, upon the rise of Hitler left his homeland to become the conductor of the Los Angeles Philharmonic Orchestra (1933–39). After a long period of poor health he resumed conducting in the U.S. and London. He was known for his interpretations of German romantic composers.

KNIGHT, GOODWIN J. (1896–1970), 31st governor of the state (1953–59), born in Utah, reared in Los Angeles. After graduation from Stanford and graduate study at Cornell, he entered legal practice, served as a judge, was elected lieutenant governor (1946), and became governor when Earl Warren was appointed Chief Justice of the U.S. Supreme Court. In general he followed Warren's policies and introduced acceptable programs of his own, but his expectation of a successful bid for reelection was upset when Sen. William F. Knowland♦ decided to run for the office, ostensibly in anticipation of a try for the presidency, leaving Knight to seek Knowland's vacated Senate seat (unsuccessfully).

Knights Ferry, see *Yolo County.*

Knott's Berry Farm, restaurant, cluster of specialty shops, and a tourist attraction located in Buena Park,♦ some 20 miles southeast of Los Angeles. Founded (1920) by Walter Knott as a roadside fruit stand, it expanded to a restaurant featuring country chicken dinners; the sale of jams (particularly boysenberry) and other foodstuffs and gifts; and an amusement area with thrilling rides but emphasizing old-fashioned Americanism as represented by a frontier ghost town, a narrow-gauge railroad, a Little Chapel by the Lake, and a Freedom Center featuring a full-scale facsimile of Independence Hall. As early as 1946 over 1,000,000 dinners were served annually.

KNOWLAND, JOSEPH R[USSELL] (1873–1966), long-time publisher of the *Oakland Tribune,* supporter of research on California history, and public figure who served in the U.S. Congress (1904–6). He was the father of William F. Knowland.

KNOWLAND, WILLIAM F[IFE] (1908–74), succeeded his father as publisher and editor of the *Oakland Tribune,* but is best known for his career in politics as a Republican. Appointed (1945) to complete the term of U.S. Sen. Hiram Johnson, he was reelected until 1958, serving as both majority and minority leader. He was known for his conservative, anti-U.N., and anti-Communist China views. Defeated for the governorship (1958), he quit politics.

Know-Nothing movement, national political organization of the 1840s and 50s whose prime purpose was opposition to foreign-born persons, mainly Roman Catholics. Begun as secret societies that emerged in the 1850s as the American party, in that decade the party was strong enough in California to get David S. Terry♦ elected to the state Supreme Court (1855) and John Neely Johnson elected governor (1856).

KOHLER, CHARLES (1830–87), German-born vintner, went to San Francisco (1853) and with his fellow countryman, John Frohling, established a cooperative vineyard society with other Germans at Anaheim (1857). He expanded his grape growing and wine making until he dominated the business throughout the state. His Pacific Glass Works was founded (1862) to produce bottles for his wine production, which amounted to 400,000 gallons a year in the 1870s.

Koni, see *Miwok.*

Konkow, see *Maidu.*

Konocti, Mount, see *Clear Lake.*

Koso, Indians of Shoshonean♦ stock who resided in the Coso, Panamint, and Death valleys. At one time there were 500 Koso, but by 1910 they were extinct. They led a meager existence in their desert territory until gold- and silver-mining activities brought the large-scale incursion of whites that resulted in their decline.

KOTZEBUE, OTTO (1786–1846), German-born captain in the Russian Navy who headed two voyages of Pacific exploration (1815–18, 1823–26), one including a month in San Francisco Bay (1816) and a shorter stay the second time. He treated his expeditions in *Entdeckungs-Reise* . . . (1821) and *Neue Reise* . . . (1830), respectively. Chamisso,♦ Choris,♦ and Eschscholtz were aboard the *Rurik,* on which the first voyage was made.

KOUFAX, SANDY (SANFORD KOUFAX) (1935–   ), Brooklyn-born baseball player. After attending the University of Cincinnati (1953–54) on a basketball scholarship he joined the Dodgers of his home town (1955). He moved with the team to Los Angeles (1958) and was a star pitcher by 1961. He pitched in the World Series against the N.Y. Yankees (1963), helping his team to win the championship while he achieved the National League record for most strike-outs in a season. He won the Cy Young Award as best National League pitcher (1963, 65, 66) but had to retire (1967) because of an arthritic elbow.

KRAMER, JACK (JOHN ALBERT KRAMER) (1921–   ), Nevada-born tennis star, reared in southern California, won the U.S. men's singles championship (1946, 47) and doubles (1947) and the British singles (1947) before turning professional. He was the world's top-ranked professional (1948–53). Later as a promoter he was instrumental in changing professional tennis from a series of challenges and one-night stands to a scheme of tournaments by a group of touring players in which professionals could appear against amateurs.

KRIPS, JOSEF (1902–74), Viennese-born symphony conductor, moved to the U.S. (1950) and became conductor of the San Francisco Symphony (1963–70). He was particularly well known for his interpretation of Beethoven.

KROEBER, ALFRED L[OUIS] (1876–1960), professor of anthropology at the University of California, Berkeley (1901–46), and founder of its Museum of Anthropology. He was the outstanding scholar of the Indians of California, about whom he wrote an important *Handbook* (1925). He was a protector and student of Ishi,♦ the Yahi called "the last wild Indian in North America," about whom his wife, Theodora Kroeber, later wrote a popular book.

KRUG, CHARLES (1830–94), Prussian-born vintner. He went to San Francisco (1852) and met Agoston Haraszthy, who persuaded him to grow grapes and make wine. After trying this in the Napa Valley, first in 1859, he established his own winery near St. Helena (1868). It has become a major firm, purchased (1943) and operated by the Mondavi family.

KUCHEL, THOMAS HENRY (1910–   ), born in Anaheim, where he practiced law until he entered state politics. He then became a U.S. Senator (1953–69) and was known as a liberal Republican. He later took up private legal practice in Los Angeles and Washington, D.C.

Kuchel and Dresel, San Francisco firm of lithographers (1853–58?), established by Charles C. Kuchel (granduncle of Sen. Kuchel) and Emil Dresel, both German-born. They issued the first view of Yosemite (1855), drawn by Thomas Ayres, and a series of views of the state's major cities and mining towns.

Kuksu cult, practiced by the Maidu, Pomo, and Wintun Indians, a religious system in which males who have been initiated in ceremonies held in a temescal♦ then dance in costumes to represent spirits of deities.

KUSKOV, IVAN, see *Russians in California.*

KYNE, PETER B[ERNARD], (1880–1957), San Francisco-born author, dropped out of school at 14. After service in the Philippines during the Spanish-American War he entered the lumber and shipping business. This commercial background served him for *Cappy Ricks* (1916), the first of many collections of short stories dealing with a kindly but shrewd retired sea captain and his experiences in a Pacific Coast lumber company and shipping line. Kyne's brief tale, *The Go-Getter* (1922), was a popular story about a canny energetic businessman.

L

L.A., nickname for Los Angeles.

Labor, in the Spanish and Mexican periods largely consisted of Indians in three capacities: as mission neophytes, as hired employees, and, occasionally, as slaves. The booming economy of the gold rush created a large, diverse, often highly paid, unstable labor force. It ranged from imported and enslaved blacks, to highly skilled European and American craftsmen who settled in San Francisco and other urban centers, generally scorning to serve as agricultural labor.◆ Although the newcomers regarded themselves as transients, they formed some unions (the San Francisco Typographical Association was the first in 1850) and participated in strikes. During the 1860s and 70s short-lived unions came and went while trying to obtain better working conditions. A Mechanics' State Council enacted an eight-hour day, challenged by a "Ten Hour League" of shipowners in 1867.

Declining opportunities in the mines often forced men to take whatever jobs they could find, even at low pay and with long hours. Conditions worsened considerably after the completion of the transcontinental railroad (1869), when the thousands of Chinese◆ imported for the construction were thrown on the labor market. By 1872 they held half the factory jobs in San Francisco. Their willingness to accept low pay for hard work led to great opposition from whites who under Denis Kearney formed the Workingmen's party◆ in San Francisco (1877) to expel the Orientals, to gain political power, and to seek constitutional changes bettering laborers' conditions in the state. The party was short-lived because the depression of the 1870s lifted in the next decade, a new state constitution (1879) provided some of the desired conditions, and an act to exclude Chinese immigrants was passed in 1882.

Emphasis now passed from political activity to union organization as Frank Roney◆ created a citywide San Francisco Trades Assembly (1881) and Patrick H. McCarthy, another Irish immigrant, brought all construction workers into the Building Trades Council of San Francisco, which he founded in 1898. The city had numerous other labor leaders, notably the steady figure of Andrew Furu-

seth,◆ who founded the Sailors' Union of the Pacific in 1891, and the radical Burnette G. Haskell, creator of an International Workingmen's Association, so that by the turn of the century San Francisco was known as a union town. Elected as mayor (1902–7) for three terms was an agreeable orchestra leader, Eugene Schmitz, since he was the candidate of a newly formed Union Labor party, manipulated by political boss Abraham Ruef.◆ Even after the party's corruption was exposed in a series of "graft trials," labor continued to have important power in San Francisco.

Los Angeles, on the contrary, was known as an open town, in large part owing to the steadfast opposition to unions led by Harrison Gray Otis and his *Los Angeles Times.* The power of his views was tremendously increased after two labor organizers, the McNamara Brothers,◆ bombed the newspaper's building (1910), killing twenty persons and injuring seventeen more. San Francisco labor later suffered a comparable setback in another *cause célèbre* when two union organizers, Tom Mooney and Warren Billings, were convicted of throwing a bomb into the midst of a civic parade to honor preparedness for war (1916).

Agricultural labor had meanwhile long remained unorganized: first the Chinese were docile and alien, then their 20th-century successors, the Japanese, were less interested in unionization than in advancement to rental of ranches or their ownership. Paradoxically, only the Industrial Workers of the World, known as I.W.W.,◆ tried to organize farm workers (c.1910 to 1920). Their most sensational event was the bloody Wheatland Riot◆ (1913). Although unemployed migratory workers as a result banded into Kelley's Army,◆ a more effective outcome of this turmoil was the opposition that led to the passage of an extremely repressive Criminal Syndicalism Act,◆ which was used in devastating fashion against unions from 1919 through the 1930s.

Opposition to organized labor reached a climax during the Great Depression when a brief but effective General Strike◆ (1934) was called in San Francisco as an outgrowth of a strike by the International Longshoremen's Association led by Harry Bridges.◆ The initiating union won an overall contract with the Employers Waterfront Association which in time brought peace to the docks, although Harry Lundeberg♦ of the Sailors' Union of the Pacific broke with Bridges over his alleged radicalism. Increased unionization, which profited from the "New Deal" atmosphere of F. D. Roosevelt's administration and specifically from its National Industrial Recovery Act (1933), even affected the long-neglected laborers in the fields. As more white workers, including migrants from the Dust Bowl of Oklahoma, flocked to California's ranches, often in futile search of jobs, labor organizers found persons far more receptive to their cause and tactics than their predecessors, mainly Chinese, Japanese, Mexican, Filipino, and Hindu.

The resultant series of strikes in the San Joaquin Valley, Imperial Valley, and elsewhere set off violent reactions, on the one side from militant employers who organized themselves as Associated Farmers♦ or from masked local vigilante bands, on the other from concerned readers moved by John Steinbeck's portrayal in *The Grapes of Wrath* (1939). Union organization in other business areas did not engender such vigorous antipathy, although it spread to such unaccustomed fields as that of the Screen Actors Guild.♦ By the 1940s labor relations became more peaceful, with fuller employment provided by wartime industry and as the place of labor in the state's economy became a recognized fact. Thus by 1947 three-quarters of San Francisco's employees were enrolled in industry-wide unions and even Los Angeles and the rest of southern California had nearly as great coverage.

Organized labor also gained great political power, clearly manifested in the election of Edmund G. Brown as governor (1958) over William F. Knowland, who championed a "right to work" or open-shop initiative. However, agricultural labor still remained unorganized, in part because the *bracero* program allowed California growers to import cheap seasonal workers from Mexico in a government-aided program. Not until the 1960s was a significant unionization achieved by Cesar Chavez.♦ Relations between his United Farm Workers and the rival Teamsters Union were ameliorated when the state legislature enacted a law (1975) providing for secret elections to let workers decide which, if any, union should represent them.

Another major development in unionization during the 1970s was the organization of previously unaffiliated individuals, such as teachers, firemen, garbage collectors, and other public employees, many of whom for the first time resorted to strikes to gain their objectives.

Labor Unions, see *Bridges, Harry; Chavez, Cesar; Furuseth, Andrew; General Strike; International Longshoremen's Union; I.W.W.; Kearney, Denis; Longshoremen; Lundeberg, Harry; McNamara brothers bombing; Mooney, Thomas; Roney, Frank; Screen Actors Guild;* and *Wheatland Riot.*

La Brea Pits, bogs of subterranean oil and tar located in Hancock Park in Los Angeles. As evidence of the geology♦ of California they contain Pleistocene and Ice Age remains of saber-toothed tigers, giant ground sloths, elephants, and other prehistoric animals, first discovered in 1906. The pits themselves were seen by Portolá (1769) and their tar (Spanish: *brea*) was used by Mexican settlers, as it had been by Indians. A great deal of oil has been pumped from the area, partly by Allan Hancock,♦ who owned the land and gave the park to the city (1916). The seeps of tar were activated anew by the San Fernando earthquake of 1971. The George C. Page Museum of La Brea Discoveries was opened in 1977.

Lachryma Montis, Sonoma home of Gen. Mariano G. Vallejo, a Victorian mansion he built in 1851 and inhabited as a patriarchal estate until his death (1890). His children sold it to the state and it now has an adjoining museum. The General gave it the Latin name "tear of the mountain" because its water came from a mountain spring. For a time he made a wine bearing that name.

LAEMMLE, CARL (1867–1939), German-born motion picture producer (1909 ff.), credited with introducing the star system. He headed Universal Pictures, producer of the first five-reel film (1912), and created Universal City, the largest studio of the day (1915), in the San Fernando Valley.

Laguna Beach, oceanside resort city of Orange County, known for its quaint shops, craft studios, and art galleries. It sponsors a summer art festival featuring dramatic tableaux with actors posed in living representations of famous paintings. The 1970 population was 14,550.

Laguna Mountains, range in the southeastern part of Cleveland National Forest in San Diego County.

La Jolla, oceanside community north of San Diego, known for its fine residences, the Scripps Institution of Oceanography, the Salk Institute, and the San Diego campus of the University of California.

The site has famous beaches and rocky caves. Its name (pronounced "la hoya") means "the hollow" in Spanish. In 1970 the population was 28,790.

Lake County, formed from part of Napa County (to the south) and incorporated (1861) with Lakeport as county seat. Mendocino County lies on the west and north, Glenn on the east and also north, Colusa and Yolo also on the east, and Sonoma on the south and west. Mt. Saint Helena♦ lies on its southwestern border. Named for and also best known for Clear Lake,♦ this is a resort area, popular for its medicinal springs. The lower part of Mendocino National Forest♦ covers the northern part of the county, where the mountains rise to more than 7,000 feet and where the Eel River is dammed to create Lake Pillsbury, a reservoir. In earlier days borax, mercury, cinnabar, and sulphur were mined in the county, but in modern times the economy depends mainly on tourists, livestock ranching, pear orchards, walnut groves, and other agriculture. The population in 1970 was 19,548. With an area of 806,976 acres, it had 15.5 persons per sq. mi.

Lake Merced, see *Merced, Lake.*

Lake Merritt, see *Merritt, Samuel.*

Lakeport, seat of Lake County, located on Clear Lake, first settled in 1859. It is a resort community with fruit packing and cannery plants. In 1970 the population was 3,005.

Lake Tahoe, located at an elevation of 6,228 feet, partly in Placer and El Dorado counties and partly in Nevada, 21.6 miles long and 12 miles wide. It is of glacial origin and its water flows into the Truckee River. Frémont♦ and Preuss♦ were the first white men to see it (Feb. 14, 1844), and Frémont, having first referred to it simply as Mountain Lake ("so entirely surrounded by mountains that we could not discover an outlet"), formally called it Lake Bonpland in honor of a French botanist who had accompanied Humboldt (Frémont gave Humboldt's name to the adjacent basin river). For political reasons the lake was officially named Lake Bigler, honoring John Bigler,♦ the state's 3rd governor, but his outspoken secessionist views caused J. S. Hittell and others to promote the ostensible original Indian name Tahoe, from the Washo word that means "water" or "lake." The legislature did not rescind the almost forgotten but official name until 1945. Of the many peaks of about 10,000 feet over-

looking the lake, Mt. Tallac♦ is particularly famous, but the whole region and Tahoe National Forest (696,000 acres), like nearby Squaw Valley, is known as a skiing, fishing, hiking, and wilderness area. The lake shore itself has become heavily populated with resorts and small houses in recent years, and the state line boundaries have attracted night clubs because of legal gambling in Nevada, in which about one-third of the lake lies.

Lakers, see *Los Angeles Lakers.*

Lakes, of natural origin are few, but numerous manmade ones are part of the state's systems for conservation and distribution of water. The largest natural body of fresh water lying wholly within the state is Clear Lake, while the largest such body, but located partly in Nevada, is Lake Tahoe. Other major natural lakes are Goose Lake in Modoc County, Eagle Lake in Lassen County, and Mono Lake in Mono County. The major reservoirs of the state from north to south are Clair Engle Lake (Trinity County), Shasta Lake and Whiskeytown Lake (Shasta County), Lake Almanor (Plumas County), Lake Oroville (Butte County), Lake Berryessa (Napa County), Folsom Lake (Placer and El Dorado counties), the Spring Valley Water Co. lakes (San Francisco and San Mateo counties), San Luis Reservoir (Merced County), Millerton Lake (Madera and Fresno counties), Lake Kaweah (Tulare County), Isabella Reservoir (Kern County), Lake Cachuma (Santa Barbara County), Lake Arrowhead and Big Bear Lake (San Bernardino County), Lake Havasu (San Bernardino County), and Lake Elsinore (Riverside County). The Salton Sea is an inland salt water sea. Nearly or entirely dry lake beds include Honey Lake of Lassen County and Searles Lake of San Bernardino County. A small but unusual lake in the center of an urban setting is Lake Merritt in downtown Oakland. *(See also individual entries.)*

Lakewood, residential city between Bellflower and Signal Hill in Los Angeles County, originally an agricultural area. In the period after World War II, real estate developers expanded subdivisions of the 1930s to create great tracts of houses. In 1970 it had a population of 83,025.

L'AMOUR, LOUIS DEARBORN (1908–), North Dakota-born author, long resident in Los Angeles, where he writes for films. Since *Hondo* (1953) he has written some 60 works of Western fiction, enormously popular in paperback editions. Among these works is *The Californios* (1974).

LAMSON, DAVID (1903–75), Stanford University Press executive, accused of murder when his wife was found dead in a bathtub of their house, seemingly bludgeoned (1933). Found guilty, he was sentenced to hang but the verdict was overturned by the state Supreme Court. A second trial ended with a deadlocked jury and two subsequent ones ended as mistrials. Charges were then dropped (1936). He wrote an account after the first trial, *We Who Are About To Die* (1935).

Lancaster, city in north central Los Angeles County on the fringe of Antelope Valley, named by early residents for their original Pennsylvania home town. The population in 1970 was 32,728.

LANDACRE, PAUL [HAMBLETON] (1893–1963), Ohio-born artist resident in Los Angeles beginning in the 1920s. He was known for his wood engravings of California landscapes.

Land grants, see *Ranchos.*

Land of Little Rain, The, fourteen sketches by Mary Austin♦ published in 1903. They present the California area "between the high Sierras south from Yosemite—east and south . . . beyond Death Valley and on illimitably into the Mojave Desert" in moving depictions of the terrain, the people—white and Indian—and the flora and fauna and the ecological relations among them.

Land of Sunshine, illustrated monthly magazine, founded (1894) in Los Angeles to promote southern California. After its first six months, editorship was assumed by Charles F. Lummis,♦ with the outlook that "Southern California grows brains as well as oranges." Until his departure (1909), he broadened the journal's scope (indicated by a change of name to *Out West,* 1902) to treat the Southwest (i.e. Arizona and New Mexico) and got notable contributors, including Mary Austin, Ina Coolbrith, Edwin Markham, Joaquin Miller, Charles Warren Stoddard, and, as illustrators, Maynard Dixon and William Keith. Although George Wharton James was one of the editors after Lummis, the magazine dwindled, particularly after 1917, until it finally expired (1935) after a merger with the state's other major early regional journal under the title *Overland Monthly and Out West* (1923).

Landmarks Club, see *Lummis, Charles Fletcher.*

LANE, FRANKLIN K[NIGHT] (1864–1921), reared in Napa and Oakland after moving (1871) from his native Canada. After graduation from Hastings College of the Law, he became San Francisco's city and county attorney. His reformist views caused President T. Roosevelt to name him to the Interstate Commerce Commission. President Wilson appointed him Secretary of the Interior, in which post he worked for conservation and for the release of Indians as individuals from government guardianship. His approval of the Hetch Hetchy reservoir♦ stirred much opposition.

LANE, LEVI COOPER, see *Cooper, Elias S.*

LANGE, DOROTHEA (1895–1965), New Jersey-born photographer, went to California (1918) and established a studio in San Francisco. There she married Maynard Dixon.♦ Her poignant photographs of Depression scenes in the 1930s, particularly of migrant laborers for the Farm Security Administration, were published in *An American Exodus* (1940), in which she collaborated with the agricultural economist Paul Taylor (1895–   ), whom she married in 1935. She later took a series of photographs of Japanese remanded to Relocation Centers.

LANGSDORFF, GEORG HEINRICH VON (1774–1852), German-born physician who accompanied Rezanov♦ on his voyage of 1806 to San Francisco Bay. There he made skillful drawings and persuaded others of the expedition to do so, in order to depict the settlements and the Indians of the region. Engravings made from his drawings appeared in his *Observations on a Journey Around the World* (1812).

LANKERSHIM, ISAAC (1819–82), German-born pioneer of southern California agriculture. He moved to California (1854) and within a decade possessed vast ranches in San Diego and Fresno counties and the San Fernando Valley. For his great crops, he built the first flour mill in Los Angeles (1878). In his enterprises he was associated with his son-in-law, Isaac Van Nuys,♦ and his son, James B[oon] Lankershim (1850–1931). His son later developed real estate through his Lankershim Land and Water Co. and became active in the banking and business life of Los Angeles.

LA PÉROUSE, JEAN FRANÇOIS DE GALAUP, COMTE DE (1741–88?), French navigator who, after service against the British in the Seven Years' War and the American Revolution, was sent by the French government on an expedition for geographic, scientific, and commercial purposes (1785). In Sept. 1786 his two vessels went from Alaska to Monterey. The first foreigners to visit Alta California since Drake in 1579, they were welcomed as French allies. For 10 days his geologists and botanists collected specimens and made drawings and he observed the fertility and mild climate of the region, while also reporting the high ideals of the missionaries but their harsh treatment of the Indians in his *Voyage autour du monde* (1787). His ships and he were lost in 1788.

LAPLACE, CYRILLE PIERRE THÉODORE (1793–1875), French naval officer in command of *l'Artémise* on scientific expeditions that took him to California's ports twice (1837, 1839). His reports with his own drawings were published as *Voyage autour du monde . . .* (5 vols., 1833–39) and *Campagne de circumnavigation* (3 vols., 1841–44).

La Purísima Concepción, eleventh of the 21 missions♦ to be founded, established near the present Lompoc on Dec. 8, 1787, the Feast of the Immaculate Conception. It was therefore given the full title *La Purísima Concepción de Maria Santísima.* The early buildings were destroyed by an earthquake and its resultant flood water (1812) so the mission was moved to the other side of the Santa Ynez River about four miles from its original site. The new buildings, erected (1815–18) with unusually thick walls intended to be earthquake resistant, had a long, low colonnade rather than the more common quadrangular form, perhaps because the linear shape was considered easier to escape from during an earthquake. The mission had a large Indian population, which revolted (1824) against the soldiers and took over the entire structure for almost a month, until defeated in a battle in which sixteen Indians were killed. After secularization, the mission was bought by John Temple♦ and it slowly crumbled away. Almost nothing was left when restoration was undertaken (1935–41), though it is the largest mission structure now standing.

La Quinta, winter resort and residential community in desert country surrounded by the Santa Rosa Mts., lying to the west of Coachella in Riverside County.

Lark, The, little magazine published (1895–97) by *Les Jeunes,* gay, whimsical aesthetes led by Gelett Burgess,♦ who created for the journal drawings of "Goops" and light verse. His best-known contribution was "The Purple Cow," followed some time later by another quatrain: Ah, yes, I wrote the "Pur-

ple Cow"—/I'm Sorry, now, I wrote it;/But I can tell you Anyhow / I'll Kill you if you Quote it! /

LARKIN, THOMAS OLIVER (1802–58), born in Massachusetts, lived in the Carolinas, went to California (1832) to join his half-brother, John R. Cooper.♦ On shipboard he met a widow, Mrs. Rachel Holmes, whom he married, she thus becoming the first woman from the U.S. to live in California, and their son, Thomas Oliver, Jr., becoming the first child of U.S. parents born in California (April 13, 1834). Larkin himself became prosperous through a store and his trade with Mexico and the Sandwich Islands. Unlike other men from the U.S., he did not become a Mexican citizen, although he quietly supported Alvarado's revolution of 1836 for a free and sovereign California. As an American he served the U.S. as consul (1844–48) and confidential agent, with a secret order from Secretary of State Buchanan (1845) to welcome California if it should again assert independence. His propaganda campaign was overwhelmed by the outbreak of the Mexican War. He served as a delegate to the Constitutional Convention of 1849 and was kept busy by his property in San Francisco and Benicia (which he helped found) and his large *ranchos.* He is said to have introduced the Monterey colonial♦ style of architecture, whose sole Mexican feature was the use of adobe. His *Papers* (10 vols., 1951–64) were edited by George P. Hammond.

LASKY, JESSE L. (1880–1958), San Francisco-born pioneer producer of motion pictures. With his brother-in-law Samuel Goldwyn,♦ he formed his first company, which became Paramount Pictures. After losing control of it in the Depression, he continued as a major film producer for other firms.

LASSEN, PETER (1800–59), Danish-born pioneer, came to the U.S. (1831), went overland to Oregon (1839), and then by ship to Fort Ross (1840) and other California settlements. Part of the time he pursued his trade as blacksmith for Sutter, but finally he settled on a *rancho* granted by Gov. Micheltorena south of the present Red Bluff. He went to Missouri (1847) and returned (1848) with settlers for his ranch, where he laid out Benton City. They became members of the state's first Masonic lodge which he established there, but his followers were drawn off by the gold rush. His pioneering in the present Tehama County and in the county honoring him led to his name being perpetuated also in a trail he established, a creek, a volcanic peak (10,453 feet high) located in a 163-square-mile national park, a national forest, and other sites. He was murdered while seeking a silver mine.

Lassen County, formed from parts of Plumas and Shasta counties, which lie south and west, respectively, with Modoc County and the state of Nevada on the north and east. It was incorporated (1864) with Susanville as the county seat. Named for the pioneer Peter Lassen,♦ the region was crossed by emigrant trails. Joseph Bruff♦ named the largest lake for his friend George Derby, but it is properly titled Honey Lake for the aphis liquid found on neighboring wild oats. The county was briefly the site of a gold rush (1855). The early settler Isaac Roop♦—for whose daughter Susanville is named—projected an independent Territory of Nataqua♦ (1856) for the region. This led to the Sagebrush War (1863) and then to the formation of the present county. The county includes a small portion of Lassen Volcanic National Park within Lassen National Forest, as well as the southern part of Modoc National Forest. The mainstays of the economy are livestock and poultry raising and lumbering. In 1970 the population was 16,796; with an area of 2,919,296 acres, it had 3.6 persons per sq. mi.

Lassen Volcanic National Park, straddling southern Shasta and Lassen counties and within the Lassen National Forest (1,200,000 acres). Lassen Peak, rising to 10,457 feet, was active between 1914 and 1921, and is the only live volcano in the continental U.S. The park contains remnants of Mt. Tehama, a vast volcano of prehistoric times, and numerous fumeroles, hot springs, lava beds, and other evidences of volcanic action.

Last spike, see *Gold spike.*

Last Tycoon, The, novel by F. Scott Fitzgerald left incomplete at his death (1940) but published as a fragment the following year. An outgrowth of his time (1937–38) as a scenario writer, it portrays a great motion picture magnate, Monroe Stahr, a founder of the film industry, and makes the story of his career and its Hollywood setting into a symbolic treatment of American life. The novel was adapted for the screen by British dramatist Harold Pinter. Fitzgerald also wrote seventeen comic stories about Pat Hobby, a corrupt author for films, which were published in *Esquire,* and his own life in Hollywood has been the subject of several memoirs and studies.

LASUÉN, FERMÍN FRANCISCO DE (1720–1803), Spanish-born friar attached to a mission at Loreto,

Baja California, from 1768 until 1773, when he went north to serve successively at San Gabriel, San Juan Capistrano, and San Diego until 1785. In that year, after the death of Serra, he was elected Father-President of all Alta California missions. During his 18-year term he built many fine churches to replace the earlier crude structures, increased the number of missions from 9 to 18, and more than doubled the Indians attached to them, their population rising to some 20,000. He was praised as a determined though gentle-mannered, pious, and capable administrator. Point Fermin of San Pedro Bay was named for him by Vancouver.

LATHAM, MILTON SLOCUM (1827–82), practiced law in his native Ohio and in Alabama before going to California (1850). He was elected to Congress (1853–55) and served as President Pierce's Collector of the San Francisco Port (1855–57) before being elected governor. He held the post only from Jan. 9 to 14, 1860, when he was chosen by the legislature to fill the vacancy in the U.S. Senate caused by the death of Broderick. As a senator he defended slavery, impugned the North, and proposed an independent California, but after the war began he usually supported war measures, although he opposed Lincoln. Failing reelection, he became a San Francisco banker and railroad magnate and later, in New York, president of that city's Mining and Stock Exchange.

Laurel, evergreen tree different from the European laurel or the true bay, although given both names in California. It grows up to 100 feet tall with many branches and a wide-spreading, dense crown. It has fragrant flowers, pungently aromatic leaves like the true bay, and yields a volatile oil. Indians used both the leaves and its fruity kernels for food and medicine. It grows near water in coastal areas and on the western slopes of the Sierra below 5,000 feet. Its commonness has led to twenty-five California place-names embodying the word laurel; it is also called pepperwood and Oregon myrtle.

LAUREL and HARDY, comedy team composed of Stan Laurel (1890–1965) and Oliver Hardy (1892–1957), born in England and Georgia, respectively, who were residents of Hollywood from 1913 and 1917, acting at the Hal Roach Studios before they began their team roles (1927). Then for more than twenty years there issued from Hollywood numerous films in which the slight, frightened Laurel and the portly, bullying Hardy were caught up in a series of situations that they wanted to cope with together;

however, they always ended in fantastic opposition to each other as they stumbled into misadventures that created dreadful shambles.

Lava Beds National Monument, reserve of 46,162 acres in Modoc and Siskiyou counties, established in 1925. The region, formed by prehistoric volcanoes, has many chasms and caves which served as fortresses and trenches for the Modoc♦ Indians in their last battles against U.S. Army forces (1872–73).

LAVENDER, DAVID (1910–　), historian of the West whose books include *The Big Divide* (1948); *Bent's Fort* (1954); *Westward Vision: The Story of the Oregon Trail* (1963); *The Rockies* (1968); *California: Land of New Beginnings* (1972); and *Nothing Seemed Impossible* (1975), a life of William C. Ralston.

La Verne, residential and citrus packing community southwest of Claremont (Los Angeles County). It was first called Lordsburg for a developer during the Santa Fe Railroad land boom of the 1890s, then renamed (1916) for a later real estate subdivider. La Verne College (founded 1891) is a coeducational Dunkard Baptist institution. The Rev. Bob Richards♦ was a faculty member while establishing pole vault records.

LAWRENCE, ERNEST O[RLANDO] (1901–58), went to the University of California, Berkeley, as a professor of physics (1928), where he invented (1929) and developed the cyclotron for his pioneering research in nuclear physics. In 1936 he became the director of the radiation laboratory named for him after his death. In 1938 he was awarded the Nobel Prize in physics.

Lawrence Berkeley Laboratory, an outgrowth of the invention of the cyclotron (1929) by Ernest O. Lawrence,♦ located in the upper hills of the University of California, Berkeley, campus. The generation of high energy beams of nuclear particles for exploring the atomic nucleus was first successfully achieved in 1931. Larger, more complex or specialized instrumentation (e.g. the Bevatron, 1954) permitted further achievements: extension of the Periodic Chart of Elements from 93 to 103; discovery of the antiproton and the antineutron; identification of new particles of matter; use of radioisotopes in biology, medicine, agriculture, and industry; and pioneering work on the atom bomb. The staff of more than 3,000 persons has included

seven Nobel Prize winners. Related laboratories for applied research and development of nuclear weapons are the Los Alamos Scientific Laboratory (N.M.), founded in 1943, and the Lawrence Livermore Laboratory, founded in 1952. In 1973 the Lawrence Berkeley Laboratory entered the fields of environmental and energy research.

Lawrence Radiation Laboratory, see *Lawrence Berkeley Laboratory.*

LAWSON, ANDREW C[OOPER] (1861–1952), Scottish-born, Canadian-educated professor of geology at the University of California, Berkeley (1890–1928), noted for his studies of the state's geology and of earthquake origins and actions.

LAZZERI, TONY (ANTHONY MICHAEL LAZZERI) (1903–46), San Francisco-born baseball player, second baseman for the Yankees (1926–37), Chicago Cubs, Dodgers, and Giants. In each of seven seasons he drove in over 100 runs.

LEA, HOMER (1876–1912), born in Colorado, educated in California public schools and at College of the Pacific, Occidental College, and Stanford, where he became interested both in China and in military tactics. In 1899 he became involved in the relief of Peking during the Boxer Rebellion and was made a general in the revolutionary army under Sun Yatsen, even though he was a frail hunchback. His writings included *The Valor of Ignorance* (1909), warning the U.S. against a Japanese attack, and *The Day of the Saxon* (1912), similarly cautioning the British Empire against Oriental threats. He returned to live in southern California, where he died.

Lead, metal commonly obtained in California with the mining of silver and zinc, first produced in the Panamint Range by Mormons (1859). Major deposits worked later came from many parts of Inyo County, but the state's total output does not amount to even 1% of U.S. production.

Leather, see *Cattle, Hide trade,* and *Tanning.*

Leather-jacket soldiers, translation of *soldados de cuera,* the name given to Portolá's troops, who wore sleeveless jackets of deerhide, horsehide, or cowhide as protection against Indian arrows. The troops were also known as great equestrians, riding horses that were equipped with leather aprons fastened to the saddles so as to protect the animals' chests and the riders' legs.

LEAVENWORTH, THADDEUS M. (1804?–93), Connecticut-born chaplain of Stevenson's Regiment,◆ with which he went to San Francisco (1847). He was *alcalde* of San Francisco (1848–49) but after investigation by Gov. Riley for alleged sympathies for the Hounds◆ and land speculators, he resigned his post. Nevertheless, a city street is named for him. He later lived on a *rancho* adjoining Vallejo's Lachryma Montis.

LEBRUN, RICO (1900–1964), Italian-born painter, moved to the U.S. (1924), where he became a commercial artist, then to Los Angeles (1938), where he taught at the Chouinard Institute and was a leading animator for Walt Disney. He also established a reputation for his bold, sculpturesque paintings of human figures which show the influence of Goya and Picasso. His subjects included the Crucifixion, Nazi concentration camps, and a fresco of Genesis (at Pomona College).

LE CONTE, JOHN (1818–91), after teaching and practicing medicine in his native Georgia and serving in the Confederate Army, went to California (1869) as a professor of physics at the new University of California, whose president he later became (1876–81). His brother was Joseph Le Conte.

LE CONTE, JOSEPH (1823–1901), studied under Agassiz at Harvard and became a professor of natural sciences in his native Georgia and at several other southern institutions, until, like his brother John, he moved to California (1869). There he served as a professor at the state university for the rest of his life, a popular and beloved teacher of geology and natural history. His scholarly work was concerned with the origins of mountain systems, but he was most widely known for his attempts to reconcile Darwinism and Christianity in some of his courses and in *Religion and Science* (1874). Among the students significantly affected by his concept of a higher and a lower nature in man was Frank Norris, who employed the theory in *McTeague* and *Vandover and the Brute*. Le Conte also wrote an *Autobiography* (1903) and a journal of experiences in the Confederate Army, *'Ware Sherman* (1937). His son, Joseph Nisbet LeConte (1870–1950), a professor of mechanical engineering at Berkeley (1892–1937), was always known as "Little Joe."

LEE, ARCHY (1837?–73), black slave who was taken to California (1857) from his native Mississippi by his master, Charles Stovall, and the next year became the subject of a major fugitive slave case. California's community of 3,000 to 4,000 free blacks financed his defense, whose attorneys included Col. Edward D. Baker, Elisha Crosby, and Edwin B. Crocker. A complicated set of hearings and trials adverse to Lee finally led to a definitive decision by a federal commissioner that Lee was free.

LEE, SAMMY (SAMUEL LEE) (1920–), diving champion born in Fresno of Korean parents. After graduation from Occidental College he became an army officer and doctor. He won the high diving competition of the Olympic Games (1948, 52) and, at age 33, was the oldest person ever to receive the Sullivan Award for the outstanding U.S. amateur athlete of the year.

LEESE, JACOB P[RIMER] (1809–92), Ohio-born merchant in the Santa Fe trade, expanded his business into a partnership with Hugo Reid◆ in Los Angeles and Monterey in 1834. Two years later he moved to Yerba Buena, and began a partnership with William S. Hinckley◆ and Nathan Spear◆ to trade hides and tallow for goods from Yankee ships. In 1836 he constructed a home that was the first substantial structure in San Francisco (at present Clay St. and Grant Ave.) near the simple canvas and board house that William A. Richardson had built the year before. Leese was naturalized (1837) and married a sister of Gen. Vallejo. Dissolving his partnership and then selling his business to the Hudson's Bay Co. (1841), he moved to Sonoma, though retaining an 8,880-acre ranch on the San Francisco peninsula. Captured with Vallejo by Edward Kern at the outbreak of the Bear Flag Revolt, he nevertheless remained a stout supporter of the American conquest of California. He was elected *alcalde* of Sonoma but later left California (1865), not to return until his old age. His daughter Rosalia was the first white native-born San Franciscan (1838), according to H. H. Bancroft.

LeFRANC, CHARLES, see *Masson, Paul.*

Legion of Honor, see *California Palace of the Legion of Honor.*

Legislative Analyst, officer of the state legislature (a post created in 1941) charged with analysis of the governor's budget and all appropriation bills, as well as investigation of the functioning and efficiency of administrative agencies. He is appointed by the Legislative Budget Committee, composed of five senators and five assemblymen.

Legislative Assembly for the District of San Francisco, grew out of a public meeting in Portsmouth

Square (Feb. 12, 1849) animated by Sen. Thomas Hart Benton's public letter to the people of California contending that with the end of the war the people had a right to be rid of military authority and to govern themselves. As commander of the Pacific Division and therefore military governor of California, Gen. Persifor Smith♦ argued that a change of government could be made only by Congress; by refusing to recognize the Assembly he held off plans for a Constitutional Convention.

Legislature, see *Assembly, Senate,* and *Legislative Analyst.*

Legislature of 1,000 Drinks, the first state legislative session (1849–50) was so called because one of its members, Sen. Thomas Jefferson Green, formerly of Texas, then of Sacramento, made several motions to ''adjourn and take 1,000 drinks'' at his expense as part of his campaign to be elected major general of the state militia. The legislature met in San Jose, then the state capital.

LEHMANN, LOTTE (1888–1976), German-born opera singer, also famous for her recitals of lieder, left her native land (1939) with the rise of the Nazis and became an American citizen (1945). She made her home thereafter in Santa Barbara where she became a teacher of master singing classes.

LEIDESDORFF, WILLIAM ALEXANDER (1810–48), native of the Virgin Islands whose father was a Danish planter and whose mother was black. He went to San Francisco (1841) in command of an American schooner after making a fortune in New Orleans as a cotton broker. In San Francisco he built the City Hotel and a large warehouse, and acquired 35,000 acres of land on the American River. He was appointed the city's treasurer, chairman of the school board that opened the first public school, and U.S. vice-consul under Thomas Larkin. Leidesdorff died of typhus, and a small downtown San Francisco street was named for him.

Lelia Byrd, see *Shaler, W. J.*

Lemon growing, see *Citrus fruit growing.*

Lemoore Naval Air Station, located at a small agricultural and former wool shipping center in Kings County, named for its founder, Dr. Lavern Lee Moore (1875).

LEONARD, ZENAS (1809–57), Pennsylvania-born trapper and mountain man. In 1833 he joined the

expedition of Capt. Bonneville♦ to the Far West and was a member of the detachment under Joseph Walker♦ that went to California. They were the first white men to make a westward crossing of the Sierra Nevada (1833–34) and perhaps the first to see Yosemite and the Sequoias. Leonard wrote of this voyage and of his visits to the California missions in his *Narrative of Zenas Leonard* (1839). He later engaged in fur trading and storekeeping in Missouri.

Letter sheets, souvenir stationery issued (c. 1849–69) in the form of pictorial writing paper (generally light blue) which often (to 1855) folded to form a self-made envelope. Lithographs and wood engravings of local scenes and situations left room for only brief letters home, the illustrations obviously being considered equally informative about the newly settled land. There were over 300 different subjects (some by prominent artists like C. C. Nahl), but probably the most commonly reprinted was ''The Miner's Ten Commandments,'' written by James M. Hutchings of *Hutchings' California Magazine.*♦ Frederick Marriott♦ was another journal publisher who got his start issuing letter sheets.

Lettuce, commercially grown in California only since about 1910, is a crop in which the state now leads the nation. In the 1920s the Salinas Valley began to be an important growing area; it now produces during the months of May through November between one-third and one-half of the nation's supply. Lettuce is also grown in the Imperial Valley, the west side of the San Joaquin Valley, Ventura County, and Pajaro Valley. The crop in 1970 was harvested on 145,600 acres and was worth $148,104,000. It has been cultivated and harvested by migratory workers, Mexican, Japanese, and Filipino, mainly. Attempts at unionization began as early as the 1920s and continued sporadically, but only met with success in the 1970s under the leadership of Cesar Chavez.♦

Leucadia, oceanside community in San Diego County. It was founded by English settlers (1885), who named it for the Ionian island on which Sappho supposedly died.

Levering Act, loyalty oath formulated by Assemblyman Harold Levering and passed by the state legislature (1950) in the aftermath of the Loyalty Oath Dispute♦ of the University of California. Unlike the university oath, the Act did not single out any group but required all state employees to swear that they did not themselves advocate or belong to an organization advocating the overthrow of the state or federal government by force or violence. In 1952 it was incorporated into the state Constitution, but in 1967 the California Supreme Court declared it unconstitutional.

Levi's, trademark for blue denim trousers, copper-riveted at points of strain. Created initially by Levi Strauss (1830–1902), a German-born merchant who went to San Francisco (1850), where the family-run firm continues to be based. It still emphasizes the basic jeans, although it also manufactures other kinds of clothing and is a leader in the nation's apparel industry.◆

LEVY, A[CHILLE] (1853–1922), Alsatian-born Jewish emigrant to California (1874) who settled as a poor boy in Hueneme. There in time he created an agricultural brokerage business, which led him to found a firm that came to be known as the Bank of A. Levy (1905). It has remained a leading institution in Ventura County.

LEWIS, GILBERT N[EWTON] (1875–1946), professor of chemistry at the University of California, Berkeley (1912–46), and contributor to its distinction in that field.

LEWIS, OSCAR (1893–), San Francisco-born author, a prolific local historian whose many studies of his native region include *The Big Four* (1938); *Silver Kings* (1947), about the capitalists of the Comstock Lode; *Sea Routes to the Gold Fields* (1949); and *Bay Window Bohemia* (1956). His locally set fiction includes *I Remember Christine* (1942), and he edited many works for The Book Club of California.

LICK, JAMES (1796–1876), born in Pennsylvania, moved to California (1847) from Chile, where he had lived for some years and had made a small fortune from piano building and other ventures. Settling in San Francisco, he became very wealthy through investments in real estate in and around the city. He built a fine flour mill in San Jose, established a vineyard in the Santa Clara Valley, bought property at Lake Tahoe and in Virginia City, Nevada, had a great *rancho* that included present Griffith Park in Los Angeles, and for a time owned Santa Catalina Island. He built San Francisco's first luxury hotel, Lick House (opened 1862), and a handsome home for himself, but lived very frugally as a bachelor. He bequeathed some of his wealth to establish a technical school with practical workshops for boys and

girls, which later merged with one founded by J. C. Wilmerding◆ and now bears both their names. He also left bequests to the Society of California Pioneers, of which he had been president, and to various other local charities and organizations, but most of his fortune went to create the observatory on Mt. Hamilton that bears his name. He is buried there in the base, which supports a large telescope.

Lick Observatory, astronomical facility funded by James Lick and presented to the University of California in 1888. Situated on the 4,261-foot peak of Mt. Hamilton,◆ east of San Jose, it serves as both a research and a graduate teaching facility of the state university, associated with its Santa Cruz campus.

LIENHARD, HEINRICH (1822–1903), Swiss settler (1846) who worked for Sutter and later in the mines and in Sacramento and San Francisco. He returned to Switzerland (1850) and later lived in Nauvoo, Ill. His recollections of California, published in German (Switzerland, 1898), were translated as *A Pioneer at Sutter's Fort* (1941).

Lieutenant Governor, elected at the same time and for the same term as the governor and with the same required qualifications for office. The position is much like that of the Vice President of the U.S., for both exist largely to take over if the chief executive dies, resigns, is incapacitated, or impeached and convicted. It is not necessary for the lieutenant governor to be of the same political party as the governor.

Lighthouses, stations for navigational aid, first developed after the gold rush brought great numbers of ships to California. Between 1852 and 1854 seven structures were built in California with congressional funds. They were located at Alcatraz and Fort Point in San Francisco Bay, on the Farallon Islands, at Point Pinos, in the harbor of Humboldt Bay, at Point Concepcion, and at Point Loma in San Diego County. Others soon followed (e.g. one in 1855 at Point Bonita, the northeast extremity of the Golden Gate). They were once administered by the U.S. Lighthouse Service but later came under the jurisdiction of the Coast Guard. Modern stations have radio beacons as well as lights and foghorns. In 1970 there were 24 stations stretching from St. George Reef, north of Crescent City, to Point Loma, south of San Diego.

Lima beans, see *Beans.*

Limantour Case, litigation arising from fraudulent land claims of José Yves Limantour, a Frenchman resident in Mexico and engaged in trade to Alta California during its administration by Gov. Micheltorena♦ (1842–45). The grants of 600,000 acres ostensibly made by that governor to Limantour included four square leagues south of present California Street in San Francisco, much of the Bay, and all of the Farallon Islands. The San Francisco city and Bay parts of the claim were upheld by the Lands Commission of 1856 and Limantour sold many quitclaims on that basis. With some of the money he fled to Mexico (1857) when the U.S. government found the documents' seals to be forged and Micheltorena's signature to have been added by him long after his governorship.

Limes, brought to California by the early mission fathers. They have been cultivated and marketed much like other citrus fruits.♦

Limestone, see *Cement.*

Lincoln-Roosevelt League, Republican party reform organization founded (1907) by Chester H. Rowell,♦ Edward A. Dickson,♦ and Francis J. Heney♦ to free the party of Southern Pacific dominance, to select convention delegates pledged to Roosevelt's policies, to elect U.S. Senators by popular vote, and to hold primaries for the nomination of all state and local offices. It achieved its ends and helped elect Hiram Johnson governor. It continued to be influential and effective for about a decade.

LINDLEY, CURTIS HOLBROOK (1850–1920), born in Marysville and educated at the University of California. He became a prominent lawyer and was best known for his *Treatise on the American Law Relating to Mines and Mineral Lands* (1897), the outstanding authority on its subject.

Lion Country Safari, tourist attraction north of San Juan Capistrano. This commercially operated 500-acre wild animal preserve is arranged so that visitors drive their cars through an area in which the animals roam free.

LISSNER, MEYER (1871–1930), San Francisco-born lawyer and political leader whose entire career was spent in Los Angeles. There he was active in political reform as an organizer of the Lincoln-Roosevelt League (1907), an associate of Hiram Johnson, and a member of the national executive committee of the Progressive party (1912–16).

Literature, began in the Spanish and Mexican periods with an infrequent book, like Palóu's life of Serra, written and printed in Mexico, and such slight works as the conventional *pastoreles* enacted at Christmas, or a brief anonymous poem like one printed by Zamorano in 1836.

More significant than the locally produced writings were those of visitors, including, first, English, French, and German explorers, later, the works of visitors including the *Personal Narrative* (1831) of James Ohio Pattie, the *Narrative of Zenas Leonard* (1839), Alexander Forbes' *California* (1839), and, most consequential of all, Richard Henry Dana's *Two Years Before the Mast* (1840), which attracted the interest of many Americans and influenced a book by one of their few local residents, Alfred Robinson's *Life in California* (1846).

Although Americans involved in the Mexican War published accounts of the region, like Frémont's *Geographical Memoir* (1848), Edwin Bryant's *What I Saw in California* (1848), and Walter Colton's *Three Years in California* (1849), not until the gold rush brought a large foreign population, mainly from the U.S., did the written word flourish locally. It appeared initially in two journals, the *Californian* (1846) and *California Star* (1847), then in the first book in English to be printed in California, written by a Pole naturalized as an American citizen, Felix Paul Wierzbicki, and bearing the descriptive title, *California As It Is, And As It May Be* (1849).

The first journal to aim at the publication of writing not merely functional or directly descriptive was the *Golden Era* (1852), and it attracted contributions from the new state's first literary figures. These included Bret Harte, who published his first important story, "M'liss," in its pages, and Alonzo Delano, the humorist, followed later by Mark Twain, Prentice Mulford, Fitz Hugh Ludlow, Charles Warren Stoddard, and Joaquin Miller, each of whom established a significant reputation in books published during the 1860s or later.

This journal was soon followed by *The Pioneer,* founded in 1854, which became well known for issuing the writings of Dame Shirley, a perceptive, romantic, and witty memoirist, and the broadly humorous George Derby. Two years later appeared another periodical of some literary pretensions, *Hutchings' California Magazine,* but the most significant literary journal did not appear until 1868, when the *Overland Monthly* was founded with Bret Harte as its editor. Not only did it print his stories, later collected in *The Luck of Roaring Camp* (1870), and his popular poem, "Plain Language from Truthful James," but during its first two years it published contributions from J. Ross Browne, Ina Coolbrith (an associate editor), Clarence King, E. R. Sill, and other leading figures of the local literary life.

The novel settings and unusual frontier attitude of mind emphasized in the *Overland Monthly* and in Harte's local color fiction were also popularized in the lustier humor of Mark Twain's "The Celebrated Jumping Frog of Calaveras County" and *Roughing It* (1872). For a time the flamboyant poetry of Joaquin Miller, like his romantically dramatic prose work, *Life Amongst the Modocs* (1873), also won many followers, abroad as well as at home. Save for Miller, most of these writers moved away after their reputations were first made through emphasis upon distinctively western materials.

They were succeeded in the 1880s and 90s by authors with different points of view. These included the cynical survey of the local scene by Ambrose Bierce, also famous for his macabre stories, and formal historians' consideration of the regional past, as exemplified by the works of Hubert Howe Bancroft, T. H. Hittell, and C. H. Shinn. The past also had its romantic interpretation in the novel *Ramona* (1884), the by-product of Helen Hunt Jackson's work to aid dispossessed and victimized Indians. Appreciation of the natural scene remained an important subject, as John Muir considered the mountains of California more fully than had the earlier Clarence King and Thomas Starr King, and as Charles Fletcher Lummis expatiated on the beauties of the Southwest, but much of the writing at the turn of the century came from younger authors with new interests.

The note of social protest was sounded by Edwin Markham in his rhetorical poem, "The Man with the Hoe" (1899), and it was heard at greater length and with more realism in the fiction of Frank Norris, one of whose novels, *The Octopus* (1901), featured a character partly modeled on Markham. Strong and striking examples of social protest, both social and individualistic, also came from Jack London in his popular novels, *The Sea Wolf* (1904), *The Iron Heel* (1907), and *Martin Eden* (1909). Less impressive than Norris and London but also popular as a novelist was Gertrude Atherton, whose fiction, often with California settings and themes, was considered daring for a woman of the time.

Quite different was Mary Austin, whose writings displayed social consciousness and mysticism, as well as the exaltation of the primitive evident in her *Land of Little Rain* (1903). She was a founder of the artistic colony at Carmel, as was George Sterling, much esteemed as a Bohemian and for such grandiose poetry as *The Testimony of the Suns* (1903). To this quiet community later came Robinson Jeffers, the far more significant poet, whose long verse tragedies like *Tamar* (1924) and intense lyrics made a deeply symbolic use of settings along the California coast. Some different aspects of the California scene, as well as those of the U.S. at large, were viewed in other ways by the socialist Upton Sinclair, whose novels, like *Oil!* (1927), were tracts aimed at reform.

The local scene appeared only occasionally in the plays of Sidney Howard, but the Napa Valley was the setting for his *They Knew What They Wanted* (1924), the major contribution to the history of California's theater♦ and the first work by a Californian to win a Pulitzer Prize. That distinguished award was not granted to another Californian until it was won by John Steinbeck for his epic novel, *The Grapes of Wrath* (1939), presenting the plight of migratory agricultural workers during the Depression. A Pulitzer Prize was also offered to William Saroyan for *The Time of Your Life* (1939), but was refused as a patronizing example of the commercialism opposed by that play and in his free-flowing stories. The Pulitzer Prize has since been given to several other Californians, whose very variety is indicative not only of the changing criteria of the judges but of the great breadth of California literature. Wallace Stegner, a professor of English at Stanford, and author of fiction, biography, and history, won the award for his novel, *Angle of Repose* (1971), drawing on the life of Mary Hallock Foote, while Gary Snyder, a San Francisco poet dedicated to cultural values of the Orient, was granted the prize for his *Turtle Island* (1974).

Other writers of distinction and diversity and winners of other national awards have included George R. Stewart, known for his fiction about the natural scene, like *Storm* (1941), and historical studies like *Ordeal by Hunger* (1936), about the Donner Party; Henry Miller, a celebrant of personal freedom, who was an older idol for members of the Beat movement of the 1950s, to which Allen Ginsberg was allied; while other leading figures include Robert Duncan, William Everson, Josephine Miles, George Oppen, and Kenneth Rexroth among poets, Richard Brautigan and Evan Connell among authors of fiction, and Scott Momaday, who has drawn upon his Indian heritage for both his fiction and his poetry. (*See also individual entries.*)

LITTLE, LAWSON (1910–68), after graduation from Stanford University won the American and British amateur golf championships two years in a row

(1934–35). As a professional he won the U.S. Open championship (1940).

Little Pete, name commonly given to Fong Ching (1865–97), a Cantonese emigrant to San Francisco. He established the corrupt Gi Sin Seer tong and controlled various rackets until he was murdered. Frank Norris wrote an article about his funeral.

LITTLER, GENE (EUGENE ALAN LITTLER) (1930–   ), San Diego-born golfer, U.S. amateur champion (1953). After turning professional (1954) he won many other championships, including the U.S. Open (1962), and in his first twenty years of play earned $921,275 in purses.

LIVERMORE, prominent family founded by the New Englander, Horatio Gates Livermore, who moved from Maine (1849), and his son, Horatio Putnam Livermore, who built dams across the American River near Folsom and thus was a leader in providing power and irrigation. That family has continued to be concerned with public utilities and with conservation. They are not related to Robert Livermore.

LIVERMORE, ROBERT (1799–1858), English sailor who jumped ship in California (1822), married Josefa Higuera (1838), was naturalized (1844), and settled in the valley that came to bear his name. There he obtained a vast grant for a ranch on which he planted vineyards and orchards, and grew rich. The city of Livermore as well as the valley were named after Robert Livermore's family, which is no relation to Horatio Putnam Livermore's family.

Livermore, city in the valley of the same name in Alameda County, long a center for vineyards (e.g. of the Wente family) and wine making, for orchards and cattle raising, and known for its annual rodeo. The University of California's Lawrence Livermore Laboratory (est. 1952) for nuclear weapons research attracted electrical engineering and electronics firms as well as an increased population which created an enlarged residential community. Both the city and the valley were named after the family of Robert Livermore. The population grew from 16,058 in 1960 to 37,703 in 1970.

Livestock, a major part of California agriculture, began with the founding of the missions. Cattle♦ were raised in large numbers on mission lands and on private *ranchos* after secularization in 1833. The padres also imported sheep,♦ the first flock being

brought into California by Rivera y Moncada in 1770. The gold rush gave great impetus to these kinds of livestock raising, virtually initiated dairying,♦ almost began production of swine,♦ greatly increased poultry♦ production, and also had a significant effect upon horse raising.♦

Lizard, tailed reptile like but unrelated to the salamander,♦ exists in California in a number of species, each with its own varieties. The eight major kinds are *alligator, gecko, gila monster, iguanid, legless, night, skink,* and *whiptail.* (1) *Alligator,* distinguished by thick, squarish scales, are found in their three varieties throughout the state. (2) *Gecko,* subtropical and usually nocturnal, distinguished by soft skin and lidless eyes, live in southern California islands, deserts, foothills, and mountains. (3) *Gila monster,* about 18 inches long, is the only venomous lizard, feeding on small mammals, other lizards, and eggs found in the mountains of San Bernardino and Imperial counties. (4) *Iguanid* include about two-thirds of all the state's lizards and have many varieties, among them the *chuckwalla* and *desert,* the only herbiverous kinds; *fringetoed lizards,* residents of the desert; *spiny lizards; western fence lizards,* the most common of all; *horned lizards,* sometimes called *horned toads;* and *tree lizards.* (5) *Legless,* under 8 inches long, feed on insects in the central and southern Coast Ranges, southern San Joaquin Valley, and southern Sierra Nevada, where they are often thought to be snakes. (6) *Night* live in some of the mountains, deserts, and islands of southern California. (7) *Skink,* small and slim, are found throughout northernmost California, in all coast areas, and scattered in southern California. (8) *Whiptail,* slim, long-tailed, and active, are found throughout California except in high mountains and humid areas. Several Indian tribes, including the Koso, Miwok, and Salinans, ate various kinds of lizards.

Llano del Rio, communal society located in Antelope Valley between the Mojave Desert and the San Gabriel Mts. Its name describes the terrain—level ground near a creek. Established (1914) by Job Harriman,♦ a leader of the Socialist Labor party, at its height it had 900 members. Economic differences, particularly occasioned by insufficient water, caused it to dwindle away (1918).

LLOYD, HAROLD (1893–1971), Nebraska-born comedian in Hollywood films for 30 years beginning in 1916. He created a character for himself as an innocent, lanky American boy with horn-rimmed glasses who gets into innumerable scrapes in his attempt to get ahead but who somehow triumphs, even though temporarily driven to frightened acrobatics atop skyscrapers or in other fantastic situations. The titles of his films reveal his persona: *Grandma's Boy* (1922), *Safety Last* (1923), *Girl Shy* (1924), *The Freshman* (1925), *The Kid Brother* (1927), and *Movie Crazy* (1932). After the long period of his film career he was known as one of its wealthiest performers, the owner of a large and lavish estate, and a leader in the order of Shriners.

Lobster, the California species is the spiny lobster, which differs from the Maine variety primarily in its lack of claws. It lives among rocks off the coast from Point Concepcion down through Baja California, and is also found near California's islands. Commercial fishing began toward the end of the 19th century and the average annual catch from 1916 through 1945 was 350,000 pounds, increased by lobsters caught off Mexico but landed in California. In the next decade catches more than doubled but then declined abruptly (1971: 224,486 pounds), partly because both commercial and sport fishermen illegally took many young, small lobsters which had not yet mated.

Locke, town in the tail of Sacramento County, north of Walnut Grove and on the Sacramento River. It was built (1915) by Chinese who worked on adjacent farms and railroads. Its main street, with two-story wooden balconied buildings, presents the classic image of an old mining town, although its residents were workers on the levees. It is still inhabited almost exclusively by Chinese.

LOCKHEED, ALLAN [HAINES] (1889–1969), California-born and self-taught aviator who was known as an exhibition flyer before he began his plane manufacturing career with a seaplane (1911), which he used in a passenger-carrying concession at the Panama-Pacific International Exposition (1915). At Santa Barbara, with his brother Malcolm (1888–1958) and John K. Northrop,♦ he established and was president of Loughead Aircraft Co., bearing the family name he later changed because it was hard to pronounce. As the Lockheed Co. located in Burbank, the firm faced large financial problems, even though it developed the first successful twin-engine passenger seaplane, and the Vega, a monplane used by Amelia Earhart and the Lindberghs. In 1929 both brothers sold their interest in the firm, which in and after World War II became a major element in the aerospace industry and in missile production. In

the 1970s the Burbank-based firm ran into great difficulties, including huge cost overruns on the construction of its C5A transport plane, the world's largest aircraft; bad international business arrangements that nearly sent the firm into bankruptcy, from which it was saved only by the U.S. Congress making its first guarantee of a federal loan to a private company; and revelation of Lockheed's large payments, considered to be bribes, to officials in Japan, Holland, and elsewhere to persuade their nations to buy the company's products.

Lodi, city in north central San Joaquin County, a market center for adjacent vineyards. It is also a community of residences as well as factories for food processing and tire-mold manufacturing. In 1970 the population was 28,691.

LOGAN, JAMES H., see *Berries*.

Loma Linda, community south of San Bernardino. Its origin can be traced to a railroad station (1875–76), but it was not incorporated until 1970. A large Seventh-Day Adventist coeducational university founded there (1905) is known for its medical, dental, nursing, and public health curricula. In 1970 the city had a population of almost 10,000.

LOMBARDI, ERNIE (ERNESTO NATALI LOMBARDI) (1908–77), Oakland-born baseball player, catcher for the Oakland Oaks (1926–30), and later in the major leagues for Brooklyn, Cincinnati (1932–41), Boston, and New York (1942–47). He twice led the National League in hitting (1938, 1942).

Lompoc, city in Santa Barbara County, located in the valley that bears the same Chumash Indian name, near Mission La Purísima. Long known for its great fields of flowers grown for seeds and its annual Flower Festival, in the 1960s and 70s it became a greatly enlarged residential community because of the founding and development of nearby Vandenberg Air Force Base.♦ In 1970 it had a population of 25,284.

LONDON, JACK (JOHN GRIFFITH LONDON) (1876–1916), born in San Francisco, the illegitimate child of William Henry Chaney (1821–1903), an itinerant astrologer, and Flora Wellman, she rearing him with her later husband, John London, in a family without fixed residence or occupation. His formal education temporarily stopped at 14 after grammar school, but he read omnivorously in books often supplied by Ina Coolbrith from the Oakland Public Library during such time as was left after earning a living in a cannery and at other odd jobs.

He also haunted the tough Oakland waterfront, providing background for later works, *Martin Eden* (1909) and *John Barleycorn* (1913), and on his sloop he and a gang raided oyster beds in the Bay, as described in *The Cruise of the Dazzler* (1902), and then turned around to join the harbor police as he also later described in *Tales of the Fish Patrol* (1915). Next he took to wider waters aboard a sealer to Japan. After returning to Oakland and more hard work in a jute mill and other jobs, he became a tramp and was jailed for the first time.

He then had a year of high school in Oakland while also making soapbox speeches as a socialist, leading to another arrest. Thereafter he tried the University of California for a few months, but became disgusted with its seemingly irrelevant instruction, as he later depicted in the novel about his fictive alter ego, Martin Eden. Soon he joined the gold rush to the Klondike (1897), getting to know the situations and kinds of people that provided the background for such fiction as *The Call of the Wild* (1903), *Burning Daylight* (1910), and "To Build a Fire" (1908), a story telling of a newcomer's death on the Yukon trail.

Upon his return to Oakland his writings, giving a Kipling-like portrait of the brutal, vigorous life of the Far North, began to be accepted by the *Overland Monthly* and the *Atlantic Monthly,* and his literary career was well started. His first collection of stories, *The Son of the Wolf* (1900), was followed with great rapidity by many other popular works, so that he suddenly found himself financially successful. He reported the Russo-Japanese War for the Hearst newspapers, made lecture tours, went on sailing voyages to the Caribbean and the South Seas, and began to build a great patriarchal estate in the Valley of the Moon.

Popular works included *The Sea-Wolf* (1904), a novel about a ruthless Nietzschean sea captain; *The Game* (1905), a novel about boxing; *Before Adam* (1906), a novel about prehistoric savages; *White Fang* (1906), a novel complementing *The Call of the Wild* in telling of a wild dog who is tamed; *Smoke Bellew* (1912), a novel about a journalist in the Yukon; *The Iron Heel* (1907), a novel depicting a fascist state eventually overthrown; and *The Valley of the Moon* (1913), a novel presenting a Utopian return to the land as solution to economic problems. In various ways this body of fiction and such nonfictional work as *The People of the Abyss* (1903), about English slum life seen first-hand, and *The War of the Classes* (1907) show his long-

standing adherence to Marxist theory, but they also demonstrate his fascination with the individualistic primitivism of Nietzschean supermen.

London's last years after the blow of having his just-completed mansion burned (1913) were occasionally frenetic as he tried to write too much, and sometimes marked by depression and lassitude, ended by a sudden, wholly unexpected death, said to be by his own hand.

"Lone woman," see *San Nícolás Island.*

Long Beach, second largest city of Los Angeles County, incorporated (1897) as an ocean resort settlement and harbor made from tidelands and sloughs. It has become an important industrial and marine center for packing and processing fish, handling petroleum derived from nearby Signal Hill♦ and offshore wells, and as a port for the U.S. Navy, which has installations on the adjacent Terminal Island♦ and San Pedro.♦ A disastrous earthquake (1933) killed 120 people and destroyed $50,000,000 of property in the city and surrounding area, but Long Beach recovered quickly. Now not only an important commercial and residential city, it is also a major convention center, its tourist attractions including the berthed British liner *Queen Mary,* converted into a Museum of the Sea, and two adobe ranch houses of the Bixby family.♦ The population in 1970 was 358,633.

LONGDEN, JOHNNY (JOHN ERIC LONGDEN) (1907–   ), English-born jockey, reared in Canada, went to California (1931) and later made his home in Arcadia. The first jockey ever to win 6,000 races, his career spanned 40 years (1927–66), and at age 59 he won his last race at Santa Anita. In 1943 he rode Count Fleet to capture the Triple Crown, winning the Belmont Stakes, Kentucky Derby, and Preakness. Only Willie Shoemaker♦ has topped his records.

Longshoremen, initially recruited informally on the docks to handle shipping during the era of the gold rush and clipper ships. As early as 1853, an abortive Riggers and Stevedores Union was formed. Not until the 1880s did real organization of waterfront workers occur, with the founding of the Wharf and Wave Federation (1888), although independent unions had earlier led strikes in San Francisco (1883) and San Pedro (1887), the two ports that have continued to be major harbors. Thereafter, organized longshoremen not only fought against employers over wages, hours, and working conditions, but they battled seamen's unions over jurisdiction and division of interests. Finally, various maritime unions of San Francisco followed the lead of the city's building trades to form a common organization, the City Front Federation (1901), from which, however, the sailors withdrew five years later. Longshoremen's strikes in San Francisco (1919) and San Pedro (1923) were lost and independent unions disappeared until the time of the Depression. Then, under the National Industrial Recovery Act's guarantee of rights to organize and bargain collectively, Harry Bridges♦ formed a new branch of the International Longshoremen's Association♦ in San Francisco (1933). A strike begun on May 9, 1933, within two months developed into a bloody fray, as employers tried to keep the docks open, but finally turned into a General Strike.♦ The union won most of its demands and was thereafter a major power in West Coast shipping. The sailors under Harry Lundeberg,♦ however, left the alliance to join the AF of L, while Bridges led his men and warehouse workers into the CIO organization of the International Longshoremen's and Warehousemen's Union. Successful negotiations with employers kept the San Francisco waterfront free of strikes from 1948 to 1971, when Bridges again led a major strike, once more retaining and consolidating the union's power.

Long tom, see *Placer mining.*

LORD, PAULINE (1890–1950), actress born in Hanford, began her career with the stock company of David Belasco in San Francisco. Her later successes included creation of the title role of Eugene O'Neill's *Anna Christie* and a major part in Sidney Howard's *They Knew What They Wanted.*

Los Angeles, most populous city in the state. Its European heritage dates back to the sighting of its San Petro harbor by Cabrillo (1542), who named it Bahia de los Fumos (Bay of Smokes) because of campfires set by one of the 28 Indian villages within present Los Angeles County, of which Yang-na is known to have been located in the present downtown area. Vizcaíno actually entered the bay (1602), but settlement began only after the Sacred Expedition.

Portolá and Crespí passed through the region (1769), camped on the river they called Porciúncula, and discovered the La Brea tar pits. Their followers founded Mission San Gabriel (1771); later Felipe de Neve established the Pueblo de Nuestra Señora la Reina de Los Angeles de Porciúncula (Town of Our Lady the Queen of the Angels of Porciúncula), whose 44 original settlers (1781) from Sinaloa's lower classes (many of them black or Indian) within 20 years grew to 315 persons resident in 30 adobes, with a new mission (San Fernando) to their north. Small and isolated, the town nevertheless was long Mexican California's most populous pueblo and was considered (1816) for its capital.

During the early 19th century some Americans arrived who were naturalized residents, among them Joseph Chapman, John Temple, Abel Stearns, William Wolfskill, and William Workman. With the outbreak of the Mexican War, the city was quickly seized by the U.S. but as quickly lost when the arbitrary and severe administration of Lt. Archibald Gillespie led to a revolt by the Angelenos. This was ended—after battles, including that of San Pasqual—by a surrender at Cahuenga Pass (1847).

In 1850 the city became the seat of the county of the same name, but the gold rush to the north left it a small frontier town of Spanish-American character. It grew, though slowly, in part because Phineas Banning helped to obtain a port at Wilmington, and faster as it finally got a Southern Pacific rail connection to San Francisco and thus to the eastern U.S. (1876), and then its own railroad, the Santa Fe (1885). Competition between the two lines led to fantastically cheap rates which attracted many midwesterners, most of them delighted by a region whose fine climate allowed oranges to be grown (and profitably) in midwinter. The widespread advertising of real estate dealers resulted in the creation of one new town, settlement, or subdivision after another. The remarkable boom finally collapsed in the late 1880s, but not before the city's population swelled from 11,000 to 50,000 in a decade.

By the end of the century the city had more than 100,000 residents, with many more in outlying territories. Prosperity and population continued to grow as oil was discovered on Signal Hill and elsewhere, as orange groves brought large profits, as the port of San Pedro flourished, and as the essential water supply was increased by the engineering feats of William Mulholland. In the 1920s, the ever-growing city was the site of further real estate booms, so that by the decade's end the population reached almost to 1,240,000. Inevitably, the city spread in all directions: main arteries like Wilshire Boulevard stretched farther and farther out from the former downtown and such onetime fashionable neighborhoods as that served by Angel's Flight, or from the original plaza area whose Olvera St. was made into one of many tourist attractions. As it sprawled outward, Los Angeles absorbed small suburbs and separate communities, to become the world's first city that grew up in the automobile age—without a real center and dependent on the private motor car to transport its citizens over its hundreds of square miles. Even independent communities like Beverly Hills were surrounded or, like Anaheim, Glendale, Long Beach, Pasadena, Santa Monica, and Venice, were closely linked by new freeways into one gigantic megalopolis.

As the area grew so did the fortunes of many of its residents, some making money from orange growing in communities like Azusa, others out of real estate sales and speculation, still others like E. L. Doheny out of oil, and new millionaires came from a myriad of other activities. The most spectacular new industry was that of motion pictures associated with Hollywood, which became not only a mecca for fans adoring the widely publicized movie stars, but also represented a glamorous and flamboyant way of life which affected the entire region. One of its many producers, Louis B. Mayer, was said to be the highest salaried businessman in the U.S.

The Depression of the 1930s affected the city, even though movies as escape entertainment continued to flourish. Economic problems, however, led to solutions as various as the EPIC political campaign of Upton Sinclair, plans like those of Dr. Townsend and Ham 'n Eggs, cults like the Mighty I Am and Mankind United, and the evangelical revivalist religion of Aimee Semple McPherson, but the city moved on to other ways as it recovered in the 1940s. It became an important shipbuilding and shipping area during the war in the Pacific and an even more significant manufacturer of airplanes by Donald Douglas, Allan Lockheed, J. K. Northrup, and others.

In the postwar years Los Angeles, both city and county, continued its phenomenal population growth, prospered with businesses ranging from fishing to fashion design, and discovered its own character and culture as exemplified by educational institutions—public, like the University of California at Los Angeles, and private, like Claremont, Occidental, Pomona, University of Southern California, and Whittier—which achieved national recognition. Other instruments of cultural life as diverse as the Hollywood Bowl, the Southwest Museum, the Los Angeles County Museums, the Music Center, the Pasadena Playhouse, and the Padua Hills Playhouse were founded or aided by champions of local culture as diverse as C. F. Lummis and the Chandler family, the last-named famous for controlling the city's major newspaper,

the *Los Angeles Times,* whose onetime militantly conservative views that had led to it being bombed by the McNamara brothers had long since given way to a cosmopolitan and responsible coverage.

Other media of communication grew as motion picture production dwindled with the development of television, a new industry for the area. Different kinds of entertainment and tourist attractions, like Disneyland and Knott's Berry Farm, also began to flourish on the outskirts of the city. Beneath the air of prosperity and pleasure were deep currents of bitterness. The poor and dispossessed—the Chicanos huddled into neighborhoods with none of the specious charm of Olvera St., or the frustrated blacks of Watts who finally erupted into rioting (1965)—at last had the effect of bringing to the city some understanding of all its citizens. A black mayor, Thomas D. Bradley, was elected in 1973. In 1970 the city covered 460 sq. mi. and had a population of 2,816,061. *(See also individual entries.)*

Los Angeles Angels, see *Angels, California.*

Los Angeles Ballet, resident company established (1974) by John Clifford, a former dancer with the New York City Ballet. Many of the ballets are modeled on those of Balanchine and performances are generally given in local theaters and college or university facilities.

Los Angeles Chargers, see *Chargers, San Diego.*

Los Angeles Coliseum, see *Los Angeles Memorial Sports Arena.*

Los Angeles County, one of the original 27 counties. The city of Los Angeles has always been its seat, but its boundaries have fluctuated, once all of Orange and parts of Kern, Ventura, San Bernardino, and San Diego counties were included, but they now bound it along with the ocean. It also includes Santa Catalina and San Clemente islands. Stretching from the Tehachapi Mts. and Antelope Valley in the north to Long Beach in the south, it includes the Angeles National Forest, in which are located the San Gabriel Mts. and Mt. Wilson. With the Transverse Ranges this makes much of the county very mountainous. The highest point is Old Baldy (properly Mt. San Antonio), over 10,000 feet. The northeast of the county includes part of the Mojave Desert and the Joshua Trees State Park. In the southwest are the San Fernando Valley and the Santa Monica Mts.

It is the most populous county in the state: the urban settlements stretch from San Fernando through Hollywood, Burbank, and Glendale beyond Beverly Hills and Los Angeles, with Santa Monica, San Pedro, and Long Beach on the ocean; inland from the mountains down to the southern borders are many other cities, including Pasadena, San Gabriel, Azusa, Claremont, Whittier, and Pomona.

This area has a long history: discovery by Cabrillo at sea and Portolá on land, the founding by Serra of Mission San Gabriel (1771), the creation of the pueblo of Los Angeles by Gov. de Neve (1781), the era of development of *ranchos,* the site of battles in the Mexican War and peace at Cahuenga, settlement by Americans, great real estate booms upon completion of rail outlets in the 1880s, and succeeding booms because of oil discoveries at Signal Hill. Orange growing, motion picture producing, and substantial shipping and manufacturing added to its former agricultural economy until a large part of the county became one vast metropolis. In 1970 the county population was 7,040,335. With an area of 2,603,904 acres, it had a population of 1,730 per sq. mi. (*See also individual entries.*)

Los Angeles County Museum of Art, (est. 1965) on Wilshire Boulevard adjacent to the La Brea Pits. It is operated and maintained by county funds, but was constructed by private donors from whom its collections also come. Built by William Pereira, its separate elements include the Leo S. Bing Theater, the Armand Hammer Wing, and the central Howard Ahmanson Building. Its works of art span all cultures, all periods, and all media.

Los Angeles County Museum of Natural History, (est. 1913) in Exposition Park contains important anthropological and paleontological collections, emphasizing the Far West, particularly California. It also has large holdings on local history, and is particularly rich in photographic records.

Los Angeles Daily News, the first daily newspaper in Los Angeles (1869–72), an outgrowth of the *Semi-Weekly Southern News* (1860) and its successors, which were Democratic in politics but pro-Union. The name was later adapted by Cornelius Vanderbilt, Jr., during his brief journalistic career, when he founded a tabloid, *Los Angeles Illustrated Daily News* (1923), which went into receivership after three years. It was then purchased by Manchester Boddy, who dropped the tabloid format and the word "Illustrated" and conducted a flamboyant campaign against local vice. Originally a Republi-

can, Boddy made his paper the only one in the city to support Roosevelt and his New Deal, after a brief flirtation with Howard Scott's Technocracy movement. Its sympathy to liberal views and labor causes led its circulation to reach over 200,000 in 1940. Although it added another 100,000 by 1947, it began to lose ground to other papers and its liberalism grew less pronounced. In 1952, after an unsuccessful try for the Democratic nomination for U.S. Senator (1950), Boddy sold the journal, which went out of existence in 1954.

Los Angeles Dodgers, see *Dodgers, Los Angeles.*

Los Angeles Dons, see *Dons, Los Angeles.*

Los Angeles Evening Express (1871–1962), daily newspaper which from 1876 to 1900 was owned by Joseph D. Lynch, who made it the companion to his morning *Herald*♦ as a Democratic organ. In 1900 Edwin Earl♦ bought it and made it a progressive Republican journal to counter Otis' conservative *Times.* Edward Dickson♦ as an editor espoused the principles of the Lincoln-Roosevelt League and promoted the career of Hiram Johnson. Dickson became an owner after Earl's death (1919) but it was sold (1931) to Hearst to be merged with the *Herald,*♦ and later with the *Examiner.*

Los Angeles Examiner (1903–), founded by William Randolph Hearst♦ to complement his *San Francisco Examiner* and to assist his campaign for the presidential nomination on the Democratic ticket. For the latter reason it cultivated union labor by taking a closed shop stand in opposition to the open shop policy of the *Los Angeles Times.* It also came to oppose the *Times* on the Owens Valley water project (1905), contending that it would enrich Harrison Gray Otis, that paper's owner, and others in his syndicate. Later Hearst adopted a more conservative and less pro-labor stance. Even before the publisher's death (1951), the paper began to decline, its sensationalism not rivaling the news coverage of the *Times.* In 1962 it left the larger morning field to the *Times,* switching its publication to the evening, and absorbing the *Herald.*

Los Angeles Free Press (1964–), first U.S. newspaper to cater to the counterculture of New Left radicalism, bohemianism, sexual freedom, and protest against the Establishment. This weekly journal had great success with many buyers (some presumably attracted by the explicitly erotic advertisements) and many imitators, including the *Berkeley Barb.*

Los Angeles Herald (1873–1962), daily newspaper founded by the father of T. M. Storke, who soon sold it. Joseph D. Lynch (1876) made it a leading Democratic journal, a companion to his *Evening Express.*♦ It was sold again in 1900 and adopted a conservative Republican stand. In 1922 it was bought by Hearst and in 1931 merged with his *Evening Express* to become the *Los Angeles Evening Herald and Express,* which in turn lost its identity when merged with the *Los Angeles Examiner* (1962).

Los Angeles Kings, National Hockey League team, founded in the expansion of 1967 which created a Western Division. Its home ice rink is the Forum,♦ which, like the team, is owned by Jack Kent Cooke, a Canadian business executive. The team's stars have been Marcel Dionne, center, a consistently high scorer, and Rogatien Vachon, goalie.

Los Angeles Lakers, National Basketball Association team, moved from Minneapolis to Los Angeles (1960). During its first 15 years in California it won 9 divisional championships and in 1971–72 not only won the NBA championship but established records for the best single season record (69-13) and the most consecutive wins (33). Star players have included Elgin Baylor,♦ Wilt Chamberlain,♦ Kareem Abdul-Jabbar (Lou Alcindor♦), and Jerry West,♦ and coaches have included Bill Sharman♦ (1971–76). Since 1965 the team has been owned by Jack Kent Cooke, a Canadian business executive, also the owner of The Forum and the Los Angeles Kings.

Los Angeles Memorial Sports Arena, located next to the Los Angeles Coliseum, was the city's first (1959) large indoor facility for sporting and other events, later challenged by The Forum in Inglewood. It was the site of the Democratic National Convention in 1960.

Los Angeles Music Center, see *Music Center.*

Los Angeles Open, the oldest state tournament for professional♦ men golfers, played each year (generally in January) since 1927. The total purse grew from the original $10,000 to $100,000 in forty years.

Los Angeles Rams, see *Rams, Los Angeles.*

Los Angeles Ranges, see *Transverse Ranges.*

Los Angeles Record, daily newspaper founded (1895) as part of the chain owned by E. W. Scripps.♦ Like the rest of his journals it was dedicated to the inter-

ests of workingmen and to liberal politics. It did not carry advertising initially. In time the paper was run by Scripps' son James, who attacked the policies of Woodrow Wilson, which were supported by the elder Scripps. As a result the *Record* was severed from the Scripps chain. Although it achieved a circulation of more than 60,000 in its last years, the paper ceased publication in 1933.

Los Angeles Sentinel, Los Angeles newspaper published by and for black readers since 1933. It was founded by Leon H. Washington and continued by his widow, Ruth.

Los Angeles Star (1851–79), weekly newspaper, initially containing some contributions in Spanish. For it Hugo Reid♦ wrote 22 articles on the Indians of Los Angeles (1852). It was a Democratic organ with anti-Union leanings during the Civil War, and for a time worked toward a division of the state on the assumption that the southern part would be sympathetic to the Confederacy. Its editor was arrested for treason and the paper was suspended (1864–68). It became a daily (1870) and was greatly improved and made nonpartisan under Ben C. Truman♦ (1873–77), but after his era of ownership it collapsed due to lack of funds. Despite its historical importance, no complete file is known to exist.

Los Angeles Times, daily morning newspaper, the leading journal of southern California, founded in 1881. The next year Harrison Gray Otis♦ bought a quarter interest, became the editor, and in 1886 became sole owner. The paper expanded as the city grew and it significantly helped promote that growth. Otis was a forceful publisher, as was his son-in-law, Harry Chandler,♦ who succeeded him. Both worked to develop the city and neighboring agricultural areas, to free the harbor from Southern Pacific control, and to obtain an adequate water supply. The *Times* also became known for its militant opposition to the closed shop; the vehemence of its views led to its being bombed by the McNamara brothers♦ (1910). Control of the family-owned newspaper and allied publishing ventures passed (1917) from Harry Chandler to his son Norman (1934), and to Norman's son Otis in 1960. The paper has grown in circulation (1,000,000 daily in 1971) and stature. Although Republican, it is not narrowly partisan and is known for the independence of its editorials and the variety of its columnists. It has won several Pulitzer Prizes, notably one in 1969 for "disinterested and meritorious public service."

Los Angeles Tribune, title of three different newspapers. The earliest was a morning daily (1886–90), which championed the Republican party. The second and most significant, also a morning daily, was founded, published, and edited (1911–19) by Edwin T. Earl♦ as a companion to his *Evening Express,*♦ and like it was a Progressive opponent of the conservative *Times.* It reached a circulation of 54,000 (1918), about one-tenth of the city's population. The third *Tribune* was a weekly for blacks published in the 1940s and 50s.

Los Gatos, residential community (est. 1850) in the Santa Cruz Mts. of Santa Clara County. Wildcats presumably once ranged there, giving the name to the creek and a land grant (*gatos* is Spanish for "cats"). It was once a lumbering and sawmill area. Josiah Royce spent part of his childhood there. It was once the site of the estate of Charles Erskine Scott Wood, and Yehudi Menuhin has a home there. Nearby a "Father" William E. Riker established (1918) a utopian colony, Holy City, which lasted into the 1950s.

Los Padres National Forest, two widely separated areas, the northern one stretching from a point above Big Sur down nearly to San Simeon and including the Santa Lucia Mts.,♦ the southern one beginning near Atascadero and stretching down near Piru and adjoining the Angeles National Forest, including the Santa Ynez and San Rafael mountains. Begun by President T. Roosevelt (1903) and twice extended, it was given its present scope and name by President F. D. Roosevelt (1936) in honor of the Franciscan fathers who had founded eight missions in or near the forest.

Lotta, see *Crabtree, Lotta.*

Loved One, The, see *Waugh, Evelyn.*

LOW, FREDERICK FERDINAND (1828–94), moved to California from his native Maine in 1849. After panning gold in the mining country he entered business, achieved the merger of all steamship lines on the Sacramento River, and became a banker in Marysville. Elected to Congress as a representative-at-large (1861) because the 1860 census showed the state entitled to a third seat, he could not be sworn in until June 1862. Elected the state's 9th governor, he was also the first to serve a four-year term (1863–67). A pro-Union Republican, he was a leader in founding the University of California, in preserving the site that became Golden Gate Park, and in trying to obtain justice for the Chinese. He was also Grant's Minister to China (1870–74). Later he returned to banking in San Francisco.

Low Desert, see *Desert.*

LOWE, THADDEUS S[OBIESKIE] C[OALINCOURT] (1832–1913), after serving as head of a U.S. balloon corps in the Civil War, moved from his native New Hampshire to Pasadena. There he tried to establish a balloon ferry to reach the 6,000-foot pinnacle of Mt. Lowe,♦ a peak near Altadena named for him. He did not succeed, but he did create a narrow-gauge railway for one open car to the top. He also tried to organize a transcontinental luxury passenger balloon line.

LOWIE, ROBERT H[ARRY] (1883–1957), professor of anthropology at the University of California, Berkeley (1917–50), known particularly for his studies of Plains Indians. The anthropology museum on the Berkeley campus is named for him.

Loyalty oath controversy, a complex, lengthy, and bitter dispute involving the faculty, administration, and Regents of the University of California. It began on March 25, 1949, when the Regents decided that all faculty and staff must take an oath affirming nonmembership and nonbelief in any organization advocating overthrow of the U.S. government by illegal or unconstitutional means. This oath, as an addition to one required by the state of its employees, was seen by the faculty as opposed to academic freedom and tenure and as singling out University members with implications of disloyalty.

The Regents' oath was altered to abjuration of membership in the Communist party, but the governing body also withheld letters of appointment and reappointment from all persons who did not sign the required oath. In an atmosphere of deep discord, representatives of the Regents and the faculty met; the latter believed that if its Academic Senate passed two motions—one approving the policy of refusing to hire Communist party members, the other calling for abolition of the oath—the Regents would accept the approval of the policy in lieu of the Regents' oath and lift that requirement. When this failed to occur and when John Francis Neylan,♦ as major proponent of the oath, disavowed an assumed understanding, the faculty became even more deeply disaffected.

The alumni then arranged that nonsigners could petition the Academic Senate's Committee on Privilege and Tenure for a hearing, but regardless of the

Committee's findings the Regents dismissed the remaining 31 nonsigners. Among them were Edward Tolman, an eminent psychologist, for whom a Berkeley building was later named, and David Saxon, who became president of the University in 1975. The dismissals led not only to condemnations by the Academic Senate and many professional societies, including the American Association of University Professors, but to court challenges.

A district court found that the Regents had abused their authority and a year and a half later (Oct. 17, 1952) the state Supreme Court ruled that the nonsigners should be reinstated. Meanwhile upon the requirement of an oath for all state employees under the Levering Act,♦ the Regents rescinded their own oath.

Loyola University, coeducational Catholic institution located in Los Angeles. It is an outgrowth (1911) of St. Vincent's College, founded (1865) as southern California's first college. In 1970 it enrolled nearly 4,000 students and had a faculty numbering almost 250.

LUBIN, DAVID (1849–1918), born in Poland, went to San Francisco from New York (1867), and with his half-brother Harris Weinstock♦ founded the Sacramento department store bearing their names. Successful in business, he entered into experimental farming, championed farmers' collectives, and with the aid of King Victor Emmanuel founded in Rome the International Institute of Agriculture (1906), which has developed into a UN organization. His son was Simon Lubin.♦

LUBIN, SIMON J[ULIUS] (1876–1936), son of David Lubin,♦ an executive of the family's Weinstock, Lubin department store in Sacramento, and a civic leader. He was instrumental in creating a state commission on immigration and housing (1913) and was its first chairman. As a result of its inquiry into the Wheatland riots♦ he worked to improve the lot of migratory laborers. He helped to create the state's department of commerce (1930), became its director, and helped to expand California's markets in Latin America.

Lucerne Valley, name given to Mussel Slough♦ (1887) after the battle there. Another place of the same name lies south of the Mojave Desert in San Bernardino County.

"Luck of Roaring Camp, The," short story by Bret Harte,♦ published in the *Overland Monthly* (Aug.

1869), and often said to be America's first local color story. It tells of hardened gold rush miners in Roaring Camp adopting the orphaned infant of Cherokee Sal, a local prostitute, and how the camp spirit is altered by the presence of little Thomas Luck, until the river rises, engulfs the camp, and drowns the child, who is being held by the miner Kentuck. It became the title piece of the book (1870) in which Harte's first stories were collected.

LUDLOW, FITZ HUGH (1836–70), New York-born author and graduate of Union College. He became notorious as "the American De Quincey" because of a frank description of his drug addiction in *The Hasheesh Eater* (1857). He visited San Francisco for four months (1863) to write sketches of his trip and of the Pacific Coast for the *Atlantic Monthly,* gathered in *The Heart of the Continent* (1870). While there he wrote for the *Golden Era* and became a friend of Stoddard and Mark Twain. He collected his stories as *Little Brother; and Other Genre Pictures* (1867).

LUGO, prominent early California family. The ancestor of the oldest branch, Francisco Salvador de Lugo (1740–1805), was with Rivera y Moncada's expedition of 1774. Several of his sons were also soldiers, and one of them, Antonio María (1778–1860), was an *alcalde* of Los Angeles. Others married into the Carrillo, Cota, and Vallejo families. A daughter of Antonio María married Isaac Williams.

Luiseño, Indians who lived in present Riverside County and derived their name from Mission San Luis Rey. They may have inhabited the island of San Clemente as well as their mainland territory. Perhaps there were as many as 4,000 Luiseño in precontact times, but only 500 remained by the time of the 1910 census. Their practices of the anniversary mourning ceremony and the girls' adolescent initiation rite were influenced by the late introduction of the toloache cult♦ and the Chinigchinich religion,♦ which they received from the Juaneño. They preferred song cycles to dances and used ground paintings in their religious ceremonies. On their Rincon, La Jolla, and Pauma reservations they have preserved some of the old customs. They were once notorious for their Pauma Massacre♦ (1846).

LUISETTI, HANK (ANGELO LUISETTI) (1916–), San Francisco-born basketball player. While at Stanford (1934–38) he was three times named All-American and led his team to three consecutive Pacific Coast Conference championships (1936–38).

He introduced the one-hand shot, scored 50 points in a single game, and set the record for points made (1,596) in a career.

Lumbering, see *Forests and forestry.*

LUMMIS, CHARLES FLETCHER (1859–1928), after education at Harvard moved from his native Massachusetts to Ohio, becoming a newspaper editor, until he arranged to walk to California (1884–85) and to record his experiences for the *Los Angeles Times.* He soon became the paper's city editor, but upon suffering a stroke (1885) he went to New Mexico to recover. There he became fascinated by the Indians of the Southwest and wrote *The Land of Poco Tiempo* (1893) about them and their region. Returning to Los Angeles, he edited (1894–1909) a promotional magazine, *Land of Sunshine,* titled *Out West* after 1902.

His journal featured writing by such local literati as Mary Austin, Edwin Markham, Joaquin Miller, and Charles Warren Stoddard, and was a booster for the state and for the Southwest, a term he popularized for New Mexico and Arizona. He organized the Sequoya League (1901) to persuade Congress that the Indians needed protection as people rather than nations with which treaties were made. He founded the Southwest Museum (1914) in Los Angeles for anthropological materials, created The Landmarks Club (1897) to restore the missions and to preserve other historic buildings, and established an important collection of Southwest material in the Los Angeles Public Library of which he was head (1905–10).

He found time for other activities, including the writing of books, among which was *The Spanish Missions and the California Pioneers* (1893), and the building (1898) with his own hands of a southwestern style dwelling, El Alisal, open to all who were sympathetic to his views. Although more a popularizer than a scholar, and flamboyantly bohemian in his interpretation of Spanish colonial culture, he did much to awaken an interest in and create an understanding of it.

LUNDEBERG, HARRY (1901–57), Norwegian-born sailor and labor leader, settled first in Seattle, then in San Francisco (1935) as the main figure of the Sailors' Union of the Pacific. He participated in the General Strike♦ (1934) but opposed Harry Bridges' radicalism and created an opposing Seafarers' International Union of North America (1938), of which he was president.

Lupine, shrub and wildflower which grows throughout California. It varies from six inches to six feet in fifty different species, the most common producing blue, purple, and lavender flowers, but yellow, pink, and white are also frequent. Some Indians boiled and ate the seeds, and the leaves have served as forage, although some species are considered poisonous to sheep. The name is also spelled lupin.

LUX, CHARLES (1823–87), German-born settler, became a butcher in San Francisco, first independently, then with Henry Miller.♦ In time they formed Miller & Lux to purchase cattle ranches, became the state's largest landowners, and successfully defended their riparian rights against James Ben Ali Haggin.♦ After Lux's death Miller tried to wrest their properties from his heirs. His American-born wife, Miranda Wilmarth Lux (1826?–94), bequeathed funds to establish a vocational school for girls in San Francisco. It lasted from 1912 to 1953 and was for a time affiliated with an institution founded by J. C. Wilmerding.♦

Lynch law, summary punishment, particularly by hanging, by a group of private persons without due process of law. It occurred in early California, as well as in other frontier areas. Vigilance committees♦ were generally more organized and often proceeded more in accord with legal processes than did lynch mobs, but the difference is in degree, not kind. The first California committee of that sort was formed in Los Angeles (1836) and was presided over by Victor Prudon, later Gen. Vallejo's secretary; after the murder of Domingo Felix by his wife and her lover, citizens took the criminals from the jail and shot them to death.

Vigilante action was more common during the early American era, particularly in the gold mines (e.g. committees were formed in Grass Valley, Jackson, Marysville, Nevada City, Sacramento, Sonora, Stockton, and Truckee), but the major organizations of this kind were those created in San Francisco in 1851 and 1856, led by such influential citizens as Samuel Brannan, William T. Coleman, and J. D. Stevenson.

Los Angeles also formed such a committee to seize and hang the bandit Juan Flores (1857). Fights over land even led masked Americans to lynch propertied people, like members of the Berryessa family. By the 1870s such summary action grew less common but mobs hanged Chinese men in both San Francisco and Los Angeles in that decade, and in the 60 years after 1875 there were 38 cases of lynching with 59 victims. Most of these occurred in non-urban areas and were related to labor troubles. But the most sensational case involved retaliation for the kidnapping and murder of Brooke Hart, the son of a San Jose merchant. The two men accused of the crime were taken from the local jail and hanged in a nearby public park (1933). Gov. Rolph made a statement approving the action. His view of vigilante action was in keeping with earlier attitudes found in Josiah Royce's *California* (1866) and H. H. Bancroft's *Popular Tribunals* (2 vols., 1877).

LYON, NATHANIEL (1818–61), West Point graduate, went to California as an army captain and engaged in punitive expeditions against Indians at Clear Lake and Pit River (1849). He was killed in a Civil War battle in Missouri. A San Francisco street is named for him.

Mc

Mc ADOO, WILLIAM GIBBS (1863–1941), born in Georgia, practiced law in Tennessee and New York, and was a leader in Democratic party politics and Wilson's Secretary of Treasury (1913–18) before moving to California (1922). There he was a leading contender for the presidential nomination of his party (1924) and a U.S. Senator (1933–38).

McALLISTER, HALL (1826–88), after practicing law in his native Georgia, went to San Francisco (1849), where he soon set up a legal firm with his father, Matthew Hall McAllister (1800–65), later the state's first U.S. Circuit Court judge (1855), and his brother, Ward McAllister (1827–95), later better known as a New York society leader. Hall McAllister's prosecution of the Hounds♦ and his aristocratic style, logical reasoning, and thoroughness made him a famous figure before juries, and he was said to have been involved in more cases, won more verdicts, and got larger fees than any other lawyer in California during his time. Two famous cases were the successful defense of Adolph Spreckels for shooting M. H. de Young, and of Charles Lux in his suit for water rights against James Ben Ali Haggin. A San Francisco street is named for him.

McCLATCHY, C[HARLES] K[ENNY] (1858–1936), succeeded his father, James McClatchey (1824–83), as editor of the Sacramento *Bee,* for which he had begun writing at age 17. With his brother Valentine Stuart McClatchey as business manager, he established the Modesto *Bee* and the Fresno *Bee* and made his *Bee* newspapers♦ very influential in their areas. His papers were independent, as he was, supporting Roosevelt's Bull Moose party, Bryan, La Follette, and Al Smith. He opposed Japanese Americans, Prohibition, and American entry into the League of Nations. An exposé of political corruption in Nevada won his Sacramento paper a Pulitzer Prize (1935).

McClellan Air Force Base, logistics and materiel command headquarters for aircraft, missiles, and space systems, located on the outskirts of Sacramento.

McCloud River, rises near Mt. Shasta, now flows 60 miles into Lake Shasta (created by Shasta Dam),

but formerly joined the waters of the Pit and Sacramento rivers. Its name is a corruption of that of Alexander McLeod, the leader of Hudson's Bay Co. trappers into California (1828).

McCLURE, MICHAEL (1932–), Kansas-born poet long resident in San Francisco and once associated with its Beat movement. His personal and passionate poetry includes *Hymns to St. Geryon* (1959), *For Artaud* (1959), and *Dark Brown* (1961). *Ghost Tantras* (1964) is verse meant for oral presentation, a development toward his dramatic writing, of which the best-known play is *The Beard* (1967), an intense erotic passage between Jean Harlow and Billy the Kid, two symbolic figures. *Freewheelin Frank, Secretary of the Angels* (1967) is an account of the Hell's Angels motorcycle gang of San Francisco.

McCOLL, WILLIAM F., JR. (1930–), San Diego-born football player. He played end on Stanford's team (1949–51), was later a professional player for the Chicago Bears, and then a medical missionary in Korea.

McCOMAS, FRANCIS [JOHN] (1874–1938), Tasmanian-born artist, went to San Francisco (1898), where he studied under Arthur Mathews. Although he also studied at the Julian Academy in France and traveled widely, he was best known for his paintings of California oaks, Monterey cypress, desert scenes, and depictions of Indian villages in the Southwest.

McCONE, JOHN A. (1902–), San Francisco-born business executive, head of shipbuilding and iron-work firms, director of the U.S. Central Intelligence Agency (1961–65), and head of the state commission appointed to investigate the riots in Watts (1965).

McCORMICK, PATRICIA [KELLER] (1930–), diving champion from southern California. During her career she won 27 American championships, and in two different Olympic Games (1952, 56) won gold medals for both springboard and platform diving, records never before achieved by any man or woman. In 1956 she won the Sullivan Award as the outstanding U.S. amateur athlete of the year.

McCOVEY, WILLIE [LEE] (1938–), Alabama-born baseball player, a left-handed first baseman and outfielder for the San Francisco Giants (1959–73), and San Diego Padres (1974–76), the Oakland Athletics (1976), and the S.F. Giants (1977–). He has been named National League Rookie of the Year (1959), Home Run Champion (1963, 68, 69), and Most Valuable Player (1969).

MacDONALD, ROSS (1915–), pseudonym of Kenneth Millar, a detective story writer since the 1940s. He was born in Los Gatos and resides in Santa Barbara. After graduating from Canadian universities and receiving a Ph.D. from the University of Michigan, he began to write tough detective novels set in southern California. The plots often involve family relations and thus play on the generation gap and the rock music culture of the 1960s. His best-known books include *The Galton Case* (1959), *The Goodbye Look* (1964), and *The Underground Man* (1971).

MacDONALD-WRIGHT, STANTON (1890–1973), Virginia-born painter, was reared, like his brother, Willard Huntington Wright, in Santa Monica. With a theorist of art from New York, Morgan Russell, he founded Synchronism, a style of near or complete abstraction emphasizing effects of light through planes of color. He was a director of the Art Students League of Los Angeles (1922–30) and a professor at UCLA (1942–54).

McDOUGAL, JOHN (1818–66), 2nd governor of the state (Jan. 9, 1851–Jan. 8, 1852). He was a native of Ohio and had distinguished himself in the army during the Black Hawk and the Mexican wars. He went to California in 1849 and as a Democrat was active in the Constitutional Convention. Elected as the state's first lieutenant governor in 1849, he became governor when Peter Burnett resigned that post. His year-long term was generally undistinguished. He championed the Chinese, whose labor was needed, but dispatched militia against the Indians. He opposed the Vigilance Committee of 1851 and later in San Francisco was a leader of the Law and Order party, which denounced the Vigilance Committee of 1856.

McDOUGALL, JAMES A[LEXANDER] (1817–67), New York-born politician, served as attorney general of Illinois (1843–46) and California (1850–51) and was therefore commonly called "General." As a lawyer he is best remembered for joining Edward D. Baker in defending Charles Cora.♦ He served in Congress (1853–55), where he argued for a transcontinental railway. A pro-Union Democrat, he was later elected to the U.S. Senate (1861–67), where he was notorious for his neglect of his post.

McELHENNY, HUGH (1928–), Los Angeles-born football player, a star halfback on the San Francisco Forty-Niners (1952–60) known for his running. He was named Rookie of the Year (1952) and twice (1952–53) named All-Pro player.

McEWEN, ARTHUR (1850–1907), Scottish-born journalist reared in the U.S. He went to San Francisco (*c.* 1866) and, after brief study at the University of California, began at 19 to write for the *Chronicle* and other journals in that city and in Nevada. He then became a militant reform-minded writer for Hearst's *Examiner,* leaving it to edit *Arthur McEwen's Letter* (Feb. 1894–June 1895), a paper devoted both to muckraking and to fiction and essays by young writers. After that financially unsuccessful venture he became a journalist in the East, returning briefly (1905) to attack Ruef♦ and Schmitz♦ in the *Bulletin.*

McGOWAN, EDWARD (1807–93), after a tempestuous political career in his native Pennsylvania, moved to San Francisco (1849) where he entered Democratic politics as a henchman of David Broderick.♦ He came to be known as "Ned McGowan, the ballot box stuffer." When his friend James P. Casey♦ shot James King of William (1856), the Vigilance Committee indicted him for complicity, but he was acquitted. He then attacked his enemies in a journal, *The Phoenix* (1857–58), and his lively, self-serving *Narrative of Edward McGowan* (1857). Later adventures involved him in lawlessness in the Fraser River mines of Canada and the organization of an Arizona Battalion of the Confederate Army before he drifted back to San Francisco as an old man.

McGROARTY, JOHN STEVEN (1862–1944), Pennsylvania-born lawyer and U.S. Congressman (1935–39) from Los Angeles. He was long the major editorial writer of the Los Angeles *Times,* but is best known for his romanticized pageant, *The Mission Play.* That drama, treating the missions from their founding (1769) to the coming of the Americans and then to the secularized and ruined buildings (1847), first produced in 1912, was for a long time presented annually at Mission San Gabriel. For his verses and other writings about his adopted state, the legislature named him Poet Laureate (1933).

McKAY, John (1923–   ), football coach of the University of Southern California (1960–75), whose teams won five times in eight Rose Bowl competitions. His son, John Jr., was a star of the team (1973–74).

McKUEN, Rod (1933–   ), popular sentimental poet, singer, songwriter, and composer. His books include *Stanyan Street and Other Sorrows* (1966), *Listen to the Warm* (1967), and *Come to Me in Silence* (1973). Born in Oakland, he lives in Beverly Hills, where he writes background music for films and television. *Finding My Father* (1976) is a prose work telling of his quest for his unknown father.

McLAREN, John (1846–1943), after study at the Edinburgh Botanical Gardens went to San Francisco as a young man. He became the assistant to William Hammond Hall♦ at Golden Gate Park, and his successor (1887) in superintending its creation and development. He is memorialized in the park's romanesque headquarters building, McLaren Lodge, and its Rhododendron Dell, as well as in John McLaren Park in southeastern San Francisco.

McLOUGHLIN, Maurice [Evans] (1890–1957), Nevada-born tennis champion, reared in San Francisco. He won the U.S. singles championship (1912–13) and became the first American to win the British men's title (1913). He was called the California Comet because of his cannon-ball serve and his generally fast style of play, a result of California's hard court surfaces in contrast to the clay or grass of the East. He also helped to popularize the image of tennis as a vigorous sport rather than just an entertainment for the rich.

McMILLAN, Dan[iel Alexander, Jr.] (1898–1975), tackle on the University of Southern California football team (1916–17) and, after war service, on the University of California "Wonder Teams"♦ (1920–21). He was later the major developer of geothermal energy♦ at The Geysers.

McMILLAN, Edwin M[atteson] (1907–   ), physicist born in Redondo Beach, a member of the faculty of the University of California, Berkeley, after 1935. He became director of the Lawrence Radiation Laboratory♦ (1958) after the death of his brother-in-law, Ernest O. Lawrence. He shared a Nobel Prize with Glenn T. Seaborg♦ for their discoveries of trans-uranium elements (1951).

McNAMARA, Eugene (*fl.* 1846), young Irish priest who on the eve of the Mexican War proposed to the President of Mexico that he colonize California with Irish Catholics to thwart the designs of the U.S., "an irreligious and anti-Catholic nation." He won the approval of the Archbishop of Mexico to bring 10,000 colonists to California, and Gov. Pío Pico granted his request for 3,000 square leagues on July 7, 1846, the day Commodore Sloat occupied Monterey, thus coincidentally ending the grandiose plan.

McNamara brothers bombing, a *cause célèbre* of organized labor. In the midst of a strike to unionize the metal trades of Los Angeles, the building of the vehemently antiunion *Los Angeles Times* was bombed on Oct. 1, 1910. Twenty persons were killed and 17 injured. William J. Burns, a private detective hired by the mayor of Los Angeles, arrested a professional dynamiter, Ortie McManigal, who implicated James McNamara. He in turn was arrested along with his brother John, an official of the striking union. Labor leaders and Job Harriman, the Socialist candidate for mayor in a pending election, believed the brothers' plea of innocence and proclaimed the case a frame-up. Suddenly the brothers reversed themselves and admitted guilt, to the dismay of their lawyer, Clarence Darrow, Harriman, the unions, and other supporters. James was sentenced to life imprisonment, John to 15 years, and 33 other union members were also convicted.

McPHERSON, Aimee Semple (1890–1944), evangelist, born in Canada, reared by her mother (Ma Kennedy) as a Salvation Army child. She was converted at a Pentecostal revival by evangelist Robert James Semple, whom she wed (1908). Ordained in the Full Gospel Assembly, she went to Hong Kong en route to China as a missionary, returning soon after her husband's death (1910) and later was married (1912–21) to a man named McPherson. Separated and later divorced from him, she began her career (1915) of itinerant preaching emphasizing fundamentalism, "speaking in tongues," faith healing, the imminent millennium, and opposition to communism. In 1918 she and her mother settled in Los Angeles, where she built a large Angelus Temple (the "Church of the Foursquare Gospel") in which she produced vaudeville-like services. Because of their drama, and her blonde good looks and costuming, she was called the Mary Pickford of revivalism. In 1926 she created a different kind of sensation by disappearing while swimming at a Los Angeles beach and turning up a month later on a Mexican desert. She claimed she had been kidnapped, while others contended she was the mystery woman who had rented a Carmel cottage with an Angelus Temple radio operator. The notoriety did not harm her church, which at her death had some 400 branches in the U.S. and Canada, 200 foreign missions, and a Bible college.

McTeague, novel by Frank Norris♦ published in 1899. In a realistic setting centered on San Francisco's Polk St. it depicts the often trivial, often squalid lives of lower middle-class people led by chance, uncontrolled emotions, and frustrated desires, into a downward course which ends in tragedy. Erich von Stroheim made a motion picture adaptation entitled *Greed♦* (1923).

McWILLIAMS, CAREY (1905–   ), born in Colorado, after graduation from USC became a Los Angeles attorney and writer and state commissioner of housing and immigration under Gov. Olson. His books include *Ambrose Bierce* (1929), a biography; *Factories in the Field* (1939), on migratory workers in the state; *Ill Fares the Land* (1942), on American agriculture and its dislocated workers; *Brothers Under the Skin* (1943), about nonwhite minorities in the U.S.; *A Mask for Privilege* (1948), about American anti-Semitism; *North from Mexico* (1949), on Spanish people in the U.S.; and *Witchhunt* (1950), about civil rights. Sociological analyses of his adopted state are *Southern California Country* (1946) and *California: The Great Exception* (1949). Associated with *The Nation* since 1945, he was its editor (1955–75).

M

MACKAY, JOHN W. (1831–1902), brought to the U.S. from his native Ireland (1840), he went to the California gold mines (1851), and then as a pick-and-shovel man to the Nevada mines (1859), where fortunate claims and speculation brought him into alliance with James G. Fair and the other developers of the Comstock Lode.♦ Like them he became a multi-millionaire, but quit mining interests in the 1880s to create the Commercial Pacific Cable Co., an international telegraph system, which laid the first transpacific cable (1902). His wife, Marie Louise, once a poor widow in Virginia City, Nevada, later lived apart from her second husband, Mackay, and became an international hostess in Paris and London.

Mackerel, spiny-finned fish related to tuna, found in two species off the California coast. The *Pacific mackerel,* living close to shore, was the most commonly caught between 1928, when canning methods were perfected, and 1947, when too much fishing threatened the species. It has been protected against undue catches since 1972. The *Pacific jack mackerel* lives about 600 miles offshore and has been the dominant type since 1947, with the major port for the catch at San Pedro and lesser ones at Port Hueneme and Monterey. Between 1967 and 1971 the annual catch averaged 52,000,000 pounds.

Mad River, rises about 40 miles south and 50 miles east of Eureka, then flows 5 miles south and about 75 miles northwest to empty into the Pacific about 10 miles north of Eureka. It was named by the governmental exploring party of Josiah Gregg♦ (1849) when he became angered by the group's failure to give him time to measure the latitude of its mouth. During Indian attacks on the river's settlers in the 1860s, Fort Lyons was built on its banks some 25 miles southeast of Eureka. The pioneer Hyampon Trail, from Humboldt Bay to the Sacramento Valley, crossed the Mad in Trinity County.

MADDEN, JOHN (1936–   ), born in Daly City, after coaching football at college teams in California, joined the Oakland Raiders' coaching staff (1967) and became its head coach in 1969, the youngest in professional football to that time. His team has won several divisional championships and the Super Bowl (1977).

Madeline Plains, large, treeless, ancient lake bed in central Lassen County, named for a girl killed by Indians (1850). There is also a town of that name on the Southern Pacific route.

Madera, seat of the county of the same name, a trade and meat-packing center for the area's agriculture and livestock raising. It was founded (1876) as a settlement on the Fresno River for transporting lumber by flume. The region was earlier explored by James D. Savage,♦ to whom a monument was erected northeast of the city. In 1970 Madera had a population of 16,044.

Madera Canal, part of the Central Valley Project.♦ It carries water from the Friant Dam on the San Joaquin River♦ to a point fourteen miles northwest of the town of Madera. It began operations during World War II.

Madera County, formed from part of Fresno County, which almost surrounds it, except for Merced and Mariposa counties to the north and Mono and a bit of Tuolumne counties to the east. The San Joaquin River forms its western and southern boundaries, and on the latter is located Millerton Lake,♦ created by Friant Dam. The county was incorporated (1893) with the town of Madera as its seat. The scene of gold mining (1849 ff.) originally, it later became a site for lumbering, mainly of sugar pine, as the county name indicates (*madera* is Spanish for "timber"). The major produce consists of grapes, cotton, fruit, nuts, and field crops. Livestock and poultry are also raised there. The Chowchilla Canal and the Madera Canal of the Central Valley Project carry water south from the Chowchilla River, which forms the county's northern boundary, and from its tributary, the Fresno River. Part of Yosemite National Park is in the county, as is part of the Sierra National Forest, in which the Devil's Postpile is located. The population in 1970 was 41,519; with an area of 1,372,864 acres, it had 19.4 persons per sq. mi.

Madonna Inn, lush motel whose construction and design was begun in 1958 by Alex Madonna on the site near San Luis Obispo where he parked the earth-moving equipment he employed for his highway construction contracts. Not far distant from San Simeon, it echoes, on the level of a supermotel, the rich decor of various styles for which Hearst Castle is known. The ornate interiors of hand-carved marble and exotic woods, often looking like kitsch products of Black Forest gnomes, include not only fanciful public rooms but more than 100 bedrooms and suites, each decorated in a different manner said to represent some elegant period style. Construction of more rooms and other features, designed by Mr. and Mrs. Madonna, continues.

Madrone (or Madroña), broadleaf evergreen shrub or tree, in the latter form reaching from 20 to 125 feet in height with a polished red trunk, dark glossy leaves, clusters of white flowers, and red berries. Found throughout the state up to 4,000-foot elevations and very colorful, it was often the subject of 19th-century California painters.

Magazines, issued as regional journals in the first decade of American statehood. They came into being because of a desire to emphasize local issues and local color for new residents and for eastern readers, and because established periodicals of the eastern seaboard not only concentrated on their own subjects but were neither rapidly nor readily obtainable.

The first consequential magazine issued from California was the *Golden Era* (1852), a weekly intended to give a view of California's life and culture through fiction, essays, poetry, and factual reports. *Pioneer* (1854), also from San Francisco, was a monthly with similar purposes and some of the same contributors, but was more exclusively literary. In 1856 two more periodical publications were begun, also in San Francisco and with similar purposes: *News Letter* was initially more a mailing sheet which carried some news, and later developed into a rather conventional newspaper; while *Hutchings' California Magazine* emphasized articles on unusual local subjects or settings (e.g. Yosemite, where the publisher ran a hotel) and scenic illustrations. A new style of journal emanated, again from San Francisco, two years later when several women established *Hesperian* as a periodical on literature and art addressed to their own sex, although often written by men who contributed to the other magazines. In 1863 it became *Pacific Monthly,* intended as much for men as for women.

As the pioneer days receded into the past, jour-

nals of the 1860s adopted new attitudes. *The Californian,* established in 1866, tended to satirize the gold rush era, but the most significant of all early California magazines, *Overland Monthly,* founded in 1868, was quickly popular and famous for the short stories of its editor, Bret Harte, romantically depicting the earlier mining era of the new state.

With the frontier era well past in the 1870s and with California firmly allied to the rest of the nation through the new transcontinental railroad, new magazines concentrated on the present day and developed a skeptical, even sharply critical tone toward current events. *The Argonaut* defended the Big Four and other established interests, but *The Wasp,* in slashing prose and vitriolic colored cartoons, attacked the railroad monopolists and Denis Kearney's labor alike, while *Thistleton's Jolly Giant* was scurrilously opposed to all Irish and Chinese immigrants.

Another *Californian* was created by the publisher of the *Overland Monthly,* which had failed, and then combined with a revival of that journal (1883); but though it had good periods and attracted such new authors as Gertrude Atherton, Jack London, Frank Norris, and later, George Sterling, the magazine was often no more than the "warmed-Overland" that Ambrose Bierce dubbed it. Two sprightly journals of San Francisco captured the *fin-de-siècle* atmosphere; *The Wave,* a weekly that lasted the final decade of the 19th century, and *The Lark,* a little magazine. The whimsical humorist Gelett Burgess was a major contributor to both. Los Angeles got its first significant magazine when the enthusiastic promoter of southwestern culture, Charles F. Lummis, founded his *Land of Sunshine* (1894), later somewhat more soberly retitled *Out West.*

During the 20th century many more magazines were founded to focus attention of different sorts on California. *Westways* (1909), initially called *Touring Topics* as the journal of the Automobile Club of Southern California, was addressed to the intelligent traveler; the *California Historical Quarterly* (1922) and the Historical Society of Southern California *Quarterly* (1935) were oriented more toward the academic and the antiquarian. *American West* (1964), although sponsored by the Western History Association, attempted a more popular appeal, while *Western Folklore* was addressed to specialized scholarly readers, as were other periodicals also issued by university presses. Many magazines came to be issued for concentration on the cities where they were published, ranging from ones that smacked of the interest of the Chamber of Commerce to those that made serious studies of local life, such as *New West, Bay Area Guardian,* and *San Francisco.*

Endless business and professional journals came to be based in California as its population grew, for there were ample opportunities to cater to special interests, ranging from industry to recreation and from sports to cults. Little magazines also flourished, not only in big cities but in so-called bohemian colonies, to print the work of contemporary poets and other experimental writers or to set forth radical or unusual ideas or minority views.

In time the distinction between magazines and newspapers grew less pronounced as both used similar formats and newsprint paper and both published reports on current events as well as more extended articles and essays on general subjects and a certain amount of creative writing in the form of fiction or verse. Thus *Rolling Stone* (1967), *Berkeley Barb* (1965), and *Los Angeles Free Press* (1964) were all exponents of counterculture ideas presented in ways that might by older standards be placed in either category of journalism, now as a newspaper, now as a magazine. Furthermore, they indicated the variety of lifestyles in California which could find large publics to subscribe to journals of conventional suburban ways, such as that to which the successful *Sunset* (founded 1898) appealed, and that for which *Berkeley Barb,* on the edge of new radicalism and new eroticism, was designed. (*See also individual entries.*)

Magic Mountain, tourist attraction northeast of Los Angeles, near Saugus, covering over 200 acres. Its features include a sky tower, an aerial tramway, a ride in a hollowed-out log (of plastic) in a flume that shoots over waterfalls, and a roller coaster.

MAGNES, JUDAH L[EON] (1877–1948), Oakland-born Jewish leader. After education at Hebrew Union College, the University of Cincinnati, and Heidelberg, and service as a rabbi, he moved to Palestine (1922). There he became the first Chancellor of the Hebrew University in Jerusalem and proposed a binational state with political parity between Arabs and Jews. A museum of Jewish history and culture in Berkeley bears his name.

MAGNIN, prominent California family, whose founder, Isaac (1842–1907), moved to the U.S. from his native Holland as a young boy. After service in the Confederate Army and life in London, he ran an art goods store and married a woman from Holland, Mary Ann Cohen (1849–1943). He, his wife, and their four children went to Oakland, then to San Francisco in 1876. Mary Ann Magnin that year opened the first Magnin store, a notions shop with fine needlework. It grew into I. Magnin & Co., specializing in direct European imports of clothing. Joseph, one of the English-born children, wanted the firm to manufacture some of its own goods, so he left the company in the first decade of the century to found the store named for him: Joseph Magnin. Emanuel John, another English-born son, succeeded his father as president of the original company, and, later, Grover, one of the four children born in the U.S., directed the firm. I. Magnin & Co. began to establish branches in California (1912) and outside the state (1925), the entire business being bought after Grover's death by a nonfamily firm. Joseph's son, Cyril (1899–), remained as president of that firm even after it was sold. He also occupied major civic offices in San Francisco and was a leader in its community affairs. The son of one of the English-born children, Edgar Magnin (1890–), became a leading rabbi of Los Angeles (1915).

MAGUIRE, TOM (THOMAS MAGUIRE) (1820–96), went from New York City, where he had been a theater bartender, to found theaters in San Francisco and the mining towns. He presented stars like Boucicault, Forrest, Joseph Jefferson, James O'Neill, Menken, and Modjeska. He also produced operas. James A. Herne♦ got his start with Maguire, and Belasco♦ served him as secretary (he was illiterate). Maguire, his fortunes waning, eventually drifted back to New York, where he died destitute.

Maiden Lane, short, narrow street of shops extending east from the center of Union Square in San Francisco. Ironically named because in the 19th century it was an alley inhabited by prostitutes, it is now a tree-lined walkway with smart boutiques and restaurants, including a building designed by Frank Lloyd Wright♦ (1948).

Maidu, Indians of the Penutian family (scornfully called Diggers by Americans because they used sticks to dig). They lived in the drainage area of the Feather, American, Bear, and Yuba rivers. Their social structure was like that of the Pomo, in that a large group held a defined tract of land while living in small allied villages, which sometimes held as many as 500 people in earth-covered dome-shaped houses. In precontact times the Maidu may have numbered as many as 9,000, but by 1910 they had been reduced to 1,000. Like the Wintun, they practiced the Kuksu cult♦ and observed a great annual mourning ceremony. The southern group of Maidu living in Sierra foothills and valley sites of the present Sacramento, Marysville, and Placerville were called Nisenan, meaning simply "People." Maidu of the northwest area were called Konkow or Concow.

Maize, grown by the Cahuilla, Paiute, and other Indian tribes. This variety of corn was an important food crop for the Europeans too, being raised at the missions and by the Russians at Fort Ross. During the gold rush Americans replaced it with wheat and barley.

Malakoff Diggins State Historic Park, site in Nevada County of a major mine excavated by hydraulic pressure to a depth of 600 feet, a length of 7,000 feet, and a width of 3,000 feet before a decision of Judge Lorenzo Sawyer (1884) prohibited further mining because the debris would pollute other properties.

MALASPINA, ALEJANDRO (1754–1810), Italian navigator, as a captain in the Spanish Navy led a scientific expedition (1789–94), one of whose purposes was to explore the Pacific Coast and to determine whether there was a Strait of Anián, or northwest passage, to Asia. During a visit to Monterey (Sept. 11–26, 1791) his two artists made charts as well as pictures of Indian and Spanish life while he collected artifacts and recorded information about the local cultures and flora and fauna. In the crew of one of his two corvettes was John Green, the first American known to have landed in California; Green died and was buried at Monterey. After returning to Spain Malaspina became the victim of a political conspiracy, his records were consigned to archives, his leadership of the great expedition was overlooked, and he faded into obscurity.

Malibu, name of unknown but Indian origin, an abbreviation of Rancho Topanga Malibu Sequit, a 22-mile-long strip of oceanfront land between Ventura and Santa Maria. Originally inhabited by Chumash, it was granted to a soldier with Anza. Later bought by Frederick Rindge,♦ who developed it into a great ranch, it was finally subdivided in the 1920s into large sites for homes, often bought by motion picture stars. The city fronts on Santa Monica Bay.

Maltese Falcon, The, see *Hammett, Dashiell.*

Mama's Bank Account, see *Norwegians in California.*

Mammoth Lakes, three small lakes located east of Devil's Postpile♦ in Mono County on the border of Fresno and Madera counties. Like nearby Mammoth Mountain, they take their name from a gold mining company and its boom town founded near there (1878). The Mammoth Lakes Recreation Area covers 200,000 acres.

Manhattan Beach, residential development on Santa Monica Bay between Venice and Redondo Beach, in Los Angeles County.

Manila galleons, large Spanish vessels, which plied between Acapulco and the Philippines from 1566 to the end of Spanish control of Mexico in 1821. They traded Mexican silver and gold for Far Eastern spices, tea, porcelain, and other luxury goods, and carried as many as 600 passengers to Spain's Pacific outpost. In 1593 the king limited trade to a single annual round trip. The length of the return voyage (six or seven months) led to search for a port on the California coast for rest, repair, supplies, and refuge from English freebooters. Although Pedro de Unamuno had entered Morro Bay in 1587, a concerted effort to find a suitable harbor led Cermeño♦ to put into Drake's Bay in 1595, while Vizcaíno,♦ exploring for a port, sailed into Monterey in 1602. Later ships sailed close to California's shore but avoided the uncharted coast, and in 1763 trade was finally carried on directly between Spain and the Philippines. The title poem of Bret Harte's *The Lost Galleon* (1867) deals with a mythic ship's voyage.

Mankind United, religious cult founded in San Francisco (1934) with a pseudo-scientific and seemingly technological program to combat so-called Hidden Rulers of all industries and governments. The cult, whose "bureaus" flourished in southern California, promised that when these evil forces were eradicated there would be full employment, long vacations, and pensions for all people. It claimed 176,000,000 members around the world at its peak (1939) but probably sold or gave away no more than 125,000 copies of its publications (1936–40). With the ending of the Depression, Mankind United faded away and its main publicizer, Arthur L. Bell, and other leaders were tried (1943) for disseminating information that interfered with the U.S. war effort. After their conviction was reversed on technical grounds, Bell created Christ's Church of the Golden Rule, which garnered several million dollars of property from followers who were thereby "freed from the bondage of ownership." The Church flourished into the 1950s.

MANLY, WILLIAM LEWIS (1820–1903), left lead mining in Wisconsin, to which he had gone from his native Vermont, to try his hand at gold mining in California by setting out along the Oregon Trail in July 1849. Upon reaching Fort Bridger he thought he could float down the Green and Colorado rivers to California, and he did make his way, with others, by rough portages to Arizona. From there he had to make a hard trek across desert country to southern California, where he finally arrived in March 1850. Of this trip he later presented a moving account, *Death Valley in '49* (1894), which had obviously been partly ghostwritten, a later abbreviated version (1927) being even further reworked. Other sketches about his trip were collected in *The Jayhawkers' Oath* (1949), its title referring to the allied party, called Jayhawkers, composed of single men who accompanied the families with which Manly traveled.

MANN, THOMAS (1875–1955), distinguished German novelist and essayist, opposed Hitler and so fled his fatherland for Switzerland (1933) and had his citizenship abrogated by the Nazis (1936). From 1938 until he returned to Switzerland (1952), Mann lived in the U.S., all but the first three of those years being spent in California at Pacific Palisades, a refuge for other German intellectuals in exile. In 1944 he became an American citizen. During the war he made broadcasts to Germany. While in California he wrote *Joseph the Provider* (1943), the last novel of his tetralogy on Joseph; *Doctor Faustus* (1947); and *The Holy Sinner* (1951).

MANSFELDT, HUGO L. (1844–1931), German-born pianist, went to the U.S. (1860) and moved to Sacramento four years later to begin a career as a distinguished music teacher. He moved to San Francisco (1872) to found his Mansfeldt Conservatory of Music. After a brief absence to study in Germany with Franz Liszt (1884–86), he continued his teaching in Oakland. His system of instruction is set forth in *Technic* (1886; rev., 1906).

MANSON, CHARLES [MILLES] (1934–   ), criminal born in Cincinnati, the illegitimate child of a teenage prostitute, by the age of 25 had served 13 years in reformatories and prisons. He moved to San Francisco's Haight-Ashbury♦ district (c. 1967) and experimented with hallucinogenic drugs and the area's communal life. In 1968 he established a commune, originally with 26 followers, 20 of them female, on a ranch in the Santa Susana Mts. The so-called Manson family was held together by drugs, group

sex, common beliefs, and the leader's charisma. As a self-appointed punisher of the affluent, Manson and some of his followers brutally murdered people otherwise unknown to them. On one night in 1969 they killed Sharon Tate, the wife of motion picture director Roman Polanski, and four of the houseguests in her Hollywood Hills home. A day later they murdered a wealthy Los Angeles grocer and his wife, both times leaving messages scrawled with blood. The trial of Manson and three followers took nine and a half months, to then the longest in California history. It ended with his being condemned to death on seven counts of murder, but the sentence could not be carried out because the state laws do not allow execution. In 1975 one of his followers, "Squeaky" Fromme, attempted to assassinate President Ford during his visit to Sacramento.

Manteca, market and food processing center and residential community for an agricultural and beef raising area of southern San Joaquin County. The population in 1970 was 13,845.

"Man with the Hoe, The," poem by Edwin Markham.♦

Manzanar, see *Japanese relocation centers.*

Manzanita, evergreen plant whose 38 species growing throughout California range from prostrate shrubs to trees 30 feet high. They have paper-thin, smooth bark colored rich red, mahogany, or chocolate; thick, leathery leaves; pink or white spring flowers; and brown and green fruit that give rise to the name, meaning "little apples" in Spanish. Raw or cooked, the berries were an important food for the Cahuilla, Wintun, Yokut, and other Shasta tribes. Both fruit and leaves have been used for medicinal purposes, and the leaves were smoked by both Indians and early settlers. The hard wood was used for dowels in some early buildings (e.g. Mission Dolores), and in later years to create such objects as canes and pipe bowls for tourists.

Maple, broadleaf deciduous tree with four varieties native to California. The *bigleaf* or *canyon* is the only large maple, reaching 65 feet in height, and noted for its clustered yellow flowers. It grows below 5,000 feet elevation. The *vine* is a dwarf maple of sprawling formation and brilliant leaves found from Mendocino County north to Oregon. The *Sierra* or *mountain* is also a dwarf, less brilliantly colored, located at elevations from 5,000 to 9,000 feet. The *California box elder* is generally 30 to 45 feet high with a broad crown of leaves that are single lobed and not the usual grape-like leaf of the maple. The trees yield lumber for flooring, furniture, boxes, veneer, ties, and spools. About 25 creeks, mainly in the northern Coast Range, are named Maple.

MARBLE, ALICE (1913–   ), champion tennis player, born in Plumas County, reared in San Francisco. As a girl she was the mascot of the San Francisco Seals. She was four times the U.S. singles champion (1936, 1938–40) and once the British champion (1939). She won the U.S. women's doubles four times (1937–40) and the British twice. She also twice won the U.S. mixed doubles championship. She was known for her strong, versatile, and aggressive game.

Marble Mountains, within the Klamath National Forest in Siskiyou County, a chain of limestone peaks from which marble is obtained. They reach their highest elevation at nearly 7,400 feet.

March Air Force Base, located near the city of Riverside, founded in 1918. It has had its present name (honoring Peyton C. March, Jr., the World War I Chief of Staff's son) since 1948. It controls most of the Strategic Air Command of the western U.S.

MARCHETTI, GINO (1927–   ), West Virginia-born football player, reared in Antioch. He became a star tackle on the University of San Francisco team (1951), which he and Ollie Matson helped lead to an undefeated season. He later played professionally for the Baltimore Colts and was voted (1969) the greatest defensive end in football history.

Mare Island, on San Pablo Bay across the Carquinez Strait and Napa River from the town of Vallejo, supposedly named by Mariano Vallejo for a favorite horse that took refuge there after falling into the water. It is the site of a U.S. Navy shipyard (est. 1854) which has built nuclear submarines.

MARICHAL, JUAN [ANTONIO] (1937–   ), born in the Dominican Republic and known for his fiery temperament, became a pitcher for the San Francisco Giants (1960–73).

Marin City, real estate development near Sausalito, begun during World War II as low-cost housing for workers in the adjacent yard where Liberty Ships were constructed.

Marin County, one of the original 27 counties, its county seat is San Rafael. It is bounded by Sonoma County to the north, and the ocean and San Francisco and San Pablo bays on other sides. The home of Miwok Indians, its first European visitor was Sir Francis Drake, who careened his ship in one of its harbors (1579). The next foreigner was Cermeño (1595) and much later Ayala used Angel Island as his base (1775). However, Spanish settlement, working up from the south, was long delayed and Mission San Rafael was not founded until 1817. The countryside was carved into *ranchos,* including one granted to William A. Richardson, who built a home at Sausalito, long an anchorage for whalers and visiting ships. The Bear Flag Revolt began in this area with the Battle of Olompali. In the late 19th century and on to the present time, the beautiful countryside close to San Francisco has developed residential regions in such communities as Ross, Fairfax, Belvedere, Sausalito, Mill Valley, and San Rafael, and preserved scenic areas such as Point Reyes, Bodega Bay, Drake's Bay, Muir Woods, Mt. Tamalpais, Stinson Beach, Bolinas Lagoon, Tomales Bay, and Inverness. Much of this country is being protected in the Golden Gate National Recreational Area, although the county has many farms for dairying, poultry, and stock raising. It is also the site of Hamilton Air Force Base and of San Quentin Prison. In 1970 the population was 206,758; with an area of 332,928 acres, it had 397.6 persons per sq. mi. (*See also individual entries.*)

Marineland, tourist attraction north of San Pedro, featuring performing whales, dolphins, and sea lions in a kind of aquatic circus. This original enterprise has been imitated elsewhere.

Mariposa Battalion, posse (Dec. 1850–May 1851) under the leadership of James D. Savage◆ and Lafayette H. Bunnell,◆ deputized as state militia by Gov. McDougal to hunt down some 350 Miwok, Yokut, and Chowchilla Indians, led by Chief Tenieya, who had attacked white miners who had invaded their lands. They finally surrendered after Tenieya's son was killed. In reconnoitering, Savage and Bunnell came upon, explored, and named Yosemite Valley, previously known only to Indians and, perhaps, to Joseph R. Walker's party.

Mariposa County, one of the original 27 counties (1850). At first it stretched over to the Coast Range and back to the Nevada state line and down to Los Angeles County, covering one-fifth of the state, but its lands were whittled away to help form ten other counties. Now it is bounded by Tuolumne County on the north and east, Merced County on the west, and Madera County on the south. The name ("butterfly" in Spanish) was given by Gabriel Moraga (1806) as Las Mariposas to an area that became the grant purchased by Larkin for Frémont. The first whites to see the region were Joseph R. Walker's party in 1833; Zenas Leonard described the great sequoia groves (1839) in his narrative of that expedition. He may also have seen Yosemite Valley, but its first explorer was James D. Savage, whose Mariposa Battalion was recruited from the mining area that grew up during the gold rush, with such mushroom towns as Ben Hur, Bootjack, Coulterville, and Hornitos, the last, as the Spanish name indicates, mainly a Mexican settlement. Bear Valley was the center of Frémont's prosperous mining activity. Since 1851 the county seat has been Mariposa, which has the state's oldest courthouse (1854). The only other sizable community is Coulterville, but both of them are still mountain towns. Wawona is an historic resort begun by Galen Clark, discoverer of the Mariposa Grove, famous for its gigantic sequoias, through one of which (Wawona) a road was cut. El Portal forms the western gate to Yosemite Valley, lying in a panhandle jutting out between the Stanislaus and Sierra National Forests. The Merced River, rising in Yosemite, flows westward through the county and forms Lake McClure. In 1970 the county had a population of 6,015; with an area of 931,112 acres, it had 4.1 persons per sq. mi. (*See also individual entries.*)

Mariposa Grant, name commonly given to Las Mariposas, an area of ten square leagues (a large part of present Mariposa County) given by Gov. Micheltorena to Juan B. Alvarado (1844), who sold it to Frémont (1847) through Frémont's agent, Larkin. Since Alvarado had not fulfilled any requirements of the grant (e.g. residence upon the land), a district court invalidated it, but Frémont's brother-in-law, William Carey Jones,♦ successfully defended his case. The U.S. Supreme Court upheld the claim despite the fact that it was also questionable because as a "floating grant" its total area was stated but its boundaries were not. In the final survey Frémont was awarded three profitable gold mining districts initially considered to be in the public domain. Obtained for $3,000, the grant made a fortune for Frémont, although he lost it in the 1860s through some complicated financial deals.

Mariposa Grove, stand of sequoias in the extreme south of Yosemite National Park, about 35 miles

from the Valley. One of the famous trees, Wawona, was tunneled for a road to pass through it, but it fell in the winter of 1968–69.

Maritime Museum, San Francisco, exhibition building on the waterfront, erected (1939) to display memorabilia and pictures of shipping on the Bay. The San Francisco Maritime State Historic Park, off the nearby wharf, is a floating display of ships representative of the kinds that once came into the Bay.

Market Street, major San Francisco thoroughfare, laid out by Jasper O'Farrell♦ (1847) and named after a street in his home city, Philadelphia. The 120-foot-wide street extends from the Ferry Building to Twin Peaks, cutting the city's conventional grid plan by its diagonal route, set at a 45-degree angle. The area on its southeast was known as South of the Slot,♦ a reference to the cable car slot that once ran up the street. Along the way are several open, park-like places, including Mechanics Square, Marine Plaza, and Hallidie Plaza. The street is a major route not only for transportation but also for the city's frequent parades.

MARKHAM, EDWIN [CHARLES] (1852–1940), Oregon-born poet, reared from the age of 4 in San Jose and near Vacaville. After attending Christian College (Santa Rosa) he became a schoolteacher in Coloma and, later, Oakland, meanwhile writing poetry. The publication of "The Man with the Hoe," in the *San Francisco Examiner* (Jan. 15, 1899), written after viewing the Millet painting owned by the Crocker family, made him suddenly famous for its rhetorical protest against the brutalizing exploitation of labor represented by a farmer "bowed by the weight of centuries." When published as the title work of a collection of poems (1899), it earned him both a critical reception and great royalties. Accordingly Markham moved to New York to be part of a larger literary scene, and temporarily continued his success with the comparable title poem of *Lincoln and Other Poems* (1901). He became a well-known declamatory reader of his own poetry and lecturer on idealistic views, but Markham's poetic achievements over a long lifetime were only fitfully comparable to his early work, as in "Swedenborg" (1924), although he wrote many volumes and edited many others. In *The Octopus* Frank Norris modeled the character Presley partly on Markham.

MARKHAM, HENRY HARRISON (1840–1923), 18th governor of the state (1891–95). After service in the

Union Army and law practice in Wisconsin he moved to Pasadena, where he made a fortune in real estate and mining. A prominent Republican, he had a term in Congress and a term as governor but was not renominated because of labor unrest and his inability to cope with an economic depression.

Mark Hopkins Hotel, hostelry on the Nob Hill site of the mansion planned by the railroad financier, completed and lived in by his widow. The retaining walls of the great house and its carriage entrance still surround the hotel (constructed 1926). Familiarly called The Mark, its glass-walled tower bar (created 1936), The Top of the Mark,♦ was long the highest public room in the city. Even though now overlooked by taller hotels, it continues to be popular.

Markleeville, seat of Alpine County, named for a pioneer settler, was founded in 1864. It flourished during the area's silver mining boom but began to decline in the 1870s. Its population in 1970 was under 400.

Mark of Zorro, The, see *Zorro.*

Mark Twain, pseudonym of Samuel L. Clemens.♦ The term, meaning "two fathoms deep," was employed in making soundings from Mississippi riverboats. An older pilot, Isaiah Sellers (*c.* 1802–64) had used it to sign some pompous articles contributed to a New Orleans journal, which Clemens so tellingly parodied in another paper of that city that Sellers never published again. Clemens may have used the name later as a kind of reparation, since he speaks well of Sellers in *Life on the Mississippi* (1883). Clemens seems first to have used the name for his own signature in the Virginia City, Nevada, *Territorial Enterprise* (Feb. 3, 1863) so that it has some associations with his residence in the Far West.

Marlin, a game fish found off the shore south from Point Concepcion. It is purple-blue with a slender striped body up to 11 feet long and an upper jaw extended outward like a round sword. Average weight is 150 pounds. Also called sailfish, they are game fighters and fishing for them is restricted to sportsmen.

Marlowe, Philip, hero of Raymond Chandler's *The Big Sleep*♦ and other detective novels.

MARPLE, WILLIAM (1827–1910), New York-born artist, resident in the mining country beginning in 1849 and in San Francisco from the 1860s to 1877.

He was known for his landscapes of the Sierra and other rugged areas.

MARRIOTT, FREDERICK (1805–84), English journalist, went to California (1849) where he mined gold and served as a correspondent for the London *Times* before founding his own journals in San Francisco. These included the *News Letter*♦ (1856), initially a letter sheet♦ of blue paper with columns of news and advertisements folded so as to leave a blank page for correspondence and another for the address. As the *News-Letter and Commercial Advertiser* it expanded into a newspaper for which Ambrose Bierce wrote his column, "The Town Crier" (1868–72), and for which he and C. W. Stoddard were for a time editors. Profits from the journal were used by Marriott to finance his long-standing hobby of aviation, particularly of a dirigible, called the *Avitor,* first flown in 1869.

MARRYAT, FRANK (SAMUEL FRANCIS MARRYAT) (1826–55), went from England to California (1850–52, 1853) to gather material for a book on an exotic place comparable to his work on *Borneo* (1848). In 1855 he published his view of California, *Mountains and Molehills,* noted for its lively and amusing observations on the gold rush and *rancho* life as well as for the author's vivid drawings. His father, Capt. Frederick Marryat (1792–1848), was a popular author of novels with naval settings who also visited the U.S., whose manners he criticized. Without first-hand knowledge of the West, Capt. Marryat wrote the melodramatic, fictive, and often plagiaristic *Narrative . . . of Monsieur Violet in California, Sonora, and Western Texas* (1843).

MARSH, JOHN (1799–1856), after graduation from Phillips Academy, Andover, in his native Massachusetts, and from Harvard (1823) was appointed a tutor to officers' children at Fort Snelling in present Minnesota. He studied medicine there, then served as an Indian agent in Wisconsin and published a Sioux grammar (1831). He fled the region when threatened with arrest for selling arms to Indians, whom he helped lead in the Black Hawk War (1832).

In time he made his way to Santa Fe and from there to Los Angeles (1836), where he became California's first practicing doctor, though he simply used his Harvard diploma to convince authorities that he was a licensed physician. His fees (mainly in cattle hides) allowed him to buy from José Noriega♦ Los Médanos *rancho* near Mt. Diablo, on which he ran cattle collected as medical fees.

Settled in California as a convert to Roman

Catholicism and as a naturalized citizen, Marsh sent word east to praise the region and to attract U.S. settlers, whom he received well but charged large sums for supplies and other aid. Having become a well-to-do cattle rancher, although disliked for his miserliness, Marsh next planned to establish himself as a lord of the manor presiding over many acres cared for by Bolbones Indians.

He married the daughter of a Massachusetts minister (1851), and for her and their daughter planned a great stone house with high English gables. But his wife died three years before the mansion was completed (1856), and Marsh became an even more lonely, cantankerous, and greedy man. Three of his *vaqueros,* angered by bad treatment and low wages, murdered him. His great new edifice was left as a memorial in the remote area, eventually to become a public monument.

MARSHALL, JAMES WILSON (1810–85), as a young man left his native New Jersey (where his great-grandfather had served as a signer of the Declaration of Independence) to live in Indiana, Illinois, and near Fort Leavenworth. In 1844 he traveled the Oregon Trail with a wagon train, wintered at Fort Hall, went to the Willamette Valley, and then south under the leadership of James Clyman♦ to Sutter's Fort. Soon after his arrival (July 1845) he obtained two leagues of land and livestock, but left them to join Frémont in the Bear Flag Revolt. After the war Marshall returned to find his cattle gone. Being without funds, he became Sutter's partner (1847) in building a small sawmill at Coloma (45 miles northeast of Sutter's Fort on the South Fork of the American River), he providing skilled work while Sutter furnished capital. Just before the mill was ready to work, the tailrace had to be deepened to allow free rotation of the wheel, and in the process, he discovered gold in the raceway (Jan. 24, 1848). Neither Marshall nor Sutter nor other associates kept the secret, and so a rush began which brought nothing but unhappiness to the partners, who soon lost their workers and their lands. Marshall became an embittered and depressed man. Although voted a pension for a time (1872–78) by the California legislature, he never reestablished himself but spent his last years in menial jobs near Coloma, where later a monument was erected to him. His original discovery is ironically memorialized: the nugget he found is called the Wimmer Nugget♦ after Peter L. Wimmer, Marshall's assistant.

MARSHALL, ROBERT BRADFORD (1867–1949), Virginia-born planner of large-scale water projects, went to California (1891) with the U.S. Geological Survey, of which he became the Chief Geographer. He originated a program (1919) to dam the upper Sacramento River and divert its water through canals into the Central Valley. This so-called Marshall Plan was the forerunner of the Central Valley Project.♦ He later helped plan and develop the state's highway system (1928–37).

MARSHALL, WILLIAM, see *Garrá Revolt* and *Pauma Massacre.*

MARTIN, BILLY (ALFRED MANUEL MARTIN) (1928–), Berkeley-born baseball player and manager. He played second base for the Oaks (1947–49), the New York Yankees (1950–53, 1955–57), and five other teams. His career as manager, which has been disputatious but athletically successful, has led him to head the Minnesota Twins (1969), Detroit Tigers (1971), Texas Rangers (1973–75), and New York Yankees.

MARTIN, GLENN L[UTHER] (1886–1955), went to Santa Ana (1905), where after work in the auto business he founded an airplane factory (1909). His planes were used for local mail delivery, perhaps the first such service. Donald Douglas was an associate in the company, which also built planes for exhibition and sport flying. After World War I he moved his company to Baltimore. His later major planes included the "China Clippers" for transpacific flight, the first twin-engine army bomber, and the first army trainer model.

MARTIN, LILLIEN JANE (1851–1943), psychologist, born in New York State, served on the Stanford faculty (1899–1916), and then founded mental hygiene clinics in San Francisco hospitals. She worked first with normal young children, later with the social rehabilitation of old people.

Martin Eden, novel by Jack London, published in 1909. Like the author, the hero is a former sailor and laborer with physical and intellectual powers who is led to educate himself and to attend the University of California. He is first inspired and later disillusioned by a college-bred society girl's cultural values which he leaves behind him as he is influenced by a Socialist poet (said to be based on George Sterling). The suicide of the poet, Martin's contempt for his former fiancée's beliefs, and his loss of affiliation with his own working class background destroy his will and lead to his suicide.

MARTINEZ, XAVIER (1869–1943), Mexican-born artist, went to San Francisco when his stepfather was made consul-general there (1893). He studied under Arthur F. Mathews♦ and in Paris under Carrière. In San Francisco and Piedmont, where he taught at the College of Arts and Crafts, he was a noted bohemian and an accomplished painter of landscapes, portraits, and evocative genre studies. He was an early member of Carmel's art colony. He married the daughter of Herman Whitaker.

Martinez, seat of Contra Costa County, located on Carquinez Strait facing Suisun Bay. It was named for Ignacio Martínez, *comandante* of the San Francisco Presidio (1822–27), on whose *rancho* it was laid out (1849). It is the site of oil refineries, canning plants, and a fishing port. The adobe of Martinez' son Vicente and the homes of John Muir and John Swett are nearby. Joe DiMaggio was born in the city. In 1970 its population was 16,506.

MARTINI, LOUIS M. (1887–1974), went to San Francisco (1900) from his native Genoa to enter the fish business with his father. After the earthquake of 1906 he began a tentative entry into the wine business. He returned to Italy to study enology, and then became a vineyardist in Napa and Sonoma counties. His son, Louis Peter, succeeded him (1960) in running what by that time was a major, family-owned business.

MARVIN, JOHN G[AGE] (1815–57), an alumnus of Wesleyan College (Conn.) and Harvard Law School, went to California (1849) where he served in the Mariposa Battalion,♦ was a founder of Tulare County, and a pioneer judge. He was the state's first Superintendent of Public Instruction (1851–53) and thereby a founder of its public school system. He was also well known for his pioneer work in legal bibliography.

MARWEDEL, EMMA (1818–93), went from Germany to the U.S. (1870) and five years later to Los Angeles, where she opened the state's first kindergarten. Later she led the kindergarten movement in the San Francisco Bay area, where her former pupil Kate Douglas Wiggin♦ was a teacher.

MARX BROTHERS, three Hollywood comedy stars, whose careers began in vaudeville: Chico [Leonard] (1891–1961), Harpo [Arthur] (1893–1964), Groucho [Julius] (1895–1977) and continued for two decades in Hollywood films, initially joined by a fourth brother (Herbert), called Zeppo, who played supporting parts as a romantic figure. The others respectively enacted a comic Italian, a zany mute harp player, and a black mustachioed pseudo-serious, wisecracking wild man. With these established characters they romped through films with surrealistically fanciful situations that befuddled the other persons caught in the plots. Their films include *Animal Crackers* (1930), *Horse Feathers* (1932), *Duck Soup* (1933), *A Night at the Opera* (1935), and *A Night in Casablanca* (1946).

Marysville, seat of Yuba County, located at the confluence of the Feather and Yuba rivers, was founded 1850 and named for Mary Murphy Covillaud, a member of the Donner Party and wife of the leading landowner of the region. It quickly became the major trading center for the northern mines during the gold rush and an important supply port. Stephen J. Field♦ was its first *alcalde.* Its population in 1970 was 9,353. On the west bank of the Feather River lies Yuba City in Sutter County, and to its northwest are the high peaks known variously as the Marysville Buttes or the Sutter Buttes.♦ Frank Bacon and Curtis H. Lindley were born in Marysville. The city's population in 1970 was 9,353.

MASON, BIDDY (1815?–91), born a slave in Georgia, was taken overland by her master to Utah (1848) and then to San Bernardino (1851) from whence her owner was prevented from taking her to Texas because he was judged to have lost his property rights by a three-year residence in a free state. As a free woman she became a nurse, with her earnings bought real estate, and became well to do and known for her charities.

MASON, RICHARD BARNES (1797–1850), 5th American military governor of California (May 31, 1847–Feb. 28, 1849), a native of Virginia and great-grandson of George Mason, the Revolutionary statesman. His army career included service in the Black Hawk War and, under Gen. Kearny, in the conquest of New Mexico and California. After succeeding Kearny as military governor he was authorized to establish a civil government. Mason drew up a code of laws, but decided not to issue them because he believed that, the Treaty of Guadalupe Hidalgo (May 1848) having concluded the war, the matter of such government was in the province of Congress. The need for a civil government and legal code became imperative because military rule was weakened by discharges and desertions, while a great civilian influx was occasioned by the gold rush. Accordingly Mason was relieved as military governor and as acting civil governor and returned to his headquarters in Missouri, where he soon died. His official report on gold deposits, issued Aug. 17, 1848, was widely printed (e.g. in Revere's *A Tour of Duty in California,* 1849) as an accurate document and attracted many. Fort Mason (S.F.) was named for him.

MASSETT, STEPHEN C. (1820–98), English-born author, went to New York City (1837) where he began his career as actor and singer. Moving to San Francisco (1849), he gave there the first theatrical performance, singing his own melodies and portraying Shakespearean characters. He dabbled in real estate, particularly in "Pipesville" near Mission Dolores. He edited the Marysville *Herald,* printing the first of the letters of Dame Shirley,♦ which he got for *The Pioneer,* being a contributor to it and the *Golden Era.* His *"Drifting About, or What "Jeems Pipes of Pipesville" Saw- and- Did* (1863) is an autobiographical account of early California theater.

MASSON, PAUL (1859–1940), French-born wine-maker, went to California as a young man (1878) to work at the pioneer Santa Clara Valley winery founded by Charles LeFranc (1852) for his Almaden vineyard, near Los Gatos and the New Almaden quicksilver mine. He was soon a partner, married LeFranc's daughter, became head of the firm, and began new vineyards in the Saratoga foothills. He sold the winery in 1936 and it has since grown under other hands but retained his name.

Matanza, Spanish word for "slaughter," term applied to the killing of cattle. It was commonly carried on at each *rancho* to obtain tallow, hides, and meat, but also occasionally became a larger event at which the animals were killed by *vaqueros* riding through the herds and slitting the beasts' throats.

MATHER, STEPHEN [TYNG] (1867–1930), born in San Francisco, a descendant of the distinguished colonial Massachusetts family. After graduation from the University of California he became an executive in the borax business. He is famous as the organizer and first director of the National Parks system (1917–29), for which he set the finest standards in the preservation of wilderness and defense of natural beauty.

Mather Air Force Base, located just east of Sacramento. Founded during World War I as a school to train pilots, it is still dedicated to that purpose.

MATHEWS, ARTHUR F[RANK] (1860–1945), artist, reared in Oakland, trained in Paris. With his wife, Lucia K[leinhaus] Mathews (1870–1955), he established a style of painting and decorative art (furniture, picture frames, and *objets d'art*) that used local scenery and flora to celebrate Californian cultural ideals in a vaguely symbolic fashion. He often displayed a romantic Hellenism that conceived of California in terms of a pastoral Greek lifestyle, but both his and his wife's paintings were marked more by pattern and design than by a developed philosophic conception. They influenced the local aesthetic life by his position as director of the California School of Design (1890–1906), where his students included Francis McComas,♦ Xavier Martinez,♦ and Gottardo Piazzoni♦ and by their journal *Philopolis.♦* His own largest works were twelve historical murals in the rotunda of the state capitol.

MATHEWS, EDDIE (EDWIN LEE MATHEWS) (1931–), Texas-born baseball player reared in Santa Barbara. He became the third baseman for the Boston Braves (1952) and moved with the team to Milwaukee and Atlanta (1966), later serving as manager (1972–74).

Mathews, Lake, reservoir southwest of Riverside, the major storage facility of the Colorado River Aqueduct. It was named (*c.* 1940) for W. B. Mathews, the first general counsel of the Metropolitan Water District of Southern California, who had died not long before.

MATHIAS, BOB (ROBERT BRUCE MATHIAS) (1930–), Tulare-born star athlete. As a 17-year-old high school student he became the youngest person ever to win the Olympic Games decathalon championship. For that he also won the Sullivan Award (1948) as outstanding U.S. amateur athlete. At Stanford University he was both a track and football star. He was also four times the U.S. decathalon champion and was again an Olympic Games champion (1952). He later played in films and was a U.S. Congressman (1966–74).

Matilija, bushy plant, 2 to 12 feet high, with gray-green foliage and large white poppy flowers. It grows wild from Santa Barbara to the Mexican border. The name is probably Chumash in origin; those Indians used the plant for medicinal purposes. Matilija Canyon (Ventura County) was the scene of the state's worst forest fire (1932).

MATSON, OLLIE (OLIVER MATSON) (1930–), Texas-born football player reared in California, where he became a star fullback for the University of San Francisco (1949–51) and an All-American. He was later a member of the U.S. Olympic track team (1952). A football player for the Chicago Cardinals, he was traded to the Los Angeles Rams for nine of their players, and became a member of that team (1959–62).

MATSON, WILLIAM (1849–1917), Swedish-born shipping magnate, went around the Horn to San Francisco (1867), where he embarked on Bay, river, and coastal trade. In 1882 he began shipping and trading to Hawaii. Later he developed California oil lands and began a Hawaiian oil company as well as expanding his Matson Navigation Co. and its investments in Hawaii. His son-in-law, William P. Roth, expanded the firm's interests and bought out the competing Oceanic Shipping Co. of the Spreckels family. Matson's grandson, William M[atson] Roth (1916–), has been a Regent of the University of California, president of California Tomorrow, and the developer of Ghirardelli Square in San Francisco.

Mattole River, rises in northern Mendocino County and runs north for about 50 miles to flow into the ocean about 35 miles below Eureka. It was named for an extinct Athabascan tribe. The Mattole Valley through which the river flows was the site of early oil discoveries in the 1860s, commemorated in the name of a town, Petrolia.

MAXWELL, GEORGE HEBARD (1860–1946), Sonoma-born lawyer and leader in championing federal programs for irrigation and land reclamation. He spent much time out of the state in the national capital and at the site of diverse conservation projects. His writings include *Golden Rivers and Treasure Valleys: Wealth from Wasted Waters* (1929).

Mayacamas Range, mountains in Napa and Sonoma counties, of which the best known is Mt. Saint Helena. Once a silver mining area, it is now known for vineyards.

MAYBECK, BERNARD (1862–1957), architect, born in New York City, worked as a boy in his father's furniture-carving shop, and at 18 went to Paris where he drifted into the Beaux-Arts to study architecture. In 1889 he moved west and settled in Berkeley. He worked briefly for Ernest Coxhead♦ and also taught architecture for a time at the University of California, inspiring and coordinating Phoebe Apperson Hearst's competition for an architectural plan for the campus.

For her he later built a vast hall on the campus to be used for entertainment, marked by a 54-foot-high laminated wood arch (1899). He also built (1902) for her a vast rubble stone castle-like home, Wyntoon, on the McCloud River, suiting the rugged northern California fishing country. Simpler buildings for plainer clients also freely adapted diverse architectural styles in a personal idiom marked by his own inventive exuberance. Often his houses were merely shingled, but details or great room height or baronial fireplace or general atmosphere gave them a Gothic feeling. Others were distinguished by his personal use of textured and interestingly colored stucco or of reinforced concrete.

He had a great sense of light (he liked clerestory windows) and of the relation of the building to its garden, frequently using a pergola to bridge the two. Those characteristics also marked his public buildings. In the First Church of Christ, Scientist, in Berkeley (1911) he freely used modern industrial materials like asbestos panels, cast concrete, and industrial steel sash in a structure marked by a poetic eclecticism that achieves a dignified but joyous feeling far above its component materials. Even more dramatic and romantic is the Palace of Fine Arts♦ he built for the Panama-Pacific International Exposition♦ (1915). Its neoclassical rotunda and colonnades curving around a lagoon are like a great Piranesi print in peach-colored plaster.

MAYER, LOUIS B[URT] (1885?–1957), Russian-born film magnate, reared in Canada, became a motion picture exhibitor and distributor in New England before going to Hollywood and entering into production. He merged firms to help create Metro-Goldwyn-Mayer (1924) and for some 25 years was an autocratic tycoon dominating stars and directors.

MAYS, WILLIE [HOWARD] (1931–), outfielder for the San Francisco Giants, born and reared in Alabama, became a member of the New York Giants team in 1951. With his team he moved to San Francisco at the end of the 1957 season and remained a star until traded to the New York Mets (1972). He broke the National League lifetime home run record (1966) and was named Baseball Player of the Decade (1970). He retired in 1973, after hitting 660 home runs in 22 years.

MEAD, ELWOOD (1858–1936), Indiana-born pioneer irrigation engineer, made his first important contribution as territorial engineer of Wyoming (1888–99) by outlining the principles of water administration that became the model for other arid and semi-arid areas. While with the U.S. Dept. of Agriculture (1899–1907) he wrote a basic report, *Irrigation Investigations in California* (1901), which led to a professorship at the University of California. He remained there until 1928, though with leaves to Australia and Palestine, and was U.S. Commissioner of Reclamation, a post he held until his death. In that capacity he supervised the beginnings of the All-American Canal and Central Valley irrigation projects, as well as the total construction of Hoover Dam, a major source for California water.♦ The lake created by the dam is the largest artificial body of water in the world, holding 32,360,000 acre-feet, or ten trillion gallons, and was named Lake Mead for him.

Mechanics' Institute of San Francisco, The, subscription library (est. 1855) whose reading rooms and book collection were originally intended for working class members. In early years it sponsored annual exhibitions to display products of the city's and the state's industries. The state Constitution provided that the Institute's president be a member of the Board of Regents of the University of California, a younger institution, until popular vote (1974) amended the Constitution. An older, comparable organization, the Mercantile Library (est. 1853), was absorbed by the Mechanics' Institute in 1906.

MEHTA, ZUBIN (1936–   ), Indian-born musician, after study in Vienna came to the U.S. (1961) and the next year became the conductor of the Los Angeles Philharmonic Orchestra, with which he remained until 1978.

MEIGGS, HENRY (1811–77), left his lumberyard in upstate New York with a shipload of timber for California (1848) at the opening of the gold rush. He not only made a small fortune but became a San Francisco civic leader. Meiggs Wharf, built in 1853 near the foot of Powell St., was but one of the investments which caused him to cover his overextended finances by forging city treasury warrants. He fled (1854) to Chile and Peru, where for a time he was even more successful as a railroad builder (repaying most San Francisco debts and persuading the California legislature to overturn an indictment against him), but once again he got into financial troubles with worthless notes.

MELLUS, HENRY (1816–60), Massachusetts-born merchant, went to California as a sailor with Dana on the *Pilgrim* (1835). He settled in Los Angeles, but in 1845 entered the general merchandise business in San Francisco with W. D. M. Howard♦ and became wealthy. In the last year of his life he moved to Los Angeles, where he was elected mayor. His brother Frank (1824–63) followed in his path as sailor and merchant.

Melones Water Project, federally funded program to build on the Stanislaus River a large dam and reservoir to supplant ones that antedate the Central Valley Project. Called the New Melones Water Project, this Bureau of Reclamation undertaking is to have a 625-foot-high dam and a 13-mile-long reservoir (with a storage capacity of 2,400,000 acre feet) about 35 miles east of Modesto. The program, expected to be completed by 1980, has been opposed by conservationists, who contend it will eliminate white water and recreational areas on the Stanislaus River, and by the state itself, which argues for a 1,100,000 acre-feet limit to protect the natural environment. A larger storage might also threaten the ability of the California Water Plan to discover sufficient surplus water in the north for diversion to southern California without harming the environment of the Delta land.

Melons, important California fruit crop. The state is the leading U.S. producer of cantaloupe: the crop in 1970 was grown on 58,000 acres and was worth $50,077,000.

Mendocino, Cape, presumably named for a Spanish viceroy, Mendoza, a promontory known to mariners of the Manila galleons in the late 16th century. It is the westernmost point of the mainland U.S. except Alaska.

Mendocino County, one of the original 27 counties (1850) but until 1859 administered by Sonoma County officials. Sonoma County lies on the south; Tehama, Glenn, and Lake on the east; Humboldt and Trinity counties on the north; and the Pacific Ocean on the west. The name derives from Cape Mendocino (presumably discovered by Cabrillo in 1542 and said to honor a Spanish viceroy, Mendoza), even though that feature is in Humboldt County.

Mendocino County has two major rivers, the Eel in the north and the Russian in the south, flowing through Coast Range valleys. The Noyo, Navarro, and Albion rivers have ocean ports, and the first a major fishing center, but these and other shipping points handled the lumber business that developed early and created such towns as Westport, Fort Bragg,♦ once a military post on an Indian reservation, Mendocino City, and Elk.

The region is noted for its redwoods and Douglas fir as well as wild rhododendron and iris on the headlands that jut above the sea, and for capes like Point Arena.♦ The old ports, reminiscent of New England towns, have become artists' colonies in recent years. The inland towns include Ukiah,♦ the county seat on the Redwood Highway; Boonville, where Boontling♦ originated; Willits; and Hopland, whose name celebrates a former major crop, hops. Round Valley, in the northeast corner, is an important Indian reservation. Tourists are attracted by the wild ocean, forest scenery, hunting, and fishing, and also by the skunk railroad.♦

In 1970 the county population was 51,101; with an area of 2,246,976 acres, it had 14.6 persons per sq. mi. Only a small, western part of Mendocino National Forest (a famous deer hunting area) is located in the county.

Mendota Pool, see *Delta-Mendota Canal.*

MENKEN, ADAH ISAACS (1835?–68), sensationally popular actress known for her role in the melodramatic *Mazeppa* (based on Byron's poem), in which she appeared in flesh-colored tights—seemingly nude—on horseback. With this play she came to San Francisco (1863), mingling there with Bret Harte, Mark Twain, and Joaquin Miller, as later, in London, she associated with Swinburne, Rossetti, and Dickens, to the last of whom she dedicated her romantic poems, *Infelicia* (1868). Among her husbands was "the Benicia Boy," John Heenan.♦

Menlo Park, residential community adjacent to Palo Alto in San Mateo County, founded (1854) by two men from Menlough, Ireland. Builders of great estates there included two U.S. Senators, Milton S. Latham, and Charles N. Felton; James C. Flood; and Faxon Dean Atherton. The former estate of Timothy Hopkins (Mark Hopkins' nephew) has long been the site of Stanford Research Institute, once part of the University, now a separate organization named Stanford Research Institute International. The most elegant part of the settlement was separated (1923) to become Atherton, which has no business district. Menlo Park had a population of 26,826 in 1970.

MENUHIN, YEHUDI (1916–), violinist born in New York City, reared in California, where he maintains a home in Los Gatos. A musical prodigy, he was a soloist with the San Francisco Symphony at age 7, made his Carnegie Hall debut at 10, and thereafter appeared with major orchestras around the world as an outstanding soloist, and often played with his sister Hepzibah, a fine pianist.

Mercantile Library, see *Mechanics' Institute.*

Merced, since 1872 seat of the county of the same name. It is a market and small manufacturing center for its agricultural region, but is best known as the gateway to Yosemite National Park. In 1970 it had a population of 22,670.

Merced, Lake, located in the southwesternmost part of San Francisco and extending to the San Mateo County line. It is a spring-fed body of fresh water by which Rivera y Moncada camped in 1774. In the 19th century it became part of the reservoirs of the Spring Valley Water Co.♦ Just to the southeast is the site of the duel between Sen. David C. Broderick and Chief Justice David S. Terry. The 36-hole golf course of the Olympic Club, private links, and the municipal course named for President Harding are located by the lake. On the ocean side of the lake are San Francisco's zoo and the Fleishhacker swimming pool and playground.

Merced County, organized (1855) from part of Mariposa County which lies on its east. Stanislaus and Fresno counties bound it north and south, while Santa Clara and San Benito counties lie to the west.

The first white exploration of the region was that of Gabriel Moraga (1805–06), who named its river in conjunction with the feast of Nuestra Señora de la Merced (Our Lady of Mercy). Succeeding travelers included Canadian and U.S. fur trappers and Frémont en route east (1844), while toll roads and the Butterfield stage route followed in the 1850s. Pacheco Pass (1,386 feet) has long been the route through the Diablo Mts. of the Coast Range, from the Santa Clara Valley to the roads south through the San Joaquin Valley. The region early became ranching country whose landholders included the Pacheco and Mejía families; and Frémont had part of his Mariposa grant here. Much of the region passed into the control of Henry Miller,♦ who made Los Banos the headquarters for his vast cattle ranches.

The entire San Joaquin Valley continues to be an agricultural, dairying, and stock raising area; Merced's major crops include alfalfa, tomatoes, sweet potatoes, almonds, and fruit. Merced has been the county seat since 1872 and is the rail and road center as well as the entry to Yosemite Valley. Major rivers are the central San Joaquin, into which flows the Merced, near the county's northern border, and the Chowchilla, along its southeastern border. The San Luis Reservoir♦ near Los Banos is a major water storage area. In 1970 the county population was 104,629; with an area of 1,267,584 acres, it had 52.8 persons per sq. mi.

Merced River, rises in Yosemite National Park in several forks which create Yosemite Falls and Bridalveil Falls, among others. From the valley the river flows southwest for 79 miles to join the San Joaquin River, north and west of Merced. Gabriel Moraga named it for Nuestra Señora de la Merced (Our Lady of Mercy) in 1806.

Mercer Caves, limestone formation near Murphys in Calaveras County. Closer to Vallecito are the Moaning Caves, a former Indian burial chamber.

Mercury, silvery metallic element, liquid at ordinary temperatures. Known also as quicksilver and obtained mostly from cinnabar, it has been mined in California since the late Mexican era. Deposits have been discovered in the Coast Range from Napa and Sonoma counties down to Santa Barbara. The two biggest mines in the U.S. were those at New Almaden♦ and New Idria (discovered 1853), southeast of Hollister, in San Benito County.♦ They closed in the 1970s.

MEROLA, Gaetano (1881–1953), Italian-born conductor, went to San Francisco (1921) as conductor of the touring San Carlo Opera Co. There he conceived the idea, which he executed the next year, of staging outdoor operas in the Stanford football stadium. In 1923 he inspired the creation of the San Francisco Opera Association and was its conductor and general director for the rest of his life. He was also instrumental in the building of the city's War Memorial Opera House (1932).

MERRIAM, Frank Finley (1865–1955), 28th governor of the state (1934–39). He began his career in Republican politics in his native Iowa and, after moving to California (1910), continued it as an Assemblyman and state Senator, a right-wing follower of Friend Richardson. From the lieutenant governorship he succeeded to the governorship on Rolph's death, quickly calling out the National Guard during San Francisco's General Strike of 1934, and thereafter was elected governor in his own right against Upton Sinclair in an intense campaign. During the Depression he emphasized economy and efficiency and introduced a state income tax. He also championed improved prisons and hospitals,

social security, and unemployment insurance, but he used highway police to break a Salinas lettuce strike. If some of his stands lost him conservative support, others lost him liberal voters, and he was not reelected.

MERRIAM, John C[ampbell] (1869–1945), professor of paleontology and geology at the University of California, Berkeley (1894–1930), a founder of Save-the-Redwoods League, and president of the Carnegie Institute.

MERRITT, Ezekiel (*fl.* 1841–48), mountain man and trapper who may have gone to California with William Walker (1833). A leader in the Bear Flag Revolt, he seized the horses of Francisco Arce♦ (June 10, 1846) in the first action of the rebellion. H. H. Bancroft considered him a "coarse-grained, unprincipled, quarrelsome fellow."

MERRITT, Samuel (1822–90), after graduation from Bowdoin College in his native Maine and the study of medicine, went to San Francisco (1849), where he was a doctor and became wealthy in real estate deals. In 1852 he moved to Oakland, became a leading citizen, and as mayor (1867–69) dammed a slough to create the downtown salt-water lake of 155 acres named for him. Though never married, he enjoyed elegant living and had a large schooner yacht, the *Casco,* which he leased to Robert Louis Stevenson for a voyage to the south Pacific (1888). Merritt founded the Oakland hospital that bears his name, and a community college was later named for him.

MERVINE, William (1791–1868), U.S. naval officer during the Mexican War,♦ sent by Commodore Sloat to occupy Monterey (July 7, 1846). In Oct. 1846 Commodore Stockton, in response to the plea carried by Juan Flaco Brown,♦ sent him to lead a relief force that initially failed in its attempt to aid the beleaguered Capt. Gillespie in recapturing Los Angeles. Mervine commanded the Pacific Squadron (1855–57).

MERYON, Charles (1821–68), French artist commissioned (1856) by F. L. Pioche♦ to create an engraving of San Francisco from five panoramic photographs. His large, handsome depiction of the city, which he never saw, included allegorical figures in the foreground, and medallions of Pioche and Jules Bayerque (another local sponsor), as well as a realistic portrayal of the city.

Mesquite, a spiny deciduous tree or shrub with long roots. It grows in desert locations. Its fruit pods provide animal fodder and have been used by Indians to make a fermented drink.

Metals, see *Minerals.*

Metropolitan Water District of Southern California, organized (1928) by the city of Los Angeles and other major cities of Los Angeles County to coordinate the distribution of water and power in their area. Their sources of water◆ include Lake Mead and that which comes via the California Aqueduct.

Mexicali, Mexican border city, literally across the street from Calexico◆ in Imperial County. It is the northern terminus of a major Mexican railroad, a free port, and location of a large brewery and a great cotton gin. It is the capital of Baja California. In 1970 it had a population of 392,324.

Mexican period of California, began in 1822 when the region was belatedly informed of the end of Spanish rule (1821) and the subsequent creation of an independent Mexican empire under Iturbide (1822). The incumbent governor who had been Spain's representative, de Sola, readily served the new nation but was soon succeeded by a native Californian, Luís Argüello, who presided over the transition to the Mexican Republic. A period of change in Mexico affected its remote Territory of California (not a Department until 1836), so that Echeandía, who succeeded Argüello, not only served his appointed term (1825–31) but with impunity ousted his successor, Manuel Victoria, to hold power (1831–33), shared with Zamorano, the printer.

Plans for secularization of the missions, suited to the more democratic Mexican government's opposition to Church monopoly, led to questionable activities, including the abortive land-grabbing scheme which sent José María Padrés and José María Híjar to project the settlement of Mexican colonists on mission lands, prevented only by Gov. Figueroa. Figueroa then issued a proclamation (1834) on the procedures for secularization.

Another major issue was whether California should have governors pledged to centralist rule from Mexico, like Chico, or native sons believing in home rule, like Alvarado, who, with his uncle Mariano Vallejo, and the help of Isaac Graham and other Americans, led one revolt (1836) and then participated in another that overthrew Gov. Micheltorena (1845).

Secularization led the governors to give much of the mission property in huge land grants to establish *ranchos* for leading families like the Carrillos, Ortegas, and Yorbas while there was very little development of the pueblos. On the *ranchos* there arose a distinctive pastoral society based on raising cattle, whose hides and tallow were traded to Americans, with whose shipping Richard Henry Dana was associated as a sailor and Alfred Robinson as a factor. This was a major example of the American impact that began with the first settler, Thomas Doak, but that included trappers, some only visitors like Jedediah Smith and James O. Pattie, some permanent settlers like George Nidever and William Wolfskill, who became Catholics and married into leading families, as did such businessmen as Abel Stearns and H. D. Fitch.

The threat of English incursion or of Russian settlement at Fort Ross was minimal next to the threat of Americans who, beginning with the Bartleson-Bidwell Party (1831), even came overland as settlers or seemed to threaten military seizure, like Commodore Thomas ap Catesby Jones in his occupation of Monterey (1842) or Frémont in his exploring expeditions. All this was prelude to the Bear Flag Revolt and the succeeding U.S. conquest of California in the Mexican War. (*See also individual entries.*)

Mexican War in California, often called the Conquest of California, followed hard on the Bear Flag Revolt (June 10–July 9, 1846). President Polk signed the congressional declaration of war on May 13, but this was not known in California until after Commodore Sloat, aware of hostilities in Texas and believing the Bear Flag Revolt needed regularization, had peacefully occupied Monterey (July 7) and San Francisco (July 12). Ill health led him to turn his command over to Commodore Stockton on July 23.

Stockton commissioned Frémont a major, put him in command of a California battalion of mounted riflemen, and dispatched him to San Diego. He also made Archibald Gillespie a captain in charge of Los Angeles, which Stockton occupied (Aug. 13). Gillespie's arbitrary rule led the Angelenos, under Capt. José María Flores, to revolt, which in turn forced Gillespie to surrender (Sept. 30). Gillespie dispatched "Juan Flaco" Brown to request of Stockton in San Francisco more troops, who soon arrived by sea under Capt. William Mervine.

An attempt to retake Los Angeles resulted in an American defeat at the Domínguez Rancho (Oct. 9), called the Battle of the Old Woman's Gun because the *Californios,* under Capt. José Antonio Carrillo, successfully used an old cannon that had been hidden in a lady's garden. Meanwhile the only engagement in the north occurred in the indecisive Battle of Natividad (Nov. 16) near present Salinas, when Californians under Manuel Castro tried to stop reinforcements being sent to Frémont.

During this time too, Frémont's force made its way south from Monterey, suppressing revolts en route and outflanking the ambush set for him at Gaviota Pass. Gen. Stephen W. Kearny, having occupied New Mexico, proceeded to California with about 100 dragoons who arrived tired, poorly fed, and ill equipped to be plunged immediately into the Battle of San Pasqual (Dec. 6), north of San Diego, where they suffered severe casualties by the Californians armed with lances and commanded by Andrés Pico. However, aided by Kit Carson's message for reinforcements and relief troops sent by Stockton, Kearny reached San Diego (Dec. 12) and, with Stockton, after an engagement at the San Gabriel River and the Battle of La Mesa, recaptured Los Angeles (Jan. 10, 1847).

Flores and Gov. Pío Pico surrendered to Frémont in the Cahuenga Capitulation (Jan. 13). With the war ended, Kearny and Stockton quarreled over the top command and establishment of a military government. Stockton soon named Frémont governor, an appointment Kearny would not recognize. Subsequent orders from Washington gave Kearny command of the land and authority to establish the government. Frémont, unaware of the orders, refused to obey Kearny, for which he was later sent to Washington for court-martial. The war itself was concluded by the Treaty of Guadalupe Hidalgo (Feb. 1848). (*See also individual entries.*)

Mexicans, the rulers of California during its Mexican period and owners of virtually all private lands, were rapidly dispossessed after the American conquest and the overrunning of the land during the gold rush. Being often free and easy about money and property or easily victimized by alien laws and race prejudice, they not only lost possessions and power but, despite an influx of Sonorans in the gold rush, they became a very small minority of the burgeoning population. By 1910 there were only 51,000 persons of Mexican descent in the state, whose total population was 2,377,549.

However, the revolution in Mexico (1910–15) and employment opportunities in California agriculture soon thereafter brought a large influx, some of them wetbacks, so that by 1945 Los Angeles was second only to Mexico City in Mexican population. The Mexicans could get only the lowest wages, were crowded into *barrios* (ghetto neighborhoods), were scorned by whites, and their young people were stigmatized as *pachucos* (juvenile hoodlums), in such cases of prejudice as the notorious Sleepy Lagoon Murder. But employers were happy to get cheap migratory farm workers under the U.S. program of importing *braceros* (1951–64), which added to the impoverished population.

Slowly they not only adapted to U.S. ways, but in the 1960s fought to get an improved status through greater opportunities to be educated in their own language, to gain easier admission to higher education, and to be recognized as a meaningful minority of persons with Spanish surnames. In part this occurred through their militant image of themselves as *Chicanos,* a name popularized in that decade as a proud adaptation of the term *Mexicanos,* and their sense of identity as *La Raza* ("the Race," or "the People"), who numbered 3,000,000, or over 15% of the population of California, in 1970.

The effective unionizing of Cesar Chavez through the use of *huelga* (strike) in grape and lettuce and other farm-working jobs also aided their image, as did the newspaper reporting in the *Los Angeles Times* of Ruben Salazar, accidentally killed in a riot (1970). (*See also individual entries.*)

MEYER, DEBBIE (DEBORAH ELIZABETH MEYER) (1952–   ), New Jersey-born swimming star, reared in a Sacramento suburb. Between 1967 and 1969 she established six world records for free-style swimming (200, 400, 800, and 1,500 meters and 440 and 880 yards). In the 1968 Olympic Games she became the first swimmer (man or woman) to win three gold medals in individual (as opposed to relay) races (200, 400, 800 meters free-style). She won the Sullivan Award (1968) as the outstanding amateur U.S. athlete.

MEYERS, WILLIAM HENRY (1815–50?), gunner aboard the U.S. warship *Cyane* (1841–44). His journal of life at sea and in California, with vivid primitive colored drawings, was partly published (1955, 1970), and his pictures of the naval conquest of California while a gunner on the *Dale* (1846) were printed in 1939.

MICHELSON, ALBERT ABRAHAM (1852–1931), Prussian-born physicist, taken by his parents to Murphys (1854) and reared there, in Virginia City, Nevada, and in San Francisco, until he went to the Naval Academy at Annapolis, Md. (1869). Later a professor at the University of Chicago known for determining the velocity of light, he was the first American scientist to receive a Nobel Prize (1907).

MICHELTORENA, MANUEL (*fl.* 1833–52), 13th Mexican governor of Alta California (1842–45) and last to be sent from Mexico. He went to the territory as a brigadier general commanding some 300 disorderly soldiers, mostly ex-convicts. He was told to exclude foreigners, especially Americans, but despite his several declarations, the incident of Commodore Thomas ap Catesby Jones♦ occurred during his administration. To gain support he granted lands to John Marsh, P. B. Reading, and others who had come overland to live in California. Micheltorena mismanaged the Monterey customs house and also had other financial problems owing to corrupt duty collectors. He promised to return former lands and income to the missions but could not carry out the program. Alvarado and Castro, incensed by the governor's troops, his currying favor with foreigners, and his Mexican centralist views, led a victorious rebellion in a battle at Cahuenga Pass (in which no persons were killed) which led to Micheltorena's expulsion. Returning to Mexico, he served in the Mexican War, became a member of the Mexican Congress (1847), and was appointed the commanding general of Yucatan (1850). While in Mexico (1852) he signed the documents, dated 1843, which were the bases of the fraudulent Limantour claims.♦

Midwinter Exposition, see *Golden Gate Park.*

MIGHELS, ELLA STERLING (1853–1934), born in California mining country and reared in Esmeralda, Nevada, a Comstock boom town, as a writer identified herself with the frontier spirit. Her works include *The Story of the Files* (1893), a compendium of early California journalism and literature, which she signed with her first husband's surname, Cummins; and *Literary California* (1918), an anthology, and *The Story of a Forty-Niner's Daughter* (1934), both of which she signed with Mighels, the surname of her second husband.

Mighty I Am, cult created by Guy W. Ballard, a one-time gold-mine promoter, and his wife Edna, a professional medium in Los Angeles (1934), and publicized by his *Unveiled Mysteries* (1934). The doctrines of the Mighty I Am, which derived its name from a chant, were called by Carey McWilliams "a weird brew of Theosophy, Rosicrucianism, New Thought, Buck Rogers and Superman." Ballard contended that a group of "Ascended Masters," including Christ and Moses but led by St. Germain, would blast followers with a "purple light" and "atomic accelerator" that removed obstructions to their will to power and wealth. The cult

became national with some 350,000 members, but after Ballard's death his widow and son were convicted for mail fraud (1940) and the organization fell apart except for a few faithful followers near Mt. Shasta, where Ballard said he had first met St. Germain.

Migration within California, evident from the first great growth of population in the mid-19th century, has been a characteristic of the state thereafter. Spanish and Mexican settlements were all near the seashore, where missions were built and pueblos founded with access by ship. Even the *ranchos* were not far from the coast. The gold rush not only brought a huge increase of population from all over the world, but it caused a great migration within California. Men moved to the foothills and mountains of the Sierra, where the gold was located, and they created cities, such as Sacramento and Stockton, as way stations to the mines and supply centers, while San Francisco, as the major harbor and great port of entry, grew largest of all.

As opportunities for individual mining slackened in the late 1850s and 60s, the Sierra Nevada counties dwindled. Changed economic opportunities led to greater migration into the lush Sacramento and San Joaquin valleys as railroad construction and drainage and irrigation projects made agriculture more rewarding. These areas supplied the increased population of the big cities and produced grain and other foodstuffs for export, so that by the 1870s California was the nation's greatest wheat-growing state.

As San Francisco continued to grow (from fewer than 150,000 people in 1870 to nearly 300,000 in 1890), many former city dwellers began to move across the Bay or down the Peninsula from which they could commute to their urban jobs by the increased services of ferries or railroads. The decade of the 80s also marked a tremendous expansion in southern California, which experienced the first of its numerous real estate booms (Los Angeles went from some 11,000 people to over 50,000) that created wholly new agricultural communities under the aegis of the region's earliest real estate promoters.

After momentary collapse, the southern California expansion grew at a greater and faster rate during the 20th century, among other things abetted by the Pacific Electric Railway Co., which built over 1,000 miles of track in the first two decades to connect ever-expanding suburban centers to the city of Los Angeles, which by 1920 had 576,673 people and for the first time surpassed San Francisco as the state's biggest city. In the Bay Area, Borax Smith's

Key Route system was playing a comparable part, though on a more modest scale. The process of urban growth accompanied by suburban expansion and widespread decentralization was significantly accelerated by the increase in automobile ownership beginning in the 1920s, with the greatest impact in southern California.

Los Angeles became a new kind of city: a minimized downtown core with a large but low-density spread of people over a very wide area linked by major boulevards. The automobile made migration to new areas easy, and by so accentuating mobility created the phenomenon, particularly Californian, of a car culture.♦ This effect was further intensified after World War II, when the state experienced a huge influx from other regions of persons with no sense of identification with one locale. Thus they, along with earlier settlers, moved easily into expanded or wholly new communities where housing was cheaper or jobs more available than in established areas.

The result was great tracts of quickly built housing and shopping centers spread over some of the state's finest agricultural land in Orange County, the San Fernando, Pomona, and San Gabriel valleys, the regions around Riverside and San Bernardino, and, to the north, the Santa Clara Valley, where San Jose earned a reputation as the world's fastest growing city. With the spread of settlement into previous nonurban areas, California also became a major developer of so-called New Towns, for over one-third of such planned instant cities in the nation were located within the state. Notable examples included the creation of Fremont in Alameda County, the smaller and more residential Foster City on the southern arm of San Francisco Bay, and developments around Irvine in Orange County.

Some more specialized kinds of migration within the state were also observable in the post-World War II era. Most striking was the shift of Japanese after their release from relocation centers, many of whom preferred to settle in the Los Angeles-Long Beach area instead of returning to their former northern California home towns. Notable too was the desire of many city dwellers to get away from large population centers and their related suburbia by going out to such removed regions as the Colorado and Mojave deserts. More limited but more extreme examples of such migration were to be seen in the trend of some young people, affected by the cultural values of hippies, to live simple, independent lives in such rural settings as Big Sur or the Mendocino coast.

National census figures on migrations within each state have been reported only since 1940, but they show that Californians have moved more frequently within their boundaries than have residents of other states and that the rate accelerates. In 1940 the percentage of such movers was 10.7 of the people in California; in 1950 it was 20.9, leaped to 45 in 1960, and kept to a high level with 39.1 in 1970. Among the results of such movement are a lack of identification with a region by its residents, a loss of both neighborliness and historical continuity, and a low level of concern with local social and political issues, even though the very movement itself leads to reapportionment in the state Senate.

Migratory labor, see *Agricultural labor.*

MILES, JOSEPHINE (1911–), poet and professor, after graduation from UCLA and graduate study at Berkeley, joined the faculty of the latter campus (1940). Her concise and observant poetry appeared in *Lines at Intersection* (1939), *Local Measures* (1946), *Prefabrications* (1955), *Civil Poems* (1966), *To All Appearances* (1974), and other volumes. She has written numerous scholarly studies of poetic diction in English and American literature from the Renaissance to the 20th century.

MILHAUD, DARIUS (1892–1974), French composer known for works that range from a short opera with libretto by Cocteau, an epic opera with libretto by Paul Claudel, ballet music, songs, and jazz treatments to chamber music. He was a professor of composition at Mills College for over 30 years.

Military installations, numerous because California is the largest and most populous state fronting the Pacific Ocean and possesses many significant industries manufacturing materiel for the armed forces. California's military importance may be traced back to the early days of American possession. For example, the old Castillo de San Joaquin, created by the Spanish to protect San Francisco, became the city's Fort Point, for defense when the Civil War was eminent. The old presidios, whose beginnings also lie in Spanish times, continue to be related to important army bases for the U.S. (such as Fort Ord in Monterey). On the other hand, many of the posts are of recent origin and were created for modern weaponry and warfare, as is evident at Vandenberg Air Force Base, a center for intercontinental ballistic missiles and satellites. The armed forces have many operational headquarters, depots, specialized stations, training centers, and various other kinds of posts but particularly important among these installations are Beale Air Force Base, Camp Pendleton, Camp Roberts, Castle Air Force Base, China Lake, Coronado, Edwards Air Force Base, Fort Baker, Fort Irwin, Fort MacArthur, Fort Mason, Fort Point, George Air Force Base, Hamilton Air Force Base, Hunter Liggett, Hunters Point, Imperial Beach, Lemoore Naval Air Station, Long Beach, March Air Force Base, Mare Island, Mather Air Force Base, McClellan Air Force Base, Moffett Field, Point Loma, Point Mugu, Port Hueneme, San Diego, Sharpe Depot, Terminal Island, Travis Air Force Base, Treasure Island, Twentynine Palms, and Vandenberg Air Force Base. (*See also individual entries.*)

Mill Valley, residential community of Marin County near Muir Woods, named for the sawmill built (*c.* 1834) by an Irish sailor resident in Sausalito. Long a summer settlement, it became a year-round home when San Franciscans moved there after the earthquake and fire of 1906. The population in 1970 was 12,942.

MILLARD, [FRANK] BAILEY (1859–1941), Wisconsin-born journalist and author, moved to California (1880), where he was, successively, city editor for the *San Francisco Chronicle, Call,* and *Examiner* and, later, managing editor of the *Bulletin.* He published Markham's "Man with the Hoe" and promoted Joaquin Miller. His own poems appeared in *Songs of the Press* (1902) and *Sunland Songs* (1933), and his other books include *She of the West* (1900), stories, and *The Lure o' Gold* (1904), a novel about the Yukon. He later edited national magazines and wrote features for the *Los Angeles Times.*

MILLER, FRANK A[UGUSTUS] (1857–1935), went to Riverside (1873) with his father, the new city's engineer, and from the family home, which took in paying guests, he developed a lavish hotel, the Mission Inn, modeled on mission architecture. After accommodating numerous visitors and celebrities, including Theodore Roosevelt and Richard M. Nixon (who was married there), it became a city-owned historic monument (1976). Miller was also active in local cultural affairs and is said to have inspired *The Mission Play* by John McGroarty.♦ Zona Gale, the Wisconsin novelist, wrote the appreciative *Frank Miller of Mission Inn* (1938).

MILLER, HENRY (1827–1916; originally named Heinrich Alfred Kreiser), born in Germany, left his homeland at 14, adopting the name of the person

whose second-hand, nontransferable ticket he had bought, and went to California in 1850. From work as a butcher he got into the cattle business, conducted (1856–87) with Charles Lux,♦ another German immigrant. He purchased and constantly increased his landholdings, many obtained with U.S. scrip bought at big discounts from army veterans and others who preferred cash to land options. He was a sharp businessman: once he got title to a large ranch under the U.S. Reclamation Act of 1850 by contending that it was swampland traversable by boat, since during a dry summer he seated himself in a rowboat and had it towed over the site by horses. By such means he came to own 1,400,000 acres and controlled ten times that area through leases and grazing arrangements for his million head of cattle and more than 100,000 sheep. His control of vast water rights for his livestock led to protracted legal battles against James Ben Ali Haggin and Lloyd Tevis, who needed irrigation for their huge ranch lands. For a long time Hall McAllister successfully defended the rights of Miller and Lux, which were not overturned until passage of the Wright Act♦ (1887).

MILLER, HENRY (*fl.* 1856–57), traveler in California unknown except for his journal, presenting an account of the decaying missions, and his drawings of missions and towns, first published in 1952 and 1948, respectively.

MILLER, HENRY (1891–), New York-born writer, began his literary career during his expatriation in Paris (1930–39). By means of intense personal narratives cast in fictive form he presented his beliefs in freedom, natural responses, individualism, understanding through emotions, the significance of natural physical relations, and the belief that "more obscene than anything is inertia." His major works of the period are *Tropic of Cancer* (France 1934, U.S. 1961), anecdotally, vividly, and humorously presenting his life in Paris with frank emphasis on sexual relations, and *Tropic of Capricorn* (France 1939, U.S. 1962), about his adolescence in New York. After travel in Greece, whose spirit he presented in *The Colossus of Maroussi* (1941), and his return to the U.S., whose values he repudiated in *The Air-Conditioned Nightmare* (1945) and a sequel, *Remember to Remember* (1947), he settled in California at Big Sur in 1944. He helped to make the region attractive to the Beat movement,♦ with which he was associated as an older idol, and he wrote of the area in *Big Sur and the Oranges of Hieronymus Bosch* (1958). In California he has written further autobiographical works, *Sexus* (1945), *Plexus*

(1949), and *Nexus* (1960), a trilogy known as *The Rosy Crucifixion,* looser and more philosophic than his earlier memoirs. His numerous other works include essays such as *The Books in My Life* (1952) and *Stand Still Like a Hummingbird* (1962), letters to various literary friends, and further personal reminiscences or commentaries on persons like Thoreau and D. H. Lawrence, whose ideas and writings have affected him.

MILLER, JOAQUIN (1837?–1913), pseudonym of Cincinnatus Hiner Miller, at first a nickname, since his early writing defended Joaquin Murieta.♦ He described his early life with romantic exaggeration, but the facts seem to be that he was born in Liberty, Ind., went west in a covered wagon in 1852, was reared in frontier Oregon, did mining in California, lived with Indians, by one of whom he had a daughter he named Cali-Shasta, and was at various times a horse thief, schoolteacher, Portland lawyer, pony express rider, newspaper editor, and Indian fighter before producing two slim volumes of verse, *Specimens* (1868) and *Joaquin et al.* (1869). The interest they aroused led him to San Francisco and its literary circle of Bret Harte, Charles Warren Stoddard, and Ina Coolbrith. Next he moved on to London, where his privately printed *Pacific Poems* (1870) and *Songs of the Sierras* (1871) delighted the Pre-Raphaelites and other cultural leaders, who acclaimed him as "the Byron of Oregon." He melodramatically lived up to the sobriquet there and in travels to Europe, South America, and perhaps the Near East. Back in the U.S., he published his moving but fanciful *Life Amongst the Modocs* (1873); *The Danites in the Sierras* (1877), a play about Mormons; *Songs of Italy* (1878), the most popular of his several dramas; *The Destruction of Gotham* (1886), a novel; and other frequently bombastic works, including the often-quoted poem "Columbus." In 1886 he returned to California, building a curious estate in the hills above Oakland, known (in his spelling) as "The Hights," and there he lived a long time, regarded variously as a bearded sage, an eccentric bard, a bohemian drinker and advocate of free love, and a last remnant of the Old West.

MILLER, JOHN FRANKLIN (1831–86), after a career as lawyer, state Senator and Union Army general in the Volunteer Infantry of his native Indiana, moved to California, where he had lived for a short time in the 1850s. He was elected as a Republican to the U.S. Senate (1881–86).

Miller & Lux, see *Miller, Henry* (1827–1916) and *Lux, Charles.*

Millerton Lake National Recreation Area, manmade lake 16 miles long created from waters of the San Joaquin River♦ as formed by the Friant Dam, about 20 miles northeast of Fresno. The Friant-Kern Canal♦ of the Central Valley Project♦ carries the water to the Bakersfield area.

MILLS, D[ARIUS] O[GDEN] (1825–1910), moved to California in 1848 after successful beginnings in banking in his native New York State. His Bank of D. O. Mills & Co., founded in Sacramento in 1859, led him to establish the Bank of California (1864) with William Ralston and other capitalists. He became a Regent of the University of California, where he endowed a chair in philosophy. Although he retained a great country estate on the San Francisco Peninsula at Millbrae (a name derived from his own), he moved to New York City in 1878, where he built many "Mills Hotels," low-cost rooming places for the poor, and died, leaving an estate of $60,000,000.

Mills College, first woman's college established west of the Rockies. It began (1852) with the seminary in Benicia run by Mary Atkins♦ which was bought by Cyrus and Susan Mills, former missionary educators. They moved the school to its present Oakland foothill campus (1871) and, after her husband's death (1884), Mrs. Mills developed it as a college. During the presidency of Aurelia Reinhardt♦ (1916–43), it first achieved real distinction. It enrolls over 800 undergraduates and emphasizes the liberal arts. Faculty have included Giuseppe Cadenasso, John Cage, Darius Milhaud, Dean Rusk, and Raymond D. Yelland. Alumnae have included Emma Nevada and Ida Strobridge.

Milpitas, city in Santa Clara County, whose name ("little cornfield") indicates its early nature. It was a *rancho,* and its ownership was disputed between Nicolás Berryessa and José María Alviso and granted to the latter. Once an isolated community, it has grown greatly since the Ford Motor Co. built an assembly plant there (1955).

Mimes, see *San Francisco Mime Troupe.*

Minarets, granite pinnacles northwest of Devil's Postpile National Monument in Madera County.

Mineral King, mountain settlement, briefly a silver mining region (1870s), east of Visalia in Tulare County. On the East Fork of the Kaweah River, it is surrounded on three sides by Sequoia National Park.

Minerals, found throughout California in great variety, the state is richer in minerals than any other part of the U.S. because it contains 600 known kinds, 45 of which are not found elsewhere. Best known and historically most significant is gold, concentrated most heavily in the so-called Mother Lode, stretching through the Sierra Nevada from Mariposa County through El Dorado County. Long before the gold rush, California's major mineral was mercury (quicksilver), whose biggest mine was at New Almaden, followed later by New Idria. Silver has never been important within the state, although Californians made fortunes from the Comstock Lode, just over the border in Nevada. The world's largest sources of borax are in Death Valley and San Bernardino and Kern counties. For a long time the state's most significant mineral has been oil, followed in more recent years by natural gas. Cement, particularly derived from Calaveras and El Dorado counties and the Mojave Desert of San Bernardino, along with sand and gravel from numerous locations, form the weightiest minerals mined in the state. Other minerals include diatomite, gypsum, molybdenum, and tungsten, all found in greater abundance within the state than elsewhere. On the other hand, iron is rather rare and copper very uncommon. Still other minerals found within the state include antimony, arsenic, feldspar, lead, manganese, mercury, potash, quartz crystal, rare-earth metallic deposits, soda ash, talc, uranium, and zirconium. *(See also individual entries.)*

Mining, see *Forty-niners, Gold mining, Gold Rush, Hydraulic mining, Mercury, Minerals, Mother Lode, Placer mining, Quartz mining,* and *Silver mining.*

Miracle Mile, name given to a commercial section of Wilshire Boulevard (L.A.) west from La Brea Ave., developed by a realtor in the 1940s.

Miss California, winner of an annual beauty contest held each June at Santa Cruz (beginning 1924) to publicize its beach resort area. The first winner, Faye Lanphier, was chosen as Miss America (1925).

Missiles, see *Aerospace industry.*

Mission Bay, enclosed harbor of San Diego, north of the city, called Puerto Falso or False Bay between the 18th century and the giving of the present name (1915). It includes an amusement park and tourist center with marine life shows.

Mission Indians, name given to various tribes which were Christianized and gathered into mission communities by the Franciscans between 1776 and the period of secularization. They were romanticized in the novel *Ramona♦* by Helen Hunt Jackson, written as propaganda for their better treatment by the U.S. government. They included Costanoan, Chumash, Fernandeño, Gabrieleño, Juaneño, and Salinan. Indians who were distant from the missions♦ were less influenced. Indians taken into mission life were called neophytes; those who were not were called gentiles.

Mission Inn, see *Miller, Frank A.*

Mission Play, see *McGroarty, John Steven.*

Mission Revival, architectural style largely inspired by C. F. Lummis,♦ who, in the 1890s, called attention to Spanish colonial ecclesiastical traditions as a basis for local design. Influence also came independently from Willis Polk's rehabilitation of Mission Dolores. A. Page Brown made the concept known through his California Building at Chicago's Columbian Exposition (1893) and a structure for San Francisco's Midwinter Fair (1894). Attempts to adapt the primitive Franciscan mission designs to modern use were generally unsuccessful, although A. C. Schweinfurth used some of the motifs to enhance his office building for the *San Francisco Examiner* and E. R. Swain adapted the arcade and tiled roof in the Golden Gate Park residence for John McLaren. The pseudo-mission style in time gave way to a so-called Spanish Colonial Revival. This intended to draw upon local traditions of domestic architecture, but since there was little available as source material, it had also to borrow from Spain, Mexico, New Mexico, and Italy. The first two influences contributed to Bertram Goodhue's buildings for the Panama-California Exposition in San Diego (1915). Foreign eclecticism is also observable in Schweinfurth's hacienda for Phoebe Apperson Hearst at Pleasanton, and many of the later residences built by George Washington Smith and Wallace Neff.

Mission San Jose, town in Alameda County that grew up (1851) near Mission San José de Guadalupe♦ on the Diablo Range foothills. The town was once an outpost into the interior valleys. Since the creation of Fremont♦ (1956), it has been incorporated into that city.

Missions, begun in 1769 for the purpose of Christianizing the Indians. *Visitador-General* Gálvez dispatched the Sacred Expedition♦ from Baja California to settle Alta California. Fathers Serra♦ and Crespí,♦ the spiritual leaders, with two land parties and two seaborne parties totaling over 100 men in all (219 had started out), under the command of Portolá♦ and Rivera y Moncada,♦ assembled at San Diego. There the first of the Franciscan missions—San Diego de Alcalá—was founded by Serra at a temporary location (July 16, 1769).

After making an exploratory trip north and spending seven months at San Diego until relief came by a long-delayed supply ship, Portolá sent Serra and others by sea to Monterey where a second mission—San Carlos Borromeo—was established (June 3, 1770), and moved (1771) to a Carmel River site. This remained Serra's headquarters and from its wooden chapel and outbuildings (the present church was not completed until 1797) he went to found other missions and to govern them all.

Conversion of members of the tribes who came to be called Mission Indians♦ was slow: by 1774 the first five missions had baptized fewer than 500 infants and enrolled under 500 members, averaging fewer than forty persons annually for each mission. Upon Serra's death (1784) Father Lasuén♦ became President-General♦ until his own death (1803). Both were able and dedicated administrators, but the missions had many problems. These included conflicts between religious and civil authorities, such as that between Serra and Fages.♦ But difficulties also came from poor supply lines, insufficient equipment and food, strained and bureaucratic relations with Mexico, and problems in converting and controlling the generally docile but sometimes hostile Indians.

Nevertheless, before he died Serra founded 9 missions and established a strong base on which 12 more were later founded, the last under Mexican rule. In all, the mission system endured 65 years.

The missions, financed by the Pious Fund,♦ were prime Spanish institutions to achieve colonial control of the frontier by means of subjugated and converted Indians who were expected in time (occasionally set at a decade) to be released from mission control and to fit into pueblos. It was even envisioned that as one group of missions would be secularized others might be established for control of more remote lands. To initiate this the Indians were educated in Spanish, taught simple building trades (e.g. making adobe bricks and roof tiles), farming, management of livestock, and such skills as blacksmithing, wine making, weaving, spinning, and tanning. Five of the missions had

an *asistencia*♦ or sub-mission located some miles away for neophytes who could not readily come to the main establishment for divine services.

All missions controlled great landholdings (e.g. in 1822 Santa Barbara held nearly 122,000 acres with orchards, vineyards, many horses, cattle, sheep, goats, and swine). The missions themselves, usually built as a quadrangle, contained a church, workshops, living and dining quarters for priests, a library, and an infirmary with outbuildings for the Indian men (unmarried women were often locked in a dormitory), and an adjacent cemetery. The buildings were architecturally attractive, even though they rarely had skilled builders. They differed in design but all featured stuccoed adobe, tiled roofs, and covered arcades. Some contained a campanile, others a campanario (a wall with open insets for bells), Moorish-styled windows with pilasters and other adornments to enhance otherwise simple facades.

By 1833 some 31,000 Indians still lived in such settings under a temporal and spiritual despotism, not always benevolent, controlled by only 60 padres and 300 soldiers. By that date almost 88,000 Indians had been baptized and over 24,000 had been married by Catholic ritual. That year the Mexican government, for political, economic, and other reasons, decided that the Indians were to live an independent life. The missions were to be secularized♦ and the chapel would simply become a parish church for a new pueblo, to whose public use the remainder of the main building would be available. The lands were to be divided for common use and each Indian family was also to be given a small private plot.

A program was worked out by Gov. Figueroa♦ (1834) which ended the mission system even though the Indians were not ready to fit into the projected program to be substituted for it. The program itself was by no means carried out as planned. Thus Gov. Pico sold the property of 15 of the secularized missions to private buyers (1845–46), generally exclusive of the church and the priest's residence, but most of these sales were later annulled. Regardless of ownership, the buildings themselves quickly fell into disrepair and were sometimes subdivided for private uses that included stores, saloons, and inns, a practice that became particularly common as the power of the church waned with the passage of California to American control. However, the U.S. government also sometimes saw to it that the mission chapels reverted to churches, and in the late 19th century some of the buildings were repaired, although often poorly and in anachronistic styles. But most of them had their roofs collapse while their adobe walls melted away. In course of time these ruins were considered romantic by artists, writers, and succeeding visitors who came as tourists.

The first reconstruction began in 1903 under auspices that included the California Historic Landmarks League, the Native Sons of the Golden West, and the Landmarks Club, and later the National Park Service and private benefactors. Nearly all missions have been well reconstructed and are now open as museums, although most of them also serve in part as churches under Franciscan auspices.

The entire chain of missions and the dates of founding (often considerably preceding completed construction of final edifices) are:

1.	San Diego de Alcalá	1769	San Diego
2.	San Carlos Borromeo	1770	Monterey
3.	San Antonio de Padua	1771	near King City
4.	San Gabriel Arcángel	1771	San Gabriel
5.	San Luis Obispo de Tolosa	1772	San Luis Obispo
6.	San Francisco de Asís (popularly called Dolores)	1776	San Francisco
7.	San Juan Capistrano	1776	San Juan Capistrano
8.	Santa Clara de Asís	1777	Santa Clara
9.	San Buenaventura	1782	Ventura
10.	Santa Barbara	1786	Santa Barbara
11.	La Purísima Concepción	1787	near Lompoc
12.	Santa Cruz	1791	Santa Cruz
13.	Nuestra Senora de la Soledad	1791	Soledad
14.	San José	1797	near San Jose
15.	San Juan Bautista	1797	San Juan Bautista
16.	San Miguel Arcángel	1797	San Miguel
17.	San Fernando Rey de España	1797	San Fernando
18.	San Luis Rey de Francia	1798	Oceanside
19.	Santa Inés	1804	Solvang
20.	San Rafael Arcángel	1817	San Rafael
21.	San Francisco Solano	1823	Sonoma

(See entries under names of individual missions.)

Miwok, Indians of the Penutian family who are also known as Moquelumnan and Mutsun. Their territory centered on the western slope of the Sierra Nevada and spread from the Cosumnes River on the north to the Fresno River on the south. Split into several groups, the northernmost were known as Koni and the southernmost as Pohonichi. Before contact with whites there were about 9,000 Miwok, but only 670 were alive at the time of the 1910 census. The Miwok believed that each person belongs to a category of beings (that is, a moiety) which is dominated by the attributes of a specific kind of animal. Membership in a category established a special relationship with other persons and species conceived as sharing the same moiety. Many other California tribes also believed in moieties and, like the Miwok, most prohibited marriage within the moiety, so that anthropologists speak of these categories as being exogamic as well as totemic.

MIX, TOM (THOMAS EDWIN MIX) (1880–1940), Pennsylvania-born rodeo star, began his motion picture career in 1910 and remained a great star until the advent of talking pictures (1928). He glamorously exaggerated the style of the Western cowboy and thus succeeded William S. Hart as a popular hero.

M'liss, novelette by Bret Harte, treating the adventures of a willful girl in the mining country, one of the earliest significant fictive treatments of life in the Mother Lode. First published in the *Golden Era* (1860), it was expanded in a second version in that magazine (1863) and then collected in *The Luck of Roaring Camp and Other Sketches* (1870).

Moaning Caves, see *Mercer Caves.*

Modesto, seat of Stanislaus County since 1872, originally named by the Central Pacific Railroad for the San Francisco banker William C. Ralston, who declined the honor, an act which led to the name (''modest'' in Spanish). The city, on the Tuolumne River, has grown to be a market and manufacturing center for its agricultural area: it has canneries, dairies, packing plants, wineries, and warehouses, as well as other industries. Among its residents have been the Gallo brothers♦ and Mark Spitz.♦ *American Graffiti*♦ was set and filmed there. In 1970 it had a population of 61,712.

MODJESKA, HELENA (1840–1909), Polish-born actress, famous for her Shakespearean roles, and hostess at a Warsaw salon of intellectuals. Through the author Henryk Sienkiewicz,♦ a member of her circle, she was persuaded to be a founder of a Utopian colony near Anaheim (1876). When it began to fail she learned English and in San Francisco resumed her theatrical career (1877). For nearly thirty years she was a very popular star throughout the U.S., and in Europe. As a naturalized American she made her home near Anaheim, a neighboring canyon and peak being named for her. The island near Newport, where she lived her last two years, was also given her name.

Modoc, Indians of northern California and Oregon. They live just south of the Klamath Indians. At the time of their discovery by Europeans, the two tribes numbered perhaps 2,000; the 1910 census counted nearly 700 Klamath and 300 Modoc. The Modoc material culture was marked by the use of tule and bulrush for a great variety of purposes, including building, raft-making, cradles, and baskets. They practiced the ghost dance of the Paiutes.♦ A fierce people, the Modocs' long enmity to the whites culminated in the Modoc War of 1872–73, a result of their unauthorized return to their own land from the reservation they had been forced to share with the Klamath. The U.S. Army pursued the Modocs, driving them to the lava beds on the south shore of Tule Lake (Siskiyou County). There about 175 of them, including a small band of 53 warriors, holed up, and from that stronghold they held off a great number of American soldiers and inflicted heavy casualties. Hopes of peaceful settlement ended when some of the Modocs killed two whites, a general and a minister who were serving as peace commissioners. The Modoc chief, Kientepoos, known as Captain Jack, betrayed by some of his own tribesmen, was caught, tried, and hanged. Joaquin Miller wrote romantically and

imaginatively about his *Life Amongst the Modocs* (1873).

Modoc County, organized (1874) from part of Siskiyou County, which lies on its west. It is bounded by Oregon on the north, Lassen County and a bit of Shasta County on the south, and the state of Nevada on the east. Its early history, including movement into and from Oregon through the Fandango Pass♦ of the Warner Mts.♦ was marked by battles with Paiute, Pit, and Modoc Indians, although the great lava beds battleground lies just over the western boundary. Most of the county is in the Modoc National Forest, and the main water source is the Pit River. Clear Lake Reservoir, with its National Wildlife Refuge, and the southern part of Goose Lake are the two main bodies of water in the county. Cattle ranching, hay, alfalfa, and potatoes, and lumbering are the main businesses. Alturas♦ is the county seat. In 1970 the county population was 7,469; with an area of 2,622,272 acres, it had 1.8 persons per sq. mi.

Modoc Plateau, region bounded on the west by the Cascade Range♦ and on the east by the Great Basin,♦ lies at an elevation of some 4,500 feet. It is the area in which Modoc County is situated.

Moffett Field, U.S. Navy air station in Mountain View (Santa Clara County), opened (1933) as a dirigible base. It was named for Rear Adm. William A. Moffett, who died in the crash of the *Akron* that year. When the dirigible program was abandoned the field became a center for aeronautical research and headquarters for Pacific aircraft patrols. It has the world's largest wind tunnel for testing aircraft.

MOFRAS, EUGÈNE DUFLOT DE (1810–c.85), French attaché of a Mexican delegation sent to inspect California and Oregon (1841–42). His findings, in which he concluded that California would soon be annexed by a major power, were issued as *Exploration du Territoire de l'Orégon, des Californies, et de la Mer Vermeille* (Paris, 2 vols., 1844).

Mohave, see *Yuma, Mojave Desert,* and *Agriculture.*

Moiety concept, see *Miwok.*

Mojave Desert, barren valley and mountain region, some 15,000 sq. mi., south of the Sierra Nevada and north of the San Gabriel, San Bernardino, and Chocolate mountains, mainly in San Bernardino County, bounded on the east by Nevada and Arizona. Often considered a wasteland, it was oc-cupied by Chemehuevi and Mohave Indians and early became a travel route along the Old Spanish Trail, later for the Santa Fe railroad, and then for a highway into Los Angeles. Although some parts are very dry and hot, farming is success-ful in Antelope Valley in the west and elsewhere. Mining of borax and of cement is a major business. Joshua Tree National Monument♦ is located there, as are some resort settlements.

Mokelumne River, rises in three forks in Alpine County, south of the southern tip of Lake Tahoe, all joining near Lodi and flowing southwest, then turning northwest to end in the Delta Lands of the San Joaquin and Sacramento rivers. Cities on the east shore of San Francisco Bay, including Oak-land, receive drinking water by aqueduct from the Pardee and Camanche reservoirs on the river near Mokelumne Hill, one of the many former mining towns that mushroomed along the river during the gold rush. Wilkes' exploring expedition (1841) named the river for a Miwok village in present San Joaquin County. The river was considered to be the dividing line between the northern and southern mines during the gold rush.

Molino Viejo, El, adobe structure near Mission San Gabriel, built (*c.*1816) by Father Zalvidea. It was the first water-powered gristmill in southern Cali-fornia, and ground flour for the mission's Indian neophytes. It later belonged to the Henry E. Hunt-ington family and in 1965 became the southern headquarters of the California Historical Society.

Mollusks, see *Abalone, Clams,* and *Oysters.*

Molybdenum, mineral found in granitic rocks and quartz veins in combination with other nonferrous elements, most commonly tungsten.♦ Discovered at 80 locations in 24 counties of the state, the most significant deposits are in the Sierra Nevada. The most consistent producer and the nation's single largest source is the Pine Creek Mine on the south slope of Mt. Morgan, northwest of Bishop in Inyo County. Molybdenite Creek and Canyon in Mono County are named for an outcropping of the min-eral. It is used in making iron and steel; in manu-facturing chemicals, pigments, catalysts, and lubri-cants; and is employed in agricultural products, aerospace and missile industries, and nuclear power activities.

MOMADAY, N[ORMAN] SCOTT (1934–   ), Okla-homa-born author whose works include *House*

Made of Dawn (1968), a Pulitzer Prize-winning novel, and *The Way to Rainy Mountain* (1969), a collection of legends of the Kiowa, his own forebears. He received a Ph.D. from Stanford with a dissertation on the poems of Frederick God-dard Tuckerman and is a professor of English there.

MONDAVI, see *Krug, Charles.*

MONEY, WILLIAM (1807–90?), Scottish-born re-former, went to Los Angeles (*c.*1840) where he practiced medicine without a license, then turned theologian to show the errors of the dominant Christian churches. His pamphlet, *The Reform of the New Testament Church* (1854), is more noted as the first book printed in Los Angeles than be-cause in it the author declares himself "Defender of the Faith" and a bishop of his own Reformed Church.

MONK, HANK, see *Overland stages.*

Mono, Indians of Paiute♦ stock, members of the Shoshonean♦ family, resident in the Great Basin east of California but with branches in the Sierra Nevada and central California in the county which took their name. According to Kroeber, the Mono population, which had been 4,000 in 1770, was reduced to 1,500 by 1910. The Mono in California, like the Miwok,♦ believed that each person belongs to a moiety or category dominated by the attributes of a specific animal, and that persons must not marry within their moiety.

Mono County, organized (1861) from parts of Cala-veras and Fresno counties. Its eastern boundary with Nevada was once so ill-defined that Aurora, its first county seat (1861–63), was belatedly found to be in the neighboring state. Its northern and south-ern boundaries were also so uncertain that parts of Mono were given to Alpine and Inyo counties (1864, 1870, respectively). The first white to tra-verse the area may have been Jedediah Smith (1827); certainly it was seen by the Bartleson-Bid-well Party (1841) as they followed the headwaters of the Stanislaus River, and Frémont crossed it going west (1843). Major routes through the Sierra include Sonora♦ and Tioga♦ passes. The re-gion was the site of a gold rush (1850s–80s) which created Bodie♦ and other mining camps and caused a hunt for a legendary lost cement mine pocked with gold. The area has much dramatic scenery, including parts of Toiyabe♦ and Inyo♦ National Forests, Mammoth Lakes,♦ and Mono Lake.♦ Bridgeport has been the county seat since 1864. The county population in 1970 was 4,016; with an area of 1,937,088 acres, there were 1.3 persons per sq. mi.

Mono Lake, roughly circular saline lake east of Yosemite and south of Bodie is so alkaline that only one kind of shrimp and one kind of fly can live in it. In the center of the lake is Paoha Island, of volcanic origin. Negit is a smaller island; on it is the state's largest rookery for the California gull.

MONROE, GEORGE (1842?–86), a black taken as a child to California from his native Georgia and, after having been a Pony Express rider from Merced to Mariposa, became a popular stage driver in Yosemite Valley, where Monroe Meadows was named for him.

MONROE, MARILYN (1926–62), Los Angeles-born motion picture star who made more than fifteen films during the 1950s, the decade to which her career was almost entirely confined. Through such films as *The Asphalt Jungle* (1950) and *Some Like It Hot* (1959) she became a major sex symbol. She was married to baseball player Joe DiMaggio and then to playwright Arthur Miller, but divorced from both. Her life was short and tragic.

Monrovia, suburban city of Los Angeles County located below the San Gabriel Mts. between Duarte and Pasadena, was named for its subdivider, William N. Monroe, a railroad engineer. Once a citrus, avocado, and papaya growing area, it is now a center for light industry.

MONTALVO, GARCÍ ORDÓÑEZ DE, see *Sergas de Esplandián, Las*.

Montara Mountains, northern extension of the Santa Cruz Mts.♦ in the northern part of San Mateo County. At the end of the mountains lies the San Andreas Lake of the Spring Valley Water Co.♦

Montecito, suburb of Santa Barbara, known for its elegant estates, fine gardens, country clubs, and golf courses. It has suffered two severe fires which destroyed many homes (1964, 1977).

Monterey, major community on the bay of that name, probably sighted by Cabrillo (1542) and named (1602) by Vizcaíno for the incumbent vice-

roy of Mexico, the Conde de Monterey. The first white settlers were Portolá and Crespí (1770), soon joined by Serra, who founded the mission (1771). The presidio dates from 1770. The town became the capital of California (1777) under Spanish and Mexican rule and was visited not only by many foreign voyagers, including La Pérouse (1784), Malaspina (1791), and Vancouver (1792), but also by invaders, including Bouchard (1818) and Thomas ap Catesby Jones (1842).

To it in time also went hide traders on ships from New England, as described by Richard Henry Dana, and settlers from the U.S. began to move in, beginning with Thomas Doak (1816) and continuing with such more substantial figures as Jacob Leese and the only U.S. consul, Thomas Larkin. But the early and long dominant settlers were the Spanish and Mexican *rancheros* of the region: soldiers, merchants, and government officials who included members of the Abrego, Alvarado, Boronda, Castro, Guttierez, Pacheco, Soberanes, and Vallejo families. They surrendered easily to the U.S. force under Commodore Sloat (July 7, 1846) which occupied the capital, where many U.S. officers were temporarily stationed, including Col. Mason and Lt. Sherman.

Under American possession Walter Colton was the first U.S. *alcalde,* and in Colton Hall the Constitutional Convention met to create a state government (1849). The town continued to be a quiet, semi-Spanish settlement; Robert Louis Stevenson, a visitor of 1879, so described it in his "The Old Pacific Capital." It developed into a residential and tourist area that also attracted writers, including Charles Warren Stoddard and, much later, John Steinbeck, and painters, among whom were Charles Rollo Peters and Armin Hansen. Visitors have long been attracted to such buildings as the Royal Presidio Chapel (1794), the Old Custom House (a State Landmark and museum), Colton Hall, the Larkin House, the Old Whaling Station (1855), and California's first theater (1847).

Its present population includes fewer of those who created its Chinatown and fewer of the *paisanos*♦ celebrated in Steinbeck's *Tortilla Flat,* but they still contribute to the city's cosmopolitan atmosphere. The onetime large business of commercial fishing, mainly for sardines but also for rockfish, abalone, and salmon, has dwindled considerably, and the numerous canneries on Cannery Row wharf (also celebrated by Steinbeck) have disappeared; the waterfront area has been converted to tourist attractions. The city is also a center for soldiers from nearby Fort Ord; for officers of the Navy Postgraduate School, located in the former Del Monte Hotel; for students in the Foreign Language Institute; and for residents of and visitors to Carmel, Pacific Grove, and the Pebble Beach area. Annual jazz festivals, as a kind of contrast to the Bach festivals of Carmel, had long attracted tourists, but in 1967 a Monterey Pop Festival went far beyond the usual event: over a three-day period it held the nation's first huge outdoor rock festival. Some 40,000 persons attended, and a great array of musical groups and performers, including the Jefferson Airplane and Grateful Dead as well as Janis Joplin and Jimi Hendrix, performed. The festival was further publicized by the film *Monterey Pop* (1969). In 1970 the city had a population of 26,302.

Monterey Colonial, architectural style developed at the end of the Mexican era. The creator was Thomas Larkin, whose house (1835–37) in Monterey, with its adobe walls, redwood frame supporting a second story, broad veranda on all sides, and low, hipped roof with shingles served as the prime model. The style made use of a basic New England structure and was not native to the *Californios,* although adopted by them.

Monterey County, one of the original 27 counties; its seat was the city of Monterey, but was transferred to Salinas in 1873. Santa Cruz County lies to the north, San Benito, Fresno, and Kings counties to the east, San Luis Obispo to the south, and the Pacific Ocean to the west. The name, first given to the port by Vizcaíno (1602), honors Gaspar de Zúñiga, Conde de Monterey, then viceroy of Mexico. The coast was probably seen by Cabrillo (1542), but the first Europeans to enter Monterey Bay were Cermeño (1595) and Vizcaíno, who had no impact on the local Costanoan Indians. The first whites to come overland and make settlement were Portolá and Crespí (1770), the former having reconnoitered the area a year earlier.

After they were joined by Serra, who went by ship, the expedition founded a presidio and Mission San Carlos Borromeo (moved to its Carmel site in 1771, where its edifice was dedicated in 1797), and Mission San Antonio de Padua. A third mission, Soledad, was founded in 1791. Further expeditions by Anza followed (1774, 1776), and Monterey became the principal settlement and seat of California's government.

It was visited by foreign voyagers such as La Pérouse (1786), Malaspina (1791), and Vancouver (1792). It was also the center for landholders who received grants of *ranchos* in the area, including members of the Alvarado, Alviso, Castro, Soberanes, and Vallejo families. English and American settlers of the region included J. B. R. Cooper, W. E. P. Hartnell, and Jacob Leese.

In the capital, Thomas Larkin served as the first and only U.S. consul, while the port was visited by American hide traders, as described by Dana, Robinson, and Thomes, until the American conquest (1846), which established Walter Colton as the first U.S. *alcalde.* In Colton Hall the Constitutional Convention met (1849) and brought the state into being. Thereafter the area grew more and more Americanized, though old Spanish buildings and traditions were proudly preserved, and two of the region's most famous residents were Scotsmen —David Jacks and Robert Louis Stevenson.

The land that forms the county stretches from the Pajaro River on the north down the coast for about 100 miles. On the west is the Pacific and an eastern boundary of Coast Range and Diablo Range mountains separates it from San Benito, Fresno, and Kings counties. On the northern coastal peninsula are Pacific Grove, Monterey, Pebble Beach, and Carmel, all residential communities, though also the major fishing area for sardine. But most of the shoreline is rugged, like Big Sur, the northern part of Los Padres National Forest, and Tassajara Hot Springs in the Santa Lucia Mts.

The larger interior cities, Salinas and King City, are trading centers for the agricultural valley, through which flows the Salinas River. The valley's major crops include artichokes, lettuce, and sugar beets, produced in the north; oil is found in the south. The county also contains three army posts: Fort Ord, Hunter Liggett Military Reservation, and the northern part of Camp Roberts. In 1970 the county had a population of 247,450. With an area of 2,127,296 acres, this gave it 74.4 persons per sq. mi.

Monterey Jack cheese, the only native California cheese, whose production was initially controlled by David Jacks,♦ whence the name.

MONTEUX, PIERRE (1875–1964), Parisian-born violinist and conductor, was the maestro of the Diaghilev Ballet Russe (1911 ff.), Boston's Symphony Orchestra (1919–24), and the Orchestre Symphonique of Paris before he became conductor of the San Francisco Symphony (1935–52). During World War II he became an American citizen (1942).

MONTEZ, Lola (1818–61), born in Ireland, named Marie Gilbert, began her career as a dancer in 1843 under her pseudonym after limited instruction in Spain. As a dancer she became well known in London and on the Continent as far off as St. Petersburg. Before beginning her career she had been married to a young English army officer stationed in India, where he deserted her. Never divorced, she had numerous affairs. Her lovers supposedly included Liszt and Dumas before her liaison with Ludwig I of Bavaria, who created her Baroness Rosenthal and Countess of Landsfeld and established her in a palace until both were exiled, in part because she urged him to take up liberal views against the ruling clerical party. She next contracted a "marriage" with a rich young Englishman and then (1851) came solo to New York, where she danced and appeared in a play, *Lola Montez in Bavaria.* Thereafter she went on tour, and in San Francisco she performed her dazzling "spider dance," acted in dramas, and again "married" a local newspaperman, Patrick Hull, in 1853. For a time she played in mining camps, then temporarily settled in Grass Valley, entertaining herself by making the child Lotta Crabtree♦ her protégée and keeping a pet bear. After a tour of Australia she made a farewell appearance in San Francisco in 1856. She later underwent religious conversion and lectured in England and the U.S., where she died at age 42.

MONTGOMERY, John B[errien] (1794–1873), naval captain in command of the *Portsmouth* of Commodore Sloat's squadron during the Mexican War, who occupied San Francisco (July 9, 1846). He raised the U.S. flag in the plaza, for which reason the onetime waterfront Montgomery St. bears his name and the plaza was given that of his sloop. (Two of his sons, who were serving aboard the ship, mysteriously disappeared from a boat while taking money from the fleet to forces ashore in San Francisco. Circumstantial evidence indicates they were murdered by crew members.) Before his California experience, Montgomery fought under Perry at Lake Erie and under Decatur against Algiers; afterwards he commanded the Charlestown, Mass., and Washington, D.C., navy yards.

MONTGOMERY, John Joseph (1858–1911), born in Yuba City, is famous for flying a glider (1883) at Otay Mesa, south of San Diego, thus becoming the first man to go aloft in a heavier-than-air craft. The site is commemorated by a monument and the Montgomery State Park. He was later a professor at Santa Clara College, but is best remembered for his youthful activity in pioneering the sport of gliding.♦

Montgomery Block, four-story brick structure erected (1853) by Henry W. Halleck♦ on Montgomery and Washington streets (S.F.) as a luxurious office building, at that time the largest on the Pacific Coast. It also housed the Bank Exchange Saloon, where Pisco Punch♦ was first concocted, and was for a while the home of the Sutro Library.♦ In time the building deteriorated and came to house rundown and raffish bohemian artists' studios and was then called "the Monkey Block." Later occupants included the exiled Sun Yat-sen, George Sterling, Maynard Dixon, Ralph Stackpole, and Diego Rivera. The edifice was demolished in 1959, and the pyramidal Transamerica Building, designed by William Pereira and completed in 1972, now stands on the site.

MOOMAW, Donn (1931–   ), football player born in Santa Ana, was a star middle linebacker for the University of California, Los Angeles (1950–52), who became a professional in the Canadian Football League. Thereafter he was graduated from the Princeton Theological Seminary and organized a Fellowship of Christian Athletes.

MOONEY, Tom (Thomas Joseph Mooney) (1882–1942), radical Socialist labor leader, went to California (1910) from his native Midwest, working occasionally as an iron molder and engaging in labor activities. He and his associate Warren Knox Billings (1893–1972) were charged with planting a bomb that killed 10 people and injured 40 more during the Preparedness Day parade held on San Francisco's Market Street (July 22, 1916) to display U.S. readiness to participate in the World War. Both were convicted. Mooney had been charged with first-degree murder and was sentenced to hang on the basis of evidence later found to be perjured. As a symbol of trade unionism and labor radicalism he was attacked by conservatives and defended by liberals, who came to include Fremont Older,♦ the national head of the American Civil Liberties Union, and many leading writers and public figures. The fairness of his trial became an international question, and as a result of an enquiry by President Wilson a review was conducted that led to Gov. Stephens' commuting Mooney's sentence to life imprisonment (1918). Over the years the case continued as a *cause célèbre*. Then, in 1939, Gov. Olson pardoned Mooney and commuted Billings' sentence. Billings was finally pardoned in 1961. Both men disappeared from public notice soon after they were freed.

MOORE, ARCHIE (1913?–), Mississippi-born boxer, originally named Archibald Lee Wright, moved to San Diego (1938) and had an active career for over 25 years. He was the world's light heavyweight champion (1952–61) and twice an unsuccessful challenger for the heavyweight championship.

MOORE, CHARLES W. (1925–), architect who came to prominence in northern California during the 1960s, when he served on the University of California, Berkeley, faculty and built homes in the area. His best-known work was the cluster of individualized condominiums at Sea Ranch♦ (Mendocino County), in which he employed a simple wood-sheathed style. He is also known for his super-Mannerist scale, emphasis on the diagonal in the exterior, and large patterns of bright color in the interior. In the 1970s, after teaching at Yale, he joined the UCLA faculty.

MOORE, JOHN JAMISON (1804?–93), Virginia-born clergyman of the African Methodist Episcopal Zion Church, went to San Francisco (1852) and lived there fourteen of the next sixteen years. He established and was principal of the state's first public school for black children. He rose to be a bishop of his church and wrote a history of it.

MORAGA, JOSÉ JOAQUIN (1741–85), second in command under Anza♦ on the 1775–76 expedition from Sonora to California. When Anza returned to Mexico, Moraga founded the presidio of San Francisco (July 1776) at a site chosen by Anza. With Palou, he established Mission Dolores,♦ where he was later buried, and he founded the pueblo of San José (1777). He remained as the first *comandante* of San Francisco's presidio and was the founder of a notable *Californio* family, allied to the Argüello and other prominent clans. His son Gabriel (1765–1823), also a member of the Anza expedition, became the leading explorer of the Central Valley (1805–17) on several expeditions that took him inland and far north in California. He thus was the originator of many place-names, e.g. Calaveras, Mariposa, Merced. He was also responsible for opening trade with the Russians at Fort Ross. Gabriel's son, Joaquin, also a soldier

in San Francisco, had a *rancho* in present Contra Costa County. It is the site of a valley and a town named for him.

MORGAN, DALE L[OWELL] (1914–71), historian of the Far West, born in Utah of Mormon descent, was the author of *The Humboldt, Highroad of the West* (1943), *The Great Salt Lake* (1947), and *Jedediah Smith and the Opening of the West* (1953). A member of The Bancroft Library staff (1954–71), he aided many scholars and was himself the editor of many works on the crossing to California and the gold rush period.

MORGAN, JULIA (1872–1957), San Francisco-born architect, the first woman to graduate from the state university in mechanical engineering and the first to be a graduate in architecture from the École des Beaux-Arts. She worked for Maybeck and then for John Galen Howard before opening her own office in San Francisco (1905); their influence can be seen in her shingle-style homes, particularly in Berkeley, and in her first major work, the rebuilding of the neoclassical interior of the Fairmont Hotel after the earthquake and fire of 1906. She later designed more than 600 residences, often marked by Tudor arches and half-timbered exteriors, which were frequently so positioned that their entries faced away from the street to afford the occupants greater privacy. Larger works, in varied idioms, include the library of Mills College, the Berkeley Women's City Club, the former Miss Burke's School in San Francisco, and, with Maybeck, the Hearst Gymnasium for Women at the University of California, Berkeley. Her major undertaking was the creation of William Randolph Hearst's estate at San Simeon,♦ construction of which extended from 1919 to *c*.1947.

Morgan Hill, farming community of Santa Clara County, founded (1892) as an outgrowth of the ranching activities of Martin Murphy.♦ It was named for his granddaughter's husband, Mr. Morgan Hill, who was the brother of Sarah Althea Hill.♦ The nearby mountain, unrelated to the town's name, is officially called Nob Hill but familiarly known in the region as Murphy's Peak.

Mormon Battalion, a group, initially numbering about 500, who went west (summer 1846), and en route were recruited into the U.S. Army at Council Bluffs, Iowa, on orders of President Polk, with Brigham Young concurring. Polk took the action to win the allegiance of an alien group and to build military strength for the Mexican War. Under Lt. Col. Philip St. George Cooke♦ they marched from Santa Fe to San Diego, partly via the Gila River, between Oct. 1846 and Jan. 1847. They built a fort at Los Angeles but were discharged without seeing battle. Thus they temporarily swelled the ranks of Mormons in California.♦

Mormons in California, arrived in three large separate groups during the 1840s and 50s. The first were determined to flee the Babylon of the U.S., in which they had been persecuted. More than 200 of them sailed from New York aboard the *Brooklyn* to arrive in Yerba Buena on July 31, 1846, docking, paradoxically, beside the U.S. naval vessel *Portsmouth*, which had come to seize California.

The Mormons, under 26-year-old elder Samuel Brannan,♦ temporarily dominated the town's population and 20 of them ventured out to found New Hope, a farm community on the Stanislaus River, the first agricultural settlement in the San Joaquin Valley. Brannan was excommunicated for taking Mormon funds for his own use and left to keep store at Sutter's Fort, where he was caught up in the gold rush; about half his original followers went to the mother settlement in Utah; and most of the remainder joined other Mormon colonies.

The second group was the Mormon Battalion,♦ which reached Los Angeles (late Jan. 1847) as a special U.S. Army detachment. Upon being mustered out in July about half the men went to Utah, the rest remaining in California to work for Sutter and to share in the gold rush. Some also helped rescue the Donner Party. One company reenlisted until March 1848, by which time most had left for Salt Lake.

The third group was comprised of Mormon Battalion members who established a settlement at San Bernardino between 1851 and 1858, leaving in the latter year for colonies in Utah and Arizona or becoming apostates. Other Mormons came separately during the gold rush, one being young Ina Coolbrith. Association with the Mormons in early days was lessened after the Constitutional Convention of 1849, when its delegates decided not to extend the new state's border east to Salt Lake. Nevertheless, a Mormon mission established in 1849 was but the beginning of the Church's spread in California which in time came to be substantial, although its communicants entered into the general fabric of society like members of any other sect. The earlier separatist era is recalled by more than 25 place-names commemorating their settlements.

MORRIS, WRIGHT (1910–   ), author born in Nebraska, where much of his fiction is set, including *Man and Boy* (1951) and *The Works of Love* (1952), lived for a time in southern California and attended Pomona College (1930–33), where *The Huge Season* (1954) is laid. He taught creative writing at San Francisco State University (1962–75) and has long been resident in Mill Valley. He is known for his short, sensitive novels, including *The Field of Vision* (1956), *Ceremony in Lone Tree* (1960), and *Fire Sermon* (1971); for his books of evocative photography and text, including *The Home Place* (1948); and for his critical studies of American culture, among them *The Territory Ahead* (1958) and *A Bill of Rites, A Bill of Wrongs, A Bill of Goods* (1968).

Morro Bay, an inner portion of Estero Bay in San Luis Obispo County, over which looms the 576-foot-high volcanic formation of Morro Rock, source of the bay's name (*morro,* Spanish for "rounded hill or bluff"). It is known to have been a campsite for Portolá's expedition (1769). The neighboring town is a recreational and residential settlement. In its State Park is a large Museum of Natural History.

MORROW, W[ILLIAM] C[HAMBERS] (1854–1923), Alabama-born author who wrote for the Southern Pacific and for San Francisco and San Jose newspapers in the 1890s. He became known for his stories in *The Ape, the Idiot and Other People* (1897), and he also wrote two novels: *A Man; His Mark* (1899) and *Lentala of the South Seas* (1908).

MORSE, C. C., see *Seed production.*

Mother Lode, name applied to the major area of gold-bearing quartz in California and, by popular extension, to the mining region running from Mariposa in the south to Georgetown, which is about 10 miles north of Coloma, the point of discovery by Marshall (Jan. 24, 1848). This area, 120 miles long, is from 2 miles down to a few hundred yards in width. The northern mines lie above the Mokelumne River, and the southern mines below it. The designation appears to have been used first in 1868 and not only suggests (incorrectly) that there is a single vein of quartz from which most of the gold came, but that there is no distinction between a quartz vein and placer deposits. Moreover, many important mines lay north of the Mother Lode.

MOTHERWELL, ROBERT (1915–   ), Washington-born painter, reared in San Francisco and graduated from Stanford University (1937). He is known for his strong, imposing, structurally patterned abstractions, which create a sense of symbolic statements.

Motion pictures, had their beginnings not only in the work of Edison and of French and English inventors, but in the experimental photographs made in California by Muybridge, which he projected through his zoopraxiscope, a device he showed Edison in 1888. The earliest commercial films projected in the nickelodeons of New York also drew upon California, since one of the popular brief scenes of celebrities included James J. Corbett, the San Francisco prizefighter. The more extensive association of films with the state began with the establishment of a studio in Los Angeles by George Van Guysling and Otis M. Gove in 1906 and the shooting of their first film on a ranch located in present Hollywood.

Meanwhile, eastern producers formed a Motion Pictures Patent Co., a monopolistic trust, which smaller filmmakers attempted to escape by moving their production to various new locations, among them several California areas, which by 1911 included Hollywood. The first full-length film completed in California was William Selig's *The Count of Monte Cristo* (1908). The Patent Co. itself was challenged in the courts by William Fox, who, many years later, after great success, was bankrupted by an antitrust suit against his own corporation. Another antagonistic producer was Carl Laemmle, who created the scheme of featured stars for his studio, including Mary Pickford.

After the Patent Co. was disbanded (1915), other independents, like Samuel Goldwyn, Jesse Lasky, Louis B. Mayer, and Adolph Zukor, became powerful forces in their own right. Some independent producers grouped together to establish their own organizations, like the Triangle Co. (1915), organized by D. W. Griffith, Thomas Ince, and Mack Sennett. One of Sennett's stars of slapstick comedy, Charlie Chaplin, and an athletic Triangle actor recruited from Broadway, Douglas Fairbanks, were so popular that they joined with "America's Sweetheart," Mary Pickford, and D. W. Griffith to establish their own producing and distributing organization, named United Artists.

Meanwhile, a few other great firms—Fox, Metro (later Metro-Goldwyn-Mayer), Paramount, RKO, and Warner Brothers among them—came to control most of the industry. Each had its own style, as each had its own stars, but all of them together tended to concentrate on certain kinds of films

that the public particularly liked. One popular type was the Western, built around such cowboy heroes as William S. Hart and Tom Mix, which appealed especially to men and boys and survived to much later days with the ruggedly independent characters played by John Wayne and others. Another major film type, geared to large audiences of women, was the romantic story featuring a great lover. Of these the most celebrated was Rudolph Valentino, followed later by more wholesomely masculine figures such as Clark Gable, Gary Cooper, Gregory Peck, James Stewart, and Spencer Tracy.

Great sex symbols among the women ranged all the way from such pert figures of the jazz age as Clara Bow and the young Joan Crawford, to the blatant Jean Harlow or the later and more comic Marilyn Monroe, to the deeply dramatic Greta Garbo and the worldly Marlene Dietrich. The last two were among many Europeans who contributed to Hollywood's films. Florid romance, compounded with grand spectacles and themes of pretentious gravity, was also cultivated by Cecil B. DeMille.

A peculiarly American creation was the slapstick comedy of funny and fantastic situations that focused on actors with great comic gifts. The leader of them all was Charlie Chaplin. Others were Buster Keaton and Harold Lloyd, as well as teams like Sennett's Keystone Cops or Hal Roach's "Our Gang" and the later Laurel and Hardy and the Marx Brothers.

A cycle of films that came in toward the end of the 1920s gloried in gangster violence, with stars like James Cagney and Edward G. Robinson, or on a more sophisticated level, the bittersweet toughness of Humphrey Bogart.

Sound films had been experimentally developed in the early 1920s by Lee De Forest but did not have commercial success until Al Jolson was seen and heard simultaneously in *The Jazz Singer* (1927). Then a whole new era began for motion picture production. The Academy of Motion Picture Arts and Sciences and its Academy Awards were also founded at that time.

The first full-length "talking picture" was *The Lights of New York* (1928), which also initiated a new cycle of subject matter: a story involving a musical comedy and its dancing chorus. The stars who were featured in these pictures included Fred Astaire, Bing Crosby, Judy Garland, Bob Hope, Ginger Rogers, Frank Sinatra, and Shirley Temple. This long-lasting genre depended also on the composers of catchy songs, the musicians who orchestrated them, and the choreographers, of whom the most lavish and fanciful was Busby Berkeley. After 1935 these and other films were further enhanced by color.

Ancillary industries burgeoned around the stars and their accompanists, the producers and directors. Among them were costume designers like Edith Head♦ and makeup creators like Max Factor.♦ The public was given a share in the glamour associated with the film world. Exotic and lavish theaters were erected, like the Sid Grauman edifices in Hollywood; and the doings of the actors and actresses were chronicled and pictured in numerous fan magazines and by newspaper columnists like Louella Parsons and Hedda Hopper.

Those who violated the curious canons of behavior approved by Hollywood and its controllers were sometimes ostracized, as Orson Welles was by the Hearst newspapers when he produced *Citizen Kane,* a symbolic biography of their founder. More seriously, in the 1940s and 50s the so-called Hollywood Ten were blacklisted for ostensible links to Communism during a period of national paranoia and concomitant patriotism.

Motion pictures continued to be popular through the decades as old formulas were updated, often with increased technical skill, and as other appealing types of production were created. The most original was the animated cartoon, which Walt Disney developed from simple short works into elaborate full-length features. Meanwhile, old types of films were often refashioned for new audiences: e.g. the genre of horror stories enacted by Lon Chaney was extended into science fiction. Fashion in comedies changed too to include more sophisticated humor like that of Mae West and W. C. Fields. Serious drama also grew more mature, as presented by such actors of stage and screen as Bette Davis, Katharine Hepburn, and Marlon Brando.

Despite these achievements and successes, the film industry was increasingly threatened by loss of its audiences to television (weekly motion picture attendance dropped from 90,000,000 in 1946 to fewer than 40,000,000 in 1958), and it responded in various ways. Some of the responses were simple: enlargement of the screen and the creation of more lavish productions suited to its grander scale; or the making of films specially suited to TV. Other responses were more thoughtful, like the move to independent production, allowing greater individuality in subject matter and interpretation.

With the passing of power from the older generation of Hollywood producers and the breaking up of most of their huge studios and their domination of chains of theaters, more specialized films could be made by younger producers with smaller budgets, freer to appeal to smaller and more cultivated audiences. Each such film was more likely to be an end in itself rather than an example of a stereotyped genre.

As all aspects of human relations and social situations came to be presented, the new films created their own mode of expression and won respect on a level with written literature and the legitimate theater. They also provided fine interpretations of the fiction of the U.S. and foreign cultures. *(See also individual entries.)*

Mount Dana, 13,050-foot peak in Yosemite National Park, named (1863) by James D. Whitney and William H. Brewer in honor of James Dwight Dana (1813–95), an eminent professor of geology at Yale.

Mount Diablo, major mountain in the East Bay, located in Contra Costa County. It rises 3,849 feet and towers high above the surrounding landscape. Other names were applied to it before the 19th century, and the origin of the present name is uncertain since the Spanish word *monte* can refer to "woods" and the devilish aspect is uncertain. However, there is a story that a party of Spanish soldiers was defeated by the Bolbones Indians (1806) led by a medicine man garbed to represent the spirit of the mountain and considered to be a *diablo* by the soldiers. Bret Harte wrote a fanciful "Legend of Monte del Diablo," about a padre's meeting with a diabolical figure who shows him the future coming of Anglo Saxons who will dig up the earth for gold and disturb the peace of the land. Actually, the mountain was the site of some coal mining in the 1860s.

Mount Hamilton, 4,261-foot peak located 13 miles east of San Jose, was named (1861) by William Brewer for his fellow climber, the Rev. Laurentine Hamilton of San Jose. It is the site of Lick Observatory.♦

Mount Lassen, see *Lassen.*

Mount Lowe, peak north of Altadena and near Mt. Wilson, 5,593 feet high, named for Thaddeus S. C. Lowe,♦ who made the first horseback ascent and developed a miniature railway which ran (1893–1939) to the summit.

Mount Morgan, see *Molybdenum* and *Tungsten.*

Mount Palomar, located in Palomar State Park in north central San Diego County, itself surrounded by Cleveland National Forest, has an altitude of 6,126 feet. On its peak is an observatory operated by the California Institute of Technology and the Carnegie Institution. Nearby is the old chapel of San Antonio de Pala.◆

Mount Saint Helena, see *Saint Helena, Mount.*

Mount Shasta, solitary peak of volcanic origin in southeastern Siskiyou County, rising to 14,162 feet. Fur trapper Alexander Henry called it Shatasla (1814) and Pete Ogden named it Sastise, both being variants of the later accepted spelling of Shasta, the name of the Indians of the area. The first climb to the top was made in 1854. The smaller west peak is called Shastina. A city named for the main mountain is located near its base between Klamath and Shasta national parks.

Mount Tamalpais, see *Tamalpais, Mount.*

Mount Whitney, highest peak in California (and highest in the U.S. outside Alaska), whose summit is 14,495 feet. Located in Sequoia National Park on the border of Inyo and Tulare counties at the headwaters of the Kings and Kern rivers, it is the southernmost peak of the Sierra Nevada. It was discovered in 1864 by a party that included William H. Brewer◆ and Clarence King.◆ They named it for their chief, Josiah D. Whitney,◆ the head of the State Geological Survey. It was first climbed by some local fishermen in August 1873.

Mount Wilson, peak near Pasadena with an elevation of 5,710 feet, known for its observatory, founded in 1904 and operated by the Carnegie Institution. The mountain was named for Benjamin D. Wilson,◆ the first U.S. mayor of Los Angeles.

Mountain Charley, see *Parkhurst, Charley.*

Mountaineering, an adventurous sporting activity undertaken by Americans not long after the era when passes had to be found and peaks scaled simply as part of the business of transcontinental migration to California and the crossing of its Sierra. Thus, Mt. Shasta was climbed as early as 1854. Appreciation of the excitement of such experiences was popularized by Clarence King in his *Mountaineering in the Sierra Nevada*◆ (1872) with its tales of his ascents of Mt. Lassen (1863) and other difficult peaks. The highest in Cali-

fornia, Mt. Whitney, was first climbed in 1873 by fishermen resident in the area. The California Geological Survey under W. H. Brewer, who scaled the mountain named for him (1864), engaged in mountaineering because of its necessity for scientific studies, but John Muir did his climbing as part of a general wilderness experience, although little is known of his precise exploits because of his reticence about his accomplishments. The early climbers concentrated on reaching the peaks in which they were interested, and they put their emphasis more on physical fitness to achieve these ends than on special skills. Perhaps the most dramatic climb of earlier days was that of Phimester Proctor,◆ who ascended Half Dome with bare feet.

Later climbers who have viewed mountaineering as a special sport have concentrated on technical problems and the development of new skills, particularly since the 1930s, when the Sierra Club organized its Rock Climbing Section. The use of bolts and of pitons of variously improved sorts drew criticism, particularly from mountaineers of the eastern U.S.; but the new method and style came to be accepted, and California climbers influenced techniques throughout the world. The climb of El Capitan by a civil engineer named Warren Harding (1957) was a major mark in this revolution and also initiated a number of other difficult ascents in Yosemite, with an emphasis on big wall climbing. By the 1970s, climbing, which had once been a highly specialized and esoteric sport for a few men, started to become a popular pursuit for many young men and women.

Mountaineering in the Sierra Nevada, sketches of exploration and experiences by Clarence King,◆ issued in the *Atlantic Monthly* and published as a book in 1872. The work not only gives an accurate account of the geology and geography of the Sierra but presents lively tales of the author's experiences in climbing the mountains of the Yosemite, Mt. Tyndall, Mt. Shasta, and Mt. Whitney. It also includes "The Newtys of Pike," a story about a family of shiftless hog ranchers, one on a local painter of the frontier, in "Cut-off Copples," an account of "The People," which explains the behavior of Californians as influenced by the climate, and "Kaweah's Run," a fictive account of an escape from highwaymen.

Mountain lion, also called catamount, cougar, panther, and puma, larger than a wildcat,◆ being 6 to 8 feet long and weighing up to 165 pounds. It has tawny gray fur. Mountain lions are found throughout the state in forested mountainous regions except for the southeast and the populous San Francisco Bay and Central Valley areas. Because they killed hogs, sheep, and cattle as well as deer, the state in 1907 began payment of a bounty for animal heads and created the post of State Lion Hunter. Bounty hunting continued until the animals became rare. Perhaps 3,000 of them were living in remote areas of the state when hunting was forbidden in 1970.

Mourning doves, the major game birds of the state (over 4,000,000 are killed annually), are found throughout California in summer, but are rarer in winter, when they migrate to Mexico and Central America. Members of the pigeon family, they are about a foot long and are soft brown with a gray-pink head and purple-pink breast. The male's mournful cry occasions the name. They feed mainly on weed seeds and grain.

Movie Crazy, film (1932) featuring Harold Lloyd as a country bumpkin trying to break into pictures as a suave lover but whose maladroitness wins him success as an unwittingly comic figure.

Mugu, Point, see *Port Hueneme.*

MUIR, JOHN (1838–1914), Scottish-born naturalist, was brought to the U.S. (1849) and reared on a Wisconsin farm before attending the state university in Madison, where he studied chemistry, geology, and botany. Inspired to make more personal study of these subjects, Muir undertook extended journeys through the U.S., often on foot. One such trip, from Indiana to the Gulf of Mexico, was reported in a journal and later edited and published as *A Thousand Mile Walk to the Gulf* (1916). A trip took him to California (1868), and there he remained. For a time (1881–91) he was a fruit grower on an orchard near Martinez which he obtained from his father-in-law. But most of his life was spent studying glacial formations of Alaska and the whole West, and the forests of the region, as well as taking the lead in creating a forest conservation movement through his own activities and through such books as *The Mountains of California* (1894), *My First Summer in the Sierra* (1911), and *The Yosemite* (1912). He was instrumental in having Yosemite named a National Park (1890) and in the establishment of a presidential commission (1896) which, mainly at his instigation, created 13 forest reservations during Cleveland's administration and many more under Theodore Roose-

velt's. These included Muir Woods, a National Monument near Mount Tamalpais consisting mainly of land donated by Congressman William Kent,♦ who requested that the 485-acre preserve, with 300-foot-tall and over 400-year-old coast redwoods, be named for Muir. Other natural features honoring him include John Muir Trail through the High Sierra, Muir Gorge in Yosemite, Muir Grove in Sequoia National Park, and Muir Pass in Kings Canyon National Park. More sites in California have been named for him than for any other person.

Muir Woods, see *Muir, John.*

MULFORD, PRENTICE (1834–91), went from his native Sag Harbor, on Long Island, in New York, to California (1856) and, among other things, mined gold and taught school before he became a regular contributor of humorous sketches to the *Golden Era* and *Californian* under the name "Dogberry." He made no lasting impression until he created a book, *Prentice Mulford's Story* (1889), telling of his life to 1872, when he left California. His later life is described in *The Swamp Angel* (1888), which presents a theosophically oriented description of his Thoreau-like retreat in New Jersey.

MULHOLLAND, WILLIAM (1835–1935), upon arrival in California from his native Ireland (1877), became a ditch tender for the antiquated Mexican water system of Los Angeles but rose to become chief engineer (1886) of a private water company. When the city took over the firm (1902) he continued in his post and began a search for new sources of water for the growing population. He proposed the Owens River (250 miles distant) in the Sierra as an ideal source. Construction of an aqueduct cost nearly $25,000,000, took from 1907 to 1913, and was hailed as a remarkable feat of engineering and the beginning of a great system of aqueducts. But it was bitterly opposed by residents of Owens Valley, who lost their own water supply. That opposition to Mulholland was nothing next to the enmity occasioned by the collapse of the project's St. Francis Dam♦ (1928), destroying much of the city of Santa Paula and killing about 400 people. The collapse was possibly the result of his miscalculation, possibly the result of sabotage.

MULLER, BRICK (HAROLD P. MULLER) (1901–62), outstanding University of California athlete (A.B., 1923), known as a speedy and powerful end on Berkeley's football Wonder Teams♦ (1920–22). He became an orthopedic surgeon and a physician for his university's football team and for the U.S. Olympic competitors (1956).

MULLGARDT, LOUIS CHRISTIAN (1866–1942), Missouri-born architect, practiced in San Francisco after 1905, building houses that made use of redwood. He also created more fanciful styles, as in his Court of the Ages for the Exposition of 1915 and the original de Young Museum.

Municipal Courts, established in all cities with populations over 40,000, are concerned with misdemeanors, city ordinance violations, civil suits under $3,000, preliminary felony hearings, and minor traffic matters. Their judges are elected to six-year terms.

MURDOCK, CHARLES A[LBERT] (1841–1928), born in Massachusetts, went to the town now named Arcata (1855) and settled in San Francisco in 1864, where he became a printer with a distinguished taste in typography. He designed and printed books by Kate Douglas Wiggin and by Herman Scheffauer, as well as Gelett Burgess' *The Lark*. He also edited the *Pacific Unitarian* (1892–1928).

MURIETA, JOAQUIN (*c.*1832–53), Mexican bandit in the Mother Lode country who presumably went to California during the gold rush and there met the common prejudice of the day against Latins, and because of some grievance is supposed to have sworn vengeance against Americans. More certain than this romantic, perhaps fictitious figure, is the fact that there were many robberies and killings in the mining region, all attributed to one person named Murieta, who was said to be the man seized and decapitated by a Texan ranger to collect a reward from the California legislature. Later legend that transformed Murieta (occasionally spelled Murrieta) into a Robin Hood began with the *Life and Adventures of Joaquin Murieta* (1854) by John R. Ridge♦ and was continued by Joaquin Miller's title poem of his second book (1869) and other popular fiction and drama, including dime novels. The Nobel Prize-winning Chilean poet Pablo Neruda even wrote a play treating Murieta as a countryman justly opposing racist *Yanquis*.

Muroc, dry lakebed site in Kern County whose name comes from spelling in reverse that of the pioneer settlers Ralph and Clifford Corum. Once used for sports car racing, during World War II it became an airplane testing station named Edwards Air Force Base (1950).

MURPHY, GEORGE [LLOYD] (1902–), Connecticut-born motion picture actor known for his song and dance roles. Active in Republican party politics, he was elected a U.S. Senator (1964–70).

MURPHY, MARTIN, JR. (1807–84), Irish-born pioneer in California who, with his father (b. 1785) and other family and friends, numbering about fifty in all, crossed the continent to California in 1844 under the leadership of Elisha Stevens.♦ Theirs was the first party to bring wagons through, the first to cross the Sierra by Donner Pass, and the first to have to winter in the mountains. That story was recounted by Moses Schallenberger.♦ Murphy was later a rancher in the Sacramento Valley, on whose land Francisco Arce♦ was seized in the first action of the Bear Flag Revolt; and, still later, he ranched at present Sunnyvale and at San Martin (Santa Clara County), which he named. One of his granddaughters married a Mr. Morgan Hill, for whom a nearby town is named.

MURPHY, TIMOTHY (1800–53), went from his native Ireland to California (1829) as an agent for the hide trade under W. E. P. Hartnell. He became a *ranchero* on a 22,000-acre grant in present Marin County.

MURPHY, TURK, see *Yerba Buena Jazz Band*.

Murphys, mining town in the Mother Lode area of Calaveras County, where the brothers John and Daniel Murphy were successful traders (1848 ff.). Albert A. Michelson lived there briefly as a child. The town, also known as the capital of E Clampus Vitus,♦ is southwest of the Calaveras Grove.

MURRIETA, see *Murieta, Joaquin*.

Museums, begun by Americans, English, and other newcomers during the gold rush with such displays of curios as those that distinguished the What Cheer House,♦ and in the next decade followed by more formal and extensive exhibits, such as the art gallery of Woodward's Gardens. The idea of a professional organization and public financing came still later with the growth of sophistication, more leisure, and better education. The Midwinter International Exposition of 1894 in San Francisco marked a flowering of the concept of museums through its numerous foreign exhibits that went far beyond the level of city, county, and state fairs and, under the aegis of M. H. de Young, left the legacy of the city's first public art gallery.

With an occasional and rather tentative exception in a large city, museums did not come to California until the 20th century, even though the mansions of the newly rich often featured art galleries, cabinets filled with unusual objects, and ostentatious displays of cultural artifacts garnered during grand tours to Europe and other foreign lands. In the 20th century museums of diverse sorts have come into being in all large population centers and at numerous historic sites and tourist attractions.

In San Francisco they include the Fine Arts Museums, comprised of the Palace of the Legion of Honor, the de Young Museum, the Asian Art Museum, and the San Francisco Museum of Modern Art. The California Academy of Sciences has a natural history museum, an aquarium, and a planetarium at its Golden Gate Park headquarters. In the old Palace of Fine Arts, created for the Panama-Pacific International Exposition of 1915, has been established an Exploratorium to provide dramatic understanding of scientific and technological concepts. Other specialized museums include a Wine Museum, an Army Museum at Fort Mason, the San Francisco Maritime Museum and its neighboring anchorage of old vessels, and several museums dedicated to the area's own past: Cable Car Barn, Old U.S. Mint, Fort Point National Historic Site, Wells Fargo History Room, California Historical Society, and Society of Pioneers.

In Berkeley are the University of California's Art Museum, Lowie Museum (anthropology), The Bancroft Library, and Lawrence Hall of Science. In that city also is the Judah L. Magnes Museum (Jewish culture and history), and in Oakland are the Oakland Museum concerned with California art, social history, and natural history and the Mills College Art Gallery.

Down the Peninsula are Stanford University's Art Gallery and its Museum, the Foothills College Electronics Museum; in San Jose the Historical Museum of Santa Clara Valley, a Rosicrucian Egyptian Museum and Planetarium; and in nearby New Almaden, a museum concerned with local mining and Indians of the region. North of San Francisco Bay is Benicia's Capitol State Park, a chapel and other displays at Fort Ross, the Silverado Museum of Robert Louis Stevensoniana at Saint Helena, the Vallejo Home at Sonoma, and the Jack London State Historic Park at Glen Ellen. Local commerical wineries also have historic displays.

En route to the mining country are Sutter's Fort in Sacramento, and the city also contains a re-developed 10-block area of old buildings, including a Railroad Museum, the E. B. Crocker Art Gallery, and the Old Governor's Mansion (a Victorian edifice). In Stockton is a Pioneer Museum and Haggin Art Galleries. The old mining towns themselves contain many lesser museums or displays, in addition to the 12-square-block restoration of Columbia, another State Historic Park.

Between San Francisco and Los Angeles there are a few museums, including Kern County Museum and Pioneer Village of Bakersfield, Hearst Castle at San Simeon, Laws Railroad Museum of Bishop, and Eastern California Museum in Independence, as well as some local historical societies' exhibits, notably that in Santa Barbara, which has also a Museum of Art and a Museum of Natural History.

Los Angeles and environs contain a greater number of important museums. Among them are several art galleries, including the Los Angeles County Museum of Art on Wilshire Boulevard, the J. Paul Getty Museum near Pacific Palisades, the Norton Simon Museum at Pasadena, and the Henry E. Huntington Library and Art Gallery. Other significant art collections are to be seen at UCLA, USC, and other universities and colleges. An institution of a related sort is the Craft and Folk Art Museum. The Southwest Museum and its associated El Alisal have major collections of Indian artifacts. Other important permanent displays on specialized subjects are found in the California Museum of Science and Industry and the Natural History Museum of Los Angeles County in Exposition Park; the Hall of Science and Travel Town in Griffith Park; and Casa de Adobe, a replica of an old hacienda.

At Long Beach is berthed the old ocean liner Queen Mary, which houses a marine museum, and in the city are a Museum of Art and the old Bixby family ranch house, furnished and equipped as it was a century and more ago. The many tourist attractions of Buena Park include a Movieland Wax Museum and a Movieworld Cars of the Stars, while at Newhall is another tribute to a film star, the William S. Hart County Park, containing the actor's home and possessions.

Between Los Angeles and San Diego are located other museums, including an Air Museum in Ontario and the Cunningham Automotive Museum in Costa Mesa. San Diego itself has an Aerospace Museum (almost entirely destroyed by fire, 1978), a Museum of Man, a Museum of Natural History, the Timken Art Gallery, and the important Fine Arts Gallery, all located in Balboa Park—sometimes called Exposition Park, from the occasion of its creation in 1915. (*See also individual entries.*)

Music Center for the Performing Arts, complex of buildings in downtown Los Angeles, designed by Welton Becket & Associates, cost $34,000,000, and opened 1964–67. It consists of the Dorothy Chandler Pavilion, an opera and orchestra hall named for Mrs. Norman Chandler,♦ a civic leader who raised half the cost of $34,000,000; the Mark Taper Forum, a setting for experimental drama; and the Ahmanson Theatre, a large auditorium.

Music in California, was initially that of Indians, who played instruments and sang, and some of whom greeted Portolá, Crespí, and their party near Santa Barbara (1769) by playing on carved bone flutes and whistle pipes. European music was introduced by the Franciscan friars, whose chants, hymns, and requiems were sung by Indian choirs. All of the missions had bells and several of the padres were known for their musical talents. Padre Durán is famous for having devised a scheme to teach his neophytes to read notes, and for creating a 30-piece orchestra (with some locally made instruments) at Mission San José.

Popular music of a lay nature was introduced by Spanish and Mexican settlers. Not only were solos, such as serenades, common, but group music became an essential element in festivities, such as *fandangos* and *bailes* for the *pastores* of Christmas Eve, and the wedding dances of which Dana wrote in *Two Years Before the Mast.*

American settlement, particularly during the gold rush, brought folk tunes from various places. Some of the most popular, like "Sweet Betsy from Pike" and "What Was Your Name in the States?" were collected in *Put's Original California Songster* (1855) and similar paperback compilations suited to parties which often traveled to the tune of "Oh, Susanna" ("I'm Going to California With My Banjo on My Knee") and founded mining camps named Fiddletown and Fiddlers Flat.

Sophisticated music flourished in more stable communities and larger cities. In San Francisco a Philharmonic Society, organized by Henry Meiggs (1852), played in a 1,200-seat Music Hall; various choral and orchestral groups were supported by German societies; Ole Bull and other concert artists appeared on tour; and special national societies presented traveling French, Italian, and Spanish opera companies, as did Tom Maguire in his Opera House and Academy of Music from the late 1850s through the next twenty years. The Tivoli Opera

House, established as a beer garden with music (1877), featured light and even grand opera right to the eve of the earthquake of 1906. Its more sophisticated rival, the Grand Opera House, was founded a year earlier. It presented both popular visitors such as Tetrazzini and the native-born coloratura soprano Emma Nevada, until it too had its curtain rung down by the catastrophe of 1906, just a few hours after Caruso had appeared on its stage.

The music of the late 19th century and the opening of the 20th also included jazz and ragtime, for the Barbary Coast provided hospitable bars and other resorts in which they could flourish. Both the popular and the elevated musical traditions were enhanced in the new century. San Francisco established a symphony orchestra of its own in 1911, with a succession of distinguished conductors who included Henry Hadley, Alfred Hertz, Pierre Monteux, Joseph Krips, and Seiji Ozawa. Los Angeles followed suit in 1919, also with outstanding maestros, including Otto Klemperer and Zubin Mehta.

The San Francisco Opera Co., created under the leadership of Gaetano Merola (1919), was the first city organization in the U.S. to have a municipally owned opera house (1932). Since 1957 its Director has been Kurt Adler. Los Angeles formed an opera company in 1924 but not until the 1960s did it build a Music Center in its downtown area, although as early as 1922 it established the huge Hollywood Bowl for outdoor performances, and in 1939 created the Monday Evening Concerts.

Several other cities (Oakland, San Jose, Fresno, Sacramento, and Stockton) and counties have orchestras. Numerous communities also have facilities for outdoor performances, such as that for the festival in Ojai (where Stokowski had a summer home), Stern Grove in San Francisco, and Carmel, which features an annual Bach festival as well as other musical productions. More intimate recitals are presented in other places, notably those staged by various wineries in their vineyards.

The 20th century also brought other support for music. Professional institutions like the San Francisco Conservatory (est. 1917) were well staffed. Several universities and colleges sponsored resident quartets and trios, as well as adding distinguished musicians to their faculties, like Ernest Bloch and Andrew Imbrie at the University of California, Berkeley, Darius Milhaud at Mills College, and Arnold Schoenberg at UCLA.

Many musicians have made their homes in California, including Charles Wakefield Cadman and

Carrie Jacobs Bond, who moved there in the early years of the century. Others, like Stravinsky and Lotte Lehmann, found refuge during the later era of European upheavals. Even more settled in California because of the success of motion pictures with sound were composers, orchestrators, musicians, and singers who were led to Hollywood to help create its popular cycles of musical comedies and diverse other film types emphasizing music, both jazz and classical. Some, like Bing Crosby and Frank Sinatra, have become international figures, famous far beyond any associations with California.

Television has also helped to sustain musicians in southern California and the state at large, which has been the home of many groups playing rock music with some distinctively local features. The state has also been the birthplace or home from youth of many distinguished performers of classical music, including singer Lawrence Tibbett, violinist Yehudi Menuhin, and other child prodigies like Isaac Stern, Ruggiero Ricci, and Ruth Slenczynska. Native-born composers include Henry Cowell, Roy Harris, Dave Brubeck, Harry Partch, and John Cage. (*See also individual entries.*)

Muskrat, aquatic rodent about 18 inches long from nose to tip of tail, exists in only two native species: the *Nevada,* the larger, and dark furred, found only in Lassen, Alpine, and Mono counties; and the *Colorado,* pale furred, also found on the very eastern edge of the state but along the Colorado River in San Bernardino, Riverside, and Imperial counties as well. To these indigenous muskrats others have been added in Kern County and elsewhere: their scent glands are used in making perfume and their pelts make popular furs. The muskrat is the state's most profitable fur-bearing animal.

Mussel Slough, site of a bloody shoot-out (May 11, 1880) arising from a conflict over land between the Southern Pacific Railroad and settlers. It is near Hanford on a branch of the Kings River, and after the tragedy it was renamed Lucerne Valley. Originally in Tulare County, a change of boundaries has put it in Kings County.

During a long period when the Southern Pacific's claim to its San Joaquin Valley land grant was in dispute, the railroad invited settlers to farm some of the disputed property with the pledge that they could buy it later at such prices as "$2.50 upward" an acre, without charge for their own improvements. But after the railroad finally acquired title,

it offered the land to any buyer, without precedence for settlers, and set prices between $17 and $40 an acre. Some of the local farmers organized a Grand Settlers League and not only refused to buy the land on which they ranched but tried to prevent others from making purchases. The railroad won ejectment suits, and a U.S. marshal accompanied an S.P. official who had the belongings of some farmers removed and tried to install two of the new purchasers.

During an encounter with members of the Settlers League near Grangeville, a horse reared and struck the marshal. Both sides, already tense, started firing. One of the would-be purchasers and four settlers were killed, two settlers later died of wounds, and a year later some farmers ostensibly hunted down and killed another potential purchaser. Five settlers were sentenced to prison, others gave up their homes, and only a few finally accepted the railroad's terms.

The Mussel Slough tragedy has been the subject of much writing, most notably Josiah Royce's only novel, *The Feud of Oakfield Creek* (1887), and Frank Norris' *The Octopus* (1901).

Mustard, probably introduced to California by the early missionaries who cultivated it in Mexico and Pimería Alta, and later grown by Russians at Fort Ross. The widespread field mustard is European in origin. More recently mustard has been grown commercially, especially since the 20th century and particularly in Santa Barbara County.

MUYBRIDGE, EADWEARD (1830–1904), English-born photographer who, as a youth, changed his name from Edward James Muggeridge. He came to the U.S. in the 1850s and after a time was engaged to do photography for the U.S. Coast and Geodetic Survey. From that job he was hired (1872) by Leland Stanford to attempt to demonstrate by photos whether a trotting horse ever has all four feet off the ground. He rigged a device whereby several cameras' shutters were tripped sequentially by strings breaking across a track, thus showing a horse with all four feet momentarily in the air. This was the first of his studies of locomotion made over a six-year period at the Senator's Palo Alto farm, and led to the illustrations of *The Horse in Motion* (1882), a work with text by Dr. J. D. B. Stillman. That study led to a more elaborate series carried out for the University of Pennsylvania (1884–86), whose resultant *Animal Locomotion* (11 vols., 1887) displayed pictures made by a battery of electromagnetically operated cameras focused on a great variety of animals and birds in action. A later work presenting thousands of photographs of nude men and women in action against a ruled background appeared as *The Human Figure in Motion* (1901). All the pictures were taken at great speeds, up to 1/6,000th of a second, so that when reproduced on a screen through a zoopraxiscope, a viewing device of Muybridge's invention, they gave the illusion of continuous motion and were among the ancestors of the modern moving picture. Muybridge was also known for his huge series of photographs documenting the coast from Alaska through Mexico, made to be viewed through a stereopticon.

My Name Is Aram, collection of short stories by William Saroyan.◆

Myrtle, evergreen plant found in two varieties in California: the *Sierra wax-myrtle,* native to the Sierra Nevada, is a shrub 3 to 6 feet tall; the *Pacific wax-myrtle,* native to the Coast Range, is a tree 10 to 35 feet tall. Both varieties bear small nuts. The *Oregon myrtle* is really a laurel.

N

NAGLEE, HENRY M. (1815–86), born in Tennessee, after education at West Point went to California with Stevenson's Regiment.♦ In San Francisco he founded one of the first banks with Richard H. Sinton (1849) and branched into other businesses, including real estate. After service as a general in the Civil War, he returned to the state and grew grapes and made wine on ranches in San Joaquin and Santa Clara counties.

NAHL, CHARLES C[HRISTIAN] (1818–78) and **NAHL,** H[UGO] W[ILHELM] ARTHUR (1820–87), German-born artists, half-brothers, descended from a family of distinguished artists, studied painting in Paris before going to California via Panama (1850). After trying their hand at mining, they settled in San Francisco (1852) where they soon became the city's leading lithographers, specializing in souvenir stationery depicting the mines, while also working as photographers. In addition, Charles created woodcuts, engravings, and drawings for local journals, his romantic style suited to such images as the dashing one of Joaquin Murieta, which he popularized. He redrew the bear for the official state flag, and his brother designed the state seal. By 1867 Charles had acquired a patron, Judge E. B. Crocker, founder of the Crocker Art Gallery.♦ Charles was also popular with other persons as the creator of vast, highly colored, romantic, Hogarth-like canvases of the local scene, including "Saturday Evening in the Mines" and "Sunday Morning in the Mines," which are said to have influenced Bret Harte to write his local color stories. Perham [Wilhelm] Nahl (1869–1935) and Virgil Theodore Nahl (1876–1930), the sons of H. W. Arthur, continued the family tradition in art, the elder as a painter and teacher, the younger as a portrayer of pioneer California and as a staff artist for the *San Francisco Examiner* from 1898 until his death.

Napa, seat of Napa County and its largest community. It is a processing and shipping center for its valley's grapes and nuts, has long-established tanneries, and newer light industry for electronics and other manufacturing. It is also a fast-growing residential area. The Napa State Hospital for insane persons is located on 1,900 tree-shaded acres where many patients work on its farmlands. In 1970 the city had a population of 35,978.

Napa County, one of the original 27 counties, is bounded by Lake County on the north, Sonoma on the west, Yolo and Solano on the east, and San Pablo Bay on the south. The name is an undefined word of an extinct Indian tribe. The first white exploration (1823) was in quest of a mission site finally selected in present Sonoma County. Early U.S. settlers included George C. Yount,♦ whose *rancho* grant (1836) adjoined present Yountville, Joseph B. Chiles, and Jacob Leese. The English surgeon Edward T. Bale, who built a sawmill and gristmill (1846) in the Napa Valley, was another early settler. This fertile, 40-mile-long narrow valley, through which the Napa River flows, became a summer resort region (1859) when Samuel Brannan founded Calistoga.♦ In one of the cottages there Robert Louis Stevenson spent the first part of his honeymoon before he and Fanny retired to a deserted silver mine nearby on Mt. St. Helena, the county's northwestern boundary and highest point (4,343 feet). The 1860s saw the development of vineyards and wineries, mostly near St. Helena, the central Valley town. In the Mayacamas Mts. are more wineries, sanitariums and the Seventh Day Adventists' Pacific Union College; and across them on the west lies a large man-made reservoir, Lake Berryessa, named for a Spanish family of early settlers, which impounds water from Putah Creek. The city of Napa, on the south, has always been the county seat. It is the major market center, and is also known for its state mental hospital. In 1970 the city had a population of 35,978, while the county had 79,140. With an area of 503,936 acres, it had 100.5 persons per sq. mi.

Napa Soda Springs, mineral water source located 8 miles east of the city of Napa and at an elevation of 1,000 feet. At this well-known site Col. John Putnam Jackson built an elaborate spa (1870), popular to the end of his life (1900), and he generally incorporated his name in advertisements of its bottled waters and of the health cure offered at the luxurious resort itself.

Napa Valley, stretches some 40 miles from near where the Napa River empties into San Pablo Bay north to the Mayacamas Mts. It is bounded on the east by the Howell Mts. and on the west by the Napa Range which forms the border with Sonoma County. The highway north from the valley's major city, Napa, is paralleled on the east by the Silverado Trail, near which the Napa River runs; Napa Soda Springs and Stag's Leap, old-time resorts, lie a little farther east in the foothills. Along the highway is Yountville and its nearby Veterans Home, the town marked by an old winery converted into a group of stores and restaurants in the vein of San Francisco's Ghirardelli Square. The town's cemetery contains the monument, with primitive carving, of the pioneer George Yount. On the 10-mile drive to the next town, St. Helena, one passes Oakville and Rutherford in the heart of the wine country and the vineyards and wineries of Robert Mondavi, Beaulieu, Inglenook, Heitz, Louis Martini, and several newer firms. On the northern outskirts of St. Helena are the wineries of the Beringer Brothers, the Christian Brothers, Charles Krug, and the Mondavi family, and Souverain Cellars in the eastern mountains. Farther along are the old mill of Edward T. Bale, the Hans Kornell Cellars, the Schramsberg Winery, and other vintners. The narrowing valley's northernmost town is Calistoga with nearby hot springs, geyser, and petrified forest. Beyond it lies the undeveloped Robert Louis Stevenson Park, crowned by Mt. St. Helena.

NAPPENBACH, HENRY (1862–1931), German-born artist, resident in San Francisco after 1885, first as a commercial lithographer, then as a popular illustrator for the *San Francisco Examiner* until 1918, when William Randolph Hearst transferred him to New York. Nappenbach also produced easel paintings.

NARJOT, ERNEST [originally ETIENNE NARJOT DE FRANCHEVILLE] (1826–98), artist, went to California from his native France late in 1849 and, except for residence in Mexico (1852–65), remained there the rest of his life, painting landscapes, genre presentations of the local scene, and decorative frescoes for public buildings.

NARVAEZ, JOSÉ MARÍA (1771–1835?), Spanish-born navigator, second pilot on a voyage to Alaska (1788) during which he stopped at California. He returned in 1808 and again in 1822, when, as captain of the *San Carlos,* he took Agustín Fernández de San Vicente♦ to California. Narvaez made a map of California in 1823.

NASH, JOHN HENRY (1871–1947), Canadian-born typographer, in 1895 moved to San Francisco, where he was associated with the Tomoyé Press (1901–11) of the bookseller Paul Elder♦ in publishing California writings and with Taylor & Taylor♦ (1911–15) before founding his own firm for fine printing (1916). From it he issued lavishly designed and elegantly made books for direct sale in limited editions, but also printed for The Book Club of California, William Andrews Clark, William Randolph Hearst, and other customers and patrons. His publications varied from *The Divine Comedy* through writings by local authors to monographs on great printers, but all were done in a grandly impressive style. Toward the end of his life he and his press and library were affiliated with the University of Oregon (1936–43).

Nataqua, Territory of, region of 50,000 sq. mi. in northeastern California, proclaimed by Peter Lassen♦ and Isaac Roop♦ in 1855 to be independent of the state. It was short-lived as a possible political entity because it was not recognized by the U.S. Congress. However, the bill creating the Nevada Territory included the region if California would cede it. This in turn led to a boundary dispute known as the Sagebrush War♦ (1863). The area is now Honey Lake Valley of Lassen County.

National Forests, the 18 federal preserves within California that include some 19,000,000 acres of land, extending from the Klamath and Modoc on the Oregon border to the Cleveland nearly on the Mexican border. They are all administered by the Forest Service of the U.S. Dept. of Agriculture. The forests are Angeles (the earliest), Cleveland, Eldorado, Inyo, Klamath, Lassen, Los Padres, Mendocino, Modoc, Plumas, San Bernardino, Sequoia, Shasta, Sierra, Six Rivers, Stanislaus, Tahoe, and Trinity. The Rogue River, Siskiyou, and Toiyabe national forests are only partly located in the state and have their headquarters outside it. All National Forests located within the state save for Plumas, Six Rivers, and Tahoe contain Wilderness Areas. (*See also individual entries.*)

National Guard in California, volunteer force of some 22,000 men in its army and some 5,000 in its air division who serve under the governor. He is their commander in chief, but in an emergency they can be called out by the federal government, from which they receive funds, weapons, and other equipment. In addition to numerous armories, their bases include Camp Roberts♦ and Fort Irwin.♦ They are used in civil disturbances, disaster relief, and civil defense training. Famous assignments occurred after the San Francisco earthquake and fire (1906), after the Wheatland Riot (1914), during the General Strike in San Francisco (1934), and during the foray over People's Park in Berkeley (1969).

National Monuments, see *National Parks.*

National Parks, founded by Congress (1872) and administered by the Dept. of Interior, were first established in California in 1890, partly at the instigation of John Muir. The five in the state in order of creation are Yosemite (1890); Sequoia (1890), including Mt. Whitney; Lassen Volcanic (1916) in the Cascades; Kings Canyon (1940), north of Sequoia; and Redwood (1968), near Crescent City. Under the same administration are the eight National Monuments: Cabrillo, Channel Islands, Death Valley, Devil's Postpile, Joshua Tree, Lava Beds, Muir Woods, and Pinnacles. Point Reyes is designated a National Seashore. The parks cover about 4,300,000 acres (1970). (*See also individual entries.*)

National Resource Lands, conservation areas for ranges, forests, and deserts, designed to preserve forage, timber, whitewater, wildlife, and recreational areas in their natural states and to allow controlled camping for the public. Their various sites include King Range in the northwest of the state and Owens Valley in the southeast.

Native Sons of the Golden West, society organized (1875) by Gen. Albert Maver Winn for "mutual improvement, social intercourse . . . and to perpetuate . . . Memories . . . of the Days of '49." Initially limited to white males born in California after July 7, 1846 (the date when Sloat raised the U.S. flag at Monterey), its constitution has since been liberalized, but the organization, once known for its open opposition to Japanese, is still considered to emphasize Anglo-Saxon Americanism. Prior to 1950 it gave fellowships to students writing works on regional history, and its parlors (i.e. chapters) still sponsor programs of local history as well as the placement of historical markers and monuments. A comparable society, Native Daughters of the Golden West, was founded in 1886. The terms "native son" and "native daughter" were once commonly used to describe any persons born in the state, regardless of affiliation with the societies, but they are now less often employed.

Natural gas, a major industrial and domestic fuel originating from organic matter deposited in marine sediment. When found with oil it is known as wet gas (propane and butane); when alone it is known as dry gas. All oil fields yield the former, which was often wasted until the 1920s; but special dry gas fields were discovered in Kern County (1920s), in the Sacramento Delta (1930s), and near Stockton (1970s). Commercial use of natural gas dates back to the 1850s, but it was not widely employed until pipelines were built for transmission to major cities during the first two decades of the 20th century. By 1947 California could no longer meet its needs and had to build many thousands of miles of transmission and distribution pipe lines to bring gas from Texas, New Mexico, Oklahoma, Utah, Colorado, and Alberta (Canada). Local fields developed since the 1930s include those in the northern Sacramento Valley up to Corning, in the Los Angeles basin, and in the Peninsular Ranges. Once the gas is tapped it is stored in underground reservoirs. By 1972 the state's residents consumed 2 trillion cubic feet of gas annually. Mexico agreed (1977) to sell substantial amounts of natural gas (about 2 billion cubic feet a day) to a consortium of six U.S. companies for use in six southern states from Florida to California after an 800-mile pipeline is completed in 1980. In addition to domestic uses, natural gas serves as a raw material in the manufacture of ammonia, hydrogen, and petrochemicals, and is widely used for the generation of electric power. Among the several utilities that provide natural gas, Southern California Gas Co.◆ is the largest distributor in the U.S.

Naval stations, see *Military installations.*

Navarro River, flows into the Pacific at Navarro Head in mid-Mendocino County through onetime lumbering country. It passes through Hendy Redwood Grove.

Nectarines, smooth-skinned variety of peaches, known for 2,000 years as an instance of bud variation, were introduced to California during the gold rush. During the 19th century they were increasingly popular for canning, drying, and fresh sale; but in this century they dropped more than 50% from their high of 1,325,000 pounds in 1895, until in the 1970s they rose again sharply. In 1970, before the highest rise, the crop was grown on 74,000 acres and was worth $10,164,000. It then accounted for 98% of U.S. production.

Needles, city on the Mojave Desert of San Bernardino County, founded (1883) as a rail center for the Santa Fe Railroad. Across the Colorado River can be seen Arizona's needle-like peaks, from which the city's name was derived. Gold, magnesite, and other mines lie to the west, in the Sacramento Mts.

Negroes in California, see *Blacks in California*.

Neophytes, see *Mission Indians*.

NEUTRA, RICHARD [JOSEF] (1892–1970), Austrian-born architect and city planner, went to California (1925) and a year later began the practice in Los Angeles that led to many large-scale housing projects as well as distinguished private homes in the 1940s and 50s. His international style used much glass, prefabricated parts, reinforced concrete supporting slabs, diagonal roofs, and warm-colored wood and stone to harmonize with the southern California setting.

NEVADA, EMMA (1859–1940), upon beginning her internationally successful operatic career changed her surname, Wixom, to the one by which she was always known and which honored both her birthplace near Nevada City and her youthful residence in the state of Nevada. After graduation (1876) from Mills College she became famous as a coloratura soprano; was praised by Verdi and Gounod; and was an intimate of Sarah Bernhardt and Christina, the Queen Regent of Spain.

Nevada Bank, see *Wells Fargo*.

Nevada City, seat of Nevada County, a major mining town beginning in 1849, first for its placer prospecting, later for quartz mines. Natives include Emma Nevada and Richard Walton Tully.

Nevada County, organized (1851) from part of Yuba County, now its western boundary. Sierra and Placer counties are on its north and south, respectively, and the state of Nevada on its east. It contained two major routes through the Sierra: one along the Truckee River and by Donner Lake to Donner Pass, the other along the San Juan Ridge between the Middle and South Forks of the Yuba River. Gold was discovered early along that river; first it was panned, then hydraulically extracted (e.g. at Malakoff Diggins), and later dredged. The towns that sprang up include Rough and Ready (the nickname of Gen. Zachary Taylor, given by a former officer of his), Whisky Bar, Jackass Flat, and North San Juan, as well as two larger settlements, Grass Valley and Nevada City. Much of the eastern part of the county lies in Tahoe National Forest. It had a population of 26,346 in 1970. With an area of 624,128 acres, there were 27 persons per sq. mi. (*See also individual entries.*)

NEVE, FELIPE DE (1728–84), Spanish governor of the Californias with the military rank of colonel, first lived in the capital of Loreto (1775–77), then in the new capital of Monterey (1777–82). He is known as "California's first lawgiver" because he issued the *Reglamento* (June 1, 1779) which codified regulations for the administration of the Californias and which, with the Viceroy's order (April 1776) directed Neve to remove the seat of government from Loreto to Monterey. The *Reglamento* formed the basis for governing the Californias throughout the Spanish period. Neve was responsible for founding the pueblos of San José (1777) and Los Angeles (1781), hoping that they would be the core of a system to rival the missions and win military dominance over Alta California. Though his legislation was never fully implemented, Neve's administrative ability was appreciated sufficiently for him to be promoted to inspector-general and later *comandante general* of the Provincias Internas (1782), a frontier region that included Mexico, Texas, and the Californias.

NEVERS, ERNIE (ERNEST ALONZO NEVERS) (1903–76), Minnesota-born athlete, attended Stanford University (A.B., 1925), where he won eleven varsity letters and was the fullback on coach Pop Warner's football teams (1923–25). He was famous for passing and line charging. He later played professional baseball, basketball, and football.

New Albion, see *Nova Albion*.

New Almaden, south of San Jose, site of the major mercury♦ mine in the U.S. Mercury's basic source, cinnabar, was known to the Indians, who used it to paint their bodies, and the ore was discovered by a white (1824) who mistook the quicksilver for silver. Mining began in 1845, and Alexander Forbes♦ soon leased the site and named it after the world's largest mercury mine (in Spain). It yielded about $1,000,000 of mercury annually, much of it wanted for amalgamating the gold then being mined in the Mother Lode. A protracted law suit over the title ended the lease of Barron, Forbes & Co. (1863) and ownership passed to a U.S. firm which employed about 2,000 Mexican and Cornish miners. Although it suffered great financial loss at times, the mine continued to operate (very successfully during World Wars I and II) until the 1970s.

NEWBY, William Henry, see *Athenaeum, San Francisco.*

NEWELL, Pete[r] (1915–   ), Canadian-born basketball coach, reared in Los Angeles, where he played for Loyola University. He became basketball coach for the University of San Francisco and Michigan State University before assuming that post at the University of California, Berkeley (1954), where his teams won the Pacific Coast Conference (1957–60) and the NCAA championship (1959). He then became the campus' athletic director (1960–68), and later was general manager of the San Diego Rockets and Los Angeles Lakers, both professional teams.

Newhall, town in Los Angeles County, north of San Fernando Pass, named (1876) a Southern Pacific station (located until 1878 at Saugus) in honor of Henry M. Newhall (1825–82), a rancher and railroad promoter of the region who belonged to a wealthy pioneer family of San Francisco. The William S. Hart ranch is located there, as are an oil refinery erected in 1875 and Magic Mountain.♦ The nearby town of Saugus was named for Newhall's birthplace in Massachusetts. Placerita Canyon is also nearby, as is Valencia, the town that serves as headquarters for the Newhall Land and Farming Co., a family corporation with large land, oil, and cattle interests, which also owns Magic Mountain.

New Helvetia, see *Sutter, John.*

New Idria, see *Mercury* and *San Benito County.*

NEWMARK, Harris (1834–1916), left Germany for Los Angeles (1853) where he became a successful businessman in general merchandise, groceries, hides, wool, and other commodities, meanwhile acquiring large real estate holdings. He was also a major civic leader, endowing Jewish charities and aiding the community at large by organizing a board of trade and founding a public library. His recollections, *Sixty Years in Southern California* (1916), give a straightforward, intimate account of the many men and events with which he was associated.

New Melones Water Project, see *Melones Water Project.*

Newport Beach, residential and resort city of Orange County on Newport Bay, includes neighboring communities, among which are Balboa and Corona del Mar. The urbanization of the Irvine Ranch and ex-tension of the San Diego Freeway led to the creation of a Newport Center with high-rise office buildings. In 1970 it had a population of 49,422.

News Letter, San Francisco journal founded (1856) by Frederick Marriott♦ as a semimonthly letter-size sheet of blue paper with columns of news and advertisements covering three pages, the fourth left blank for a personal message and, after folding, for a mailing address. It was long popular as a means for settlers to send home news about California. Later it was expanded into a more conventional weekly newspaper, the *News-Letter and Commercial Advertiser,* of which Ambrose Bierce became the editor (1868–72), writing for it a caustic column, "The Town Crier." Although Marriott continued as publisher until he was succeeded by his son in 1915, the paper dwindled in importance, was finally merged with *The Wasp♦* (1928), and drifted to inanition and death in 1941.

Newspapers, began in California at the end of the Bear Flag Revolt with *The Californian,* a weekly issued first (1846) from Monterey, then from San Francisco (1847). At the beginning of the gold rush it merged with Sam Brannan's weekly *California Star* (1848), itself quickly absorbed (1849) by *The Alta California,* which became the city's first daily (1850) and lasted until 1891. It was initially edited by Edward C. Kemble. As historian of the state's newspapers to 1858, he described the numerous competitors. Many were weak and temporary; but others, like the *Pacific News* of San Francisco and the *Sacramento Union,* were of some consequence.

In that era even towns as small as Downieville and Knights Landing had their own weeklies, and the larger settlement of Placerville had twelve journals that came and went during the 1850s. Because of the cosmopolitan population attracted by gold, a large number of foreign-language papers was issued. Relatively well-established examples included *L'Echo du Pacifique,* with its weekly *Courrier de San Francisco;* the *California Staats-Zeitung* and *California Demokrat;* and, in Sacramento, a *Chinese News.* The most significant was the first Spanish-language journal of Los Angeles, *El Clamor Público,* designed for a town that still retained much of its Spanish heritage, which northern California had not.

As wealth, leisure, and stability increased, more newspapers were founded to appeal to special interests. Among them were religious, political, and temperance journals, and the black weekly *Mirror of the Times* (1856–58). But the greatest development was in basic journals of the larger cities. The earliest major daily was the *San Francisco Bulletin,* founded in 1855 by James King of William, the reform-minded editor killed the next year by Supervisor James P. Casey, whom he had exposed as an ex-convict. The *San Francisco Call,* founded in 1856, is most famous for having had Mark Twain as a reporter during its first decade; but it actually continued as a consequential publication for over a century. The *San Francisco Chronicle,* established in 1865 as a theatrical news sheet, grew to be a successful and sensational daily in competition with the *Bulletin* and the *Call,* each of whose circulation it surpassed in the 1870s. A major competitor appeared when the *San Francisco Examiner,* founded in 1863, was taken over by William Randolph Hearst in 1887. Its eight pages made it the largest journal in the state, and on page one it introduced news instead of want-ads, while inside it printed not only sensational reporting but special columns and other features.

In Los Angeles journalism long remained more conservative, in keeping with the city's own atmosphere. The first daily, the *Los Angeles Daily News,* did not appear until 1869 and it did not last long, and even the *Los Angeles Star,* which was made a daily in 1870, collapsed within seven years. A major paper was not established until Harrison Gray Otis in 1882 took over the year-old *Los Angeles Times* and made it a great force in the city's growth, dedicated to the development of a good harbor, a satisfactory fresh water supply, and increased population in the surrounding southern California area. Its conservative views were countered by the *Los Angeles Evening Express* which Edwin Earl took over (1900) and, with the aid of Edward Dickson, made into a voice of the Lincoln-Roosevelt League of liberal Republicans. In time both that paper and the older *Los Angeles Herald* were purchased by Hearst and eventually merged with the *Los Angeles Examiner* (1962), but the *Times* remained the city's great paper and it eventually overwhelmed the Hearst journal. The *Times'* most significant competitor was the *Los Angeles Record,* founded (1895) by E. W. Scripps as one of his politically liberal chain that also included the *San Francisco News* (1903–65). A temporary attempt to challenge established papers in both cities was made by the young Cornelius Vanderbilt, Jr., who published his tabloid *San Francisco Illustrated Daily Herald* and *Los Angeles Illustrated Daily News,* but they did not survive.

Outside the two major cities some papers that were established by E. W. Scripps flourished in San Diego, Sacramento, and Fresno, but the great chain in the Central Valley was that of the *Bee* newspapers established by James McClatchey, first in Sacramento and Modesto, and taken up by his heirs in Fresno. In Oakland the leading newspaper was the *Tribune,* founded in 1874 by a San Francisco journalist but tremendously strengthened as a publication with political power after it was bought by the Knowland family in 1915. Another significant journalistic voice in the state was the *Santa Barbara News-Press,* which T. M. Storke made liberal and independent during his long career. Still another newspaper power in California has been the Copley Press, a chain of newspapers founded in San Diego (1928) and expanded widely not only in southern California but in 1966 in northern California by purchase of the *Sacramento Union,* a daily dating back to 1851 which had once employed Mark Twain as a correspondent.

Many smaller papers were founded in the mid-20th century to appeal to special groups, the two large ones for blacks being the *Los Angeles Sentinel* and the *Sun Reporter* of San Francisco. But perhaps the most unusual journalistic development of recent years has been the successful creation of widely circulated counterculture papers, of which the most striking are the *Los Angeles Free Press* and the *Berkeley Barb. (See also individual entries.)*

NEWTON, Huey P. (1942–), born in Louisiana and brought to California as a child, with Bobby Seale became a founder of the Black Panther party♦ (1966). Arrested (1967) as the result of a fracas between police and blacks in which he was wounded, Newton became the focus of a "Free Huey" campaign. After a lengthy trial he was found guilty of voluntary manslaughter, a conviction reversed by a court of appeals. But when he was charged with murder in another case (1974) he fled to Cuba (1974), from which he returned (1977) to stand trial.

New Towns, planned urban developments created in previously unpopulated areas, intended to be largely self-sufficient economically and socially. An alternative to metropolitan congestion and to nearby relatively unplanned suburbs and subdivisions, the New Towns have a heritage that goes back to early 20th-century garden cities in England and to such U.S. experiments of the 1920s as that of Radburn, N.J. The first example in California was Baldwin Hills Village (1941) in Los Angeles, which separates pedestrian and auto routes and has a community park that all houses face. Planned towns varying considerably in size and character began to be built frequently during the 1960s, and in the next decade California contained 30% of all such new construction in the nation. Notable projects include Foster City, a development built on filled land with canals and boat harbors, located on the southern arm of San Francisco Bay near Palo Alto; Valencia, a community planned for 250,000 people on the Newhall Ranch near Los Angeles; a city which is to be created on the Irvine Ranch in Orange County, near the local campus of the University of California; and a planned metropolis of 160 sq. mi. in the Mojave Desert, to be called California City.

NEYLAN, JOHN FRANCIS (1885–1960), New York-born lawyer and newspaperman, went to California (1910), and after working on the San Francisco *Call* and *Bulletin*, attracted Gov. Hiram Johnson's attention and became a member of his administration. He was later publisher of Hearst newspapers in San Francisco and Hearst's general counsel. As a liberal he defended Anita Whitney♦ (1925) but later became a conservative foe of Roosevelt's New Deal and, as a Regent of the University of California, led the militantly anti-Communist program to require a loyalty oath of the faculty (1949 ff.).

NG POON CHEW, see *Chew, Ng Poon.*

NIDEVER, GEORGE (1802–83), Tennessee-born frontiersman, left his Arkansas home to become a mountain man (1830) and in 1833 was a member of the detachment of Bonneville's trapping and exploring party under Joseph R. Walker♦ which was the first to cross the Sierra Nevada into California. He later hunted with Yount, sought sea otter on the Channel Islands, was part of Frémont's company in the march to Los Angeles (1846), and finally settled in Santa Barbara. He helped remove the Indians of San Nicolás, one of the Channel Islands (1835), and returned (1853) to discover the legendary "lone woman" who had became separated from the group years before. His reminiscences were published in 1937.

NIEBAUM, GUSTAVE FERDINAND (1842–1908), Finnish-born sea captain, after sailing a ship of his own to Alaska (1864) settled in San Francisco, where he became a partner in the Alaska Commercial Co.♦ Having made a fortune, he retired to his 1,000-acre estate in the Napa Valley where he established the Inglenook Vineyards (1887), eventually absorbed by the winery of Louis Petri (1964).

Nisei, see *Japanese in California.*

Nisenan (or **Nishinan**), southern group of Maidu Indians.♦

NIXON, RICHARD M[ILHOUS] (1913–), born in Yorba Linda, the second of five sons, to a rather poor family, was reared in Whittier where he went to college. He practiced law there after receiving a legal degree from Duke. Following naval service in World War II he was elected as a Republican to Congress (1946–50) and then to the Senate (1950). His Senate campaign against Helen Gahagan Douglas was notorious: he attacked her for ostensibly being "soft" on communism. He was elected as Eisenhower's Vice President (1953–61) and was narrowly defeated by Kennedy for the presidency (1960). He then ran for governor of California and was defeated by Brown (1962). The next year he moved his home and political base to New York and campaigned hard for the presidency, which he achieved (1969). His administration, though noted for the recognition of China, détente with Russia, and the end of the war in Vietnam, became bogged down in ever-growing scandals and corruption. Within two years of his reelection by a great majority, articles of impeachment were voted against him by the Judiciary Committee of the House of Representatives (1974), and when he confessed that he had not told the truth about his knowledge of espionage against Democratic party headquarters in the Watergate Complex (Washington, D.C.) he lost almost all support. As a result he resigned his office (1974) and moved to his erstwhile "Western White House," Casa Pacifica in San Clemente. At that retirement site he made five long television interviews with David Frost (1977), wrote his memoirs, and instituted suits to claim ownership of the revelatory tapes that had covertly recorded his conversations while he was President. About his earlier problems he wrote *Six Crises* (1962).

Nob Hill, site in San Francisco, originally called California Street Hill, said to have acquired the present name from the term "nabob" applied to the wealthy men who built ostentatious homes there after the cable car made it accessible (1873). At the summit or close to it, large properties were bought by Leland Stanford, Mark Hopkins, James G. Fair, and Collis P. Huntington, who built mansions there. They are now recalled in the names of hotels built in place of the first three mansions and across the street from the site of the fourth. The James Flood house survives in remodeled form as the Pacific Union Club, the Charles Crocker property is now the site of Grace Cathedral, and David D. Colton's house, later Collis P. Huntington's, has yielded to Huntington Park. The marble portico called Portals of the Past, now located on Lloyd Lake in Golden Gate Park, was the surviving remnant from the 1906 earthquake and fire which destroyed the A. N. Towne mansion on the corner of California and Taylor streets.

NOÉ, José de Jesus (1805–72?), came from Mexico to California in the Híjar♦ and Padrés colonizing group (1834). He settled in San Francisco and became its last Mexican *alcalde* (1846). From Pío Pico he received a land grant to the San Miguel *rancho* (1845) of about 4,000 acres in San Francisco, including Twin Peaks. A city street is now named for him.

NOGUCHI, Yone (1875–1947), Japanese poet who as a young man went to California where he became a protégé of Charles Warren Stoddard and Joaquin Miller and an affiliate of Les Jeunes.♦ His curiously personal poetry, written in uncertain English, was published as *Seen and Unseen; or, Monologues of a Homeless Snail* (1897), a book praised by some bohemians but travestied by Norris in *The Octopus*. *From the Eastern Sea* (1903) collects more conventional lyrics written in England, to which he had moved. In them he expressed his longing for Japan. He then returned home and had a long, distinguished career as literary critic and professor as well as poet. His son is Isamu Noguchi, the sculptor.

NOMELLINI, Leo (1924–   ), Italian-born football player, first at the University of Illinois, where he was All-American tackle (1946–49), then with the San Francisco Forty-Niners (1950–63), playing in 174 consecutive games as a great lineman.

Nomlaki, Indians of the Wintun tribe.

NORDHOFF, Charles (1830–1901), Prussian-born journalist and author, reared in the United States. He traveled in California and Hawaii (1871–73) and as a result wrote *California for Health, Wealth and Residence* (1872), an enormously popular work which stimulated much settlement, and *Peninsular California; Some Account . . . of Lower California* (1887). He lived for a time in Ojai,♦ originally named for him, and spent his last years in Coronado. His son was Walter Nordhoff,♦ and his grandson was Charles B. Nordhoff (1887–1947), the popular novelist best known for *Mutiny on the Bounty* (1932), written with James B. Hall.

NORDHOFF, Walter (1858–1937), rancher in Baja California, and son of Charles Nordhoff.♦ Walter Nordhoff retired to Santa Barbara where he wrote a popular historical novel, *The Journey of the Flame* (1933), published under the pseudonym Antonio de Fierro Blanco, concerning the adventurous travels of the fictive Don Juan Obrigón, born in Baja California in 1798, who tells his tale in 1902, age 104.

NORIEGA, José (1792–1870?), supercargo of the vessel that brought the colonists of Híjar and Padrés♦ (1834) to California. He became the grantee of Los Médanos (Sandbanks) *rancho* (Contra Costa County, later owned by John Marsh♦), an *alcalde* of San Jose, and was captured at the opening of the Bear Flag Revolt with Francisco Arce.

Normal Schools, state institutions created for the training of teachers, began with one in San Francisco (1861), soon followed by others in San Jose (1871), Los Angeles (1882), Chico (1889), and other population centers. In time they came to be called Teachers Colleges and later developed into colleges and universities, including UCLA and branches of the State University and College system.

NORRIS, Charles G[ilman] (1881–1945), brother of Frank Norris and husband of Kathleen Norris, also a novelist, each of whose works, including *Salt* (1918), *Brass* (1921), *Seed* (1930), and *Flint* (1944), treats a single different major social problem of the time.

NORRIS, [Benjamin] Frank[lin] (1870–1902), was born in Chicago but moved with his parents to San Francisco (1884) and always thought of himself as a Californian. To develop his artistic talent he was sent to an art school in France (1887), but spent his spare time writing medieval romances. Brought back to the U.S., he became a student at the University of California (1890–94), meanwhile writing stories and sketches for student and local publications. While a special student at Harvard (1894–95), and under the influence of Zola's fiction, he turned from youthful romanticism to a naturalistic view of man and began the novel that became *McTeague,* treating middle and lower-class life mainly as seen on San Francisco's Polk St. During the same period he wrote the novel posthumously published (1914) as *Vandover and the Brute,* depicting the degeneration of a young San Francisco society man and aspiring artist.

After a journalistic stint in South Africa (1895–96), Norris settled in San Francisco as an editor of

The Wave,♦ in which he printed much of his own writing, like *Moran of the Lady Letty* (1898), the adventure story of a shanghaied San Franciscan; that Kiplingesque romance still attracted him is also evident in *Blix* (1899), a light local-color novelette set in San Francisco and fancifully portraying his own wooing of a local society girl.

Settling in New York to work as a publisher's reader and magazine contributor, Norris also made trips home to gain background for an "Epic of the Wheat," a trilogy of novels employing a naturalistic philosophy, realistic detail, and a concern with the impact of socio-economic and natural forces on individuals. The first of these works, often considered, along with *McTeague* (1899), as his finest fiction, was *The Octopus* (1901), presenting the struggle of oppressed wheat ranchers against the grasping power of the monopolistic railroad. The climax of the novel was based on the Mussel Slough tragedy. It was followed by *The Pit* (1903), a tale of speculation on the Chicago wheat exchange. Norris had intended to write a third novel (to be entitled "The Wolf") in which he would deal with the consumption of wheat in a famine-stricken European village, but he died suddenly, following an appendectomy.

He did leave articles on his theories of fiction, gathered as *The Responsibilities of the Novelist* (1903), in which he contended that the best novel is one which "proves something, draws conclusions from a whole congeries of forces, social tendencies, race impulses, devotes itself not to a study of men but of man."

NORRIS, KATHLEEN (1880–1966), wife of Charles G. Norris, was even more popular than he was as a novelist. She wrote dozens of domestic comedies and tragedies which, like the first, *Mother* (1911), were always marked by wholesome sentiment.

North Beach, section of San Francisco so named because in the 1850s it was actually the beach of a Bay inlet between Telegraph Hill and Russian Hill. It has long been an area of Italian settlement (its main thoroughfare proudly named Columbus Ave.), but part of it was also known as the lurid nightlife section of the city called the Barbary Coast.♦ In the 1950s part of the neighborhood was the home of the Beat movement,♦ and more recently the intersection of Columbus and Broadway has became the site of tawdry bars featuring nude shows.

Northeast Intermontane Region, see *Desert.*

Northern California, a general geographic term traditionally applied to the part of the state that lies north of the Tehachapi,♦ is sometimes given a greater sense of separateness by capitalizing the defining adjective. The region includes 43 counties: Del Norte, Siskiyou, Modoc, Humboldt, Trinity, Shasta, Lassen, Mendocino, Tehama, Plumas, Glenn, Butte, Sierra, Lake, Colusa, Sutter, Yuba, Nevada, Placer, El Dorado, Sacramento, Yolo, Napa, Sonoma, Marin, Solano, Amador, Alpine, Calaveras, Tuolumne, San Joaquin, Contra Costa, San Francisco, San Mateo, Alameda, Santa Clara, Santa Cruz, Stanislaus, Merced, Mariposa, Madera, Monterey, and San Benito. Fresno County is sometimes considered to belong to this group but is as often added to the 14 counties that are accepted as comprising southern California.♦

The gold rush made northern California by far the most populous part of the new state, for the mining area attracted some 120,000 people by 1852 and San Francisco quickly became the metropolis of California, incomparably larger than the older Los Angeles. Not until the 1920s did southern California's population finally surpass that of northern California, which continued to receive proportionately greater representation in the state legislature until the reapportionment following the U.S. Supreme Court decision (1964) establishing a one-man-one-vote criterion. After that some northern California legislators proposed a division of the state at the Tehachapi boundary, an idea earlier put forth by some southern Californians, who now oppose it.

One of the major disputes between the two sections has concerned the large-scale redistribution of water♦ from the north to the south since it is feared that there may not be enough for both, particularly in drought years. The economy of northern California is diverse, as are its several geographic environments, and the major industries include agriculture, electrical machinery, food processing, lumber, petroleum refining, shipping, and wine making. In 1900 the region's population was about 1,700,000; by 1970 it had increased to approximately 7,550,000.

Northern mines, see *Mother Lode.*

NORTHROP, JOHN K[NUDSEN] (1895–), aeronautical engineer and designer, began his career with Loughead Aircraft Co. (1916) in his home city of Santa Barbara and became a co-founder of its successor firm, named Lockheed.♦ He established his own engineering and manufacturing firm, Avion Corp. (1928), which became Northrop Corp. (1932) and, later, part of Douglas Aircraft. For it he designed distinctive airplanes. He also contributed to the Air Force and to guided missile and atomic energy projects.

Northwestern Pacific Railroad, see *Santa Fe Railroad.*

NORTON, JOSHUA ABRAHAM (1818–80), known as Emperor Norton, born in London, after business ventures in South Africa went to San Francisco (1850) where he became a commission merchant. An unsuccessful attempt to corner the rice market (1853) bankrupted him and drove him mad so that he came to believe he was "Norton I, Emperor of the United States," to which title he later added "Protector of Mexico." He affected a plumed or cockaded top hat, a quasi-military suit with epaulettes, and a sword, but he comported himself with great dignity as he wandered the city, generally accompanied by his dogs, Bummer and Lazarus. He was sympathetically received by the subjects in his capital, his promissory notes were honored for goods and petty cash, and people were tolerant of and amused by his various proclamations, of which the most famous was the command to build bridges across the Bay (1869). There were occasional hoaxes, such as a suggestion that he wed Queen Victoria, and some specious messages were issued in his name, but his own texts and actions generally had a grand solemnity.

Norwalk, city in southwestern Los Angeles County, like its neighbors Downey and Bellflower was once a farming and dairying area. After World War II the great population boom of Los Angeles and Orange counties made it a major tract housing center. In 1970 the population was 91,827.

Norwegians in California, although a few came to Mexican California, the first real influx began during the gold rush with the arrival of companies from Norway and the Midwest organized for mining, or with sailors deserting ships. Many of them drifted into small farming, business, shipbuilding, and fishing. Four particularly prominent Norwegians were Peder Sather, an Oakland banker, George C. Johnson, the major hardware supplier of the Pacific Coast, Capt. John G. North, a builder of bay and river steamboats in his Potrero shipyard of San Francisco, and John Albert Thompson, who regularly snowshoed across the Sierra Nevada to deliver mail. Another famous Norwegian, slightly later, was Andrew Furuseth,♦ a San Francisco labor leader for sailors, as was the still later Harry Lundeberg.♦ During the 20th century, in addition to traditional activities, a good many Norwegians have become fruit and grape growers. The San Francisco-born author, Kathryn Anderson McLean (1909–),

under the pseudonym of Kathryn Forbes, wrote *Mama's Bank Account* (1943), humorous sketches of her Norwegian grandmother's life in San Francisco, dramatized by John Van Druten as *I Remember Mama* (1944) and by others as a television series.

Notre Dame, College of, Catholic women's liberal arts institution, founded in 1855, long located in Santa Clara, was moved in 1923 to its present site on the former country estate of William C. Ralston in Belmont (San Mateo County). In 1970 it had 1,060 students.

Nova Albion, name coined by Francis Drake that he had incised upon a plate of brass and posted at his landing place in California (1579) when he took possession of the region for Queen Elizabeth. According to *The World Encompassed* (1628), presumably written by Drake's chaplain, Francis Fletcher, he did this for two reasons: "the one in respect of the white bancks or cliffes, which lie toward the sea [as in England]: the other that it might have some affinitie, even in name also, with our owne country, which was sometime so called." The title was employed by Vancouver and others who wished to ignore Spanish claims to the area.

Noyo River, rises west of Willits and flows into the Pacific 35 miles farther west, just below Fort Bragg. Its Pomo name may mean "creek." The town of that name was once a redwood lumber harbor served by the Skunk Railroad♦ and is now a fishing center.

Nuclear energy, as a source of power came into being in California because increased needs of a growing population could not be met by diminishing gas and oil supplies, limited hydroelectric♦ plants, and the very small use of geothermal energy.♦ The development of nuclear power has nevertheless been limited because of public opposition to its plants as a potentially explosive or radioactive danger, and because the water they must evacuate into the ocean is so hot as to endanger nearby marine life. The first nuclear power plant was opened by Pacific Gas and Electric Co. at Humboldt Bay in 1963 but closed (1976) to study its possible damage from earthquakes. The second, completed in 1968 by Southern California Edison, is at San Onofre,♦ a third is at Rancho Seco in Sacramento County, and others have been projected or partly constructed at Diablo Canyon, just south of San Luis Obispo, and at Sundesert, near Blythe in

Riverside County. In 1976 the state's voters rejected an initiative proposition to prohibit the construction of new nuclear power plants and lower the operating levels of existing ones, but administrative and legislative disputes have continued on these subjects.

Nueva California, see *Alta California.*

Nugget, see *Color* and *Gold mining.*

Nurseries, horticultural, introduced by Americans during the gold rush to improve the fruits and plants brought to California by the padres. The good climate and demand for fruit, grapes, and plants caused eastern nurserymen to set up agents, and by 1852 they were growing their own stock. By 1856 substantial nursery businesses flourished around San Francisco Bay. Notable early nurserymen included Louis Pellier, who introduced the prune♦ to California (1856), and George C. Roeding, a Fresno entrepreneur, who introduced the Smyrna wasp (1899), necessary to grow figs.♦ At his Santa Rosa nursery Luther Burbank♦ developed many hybrids and created new varieties of fruit, vegetables, and plants. To protect native stock, the state established a quarantine (1892) against importation of fruit trees, and to maintain standards the Nurserymen's Association of California was created (1915). The present-day major regions of flower growing are Monterey and Santa Clara counties in the north; Ventura, Orange, and San Diego counties in the south; and valleys north of the city of Santa Barbara. Since 1929 Lompoc Valley has displaced France as the major U.S. source of seeds. California also accounts for most of the nation's supply of cut flowers.

Nut Tree, restaurant on U.S. 80 near Vacaville, with tourist attractions, operated by descendants of the Iowa rancher who established (1855) on its Emigrant Trail site a fruit ranch marked by a large black walnut tree. The popular stopping place features California foods, and has gift shops, a toy railroad, and an airport.

Nuts, except for those which are native, like pine nuts, were introduced to California by the padres in their mission gardens but began to be more widely grown after the gold rush. Commercial production came relatively late and emphasis has been on walnuts and almonds. The native hardshell black walnut gives its name to several sites in the state, e.g. Walnut Creek in Contra Costa County. But the softshell English walnut, which was cultivated on the ranch of William Wolfskill,♦ was not raised commercially on a large scale until the 1860s with plantings by Joseph Sexton of Santa Barbara and Felix Gillet of Nevada City, and in the 1880s by Harriet Strong in Whittier. California is now the foremost producer and grows 99% of the commercial U.S. crop. A cooperative agency, the Diamond Walnut Growers, was established in Stockton (1912) and now handles half or more of the California crop. The San Joaquin Valley from Stockton to Modesto and the Chico area are the main centers for a crop that in 1970 was raised on 146,000 acres and was worth $51,912,000. Almond growing is mainly carried on in the same regions as well as in the Salinas Valley near Paso Robles, but there are orchards in all save nine of California's counties. Production has increased from 525 tons in 1885 to 124,000 tons in 1970. They were grown on 170,000 acres and were worth $80,000,000 in the latter year. The California Almond Growers Exchange in Sacramento (est. 1910) handles 70% of the crop. California accounts for over half of the world production. Since 1970 pistachio trees have been planted quite heavily in the southern San Joaquin Valley; 27,000 acres are said to be devoted to their cultivation.

NUTTALL, THOMAS (1786–1859), curator of the Botanical Garden, Harvard College, and a member of Nathaniel B. Wyeth's expedition to Oregon (1832), visited California (1836), where he identified cacti and other flora, and returned to Boston aboard the *Alert* on the same voyage as Richard Henry Dana, Jr. (He was not related to Zelia Nuttall.)

NUTTALL, ZELIA (1857–1933), California-born archaeologist, descended from a Mexican family and John Parrott,♦ a rich San Francisco banker. She was married briefly to Alphonse Pinart, a French ethnologist, who interested her in anthropology. Most of her life was spent as an expatriate in Europe and Mexico, where her scholarship led to the identification of two pre-Columbian codices, to published research on Drake, and to archaeological discoveries.

OAK, HENRY L[EBBEUS] (1844–1905), principal assistant to H. H. Bancroft♦ in administering his library and in the composition of the historian's volumes on California. Oak later attacked his former employer for failing to give him proper credit.

Oak, tree of which many varieties flourish in California, these being divided into deciduous and evergreen. Of the deciduous the most common are: *valley* (or *weeping*) *oak,* generally 40 to 75 feet high, with a round-topped crown, russet leaves in autumn, and a dark brown or ash-gray bark, found below 4,000-foot elevations from the Eel River to Los Angeles, the most famous specimen being the 1,000-year-old one in Chico (toppled 1977) named for the British botanist Sir Joseph Hooker who thought it was the world's largest (over 100 feet high with a branch spread over 150 feet); *blue* (or *mountain white* or *rock*) *oak,* rarely over 40 feet tall, with a rounded crown, a blue tint to its leaves, and a gray to white trunk, growing on the Coast Range and the western slope of the Sierra up to 3,500 feet; *California black oak,* 30 to 85 feet high, with leaves that change from soft pink to dark yellow-green as spring turns to summer, and a dark bark, grows in elevations to 8,000 feet throughout the state; and *Oregon white* (or *Garry* or *Post*) *oak,* is found in the Bald Hills and down to Santa Rosa.

The evergreen or live oaks include: *tanbark* (or *tan*) *oak,* with light green leaves shiny on top and cotton-like below, a smooth trunk whose bark is used for tannin in leather curing, grows in coastal mountains of the whole state below 4,500 feet; *coast live* (or *live*) *oak,* usually less than 70 feet tall, with leaves like holly and bark like birch, grows below 3,000 feet from Sonoma to Mexico; *maul* (or *canyon live*) *oak,* somewhat similar in appearance, found throughout the state; *Sadler* (or *deer*) *oak,* a scrub tree under 8 feet, found in mountains of northwestern California; *Engelmann oak,* with gray-green leaves and a scaly gray bark, native to southern California areas below 4,000 feet; *California scrub oak,* with varied leaf forms, rarely over 8 feet tall, flourishes in the southern part of the state; *giant Chinquapin oak,* grows to 50 feet in height, with tough leaves dark green above and gold below, and a red bark, flourishes mostly in the northern Coast Range; and *huckleberry live oak, interior live oak,* and *Brewer oak.*

The acorns of all oaks furnished food for Indians. Because they are such common trees the word oak is incorporated into some 150 of the state's place-names; *roble,* Spanish for "deciduous oak," and *encina,* Spanish for "live oak," also furnish many place-names.

Oakland, largest city of Alameda County and the metropolis of the east shore of San Francisco Bay, built on land that was once inhabited by Costanoan Indians. The site's first white visitors were in the exploring party of Fages and Crespí (1772), followed by Anza (1776). The land was granted to Luís María Peralta (1820), but his heirs lost it to squatters and others who came during the great gold rush, some of them engaging in farming or lumbering of the oaks and redwoods on the old Rancho San Antonio. The most enterprising of all was Horace W. Carpentier♦ who, with associates, cunningly laid out and incorporated the town of Oakland (1852), reserving the whole waterfront for himself.

Outlying settlements (Clinton and Brooklyn) became affiliated with the new town whose early developers included Dr. Samuel H. Merritt, a mayor (1867–69) and developer of the salt water tidal lake in the middle of town that bears his name. Other distinguished early settlers included the Dutchman James de Fremery, whose homesite is now a park bearing his name, George C. Pardee,♦ the state's governor (1903–7), and Josiah Stanford, brother of another governor, Leland Stanford. Bret Harte lived in Oakland as a young man (his stepfather, Col. Andrew Williams, was the city's fourth mayor), and the region in which he resided has been preserved and refurbished as Bret Harte Boardwalk. His friend Ina Coolbrith became the city's first librarian, in which capacity she aided and encouraged young Jack London. Another literary resident (1892–99) was Edwin Markham, and in the hills behind the city Joaquin Miller built his estate, The Hights.

The city grew to be a major transportation center,

since it was the western terminus for the transcontinental railway (1869) whose passengers and freight had to cross the Bay to San Francisco on the ferries, which first came into being in 1850. Over the years Oakland developed into a major port and shipbuilding center and came to include a large U.S. Army Port of Embarkation and an equally great Naval Supply Depot. It also developed major industrial and manufacturing plants for shipbuilding, machinery, food processing, and chemicals and became the headquarters for the varied enterprises founded by Henry J. Kaiser.

Its large population has called into being such metropolitan edifices as a Coliseum for its professional athletic teams, including the Raiders (football) and Athletics (baseball); a large and striking Museum displaying exhibits on the ecology, history, and art of California; and a fine zoo in Knowland Park. That facility bears the name of the city's modern political leaders, Congressman Joseph Knowland and Sen. William Knowland, publishers of the *Oakland Tribune*. Another major figure identified with the city was Chief Justice Earl Warren.

Natives of the city include Arthur Brown, Jr., Donald Budge, Robert Duncan, Wesley Hohfeld, Sidney Howard, Ernie Lombardi, Judah Magnes, Nance O'Neil, and Harry Partch.

As the western terminus of the first transcontinental railroad the city early had a small population of black families, whose male heads were sleeping car porters, but during World War II local industry attracted a great influx of blacks from the South. This created a ghetto, problems of crime, and militant radicalism like that of the Black Panthers. By 1970 almost 35% of the population was black and in that decade they were represented by a black superintendent of schools and a black mayor.

Educational institutions include Mills College, the California College of Arts and Crafts, and the College of Holy Names. In 1970 the population was 367,548.

Oakland Athletics, see *Athletics, Oakland.*

Oakland Raiders, see *Raiders, Oakland.*

Oakland Tribune (1874–), daily newspaper owned and published (until 1911) by a former San Francisco journalist, William E. Dargie, who until 1891 called it the *Oakland Daily Evening Tribune*. In 1906 he added a Sunday edition. It was bought by Joseph R. Knowland♦ in 1915 and thereafter published by him, his son, William K., and his grandson, Joseph R., who kept it the leading East Bay journal and still an evening paper, noted for its thorough coverage of East Bay news. When the Knowland family sold it (1977), it became a morning publication.

Oaks, Oakland, baseball♦ team in the Pacific Coast League that was the city's club (1903–58) until the advent of the Athletics and the entrance of that team into the major leagues.

Oats, field crop probably first cultivated in California by the early padres at the missions. Although the grain is an important food for horses, it has nevertheless remained relatively unimportant in California and the state does not rank among the nation's leading producers. The Kadota oat, introduced by the University of California (1922), has replaced the previously common strain, California red. The 1970 crop, grown on 101,000 acres, was worth $3,889,000.

O'BRIEN, PARRY (1932–), Santa Monica-born track star, before graduation from the University of Southern California developed a new technique for throwing the shot and established a world's record (1953), but in 1959 broke his own record with a put of 63′ 4″. He won the Sullivan Award (1959) as the outstanding amateur athlete of the U.S.

O'BRIEN, WILLIAM S[HONEY] (1826–78), Irish-born, went directly to California (1849) where he met James C. Flood♦ while mining on Feather River. O'Brien and Flood later opened the Auction Lunch Saloon in San Francisco which attracted many stockbrokers from whom they got tips on mining. Thereupon the two entered the brokerage business themselves. With John W. Mackay♦ and James G. Fair,♦ also Irishmen, they got control of the Comstock Lode♦ and all four (called the Silver Kings♦) became multimillionaries. They also founded the Nevada Bank that later became Wells Fargo.

Observatories, see *Griffith Park, Lick Observatory, Mount Wilson,* and *Mount Palomar.*

O'CAIN, JOSEPH, see *Russians in California.*

Occidental and Oriental Steamship Company, see *Southern Pacific Railroad.*

Occidental College, nonsectarian, coeducational liberal arts college founded (1888) by Presbyterian clergy and laymen. It is located in northeast Los Angeles and has an undergraduate enrollment of about 1,700 students. Distinguished alumni include Dean Cromwell, Robinson Jeffers, Homer Lea, Sammy Lee, Lawrence Clark Powell, and Ward Ritchie.

Oceanside, residential beach city of San Diego County, the nearest community to the Marine Corps base of Camp Pendleton. Also nearby are citrus, flower, and vegetable ranches; Mission San Luis Rey; and Mt. Palomar Observatory. In 1970 it had a population of 40,494.

O'CONNELL, DANIEL (1849–99), Irish-born journalist and author, went to California in the late 1860s. In San Francisco he and Henry George founded the short-lived daily *Evening Post,* and later he edited the *Chronicle, Bulletin,* and *Wasp.* He was a founder of the Bohemian Club and wrote *Songs from Bohemia* (1900).

Octopus, The, novel by Frank Norris,♦ published in 1901. Intended as the first volume of a trilogy, "The Epic of the Wheat," it presents a broad panorama of wheat growing in the San Joaquin Valley and the fight of the ranchers against the monopolistic railroad, stigmatized as a monstrous and malevolent octopus. The story comes to a climax in a fictive rendering of the Mussel Slough♦ tragedy. Despite the realistic portrayal of men in deadly conflict, they are viewed as mere "ephemerides" in the great cycle of the seasons as the wheat continues to grow, for the power of nature is seen as far vaster than that of human life.

ODETS, CLIFFORD (1906–63), rose from the Bronx to make a New York reputation as a proletarian playwright during the Depression with *Waiting for Lefty* (1935) and *Awake and Sing* (1935). Much of his later career was spent in Hollywood, where he adapted his plays, *Golden Boy* (1939), about a slum boy searching unhappily for a meaningful success; *The Country Girl* (1954); and *The Big Knife*♦ (1955). He also wrote original scenarios and directed some films.

O'DOUL, LEFTY (FRANCIS JOSEPH O'DOUL) (1897–1969), San Francisco-born baseball player, began his career as a left-handed pitcher with the Seals, went to the N.Y. Yankees (1919–23), then, after hurting his arm, became an outfielder and

great batter for Philadelphia and Brooklyn. He twice won the National League batting championship. He later managed various teams, including the Seals for 17 years, winning three pennants. His protégés included Joe DiMaggio and Willie McCovey. He helped introduce baseball to Japan. In 1949 he won the Bing Crosby golf tournament.

O'FARRELL, JASPER (1817–75), Irish-born civil engineer, went from Chile to California (1843), where he was appointed Surveyor-General of Alta California. He continued his work under the Americans and his mapping of San Francisco (1847) located Market St. and established many street names of the area bounded by Post, Leavenworth, and Francisco streets and the Bay. One street in the gridiron plan he extended for the city was later named for him.

Offshore drilling, see *Oil.*

Of Mice and Men, novelette by John Steinbeck, published and dramatized by him in 1937. Blending realism and sentimentality, it presents the close relationship between two itinerant farmhands, George, a sensible but hopeful worker, and Lennie, a feeble-minded but loving and childlike man with a morbid need for stroking soft things. They yearn for a farm of their own but are perpetually deprived of it and finally meet tragedy when Lennie accidentally kills a woman and George has to kill him before he is lynched by a mob of local ranchers.

OGDEN, PETER SKENE (1794–1854), fur trader, probably the first Canadian to go to California (1826). He returned (1829–30) leading a large brigade, coming down through Idaho and Nevada to the Colorado River and the Gulf of California, then trapping up the San Joaquin and Sacramento rivers en route to the headquarters in Oregon of the Hudson's Bay Co. for which he worked.

"Oh, My Darling Clementine," popular song about a forty-niner's daughter, whose words first appeared as "Down by the River Lived a Maiden" (1863), by H. S. Thompson. The first printing of the words in a musical setting appeared as "Oh, My Darling Clementine" (1884), by Percy Montrose. A variant, "Clementine," appeared the next year with words and music credited to Barker Bradford.

Oil, the most valuable mineral extracted in California, was known to Indians, who used tar pools like the La Brea pits♦ for such purposes as caulking their boats. Oil seeps, mainly south of the Tehachapis, provided Spanish and Mexican settlers with a roofing substance for their adobes. Serious interest in oil for larger purposes followed in the decade after the gold rush, for the world's first commercial oil well had been drilled in Pennsylvania in 1859. It was followed a few years later by an unsuccessful well in the Mattole Valley near Eureka.

However, a California boom began in the 1860s when a onetime whale oil merchant, George S. Gilbert, drilled wells and built a refinery in the Ojai Valley that the esteemed Professor Benjamin Silliman, Jr., of Yale declared would yield "fabulous wealth." This prophecy led to a land-buying and well-drilling boom by Thomas A. Scott, Thomas R. Bard, and others who formed numerous companies to explore likely sites up and down the coast. Although the first (and very brief) gusher was brought in at Ojai (1867) and several wells were developed in Pico Canyon♦ near Mission San Bernardino, the oil was too crude and too filled with tar for primitive refining techniques to yield a product comparable to that which Standard Oil Co. imported into the state from its eastern wells.

More successful wells were also dug during the 1860s on the west side of the San Joaquin Valley near Maricopa and McKittrick, which became a major source for oil. The demand for oil to be used as a lubricant, to burn for manufacturing, to power locomotives, to refine as kerosene for illumination, and to serve other purposes was so great that production was hugely profitable and kept increasing. In 1880 the state produced 40,000 barrels of oil; in 1895 it produced 1,245,000 barrels. Local producing companies, like that of Sen. Felton♦ and Lloyd Tevis,♦ merged with large eastern firms like Standard Oil Co., which controlled the distribution within the state of high-grade oil produced outside California.

Other important local companies formed toward the turn of the century included Union Oil, founded by Bard (1890), Associated Oil, created by several San Joaquin Valley producers (1901) but bought out by Southern Pacific Railroad, and one formed by Edward L. Doheny,♦ who discovered oil near Los Angeles (1892), thus precipitating the city's first boom—more than 1,000 wells were drilled in the northwest part of Los Angeles by 1900. Other fields were discovered elsewhere in Los Angeles County, as well as in Santa Barbara, Ventura, Kings, and Kern counties, so that production of high quality oil increasingly mounted to make the state the major producer. In 1900 California produced 4,320,000 barrels; in 1910 its production

was 77,698,000 barrels; and in 1920 the amount had swollen to 105,721,000 barrels.

By the 1920s the development and ubiquitous use of automobiles throughout the state and the nation led to a huge demand for gasoline, once the least important part of the oil business. Accordingly, more and more refineries came into being, many of them located in the San Francisco Bay area, as even more discoveries of rich fields were made in the 1920s. Greatest of these was Signal Hill♦ (1921), which soon yielded a quarter of a million barrels of oil daily. The value of oil produced in that decade alone exceeded by 20% the value of all the gold ever mined in the state, and the value of the refineries' output was twice that of the state's next largest business, fruit and vegetable canning and preserving.

Such big business opportunities led to corrupt activities. The most sensational event was the conviction of Secretary of Interior Fall (1923) for having accepted a bribe of $100,000 from Doheny to open the rich government reserve field of Elk Hills♦ to private drilling. Bribery along with chicanery of various sorts marked the stock rigging and speculation in shares of the firm that bore the name of C. C. Julian.♦ Nevertheless, the oil business continued to boom in the 1930s as a new field was developed in Wilmington (1936), making the nearby port of San Pedro a vast shipping center as the U.S. Navy drilled on its land at Kettleman Hills♦ and as further discoveries were made in the San Joaquin Valley and elsewhere.

The need for fuel in World War II, both for direct military uses and for war-related industries, led to further production and refining as well as increased shipping out to Pacific battlefields. The booming postwar economy continued to demand additional amounts of oil and of natural gas♦ and tideland drilling, which dated back to wells in Summerland near Santa Barbara (1887), now was extended in that area to offshore drilling from platforms in the Santa Barbara Channel (1958). A serious spill there (1969) fouled beaches and killed wildlife, leading to an outcry for regulation and for environmental protection. But the dependence on imports, mainly from the Middle East, and the recognition that these could be stopped quickly, as they were during the Arab-Israeli War of 1973, brought about increased emphasis upon the production of native sources of energy, thus again leading to a boom in the oil industry.

Ojai, town in the small Ventura County valley from which it derives its name, a Chumash word

308

meaning "moon." Originally (1874–1916) the town was named for Charles Nordhoff,♦ an enthusiastic settler and booster. Although it is in an agricultural area, mainly of citrus trees, the town itself is best known for its sequestered atmosphere, harmonized architecture, and cultivated and educational interests, including an annual music festival. Thacher School is located there and residents have included Leopold Stokowski and the mystic Krishnamurti. The "Shangri-La" setting of the motion picture *Lost Horizon* was filmed in Ojai Valley.

Okies, pejorative name given to impoverished migrants to California from Oklahoma and other "Dust Bowl" states during the Depression of the 1930s. They flocked mainly to the Central Valley and other agricultural regions of the state in search of work. Severe friction occurred between the poverty-stricken migrants, who were forced to live on a marginal economy and in squalid shacks, and the farm owners, who feared unionization and the social views of the newcomers. The classic depiction of the Okies and their situation is Steinbeck's *The Grapes of Wrath*.♦ Dorothea Lange and Paul Taylor collaborated on a major pictorial record, *An American Exodus* (1940).

Old Baldy, common name given to Mt. San Antonio, the highest point (10,064 ft.) of the San Gabriel Range, so called because its windswept peak is without vegetation, though the mountain was in fact named for the mission.

Old Block, pseudonym of Alonzo Delano.♦

OLDER, FREMONT (1856–1935), born in Wisconsin, where he was mostly self-educated, went to California in 1873. He worked as a compositor for newspapers in Nevada and in the San Francisco Bay area, drifted into reporting and editing, taking over editorship of the *San Francisco Bulletin*♦ (1895), and made the paper a great success with sensational stories aimed at social and political reform. He worked closely with Mayor James D. Phelan,♦ exposed Phelan's successor Eugene Schmitz♦ and the city's boss, Abe Ruef,♦ and crusaded on behalf of the gubernatorial campaign of their prosecutor, Hiram Johnson. Older's concern with penal reform led him to campaign for Ruef's parole, to aid ex-convicts, and to oppose the death penalty. He also championed labor unions, and showed that some testimony against Mooney and Billings was perjured. Forced from the *Bulletin* for

those views (1918), he was hired by William Randolph Hearst to edit the *Call*, returning to his old paper (1929–35) when Hearst bought and merged the two. He wrote his autobiography in *Growing Up* (1931) and *My Own Story* (1919). His wife, Cora Older (1873–1968), not only shared his reform interests, but wrote about their activities and about California history.

Old Saint Mary's Church, Gothic-revival edifice located on the edge of San Francisco's Chinatown at California St. and Grant Ave., was built (1853–54) of brick brought around the Horn and granite cut in China. It served as the cathedral for the West Coast until a new St. Mary's was built (1894) on Van Ness Ave., which after destruction by fire (1960) was succeeded (1971) by the present Cathedral on Geary Blvd., distinguished by a roof of hyperbolic paraboloids.

Old Spanish Trail, name given to a caravan route to Los Angeles from Santa Fe and Taos. An attempt to reach the California missions by that route was made by two friars, Silvestre Escalante and Francisco Dominguez, in 1776, and although they only got as far as the Colorado River on the Utah-Arizona border, their trek is known as the Crossing of the Fathers. The first party to make it through was that of Antonio Armíjo (1829), who brought goods to trade for horses and mules. William Wolfskill♦ made the trip in the winter of 1830–31. Caravans and flocks of sheep thereafter made frequent crossings until the late 1860s. The route went from Santa Fe to the present Durango in Colorado, across southernmost Utah, then down along the Virgin River and Colorado River, crossing into California by present Needles and into San Bernardino, although Wolfskill varied his path by making a loop northwestward in Utah.

Old Woman Mountains, range in eastern San Bernardino County, so named because its highest pinnacle looks like an old woman.

Olives, brought to California by Portolá (1769) as cuttings and seeds, were raised by the mission fathers, mainly for oil used in religious services, but also for eating. By 1800 Mission San Diego was said to have 500 trees. In the 1840s *rancheros* had some groves, extended to northern parts of the state by Americans during the gold rush. After the 1870s growing became a large business as the olive began to be valued as a food as well as for its oil. Over 75% of the crop was pickled until 1910, when improved techniques were evolved. By 1925 production had reached 19,000,000 pounds, and by 1970 the crop (mainly from Tulare, Butte, and Tehama counties) was worth over $12,000,000.

OLMSTED, FREDERICK LAW (1822–1903), Connecticut-born landscape architect and conservationist, early established a reputation as an observant commentator on alien areas in *Walks and Talks of an American Farmer in England* (1852), *A Journey in the Seaboard Slave States* (1856), *A Journey Through Texas* (1857), and *A Journey Through the Back Country* (1860). He was equally well known for his landscape planning—he was chief architect of New York's Central Park (1858). In 1863 he became superintendent of Frémont's Mariposa estate and soon was instrumental in having Yosemite named a state reservation. He designed the landscaping for the University of California and other California sites before returning east (1865); at a later time he drew the land plans for Stanford University.

Olompali, Battle of, engagement in the Bear Flag Revolt♦ at a *rancho* with a Miwok name north of San Rafael (June 24, 1846). It occurred when some Americans attempted to seize horses from a corral of the *Californios,* who in turn were planning to recapture Sonoma, some fifteen miles away. This was the Revolt's only battle with deaths on both sides, and it resulted in the Americans holding and extending their control of the area north of San Francisco Bay. At an ancient Indian settlement of Olompali, excavations (1975) yielded a 16th-century sixpence thought possibly to be the one posted by Francis Drake with his plate of brass.

OLSON, CULBERT L. (1876–1962), 29th governor of the state (1939–43), born in Utah where he began his career as a lawyer and liberal Democratic politician. He continued it in California after 1920. He supported Upton Sinclair, but when elected governor was a follower of Roosevelt's New Deal. He pardoned Mooney and sponsored prison reforms, but the Depression and then wartime issues took much of his energy and he lost the backing of liberals.

Olvera Street, downtown Los Angeles lane, restored (1929–30) in the style of an old Mexican street. It features Mexican products, food, and pageantry, and is a tourist attraction. It is named for Agustín Olvera, a nephew of Ignacio Coronel,♦ who as a boy went with Coronel to California

among the Híjar and Padrés colonists. He fought against Frémont's forces and was one of the commissioners who signed the treaty of Cahuenga. He was later a county judge and supervisor.

Olympic Club, The, gentleman's athletic and social organization in San Francisco, founded (1860) as an outgrowth of a gymnastic group sponsored by Charles and Arthur Nahl.♦ Since 1912 it has been housed in a large building on Post St., and a few years thereafter it added the golf facilities of Lakeside Country Club at Lake Merced to which ladies are welcome. At varying times its sports and teams have included baseball, basketball, boxing, crew, cricket, fencing, golf, polo, soccer, swimming, tennis, track, and wrestling. It long had a salt water pool in its downtown clubhouse and still sponsors a New Year's Day dip in the Pacific.

Olympic Games, athletic contests of international teams revived (1896, in Athens) as an extension of those held in ancient Greece, have come to be divided into summer and winter competitions with each featuring sports appropriate to the seasons. In the summer of 1932 track and field and related sports were held in the Coliseum at Los Angeles and in 1960 winter competition was held at Squaw Valley.♦ Between 1896 and 1972 Californians won more than 100 gold medals (first place prizes) and Mark Spitz♦ alone won 9 of them. The U.S. Olympic Committee selected (1976) Los Angeles as the American city to be the site of the games in the summer of 1984, virtually assuring that as the final location.

O'MALLEY, WALTER F. (1903–   ), born in New York, during a successful legal career became a director of the Brooklyn Dodgers, whose controlling interest he bought (1944). As president of the club he moved it to Los Angeles at the end of the 1957 season. Under his leadership Branch Rickey hired Jackie Robinson, the first black to play on a major league team (1945).

Once in a Lifetime, play by Moss Hart and George S. Kaufman (1930), made into a film (1932), presents a vaudeville trio trying to achieve success in Hollywood, whose motion picture world is treated farcically with broad burlesque.

O'NEIL, NANCE (1874–1965), stage name of the Oakland-born actress Gertrude Lambert, who lived and worked in New York from 1896 on. There she became famous for her roles as Hedda Gabler, Lady Macbeth, Camille, and Juliet.

O'NEILL, EUGENE (1888–1953), distinguished American dramatist who owned a large residence, Tao House (1937–44), on a secluded estate near Danville at the base of Mt. Diablo where he lived quietly during the war years. There he wrote *The Iceman Cometh* (1946), *Long Day's Journey into Night* (1956), *Hughie* (1958), and the eleven-play cycle. A Tale of Possessors Self-Dispossesed, most of which he destroyed in manuscript. His works that were produced were esteemed as major dramas but, like the author himself, bore no relation to the California scene in which they were created. Tao House, a National Historic Shrine, was purchased in the 1970s by the State Department of Parks and Recreation and plans have been made for it to be a performing arts center.

Onions, vegetable first grown at the missions, became an important commercial crop during the later gold rush era, when they were raised mostly in the Sacramento-San Joaquin Delta. Imperial, San Joaquin, Kern, and Monterey counties are now the major producers, their acreage for onions having been increased over 75% between 1950 and 1970, when the crop was grown on 23,800 acres and was worth $19,700,000.

Ontario, town founded (1882) on the *rancho* of Cucamonga♦ in southeastern San Bernardino County by George Chaffey♦ and named for the Canadian province from which he came. It was conceived as a model agricultural community with a mutually owned irrigation and hydroelectric power program. The city has developed beyond its citrus groves and vineyards and now has aircraft and other manufacturing plants. It also has an auto racing speedway. In 1970 the population was 64,118.

Opera, see *Music.*

OPPEN, GEORGE (1908–   ), poet reared and resident in California, a member of the Objectivist school, whose *Of Being Numerous* (1968) was awarded a Pulitzer Prize. His *Collected Poems* appeared in 1975.

Opossum, nocturnal marsupial, specimens of which were introduced into San Jose from Tennessee as pets (*c.*1910). Succeeding wild generations became established in areas from coastal slopes to the ocean and from San Francisco Bay to the Mexican border, mostly near streams where deciduous trees provide cover and some food. They also eat reptiles, frogs, eggs, birds, and garbage.

Orange County, formed (1889) from part of Los Angeles County with Santa Ana as its seat. Its boundary on the Pacific stretches from Seal Beach south almost to San Onofre; to its east in the Santa Ana Mts. lies Riverside County; and Los Angeles and San Diego counties flank it north and south. The first whites to visit the region were in Portolá's party (1769), followed by Padre Lasuén who selected the site for a mission at San Juan Capistrano (1775), Serra who dedicated it (1776), and Anza. The major settlement was around the mission, but in the 19th century there arose *ranchos,* among them those of the Peralta, Yorba, and Sepulveda families which were later brought together to form the vast Irvine Ranch.♦

Americans also came by sea to engage in hide trading as described in *Two Years Before the Mast* by Richard Henry Dana, whose daring dislodgment of hides caught on a high cliff is commemorated by the place-names Dana Point and Dana Cove. The earliest large settlement of the 19th century was at Anaheim♦ (1857), begun as a cooperative farming community of Germans and later the site of a Polish colony in which Sienkiewicz♦ and Modjeska♦ shared. It was soon followed by the seaport on Newport Bay.

In the 20th century the county has grown spectacularly and has become the most populous of the state next to Los Angeles. The cause of much of that growth lies in its urban developments, which have spread out very widely. Before that occurred, Orange County was appreciated for the fruit that gave it its name, and for the productive plain, watered by the Santa Ana River, where oranges and other citrus fruits could be successfully raised. Fruits, flowers, and vegetables later became major crops.

The county also flourished as a residential and resort area, and its fine ocean shoreline led to the growth of such communities as Seal Beach, Huntington Beach, Newport Beach, Balboa, Laguna Beach, and Costa Mesa. Some of those places also developed industry, like the great oil production of Huntington Beach and the aerospace and light manufacturing industries, near Newport Beach. Larger cities grew up inland as businesses and homes replaced orange groves in La Habra, Buena Park, Fullerton, Anaheim, Garden Grove, Santa Ana, Tustin, and Westminster. Attention has been drawn to the county too because Richard Nixon was born in Yorba Linda and, while President, bought a private estate in San Clemente which he made his "Western White House."

Great numbers of tourists visit the county for

such attractions as Disneyland♦ and Knott's Berry Farm,♦ as well as a Movieland Wax Museum, a Japanese Village and Deer Park, and a drive-in Lion Country Safari. The county also has a campus of the University of California on the old Irvine Ranch, a State University at Fullerton, and the Bowers Museum of early Californiana in Santa Ana. In 1970 the county population was 1,420,386. With an area of 500,480 acres, it had 1,816 persons per sq. mi.

Orange growing, see *Citrus fruit growing.*

Orchards, see *Fruit growing.*

ORD, E[DWARD] O[THO] C[RESAP] (1818–83), sent to California (1847) as a lieutenant in the Mexican War, remained there except for occasional service elsewhere and as a major general under Grant in the Civil War. He made the first city map of Los Angeles (1849). He became commander of the army's Department of the Pacific (1868), and Fort Ord is named for him. His brother James went to California as a surgeon with the army (1847) and married into the de la Guerra family.

Oregon myrtle, see *Laurel.*

Oregon Trail, name given an overland route to the Pacific Coast, originally to Oregon, later including a pathway south from Fort Hall on the California Trail,♦ which became the name for the entire route, as heavier travel was destined there.

Orland, see *Glenn County.*

Orocopia Mountains, range in southeastern Riverside County below Joshua Tree National Monument, the name suggesting a cornucopia of gold.

Oroville, seat of Butte County, a gold rush town founded (1850) as Ophir City and renamed six years later. It was a trade center because of its location at the confluence of the North and Middle forks of the Feather River. During mining days it had a huge Chinatown, of which a fine temple remains. The region was once inhabited by Yahi Indians, of whom the last, Ishi,♦ was found starving in the neighborhood (1911). Dredging damaged much of the land, but it has long been a lumbering area and an agricultural region for citrus and other fruits and for olives, which has made the city a canning center. A 770-foot-high dam on the river has created Lake Oroville for the California Water

Plan. The lake enhanced recreational facilities for tourists, but it also swept away such mining settlements as Bidwell's Bar. In 1970 the city had a population of 7,536.

ORTEGA, prominent early California family, whose Mexican-born founder was José Francisco Ortega (1734–98), a sergeant on Portolá's expedition (1769) who led the first Spanish party to see San Francisco Bay. He was proposed by Serra to replace Fages as *comandante* of California when Serra and Fages clashed, but the viceroy only advanced him to lieutenant. Ortega founded the San Francisco presidio (1776), and aided in founding Mission Santa Barbara, for which he received the land grant of Rancho El Refugio, just to the north. From the beach there the family carried on trade with foreign ships. He married María Antonio Victoria Carrillo, and their son Ignacio came to own Rancho San Ysidro near Monterey, part of which passed to his son-in-law, John Gilroy.♦ The Ortegas married into the Bandini, Carrillo, Castro, de la Guerra, and Vallejo families. T. M. Storke♦ was descended from the Santa Barbara branch of the family. A presumably unrelated Captain Francisco de Ortega made a voyage by ship from Mexico to explore Baja California in 1632.

ORY, KID (EDWARD ORY) (1886–1973), Louisiana-born jazz musician, played the slide trombone, string bass, cornet, and alto saxophone. While in Los Angeles (1919–24) his was the first all-black small orchestra to make records; and his later recordings with Louis Armstrong's "Hot Five" included his "Muskrat Ramble." He had his own night club in San Francisco (1954–61) after a period spent in Los Angeles appearing in films.

OSBOURNE, [SAMUEL] LLOYD (1868–1947), born in San Francisco, accompanied his mother and stepfather, Robert Louis Stevenson, on their honeymoon, described in Stevenson's *The Silverado Squatters,*♦ and later went with them to Scotland, to Switzerland (where he and R.L.S. collaborated on texts for his toy press), to England, back to the U.S., and then to Vailima in Samoa. When he was a young man he and his stepfather wrote the novels *The Wrong Box* (1889); *The Wrecker* (1892), partly descriptive of San Francisco; and *The Ebb-Tide* (1894). Later he wrote less successful fiction and plays of his own as well as collaborating with his nephew, Austin Strong.

Oscars, see *Academy Awards*.

O'SHAUGHNESSY, MICHAEL MAURICE (1864–1934), Irish-born civil engineer, went to San Francisco as a young man and, after designing a water system for the city following its earthquake and fire (1906) and constructing a huge dam near San Diego, became (1912) San Francisco's City Engineer. In that capacity he laid out the municipal railway streetcar system with its Twin Peaks Tunnel and Stockton Street Tunnel, and constructed the Hetch Hetchy water system,♦ one of whose dams bears his name, as does a San Francisco boulevard.

Ostrich Farms, originated in the U.S. by Billie Frantz (1882), a successful chicken farmer near Anaheim, with birds imported from South Africa. By 1910 there were ten such farms in southern California with almost 1,100 ostriches and the fad had spread to Arizona and Texas, which also had the requisite warm, dry climate. The ostriches were raised for their feathers (used in boas, stoles, and fans), but the farms were also a tourist attraction as the birds were trained to draw small carriages in which people could ride, or even to be saddled for riders. After ostrich plumes went out of fashion the farms began to disappear. Only two California farms (with 148 ostriches) survived in 1920, and by 1940 none seems to have been in operation in the U.S.

O'SULLIVAN, TIMOTHY H. (1840–82), brought to U.S. from Ireland at age 2, as a boy was apprenticed to the photographer Mathew Brady and later assisted him in taking pictures on Civil War battlefields. He became the photographer for the U.S. Geological Survey under Clarence King (1867–69), recording the Sierra and other scenes of California and the West, including Nevada and Utah deserts and Comstock mines. Later he was a photographer for official expeditions in Panama, on the Colorado River, and for the Treasury Department.

OSUNA, prominent early California family whose founder, Juan Ismerio de Osuna (1746–90), was a soldier on the Sacred Expedition. One of his sons, Juan María Osuna (1785–1851), a soldier and landholder in San Diego, was a leader in the revolution against Gov. Victoria♦ (1831).

OTIS, HARRISON GRAY (1837–1917), moved to California (1876) from his native Ohio to continue a journalistic career, becoming part owner (1881) of the *Los Angeles Times,*♦ then its sole owner and publisher, and the president of the Times-Mirror Co. in 1886. He was a major developer of southern California, a conservative Republican, and a strong opponent of the union shop, the cause of the McNamara brothers bombing♦ of the *Times* (1910). He was an officer in the Civil War and general in the Philippines in the Spanish-American War. His son-in-law, Harry Chandler,♦ succeeded him as publisher of the *Times*.

Otis Art Institute, school founded (1917) in the former home of Harrison Gray Otis,♦ which was presented by his family to Los Angeles County after his death. In 1954 the school added a graduate program with a Master of Fine Arts degree. Millard Sheets was the director from 1953 to 1959.

Otter, large member of the weasel family, whose sea variety resembles a seal and reaches 4 to 5 feet in length. Its brown fur, brightened by silvery hair, was sought as early as the 1870s, when the Spanish got skins by barter with Indians and traded them in China. By the opening of the 19th century American ships began smuggling skins out of California (the aptly named *Otter* of Ebenezer Dorr♦ put into Monterey, 1796), and Russians with skilled Aleut hunters joined some Americans to kill the animals and then established their own Fort Ross, partly for that purpose. Americans who came overland, like Nidever, Yount, and Wolfskill, also engaged in hunting until the late 1840s, when changes of fashion made the otter less desirable. But otters had been so hunted (the Russians are said to have taken at least 5,000 annually) that they almost disappeared by 1874. State and federal laws protected the few that remained, and now perhaps more than 1,000 live off the coast between San Mateo and Santa Barbara counties, although they are still considered among the state's most endangered creatures. River otters, also extensively hunted in earlier days, particularly by mountain men who came from the U.S., are now found in streams and marshes in the northern part of the state, although the Sonora species inhabits the Colorado River only.

OTTO, JIM (1938–), center on the Oakland Raider football team (1960–74), was named All-Pro for 12 consecutive years.

"Outcasts of Poker Flat, The," local-color short story by Bret Harte,♦ published in the *Overland Monthly* (Jan. 1869) and collected in *The Luck of*

Roaring Camp and Other Sketches (1870). It tells of the ousting of two prostitutes—"the Duchess" and "Mother Shipton"—the gambler John Oakhurst, and the drunken sluice-box robber, Uncle Billy, from the mining camp of Poker Flat. In the mountains the exiles meet "The Innocent," Tom Simson, and his fiancée, Piney, who are eloping, and when all of them are trapped in the snow, Mother Shipton does not eat so that Piney may have her rations, Oakhurst kills himself to give Tom the one chance to be saved, and the Duchess lies down with Piney as the two die together. There is a town named Poker Flat in Sierra County.

Out West, see *Land of Sunshine.*

Overland Mail Company, see *Butterfield, John.*

Overland Monthly (1868–75, 1883–1935), regional magazine founded in San Francisco by Anton Roman as a monthly, with Bret Harte, Noah Brooks, and William C. Bartlett as editors. Harte not only quickly became the real editor, but brought the journal fame when he printed his "The Luck of Roaring Camp" in the second issue (Aug. 1868). He followed it with "The Outcasts of Poker Flat" (Jan. 1869), "Tennessee's Partner" (Oct. 1869), "Plain Language from Truthful James" (Sept. 1870), and other writings that made both the magazine and the author successful.

After nine months Roman sold the publication to John H. Carmany and for a time it continued to do well. During the first two years the *Overland* also published work by J. Ross Browne, Ina Coolbrith (an associate editor), Clarence King, Prentice Mulford, E. R. Sill, and C. W. Stoddard. In Feb. 1871 Harte left and the editorship was assumed by Bartlett, Benjamin P. Avery, and others. In 1875 it collapsed, but it was revived (1883) in association with Roman's new journal, *The Californian.*

Despite contributions from Joaquin Miller and others who had written for the earlier journal, the new magazine so obviously rested on its former reputation that Bierce dubbed it "the warmed-Overland Monthly." It limped along until the turn of the century, when it was greatly improved by writings of Gertrude Atherton, Jack London, Edwin Markham, Frank Norris, and, slightly later, George Sterling. In 1923 it absorbed *Out West,* of Los Angeles, another moribund magazine, but it finally died of inanition. *(See also individual entries.)*

Overland stages, transportation by stagecoach was begun in 1858 on a semiweekly basis with a 25-day travel schedule by John Butterfield♦ via a southern route from Missouri through Arkansas, El Paso, and San Diego to San Francisco. In 1861 the Civil War created a need for a central route through lands more securely identified with the Union. Under Ben Holladay♦ a route was established from the Missouri River to California to carry mail and passengers in 20 days. Holladay also established branches to Oregon and Montana but then sold his business to Wells, Fargo♦ (1866). The Concord stagecoaches seated 9 or 10 persons inside and more outside with the driver, who managed 4 to 6 horses. With changes of teams a coach covered 100 miles in 24 hours. Horace Greeley and Mark Twain were among the famous passengers, as they described in *An Overland Journey* (1860) and *Roughing It* (1872), respectively. Their driver was Hank Monk, the dean of the "whips," famous for the speed and skill with which he covered the mountain roads. Some stagecoach drivers on local routes rather than the transcontinental one were famous too, among them "Mountain Charley" Parkhurst♦ and Clark Foss.♦

Overland Trail, see *California Trail.*

OWENS, RICHARD (1812–1902), Ohio-born frontiersman whose name was originally Owings, accompanied Frémont on his expedition of 1845–46 to California. Owens Valley, through which he was one of the first whites to travel, was named for him by Frémont, who also gave his name to a river, a lake, and a peak. Frémont called Owens "cool, brave, and of good judgment" and made him a captain in his California Battalion♦ during the Bear Flag Revolt. Owens also served as Secretary of State during Frémont's brief governorship. His later life was spent in Taos.

Owens Valley, bounded by the Sierra and the Inyo Range (Inyo County), stretches about 100 miles and is 5 to 12 miles wide. It lies in the area south of Lone Pine. In the 1870s it was the site of silver, lead, and zinc mines, whose ore was carried across Owens Lake, the end of the Owens River. In 1872 the valley was the site of a major earthquake. The lake has disappeared since the river was diverted by a great aqueduct built by William Mulholland♦ to carry water some 250 miles to Los Angeles, impounding it en route by the St. Francis Dam,♦ which collapsed disastrously. To the north lie Manzanar, a Japanese Relocation Center,♦ and Independence, the county seat, which has an Eastern California Museum with Owens Valley memorabilia.

Oxnard, city on the coast of Ventura County, named (1898) for the owner of a beet sugar refinery. It is still an agricultural, dairying, and food processing center, but is also an entry to military installations at Port Hueneme and Point Mugu. In 1970 it had a population of 71,225.

Oysters, known to have been eaten by the Costanoan and other Indians because the shells have been found in their kitchen middens, were first commercially produced and harvested during the gold rush. In that period, when they were accounted a delicacy to be shipped from the eastern U.S. or from Washington, someone in Placerville with gourmet tastes concocted the dish known as Hangtown♦ Fry, consisting of scrambled eggs with fried oysters and bacon. A dish created in San Francisco and popular there was the Oyster Loaf, a toasted loaf of scooped-out French bread filled with fried oysters.

In 1869 the transcontinental railroad made possible the shipment of live stocks from the East Coast and the consequent building up of beds in the south end of San Francisco Bay. The industry was so lucrative that daring young men (including Jack London) became oyster pirates, eluding the specially established Fish Patrol.

From 1895 to 1904 oysters were the single most valuable fishery product of the state, averaging a gross of $500,000 annually during that decade. Production declined after that and finally pollution in San Francisco Bay entirely ended oystering in the late 1930s. However, in that decade the Dept. of Fish and Game introduced the *Pacific oyster* from Japan for cultivation in Morro Bay, Humboldt Bay, and Drake's Estero near Point Reyes.

The native *Olympia oyster,* a very small and very sweet species, has been too scarce to be more than a luxury, although the crop from Humboldt and Tomales bays is much esteemed. Between 1915 and 1956 the harvest of all species averaged 256,000 pounds annually, but by the end of the 1950s it rose to 1,659,699 pounds and has continued high.

OZAWA, SEIJI (1935–), Japanese musical director, studied with Leonard Bernstein and others and became the conductor of the San Francisco Symphony Orchestra (1968–75), at the same time occupying a comparable post in Boston.

P

PACHECO, a prominent early California family whose founder was Juan Salvio Pacheco, a soldier in Anza's second expedition (1775–76). A son, Ignacio (1760–1829), was an *alcalde* of San Jose, and Ignacio's son, the second Ignacio (1808?– 64), was a soldier and *ranchero* who was seized by Frémont at the outset of the Bear Flag Revolt and who later served as an *alcade* of San Rafael and founded the town of Ignacio (Marin County). Other prominent members of the family include Salvio Pacheco (1793–1876), a *ranchero* in present Contra Costa County, where Pacheco Valley bears his name; Juan Perez Pacheco, on whose land in Merced County♦ is located Pacheco Pass; and Gov. Romualdo Pacheco, whose daughter married a son of Lloyd Tevis. Juan Pablo Pacheco (1786–1829) settled on Rancho Santiago de Santa Ana (present Orange County) and founded the family's southern branch.

PACHECO, Romualdo (1831–99), 12th governor of the state (Feb. 27–Dec. 9, 1875), born in Santa Barbara, was the first native son to hold the office and the only one of Spanish descent to be a California state governor. He came to the post from the lieutenant governorship when Newton Booth was elected to the U.S. Senate. The Republicans did not renominate him, but he was elected to Congress (1876–83) and served as Envoy Extraordinary to Central America (1890–93). His father, whose name he bore, was an aide of Gov. Victoria and was killed at Cahuenga Pass♦ (1831) defending his government against José Antonio Carrillo and Echeandía.

Pachuco, pejorative applied in the 1940s and 50s to young Mexican men accused of gang activities in Los Angeles and other urban areas. They affected a swaggering lifestyle with extreme clothing, castigated as "zoot suits," in whose pockets they sometimes carried switchblade knives. In 1943 new veterans of the navy and marines got into a riot with them in Los Angeles. They were also the subject of violent prejudice in the cases that grew out of the Sleepy Lagoon Murder.♦

Pacific Avenue, San Francisco street that begins near the Bay, passes through the old Barbary Coast area, now on the fringe of the new office complexes behind the Embarcadero and the historic small buildings of Jackson Square, then continues westward past Grant Ave. and Chinatown out to the elegant residential area of Pacific Heights.

Pacific Coast Appeal, see *Elevator, The*.

Pacific Coast Conference, see *Football*.

Pacific Coast League, professional baseball♦ association including California minor league teams (1903–58), evolved from the California League♦ and was replaced by the introduction of major league teams to the sport in California (1958). After 1958 Sacramento was the only California team left in the minor league.

Pacific Coast Stock Exchange, organized (1957) as a result of the merger of the San Francisco Stock Exchange (est. 1882) and the Los Angeles Stock Exchange (est. 1889). About 10% of its listings are local; the remainder are also traded on the New York or the American stock exchanges. The name was changed to Pacific Stock Exchange in 1975; it continues to have headquarters in San Francisco and Los Angeles.

Pacific Crest Trail, see *Trails*.

Pacific Electric Railway Company, interurban transportation system that once covered the entire Los Angeles Basin. It was incorporated (1901) by Henry E. Huntington♦ after he sold out his inherited Southern Pacific holdings and moved from San Francisco to Los Angeles, where he, E. H. Harriman, and other associates used their capital to buy the area's first electric rail system (begun 1895), owned by Moses Sherman and Eli Clark, which linked Los Angeles with Pasadena and Santa Monica. Huntington's system not only competed successfully against the Southern Pacific's steam railroad service, but greatly expanded its own original area by building a spur to Long Beach (1902) and by buying out small independent lines in the region. By 1910 Huntington controlled most of the trolley service in southern California and, having achieved this near monopoly, sold out to the Southern Pacific.

The railroad then consolidated the purchased lines with its own rails and named William Herrin♦ the new president (1911). He was succeeded by Paul Shoup, president for three decades. The united system was the most extensive interurban railway in the U.S., continuing to expand into the 1920s to become a $100,000,000 investment. By that time it operated over 1,000 miles of track, and its famous big red cars were made up into trains that went into and out of Los Angeles more than 1,000 times a day, carrying over 100,000,000 passengers annually.

Freight was carried as well, but over 75% of the line's revenue came from passengers who could travel easily and cheaply (fares averaged less than three-quarters of a cent a mile) to the ever-expanding suburban centers of Los Angeles where Huntington owned new real estate developments. At its height the system covered an area from the San Fernando Valley to the San Gabriel Mts., down the coast from Santa Monica to Balboa, and as far east as San Bernardino and Redlands.

Competition from private automobiles began to cut into the traffic in the late 1930s, but the system made a comeback during World War II. Directly after the war there was a rapid decline in public use and the system was allowed to deteriorate until passenger service was almost entirely discontinued in 1950. In 1954 the rail line sold out to Metropolitan Coach Lines. In 1957 the citizens of Los Angeles voted to establish a Metropolitan Transit Authority, which, in the following year, bought out the remaining trolley lines and finally ran the last big red car in 1961 on the Los Angeles–Long Beach line.

Pacific Exploring Expedition, see *Wilkes, Charles.*

Pacific Gas and Electric Company, one of the largest public utility firms in the U.S., based in northern California. Its history began with the San Francisco Gas Co., founded (1852) by Peter Donahue and his brothers. Another forerunner was the California Electric Light Co., founded (1879) as the nation's first utility to provide electricity to the public from a central generating station. By a merger (1896) these firms and the Edison Light and Power Co. were combined to create the San Francisco Gas and Electric Co. In 1901 another merger incorporated utility firms of Oakland, Sacramento, Fresno, and Stockton to create the

California Gas and Electric Co., which in turn joined the San Francisco Gas and Electric Co. and some smaller firms to found the Pacific Gas and Electric Co. in 1905.

The new corporation was capitalized at $30,000,000 and the stock financing was arranged by the brokerage house of N. W. Halsey, who then became the first president of P.G.&E. He was succeeded by Frank G. Drum (1907–20), formerly of the California Gas and Electric Co. Another leader of the firm's early years was A. F. Hockenbeamer (president, 1927–35). The corporation became the state's first utility to be listed on the New York Stock Exchange and went on to greater growth by absorbing smaller utilities from the Oregon border on the north to the Nevada border on the east and down to Fresno. Its last great acquisitions occurred (1930) when it absorbed the San Joaquin Light and Power Co. (founded 1910) and the Great Western Power Co., against which it had fought since that company had come into being in 1915.

In time P.G.&E. became a consolidation of hundreds of smaller utilities in northern and central California and thus essentially a monopoly in a huge area of the state, but along the way it became involved in numerous political battles involving public power. The earliest major fight related to the Hetch Hetchy♦ reservoir, whose federal funding by the Raker Act of 1913 forbade private companies from distributing electricity generated by the project. Nevertheless, a series of decisions by the Board of Supervisors of San Francisco, followed by a popular vote of the city's citizens, led to P.G.&E. being granted the contract to distribute Hetch Hetchy power (1925). The 1920s also saw the beginning of a long conflict with the nascent Central Valley Project♦ about the distribution of the power it would generate from government financed dams and canals. Eventually P.G.&E. negotiated contracts for its own distribution lines, which culminated in an agreement (1951) to purchase federally financed power in return for letting its lines be used to deliver power from the Shasta Dam as needed by the independent Sacramento Utility District.

By 1968 P.G.&E. service extended over 94,000 sq. mi., transmitted electricity over 85,000 miles of lines, and had 27,000 miles of gas mains. There were more than 4,500,000 customers, and annual revenues were over one billion dollars. It owned nearly 100 power plants, from Pit River on the north to Kern River on the south, and, in addition to its basic hydroelectric power system, it also generated nuclear energy at Humboldt Bay and geothermal energy at The Geysers.

Pacific Grove, residential town on the Monterey Peninsula, founded as a tent city (1875) by the Methodist Church, was the site of the first Chautauqua in the western U.S. (1879), the forerunner of annual summer educational programs. It retains something of that religious and cultural ambience. It is also known for the Hopkins Marine Laboratory,♦ Asilomar,♦ and the annual autumn migration of Monarch butterflies, which swarm from Alaska and Canada and cling to the trees of the town's pine grove. Sand and feldspar are mined nearby. In 1970 the population was 13,505.

Pacific Heights, elegant residential area of San Francisco, known for its fine homes and dramatic Bay views. Its boundaries are not clearly defined but are generally considered to extend from Van Ness Ave. to Arguello St. and from California to Union streets, although Union St. is also thought of as the main shopping street of Cow Hollow.♦

Pacific Lighting Corporation, public utility holding company, founded (1886) by two heads of San Francisco's Pacific Gas Improvement Co. Its interests were concentrated in southern California, and it acquired the Los Angeles Gas Co., the Los Angeles Electric Co., Southern California Gas Co., and, finally (1924), the Southern Counties Gas Co. In 1937 it sold its electric properties to the city of Los Angeles and obtained a long-term, ongoing contract from the city for distribution of gas through its major subsidiary, Southern California Gas Co.♦ The holding company also has some non-utility businesses.

Pacific Mail Steamship Company, founded (1848) by W. H. Aspinwall♦ to operate steamers from Panama to the Columbia River under a government mail contract. The discovery of gold in California made his line very successful until Cornelius Vanderbilt opened a competitive route across Nicaragua (1851), but they agreed (1859) to divide the business, Vanderbilt taking the Atlantic half and Aspinwall the Pacific half. In 1865 Pacific Mail bought out Vanderbilt and entered into rate fixing agreements with the Central Pacific Railroad, whose transcontinental tracks were a great threat and caused the steamship company to emphasize service to Japan and China and thus to become known as a major means for the Chinese♦ to migrate to California.

Pacific Monthly, see *Hesperian.*

Pacific News, tri-weekly journal of San Francisco, the only competitor of the earlier *Alta California,♦* ran from Aug. 25, 1849, to May 7, 1851. A democratic organ, its editors included Ferdinand C. Ewer.♦

Pacific Palisades, residential community in northwest Los Angeles overlooking the ocean. Founded (1921) by a Methodist organization, it later was the settlement closest to Will Rogers' ranch, and in the 1940s its terraced sites became home for a colony of cultivated German exiles, including Thomas Mann and Lion Feuchtwanger. Other cultural leaders among the German émigrés lived nearby: Bruno Walter and Franz Werfel in Beverly Hills, Arnold Schoenberg in Brentwood, and Igor Stravinsky in Hollywood. The Getty Museum is adjacent to Pacific Palisades.

Pacific School of Religion, interdenominational seminary, founded in San Francisco (1866), soon moved to Oakland, and has been located in Berkeley since 1901. It is the oldest theological school in California and is now a part of the Graduate Theological Union.♦ Its library contains the fine John Howell Collection of Bibles.

Pacific Stock Exchange, see *Pacific Coast Stock Exchange.*

Pacific Union Club, exclusive gentleman's social club in San Francisco, incorporated (1881) as a consolidation of the Pacific Club (founded 1852) and the Union Club (founded 1854). Since 1911 it has been housed in the brownstone mansion originally built for James C. Flood♦ (1886), which was remodeled by Willis Polk,♦ who added two wings.

Pacific Union College, Seventh-Day Adventist institution founded in 1882 and located at Angwin, overlooking Napa Valley. In 1970 it had 136 faculty members and an enrollment of 1,613. The students are training to be ministers or teachers, or are studying for medical and other technological programs.

PACKARD, DAVID (1912–), born in Colorado, graduated from Stanford (1934), where he also took a degree in electrical engineering and, as a student of Frederick Terman, was encouraged to apply his knowledge by joining his classmate William R. Hewlett♦ to found Hewlett-Packard (1938), a leading developer and manufacturer in the field of electronics.◆ He served for a time as Deputy Secretary of Defense in the Nixon administration.

PADDOCK, CHARLES [WILLIAM] (1900–43), Texasborn track star, gained fame as a sprinter at the University of Southern California. He won the Olympic Games 100 meter run (1920) and in 1921 set world records in the 100 yard (9.5 sec.), 100 meter (10.4 sec.), 200 meter (20.8 sec.), and 220 yard (20.8 sec.) races. In one afternoon he set four world records: the 100 meter, 200 meter, 300 yard, and 300 meter races. He was famous for making spectacular finishes, jumping through the tape.

PADRÉS, JOSÉ MARÍA, see *Híjar, José María.*

Padres, Spanish for "Fathers," applied to men in religious orders who, in early California, were Franciscans,◆ the founders of the missions.

Padres, San Diego, baseball team in the Western Division of the National League. The name was first used (1936) by a local team of the Pacific Coast League, in reference to the Spanish fathers who founded California's first mission at San Diego, but later adopted by the new team (1969). Although it finished last in every season to 1974, in that year it was bought for $10;000,000 by Ray Kroc, an Illinois resident, head of MacDonald's hamburger restaurants. They play in the San Diego Stadium, which seats over 47,000 people.

Padua Hills Theater, a complex of restaurants, handicraft shops, and a theater for drama and dance, all featuring Mexican material. It was founded in 1932 and is located near Claremont.

PAGES, JULES (1867–1946), San Francisco-born artist of French descent, whose father, Jules F. Pages (1843–1910), was a local engraver. The younger Pages began his career as a newspaper illustrator but became a well-known painter during his long expatriation (*c.* 1900–41) in France.

Paicines, see *Hollister.*

Paisano, name applied by Steinbeck in his *Tortilla Flat* (1935) to a resident of an uphill district of Monterey: "He is a mixture of Spanish, Indian, Mexican and assorted Caucasian bloods. His ancestors have lived in California for a hundred or two hundred years. He speaks English with a paisano accent and Spanish with a paisano accent. When

questioned concerning his race, he indignantly claims pure Spanish blood. . . . His color, like that of a well-browned meerschaum pipe, he ascribes to sunburn."

Paiute (or **Piute**), Indians of the Shoshonean◆ family who lived in the extreme northeastern portion of the state, the main body of their territory extending into Nevada. In addition to the northern Paiutes, the eastern Mono◆ Indians resident in the present county of that name were of Paiute stock, and the Chemehuevi◆ are southern Paiutes. Wovoka, or Jack Wilson, a northern Paiute of Nevada, originated the Ghost Dance movement in 1889. This movement included belief in an apocalypse and the establishment of a new world characterized by sexlessness, in which the dead would return, believers would remain alive, and nonbelievers would be turned to stone. The ghost dance itself incorporated men, women, and children revolving in three concentric circles. The dance spread to the Modoc and from them to tribes in northwestern California. Some Paiutes fought as members of Frémont's forces during the Mexican War. The Paiute figure in Mary Austin's poetic drama, *The Arrow Maker* (1911), and they are autobiographically treated in *Life Among the Piutes* (1883) by Sarah Winnemucca.◆ The tribal name is often spelled Piute in the numerous California placenames, e.g. Piute Creek in Lassen and Fresno counties and Yosemite and Piute Mountain in Mono and Kern counties and Yosemite. Two heroic Paiutes, Tinemaha and Winnedumah,◆ have places named for them in Inyo County.

Pajaro Valley, small agricultural area between Monterey Bay and the Santa Cruz Mts., watered by the river of that name, which was so called by Portolá's soldiers because they encountered there a bird (*pájaro*) stuffed by Indians (1769). The valley has long been noted for its apples, pears, strawberries, and vegetables. The river forms the boundary between Santa Cruz and Monterey counties and between Santa Clara and San Benito counties.

Pala, see *San Antonio de Pala.*

Palace Hotel, luxury hotel located on Market and Montgomery streets, San Francisco, constructed by William C. Ralston and opened in 1875. It was famous for the glass-roofed Palm Court, six stories high, into which carriages drove. It had also five hydraulic elevators, elaborate furnishings, bay-windowed bedrooms, superior service, and fine food. After Ralston's death Sen. Sharon became the owner. Destroyed by the earthquake and fire of 1906, an elegant new building designed by George W. Kelham, with an imposing glass-roofed Garden Court dining room, replaced it. Sharon's heirs owned the hotel until 1954, when it passed out of local hands into a chain. Innumerable distinguished guests stayed in both edifices. King David Kalakaua of Hawaii died in one (1891) and President Warren G. Harding in the other (1923).

Palace of Fine Arts, building in the romantic style of Hellenism designed by Maybeck◆ for the Panama-Pacific International Exposition (1915). It has a great Corinthian colonnaded gallery at whose center is a domed octagonal temple of arches and columns. The only building of the exposition retained on the site, it began to go to pieces but was reconstructed with permanent materials in the 1960s through a combination of private and public funding and has since been called the Palace of Arts and Science. It houses an Exploratorium◆ featuring exhibits which the visitors may operate or experience directly to comprehend scientific principles.

Palmdale, settlement near Antelope Valley◆ of Los Angeles County, founded by German Lutherans (1886) and named for the yucca palm, a Joshua tree. This site on the edge of the Mojave Desert (*c*. 35 miles north of central Los Angeles) is known not only for its nearby preserve of poppies, but as the center of a 120-mile-long area of land that has risen perceptibly (some 10 inches) during the 1960s and 70s. The bulge may indicate the location of a blocked section of the San Andreas Fault whose eventual separation would cause a severe earthquake.

Palm Springs, elegant winter resort in the Colorado Desert near the San Bernardino National Forest. Since the 1930s the community has attracted celebrities, particularly from Hollywood, including Bob Hope, Frank Sinatra, Liberace, Elvis Presley, and Red Skelton. In addition, Eisenhower, Kennedy, Johnson, and Nixon have vacationed there and Ford established a home there. In 1960 Bob Hope founded an annual Desert Classic open golf tournament to raise funds for local charities. The aerial tramway (opened 1963) between Palm Springs and the Mt. San Jacinto wilderness is the world's largest (80 passengers to a car) and longest (2½ miles) single-lift tram.

Palm trees, exist in some 1,200 species of which but one—*Washingtonia filifera*, the *California, desert,*

or *Washington*—is native to the state. This ornamental tree grows from 20 to 75 feet tall in southern California, where many places are named for it, e.g. Palm Springs, Thousand Palms. Indians are said to have eaten its fruit and to have thatched huts with its fronds. Mission fathers introduced the *date*◆ *palm,* although substantial growing of the fruit did not occur until 1902, in the Coachella Valley. The Joshua tree is sometimes inaccurately called a yucca palm. Many other true palms have been introduced to the state, yet they number but a few of all the varieties found in the tropics.

Palo Alto, city in Santa Clara County at the base of the San Francisco Peninsula as it merges into Santa Clara Valley, is known principally as the home of Stanford University and its allied research organizations and as the center for neighboring electronics and aerospace businesses inspirited by the University. East Palo Alto is a predominantly black community. The name is Spanish for "tall tree," a redwood mentioned by Palou, a member of the Anza expedition (1774), and was adopted by Leland Stanford for his country estate (1876) and later applied to the town (1892), laid out by Timothy Hopkins. Alan Cranston was born in the city. In 1970 the population was 55,835.

Palomar, see *Mount Palomar.*

Palo Verde Valley, in southeast Riverside County, bounded on the east by the Colorado River and on the south by the Palo Verde Mts. of Imperial County. To the north is its main town, Blythe (pop. 1970, 7,000), named for the San Francisco financier who was its developer. Once planted in cotton, it now also produces lettuce, melons, alfalfa, and barley, and serves for livestock grazing.

Palos Verde, oceanside peninsula between Redondo Beach and San Pedro, once a *rancho* of the Sepúlveda family, was developed in the 1920s as an elegant subdivision of estates. Lloyd Wright's Wayfarer's Chapel is located there, as is Marineland.

PALÓU, FRANCISCO (*c*.1722–*c*.89), Majorca-born missionary, studied under Junípero Serra at Palma's Convento de San Francisco, where he also prepared to teach. He went with Serra to Mexico City (1749), and there they were together at the College of San Fernando and as missionaries in Jalapan. When the Jesuits were expelled from Baja California, Palóu was among the Franciscans to go there under Serra's leadership. Palóu succeeded Serra as

President on the peninsula when Serra went north to Alta California on the Sacred Expedition (1769). When the Franciscans in turn were replaced by Dominicans in Baja California, Palóu marked its boundary line and went on to Monterey (1773). He went to San Francisco on two expenditions (1774 and 1775) under Rivera y Moncada, and then, in an expedition led by Moraga (1776), he established Mission Dolores there. He headed it for nine years until he moved to Monterey upon becoming President-General♦ when Serra died (1784). The next year he became president of the College of San Fernando in Mexico, where he remained the rest of his life. He was the author of Serra's biography, *Relación Histórica de la Vida y Apostólicas Tareas del Venerable Padre Fray Junípero Serra* (Mexico, 1787; trans., 1913) and *Noticias de la Nueva California* (1857; trans. by Bolton in 4 vols., 1926).

Panama-California Exposition, held in San Diego (1915–16) to celebrate the completion of the Panama Canal. It emphasized Pan-American themes in the displays and in the architecture of its dignified Spanish-style buildings, which still stand on the lushly gardened site of Balboa Park.♦ Unlike the usual practice in constructing expositions, its buildings were designed as permanent structures for civic and cultural use.

Panama-Pacific International Exposition, held on San Francisco's bayside Marina (Feb. 4–Dec. 4, 1915) to celebrate the opening of the Panama Canal (July 1915) and to show the world that in less than a decade the city had recovered from the devastation of its earthquake and fire (1906). Over 19,000,000 persons visited the buildings, which were constructed in a kind of Spanish and Italian baroque style. The most famous examples were the central Tower of Jewels and the Palace of Fine Arts, the latter by Maybeck.♦

Panamint Range, mountains on the western side of Death Valley whose highest point is Telescope Peak (14,494 ft.). They form the eastern boundary of Panamint Valley, the site of a 60-mile-long Ice Age lake. The name is that of a tribe of Shoshonean Indians. Some gold mining was done there in the 1870s, and it is the site of part of the end of Norris' novel *McTeague*.

Panning gold, see *Placer mining*.

Panoche Valley, cattle pasturing area southeast of Paicines in San Benito County, from which it is reached by Panoche Pass. Panoche Creek flows through it and through the adjacent area of Fresno County. The name is that of a sweet substance extracted by Indians from reeds and wild fruit.

Panza Range, mountain chain in Los Padres National Forest.♦

Paper making, began with the first mill established in 1856 by Samuel P[enfield] Taylor near Olema (Marin County) on what is now known as Paper Mill Creek in Samuel Taylor State Park.♦ Rags for the manufacture were collected by Chinese in San Francisco and shipped to Taylor's warehouse on Tomales Bay. As popular journalism grew along with needs for more and more paper, and as new techniques of manufacturing were introduced with the use of wood pulp instead of rags, new mills were founded in the 1870s and 80s in Stockton, at Soquel, and elsewhere. By 1899 printing was one of the ten major industries of the state and more paper supplies were required. In that year financiers of the Oregon-based Crown Paper Co. opened the Floriston Pulp and Paper Co. on the Truckee River near Lake Tahoe. Operating until 1930, it was a major supplier of the central and southern California markets. In 1906 the paper selling firm founded by Anthony Zellerbach moved into large-scale manufacturing, and in the ensuing decades it came to dominate the business by purchasing other pulp and paper makers, entering into national sales, merging with a major competitor in boxboard products and another that manufactured newsprint and other types of paper in Oregon, and establishing new plants in Stockton and southern California. However, other established firms, like those founded by such old families as the Fleishhackers and Moffitts, continued to be active, and competition also came from other parts of the nation.

PARDEE, GEORGE COOPER (1857–1941), 21st governor of the state (1903–07), and first native-born to be elected to that office, was a graduate of the state university. A mayor of Oakland, regent of the University, and active in Republican politics, he was also an oculist. He devoted much time to matters of conservation of natural resources. A reservoir of the Mokelumne River, from which Oakland gets its drinking water, was named for him.

PARK, DAVID (1911–60), Boston-born painter, resident in San Francisco and Berkeley after 1929. There he taught at the California School of Fine

Arts and, in his last five years, at the University of California. He was a leader of a Bay Area group that turned from abstract expressionism to richly colored figurative painting emphasizing the human form.

PARKER, CARLETON H[UBBELL] (1878–1918), born in Red Bluff and reared in Vacaville, after graduation from the University of California (1904) and a doctorate from Heidelberg (1912) became a professor at his alma mater and later Dean of the College of Commerce at the University of Washington. He specialized in labor relations, particularly of migratory workers, relating conflicts to psychological maladjustment as well as to economic conditions in his *The Casual Laborer and Other Essays* (1920). After the Wheatland Riot,♦ Gov. Hiram Johnson created an Immigration and Housing Commission and named Parker Executive Secretary. For it Parker wrote an important report on the incident. His wife Cornelia Stratton Parker, wrote his biography, *An American Idyll* (1919), a significant book in itself.

Parker Dam, see *Havasu, Lake.*

PARKHURST, CHARLEY [DARKEY] (1812–79), native of New Hampshire, was a rough stagecoach driver, generally called "Mountain Charley" or "Cock-eyed Charley," who was a noted whip of the Santa Cruz Mts. area in the post-gold-rush era. Only after "his" death was it discovered that Charley was a woman, and, therefore, as a voter in 1868, perhaps the first woman to exercise the franchise in California. She is memorialized along her route by Mountain Charley Road.

Parks, areas of land set apart for public use, are of various sorts and widely distributed throughout the state. The federal government is responsible for five National Parks—Kings Canyon, Lassen Volcanic, Redwood, Sequoia, and Yosemite—and it preserves unusual terrain of specialized sorts in the eight National Monuments within California. Furthermore, there are eighteen National Forests, which include Wilderness Areas, and there are also National Resource Lands and the Golden Gate National Recreational Area. Besides these federal reserves, there are State Forests and Parks, the latter inaugurated so early as 1864. In addition, the state maintains many beaches and also cares for State Historic Parks or monuments, such as Fort Ross and San Simeon, recreation areas, scenic or scientific reserves, and even state wayside camps.

Several cities also contain well-known urban parks. The two largest within city limits are Griffith Park in Los Angeles and Bidwell Park in Chico. Other notable parks are the Golden Gate in San Francisco, Balboa in San Diego, Lakeside of Lake Merritt in Oakland, and Alum Rock in San Jose. Small but significant city plazas include Portsmouth Square and Union Square in San Francisco and Pershing Square in Los Angeles. San Francisco also contains a park-like military reservation, the Presidio, which is to be added to the Golden Gate National Recreational Area. Across the Bay is the large East Bay Regional Park. (*See also individual entries.*)

Parks and Recreation, Department of, under the jurisdiction of the State Resources Agency, operates over 200 units, of which the major elements are State Parks.♦

PARROTT, John (1811–84), Virginia-born financier, after long residence in Mexico, including business as a trader and service as U.S. consul at Mazatlan (1838–50) and two earlier visits to California, moved to San Francisco, where he made a fortune in shipping and built a great country estate for himself at San Mateo.

PARSONS, LOUELLA [OETTINGER] (1881–1972), Illinois-born newspaper columnist, moved to California for her health and, as a writer for the Hearst newspapers, became the first syndicated Hollywood correspondent treating the film industry (1925–65). In the 1930s and 40s she was said to have had 20,000,000 readers so that her judgments of individuals and their films significantly affected their popularity. She portrayed herself in *Hollywood Hotel,*♦ a film about her radio program of that name.

PARTCH, HARRY (1901–), Oakland-born composer, largely self-taught, has formulated his own theory of music for a 43-tone scale and for instruments he has invented. His compositions include "Rivers of Babylon" (1930), "Barstow" (1941), "Plectra and Percussion Dances" (1949–52), "Rotate the Body in All Its Planes" (1963–64), and "And on the Seventh Day Petals Fall in Petaluma" (1963–64). His book, *Genesis of a Music* (1947), calls for an alternative musical culture.

Pasadena, city northeast of downtown Los Angeles, at the foot of the San Gabriel Mts., founded in 1875 and given a Chippewa name pertinent to its valley site. Along its Arroyo Seco♦ Charles Fletcher Lummis♦ and other writers and artists built homes and studios at the end of the century. The city not only was the site of resort hotels like the Raymond,♦ but became a conservative residential community with many large estates like those also found in the neighboring San Marino.♦ It is known for an annual Rose Bowl♦ football game and attendant New Year's Day floral parade. Other major features include the California Institute of Technology, Pasadena Playhouse, the Norton Simon Museum of Art, the Civic Auditorium, the Ambassador College Auditorium, and the nearby Huntington Library. The population in 1970 was 113,327.

Pasadena Playhouse, dramatic arts school and theater founded in 1916. It continually produced plays, many featuring actors who became prominent in motion pictures, until it went out of business (1970).

Paso Robles, small city in San Luis Obispo County. It was named for the pass through the oaks found by Font (1776) through which El Camino Reál later ran. The town (founded 1886) is in the midst of wheat, cattle, and almond country, and is also the nearest settlement to Camp Roberts. Long known for its medicinal hot springs, it once had an elegant resort spa (1889–1941). In 1970 the population was 7,168.

Pastures of Heaven, volume of related short stories by John Steinbeck.♦

PATIGIAN, HAIG (1876–1950), Armenian-born sculptor, brought to the Fresno area (1881) and early became a San Francisco newspaper illustrator. Later he became a sculptor, and his large pieces include allegorical figures for the Panama-Pacific International Exposition (1915), the statue of Thomas Starr King in Statuary Hall of Washington, D.C., and the vast, symbolic owl that serves as the totemic figure at the Grove of the Bohemian Club, the organization of which he was president three times.

PATTIE, JAMES OHIO (1804?–50), Kentucky-born mountain man, who in 1824 set out with his father, Sylvester, on a beaver-trapping expedition from the Missouri River into New Mexico and on to the California and Arizona frontiers, where they had a bloody battle with the Mohaves. In 1827 they undertook another expedition, but because they entered

California without permission they were jailed at San Diego, where the elder Pattie died. The younger Pattie, however, was employed by Gov. Echeandía as a translator and claimed that Echeandía also had him vaccinate the people of the area with the vaccine Pattie had brought as protection against smallpox. These dramatic adventures and his ostensibly patriotic refusal of land and cattle in recompense on the condition that he become a Catholic and a Mexican citizen derive from his *Personal Narrative* (1831), a work very likely quite fictional, edited, or perhaps largely written by Timothy Flint, a New England minister and romantic novelist. Pattie is thought to have returned to California during the gold rush.

PATTON, GEORGE S[MITH, JR.] (1885–1945), army general, born in San Gabriel and reared there on the ranch of his grandfather, Benjamin D. Wilson,♦ after graduation from West Point commanded a tank brigade in France during World War I. He became a legendary and flamboyant character who in World War II commanded the Third Army, which swept through northern France into Czechoslovakia.

PATTON, MEL[VIN EMERY] (1924–), Los Angeles-born track star, while a student at USC (1943–49) became one of the all-time great sprinters. He was the first man to run the 100-yard dash in 9.3 seconds (1948) and in the same year was the 200-meter champion in the Olympic Games.

Patwin, Indians of the southern Wintun♦ group extending through the present Yolo, Sutter, Sacramento, and Solano counties, who practiced the Kuksu cult♦ with its secret ceremonial dances.

PAUL, RODMAN W[ILSON] (1912–), Pennsylvania-born historian of the Far West, has been a professor at the California Institute of Technology since 1947. His books include *California Gold* (1947); *Mining Frontiers of the Far West* (1963); and *A Victorian Gentlewoman in the Far West* (1972), a biography of Mary Hallock Foote.

PAULING, LINUS [CARL] (1901–), Oregon-born professor of chemistry at the California Institute of Technology (1927–64), where he had received his Ph.D., and at Stanford (1969–74) and elsewhere. His discoveries about the chemical bonds and about molecular structure led to the award of a Nobel Prize (1954). He also won the Nobel Peace Prize (1962). In 1973 he became president of the Linus

Pauling Institute for Science and Medicine located near Stanford University.

Pauma Massacre, an uprising of Luiseño♦ Indians shortly after the Battle of San Pasqual (1846) in which eleven *Californios* who had fled from the battle scene were killed on the Pauma Rancho, between Mission San Luis Rey and Warner's Ranch in present San Diego County. Among the murderers were Antonio Garrá and William Marshall, both later involved in Garrá's Revolt.♦

Pautah, former county of California (1852–59) lying within the present state of Nevada. It was contiguous with Sierra, Nevada, Placer, El Dorado, Alpine, and Mono counties and it contained a triangle of land extending as high as Lassen County but east of it. That extension of the state's mining lands was not ceded to California by Congress and so had to be returned to what was then the Territory of Utah.

PAYERAS, MARIANO (1769–1823), Majorca-born Franciscan missionary, went to California (1796) and was named President-General♦ (1815–19) and then Commissary Prefect (1820–23) of the order. He wrote biographical sketches of the missionaries who served under him.

Peace and Freedom party, political party created mainly in opposition to the Vietnam War, qualified for the state ballot in 1968. Eldridge Cleaver was its nominee for President of the U.S. The party, begun in California, was on the ballots of 15 other states that year.

Peaches, major deciduous fruit crop of California, first grown at the missions but not raised in quantity until after the gold rush. The major growing area was once the Feather River Valley but since then the largest orchards have been in the Modesto and Fresno areas of the San Joaquin Valley. The crop in 1970 was grown on 82,000 acres (59,300 for cling, 23,000 for freestone) and was worth $77,356,000.

Pears, fruit crop first grown at the missions but not raised in quantity until after the gold rush. The leading orchard area was long the Santa Clara Valley, but Sacramento and Lake counties now surpass it. In 1970 the crop was grown on nearly 40,000 acres and was worth $36,120,000. California raises more pears than any other state.

Peas, vegetable widely grown in California, its production having more than doubled—from 5,220

acres in 1941 to 10,740 in 1965. During the 1960s production averaged over 17,000 tons of processed peas annually. Once peas were usually canned, but now over two-thirds of the crop is frozen.

Pebble Beach, elegant residential community on Monterey Bay's Seventeen Mile Drive♦ known also for its luxurious Lodge of the old Del Monte Hotel♦ and golf course on which the annual Bing Crosby tournament is played. Other places in California bear the same name.

PECK, GREGORY (1916–   ), born in La Jolla, after attending the University of California, Berkeley, and engaging in a stage career, became a motion picture actor (1944). He steadily continued in starring roles enacted in an understated style. His films include *Duel in the Sun* (1946) and *The Gunfighter* (1950), westerns, and *To Kill a Mockingbird* (1962), for which he won an Academy Award. In the 1970s he began to produce films. He has also been a civic leader in humanitarian activities and president (1967–70) of the Academy of Motion Picture Arts and Sciences.

PEIXOTTO, distinguished family of Sephardic Jewish background, whose local founder, Raphael (1849–1905), went to San Francisco in 1869. His children were Edgar (1867–1923), an attorney; Ernest (1869–1940), an artist, book illustrator, and author associated with Les Jeunes;♦ Eustace (1887–1963), an army general; Sidney (1866–1925), a social worker; and Jessica (1864–1941), a professor of economics at the University of California.

Pelicans, see *Shore birds.*

PELLIER, LOUIS, see *Prunes.*

PELTON, LESTER ALLEN (1829–1910), Ohio-born inventor, went to California (1850) to mine gold but soon became a millwright and carpenter in Yuba County. After years of experimentation he patented the Pelton Water Wheel, which split a jet of water in two, thus ensuring that it would strike the wheel's buckets in such a way that the entire impact of the water would drive in one direction without diffusion of energy. The device improved mining machinery and was subsequently used for purposes ranging from developing electric power to driving large sewing machines. His company was based in San Francisco, but he lived in Oakland.

Pendleton Marine Base, see *Camp Pendleton.*

Peninsula, see *San Francisco Peninsula.*

Peninsular Ranges, extend south from the end of the Transverse Ranges—that is, from San Gorgonio Pass♦ through the Santa Ana, San Jacinto, and Santa Rosa mountains deep down into Baja California. Their highest peak is Mt. San Jacinto (10,804 ft.), behind Palm Springs. The Los Angeles Basin is one of the valleys between the ranges.

Penutian, family of Indian tribes related by linguistic affiliations, consists of groups whose central territories lay where the Sacramento and San Joaquin rivers join to empty into San Francisco Bay. The name is a combination of variant forms of the word "two," "pene" among the Wintun,♦ Maidu,♦ and Yokut tribes,♦ and "uti" among the Miwok♦ and Costanoan.♦ The Penutian family not only inhabited the central part of the present state of California but ranged over more than half of its terrain.

People's Park, name given to a square block of unused University of California land near the Berkeley campus which had been intended for a dormitory and playing fields, but was seized by students and "street people" for their own use. Their ouster and attempt to retake the heavily fenced land led to a battle (May 1969) with National Guard troops and sheriff's deputies in which one person was killed and another blinded.

Pepperdine University, coeducational liberal arts institution affiliated with the Churches of Christ, has campuses in Los Angeles, Malibu, Santa Ana, and Heidelberg (Germany). It was founded in 1937 and named for its benefactor, a local businessman with conservative views.

Peppers, the red or chili variety are much used in Mexican cooking and therefore were probably cultivated by the fathers at the missions. They had certainly been widely grown in 19th-century California before the coming of the Americans, who commented upon them. The state accounts for most of the U.S. supply. In 1970 the crop was grown on 4,900 acres and had a value of $4,791,000.

Pepperwood, see *Laurel.*

PERALTA, a prominent early Bay Area family founded by Luís María Peralta (1759–1851), a native of Sonora who went to California with Anza (1775–76). He later held military and civil posts in San Jose, where he settled with his wife, María Loreto Alviso, whose family also went to California in the army with Anza. De Sola granted Peralta the Rancho San Antonio (1820) with over 13 miles of the East Bay shoreline from the present city of San Leandro to that of Albany and stretching east to the summits of the Contra Costa hills, an area of about 44,000 acres. Of his 17 children, 5 daughters and 4 sons—Hermenegildo, José Domingo, Antonio María, and José Vicénte—lived to maturity. In 1842 each of the men received part of the land, though they lost most of it after the gold rush. Antonio, for example, sold the peninsula of Alameda (1853) for $7,000, and the property on which Oakland now stands was simply seized in the 1850s by U.S. land speculators, of whom the most notorious was Horace W. Carpentier.♦

Perch, small spiny-finned fish, of which many varieties are found in California. The *yellow perch,* the only true fresh-water perch, was introduced in 1891 and is found mainly in Copco Lake, just south of the Oregon border and its Klamath River outlet. The *Sacramento perch,* actually a sunfish, is now rare. Over a dozen different kinds of surfperch are found off the coast. They have been fished since Indian days; the annual catch in California's ocean waters during the 1970s has ranged from 272,470 to 132,135 pounds.

PEREIRA, WILLIAM (1909–), Chicago-born architect, long resident in southern California. His works include the Los Angeles Museum of Art and the master planning for the Irvine campus of the University of California, as well as the pyramid skyscraper that is the San Francisco headquarters of Transamerica Corporation.

PÉREZ, JUAN (17??–75), onetime pilot of Manila galleons, became captain of the *San Antonio,* a vessel of the Sacred Expedition of 1769 under the overall command of Portolá.♦ The ship left Cape San Lucas February 15, reached San Diego April 11, and then returned south to San Blas for supplies to succor Serra and others after their arduous trip. Upon the ship's return Pérez took it north to Monterey (1770). In 1773–74 he explored the northwest coast to present British Columbia, claiming Nootka Sound for Spain.

Periodicals, see *Magazines* and *Newspapers.*

Peripheral Canal, projected addition to the state program to move water♦ from north to south. It envisions a 43-mile-long, 500-foot-wide canal extending from a point below Sacramento to one above Tracy. It will move Sacramento River water around the southeastern edge of the Delta to the State Water Project and the Central Valley Project farther south. Along the way the canal would release enough water to keep the Delta from becoming brackish.

PERKINS, CHARLOTTE (1860–1935), grandniece of Harriet Beecher Stowe, moved for her health's sake from her native Connecticut to California (1885) and lived mostly in Pasadena. Her first writings were poems published as *In This Our World* (1893) and *Suffrage Songs and Verses* (1911), but as a feminist and sociologist interested in Fabian Socialism she became a leader in women's movements and wrote an influential treatise, *Women and Economics* (1898). She is sometimes known by the surnames of her husbands, Stetson and Gilman.

PERKINS, GEORGE CLEMENT (1839–1923), 14th governor of the state (1880–83), went to California (1855) from his native Maine to mine gold but soon entered business and by shrewd investments became an owner of the Pacific Coast Steamship Co., whose vessels went up to Alaska and down to Central America, and of other important businesses. His political career as a Republican began as a state senator when he was thirty. He continued as governor (1880–83) in an administration much concerned with prison affairs. During a long period in the U.S. Senate (1893–1915), he concentrated on maritime matters, supported the building of the Panama Canal, and opposed the naturalization of Japanese.

PÉROUSE, COMTE DE LA, see *La Pérouse, Jean François de Galaup, Comte de.*

Perris Valley, located in Riverside County and an offshoot of the San Bernardino Valley, was named for the chief engineer of the California Southern Railroad, an early resident. A lake and a town also bear his name. The lake is the terminus of the California Aqueduct.◆

PERRY, JOE [FLETCHER] (1927–), Arkansas-born football player reared in Compton, was the fullback for the San Francisco Forty-Niners (1948–60, 63). With Y. A. Tittle◆ and Hugh McElhenny,◆ he gave the team a famous backfield.

Perry Mason, fictional southern California lawyer and sleuth who was the hero of a long series of detective novels by Erle Stanley Gardner.◆ His adventures and brilliant courtroom actions were featured in a radio series (1943–55) and two television programs (1957–66, 1973–74).

Pershing Square, a downtown Los Angeles park named for the World War I general in 1918, was mainly inspired by the planning of Frederick B. Eaton. It is bounded by Hill, Olive, Fifth, and Sixth streets.

Persimmon, fruit from the *Diospyros virginiana* tree, introduced to California during the gold rush. The Japanese variety (*D. kaki*) was introduced in the 1870s. For a long time the crop was small, since only 3,300 trees of both kinds were bearing by 1910. Large plantings were made later in southern California and in Placer and Butte counties, so that by 1930 there were 98,300 trees. The harvest in 1970 was 1,400 tons, worth $188,000, and provided most of the U.S. supply.

Petaluma, city in Sonoma County long known as a poultry center. A young Canadian, Lyman Ryce, introduced white leghorns and invented incubators there in 1878. It is also a dairy center known for cheese making. Nearby Gen. Mariano Vallejo built the headquarters of his Rancho Petaluma (*c.* 1836), the largest adobe in northern California. In the 1970s the city began to be a suburban residential area (in 1970 it had a population of 24,870), and it restricted future growth by a plan (enacted 1972) that limited new housing to 500 units a year and established a 200-foot-wide green belt around the city as a boundary against future development.

PETERS, CHARLES ROLLO (1862–1928), San Francisco-born painter, studied under Jules Tavernier and, in France, became noted for his "nocturnes," canvases depicting moonlight on the missions and other old Spanish buildings and local California sites.

PETRI, LOUIS A. (1912–), grandson of a small vintner and wine merchant in the San Joaquin Valley, expanded his business by organizing the Allied Grape Growers, from which he bought his grapes. His Petri Wine Co. bought Italian-Swiss Colony (1953) and Inglenook (1964) and then, as United Vintners, led all winemakers in production capacity until surpassed by Gallo. He pioneered in shipping wine by railway tankers and in large-scale retailing. His firm was bought by Heublein (1969).

Petrified Forest, commercially operated preserve west of Calistoga (Sonoma County), in which giant redwoods (one 126 feet long) are found that were once converted to stone by a prehistoric flow of volcanic mud and ash from Mt. St. Helena. Much earlier, lava flowed into the soil in which the forest eventually grew. The trees were discovered by a Charles Evans, whom Stevenson met and wrote about in *The Silverado Squatters.* Another Petrified Forest is in the El Paso Mts. of eastern Kern County.

Petroglyphs, decorated rocks in caves, on boulders, and at other sites. They were made by prehistoric Indians. In the area east of the Sierra crest they are generally simple geometric forms or stylized presentations of mountain sheep, snakes, and bird tracks pecked out of the rocks. In the northern Coast Range they are grooved and rubbed, often in cup shape. In southwestern California they are generally geometrical forms in linear arrangements, especially chains of diamonds, and are painted red. In the coastal area and the eastern mountains surrounding the lower San Joaquin Valley, they often depict human forms and are painted red, yellow, and black. Petroglyphs are not found in the Anderson, Sacramento, and San Joaquin valleys, nor in the general area between Redding and Eureka. A large number of relatively modern petroglyphs have been found north of Bishop in the area of the Inyo-Mono counties border.

Petroleum, see *Oil.*

Phalaropes, see *Shore birds.*

Pheasants, game birds introduced to California from Mongolia. The members of the ringneck species are found in the marshlands of the Sacramento Valley and in the Tule Lake area, just south of the Oregon border.

PHELAN, JAMES D[UVAL] (1861–1930), began his career in the family banking business established by his father, who went to California in the gold rush. The younger Phelan served as a reform mayor of San Francisco (1897–1901), combating the city's boss-run and corrupt government and emphasizing urban beautification in parks and playgrounds. Elected to the U.S. Senate (1915–21) as a Democrat, he strongly supported the policies of Woodrow Wilson until the end of World War I, but he also vigorously advocated the exclusion of Orientals from the U.S. He was a well-known patron of the arts and left part of his fortune and his country estate, Villa Montalvo, in Saratoga, to aid California writers and artists.

Philippinos, see *Filipinos in California.*

Philopolis, monthly magazine published in San Francisco (1906–16) by Lucia and Arthur F. Mathews.♦ In it they promulgated their aesthetic and ethical ideas of a wholesome civic spirit and proposed a program of urban planning to rebuild the earthquake-shattered city. Their Philopolis Press issued well-made books on art, literature, and California culture.

Phoenixiana, collection of 30 humorous tales and travesties on California affairs written by George H. Derby.♦ They were printed in a San Francisco journal, *The Pioneer,* and collected in that volume (1855) under the author's pseudonym, John Phoenix.

Photography, began in California with the gold rush, just a decade after the French innovator, Daguerre, announced his process (1839) and S. F. B. Morse in the same year made the first daguerreotypes in the U.S. The unusual scenes and events of the gold rush attracted such documentary photographers as Robert H. Vance,♦ William Shew,♦ and George Fardon, as well as W. H. Rulofson,♦ who entertained the idea of making portraits of all distinguished visitors from 1849 on.

The landscape views that Carleton E. Watkins♦ made from glass plates were much admired as art. Watkins photographed the natural scene and the decaying missions as well as the conventional views of gold mining and the new towns and cities that mining brought into being. To reach his remote subjects he sometimes used a dozen mules to pack the camera, very large glass plates, and the tent in which he coated and developed them. He also employed a stereoscopic camera for dramatic landscapes, as did Eadweard Muybridge,♦ the state's most prominent photographer, particularly distinguished for his studies of animal and human locomotion that were a forerunner of motion pictures.

I. W. Taber♦ was another leading photographer; he concentrated both on portraits and on souvenir albums of the scenes, businesses, and ways of life peculiar to the West Coast. In the last decade of the century, A. C. Vroman♦ employed the point of view of the new field of anthropology in his sharply presented but sensitively conceived pictures of Indians in the Southwest, also the point of view of

Edward Curtis.♦ Later both Vroman and George Wharton James♦ adopted the archaeologists' attitude in documenting the moldering missions with great detail. Meanwhile, A. W. Ericson♦ created a documentary history of lumbering.

At the turn of the century a major aesthetic contribution to photography was made by Arnold Genthe,♦ who created portraits of eminent San Franciscans, which by their soft focus and sensitive employment of dark and light patterns not only caught the character of the subject but displayed the selective eye of a painter. In the same way he captured the atmosphere of the city's Chinatown and the spirit of San Francisco on the eve of the earthquake and fire and during the drama of that great event. Francis Brugière♦ held views similar to those of Genthe, initially concentrating on dramatic subjects such as the Panama-Pacific Exposition buildings and actual stage productions and later on abstract designs in color. By the 1920s photography as an art form rather than as a medium of documentation was a well-established concept. One of its leading practitioners was Edward Weston, who soon abandoned soft focus for sharp, clear depiction of the forms and textures that interested him, whether in nature or in manufactured objects, which he observed very close up so as to present their essential patterns and rhythms. Imogen Cunningham,♦ through a long career, also created photographs based on similar concepts.

Ansel Adams♦ was a major figure from the 1930s on, mainly for his sharp-eyed spacious, frontal views of the natural scene, displayed realistically with a kind of epic grandeur, but also for his influence upon other photographers. He taught at the California School of Fine Arts and the Art Center in Los Angeles, and collections of his prints were published. Another important figure of the time was Dorothea Lange,♦ noted particularly for her sympathetically understanding but sharp portrayals of people during the Depression.

Younger Californians have employed a diversity of other, and often more experimental approaches. Among these is the work of Edward Ruscha, which presents tawdry aspects of the southern California scene in a style that looks like journalism but incorporates the satire of pop art. By the 1970s a great interest in photography as an art form occasioned the opening of numerous galleries which sold prints at prices formerly considered appropriate only for paintings and drawings, and, along with retrospective exhibitions of major photographers, Californian and foreign, there arose a great interest in new and experimental photographers.

PIAZZONI, GOTTARDO (1872–1945), Italian-Swiss-born artist, brought to California (1886), where he studied under Arthur Mathews. He also studied at the Académie Julian in Paris. In addition to smaller paintings he was known for his large murals, such as those in the San Francisco Public Library, which in simple and somber colors and rhythmic patterns depicted California hills and valleys. He was also an influential teacher at the California School of Fine Arts (1919–35).

Picacho, deserted mining town on the Colorado River in Imperial County, named for the redundantly titled Picacho Peak (*picacho* is Spanish for "peak") near it, had rich gold placers worked by Mexicans in the 1860s and by Americans thereafter. Nearby is a State Recreation Area. An abandoned mercury mine near New Idria in San Benito County also bore this name.

PICKETT, CHARLES EDWARD (1820–82), moved from his native Virginia to Oregon (1842) and then to California (1846) where he became a journalist, a dabbler in the law, a political and polemical pamphleteer, and an agitator for the Confederacy. The subjects of his quixotic attacks included Ralston, Stanford, the Silver Kings, and Stephen J. Field. Bancroft called him San Francisco's Diogenes, and he was also known as Philosopher Pickett.

PICKFORD, MARY (1893–), stage name of Gladys Mary Smith, whose theatrical career began in stock companies of her native Toronto and under Belasco in New York. In 1913 she began a tremendously successful motion picture career under the direction of D. W. Griffith. She became "America's sweetheart," playing child parts and sentimental roles as an ingenue, including adaptations of Bret Harte's *M'liss* and Kate Douglas Wiggins' *Rebecca of Sunnybrook Farm,* although she later essayed a mature part with her husband (1919–35), Douglas Fairbanks, in *The Taming of the Shrew* (1929). For many years the two of them were considered the social leaders of Hollywood, at their estate, Pickfair. With Chaplin and D. W. Griffith they established (1919) their own film production and distribution company, United Artists, in which she remained a principal stockholder until 1950.

Pick handle brigade, see *Coleman, William T.*

PICO, prominent early California family whose founder was Santiago de la Cruz Pico, a soldier who, with his wife (listed in a census as a "mulata") and seven children, went to San Francisco with the Anza expedition (1776). After nine years at the San Diego presidio he settled in Los Angeles (1786). Three of his sons were granted Rancho San José de Gracia de Simi (1795) on the condition that he and his family continue to live in the underpopulated Los Angeles pueblo. Two other sons, José Dolores (1764–1827) and José María (1765–1819), founded branches of the family at Monterey and San Diego, respectively. José María became the more prominent. José María's sons included Pío,♦ twice governor of California, and Andrés (1810–76), commander of the *Californios* at the Battle of San Pasqual, for two days their last governor, and later a state senator, and his daughters married into the Alvarado, Argüello, Carrillo, and Ortega families. One of José Dolores' thirteen children, Salomon, became a highwayman, supposedly as a protest against American occupation. Mt. Solomon (*sic*) and Solomon Canyon (south of Santa Maria) are named for the scenes of his operations. He was later executed in Baja California (1860), presumably for other crimes. His many respectable siblings and cousins lost their fortunes and great *ranchos* through costly land disputes under U.S. rule.

PICO, Pío [DE JESUS] (1801–94), the 5th and last (14th) Mexican governor of Alta California. His very brief first term (Jan. 27–Feb. 18, 1832) followed the ouster of Manuel Victoria and was an appointment made by the provincial *diputación* after its disagreement with Echeandía, the military governor of California, but was quickly terminated when Echeandía not only refused to resign but dissolved the *diputación*. His second term (March 1845–July 1846) followed the ouster of Micheltorena when the *Californios* decided they wanted a native governor. He set up his administration in Los Angeles but, lacking influence in the north, had to let José Castro, the military commander who had driven out Micheltorena, run the customs and treasury from Monterey. Pico, however, was lavish in disposing of land grants for *ranchos,*♦ even to an adventurer like Eugene McNamara.♦ The friction between Pico and Castro kept the governor from accomplishing much and made it easy for the Americans to defeat them and to drive them into exile in Mexico. Pico returned to California (1848), first to the ranch of his brother-in-law, John Forster,♦ then to Los Angeles.

Pico Canyon, near Newhall in Los Angeles County, was named for Andrés Pico, who produced coal oil in the region. "Old Pico," a pioneer well which is now a National Historic Landmark, was drilled there in 1876.

Pico House, leading Los Angeles hotel of an early period, erected by Pío Pico (1870) as a luxurious three-story Romanesque building on the corner of Main St. and the Plaza.

Pico Rivera, city in east Los Angeles, residential tract area that sprang into being after World War II on a convenient site off the San Gabriel Freeway. In 1970 it had a population of 54,170.

Pictographs, see *Petroglyphs*.

Pigeon, wild bird, often called a dove, found throughout most of California. The *mourning dove*♦ is the most common variety. The *band-tailed pigeon* inhabits the Sierra Nevada and also lives in the Coast Range during the summer, feeding on nuts and berries. Once widely hunted, it now has some protection from federal legislation (1913). The common pigeon, seen in Union Square, San Francisco, and numerous other parks and public places, is descended from the *European rock dove*.

Pigs, see *Swine*.

Pike, a type of westering immigrant traditionally said to be from "Pike County," although that area was variously ascribed to Missouri, Arkansas, southern Illinois, northern Texas, or any frontier region. A man from Pike was considered to be a loutish, ignorant, distrustful, but acquisitive backwoodsman who was the butt of jokes and became a typical character in 19th-century American humor. Bayard Taylor, in his *Home and Abroad* (1860) described the Pike as "the Anglo Saxon relapsed into semi-barbarism. He is long, lathy, and sallow; he expectorates vehemently; he takes naturally to whisky; he has the 'shakes' his life long at home, though he generally manages to get rid of them in California; he has little respect for the rights of others; he distrusts men in 'store clothes,' but venerates the memory of Andrew Jackson." The Pike character was introduced in the works of George Derby, but he also appears in many other California writings, including "The Newtys of Pike" in Clarence King's *Mountaineering in the Sierra Nevada* and as a hired man in Stevenson's *The Silverado Squatters*. As a folk hero of the forty-niners he appears in a popular song: "My name it is Joe Bowers,/And I've got a brother Ike;/I come from old Missouri—/Yes, all the way from Pike." Closely related in song and folklore of the gold rush, but more appealing by far, was Sweet Betsy from Pike.

Pimería Alta, see *Kino.*

PINCKERT, ERNIE (ERNEST PINCKERT) (1908–77), football player, was a star blocking back on coach Howard Jones'♦ University of Southern California teams (1929–31) and played in two Rose Bowl games (1930, 32). He was twice named an All-American fullback and was elected (1957) to the National Football Hall of Fame.

Pine nuts, or **piñons,** edible seeds of the *one-leaf* and the *four-leaf* (or *Parry*) *piñon,* obtained by placing their mature cones close to low fires so that they open and the shell-covered nuts can be extracted. They were a basic part of the diet of many Indian tribes.

Pines, coniferous evergreen trees, of which there are many varieties in California. The best known are *beach pine,* found along the coast from Point Arena to the Oregon border, grows 10 to 20 feet tall; *bishop pine,* a coastal tree from Santa Barbara to Fort Bragg at elevations up to 1,000 feet, grows 40 to 80 feet tall; *bristlecone pine,* found in the eastern mountains of central California up to 11,500 feet, is the longest living species in the U.S. (one, in Inyo National Forest, is over 4,600 years old); *Coulter* (or *big cone*) *pine,* native to the southern Coast Range up to 7,000 feet, grows to 70 feet; *digger pine,* found in dry, rocky areas of the Coast Range, the Sierra, and the Klamath, Santa Lucia, and Tehachapi mountains, is generally 40 to 50 feet tall; *four-leaf* (or *Parry*) *piñon,* native of the Peninsular Ranges up to 5,500 feet, grows to 30 feet and bears pine nuts; *foxtail* (or *hickory* or *Balfour pine*), found in the Sierra and Klamath mountains, reaches heights of 45 feet; *Jeffrey pine,* found mainly at 6,000–9,000 foot elevations in the Sierra, the San Jacinto, and the San Bernardino mountains, grows to 120 feet or more; *knobcone pine,* native to dry, rocky areas below 4,000 feet from Monterey to Oregon, in the western central Sierra, and on the San Bernardino and Santa Ana mountains, ranges from 5 to 30 feet in height; *limber pine,* lives at high elevations to 11,500 feet in the northeast of the state, the eastern Sierra, and the southern California mountains, growing from 10 to 60 feet tall; *lodgepole* (or *tamarac*) *pine,* found in the Klamath, the Sierra, and the San Jacinto mountains, grows from 50 to 80 feet or more; *Monterey pine,* flourishes in coastal areas from Santa Cruz County to the Chan-

nel Islands, grows from 30 to over 100 feet tall, is easily transplanted or grown from seed so is much used for reforestation, landscaping, and as a Christmas tree; *one-leafed piñon,* grows on the western side of the southern Sierra and on desert mountains to 9,000 feet, is generally 8 to 20 feet tall, and produces pine nuts; *ponderosa* (or *yellow*) *pine,* found from the coast up to 8,500 feet, is, with the *Jeffrey,* the most widespread variety, and grows from 60 to 225 feet tall; *sugar pine,* a common variety found throughout the state, grows from 70 to 200 feet tall; *Torrey pine,* found only in San Diego County and on Santa Rosa Island, is a rare species protected at Torrey Pines State Park;♦ *western white* (or *silver* or *mountain* or *Idaho white*) *pine,* grows from the Sierra to the Klamath Mts. at elevations to 10,000 feet, and reaches a height of 200 feet; and *whitebark pine,* grows at or near the timber line of the Sierra where it may be found dwarfed or even prostrate. *Ponderosa* and *sugar* are the most heavily logged of these 17 varieties, yielding 16% and 8%, respectively, of the wood cut for mill use, and are also used for veneer and plywood. More than 200 physical features and settlements incorporate "pine" in their place-names. The Spanish word *piñons* provides names for 15 geographic features south of Monterey.

Pinnacles National Monument (est. 1908), an area of ancient volcanic origin. It has eroded spires and crags, and lies in the Gabilan Range, 35 miles north of King City.

Pinos, Point, see *Point Pinos.*

PIOCHE, FRANÇOIS LOUIS ALFRED (1818–75), French-born banker and real estate and railroad financier of San Francisco from 1849. After his investments became overextended he committed suicide. In 1856 he commissioned a handsome engraving of his adopted city by the French artist Charles Meryon.♦ A Nevada mining town was named for him.

Pioneer, monthly literary journal (1854–56) founded and edited by Ferdinand C. Ewer as the first magazine dedicated to the culture of California. Its most famous series was the collection of letters from Dame Shirley by Louise Clapp.♦ Other major contributors included George Derby, whose sketches were signed John Phoenix; Stephen Massett, whose columns were signed Jeems Pipes of Pipesville; Edward Pollock, known for his lofty poetry; and John Swett, later famous as a founder of the state's public education system. The *Pioneer*'s symbolic cover picture, depicting a newly arrived family joyously looking down from the Coast Range on the Pacific, was later adopted by the California Historical Society as its emblem.

Pioneer Register, index of 372 close-packed pages, compiled by H. H. Bancroft♦ for his *History of California* (7 vols., 1886–90), which lists the names and his page references to persons in California from its European discovery to 1848, as treated in the first five volumes of his work. It has been reprinted (1964) in a single volume.

Pioneers, Society of California, see *Society of California Pioneers*.

Pious Fund, endowment established in the 17th century to aid missions in Baja and Alta California. Originally under Jesuit jurisdiction, it was transferred by Viceroy Gálvez to the Franciscans but held in trust by the government. In 1842 the principal was sequestered by President Santa Anna, who promised to pay the interest. He did so (very irregularly) until California was ceded to the U.S. in 1848. With the aid of J. T. Doyle,♦ Archbishop Alemany♦ was instrumental in persuading the U.S. government to have the matter submitted to an international arbitration commission, which arranged (1875–76) an award of half the interest since 1848 ($43,000 Mexican gold per year). By 1890 the debt had been cleared to the year 1869. When Mexico then refused either annual payments or payment of new interest, the Hague Tribunal arranged (1902) a single settlement of $1,427,682 Mexican for the past and a commitment of future annuities. These annual payments were discontinued at the time of the Mexican Revolution, but a final lump sum of $719,546 U.S. was paid in 1967.

Piru, Lake, a reservoir on the border of Los Padres National Forest in southeastern Ventura County, near which are located a river, a canyon, and a town bearing the same name. It may derive from a Shoshone word for a kind of plant.

Pisco punch, alcoholic drink popular in San Francisco between the 1850s and Prohibition. The saloon most associated with it was the Bank Exchange, which kept secret the recipe. It contained Peruvian (Pisco) brandy, fresh pineapple, lemon juice, gum syrup, and distilled water.

Pismo Beach, oceanside residential and tourist resort town in San Luis Obispo County, famous for

its clams.♦ Anza camped near the site (1776), which was named for an Indian term for tar. The population in 1970 was 4,043.

PISSIS, Albert (1852–1914), born in Guaymas, Mexico, lived in San Francisco after 1858 and, following Beaux-Arts training, became a leading local architect. His buildings include the classic Hibernia Bank (1890). His brother Emile (1854–1934) was a painter and designer of stained glass windows.

Pit River, named by Hudson's Bay Co. trappers for the local Indian practice of digging pits along its banks to maim their enemies. It runs across the plateau of Modoc, Lassen, and Shasta counties from the lava beds into Shasta Lake,♦ whose dam impounds water from the Sacramento and McCloud rivers. The lake is a major source of state water.♦ The river's flow is quite even through the seasons because porous volcanic rocks hold the run-off from rain and snow. The river was a route both for the Applegate Cut-off Trail of the 1840s, from the Humboldt River in Nevada to Oregon, and for the Lassen Trail, a route from the east into northern California. During the 19th century a mistaken notion about the origin of the name often led to the spelling Pitt.

Pitzer College, see *Claremont Colleges*.

Piute, see *Paiute*.

PIXLEY, Frank [Morrison] (1825–95), New York-born lawyer and journalist who, after graduation from Hamilton College and practice in Michigan, went to California (1849). He was Gov. Stanford's attorney general (1862–63) and President Grant's attorney general (1869). He edited the *Daily Herald* of San Francisco, contributed to the *Sacramento Union,* and was chief editorial writer for the *San Francisco Chronicle* before becoming a co-publisher and the editor of the *Argonaut*♦ (1877–93). He attracted important writers, including Gertrude Atherton, Ina Coolbrith, and Arthur McEwen; supported Stanford and the railroad; inveighed against Oriental immigration and the Catholic Church; and made many enemies, including Bierce, who proposed as his epitaph "Here lies Frank Pixley—as usual." A Tulare County town and a San Francisco street were named for Pixley.

Placer County, formed (1851) from parts of Yuba and Sutter counties, which lie, respectively, on its north and west. Nevada County is also on the north,

Sacramento and El Dorado on the south, and the state of Nevada on the east. Auburn,♦ once the capital of Sutter County, has always been the Placer County seat. Placer is a Spanish term for ore deposits worked by surface mining.

Early white explorers included Carson and Frémont, who were soon followed by settlers who went there via the California Trail and through the county's Emigrant Gap.♦ Gold was found early, leading to the creation of many mining camps along the North and Middle forks of the American River and the Yuba and Bear rivers, which form the county's northern boundary. The camps included not only Auburn, but Ophir, Gold Run, Newcastle, Dutch Flat, Iowa Hill, Yankee Jim's, Last Chance, and Michigan City, many of which are now ghost towns. Their names suggest the colorful diversity of the gold rush, as do such place-names as Shirt-tail Canyon, Humbug Creek, and Mosquito Ridge. The county is also known for Donner Pass, on its northern border, and for Lake Tahoe, whose western shoreline forms the county's eastern boundary. Squaw Valley♦ lies within Tahoe National Forest on the Truckee River.♦

In the 1860s the Central Pacific Railroad passed through Placer and made Colfax a major station. The southeastern part of the county is known for its orchards, fruit ranching having been begun by French settlers in 1846, though today orchards produce less than livestock and poultry farming do. In 1970 the population was 77,632. With an area of 916,992 acres, it had 54.2 persons per sq. mi.

Placer mining, the most common form of mining during the gold rush period, in which the gold mixed in the gravel and sand of a river bed is shaken free. At first a pan (or *batea,* as the Mexicans and Spanish called it) was used for this purpose; it was shaken under the stream of water, which washed away the lighter debris while allowing the heavy metal to fall to the bottom. A more sophisticated means of placer mining employed the rocker, a cradle-like device with a sieve at its head into which one man poured the rubble from the riverbed while another rocked the implement as water flowed through it so that gold would be caught behind cleats on the bottom while the dirt passed through the open end of the box. A further development was the long tom, a sloping trough about 12 feet long and wider at the top than the end. Its bottom was made of perforated sheet iron hung above a wooden box with cleats (called riffles) across its base. One man piped water into the upper opening of the trough, another shoveled in dirt, and a third stirred it so that

the heavy gold would drop into the riffle box. A still further development took the shape of a sluice box, a long trough or series of riffle boxes through which the debris could be washed several times in order that each would catch successively finer particles of gold. Hydraulic mining♦ was a later development. Quartz mining,♦ begun in 1849, being expensive and complex, was not common until the late 1850s.

Placerita Canyon, site near Newhall and Saugus in Los Angeles County, where Francisco López made the first commercially significant gold discovery (1842) in the present state. A sample was carried to the U.S. by Alfred Robinson, but it had no effect there, though the discovery did start a small rush, both locally and from Sonora (Mexico). The canyon was later the scene of robberies by Tiburcio Vásquez. It is now a State Park.

Placerville, county seat of El Dorado County,♦ came into being soon after Marshall's discovery of gold at nearby Coloma (1848). During that first year it was known as Old Dry Diggins, but after the summary execution of three gold thieves it was informally called Hangtown♦ (1849). An important stopping point on a major overland trail, it enjoyed a population boom, becoming a supply center, a station on the Central Pacific Railroad, and the western end of the Pony Express. Among its early residents were Mark Hopkins, a grocery store owner, Philip Armour, a butcher, and John Studebaker, a builder of wheelbarrows. Hopkins went on to become a railroad magnate, Armour a great meatpacker, and Studebaker a wagon and automobile manufacturer. The population in 1970 was 5,416.

"Plain Language from Truthful James," comic ballad by Bret Harte.♦ Published in the *Overland Monthly* (Sept. 1870), it was first collected in his *Poems* (1871) but meanwhile was widely pirated in the U.S. and England as *The Heathen Chinee* or *That Heathen Chinee*. Set at "Table Mountain, 1870," in the Calaveras County mining country according to the subtitle, the tale describes a euchre game in which Truthful James and his friend Bill Nye plan to cheat the Chinese gambler Ah Sin, but are themselves "ruined by Chinese cheap labor," being bested by the "ways that are dark" of the wily Oriental. The poem was a popular expression of the antipathy to Chinese♦ in California, though Harte himself vigorously opposed racial persecution.

Plane tree, see *Alder.*

Plantin Press, The, founded (1931) in Los Angeles by the Polish-born Saul Marks (1905–74) and his wife Lilian to produce typographically distinguished books in limited editions. The first published was *A Gil Blas in California,* by Dumas♦ (1933).

Plate of Brass, see *Drake, Francis.*

PLEASANT, MAMMY (MARY ELLEN PLEASANT) (1814?–1904), a black who went to San Francisco about 1849. Many stories are told of her: it is said that she came from Boston, where she had been acquainted with William Lloyd Garrison and had aided his work. In San Francisco she ran a boardinghouse, and supposedly a bawdy house, using her money to aid runaway slaves and other oppressed people of her race. In the course of time Mrs. Pleasant became the housekeeper of a local banker, Thomas Bell, whom she ostensibly dominated and whose home she turned into a "House of Mystery." She interfered in the affairs of another wealthy San Franciscan, William Sharon,♦ her onetime boarder; she was responsible for a forged marriage contract used by Sarah Althea Hill♦ in an unsuccessful attempt to claim a share of Sharon's fortune. A small park on Bell's San Francisco property is named for her.

Pleasanton, community in southern Alameda County near Livermore,♦ has grown rapidly in recent years with the development of rock, sand, and gravel quarry businesses and research laboratories. It is also a residential community. It was the site of an elaborate mansion built by A. C. Schweinfurth and Julia Morgan for Phoebe Apperson Hearst. Ironically, her great-granddaughter Patricia Hearst was incarcerated in a state prison nearby.

Plumas County, formed (1854) from part of Butte County, has always had Quincy as its county seat. It is bounded by Lassen County on the north and east, by Sierra and a bit of Yuba counties on the south, and by Tehama and Butte counties on the west. (*Plumas* was the original Spanish name of the Feather River.) It became an important point of entry to California after the discovery (1851) by James Beckwourth♦ of the pass named for him. Because that pass is the lowest (5,212 feet) across the Sierra, it had a share, though rather belated, in the gold rush, particularly along the Middle and North forks of the Feather River. Among the mining camps in the latter area was Rich Bar, from which Dame Shirley♦ dated her letters in 1851–52. Another famous temporary resident was Lotta

Crabtree, who grew up in La Porte. A central town for the mines was American Ranch, later named Quincy after its owner's home town in Illinois. The county's later economic resources included copper mining, lumbering, dairy farming, and field crops. Hydroelectric power was first developed by the damming that created Lake Almanor (1917), which was named for parts of the names of the three daughters of Guy Earl, a founder of Great Western Electric Power Co.♦ Much of the county lies within the Plumas National Forest, headquartered near Johnsville, where ski contests were held as early as 1860. In 1970 the county's population was 11,707. With an area of 1,643,948 acres, it had 4.6 persons per sq. mi.

Plums, see *Prunes.*

PLUNKETT, JIM (JAMES WILLIAM PLUNKETT) (1947–), San Jose-born football player, was the quarterback on Stanford's team (1968–70). He set an NCAA record for passes in a career (7,877 yards), led his team to a Rose Bowl victory over Ohio State (1971), and was awarded the Heisman Trophy (1970) as the best college player in the U.S. He joined the Forty-Niners in 1976.

Poblador, Spanish word for founder or settler of a pueblo.♦

Poet Laureate, a lifetime title created by the legislature (1915) to honor Ina Coolbrith,♦ in part for her contributions to the Panama-Pacific International Exposition. She held the post until her death (1928). Subsequent laureates have been Henry Meade Bland (1929–31), John Steven McGroarty (1933–44), Gordon W. Norris (1953–61), and Charles B. Garrigus (1966–).

Poetry Center, San Francisco, organization founded (1953) during the San Francisco Renaissance♦ to encourage the creation and reception of contemporary poetry. Affiliated with San Francisco State University, it has sponsored frequent readings both by prominent local poets such as Ginsberg, Snyder, Ferlinghetti, and McClure and by obscure ones, as well as by distinguished visitors. It has created an American Poetry Archive and Resource Center for its more than 1,000 tape recordings and sponsors a Poetry in the Schools program.

Point Arena, see *Arena, Point.*

Point Arguello, coastal headland north of Point Concepcion in Santa Barbara County, was named by Vancouver (1792) for José Darío Argüello. Vandenberg Air Force Base is located there.

Point Concepcion, original name of the turning point on the coastline north of Santa Barbara. The cape was discovered by Cabrillo (1542) who called it *Cabo de Galera* because he thought it looked like a seagoing galley. Vizcaíno sighted it (1602) on Dec. 8, the feast day of *Purisima Concepción* (Immaculate Conception) and therefore gave it the present name, which is still used for the local post office. The name of the cape itself has been anglicized to Point Conception.

Point Dana, see *Dana Point.*

Point Dume, ocean headland just north of Malibu, named by Vancouver, but with a misspelling, to honor Francisco Dumetz, the Spanish friar who had entertained him at Mission San Buenaventura.

Point Lobos, 1,250 acres on the south shore of Carmel Bay, designated a State Reserve (1933). The headland has a great grove of Monterey cypress and the offshore rocks are inhabited by sea lions and pelicans, while in the waters are sea otter and migrating gray whales. There was a whaling station active at the site from 1861 to 1884.

Point Loma, settlement south of San Diego, site of an old lighthouse, hide houses like that in which Dana lived (as described in *Two Years Before the Mast*), and former Fort Rosecrans. It was also the name and location of a theosophic community (1897–1942), long led by Katherine Tingley,♦ who was known as the Purple Mother. The grounds and remaining buildings became the campus of California Western University. The area also houses the West Coast naval base for submarines and the navy's laboratories for undersea and electronics research.

Point Mugu, settlement on a lagoon of the same name south of Port Hueneme♦ in Ventura County. It is the site of a navy missile test center. The name Mugu, from the Chumash word for "beach," was cited by Cabrillo (1542) as that of an Indian village. It may be the state's oldest place-name.

Point Pinos, headland of Monterey Bay adjacent to Pacific Grove, was sighted by Cabrillo (1542),

but given its present name by Vizcaíno (1602) because of the pine-covered promontory. One of the state's first lighthouses♦ was built there, and its present structure is part of a Lighthouse Reservation. Asilomar♦ is nearby.

Point Reyes, peninsula some 30 miles north of San Francisco, in Marin County, named Punta de los Reyes by Vizcaíno (Jan. 6, 1603) after the feast day of the Three Kings (Epiphany). Along it are Drake's Bay,♦ where some historians contend that the *Golden Hind* was careened and a plate of brass erected; Bodega Bay♦ and Tomales Bay; and the simple summer town of Inverness.♦ A large part is preserved as a National Seashore (founded 1962) and is now included in the Golden Gate National Recreational Area. It is the site of the state's heaviest fogs and is the coolest point of the continental U.S. in midsummer.

Point Sal, see *Sal, Hermenegildo.*

Poison oak, shrub of the same genus as poison ivy and poison sumac, grows near oak trees and has a leaf that resembles theirs but becomes brilliant red in autumn. One can be poisoned by touching it or even by indirect contact from animals, clothes, etc. that have touched it and from the smoke of the burning plant. Almost all people are painfully affected; the skin turns red, itches, swells, and blisters. Only California's deserts and high mountains are free of it.

Polecat, see *Skunk.*

Poles in California, probably arrived first as settlers with the Russian-American Co., but individual Poles were not associated with the region until the time of Dr. Felix Wierzbicki,♦ who came with Stevenson's Regiment (1847) and wrote the first English book printed in the state. Other early settlers include Capt. Alexander Zakrzewski (1799–1866), a San Francisco lithographer and cartographer; John Theophil Strentzel (1813–90), a pioneer horticulturist and the father-in-law of John Muir; and Rudolf Piotrowski (1814–83), a colonist from Sebastopol who became the state's commissioner of immigration. The gold rush and political upheaval at home drew more Poles to California during the 1850s. The most famous Polish group to settle (briefly) in California was that which included the actress Modjeska and the novelist Sienkiewicz.♦ They founded a utopian colony in Anaheim. Prominent Polish people later associated with the state include Christian Brevoort Zabriskie (1864–1936), son of a forty-niner and an executive in borax mining in Death Valley; and Prince André Poniatowski, who married Beth Sperry (1894) of the Stockton flour-milling family. Polish settlement in the 20th century, which included many Jews, went mainly from New York and Chicago to Los Angeles, and included persons prominent in the motion picture business, like Samuel Goldwyn.

Politics, initially evident in the era of Mexican government, when a struggle occurred between governors like Chico, pledged to centralist rule from Mexico, and native sons like Alvarado and Vallejo, who believed in home rule. Allied to this issue was that of secularization of the missions, whose lands would pass to those *rancheros* and to the American merchants associated with them. Conflicts were so intense that in the period 1835–36 alone the governorship was occupied successively by Castro, Gutiérrez, Chico, Gutiérrez (2nd term), and Alvarado.

Under U.S. government the new state was initially dominated by Democrats who split into two factions: the Southerners under William M. Gwin and others under Tammany-trained anti-slavery leader David Broderick. The Democratic split allowed the American party of the Know-Nothing movement to gain important state offices, including the governorship, in the election of 1855. During the Civil War California was strongly pro-Union and a new political grouping, the Union party, was temporarily a major force.

In the 1870s, state politics reflected California's changing economic conditions. The decline of mining and a general depression were exacerbated by a great increase in the supply of labor when thousands of Chinese construction workers were thrown on the market by the completion of the transcontinental railroad (1869). A Workingmen's party led by Denis Kearney took as its slogan "The Chinese must go!" and demanded the rewriting of the state Constitution to regulate the omnipotent railroad and the powerful banks and to alter the tax laws adverse to farmers. The party declined rapidly after a state Constitutional Convention (1878) enacted many of the desired changes, a federal law (1882) banned further Chinese immigration, and the state economy began to prosper again.

By the 1880s the Southern Pacific Railroad began to be the dominant force in state politics, gaining great power in both the Republican and Democratic parties. Despite the revelation by the widow of David Colton of the railroad's chicanery, and despite the indictment of San Francisco's Democratic boss, Christopher Buckley, William F. Herrin, the railroad's lawyer, kept its political machine omnipotent well into the 20th century. Both farmers and urban workers and some industrialists, including the rival Santa Fe and Western Pacific lines, as well as William Randolph Hearst, rose to oppose the Southern Pacific. The national reform movement of Progressivism in California led to a coalition of reformers under Dr. John R. Haynes. It added initiative, referendum, and recall provisions to the Los Angeles city charter, while in San Francisco the reform movement, led by Fremont Older and Rudolph Spreckels, exposed the corruption of Mayor Eugene Schmitz and his political boss, Abraham Ruef.

On the state level the Lincoln-Roosevelt League helped to elect Hiram Johnson, the graft-prosecuting attorney, to the governorship (1911) and later to the U.S. Senate (1916). During Johnson's governorship many political reforms were instituted, including cross-filing in primaries (intended to thwart established political machines), direct election of U.S. Senators by popular vote rather than by the legislature, and the creation of a more effective railroad commission, but the Progressive movement was weakened during Johnson's second term.

During the postwar era of the 1920s a large part of the public sought prosperity rather than reform and its attendant instability, so the dominant Republican party favored business and opposed radicalism, including labor unions. Even after the stock market collapse of 1929 and the coming of the Depression, Republicans continued to hold political power, with "Sunny Jim" Rolph in the governorship (1931–34), happily vetoing a state income tax but upholding the creation of a sales tax which fell heavily on poorer people. But the impact of Roosevelt's New Deal did sweep a Democrat, McAdoo, into the U.S. Senate (1932).

The death of Rolph opened the governorship to a tough fight in 1934 when Upton Sinclair, a longtime Socialist, won the Democratic nomination and campaigned on an EPIC (End Poverty in California) platform, which included cooperative ownership of farms and factories. The press and the motion picture industry conducted a campaign to vilify Sinclair, and he lost the election to Frank Merriam, a conservative Republican. Even so, reform movements continued to have a wide appeal. Most notable were the Townsend Plan of $200 pensions for all persons over 60 and the even more fanciful Ham 'n Eggs program. Four years after Sinclair lost the gubernatorial campaign it was won by Culbert Olson, a liberal Democrat, who created a local New Deal for California, while Sinclair's running mate in the EPIC campaign, Sheridan Downey, with the aid of the pension planners he endorsed, defeated his Democratic rival, McAdoo, and went to the U.S. Senate.

After one rather unsuccessful term Olson lost the governorship to Earl Warren, who stayed in office for a decade (1943–53). Warren projected a tone of nonpartisanship, even though he ran for the vice-presidency on the Republican ticket in 1948. Upon Downey's death in 1950 Warren appointed Congressman Richard M. Nixon to the Senate, giving the state two Republican Senators, since on Hiram Johnson's death in 1945 Warren had appointed William Knowland, the *Oakland Tribune* publisher, to the other seat. After Warren had gone on to the U.S. Supreme Court and the governorship had passed to lieutenant governor Goodwin Knight (1953), his two senatorial appointees vied for the Republican nomination for the presidency. In his attempt, Knowland forced Knight to run for his Senate seat while he himself campaigned for the incumbent Knight's governorship as a power base, the result being the loss of both posts, the former to Clair Engle and the latter to Edmund G. (Pat) Brown, thus bringing the Democrats back into power.

But the Republicans came back into office in the 1960s when Ronald Reagan, projecting the image of a conservative citizen candidate, followed by the successful senatorial campaign of his fellow motion picture star, George Murphy, by beating Brown for the governorship.

During the turbulent decade beginning in the mid 1960s new political forces burst upon the state scene, such as the Peace and Freedom party, campaigning mainly against the Vietnam War, and the Black Panther party, a militant organization of blacks. The events that called them into being and that also caused them to be opposed by conservatives had their impact upon elections to major state offices, too, so that in the mid-1970s the voters on the one hand elected a very young man with a liberal image, Edmund G. (Jerry) Brown, Jr., to the governorship, and on the other, sent S. I. Hayakawa, a 70-year-old novice in politics, known for his conservatism, to the Senate. (*See also individual entries.*)

POLK, WILLIS [JEFFERSON] (1865–1924), Kentucky-born architect, in 1889 went to San Francisco, where he was associated with Les Jeunes,♦ a bohemian group. After working for a period in Chicago under Daniel Hudson Burnham,♦ he began his real California career (1904). He headed Burn-

ham's San Francisco office, working on his city plan, and constructing buildings of his own after the earthquake and fire of 1906. He is known for his varied designs. They include intimate but elegant brown shingle homes like his own on Russian Hill; the graceful remodeling of the James Flood house into the Pacific Union Club; the rehabilitation of Mission Dolores (1917); and the very different work of the same year, the Hallidie Building, named for the inventor of cable cars, which was marked by a front built almost entirely of glass with limited metal decoration.

POLLACK, EDWARD A. (1823–56), Pennsylvania-born lawyer and poet, in 1852 went to San Francisco, where he contributed to the *Pioneer* and planned a national epic. His poems were posthumously collected in 1876.

Pollution, a problem of life in California in various ways and to different degrees ever since the advent of substantial population after the American conquest. The potential existed from the beginning of human settlement, as Cabrillo recognized in 1542 when he observed a pall of smoke hanging over San Pedro Bay, an early example of smog♦ caused by Indian campfires burning under an inversion layer of warm air. Similarly, Crespí in 1769 noted asphalt or oil seeping into the ocean near Carpenteria. But such instances were so trivial that they had no effect upon the environment. Not until the last half of the 19th century did pollution become pronounced.

One of the most dramatic examples was occasioned by hydraulic mining,♦ in which large, heavy-powered hoses washed away hillsides, dumping debris into rivers that flowed into the Sacramento Valley and rendering their water unfit for animals or humans to drink or to use for irrigation. It also poisoned fish and spread detritus over agricultural lands. The result was a feud between farmers and miners which was finally settled when Judge Lorenzo Sawyer ruled (1884) that tailings could not be disposed of in rivers, thus effectively terminating the hydraulic process. Nevertheless, twenty-five years or more passed before the damage to the land was eradicated.

Also, from the earliest days of their settlement, Americans filled in San Francisco Bay along the city's shoreline, and even after the earthquake of 1906 they were still busily quarrying the east side of Telegraph Hill. The Bay was further damaged by the discharge of open sewage and of industrial wastes, so that the oyster beds and native crab and shrimp were contaminated and then died out. The huge population growth, great economic expansion, and vastly increased industrialization of the state in the 20th century tremendously compounded the problems of pollution.

The seriousness of smog was first evident in Los Angeles on July 26, 1943. Its effect over the following years on the quality of life in the state and on farm products led to the creation of local and regional smog control districts, as well as the regulation of motor vehicles. Similarly, the growing pollution of wells and of ocean, bay, river, and lake waters was made dramatically evident in midcentury by the incident at Montebello (1947) when that Los Angeles County town had its water supply poisoned by a toxic weed killer which had been dumped down a drain and had then seeped into household well waters. The legislature in 1967 created a state water quality board and nine regional ones. Federal aid was increased, and public concern manifested itself through such organizations as Save San Francisco Bay Association (founded in Berkeley, 1961), which worked to stop the filling of the Bay because the fill had impaired the capacity to handle sewage properly. The organization was instrumental in the creation of the state's Bay Conservation and Development Commission (1965). The state also made agreements with Nevada to control sewage disposal into Lake Tahoe.

Meanwhile, concern over the wide and growing use of pesticides prompted regulations to prevent the continued harm to fish and birds that had almost eliminated the pelican along the ocean shores. The spill of oil♦ from offshore drilling into the Santa Barbara Channel (1969) dramatized the dangers of pollution and led to the formation of citizens' groups such as GOO (Get Oil Out) and the concern of foundations like California Tomorrow.♦ New legislative action was also engendered by the increased interest in the environment, and in state and local elections voters were presented with propositions on diverse issues related to pollution, including the limitation of power plants for nuclear energy.

Pomegranate, fruit whose seeds were carried to California on the Sacred Expedition♦ (1769). The crop remained small for centuries; even as late as 1910 the state had only 1,800 bearing trees. The crop increased about tenfold later in the century. In 1970 the state marketed 3,600 tons, worth $418,000, accounting for most of the U.S. supply.

POMEROY, EARL (1915–   ), historian of the Far West, born and educated in California, has been a professor at the University of Oregon (1949–76) and the University of California, San Diego (1976–   ). His books include *In Search of the Golden West* (1957), which is about tourists in the western U.S., and *The Pacific Slope* (1965).

Pomo, Indians resident in village communities of the Russian River valley and in nearby parts of Mendocino, Lake, and Sonoma counties and in small parts of Colusa and Glenn counties. They held land communally for hunting, fishing, and food gathering, and practiced the Kuksu cult.♦ The ancient population (about 8,000), which was split into seven divisions with distinct languages, had about 75 principal villages. The 1910 census counted 1,200 Pomo. Besides weaving fine baskets, they made money for themselves and for neighboring tribes from ground and polished clam shells and magnesite beads. A vocabulary of their language was compiled by Father Engelhardt.♦ In 1970 they had seven reservations, on which most of them lived.

Pomona, city in Los Angeles County, appropriately named for the Roman goddess of fruit because it was early a center for citrus growing. It has long been merged into the urban complex of Los Angeles, and although the county's huge annual fair (since 1922) is held there, and the California State Polytechnic University breeds and displays Arabian horses, it is now known also for manufacturing missiles and airplane parts. The site of the Palomares Adobe (c.1837) is on a former *rancho* of the family of that name. In 1970 the city had a population of 87,384.

Pomona College, see *Claremont Colleges.*

PONIATOWSKI, ANDRÉ, see *Sperry, Simon Willard.*

Pony Express, began on April 3, 1860, to carry mail swiftly to California from its starting point, St. Joseph, Mo. The route (1,966 miles) in general followed the Oregon Trail but went south to Salt Lake and through Carson City and Placerville to end at Sacramento. The riders changed mounts at stations about 15 miles apart, though the young men themselves were relieved at less frequent intervals. The service at first was weekly, then semi-weekly. In summer the trip took 10½ days. The fastest trip—6 days—from Fort Kearny, Neb., to Fort Churchill, Nev. (then the two telegraph termini), carried the news of Lincoln's assassination. The express lasted a little over 18 months, until the completion of a transcontinental telegraph (Oct. 24, 1861). Initially the postage was $10 an ounce, later reduced to as low as $2. Wells, Fargo had a local pony express (1852 ff.) for the mining towns alone, operated the Salt Lake–Sacramento part of the transcontinental enterprise (April–Oct. 1861), created its own line between San Francisco and Placerville (July–Oct. 1861), and had an express between Virginia City and Sacramento (Aug. 1862–March 1865).

Poplar, tree that grows widely throughout California where water is available. Its varieties include the *aspen,*♦ found in the Sierra; the *black cottonwood,* found at elevations below 9,000 feet, which can grow to 125 feet with a 6-foot trunk, thus providing good lumber; and the *Fremont cottonwood,* found along valley rivers and streams and up to 3,000-foot elevations, which reaches a height of 75 feet and a diameter of 2 feet, and is valued for preventing soil erosion of river banks. The Spanish word for poplar, *alamo,* is often found as a place-name, particularly in desert areas, where cottonwoods were both landmarks and indicators of water, e.g. the Alamo River, which runs from the Salton Sea east of El Centro to Mexico.

Poppy, wildflower native to California and once quite widespread. Adelbert von Chamisso♦ named it *Eschscholtzia californica* in honor of Johann Friederich Eschscholtz, the surgeon on the same Russian expedition that brought him to California (1816). In 1903 the state legislature, noting that its golden color symbolized the mineral wealth and the sunshine of the state, named it the state flower. A Poppy Preserve is located in Antelope Valley.♦

Population, at the time of U.S. occupation California had fewer than 100,000 Indians and perhaps some 14,000 *gente de razón.* The gold rush made California cosmopolitan, created cities like San Francisco and Sacramento, and moved people inland into the Sierra mushroom towns which grew rapidly and were as quickly deserted—examples of the state's tendency to internal migration.♦ A decade later, at the time of the first census (1860), over half the people lived in the Sacramento Valley or in nearby mining regions and about a quarter in the San Francisco Bay area. The southern part of the state was little changed from Mexican days, with Los Angeles, its largest community, claiming only 4,385 to San Francisco's 56,802 out of the total of almost 308,000. Even by 1880, when the state had 864,694 people, almost two-thirds of them

lived north of the Tehachapis. But in that decade with the development of railroads and rate wars to attract residents, Los Angeles mushroomed from 12,000 in 1884 to 50,000 in 1887.

In the 20th century California's population growth was at least twice that of the rest of the nation, with southern California♦ growing ever larger because of successive booms (tourism, citrus growing, oil production, motion picture production) until in the 1920s it surpassed northern California.♦ The population of the state more than doubled in the first two decades, from 1,485,053 in 1900 to 3,426,861 in 1920. That was a prelude to the growth that continued to the early 1970s, when for the first time it temporarily tapered off to match the rate of the nation at large. The boom of the war years and the two decades thereafter brought about a near tripling of population, from 6,907,387 in 1940 to 19,953,134 in 1970, by which time it had surpassed New York to become the most populous state of the union. Over 7,000,000 of these people lived in Los Angeles County, and about 60% of all the state's people lived in its eight southernmost counties. In 1970 the state contained nearly 10% of all Americans. Of them, about 89% were white (of whom 15.5% had Spanish surnames), and about 7% were black. U.S. Census estimates of July 1, 1977, showed a 9.6% increase to 21,896,000. (See the Chronological Index for more population figures.)

Porciúncula, name for the Los Angeles River, abbreviated by Costansó (1770) from that which Portolá gave to it (1769)—*Nuestra Señora la Reina de los Ángeles del Rio de Porciúncula*—when he camped by it on the feast day (Aug. 2) of Our Lady of the Angels of the Portiuncula Chapel of the Franciscan order near Assisi, Italy. On the other hand, in common parlance the pueblo♦ soon came to be called simply Los Angeles, though named for the river and for the Virgin (la Reina) rather than for the angels.

Port Chicago, 20th-century industrial settlement on the south shore of Suisun Bay. A U.S. Navy ammunition depot and two Liberty ships it was loading blew up (July 17, 1944) there, killing 322 people and injuring many more.

Port Costa, site on Carquinez Strait once used for the oceanic shipment of grain brought from the Central Valley in small boats. Large ferryboats also plied the strait, carrying entire railroad trains. The present town recalls its past in antique stores and other appeals to tourists.

PORTER, Bruce (Edmund Cushman Porter) (1865–1953), a member of San Francisco's Les Jeunes.◆ He helped interest his friend Frank Norris in mystical phenomena and was a contributor to the city's cultural life. He married the daughter of William James (1917). His artistic activities included landscape designing, painting of murals, and creation of stained glass windows.

PORTER, R[obert] Langley (1870–1965), Canadian-born doctor, in 1891 went to California, where he served on the faculty of Stanford University, then as Dean of the Medical School of the University of California in San Francisco. His contributions to psychiatric treatment led the latter university to name its institute in this field in his honor.

Porterville, city in Tulare County, founded (1864) as a stage stop and market center for the nearby agricultural area of orange, fruit, vegetable, and cotton growing and dairy ranching. Its residents have included authors Dorothy and Howard Baker and basketball star Bill Sharman. In 1970 it had a population of 12,602.

Port Hueneme, seaport town with a fine harbor, south of Oxnard, bears the name of a Chumash village, given to it in 1856. It is the only deep-water port between San Francisco and Los Angeles. A major armed forces shipping point in World War II, it is the base for the Naval Construction Battalion (Seabees), and just south, at Point Mugu, is a naval Air Missile Test Center. The town itself is a fish canning and citrus packing center and has a major commercial fishing port. Leading early settlers included A. Levy.◆ The population in 1970 was 14,295.

Portland cement, see *Cement.*

PORTOLÁ, Gaspar de (c. 1723–86), first Spanish governor of the Californias, was born in Catalonia of a noble family. After military service in Italy and Portugal as a captain of dragoons, he was appointed governor of Baja California (1767), where he was assisted in the transfer of the missions from the Jesuits to the Franciscans.

In 1769 he volunteered to command the expeditionary force planned by *Visitador-General* José de Gálvez to found settlements in Alta California and thus secure the area, increase the revenues of New Spain, and bring the Christian faith to the Indians. The Sacred Expedition◆ was split into four parties: two traveled by sea, on the *San Carlos*

(departed Jan. 10) and the *San Antonio* (departed Feb. 15), and two by land, under the separate commands of Capt. Fernando Rivera y Moncada and Portolá, who left on March 24 and May 15, respectively.

Portolá was the last to reach San Diego (June 29, 1769), and on July 14 he led a party north in search of Monterey Bay, the existence of which was known from Vizcaíno's report. He sent the *San Antonio* south to San Blas for supplies and left behind the exhausted or sickly members, including Junípero Serra, who, at San Diego, soon founded the first mission. Portolá's party, on reaching Monterey Bay, did not recognize it, and so continued north, arriving at the Gulf of the Farallones on Oct. 31. On Nov. 2, 1769, Sgt. Ortega and others discovered San Francisco Bay, but Portolá and his men, wearied by the hardships of their journey, did not appreciate the discovery.

They returned to San Diego Jan. 1770 and would have gone back to Mexico except for the determination of Serra, who insisted that the needed supplies would arrive in time to save them. Thereupon Portolá made a second trek north, arriving at Monterey Bay May 24. Mission Carmel and the presidio of Monterey were founded there on June 3. As commander in Alta California Portolá was its governor (*gobernante*) from March 1769 to July 1770, although Matías de Armona◆ technically carried the title.

Portolá left Lt. Fages in temporary command of the garrison at Monterey and embarked on the *San Carlos* for San Blas. He then went to Mexico City, where he was hailed as a hero and promoted to lieutenant-colonel. In 1777 he was appointed governor of Puebla, his last post in New Spain, and in 1785 he returned to his homeland.

Portola Valley, rural residential community in San Mateo County, once a lumbering area. It is named for the region's early explorer but pronounced in an American style. Early residents included Andrew S. Hallidie,◆ the inventor of the cable car, who built an aerial tramway to his isolated home.

Portsmouth Square, San Francisco park, originally named the Plaza of Yerba Buena. It is bounded by Clay, Washington, and Kearny streets and an alley (Brenham Place) just below Grant Ave. and was the Mexicans' site for the town's custom house. The plaza was originally almost on the waterfront, and John B. Montgomery anchored the U.S.S. *Portsmouth* nearby (July 8, 1846) when he took possession of the settlement for the U.S. Hence its modern name. To memorialize Robert Louis Stevenson, who often sat there, the little square contains a monument (1897) with a granite plinth, designed by Bruce Porter, which is incised with some of the author's text, and is topped by a bronze sailing ship sculpted by George Piper. The square has been redesigned, with a garage beneath it and a large hotel intruding upon it. It is now mainly used as a recreational area for the Chinese who live nearby.

Ports O' Call Village, tourist attraction at the port of Los Angeles, founded in 1962. It consists of winding lanes along which have been built facsimiles of buildings modeled on those of New Bedford, Mass., and various other seaports. Shops and restaurants occupy them.

Portuguese in California, at first were explorers, in keeping with the tradition of Henry the Navigator (1394–1460). Cabrillo,♦ the European discoverer of California, and Cermeño♦ were both Portuguese, though they sailed Spanish vessels. Extensive settlement began during the gold rush, yet the Portuguese did not go to the mines. Instead they went into commercial fishing. Initially, they were whalers, but then developed the tuna catching and canning business. Many became truck farmers and dairymen around San Leandro, and J. B. Avila, who was born in the Azores, introduced those islands' native crop, the sweet potato, and came to be called the "Father of the Sweet Potato Industry." Many other settlers also came from the Azores rather than from Portugal's mainland.

Postsecondary Education Commission, see *Coordinating Council for Higher Education.*

Potash, potassium oxide, a brittle gray mineral, is mined in California only at Searles Lake,♦ in the Mojave Desert. That deposit, which has been exploited since 1916, contributes less than 10% of the nation's output; it is used mainly in fertilizers for farming.

Potatoes, staple vegetable not brought to California by the founding padres of the missions but by La Pérouse♦ (1786) who had discovered them in Chile. Thereafter potatoes were cultivated at the missions as a basic food, and later they were extensively raised for the people who came with the gold rush. Ten Burbank potatoes, the first of Luther Burbank's creations, were taken by him to California

(1857) as his basic capital. In this century California has been a major grower of a late spring potato crop in Kern County. Other important potato raising areas are Tulare, Madera, Fresno, and Kings counties. For a time George Shima♦ controlled the potato market. In 1970 the crop was grown on 87,500 acres and was worth $98,880,000. The sweet potato (introduced by the Portuguese♦) in 1970 was grown on 7,800 acres and the crop was worth $6,492,000.

Potato King, see *Shima, George.*

Poultry, reared from the mission days in California, did not become a large commercial undertaking until after 1875, when a Canadian, Lyman C. Ryce, invented an incubator and brooder in Petaluma. That Sonoma County city later became the great center for poultry production; it advertised itself as "The World's Egg Basket." Poultry farms abound through the state, particularly in southern California. In 1969 there were almost 50,000,000 chickens and about 1,245,000 turkeys raised, and about 8,380,000 eggs produced. In the 1970s the state ranked first in number of chickens raised and second in number of turkeys.

POWELL, H. M. T. (*fl.* 1849–52), diarist who chronicled his overland trek from Greenville, Ill., via Santa Fe to San Diego (1849–50), thence to San Francisco, the mines, and home by ship to the Isthmus. His text is accompanied by his own fine sketches of Los Angeles (the first known drawings of the town), San Diego, Santa Barbara, and several missions. It was first published as *The Santa Fe Trail to California,* in a lavish edition printed by The Grabhorn Press for The Book Club of California (1931).

POWELL, Lawrence Clark (1906–), chief librarian of the University of California at Los Angeles (1944–61) and founding dean (1960–66) of its School of Library Service. He is known for his enthusiastic dedication to books. His own essays have been published in such volumes as *Islands of Books* (1951), *A Passion for Books* (1959), and *Books in My Baggage* (1960). He has also written many literary studies, including his doctoral thesis at the University of Dijon (1932), one of the first works on Robinson Jeffers; *Southwestern Book Trails* (1963); and *California Classics* (1971).

POWELL, William J. (1802?–48), naval surgeon aboard the sloop of war *Warren* in the conquest of

California (1846). Near Portsmouth Square he founded a sanitarium for sailors, and a San Francisco street was named after him.

POWERS, STEPHEN (1840–1904), born in Ohio and graduated from the University of Michigan (1863), was a newspaper reporter. He toured Europe before he embarked on a trek, walking from North Carolina to San Francisco (1868). For the next six years he traveled part of California on foot; engaged in ranching; studied Indian tribes; and published poems, stories, and articles about the Indians in the *Overland Monthly.* He served (1875–76) as "special commissioner" for Philadelphia's Centennial Exposition, collecting materials illustrative of California Indians. He then returned to his native state (1876). In 1884 he moved to Florida, where he died. His writings include *Afoot and Alone; A Walk from Sea to Sea* (1872) and *Tribes of California* (1877).

Prairie Creek State Park, see *Redwood National Park.*

Prairie schooner, name applied to an ox- or mule-drawn covered wagon♦ used to cross the plains. From a distance it looked rather like a ship at sea. This variant of the old Conestoga wagon was commonly used by parties en route to California during the gold rush and succeeding years.

Preparedness Day Parade, see *Mooney, Tom.*

President-General, chief official of California's missions. He was appointed by the apostolic college in Mexico, to which he belonged. Beginning in 1812 some of his powers were assumed by a Commissary Prefect appointed by the Commissary General of the Indies, a Franciscan resident in Spain. The Presidents-General were Serra (1769–84), Palóu (1784–85), Lasuén (1785–1803), Tapis (1803–12), Señán (1812–15, 1820–23), Payeras (1815–19), Sarría (1823–25), Durán (1825–27) Sánchez (1827–31), and Durán (1831–33). In the years just before and during secularization two Presidents served, one for the southern missions from San Miguel to San Diego (Durán, 1833–38, and Jimeno, 1838 ff.) and the other for the northern missions from Soledad to Sonoma (García Diego, 1831–35; González Rubio, 1835–43; and José Anzar, 1843 ff.). *(See also individual entries.)*

Presidios, frontier military fortifications built at strategic points to guard the land against foreign incursions and to protect neighboring missions from hostile Indians. There were four of them. They overlooked major ports, but were only simple enclosures for limited arms and poor garrison quarters, manned by no more than 400 soldiers during the Spanish period. They were at San Diego (1769), Monterey (1770), San Francisco (1776), and Santa Barbara (1782). Each had a chapel separate from its nearby mission.

Press and Union League Club, San Francisco social organization. An outgrowth of a club for newspapermen (est. 1888), it has long had members of other professions, and since 1973 it has admitted women.

PREUSS, CHARLES (1803–54), German-born cartographer who accompanied Frémont on his first expedition to the Rockies and his first to California (1843–44). He also drew the map of Oregon, California, and the Rockies to which Frémont's *Geographical Memoir* served as text. His recollections of exploring with Frémont were published in 1958; they also briefly describe his participation in Frémont's disastrous fourth expedition.

PRÉVOST, LOUIS, see *Silk.*

PRICE, NIBS (CLARENCE MERLE PRICE) (1891–1968), athletic coach at the University of California, Berkeley (1919–54). First he coached football (one of his teams went to the Rose Bowl), then basketball (six of his squads won Pacific Coast Conference titles).

Prickly pear, see *Cactus.*

PRIESTLEY, HERBERT I[NGRAHAM] (1875–1944), professor of Mexican history at the University of California, Berkeley (1917–44), and a member of The Bancroft Library staff after 1912 and its director from 1940 to 1944. His works include *The Mexican Nation, A History* (1923).

Printing, see *Allen Press; Auerhahn Press; Bartlett, Washington; Book Club of California; Bosqui, Edward; Browne, Clyde; Doxey, William; Grabhorn Press; Kemble, John; Murdock, Charles; Nash, John Henry; Plantin Press; Ritchie, Ward; Roman, Anton; Taylor & Taylor; Wilson, Adrian;* and *Zamorano, Agustin.*

Prisons, state penal institutions. They include reception centers at Vacaville and Chino; a male maximum-security prison at Folsom (est. 1880); the state's oldest (1852) and largest prison for men at San Quentin, housing all men under sentence of death (reinstituted 1977); a minimum-custody institution at Chino for young men and first offenders; Deuel Vocational Institution, near Tracy, for males too young to be in adult institutions but too old for juvenile detention; the California Medical Facility at Vacaville; the Men's Colony near San Luis Obispo for persons needing psychiatric treatment and for the old and sick; a minimum-security prison farm near Soledad; the California Institution for Women near Corona; and a medium-security campus-like institution near Pleasanton for young women offenders. Prior to the creation of San Quentin, the state's prisoners were confined in dismantled ships anchored off Angel Island in San Francisco Bay.

Prizefighting, see *Boxing.*

Pro Bowl, annual All-Star professional football game played in the Los Angeles Memorial Sports Arena♦ each January at the end of the regular season. Begun in 1951, it initially was played by teams representing the Eastern and Western Conferences of the National Football League; later it pitted a team from the American Conference of the NFL against one from its National Conference.

PROCTOR, A[LEXANDER] PHIMESTER (1860–1950), Canadian-born sculptor and mountaineer. Reared in Colorado, he became famous for climbing Half Dome barefoot on his first trip to Yosemite (1884). A longtime resident of Palo Alto, he was a successful sculptor of animals and of frontier figures in a rugged style.

Progress and Poverty, economic treatise by Henry George♦ published in 1879. It argues that individual poverty increases even while the nation grows more prosperous because the benefits of social advance accrue to landlords and not to laborers. In order to have the community-created value returned to the community, George advocated a Single Tax amounting to most or the entirety of income gained through the appreciation of land values, thus also permitting the abolition of other taxes.

Progressive party, national political party, commonly called Bull Moose, founded in 1912. Theodore Roosevelt was its presidential candidate and Hiram Johnson his running mate, even though there was no formal third party organization in California. The Lincoln-Roosevelt League♦ backed it, and liberal Republican supporters included Edward A. Dickson, Francis J. Heney, Chester Rowell, and Harris Weinstock. In 1913 a state party was organized, and it was temporarily effective, but it began to dwindle away in 1916.

Promontory Point, see *Gold Spike.*

Prong-horned antelope, see *Antelope.*

Providence Mountains, a range located between desert valleys in northeastern San Bernardino County.

Provincias Internas, see *Neve, Felipe de.*

Prunes, dried sweet plums, were introduced to California by French-born miner and San Jose nurseryman Louis Pellier and his brothers (1856). This so-called French prune was dried without spoiling and without seed removal. The crop was initially centered in the Santa Clara Valley, where land used for its cultivation increased from 5,400 acres (1880) to a high of 171,400 acres (1929). In 1970 plum trees occupied about 97,900 acres, mainly in the Santa Clara, Sacramento, and Santa Rosa valleys; in Tulare, Fresno, and Kern counties; and in Placer County foothills. In 1970 the crop, worth about $57,400,000, represented over 90% of U.S. production.

Public Instruction, Superintendent of, see *Superintendent of Public Instruction.*

Pueblos, the earliest towns with civil governments, founded in keeping with the *Reglamento* of Gov. Felipe de Neve.♦ The towns attracted settlers *(pobladores)* by granting them land and supplies. Each town was governed by a civil officer, an *alcalde,*♦ and a board, an *ayuntamiento.*♦ Neve himself established San José de Guadalupe (present San Jose) in 1777 with 14 families from the Monterey and San Francisco presidios; it was the first pueblo in Alta California. It was followed the same year by El Pueblo de Nuestra Señora la Reina de Los Ángeles del Rio de Porciúncula (present Los Angeles). The third early pueblo was Branciforte,♦ founded in 1797. Other pueblos, all associated with neighboring missions, included San Luis Obispo (1772), San Juan Capistrano (1776), San Juan Bautista (1797), and Sonoma (1823). Early military towns were associated with presidios: San Diego (1769), Monterey (1770), San Francisco (1776), and Santa Barbara (1782).

Puma, see *Mountain lion.*

Publishing, see *Book publishing, Magazines, Newspapers,* and *Printing.*

Purísima Mission, see *La Purísima Concepción.*

"Purple Cow, The," poem by Gelett Burgess.♦ It was first published in *The Lark.*♦

Putah Creek, stream running through Lake, Napa, Yolo, and Solano counties. It was named after a branch of the Patwin Indians, though sometimes the name is mistakenly thought to have come from the Spanish word *puta,* meaning "harlot." Monticello Dam, which controls the creek, has created Lake Berryessa in Lake County.

PUTNAM, ARTHUR (1873–1930), Mississippi-born sculptor, went to San Francisco in 1894. There he was best known for his bronzes of mountain lions and pumas. He was also the creator of decorative designs ("The Winning of the West") for the standards of Willis Polk's electric light fixtures on Market St. and of a rakish plaster of Paris frieze of nude female dancers for a Barbary Coast bar. He taught Ralph Stackpole, and, like his pupil, he spent his last years in France.

Q

Quail, small game birds, of which there are three types in California. The *valley quail* (the official symbolic bird of the state) is by far the most common, found in about 70% of the state. It feeds on insects, weeds, and, occasionally, grain. The male is distinguished by a crest of five or six black feathers. The *mountain quail* lives in northern and mid-California coastal ranges and in mountains other than those in desert areas, and feeds mainly on berries. The male is distinguished by a long crest of two narrow black feathers. The *desert* or *southern gambel quail* resembles the *valley quail,* lives only in the southeastern part of the state, and feeds on leaves, twigs, shoots, buds, seeds, grain, and wild fruit. First hunted for food by the Maidu and, perhaps, the Salinan and Gabrieleño Indians, they were over-hunted for markets by post-gold-rush settlers despite a state limitation law (1852), but in more recent times hunting has been limited to certain seasons. Even so, during those times well over 3,000,000 are killed annually.

Quaking aspen, see *Aspen.*

Quartz mining, the extraction of gold from quartz veins, or lodes. It began in Mariposa (1849). The mined material had to be pulverized by a stamp mill, or *arrastre,*◆ and the gold then salvaged by a chemical process or a mechanical contrivance. It was most common after the late 1850s.

Queen Mary, former Cunard luxury liner. Since 1967 she has been docked at Long Beach as a tourist attraction. In the ship are a restaurant, a hotel, shopping facilities, and a Museum of the Sea.

Quicksilver, see *Mercury.*

Quincy, seat of Plumas County, named by its founder (1854) for his hometown in Illinois. Located in American Valley, it is near the old Feather River mining region.

Quintal, Spanish unit of weight used in early California, equal to 220.462 pounds.

Quivira, settlement sought by Coronado (1540) during his quest for the fabled Seven Cities of Cibola, has been identified with an Indian village in the Kansas-Nebraska region. A map by Abraham Ortelius (1564) placed it near the northwestern American coast and one by Mercator (1569) located it directly on the northwest coast close to the legendary Strait of Anián◆ in an area then generally considered an extension of California.

R

Rabbit, many varieties live wild in California. The *Washington snowshoe rabbit,* which inhabits the higher mountains of northern California and the Sierra south to Tuolumne County, is cinnamon-brown in summer and totally white in winter. All other types are black on their upper body and white underneath during fall, but their fur takes on different colors at other seasons. The main species include *black-tailed jack rabbit,* inhabiting open land in major valleys, coastal areas, and the deserts; *Audubon cottontail rabbit,* able to survive in almost equally various regions, found in the Central and Salinas valleys, on the coast south from Ventura County, and in the desert; *brush rabbit,* dwelling in chaparral or other dense cover along the coast and its ranges, and the western Sierra; *Nuttall cottontail rabbit,* an inhabitant of sagebrush land east of the Sierra; *pigmy rabbit,* found only where sagebrush dominates in the northeast of the state; and the *white-tailed jack rabbit,* at home above the timber line on the eastern side of the Sierra to Mt. Whitney. Many California Indians ate rabbits and used their fur for blankets, and some tribes (e.g., Paiute) even had a "rabbit boss" to lead hunts. The herbivorous animals were also commonly eaten by early settlers and miners, but their destruction of grain crops led farmers to hold great rabbit drives and killings, as dramatically depicted in Frank Norris' *The Octopus.* In the 20th century, rabbits have also been raised commercially for food and pelts.

Raccoon, small nocturnal carnivore, found throughout the state except in the extreme northwest and northeast, deserts, and highest mountains. Living near water, in daytime they generally inhabit hollows of trees. They feed on fowl, eggs, fish, fruit, grain, and garbage.

Radio, experimentation began with wireless broadcasting between San Pedro and Catalina Island (1901), soon followed by stations to transmit between San Francisco and Oakland, and by a San Jose station (1909). Stations and receiving sets remained primitive until the 1920s, when the medium became common and the industry grew great. Networks, both regional and national, were formed to broadcast major shows to numerous stations. Soon stars, sometimes also in motion pictures, became known for their special programs, which often originated from the regional center of drama, Hollywood. The heyday of radio ended in the 1950s with the advent of television.♦ Large network programs began to disappear early, but specialized programs (news accounts, various kinds of music, talk shows) were developed by separate stations, often directed to automobile drivers temporarily without access to televison. Despite the popularity of the newer medium, there were only about one-tenth as many televison stations as there were radio stations in 1970, the latter then numbering 4,319 AM and 2,184 FM stations.

Raiders, Oakland, professional football team, established (1960) as part of the American Football League, whose championship it won (1967), although it lost in the Super Bowl. In 1970 it joined the National Football League and won many Western Division championships, and in 1977 it won the Super Bowl.

Railroad land grants, territory within the public domain given by Congress (1862 ff.) to builders of transcontinental railroads, to encourage needed transportation and allow the railroads to sell land cheaply and thereby assist settlement. The land grants extended up to 20 miles on either side of the tracks and were divided in a checkerboard pattern to prevent monopolistic control of all territory by the recipient railroad. Congress also granted so-called lieu lands up to 20 miles farther out (or even elsewhere) when the original areas were already privately owned. All grants eventually came to the Central Pacific or Southern Pacific, giving them the reputation of an octopus throttling the state. This concept was illustrated most dramatically by the tragic shootout at Mussel Slough♦ (1880) and in Frank Norris' *The Octopus.*

Railroads, see *Central Pacific, Northwestern Pacific, Santa Fe, Southern Pacific, Union Pacific,* and *Western Pacific.*

Rainfall, occurs primarily between October and March but is most concentrated from December through February, since at other times of the year a high-pressure area prevails and sends toward the coast hot winds that deflect the moisture-filled ones moving onshore from the Pacific Ocean. Within this seasonal rainfall, great variation occurs between an annual average that runs as high as 80 inches in Del Norte and Humboldt counties, and as low as 3 inches in Imperial and eastern Riverside counties. This variation is caused not only by latitude but by distance from the ocean and elevation in the mountains. Nevertheless, rainfall can vary as much as 700% from year to year. One of the famous wet winters was that in which Sacramento received 36 inches in 1850, followed by less than 5 in 1851. The heaviest annual rainfall recorded was 153.54 inches in 1909 at Monumental, Del Norte County; the heaviest monthly was 71.54, also in 1909, at Helen Mine, Lake County; the heaviest in twenty-four hours was 16.71 in 1916 at Squirrel Inn, San Bernardino County. The longest drought was that in which no measurable rain was recorded at Bagda, San Bernardino County, between Oct. 3, 1912, and Nov. 8, 1914. Since the rainfall is heaviest in the northwest and the state's farmlands and largest population lie far to the south, elaborate projects of aqueducts, dams, and reservoirs have been devised to transfer the state's water.♦

Raisins, see *Grapes*.

RALSTON, WILLIAM C[HAPMAN] (1826–75), Ohio-born financier, moved to San Francisco (1854) and, having made a reputation in banking, a decade later founded the Bank of California with D. O. Mills♦ and others. He conducted its affairs so dramatically and so effectively that he made it the leading bank in the Far West and was himself made president of it (1872). His enthusiastic dedication to his adopted city, state, and region led him to finance on his own and with the bank's funds a great variety of businesses: steamship lines, railroads, mines in the Comstock Lode, the Palace Hotel, a theater, and woolen and silk mills. Thus, he was a leading power in the business world, but he was concomitantly a force in politics and cut a great social figure at his country estate in Belmont and elsewhere. He overextended himself and his bank in speculative financing, which became more extreme toward the end of his career as he attempted to recoup funds. Despite his reputation as a financial genius and the aid of other institutions and individuals intent on keeping his great bank secure, in August 1875 a run on its deposits forced it to close its doors. At that tense time he left for

a swim in the Bay, a frequent recreation of his, and was drowned. Whether this occurred by accident or design was never known, although after his death his questionable manipulation of funds was discovered, as was his own insolvency which left his estate deep in debt.

Ramona, romantic novel by Helen Hunt Jackson,♦ published in 1884. Set on the southern California ranch of Señora Moreno, it tells of the love between the Señora's adopted daughter, Ramona Ortegna, a half-Indian, half-Scottish girl, and Alessandro, a noble full-blooded Indian, and of their elopement, because of the Señora's refusal to allow Ramona to wed an Indian. They are driven from place to place by the marauding Americans who grab Indian land, and Alessandro is killed by one of them. Ramona and their child are found by Señora Moreno's son Felipe, who brings her home to the ranch that is now his since his mother's death; but after a brief, halcyon period he has to sell the ranch to the Americans and they emigrate to Mexico. The novel created a legend about the Ramona country and such sites as the one where this fictitious girl was wed. Myths were encouraged by local boosters like George Wharton James,♦ three motion picture versions, and an annual pageant by Garnet Holme staged outdoors at Hemet in Riverside County, as well as by communities named Ramona, such as one in San Diego County.

Ramparts (1962–76), San Francisco magazine established as a liberal Catholic lay journal, first quarterly, then bimonthly, and thereafter monthly. Financially unsuccessful, it lost its Catholic purpose, became increasingly radical, and concentrated on Cuba, civil rights, and Vietnam, while it also became interested in sensational exposés.

Rams, Los Angeles, professional football team, was the first major league sports team permanently established in California. It was transferred from Cleveland (1946). A member of the National Football League, whose championship it won (1951), it has also several times won the Western Division title.

Ranchería, special settlement for Indians, sponsored by a mission but lying some distance from it. It served as a kind of Indian reservation♦ with a church, but did not necessarily include cultivated land. The term is still used for Indian reservations in California.

Rancheros Visitadores, Los, men's social group of some 600 members, founded in Santa Barbara (1930). It holds an outing each May that includes a long horseback ride (highlighted by a blessing of men and mounts at Mission Santa Inés) conducted in the spirit of early California and cowboy life.

Ranch House Style, popular style of homes in the period following World War II, drawing upon a mixture of elements, in part from the real Mexican American ranch houses of the 19th century. The resemblances to the earlier versions included a one-story design, a sense of relation to the land, informal interior space, use of wood and stucco, and often a courtyard or a very limited employment of a covered walkway. However, instead of being large residences, the homes of the 20th century were often placed on small lots and duplicated in mass production for large-scale suburban real estate developments. From California the type spread to many other places.

Ranchos, large landholdings granted to individuals during Spanish and, later, Mexican rule. They were presented by the crown, later the state, either as a reward for loyal service or as a means of attracting settlers to undeveloped areas. An initial grant of a small piece of property near Mission San Carlos was made (1775) by Rivera y Moncada to a retired soldier, Manuel Butrón, but the system really began with three extensive grants made by Gov. Fages (1784) to three other retired soldiers: Juan José Dominguez (Rancho San Pedro, 43,000 acres); Manuel Nieto (Rancho los Nietos, all land between the Santa Ana and San Gabriel rivers from the mountains to the sea); and José María Verdugo (Rancho San Rafael, 36,000 acres from Arroyo Seco to Mission San Fernando). Each grantee had to build a permanent dwelling and farm or raise stock on the land, whose title remained with the crown.

Outright grants began in the Mexican era. Before secularization of the missions (1834), only 50 *ranchos* were created. In the next 13 years before American conquest, over 600 more grants were made, including, in the final year of 1846, 87 presented by Gov. Pío Pico, often to friends. In keeping with the Law of Colonization passed by the Mexican Congress (1824) to encourage settlement, an individual might petition for a square league (about 4,400 acres) of irrigated land, 4 leagues of land dependent on rainfall only, and 6 leagues for grazing cattle, i.e. a legal maximum of 11 square leagues, or 48,400 acres. To claim land, the peti-

tioner had to request property in the public domain, to define it by verbal description and a *diseño,*♦ and to show cause why he should receive it. On these bases the territorial assembly advised the governor of California, who made the final decision on the grant.

Thus were created great landholding families of *rancheros*—e.g. in the south: the Carrillos, with 320,000 acres; the de la Guerras, with 326,000 acres; and the Picos, with 532,000 acres; in the north, with comparable holdings, the Alvarados, Castros, Peraltas, and Vallejos. Foreigners—that is, Americans who had assumed Mexican citizenship and the Catholic faith, like William G. Dana, Henry Fitch, and Abel Stearns—became great landowners, too.

Most *ranchos* were located near the coast, often on old mission lands, even though the Law of 1824 prohibited grants within 10 leagues of the coast without special permission from the central government in Mexico City. All grants were suspect after the American conquest, despite the promise of the Treaty of Guadalupe Hidalgo to respect all Mexican land titles. The vague Mexican boundaries encouraged the rapacity of American settlers or squatters, whose claims to *rancho* lands were upheld in a report made by Henry W. Halleck,♦ later a lawyer for American land grant cases before the Land Commission created (1851) by a U.S. act sponsored by Sen. Gwin. Then the old *ranchos* were broken up and the *Californios* lost their large landholdings.

Rancho Santa Fe, small, fine residential settlement north of San Diego. Originally (1906) a eucalyptus tree farm of the Santa Fe Railroad, it was sold to a real estate promoter who created an elegant planned community (1920s) in the Spanish Colonial Revival style.

Rand Corporation, nonprofit organization located in Santa Monica which derives its name from R and D, an abbreviation of Research and Development. Founded (1946) as a U.S. Air Force project to continue the kind of planning conducted in World War II, it has been independent since 1948, but its programs of strategic planning and scientific research are carried out mainly for government agencies, from which it also receives most of its funding.

Rand Mountains, part of the so-called Rand District in eastern Kern County, named for the rich gold-mining Witwatersrand (nicknamed the Rand) of

347

South Africa. The Mojave Desert hill area was the site of a major gold discovery in 1895. A Desert Museum of mining is located in Randsburg.

RAPHAEL, Joseph (1872–1950), California-born painter, after study in Paris (1903 ff.) lived much of his life in Europe. He was also known for paintings and watercolors of California scenes in the Impressionist style.

Rattlesnake, see *Snake*.

Rattlesnake Dick, see *Barter, Richard*.

Raymond Hotel, elegant resort hotel of Pasadena (1886–95) run in conjunction with the Crawford House of New Hampshire, whose employees left that White Mountain resort to work in California during the winter.

READING, Pierson B[arton] (1816–68), New Jersey-born pioneer who moved to California with the Bartleson-Bidwell Party♦ (1845). He worked for Sutter as a clerk and head trapper and was active in the Bear Flag Revolt. As an explorer, he came to know present Tehama and Shasta counties, and got a large grant along the Trinity River on which he discovered gold. Although he once ran for governor (1851), the latter part of his life was spent as a rancher. Reading Peak in Lassen National Park is named for him; the city of Redding♦ is not.

REAGAN, Ronald (1911–), 33rd governor of the state (1966–75), born in Illinois, after graduating from college there, became a sports announcer in Iowa for five years until he moved to California and entered motion pictures (1937), later becoming a popular hero on screen and television. He served in the air force in World War II and was later president of the Screen Actors Guild for six terms, moving toward politics and the Republican party. He was elected governor without having held any previous political office, and both his first and second terms were marked by a conservative program emphasizing economy, particularly in the areas of higher education, social welfare, and medical aid. In 1976 he ran for the Republican presidential nomination and came close to capturing it from the incumbent, President Ford.

REALF, Richard (1834–78), English-born poet, went to the U.S. at the age of 20 and as a newspaperman was so impressed by the abolitionist John Brown that he became the secretary of state

in Brown's provisional government, set up in Canada (1858). Arrested after Brown's attack on Harpers Ferry, Realf later served as a U.S. Army officer in the Civil War. In 1878 he went to California in bad health and soon committed suicide in Oakland. His verse was posthumously collected as *Poems by Richard Realf, Poet, Soldier, Workman* (1898).

Reapportionment, has affected the Senate of the state more than the Assembly, although historically both have had their numerical representation based upon population as recomputed each decade. Although this resulted in much gerrymandering, it was considered an equitable procedure until the great growth of Los Angeles led politicians from some other areas to propose a new scheme. While the Assembly continued under the traditional form of representation, in 1926 a so-called Federal Plan reapportioned the Senate seats at no more than one to a county, with no more than three counties to a senatorial district. Because representation was thus by area rather than by population, this procedure created the greatest disparity of representation in the U.S. Los Angeles County, with a population of more than 6,000,000, had the same single vote as the district of Alpine, Mono, and Inyo counties, with a population of about 14,000. In 1964 the U.S. Supreme Court ruled that both houses of a state legislature must be apportioned on the basis of population, or "one-man/one-vote." Accordingly, in 1965 new senatorial districts were created with no more than a 15% deviation among them.

REBER, John (1887–1960), Ohio-born, self-taught engineer who conceived of the so-called Reber Plan to divide San Francisco Bay by earthwork dams (topped by highways and railways) to form a salt-water bay and two fresh-water lakes. The plan was seriously considered for some time.

Recall, governmental procedure to remove a public official from office by a popular vote invoked by a specified number of the electorate, was introduced to California mainly by Dr. John R. Haynes.♦ The first city in the world to incorporate this process in its charter was Los Angeles (1903). The Senate and Assembly enacted this procedure for the state (1911).

Recreation, activities carried on for pleasure, relaxation, play, and self-expression, have been not only very common but unusually varied in California because a generally pleasant climate and the choices of appealing terrain allow diverse outdoor pastimes to be pursued most of the year.

During the Spanish and Mexican periods, many recreational activities were related to horsemanship. The settlers were enthusiastic equestrians who enjoyed testing their skills in competitions, such as one requiring a galloping rider to seize a chicken half-buried in the ground and wrest it aloft by the neck. Another brutal entertainment involved pitting a bear and a bull against each other in a temporary arena.

The settlers of the early American period were often too busy or too tired from outdoor exertions to be attracted to recreations other than socializing at bars, gambling houses, and theaters. As arduous labor in mines and ranches came to be balanced by urban life, by more stable and increased wealth, and by greater leisure, Sunday outings to places like Woodward's Gardens were enjoyed, and even greater outdoor forms of recreation began to grow in popularity. The first formal track for horse racing was opened in San Francisco in 1850; by 1894 there were 40 in the state. Camping trips afforded economical vacations to scenic spots as early as the latter 1850s, and sporting outings on San Francisco Bay at the same time led to the organization of clubs to sponsor yachting. Fishing and hunting, initially carried on for individual need for food or for larger commercial purposes, also came to attract sportsmen. Similarly, skiing and mountaineering, once practical activities, began to be pursued for pleasure, although they did not become widely popular for some time.

Nevertheless, as the culture became more urban, simpler outdoor activities grew in popularity. In the 1880s bicycling became a national fad when equal-sized wheels and air-filled rubber tires made riding easy and allowed both men and women to enjoy the vogue of cycling in the city parks, where other forms of recreation were available, including visits to special events and exhibits, such as museums. Other special events included performances of music, ranging from opera and symphony to band concerts and jazz.

With the development of the automobile in the 20th century, recreation could consist simply of making excursions to various parts of the state. Concomitantly, organizations such as the California State Automobile Association and the Automobile Club of Southern California pressed for improved roads, while greatly increased numbers of sites were opened to visitors with the expansion of National and State Parks and Forests. More social and more

sedentary pastimes for the upper classes were provided by the creation of country clubs, the first and perhaps the most stylish located at Burlingame (1893). The clubs also fostered golf, tennis, and swimming, sports that soon came to have far greater followings at municipal links, courts, and pools.

Spectator sports also attracted great numbers of people, at first mainly to college football and basketball and to professional baseball, but in time all athletic competition in major sports had large audiences of enthusiastic fans. Other, though less frequently scheduled competitions that appealed to great crowds included boxing and rodeos. The largest steady box office attractions were motion pictures, although in time they came to feel the competition from radio and television programs that could be enjoyed at home.

Following World War II more emphasis was placed on outdoor activities, some of which were peculiarly Californian. A whole beach culture arose, and with it increased interest in water skiing and surfing, but wild rivers also appealed to people who enjoyed raft trips on the "white water" of the Stanislaus River and a stretch of the Sacramento. The long-standing emphasis on automobiles grew into a veritable car culture, which found expression in converted vans that became virtually residences on wheels, in campers and other recreational vehicles, in motorcycles, and in such specialties as dune buggies for beach and desert exploration. A simpler emphasis on mobility and one geared to a younger generation brought about the popularity of skateboarding. Far more venturesome and technologically sophisticated locomotion was represented by the many Californians who took up aviation for sport, experimented with sky diving, and even originated hang gliding. (*See also individual entries.*)

Red Bluff, seat of Tehama County, on the banks of the upper Sacramento River, grew up near the California-Oregon Trail and became a center for miners en route to the Trinity diggings and a shipping point for locally raised wheat, grapes, fruit, and lumber. Nearby an adobe (now part of a State Historic Park) was built by William B. Ide♦ (c. 1840s). In the late 1860s a house in town was occupied by the family of the late John Brown, the abolitionist of Harpers Ferry. The population in 1970 was 7,676.

Redding, seat of Shasta County, on the upper Sacramento River along the old California-Oregon

Trail. A former nearby town was named Reading for the pioneer Pierson B. Reading, but the present city was laid out by and named for B. B. Redding, a land agent of the Central Pacific Railroad (1872). It has long been a shipping center for farms, fruit orchards, and mines in the area. Shasta Dam is just to its north, and the Shasta-Trinity National Forest is nearby. In 1970 it had a population of 16,659.

Redlands, city in southwest San Bernardino County, named for the colored soil on which are raised citrus fruits and other crops. It is also a residential and manufacturing center, and located there are Redlands University,♦ a park of exotic plants, a Lincoln library, an outdoor bowl for concerts and theater, and the San Bernardino *Asistencia* of Mission San Gabriel. In 1970 the population was 36,355.

Redlands University, founded (1909) as a college in the city of Redlands by Baptists, it has grown to be a liberal arts institution, with a faculty of nearly 200 and a student body of almost 2,000 in 1970.

REDMOND, GRANVILLE (1871–1935), painter of California landscapes. Born in Philadelphia and reared in San Jose, he studied with Arthur Mathews and at the Académie Julien. He long lived in the Los Angeles area. A deaf mute, his canvases often depict unpeopled, quiet, bucolic scenes.

Redondo Beach, resort and residential community on southern Santa Monica Bay in Los Angeles County. It was the site of the first surfing♦ (1907) in California. In 1970 the city had a population of 56,075.

Red Pony, The, novelette by John Steinbeck,♦ published in 1937 as related stories in *The Long Valley.* It tells of a Salinas Valley farmboy, Jody, experiencing life as he cares for and loses his beloved red pony.

Redwood City, county seat of San Mateo County, founded in the 1850s, as the name indicates, as a lumber center and port. The Bay harbor now ships goods varying from its local cement to home-grown chrysanthemums. It is also the site of light industry and of Marine World, a tourist attraction. In 1970 it had a population of 55,686.

Redwood Empire, name coined in the 1920s by a tourist association and thereafter popularized to draw attention to the coastal area north from San Francisco to the state border and on to Grants Pass, Oregon, along what is called the Redwood Highway.

Redwood National Park, forest preserve of 58,000 acres between Crescent City and Orick (Del Norte and Humboldt counties), encompassing the separately administered Del Norte Coast, Jedediah Smith, and Prairie Creek state parks (27,468 acres). An additional 48,000 acres was added to the Park (1978) and a border area (30,000 acres) may be added if the Secretary of Interior and Congress find that adjacent timber cutting threatens the Park.

Redwoods, trees that grow in forests and groves of the Coast Range from Monterey north into Oregon (*Sequoia sempervirens*) and in the Sierra Nevada (*Sequoia gigantea*). Major stands in the former area include Muir Woods and in the latter, Yosemite and Wawona, Sequoia National Park, Mariposa, and Calaveras. The Sierra redwoods live longer (3,200 years maximum) than the coastal ones (2,200 years maximum) but both are outlived by the bristlecone pine (4,600 years maximum). However, they are the world's tallest trees, one having reached 367 feet. The first white man to see the coast redwoods was Crespí in 1769. Palo Alto, the lone tree near Stanford University, was named by Portolá. The Russians in the early 19th century were the first to grow seeds and seedlings abroad. Commercial logging, dating from the late mission period (some redwood was used in northern missions), has grown to an industry that in 1970 supported 20,000 workers and produced about $250,000,000 worth of materials. Conservation efforts dating back to the mid-19th century include the Save-the-Redwoods League, founded in 1918, instrumental in funding and creating over 135,000 acres of state parks, and the Sierra Club, which has been a leader in the campaign for a great national park. (*See also individual entries.*)

REESE, MICHAEL (1817–78), German-born financier who moved to San Francisco (1850), where he substantially increased his fortune. He was known as a miserly bachelor, but he did aid the University of California library, and his heirs contributed to a hospital in Chicago then named for him.

REEVES, DAN[IEL FARRELL] (1912-71), New York City financier who bought the Rams♦ football team of Cleveland and moved it to Los Angeles (1946) as the first major league professional sports team to go to the West Coast. He also developed the first full-scale scouting system and used television extensively to broaden interest in professional football.

Referendum, governmental procedure to submit legislatively enacted measures to confirmation or rejection by popular vote, was introduced to California mainly by Dr. John R. Haynes.♦ The first city in the world to incorporate the process in its charter was Los Angeles (1903). A state constitutional amendment (1911) allowed this procedure to be invoked upon demand of a petition signed by 5% of the electorate who voted in the preceding gubernatorial race.

REGAN, AGNES GERTRUDE (1869–1943), born in San Francisco of parents who were forty-niners, her father serving, as had her uncle, Richard Tobin, as secretary to Archbishop Alemany. She was for 30 years in the San Francisco public school system and then for 20 years the secretary of the National Council of Catholic Women.

Regidor, councilman in the Spanish system of local government, served with the leading civil officer, the *alcalde,* on the municipal board, the *ayuntamiento.*

Reglamento, see *Bucareli, Antonio,* and *Neve, Felipe de.*

Regulators, see *Hounds.*

REID, HUGO (1810–52), Scottish-born trader who went to California (1832) from Mexico and formed a firm with Jacob Leese♦ to trade local hides for imported manufactured goods. He married a cultivated Indian woman (a neophyte of Mission San Gabriel), served on the *ayuntamiento* of Los Angeles, became a large landholder of Rancho Santa Anita, and was a member of the Constitutional Convention of 1849. He wrote 22 "letters" about California Indians for the *Los Angeles Star* (1852).

REINHARDT, AURELIA [ISABEL] HENRY (1877–1948), San Francisco-born educator who, after graduation from the University of California (1898), a Ph.D. from Yale, translation of Dante's *De Monarchia,* and teaching English at the forerunner of the University of Idaho, became president of Mills College (1916–43). A feeble institution when

she took over, it was enormously enhanced by her dynamic energy and reputedly rather dictatorial manner.

Relocation camps, see *Japanese relocation centers.*

Representation, see *Reapportionment.*

Republic of California, see *Bear Flag Revolt* and *Alvarado, Juan B.*

Requa, town at the mouth of the Klamath River in southern Del Norte County, named for the clan of Indians still prominent in the mid-20th century. Jedediah Smith's starving party was fed by the Indians near there (1828).

Reservations, see *Indian reservations* and *rancherías.*

Resorts, see *Hotels* and *Spas*; also *Arlington Hotel, Coronado, Del Monte Hotel, Palm Springs,* and *Raymond Hotel.*

REVERE, JOSEPH WARREN (1812–80), native of Boston and grandson of Paul Revere, began a naval career in 1828, and in 1845 was assigned to California aboard the *Portsmouth.* He raised the U.S. flag at Sonoma and later, after resigning from the navy in 1850, was a rancher in that area, also serving as an agent for naval timber land and as a trader with Mexico. While in Mexico City (1851), he temporarily served in its army as a colonel and organized its artillery. At the outset of the U.S. Civil War, he entered the Union Army and rose to brigadier general, but after trial and dismissal for moving his ill-supplied forces to the rear at Chancellorsville, he was allowed by President Lincoln to resign. He is best remembered for *A Tour of Duty in California* (1849) and the anecdotal autobiography, *Keel and Saddle: A Retrospect of Forty Years of Military and Naval Service* (1872).

REXROTH, KENNETH (1905–   ), born in Indiana, moved around the country, and was generally self-educated. He settled in San Francisco (1927), where he has been a force in literary and general cultural movements. He was an older leader of the Beat movement♦ and has been allied with many other antiestablishment activities. His many publications include *The Art of Worldly Wisdom* (1949), surrealistic poems; *Natural Numbers: New and Selected Poems* (1964); *An Autobiographical Novel* (1966), a prose account of his youthful experiences;

Bird in the Bush (1959), essays; and *One Hundred Poems from the Chinese* (1956).

REYNOLDS, BOB (ROBERT REYNOLDS) (1914–), Oklahoma-born football player, was a tackle on the Stanford teams (1932–35) known as the Vow Boys.♦ His teams competed in the Rose Bowl three times, in two of which he played the entire 60 minutes.

REYNOLDS, MALVINA (1901–78), folk singer and radical crusader for social causes, born South of the Slot in San Francisco. A longtime resident of Berkeley, she was an active supporter of FSM and of anti-Vietnam War movements. Her songs included "Little Boxes," about "ticky-tacky" rows of houses spreading over the landscape, and were sung by Joan Baez and other leading vocalists.

REZANOV, NIKOLAI PETROVICH (1764–1807), a founder of the Russian-American Co. after youthful service in the army and as a civil administrator. Still in his twenties, he was sent by Catherine II to Siberia to investigate imperial expansion into the American Northwest. His mission led to the establishment of the Russian-American Co. to develop this area, and in 1803 he headed an expedition for the state and the company to open Japan to Russian trade, to investigate supply routes to the Russo-American posts by sea instead of through Siberia, and to put the company on a better footing. The voyage was a hard one. He had just lost a beloved wife, he and the ship's captain quarreled seriously, the year at sea was difficult, and he was imprisoned in Japan.

In August 1805 he finally visited the Alaskan colonial seat of New Archangel (modern Sitka), where he experienced a winter of scurvy and near starvation. Buying the American vessel *Juno,* he sailed south on a mission for food and diplomatic relations. He reached San Francisco in April 1806. His attractive personality not only made him an intimate of the initially suspicious commander of the presidio, Don José Argüello,♦ but captivated his 15-year-old daughter, Doña Concepción. As he made clear in his official report, Count Rezanov became engaged to her for reasons of state. Supplied with food received in trade for goods he had brought with him, Rezanov sailed in May to New Archangel and that fall went on to Okhotsk for return to his native St. Petersburg, but his poor health could not withstand the rigors of crossing Siberia, where he died aged 43.

Doña Concepción's long wait for him and her later life as a Dominican nun made her a romantic figure for such interpretations as one in a poem by Bret Harte and another in a fictionalized history by Gertrude Atherton.

RHODES, EUGENE MANLOVE (1869–1934), novelist noted for his depictions of ranch and range life of New Mexico, had brief associations with California as a student for two years at the University of the Pacific in San Jose and in the last three years of his life, when he moved to California for his health.

RHODES, WILLIAM H[ENRY] (1822–76), born in North Carolina, educated at Princeton, after graduation from Harvard Law School (1846) practiced law in his native state, in Texas, and in California, to which he moved in 1850. There he also continued the writing begun with *The Indian Gallows and Other Poems* (1846) by contributing to the *Golden Era* under the name Caxton and writing science fiction stories like "The Case of Summerfield" (1871). His writings were gathered posthumously as *Caxton's Book* (1876).

RICCI, RUGGIERO (1920–), San Francisco-born child prodigy, came to prominence as a violinist in the wake of Yehudi Menuhin's success. Since his New York debut (1929) he has been an internationally recognized concert violinist.

Rice, cultivation was attempted as early as 1860, but the first successful crop was not grown until 1912 in Biggs (Butte County). Large-scale planting began just before American entry into World War I, with 60,000 acres producing 1,800,000 bags in 1916. This rose to 247,000 acres yielding 7,000,000 bags by 1946. Heavy clay lands in Butte, Colusa, Glenn, Sutter, Yolo, and Yuba counties in the Sacramento Valley and Fresno, Kern, Merced, San Joaquin, and Stanislaus counties in the San Joaquin Valley hold irrigation water well for rice cultivation. The two varieties of rice grown in California are pearl (short grain), whose seed came from Japan, and Calrose (medium grain), locally developed and by the 1970s accounting for 60% of the crop. In 1970 the production from 331,000 acres was valued at nearly $90,000,000. Three-quarters of the crop is handled through two marketing cooperatives: the Rice Growers Association of California (est. 1921) and the Farmers Rice Cooperative (est. 1924), both with headquarters in Sacramento. A major portion of California's rice production is shipped to Puerto Rico and South Korea. Rice accounts for 30% of all tonnage shipped from Sacramento.

RICHARDS, Bob (Robert F. Richards) (1926–   ), Illinois-born track star, while a faculty member at La Verne College and an ordained minister, competed as a pole vaulter in the Olympic Games of 1948, 52 and 56, placing first in the latter two. His own record was 15', 7" (1957). He was also U.S. champion in the decathlon (1951, 54, and 55). In 1955 Reverend Richards won the Sullivan Award as the outstanding amateur athlete of the U.S.

RICHARDSON, Friend William (1865–1943), 25th governor of the state (1923–27), born of a Quaker family (hence his first name) in Michigan. They moved to San Bernardino, where he later began his newspaper publishing career. His one-term administration was noted for its conservative opposition to the Progressive wing of the Republican party and for its great emphasis on business-like economies. A redwood-forested State Park in southernmost Humboldt County was named for him.

RICHARDSON, Mary Curtis (1848–1951), New York City-born painter, moved to San Francisco (1850), studied under Virgil Williams, and became known for her portraits and for outdoor scenes in the Impressionist idiom.

RICHARDSON, William A[ntonio] (1795–1858), went to San Francisco from his native England as first mate on a whaler (1822), stayed, was baptized a Catholic, married the daughter of the presidio *comandante,* Ignacio Martínez, and adapted her given name, Maria Antonia, for his middle one. Vallejo appointed him Captain of the Port (1835–44), and he built the first habitation (a tent and later a board house, 1835, then an adobe, 1836) in the present city, then called Yerba Buena, at the site of the present Grant Ave. between Clay and Washington streets. His large Rancho Saucelito ("willow grove" in Spanish) bordered on the bay named for him, whose entrance is flanked by the modern town of Sausalito◆ and Tiburon in Marin County.

Richardson Bay, see *Richardson, William A.*

Richmond, city of Contra Costa County, an industrial and shipping center on San Francisco Bay. Founded when the Santa Fe Railroad selected it as the western terminus (1899), it grew enormously during World War II when Henry J. Kaiser established shipyards there that launched nearly 750 vessels. It remains a shipping, warehousing, manu-

facturing, and oil refinery center. A separate cove, Point Richmond, has a fine settlement of residential homes, many occupied by professors from Berkeley. The city is also the terminus of the Richmond San Rafael Bay Bridge (opened 1956). In 1970 the city had a population of 79,043.

Richter Scale, see *Earthquakes.*

RICKETTS, Edward (1896–1948), operator of a small commercial marine biological laboratory on Cannery Row, Monterey, and friend of John Steinbeck, whose ideas he influenced. His study of marine life, *Between Pacific Tides* (1939), preceded the trip he and Steinbeck made into the Gulf of California, which they wrote about in *Sea of Cortez* (1941) and, with a tribute to his friend, in *The Log from the Sea of Cortez* (1951).

RIDGE, John R[ollin] (1827–67), Georgia-born son of a leading Cherokee Indian and a white woman, after a turbulent youth moved to California (1850) during the gold rush. There he drifted into journalism, writing poems and articles for the *Golden Era* and *Hesperian* signed "Yellow Bird," a translation of his Indian name. His best-known work was *Life and Adventures of Joaquin Murieta* (1854), a romantic fictional treatment of a Mexican bandit of the gold mines whom he made into a noble Robin Hood, a character also enhanced by the illustrations of C. C. Nahl that accompanied the pamphlet. In later years Ridge supported the Confederacy in his writings. His romantically conventional *Poems* were posthumously collected (1868).

Ridge Route, twisting part of the Los Angeles to Bakersfield highway, extending 48 miles between Castaic and the Grapevine◆ on a mountainous crest of the Tehachapis. Opened in 1915, it was superseded (1933) by the first route of Highway 99.

RIEGELS, Roy (1908–   ), football player who was center on the University of California, Berkeley, team (1927–29) and its captain. A fine player, he is remembered for a bizarre incident during the Rose Bowl game against Georgia Tech (1929) in which he recovered a fumble and by mistake ran 60 yards toward his own goal, was finally turned around a yard from it by a teammate, and there downed. In the next play, Georgia Tech made a safety goal that provided the winning point in the game. He later became a high school coach.

Riffles, see *Placer mining.*

RIGGS, BOBBY (ROBERT LARIMORE RIGGS) (1918–), Los Angeles-born tennis star, was the U.S. singles champion (1939, 1941) and the singles, men's doubles, and mixed doubles champion of England (1939). He turned professional (1941) and became the top-ranked player (1946–47). At the age of 55 he returned to prominence by challenging younger leading professional women tennis players, climaxed by a match (1973) against Billie Jean King♦ that became a *cause célèbre* for women's liberation as well as for tennis when she defeated him in straight sets.

RIGNEY, BILL (WILLIAM JOSEPH RIGNEY) (1919–), baseball player and manager, born in Oakland, became an infielder with the Giants (1946–53) and their manager (1956–60, 1976), and was manager of the Los Angeles Angels (1961–69) and the Minnesota Twins (1970–72).

RILES, WILSON (1917–), born in backwoods Louisiana, orphaned at 11, as a boy moved to Arizona to be with relatives, and there, after college, became a public school teacher and administrator. Moving to Los Angeles (1954), he joined California's Department of Education and, as the first black elected to a state constitutional office, became the Superintendent of Public Instruction♦ (1971).

RILEY, BENNET (1787–1853), 7th American military governor of California (April 12-Dec. 20, 1849), after a distinguished military career, particularly in the Mexican War, was made commander of the Pacific Division and therefore ex officio governor of California. Unlike his predecessor, Persifor Smith, he assisted civil government, calling for a convention to create a constitution in anticipation of a territorial government, and divided California into ten districts for representation. After the convention Riley called for a gubernatorial election, won by Peter Burnett, his former appointee as judge for San Francisco, who succeeded him as civil authority. Riley's given name is often misspelled "Bennett."

Rim of the World Drive, mountainous road in San Bernardino County, winding for 40 miles to give panoramic views of Lake Arrowhead, Big Bear Lake, and other sights.

Rincon Hill, site south of Market St. in San Francisco, named from the Spanish word meaning "a small sequestered piece of land." First settled in 1849, it became in the next two decades a stylish residential area, like the adjacent South Park,♦ for business leaders including William C. Ralston and Henry Miller. It was esteemed because it was freer of low-lying fogs and close to but removed from the business district. Cut away to let a street through (1866), it was already a poor neighborhood when Jack London was born nearby. C. W. Stoddard lived there and R. L. Stevenson visited him (1879), as the elite had moved on the new cable cars up to Nob Hill. The hill almost disappeared when approaches to the Bay Bridge covered it in 1936.

RINDGE, FREDERICK HASTINGS (1857–1905), Massachusetts-born rancher, owner of the great *rancho* of Malibu,♦ of which he wrote warmly in *Happy Days in Southern California* (1898) and which was kept mainly as a private estate by his widow, May, almost until her death in 1941.

RIPLEY, ROBERT [LEROY] (1893–1949), journalist and cartoonist, born in Santa Rosa, in 1918 created his newspaper feature, "Believe It or Not," setting forth unusual and tantalizing facts. It was widely syndicated and gathered into books, and its title became a popular expression. Ripley is buried in Santa Rosa, and a Ripley Memorial Museum located there is made of redwood cut from a single tree.

RITCHIE, WARD (1905–), Los Angeles typographer, after graduating from Occidental College and learning to print at the press of Clyde Browne,♦ went to Paris to study further with François-Louis Schmied (1930–31). Returning to California, he then collaborated on the Primavera Press and founded the Ward Ritchie Press (1932), which soon became and remained a leading Los Angeles fine printing firm for limited editions and some larger commercial publications.

RIVERA, DIEGO (1886–1957), Mexican mural painter who visited San Francisco (1934), where he influenced local painters to work on frescoes, of which he contributed several examples, including one in the San Francisco Art Institute. He later painted mural panels for the City College of San Francisco (1940) that were finally installed in its theater in 1961.

RIVERA Y MONCADA, FERNANDO (1711–82), captain of the garrison at Loreto (Baja California) sent (March 24, 1769) by *Visitador-General)*

Gálvez to lead a company of cuirrasiers, accompanied by Father Crespí, to march north for the establishment of missions and presidios in Alta California. His contingent in this Sacred Expedition◆ was soon followed by a comparable one under Portolá, the major commander. Having become the first leader of an overland party to reach Alta California, he accompanied Portolá to Monterey and was then sent back to Baja California for supplies. In 1774 Rivera y Moncada returned and replaced Fages as military *commandante* of Alta California when the latter quarreled with Serra. Although he thus became the successor to Fages as governor, Rivera y Moncada did not heal the breach with the missionaries and was not an able administrator. Serra excommunicated him (1776) when he entered the church at San Diego to seize an Indian who had taken sanctuary there after it was assumed he was the leader of those who had destroyed the mission and killed its padre. In 1777 Rivera was replaced by Felipe de Neve and returned to Loreto to become lieutenant governor of Baja California. On a later overland expedition to Alta California, he was killed by Yuma Indians.

Rivers, basic sources of the elaborate system for the distribution of water in California, are far more plentiful in the upper part of the state than the lower. Important rivers in the north include the Klamath, Smith, Mad, Eel, Trinity, Pit, and McCloud. The major river of the state, the Sacramento, flows south from Siskiyou County to Suisun Bay. Its tributaries include the McCloud, Pit, Feather, Yuba, Bear, and American rivers. South of the Delta, into which flows the Mokelumne River, the great river is the San Joaquin, and into it flow the Calaveras, Stanislaus, Tuolumne, Merced, Chowchilla, Fresno, and Kings rivers. Other major rivers of California include the Russian, Salinas, Truckee, Kern, Kaweah, Santa Ynez, Mojave, Santa Ana, and San Gabriel, and on the southeastern border of the state lies the Colorado River. *(See also individual entries.)*

Riverside, seat of Riverside County, in whose northwest corner it lies, dates back to the Indians whose nearby pictographs are still visible and to Anza's crossing of the Santa Ana by his bridge there (1774). It was later part of Don Juan Bandini's Rancho Jurupa. Settlement began with the silk making colony of Louis Prevost (1869), followed by a canal and township development with the present name (1871). It was initially an agricul-

tural center, particularly of citrus ranches where the navel orange◆ was developed. The city has grown rapidly, particularly since 1950, to become a commercial and industrial metropolis. It is also an educational center with several universities, including a campus of the University of California that developed from its Citrus Experiment Station. Major sites include the cross on Mt. Rubidoux,◆ where Easter sunrise services are held; the World Peace Tower honoring Frank A. Miller,◆ builder of the resort, Mission Inn; and the Inn itself. In 1970 the population of the city was 140,089.

Riverside County, formed (1893) from parts of San Bernardino and San Diego counties that lie on its north and south. Imperial County is also on its south, Orange County on its west, and the Colorado River in Palo Verde Valley and the state of Arizona on its east. The city of Riverside has always been the county seat.

Serrano, Temecula, Cahuilla, and other Indians lived there, and the county still has large reservations. The first whites to travel through the area were Fages (1772) and Anza (1774), who discovered San Carlos Pass through the San Jacinto Mts. The first Americans were traders who pioneered the Emigrant Trail (1831). Early settlers included the Yorba and Estudillo families, Don Juan Bandini, Benjamin D. Wilson, Abel Stearns, and Louis Rubidoux.

The mountainous western region includes the San Bernardino and San Jacinto ranges with San Gorgonio Pass between them, and also between the San Bernardino National Forest and Joshua Tree National Monument (above the northern tip of Salton Sea). Mt. Rubidoux (7,731 feet) lies just west of the city of Riverside. This western region is offset by a central area of desert country with such resorts as Palm Springs and La Quinta. Farther to the east lie the Chuckwalla Mts. and Valley, and beyond them, Blythe. The central area of Coachella Valley is the great agricultural region whose city of Indio is known as the major site for the growing of dates. In the western part of the county lie the cities of Banning, an early center named for its developer, who founded transportation routes there, and Hemet, an agricultural and residential community known for its pageant about Ramona.

The main city is Riverside, long famous for its Mission Inn and the home of a University of California campus that began as an experimental station for citrus growing in the region which developed the navel orange. In 1970 the county had a population of 459,074. With an area of 4,592,832 acres, it had 64 persons per sq. mi. *(See also individual entries.)*

RIX, JULIAN [WALBRIDGE] (1850–1903), Vermont-born, self-taught painter, taken to San Francisco at the age of 4. Closely associated with Jules Tavernier, he was a well-known contributor to San Francisco's artistic life in the 1870s and 80s. His oils and watercolors depict local scenes poetically illuminated by atmospheric light.

ROACH, HAL (1892–), New York-born producer of films who began his Hollywood career (1914) with a picture featuring Harold Lloyd. He also brought Laurel and Hardy together, created the long-lasting *Our Gang* films depicting children humorously, and produced comedies ranging from slapstick to the sophisticated Topper series. In 1948 he entered into television production.

Roadrunner, bird of the cuckoo family, so named because it rarely flies on its short wings but instead runs at speeds of up to 30 miles an hour on its strong legs, its head down and its long tail extended. It is found mostly in dry or desert country.

ROBERTS, FREDERICK MADISON (1880–1952), born in Ohio and reared in Los Angeles, was a newspaper editor there and in Colorado before and became California's first black to be elected a state Assemblyman (1918–34).

ROBERTS, THEODORE (1861–1928), San Francisco-born actor who began his dramatic career at the Baldwin Theatre (1880) and continued for nearly half a century depicting rugged, outdoor Americans on the stage and, in his last years, in films. His sister, Florence Roberts, also had a prominent career on the stage.

Roberts, Camp, see *Camp Roberts.*

ROBIDOU, see *Rubidoux.*

ROBINSON, ALFRED (1807?–95), went to California (1829) from his native Massachusetts as the resident representative of Bryant, Sturgis & Co., the important hide-trading and shipping firm. After conversion to Catholicism, he married an heiress of Santa Barbara's de la Guerra family,♦ as vividly described by Dana in *Two Years Before the Mast.* In 1842 he went east with dispatches from Commodore Thomas ap Catesby Jones and carried about 20 ounces of gold from southern California,

the first to be sent to the U.S. His anonymous *Life in California* (1846) is a primary source book. To it he added as a supplement the account of Indian religion in California written by Father Boscana.♦ After 1849 Robinson was an agent for the Pacific Mail Steamship Co.,♦ both on the East Coast and in southern California, while he managed the de la Guerra properties. A collection of his *Letters* was published in 1972.

ROBINSON, EDWARD G. (1893–1973), Rumanian-born motion picture star whose career of nearly fifty years began in Hollywood in 1923. His most famous role, that of a gangster in *Little Caesar* (1931), established a type in which he was later often cast.

ROBINSON, FRANK (1935–), Texas-born baseball player and manager, reared in Oakland, was an outfielder with several teams, including the Los Angeles Dodgers (1972) and California Angels (1973–74). He became the latter team's manager, the first black man to be appointed to such a post by a major league team. He was selected Most Valuable Player by the National League (1961) and by the American League (1966), the only person ever chosen by both leagues.

ROBINSON, JACKIE (JACK ROOSEVELT ROBINSON) (1919–72), Georgia-born athlete reared in Pasadena from the age of one. At the University of California, Los Angeles, he was a star halfback, leading basketball scorer, champion broad jumper, and fine baseball player. He played professional football briefly, then became the first black on a major league baseball team when he joined the Brooklyn Dodgers (1945–56), mainly as a second baseman, and was named Rookie of the Year and Most Valuable Player (1949). He was later active in civil rights matters.

ROBINSON, WILLIAM (1822?–1902), moved from his native Virginia to California, supposedly in 1847, and in time became active in Stockton for the civil rights of his fellow blacks. He was also a Pony Express rider from Stockton to the mines.

ROBINSON, W[ILLIAM] W[ILCOX] (1891–1972), born in Colorado but reared and resident in southern California, of which he became a leading local historian while working for a title insurance firm. His many publications include *Ranchos Become Cities* (1939) and *Land in California* (1948) and, with Lawrence Clark Powell, *The Malibu* (1958).

Rock cod, see *Cod.*

Rocker, see *Placer mining.*

Rockfish, see *Bass* and *Cod.*

Rock music, flourished in California during the 1960s and 70s when many nationally popular groups got their start in the state and established styles and trends for the rest of the country. Begun in the early 1960s with southern California groups, notably The Beach Boys,♦ a "California Sound" was developed, although its musical characteristics were not so distinctively regional as its lyrics celebrating surfing, car culture, and other aspects of local life.

More musically and stylistically innovative were the bands that arose in San Francisco to make rock music part of the counterculture or hippie♦ way of life so that in the mid-1960s they quickly found an enthusiastic following among young people, as well as serious social and artistic analysis by Ralph Gleason.♦ The heavy beat, loudness, fanatical delivery of both music and lyrics, sexual overtones, and drug-like stimulation were representative of youthful opposition not only to jazz♦ and other rhythms enjoyed by an older generation but to an entire sense of established adult values. The narcotic associations were enhanced by electronic effects and the use of strobe lights (seemingly originated in California) so that a style of "psychedelic" or "acid" rock was created.

Among the San Francisco bands that played such vibrantly insistent and anarchically exciting music at the Fillmore Auditorium,♦ under the aegis of the producer Bill Graham, were the Jefferson Airplane♦ and the Grateful Dead♦ and Big Brother and the Holding Company. The last group became a major attraction only after being joined by the singer Janis Joplin (1943–70), whose intensity caused her to be called "a rock version of Edith Piaf." All of these bands got national attention at the Pop Festival in Monterey♦ (1967), the first of several in California that culminated in the tragic violence of the one held at Altamont♦ in 1969 which disenchanted many sympathizers with the counterculture.

Thereafter the bands that emerged in the Bay Area were less inclined to psychedelic sound and more to other styles. Newly popular groups included Creedence Clearwater Revival, which synthesized rock and country blues, the Mamas and the Papas, who put more stress on vocal harmony, and Santana, a band combining Latin American, African, and basic blues rhythms.

Meanwhile, Los Angeles groups attained great

followings at clubs on the Sunset Strip♦ and also nationally for various kinds of rock music. Particularly popular were The Byrds and The Doors, whose lead singer, Jim Morrison (1943–71), was a powerfully charismatic figure. Even more exotic and more popular was Frank Zappa,♦ whose progressive rock assimilating other musical forms was also marked by his outrageous stage shows and lyrics of social invective against prevailing culture.

ROCKWOOD, CHARLES ROBINSON (1860–1922), Michigan-born railroad engineer for whose California Development Co. George Chaffey♦ designed an irrigation system for the Imperial Valley (1901 ff.). Rockwood later tried to improve it by creating a by-pass, the Rockwood Cut, that avoided the canal and its gate built by Chaffey, which had failed to provide enough water in years when the Colorado River was low. The ironic result was that when the river flooded (1905) water gushed into the valley, and within two years it turned a dry sink into the Salton Sea.♦

Rodeo, in the Spanish and Mexican periods simply a periodic roundup of cattle by *vaqueros* to inspect the herds, cull those to be slaughtered, care for diseased stock, separate them by ownership, and brand calves and newly acquired cattle. The first rodeos conducted by missions were often held on Saturdays to slaughter cattle for the coming week's provisions, but more elaborate roundups for one or more *ranchos* were not only business affairs with appointed *jueces del campo,* field officers to settle ownership disputes, but social occasions enlivened by lassoing and other displays of skill. In the 1850s American laws began to regulate the business of rodeos. In the 1880s they started to become sporting affairs. Since 1900 the events, sponsored by cities, counties, and the state, have become circus-like competitions including professional riders who engage in roping, steer wrestling, and bareback and bull riding.

RODIA, SIMON [SEBASTIANO] (1873–1965), Italian immigrant folk artist, who settled in Watts,♦ where he paid a tribute to his adopted land by creating monumental towers (1921 ff.) of filigree steel, the tallest rising to 99 feet from a base of reinforced concrete adorned with glass, broken tile, shells, and pottery fragments. Disputes about their safety disgusted him, and he left his long labor of love to settle and die in Martinez. The towers were later declared a monument by the Los Angeles Cultural Heritage Board.

ROEDING, GEORGE CHRISTIAN (1868–1928), San Francisco-born horticulturist who founded the California Association of Nurserymen (1911) and significantly enhanced the state's fruit crop by making Smyrna-type figs grow there through the introduction of a Middle Eastern wasp needed to fertilize the tree's formerly barren flowers. His father, Frederick Christian Roeding (1824–1910), a banker with great landholdings in the San Joaquin Valley, gave 157 acres in Fresno to create its Roeding Park.

ROGERS, GINGER (1911–   ), Missouri-born actress and dancer whose Hollywood career included light comedies; she co-starred with Fred Astaire in eight musicals during the 1930s.

ROGERS, ROY (1912–   ), Ohio-born motion picture actor who succeeded Gene Autry as a singing cowboy of the films. He starred in 89 pictures, creating an image of a good, clean American cowboy devoted to his horse, Trigger. That image was enhanced by his appearances on television and in person at rodeos and fairs, accompanied by an ideal cowgirl mate, his wife, Dale Evans. His financial success led to his franchising a chain of Roy Rogers Family restaurants and the ownership at one time of an inn at Apple Valley, where a museum about him is located.

ROGERS, WILL[IAM] (1879–1935), born in Oklahoma of part Indian heritage, after brief schooling became a cowboy in the Texas Panhandle and drifted into a Wild West show as a rough rider and roper, traveling in South Africa and Australia before beginning a successful U.S. career as a performer. He developed an act in which he performed lariat tricks while carrying on a deadpan humorous monologue on current events, achieving great popularity with the Ziegfeld Follies for his simple, laconic folk style, which stood in sharp contrast to the lush libertinism of the rest of the program. From this career he developed into a motion picture actor, moving in 1919 to California, where he also wrote a humorous syndicated column and a variety of books expressing his "cowboy philosophy" in relation to political and other current issues. He died in an airplane crash in Alaska. A State Park in the Santa Monica Mts. is named for him, as is a nearby State Beach on Santa Monica Bay.

Rogue River National Forest, preserve located mainly in Oregon but crossing the state line into the northernmost part of Siskiyou County.

ROLLE, ANDREW F. (1922–   ), historian of California who holds the chair named for Robert G. Cleland at their alma mater, Occidental College. His books include *An American in California* (1956), the life of William Heath Davis; *Occidental College* (1963); and *California: A History* (1963).

Rolling Stone, biweekly San Francisco journal, founded in 1967 by Jann Wenner and Ralph J. Gleason.♦ Initially it concentrated on rock music; it then also became concerned with politics and social issues as seen from a counterculture point of view. Later it turned toward investigative journalism, although music remains the primary concern. The magazine moved to New York in 1977.

ROLPH, JAMES (1869–1934), rose to prominence in his native San Francisco because of his handling of relief after the earthquake and fire of 1906 and because the pleasant personality and genial friendliness that caused him to be nicknamed "Sunny Jim" were appealing to a city tired of the period of tawdry graft under Mayor Schmitz and Abe Ruef. First elected mayor in 1911, his five terms (to 1930) won wide approval because he supported a handsome civic center, good parks, more schools, a municipal streetcar system, and public water and power programs. His later years revealed his limited mind, his turnabout to support a private utility company's development of Hetch Hetchy power, and his inability to carry out complete municipal ownership of street railways. But the public still liked his style, and he was elected the state's 27th governor (1931–34). He soon found the problems of the Depression and the scope of this office beyond his powers. He fought with the legislature and other state officers and was held up to opprobrium for condoning the actions of a mob that took two accused kidnappers and murderers from a San Jose jail to lynch them.

ROMAN, ANTON (1828?–1903), German-born publisher who went to California (1851) and at first mined gold in the Shasta area. He then opened a bookstore there and later in San Francisco (1857), which in 1860 he developed into a book publishing firm. He issued Bret Harte's first book, *Outcroppings* (1865), an anthology, and, on the advice of Charles Warren Stoddard, another of his authors, selected Harte to edit his journal, the *Overland Monthly* (1868). Ill health forced him to sell the magazine before its first year was out, but he soon resumed his bookselling and publishing until 1888 and founded another magazine, *The Californian*♦ (1880–83).

ROMÉU, José Antonio (1742?–92), 6th Spanish governor of the Californias (1791–92), had earlier served with Fages in the campaign against the Sonora Indians. Roméu assumed the governorship at Loreto in April 1791, arrived in Monterey as an invalid in October, and died the following April. Sickness kept him from instituting seriously needed financial reforms. During his short administration the missions of Santa Cruz and Soledad were founded.

RONEY, Frank (1841–1925), Irish-born labor leader, came to New York (1867) and moved to San Francisco (1875), working as an iron molder. He joined the Workingmen's party but was against Denis Kearney's emphasis on opposition to Chinese labor, placing his own stress on organizing unions according to trade lines, creating city-wide local federations and national affiliations. He became president of the San Francisco Trades Assembly (1881) and also combated local labor problems by creating a Seamen's Protective Association to safeguard sailors against maltreatment by shipowners, boardinghouse keepers who practiced shanghaiing, and captains. His autobiography was published posthumously (1931).

ROONEY, Mickey (1922–), Brooklyn-born child vaudeville performer who continued to portray youngsters as a Hollywood star in the 1930s and 40s because of his small stature, fresh face, and youthfully exuberant energy. He was featured in a long series of films about Andy Hardy.

ROOP, Isaac [Newton] (1822–69), Maryland-born pioneer of the Lassen County♦ area who founded Susanville (1854) and named it for his daughter. Roop projected an independent Territory of Nataqua♦ (1856) and thus was the cause of the Sagebrush War♦ (1863). He was provisional governor of the Territory of Nevada (1859–61).

ROSALES, Vicente Pérez, see *Chileans in California.*

ROSE, Ralph (1885–1913), Healdsburg-born athlete who set his first world record by putting the shot at the University of Michigan (48′ 7″) in 1904. He was the Olympic Games champion of 1904 and 1908, and in 1909 became the first man to put the shot over 50 feet, a record (51′) that lasted nearly 19 years.

Rose Bowl, see *Roses, Tournament of.*

ROSECRANS, William Starke (1819–98), Ohio-born army officer who was graduated from West Point and as a Union general in the Civil War was considered a leading strategist despite his defeat at the battle of Chickamauga. He moved to California (1867) and settled in Los Angeles and then in San Diego, where a fort was posthumously named for him. He was elected to Congress (1881–85). A descendant of his married Adolph Spreckels' daughter.

ROSENBERG, Aaron (1912–), New York-born football player reared in Los Angeles, was a guard on the University of Southern California teams (1931–33) which twice competed in the Rose Bowl. He was twice selected as an All-American. He later became a successful motion picture producer.

ROSENTHAL, Toby (Tobias Edward Rosenthal) (1848–1917), German-born painter, reared in San Francisco, trained and long resident in Munich, was famous for his dramatic canvases depicting incidents in historical literature, such as the death of Elaine (based on Tennyson's "Launcelot and Elaine"), or humorous storytelling genre scenes, often of childish escapades, popularly reproduced as chromolithographs.

Roses, Tournament of, annual New Year's Day event in Pasadena, initiated in 1890 and marked by a parade of elaborately decorated floral floats that advertise the good climate and lush horticulture of midwinter California. In 1902 the parade was followed by a football game, and in succeeding years other sports (including chariot races) were tried until in 1916 there began a postseason championship intersectional football game, played since 1946 between the Pacific Coast Conference and Big Ten Conference winning teams. In 1923 the new stadium and the game played in it were called the Rose Bowl, the original of many other "bowl" regional championships.

Ross, small suburban town of Marin County, noted for its quiet community spirit in cultural and conservation activities.

Roughing It, autobiographical narrative by Samuel Clemens,♦ published under his pseudonym Mark Twain in 1872. The work, based on actual experience but fancifully and almost fictively treated, tells of his 19-day stagecoach trip from St. Louis to Carson City, Nevada, in 1861, his service as secretary to his brother, the secretary to the territorial governor of Nevada, his reporting for the *Territorial Enterprise* of Virginia City, his experiences in mining and other adventures in a strange new land, his brief visit to the gold mining country of California, his work as a reporter in San Francisco, and his visit to the Sandwich Islands (1866). The work, replete with tall tales and hearty humor of the frontier spirit, uses his own persona as a means of showing how a greenhorn is changed into a representative of the Far West.

Round Valley, circular Coast Range basin in Mendocino County, site of a reservation (est. 1856) for various Indian tribes. It is also a cattle and hop-raising region. Other valleys of this name are located in Mono and Plumas counties.

ROWELL, CHESTER [HARVEY] (1867–1948), born in Illinois, graduated from the University of Michigan, and after further studies in Europe became editor of the *Fresno Republican* (1898–1920). He made it a political force, using it to set forth the views of the Lincoln-Roosevelt League♦ to combat the power of the Southern Pacific in state politics. After a period of government service on state boards and commissions, he became editor of the *San Francisco Chronicle* (1932–35) and its major editorial columnist (1935–47).

Rowing, see *Crew.*

Roxburghe Club, San Francisco society of bibliophiles founded in 1928. It meets monthly for dinners, issues keepsakes, and is similar in character and purpose to the Zamorane Club of Los Angeles, with which it holds a biennial joint meeting. Bibliographies of its publications have been printed.

ROYCE, JOSIAH (1855–1916), the son of the forty-niner, Sarah Royce, was born and reared in Grass Valley until age 11. After schooling in San Francisco, he studied under Joseph LeConte and Edward R. Sill at the University of California, from which he graduated in 1875. After a year in Germany and a Ph.D. from Johns Hopkins, he became an instructor of English at Berkeley (1878–82), from which he went to Harvard, where he remained the rest of his life as professor of philosophy and a distinguished idealist and monist in his own philosophy. Not long after leaving California, he wrote two works concerned with it. The first was *California . . . A Study of American Character* (1886) treating the period 1846–1856 in terms of the American as conqueror, the struggle for order, and

social evolution. The second was *The Feud of Oakfield Creek* (1887), his only novel, concerned with the Mussel Slough♦ tragedy.

ROYCE, SARAH ELEANOR BAYLISS (1819–91), born in England, reared in New York State, as a young wife made an arduous overland trek to California (1849) with her husband and 2-year-old daughter, going alone and slowly (April–Oct.), partly because they would not travel on the Sabbath. She later recalled this journey in a moving and spiritual account written solely for the use of her famous son Josiah♦ when he was preparing his study, *California,* but published as *A Frontier Lady* (1932).

Rubicon River, flows through northern El Dorado County. Slightly farther east, the name is applied to a Point projecting into Lake Tahoe. Desolation Valley lies at the river's headwaters.

RUBIDOUX [originally **ROBIDOU** or **ROBIDOUX**], LOUIS (1796–1868), member of a family of fur trappers of French descent from St. Louis, like the others became a trader in Santa Fe. He finally settled in present Riverside County (1844), where he ranched on land that included Mt. Rubidoux, since 1909 the site of an annual Easter pilgrimage for sunrise services. One of his brothers, Joseph (1783–1868), also went to California, serving with Kearny's expedition and being wounded in the battle of San Pascual. Louis Rubidoux later became a judge.

RUEF, ABE (ABRAHAM RUEF) (1864–1936), born in San Francisco, where he practiced law after graduation from the state university and Hastings College, and where he soon entered Republican party politics. Failing to gain leadership, he then entered the new Union Labor party. Quickly becoming its boss, he propelled his candidate, E. E. Schmitz,♦ to election as mayor (1902–7). The two of them controlled patronage, receiving retainers from large corporations that thereby brought Ruef close to powerful Republican businessmen and to opportunities for substantial graft. Francis J. Heney♦ and Fremont Older,♦ aided by Rudolph Spreckels♦ and James D. Phelan,♦ exposed the broad corruption of Mayor Schmitz and Boss Ruef, and of their party and henchmen. They revealed the bribes Ruef accepted as well as the ones he gave to supervisors in connection with favored franchises for a telephone company, a street railway, a water company, and real estate developers, as well as his extortion related to liquor licenses. The exposés led to a trial in which Heney and Hiram Johnson♦ were attorneys for the prosecution and Ruef was defended by Samuel Shortridge.♦ Ruef was convicted, and when pardoned after less than five years in prison, he returned to his native city to become an active real estate broker.

RULOFSON, WILLIAM HERMAN (1826–78), born in Canada, went to San Francisco (1849) to conduct there and in mining towns a thriving business as a daguerreotypist and photographer. His firm, Bradley and Rulofson, in 1864 bought out the studio of Robert H. Vance.♦ Rulofson collaborated with Ambrose Bierce in writing *The Dance of Death* (1877), a travesty of a work by the wife of J. Milton Bowers.♦

Rumford Act, state law prohibiting discrimination in real estate dealings, sponsored by Assemblyman Byron Rumford, Sr. (1948–66), enacted (1963) and then revoked by an amendment to the state Constitution (1964). The revocation was overturned by a U.S. Supreme Court decision (1967).

RUSCHA, EDWARD JOSEPH (1937–), Nebraska-born artist, studied at the Chouinard Art Institute and in the 1960s became a Los Angeles exponent of Pop Art. His works include a colorful silk screen print depicting a vast sign advertising Hollywood and straddling its hills, and three books: *Some Los Angeles Apartments* (1965), *Every Building on the Sunset Strip* (1966), a 27-foot-long sequence of photos viewing the supposedly glamorous avenue as a rundown Main St., and *Thirty-four Parking Lots* (1967).

Russ House, early San Francisco hotel built by Immanuel Charles Christian Russ (1795–1857), often called "Colonel," a German settler in California who had come in Stevenson's Regiment♦ (1847). After a career in the mines as gold digger and justice of the peace, he built the hotel. It was located on Montgomery, Pine, and Bush streets, the site of the Russ Building, an office structure that was the largest on the Pacific Coast when completed in 1927 and the city's tallest until the 1960s.

RUSSELL, BILL (WILLIAM FELTON RUSSELL) (1934–), Louisiana-born basketball player and coach, reared in Oakland. At the University of San Francisco, the team on which he played center won 55 games and became NCAA champions (1955–56). As a professional player for the Boston Celtics,

he was 11 times voted to the National Basketball Association all-star team (1956–69) and five times named the Most Valuable Player in the league. During his career he averaged 15.1 points per game. As player-coach of the Celtics, he was the first black to coach a major league sports team.

Russian-American Company, see *Russians in California; Rezanov, Nikolai;* and *Fort Ross.*

Russian Hill, fine residential district of San Francisco, supposedly named for a burial place of Russian sea otter and seal hunters on its crest. Before the earthquake of 1906 some of the city's artistic colony lived there, including Gelett Burgess and Willis Polk. It still has some meandering lanes, simple shingled homes, and large gardens among the big houses and elegant apartment buildings. Landscaped Lombard St. is famous for its curving road down a deep descent. Two blocks off, on Chestnut St., stands the San Francisco Art Institute.

Russian River, rises near Willits and flows south and slightly east for about 58 miles to Healdsburg, where it is joined by another branch originating 11 miles northwest, then flowing south some 8 miles and generally west for about 13, to end in the Pacific near Jenner. The major settlements are Healdsburg and Guerneville, but the region is best known for its summer resorts, as the site of the private Grove at which is held the annual encampment of the Bohemian Club,♦ and for the Armstrong Redwoods State Park. The river, once called San Ygnacio, was named Slavianka ("Slav woman") by the Russian colonists, for whom it was then called Rio Ruso by the local Mexican settlers.

Russians in California, first were feared by the Spanish when *Visitador-General* Gálvez used the possible threat of their movement south from the Aleutian Islands as one reason to promote the Sacred Expedition♦ (1769) north to Monterey under the command of Portolá. By the end of the century the Russian-American Co. had moved only as far south as Alaska, although in 1803–04 the American ship captain Joseph O'Cain and some Aleuts were sent by Baranov to hunt otter off the California coast.

Then in 1806 Count Rezanov,♦ as the official representative of the Russian-American Co., went to San Francisco to get supplies for the Sitka colony and to investigate potentialities for the fur trade. Based on his view of the region, Ivan Kuskov, an officer of the company, came to Bodega Bay♦ to trade and to hunt otter (1808, 1811), and returned (1812) to found Fort Ross.♦ With this headquarters, the Russians ignored Spanish protests about trespassing on their terrain and even moved south, establishing a seal-hunting station on the Farallones. Furthermore, two Russian naval exploring expeditions under Kotzebue♦ also visited California (1816, 1826). Nevertheless, lack of support from Russia finally led to the liquidation of the enterprise, and the company's holdings were then sold to Sutter♦ (1841) for $30,000.

Recollections of the California outpost of the Russian empire survive in some place-names, notably Russian River (a translation of the Mexicans' Rio Ruso, although the Russians themselves called the river Slavianka, "Slav woman") and San Francisco's Russian Hill, presumably the burial site of some Russian fur hunters. During the rest of the 19th century few Russians went to California, since emigration from the homeland was forbidden; fewer than 600 were assumed to be in California by 1870. At the time of the 1905 Revolution some Russians went to California. Many more traveled via China, as well as via western Europe, after the Russian Revolution, and still others came during and after World War II. As a result, Russian colonies have arisen in San Francisco and elsewhere, and the Russian-related population of the state was estimated to be over 66,000 in 1950.

RYAN, [Lynn] Nolan (1947–), Texas-born baseball player, traded from the New York Mets to the California Angels (1972), is the greatest strikeout pitcher in major league history (383 batters in 1973). His fastball (mechanically timed at over 100 mph) is the speediest recorded.

RYAN, T[ubal] Claude (1898–), Kansas-born airplane manufacturer, reared in southern California, who founded the Ryan Flying Co. in San Diego (1922). His firm established the first year-round daily plane passenger service in the U.S. with flights between San Diego and Los Angeles. It also designed and built the monoplane the *Spirit of St. Louis,* which Lindbergh flew across the Atlantic (1927). Ryan's later firm, Ryan Aeronautical Co. (1928 ff.), became an important manufacturer of U.S. military planes and developed the first jet to take off vertically. The San Diego airport is named for him.

RYCE, Lyman, see *Petaluma.*

S

Sablefish, see *Cod.*

Saber-toothed tiger, see *State symbols.*

Sacramento, seat of the county whose name it bears and the state capital since 1854. It was first settled (1839) by John A. Sutter,♦ whose reconstructed fort and the adjacent State Indian Museum are major tourist sights. The fort was a welcome terminus for early transcontinental travelers, but after the discovery of gold (1848), hordes of miners overran Sutter's property and created an instant city on the banks of the Sacramento River, which served as a great port and supply center for mines nearby and distant.

Floods and fires devastated the community into the early 1850s but gradually levees and brick buildings rehabilitated the site, which has recently been redeveloped as a ten-block mall called Old Sacramento. As the city began to grow more secure in the 1850s, it became not only a Pony Express terminus but the depot of the state's first railroad (1856), constructed by Theodore Judah♦ to nearby Folsom. With backing from local storekeepers Charles Crocker, Mark Hopkins, Collis P. Huntington, and Leland Stanford, who came to be known as the Big Four,♦ Judah then planned the transcontinental railroad they took over. They and other magnates, such as the merchant and banker D. O. Mills, soon erected great mansions before they moved on to the even more metropolitan San Francisco. Some of their residences survive as the Crocker Art Gallery, Old Governor's Mansion, and Stanford Home.

The city continued to grow as a supply center for the agriculturally rich Sacramento Valley and for nearby communities like Davis, the home of a University of California campus, or Carmichael, where the new Governor's Mansion is located. It is also a major transportation center and manufacturing community, associated mainly with food processing. But its biggest business is state government. This is centered on the neoclassical old Capitol Building (1861), with its 237-foot-high dome overlooking Capitol Park. Spread out from it are numerous office and other governmental buildings, including the State Archives♦ and the State Library,♦ the latter with a great collection of Californiana. Natives of the city include Herb Caen, Albert Elkus, Stanley Hack, Sibyl Sanderson, and Ruth Slenczynska. In 1970 the population was 254,413.

Sacramento Bee, see *Bee.*

Sacramento County, one of the original 27 counties (1850), whose seat has always been the city of the same name, also derived from that of the river honoring the Holy Sacrament. Sutter and Placer counties lie on its north, El Dorado and Amador counties on its east, San Joaquin and Contra Costa counties on its south, and Yolo and Solano counties on its west; it has a long tail into Solano and Contra Costa counties.

The region, first inhabited by Patwin and Miwok Indians, was partially explored by Pedro Fages (1772), Gabriel Moraga (1808), and Father Durán (1817). Jedediah Smith was the first American to travel through the region. White settlement began with John A. Sutter♦ (1839), who obtained a great grant of eleven leagues (1844) surrounding his Sutter's Fort in what is now the heart of the capital city. Soon William Leidesdorff obtained another vast grant, which at his death (1848) was bought cheaply by Joseph L. Folsom, who made a fortune from land and trade there and is memorialized in the name of the city, prison, and dam located on his former ranch. The impact of Americans became dramatically evident in the first engagement of the Bear Flag Revolt,♦ when Ezekiel Merritt♦ seized the horses of Lt. Francisco Arce♦ on the ranch of Martin Murphy, Jr.,♦ between present Galt and Elk Grove.

The earlier era was definitely ended by the gold rush that brought a stampede of men to the American and Cosumnes rivers, the sudden creation of many jerry-built mining towns, and the establishment of Sacramento as a major trade and supply center. Accordingly, Sacramento was the terminus of the first railroad built in the state (1856), and although it went no farther than Folsom, its engineer, Theodore Judah, soon envisioned a transcontinental line. This was financed and then taken over by local storekeepers Charles Crocker, Mark

Hopkins, Collis P. Huntington, and Leland Stanford. Before its creation, the Pony Express provided fast contact with the world beyond the county. In early days, other communication and transportation were by river boats, which since 1963 have been augmented by a 42-mile channel to the west of the Sacramento River that connects the capital city with San Francisco Bay.

The Delta◆ between the San Joaquin and Sacramento rivers, through which the Central Valley Project◆ water is carried, is marked by very rich soil. Isleton is the center of asparagus growing, and other crops of the area include tomatoes, rice, pears, corn, sugar beets, and alfalfa. Dairying and cattle raising are also major activities of the county. Food processing is the leading industry, followed by chemical production.

The county has only one major city, Sacramento, whose business is government. Many other communities, like Carmichael, where the Governor's Mansion is located, have been collected into suburbs, although an occasional small town, like Locke,◆ in the county's tail, remains anachronistically remote. In 1970 the county population was 634,190. With an area of 623,936 acres, it had 650 persons per sq. mi.

Sacramento Delta, see *Delta Lands*.

Sacramento Mountains, range in San Bernardino County just west of Needles and north of Lake Havasu.

Sacramento Record, see *Sacramento Union*.

Sacramento River, rises in Siskiyou County at a small lake by Mt. Eddy in the Klamath Range and flows east and then southwest to Lake Shasta.◆ From there it travels 152 miles south to the junction with the American River,◆ then 42 miles southwest through the Sacramento Valley, to join the San Joaquin River at the Delta Lands. Finally, it empties into Suisun Bay near Pittsburg after a 400-mile course. Carrying one-third of the annual runoff of all California streams, the Sacramento has the largest flow of any river in the state. Its tributaries include the McCloud, Pit, Feather, Yuba, and Bear rivers. The name (Spanish for "Holy Sacrament") was given by Gabriel Moraga to Feather River (1808) but shifted to the present river, which had previously been called San Francisco and Buenaventura or Bonaventura. Moraga also called the upper reaches of the Sacramento the Rio Jesus María. Russians were the first to navigate the river

for commercial purposes, and during the gold rush it became a common route for people and supplies bound for the mines. Later it was a subject of political battles between hydraulic miners, who dumped debris into it, and farmers, who needed pure water for irrigation, leading to a ban (1884) on such pollution. It has long been a major source of the state's water◆ programs. A Deep Water Channel was built to the city of Sacramento by the U.S. Army Corps of Engineers (1963).

Sacramento Star (1904–25), daily newspaper founded by E. W. Scripps as part of his chain, although never as successful as most of his other papers. It was independent in politics and appealed primarily to working-class readers. It was sold to C. K. McClatchey for incorporation into his *Sacramento Bee*.

Sacramento Union (1851–), daily newspaper founded as the *Daily Union* by former printers of the city's *Transcript* when that journal threatened them with a wage cut. Within two years it changed hands twice to become a vigorous anti-Central Pacific Railroad journal, causing the Big Four railroad barons to start their own *Record* in opposition and to refuse to carry or ship the *Union* on their trains. In 1875 the older paper was absorbed by the newer under the name *Record-Union,* but under new ownership at the beginning of the 20th century it resumed its earlier name. In 1930 it took its present title as an independent journal that was bought by the Copley◆ chain (1966). Its most famous contributor was Mark Twain, who, as its traveling correspondent, wrote 25 letters to the newspaper from the Hawaiian Islands (1866).

Sacramento Valley, northern part of the Central Valley◆ drained by the Sacramento River, extends through Shasta and Tehama counties (that northernmost section being called Anderson Valley), and Glenn, Butte, Colusa, Sutter, Yuba, Placer, and Yolo counties into the Delta◆ and Sacramento and Solano counties.

The area was originally inhabited by the Wintun Indians and was first seen by the Spanish from Mt. Diablo when the party of Fages and Crespí explored the interior. The first important expedition into the region was that of Moraga (1808), who gave the name Sacramento to what is now called Feather River. The earliest visitors included Jedediah Smith (1828), whose beaver trapping was soon followed by that of the Hudson's Bay Co. and extended into the next decades. Settlement began with the huge land grant given to Sutter (1839–41). The discovery of gold brought great hordes of people through the valley to the mines and caused the founding and speedy growth of Sacramento, Marysville, Yuba City, and Shasta as supply centers, so that by 1850 about half the state's population of 100,000 lived in the valley.

Agriculture also became important in the 1850s, when cattle and sheep raising became significant undertakings, while dairy products were produced for the cities. About half the farm acreage of the 1850s was devoted to raising barley, hay, alfalfa, and wheat, although vegetables were also grown and the first commercial fruit orchards began to yield by 1858. The relatively diversified agriculture of those early years was increasingly replaced after 1867 by concentration on wheat, which in the 1870s and 80s dominated the region's economy. By 1882 1,000,000 acres were planted in wheat grown on huge ranches. The vast holdings of Dr. Hugh Glenn◆ were the largest controlled by any individual, and 25% of all the land was owned by only 82 people. Lumbering became an important industry around Red Bluff, Chico, and Oroville, and grape growing was elsewhere another major business.

With increased irrigation made possible by the Wright Act◆ (1887), the development of local canneries (successfully begun in 1882), and improved techniques of shipping by rail, the raising of apples, peaches, apricots, pears, almonds and walnuts, and other fruits became profitable and common. Four later but major valley crops were asparagus, tried as early as 1852 near Sacramento but later concentrated in the Delta; sugar beets, introduced in the 1870s but commercially significant only in the 20th century; tomatoes, developed on a large scale in the 1920s; and rice, introduced early near Biggs (Butte County) and greatly increased during World War I. Other major crops include almonds, hops, barley, olives, alfalfa, safflower, sorghum, prunes, peaches, and pears. The area's large yield depended upon the great increase in irrigation, as acreage that employed it mounted from 206,000 acres in 1902, to 650,000 in 1919, to nearly 1,000,000 in 1950. In part this was a product of the Central Valley Project, which also aided flood control and electrification in the valley.

Sacred Expedition, name given to the first expedition (1769) from Baja California to establish missions in Alta California, in part ostensibly to counter potential Russian colonization there. It was dispatched by *Visitador-General* José de Gálvez,◆ led by Portolá,◆ and under the religious authority of Father Serra.◆ The expedition went by land from Loreto to the site of the first mission, San Diego, in two parties. The first detachment, under Capt. Rivera y Moncada◆ and Father Crespi,◆ consisted of 27 soldiers in leather jackets◆ driving a herd of horses, mules, and cattle. It left March 24 and arrived at San Diego May 14. The second party, under command of Portolá and Serra, was less burdened with livestock and made the trip between May 15 and July 1. Supplies, seedlings, and other equipment for farming and settlements went aboard three small, locally built ships, the *San Antonio* (under command of Juan Pérez◆), the *San Carlos,* and the *San José.* They sailed from Cape San Lucas and La Paz with Lt. Fages◆ and the engineer, Costansó,◆ the first ship arriving after 45 days on April 11, the last one lost at sea with all hands. About half of the 300 men on the whole expedition died en route. Nevertheless, after founding the first mission, parties made their way north, blazing the route for El Camino Reál,◆ visiting San Francisco Bay, and founding a mission at Monterey (1770). The expedition was documented in the official *Estracto de Noticias del Puerto de Monterrey, de la mission, y presidio . . .* (1770), in the *Diario Historico* (1770) of Miguel Costansó, the *Diario* of Portolá, and accounts by Fages and Crespí.

Safflower, an East Indian plant cultivated in California only since 1949. Its seeds yield an edible oil low in cholesterol and also useful in paints. It is grown mainly in the Trough area of Fresno and Kings counties.

Sagebrush, bushy plant generally less than 5 feet tall, mainly *Artemisia,* grows mostly in the northeast corner of California (hence the reason for calling a land dispute there the Sagebrush War◆), on the eastern side of the Sierra and over into Nevada, and in the mountains of southern California. It is a smaller, more open ground cover than chaparral. The humorists of Virginia City, Joseph T. Goodman, Dan DeQuille, and Mark Twain, were sometimes called "the sagebrush school."

Sagebrush War, name given to a dispute of the 1860s over the precise boundary lines of Nevada and the northeasternmost part of California, an area previously involved in the short-lived (1856–57) Territory of Nataqua,◆ projected by Isaac Roop.◆ When California reasserted jurisdiction over the ostensibly separate area, Roop continued to claim independence. His cabin in the capital of Susanville, named for his daughter, was itself called Fort Defiance. From it he defied the Sheriff of Plumas County in the gun battle that was the only actual shooting campaign of the war (Feb. 1863). An armistice resulted in redrawing the California-Nevada boundary line to include Roop's territory of Honey Lake Valley in Lassen County, with Susanville as its seat.

Sage hen, see *Grouse.*

SAHL, Mort[on Lyon] (1927–   ), Canadian-born comedian, lived in southern California where he attended Compton Junior College before graduating from USC. He made a reputation as a night club entertainer at the Hungry I in San Francisco beginning in 1953, and was known for his witty and acerb monologues commenting on the current scene and satirizing political affairs and accepted institutions.

Sailfish, see *Marlin.*

Saint Francis Dam, built in San Francisquito Valley near Saugus, Los Angeles County (1926), by William Mulholland◆ to impound water brought by aqueduct from Owens Valley. It was 180 feet high and 600 feet long, and when it suddenly gave way on the night of March 12, 1928, it sent a tidal wave of water through the Santa Clara Valley, finally issuing into the ocean between Ventura and Oxnard. It swept through the city of Santa Paula at a height of 25 feet, carrying everything before it. About 400 people were killed, and homes, other buildings, bridges, railways, livestock, farmland, and orchards were destroyed along the 54-mile route covered by the water in less than 5½ hours.

Saint Francis Hotel, a major hostelry of San Francisco, it occupies one block of Powell St. facing Union Square, and was originally designed of Colusa gray stone by Walter Bliss and Arthur Faville (1904). After being gutted by the fire following the earthquake of 1906 it was reconstructed and a third wing was added. It was more fashionable before it was enlarged by an overshadowing tower built by William Pereira (1972). Previously it had a notable Mural Room with paintings by Albert Herter, and was the scene of stylish luncheons with menus by a notable chef, Victor Hirtzler, memorialized (1972) by a tower restaurant named for him. The city's first St. Francis Hotel was at Clay and Dupont (Grant Ave.) streets.

Saint Helena, Mount, part of the Mayacamas Range, rises 4,343 feet to overlook the Napa Valley. "Three counties, Napa, Lake, and Sonoma, march across its cliffy shoulders," according to its most famous visitor, Robert Louis Stevenson. He spent his honeymoon on its slopes at the site of an abandoned silver mine (1880), described it in *The Silverado Squatters,* and recalled its flat-topped profile in his Spyglass Hill of *Treasure Island.* The nearby city of St. Helena is the major settlement of the central Napa County.◆ The Silverado Museum, dealing with the life and works of Stevenson, is located there.

Saint Ignatius College, see *University of San Francisco.*

Saint Mary's Church and Cathedral, see *Old Saint Mary's Church.*

Saint Mary's College, liberal arts Catholic institution, had its beginnings in San Francisco (1855), moved to Oakland (1889) and then to its present campus at Moraga (1928) in the hills behind Oakland. Its art gallery has an important collection of paintings by William Keith. Long a men's college, it is now coeducational. Alexander Patrick Doyle was its first graduate (1875) to become a priest. Since 1868 it has been administered by the Christian Brothers.◆

Saint Vincent's College, see *Loyola University.*

SAL, Hermenegildo (*fl.* 1776–1800), Spanish-born soldier who went to California with Anza's expedition (1776). In time he became *comandante* of the San Francisco presidio, secretary to Gov. Borica, and a founder of the missions at Santa Cruz and San Jose. Point Sal, on the Santa Barbara County coast, was named for him by Vancouver (1792) in appreciation of Sal's aid. The state's first gypsum was produced at Point Sal (1880).

Salamander, amphibious tailed reptile that resembles the unrelated lizard.◆ More than 20 varieties live in California, members of 4 families: *ambystomid, lungless, newt,* and *slender. Ambystomid salamanders,* found throughout the state, are large and have smooth skins, small eyes, and flat-sided tails. Best known is the *Pacific giant,* largest of native salamanders, sometimes reaching 12 inches and found in the upper Sacramento Valley and the northern mountains and Coast Range, where it lives mostly underground. Although rarer as a native, the *tiger,* often called a water dog, is imported as fish bait and is also found in the Central Valley.

Lungless salamanders breathe through their skins, and are land-dwelling (often tree-climbing), and nocturnal. Found throughout much of the state, particularly in the north, they are the most common species and are represented by many varieties.

Newts, which have rough, rather dry skins, live mainly on land, entering the water to breed during winter and spring. They are also seen in daylight more often than other salamanders and inhabit the Coast Range, northern mountains, Sierra Nevada, and southern California mountains.

Slender salamanders, as the name indicates, are noted for their tiny, slim bodies. Found in the Coast Range, the Sierra Nevada, and other mountains, they are also the best known of all species because they often live in cultivated gardens.

Salinan, Indians resident south of the Esselen and west of the Yoku tribes in the mountains from Santa Lucia Peak to an area inland from San Luis Obispo. They probably numbered 2,000 in mission days, but Kroeber thought only 40 survived *c.*1950. They were of the Hokan family and practiced the Toloache♦ cult and Kuksu♦ rites.

Salinas, seat of Monterey County, its beginnings date from 1856 and its name derives from the salt marshes at the mouth of the river bearing the name. It is a market and food-processing center for lettuce, sugar beets, and other vegetables and fruits. An annual rodeo has been held every July since 1910. John Steinbeck was born there in 1902. In 1970 the population was 58,896. Its setting, the Salinas Valley, lies in the Coast Range west of the Gabilan Mts., and its fertile farmlands include the towns of Spreckels, Soledad (and its mission), and King City.

Salinas River, flows northwest for 170 miles from the midpoint of San Luis Obispo County into Monterey Bay. It is unusual both in flowing north and in being the largest submerged river in the U.S., most of its water lying below the surface.

Salinas Valley, extends 90 miles northwest from the mountains near San Luis Obispo between the Gabilan and Santa Lucia ranges to the Pacific Ocean at a point about 15 miles north of Monterey. The fertile valley, named for the salt deposits near the Salinas River mouth, has a Mediterranean climate. Inhabited by Costanoan and Salinan Indians, the long, narrow valley had Portolá as its first white visitor (1769) on a route later followed by El Camino Reál. The Spanish founded the missions of San Antonio de Padua and Soledad, and nearby the fathers planted corn and wheat and raised sheep, swine, and poultry, engineering some irrigation for their fields. Settlement was slight until after Mexican independence (1821), when most of the valley was carved into 32 generous grants for *ranchos.*

The area's economy was dominated by cattle raised for the hide and tallow trade until the gold rush, when it was wanted for beef. A severe drought (1860–62) reduced herds and caused ranchers to switch to wheat growing, depending on the Southern Pacific (which reached Salinas in 1872) for transportation. The economy was again altered in the late 1880s and 1890s, when Claus Spreckels♦ built huge refining factories at Watsonville and in the valley for the sugar beets that brought a greater yield per acre than wheat. This, in turn, affected the established dairy business, since herds were fed on beet pulp and tops. Irrigation from wells and by canals aided farm development after 1890.

Beginning in 1920, lettuce growing replaced much of the sugar beet crop, and Salinas was called the U.S. lettuce capital. Artichokes also became a big crop near the coast, and almonds inland. Migratory workers, particularly Filipinos, Mexicans, and Japanese, were hired to harvest the crops. Their poor working conditions led to serious labor strife in the 1930s and, later, to unionization under Cesar Chavez.♦ In his novels John Steinbeck♦ has presented moving fictional accounts of his native Salinas Valley area throughout its history.

SALINGER, PIERRE [EMIL GEORGE] (1925–), San Francisco-born journalist, press secretary to President Kennedy. Appointed U.S. Senator by Gov. Pat Brown upon Clair Engle's death, he served only from August through December 1964 before being defeated for election by George Murphy.

Salk Institute for Biological Studies, research laboratory in La Jolla, founded and headed (1963) by Dr. Jonas E. Salk, creator and developer of the first vaccine (1953) for poliomyelitis.

Salmon, ocean fish that thrive from Morro Bay to the Oregon border and then ascend the Klamath, Eel, Sacramento, Trinity, and San Joaquin rivers to spawn and die while their young spend up to a year in those fresh waters. The *king salmon* (*Chinook*) grow to 50 pounds and the *silver salmon* to 15 pounds. John A. Sutter and Nathan Spear began commercial fishing of salmon, formerly a staple of Indian diet, by using nets on the Sacramento River (1840), a practice that became common during the gold rush. By 1850 three companies were smoking and salting the fish. The first cannery was established on the Sacramento River (1864), which had twenty by 1882. In 1880 some 12,000 tons of salmon were caught, but such unduly large catches, along with pollution and the disturbance of rivers by mining, logging, and construction, have ended commercial fishing in rivers and reduced the ocean catch to some seven to eight million pounds annually. *Steelhead salmon* is actually a trout.

Salmon Mountains, range running down the Klamath National Forest in Siskiyou County and along the northern border of Trinity County. The Salmon River runs through the mountains.

Salt, first obtained by Indians from saline waters, seaweed, salty grass, and solid deposits, later by the Spanish and Mexicans and early U.S. settlers from tidal pools, particularly along the southeast shore of San Francisco Bay. Although techniques have been improved, they still depend on solar evaporation of sea water. Similar means are used to obtain salt at such other major sources as Monterey, San Pedro, and San Diego bays and at Searles Lake and other inland sites. Most of the salt is used for the chemical industry and as a preservative rather than for human consumption.

Salton Sea, was a sandy ancient lake bed—the Salton Sink—until 1905, when the Colorado River overflowed the irrigation system of Charles Rockwood,♦ rushed into Imperial Valley,♦ and filled the sink to a depth of 83 feet and a length of 45 miles. The flood, finally stopped in 1907, has left a lake with no outlet but some drainage from irrigation ditches. It is 30 miles long and 8 to 14 miles wide, and lies about 235 feet below sea level. The ancient lake bed was named for the Coachella Indians (variously spelled); the modern name presumably derives from the word "salt." Harold Bell Wright's novel, *The Winning of Barbara Worth* (1911), treats the subject of the flood.

SALVATIERRA, JUAN MARÍA DE (1648–1717), Italian-born Jesuit, sent to inspect the missions of Pímeria Alta♦ and to establish missions in Baja California (1690). At Loreto (1697) he erected the first Jesuit mission and founded the first permanent settlement in Baja California. He continued to labor in the region under adverse circumstances, being

rewarded eventually by the establishment of five missions and by his appointment as Provincial of the entire Jesuit order in New Spain. His biography was written by Venegas.♦

SALVATOR, LUDWIG (1847–1915), Austrian archduke who wintered in Los Angeles (1876) and wrote *Eine Blume aus dem Goldenen Lande* (1878), which introduced the region to many Europeans. The work was translated as *Los Angeles in the Sunny Seventies* (1929).

SAMISH, ARTIE (ARTHUR H. SAMISH) (1899–1974), lobbyist in Sacramento for liquor and other industries, whose long career in controlling politics ended (1955) when he was found guilty of income tax evasion and imprisoned. U.S. Sen. Kefauver called him "a combination of Falstaff, Little Boy Blue and Machiavelli, crossed with an eel." Samish wrote an autobiography, *The Secret Boss of California* (1971).

Sam Spade, detective in Dashiell Hammett's *The Maltese Falcon*♦ (1930), a tough loner dedicated to his work but sensitive to the character of other people. Humphrey Bogart portrayed him in the film.

Samuel P. Taylor State Park, preserve of 2,576 acres near San Anselmo, Marin County. It is the site of the Pioneer Paper Mill (1856–93) run by Taylor, a forty-niner from New York, who established the state's first papermaking mill.♦

San Andreas, since 1866 the seat of Calaveras County, is one of several state sites named for the disciple St. Andrew. It was a lively mining town during the gold rush. A valley in San Mateo County was given this name by Palóu, and from it a lake was named that is the most northern of the Crystal Springs Lakes. The valley is on the rift for which a major earthquake fault is named.

San Andreas Fault, the state's longest and best-known zone for earthquakes,♦ extending from the area of Point Arena in Mendocino County south for some 650 miles near the Coast Range, with branches into the Pacific Ocean and Baja California. In width it varies from about 100 yards to a mile or more. Among the major quakes caused by the fault are Tejón Pass (1857), San Francisco (1906), and Imperial Valley (1940).

San Anselmo, residential community in Marin County, in which is located the San Francisco

Theological Seminary.♦ To the town's west lies Samuel P. Taylor State Park,♦ a redwood grove that is the site of the state's first paper mill.

San Antonio, Mount, see *Old Baldy.*

San Antonio de Padua, third of the 21 missions,♦ founded by Serra (July 14, 1771) on a site in present Monterey County (about 20 miles southwest of King City) proposed by Portolá. The present structure is a restoration of the large quadrangular edifice built 1810–13. It is now surrounded by Hunter Liggett Military Reservation.

San Antonio de Pala, *asistencia* of Mission San Luis Rey,♦ located at the foot of Mt. Palomar, about 20 miles inland from its mission. Founded (1815) by Father Peyri for the Pala Indians, it was secularized in the 1830s and then returned to the Church (1903). It has since served as parish church for neighboring Indians.

San Benito County, founded (1874) from part of Monterey County, which lies on its west and south, with territory added (1887) from Merced and Fresno counties, lying on its east. Hollister has always been the county seat. The region was inhabited by Costanoan Indians, for whom was built (1797) Mission San Juan Bautista.♦ The settlement became the *rancho* headquarters of José Castro,♦ later sold to Patrick Breen,♦ its first non-Spanish-speaking resident. The town that developed around the deserted mission is an outstanding example of a Spanish-Mexican–early U.S. community and is now a Historical Park. A few miles east lies Hollister,♦ a wholly American city and the county's fruit- and vegetable-packing center. It is named for the landowner who was a leader in moving sheep across the continent to California. The area is famous for frequent earthquakes from the San Andreas Fault. In the Gabilan Mts., which form the boundary with Monterey County, lies Fremont Peak (also called Gabilan and Hawk's Peak), where Frémont briefly defied Castro's troops in 1846. To the south lies the Pinnacles National Monument♦ and to the east, Panoche Valley. The larger central valley is watered by San Benito River. To the southeast in the Diablo Range lie the New Idria mines (named from an Austrian mine) of quicksilver. In 1970 the county had a population of 18,226. With an area of 893,824 acres, it had 13.1 persons per sq. mi.

San Benito Valley, lower region of the Santa Clara Valley around Hollister.

San Bernardino, seat of San Bernardino County, dates back to the *asistencia* of Mission San Gabriel (1810), several times destroyed by disaffected Paiutes. A Mormon settlement (1851) antedated establishment of the city itself (1854). It grew to become a residential community and center for packing citrus fruit. In 1970 the population was 104,251.

San Bernardino County, organized (1853) from parts of Los Angeles and San Diego counties. Inyo County lies on its north, Kern and Los Angeles counties on its west, Orange and Riverside counties on its south, and the states of Nevada and Arizona on its east. The populous southwest corner contains not only the county seat of San Bernardino but communities closely connected to the eastern areas of Los Angeles: Upland, a former citrus orchard area; Montcalm; Ontario, outgrowing its agricultural background when it developed a speedway; Cucamonga, an old-time grape growing and wine making area; Fontana, the site of the state's largest steel plant; Rialto, a citrus packing, industrial, and residential city just west of San Bernardino; and Loma Linda and Redlands, each a residential city with a university.

To the north and east of this most populated area lies San Bernardino National Forest, in whose San Bernardino Mts. are located Lake Arrowhead and Big Bear Lake. North of the forest is the Mojave Desert, whose main transportation centers include Barstow, at the base of the Calico Mts., and Victorville, a market town for the nearby tourist area of Apple Valley. In the northwest is Searles Lake, a major source of borax. East of the forest are Yucca Valley, Joshua Tree, and Twenty-nine Palms, desert communities and resorts, with the tip of Joshua Tree National Monument just reaching into the county. Part of the eastern desert region is occupied by a large marine corps base. On the far eastern border lies the transportation center of Needles and below it, on the Colorado River boundary, Lake Havasu. Between them are the Sacramento and Chemehuevi mountains.

The county's early history includes the explorations of Fages (1772) and Garcés (1776) through Cajón Pass, but even the desert land to the east was part of the route of the Old Spanish Trail from Santa Fe to Los Angeles. Settlers from the Mormon Battalion were early residents of San Bernardino Valley. The economy is varied, including citrus and other fruit growing, vegetable and alfalfa production, livestock and poultry farming, cement and steel manufacture, and diverse other industries. The population in 1970 was 682,233. The largest county not only of California but of the U.S., it contains 12,876,032 acres, giving it a population of 33.9 per sq. mi. in 1970. (*See also individual entries.*)

San Bernardino Mountains, see *Transverse Ranges*.

San Bernardino National Forest, preserve of 812,000 acres, including Lake Arrowhead,♦ Big Bear Lake,♦ San Gorgonio Mt.,♦ and other forest areas.

San Buenaventura, ninth of the 21 missions♦ to be founded and the last established by Serra (1782), located in the present city of Ventura. It was named for a 13th-century Italian Franciscan. The original wooden structure burned down and was replaced by a stone building (1809), which was badly damaged by an earthquake (1812) but rebuilt (1816). After secularization and severe remodeling, the building was returned to the Church (1862) and finally faithfully restored (1929), but without its quadrangle and an outlying chapel.

San Carlos, see *Ayala, Juan*.

San Carlos Borromeo de Carmelo, second of the 21 missions,♦ commonly called Mission Carmel, was named for St. Charles Borromeo, a 16th-century Italian cardinal. The original mission was founded by Serra at Monterey (1770), but the location was shifted to Carmel the next year because of liaisons between the Indian women neophytes and soldiers in the Monterey presidio. A presidio chapel was built (1775) and replaced by the larger permanent building (1794), which is still standing and was served until 1840 by the mission fathers of Carmel. The mission itself was used by Serra as his headquarters, although its temporary wooden structure and succeeding adobe ones were not so handsome as those of other missions. After the death of Serra (1784), the present fine edifice of native sandstone (the seventh one) was built (1793–97). In it, both Serra and Crespí are buried. It is particularly known for the deep star-shaped window above the main door and for its Moorish tower. Like other missions it fell into ruins after secularization, but some inaccurate restoration was conducted by Father Casanova (1884) and a thorough and authentic rebuilding was carried out in 1936.

SÁNCHEZ, José Bernardo (1778–1831), Spanish-born missionary in California, served at San Diego (1804–20), Purisima, and San Gabriel before becom-

ing president of the missions (1827–31). At San Gabriel he befriended Jedediah Smith,♦ who in recompense called the entire Sierra Nevada "Mt. Joseph."

Another José Sánchez arrived with Anza and became *comandante* of the San Francisco presidio. He was the founder of a family that included Francisco Sánchez (1805–62), several times *alcalde* of San Francisco and a major *ranchero* south of the city, whose adobe at Pacifica is a historic monument open to the public.

San Clemente, Orange County beach resort community about 50 miles south of Long Beach, a residential town developed (1925) by a real estate dealer in a pseudo-Spanish style. It is best known as the California residence of Richard Nixon and during his presidency was often called the "Western White House." Nearby are Dana Point and San Juan Capistrano. Just across the border in San Diego County lie the marine corps' Camp Pendleton♦ and the San Onofre nuclear generating station.♦ The island of this name, one of the Catalina Islands,♦ lies 60 miles offshore and is part of Los Angeles County.

San Clemente Island, see *Catalina Islands*.

Sand and gravel, mineral products produced in greater quantities in California than anywhere else in the U.S. (1942–72), the first consisting of rock fragments ranging from .003 to .25 inch in size and the latter from .25 to 3.5 inches. Of the sand and gravel mined in the state, 90% is used either for mixing Portland cement♦ or for asphaltic compounds, both utilized by the building and paving industries. The remaining 10% consists of silica sand, which meets rigid chemical specifications for its use in glass making, sand blasting, and foundry processes. Continuing increases in population have led to constantly added production, so that California turned out as much sand and gravel between 1954 and 1964 as it had in the previous 61 years: about 1,000,000,000 tons. Current production is over 100,000,000 tons annually, with a value approaching $200,000,000.

Sand and gravel, dating mostly from the Quaternary era, is obtained from stream and alluvial deposits, canyon mouths, dunes, beaches, and marine beds. Since neither can be transported economically for more than about fifty miles, most production is near major cities, such as the Niles-Centerville and Livermore-Pleasanton areas; Sunol Creek and Santa Clara County creeks for the San

Francisco Bay area; and Tujunga Creek and San Gabriel River for Los Angeles. Silica sands are found near Mt. Diablo in the East Bay, in Amador County, and at several sites in southern California. Beach sands, particularly from areas immediately southwest of Pacific Grove and north of Monterey, provide materials for sand blasting and foundry work.

Sanddab, fish of the flounder family, found off the coast north of San Quentin Bay. Rarely larger than 12 inches, they live in water 120 to 300 feet deep. For forty years the catch has ranged between 500,000 and 700,000 pounds annually.

SANDERSON, JEREMIAH BURKE (1821–75), moved to San Francisco (1854) from Massachusetts and became a leader of the black community as a pastor of the African Methodist Episcopal Church and the head of schools for both children and adults.

SANDERSON, SIBYL [SWIFT] (1865–1903), Sacramento-born daughter of a state Supreme Court Justice, educated in Paris, became a famous soprano in operas produced in Paris, Brussels, St. Petersburg, New York, and Milan. Among her roles was the one in *Thaïs,* by her friend Massenet, and the title role in *Phryné,* created for her by Saint-Saëns.

Sand Hills, dunes in southeastern Imperial County between the Chocolate Mts. and Imperial Valley, rising at a few points to 300 feet in their 40-mile range.

San Diego, the city's site on the bay discovered by Cabrillo (1542), was named by Vizcaíno (1602) for his flagship, the *Saint Didacus.* It was first settled by the Sacred Expedition♦ (1769), led by Portolá and under the religious authority of Father Serra, who immediately established San Diego de Alcalá, the forerunner of the present mission, founded in 1774. Although the first mission, presidio, and community of Alta California, San Diego did not grow or prosper as much as the capital, Monterey, and by 1800 the non-Indian population had reached only 167. The first Americans to see it were William J. Shaler♦ and R. J. Cleveland, who illegally put in in their ship, *Lelia Byrd,* there (1803), but despite official Mexican opposition others came from the U.S., among them the mountain men James O. Pattie and Jedediah Smith in the 1820s and many hide traders and seamen like Richard Henry Dana in the 1830s. The city was seized by U.S. Marines

aboard the *Cyane* (July 29, 1846), but its possession alternated between the Americans and the *Californios* until after the climactic Battle of San Pasqual♦ in December. The era of the Spanish and the Mexicans, residents of what is now called Old Town, thus came to an end, but there was intermarriage between old families like the Carrillos♦ and Americans like Henry Delano Fitch. Other prominent early U.S. residents included George Derby and William Heath Davis.

The city remained relatively quiet until the arrival of the Santa Fe Railroad transcontinental tracks (1885), but the population, which soon reached 40,000, dwindled after the collapse of the first boom, although from those days date the great resort hotel at nearby Coronado♦ and other developments of the Spreckels family.♦ Other community leaders included E. W. Scripps♦ and his sister Ellen.♦ In the 20th century the city has grown enormously, and has added many cultural attractions, including one of the world's great zoos.♦ The Panama-California Exposition (1915–16), held in Balboa Park,♦ which was landscaped by Kate Sessions,♦ not only celebrated the completion of the Panama Canal but marked the rise of the modern city, which profited from the establishment of major army and navy bases during World War I.

Since then the city has not only expanded physically but has had a huge economic and population growth. It has become a major center for aircraft plants and the aerospace industry, for electronics companies, scientific laboratories, and oceanographic research and fishing conducted out of its great natural harbors. San Diego has grown, projecting north through Point Loma♦ to include La Jolla;♦ deep into the south beyond Coronado;♦ and far into the interior, whose densely populated satellite communities include El Cajon and Chula Vista. Within these expanded borders are a campus of the University of California and one of the California State University. Most of this expansion occurred during World War II or in the decades after it. Population just before the war was under 150,000; in 1960 it was 573,224; in 1970 it was 697,027, and two years later this had grown to 746,500, making San Diego the eleventh largest city in the U.S.

San Diego Chargers, see *Chargers, San Diego.*

San Diego County, one of the original 27 counties (1850), whose seat has always been San Diego,♦ is bounded on the north by Orange and Riverside counties, on the east by Imperial County, on the west by the Pacific Ocean, and on the south by Mexico. Its early history is essentially that of its major city, the initial settlement (1769) of the Sacred Expedition, where the present state's first mission and presidio were founded.

The present city has spread north to include La Jolla,♦ with its University of California campus; east to El Cajon; and south to encompass Point Loma♦ and the resort and naval school at Coronado,♦ and to extend through the agricultural and suburban area of Chula Vista almost to the Mexican border town of Tijuana. Fine beaches with resorts and residences stretch north through Del Mar, Leucadia, Carlsbad, and Oceanside to Camp Pendleton,♦ the marine base once a *rancho* of the Pico and Forster families, on the county border. Just short of that border is a nuclear-generated commercial power plant at San Onofre.♦ In the central inland area lie Escondido, a residential and vineyard community on the old ranch of William Wolfskill;♦ the town of Ramona;♦ and San Pasqual,♦ the site of a major cavalry battle (1846) between the forces of Gen. Andrés Pico and Gen. Kearny. Farther inland in the mountains lies the Cleveland National Forest,♦ with the observatory on Mt. Palomar♦ in its northern segment. Surrounding it are numerous small Indian reservations. To the east are Cuyamaca Rancho State Park,♦ the old mining town of Julian,♦ and Warner's Ranch.♦ Farther off, stretching to the county's eastern border, is the Anza-Borrego Desert State Park.♦ Up to the desert the land lies in the Peninsular Ranges.

The economy of the county is partly industrial (aircraft, military weapons, and machinery), partly agricultural (dairying, tomatoes, avocados), and partly naval and commercial shipping and fishing. In 1970 the county population was 1,357,854. With an area of 2,727,488 acres, it had 318.6 persons per sq. mi.

San Diego de Alcalá, first of the 21 missions,♦ founded by Serra (July 16, 1769) as a log structure with a thatch roof on Presidio Hill and named for St. Didacus of Alcalá, Spain. Moved into a similar building on its present site (1774), it was burned by Indians (1775), rebuilt (1780), and destroyed by an earthquake (1803). A major quadrangular adobe around a 120-square-foot patio was built in 1813, but after secularization (1834) it fell into disrepair. Returned to the Church (1862), it was decrepit until a reconstruction (1931) rebuilt only a small part of the mission, which once had had a monastery, residences, and shops. A sub-mission built

60 miles east in the Santa Ysabel Valley as the *asistencia* Santa Ysabel (1818) also fell into ruins, but its chapel was rebuilt in 1924.

San Diego Herald (1851–60), the second-earliest newspaper of southern California (the Los Angeles *Star* preceded it by 12 days), is best remembered for the six issues produced by George H. Derby♦ in 1853 during the absence of the editor, J. J. Ames, when the humorist filled the weekly paper with hoaxes and wit.

San Diego Padres, see *Padres, San Diego.*

San Diego Sun (1881–1940), daily newspaper purchased by E. W. Scripps♦ in 1892 and sold in 1939, when it was merged with a competitor to become the *San Diego Tribune-Sun.*

San Diego Union, daily newspaper founded in 1868. John D. Spreckels owned it for 38 years prior to his death in 1926; two years later it was acquired by the Copley♦ chain.

Sand lot agitation, see *Kearney, Denis.*

Sandpipers, see *Shore birds.*

San Fernando College, Franciscan order's Mexican apostolic training center (est. 1734) at which Serra and other mission fathers of California received their preparation. The members were called Fernandinos. After 1833 they presided only over the missions from San Miguel to San Diego, the northern ones being under the jurisdiction of other Franciscans from the College of Zacatecas in Mexico.

San Fernando Rey de España, seventeenth of the 21 missions♦ to be founded, established by Lasuén at a point just west of the city that took its name, a site intended to be midway between missions San Buenaventura and San Gabriel but far closer to the latter. The name commemorates Ferdinand III of Castile, founder of the University of Salamanca and many churches, canonized (1671) four centuries after his death. The second and very large mission building (1806) was a quadrangle constructed around a patio, but an earthquake (1812) demolished it and left only a major outer building, the Convento, a colonnaded structure almost 250 feet long. Deterioration after the secularization of the mission was repaired in several restorations between 1879 and the 1930s, and now not only the Convento but also the old church, the campanario, and shops have been reconstructed. The mission site is also known for a small gold rush (1842), when the first California ore, found on a mission *rancho,* was sent to a mint in the U.S.

San Fernando Valley, located north of central Los Angeles, originally the home of Indians now called Fernandeños, was traveled by Portolá and Crespí (1769) and became the site of the mission (1795) from which it derived the name that replaced the earlier Encino Valley. Cahuenga Pass, at its southeast corner, was the site of a battle (1831) that defeated Gov. Victoria, of another that overthrew Gov. Micheltorena (1845), and of the treaty (1847) that ended the American conquest of California. In later years the valley was cultivated for sheep, cattle, and wheat ranching, but pastoral isolation ended with the coming of the Southern Pacific Railroad from Los Angeles (1874) and the real estate development which that year founded the town bearing the valley's name. Subdivisions began in the 1880s, and the population expanded further when the aqueduct engineered by William Mulholland♦ brought Sierra water to the valley (1913). Citrus and olive orchards and other rural settings gave way to major settlements, including Burbank, Glendale, North Hollywood, Studio City, Sherman Oaks, Van Nuys, Encino, Tarzana, Canoga Park, Newhall, Valencia, Northridge, Chatsworth, and Sylmar. Most of the valley, except San Fernando itself, was annexed to Los Angeles (1915), to become a huge suburban area with its own state university (begun 1956), industry, businesses, and homes. A severe earthquake, centered near Sylmar (1971), has not stopped development.

San Francisco, the city and county are coterminous, the latter being one of the original 27 (founded 1850). It included present San Mateo County until 1856, when the Farallon islands were annexed to the city. The city, nearly surrounded by the ocean and the Bay (first sighted by Ortega in 1769 and first entered by Ayala and Cañizares in 1775), lies on the northern tip of its peninsula and covers just 46.38 sq. mi.

The home of Costanoan Indians, it got its first white settlement with Anza's expedition (1776) on sites where Moraga and Palou late that year began the presidio (still containing about 1,400 acres) and the mission called Dolores. Near the presidio was later established (1794) the protective Castillo de San Joaquín, the site of the Americans' Fort Point, now overshadowed by the approach to the Golden Gate Bridge. Later settlement occurred to the

southeast when William A. Richardson and Jacob P. Leese built homes on the cove they called Yerba Buena (1835ff.), beginning an American colony on the site of the present downtown financial district. The rest of the present city area, with its 43 hills, was occupied largely by *ranchos,* including a large one owned by Francisco de Haro, the first *alcalde* (1835), who ordered the first land survey, made by Vioget (1839). Land grants were so generous that during the early U.S. rule there was even a belief that much of the city area had been and might still be owned by the fraudulent claimant, José Limantour. Centrally located in Yerba Buena was the plaza that, upon American occupation in 1846, was named Portsmouth Square for the U.S. sloop on which Capt. John B. Montgomery put into harbor when he took possession of the area (July 9, 1846). The nearby street named for him is a reminder that the Bay water came up to that point. It was there, too, that Samuel Brannan and his 238 colonists arrived at the end of the month in their disappointed search for a region outside U.S. dominion, a quest that temporarily made the new American settlement largely a Mormon town, a great contrast to the population of 1845 that Bancroft later estimated at 300, half of them *gente de razon,* 50 foreigners, and 100 Indians and Kanakas.

The gold rush caused radical and sweeping changes as San Francisco became the great port for men from around the world hurrying to the mines. Suddenly the city became a cosmopolitan metropolis as a thousand tents covered the sheltered sand dunes of Happy Valley (where only 25 years later the luxurious Palace Hotel was opened); shanties clustered at the base of Telegraph Hill (much of it quarried to fill in the nearby Bay); wharves built by speculators like Henry Meiggs thrust out into the surrounding waters; and the dignified Old St. Mary's Church (Roman Catholic) was built of brick brought around the Horn from New England and granite from China; while saloons, theaters, gambling houses, and other businesses were housed in jerry-built wooden buildings, more than once swept by large and devastating fires. Soon definite districts evolved in the ever-growing city, which by 1860 numbered 56,000 residents: South Park and its adjacent Rincon Hill, a stylish settlement; the area remodeled a century later as Jackson Square, a locale of sturdy warehouses, banks, and office buildings like the Montgomery Block; North Beach for Italian newcomers; the Barbary Coast for a notorious nightlife; Chinatown for the nearly 3,000 persons attracted by the gold mines and soon to be so enormously swollen by workers on the transcontinental railroad, against whom angry white labor leaders and nativist politicians would raise the cry, "the Chinese must go"; Union Square, which was to become the city's central hotel and elegant shopping district; Nob Hill, opened in the 1870s by the invention of cable cars to become the citadel of the new nabobs, whose names are now preserved by the hotels built on the sites of their former homes; and Market St., the great angled boulevard that swept from the central waterfront where the Ferry Building was constructed in 1877 up to Twin Peaks.

All this was changed by the great earthquake of April 18, 1906, followed by a disastrous fire that swept over the older and most populated parts of the city out to Van Ness Ave., the major new stylish residential street, and forced thousands to seek refuge on the green lawns of Golden Gate Park, the vast landscaped area created on former sand dunes. The city was rebuilt with remarkable vigor and speed as a great new Civic Center was erected in Beaux-Arts style near the base of Van Ness Ave., new residential regions were opened beyond that avenue in Pacific Heights and in the Western Addition to accommodate over 400,000 people, and the recovery was celebrated in the Panama-Pacific International Exposition of 1915, whose one permanent contribution to the local scene was the Palace of Fine Arts.

Long and familiarly known as "The City," because it was the state's only metropolis, San Francisco in the second decade of the 20th century began to lose its primacy of population and dynamism to Los Angeles, and the southern California city without a natural port even began to outstrip the one with an unparalleled great harbor. Nevertheless, San Francisco was a major military, manufacturing, and shipping center during World War II, and many of the people who passed through en route to war zones or who came for temporary employment in shipyards and other plants decided to make San Francisco or its environs their new home. The San Francisco–Oakland Bay Bridge, which did away with the traditional ferries when opened in 1936, daily became clogged with commuters who worked in the city and lived in the East Bay, whose population multiplied rapidly and was counted as part of the greater San Francisco Bay area.

To care for its own added population, both daytime commuters and permanent residents, downtown San Francisco in the 1960s became the scene of a tremendous building boom, with skyscraper after skyscraper rising on the old filled land and

climbing up the hills to create a strikingly changed landscape, often described, invidiously, as "Manhattanization." But with this building also came handsome new developments for altered ways of life, including the numerous great structures for dwellings and for commerce, such as that of the Golden Gateway, located in a former wholesale produce market area close to the heart of old Yerba Buena, and the ingenious remodeling of one-time manufacturing plants into attractive and sophisticated shopping complexes, like Ghirardelli Square, at the foot of Russian Hill, another very early city settlement, and near the popular tourist attraction of Fisherman's Wharf.

Tourists and residents alike find the city appealing for its urbane traditions and its diverse cultural institutions, among them the Palace of the Legion of Honor; de Young Museum; Asian Art Museum; San Francisco Museum of Modern Art; Opera House, for symphony and ballet (and the place where the UN was founded); San Francisco University and Sutro Library; Natural History Museum, with its Steinhart Aquarium; California Historical Society; Maritime Museum; San Francisco State University; and many other places and activities, including one of the state's major zoos.♦ There are also numerous little theaters and art galleries, as well as many poetry readings and other specialized performances. In 1970 the city had a population of 715,672, down from 740,000 a decade earlier, but with an area of only 29,056 acres, it still had a heavy concentration of people, 15,903.8 per sq. mi.

San Francisco, popular film (1936) of local color, whose plot involves a romance between a Barbary Coast café owner and a parson's daughter who sings the title song. The picture concludes with a melodramatic treatment of the earthquake and fire of 1906.

San Francisco Art Institute, begun (1871) as an association to promote art, opened the California School of Design (1874) as the first art school west of the Mississippi. Known temporarily as the Mark Hopkins Institute of Art (1893–1906) because it was for a time housed in the late tycoon's Nob Hill mansion, it was later titled the California School of Fine Arts (1917–61), and has long been a college offering the B.A. and M.A. degrees and is affiliated with the University of California. Its directors have included Virgil Williams (1874–86) and Arthur Mathews (1890–1906). Artists who have been faculty members or students include R. D. Yelland, William Keith, Xavier Martinez, Gottardo

Piazzoni, Charles Rollo Peters, Maynard Dixon, Clyfford Still, Mark Rothko, David Park, Richard Diebenkorn, Elmer Bischoff, and Nathan Oliveira.

San Francisco Ballet, founded (1937) by the three Christensen brothers: William (1902–), who later left to direct Ballet West in Utah; Harold (1904–), who long headed the San Francisco company's school; and Lew (1909–), once a dancer with George Balanchine and since 1951 director of the San Francisco troupe. The company, with an eclectic repertoire, is known for its own style of great verve and a graceful elegance.

San Francisco Bay, a name first applied by Cermeño to Drake's Bay (1595), while the name of Drake was loosely affiliated with the bay now called San Francisco. There have been contentions that Drake actually sailed into that bay (1579), but it is generally assumed that the first whites to discover it were a detachment of Portolá's expedition (Oct. 31, 1769) led by José Ortega on a march to the north. The name was not formally used before it appeared on the map drawn by Cañizares as a result of the explorations he and Ayala made (1775).

The Bay at low tide has a shore line of about 100 miles enclosing some 450 square miles of water. It extends from the Golden Gate, named by Frémont (1846), for nearly 40 miles southeast along the San Francisco Peninsula and for about 10 miles northeast to the entry into San Pablo Bay, itself separated by Carquinez Strait from the more easterly Suisun Bay, into which the Sacramento and San Joaquin rivers flow. At its greatest width, San Francisco Bay measures 13 miles. It has depths to 36 fathoms (216 ft.), but about 70% of it is less than 12 feet deep, leading to construction of many long wharves and piers and to the use of fill from the time of the first American settlers, who found a shoreline at the present Montgomery St. of San Francisco.

The state's Bay Conservation and Development Commission regulates fill. The Bay has numerous islands (the Farallones lie about 30 miles off Golden Gate), of which the most important are Alcatraz, Angel, Treasure, and Yerba Buena. The bridges that cross the Bay are Golden Gate, San Francisco–Oakland, Richmond–San Rafael, San Mateo, and Dumbarton, but some ferries still survive, although smaller and trivial by comparison with those that preceded the building of the big bridges. The most important fish caught in the Bay is striped bass. (*See also individual entries.*)

San Francisco Bay Conservation and Development Commission, established (1965) by the state legislature and granted increased powers (1969) to regulate land fill in the Bay and otherwise preserve its integrity. It is generally called BCDC.

San Francisco Bulletin (1855–1929), established as the *Daily Evening Bulletin* by James King of William,♦ who soon made it the city's most respectable and leading reform journal. He inaugurated the practice of printing announcements of Sunday school church services in his Saturday papers, and his editorial policy opposed the political machine of David Broderick. When he revealed that Supervisor James P. Casey♦ was an ex-convict he was killed by Casey, who in turn was executed by the Vigilance Committee created to cope with the issue. At this time the paper had the city's greatest circulation, a lead held by King of William's successors (including T. H. Hittell), who opposed Ralston and big business. In the 1870s and 80s it was overtaken by the *Chronicle* and dwindled, until in 1895 Fremont Older♦ became its editor and made it a reform organ again, leading the attack on Ruef and Schmitz and supporting Hiram Johnson for governor (1910). After Older's liberalism forced him from the paper (1918), it drifted again until sold (1929) to Hearst, who merged it with the *Call*♦ as an evening paper (1929) and brought Older back to edit the combined paper until his death in 1935.

San Francisco Call (1856–1965), newspaper issued each weekday, initially as the *Morning Call*. It emphasized reforms in city government, but the early days are best remembered because Mark Twain was its Washoe correspondent (1863) and local reporter (1864). Later allied to the evening *Bulletin,* during the 70s it conducted a circulation war with the *Chronicle* to control morning readership, sensationally emphasizing the danger of Denis Kearney and opposing Ralston's attempt to have the city buy his Spring Valley Water Co.♦ Its crusading campaigns ended when the paper was sold (1895) to John D. Spreckels, who installed Charles Shortridge as manager. Although modernized in format, the paper became extremely conservative. M. H. de Young bought it (1913) to eliminate this rival to his morning *Chronicle,* but sold it the same year to Hearst, who made it an evening journal. Fremont Older, the city editor before 1895, was brought over from the *Bulletin* to make the *Call* a crusading journal again. In 1929 Hearst merged it with the *Bulletin,* both then managed by John Francis Neylan. In 1940 Edmund Coblentz was put in charge of the *Call-Bulletin,* which absorbed the *News* (1959) and was itself absorbed into Hearst's morning paper, the *Examiner* (1965).

San Francisco Chronicle (1865–), founded by Charles de Young,♦ soon joined by his brother M. H. de Young, as the *Daily Dramatic Chronicle,* a four-page theater program sheet with a news supplement. It managed to scoop local newspapers on the story of Lincoln's assassination and also contrived to create interesting rewritten versions of accounts from the Associated Press, thereby growing into the *Daily Morning and Evening Chronicle* (1868), which was initially edited by Henry George.

A bitter fight to wrest control of the morning circulation from the *Call* led to sensational stories inveighing against Denis Kearney and the Workingmen's party and its candidate, Rev. Isaac Kalloch,♦ who in turn excoriated de Young from his pulpit. Charles de Young then shot Kalloch in cold blood, and Kalloch's son in turn killed de Young (1880). Under M. H. de Young the journal became somewhat more temperate, among other matters ceasing attacks on the Southern Pacific. It vied with Hearst's *Examiner* to be the city's main newspaper, representing the Republican point of view, attempting leadership in local cultural activities, such as sponsorship of the Midwinter Fair of 1894, and adding local literary figures to its staff, like Prentice Mulford and Charles Warren Stoddard.

After de Young's death (1925) his son-in-law, George Cameron, became publisher. The paper was for a time a liberal journal, modeling itself on *The New York Times* and also cultivating outstanding local columnists, including Herb Caen. At Cameron's death, control passed (1955) to de Young's grandson, Charles de Young Thieriot, who made it and its television station, KRON, financially successful, with the newspaper assuming the sensational style of Hearst journalism. It routed the latter, achieving dominance of the morning field when the *Examiner* became an afternoon daily, but the two papers have issued a joint Sunday paper with separately edited sections since 1965.

San Francisco Conservatory of Music, independent professional institution founded in 1917. It enrolls about 100 undergraduate students and a few graduates, and its faculty includes members of the San Francisco Symphony. Ernest Bloch♦ was its director (1925–30), a post later held by Albert Elkus (1951–57).

San Francisco de Asís, sixth of the 21 missions,♦ named for the founder of the Franciscan order, St.

Francis of Assisi, but generally known as Mission Dolores because in 1776 its founder, Palóu, chose for it a site in San Francisco alongside a stream that Anza had named Arroyo de los Dolores for Our Lady of Sorrows. The creek and its adjacent lake have long since been filled in, but the name persists. The original log structure roofed with thatch was supplanted by the present chapel, built (1782–91) on a site more than a block away. Like other missions, the chapel was at one time part of a quadrangle that disappeared over the years. Its importance is also suggested by the creation of an *asistencia,* San Rafael Arcángel,♦ but for a long time the simple, almost neoclassical adobe church, rehabilitated by Willis Polk (1917), has been overshadowed by the large, elaborate basilica built just to its north (1916). On the south is the more suitable little cemetery in which are buried such notables as Gov. Argüello and the first and last *alcaldes* of San Francisco, Francisco de Haro and José Noé. The region in which the chapel is located is called the Mission district of the city.

San Francisco earthquake and fire, began with a tremor at 5:13 on the morning of April 18, 1906, the greatest of many quakes and conflagrations to rack the city. The initial two-minute earthquake probably measured 8.3 on the Richter scale♦ devised afterward. Although the tremor itself destroyed some buildings, like the jerry-built new City Hall, about 80% of the property damage was caused by fires created by the knocking over of chimneys, etc., and by the lack of water in broken lines to fight the initial flames. In three days, the fires destroyed about a third of San Francisco's buildings in 490 blocks of about a four-square-mile radius, between the Bay side financial district and the residential area roughly bounded by Van Ness Ave. The twin disasters of quake and fire caused 500 deaths, thousands of injuries, and the destruction of over 28,000 buildings, with losses of $400,000,000 in the city alone. The quake also damaged every city from Eureka to Salinas, particularly Santa Rosa and San Jose, as the earth was ruptured from San Juan Bautista to the Mendocino coast. The national guard and army troops under Gen. Funston♦ worked with city officials of San Francisco to prevent looting and to provide communications, tent housing in parks, sanitation, and food.

San Francisco Examiner (1863–), established as the *Democratic Press* (1863–65), whose vigorous championing of the Confederacy led a mob to break into its offices after Lincoln's assassination and culminated in its concomitant decision to adopt the new name *Daily Examiner* (1865–80). For a time, the same owners continued their evening daily as an ultraconservative Democratic organ. George Hearst bought it (1880), made it a morning paper, and used it to aid his political purposes, but after election to the U.S. Senate he transferred the paper to his son, William Randolph Hearst, who had become fascinated by journalism.

The young Hearst installed Arthur McEwen♦ as editor (1887–94) and gathered a group of outstanding writers as staff members or contributors, including Ambrose Bierce (who wrote a column of "Prattle"), Edwin Markham (whose "The Man with the Hoe" appeared in the paper, 1899), Ernest Lawrence Thayer (whose mock-heroic poem "Casey at the Bat" appeared in the paper, 1888), Joaquin Miller, and Winifred Black Bonfils, who wrote sob-sister stories such as "Annie Laurie." Hearst made the *Examiner* the first eight-page paper in California, put news instead of ads on the front page, and made all reporting sensational and exciting. As a result, the paper surpassed the circulation of the rival *Chronicle* (1893) and came to be called the "Monarch of the Dailies" after a circulation stunt that depended on the capture for a San Francisco zoo of a live grizzly bear named Monarch.

After Hearst bought the *New York Journal* he gave less personal attention to the San Francisco paper, but it profited by getting syndicated features such as Richard Outcault's comic strip about a tough "Yellow Kid," which caused the term "yellow journalism" to be applied to all Hearst papers. The *Examiner* continued the same policies until Hearst's death (1951). Later the paper declined and the *Chronicle* surpassed it in circulation. It then became an afternoon daily, joining (1965) with its rival to issue a Sunday paper that combined separately edited sections.

San Francisco Forty-Niners, see *Forty-Niners, San Francisco.*

San Francisco Giants, see *Giants, San Francisco.*

San Francisco Illustrated Daily Herald, tabloid newspaper founded (1923) by Cornelius Vanderbilt, Jr., as part of a chain begun with his *Los Angeles Illustrated Daily News.* It lasted for a year.

San Francisco Maritime Museum, see *Maritime Museum.*

San Francisco Mime Troupe, nonprofit, collectively run theater group organized in 1961. Its company of

actors and accompanying musicians perform free in the city's parks, passing the hat for contributions. It frequently satirizes local issues. Two mimes unrelated to the Troupe, Robert Shields and his wife, Lorene Yarnell, had their own act in Union Square during the early 1970s until their success led them to night clubs, television, and films.

San Francisco News (1903–65), founded by E. W. Scripps♦ as part of his chain of newspapers, was given the name *Daily News,* sold for a penny, was devoted to labor issues, and concentrated its circulation in the South of Market area. In 1915 the predominantly Mission district paper became a citywide journal but continued to advocate the publicly owned Hetch Hetchy water system, a publicly owned municipal transit system, and woman's suffrage. It adopted the shortened name of *News* in 1927. During the 1930s and 40s it continued to emphasize labor and liberal views. It was merged with Hearst's *Call-Bulletin* (1959) and totally lost its identity upon the resulting paper's merger with the *Examiner* (1965).

San Francisco–Oakland Bay Bridge, world's longest steel bridge, built on two levels for vehicles only, extending 8¼ miles from the Rincon Hill♦ approach in San Francisco to the Toll Plaza in Oakland. The western part consists of twin suspension bridges joined at a central point, spanning 10,450 feet to Yerba Buena Island.♦ There the roads pass through a double-tiered tunnel to reach the eastern segment, consisting of a 1,400-foot cantilevered span succeeded by truss bridges, for a total of 19,400 feet. Construction was begun in 1933, and the bridge was opened in 1936.

San Francisco Peninsula, demarcated by the Pacific Ocean, Golden Gate entrance to the Bay, and the lower or southern San Francisco Bay. Its northern tip is the city and county of San Francisco, and the remainder lies in San Mateo County and a small portion of Santa Clara County. It extends, approximately, from East Palo Alto on the Bay side and San Gregorio on the ocean to the approach to the Golden Gate Bridge.

San Francisco Poetry Center, see *Poetry Center.*

San Francisco Renaissance, name given to the anti-Establishment movement in the arts that was best expressed in Beat♦ writing in the mid- to late-1950s. Its major literary figures included Allen Ginsberg, Jack Kerouac, Gregory Corso, Gary Snyder, Lawrence Ferlinghetti, and Michael McClure. It also emphasized jazz and initiated poetry readings to music in the North Beach♦ settings where it flourished. Simultaneously but more distantly associated with it were exhibitions of abstract expressionist paintings or sculptural assemblages, the latter derived from surrealism. Numerous small presses grew up to issue poetry and some prose, the most significant being City Lights, a paperback bookstore founded by Ferlinghetti. Like neighboring North Beach coffee houses, it served as a gathering place for poet performers and other creators of the movement.

San Francisco Solano, last of the 21 missions♦ to be founded, was established (1823) in the present town of Sonoma. Named for a Spanish missionary to Peru, the mission was the only one created during the Mexican era of California. After secularization, Mariano Vallejo not only supported the pueblo as a buffer against the Russians but administered the mission until its church collapsed. The present chapel was then built as a parish church (1840) and was reconstructed (1911–13) to become a museum in a State Historic Park.

San Francisco Theological Seminary, graduate theological school of the Presbyterian Church, founded (1871) in the city for which it is named. It has been located since 1892 in San Anselmo, Marin County, and is affiliated with the Graduate Theological Union in Berkeley.

San Francisco, University of, see *University of San Francisco.*

San Gabriel, residential suburb of Los Angeles, also a center for manufacturing aircraft and electronic parts. It attracts tourists to its mission, adobes, the "birthplace" of Ramona, and the site of the battle (Jan. 8, 1847) between the forces of Gen. José Flores and Kearny and Stockton that opened up the occupation of Los Angeles. Gen. George S. Patton was born there. In 1970 the population was 29,176.

San Gabriel Arcángel, fourth of the 21 missions,♦ founded (1771) on a site about nine miles east of present downtown Los Angeles, moved a little farther east (1775) to present San Gabriel. The church (built 1791–1805) has a long side wall as its real façade, marked by high oblong windows between capped buttresses, perhaps influenced by the cathedral at Cordova. It had the largest crops of any mission and a great vineyard and winery. Father Boscana♦ is buried there.

San Gabriel Mountains, see *Transverse Ranges.*

San Gabriel Valley, bounded by the Verdugo Mts. and the San Rafael, Montebello, and Puente Hills on the south, the San Jose Hills on the east, and the San Gabriel Mts. on the north, it extends from about Tujunga nearly to Pomona. First visited by Portolá (1769), it was settled by the founding of Mission San Gabriel (1771), now standing on its second site (1776). In addition to the mission city, it contains Pasadena, Alhambra, El Monte, Azusa, and Covina.

San Gorgonio Mountain, within San Bernardino National Forest, towers 11,502 feet, and between it and San Jacinto peak runs San Gorgonio Pass.

San Gorgonio Pass, a major entry and transportation route to southern California, located between the San Bernardino and the San Jacinto mountains, thus a dividing point between the Transverse Ranges♦ on the north and the Peninsular Ranges♦ on the south. Near Banning in Riverside County, its elevation is 2,559 feet. Because of the desert to the east, it was little used before the time of trains and automobiles. The name comes from the nearby Mission San Gabriel ranch honoring Gorgonius, a 3rd-century martyr.

Sanitary Commission, organization for the Union forces during the Civil War, whose purposes were comparable to those of the modern Red Cross. Although a national organization, it received one-quarter of its funds from California, beginning in the fall of 1862. Thomas Starr King was a major spokesman, although Gov. F. F. Low was president of the California branch of the organization. Ingenious methods were used to raise money. These included auctions at which the same item was sold and returned for sale several times over. The most notable example, commented upon by Mark Twain, among others, was a sack of flour, first sold at Austin, Nev., and then auctioned off across California, to bring in a total of $40,000. A Point Reyes cheesemaker created a wheel weighing 3,850 pounds, which was sold for a dollar a pound. Elegant dances with substantial admission fees were also held to help raise the $1,234,000 contributed by California.

San Jacinto Basin, name applied to the lowland area of Riverside County, lying south of Riverside, with the San Jacinto Mts. on the east and the Santa Ana Mts. on the west. An agricultural and dairying region, it is also the site of March Air Force Base. The largest city is Hemet.

San Jacinto Fault, see *Earthquakes.*

San Jacinto Mountains, see *Peninsular Ranges.*

San Joaquin County, one of the original 27 counties (1850), bounded on the north by Sacramento and Yolo counties, on the west by Yolo, Contra Costa, and Alameda counties, on the south by Stanislaus County, and on the east by Stanislaus, Calaveras, and Amador counties. The river after which the county is named flows from the midpoint of the San Joaquin Valley to Stockton and into the Delta. To the north, the Mokelumne River dips in from the Camanche Reservoir, the Calaveras River comes in from the east to northern Stockton, and the Stanislaus River forms the county's southern border. The Mendota Canal cuts across the southwestern corner.

Extending from the bay counties on the west to the Sierra, San Joaquin was a major route to the mines, the Mariposa Road being a leading route to the southern part of the Mother Lode country. Although the first white settlers were the French-Canadian trappers of the Hudson's Bay Co. who established French Camp, it was Stockton just to the north that, after its founding (1847) by Charles M. Weber,◆ became the main community and the county seat.

On its north lies Lodi, founded (1869) with the coming of the Southern Pacific and thereafter a market and food-processing center. To its east is Holt, named for the builder of Caterpillar tractors. On Stockton's south lie Tracy, Banta, and Manteca, residential and market communities for the surrounding agricultural areas, with businesses of food processing and farm equipment, but also noted for nearby ranches of beef cattle. The county is also a leader in the production of dairy products, vegetables, grapes, and sugar beets. In 1970 its population was 289,564. With an area of 905,280 acres, it had 205 persons per sq. mi.

San Joaquin River, rises near the southeastern border of Yosemite National Park and flows southwest to a point a little north and 26 miles west of Fresno. There it begins a crooked but generally northwest course for 100 miles through the San Joaquin Valley before turning northwest to end in the Delta lands at the confluence with the Sacramento River. Friant Dam, 20 miles northeast of Fresno, part of the Central Valley Project◆ for directing the state's water,◆ impounds the river into Millerton Lake and then, by the 160-mile Friant-Kern Canal, carries the water south to the San Joaquin Valley's driest areas. Stockton, connected to San Francisco Bay by the river and a deep-water channel about 80 miles long, has become an important inland seaport and the major one on the river. The first whites to see the river were Crespí and Fages (1772), and it was named for St. Joseph by Moraga (1805 or 1806). Gold mining took place along the river's tributaries, but after disputes between farmers and hydraulic miners, the latter were prohibited (1884) from dumping debris that would pollute its waters. Salmon fishing was at one time a major activity but was ended by state law in 1957.

San Joaquin Valley, the southern part of the Central Valley, or the drainage area of the San Joaquin River, lies between the Sierra Nevada and the Coast Range, extending from the Sacramento River south to the Tehachapi Mts. It includes all of San Joaquin County, most of Stanislaus, Fresno, Merced, and Kings counties, about a third each of Kern, Tulare, and Madera counties, and a small part of Contra Costa County. The valley was inhabited by Yokuts and Miwok, and Pedro Fages was the first known white man to enter it in pursuit of army deserters (1772), but it remained little known since missions were not built there. Gabriel Moraga named the river (1805?) for St. Joachim, father of the Virgin, and the valley, which took its name from that, became known to Jedediah Smith and other American trappers and to the Hudson's Bay Co., which established a post near the present Stockton, and was explored by Frémont (1844–45).

Settlement began after the gold rush with cattle ranches, succeeded by wheat farming, for which the flat fields, weed- and stone-free soil, and light rainfall were suitable. Disputes over land ownership, particularly relating to grants given the Southern Pacific, were common after the 1860s, the most disastrous resulting in the Mussell Slough tragedy. Henry Miller and his partner, Charles Lux, came to control large areas, extending 68 miles on the west side of the Valley, including thousands of acres in Kern County and 200,000 acres on the east side.

During the late 19th century, irrigation systems were constructed because early water laws forbade use of stream waters by any ranchers except those who owned land along the banks. Small irrigation systems were merged in the 20th century, culminating in the great Central Valley Project. Water for the valley made possible diversification of crops beyond wheat. Vineyards were introduced in the 1850s; almond and peach trees were planted in the 1870s and 1880s, respectively; rice was grown experimentally in 1910 and commercially by 1915; and cotton, first planted successfully in 1910, was a main crop by 1920. Cattle raising has continued as a major business, dairy products are important, and other crops include tomatoes, potatoes, alfalfa, sugar beets, olives, and various fruits. Oil, its existence known as early as 1868, has been discovered in large fields, particularly along the Kern River, and a pipeline to Pt. Richmond was built as early as 1902. The valley's largest cities are Stockton, Fresno, and Bakersfield. (*See also individual entries.*)

San Jose, seat of Santa Clara County, located just beyond the southernmost reach of San Francisco Bay, was founded by José Joaquin Moraga (1777) as the first pueblo within the present state. It was given the name Pueblo de San José de Guadalupe, the modifier referring to the nearby river named by Anza (1776) for his expedition's patron saint. Although generally called simply the Spanish equivalent of St. Joseph, the city was always spelled with an accent on its final letter until Americans overwhelmed the original Spanish-speaking settlers. The mission of the same name was not founded until 1797 and lies some 15 miles northeast, while Mission Santa Clara was established at the time of the pueblo but became part of the adjacent city of Santa Clara, developed during the gold rush, though long connected by the Alameda, a broad tree-lined road.

San Jose remained a quiet pueblo which by 1848 had about 700 inhabitants and was the major community north of Monterey. Early newcomers from the U.S., like the Martin Murphy family and descendants of Donner Party members, began an American settlement which grew tremendously during the gold rush, when it provided a supply center for miners. Thus San Jose became the first state capital (1849–51) and the site of the first meeting of its governing body, known as the Legislature of 1,000 Drinks.♦ By 1850 the newly incorporated city had a population of 3,000, and early Spanish settlers, like the Peralta family, were being outnumbered by newcomers. Among them were Gen. Henry M. Naglee, the French agriculturalist Louis Pellier, and the poet Edwin Markham.

The nearby fertile Santa Clara Valley became a major area for fruit orchards, vineyards, vegetable farming, and cattle raising, all of which made the city an important packing and shipping center. Even as it grew greatly and became known for its canneries (the first was established in 1871), it still remained a kind of outpost of San Francisco. At the beginning of the 20th century, the city had 21,500 residents; it continued to grow slowly but substantially during the next four decades.

The period after World War II changed the character of San Jose strikingly. At the end of the war it had a population of about 57,000; by 1950 there were 95,000 inhabitants; and by the mid-1970s it had reached a population of 535,000. In this period San Jose earned the reputation of being the world's fastest-growing city. Although it was the fourth largest city in the state, it consisted essentially of suburbs and special centers, without a significant downtown. Its food-related businesses of processing, packing, freezing, canning, and drying expanded enormously. But the city also attracted large new enterprises extending not only into food machinery but into computer manufacturing, chemical production, and equipment for the use of atomic power.

The city is also known as the home of California's first state college (est. 1857), which has grown into the full-fledged California State University at San Jose, with an enrollment of 27,000 in 1970. Tourists as well as residents are attracted to the city's five-and-a-half acre Municipal Rose Garden, its Rosicrucian Egyptian Temple and Museum, a planetarium, nearby Alum Rock Park,♦ the Winchester House,♦ and a modern Frontier Village. Prominent residents of San Jose have included Henry Meade Bland and A. P. Giannini.

San José de Guadalupe, fourteenth of the 21 missions♦ to be founded, was established by Lasuén (1797) at an inland site about 15 miles northeast of the present city of San Jose, on the slope of the Diablo Range. It is named for Joseph, husband of the Virgin Mary, and is known as Mission San Jose, the name of the town founded nearby (1851). The location was selected as a base for expeditions against hostile Indians as well as a place to convert them. The tile-roofed adobe church, monastery, and other buildings constructed in 1805–9 were destroyed by an earthquake (1868), and only part of one wing has been reconstructed (1916, 50). The Father for many years was Narciso Durán,♦ who taught his charges, including the notorious Estanislao, to read music and to play in an orchestra. Although the city of San Jose (originally the pueblo of San José de Guadalupe) is in Santa Clara County, the mission is in Alameda County.

San Jose Mercury (1851–), founded as the *Weekly Visitor,* was also named the *Santa Clara Register* and *San Jose Telegraph* before assuming its present name (1860) and attempting daily publication twice

(1861–62 and 1869). Charles Shortridge owned and published the paper (1885–99), whose control passed (1901) to E. A. and J. O. Hayes, leaders of the Good Government League and owners of the local *Herald,* with which they merged it (1913) to form a strong daily. The single name, *Mercury,* was resumed in 1950.

San Juan Bautista, fifteenth of the 21 missions♦ to be founded, was established by Lasuén (1797) at a site west of present Hollister in the northernmost part of San Benito County, and named for St. John the Baptist. The first church (1798) was damaged by earthquakes and the present one (1803–12), severely injured by the great quake of 1906, was reconstructed in 1949–50. Cruciform in shape, it has a modern (1865; remodeled, 1929) low corner belfry. Behind the altar is a colorful reredos with niches for statues of saints that was painted by Thomas Doak♦ (1818). Only one wing of the adjoining quadrangle remains, but the mission faces the town of the same name (begun in 1814), around whose plaza cluster the Plaza Hotel (begun as barracks); the Castro house (1840), originally the home of Gov. Castro and later of Patrick Breen, who converted it to an inn; the Zanetta House (1868), home of the Plaza Hotel's owner and built of adobe bricks made for the mission Indian girls' dormitory; and the Plaza Stable (1874), which served the many stage lines that converged there as a stopping point. All these buildings except the mission form a State Historical Park (1935).

San Juan Capistrano, seventh of the 21 missions♦ to be founded, had its site selected by Father Lasuén (1775) in present Orange County and was formally dedicated by Serra (1776) with its first church built (1777), named for St. John of Capistrano, a 14th-century Italian theologian. The large mission built between 1796 and 1806 was severely damaged by an earthquake in 1812 and again in 1918. Only a portion of the church and its elaborate out-buildings has been restored, but the ruins are a romantic tourist attraction of the town of its name, which has been built in Spanish style and is known for the legend of the swallows,♦ who are said to flock to it the same day each year. Boscana♦ was the mission's Father (1814–26).

San Leandro, city directly south of Oakland, named for a *rancho* owned by the Estudillo family, was founded in 1854. Long a farming area with a large Portuguese population, it has become a residential suburb and manufacturing center and one of the fifty most populous communities of the state. The artist Borein was born there. In 1970 the population was 68,698.

San Lorenzo River, a 25-mile stream flowing through Santa Cruz County's redwood region. It was seen and named by Portolá's party led by José Ortega (1769).

San Luis Canal, see *Central Valley Project* and *Westlands.*

San Luis Dam, constructed jointly by the state and federal governments (1958) near Pacheco Pass and Los Banos (Merced County), to store water from the Delta-Mendota Canal♦ and the California Aqueduct♦ in its San Luis Reservoir.

San Luis Obispo, seat of the county of the same name, developed around the mission and grew into a merchandising and marketing center for nearby ranches. It lies at the foot of the Santa Lucia Mts. and is at a major junction of highways 1 and 101. California State Polytechnic College (est. 1901), located there, is a predominantly agricultural and engineering institute. The population in 1970 was 28,036.

San Luis Obispo County, one of the original 27 counties (1850), has always had the city of the same name as its seat, the appellation deriving from that of the mission♦ founded in 1776. The county is bounded by the ocean on the west, Monterey County on the north, Kern County on the east, and Santa Barbara County on the south. The region was the home of Chumash Indians, and the first whites to see it were Pedro de Unamuno♦ and Sebastian Cermeño,♦ who landed their Manila galleons there in 1587 and 1605, respectively. The first to come by land were Portolá (1769), Fages and Serra (1772), and Anza (1774, 1776). In 1797 Mission San Miguel♦ was founded near the county's northern border, and to it was attached the *asistencia* of Santa Margarita, located at Cuesta Pass♦ at the northernmost point of Los Padres National Forest.

Much of the coast is relatively isolated between the steep Santa Lucia Mts.♦ and the sheer ocean cliffs. In the north it is dominated by the great Hearst Castle at San Simeon,♦ overlooking miles of privately held ranch lands. To the east across the mountains lies the man-made reservoir of Lake Nacimiento. Farther south on the coast are the towns of Morro Bay♦ and Pismo Beach.♦ Inland along Highway 101 lie the county's few moderately sizable settlements: Paso Robles♦ (and its adjacent Camp Roberts♦), Atascadero, and San Luis Obispo.♦ At its southern extremity is the town of Nipomo, the home of William G. Dana.♦ In the southeast of the county is the isolated Carrizo Plain♦ and the Caliente Range, which, with the Cuyama River, form the southern border. The county's main business is cattle ranching, with poultry, vegetables, field crops, and oil also of importance. In 1970 it had a population of 105,690. With an area of 2,037,696 acres, it had 33.2 persons per sq. mi.

San Luis Obispo de Tolosa, fifth of the 21 missions,♦ founded by Serra (Sept. 1772) on a site where Portolá had killed many bears for meat (1769) and where subsequent hunts were carried out to help feed other missions. The new mission was named for St. Louis, the royal bishop of Toulouse. Indian enemies of the mission's neophytes burned many of the log buildings (1776) by shooting flaming arrows into the thatched roofs. This led to reconstruction that employed curved roof tiles of a Spanish style, soon imitated in all other missions as well as in this mission's new adobe building. Its façade incorporated a belfry (1792–94) that was damaged by earthquakes, then modernized, and reconstructed in its original form beginning in 1933.

San Luis Rey de Francia, eighteenth of the 21 missions♦ to be founded, was the last one established (1789) by Lasuén. Named for Louis IX of France, who was sanctified (1297) for his crusades against the infidels, the mission was intended as a more-or-less midway point between missions San Diego and San Juan Capistrano. It is about 5 miles east of the present town of Oceanside. Father Antonio Peyrí built the first little adobe church (1802) and then designed and oversaw construction (1811–15) of this, the largest of the missions. The cruciform church with a dome over its crossing was intended to accommodate 1,000 worshippers. The somewhat Moorish façade is marked by an elaborate tower and accented in red by painted cornices, pediments, and pilasters. Off the nave is an octagonal mortuary chapel surmounted by a small dome. Adjoining the church are an arched and colonnaded quadrangle containing a monastery and other facilities facing a large patio. Below these structures are an elaborate arch and broad staircase leading down to sunken gardens and an outdoor laundry. After the usual decay following secularization, reconstruction was begun (1893) on the edifice, which had been returned to the Church and made into a seminary.

During its heyday it had more cattle, sheep, and horses on its lands than any other mission, and it attracted more neophytes both to its mission and to its *asistencia* of San Antonio de Pala.♦

San Marcos Pass, route through the Santa Ynez Mts., northwest of Santa Barbara. Frémont was guided by an early English settler, William Benjamin Foxen (who lived in nearby Foxen Canyon), through this pass on Christmas Eve 1846, thereby avoiding Gaviota Pass farther north, where the *Californios* were thought to be waiting to ambush him. Thus, he occupied Santa Barbara peaceably on Christmas Day.

San Marino, independent municipality adjacent to Pasadena, developed around the estate of that name owned by James de Barth Shorb, son-in-law of Benjamin Wilson. The property was bought by Henry E. Huntington♦ (1903) as the site of his mansion and, later, of his library and museum.

San Mateo, residential community on the San Francisco Peninsula in the county of its name, derived from an arroyo named by Anza (1776). It is also a center for shopping and light industry and the terminus of a low-lying south Bay bridge (1929). In 1970 the population was 78,991.

San Mateo County, created (1856) from the southern part of San Francisco County and extended (1868) by annexation of part of Santa Cruz County. Except for the first year, the county seat has always been Redwood City. The county is bounded on the north by San Francisco at the tip of the Peninsula, on the west by the ocean, on the south by Santa Cruz County, and on the east by lower San Francisco Bay and Santa Clara County. Daly City and South San Francisco, just over the border from San Francisco, are a modest residential suburb and a big manufacturing and meat packing center, respectively.

After the adjacent city airport, the San Francisco Peninsula changes character, becoming on the Bay side a continuous series of residential communities with an early history as small towns surrounded by country houses and estates. Millbrae, geographically the first of these communities, was originally the 1,100-acre ranch and great summer house of D. O. Mills; Burlingame, San Mateo, and Hillsborough, three intertwined communities, have had a history of millionaires' homes, ranging from those of very early settlers like W. D. M. Howard, Alvinza Hayward, and John Parrott, through those of the next generation of wealthy families like the Crockers, Newhalls, and Tobins, down to some of their descendants and other present-day members of the exclusive Burlingame Country Club. Nearby is Belmont, where William C. Ralston had his mansion, taken over by Sharon and now the site of the College of Notre Dame. Farther down the Peninsula, almost at its end, lie the similar communities of Atherton and Menlo Park, whose early owners of great landholdings included James King of William, Faxon Dean Atherton, and Milton S. Latham, followed by newer figures like James C. Flood, who built the most ostentatious of all these houses.

In the Montara Mts. and other hills overlooking these communities are the reservoirs of the Spring Valley Water Co., at whose northernmost lake Sen. Broderick had his fatal duel with Judge Terry. In the Santa Cruz Mts. toward the southern end of the county lie Woodside and Portola Valley (celebrating its explorer of 1769), more rustic but also social communities, which were begun as logging camps for the great redwoods whose lumber was shipped from the now irrelevantly named Bayside port of Redwood City.

The ocean side of the county has a quite different character with its foggy climate, rugged headlands, and rocky shoreline interspersed with small beaches, an area in which were developed isolated dairies and farms for artichokes and other truck gardening at Half Moon Bay and Pescadero. Suburbia has infiltrated even this remote region. The southern border of the county includes the Stanford Research Institute, but the University itself lies just on the other side of the boundary line at San Francisquito Creek. At the demarcation point long stood the towering redwood beside which Rivera y Moncada and Palou camped (1774), as did Anza (1776), which gave the name to the modern city of Palo Alto ("tall tree"), lying just across the border. Nearly east of there on the Bay shore is Dumbarton Bridge (1927), the first automobile route to span San Francisco Bay.

Since World War II the county's population has expanded enormously, with many subdivisions along the Bayshore Highway. Many of the new residents are commuters to San Francisco, but the county has its own manufacturing plants, many for electronics and food processing, as well as large retail enterprises. It is also a major area for nurseries and flower growing; cement manufacturing is a big business, too. The population in 1970 was 556,601. With an area of 285,284 acres, it had 1,245.1 persons per sq. mi. (*See also individual entries.*)

San Miguel Arcángel, sixteenth of the 21 missions♦ to be founded, was established by Lasuén (1797) in the northernmost part of San Luis Obispo County, about 40 miles south of Mission San Antonio and 40 miles north of Mission San Luis Obispo. Two earlier churches were replaced by the present one (1816–21), whose monastery colonnade is marked by different-sized and -shaped arches, and whose church has an interior brightened by *trompe l'oeil* murals by the Spanish artist Estévan Munras and by patterned designs painted by Indians under his direction. The remaining buildings have weathered time better than most missions and needed only renovation rather than reconstruction (1901, 1928).

San Miguel Island, see *Santa Barbara Islands.*

San Nicolás Island, most removed of the Catalina Islands,♦ 76 miles southwest of Los Angeles Harbor, discovered by Vizcaíno (1602), famous for the "lone woman" who eluded the transfer of other Indians to the mainland (1835) and was finally rescued (1853) by George Nidever.♦ The island is part of Ventura County.

San Onofre Nuclear Generating Station, located just south of the Orange County–San Diego County line, near San Clemente, is a commercial power plant established (1968) by Pacific Gas and Electric Co. on federal land.

San Pablo Bay, northeast of San Francisco Bay, its entry is beyond the city of Richmond and its eastern terminus is Carquinez Strait. Its major city is Vallejo,♦ and near it lies Mare Island.♦

San Pasqual, Battle of, occurred on Dec. 6, 1846, east of the present town of Escondido (San Diego County) when the cavalry of Gen. Andrés Pico was engaged by Gen. Kearny♦ immediately upon his arrival from Santa Fe, even though his force of 100 dragoons was exhausted by its march across the desert. The brief, intense battle involved the use of American sabers against the *Californios'* lances. Twenty-one Americans were killed and many others wounded, including Kearny, and perhaps a dozen *Californios* were wounded before both sides withdrew. Taking refuge on a hill above the valley site of the battle, Kearny awaited reinforcements until Dec. 11, his men being forced to eat their mules to avoid starvation. Kit Carson, Edward F. Beale, and an Indian ally sneaked out and got forces sent by Commodore Stockton, and the Americans, making their way to San Diego, later gained control of the area.

San Pedro, harbor of Los Angeles, 25 miles south of its downtown area, created by dredging San Pedro Bay. That site had served as an anchorage for sailing vessels, as described in *Two Years Before the Mast,* but it was first developed in the 1850s by Abel Stearns and Phineas Banning. A much more substantial development begun in the 1890s was for a long time vigorously opposed by Collis P. Huntington because the Southern Pacific hoped to develop its own properties at Santa Monica. By 1909 the larger harbor was joined to Los Angeles by the city's "shoestring" extension to the ocean. With Wilmington (originally New San Pedro) and Terminal Island,♦ this harbor has become a major seaport where ships costing billions of dollars were constructed during World War II. With Long Beach♦ as a major city and harbor next door, the area is one of the five major ports of the U.S., known too as the one where more fish are landed than at any other single place in the nation.

San Quentin, the state prison♦ that is the oldest (founded 1853) and largest (inmate maximum of 5,000 set in 1960) in California. Operated until 1860 on a private contract, it has since been the major penitentiary for men, although there were women prisoners prior to 1927. All men condemned to death are sent there because it is the only place in the state with a gas chamber. Famous inmates have included Black Bart, Abe Ruef, Tom Mooney, and J. B. McNamara. The longest trial in the state's history (507 days in 1975–76) was that of the "San Quentin Six," six black prisoners involved in an alleged escape attempt from San Quentin (Aug. 21, 1971), said to have been led by the revolutionary inmate, George Jackson, one of the Soledad Brothers♦ who was killed in the melee that also resulted in the deaths of three guards and two trusties. Three of the defendants were convicted and three were acquitted. The prison name is that of its site in Marin County on San Francisco Bay, itself named for an escaped Indian neophyte captured there (1824). He had been christened with the cognomen of a Roman officer who left the army to become a Christian missionary. Near Point San Quentin was found the "Plate of Brass" (1936) that at one time was believed to have been originally erected by Francis Drake (1579).

San Rafael, seat of Marin County and site of a mission established (1817) as an *asistencia* for Mission Dolores, razed (1870) and since rebuilt. A pleasant residential and retail shopping town, it is also noted for the County Civic Center designed by Frank Lloyd Wright, the nearby Dominican College, and San Quentin Prison. The population in 1970 was 38,977. Mountains of this name are part of the Los Padres National Forest in Santa Barbara County, and hills of the same name are in Los Angeles County.

San Rafael Arcángel, twentieth of the 21 missions,♦ founded (1817) by Father Sarría as a hospital *asistencia* for Mission Dolores, whose neophytes suffered from diseases brought by soldiers and settlers. It was named for St. Raphael, patron of good health. Located in the sunny climate of the present city of San Rafael, the simple adobe building was basically a sanitarium and monastery. Razed in 1870, a replica was built in 1949.

San Rafael Wild Area, a preserve of 75,000 acres in the San Rafael Mts. of the Los Padres National Forest along the Sisquoc River, north of Santa Barbara. It is a sanctuary for the condor.♦

San Simeon, site of the lavish estate of William Randolph Hearst♦ in the Santa Lucia Mts., built on the 240,000-acre ranch of his father, George Hearst, overlooking a private ocean frontage of more than 50 miles, north of Morro Bay. Beginning in 1919 and continuing throughout his life, William Randolph Hearst built a grandiose group of edifices designed by Julia Morgan.♦ The major one is marked by a cathedral-like façade with two bell towers in a vaguely Spanish renaissance style. It contains about 150 rooms, most of them vast and stately, often built with paneling and stonework from European palaces and churches, all furnished with an enormous aggregation of *objets d'art.* The lavishly landscaped grounds included a zoo said at one time to be the world's largest in private ownership. Hearst's heirs presented the cultivated area and its buildings, known as La Cuesta Encantada (The Enchanted Hill), to the state, which opened it to the public in 1958.

SAN VICENTE, Fernandez de, see *Fernandez de San Vicente.*

Santa Ana, seat of Orange County, founded in 1869. It is a residential, retail trade, and manufacturing city that has experienced the same phenomenal growth as its county. Before World War II it had about 30,000 residents; in 1970 the population was 156,601. The Charles W. Bowers Memorial Museum contains early California artifacts. In 1933 the city suffered a severe earthquake.

Santa Ana, hot, dry wind like a sirocco that blows north and northeast, mainly in the late summer and early fall. The name is derived from the Santa Ana Canyon in Orange County, but the wind, associated with fire hazards, is common in other southern California mountain and canyon areas, such as Bel Air, behind Beverly Hills, and Montecito, behind Santa Barbara.

Santa Ana Mountains, see *Peninsular Ranges.*

Santa Anita Park, located in Arcadia,♦ since its founding (1934) has been one of the major thoroughbred horse-racing tracks of the U.S. It introduced a starting gate, photographed finish, electrical timer, and totalizer. Like Tanforan, Santa Anita was ignominiously used as an assembly and internment center for Japanese soon after American entry into World War II (1942). It is located on the land grant that once belonged to Hugo Reid♦ and later to Elias Baldwin.♦

Santa Barbara, tenth of the 21 missions♦ to be founded (1786), was established by Lasuén on a site overlooking the presidio of the present city of Santa Barbara. It was named for the Roman virgin who was beheaded by her pagan father for embracing Christianity. The initial log structure with its thatched roof was successively replaced by two larger adobe buildings, the last (finished 1794) destroyed by an earthquake (1812) and finally replaced by the present stone edifice (1815–33), with its classical façade and twin towers. It stands at one corner of a large quadrangle that includes a monastery. Damaged by an earthquake (1925), it was repaired in the next two years and had its façade further rebuilt in 1950. A theological college, St. Anthony's Seminary, was constructed (1956–58) behind the original mission.

Santa Barbara County, one of the original 27 counties (1850), whose seat has always been the city of Santa Barbara, derived its name from the ocean channel between the mainland and the island that was so called by Vizcaíno (1602). The county is bounded by the ocean on the west and south, by Ventura County on the east, and by San Luis Obispo County on the north.

The Indians who lived there were Chumash, and their settlements included the one called Carpenteria, where Cabrillo saw asphalt springs (1542) and Crespí saw Indians building a canoe and caulking it with local tar (1769). Crespí and Portolá camped at various places in the present county on their way north to found missions, and their route was followed by Serra on his way back to Mexico (1772) and by Anza in 1774 and 1776. The first settlement was the presidio established by Gov. de Neve and Lt. José Francisco Ortega and dedicated by Serra (1782). The first mission was consecrated in 1786, but it was several times replaced (one building was destroyed by the earthquake of 1812) before an edifice of the present design was dedicated in 1820. It, too, had to be almost wholly reconstructed after another earthquake in 1925.

The county has more missions than any other, containing also La Purisíma Concepción, built at present Lompoc (1815–18), and Santa Inés, constructed in 1813–17. The major settlement has always been the port of Santa Barbara, whose Spanish heritage, represented by the de la Guerra, Carrillo, Ortega, and other old families, has been described by Richard Henry Dana, Alfred Robinson, and William Henry Thomes, among others. That heritage has also been preserved by the restoration of old adobes and by the reconstruction of the city after the 1925 earthquake in a Spanish style employed by George Washington Smith and others. The notable public structures include El Paseo, a pseudo-Spanish section built around the de la Guerra house, and the spaciously impressive County Court House. The city's background is also recalled during an annual midsummer Fiesta celebrating Old Spanish Days (begun 1924) and by such festivities as the horseback expeditions of the Rancheros Visitadores, initiated by the local artist Edward Borein.

The area's American history dates back to the visits of New England traders engaged in the hide and tallow business and the subsequent conquest during the Mexican War, when Frémont evaded an assumed ambush by *Californios* at Gaviota Pass by coming through San Marcos Pass to take the city peacefully on Christmas Day, 1846. This diverse but vividly recalled historic background is among the attractions that have long brought tourists to the area. Thus, the area has developed many resorts, such as the onetime Arlington Hotel, owned by W. W. Hollister, a pioneer rancher of the region, and the Potter Hotel (1901–21). The long coastline that turns at Point Concepcion, with its scenic views, safe beaches, and good climate, is also a major attraction. The cultural life of the main city, with a fine art gallery, theater, and music, a good newspaper, the *Santa Barbara News-Press,* long published by T. M. Storke, also appeals to discriminating visitors and cultivated residents.

Communities other than the county seat that bring persons to the region include Solvang, a Danish settlement; Lompoc, where great fields of flowers furnish a large part of the world's horticultural seeds; Santa Maria, the city on the county's northern border that provides homes and commerce for nearby Vandenberg Air Force Missile Base; Goleta, the site of the University of California's Santa Barbara campus; and Montecito, an elegant residential community just outside Santa Barbara. In the county's interior lie the rugged Sierra Madre and San Rafael mountains, home of California's condors and part of the Los Padres National Forest, which also nearly surround the man-made Lake Cachuma. Between this reservoir and the coastal communities lie the dramatically precipitous Santa Ynez Mts. Offshore are the Santa Barbara Islands, of which San Miguel, Santa Rosa, and Santa Cruz belong to the county. Among the region's oilfields is Ellwood, just west of Goleta, which was the site of the only direct enemy attack on the continental U.S. during World War II, made when a Japanese submarine surfaced and shelled the petroleum installation (Feb. 23, 1942). A more disastrous event was the serious blowout of an oil well being drilled from a platform 5 miles offshore (Jan. 28, 1969), which led to a spreading spill stretching as far as 20 miles along the coast and 40 miles to sea, some of it coming in to foul beaches and kill birds. The city has also suffered two great fires which destroyed many residences (1964, 1977).

The county's economy is based not only on tourists and mineral production, including oil, natural gas, and diatomite, but on manufacturing (much of it related to Vandenberg Air Force Base's activities) and agriculture, including livestock and poultry raising, vegetable farming, citrus and avocado growing, sugar-beet raising at Betteravia, and flower and seed production. In 1970 the county seat had a population of 70,215, and the county itself had 264,324. With an area of 1,752,064 acres, it had 96.6 persons per sq. mi. *(See also individual entries.)*

Santa Barbara Island, see *Channel Islands National Monument* and *Catalina Islands.*

Santa Barbara Islands, four islands about 25 to 30 miles off the coast from Point Concepcion to Port Hueneme of Santa Barbara and Ventura counties. They are from north to south San Miguel, Santa Rosa, Santa Cruz, and Anacapa. The largest is Santa Cruz, 23 miles long and 2 to 6½ miles wide.

All are mountainous and were once volcanic. They have flora (Santa Cruz pine) and fauna (dwarf fox and spotted skunk) different from those of the mainland. The Indians were Chumash and were said to have been killed in great numbers by Russians and Aleuts who used the islands for fishing and seal and otter hunting. San Miguel was discovered by Cabrillo♦ (1542), who is thought to have been buried there. It was later leased by George Nidever,♦ then seized by one Capt. Waters because it is not mentioned in the Treaty of Guadalupe-Hidalgo,♦ and is now privately owned as a ranch. Santa Rosa was the site on which was found the incised rock thought to be Cabrillo's tombstone. The island was granted as a *rancho* to the Carrillo family (1843), and is now a privately owned cattle ranch. Santa Cruz (called San Salvador by Cabrillo), the first landing place of the Sacred Expedition, was once a penal colony, then a private land grant, and now a private cattle ranch with wild boar stocked for hunting. Anacapa consists of three segments and is the most barren of the islands. It and Santa Barbara Island (of the Catalina group♦) comprise the Channel Islands National Monument, a federally owned ecological preserve.

Santa Barbara News-Press (1937–), daily evening newspaper founded by T. M. Storke♦ when he merged the *News* (which he had owned since 1913 when he affiliated it with the *Independent,* which he had issued since 1901) and the *Morning Press,* which he bought in 1932. The lineage of the papers can be traced back to 1855, making the final merger a continuation of the oldest surviving daily in southern California. Shortly before his death (1971) Storke sold the paper, which he had made into a distinguished independent news medium.

Santa Catalina, island 27 miles offshore southwest of Wilmington, the Los Angeles harbor, is 21 miles long and from one-half to 8 miles wide, with rugged mountains rising to 2,100 feet. Discovered by Cabrillo (1542) and named by him for his ship, the *San Salvador,* it was renamed (Nov. 1602) by Vizcaíno, who anchored there at the time of the feast of Santa Catalina (St. Catherine) of Alexandria. The original inhabitants, Gabrieleños, were exterminated, mainly by Russian sea otter hunters (*c.*1810). Capt. William Shaler♦ was presumably the first American visitor (1805), and the island came into American possession when Gov. Pico granted it to a Santa Barbaran, Thomas Robbins (1846). It has remained a private possession, later owners including James Lick, the sons of Phineas Banning, and William Wrigley, Jr. Wrigley and his son Philip developed part of it as a tourist attraction, building up the town of Avalon with a great casino, promoting deep sea fishing, and making it the site of spring training for his baseball team, the Chicago Cubs; but most of the interior and much of the coastline are preserved as open land. The island is part of Los Angeles County and is one of the four Catalina Islands.♦

Santa Clara, city adjacent to San Jose that grew up around its mission and then by the infiltration of gold miners who took up ranching and residence there. It has continued not only as a residential area but as a center for dried-fruit processing, packing plants, and light industry, generally related to the produce of Santa Clara Valley. The valley, consisting of some 200 square miles, is a rich farming land with Pajaro Valley on its west and Salinas Valley on its south. Famous for its fruit orchards, vineyards, tomatoes, walnuts, barley, and cattle raising, since World War II it has been more and more seriously invaded by subdivisions and tract housing, and recently by a Disney-like amusement park, "Great America." The University of Santa Clara is located on the old mission's site. In 1970 the city population was 87,717.

Another and smaller Santa Clara Valley between the San Rafael Range and the Sierra San Fernando lies in Ventura County and is the site not only of the earliest oil strike in the state (1866) but of citrus orchards and other farms. It was the site of a disastrous flood caused by the collapse of the Saint Francis Dam♦ (1928).

Santa Clara, University of, coeducational Jesuit institution not restricted to Catholics, founded (1851) as a college, renamed University in 1912, initially an outgrowth of the old Mission Santa Clara de Asís.♦ In 1970 it enrolled about 5,700 students.

Santa Clara County, one of the original 27 counties (1850), has always had San Jose as its seat. The county is bounded on the north by Alameda County, a tip of San Francisco Bay, and San Mateo County; on the west by San Mateo and Santa Cruz counties; on the south by San Benito County; and on the east by Stanislaus and Merced counties.

Costanoan Indians dwelt there, and early explorers included Portolá (1769), who camped on the northern boundary under the Palo Alto redwood, Fages (1772), and Anza (1776), blazing trails that

would become El Camino Reál. Mission Santa Clara de Asís was founded in 1777, as was the pueblo San José de Guadalupe, established by José Joaquín Moraga, later that year. A tree-lined road, the Alameda, connected them. A separate town of Santa Clara grew up around the mission, whose secularized buildings in time became the home of Santa Clara College (est. 1851). Later settlers were attracted to the present county by the development of the New Almaden mine, from which great quantities of mercury were extracted beginning in 1845. Early settlers included those who obtained ranching lands on which communities developed, among them Juan Ignacio Alviso, who created a port in the Alviso Slough for San Jose and the mission; John Gilroy, a Scottish rancher whose surname is borne by a town near his lands; José María Alviso (Juan Ignacio's son), on whose Rancho Milpitas ("little cornfield") a town of that name developed; Martin Murphy, who ranched near the present Sunnyvale and San Martin, who, like two other newcomers of 1844, Elisha Stevens and Moses Schallenberger, settled in the area.

The tradition of farming, begun early, has been a mainstay of the region, whose Santa Clara Valley has long been famous not only for the plums introduced there by Louis Pellier (1856) and once the source of about one-third of the world's prunes but for other fruits, vegetables (particularly tomatoes), livestock, and poultry. More and more of the county's rich farmland has been taken over by tract housing, shopping centers, and manufacturing as a result of the phenomenal growth of the area in the years following World War II.

San Jose and Santa Clara, as well as the northern area, including the communities of Palo Alto, Mountain View, Los Altos, and Sunnyvale—the latter long known for its Moffett Field—have burgeoned. Development of the residential and wine-growing areas in the Santa Cruz Mts., on the county's western borders, has been less great, so that Saratoga and Los Gatos retain their old independence, and have not yet become suburbs of San Jose, like Campbell, where the Winchester House is located, and Cupertino, into which electronics and aerospace industries have penetrated. Population has crept into the Diablo Range on the valley's east, whose high point is Mt. Hamilton, with its great Lick Observatory. The southern part of the county is far less affected, continuing in relative isolation with Hecker Pass, the route through the western mountains to Santa Cruz and Pacheco Pass, the entry into the interior San

Joaquin Valley. The county is known not only for its agriculture and its varied manufacturing plants, including those for electronics, military supplies, and food processing, but for its numerous institutions of higher education, including Stanford University, the University of Santa Clara, and San Jose State University. In 1970 the county had a population of 1,066,174. With an area of 832,256 acres, it had 820.1 persons per sq. mi. *(See also individual entries.)*

Santa Clara de Asís, eighth of the 21 missions♦ to be founded, named for St. Claire of Assisi, who established the order of nuns often called Poor Claires. The first church, a simple log structure, was built (1777) on the Guadalupe River in the present town of Santa Clara. Other buildings replaced this one in 1779, 1784, and 1818–19. The final adobe church was constructed in 1825 and after secularization (1836) was returned to the Church, but was transferred from the Franciscans to the Jesuits to serve as a college (1851), now the University of Santa Clara. Destroyed by fire (1926), a somewhat elaborated reconstruction of stucco and concrete was completed in 1929. It continues to be part of the University.

Santa Cruz, twelfth of the 21 missions♦ to be founded, was established (1791) by Lasuén on a site overlooking the present city of its name. Construction of the mission and its quadrangle was completed in 1795. The establishment of the nearby pueblo of Branciforte♦ (1797) endangered the mission as settlers encroached on its lands, molested the Indians, and stole much of the property when the buildings were temporarily deserted because of a feared invasion by the pirate Bouchard♦ (1818). Not surprisingly, it was the first mission to be secularized (1834), and the untended buildings disintegrated. A small replica of the mission's chapel was built (1931) and houses some mission relics.

Santa Cruz, beach resort and residential city, seat of the county of the same name. Its history dates back to the expedition of Portolá (1769), the founding of the mission (1791), and the establishment of the pueblo of Branciforte (1797). The present city grew up beside the mission plaza. Even before it was chartered (1866), it was an important port on Monterey Bay, from which lumber cut from the big redwoods of neighboring forests was shipped. It was also a center for neighboring *ranchos,* and tanneries for regionally raised cattle hides have

prospered since 1850. The city has also had some manufacturing, beginning with the production of miners' picks during the gold rush. Other city features are the municipal pier near which the annual Miss California pageant♦ is held. Famous begonia nurseries are located in nearby Capitola. The University of California has a major campus on the adjacent land once owned by the Cowell♦ family. In 1970 the city had a population of 32,076.

Santa Cruz County, one of the original 27 counties (1850), during its first months (Feb.-April 1850) was called Branciforte. The city of Santa Cruz♦ has always been its seat. The ocean lies on the county's west, Santa Clara County on its east, and Monterey County and a small strip of San Benito County on its south. On the north is San Mateo County, into which was absorbed the town of Pescadero and the area south of the town (1868), which now lie on the west of Santa Cruz County, their original home.

The native Indians were Costanoan. Cabrillo was probably the first white to see Monterey Bay♦ (1542), whose northern portion is in the county. Cermeño (1595) and Vizcaíno (1602) were the first to bring ships into the bay. The first whites to traverse the area were Portolá, Crespí, and their party (1769), but the initial settlement was that of the first mission (1791), from which the county derived its permanent name. Near the mission, the pueblo of Branciforte♦ (1797) was established, and it continued a separate existence on the opposite side of the San Lorenzo River until absorbed (1907) into the city of Santa Cruz, which had come into being in 1866. The big redwood stands north of the city were the early sites of sawmills and paper manufacturers. Near Davenport lime kilns were established, and south of it cement plants and tanneries were set up.

In time the giant trees came to be protected, initially by the Big Basin Redwoods State Park, the first state reserve to be created (1902), later by a park named for Henry Cowell,♦ on whose ranch the University of California developed a campus (1961), and by the Forest of Nisene Marks State Park. This area of the Santa Cruz Mts., through which Mountain Charley (Parkhurst)♦ and other stagecoach drivers once made their way, was opened to Santa Clara County by Hecker Pass♦ (1928), but it preserves a sense of rustic retreat in forest settlements that include Brookdale, Boulder Creek, and Felton. Along the ocean shore south of Santa Cruz lie larger communities, also mainly residential, such as Capitola (known for its begonia nurseries), Soquel (once a lumber town, now an orchard and home area), and Aptos (a beach resort and residence site). Inland in the Pajaro River Valley lies the county's second largest city, Watsonville,♦ where apples are grown and packed, along with other fruit and garden crops. The county has an area of 281,472 acres. With a total population of 123,790, it had 281.5 persons per sq. mi. in 1970.

Santa Cruz Island, see *Santa Barbara Islands.*

Santa Cruz Mountains, part of the Coast Range, extending from the southern part of the San Francisco Peninsula through Santa Cruz County, ending above the Gabilan Range.♦ Hecker Pass♦ is a major east-west route through them. Mountain Charley (Parkhurst)♦ was a famous stagecoach driver in the range. Saratoga♦ is not only an important residential community, but is the center of an area of major vineyards and wineries.

Santa Fe Railroad, an outgrowth of the Atchison, Topeka, & Santa Fe Railroad (founded in Kansas, 1860), whose westward expansion through Colorado and New Mexico into Arizona (where in 1883 it made a connection with the Southern Pacific) led its owners to search for a Pacific outlet. After a track to Guaymas, Mexico, was built (1882), it joined the line of its long-time opponent, the Southern Pacific, at San Bernardino (1885), and bought the Southern Pacific track from Needles to Mojave. The railroads continued to compete in a great rate war, but the Santa Fe expanded with its own track to Los Angeles (1887), constructed its "Surf Line" to San Diego (1888), and built a line up the San Joaquin Valley to Pt. Richmond (1900) and into San Francisco and Oakland (1904). The opposing lines joined to create the Northwestern Pacific Railroad (1907–29) for service into the northern part of the state, eventually surrendered wholly to the Southern Pacific.

Santa Fe Trail, see *Old Spanish Trail.*

Santa Inés, nineteenth of the 21 missions♦ to be founded, was established (1804) at a site where the town of Solvang♦ now stands, about 25 miles east of Mission La Purísima. Named after St. Agnes, a Roman girl noted for her purity, it gave the name to the Santa Ynez Valley, Mountains, and River that use a variant spelling. After the original structure was destroyed by an earthquake (1812), the present mission was built (1813–17), with Joseph Chapman♦ as one of the workmen. It suffered from the revolt of Indian neophytes begun at La Purísima♦ (1824), and although repaired, it deteriorated greatly after secularization. Reconstruction has been carried on intermittently since 1904, but only the church, the campanario, and a small part of a once-substantial quadrangle survive. It now figures in the annual ceremony of the Rancheros Visitadores.♦

Santa Lucia Mountains, largest of the southern Coast Ranges, extend about 125 miles from Monterey Bay to Estero Bay and rise almost to 6,000 feet. They include Carmel Valley,♦ Big Sur,♦ northern Los Padres National Forest,♦ Ventana Wild Area,♦ Tassajara Hot Springs,♦ Hunter Liggett Military Reservation,♦ and San Simeon.♦ They were named by Vizcaíno.

Santa Maria, northernmost city in Santa Barbara County, located on the river and in the valley of the same name, is the market center for the region's grain, beans, flower seeds, and dairy products. Nearby oil discoveries and Vandenberg Air Force Missile Base have brought great increases in population, which in 1970 was 32,749.

Santa Monica, independent municipality south and west of Los Angeles on the oceanfront, incorporated (1886) after a real estate development was begun there (1875). It lies below the southern extremity of the Santa Monica Mts. (named for the mother of St. Augustine, probably by Portolá in 1770) and fronts on Santa Monica Bay. The city early became a residential and resort area with a popular amusement park. A different development occurred with the establishment in the 1920s of the Douglas Aircraft Co., great builders of commercial and military planes. It is also the site of the Rand Corp.♦ Natives of the city include Parry O'Brien and Shirley Temple. In 1970 the population was 88,289.

Santa Monica Mountains, part of the Transverse Ranges,♦ extending about fifty miles from the Los Angeles River to the Oxnard plain. Hollywood lies on its foothills, and the mountains themselves include Griffith Park, Will Rogers Park, and other public areas.

Santa Paula, city in Ventura County, both a residential community and a packing center for nearby citrus and avocado ranches. It is also an oil refinery center, and its California Oil Museum was the founding site of the Union Oil Co. The town name dates back to a mission ranch in 1834 and has been given to a nearby peak in Los Padres National Forest, its adjacent creek, and a canyon, but the city grew up in early 1870s. In 1970 it had a population of 18,001.

Santa Rosa, seat of Sonoma County, is a major market and merchandising center for ranches of Sonoma Valley. Wineries and fruit processing plants are located there also. In the 1960s and 70s the city grew enormously as a residential suburb. Its most famous landmarks are the house and gardens of the experimental horticulturist, Luther Burbank.♦ The small-town atmosphere was featured in Alfred Hitchcock's film *Shadow of a Doubt* (1943) set there. Natives of the city include Robert Ripley, memorialized by a local museum. In 1970 the population of the city was 50,006.

Santa Rosa Island, see *Santa Barbara Islands*.

Santa Rosa Mountains, see *Peninsular Ranges*.

Santa Susana Mountains, see *Transverse Ranges*.

Santa Ynez Fault, see *Earthquakes*.

Santa Ynez Mountains, lying back of the Santa Barbara coast, part of the Transverse Ranges.♦ The name derives from Mission Santa Inés, which lies within the Santa Ynez Valley, as do Solvang♦ and Lake Cachuma.♦

Santa Ysabel Chapel, see *San Diego de Alcalá*.

Saratoga, residential community in the Santa Cruz Mts. of Santa Clara County. Once a lumbering center for nearby redwoods and then a spa (hence the name, which recalls the New York resort), it has long had distinguished vineyards and wineries, including that of Paul Masson. Since 1930, Villa Montalvo, the home of Sen. Phelan, has been a creative arts center for writers and painters. In 1970 the population was 27,110.

Sardines, most commonly used as bait to catch salmon until the beginning of the 20th century, when they were netted for food. By 1904 Monterey's Cannery Row was calling itself "the sardine capital of the world." In season, it was packing four tons of fish a day for eating while rendering the head waste for oil and as fertilizer. Before 1940 a billion pounds a year were landed, but since then the fish have become so scarce that only 7,000,000

pounds were caught in 1963, and a moratorium on fishing was set in 1967.

SARGENT, AARON AUGUSTUS (1827–87), Massachusetts-born leader in Republican party politics of California, to which he moved in 1849. There he became a lawyer, state Senator, U.S. Congressman (1861–63, 69–73), and U.S. Senator (1873–79). He was later Minister to Germany and then to Russia.

SAROYAN, WILLIAM (1908–), born in Fresno of Armenian parents, he has drawn upon his cultural and personal background for his fiction, drama, and sketches, which are also informed by a rich, impressionistic imagination. Part of his youth was spent in an orphanage because of his widowed mother's poverty. He quit school at age 12 to become a telegraph messenger boy and began publishing stories in 1934. That year there appeared the first of his many collections, *The Daring Young Man on the Flying Trapeze,* marked by an exuberant, sentimental, and rhapsodic exaltation of diverse characters, all presented in radiant moments of revelation. The stories were all marked by his dynamic, self-assured style, which he described as being of the "jump-in-the-river-and-start-to-swim-immediately" nature. Other stories have poured out in such volumes as *Inhale and Exhale* (1936), *Little Children* (1937), *The Trouble with Tigers* (1938), *Peace, It's Wonderful* (1939), and later collections. Some of his short fiction is more distinctly autobiographical, particularly *My Name Is Aram* (1940), revealing the experiences of Armenian children in California.

Much of his other work, often similar in style and technique to fiction, is clearly autobiographical, including *The Twin Adventures* (1950), incorporating *The Adventures of Wesley Jackson* (1946), a whimsical telling of the World War II adventures of a Saroyanesque army private, counterpointed by the ostensibly actual "Adventures of William Saroyan," concerning the author's way of writing a novel; *The Bicycle Rider in Beverly Hills* (1952); *Here Comes, There Goes, You Know Who* (1962); *Not Dying* (1963); and *One Day in the Afternoon of the World* (1964). He has also written novels that are more clearly fictional, including *The Human Comedy* (1943), *Rock Wagram* (1951), *Mama, I Love You* (1956), *Papa, You're Crazy* (1957), and *Boys and Girls Together* (1963).

He is the author of a great number of plays whose manner and attitude are much like those of his fiction. The best-known of these is *The Time of Your*

Life (1939), for which he refused a Pulitzer Prize (he considered it a patronizing bit of commercialism). The three-act play, set in a San Francisco waterfront bar, reveals the essential, innate virtue of very diverse people who gain the opportunity to pursue their hopes and dreams when a wealthy drunk gives them money. Other dramas include *My Heart's in the Highlands* (1939), a loose, short play also presenting the belief that aspiration means more than worldly achievement; *Love's Old Sweet Song* (1941); *Razzle Dazzle* (1942); *Jim Dandy, Fat Man in a Famine* (1947); and *Don't Go Away Mad* (1949).

SARRÍA, VICENTE FRANCISCO DE (1767–1835), Spanish-born missionary who went to California (1809) and became President-General♦ of the missions (1823–25). He founded the mission at San Rafael (1817) and helped put down the Chumash revolt at Santa Barbara (1824).

Sather Gate, major city entrance to the Berkeley campus of the University of California, which, as a gathering place for social and political ferment, particularly on the adjacent Sproul Hall steps during the Free Speech Movement,♦ is a symbol of student social action. The gate was erected (1913) in memory of Peder Sather (1841–86), a banker and trustee of the College of California, by his widow, Jane Sather. Her own memorial (also her gift to the Berkeley campus) is Sather Tower, more commonly called the Campanile, modeled on the bell tower of St. Mark's Cathedral in Venice, completed in 1918, and, like the Gate, designed by John Galen Howard.

Saugus, see *Newhall.*

SAUNDERS, CHARLES FRANCIS (1859–1941), Pennsylvania-born settler in Pasadena, where he wrote appreciative books about his new homeland, including *Under the Sky in California* (1913) and *Finding the Worthwhile in California* (1916).

Sausalito, waterfront town of Marin County on San Francisco Bay, named for the land grant of its first settler, William A. Richardson,♦ who in 1838 obtained the Rancho Saucelito ("willow grove" in Spanish). Once a harbor for whalers and other visiting vessels, its overlooking hills with their winding streets have long been a quiet residential area attracting artists as well as tourists. During World War II, the serene atmosphere was disrupted by a big shipbuilding yard. The population in 1970 was over 6,000.

SAVAGE, JAMES D. (1823–52), frontiersman who went to California (1846) and, because he lived among some Indians as a trader, came to be known as the "Blond King of the Tulare." With Lafayette H. Bunnell♦ he led the Mariposa Battalion,♦ a deputized body of state militia who undertook a punitive expedition (1851) against Indians who had killed whites in the area of Fresno and Mariposa. In the process of reconnoitering, he and Bunnell entered and named Yosemite Valley, the first whites after Joseph R. Walker's party to view it. Savage was killed in a fight with a ranger whom he accused of attacking some peaceful Indians.

Save-the-Redwoods League, see *Redwoods.*

Savings and Loan Associations, in part an outgrowth of savings banks like the San Francisco Accumulating Fund Association (est. 1854), differ from commercial banks in that they can make loans only on tangible security and cannot issue commercial paper. They differ also from such an association as the California Building and Loan Society (est. 1865), in which funds are loaned only to members who make periodic fixed payments to the society. Savings and loan associations grew in the latter part of the 19th century, but their huge increase in number of institutions, in branch offices scattered throughout all cities in the state, and in value of deposits has occurred in this century, particularly since World War II. California now has more savings and loan associations than any other state, but the number of separate institutions has decreased through mergers that have resulted in several associations, each having more than a billion dollars in assets.

Sawmills, see *Forests and forestry.*

SAWYER, LORENZO (1820–91), left his law practice in Wisconsin to move to California during the gold rush (1850). There he pursued his career and became a state Supreme Court Justice (1863) and U.S. Circuit Court Judge (1870–91). In the latter capacity he rendered an important decision against a mine at Malakoff Diggins♦ prohibiting further hydraulic mining there or elsewhere in the state to prevent pollution of properties not owned by the mining company. His *Way Sketches* (1926) describes his travels to California.

Scandinavians in California, were Danes,♦ Finns,♦ Norwegians,♦ and Swedes♦ who began to arrive mainly during the gold rush but substantially increased in population later in the 19th century. In 1850 there were only about 380 Scandinavians in the state, but by 1870 the census showed 4,781.

Scenic attractions, are various, and distributed throughout most of the state. They range from dense forests in the northwest to barren deserts in the southeast. Among them, roughly north to south, are Redwood National Park, Six Rivers and Trinity National Forests, the Mendocino Coast, Mt. Shasta, Shasta National Forest, Trinity National Recreational Area, Lassen Volcanic National Park, Lava Beds National Monument, Glass Mountain, Lassen and Modoc National Forests, Plumas National Forest, Lake Tahoe, Fort Ross, Clear Lake, Russian River, Point Reyes, Napa Valley, Valley of the Moon, Muir Woods and Mt. Tamalpais, San Francisco Bay, Monterey Bay, Big Sur, the Delta, Sierra Nevada Mts., Calaveras Grove, Mercer Caves and Moaning Cave, Devil's Postpile, Mariposa Grove, Mono Lake, Bristlecone Pine Forest, Kings Canyon National Park, Mt. Whitney, Sequoia National Park, Death Valley, Lompoc flower fields, Santa Barbara area, Angeles National Forest, Lake Arrowhead and Big Bear Lake, Antelope Valley Poppy Preserve, Palm Springs, Joshua Tree National Monument, southern California beaches, Salton Sea, and Anza-Borrego State Park. (*See also individual entries.*)

SCHAFER, FREDERICK (1839–1927), German-born artist, resident in San Francisco and, after 1877, in Oakland. He is known for his dramatic landscapes of western mountain scenes.

SCHALLENBERGER, MOSES (1826–1909), traveled overland to California (1844) in the party led by Elisha Stevens,♦ notable because it was the first to get wagons over the Sierra (via Donner Pass, which the group discovered) and because Schallenberger and others were forced by November snow to winter at the lake site where the Donner Party starved two years later. An account first published in a local history (1888) was edited (1953) by George R. Stewart as "Overland in 1844," and he showed that it had been written mostly by Schallenberger.

SCHEFFAUER, HERMAN [GEORGE] (1878–1927), San Francisco-born author of German descent. He made a reputation in California as a poet before he went to Germany (1910) to work there as a journalist and translator. He was a protégé of Bierce, wrote poetry somewhat in the vein of his friend Sterling, and, like Sterling, took his own life. His poems written in California include *Of Both Worlds* (1903); *Looms of Life* (1908); *The Sons of Baldur* (1908), a Bohemian Grove play; and *Drake in California* (1912).

SCHENCK, JOSEPH (1877–1961), Russian-born motion picture executive who, with his brother Nicholas (1881–1969), was a head of the theater-owning firm of Marcus Loew. He left (1917) to produce films for Lewis Selznick. He was later president of United Artists and, with Darryl Zanuck,♦ headed the Twentieth-Century-Fox studio. Although jailed (1941–47) on income tax evasion charges, he later won a Motion Picture Academy Award for "services to the industry."

SCHINDLER, RUDOLPH M. (1887–1953), Viennese-born architect, came to the U.S. and worked with Frank Lloyd Wright (1914–17). He established his own practice in southern California (1922) and specialized in houses, using concrete or stucco and glass in a modern, austere style.

SCHLIEMANN, HEINRICH (1822–90), German-born archaeologist, famous for discovering the site of Troy (1871 ff.). As a young man he went to California (March 31, 1851–April 8, 1852). There he visited the mines, resided in Sacramento, where a brother of his had lived and died, and established a successful bank in San Francisco. His wealth allowed him to declare that "among those who leave this Country [California] there is hardly one in a hundred thousand who has done as well as myself."

SCHMITZ, EUGENE E. (1864–1928), native San Franciscan who went from his occupation as a theater orchestra leader to the city's mayoralty (1902). Because of his attractive presence, his presidency of the local musician's union, and his Irish-German Catholic heritage, he convinced political boss Abe Ruef♦ that he (Schmitz) would be a good candidate for the newly formed Union Labor party ticket. With the support of Republican big businessmen, he was twice reelected (to 1907). Then, in the reform movement that came as an aftermath of rebuilding the city shattered by the earthquake and fire of 1906, Schmitz and Ruef were charged with acceptance of bribes, extortion, and other corrupt acts. The series of graft trials that ended Schmitz' mayoralty led to his conviction and sentencing to San Quentin for five years.

A higher court overturned the conviction, and Schmitz was later elected to the city's Board of Supervisors.

SCHOENBERG, ARNOLD (1874–1951), Austrian composer known for his twelve-tone compositions and atonality, also a distinguished teacher. With the rise of Hitler he moved (1933) to southern California, where he spent the rest of his life. He taught at USC (1935–36) and at UCLA (1936–44). The former university inherited his archives, which it placed in a research and recital institute named for him, while the latter university named its music building for him. His works include *Ode to Napoleon* (1942), a Piano Concerto (1942), and *A Survivor from Warsaw* (1947).

SCHOLLANDER, DON[ALD ARTHUR] (1946–), North Carolina-born swimming star, moved to Santa Clara in 1961. Two years later he became the first person to swim 200 meters in less than two minutes (1:58.8). In the Olympic Games of 1964, he won two gold medals for the 100- and 400-meter freestyle individual races and two on the relay teams in the 400- and 800-meter races, thus receiving more medals than any other swimmer had won in one Olympic Games contest up to that time. He was the youngest person to be given the Sullivan Award (1964) as the outstanding U.S. amateur athlete.

SCHRAM, JACOB (1826–1904), German-born vintner, moved to the U.S. (1840) and established a winery, Schramsberg (1862), north of St. Helena. Its products were celebrated by Robert Louis Stevenson in *The Silverado Squatters.* The firm was revived about a century after its founding, and President Nixon took its champagne to Peking for the banquet he gave there when the U.S. reestablished diplomatic relations with China (1972).

SCHULBERG, BUDD [WILSON] (1914–), son of a motion picture producer, was reared in Hollywood, which he satirized in his novel, *What Makes Sammy Run?* (1941). It is about a dynamic and vicious opportunist. He has also written other novels and stories and adapted them for films, and he revealed the attitudes of blacks in Watts after the riot there in his nonfictional *From the Ashes—Voices of Watts* (1967).

SCHULZ, CHARLES [MONROE] (1922–), cartoonist born in Minneapolis, has been a longtime resident of Santa Rosa. In 1950 he created the comic strip *Peanuts,* a fancifully wry and whimsical commentary on human behavior as seen through the tragi-comic adventures of some children, an imaginative dog, Snoopy, and a querulous bird. Adults never enter their world directly. The strip, a series of cartoon books, beginning with *Peanuts* (1952), and occasional TV specials have been enormously popular.

SCHUMANN-HEINK, ERNESTINE (1861–1936), Austrian-born opera singer known mainly as a contralto in Wagnerian roles. After great success in Germany and England, she came to the U.S. (1898) and bought a home in San Diego (1906). She was known for her concerts to U.S. servicemen during World War I, when her own sons served in opposing armies, and for her stand against Hitler. An ardent American (she named one of her children George Washington), she became a popular cultural idol through numerous "farewell" tours, radio appearances, and a motion picture role.

SCHWEINFURTH, A. C. (1864–1900), Boston-born architect associated with A. Page Brown in New York. He moved to San Francisco (1892) where he built the hacienda of Phoebe Apperson Hearst near Livermore, the Examiner building (1898), and the Unitarian church (1898) near the University of California's Berkeley campus.

Scotia, a self-contained community in Humboldt County, was established by William C. Ralston as a lumber camp for a logging enterprise. It still remains a company town. The name was given by Canadian settlers to honor their former home, Nova Scotia.

Scots in California, were represented by the earliest non-Hispanic settler, John Gilroy◆ (1814), who wed an Ortega. He is remembered by the town that bears his name. An early visitor to California was the natural scientist David Douglas◆ (1823), for whom the Douglas fir is named. Hugo Reid,◆ who was called a "Scotch paisano," arrived in 1832 and married a cultivated Indian woman. Like other people from all over the world, more Scots came during the gold rush, including the founder of Downieville◆ and John Borthwick,◆ both of whom left records of their mining experiences. Later prominent Scots include John Muir, the naturalist; William Keith, the painter; Andrew Hallidie, inventor of the cable car; Robert Dollar, founder of a major steamship line; David Jacks, a large landholder;

William Mulholland, developer of the Los Angeles water system; and John McLaren, creator of Golden Gate Park. The most notable Scottish visitor was Robert Louis Stevenson, who honeymooned with his wife on Mt. St. Helena (1880) and wrote about his experiences and "The Scot Abroad" in *Silverado Squatters*. The quiet resort town of Inverness was developed by a Scot. The Scots have never been a large element in California; they were said to number only 883, or 4.1% of the population, in 1850. Though their number rose to 9,299 in 1890, by 1950 their representation was calculated to have declined to about 2.5% of the state's population.

SCOTT, HENRY T[IFFANY] (1846–1927), Maryland-born entrepreneur and social leader in San Francisco. There he made a fortune in the iron business as president of the Union Iron Works, and he later became president of Pacific Telephone and Telegraph Co. He founded Hillsborough. His brother was Irving M. Scott.◆

SCOTT, IRVING MURRAY (1837–1903), Maryland-born engineer, went to San Francisco (1860) to work for Peter Donahue.◆ He became a partner five years later. Scott designed mining machinery used on the Comstock Lode in Nevada, and at their Union Iron Works he developed a shipbuilding business◆ which constructed major battleships (1889 ff.). His achievements led him to be asked for advice on warship construction by the government of Russia, for which he made a trip to St. Petersburg (1898). He was a Regent of the University of California, a Trustee of Stanford, and president of the Mechanics' Institute. His brother was Henry T. Scott.◆

SCOTT, WALTER, see *Death Valley Scotty*.

SCOTT, WILLIAM ANDERSON (1813–85), Tennessee-born Presbyterian clergyman. After a pastorate in New Orleans he went to San Francisco (1854), where he became a noted cultural leader, but he was such a Southern sympathizer that at the outbreak of the Civil War he had to leave. After living in England and New York for a time, he returned (1870) to San Francisco, where he founded St. John's Church. He is remembered for having married Robert Louis Stevenson and Fanny Osbourne, but is better recalled as an eloquent and learned divine and a founder of the San Francisco Theological Seminary.

Scott Valley, located in Siskiyou County, is the largest valley (20 miles long and up to 5 miles wide)

in the Marble Mts. of the Klamath Range. It was named, like Scott Bar, Scott Mts., and Scott River, for a miner who discovered gold there (1850). Its economy has long since been based on hay raising and livestock ranching.

Screen Actors Guild, labor union founded in Hollywood (1933) when producers threatened actors with an industry-wide pay cut. In 1935 the Guild became affiliated with the AFL, and two years later it won its first union shop contract. In 1960 it called its first large strike (one month long) against major studios over the matter of payment to actors for residual rights of films used on television. It was ended by compromise. Presidents of the Guild have included Robert Montgomery, James Cagney, George Murphy, and Ronald Reagan.

SCRIPPS, E[DWARD] W[YLLIS] (1854–1926), newspaper publisher, born in Illinois. He began his journalistic career in Ohio, where he established the first chain of dailies in the U.S. He founded the United Press (1907), a news-disseminating agency, and from a column of miscellany gathered by his half-sister, Ellen Browning Scripps (1836–1932), organized the Newspaper Enterprise Association (NEA) to supply his papers and others with feature materials. In 1891 he and Ellen moved to a 2,000-acre estate, Miramar, near San Diego, where he established a chain of papers in San Francisco, Los Angeles, Fresno, Sacramento, and San Diego, as well as the Pacific Northwest, that were independent in politics, liberal in social views, and supportive of unions. He wrote *Damned Old Crank,* an autobiography (ed. by C. R. McCabe, 1951). With his half-sister, Ellen, he endowed the Scripps Institution of Oceanography. She herself had an independent fortune, made in San Diego real estate, and with it founded Scripps College. She was a generous benefactor in her community and elsewhere. E. W.'s son, Robert Paine Scripps (1895–1938), in association with Roy Howard, perpetuated the newspaper chain. He also continued the family's liberal tradition by championing Mooney and Billings and supporting Sen. La Follette for President.

Scripps College, see *Claremont Colleges* and *Scripps, E. W.*

Scripps Institution of Oceanography, part of the University of California, San Diego, located at La Jolla. It began with research conducted from Berkeley (1892). That work led to the founding of the San Diego Marine Biological Institution (1903) and later (1912) to the present organization, named after Ellen B. Scripps and her half-brother, E. W. Scripps,♦ the newspaper publisher, who were long the major contributors to the Institution.

Sea bass, see *Bass.*

SEABORG, GLENN T[HEODORE] (1912–   ), chemist born in Michigan, received his A.B. from UCLA and his Ph.D. from Berkeley. He began his career in Berkeley's Department of Chemistry (1937), then became an associate director of the Lawrence Radiation Laboratory♦ and chancellor (1958–61). He also served as chairman of the Atomic Energy Commission (1961–71). He was co-discoverer of many transuranium elements, and for that work he with Edwin McMillan,♦ a physicist, was awarded the Nobel Prize in chemistry (1951).

SEAGREN, BOB (ROBERT LLOYD SEAGREN) (1946–   ), Pomona-born pole vaulter who, while a junior college student, set a world record of 17′ 5½″. He broke that record while a student at the University of Southern California and again in 1972, when he reached 18′ 5¾″.

Seagull, see *Gull.*

Seal, fur-bearing aquatic mammal found off the shores of California. The *Pribilof* migrates to the coast during the winter, but the *Guadalupe* is far more common. It began to be hunted for its skin early in the 19th century by Russians and Americans in the same way they hunted sea otter.♦ The Russians, using Fort Ross as their headquarters, established a sealing station on the Farallones, and 73,402 seals were reported killed there between 1810 and 1812. That slaughter led to near extermination, and finally, in 1833, only 54 were found and the hunting was ended. The onetime commonness of both species is suggested by seven sites named Seal Rocks, the best known lying off the coast of San Francisco, and various places, such as Point Lobos in Monterey County and in San Francisco, derived from *Lobo Marino,* Spanish for both "seal" and "sea lion." The *Guadalupe,* which has been protected by state law since 1911, is slowly making its way back, first off Guadalupe Island of Baja California and, more recently, in summers off the Santa Barbara Islands. The waters off the state are also the home of sea lions♦ and two other kinds of non-fur-bearing seals: the *north elephant seal,* which breeds only off the coast of Mexico, and the more common

harbor seal, only about five feet long, which lives in harbors and bays of the state.

Seal, see *State symbols.*

SEALE, BOBBY (1936–   ), born in Texas, was reared in Oakland, where he and Huey Newton came to organize the Black Panther party♦ (1966). At first the organization urged violence, but gradually its militancy was phased out. Seale then attempted to achieve some of its goals peacefully. He ran for mayor of Oakland (1972) and sponsored community programs of free medical care, free breakfasts for children, and aid to senior citizens. He wrote an autobiography, *A Lonely Rage* (1978).

Sea Lion, seal that is non-fur-bearing, is of two types: the *stellar* (about 14 feet long), which lives off the coast from the Oregon border to the Santa Barbara Islands, and the *California* (only 8 or 9 feet long), which lives off the entire length of the coastline. Both were hunted for their hides and oil and because commercial fishermen thought they damaged their catch. Now protected by law, they flourish on the Seal Rocks off San Francisco and elsewhere. They are the creatures called "trained seals."

Seals, San Francisco, minor league baseball♦ team in the Pacific Coast League. It was the city's club (1903–58) until the transfer of the major league Giants to San Francisco. Lefty O'Doul♦ was one of the Seals' great stars. The same name was later given to the Oakland ice hockey team.

Sea of Cortés, see *California, Gulf of.*

Sea of Cortez, an account of research in marine biology and of reflections on life arising from voyaging in the Gulf of California. It was written by John Steinbeck and Edward F. Ricketts♦ and published in 1941.

Sea otter, see *Otter.*

Sea Ranch, low-density residential development on a southern Mendocino County coastal-plain site of 5,000 acres. Its master plan, designed by Lawrence Halprin, preserved the sense of open land and the integrity of the area. The simple wooden houses, built by Charles Moore and Joseph Esherick during the late 1960s, were either small condominiums or free-standing homes organized in small groups.

Searles Lake, site of a large saline lake created in the late Quaternary era and since evaporated. It is located in the Mojave Desert in northwestern San Bernardino County. It was named for brothers who discovered borax there (1863). The "lake" has long been the state's only source of potash.

SEAVER, TOM (GEORGE THOMAS SEAVER) (1944–), Fresno-born baseball player. After becoming an All-American pitcher at the University of Southern California, he joined the New York Mets (1967–77) and was voted Rookie of the Year in the National League. He was given the Cy Young Award as best pitcher in the league (1969, 73, 75).

Seaweed, marine algae whose brown species grow north of Point Concepcion and red species grow south of the Point. The largest brown variety is the *giant bladder kelp,* stretching from ocean depths of 30 to 60 feet up to the surface. It is harvested commercially for chemicals, vitamins, and medicinal use. The major red variety is the *agar-weed,* about a yard long and growing not far below the surface, harvested for laboratory use. Flowering seaweeds include *sea lettuce, sponge weed,* and *surf grass.*

Sea World, tourist attraction located on an 80-acre site at Mission Bay Park, San Diego, since 1964, features performing whales, dolphins, and sea lions, as well as a Japanese village where oyster diving is performed.

Sebastopol, town in Sonoma County with apple orchards. It was named about the time of the Anglo-French siege of the Russian port during the Crimean War (1854). Luther Burbank had an experimental farm at the site, which is just west of Santa Rosa. In 1970 the town had a population of 3,993.

Secretary of State, elected at the same time and for the same term as the governor, he keeps all state records, charters all state corporations, commissions all notaries public, and supervises all state elections. For over fifty years (from 1910), only two men held the office: Frank C. Jordan and Frank M. Jordan, father and son, both Republicans. Edmund G. Brown, Jr., was Secretary of State (1970–74). He was succeeded by March Fong Eu, the first woman in the post.

Secularization, program to turn the missions into parish churches, replace the friars by parish priests (the latter being secular clergy, as distinct from the Franciscans' clergy of an order), release Indian neophytes from mission jurisdiction, and convert mission property into pueblos in which each Indian family would receive some land and livestock. Decrees of secularization were issued in Spain (1813, 1820) and were favored by Mexican republicans but had no immediate effect in California. Gov. Echeandía issued the first California decree of secularization (1826) permitting married Indians to leave the missions, but few took advantage of this opportunity. Finally, Gov. Figueroa issued a proclamation (Aug. 4, 1834) ordering ten missions to be secularized that year, six in 1835, and the last five in 1836, with half the property to be handled by lay administrators and half given to the neophytes, with the friars to continue religious jurisdiction of the missions until curates might become available. Gov. Micheltorena disposed of all remaining mission property, except that of Santa Barbara, by an order issued in 1844. Since the former neophytes generally could not cope with the land independently, and since the land was coveted by others, the result was that all the property passed through the lay administrators to *rancheros* and other non-religious persons.

Seed production, a major element of California agriculture, began with the planting of a commercial seed crop of head lettuce by R. W. Wilson in 1873. C. C. Morse, born in Maine, who settled in the Santa Clara Valley, purchased Wilson's business (1896) and, after merging with the Detroit firm of D. M. Ferry (1930), became one of the world's largest vegetable and flower seed producers. The company operates the world's largest seed-cleaning mill at Mountain View. California's production of flower seeds, centered in the area of Lompoc, accounts for about 85% of the nation's output. Other major seed crops include alfalfa, Ladino clover (from Glenn County), and safflower, in all of which California leads the nation. Vegetable seed production is concentrated in the Central Valley, and melon seed production is carried on mainly in the Sacramento Valley.

SEGRÈ, EMILIO, see *Chamberlain, Owen.*

SELZNICK, DAVID O[LIVER] (1902–65), son of an early motion picture producer, Lewis Selznick (1870–1932), and son-in-law of another, Louis B. Mayer. He became head of his own film-making company in Hollywood (1935), from which he produced numerous lavish films. The most sensational was *Gone With the Wind* (1939).

SEMPLE, ROBERT B[AYLOR] (1806–54), Kentucky-born printer who traveled to California with Lansford Hastings' party in 1845. He was a leader of the Bear Flag Revolt in 1846. Later that year, he and Walter Colton♦ founded *The Californian,*♦ the first California newspaper, in Monterey. They moved it to San Francisco in 1847. He was later a founder of Benicia and president of the Constitutional Convention of 1849. Though Semple was significant because of his varied achievements, he was also impressive because of his unusual height— 6′ 6″.

SEM-YETO, see *Solano County.*

SEÑÁN, JOSÉ FRANCISCO DE PAULA (1760–1823), Spanish-born Franciscan missionary, was in California *c.*1787–95 and 1798–1823. He was President-General♦ (1812–15, 1820–23).

Senate, upper house of the state's bicameral legislature, composed (1977) of 40 members. Half of them are elected every 2 years for 4-year terms. From 1926 to the reapportionment♦ of 1965, representation was by area rather than by population, but since then the districts have been established on a basis of one-man/one-vote. The lieutenant governor presides, but the Senate elects its own president pro tempore, who has great control over the actual proceedings through committees and on the floor. The first Senate session consisted of 16 members and met in San Jose (1849).

Senators, U.S.[1]

Gwin, William M.	1850–55[2], 1857–61	Dem.
Frémont, John C.	1850–51	Dem.
Weller, John B.	1851–57	Union-Dem.
Broderick, David C.	1857–59	Dem.
Haun, Henry P.[3]	1859–60	Dem.
Latham, Milton S.[4]	1860–63	Dem.
McDougall, James A.	1861–67	Dem.
Conness, John	1863–69	Dem.
Cole, Cornelius	1867–73	Union-Rep.
Casserly, Eugene	1869–73	Dem.
Hager, John S.[5]	1874–75	Dem.
Sargent, Aaron A.	1873–79	Rep.
Booth, Newton	1875–81	Dem.
Farley, James T.	1879–85	Dem.
Miller, John F.	1881–86	Rep.
Hearst, George[6]	1886; 87–91	Dem.
Williams, Abram P.[7]	1886–87	Rep.
Stanford, Leland	1885–93	Rep.
Felton, Charles N.[8]	1891–93	Rep.
Perkins, George C.[9]	1893–1915	Rep.
White, Stephen M.	1893–99	Dem.
Bard, Thomas R.	1899–1905	Rep.
Flint, Frank P.	1905–11	Rep.
Works, John D.	1911–17	Rep.
Phelan, James D.	1915–21	Dem.
Johnson, Hiram W.	1917–45	Rep.
Shortridge, Samuel	1921–33	Rep.
McAdoo, William	1933–38	Dem.
Storke, Thomas[10]	Nov. 1938–Jan. 39	Dem.
Downey, Sheridan	1939–50	Dem.
Knowland, William F.[11]	1945–59	Rep.
Nixon, Richard M.[12]	1950–53	Rep.
Kuchel, Thomas H.[13]	1953–69	Rep.
Engle, Clair	1959–64	Dem.
Salinger, Pierre[14]	Aug.–Dec. 1964	Dem.
Murphy, George	1964–71	Rep.
Cranston, Alan	1968–	Dem.
Tunney, John	1971–77	Dem.
Hayakawa, S. I.	1977–	Rep.

1. Until the 17th Amendment to the U.S. Constitution was ratified (1913), U.S. Senators were elected by the state legislature.
2. Seat vacant 1855–57.
3. Appointed to Broderick vacancy.
4. Elected to Broderick vacancy.
5. Elected to Casserly vacancy.
6. First appointed to Miller vacancy; later elected.
7. Elected to Miller vacancy.
8. Elected to Hearst vacancy.
9. Appointed to Stanford vacancy; reelected.
10. Appointed to McAdoo vacancy.
11. Appointed to Johnson vacancy; reelected.
12. Appointed to Downey vacancy; reelected.
13. Appointed to Nixon vacancy; reelected.
14. Appointed to Engle vacancy.

SENNETT, MACK (1884–1960), Canadian-born motion picture producer and director who went to Los Angeles (1912). During his long Hollywood career, initially for the Keystone Film Co., he presented a troupe of Bathing Beauties as well as such comedians as Charlie Chaplin, Fatty Arbuckle, Mabel Normand, Chester Conklin, and the zany Keystone Cops, whom he cast in outrageous slapstick burlesques.

SEPÚLVEDA, a leading southern California family whose founder, Francisco Xavier Sepúlveda (1742–88), came from Mexico as a soldier and was the first adult Spaniard buried at Mission San Gabriel. His son Juan José (1764–1808) founded one branch of the family, possibly on Rancho Los Palos Verdes (between Redondo Beach and San Pedro), while another son, Francisco (1775–1853), established the family at Los Angeles (1815), of which he was acting *alcalde* (1825) and where he received the San Vicente y Santa Monica grant (1839). Francisco's daughters married into the de la Guerra family,♦ and his son José Andrés (1803–75) was granted (1837) the vast Rancho San Joaquín by Gov. Alvarado in present Orange County, where he built a great home named Refugio before selling the land (1864). It became part of the Irvine Ranch.♦ José's son Ygnacio (1842–1916) had a career in Mexico under Maximilian and later as U.S. *chargé d'affaires,* as well as being an assemblyman and superior court judge in Los Angeles. A canyon and a boulevard in Los Angeles bear the family name.

Sequoia National Park, located in Tulare County on the western side of the Sierra, was established in 1890. Its 604 square miles are just south of Kings Canyon National Park and contain Mt. Whitney♦ and a grove of giant redwoods, of which the largest is the General Sherman, 275 feet high and nearly 40 feet in diameter. It was called the Karl Marx when the Kaweah Colony♦ claimed it, but was renamed when the park was taken over by the government. The Kaweah River♦ rises in or near the park, and Sequoia National Forest lies just to the south.

Sequoias, see *Redwoods*.

Sergas de Esplandián, Las, Spanish romantic narrative ("The Exploits of Esplandian") written by Garcí Ordóñez de Montalvo and published in Seville (1510) as a sequel to the popular Portuguese poem, *Amadís de Gaula*. It recounts the fictional adventures of Esplandián, the son of Amadís. Among the places he visits is one "on the right hand of the Indies, . . . an island called California, very near to the Terrestrial Paradise, which was peopled with black women, . . . accustomed to live after the fashion of Amazons. . . . Their arms were full of gold." The land was ruled by a queen named Calafia. The etymology and the meaning of the name "California" have never been established, but Edward Everett Hale, the author of *The Man*

Without a Country, in 1862 first contended in a meeting of the American Antiquarian Society and declared in an article in the *Atlantic Monthly* (March 1864) that the state's name was derived from a Spanish explorer's association of the terrain of Baja California with the island mentioned in Montalvo's fiction, an origin now generally accepted. The explorer has not been identified. He might have been Fortún Jiménez, who landed in Baja California on an expedition sent by Cortés♦ (1533), or Francisco de Bolaños, who explored both sides of the Baja California peninsula (1541). In any case, when Cabrillo used the name (1542), he did so as if it had been previously employed.

SERRA, Junípero (1713–84), missionary and padre, was born on the island of Majorca and baptized Miguel José Serra. After study at the Lullian University in Palma, noted for its missionary tradition, he was ordained under the name of Junípero and remained at the school, where he taught philosophy for fifteen years. In 1749, with a former student and friend, Father Francisco Palóu, he was sent to Mexico as a missionary. Upon arrival at Vera Cruz, he decided to walk to the capital, an act in keeping with his ideal of self-punishment, and en route he was bitten by a snake or an insect. As a result, he was permanently lamed, and for the rest of his life his leg was openly ulcerous and swollen. Nevertheless, he pursued without rest his dedication to missionary work, first at the College of San Fernando,♦ a Franciscan training center, and later in villages near the capital. His intensity was so great that he often scourged himself, sometimes while delivering a sermon, and drove himself to the utmost exertions, even though he was a small man, about 5′ 2″.

In 1769 Serra was made Father-President of the missions in Baja California. That year, he went as the religious leader on the Sacred Expedition,♦ sent to Alta California by Gálvez under the military leader Portolá. Arriving in San Diego, Serra founded the first of the nine missions♦ of Alta California which he was to establish and supervise the rest of his life. In 1770 Serra made his way north by sea with Costansó♦ and Fages♦ to establish his second mission, San Carlos Borromeo, first at Monterey and moved the next year to the Carmel River. It became Serra's headquarters, and from it he established other missions. In fact, he planned even more than Fages would allow—there were not enough soldiers to protect them all. This so angered Serra that he made the long and difficult journey to Mexico City (1772–73) to plead for more support for his missions and for the removal of Fages. The transfer of Fages did occur in 1774, but Serra got along even less well with the new governor, Capt. Fernando Rivera y Moncada. Nevertheless, he continued to labor zealously in the founding of new missions and the conversion of the Indians, working without rest up to the moment of his death.

Serra's biography was written by his friend and follower, Palóu, as *Relación Histórica de la Vida y Apóstolicas Tereas del Venerable Padre Fray Junípero Serra,* published in Mexico City in 1787 and first translated into English in 1913. Palóu also treated Serra in his *Noticias de la Nueva California,* which he finished in 1783 but which was not published until 1857 and not translated into English until 1926. Serra's birthplace in Majorca was given to the city of San Francisco (1932).

Serrano, Shoshonean Indians of several groups, one named Tejon, another called Serrano, meaning "Sierrans" or "mountaineers." They lived in and south of present Kern County, through the San Bernardino Range and the San Gabriel Mts. They had a hereditary chief, built tule houses, including special ones for ceremonies, and, like the Miwok,♦ did not sanction marriage between persons belonging to the same totemic moiety.

Serrano Decision, state Supreme Court ruling (1971) that the system of financing schools primarily through property taxes was unconstitutional. The decision was the outcome of a suit brought by John Serrano, Jr. (1971), against the state treasurer on the grounds that his son, John Anthony Serrano, was receiving a poorer education in the Mexican quarter of East Los Angeles than he could obtain elsewhere because the low value of taxable property in his school district did not provide the quality of schooling available in richer communities. Although in another case the U.S. Supreme Court ruled (1973) it was not federally unconstitutional to finance school systems by property taxes, the Serrano ruling holds in California, and attempts to equalize funding of school districts have led to increased use of state income tax money to try to meet the requirement that disparities should be reduced to less than $100 per child per year.

Sespe, *rancho* in the Santa Clara Valley of Ventura County near Santa Paula, considered for a mission site by Serra and Palóu (1769). It was granted as a *rancho* (1834) to Carlos Antonio Carrillo of Santa Barbara. After his widow's death, it

was bought by Thomas W. More (1854), who had married into the Ortega family, but it passed out of their family's control in 1888. The name, from Chumash, is also applied to a creek, a gorge, hot springs, a town, and oil fields. In the nearby mountains lies the Sespe Condor Sanctuary.

SESSIONS, KATE OLIVIA (1857–1940), born in San Francisco, after graduation from the University of California established a horticultural nursery in San Diego. It was the beginning of that city's Balboa Park.♦ She also introduced and popularized many new plants and trees in the area.

Seventeen Mile Drive, scenic route along the shoreline of the Monterey Peninsula. It is located on private land owned by the Del Monte Properties Co. Pebble Beach♦ lies along the drive.

77 Sunset Strip, hour-long television series (1958–64) presenting crimes investigated by two private detectives whose office was located on the famous Hollywood street that provided background and a title to the program.

SEVERANCE, CAROLINE MARIA SEYMOUR (1820–1914), a leader in woman's rights, anti-slavery, and liberal religious movements in Ohio and Boston. She created Boston's New England Woman's Club (1868), a forerunner of the similar societies she established after moving to Los Angeles (1875). The longest-lasting was the Friday Morning Club (1891), dedicated to cultural and social betterment, including civic reform. Among its members and her followers was Katherine P. Edson.♦ She was also the organizer of the Los Angeles Free Kindergarten Association (1885) and local organizations for woman suffrage and international peace.

S.F., nickname for San Francisco.

Shad, herring-like fish, imported and planted by the California Fish Commission (1871) in the Sacramento River. It soon became common there and in the San Joaquin River, and by the second decade of the 20th century the commercial catch exceeded 4,500,000 tons annually. However, the use of gill nets also killed off striped bass. For that reason gill netting was prohibited (1957), and the commercial fishing of shad was ended.

Shadow of a Doubt, motion picture by Alfred Hitchcock♦ filmed in Santa Rosa.♦

SHALER, WILLIAM (c. 1773–1833), Connecticut sea captain who, with his partner and first mate, Richard J. Cleveland (1773–1860), put into California ports, despite Spanish laws against visitors, and illegally traded in otter skins. At San Diego, Cleveland was jailed and their ship, the *Lelia Byrd*, fired upon (1803). Shaler's "Journal of a Voyage Between China and the North-Western Coast of America" (*American Register*, 1808) was the first extensive account of California published in the U.S. by an American visitor. Cleveland set forth his own account in *A Narrative of Voyages and Commercial Enterprises* (2 vols., 1842).

Sharks, found in large numbers along the California coast in seven varieties. Over 650,000 pounds of the fish are caught annually, and they are utilized mostly for the high vitamin A content of their livers. The town of Tiburon (Marin County) derives its name from the Spanish word for "shark."

SHARMAN, BILL (WILLIAM SHARMAN) (1926–   ), Texas-born basketball player and coach, reared in Porterville. He played with the University of Southern California and was named an All-American forward. After playing professional baseball briefly, he returned to basketball. His professional basketball career with the Boston Celtics (1951–61) was marked by great shooting and free-throw accuracy (.883 in one season). His subsequent career included coaching four California teams—the Los Angeles Jets, the San Francisco Warriors, the Los Angeles Stars, and the Los Angeles Lakers—and winning titles in three leagues.

SHARON, WILLIAM (1821–85), Ohio-born financier, appointed (1864) by William C. Ralston♦ as the Virginia City, Nevada, agent of the Bank of California. The first Comstock boom was then ending, and he tempted mine- and mining-share owners to borrow heavily at the low rates he offered and then foreclosed, obtaining the mines for the bank and important interests for himself. However, he was bested by the Silver Kings and defeated by one of them—Fair—in his first race for the U.S. Senate. Nevertheless, he made a great fortune, acquired many of Ralston's properties—including the Palace Hotel, after Ralston's death—and was elected from Nevada to the U.S. Senate (1875–81). His liaison with Sarah Althea Hill♦ led to great notoriety after his death. She sued his estate, claiming a wife's share under the terms of a "marriage contract" presumably forged by Mammy Pleasant.♦ Sarah Hill was represented by David S. Terry,♦ who married her, but in an altercation he was killed by David Neagle, the bodyguard of Justice Stephen J. Field, who had found the marriage document to be fraudulent.

SHARP, JOSEPH HENRY (1859–1953), Ohio-born painter, after study in Europe, returned to the U.S. Beginning in 1901, he lived in Montana and New Mexico near the Indians whose way of life and portraits he painted. He later settled in Pasadena.

Sharpe Depot, U.S. Army installation at Lathrop, just south of Stockton. It is used for repair of tanks, autos, amphibious crafts, and helicopters, and to house troops and to make shipments to the Pacific.

Shasta, Indians of Hokan stock resident on the Klamath River and its southern tributaries. In ancient times they numbered about 2,000 and were located in some 50 settlements in California and more in present Oregon. The 1910 census counted only 255, some of them perhaps not even ethnically Shastan. Shasta houses and other artifacts show their culture to have been like that of the Yurok and Karok, but simpler. They built dams to trap fish and trained dogs for hunting. The name, once variously spelled, probably derived from that of a great chief. It has been applied to springs, a lake, a mountain, a river, a national park, a dam, a city, and a county. (*See also individual entries.*)

Shasta, Mount, see *Mount Shasta.*

Shasta County, one of the original 27 counties, whose seat was first Reading's Ranch (1850–51), then the town of Shasta (1851–88), and thereafter Redding. It is in the northernmost part of the Sacramento Valley. Siskiyou County and westernmost Modoc County lie to the north, Lassen to the east, Tehama to the south, and Trinity County to the west. The first whites to venture into the region were trappers, like Jedediah Smith, the Hudson's Bay Co. members, and Pierson B. Reading.♦ Reading obtained a large Spanish land grant (1844) and discovered gold (1848), precipitating a rush of miners. However, the gold did not last. Lumbering became important to the economy, as did cattle ranching and the growing of field crops.

Over half the county is covered by National Forests, Shasta in the northwest and part of

Lassen in the southeast. In Shasta is the Whiskey-town-Shasta-Trinity National Recreation Area,♦ including Shasta Lake,♦ which was created when the 602-foot-high Shasta Dam was built to control the waters of the Sacramento, McCloud, and Pit rivers as part of the Central Valley Project. A tributary of the Pit is Burney Creek, whose 165-foot falls form a State Park within Shasta National Forest. Nearby lie Lake Britton, another reservoir, and Hat Creek. In the southeast corner of the county is Lassen Volcanic Park, with the only active volcano in the continental U.S. Castle Crags♦ are granitic spires, the site of a battle between whites and Modocs (1855) in which Joaquin Miller claimed to have participated.

There are few sizable communities, the largest being Redding♦ and the next largest nearby Shasta. In 1970 the county had a population of 77,640; with an area of 2,427,648 acres, it had 20.5 persons per sq. mi.

Shasta Dam, see *Shasta Lake.*

Shasta Lake, four-pronged body of water 14 miles north of Redding. Formed by Shasta Dam, it is the major northern reservoir of the Central Valley Project which controls the state's water, and it stores the flow of the Sacramento, McCloud, and Pit rivers. It is also a federal Recreational Area. Keswick Dam lies nine miles south. *(See also individual entries.)*

Shasta-Trinity National Forests, a preserve of 2,853,000 acres, including Mt. Shasta, Shasta Lake, Clair Engle Lake, and the Trinity Alps.

Shastina, see *Mount Shasta.*

SHAUGHNESSY, CLARK (1892–1970), Minneapolis-born football coach. After 25 years of coaching elsewhere, he went to Stanford (1940). There, with Frankie Albert as his quarterback, he perfected the T-formation, which became a mainstay of modern football. He had a perfect season culminating in a Rose Bowl victory, but after one more year at Stanford he left for other universities, returning later to California to coach the Los Angeles Rams (1948–49).

SHAW, BUCK (LAWRENCE T. SHAW) (1899–   ), Iowa-born football coach. After playing football at Notre Dame under Knute Rockne, he began the coaching career that took him to the University of Santa Clara (1936–42), where he had a dis-

tinguished record. He coached the San Francisco Forty-Niners (1946–54) and other teams until 1960. On retirement, he became a Regent of the University of Santa Clara.

Sheep, first imported into Alta California by Rivera y Moncada (1770) and bred by the mission fathers, but more for wool to clothe Indians than for meat. The stock was small and of poor strain, raised on ill-fenced and mediocre grazing lands under Indian care, and yielded little wool. Never important during the *rancho* era, sheep raising grew greatly during the gold rush because of the demand for lamb and mutton. In 1851 William W. Hollister,♦ in association with ranchers Bixby and Flint, drove some 6,000 sheep from St. Louis to San Diego County over a 20-month period. By 1872 about 23,000,000 pounds of wool were being produced in the state, and by 1876 there were about 7,700,000 sheep. Basque and Mexican sheepherders were employed by the American ranchers, but the number of sheep declined from the high of the 1870s to 3,350,000 in 1889, to 3,000,000 in the period 1920–1940, and down further as the influx of people into the state made the land more valuable for other uses. In 1970 there were only 1,317,000 sheep and lambs reared, mostly in Fresno, Glenn, Kern, Mendocino, Sonoma, and Tehama counties. For over a century sheep have been driven from gathering points in San Gabriel and San Bernardino along trails north by Bakersfield, across various Sierra passes to graze on its eastern slopes, and then down the western side to home ranches in the fall. Wild sheep, called *mountain* or *bighorn,* have been protected since 1883, but they continue to be rare. Perhaps fewer than 2,500 exist today. Most live in Anza-Borrego State Park and the Picacho Recreation Area.

SHEETS, MILLARD (1907–   ), landscape artist and muralist, born in Pomona, with which area he has later been identified. He was also a professor (1932–54) at Scripps College and director of the Otis Art Institute (1953–59).

Shell mounds, campsites of prehistoric nomadic Indians, common along the San Francisco Bay shoreline. Over 425, virtually all of which have been obliterated, have been noted in the area, and from them have come, in addition to discarded remnants of shellfish, many artifacts and some human skeletons. One of these kitchen middens, in present Richmond, was estimated to have been 30 feet high, 460 feet long, and 250 feet wide.

Some of the sites remained inhabited until the Spanish period, and the upper layers of mounds in these areas have yielded European medals, a crucifix, and other foreign objects.

SHEPARD, MORGAN, see *Elder, Paul.*

SHERMAN, WILLIAM TECUMSEH (1820–91), Ohio-born military leader. After graduation from West Point, he served in the Mexican War as aide to Gen. Kearny and adjutant to Col. Richard B. Mason♦ and Gen. Persifor Smith;♦ whose headquarters were in Monterey. His duties were light, so he could also conduct business in Coloma (1848–49). In Jan. 1850 he was relieved and sent east with dispatches for Gen. Scott, also preparing reports that became the basis of President Polk's message on gold discoveries in California. He returned to San Francisco (1853) to manage the branch of a St. Louis bank, but when a depression caused the bank to close he returned east (1857). A few years later he became a leading Union general in the Civil War, succeeding Grant as supreme commander in the West (1864) and again succeeding him as commander of the army after the war (1869). A former soldier who had served under him named the world's largest redwood in Sequoia National Park♦ the "General Sherman" in his honor. Legend contends that, as a young lieutenant in Monterey, he had a romance with a Señorita María Ygnacia Bonifacio, and that when he was ordered east they planted a rose in her garden, but his vow to return when the flowers bloomed was unfulfilled, and she remained unmarried for the rest of her life.

SHEW, WILLIAM (1820–1903), New York-born photographer who pursued his business in San Francisco, sometimes with his brothers Jacob and Myron, from the gold rush until his death. He concentrated on studio portraits of people in all walks of life.

SHIMA, GEORGE (1863–1926), Japanese-born farmer, went to California (1889) as a poor laborer. In time, he was able to lease 15 acres of San Joaquin Delta land. Then, in partnership with other Japanese farmers, he expanded his control. The land was rich, and Shima concentrated on potato growing. By 1913 he controlled 28,000 acres and 85% of the state's potato crop, and had become known as the "Potato King." He moved from Stockton to Berkeley, where he met great prejudice, at least at first. By the time of his death, he had amassed an estate worth some $15,000,000.

SHINN, CHARLES HOWARD (1852–1924), born in Texas, reared in California during the post-gold-rush era. After some school teaching and newspaper work, he went east to Johns Hopkins. There he wrote the papers revised as *Mining Camps: A Study in American Frontier Government* (1885), treating the growth of law in mining camps and its relation to earlier mining laws and to Spanish California government. He returned to California to become the business manager of the *Overland Monthly* (1885–90), then edited by his sister Milicent, and wrote *The Story of a Mine* (1896), about the Comstock Lode. He was later a member of the state university's Agricultural Experiment Stations (1890–1901), a conservationist, and a leader in the federal Forest Service (1901–11).

SHINN, MILICENT WASHBURN (1858–1940), after graduation from the University of California, where she was deeply influenced by Edward Rowland Sill, became the editor of the revived *Overland Monthly*♦ (1883–94), for which she wrote a good deal of prose and poetry. She returned to Berkeley for graduate study on child development and became the first woman to receive a Ph.D. from the University. Her research led to a popular book, *The Biography of a Baby* (1900), but the remainder of her life was removed and quiet. Her brother was Charles H. Shinn.♦

Shipbuilding, had its beginnings in 1719, the date when Father Ugarte constructed *El Triunfo de la Cruz* in Baja California. Then, in 1775, Ayala fashioned a redwood dugout for exploring San Francisco Bay. The first substantial shipbuilding in Alta California was done by the Russians at Fort Ross. There, sometime prior to 1824, they launched four small vessels for the Spanish. The larger 60-ton schooner *Guadalupe* was built (1831) at San Pedro for Mission San Gabriel by Joseph Chapman. The gold rush led to the building of ships, mainly riverboats, at Benicia, Sausalito, and Sacramento. The first ocean-going steamer, the *Del Norte,* was not built until 1864.

Meanwhile, shipyards for lumber-carrying ships were constructed at Humboldt Bay, which until the 20th century shared with San Francisco the position of leadership in the business. The latter port often installed boilers and engines in hulls built to the north. The industry was given great impetus in 1883, when, under Irving Scott, the Union Iron Works shifted from the construction of mining equipment to shipbuilding in the Potrero district of San Francisco near Hunters Point,♦ a drydock area established by William C. Ralston.

The first steel vessel built on the West Coast, the *S.S. Arago* (1885), came from the Union Iron Works yards, which also superseded the outgrown Mare Island facility of the navy in building the cruiser *Charleston* (1889). Between 1887 and 1902 that firm built 75 warships, including the crusier *Olympia,* Dewey's flagship at Manila Bay, and the battleship *Oregon.* In 1905 the Bethlehem Steel Corp. acquired the Union Iron Works yards from their owners, the Scott family, and began to build steel destroyers and submarines for both American and British use in World War I.

At the beginning of the 20th century, Los Angeles and San Diego also became large shipbuilding centers. One of the state's two leading industries during World War I, shipbuilding declined for many years until the coming of World War II. Then the construction of so-called Liberty and Victory ships reanimated old yards and occasioned the creation of new ones in Los Angeles, Richmond, Sausalito, South San Francisco, and other sites. As a result the labor force mushroomed from 4,000 (1939) to 282,000 (1943), including many women during the wartime period. The main new entrepreneur was Henry J. Kaiser,♦ whose yards at Richmond, Oakland, Sausalito, Vallejo, and San Pedro operated around the clock, constructing a Liberty ship every 25 days and launching a new freighter every 10 hours. This production was made possible by his creation of assembly-line techniques, prefabrication of standardized parts, and development of the concrete vessel.

The industry continued into the 1950s as a major economic power, but development of large cargo-carrying planes, changing demands in weaponry, and eventual cuts in defense spending made shipbuilding a minor business of the state in the 1970s.

Shipping, see *Clipper ships; Ferries; Hide trade; Matson, William;* and *Pacific Mail Steamship Company.*

Shirley Letters, The, see *Clapp, Louise.*

SHOCKLEY, William B[radford] (1910–), English-born scientist, received his B.S. from the California Institute of Technology and Ph.D. from MIT. A co-inventor of the transistor, he won a Nobel Prize in physics (1956), set up a manufacturing firm in Palo Alto, became a professor at Stanford, and later aroused much controversy because of his publication of theories of genetics that seemed to find whites intellectually superior to blacks.

SHOEMAKER, Willie (William Lee Shoemaker) (1931–), Texas-born jockey, reared in El Monte and longtime resident of Santa Monica. He is the leading jockey of all time, having ridden more winners in more major races (by 1975, over 555) than any other, including the Kentucky Derby (1955, 59, 65), Preakness (1963, 67), and Belmont Stakes (1957, 59, 62, 67). He holds the all-time record for first-place finishes in a single season (485 in 1953) and was 10 times the leading money winner among jockeys. By 1970 he had ridden 6,033 winners.

Shopping centers, a California innovation, developed mainly in the Los Angeles area as an outgrowth of its suburban branches of downtown stores. They were created as early as the 1920s on Wilshire Blvd. and other major thoroughfares because inadequate public transportation, poor parking for private automobiles, and heavy traffic made shopping in the center of the city difficult and unpleasant. From the branch stores of major retail firms, shopping centers began to develop until the downtown of the city provided only 35% of its department store sales in 1951.

Relatively cheaper land in outlying areas, easy access by freeways, and the dispersion of residential districts made the centers a great success. Early examples in the Los Angeles area included the Crenshaw district south of Hollywood and Lakewood Center, while Stonestown near Lake Merced in San Francisco was a forerunner of the movement in the north. The fully developed center has long outgrown the mere branch of a department store to include such various facilities as motion picture theaters, grocery stores, banks, bars and restaurants, and numerous service and professional firms.

Beyond providing merchandise for sale, the shopping center has become a community center offering art exhibitions, concerts, recreational opportunities, and other diversions in a secure and concentrated space, sometimes encapsulated under huge protective roofing. It thus combines something of the appeal of an old-time small-town atmosphere with the ambience of a huge marketplace where one can window shop or purchase a great variety of novelties and staples. The largest centers include the great mall of Eastridge in San

Jose (the surrounding valley has a great many other such combines) and Fashion Island on the old Irvine Ranch in Orange County.

Shore birds, technically considered to be only those of the suborder *Charadrii,* rather than all birds nesting or sighted on the coast, although some shore birds are migrants and some are permanent residents. Those that frequent tidal flats and salt water marshes include the *Willits* and *marbled godwits,* the *American avocet,* and the *Wilson phalarope.* The latter, along with the *northern phalarope,* are also found in lagoons, bays, and estuaries. *Brown pelicans* and *rails* are found in the flats and marshes too, while *cormorants* and *gulls* inhabit both areas and also move from salt to fresh water sites. Sea beaches, reefs, and coastal waters are breeding places for the *snowy plover* and the *least tern.* They are also locations for the *godwits, whimbrels* (all types of *sandpipers* or allies), *surfbirds, black turnstones,* and *black oystercatchers,* as well as *gulls, brown pelicans, terns, cormorants, grebes, loons,* and *scooters.* Only *wandering tattlers* and *phalaropes* inhabit the open seas as well. *Pelicans* have long been so common as to be the source of several California place-names, e.g., Pelican Bay on the Oregon border and Alcatraz Island in San Francisco Bay.

SHOREY, WILLIAM T. (1859–1919), native of Barbados, moved to California (*c.*1883), where for a long time he was captain of a whaling ship on which he is said to have had an entire crew of his fellow blacks.

SHORTRIDGE, SAMUEL M[ORGAN] (1861–1952), Iowa-born attorney and Republican party leader, resident in California after 1875 and its U.S. Senator (1921–33). His sister was Clara S. Foltz,♦ and his brother Charles owned the *San Jose Mercury*♦ and later managed the *San Francisco Call* for the Spreckels family.

Shoshone, Indian tribe that lived in an area stretching in a wide arc from the terrain of the northern Paiute in the northeast of present California down its eastern border (except for Washo lands around Lake Tahoe) into the large regions of Mono and Koso territory to the state's southeastern fringe, occupied by Yuma Indians. The most southerly tribes included the Chemehuevi, Serrano, Cahuilla, and the coastal Fernandeño, Juaneño, and Luiseño. Thus, they ranged over about one-third of the state's terrain. (*See also individual entries.*)

SHREVE, GEORGE R. (1861–1914), jeweler and silversmith, continued the San Francisco store founded (1852) by his father, George C. Shreve, originally of Boston. Their silverware was marked by distinctive styles, including hammered straps with spaced studding and the use of sinuous Art Nouveau motifs.

Shrimp, a crustacean found throughout California coastal waters. A distinctive small variety thrives in San Francisco Bay, and commercial fishing for that type has been carried on, mainly by Italians, since 1869. Chinese began catching shrimp in San Francisco and Tomales bays about 1871, followed by Japanese, but anti-Oriental laws restricted them to the area south of the Ferry Building. Most shrimp are now frozen, but a small amount of the fresh catch is relished as a delicacy.

SHUBRICK, WILLIAM BRANFORD (1790–1874), U.S. Navy commodore, dispatched to Monterey to replace Sloat (July 1846) in his command of naval forces in California. He, in turn, was soon replaced by Commodore James Biddle, but went south to blockade Mazatlan, until he was recalled (July 1847) to command in Alta California. He later returned to seize Mazatlan.

SIENKIEWICZ, HENRYK (1846–1916), Polish author, winner of a Nobel Prize (1905), best known for his novel *Quo Vadis?* (1895), as a young man moved to California (1876–78). After a stay in San Francisco, he went to Anaheim as a participant in a Utopian colony which also included the actress Helen Modjeska.♦ He wrote newspaper "Letters" and several stories about the region, but he soon returned to Poland.

Sierra Buttes, see *Sierra County.*

Sierra Club, organization with headquarters in San Francisco, founded (1892) "to explore, enjoy, and render accessible the mountain regions of the Pacific Coast; to publish authentic information concerning them; to enlist the support and cooperation of the people and the government in preserving the forests and other natural features of the Sierra Nevada." Over the years it has sponsored mountain camping and hiking trips, published books, worked for ecological purposes, and extended its interest to other regions. John Muir was its first president.

Sierra County, organized (1852) from part of Yuba County. Plumas and Lassen counties lie on its north, Plumas and Yuba counties on its west, Nevada County on its south, and the state of Nevada on its east. The western half of the county is mountainous and forested, containing 45 mile-high lakes, of which the largest is Gold Lake, and an estimated 700 miles of trout streams. Here, too, along the Yuba River, are located the northern-most mining town; Goodyear's Bar; Downieville,♦ the county seat; and Sierra City, where E. Clampus Vitus♦ was founded (1857). Farther north is Poker Flat. Eastward, by the North Fork of the Yuba River and near the lake region, lie the Sierra Buttes, peaks rising to 8,500 feet. Beyond them is Yuba Pass (6,713 feet) on an emigrant route and Mt. Ina Coolbrith. Plumas, Tahoe, and Toiyabe national forests form large parts of the county. Livestock raising and lumbering are the main businesses. In 1970 the population was only 2,365. With an area of 612,800 acres, there were 2.5 persons per sq. mi.

Sierra Madre, range lying east of the Santa Ynez Mts., in rugged and unpopulated terrain. This Spanish term for "Mother Range" was used by Font and others for various mountain chains. A town of this name, originally an orange grove settlement, lies at the foot of the San Gabriel Mts. near Pasadena.

Sierra National Forest, on the western slope of the Sierra Nevada in Madera and Fresno counties, lies between Kings Canyon and Yosemite national parks. Devil's Postpile National Monument in northeastern Madera County and Huntington Lake in northwestern Fresno County are both parts of the Forest.

Sierra Nevada, mountain range extending for some 400 miles from Lassen Peak on the north to Tejón Pass, with a width ranging from less than 50 miles in the south to over 80 miles near Lake Tahoe. Its highest peak is Mt. Whitney; its major sites include Yosemite, Sequoia, and Kings Canyon National Parks, Lake Tahoe, and the Calaveras Grove. The Yokut, Miwok, and Maidu lived on the western side and the Washoe and Mono on the eastern side of the range.

Capt. Fages and Father Crespí were the first whites to see the Sierra (1772). The first white person to cross it (going east) was Jedediah Smith (1827); the first party to make a westward crossing included Joseph Walker and Zenas Leonard (1833–34). Early travelers through the passes included Joseph Chiles, the Bartleson-Bidwell Party, and the Donner Party. Official explorations were made by Frémont. Boom settlements in the foothills and lower mountains grew up throughout the Mother Lode area during the gold rush.

Mail was carried across the Sierra by Snowshoe Thompson before the Pony Express and stagecoaches were able to get through. Later, rail crossings were made by the Central Pacific over Donner Pass (1868) and by the Southern Pacific across Tehachapi Pass (1876), followed by the Western Pacific crossing at Beckwourth Pass (1909).

Major later explorers of and writers about the region include the California State Geological Survey (1863), members of which were W. H. Brewer, Clarence King, and J. D. Whitney; and John Muir. National and State Parks and Forests now protect much of the land and its forests of sequoia, pine, fir, and cedar trees, logged elsewhere. The High Sierra is the wilderness area from Tioga Pass to Walker Pass, mostly at the timberline level, with access only by trails. This has long been the region for hiking parties sponsored by the Sierra Club. The southernmost part of the Sierra Nevada is called the Southern Prongs. (*See also individual entries.*)

Sierra Pelona, range of mountains and adjacent valley in the Angeles National Forest. The second word in Spanish means "bald."

Signal Hill, independent community adjacent to Long Beach,♦ once the *rancho* of John Temple (1844 ff.) and known then as Los Cerritos (the "little hills"), and later of the Bixby family.♦ It was renamed when it became the signal point of the coast survey (1889), just as its 300-foot eminence had once served the Indians and then the Spanish as a beacon place. In 1921 a great oil field was discovered there. It was soon bristling with derricks, from which over 250,000 barrels of oil gushed forth daily.

Silk, production was first attempted (1854) by a French botanist, Louis Prévost, who introduced mulberry bushes and silkworms. Despite a state bounty paid for the plants and cocoons and Prévost's establishment of a California Silk Association at Riverside, sericulture did not thrive. His project dwindled away after his death (1869) in the very year that the ill-fated Wakamatsu Colony♦ of Japanese was founded. However, enough interest remained for Anton Roman to publish T. A. Kendo's *Treatise on Silk and Tea Culture . . . Adapted to . . . California* (1870).

SILL, EDWARD ROWLAND (1841–87), upon graduation from Yale (1861), to aid his frail health emulated Dana by sailing around the Horn to California, where he held odd jobs until 1866. After a year at the Harvard Divinity School and a turn at journalism in New York, he returned to California to teach English at the Oakland high school (1871–74) and at the University of California (1874–82). He was known as an inspiring teacher and the author of classic verse often concerned with religious doubt, privately issued as *The Venus of Milo* (1883), followed by posthumous collections of *Poems* (1902) and *Prose* (1900). Joseph LeConte named a peak for Sill (1896) in Kings Canyon National Park.

Silverado Squatters, The, personal narrative by Robert Louis Stevenson,♦ published in 1883. It describes the trip he, his bride, and her twelve-year-old son Lloyd Osbourne♦ made in 1880 as a honeymoon through the Napa Valley to Mt. St. Helena,♦ where they lived in an abandoned cabin of a silver mine. The work contains charming depictions of the region and amusing character sketches of local persons.

Silver Kings, see *Bonanza Kings* and *Comstock Lode.*

Silver mining, begun as a chance adjunct to the mining of gold during the 1850s, was almost ignored in the rush to find the more valuable metal and at that time was never sought only for itself. Not until the discovery of the Comstock Lode♦ in 1859, just twenty miles east of the state border, near Washoe in Nevada, did silver become a significant metal for California.

Then the Territory of Nevada became a kind of suburb of San Francisco, as its initial discovery of silver and the resultant boom came to be controlled largely by the Bank of California under William C. Ralston♦ and the management of William Sharon.♦ After 1873 another group of Californians—James G. Fair, James C. Flood, John W. Mackay, and William S. O'Brien—became the Silver Kings who dominated the mines of Virginia City, while Adolph Sutro,♦ later mayor of San Francisco, devised the scheme of digging a great tunnel to reach the deeply embedded ore with increased safety.

Not long after the discovery of the Comstock Lode,♦ a significant amount of silver was found on the western side of the California-Nevada border. Some was discovered in the eastern Sierra of Alpine

County; some on Mt. St. Helena in Napa County, where Stevenson honeymooned and about which he wrote *The Silverado Squatters;*♦ some in Silverado Canyon in Orange County; and some at Esmeralda in Mono County. The biggest strikes were in the Death Valley area and led to the creation of major camps at Cerro Gordo, Darwin, and Panamint City in Inyo County. Cerro Gordo was the site of mines that yielded millions of dollars' worth of silver between 1868 and 1877 and provided an economic stimulus to Los Angeles. In the early 1880s, silver was mined in the Calico Mts. of the Mojave Desert.

The state's biggest silver discovery occurred in 1919 at Randsburg, south of China Lake, in the Mojave Desert area of San Bernardino County. The Rand Mine, commonly called Big Silver, produced about $15,000,000 in less than a decade. At its peak in 1924, it led the state and accounted for about 8% of the nation's silver production. Some 75 geographic features (lakes, mountains, etc.) and towns of California incorporate the word "silver" in their names, but most of them are so called for their appearance rather than for the presence of the metal.

Simi Hills, like the peak of the same name and the adjacent valley, are located in southeastern Ventura County and derive their name from a Chumash word for "settlement." A growing city of that name is located on the San Fernando Valley Freeway.

SIMON, NORTON (1907–   ), Portland-born, San Francisco-reared business executive whose financial interests have expanded broadly from his food-packing firm, headquartered in his home city of Los Angeles. He has created one of the greatest collections of paintings and sculpture assembled by an individual in recent times, located since 1975 in the museum named for him in Pasadena.

SIMPSON, O[RENTHAL] J[AMES] (1947–   ), San Francisco-born football player, played running back for San Francisco City College (1965–66), scoring 54 touchdowns, and for the University of Southern California (1967–68), where he established a record of 1,709 yards gained in a single season. As a senior, he won the Heisman Trophy as the best college player in the nation. He later played professional football for the Buffalo Bills until he returned to his home town to join the Forty-Niners (1978).

SINATRA, FRANK (1915–   ), born in New Jersey, became a singer on radio programs with popular orchestras, and rose to such success as to be idolized by young girls. In the 1940s he became a popular Hollywood film star as a singer, and later an actor noted for his depiction of hard-boiled characters. Even as he aged and after he retired briefly in the 1970s, he continued to be a major singer of romantic popular music and to have a huge following.

SINCLAIR, UPTON [BEALL] (1878–1968), first visited California (1909) at the instigation of George Sterling♦ and Gaylord Wilshire♦ and settled permanently in Pasadena (1917) after a substantial career in the East. Born in Baltimore of a prominent but impoverished family, at age 15 he began to write dime novels to pay for his education, which included graduation from the College of the City of New York and further study at Columbia University. Among his more serious early works were six novels, including *King Midas* (1901) and *The Journal of Arthur Stirling* (1903). Their tone is indicated by his statement that Jesus, Hamlet, and Shelley shaped his thought, and that he was disillusioned when the world did not meet him with the love and trust he felt. An investigation into the stockyards of Chicago led to *The Jungle* (1906), a realistic novel exposing capitalist corruption and brutality, related to his recent conversion to socialism. He used his large royalties to found a utopian cooperative, the Helicon Home Colony, at Englewood, N.J. (1906–7).

After moving to California, he continued his prolific literary career with more than 100 works, mainly novels and tracts, animated by a kind of Christian socialism and marked by simplistic arguments against specific evils of capitalism and prevailing socioeconomic situations. These works, which achieved great international popularity, included *King Coal* (1917), a novel about the recent Colorado coal strike; *The Profits of Religion* (1918), arguing that organized religion is a capitalist tool teaching the poor that their status is God-given; *Jimmie Higgins* (1919), a pacifist novel; *The Brass Check* (1919), on the antidemocratic nature of the modern press; *The Goose-Step* (1923), on the failings of U.S. higher education; *The Goslings* (1924), a sequel, on U.S. schools; *Oil!* (1927), a fictional treatment of the oil scandals of the Harding administration; *The Wet Parade* (1931), a novel supporting liquor prohibition; and a series of 10 novels ranging from *Between Two Worlds* (1941) to *The Return of Lanny Budd* (1953), which treated American and international history from 1913 to the period after World War II by weaving the protag-

onist's actions into true contemporary events through association with their actual leaders.

Meanwhile, despite his tremendous literary output, Sinclair found time for work on many social issues, including running on the Socialist party ticket for Congress (1920), for the U.S. Senate (1922), and for governor (1926). His greatest campaign was fought for the governorship in 1934 on the Democratic party ticket, whose nomination he won against George Creel during the Depression by offering a program to End Poverty In California, known as the EPIC plan.♦

Siskiyou County, organized (1852) from the northern part of Shasta County and part of Klamath County, which contributed more land when Klamath was dissolved (1874). Yreka has been the county seat from the beginning. On the north, Siskiyou is bounded by the state of Oregon, on the east by Modoc County, on the south by Shasta, Trinity, and Humboldt counties, and on the west by Del Norte County. Most of the county is covered by national forests—Klamath on the west and east, Shasta between them, Modoc in the northeast, and Rogue River in the northwest.

Through the heavily timbered land run numerous mountain chains, including the Salmon Mts. of the southwest and the Marble Mts. above them. Both are encompassed by the Klamath Mts., with the Salmon, Klamath, and Scott rivers flowing through them. In the central Shasta Valley runs the Shasta River and to its north the Yreka River; on the west, in Scott Valley, flows the Scott River. The headwaters of the Sacramento River rise in the county, and its tributaries include the McCloud River in the south of the county. Other major natural sites are Marble Mountain itself; the Lava Beds that form a National Monument in the northeast part of the county; the Tule Lake National Wildlife Refuge north of them; and Glass Mountain, a peak of black obsidian south of them. The most striking sight of all is Mt. Shasta, the extinct volcano, rising 14,162 feet, standing out above the Cascade Range.

Originally a land inhabited by Modoc and Klamath Indians, it was first entered by white fur trappers from Hudson's Bay Co. (1827 ff.) and the U.S., followed by settlers coming from Oregon, and culminating in substantial movements in the 1840s and during the gold rush. As discoveries were made, hordes of men poured into jerry-built camps along the Salmon and Klamath rivers. Later years in this region were fairly quiet, since mining was exhausted and the only significant activities were lumbering in the forests and growing field crops, raising potatoes and other vegetables, or ranching with livestock in the Shasta, Scott, Butte, and Tule Lake valleys. However, in 1872–73 the county attracted national attention because the Modoc, under their leader, Capt. Jack, revolted against the U.S. and held its army at bay.

Even in the late 20th century the county has not developed any sizable communities, the largest being Yreka; Dunsmuir, a railroad and supply center; and Weed, a lumber town between them. With an area of 4,008,640 acres and a population in 1970 of 33,225, the county has a density of only 5.3 persons per sq. mi. (*See also individual entries.*)

Siskiyou Trail, see *Hudson's Bay Company.*

Six Companies, coordinating body of Chinese district associations, headquartered in San Francisco but serving all California. The companies, called Tongs, each composed of people from a particular area of China, were organized in the 1850s as the Chinese Benevolent Association, and under that name have had as many as eight groups. Initially they were in the business of bringing Chinese to the U.S., with employment guaranteed in exchange for repayment of passage money and a percentage of wages, the settlers also being assured of being returned alive or for burial to China. Before the Manchu government had established a U.S. consulate, the Six Companies informally represented China. Later it became the spokesman for Chinese in California, fighting immigration restrictions, arbitrating disputes among its own people, handling fund drives, and organizing relations with Caucasians, who sometimes considered it to be a powerful body in bringing in cheap labor and at other times feared it as a sinister society.

Six Rivers National Forest, located on the western slope of the northern Coast Range and drained by the Smith, Klamath, Trinity, Mad, and Van Duzen rivers and the North Fork of the Eel. It lies just west of the Klamath, Trinity, and Mendocino National Forests. The forest was named by Peter B. Kyne◆ and incorporated in 1946.

Skateboarding, pastime and sport originated in southern California (1963), by an unknown creator of a simple vehicle consisting of a small, short board with round ends to whose underside were mounted two pairs of roller skate wheels. The initial fad for skateboards was confined to children and lasted only about two years, though it became nationwide. The interest revived about 1975, again in

southern California, with the introduction of fiberglass boards whose polyurethane wheels allowed riders to move at great speeds and to perform athletic movements resembling those achieved on surfboards. Older persons took to the boards and achieved remarkable feats, including long jumps and acrobatic routines. Professional teams and championship tournaments soon came into being, as did a popular literature of magazines and manuals on the subject.

Skiing, popular winter sport, whose American origins began (1850) at La Porte (Plumas County) when miners improvised so-called "long snowshoes" to travel over the heavy snow surrounding their mining camp. Those skis were initially made from barrel staves, but a better version was made probably by Scandinavian sailors who had come to the mines after jumping ship in San Francisco and who recalled professional skis from winters at home. The name "snowshoe" was used for all models, even though they were unlike the woven rawhide web footgear used by Indians in other parts of the country. Their most famous user was "Snowshoe" John Albert Thompson.◆ They were also used in the La Porte area for sport in the early 1850s, and the first formal skiing competition in the U.S. was sponsored by the Alturas Snow Shoe Club, founded in 1867. The popularity of the modern sport dates mainly from the 1930s and increased greatly in California after the winter Olympic Games of 1960 were held at Squaw Valley.◆ The first Californians to achieve national championships were Roy Mikkelsen (jumping, 1935) and Sig Uwland (1938). Skiing on water began as a sport in France during the 1930s, was introduced to California within a few years, and became very popular after World War II. It is pursued particularly in protected coastal waters, such as those of Long Beach, or in recreational area lakes, such as Lake Mead. Danny Churchill of Downey set a speed record for men of 126.4 mph at Oakland (1972).

Skipjack, see *Tuna.*

Skunk, small omnivorous member of the weasel family, found in California in several varieties. These include diverse spotted types (sometimes called polecat) that have two white spots on the lower back near the tail and are found in most of the state west of the Sierra, and striped types, also found throughout the state except in the southeast.

Skunk Railroad, name given to the California Western Railroad from Fort Bragg to Willits in Mendocino County,♦ because the old-fashioned equipment of this tourist attraction formerly included a pungent diesel engine. The 40-mile scenic ride is popular with railroad enthusiasts, as the former logging line loops over bridges across the Noyo River.

SLA, see *Symbionese Liberation Army.*

SLACUM, William A. (*fl.* 1836–37), U.S. naval lieutenant, sent by President Jackson to reconnoiter the west coast of North America for possible acquisition, at least of San Francisco Bay. Slacum spent much of his time in the Willamette Valley, where he became associated with Ewing Young in the cattle trade. He wrote an enthusiastic report for Congress.

Sleepy Lagoon Murder, *cause célèbre* of Chicano mistreatment, involved the death of a Mexican-American boy, José Diaz (Aug. 2, 1942), at a moldering reservoir in east Los Angeles. After heavy drinking, Diaz feel asleep on a road, where he may have been accidentally run over rather than killed in a gang war, as postulated by the police. A dragnet led to the arrest of 300 teenage Chicanos, the indictment of 23, and the conviction of 12 for murder and 5 for assault. Newspaper, public, and judicial bias, as well as police prejudice and blatant mistreatment, lay behind the jury verdicts, which were overturned by an appellate court.

SLENCZYNSKA, Ruth (1925–), Sacramento-born musical prodigy, had her first piano recital at Mills College at age 4. She later studied with major pianists, attended the University of California, Berkeley (1941–44), and performed with major orchestras in the U.S. and Europe. She wrote an autobiography, *Forbidden Childhood* (1957).

Slidell mission, occurred when President Polk appointed John Slidell, a Louisiana politician and former Congressman, as Commissioner to Mexico (1845) to negotiate the acceptance of Texas as part of the U.S., with its boundary at the Rio Grande, and the purchase of New Mexico and California. Polk was prepared to offer up to $40,000,000, but President Herrera refused to receive Slidell.

SLOAT, John Drake (1781–1867), 1st American military governor of California (July 7–29, 1846),

a native of New York, was a midshipman in the navy (1800–1801), entered the merchant service, and returned to the navy in the War of 1812, later serving with the Pacific Squadron in 1821–23. Rising in rank to captain, he was appointed in 1844 to command the Pacific Squadron and spent from Nov. 1845 to June 1846 at Mazatlan, avoiding bellicose actions but with instructions to move swiftly to forestall British seizure of California in the event of war between Mexico and the U.S. Upon learning unofficially of hostilities in Texas, he sailed to Monterey, but without formal notice of the declaration of the Mexican War,♦ he waited five days, until July 7, 1846, to go into the harbor and take possession without opposition, having sent an officer to do the same in San Francisco. After being joined by Commodore Stockton (July 15), Sloat, in ill health, designated him as commander of the American military forces in California and departed for the East on July 29. He continued in the navy, going on the reserve list in 1855 but being promoted to Rear Admiral (1866) in retirement.

Sluice box, see *Placer mining.*

SMITH, Andy (Andrew Lathem Smith) (1883–1926), Pennsylvania-born football coach, was an All-American fullback at the University of Pennsylvania (1904). After coaching at his alma mater and Purdue, he went to the University of California, Berkeley (1915–26), where he raised football to a major sport by coaching his Wonder Teams,♦ which went through five seasons without losing one of their 44 games.

SMITH, Clark Ashton (1893–1961), poet born in Placer County and longtime resident in Auburn, whose *Odes and Sonnets* (1919) and other volumes show the influence of his mentor, George Sterling. Late in life, he became a prominent writer of science fiction.

SMITH, Ernie (Ernest Frederick Smith) (1909–), South Dakota-born football player, reared in Gardena, was a tackle on the University of Southern California teams coached by Howard Jones (1931–32) that won two Rose Bowl games and went undefeated and untied in the second season. He later played professionally for the Green Bay Packers.

SMITH, Francis M[arion] (1846–1931), went from Michigan to California (1867), and in 1872, in Nevada, discovered borax,♦ which he shipped to Oakland for refining. From this, and the mines he bought from William T. Coleman, he made a fortune and an international business, as well as gaining the nickname "Borax Smith." He later diversified his interests into East Bay real estate, aided by his Key Route interurban trains and ferries,♦ but he overextended his finances and lost his fortune in 1913.

SMITH, GEORGE WASHINGTON (1876–1930), Pennsylvania-born architect and painter, trained at the Beaux-Arts in Paris. He lived in Santa Barbara the last fifteen years of his life and designed many homes in a Spanish style.

SMITH, HARRY (1918–), Missouri-born football player, was a guard on the University of Southern California team (1937–39) that won two Rose Bowl games. He was twice named an All-American.

SMITH, JEDEDIAH STRONG (1799–1831), New York-born fur trapper, reared in Ohio and Illinois, became a mountain man and explorer. He opened the South Pass (Wyoming) route to the Far West and, as a co-owner of the Rocky Mountain Fur Co., went with his beaver-trapping companions from Salt Lake in 1826 across the Mojave Desert to California. At Mission San Gabriel, he was well received by Father José Bernardo Sánchez,♦ for whom he later named the entire Sierra Nevada range as Mt. Joseph. He and his party, ousted by Gov. Echeandía as possible spies, retired to the San Joaquin Valley to trap beaver and then, en route east, became the first white men to cross the Sierra (1827). That summer he returned, though on the way ten of his men were killed by Mohave Indians. Father Durán at Mission San José first jailed and then remanded him to gain permission from Echeandía in Monterey, and for a second time he was ousted. In the spring of 1828, he led the first overland expedition of whites to Oregon, in which all but two were massacred by Umpqua Indians. Three years later, while still a young man, he was killed by Comanches in New Mexico. The Smith River in the extreme northwest corner of California honors him, as does the Jedediah Smith State Park of the Redwood National Park.♦

SMITH, "PEGLEG," see *Smith, Thomas Long.*

SMITH, PERSIFOR FRAZER (1798–1858), 6th American military governor of California (Feb. 28–April 12, 1849), was born in Philadelphia, and after graduation from the College of New Jersey (renamed Princeton, 1896) moved to New Orleans, where he practiced law and led a local regiment in the Seminole War. He had a distinguished military career in Mexico during the Mexican War, rising to major general and military governor of Mexico City. During his brief command of the Pacific Division, and thus military governorship of California, he sent aid to American emigrants struggling overland to California, but he improperly proclaimed that all foreigners in California except U.S. citizens would be treated as trespassers in gold mining. Even though he was a military commander and not a civil governor, Smith refused to recognize the Legislative Assembly for the District of San Francisco,♦ thereby further contributing to governmental restlessness. After leaving California, he held other military command posts.

SMITH, SARAH BIXBY, see *Bixby.*

SMITH, STEVE[N] (1951–), Torrance-born pole vaulter who established a world indoor record of 17′ 6¾″ (1973), which he broke with a new record of 18′ 5″ (1975).

SMITH, THOMAS LONG (1801–66), fur trapper and mountain man, known as "Pegleg" Smith because, after being wounded by an Indian, his left leg had to be amputated (1827) and thenceforth he wore a wooden leg. He nevertheless continued his life in the wilderness and made forays into California in the 1830s to trap beaver and steal horses from the missions. He returned to California during the gold rush, supposedly to work a mine he had earlier discovered in the area of Borrego Valley, a find which became as legendary as the tall-tale-telling frontiersman himself. A monument has been built to him in the area of his mythic mine.

SMITH, TOMMIE (1944–), Texas-born track star, reared in Lemoore (Kings County), by 1967 held or shared nine world records, including those for the 220-yard sprint (19.5 sec. on straightway, 20.0 on curve) and the 200-meter sprint (19.7). After winning the 200-meter race (19.8) at the Olympic Games (1968), he gave the clenched fist Black Power salute on the official victory platform and for that irregular act was suspended from the U.S. team.

Smith River, name applied to the lower Klamath River of Del Norte County in honor of Jedediah Smith.♦ At various earlier times the name was applied to the Eel, Rogue, San Joaquin, and Stanislaus rivers.

Smog, term created to describe a combination of smoke and fog, was first noticed in California on a large scale in Los Angeles on July 26, 1943. It has since become common there, particularly in summer, and in many other parts of California, especially along the coast. Los Angeles is a greatly troubled area, not only because its dense population creates pollution, but because smoke and smog-producing chemicals are trapped at ground level by an inversion layer of warm air which puts a lid on them. The smog is held down in the basin, which is partly surrounded by the San Gabriel Mts., so that weak summer breezes cannot blow it away but leave it to be intensified by the sun's warm rays.

The first manifestation of smog in California occurred at the same site 400 years earlier, when Cabrillo in 1542 observed smoke from Indian campfires rise only a few hundred feet and then spread out at the base of the mountains, causing him to name the modern San Pedro Bay "La Bahia de los Fumos." The geographic conditions of Los Angeles, unhappily, are found in other coastal basins, particularly around San Diego and at San Francisco, where, however, the common cold fog◆ helps to counter the atmospheric conditions. The populous areas of the Central Valley have also become smog centers.

Over 100 causes of smog have been identified (smoke from incinerators, factories, etc.), but automobiles are considered to be responsible for about 60% of it. To counter smog, the most serious form of the state's pollution,◆ control districts have been created for Los Angeles County (1947) and the San Francisco Bay area (1955), as well as for other regional districts (1967). To cope with automobiles, the state legislature created a Motor Vehicle Pollution Control Board (1960) as an adjunct to the Department of Public Health and, later, a more powerful Air Resources Board (1967) to set regional air quality standards and thus attempt to arrest or reverse the damaging effects of smog upon the quality of life in the state. These include harm to human health and damage to some $8,000,000 worth of agricultural produce annually.

Smoketree, desert tree, ash-gray in color, growing up to 25 feet, with a multibranched crown, features that cause it to resemble rising smoke and therefore account for its name.

SMYTH, WILLIAM (1800–77), English naval officer and artist on the expedition of Beechey◆ to California (1826–28), whose pictures illustrated his captain's *Narrative* and *California* (1839) by Alexander Forbes.

SMYTHE, WILLIAM ELLSWORTH (1861–1922), moved from his native Massachusetts to Nebraska, New Mexico, and California (1893), crusading for scientific irrigation to create and control agriculture on small farms. His ideas, coupled with progressive democracy, were practiced in colonies in southern California and Idaho. He promulgated his theories in *The Conquest of Arid America* (1900) and *Constructive Democracy: The Economics of a Square Deal* (1905). He also wrote a history of San Diego.

Snake, reptile with 34 varieties native to California. The most famous and most dangerous is the rattlesnake, a member of the viper family. Its name refers to its tail, which is composed of hollow, horn-like segments that rattle when shaken. The older the snake, the longer the rattle, one link being added at each molting and replacement of skin. The six indigenous types of rattlesnake are the *Mojave,* 24 to 51 inches long, found in the desert from which its name derives; the *red diamond,* 30 to 65 inches long, with a red or pink color, found mainly in the rocky brushlands on both sides of the Peninsular Ranges; the *sidewinder,* 17 to 31 inches long, which crawls sideways with its body in an S shape and is found in the desert south of Mono County; the *speckled,* 24 to 52 inches long, found throughout the desert and in the Peninsular Ranges; the *western,* 15 to 62 inches long, found throughout the state except in desert areas; and the *western diamondback,* 30 to 89 inches long, found in the low desert south of the Little San Bernardino Mts. but comes into the Mojave Desert only near the Nevada line. All rattlesnakes eat rodents and lizards, and sometimes birds or rabbits. Most California Indians were reluctant to kill rattlesnakes, and the Maidu, Mohave, Shasta, Yokut, and Yuki had special shamans devoted to preventing or curing bites from rattlesnakes. The frequency of white encounters with the snakes is suggested by the nearly 200 geographic features that incorporate the name.

Other varieties of snakes are generally harmless. The local boas, though of the same family as the notorious *boa constrictor,* are not dangerous. The *rosy boa,* 24 to 42 inches long, feeds on birds and small mammals found in its regions, the Mojave desert, southern California mountains, and on the coast of San Diego County; the *rubber boa,* 14 to 30 inches long, lives on lizards and small mammals in the mountains of the northern part of the state. The *colubrids* are of three types: the *ringneck,* found throughout the state, except in the Central Valley and the eastern mountains; the *sharp-tailed,* found in the Siskiyous and Cascades, on the western slope of the Sierra, and in the Coast Range from Humboldt to San Luis Obispo counties; and the *spotted leaf-nosed,* found in deserts; They feed, respectively, on lizards, frogs, and other snakes; on slugs; and on reptile eggs.

Garter snakes of eight varieties are found throughout the state. The most aquatic of local snakes, they eat fish, frogs, salamanders, small rodents, and bird eggs. *Gopher snakes* can grow to eight feet and are found throughout the state. One or another of the *king* snake's three varieties is found throughout the state. They feed on lizards, other snakes (including rattlers), rodents, frogs, and birds. *Lyre snakes* are of three varieties: the *California lyre,* found south of the Tehachapi; the *night snake,* found in the Central Valley, southern California, and part of the desert; and the *Sonora,* found in the eastern desert. All are venomous but probably not dangerous to man. They feed on small mammals and lizards. Some of the wide variety of *racer snakes* are to be found throughout the state, a few being called *whipsnakes.* The *gopher snake* belongs to that family. The *western snake,* found throughout southern California except in the higher mountains, is very small, resembles an earthworm, and feeds on ants and termites.

SNIDER, DUKE (EDWIN DONALD SNIDER) (1926–), Los Angeles-born baseball player, was an outfielder with the Dodgers (1947–62), the N.Y. Mets (1963), and the Giants (1964). He hit 40 or more home runs in five consecutive years (1953–57) and drove in over 100 runs in each of six years.

Snow, generally found only in the mountainous parts of the state and in its northern latitudes, is crucial to all of California because it is the significant source of water for hydroelectric power and irrigation. Almost half the state's natural run-off depends upon the Sierra Nevada, which has one of the heaviest snowfalls in the U.S. Since temperatures in those mountains are warm in summer, little snow remains, even on the highest northern slopes and in the deepest ravines, although Mt. Tallac♦ is famous for its perennial cross of snow. The lofty, isolated Mt. Shasta in northeastern California also generally has its peak crowned with snow throughout the year.

The amount of snow in California's mountains varies from the Peninsular Ranges, with only a few inches, to the 8,000-foot level of the Sierra Nevada in Alpine County, at whose Tamarack an average of 445 inches falls each year. Tamarack is also the site of the greatest seasonal fall recorded in the state (884 inches; nearly 74 feet), the greatest monthly snowfall (390 inches in Jan. 1911), and the greatest depth on the ground at one time (454 inches on March 9, 1911). The snow by which the Donner Party was trapped is estimated to have been about 156 inches deep at their camp by Donner Lake.

When the adjacent Donner Pass became the route for the transcontinental railroad, snowsheds♦ had to be built, but they have sometimes been wrecked by slides, and in the winter of 1889–90 the nearby tracks were blocked for four months. Latter-day highways are often briefly blocked too, but the heavy snowfall has made the region popular in recent years for skiing and other winter sports, and caused Squaw Valley to be selected as the site of the Winter Olympic Games of 1960. Snow beyond the mountains is unusual and is a great rarity in coastal areas. San Francisco has experienced a measurable snowfall only about ten times from the beginning of record keeping until the mid-1970s.

Snowsheds, structures built by the Central Pacific Railroad♦ (1867) to protect its track over the Sierra Nevada, initially with pitched A-frame roofs and after 1869 with level roofs. To meet passenger objections to blocking of scenic views, the Central Pacific double-tracked the snowshed area (1880), using the shed-line only in winter.

SNYDER, GARY (1930–), San Francisco-born poet, educated at the University of California, Berkeley, where he studied anthropology and Oriental culture, which have strongly affected his writing. His experiences as a logger and sailor have also been influential, as have been the many years he lived in Japan. His poetry is built upon contrasts between eastern and western values, and between the land and urban, mechanized society. Among his collections of poetry are *Riprap* (1959), *Myths and Texts* (1960, 1965), *Cold Mountain Poems* (1958), *The Back Country* (1967), and *Turtle Island* (1974, Pulitzer Prize). His essays are gathered in *Earth House Hold* (1969).

Soaring, see *Gliding.*

SOBERANES, prominent early California family whose founder, José María Soberanes, arrived with the Sacred Expedition (1769) as a soldier. With his father-in-law, Joaquin Castro, he became the owner of a large *rancho* near Monterey, where many of his descendants later lived. A son, Mariano de Jesus (1794–1859), married a daughter of Ignacio Vallejo. Other marriages allied the Soberanes with the Bale, Carrillo, Castillo, Dana, and Hartnell families.

Society of California Pioneers, The, organization founded (1850) to preserve records of early California in manuscript and printed form. Its members are restricted to males descended from persons who were in California prior to 1850. Its headquarters, containing a museum and library, are located near San Francisco's Civic Center.

"Society Upon the Stanislaus, The," humorous poem by Bret Harte, published in 1868 to satirize false erudition, such as the declaration of J. D. Whitney♦ that a modern skull found in Calaveras♦ was prehistoric.

SOLÁ, PABLO VICENTE DE (1761–1826?), last Spanish (1814–22) and first Mexican (April 11–Nov. 22, 1822) governor of Alta California, served as a lieutenant colonel in Guadalajara before being appointed governor because of his outspoken royalist sympathies at a time when Spanish control of the New World was threatened from all sides. Welcomed to Monterey (Aug. 30, 1815) with elaborate festivities, Solá tried to implement the Spanish policy of excluding foreign military and commercial interests, but economic need caused him to continue the illicit exchange of wheat for Russian manufactured goods. In 1818 two privateers commanded by the Buenos Aires pirate Hippolyte de Bouchard♦ attacked Monterey, forcing Solá and others to retreat to the interior temporarily. This first attack by a foreigner on California was symbolic of more peaceful incursions. The first non-Spanish resident of Alta California, John Gilroy,♦ had arrived in 1814 and settled on a ranch at the site of the town which bears his name, followed in 1816 by the first American, Thomas W. Doak.♦ Solá's greatest accomplishment was the encouragement of education by the founding of primary schools at each of the four presidios and two pueblos. When the Spanish rule of Mexico was ended in 1822, Solá took the oath of allegiance to Iturbide, becoming the first Mexican governor of Alta California. The junta he created at Monterey soon selected him as the deputy from California to the Mexican Congress, and he thereupon departed for Mexico City, never to return.

Solano County, one of the original 27 counties (1850), whose seat at first was Benicia, transferred (1858) to Fairfield. The western boundary is Napa County and part of San Pablo Bay off Sonoma County; Putah Creek marks the northern division from Yolo County, the county which also forms the eastern boundary, along with the tail of Sacramento County; and the southern boundary is formed by the Sacramento River, Suisun and San Pablo bays, and Carquinez Strait.

Gen. Mariano Vallejo battled the local Soscol Indians (1835), but then made a friend of their chief, the majestically tall Sem-Yeto, who was baptized and renamed Solano after Mission San Francisco Solano at Sonoma. Solano was also chief of the Suisun Indians and led both tribes to protect the mission and other white properties against wilder Indians. Gen. Vallejo accordingly asked that the new county be named for him (1850).

Vallejo held the great Soscol land grant stretching north from Carquinez Strait, and on that ranch land were established two cities that each became the state capital briefly: Benicia (1847), intended to be a port rivaling San Francisco, and Vallejo (1850), which flourished because the adjacent Mare Island soon became a major naval base. Another early settler was Juan Manuel Vaca, who moved to California from New Mexico with William Workman (1841) and the following year settled in the area, where he is memorialized by Vacaville.

The first settlers from the U.S. were the brothers of William Wolfskill, who began cattle ranching and fruit farming there in the 1840s. Other early settlers included John Bidwell, whose great land grant lay along the west bank of the Sacramento River, and Lansford Hastings, who built a home on Suisun Bay. The early urban promise suggested by two capital cities has never been fulfilled, but the county has long been an important agricultural region. Its major produce consists of sugar beets, tomatoes, fruit and nuts, and field crops. In the southeast are sloughs that attract ducks and other migratory fowl. Beyond them lies the rich delta land of Sacramento County, some of whose produce is shipped from Solano's Rio Vista, located on a deep-water canal.

The town lies at the center of huge natural gas fields, whose product is about equal in value to all of the county's agricultural output. Another important economic force has been Travis Air Force Base, while food processing is the major industry. In 1970 the county had a population of 171,989. With an area of 528,384 acres, this gave it 208.9 persons per sq. mi. *(See also individual entries.)*

Soldados de cuera, see *Leather-jacket soldiers.*

Sole, a flatfish similar but unrelated to the true European sole. It is found on the ocean bottom near shore, mostly on the northern coastline. In the 1960s the annual catch averaged 20,000,000 pounds.

Soledad Brothers, three unrelated black prisoners confined in the Correctional Facility of that name in the Salinas Valley: George Jackson (1941–71), Fleeta Drumgo, and John Clutchette, accused of killing a white guard (Jan. 1970) in reprisal for the shooting of three black inmates. The revolutionary prison letters of Jackson, *Soledad Brother* (1970), attracted much attention, which was heightened when George's 17-year-old brother Jonathan seized and held five hostages, including a judge, at a San Rafael courthouse, intending to trade them for the release of the Brothers. The melee ended with the death of young Jackson, the judge, and others, and the unproven charge that Angela Davis♦ had smuggled in the fatal gun. George Jackson was killed at San Quentin,♦ ostensibly while trying to escape, and his two "Brothers" were acquitted of the murder of the guard.

Soledad, Nuestra Señora de, thirteenth of the 21 missions♦ to be founded, was dedicated (1791) by Lasuén and named for the Virgin as Our Lady of Solitude because neighboring Indians identified themselves by a word that sounded like "Soledad," a name later given to a farming community founded nearby in the Salinas Valley. An adobe church with a thatched roof was completed in 1797 and enlarged in 1805 but was later damaged several times by flooding of the Salinas River. The church is the burial place of Gov. Arrillaga (1814). A chapel built there in 1832 was the site of the death of Father Sarría. That chapel was rebuilt in 1954 and a residence wing was restored in 1963, but much of the remaining mission is a deteriorating pile of adobe. A State Correctional Facility is also located at Soledad.

SOLÍS, Joaquín (*fl.* 1829), sent from Mexico to California as a convict pardoned because he accepted resettlement. He joined José María Herrera, a financial agent of the government, in leading a bloodless revolt (1829) against Gov. Echeandía. Begun in Monterey as a protest by soldiers who had not received their pay, the revolt ended with a confrontation in Santa Barbara, after which Solís was arrested and sent to San Blas, where he was freed.

Solvang, Danish community in the Santa Ynez Mts. of Santa Barbara County, founded (1911) by the Danish-American Corp., including Danish professors from Illinois, who established a now defunct college. The name means "sunny field." An annual Danish Days celebration is held in summer to attract tourists. Mission Santa Inés is located there.

Song, State, see *State symbols.*

Songs, in the English language were introduced to California by settlers who brought their own folk music and created variants or new versions suited to the great influx of settlers in the 1840s and 50s. Among the latter were "Sweet Betsy from Pike," "What Was Your Name in the States?" and the version of "Oh Susanna" that declared "I'm going to California with my banjo on my knee." Such works were collected in *Put's Original California Songster* (1855), which also included lyrics about local phenomena, such as "Sacramento Gals" and "When I Went Off To Prospect."

Other songbooks were popular both in the state and in the miners' old regions to convey a sense of the new life, but in California the newcomers also sang tunes and used words of their native tongues: French, German, Italian, Mexican, and others. In the more settled years that followed, there were few indigenous songs, although some new works, like "Oh, My Darling Clementine,"♦ had local references. Poetry by local writers often emphasized the musicality of their verse, with such titles as Joaquin Miller's *Songs of the Sierras* and *Songs from the Sun-lands.*

The lure of California for tourist and new resident alike toward the end of the 19th century and the beginning of the 20th was expressed in songs as well as other forms of writing, a quintessential and very popular example being "A Perfect Day," by Carrie Jacobs Bond♦ (1910), celebrating the beauties of the writer's home area in Riverside and those of the Mojave Desert. Somewhat similar in tone was "I Love You, California,"♦ first issued in 1913 and made the state's official song in 1951. Of later dates and style were the analogous songs, "California, Here I Come,"◆ (1921), popularized by Al Jolson, and "I Left My Heart in San Francisco," made the city's official song in 1969, just 16 years after it was composed. Smaller communities were also eulogized in songs, often assisted by local chambers of commerce, so that there has been "Pasadena, Where the Grass is Greener," "When the Swallows Come Back to Capistrano," published in 1938 to commemorate a phenomenon popularizing the town of San Juan Capistrano, "Do You Know the Way to San Jose?" and "Twenty-six Miles," glorifying the insular attractions of Santa Catalina Island, which lies that distance offshore.

Although not lauding the state or its communities, but certainly identified with the area, are college songs, including "The Golden Bear" of the University of California, written by Charles Mills Gayley in 1895, "Come Join the Band" of Stanford University, and "Fight On for Old S.C." of the University of Southern California. In more recent times, the images of California popularized in song have been diverse, ranging from Woody Guthrie's lyrics (1937) of the Depression, declaring that the state might be a Garden of Eden for some people but not for those who "ain't got the Do-Re-Mi," to the euphoric celebration of "California Girls" and the state's sunny culture by the Beach Boys. The latter group achieved great popularity, as did the vocalists associated with some rock music◆ bands, but some singers who were featured in films, like Bing Crosby and Frank Sinatra, became international figures.

Sonoma County, one of the original 27 counties, whose initial seat was the town of that name (1850–54) but has been Santa Rosa◆ since then. Marin County and a bit of San Pablo Bay lie on the south, the Pacific Ocean on the west, Mendocino County on the north, and Lake and Napa counties on the east. It was the home of coast Miwok, and the first white exploration was by Lt. Francisco de Bodéga y Cuadro (1775), for whom the county's southern coastal point of Bodega Bay◆ is named.

The first white settlers were the Russians (1809), who three years later built Fort Ross.◆ The *Californios*' concern at this intrusion led to the explorations of Gabriel Moraga, the establishment of a mission, San Francisco Solano◆ (1823), and the founding of the pueblo of Sonoma (1835) by the great man of the area, Gen. Mariano Vallejo.◆ He built the settlement around the town plaza (made a State Historical Monument in 1958), with its Casa Grande (the Vallejo family mansion), long

since burned down; the homes of other family members and relatives, including the General's brother-in-law, Jacob P. Leese; the mission, the house of the mission fathers; and a barracks for soldiers.

The town was seized at the start of the Bear Flag Revolt◆ (1846), leading to the arrest and imprisonment of Vallejo and the raising of the California Republic's Bear Flag by Capt. William B. Ide. The Russians had long since given up their settlements because of the power represented by the presence of the Spanish and because they had exhausted the sea otter catch. Their land and buildings had been owned since 1841 by John A. Sutter. After the U.S. victory in the Mexican War, Vallejo moved back to the great *ranchos* that had made him the manorial lord of the region. Near present Petaluma◆ he had built a two-storied, balconied adobe, once the grandest home in northern California, and at Sonoma he built a Victorian gothic house, Lachryma Montis, his home from 1850 to his death in 1890 and now part of a State Historic Park.

Other early settlers of the region included Agoston Haraszthy,◆ two of whose sons married two daughters of Vallejo. Haraszthy developed the state's first large vineyards (1858 ff.), and the county has become second only to Napa as a wine producer, whose well-known wineries include that of Asti's Italian-Swiss Colony.◆ Agriculture of other kinds has become a major economic base of the county, with emphasis mainly on livestock and poultry ranching, although apple and other fruit and nut growing are also important. The county derived some of its agricultural fame from the many experiments carried out by Luther Burbank◆ at Santa Rosa.

The county is also famous for its great stands of redwood trees along the Russian River◆ and the Redwood Highway, including public sites like the Armstrong State Park and private ones like the Bohemian Grove. The hot springs and fumaroles (steam geysers) of the area are most notable in the region of Healdsburg◆ and The Geysers,◆ where the world's largest geothermal generating plant is located. Another natural phenomenon is the Petrified Forest,◆ which is not far from the county's highest peak, Mt. St. Helena,◆ both vividly described by a summer resident, Robert Louis Stevenson. Another famous author who lived in the region was Jack London, who described it in *The Valley of the Moon* (1913) and built at Glen Ellen his great Wolf House. It burned down as he was about to move into it and is now part of a State Historic Park. In 1970 the county had a population of

204,885. With an area of 1,026,240 acres, it had 127.7 persons per sq. mi.

Sonoma Valley, extension to the southeast of Santa Rosa Valley, is also called the Valley of the Moon, although the name of the Indian tribe from which it is derived probably had no such meaning. Its mission was founded in 1824 and the town in 1835. Since the days of Agoston Haraszthy,♦ it has been a major vineyard area. Orchards and grazing lands are also common. It is the site of Jack London's great ranch at Glen Ellen.

Sonora, seat of Tuolumne County, derived its name from the large settlement of Mexicans who mined there successfully during the gold rush until most were driven out by Americans. Some 5,000 people were said to be residents of the town in late 1849. In 1970 the population was about 3,000.

Sonora Pass, see *Tuolumne County.*

Sonora Trail, overland route from northern Mexico to California in the gold rush, following generally the trail of the second expedition (1775–76) of Anza.♦

Sonorans in California, attracted from the northern mining district of Mexico to the California mines during the gold rush; some 5,000 settled in the Mother Lode region (1848–50). These Mexican miners established the town of Sonora, and there and at other settlements they met gross antipathy, discrimination, and vigilantism. Just as the Hounds♦ harried them in San Francisco, so Americans in general used a variety of means to oust "foreigners" from the mining country. Feelings ran so high that in Downieville♦ they even hanged a woman (1851) named Juanita who had stabbed a miner who broke into her cabin as an aftermath of a July 4th celebration. The imposition of the Foreign Miners' License Tax♦ was instrumental in causing most of the Sonorans to return home, although some stayed to mine quicksilver at New Almaden.

SONTAG, JOHN (1861–93), with his younger brother George, was employed by and later embittered toward the Southern Pacific for alleged bad treatment when injured on his job as brakeman. In revenge the brothers joined with a farmer, Chris[topher] Evans (1847–1917), also embittered against the railroad, and held up or dynamited trains, seizing funds in transit. During these esca-

pades (1889–92), they killed and wounded several policemen. John was shot to death by a sheriff's posse in Tulare County, and George and Evans were jailed but escaped, only to be recaptured. The character of Dyke and his opposition to the railroad, depicted by Norris in *The Octopus,* were based partly on the Sontag case and conveyed some sense of why his exploits were often admired. Evans and the younger Sontag were eventually pardoned (1911), and the former's wife appeared in a popular melodrama depicting the group as heroic Robin Hood figures.

Sorghum, major field crop grown as grain for livestock. Production centers are Sacramento, San Joaquin, and Imperial valleys and the Delta. In 1970 it was grown on 396,000 acres and was worth $41,905,000.

Soscol, see *Solano County.*

SOULÉ, FRANK[LIN] (1810–82), born in Maine, after graduation from Wesleyan College (Conn.) and newspaper work, moved to California (1849). After a year of mining he became editor of the *Alta California*♦ (1851); the *Chronicle* (1853–56), a San Francisco evening paper; and the *San Francisco Times* and *Call* in the 1860s. He also held governmental posts in his adopted city, about which he compiled, with John H. Gihon and James Nisbet, *The Annals of San Francisco*♦ (1855), collecting data on the city's foundation and development.

Sourdough, a bread dough made of flour and water, fermented without yeast, or, by extension, the loaf of bread itself, also often called French bread, long a gourmet specialty of San Francisco. It was introduced to the city and to the mining towns during the gold rush by settlers from France and Mexico, the latter having got it originally from France. Miners often kept a bit of the sourdough leaven (called "mother") for starting fermentation again easily in their remote cabin settlements. The same practice prevailed during the Klondike gold rush (1897–98) and led to its prospectors being called "sourdoughs." The quality of San Francisco's bread is often said to depend on local fog and a special style of brick oven, but that seems to be simply folklore.

South Bay, name given to the oceanfront area of Los Angeles County, including Manhattan Beach, Hermosa Beach, and Redondo Beach, and extending inland behind them. It is also called southern Santa Monica Bay. The name "South Bay" is also applied to the arm of San Francisco Bay extending down the Peninsula.

Southern California, a very general geographic term referring to the part of the state that lies south of the Tehachapi Mts.,♦ is often given a greater sense of separateness by capitalizing the defining adjective. It encompasses 14 counties: Mono, Kings, Tulare, Inyo, San Luis Obispo, Kern, San Bernardino, Santa Barbara, Ventura, Los Angeles, Orange, Riverside, San Diego, and Imperial.♦

Cleavages evident during the Mexican period, e.g. between Echeandía and Zamorano or Pío Pico and José Castro, continued under the U.S. government, so that southern Californians moved for separate statehood at the first Constitutional Convention (1849). Following its relative isolation, with the gold rush concentrated in the north, the six so-called Cow Counties♦ gained the state legislature's approval to create an unrealized Territory of Colorado (1859).

Beginning in the 1880s, southern California experienced a series of land booms, aided by direct rail connections with the East, as people entered in ever larger numbers mainly for health, to grow citrus, to invest in real estate, and for retirement in an attractive climate. The population, which had been about 6,000 in 1850, grew to 60,000 by 1875 and exploded to 325,000 in 1900.

The great expansion of old communities which made Los Angeles♦ the state's largest city and the third largest in the U.S. also created one new city after another. The vast increase led to a need to import water♦ from northern California and the Colorado River, and also required a more equitable redistribution of seats in the state's legislature.

The economy is various, but major industries include aerospace, agriculture, apparel, electronics, motion pictures and television, petroleum, and tourism. The population (1970) is about 12,400,000, all but about 3% having been added since 1900.

Southern California Edison Company, a public utility firm whose parent company, West Side Lighting Co. (founded in Los Angeles, 1896), absorbed the Los Angeles Edison Co. (1897) and other smaller utilities until only Henry E. Huntington's Pacific Light and Power Co. and the Los Angeles Gas and Electric Co. remained outside of it in southern California. It took its present name in 1909, when it was reorganized and capitalized at $30,000,000, and in 1917 it merged Huntington's

company into its system. Thus, it became a $100,000,000 corporation whose service extended throughout the Santa Ana, San Gabriel, and Los Angeles valleys, from San Juan Capistrano in the south to Santa Barbara and the edge of Fresno County in the north, and from the Pacific Ocean in the west to Redlands in the east. To serve its large market, the company developed hydroelectric plants♦ on the Kern and San Joaquin rivers far to the north and in 1920 began its huge Big Creek project in Fresno County. Since its inception in 1909, it has been involved with the city of Los Angeles over municipal ownership of the electric-power distributing system. The city's electorate (1910 and 1914) decided that electricity generated by the publicly financed Owens Valley water project♦ would also be municipally owned, and so the company had to sell its lines to the city (1916–21). It also attempted to construct its own dam on the Colorado River, a project supplanted by the federally financed Hoover Dam, although the company did enter into a contract with the government to transmit and sell the energy produced. It now supplies most of southern California outside Los Angeles and San Diego County with its electricity, while along the Nevada state line its service stretches nearly to Lake Tahoe. In 1975 it operated 36 hydroelectric plants, 12 fossil-fueled steam electric generating plants, two combustion turbine plants, one diesel electric generating plant, and the nuclear generating station at San Onofre.♦

Southern California Gas Company, private utility firm, a division of Pacific Lighting Corp.,♦ had its beginnings in the Los Angeles Gas Co., created in 1867 to light the streets of the little city of Los Angeles. A century later, the company had become the largest distributor of natural gas♦ in the U.S.

Southern California Historical Society, see *Historical Society of Southern California.*

Southern California Mountains, see *Transverse Ranges.*

Southern Cascade Mountains, see *Cascade Range.*

Southern mines, see *Mother Lode.*

Southern Pacific Railroad, founded (1865) to build a line from San Francisco to San Diego and to the state's eastern border, for which it received a congressional land grant of ten sections (i.e. square miles) in an alternate checkerboard pattern for each mile of track that it laid. The Big Four◆ came to control the company and, upon completion of their Central Pacific Railroad (1869), began work on the new line. By 1877 they had not only linked the two California cities but had extended their track to Yuma. Later expansion included a link in New Mexico to the Santa Fe Railroad, achieving a new transcontinental line (1881); acquisition of the "Sunset" route to New Orleans (1883); a track from San Francisco to Portland (1887); and alternate routes to Los Angeles (1901).

The Southern Pacific first leased (1884) and later bought (1899) Central Pacific stock in order to assure the control of both rail systems by the Big Four. The Southern Pacific was condemned for its monopoly, which extended to river traffic through its California Steam Navigation Co. to its oceanic Occidental and Oriental line; and rate agreements with the Pacific Mail Steamship.◆ As a force in state politics, it gained control of the commission elected to regulate railways and of other offices of government. The railroad was also hated for its policy of freight charges based on whatever the traffic would bear and for the special rates it allowed to large shippers like Standard Oil. Opposition became most vehement when the railroad had San Joaquin Valley settlers evicted from their farms, leading to the battle of Mussel Slough,◆ fictionalized by Frank Norris, and to attacks like that of John Sontag.◆

Not until Claus Spreckels built the San Francisco and San Joaquin Railroad (1893–97), which was purchased by the Santa Fe Railroad (1898), was there any alternative to the dominant Southern Pacific in northern California, and only the Santa Fe challenged it in the south. However, the end of the line's power came only when Hiram Johnson was elected governor (1910) and proceeded to remove railroad supporters from state offices. For some years after 1900, Edward H. Harriman's Union Pacific Railroad◆ controlled Southern Pacific stock and thus, after 1910, its subsidiary, Pacific Electric Railway,◆ until this was declared to be a violation of the Sherman Anti-Trust Act. During the 20th century the railroad acquired more lines outside the state, entered the truck and bus business, and employed new techniques (e.g. refrigerator cars to convey perishable foods), which let it continue a successful business that profited greatly from its continuing vast landholdings in California.

Southern Prongs, southernmost ranges of the Sierra Nevada, linking it with the southern Coast Range and the Transverse Ranges. They include the Greenhorn Mts. on the west, Kiavah Mts. on the east, and Piute Mts. in the middle, with the Tehachapi Mts. on the south, so that Tehachapi Pass and Tejón Pass are part of the Prongs.

South Gate, city south of Los Angeles between Watts and Downey, founded (1918) as a gardened entry area to the Cudahy Ranch on the old *rancho* of the Lugo family. It grew rapidly after World War II as a residential tract area near industrial plants. In 1970 it had a population of 56,909.

South of the Slot, popular name for the district south of the eastern reaches of Market St. in San Francisco, in reference to the slot that formerly held the cable for its street cars. Among the many San Franciscans who gloried in this area as their birthplace were David Belasco, Sidney Grauman, Jack London, James Rolph, and David Warfield.

South Park, residential development south of Market St., San Francisco, created (1852) in the style of a London square by George Gordon,◆ a Yorkshireman whose local success as a businessman was shadowed by the actions of his wife, a former barmaid, who supposedly made their daughter an alcoholic. Gertrude Atherton fictionalized their story in *A Daughter of the Vine* (1899). The fashionable oval deteriorated into a slum as 20th-century industry encroached on it and freeway approaches to the Bay Bridge covered the adjacent Rincon Hill.◆

Southwest Museum, founded by Charles Lummis' Southwest Society (1907), was opened in 1914 and located in Highland Park, northeast Los Angeles. It contains relics and examples of the arts and crafts of Indians from Alaska to Yucatan and from the plains of the U.S. to its West Coast. The museum also has a research library whose collections are broader than anthropology alone. Lummis' home, El Alisal,◆ and La Casa de Adobe◆ are parts of the museum.

Spa, site where mineral springs are found. The word itself derives from the place-name of a famous Belgian resort and, by extension, is applied to vacation hotels visited for medicinal or thermal purposes by persons seeking to improve their health. California had many such places, which were particularly popular during the last four decades of the 19th century. Among the major resorts were Aetna Springs, Calistoga, The Geysers, Napa Soda Springs, Paso Robles, and Tassajara Hot Springs.

Spas became popular again in the 1960s with a new back-to-nature movement at these and other locations, including Murietta Hot Springs (Riverside County) and Escondido and Carlsbad (San Diego County). (*See also individual entries.*)

Spanish Colonial Revival, see *Mission Revival.*

Spanish period of California, began with the discovery of Baja California under the aegis of Cortés (1533) and with the discovery of Alta California by Cabrillo (1542). The next European to land in Alta California was Francis Drake (1579), but despite his claim to the land for England, it remained in the orbit of Spain, like the Pacific Ocean itself, over which sailed the Manila galleons, whose search for a good harbor north of Acapulco led Cermeño (1595) and Vizcaíno (1602) to explore Alta California's shore for satisfactory ports.

Nevertheless, the colonization of the region remained only a dream for more than 150 years after the last of these explorers visited Alta California by sea, even though Baja California became the site of Jesuit missions founded by Fathers Kino, Salvatierra, and Ugarte. Not until 1769 did a viceroy under the promptings of the *visitador-general,* José de Gálvez, begin colonization by dispatching the Sacred Expedition to Alta California under the command of Gaspar de Portolá and the religious leadership of the Franciscan Father Junípero Serra. A second overland party, led by Capt. Rivera y Moncada and Father Crespí, and ships to carry supplies for agriculture and settlement, made a rendezvous with Portolá and Serra at San Diego. At that site was founded (1769) the first of the 18 missions established in Alta California that century, with three more dedicated by 1823.

A new route for supplies and settlers from Sonora was pioneered by Anza (1774), who the next year founded Alta California's first presidio at San Francisco, whose Bay had been explored by Ayala (1775). By 1777 Alta California was important enough to cause Gov. Felipe de Neve to tranfer his capital from Loreto to Monterey. Neve also codified the laws of the region and established its first pueblos. Nevertheless, Alta California was only a poor, remote outpost, with perhaps 600 residents other than Indians in 1781 and only some 3,000 by 1821; its pueblo of Los Angeles had only about 30 small adobe homes by 1800. The missions did prosper and convert many Indians, but the Spaniards did not attempt to locate their settlements or extend their influence beyond the coastal area, and their eastern boundary was never determined. Very few grants were made into *ranchos,* and these were all near the coast, even though Gabriel Moraga explored the little-known interior valleys and mountains. The few settlements fringing the ocean were described as crude and impoverished by such visitors as Vancouver and Rezanov. Their respective nations of England and Russia coveted this almost undefended and isolated territory, as did the few Yankee sailors on U.S. merchantmen who put into shore illegally for supplies or a bit of trading.

Meanwhile, Spain had increasing difficulty in holding on to California's homeland of Mexico, which fought for independence and finally achieved it (1821). California was almost unaffected by the wars for independence, except for such trivial incidents as the attack of Bouchard, just as it was unaffected by its nominal position as part of the empire of Iturbide. However, through remote events, in 1822 it declared itself part of the independent nation of Mexico. Thus began the Mexican period of California. (*See also individual entries.*)

Spanish Trail, see *Old Spanish Trail.*

SPARKS, WILL (1862–1937), Missouri-born painter, newspaper artist, and editorial writer for Fresno, Stockton, and San Francisco papers. He lived in California the last fifty years of his life and painted numerous canvases of the missions and mining towns.

SPEAR, NATHAN (1802–49), Massachusetts-born trader and merchant who went to Monterey (1831) after spending much time in the South Seas and on the Hawaiian Islands. One of the first residents of Yerba Buena, he took possession of the island of that name, where he pastured goats, causing it for a long time to be called Goat Island. He was associated with Sutter and Jacob Leese♦ in diverse business enterprises. His nephew was William Heath Davis.

Special Districts, see *Districts.*

SPERRY, SIMON WILLARD (1822–86), born in New Hampshire, moved to Stockton in 1856. There with his cousin, Austin Sperry, he founded the early Sperry Flour Mill, on which the family fortune was based. His daughter Ethel (1863–1934) married the San Francisco banker William H. Crocker;♦ another daughter, Elizabeth, married Prince André Poniatowski (1864–1954), a Polish nobleman. The brothers-in-law were early developers of hydroelectric power from the Mokelumne River. Poniatowski also founded the race track at Tanforan.♦ S. W. Sperry briefly owned the Calaveras Grove,♦ which became the property of his brother, James L. Sperry, who developed it. The Sperrys' company, the largest miller of flour♦ on the Pacific Coast, was sold to a national concern in 1929.

Spinach, vegetable whose California crop accounts for most of the nation's supply. Over three-quarters of it is grown in the central coastal region or in the central interior valleys, the remainder being harvested in southern California. Well over half the processed crop is now frozen.

SPITZ, MARK [ANDREW] (1950–), Modesto-born champion swimmer, set 35 U.S. records and 23 world records. As a U.S. Olympic team member, he won 2 gold medals in 1968 and 7 in 1972.

Splendid, Idle Forties, collection of short stories by Gertrude Atherton.♦

Sports, athletic activities engaged in for recreation and competition, have long been so prominent in California life that they are considered peculiarly representative aspects of the state's culture. Their popularity and importance have grown mainly in the 20th century. During the times of Spanish and Mexican settlement, sports were related to horse raising♦ and horseback riding, as extensions of daily life. In the gold rush era, Americans and other foreigners introduced a wider range of sports to relieve the tedium of their labors; boxing♦ was particularly popular during the rest of the century. The larger cities not only enjoyed prizefights but began to introduce games for participants and spectators, so that as early as 1859, San Francisco had a baseball team.♦

Increased wealth and leisure allowed some Californians to develop other recreational pastimes, including yachting,♦ introduced in the 1850s and 60s; tennis,♦ imported from England in 1879; and golf,♦ for which the first course was built in southern California in 1891. All of these sports were considered the playthings of the rich, as was swimming♦ in tanks (later called pools) at exclusive country clubs or private estates.

Colleges, which were generally thought to be mainly for well-to-do young men, encouraged their students to participate in these and other sports and aroused great interest in their major competitive teams. Football,♦ introduced as soccer in 1877, was developed into an American version, and inter-

collegiate contests began in 1889. Similar competition occurred in baseball (introduced at the University of California in 1892) and in basketball♦ and track and field sports,♦ both established in 1893.

During the first decades of the 20th century, interest in diverse sports was greatly increased as Californians became champions, partly because their benign climate permitted year-round practice. Indeed, with such a figure as Maurice McLoughlin♦ in tennis, they began to develop distinctive regional styles of play. The opportunity to enjoy outdoor sports in winter and the importance of sports in general were widely publicized through the intersectional football games of the Tournament of Roses,♦ established in 1916 as a New Year's Day event that grew into the first of the postseason football championships, the Rose Bowl competition. California's interest in and support of all forms of athletics was further emphasized when the Olympic Games were held in Los Angeles in 1932.

The tremendous appeal of amateur competition and of collegiate rivalries also stimulated more professional games, ranging from individual sports, like golf, to those for teams, like ice hockey,♦ introduced in 1928. By 1946 a professional football team had moved to the state, and in the 1950s California got major league baseball teams. The post-World War II era also brought about a great boom in both recreational and spectator sports, which appealed to the many young people who comprised an increasingly large part of the population as well as to persons of retirement age who moved to California for easier living.

Sports-oriented styles of life became increasingly evident as residents cultivated various forms of recreation.♦ The Winter Olympic Games held at Squaw Valley in 1960 aroused great interest in skiing, previously very little known in the state. A new beach culture,♦ particularly for young people, greatly increased interest in such ocean sports as water skiing,♦ surfing,♦ and skin diving, while older persons made swimming pools commonplace for even modest homes in much of southern California. More venturesome forms of sporting activities ranged from mountaineering♦ and river rafting to hang gliding♦ and the racing of automobiles, the latter activity part of the state's growing addiction to what has been called a car culture.♦

SPRECKELS, prominent California family, founded by Claus Spreckels (1828–1908), who came from his home in Hanover, Germany, to the U.S. (1848) as a penniless immigrant to work as a grocery boy. Moving to San Francisco in 1856, he opened a grocery store and became interested in sugar refining, acquiring a small plant of his own (1863). By studying European ways of production on a return trip to his homeland, and by shrewd business methods, he came to control all of San Francisco's refineries and established the state's sugar-beet industry.

He then financed the Hawaiian kingdom and controlled much of its cane production and shipping. He also founded a railroad for shipping his produce by a means other than the monopolistic Southern Pacific;♦ organized independent gas, light, and power companies to combat the established public utility firms of San Francisco; and created a street railway line in opposition to the established firm.

His four sons were John D[iedrich] (1853–1926), Adolph [Bernard] (1857–1924), Claus A[ugustus] (1858–1946), and Rudolph (1872–1958). The father and the two older brothers feuded with the two younger ones over control of the family businesses and continued their fight by financing rival gas and electric companies, among other things, until a reconciliation was at last reached in 1905. John D. founded the Oceanic Steamship Co. (1881) for passengers and mail to Hawaii and New Zealand, but having been attracted by San Diego, he established his main interests there in coal depots and wharves, ownership of the city railroad, publication of the *Union,* and development of the neighboring resort of Coronado. He also owned the *San Francisco Call* (1897–1913), the morning rival of the *Chronicle.*

Adolph was in the family sugar business, and his fury at the *Chronicle*'s allegation that it defrauded stockholders led him to shoot M. H. de Young♦ (1884). At age 50 he married Alma de Bretteville, with whom he donated the California Palace of the Legion of Honor art museum♦ to San Francisco (1924).

Rudolph early made an independent fortune in the sugar and gas company businesses, over which he fought his father. But he was mainly interested in good city government and became a progressive reformer, spearheading the attacks on the corruption of Abe Ruef♦ and Mayor Schmitz.♦ He later became an investor in radio manufacturing, but lost his entire fortune in the Depression.

Claus Augustus, also in the family sugar business, allied himself with Rudolph in family feuds but was little interested in business or politics. In later life he became an expatriate in France.

Spring Valley Water Company, a private utility firm begun under a state charter (1858), was designed to supply water to San Francisco. Its name derived from a site between Mason and Taylor and Washington and Broadway streets, but was associated with its larger source, the 11 miles of Crystal Springs Lakes and their surrounding watershed on the peninsula mountain ridge south of San Francisco, from which it started delivering water in 1862. William Ralston♦ controlled the firm and opposed municipalization until he tried to sell the system at an exorbitant price when he was in financial difficulties (1875). This made the company unpopular and it was long attacked as a monopoly by the *San Francisco Call,* yet voters declined to purchase the system until 1929. On the southern end of its reservoir lakes, the company erected a small Greek temple dedicated to George Sterling, although water was his least favorite liquid. Lake Merced (S.F. County) and San Andreas Lake (San Mateo County) were stopping places for Portolá (1769) and Rivera y Moncada (1774), respectively. Adjacent to Lake Merced is the site of the duel between Sen. Broderick and Chief Justice Terry (1859). Another Spring Valley, on the outskirts of San Diego, was the site of H. H. Bancroft's ranch home.

SPROUL, Robert Gordon (1891–1975), 11th president of the University of California, born in San Francisco, was educated at the institution (Berkeley, B.S., 1913), with which he was thereafter associated, first as comptroller and vice president for business and financial affairs, then as its longtime president (1930–58). During his administration, UCLA developed from a "Southern Branch" to a full-fledged university of great distinction; the Davis campus moved into general education; campuses were founded at Santa Barbara and Riverside; the Berkeley faculty was rated by the American Council on Education as second most distinguished in the U.S.; outstanding scholars, like Ernest Lawrence, were attracted and developed great facilities, such as the cyclotron; enrollment increased from some 19,000 to over 46,000; the libraries grew from 1,035,181 to 3,997,245 volumes; and state appropriations increased from $7,256,000 to $72,879,000. His whole administration was affirmative except for the last years, which were marred by the Loyalty Oath Controversy.♦

Spruce, coniferous evergreen, some of whose species are cultivated as ornamental trees and shrubs. The natives are the *Tideland* or *Sitka,* 75 to 180 feet tall, found near the California coast north from

Mendocino County, and the *weeping* or *Brewer,* 20 to 95 feet tall, found only in the Klamath Mts. *Big-cone spruce,* found on southern California ranges, is not a true spruce but belongs to the family of the *Douglas fir,*♦ and the *Williamson spruce* is actually a hemlock. Some Indians used spruce strips in basket weaving.

Squash, edible fruit of a vine, related to the pumpkin and a common vegetable in its many forms, is basically divided between summer and winter varieties. Grown mainly in the Central Valley, the state's crop accounts for most of the national product.

Squaw Valley, on the Truckee River near Lake Tahoe, was developed as a winter resort (1948) and became the site of the winter Olympic Games (1960). It long served in part as a conference center run by the State Division of Beaches and Parks until it was sold (1974) for a resort and real estate development.

Squibob Papers, collection of 27 brief comic sketches and some poetry by George H. Derby,♦ accompanied by his humorous drawings. The book was posthumously published in 1865.

Squid, cephalopod with tentacles found in several varieties along the entire California coast. They are caught mainly when spawning, at depths of from 10 to over 100 feet during winter off La Jolla, Catalina, and other southern California waters and the rest of the year in Monterey Bay. Attracted by light, they are then easily netted or even pumped right from the water. Annual catches average 24,000,000 pounds. Most of it is frozen or canned and shipped abroad.

Squirrels, abounding throughout California, are of two general kinds: tree and ground. Of the tree squirrels, the largest and most beautiful is the *gray,* salt-and-pepper above and white beneath and about 22 inches long. It lives in the state's pine areas and the Sacramento Valley, feeding on acorns and other nuts. The *northern flying squirrel,* also of the tree classification, lives in almost all wooded mountainous areas of the state. About 11 inches long, it is lead gray above and dull white beneath and glides by using the fur-covered skin between its fore and hind legs. It feeds on nuts, seeds, forest vegetation, birds' eggs, and adult insects. Other tree squirrels are the *Douglas,* about 14 inches long, its back dark brown with a reddish tinge and its underside white or buff, which lives

in the Sierra forests, feeding on pine cone seeds; and the *fox,* not a native, but now established on the San Francisco Peninsula and around Fresno. It is about 20 inches long, its back and sides reddish gray, and its underside reddish yellow.

The most common ground squirrel is the *Beechey* (also called the *Douglas, fisher, San Diego,* and *digger*), which lives everywhere in the state except east of the Sierra, in the highest mountains, and in the Colorado and Mojave deserts. About 16 inches long, its fur is gray with lighter flecks and it has a dark patch from its head to the center of its back. It feeds on seeds, acorns, roots, and fruits and is a serious pest because it eats farm crops, wrecks irrigation canals, and has carried serious disease. The *golden-mantled ground squirrel,* about 11 inches long, has an orange-colored head and a white stripe bordered by black bands on either side of its back. It eats mostly grains, berries, pine nuts, roots, and bulbs and it too carries disease. Another disease carrier is the *Belding ground squirrel,* found in most of the Sierra. About 10 inches long, it is reddish brown or brownish gray above and buff or buff-white below, with a short tail. It eats grasses and herbs.

Other ground squirrels include the *round-tailed,* about 10 inches long, colored gray or cinnamon with white cheeks, a resident of the desert; the *Townsend,* short-tailed, buff gray, about 9 inches long, resident in Inyo and Mono counties; the *Mojave,* pinkish-cinnamon above and a white tail and underside, and some 9 inches long, living in the desert; the *San Joaquin antelope,* yellow-brown with a white stripe on either side, the same size and living in the lower San Joaquin Valley; the *antelope,* also the same size, grayish-brown with a white stripe on either side, feeding on seeds and insects of the Mojave and Colorado deserts; and the *rock,* gray-buff or darker in color, living in a small part of the Mojave Desert and eastern San Bernardino County. Chipmunks♦ are related to squirrels.

SRI International, see *Stanford Research Institute.*

STACKPOLE, Ralph (1885–1973), Oregon-born sculptor, resident in San Francisco (1901–49) and later an expatriate in France. His works ranged from figures, often monumental—like the theme sculpture "Pacifica" for the Golden Gate International Exposition—to abstract designs. His son Peter is a photographer; he is particularly noted for pictures he took of the Bay Bridge when it was under construction.

Stagecoach, see *California Stage Company, Concord Coach,* and *Overland stagecoach.* See also *Foss, Clark; Monk, Hank; Monroe, George;* and *Parkhurst, Charley.*

STAGG, [AMOS] ALONZO (1862–1965), New Jersey-born football player and coach, graduated from Yale, where he starred as a baseball pitcher and as an end in football, was named to the first All-American team. He became the football coach at the University of Chicago (1892) and remained there for 41 years, until he reached mandatory retirement age (70). He then went to California to coach the College of Pacific football team (1933–46); assisted his son in coaching at Susquehanna University in Pennsylvania (1947–53); and was an advisory coach at the junior college of his home town, Stockton (1954–60). He originated or was a leading advocate of many modern football tactics, including the huddle, shift, forward pass, and basic T-formation.

STANFORD, JANE [ELIZA] LATHROP (1828–1905), born in Albany, N.Y., married (1850) Leland Stanford,♦ then a young lawyer in a nearby town. In 1855 they moved to California, where he had already been successful in business and politics. She was a co-founder of Stanford University, which opened only two years before the death of her husband (1893). She assumed all powers later given to trustees and had to cope with the University's severe financial problems, which were caused by tremendous taxes on her husband's estate. On these and other university affairs she worked closely with the president, David Starr Jordan.

STANFORD, LELAND (1824–93), born in Watervliet, N.Y., after a fair education at age 21 went into law, which he practiced there and in Wisconsin until moving in 1852 to California's mining country, to join his five brothers in a retail grocery store. The business was moved successfully to Sacramento, where he became a founder of the Republican party in California. Already one of the Big Four♦ and president of the Central Pacific Railroad, he was also elected governor. During his two-year term (1862–63), he was a staunch Union supporter and an equally strong advocate of railroad interests, obtaining several public grants. As the public figure of the railroad builders, Stanford drove the last spike (made of gold) on May 10, 1869, at Promontory Point, Utah. He not only remained president of the main company until his death but was also president of the Southern Pacific Co. (1885–

90), the holding company for the system's various properties, which also ran the railway of that name, and he took an active though hidden part in the state's politics.

He was elected U.S. Senator along party lines by the state's legislature (1885) and was reelected in 1891, remaining in office the rest of his life, even though he contributed little to legislation or debate. During the years of his first term he also gave much time to the endowment, establishment, and building of the university he and his wife Jane♦ named in honor of their son, Leland Stanford, Jr., who had died in 1884 at age 15. He also enjoyed the life of a country squire, cultivating vineyards on his extensive Tehama County land, and training trotting horses on the Palo Alto ranch (which became the site of the university), even engaging Eadweard Muybridge to make elaborate series of photographs as studies of animal locomotion.

Stanford Research Institute, independent, non-profit research institution founded (1946) for work with governmental agencies and industrial organizations. Its main fields have been engineering, management, physics, life sciences, agriculture, electronics, industrial economics, and electrochemistry. For over twenty years it was an adjunct of Stanford University and now maintains its large headquarters at nearby Menlo Park Project and marketing offices are located in England, Europe, Japan, and Saudi Arabia. Affiliation with the University was severed (1970), and the name changed (1977) to SRI International.

Stanford University, founded by Leland Stanford♦ and his wife Jane♦ in 1885 as a memorial to their 15-year-old son, who had died the year before. Initially chartered as Leland Stanford Junior University, it was entirely funded by the founders and located on the ranches at Palo Alto (8,000 acres once belonging to George Gordon♦ and 1,200 acres once belonging to Peter Coutts,♦) thus giving the campus its nickname, "the Farm." Frederick Law Olmsted laid out the long Palm Drive entryway and landscaping that set off the initial arcaded quadrangle of sandstone, which borrowed architectural motifs from the tile-roofed missions of California and Romanesque traditions.

The first class, which enrolled in 1891, numbered 559 students, Herbert Hoover among them, and was instructed by a faculty of 17 under the administration of David Starr Jordan, the president from 1891 to 1913. The student body was coeducational from the outset, although for more than fifty years women were limited to 500 in an ever-growing enrollment that soon branched out into graduate professional education.

After Sen. Stanford's death in 1893, his wife exercised the effective powers of sole trustee for a decade, a period marked by a benevolent though autocratic rule. She employed her personal fortune to keep the institution open during the time when her husband's estate was tied up, while also intruding into academic affairs by achieving the ouster of Edward A. Ross, a professor of economics who championed liberal causes. A more positive result of the affair was the granting of governing powers to an enlarged board of trustees.

The campus was hard hit by the earthquake of April 18, 1906, which toppled the tower of the Memorial Church, which honors Leland Stanford and is distinguished by a Venetian mosaic façade, depicting the Sermon on the Mount. The university quickly recovered and continued to augment its distinguished academic programs as the leading private university of the state and one of the top such institutions in the country. In 1908 it absorbed Cooper Medical College, founded by Elias S. Cooper,♦ which continued to be located in San Francisco until its faculty and facilities, renamed the Medical Center,♦ were moved to the campus site in 1959. From this medical background came Jordan's great successor, Dr. Ray Lyman Wilbur, the first alumnus to be president and the third in office (1915–43). When he assumed the post, the university had 26 departments of instruction and 125 faculty members. After World War I the university became the home of the great library on war, revolution, and peace established by collections gathered by Herbert Hoover and latterly known as the Hoover Institution.♦ It was housed in a tile-topped, 285-foot-high Hoover Tower, which is a campus landmark comparable to the Campanile at Berkeley.

In the years after World War II, Stanford not only grew physically to accommodate a substantially increased student body but significantly and rapidly augmented its academic distinction, particularly in the areas of science and engineering. The latter was fostered by the prime mover of the state's developments in electronics, Frederick E. Terman,♦ the provost under a new, dynamic president, J. E. Wallace Sterling. Important additions for research included the Stanford Research Institute (no longer affiliated with the university) and a Linear Accelerator, a two-mile-long atomic energy center, opened in 1967. The humanities and social sciences were also cultivated by the founding of a creative writing school under Wallace Stegner;♦ the refurbishing and invigorated collecting of the Art Gallery and Stanford Museum; and the inspiration derived from the neighboring Center for the Advanced Study of the Behavioral Sciences.

By 1975 the university enrolled 11,400 students (nearly 5,000 in graduate studies) in 7 schools (including law, medicine, and business), 70 academic departments, and 27 associated institutes, including Hopkins Marine Laboratory♦ at Pacific Grove, as well as on affiliated campuses abroad. Long the traditional athletic rival of Berkeley in such contests as the Big Game,♦ it has also been well established as its academic peer.

Stanislaus, name of a river and a county derived from that of Estanislao, an Indian educated by Padre Durán at Mission San José and there given the name of a Polish saint. He ran away (1827 or 1828), and the Spaniards came to believe that he and other escaped neophytes were planning a general uprising against the mission program. Military expeditions, including one under Mariano Vallejo (1829), put the armed Indians to flight after killing many of them, both warriors and women. The major engagement occurred at the river, which was thereafter named for the Indian leader, the county subsequently taking its name from the river. The river rises in the Sierra in three branches that join about 60 miles northeast of Modesto, and 13 miles west of that city it joins the San Joaquin River. It forms the boundary between Calaveras and Tuolumne counties. Stanislaus National Forest, covering over 1,000,000 acres, lies northwest of Yosemite, in Tuolumne County.

Stanislaus County, organized (1854) from part of Tuolumne County, derived its name from the river Stanislaus,♦ which forms part of the dividing line from San Joaquin County, lying generally on its north and west. The Diablo Range separates it on the southwest from Santa Clara County. Merced County lies to the south, and Calaveras and Tuolumne counties to the east and north. The county seat had four locations before being settled in Modesto (1872).

The earliest white explorer was Gabriel Moraga,♦ who visited the area in 1806, 1808, and 1810. There were a few settlers before the gold rush attracted great numbers to the Stanislaus,♦ Tuolumne,♦ and San Joaquin rivers.♦ These settlers engaged in placer mining and built towns like Knights Ferry, a trading center on the Stanislaus, which was a major crossing point to the Mariposa mines and the county seat (1862–72); and La Grange, on the Tuolumne River, initially a French settlement, later the county seat (1855–62).

Modesto♦ grew up later as a San Joaquin Valley farming community when the railroad reached there. South of it, also on the main Southern Pacific line, is Turlock, another farming and food-processing community, depending on the great irrigation program begun in 1887. Between them is Ceres, still another farming center, known for its date palms. On the west side of the San Joaquin River lies Newman, named for an early merchant who donated land to the second Southern Pacific crossing in 1887. Still farther west, the Delta-Mendota Canal♦ carries water south, just as the Hetch Hetchy Aqueduct carries Sierra water to San Francisco. The Melones Project,♦ on the Calaveras and Tuolumne counties border, provides water for northern Stanislaus County. Other water resources are Farmington and Woodward reservoirs in its northeastern triangle and Modesto Reservoir and Turlock Lake in the southeast.

The county is a major producer of peaches, walnuts, and apricots, but also raises many other crops, including various fruits and vegetables, grapes, and field produce. It is also an important livestock and poultry area. In 1970 it had a population of 194,506, which, with a total acreage of 967,040, gave it 128.7 persons per sq. mi.

Star Is Born, A, screenplay by Dorothy Parker and others, dealing with the breakup of a marriage between two Hollywood stars, the woman first achieving success, and the man sinking into alcoholism. In 1937 it was a popular film with Frederic March and Janet Gaynor in the starring roles; in 1954 Moss Hart readapted it as a musical for James Mason and Judy Garland, with songs by Harold Arlen and Ira Gershwin; and in 1976 a rock music version was made starring Barbra Streisand.

STARKEY, JAMES R[YLANDER] (1821–70), born a slave in North Carolina, moved to San Francisco in 1852. Although he became literate only as an adult, he soon wrote articles on the life and rights of blacks for their journals and was a founder of the Athenaeum.♦

State Archives, official depository located in Sacramento. It contains some Spanish land-grant documents, records of the state constitutions of 1849 and 1879, and various papers of the executive and legislative branches of the government.

State Board of Equalization, see *Board of Equalization.*

State Colleges, see *State Universities and Colleges.*

State Fair, initially held in San Francisco (1854), a governmental development of a project initiated by James L. L. Warren.♦ It displayed California's resources, essentially agricultural products and livestock, and was settled permanently in the capital, Sacramento, in 1859. There, from about late August to Admission Day (Sept. 9), is held an annual exposition under the auspices of the State Board of Agriculture, including displays of the state's activities and achievements of a wide variety, as well as an amusement sector.

State Flag, based on the original banner of the Bear Flag Revolt♦ designed by William C. Todd, and first raised at Sonoma on June 14, 1846. The modern official flag, approved by the legislature (1911), depicts, on a white background, a single brown star in the upper left field, a brown grizzly bear moving toward the star across green earth, the words "California Republic" in black below it, and, across the base, a broad red stripe.

State Forests, timberland (70,000 acres) administered by the California Division of Forestry for conservation, demonstration, and research purposes.

State Historic Parks, see *State Parks.*

Statehood, granted to California on Sept. 9, 1850, by President Polk's signature on the bill for admission (a date thereafter celebrated as Admission Day), even though Californians had lived under a state government since Nov. 13, 1849, the date of ratification of the Constitution. It had elected officials, including two U.S. Senators, but it could not have congressional representation until approved by the federal government. The year's wait had been caused primarily by the debate over the balance between slave and free states.

State Library, founded (1850) with books from Frémont, has long been under the administration of the State Department of Education, and coordinates various aspects of the state's public library system. In its building, across from the Capitol, is located a California Section that not only has a large collection of Californiana but includes an index of the *San Francisco Chronicle* since 1904 and an Information File of some 800,000 references. The Sutro Library♦ is part of the State Library, but it is housed in San Francisco.

State Parks, inaugurated when Congress transferred (1864) Yosemite Valley and the Mariposa Grove to California's jurisdiction. The state returned them (1905) for incorporation into the surrounding Yosemite National Park♦ (1890). The first of the still-preserved parks, California Redwood Park, at Big Basin, Santa Cruz County, was founded in 1902. The largest park is the Anza-Borrego Desert State Park.♦ In 1970 the State Park system included 148 parks and beaches containing 800,000 acres, including 211 miles of ocean frontage. Also under the administration of the Dept. of Parks and Recreation are 15 State Historic Parks and 19 State Historical Monuments, including Fort Ross; Bidwell Mansion; sites in Sonoma, Columbia, San Juan Bautista, and Monterey; the Palace of Fine Arts site in San Francisco; San Simeon; the home of Charles Lummis; Mission La Purisima in Lompoc; Sutter's Fort; San Pasqual Battlefield; and the home of Will Rogers. The agency also runs conferences at Asilomar and Squaw Valley.

State symbols, officially designated at various dates by the legislature, except for the earliest: the Great Seal. This seal, adopted (Oct. 2, 1849) by the Constitutional Convention, was designed by Major Robert S. Garnett, a Virginia-born army officer stationed in Monterey. It depicts Minerva (goddess of wisdom, sprung full grown from Jupiter's brow, just as California was conceived as being born a full-fledged state, without infancy as a territorial government) seated on a mountainside, a small grizzly bear, wheat, and grapes at her feet, San Francisco Bay with ships and the Sierra Nevada in the background, a miner at work, the motto "Eureka," and 31 stars (representing the number of states upon the admission of California) above Minerva's helmet and spear. The whole circular picture is framed by the words "The Great Seal of the State of California." Other symbols include the golden poppy *(Eschscholtzia californica)* as the state flower (1903); a variation of the Bear Flag♦ as the state flag (1911); the valley quail *(Lophortyx californica)* as the state bird (1931); the golden trout *(Salmo aguabonita)* as the state fish (1947); purple-blue and gold as the state colors (1951); "I Love You, California," with words by F. B. Silverwood and music by A. F. Frankenstein, as the state song (1951); the redwood (both *Sequoia semper-*

virens and *Sequoiadendron giganteum*) as the state tree (1953); the grizzly bear as the state animal (1953); gold as the state mineral (1965); the saber-toothed tiger *(Smilodon)* as the state fossil (1968); the dog-face butterfly as the state insect (1973); the desert tortoise as the state reptile (1973); and the gray whale as the state marine mammal (1976).

State Universities and Colleges, an outgrowth of the normal schools founded in San Francisco (1857) to provide instruction of and practice in teaching. The earliest continuing one has evolved into the California State University at San Jose, while one opened in Los Angeles (1882) developed into the Los Angeles campus of the University of California, a separate system of higher education within the state. In 1970 there were 19 institutions in the State University and College complex, with more than 267,000 students, including those who attend part time. The complex accepts the top third of the state's high school graduates and offers them vocational and liberal arts programs leading to A.B. and M.A. degrees, with some opportunities for doctoral degrees in conjunction with the University of California. Supported by state funds (the 1970–71 budget was $310,000,000), it is governed by a Board of Trustees appointed by the governor and administered by a chancellor, with each campus having its own president. In 1970 the universities were Chico, Fresno, Fullerton, Hayward, Humboldt, Long Beach, Los Angeles, Northridge, Pomona Polytechnic, Sacramento, San Diego, San Francisco, San Jose, and San Luis Obispo Polytechnic. The colleges were Bakersfield, Dominguez Hills, San Bernardino, Sonoma, and Stanislaus.

Statuary Hall, national shrine created in the former hall of the U.S. House of Representatives, Washington, D.C. (1864), to accommodate not more than two statues of distinguished persons representing each state. California selected Junípero Serra as one representative. In the adjacent Hall of Columns is a statue by Haig Patigian of Thomas Starr King, the second representative. There are no Californians in the Hall of Fame, a national shrine maintained by New York University.

Steam beer, see *Breweries.*

STEARNS, ABEL (1798–1871), went from his native Massachusetts to live in Mexico for three years, where he was naturalized, before moving to Los Angeles (1829). There he became the leading trader; his marriage into the Bandini family made him the largest landowner and cattleman in southern California. He was a leader in the movements that overthrew governors Victoria (1831) and Micheltorena (1845). He worked secretly with Larkin to achieve U.S. control of California, although, as a Mexican official, he was neutral during the Bear Flag Revolt.

STEBBINS, HORATIO (1821–1902), Massachusetts-born clergyman, called by the Unitarian Church of San Francisco to take the pulpit vacated by Thomas Starr King's death (1864). He was a strong cultural force and public figure, serving on the governing boards of both the University of California and Stanford University. He wrote *Thirty-one Years in California* (1895). His daughter, Lucy Stebbins, was the Dean of Women at Berkeley (1913–36).

STEELE, JOHN (1832–1905), traveled overland to California from New York State (1850) and remained there for three years. He recounted his adventures in *Across the Plains* (1889 in newspaper, 1930 as book) and *In Camp and Cabin* (1901).

Steelhead, see *Trout.*

Steelmaking, an industry begun when the Union Iron Works was founded (1851) in San Francisco by Peter Donahue♦ to build mining machinery and, later, ships and locomotives. In the early years, the steel plants of California depended on scrap iron and steel manufactured elsewhere, since iron mining♦ and pig iron production in the Sierra Nevada and near Mt. Shasta were unsuccessful. In the early 20th century the industry came to be dominated by two steelmakers: Bethlehem, which purchased the Union Iron Works (1902), and Columbia (founded 1908), which had its first plant at Pittsburg and, later, facilities at Torrance (1923), until Bethlehem bought out Columbia (1929). The production and fabrication of iron and steel remained small, despite a temporary increase during World War I, until the 1940s. Then Henry J. Kaiser created the state's first complete steel mill, including blast furnaces, at Fontana, 50 miles east of Los Angeles, importing coal from Utah and iron ore from San Bernardino and Riverside counties.

STEFFENS, [JOSEPH] LINCOLN (1866–1936), California journalist and social commentator,

reared in Sacramento, as movingly recalled in *Boy on Horseback* (1935). After graduation from the University of California and study of philosophy in Europe, he became a muckraking editor, exposing governmental corruption in a book, *The Shame of the Cities* (1904). His best-known work is his *Autobiography* (1931). It is skeptical about conventional American society but hopeful of new social systems, such as that of Russia, about which he declared, "I've seen the future and it works."

STEGNER, WALLACE [EARLE] (1909–   ), Iowa-born author and professor, taught American literature and creative writing at Stanford University (1945–71). His own numerous works, mainly on the West, include the novels *The Big Rock Candy Mountain* (1943), about a Far Westerner searching for a promised land of fortune after the frontier period had ended; *A Shooting Star* (1961), presenting ways of life and values among established, wealthy northern Californians; *Angle of Repose* (1971), winner of a Pulitzer Prize, and adapted as an opera by Andrew Imbrie and Oakley Hall, presenting a fictional rendering of the life of Mary Hallock Foote; and *The Spectator Bird* (1976), viewing the life of an aging literary agent retired in California. Stegner's sensitive nonfiction includes *Mormon Country* (1942); *Beyond the Hundredth Meridian* (1954), about John Wesley Powell's western explorations; and *Wolf Willow* (1962), recalling the "last plains frontier," where Montana and Saskatchewan meet, an area in which the author spent his youth.

STEIN, GERTRUDE (1874–1946), experimental writer, born in Pennsylvania, was associated with California because she and her family lived there (1880–92). Despite her cavalier remark about her home city of Oakland ("There's no there there"), she later drew upon the area in some of her writing. She was also allied to it because her brother remained in business in San Francisco, the home city too of Alice B. Toklas,♦ her constant companion during their long years of expatriation in France, where Stein had a famous salon.

STEINBECK, JOHN [ERNST] (1902–68), born in Salinas, center of the region in which most of his fiction (and his best) is set. After attending Stanford University (1919–20, 22–23, 24–25) and working at odd jobs, he began his literary career with *Cup of Gold* (1929), a romantic novel based on the life of the buccaneer Sir Henry Morgan. His first significant and representative work was *The*

Pastures of Heaven (1932), stories of a farm community in a California valley. The title is ironic, as the people suffer an inability to have meaningful relationships with each other or with their natural setting. Another early book, *To a God Unknown* (1933), treating a California farmer's pagan, mystical obsession with nature, was followed by his first great success, *Tortilla Flat* (1935), a warmly humorous fictional depiction of the *paisanos* of Monterey. While that work displayed his tenderness and sentimentality, his next book, *In Dubious Battle* (1936), showed his other dominant characteristic, a strong and realistic presentation of partisan passions crushing men of good will. It is a novel about a strike of migratory fruit pickers and the attempts of communists to organize them. Steinbeck's *Of Mice and Men* (1937) is a novelette about itinerant farmhands that fused the two veins with great popular success. It was also the first of his fiction that he successfully dramatized.

After producing another collection of stories, *The Long Valley* (1938), presenting human relations with the land and its crops and animals, most movingly in "The Red Pony," a tale of a boy and his horse, Steinbeck wrote his greatest work, *The Grapes of Wrath* (1939). That novel, for which he received a Pulitzer Prize and which led to much condemnation from ranch employers as well as great public appreciation, was a saga of the dispossessed during the years of the Great Depression. It traced an appealing refugee family, the Joads, from their Oklahoma dust bowl home through the tribulations of their movement to California and their pathetic struggles to find work on the farms of the state, run by an almost feudal system in exploitation of labor.

The following decade of Steinbeck's writing was one of great but scattered activity without a major accomplishment. His books of that period include *The Forgotten Village* (1941), a script for a film about Mexican village life; *The Sea of Cortez* (1941), written with his friend Edward F. Ricketts,♦ the marine biologist with whom he voyaged in the Gulf of California and who influenced his nonteleological thinking and his organic view of human society; *The Pearl* (1948), a parable about a Mexican fisherman whose discovery of a rich jewel brings evil to his family; and journals of his World War II experiences; as well as a novelette, *The Moon is Down* (1942), about Norwegian resistance to German occupation. Other works of the time include *Cannery Row* (1945), a whimsically charming tale of idlers in Monterey and their relationship to a character based on Ricketts,

itself a work in the vein of *Tortilla Flat*, as was the later *Sweet Thursday* (1954); and *The Wayward Bus* (1947), a novel showing the frustrations of contemporary American society represented in microcosm by the stresses of a group of passengers aboard a rural California bus.

Steinbeck issued his first major novel in over a decade with *East of Eden* (1952), a family saga from the time of the Civil War to World War I, in which a version of the Cain and Abel story, partly set in the Salinas Valley, depicts man's struggle between good and evil. Although he published lesser works, such as a comic fantasy, *The Short Reign of Pippin IV* (1957), and an account of his tour of the U.S. with his poodle, *Travels with Charley in Search of America* (1962), he issued only one other work of importance, *The Winter of Our Discontent* (1961), a novel treating the moral collapse of a modern New Englander under the strains of 20th-century corruption. However, for the achievements of his entire literary career, he was awarded a Nobel Prize (1962). He was the first California author to be so honored.

STELLMAN, Louis J[OHN] (1877–1961), Baltimore-born journalist who worked for Los Angeles and San Francisco newspapers beginning in the 1890s. He was the author of articles about the latter city, *Port o' Gold* (1922), *Mother Lode* (1934), and *Sam Brannan* (1954), but is best remembered for his avocation, photography. His sympathetic photographs of his adopted city, *The Vanished Ruin Era* (1910), and of its post-Genthe and post-earthquake Chinatown, were collected by Richard Dillon in *Images of Chinatown* (1976).

STENGEL, CASEY [CHARLES DILLON STENGEL] (1891–1975), born in Kansas City, was a professional baseball player with various teams between 1910 and 1925. In the latter year he began his great career as a manager. He managed several teams, including the Boston Braves (1938–43), the New York Yankees (1949–60), and Oakland Oaks (1946–48). His permanent home was Glendale.

STEPHENS, HENRY MORSE (1857–1919), English-born professor of history at the University of California, Berkeley (1902–19). He was noted as a popular lecturer on modern Europe and a faculty leader.

STEPHENS, WILLIAM DENNISON (1859–1944), 24th governor of the state (1917–23), moved to Los Angeles from his native Ohio and was elected to Congress (1910–16), first as a Republican, then as a Progressive.♦ When Hiram Johnson was elected to the Senate, Stephens was appointed lieutenant governor and thus succeeded him. He emphasized economy and efficiency and war issues. He also suppressed the I.W.W., but commuted Mooney's death sentence to life imprisonment.

STERLING, George (1869–1926), California poet, born in Sag Harbor, N.Y., went to Oakland (1890) to work for his uncle, a real estate developer. Soon he met Ambrose Bierce, Joaquin Miller, and Jack London and, accepting Bierce as his master, began to publish poetry marked by romantic imagery and themes and by an accomplished but facile sonnet style. His early works include *The Testimony of the Suns* (1903), *A Wine of Wizardry* (1909), and *The House of Orchids* (1911). In 1905 he became one of the first to move to Carmel, a setting suited to his bohemian style of life, celebrating the idealistic and beautiful. His appreciation of the local scene anticipated Jeffers, whom he championed in *Robinson Jeffers, the Man and the Artist* (1926), but he wrote of its seacoast sometimes grandly, as in "On a Western Beach," and sometimes humorously, as in "The Abalone♦ Song." Similar were the celebrations of his adopted city of San Francisco, which he called "The Cool, Grey City of Love." He was also a major contributor to the life and dramatic productions of the Bohemian Club, his last home, where he committed suicide. He is said to be the prototype of Brissenden in London's *Martin Eden.* Monuments to him include a Greek temple at the Crystal Springs Lakes of the Spring Valley Water Co.♦

STERN, Isaac (1920–), Russian-born violinist, brought to San Francisco at age one and there attended the San Francisco Conservatory. He made his debut with the San Francisco Symphony orchestra at age 11. He has since appeared as soloist and accompanist throughout the U.S. and Europe and has made sound tracks for motion pictures.

STETSON, Charlotte Perkins, see *Perkins, Charlotte.*

STEVENS, Elisha (1804?–84), trapper and frontiersman, led a large party, including the family of Martin Murphy,♦ overland to California (1844). It was noted for taking the first wagons ever to cross the Sierra, going via Donner Pass, which the party discovered, and because some members, men and women, were forced by November snow

to winter at the lake where the Donner Party later starved. Their snowbound experience was recorded by young Moses Schallenberger.♦

STEVENSON, Jonathan D., see *Stevenson's Regiment.*

STEVENSON, Robert Louis (1850–94), Scottish-born writer, on a holiday trip to France in 1876 met Fanny Van de Grift Osbourne, a married woman from Oakland, with whom he fell in love. He pursued her to California in 1879. While there, although he was often seriously ill, he was near her in Monterey, San Francisco, and Oakland, until after her divorce, when they were married (May 1880). They honeymooned in the cabin of an abandoned silver mine on the slope of Mt. St. Helena, accompanied by her twelve-year-old son, Samuel Lloyd Osbourne.♦ Recuperated and returned to the good graces of his parents, Stevenson, his wife, and his stepson set off for his native Scotland, moving later to Switzerland, France, and England, constantly in search of a climate favorable to his tubercular ill health. Finally they returned to the United States for a winter at Saranac, N.Y. Then, on a yacht leased from Samuel Merritt,♦ an Oakland doctor, they set sail (1888) for the South Seas, settling in Vailima, Samoa, where he spent his last years.

During that period he collaborated on novels with Osbourne, one of them, *The Wrecker* (1892), presenting a romantic description of San Francisco. However, Stevenson's more important writings related to California include an account of his voyage as a second-class passenger across the Atlantic in *The Amateur Emigrant* (1894), his trip across the continent by crowded railway in *Across the Plains* (1892), and his charmingly romantic description of life at Mt. St. Helena in *The Silverado Squatters*♦ (1883).

Other writings about California include "The Old Pacific Capitol" and "The New Pacific Capitol," describing Monterey and San Francisco, respectively. These and lesser writings were gathered in *From Scotland to Silverado* (1966). His stay in California is memorialized in a Stevenson House in Monterey, a state museum containing memorabilia, and the Silverado Museum in St. Helena, featuring rare books and manuscripts.

Stevenson's Regiment, name applied to the First Regiment of New York Volunteers, whose commander was Col. Jonathan D. Stevenson, a Democratic ward politician of New York City recruited by Secretary of War Marcy to lead to California a military force for service in the Mexican War and promised discharge there for later settlement as part of an Americanization program. The 917 enlisted young men, mostly from New York City, were led by only a few regular army men among the 38 officers. The regiment comprised a motley group ranging from temperance men through clerks, printers, mechanics, and farmers to hoodlum types, all of whom considered themselves to be adventurers. Arriving by ships in San Francisco (March and April 1847) too late for military service except for a few companies sent south, they were used for garrison duty and disbanded in 1848. Stevenson and some other Tammany Hall followers then formed volunteer firefighting companies to serve also as political clubs in aid of David Broderick.

Another group, led by Lt. Sam Roberts, formed the Regulators, self-appointed vigilantes commonly called Hounds because their program for "order" consisted of hounding Spanish American and other minorities out of the state. In addition to those notorious members, the regiment included some distinguished contributors to California life, including William G. Marcy, the son of the Secretary of War; Gen. John B. Frisbie, secretary of the first Constitutional Convention; I. C. Christian Russ, a noted hotelkeeper; Edward G. Buffum and Edward Gilbert, editors of the *Alta California*; Rev. Thaddeus Leavenworth, the regimental chaplain and San Francisco's *alcalde* in 1848–49; G. D. Brewerton; Joseph L. Folsom; Henry M. Naglee; Alfred Sully; and Felix Wierzbicki. *(See also individual entries.)*

STEWART, GEORGE R[IPPEY] (1895–), Pennsylvania-born educator and author, a professor of English at the University of California, Berkeley (1923–62), many of whose writings deal with California and the Far West. Among his nonfiction works in this area are *Bret Harte* (1931); *Ordeal by Hunger* (1936), about the Donner Party; *John Phoenix, Esquire* (1937), a life of George H. Derby; *Take Your Bible in One Hand* (1939), a life of W. H. Thomes; *The California Trail* (1962), treating the main overland route during the 1840s and 1850s; and *Committee of Vigilance* (1964), about San Francisco's first vigilance committee. His novels with a western background include *East of the Giants* (1938), concerning California before the gold rush; *Storm* (1941), presenting the dramatic events that occur in California and eastward across the continent because of a severe storm; *Fire*

(1948), in which a forest fire is the protagonist; *Earth Abides* (1949), about life in California after a disaster has killed all but a few people there and throughout the world; and *Sheep Rock* (1951), the ages-long history of a Nevada site. Among his other works is *Names on the Land* (1945), the classic account of the history of place-naming in the U.S.

STEWART, JAMES (1908–), Pennsylvania-born actor, after a successful beginning on the stage went to Hollywood (1935), where he played numerous roles as a boyishly good-looking but unpretentious young American hero, at once likable and dedicated to idealistic values. His successes include *Mr. Deeds Goes to Town* (1938), *Mr. Smith Goes to Washington* (1939), and *The Philadelphia Story* (1940). His acting career has extended into the 1970s.

STEWART, WILLIAM M[ORRIS] (1827–1909), left his studies at Yale for California to mine gold (1850) and made enough money to resume legal study in Nevada City and be admitted to the bar (1852). He was attracted to Nevada by the silver mines (1859), and the rest of his life he served that state as its U.S. Senator (1862–75, 1887–1905). He and John T. Doyle represented the Roman Catholics in California in the case concerning the Pious Fund.♦

STILL, WILLIAM GRANT (1895–), Mississippi-born musician, after study in New England became an arranger for major jazz band leaders and then composed the first major symphony (*Afro-American Symphony,* 1931) by a black musician in the U.S. He also established a precedent for blacks by conducting his own music at the Hollywood Bowl (1936). He settled in Los Angeles (1934), where he continued to compose orchestral and symphonic works.

Stinson Beach, sandy ocean site of Marin County, northwest of Muir Woods, made a State Park (1961), is a popular recreation area near San Francisco. The finish line of the annual Dipsea race♦ is there.

Stock exchange, see *Pacific Coast Stock Exchange.*

STOCKTON, ROBERT FIELD (1795–1866), second American military governor of California (July 29, 1846–Jan. 19, 1847), began his naval career in 1811 and served in the War of 1812 and the Algerian War, later helping in the settlement of Liberia. As commander of the *Congress,* he delivered to Texas the papers annexing it to the U.S. and continued on to arrive at Monterey (July 15, 1846). There he reinforced the squadron of Commodore Sloat, who because of ill health soon retired after having appointed Stockton commander of American military forces in California.

Stockton promptly issued a proclamation threatening California leaders and created a California Battalion of Mounted Riflemen, commissioning Frémont and Gillespie♦ as high-ranking officers. Without resistance he captured Santa Barbara and Los Angeles, declared California to be U.S. territory, named himself governor and commander in chief, and planned a triumphal meeting with Gen. Taylor in Mexico. But a revolt in Los Angeles lost him that city until Gen. Kearny provided him with enough forces to recapture it and to achieve the total surrender of the *Californios* (Jan. 13, 1847) by a treaty signed at Cahuenga.

His next battle was with Kearny; it concerned the authority of military and civil government. Stockton soon departed, but he seems to have exceeded his authority in establishing a civil government and in naming Frémont as his successor as governor. In 1850 he resigned from the navy, but the legislature of his native New Jersey elected him to the U.S. Senate, in which he served from 1851 to 1853.

Stockton, seat of San Joaquin County, located at the head of tidal water of the San Joaquin River where the Calaveras River flows into it. Founded (1847) by Capt. Charles M. Weber on an old Hudson's Bay Co. settlement, Rancho del Campo de los Franceses, he first named it Tuleberg, then, in 1848, renamed it for Commodore Stockton. The gold rush made it an important communications and trade center for the southern mines, and it remains so for Yosemite Valley. It is also surrounded by rich agricultural lands. In addition to the pioneering Weber family, persons associated with Stockton include David S. Terry, buried there after being killed at nearby Lathrop; James Ben Ali Haggin, a wealthy landowning rancher; "Juan Flaco" Brown, the Paul Revere of the U.S. conquest of California; Simon Willard Sperry, an early flour miller; Harriet Adams, an explorer; Benjamin Holt, inventor of the caterpillar tractor; Carl E. Grunsky, an irrigation engineer; and the modern architect William Wurster. The city is a major inland port with a 75-mile-long deep-water channel to San Francisco Bay, and also a center for pleasure boating. Its industry is various, including farm machinery, food processing, and wood products. The city is the home of the University of the Pacific, the first institution of higher learning to be chartered in the state (1851), and the Haggin Art Gallery and County Pioneer Museum. In 1970 it had a population of 107,644. *(See also individual entries.)*

STODDARD, Charles Warren (1843–1909), taken to San Francisco (1855) from upstate New York, began to contribute poetry in 1861 to the *Golden Era* under the pseudonym Pip Pepperpod, and under the editorship of Bret Harte had his work collected in *Poems* (1867). Unstable in physical and mental health, he was led by his questing to the Hawaiian Islands and Tahiti and into the Catholic church. The travels resulted in *South-Sea Idyls* (1873), and he interested R. L. Stevenson in the region when he befriended the Scot in San Francisco (1879–80), and probably later also interested him in Father Damien as a result of his *The Lepers of Molokai* (1885). Stoddard spent many years in the East as a professor of English, first at the University of Notre Dame (1885–86) and then at the Catholic University of America (1889–1902). He told of his conversion in *A Troubled Heart* (1885). His last years were spent in California, where he wrote *In the Footsteps of the Padres* (1902) about the missions, and a novel, *For the Pleasure of His Company* (1903). His sweet personality and whimsical humor made him many friends, including Mark Twain, whom he briefly served as secretary; Thomas Starr King; Bret Harte; and Ina Coolbrith, who edited a posthumous collection of *Poems* (1917).

STOKES, Darius P. (*fl.* 1853–56), Baltimore-born clergyman of the African Methodist Episcopal Church in San Francisco, Sacramento, and Marysville, and a leading black citizen.

STONE, Irving (1903–), novelist and biographer, born in San Francisco and educated at the University of California, Berkeley, but long resident in southern California. His numerous, very popular books are mostly in the genre of fictionalized lives of remarkable persons, often artists or adventurers. Those with California themes include *Sailor on Horseback* (1938), about Jack London; *Immortal Wife* (1944), about Jessie Frémont; and *Men To Match My Mountains* (1956), about pioneers of the state.

STONEMAN, George (1822–94), 15th governor of the state (1883–87), born in New York, after graduation from West Point (1846) was immediately sent to California in the expedition under Gen. Kearny.♦ After a military career of great distinction, particularly in the Civil War, he retired (1871) to grow oranges near Los Angeles. Elected governor as a Democrat, he opposed the political power of the railroads and worked for irrigation projects.

STORKE, THOMAS MORE (1876–1971), Santa Barbara civic leader, descended from the Ortega family and a Yankee gold rush pioneer. In 1901 he bought a newspaper that dated back to 1855 and through subsequent mergers created the *Santa Barbara News-Press*♦ (1937), which he edited in such a way as to bring him both journalistic and financial success. He was appointed U.S. Senator (1938) to finish McAdoo's term. His articles exposing the covert local John Birch society won him a Pulitzer Prize. *California Editor* (1958) is his autobiography.

Strait of Anián, see *Anián, Strait of.*

STRAUSS, JOSEPH B[AERMANN] (1870–1938), Ohio-born engineer specializing in bridge building, who opened a San Francisco branch of his Chicago firm in 1904. Over the years he designed and built more than 400 bridges, including his greatest monument, the Golden Gate Bridge♦ (1937), which he had advocated since 1917. Next to its Toll Plaza is a bronze statue of Strauss by Frederick W. Schweigardt (1941).

STRAUSS, LEVI, see *Levi's.*

STRAVINSKY, IGOR [FEDOROVICH] (1882–1971), Russian composer and major creator of modern music, came to the U.S. (1937) after previous residences in Switzerland and France, and became an American citizen in 1945, from 1940 to 1969 residing in Hollywood. During his long California residence his compositions included *Danses Concertantes* (1941), commissioned by the Werner Janssen Orchestra of Los Angeles, and the Babel episode of a cantata based on Genesis, first performed in Los Angeles (1945).

Strawberry, a wild variety native to sandy coastal areas from Cape Mendocino south, was first described by Chamisso, Beechey, and other explorers, and was esteemed because it had both a fall and a spring crop. A wild alpine type was later found in the Sierra Nevada. Many other varieties were in-

troduced after American occupation. They are now the most popular of California berries.♦ More are grown there than in all the rest of the U.S.; in 1970 nearly 9,000 acres were planted with strawberries.

Streets of San Francisco, The, hour-long television crime drama initiated in 1972. It featured cases involving a veteran police lieutenant, a detective, and his partner, an impulsive college graduate, whose investigations are carried out against a background of the city's scenes.

Strip, The, see *Sunset Boulevard.*

STROBRIDGE, IDA MEACHAM (1855–1932), born near Oakland and educated at Mills College, lived in the Pasadena art colony of Arroyo Seco,♦ where she ran her Artemesia Bindery. From it she issued her *The Land of the Purple Shadows* (1904), *In Miners' Mirage-Land* (1904), and *The Loom of the Desert* (1907), stories and sketches of the difficult but mystically beautiful life of a woman settler on the desert. Some of her works were illustrated by Maynard Dixon.

STRONG, HARRIET WILLIAMS RUSSELL (1844–1929), born in Buffalo, N.Y., but because of her father's mining activities moved to Plumas, California (1854), and then to Nevada during the silver boom, where she married a superintendent of a Comstock Lode mine (1863). After her husband's death (1883), she became a major grower of walnuts and of pampas grass (used for decor) on her ranch near Whittier. She also became known as a feminist, a cultural leader, and an advocate of improved water supply systems.

STRONG, JOSEPH DWIGHT, JR. (1854–99), son of a prominent San Francisco minister, became a well-known painter and bohemian of that city. Married to Isobel Osbourne, the daughter of Mrs. Robert Louis Stevenson, he lived at Vailima and, later, in Hawaii, depicting both areas as well as painting portraits of Stevenson, Stoddard, and other literary figures.

STROUD, ROBERT (1890–1963), murderer condemned (1909) to life imprisonment, transferred from Leavenworth to Alcatraz (1942) in the year that he published his classic study, *Stroud's Digest of the Diseases of Birds.* A sympathetic biography by Thomas E. Gaddis, *Birdman of Alcatraz* (1955), was made into a popular film (1962).

STUART, JAMES EVERETT (1852–1941), after study under Thomas Hill, William Keith, Virgil Williams, and Raymond Yelland, became a well-known painter of landscapes, mainly of the western U.S. Many depicted Indian encampments or concentrated on the mountains and missions of California, his home state after 1860.

Sugar refining, begun by George Gordon♦ in 1856 but far more significantly developed (1863 ff.) by Claus Spreckels,♦ whose companies handled Hawaiian cane and achieved a virtual monopoly except for some production by William T. Coleman.♦ Spreckels' business was first aided by a Reciprocity Treaty (1877) that allowed Hawaiian sugar to enter the U.S. duty free and then further by U.S. annexation of Hawaii (1898). Production in California from beets began in the 1870s and was first successfully achieved by Spreckels at Salinas in the 1890s. Other early refiners included Henry T. Oxnard, who established his plant in the 1890s at the site of the town named for him. By 1917 there were 137,000 acres planted in sugar beets, and 210,000 tons of sugar were produced from the crop. After World War II cultivation was extended to the Imperial Valley and to Yolo, San Joaquin, and Fresno counties, making California the largest producer of sugar, the demand for which was increased after the ban on imports from Castro's Cuba in the 1950s. In 1970 320,800 acres of sugar beets were harvested in California, yielding $117,114,000 of produce for local refining.

Suisun Bay, northeast of San Pablo Bay, to which it is linked by Carquinez Strait. Grizzly Bay and Honker Bay form its northern and eastern arms, respectively, and the Delta formed by converging waters of the Sacramento and San Joaquin rivers flows into it on the east. Its islands are Brown, Chipps, Roe, Ryer, and Seal. First explored (1775) by Cañizares,♦ it bears the name of a Wintun tribe, one of whose later chiefs was Sem-Yeto. He was baptized Francisco Solano and helped Vallejo hold the region against wilder Indians. Situated in Solano County, Port Chicago is on its south side. The salt water marshes of Suisun Slough, a waterfowl feeding area, lie on its north, in part forming Grizzly Island. The bay has harbored a large "mothball fleet" since World War II.

Sullivan's Travels, motion picture (1941) satirizing Hollywood, presents a famous film director setting off as a tramp to discover the meaning of poverty, while a studio entourage surreptitiously follows him in the misadventures that lead him to conclude the public only wants comedies.

SULLY, ALFRED (1820–79), Pennsylvania-born son of the portrait painter Thomas Sully, went to California as a professional army officer in Stevenson's Regiment.♦ Stationed in Monterey (1849–52), he sketched pictures of the town and married into a prominent local Spanish family. After 1853 his life was spent elsewhere.

Sunkist, see *California Fruit Growers Exchange.*

Sunnyvale, residential and manufacturing community on the San Francisco Peninsula in Santa Clara County. Its first settler was Martin Murphy, Jr.♦ (1850), but it was named (c. 1900) by a real estate developer. Nearby Moffett Field♦ attracted a missile center development by Lockheed and other electronics firms, so that it grew rapidly after World War II. It is now one of the state's fifty most populous communities. In 1970 it had a population of 95,408.

Sun Reporter, San Francisco newspaper published by and for black readers since 1945. It has long been published by Dr. Carlton Goodlett.

Sunset, monthly magazine founded (1898) by the Southern Pacific as a journal dealing with life in California and the Far West, thus attracting people and business to that region. In 1931 it was acquired by the Lane family, which has made it a major family magazine, treating a regional lifestyle, often suburban, emphasizing home and garden, cookery, recreation, and travel. In 1972 it had a circulation of over 1,000,000 and was also a publisher of numerous Sunset Books, which dealt in greater depth with the same subjects that the journal covered.

Sunset Boulevard, a major traffic artery of Los Angeles, running east-west from an area near Elysian Park through Hollywood, Beverly Hills, and Bel Air to the ocean near Pacific Palisades. A two-mile stretch of the road midway through the county territory is known as The Strip. This area is now famous for businesses catering to night life, although originally it featured expensive gift shops, boutiques, and fine restaurants, many of them housed in a local version of high-styled Georgian-Colonial architecture. Later the area deteriorated and was frequented by adolescents in search of excitement. The film *Sunset Boulevard* (1950), directed by Billy Wilder, is a sardonic portrayal of an aging screen actress (played by Gloria Swanson) lost in fantasies of her past stardom. It depicts Hollywood's palmy days with strong satire.

SUÑOL, ANTONIO MARÍA (1800–65), Spaniard in the French naval service, deserted his ship in Monterey harbor (1818) to live in San Jose. He married into the Bernal family and settled on a *rancho* near present-day Fremont (Alameda County), where a Regional Park and town are named for him. A daughter of his married the French vintner Pierre Sansevain, nephew of Jean Louis Vignes.◆

SUN YAT-SEN (1866–1925), Chinese revolutionary leader, born in China of a Christian family and educated in Honolulu for a time, was dedicated to the overthrow of the Ch'ing dynasty and the establishment of a Chinese republic. He had to flee his homeland and work overseas to finance his program, and during that period he lived in San Francisco (1896 for a month; then 1904–5). There he founded a newspaper, *Young China*, to disseminate his views. In 1911 he was elected the first president of the Chinese Republic. An elegant, stylized statue of him (in rose granite and stainless steel) by Beniamino Bufano stands in St. Mary's Square, on the edge of San Francisco's Chinatown.

Superintendent of Public Instruction, elected at the same time and for the same term as the governor, is the chief executive of the state's educational laws and also of the educational policy set by the State Board of Education, a body appointed by the governor. The Superintendent administers the State Department of Education.

Superior California, name occasionally given to that part of northern California which lies north of the San Francisco Bay area.

Superior Courts, major trial courts of the state, one being located in each of the state's 58 counties. Judges are elected, on a nonpartisan basis, to six-year terms.

Superstition Hills, sandy elevations southwest of the Salton Sea in Imperial County, were so called because the formations, shifting with the winds, were thought by whites to be the cause of the local Indians' superstitions about evil.

Supreme Court, has a chief justice and six associate justices who are appointed by a governor, con-

firmed by a Commission on Judicial Appointments, and approved by statewide election to 12-year terms. The Court's jurisdiction is both appellate and original, and it holds at least four sessions in San Francisco, four in Los Angeles, and two in Sacramento. The first chief justice was S. C. Hastings, founder of the college named for him. The first woman to serve as chief justice (1977) is Rose Bird.◆

Surfing, the sport of riding a board on the forward portion of an ocean wave, originated in the Pacific islands. Capt. Cook described the natives' skill at Oahu in 1778. From Hawaii the sport was exported to California when George Freeth (1883–1918), an Anglo-Hawaiian, brought his surfboard to Redondo Beach (1907) and rode it in exhibitions sponsored by Henry E. Huntington as promotion for his real estate development there. The sport did not become popular in California for some years, and even the Hawaiian Islands did not have a surfing club until 1920. Later the large, heavy wooden board was replaced by a lightweight, more easily maneuverable board made of synthetic materials, devised by Bob Simmons, a Californian who had attended the California Institute of Technology. This helped to popularize the sport in the 1950s, and southern California came to be one of the best and most frequented regions for surfing. Rules for international competition were set at a world championship meet in San Diego (1966). Leading surfers from California include Corky Carroll (U.S. champion, 1966–67), Mike Doyle, Joyce Hoffman (woman's world champion, 1966–67), and Margo Godfrey (woman's world champion, 1968). The popularity of the sport led to music being written about it, such as *Surfin'* (1961) by The Beach Boys.◆

Susanville, see *Lassen County*.

Suscol, see *Solano County*.

SUTRO, ADOLPH (1830–98), born in Aix-la-Chapelle (Aachen, Prussia), went to Baltimore (1850) and the next year to San Francisco. He ran a tobacco store for a time and then was attracted to Nevada (1860) by the Comstock bonanza. After making some money in mining, he conceived the idea of a great tunnel under the Comstock Lode to allow better access to the mines and improved ventilation and drainage for the miners. His plan attracted the Silver Kings, who contracted to use the projected tunnel for a fee of $2 per ton of ore mined. Deciding that this was too expensive and they might make the profits themselves, they then turned against him. He found new sources of capital, and after expending $6,500,000 on his project, in 1869 he completed a tunnel 10 feet high, 12 feet wide, and 3 miles long, with 2 miles of lateral branches. From his contracts he made a fortune, but sold the tunnel in 1879. He next invested in San Francisco real estate, coming to own one-twelfth of the property in the city. On 1,000 acres facing the ocean beyond the Golden Gate, he had his own mansion. He also ran the Cliff House, a popular early hotel and restaurant, and the Sutro Baths—salt water swimming pools—there. He was a reform Populist mayor of San Francisco (1894–96), and his varied cultural interests included formation of the Sutro Library.◆

Sutro Library, book collection formed by Adolph Sutro◆ in the early 1880s. By 1895 it contained some 250,000 volumes, then said to be the largest private collection in the U.S. It included about 3,000 incunabula and many manuscripts, among them some 10,000 private papers of Sir Joseph Banks. About half the library was lost in the San Francisco earthquake and fire of 1906, only 42 incunabula, the Banks papers, 90,000 volumes, and a large pamphlet collection surviving. Sutro's heirs gave the collection to the state library in 1913 with the proviso that the collection be housed in San Francisco, and it has for some years been at the University of San Francisco.

SUTTER, John Augustus [Johann August Suter] (1803–80), born in Germany, reared partly in Switzerland, in whose army he served, ostensibly as an officer, after contracting an uneasy marriage and failing in his dry-goods business, fled to New York (1834). He then went to St. Louis, with traders to Santa Fe, overland to Oregon, and then sailed to Honolulu and Sitka before arriving in San Francisco (1839). After he became a Mexican citizen, Gov. Alvarado gave him the largest possible land grant (11 square leagues, or 48,400 acres) at the junction of the Sacramento and American rivers, presumably because the Governor wanted to check the power of his uncle and political rival, Vallejo, in the northern region.

On his vast *rancho*, at the center of that region, in which he also was given power to enforce California's laws, he used Indian labor as serfs. There he not only planted wheat, orchards, and vineyards, but began to establish a kind of barony he named

Nueva Helvetia. Its center was a fort with outer walls 3 feet thick and 15 feet high, having bastions for cannon at two corners. The inner part of the quadrangle contained quarters for the craftsmen who equipped his self-sufficient domain, which was governed from the fort's central two-and-a-half-story building. It was headquarters not only for his *rancho* but also for a trading business and for the reception of American settlers, beginning with John Bidwell (1841), who ran Sutter's Hock Farm on the Feather River for some time.

In 1841 Sutter extended his domain by buying all the Russian properties at Bodega and Fort Ross for $30,000. The military aid he temporarily rendered to Gov. Micheltorena (1845) led to his receiving a new grant of 22 square leagues of land. Even though Sutter soon gave his support again to Alvarado, Micheltorena's opponent, he thereafter used the title "General," because of his aid to Micheltorena, although the rank was no more real than that of "Captain of the Royal Swiss Guard," which he liked to say he had once held. Although Frémont was temporarily suspicious of him and briefly seized his fort, Sutter supported the Americans in the conquest of California and was supported by them, becoming a delegate to the Convention that wrote the state's Constitution.

The building of a sawmill on his American River land proved his undoing when James Marshall,◆ his partner in the venture, discovered gold (Jan. 1848) and began the great gold rush. His workmen deserted him, his *rancho* was ruined, and squatters took over and despoiled his properties. By 1852 he was bankrupt and lacked the finances needed to reclaim the properties, all of which, save the Micheltorena grant, were confirmed to him by the U.S. For a time (1862–78) the state legislature gave him a pension of $250 a month, but his long petitioning of Congress, which led him to move to the Moravian colony of Lititz, Pa., so that he might be at the capital in winter, never succeeded, and he died impoverished. His name is commemorated in a county and in many other ways, and his rebuilt Fort is now a State Historical Monument in downtown Sacramento.

Sutter Buttes, volcanic hills of northern Sutter County rising sharply from the Sacramento Valley floor. They were known to the Spaniards, Jedediah Smith, and Hudson's Bay Co. trappers, but it was Frémont, when camping there (May 1846), who seems to have named them Buttes. Butte County and Butte City (Glenn County) derive their names from these formations. They themselves are often called the Marysville Buttes for the nearby city in Yuba County.

Sutter County, one of the original 27 counties (1850), in its first six years had four different seats of government, including Auburn, which in 1851 was made the seat of Placer County, created that year in part from Sutter. Yuba City became Sutter's county seat (1856) and has remained so. Butte County lies on its north, Yuba and Placer on its east, Sacramento and Yolo on its south, and Yolo and Colusa counties on its west, with the Sacramento and Feather rivers forming its western and eastern borders, respectively. The Maidu Indians originally occupied the region.

Gabriel Moraga was the first white man to explore the area during his second expedition (1808), followed by Luís Argüello during a reconaissance for potential mission sites (1817). The first American to see the region was Jedediah Smith (1828), and it also became known to Hudson's Bay Co. trappers on their expeditions south.

John A. Sutter, for whom the county is named, settled it by establishing (about 8 miles below present Yuba City) on the west bank of Feather River his Hock Farm (1841), a name that is a corruption of the German *hoch*, meaning "upper," to indicate its northern location. For a time John Bidwell ran this stock ranch for Sutter. Two years after Sutter's settlement, Nicolaus Allgeier, a German-born trapper with Hudson's Bay Co., received from him some nearby land for ranching, the site of the present Nicolaus, once the county seat, now a major town.

The gold rush attracted many miners to Feather River.♦ Among the newcomers was Samuel Brannan,♦ who helped lay out Yuba City,♦ at the confluence of the Feather and Yuba rivers, across the way from Marysville in Yuba County. The gold rush indirectly caused the ruination of the elaborate estate to which Sutter retired after miners had overrun his Nueva Helvetia property, for floods in 1862 washed debris from mines over his gardens, vineyard, and orchard, and in that decade he left California for good.

Floods have continued to plague this flat farming land, but its most dramatic geographic feature consists of a volcanically formed mountain range, the Sutter Buttes,♦ which rise over 2,000 feet. South of it is the Sutter National Wildlife Refuge. The marsh and slough land is good for the raising of rice. Other major produce includes prunes, other fruits, nuts, vegetables, grain, and field crops. Cattle and poultry are also raised there. Food-

processing plants are the main form of manufacturing. In 1970 the county had a population of 41,935; with an area of 385,664 acres, this gave it 69.6 persons per sq. mi.

Swallows of San Juan Capistrano, according to legend, annually leave their mud nests on the mission buildings on Oct. 23 (St. John of Capistrano died on that date in 1456) to migrate south and return exactly on the next March 19 (the Feast Day of St. Joseph). The birds do seem to come and go in sufficient numbers on those dates to make this folklore appear to be accurate, but, like swallows elsewhere, they migrate on other days of those months to feed on insects that are found most easily in warm weather. The legend is bolstered by Leon René's popular song, "When the Swallows Come Back to Capistrano" (1938), and by annual press releases confirming the happenings. In recent years the swallows have become fewer because land that once was open has been filled by subdivisions, whose new residents drive off the birds and destroy nests and eggs because they believe that the swallows befoul the area.

SWAN, JOHN A[LFRED] (1817–96), English-born sailor, settled in Monterey (1843), where he ran a boardinghouse, store, and saloon. His adjacent warehouse became California's first theater: it was used for productions by members of Stevenson's Regiment.♦ Swan recounted his gold rush experiences in *A Trip to the Gold Mines . . . in 1848* (1960).

Swedes in California, arrived mainly during the gold rush, but a Dr. G. M. Waseurtz af Sandels, a visitor (1842–43), wrote an account of the region. Later settlers (who numbered about 160 in 1850 and about 1,400 in 1860) arrived not only from the mother country but also from the Midwest and as Mormons. Many entered the familiar occupations of lumbering, carpentry, seafaring, and farming. Lumbering led to a large settlement in Humboldt and Mendocino counties. Besides manning ferryboats and river steamers, some became captains of oceangoing vessels, of whom the most prominent was William Matson, head of the large shipping line bearing his name. Stock breeding and fruit farming also attracted many new arrivals, and with the use of irrigation, a special Swedish colony began to raise fruit, vegetables, and field crops around Turlock (1901). Major Swedish population centers of the state are now in Los Angeles and the

East Bay of the San Francisco area. Almost 20 place-names in the state incorporate the word "Swede," probably often pointing only to some Scandinavian association.

SWETT, JOHN (1830–1913), moved to California (1853) from his native New Hampshire and in San Francisco continued his career as a public school teacher, later serving as city superintendent of schools. He struggled against Boss Chris Buckley to keep politics out of education.

SWIFT, JOHN FRANKLIN (1829–91), born in Missouri, moved to California in 1852. He wrote about his later travels to the Holy Land in *Going to Jericho* (1868) in the vein of Mark Twain's *The Innocents Abroad*. Like Twain, too, he wrote about Nevada's bonanza days in his novel, *Robert Greathouse* (1878), but the rest of his career differed from that of his fellow Missourian in that he practiced law, was active in Republican party politics, and was Minister to Japan from 1889 until his death.

Swimming, a popular amateur sport, particularly in those parts of California where the weather is warm much of the year. Swimming pools have become commonplace even for modest homes in much of southern California. As a competitive sport it is judged essentially on the basis of time, rather than style or tactics, which are valued in other competitions. Among the California champions, the greatest early men's star was Johnny Weissmuller, who won three Olympic gold medals in 1924 and two in 1928, established 24 world records, and was the first person to swim 100 meters in less than 1 minute and 400 meters in less than 5. The greatest latter-day champion is Mark Spitz, who won 9 Olympic gold medals (1968, 1972) and established 27 world records (1967–72). Other great swimmers from the state include Patricia McCormick, Debbie Meyer, Chris Von Salta, Don Scollander, and Sammy Lee, a diving champion. Among the popular long-distance swims to test endurance in cold, rough water are those to and from Alcatraz Island in San Francisco Bay and to and from Catalina Island, with a record for the 31-mile crossing established at 8 hours, 50 minutes by David Cox (1972). Other popular ocean events are the Olympic Club's annual New Year's Day swim and the Dipsea Race. (*See also individual entries.*)

Swine, introduced to California when they were imported for the missions by Father Serra. Pigs were later raised at Fort Ross by the Russians, but there were few hogs (pigs weighing over 120 pounds) in the region until the gold rush. In 1850 there were only 2,700 head, but by 1860 the state had 456,000 hogs. This rose to 603,000 by 1880, when hog raising was concentrated in the northern half of the state. One of the farmers was Philip D. Armour, who, near Auburn, began the career that led him to become head of the nationwide Armour Packing Co. But the state has never been a big raiser of hogs, even though their number increased from 500,000 in 1900 to 1,000,000 in 1940. In 1970 there were 1,593,000 pigs slaughtered, most of them imported, but hog raising on a large scale has been carried on more profitably in the Middle West, which provides more good pastureland and corn for feed.

SWINNERTON, JAMES G[UILFORD] (1875–1974), Eureka-born artist whose earliest works were comic strips of an antic bear and a western child, Little Jimmy. He continued to draw for the Hearst papers, but settled in Palm Springs, where for some sixty years he was a painter of the desert scene there and throughout the Southwest.

Swiss in California, began with the man who remains the most famous of all: Johann August [John A.] Sutter.♦ Three other prominent early settlers were two surveyors—Vioget♦ and Julius Kellesberger, who drew the original plan of Oakland (1852)—and Heinrich Lienhard.♦ The real settlement movement began with the gold rush, attracting German-, French-, and Italian-speaking Swiss, the last, from Ticino, in the majority. Although many tried mining, as experienced farmers they often turned to dairying, so that in 1870, when only 20% of all Californians were engaged in agriculture, nearly 63% of all the Italian Swiss were so employed. Many settled in Marin and Sonoma counties and in the Salinas and San Joaquin valleys as dairymen and cheese makers. Some grew grapes and made wine, as they had at home, but the Italian-Swiss colony♦ at Asti was populated more by the former than by the latter. Many also engaged in the restaurant business. Modern Swiss in California include the artist Piazonni♦ and the composer Ernest Bloch.♦ The high point of population came after World War II, when there were about 30,000 Swiss in California, but their earlier impact is suggested by the fact that over 20 place-names in various parts of the state incorporate the word "Swiss."

Swordfish, migratory gamefish found from June through September in California waters, generally

437

south of Point Concepcion. They are angled for by sportsmen and harpooned by commercial fishermen, the annual catch fluctuating from 23,000 pounds to more than 1,000,000 pounds.

Sycamore, see *Alder*.

Sydney Ducks, ex-convicts or escaped convicts from Australia who came to California during the gold rush, many of whom settled in shanties at the base of Telegraph Hill, San Francisco, in their socalled Sydney Town. Along with the Hounds,♦ they were responsible for many robberies and also for arson, which enabled them to loot gutted buildings. In retaliation, the first Vigilance Committee was formed (1851); some of the criminals were hanged and others banished. Many returned to Australia during its gold rush (1851).

SYKES, JOHN (1773–1858), British naval officer who was with the expedition of Vancouver♦ to the Pacific (1790–95). On it, he made a great many pencil and watercolor sketches of California and other regions.

Symbionese Liberation Army, underground revolutionary organization of terrorists, at first probably headquartered in the East Bay area. It took credit for the murder, with cyanide-filled bullets, of Marcus Foster, Superintendent of Schools in Oakland (Nov. 1973) because of his plan for identification and surveillance of students in the city's high schools. It kidnapped (Feb. 4, 1974) Patricia Hearst, a student at the University of California and granddaughter of William Randolph Hearst,♦ from her Berkeley apartment. As ransom, her parents, Mr. and Mrs. Randolph Apperson Hearst, instituted an elaborate program of food distribution to poor people in the state. Instead of being freed to return, Miss Hearst announced that she had willingly joined her captors, taken the name of Tania, and participated in some of their crimes, including a bank robbery. Six leaders of the SLA were killed during a shootout and fire in Los Angeles (1974), but Patricia Hearst and three associates remained fugitives for nineteen months. She was captured in 1975, tried, convicted, and sentenced to seven years in prison.

Symbols, State, see *State symbols*.

Symphony, see *Music*.

T

TABER, I[SAIAH] W[EST] (1830–1912), born in Massachusetts, after experience as a whaler sailed to California (1849), where he entered into Pacific trade before becoming a gold miner, rancher, and then dentist for four years until he finally found his true vocation as a photographer. He practiced first in New York, then with Bradley and Rulofson in San Francisco (1864), and at last on his own (1871). He became the leading photographer of noted people, both local and visiting, and of the Pacific Coast scene.

Table Mountain, see *Tuolumne County.*

Taft, urban center for oil fields in Kern County, founded in 1909 and named for the newly elected President of the U.S.

TAGGARD, GENEVIEVE (1894–1948), born in Washington, reared in Hawaii, graduated from the University of California, Berkeley (1919), began her career as a poet in the metaphysical vein. She was deeply concerned with liberal social views while in California. *Traveling Standing Still* (1928) is a collection of her early poems. After 1929 she taught at Mount Holyoke, Bennington, and Sarah Lawrence colleges.

Tahoe, see *Lake Tahoe.*

Tallac, Mount, peak (9,785 ft.) overlooking Lake Tahoe, whose Washo name means simply "big mountain." The crevices of the mountain form a huge cross, generally snow-packed the year round, as Longfellow noted in a poem. At the mountain's lakeside base, E. J. ("Lucky") Baldwin built a luxurious summer resort (1880–1914).

Tamalpais, Mount, highest mountain (2,604 ft.) on the west side of San Francisco Bay, located in Marin County. It overlooks Muir Woods♦ and, like that site, was once owned by the conservation-minded Congressman William Kent.♦ The name, first used in the 19th century, presumably relates to the Miwok Indians, called Tamal by the Spanish. Each May (since 1913) a Mountain Play is enacted in the amphitheater presented by Kent. The moun-

tain is part of the Golden Gate National Recreational Area.

Tamarisk, small ornamental tree imported from Asia to provide shade and a hedge against wind in desert areas.

Tanforan, see *Horse racing.*

Tanning, begun by the mission fathers for leather goods they needed, was dependent for tannin upon the tanbark oak found throughout the Coast Range mountains from Oregon to Santa Barbara. The tree is also found in the Sierra from Lassen through Mariposa counties. Dana observed that the *Californios* sold cowhides to be shipped to Boston for tanning and making into shoes, which they then had shipped back around the Horn, rather than trying to develop their own manufacture. The Russians at Fort Ross were somewhat more sophisticated at tanning than the mission fathers. The first U.S. tannery was founded by Cyrus Alexander in present Alexander Valley (Sonoma County) in the 1840s. During the gold rush, tanneries grew up around San Francisco Bay, where local cowhides were made into saddles, harness, machine belting, and other heavy leather goods, as well as boots and shoes. A particularly fine glove leather was made in Napa, and soft leathers in general took its generic regional name. The largest early tanneries were located on the San Lorenzo River in Santa Cruz County. Between 1857 and 1890 the state's tanneries grew from 18 to 62. Thereafter, they declined as shoe manufacture became centralized on the eastern seaboard and as the need for harness declined. In 1951 there were 26 tanneries in California; by 1967 they had dwindled to 15.

TAPIS, ESTÉVAN (c. 1756–1835), Spanish-born Franciscan missionary, went to California (1790) and remained at Santa Barbara until he became President-General♦ (1803–12).

Tar, see *Asphalt.*

Tarzana, see *Burroughs, Edgar Rice.*

Tassajara Hot Springs, mineral waters used for medicinal purposes by Costanoan Indians and by the Spanish. The springs are in a northern Los Padres National Forest site beyond Carmel Valley in Monterey County. In 1904 a resort hotel and baths were constructed there. The resort has become a Zen center. The name is Spanish for a place where jerky is cut and dried, and it appears in other California locations.

TAVERNIER, JULES (1844–89), after enjoying a career as painter and magazine illustrator in his native France and in England, went to the U.S., spending some time in San Francisco and Monterey in the 1870s. He led a bohemian life and painted some charming local scenes.

TAYLOR, ALEXANDER S. (1817–76), born in South Carolina, went as a sailor to Monterey, where he settled (1848–60). Later he moved to Santa Barbara, where he married into the Ortega family. At both places, he collected Spanish historical documents. He gave many of those papers to the Catholic diocese of San Francisco, after having used them to write studies of California's past, its Indians, and a manuscript bibliography of Californiana. Bancroft considered his scholarship "well nigh valueless."

TAYLOR, BAYARD (1825–78), man of letters who, as a young writer of literary and travel articles for the *New-York Tribune*, was sent to report on California during the gold rush. He voyaged to and from the West Coast via Panama and visited San Francisco, Monterey (where he attended the Constitutional Convention), and the mines (July-Dec. 1849). He wrote frequent letters to the paper that formed the basis of his book, *Eldorado; or Adventures in the Path of Empire* (1850).

TAYLOR, EDWARD ROBESON (1838–1923), moved to San Francisco (1862) from his native Midwest and after professional study became both a physician and a lawyer. He was also active in Democratic party politics and was mayor of San Francisco (1907–9) as well as a leader in cultural affairs of the city and a poet. The printing firm of Taylor & Taylor♦ was founded by his sons.

TAYLOR, ELIZABETH (1932–), English-born actress, brought to California during World War II by her parents and there cast in the part of an English child in *Lassie Come Home* (1942), leading to further adolescent roles, including *National Velvet* (1944). As a mature actress, she became famous as a sultry beauty playing romantic and troubled characters, not far removed from her headline-recorded life as a figure of glamour, often married, and involved in international and luxurious situations. Films with her fifth husband, Richard Burton, include *Cleopatra* (1963) and *Who's Afraid of Virginia Woolf?* (1966). Beside her abilities as an actress, she is also known as a major latter-day representative of the Hollywood star.

TAYLOR, PAUL, see *Lange, Dorothea.*

TAYLOR, SAMUEL P., see *Samuel P. Taylor State Park.*

TAYLOR, WILLIAM (1821–1902), Virginia-born Methodist minister who moved to San Francisco (1849) and remained there as an evangelical divine for seven years. He was known for his flamboyant sermons delivered in Portsmouth Plaza, saloons and gambling houses, as well as in his own chapel. He wrote of this in *Seven Years' Street Preaching in San Francisco* (1857). Later missionary work took him all over the world, and from Australia in 1863 he sent back the seeds from which grew some of the first eucalyptus in California. Late in life he returned to retire in California.

Taylor & Taylor, fine printers of San Francisco, founded (1896) by Edward DeWitt Taylor, who was joined (1905) by his brother Henry H. Taylor and, from 1911 to 1915, by John Henry Nash.♦ They printed for publishers, booksellers, clubs, and private distribution a wide variety of texts, including many by such California authors as Gelett Burgess, Wallace Irwin, Joaquin Miller, George Sterling, Charles Warren Stoddard, and their own father, Edward Robeson Taylor.♦ Their classically pure typography is also evident in a handsome type specimen book issued in 1939. The firm was liquidated in 1960.

Tea, entered into California commerce during the Mexican period, when American traders exchanged furs for China tea, then brought it by ship to the eastern U.S. Demand for tea in California occurred after the gold rush, and San Francisco became a regional distributing center in the 1870s and 80s with the establishment of importing businesses by local families such as Schilling, J. A. Folger, and M. J. B.[randenstein]. Others attempted to cultivate the plant in California, particularly in the Sierra foothills, and hoped to have local Chinese care for it, but sporadic attempts (1860s to 1880), including that of the Wakamatsu Colony,♦ were unsuccessful.

TEAGUE, CHARLES COLLINS (1873–1950), agricultural entrepreneur, born in Maine, reared in Kansas, moved to southern California (1893) to begin a career of raising lemons that culminated in his becoming probably the world's largest producer. He was president of the California Fruit Growers Exchange♦ (1920–50) and for thirty years was president of the California Walnut Growers Association. His memoirs are entitled *Fifty Years a Rancher* (1944).

Tehachapi Mountains, southern terminus of the Sierra Nevada and end of the Central Valley in Kern County, generally considered to be the dividing line between northern and southern California. The six passes through the mountains, first explored by Fages, include, from east to west, Walker Pass, named for Joseph Walker;♦ Tehachapi Pass (4,025-ft. summit), a major engineering feat of the Southern Pacific Railroad (1876), whose tracks loop so that the caboose of an 85-car freight train is directly above its engine in a tunnel below; and Tejón Pass,♦ a name once given to a gap east of the present pass of that name, which itself was formerly called Cañada de las Uvas and is now the route into what is called Grapevine Canyon.♦

Tehama-Colusa Canal, part of the Central Valley Project,♦ diverts water from the Sacramento River in the area near Red Bluff (Tehama County) and brings it down the west side of the Sacramento Valley.

Tehama County, organized (1856) from sections of Shasta, Butte, and Colusa counties. It is bounded by Mendocino and Trinity counties on the west, Shasta County on the north, Plumas and Butte counties on the east, and Butte and Glenn counties on the south. The first white explorers were Luís Argüello (1821), Jedediah Smith (1828), and Hudson's Bay Co. trappers (1830 ff.). The route of the last was followed by emigrants from Oregon. Early settlers included Peter Lassen, Pierson Reading, William B. Ide, Job Dye, and Robert H. Thomes.

Lumbering has always been an important activity in the timberlands, some of which now are reserved in the part of Trinity National Forest that lies on the county's west and the part of Lassen National Forest that lies on its east. The Yolla Bolly Mts. are on the western border. Fruit and nut crops are also important, as are field crops for livestock. At one time Leland Stanford had near Corning his Vina Ranch, formed partly from the original Lassen

grant, on which he planted one of the world's largest vineyards.

Down the middle of the county runs the Sacramento River, and on or near it lie the major urban settlements of the county: Red Bluff, the seat of government since 1857; Corning, the center of olive growing and packing; and Tehama, the county seat in the first year of government. The county in 1970 had a population of 29,517 on its 1,909,888 acres, which gave it 9.9 persons per sq. mi. (*See also individual entries.*)

Tejón Pass, on the Los Angeles County border just below Kern County, was discovered by Pedro Fages (1772) while pursuing deserters from the army, but was given its name (Spanish for "badger") by the expedition of Lt. Francisco Ruiz (1806). This pass through the Tehachapi Mts.♦ into Grapevine Canyon♦ in Kern County and north into San Joaquin Valley was long guarded by Fort Tejón.♦ It was on the route used by the Butterfield stagecoach line (1858 ff.) between Los Angeles and San Francisco. The region was hit by one of the state's worst earthquakes in 1857. Another gap to its east was once called Tejón Pass, when the present one was called Cañada de las Uvas. In that area, Edward F. Beale,♦ as Superintendent for Indian Affairs in California, established a reservation of about 25,000 acres for some 2,500 Indians, a model system.

Telegraph Hill, named for the semaphore erected (1850) to signal the arrival of ships in the Bay, rises 274 feet above the northeast San Francisco shoreline. Rugged in appearance because so much of the hill has been quarried away, it overlooks North Beach♦ and the old Barbary Coast♦ and has itself been a colorful area whose past bohemian residents included Gelett Burgess. From its summit rises the 210-foot Coit Tower♦ erected (1933) with funds bequeathed by Lillie Hitchcock Coit.♦

Television, experimentation in California was begun in 1925 by KPO, San Francisco, with still picture transmission, soon followed by further trials by Philo T. Farnsworth in San Francisco (1927–31) and Harry Lubcke in Los Angeles (1931), the latter using all electric equipment and establishing the first transmitter, W6XAO, on an hour-a-day program (1931). In 1933 the station broadcast films of the Long Beach earthquake within two weeks after the event. Receiving sets (for black and white images) became readily available only in 1946, and not until then was there widespread public interest in television. The first regular commercial station, KTLA, was established in Los Angeles (1947), followed by KPIX in San Francisco (1948) and by KFMB of San Diego in 1950. Until that date at least 80% of television shows, including serials, were presented live, but the success of two filmed series—*Dragnet*♦ and *I Love Lucy*—occasioned an exodus from New York to the Los Angeles area, where motion picture studios and a wider variety of settings were available. In the 1950s the established producers began to cooperate with television by creating films specially for the new medium, particularly Westerns, which became enormously popular. At the same time, the major studios began to sell their old films as staples for viewing by new audiences. Another development of the decade was the founding (1954) in San Francisco of KQED, an independent, noncommercial station that won needed support through annual televised auctions of contributed goods, a program that appealed to many viewers, and the station's success provided a model for other public television enterprises. Since 1966 almost all broadcasting has been in color. In 1973 California had 49 stations, including ones in communities as small as Alturas and Coalinga.

TELLER, EDWARD (1908–), Hungarian-born physicist, moved to the U.S. (1935), became a U.S. citizen (1941), and, during World War II, both at the Manhattan Project of the University of Chicago and at the University of California's Los Alamos Laboratory (1943–46), he was involved in planning the atomic bomb. Then and later, he was also instrumental in developing the hydrogen bomb. He was a professor of physics at the University of California, Berkeley (1953–75), and director of the Lawrence Livermore Radiation Laboratory. Upon retirement, he became a senior research fellow at the Hoover Institution. His books include *Our Nuclear Future* (1958) and *The Legacy of Hiroshima* (1962).

Temblor Range, southern continuation of the Diablo Range,♦ lying on the border of San Luis Obispo and Kern counties, runs along the San Andreas Fault line, west of Bakersfield.

Temescal, a low, small, sloping log structure, brushroofed, with an excavated earth base, in whose center an open fire was built. Around it Indian men lounged, both for social and ceremonial reasons and to enjoy the intense heat, from which they would go, perspiring, to plunge into a cold river or lake. The name *temascal* (Mexican, derived from Aztec for "bathhouse") was given by the Spaniards to these structures, which were found among various tribes. In its modernized spelling, Temescal is a place-name in at least ten locations, including Alameda, Los Angeles, and Riverside counties.

TEMPLE, JOHN (1798–1866), born in Massachusetts, moved to California from Hawaii (1827) as a trader, and opened the first general store and later the first office building in Los Angeles, the latter bought by the county for its first courthouse. He became a naturalized Mexican, married into the Cota family, built an adobe mansion on his Rancho Los Cerritos (1844) on the site of the present Signal Hill, and, after its secularization, bought Mission La Purísima Concepción (1845). He added to his fortune by contracting with the Mexican government to operate its mint in Mexico City. His last years were spent in San Francisco, but he is remembered as a pioneer of Los Angeles, whose Temple St. commemorates him. His brother, Francis Pliny F. Temple (1821–80), joined him in business, was later a banker with I. W. Hellman,♦ and married the daughter of William Workman,♦ with whom he established a bank that failed. Thereafter he was impoverished.

TEMPLE, SHIRLEY (1928–), born in Santa Monica, was cast in Hollywood movies at age 3 and at 6 was a sensationally popular star noted for her winsome personality, cute smile, blonde curls, and genuine talent as actress, singer, and dancer. Her films include *Little Miss Marker* (1934), *The Littlest Rebel* (1935), and *Rebecca of Sunnybrook Farm* (1938). In 1950 she retired from films and married Charles A. Black, a socially prominent San Francisco businessman. She became active in Republican party politics, was appointed to United Nations posts, then Ambassador to Ghana, and later Chief of Protocol of the U.S. (1976).

TENNEY, JACK B. (1898–1970), Assemblyman from Los Angeles (1936–54), formerly a songwriter ("Mexicali Rose"), was known for his chairmanship of a state un-American activities committee (1941–49). His flamboyant public hearings and charges of alleged communist infiltration were so extreme that eventually legislators (some of whom he accused) and the public turned against him. With relatively little change, the "Tenney Committee" then became the "Burns Committee" of State Senator Hugh M. Burns.

Tennis, a sport which in its modern form was created in England (1873) and introduced into California (1879) by William Young, who had moved to Santa Monica from his native England. The game soon became popular in the state but was initially considered to be an upper-class recreation identified with wealthy communities and elegant resorts, such as Del Monte. By 1887 interest was sufficiently widespread to warrant a statewide tournament, won by William Young, that is believed to have been the first state championship in the U.S.

The nation's first intercollegiate matches were also held in California, between Stanford and the University of California (1892). As the game began to be more widely played, more hard-surface courts were built, in contrast to the grass or clay surfaces common in the East. Thus, a different kind of bounce and a different style of harder play was developed in the state. Maurice McLoughlin represented this style and became known as the California Comet when he won the U.S. singles championship (1912–13) and became the first American man to win at Wimbledon (1913). He also helped to end the image of tennis as a rich man's game, since he had learned to play on the public courts of Golden Gate Park.

California women early proved tennis to be a game for them, too, as May Sutton won the U.S. national competition (1904) and also became the first American woman to win a British championship (1907). She was soon followed by Hazel Hotchkiss, who won all the women's U.S. championships three years running (1909–11). In the 1920s and 30s the world's competition among women was dominated by two Californians, Helen Wills and Helen Jacobs.

In those decades and subsequent ones, many other leading U.S. players who won not only U.S. but English and foreign championships have also come from California, where the climate is congenial to year-round outdoor competition. Among the men were Donald Budge, Pancho Gonzales, Jack Kramer, Bobby Riggs, and Elsworth Vines, while the women included Pauline Betz, Maureen Connolly, Billie Jean King, and Alice Marble. (*See also individual entries.*)

TERMAN, FREDERICK E[MMONS] (1900–), son of Lewis M. Terman, a distinguished professor of psychology at Stanford, received his A.B. and electrical engineering degrees there and a Sc.D. from MIT before joining the electrical engineering faculty of Stanford (1925). In time he became its

dean and the University's provost and vice president. In these capacities he encouraged his students, such as William R. Hewlett♦ and David Packard,♦ to relate research to manufacturing and business, located at Stanford Industrial Park, where plants could be close to classrooms and laboratories. Thus he became a prime mover of the state's great development in electronics.♦

Terminal Island, partly man-made site offshore from San Pedro♦ between Wilmington and Long Beach, initially extended and developed from Rattlesnake Island by Phineas Banning and connected by a bridge to the mainland. Once a bathing resort, it became a fishing port and packing and processing area as well as a U.S. Navy shipyard.

Territorial Enterprise, see *Clemens, Samuel; Comstock Lode; Daggett, Rollin;* and *De Quille, Dan.*

TERRY, DAVID S[MITH] (1823–90), moved to California (1849) from Texas, where he had served as a lieutenant in the Mexican War. Elected by the Know-Nothing party♦ to the state Supreme Court (1855), he became Chief Justice (1857), even though he had meanwhile been jailed for stabbing a member of the Vigilance Committee, which he opposed. He aligned himself politically with Sen. William Gwin♦ and the southern faction of Democrats, as befitted a man born in Kentucky who had volunteered in the war for Texan independence. That alignment caused him to be denounced by Sen. David Broderick♦ and led to a pistol duel at Lake Merced (1859) in which Broderick was mortally wounded. During the Civil War, Terry fought for the Confederacy, later living for a time in Mexico before returning to California (1869) and legal practice. He became the lawyer for Sarah Althea Hill in her suit against William Sharon♦ and married his client. When U.S. Supreme Court Justice Stephen J. Field♦ found her documentation fraudulent, Terry threatened Field and thus occasioned the U.S. Attorney General to assign a bodyguard, David Neagle, to Field. When Field and Terry met by chance in a railroad restaurant at Lathrop (near Stockton), Terry struck Field and was in turn gunned down by Neagle. W. F. Herrin♦ defended Neagle and got him acquitted of a murder charge.

TEVIS, LLOYD (1824–99), moved to California (1849) from his native Kentucky and established a law practice with his brother-in-law, James Ben Ali Haggin.♦ They represented George Hearst, and also fought a long, unsuccessful court battle against the riparian control of Miller and Lux. Their court claims were eventually upheld by the Wright Act's interpretation of the control of water.♦ Tevis was president of Wells Fargo and a major stockholder through his Pacific Express Co., Spring Valley Water, Sutro Tunnel, Bank of California, and Anaconda and Homestake mines interests. A San Francisco social leader, he lived in South Park.♦ One of his sons married a daughter of Gov. Pacheco, and the family has continued to be prominent in social, cultural, and financial affairs.

Textiles, woven or knit cloth manufactured in California, must compete with that from other parts of the U.S. that have cheaper labor costs. For this and other reasons, it depends on native production of raw materials. Cotton♦ has been successfully and widely grown there only in the 20th century, although cotton mills were first founded in the 1860s. Wool textile making of the simplest sort dates back to the time of the missions, but a real woolen goods industry first flourished only during the Civil War, when a short supply in the East and high shipping costs warranted large local production. The end of the war and the completion of the transcontinental railroad (1869) changed the situation for the worse within a decade. Then sheep-grazing lands began to be used for increased agriculture. Attempts to grow silk also came to an end in the 1870s. Thus textile manufacturing has not been a major business, although it was much expanded in the 1960s with the growth of California's apparel industry.♦ Still, by comparison with other manufactured products such as lumber and metal, textile production remains relatively small.

THALBERG, IRVING (1899–1936), Brooklyn-born producer of Hollywood films. He was brought to California by Carl Laemmle, whose Universal City he essentially ran from 1919 to 1923. He later ran Metro-Goldwyn-Mayer (1923–33) and then worked as an independent producer. His major films included *The Big Parade, Ben-Hur, Broadway Melody, Grand Hotel,* and *Mutiny on the Bounty.* He was the prototype of Monroe Stahr in F. Scott Fitzgerald's *The Last Tycoon.*♦

Theater, in the Spanish and Mexican periods was related to Church rituals and festivals, such as the popular *Navidad* acted at Christmas or the more refined *Pastorela,* a Nativity play suggested by the Gospels. During the occupation following American conquest, amateur theatricals, such as minstrel shows, were put on by troops at Sonoma and elsewhere. At Monterey, a saloon owned by John A. Swan was used for this purpose and then remodeled to become California's first theater (1847), whose first real play was Nathaniel H. Bannister's patriotic comedy, *Putnam, the Iron Son of '76,* originally produced in New York three years earlier.

The gold rush brought many more theaters, producers, and actors to San Francisco (Washington Hall, its first theater, opened on Jan. 16, 1850), Sacramento, and the larger mining towns. The first star was Stephen C. Massett, who in June 1849 gave performances in San Francisco of snatches from Shakespeare interspersed with his own songs. He later recalled them in his theatrical memoirs, issued under his pseudonym, "Jeems Pipes of Pipesville." More formal productions were staged by a druggist, Dr. D. G. Robinson, and Tom Maguire, who did well enough as a San Francisco impressario to branch out into mining towns and to book into them such stars of New York and London as Junius Brutus Booth, Sr. and Jr., Edwin Forrest, and Laura Keene, as well as productions of opera, minstrels, and burlesques. The most sensational was Lola Montez, who developed the career of the younger local star, Lotta Crabtree. Another favorite was the notorious Adah Menken, who enacted the role of Mazeppa in a melodramatic adaptation of Byron's poem, wearing flesh-colored tights that made her appear to be nude. The stage was so popular in San Francisco that journals were published as combination theater programs and news sheets, the most successful being issued by the de Young brothers, who later developed it into a regular newspaper.

In the 1860s and 70s new theaters were constructed, the most important being the California Theatre, financed by William Ralston, and the Baldwin Academy of Music (commonly called Baldwin Theatre), which was part of the hotel Lucky Baldwin built (1876) and named for himself. Baldwin's theater was run by Tom Maguire, who, in turn, had James A. Herne as his stage manager and David Belasco as an actor and associate. Both of them went on to successful careers as playwrights and producers in New York. In addition to these locally bred theatrical figures and Joaquin Miller, who wrote for the stage in the 1870s, theaters in San Francisco and elsewhere in the state attracted such cosmopolitan stars as Modjeska (she settled in Anaheim for a while), Joseph Jefferson (with his perennial *Rip Van Winkle*), James O'Neill (with his equally hardy *Count of Monte*

Cristo), Sarah Bernhardt, Ellen Terry, Julia Marlow, and the Barrymores.

Los Angeles did not have a real theater until 1860. It did not have a lasting stage until late in the century, when Oliver Morosco established his Majestic and Burbank theaters for stock productions, touring companies, vaudeville, and opera. At the turn of the century English and American stars were booked into San Francisco, Los Angeles, and the larger of the lesser cities as part of a syndicate that controlled touring companies of actors and their dramas. As counterpoise, the cities developed their own stock companies in the early 20th century, with groups of local actors presenting both classically established plays and recent Broadway hits. A compromise between home production and syndicate tours was found in vaudeville houses that booked not only traveling variety acts interspersed with local attractions but also some legitimate actors presenting truncated versions of their regular repertoires.

California also developed its own dramatic figures, including Belasco's star David Warfield, other popular actors like Frank Bacon, Holbrook Blinn, Blanche Bates, and Nance O'Neill, and the dramatists Richard Walton Tully, Sidney Howard, and Dan Totheroh. It also created its own special dramatic pageants, including one about Ramona as well as others for production at Mount Tamalpais and the Hollywood Bowl.

But even as the state contributed to the national theater and developed its native traditions, that theater itself was being threatened by a new form of drama that was to make its home in Hollywood. Motion pictures, which had originally been mere novelties at vaudeville houses or simply a cheap form of entertainment at their own sleazy theaters, came more and more to be the dominant form and to drive out acting on the stage. Even as early as 1917, San Francisco had far more motion picture houses than regular theaters, and the trend became further pronounced during the 1920s and subsequent decades.

In protest against Hollywood films and poor touring productions of Broadway hits, there grew up in the major cities little theaters for experimental presentations to appeal to the more cultivated or sophisticated elements of the public. Among the most lasting were the Pasadena Playhouse and the specialized Padua Hills Theatre. But although the stage received significant help during the Depression from the Federal Theatre of the national Works Progress Administration, the general public no longer looked to it as the major form of art and

entertainment but turned increasingly to the motion picture. (*See also individual entries.*)

Theological Union, see *Graduate Theological Union.*

Thermalito Bay, see *Butte County.*

THIEBAUD, WAYNE (1920–   ),   Arizona-born artist, educated at Sacramento State College, where he later taught before joining the faculty of the University of California, Davis (1960). He is known for his colorfully patterned pseudo-realistic paintings of pastries.

Thistleton's Jolly Giant, scurrilous, vitriolic, and racist San Francisco weekly journal (1837–82) that became a monthly in its dying days. It was violently anti-Catholic and anti-Irish, and was opposed to the Chinese in both the flamboyant text and the crude colored cartoons it featured.

THOMAS, JOHN HUDSON (1875–1945), Berkeley-born architect, educated at Yale and the University of California. Working in his native city, he built in various parts of the state residences marked by striking structural elements such as overscaled columns in the tradition of the Austrian Secessionist architects, but sometimes employing a timber style akin to Maybeck's.

THOMES, ROBERT HASTY (1817–78), left his native Maine and became an emigrant to California with the Bartleson-Bidwell Party♦ (1841). After residence in San Francisco and Monterey, he settled as a converted, naturalized Californian on a large *rancho* in Tehama County. He was a remote relative of W. H. Thomes.

THOMES, WILLIAM HENRY (1824–95), shipped as a common sailor from his native New England to California in 1842 to engage in its hide and tallow trade, ostensibly in emulation of Dana's experiences which had recently been reported in *Two Years Before the Mast.* His own adventures at sea and ashore later formed the basis of his account for juvenile readers, *On Land and Sea* (1883), whose setting and incidents are not unlike those reported by Dana, although heightened by more romance and fictional flavor. When his ship was to sail home in 1845, Thomes and a friend deserted. Their adventures were the basis for an even more fictitious work, *Lewey and I* (1884), though he may, as he claims, have been impressed into the Mexican

Army during the Bear Flag Revolt. At the end of 1846, he left California for home but sailed back in 1849 to seek gold. Having no luck, he left again in 1851 on a voyage reported (with some fiction) as *A Whaleman's Adventures in the Sandwich Islands and California* (1872) and *The Gold Hunter's Adventures; or, Life in Australia* (1864), written, like the other books, for boys. Back in Boston, he began his career of journalist and writer of fiction and fictionalized autobiography, but he paid several sentimental return visits to California.

THOMPSON, ALPHEUS B. (1795–1869), Maine-born mariner, active in the hide trade of California during the 1830s. He later became a *ranchero* but made his home in Santa Barbara after 1834, when he married a daughter of the Carrillo family.

THOMPSON, JOHN ALBERT (1827–76), native of Norway, originally named Tostensen, was brought to the U.S. as a child. He went to California in 1851 to mine and ranch. Recognizing the difficulty of getting mail across the Sierra in winter, he constructed skis such as he had known in Norway, but called them "snowshoes." With them he began his business of carrying as much as 100 pounds a trip (including the first ore from the Comstock Lode to be assayed) for 20 years, a service that earned him the name Snowshoe Thompson.

THOMPSON, SNOWSHOE, See *Thompson, John Albert.*

THORNTON, J[ESSY] QUINN (1810–88), overland emigrant to Oregon (1846) who met the Donner Party en route and published a long account of it in his two-volume work, *Oregon and California in 1848* (1849), which is also notable for its early information on the gold mines. He later became a Supreme Court Justice of Oregon.

Throop Polytechnic Institute, founded in Pasadena (1891) to teach engineering, arts and crafts, and the humanities to men and women. In 1920 it was reorganized as the California Institute of Technology.♦

THURMAN, HOWARD (1900–), Florida-born clergyman of the Baptist Church, a leading pastor both for his fellow blacks and for all liberal persons, in keeping with the name of the San Francisco congregation to which he ministered (1944–53): Church for Fellowship of All Peoples. He has held

visiting teaching posts at several universities and colleges and has written numerous books, including *Deep River* (1946), *The Inward Journey* (1961), and *The Search for Common Ground* (1971).

TIBBETS, LUTHER CALVIN, see *Citrus fruit growing.*

TIBBETT, LAWRENCE (1896–1960), Bakersfield-born opera singer, made his debut at the Metropolitan Opera House, N.Y., in 1923 and became famous as a baritone and dramatic actor. He was also successful in motion pictures.

Tiburon, waterfront residential town in Marin County on the peninsula that juts out into Richardson Bay. Belvedere lies west of its cove and Angel Island is nearby in San Francisco Bay. The name, known in the 1820s, comes from Punta de Tiburon (Shark's Point).

Tijuana, Mexican border city just south of San Diego, is a popular tourist area offering jai alai games, horse and dog racing, bullfights, and other colorful foreign attractions. In 1970 its population was 340,583.

TILDEN, CHARLES LEE (1857–1950), born in a mining camp in Calaveras County but reared in San Francisco, after graduation from the University of California and Hastings College (1881) and legal practice, became a successful business entrepreneur. At one time his cable company, lumber, canning, and banking interests made him San Francisco's largest individual taxpayer. He later moved to Alameda and became a founder of the East Bay Regional Park system (1934). Its Tilden Regional Park is named for him.

TILDEN, DOUGLAS (1860–1935), first native Californian to become internationally famous as a sculptor. He is best known for his dramatically modeled athletic male figures, such as the Mechanics Monument (1899) on Market St., San Francisco (a memorial to Peter Donahue), and the statue of rugby players on the University of California's Berkeley campus. He also created a monumental statue of Serra which stands in Golden Gate Park. A mute, he taught for a time at the California Institute for the Deaf.

Time of Your Life, The, play by William Saroyan.♦

TINEMAHA, see *Winnedumah.*

TINGLEY, KATHERINE AUGUSTA WESTCOTT (1847–1929), Massachusetts-born theosophist, established at Point Loma♦ the headquarters of her arcane society; a community also dedicated to social reform, philanthropy, and cultural activities; a child's school; and a university.

Tioga Pass, mountainous entrance to Yosemite from the east via Tuolumne Meadows, is the highest automobile pass in the state (9,941 ft.). The Tioga Road, originally the Great Sierra Wagon Road (1883) to gold and silver mines in the area, became a scenic route transferred to the Dept. of the Interior (1915). The name is Iroquois (meaning "where it forks"), used in New York and Pennsylvania, and borrowed for a California mine name by a white miner.

Tish-Tang-A-Tang, name of a ridge, point, and creek in Humboldt County, on the southeast border of its Hoopa Valley Reservation. In the Hupa language it is said to mean "a neck of land projecting into a river."

TITTLE, Y[ELBERTON] A[BRAHAM] (1926–), Texas-born football player, after being a star quarterback at Louisiana State University (1944–48), played that position with the San Francisco Forty-Niners (1951–60) and the New York Giants (1961–64). He was among the greatest passers in professional play.

Toad, tailless amphibian, more terrestrial than the related frog,♦ is found in many species throughout the state, feeding on insects, while some types also eat snails, scorpions, spiders, centipedes, small lizards, crayfish, and other toads. The *western toad* lives throughout California except in the desert south of Death Valley and the central high Sierra Nevada, which is the home of the *Yosemite toad*. The *Great Plains toad* and *Woodhouse's toad* live in Colorado River bottom lands and in irrigated lowlands of Imperial and Riverside counties. The *red-spotted toad* lives in the southern desert area, and the *southwestern toad* is found in the southern Coast Range, the Transverse Mountains, and along the Mojave and Colorado rivers. The latter region is also the home of the *Colorado River toad*, the only one that eats mice. Three varieties of *spadefoot toads,* marked by a single black sharp spade on one hindfoot, are found in the Central Valley, the southern Coast Range, and the eastern state border, spending much of their time underground. A *horned toad* is a lizard.♦

Tobacco, introduced to California missions and ranches by the Spanish and at Fort Ross because the native wild plant was harsh and toxic. Production was increased, particularly in the San Francisco area, by Americans during and after the gold rush. However, though the business flourished in the earliest days and again during the Civil War when imported leaf was hard to get, it was never very successful agriculturally or commercially. Production rose to 64,000 pounds in 1864 but declined sharply in the 1870s and did not rise significantly again until the period of World War I, when 490,000 pounds were raised in the state. Despite temporary successes (such as the growing of Turkish tobacco in Fresno County after World War II), farmers find it an uncertain crop that is uncompetitive since it must be transported to eastern factories.

TOBIN, prominent California family, founded by Richard Tobin (1832–87), who was born in Ireland and reared in Australia and Chile before being taken to San Francisco in 1847. His knowledge of Spanish helped him to become the secretary to José Sadoc Alemany,♦ California's first archbishop, a post he held before becoming a lawyer and businessman. His brother, Robert J. Tobin, arrived in San Francisco in 1848, entered politics, and was elected an alderman (1855). The two of them went on to found the Hibernia Savings and Loan Society (1859), soon San Francisco's largest savings bank.

Richard married Mary Ann Regan, born in Chile of Irish extraction, and they had twelve children. Among them were Alfred (1864–1900), who followed in his father's footsteps as counsel for the Hibernia Bank; Agnes (1864–1939), who translated Petrarch, Dante, and Racine, wrote poetry of her own, and, as an expatriate in London, was a friend of Conrad, Yeats, and Pound; Richard Montgomery (1866–1952), a member of the U.S. Peace Commission at Versailles after World War I and Ambassador to the Netherlands (1923–29); Joseph Sadoc (1869–1918), a lawyer and a supervisor of San Francisco (1900–02); and Edward J. (1872–1961), a longtime president of the family bank until he was succeeded (1933–52) by his brother, Richard Montgomery.

Robert J. Tobin's son, Joseph Oliver (1877–), succeeded his cousins as bank president. He married Constance de Young, a daughter of M. H. de Young.♦ The relationship to the family that founded the *San Francisco Chronicle* was further cemented when the daughter of Abigail Parrott and Edward J. Tobin, Barbara Mary, in 1938 married Charles de Young Thieriot (1915–77), the nephew of Joseph O. and Constance Tobin.

TODD, WILLIAM L. (*fl.* 1845–46), a nephew of Mary Todd Lincoln, moved from his native Illinois to California (1845) and the next year joined the leaders of the Bear Flag Revolt at Sonoma. For their cause he designed and painted the Bear Flag.♦

Toiyabe National Forest, located mostly on the eastern side of the Sierra Nevada in the state of Nevada (where it has its headquarters) and partly in Mono and Alpine counties. The California part was created (1946) from the northern section of Mono National Forest and given an Indian name meaning "big [or "black"] mountain."

TOJETTI, DOMENICO (1807–92), Italian-born artist, resident after 1859 in San Francisco, became known for his literary and allegorical paintings. His sons Virgil (1850–1901) and Edward were also painters.

TOKLAS, ALICE B[ABETTE] (1877–1967), San Francisco-born friend, constant companion, and secretary after 1907 of Gertrude Stein, who made her the ostensible author of *The Autobiography of Alice B. Toklas* (1933), actually Gertrude Stein's own memoir. Miss Toklas finally wrote her own brief recollections, *What Is Remembered* (1963), and two cookbooks containing reminiscences, too.

TOLAND, HUGH H[UGER] (1806–80), physician born in South Carolina and a graduate of a Kentucky medical school, moved to California in the gold rush. He was a doctor for James King of William,♦ and his treatment of the wounded editor led to accusations of malpractice. He founded Toland Medical College (1864) in San Francisco with most of the staff of Elias S. Cooper.♦ He later gave his school to the University of California to found its medical facilities (1873) with a chair named for him, whereas the Cooper faction became the nucleus of the Stanford University Medical School.

Toloache cult, originated among the Gabrieleño Indians of San Clemente and Santa Catalina islands, spread to the nearby mainland and thence to southern and central California Indian tribes, including the Juaneño, Chumash, and Yokut. Consumption of the narcotic jimson weed (toloache) by young boys was part of the ritual. It induced them to have visions of animals while priests addressed them on proper behavior and threatened them for trans-

gressions with punishment from animals depicted in a sand painting, those creatures being the messengers of Chinigchinich,♦ a prophet or god.

Tolowa, Indians of the Athabascan♦ family, who resided in the drainage basin of the Smith River in present Del Norte County. Their prehistoric population of 1,000 was reduced to 150, according to the census of 1910. They were the principal dealers in dentalia shells, the main currency of northwestern California Indians. Their culture resembled those of the Hupa♦ and the Yurok.♦

Tomales Bay, see *Bodega Bay.*

Tomatoes, though not widely cultivated in California until the 20th century, have long since been the major vegetable crop of California, which produces far more for the nation's consumption than any other state. In 1970 tomatoes for processing were grown on 141,000 acres and had a value of $83,543,000, while tomatoes for the fresh market were grown on 35,700 acres and had a value of $80,504,000. The former are raised mainly in the Delta lands and Yolo County, the latter primarily in San Diego and Orange counties. Major canneries are located in Tracy, Stockton, Sacramento, San Jose, and Oakland. The University of California, Davis, has developed canning varieties of tomatoes that can be harvested mechanically with such requirements as consistency, firmness, and good solids content, and one strain (No. 82) is more square than round, which makes it easier to handle.

Tomoyé Press, see *Elder, Paul.*

Tongs, see *Chinese* and *Six Companies.*

TOOMEY, BILL (WILLIAM ANTHONY TOOMEY) (1939–), Philadelphia-born track star, settled in Santa Barbara as a schoolteacher while training for the decathlon. He was four times (1965–68) the American decathlon champion and won the Olympic Games gold medal in the fourth year.

Topanga Canyon, located in the Santa Monica Mts., descends to the beach of the same name between Malibu and Santa Monica in Los Angeles County. It bears a Gabrieleño Indian name. In it is a State Park.

Topatopa Mountains, in Ventura County, lie behind the Ojai Valley and are part of the Transverse Ranges.♦ They get their name from a Chumash word meaning "many gophers."

Top of the Mark, see *Mark Hopkins Hotel.*

TORQUEMADA, JUAN, see *Vizcaíno, Sebastián.*

Torrance, industrial and tract-home city of Los Angeles County, approximately midway between the Los Angeles Airport and San Pedro. A tourist attraction, a Bavarian beer garden, is located there. In 1970 the city's population was 134,584.

Torrey Pines State Park, south of Del Mar, San Diego County, to whose steep cliffs cling a species of pine, 15 to 40 feet tall, found only there and on Santa Rosa Island. The old, twisted, and rangy trees were identified as a separate species by Joseph Le Conte and later named for Professor John Torrey (1796–1873) of Columbia University, Le Conte's mentor, who had reported on the plant collections of Frémont's first two expeditions and visited California (1865, 1872).

Tortilla Flat, novel by John Steinbeck,♦ published in 1935. Presenting *paisanos*♦ of Monterey, the story sentimentally depicts their easy-going way of life, innocently amoral and warmly companionable.

Tortoise, a land-living turtle,♦ of which only three species exist in the U.S. The only one native to California is the *desert tortoise,* which ranges through the Mojave Desert and the uplands east of Salton Lake. It is also found in southern Nevada and extreme southwestern Utah and western Arizona, as well as parts of Mexico. It grows 6 to 14$\frac{1}{2}$ inches long and has a high-domed shell. Commercial collecting for the pet trade has made it an endangered species protected by law. In 1973 it was named the official state reptile. The *Texas tortoise* has been inadvertently introduced into California by pet owners in recent years.

Totemic moiety, see *Miwok.*

TOTHEROH, DAN (1895–1976), San Francisco born playwright who, after graduation from the University of California, directed its Greek Theatre, in which he first produced his *Wild Birds* (1922), a tragic tale about an orphan girl and a reform-school boy. It became a successful Broadway production. Other plays include *Distant Drums* (1932), about the pioneer West, and *Mother Lode* (1934). He also wrote novels.

Tourist attractions, sites throughout the state that are as various as the diverse interests of the travelers themselves. Excluding the cities, with their parks, zoos, museums, and other appealing features, like San Francisco's cable cars and Los Angeles' Olvera St., the major interests include numerous scenic attractions.♦ Among them are the national and state parks, national and state forests, and national and state monuments. Particularly popular places include Lake Tahoe, Yosemite, Muir Woods, the wineries of Napa Valley, Big Sur and Carmel, the beaches of southern California, and Death Valley. Favorite historical buildings include the missions, Fort Ross, various adobes at Monterey and elsewhere, and the gold rush settlements of the Mother Lode region, such as Columbia. Modern edifices visited by many travelers include the Hearst Castle at San Simeon and Death Valley Scotty's Castle. There are also many commercial attractions: Busch Gardens, Disneyland, Great America, H.M.S. *Queen Mary,* Knott's Berry Farm, Lion Country Safari, Magic Mountain, Marineland, and Universal City. (*See also individual entries.*)

Tournament of Roses, see *Roses, Tournament of.*

Town Hall, Los Angeles organization, open to general membership, whose programs, similar to those of the Commonwealth Club of San Francisco, are carried on in weekly forums and study groups devoted to special topics.

Townsend Plan, financial program conceived during the Depression (1933) by Dr. Francis E. Townsend, an elderly unemployed physician of Long Beach. Dr. Townsend founded an organization called Old Age Revolving Pensions, Ltd., proposing that all U.S. citizens over age 60 receive a pension of $200 a month (financed by a federal sales tax) that would have to be spent within 30 days, thereby creating prosperity by stimulating the circulation of money. The plan was embraced by many elderly persons who organized Townsend Clubs, and politicians wooed their votes or devised variants of the Townsend idea, such as the Ham 'n Eggs scheme.♦ It even affected national politics and probably helped to stimulate President Roosevelt's Social Security program.

Toyon, evergreen shrub or tree sometimes reaching 30 feet in height, flowering in June and July and producing berries ranging from scarlet to yellow from October through January, and hence acquiring the names "Christmasberry" and "California holly." It grows in the Sierra and the Coast Range and its foothills, and is frequently planted in gardens. Indians cooked the berries and ground them into meal, and the Spanish used them to make a drink.

Track and Field Sports, introduced as organized competitions by teams of the Olympic Club, the nation's oldest athletic association of its kind (1860 ff.), and the Los Angeles Athletic Club (est. 1880). Colleges and universities soon joined the movement: the University of California fielded its first team in 1893 and Stanford organized one in 1894 under W. M. Hunter. As early as 1904, world records had been set by two Californians: Norman Dole of Stanford in the pole vault and Ralph Rose of Healdsburg in the shot put. Under the guidance of such outstanding coaches as Walter Christie, Dean Cromwell, Brutus Hamilton, and R. L. Templeton, California colleges and clubs have produced a great many Olympic champions and world record holders. Among the most famous have been Charles Dumas, Ben Eastland, Lee Evans, Bud Houser, Rafer Johnson, Bob Mathias, Perry O'Brien, Charles Paddock, Bob Richards, Bob Seagren, Steve Smith, Tommie Smith, Bill Toomey, Cornelius Warmerdam, and Mal Whitfield.

Fine coaching has been assisted by popular interest and support, excellent facilities, and good year-round weather to develop track stars and leading teams. After the NCAA held its first national competition in 1921, California colleges and universities often won championships, holding the title 36 times in the first 55 years. Noncollegiate track clubs, such as the California Striders, have also been very successful in their national Amateur Athletic Union championship. Women competitors from California have also set national records. The major event in the state's history of track and field was the location of the Olympic Games in Los Angeles (1932), where some 400,000 spectators watched the competition during the Tenth Olympiad, although only one local participant, William Miller of Stanford, won a gold medal, for the pole vault. (*See also individual entries.*)

Tracy, market and food-processing center in southwestern San Joaquin County, also a transportation junction. A huge pumping plant provides water for the Delta-Mendota Canal of the Central Valley Project and the long California Aqueduct.♦ The population in 1970 was 14,724.

TRACY, SPENCER (1900–67), Wisconsin-born actor, after a stage career went to Hollywood (1930) and there for more than 30 years was cast in numerous major films. He was outstanding for his professional talents, expressed in diverse roles that drew upon his own honest, manly, unglamorous, sincerely decent, and humorous personality. His films include *Captains Courageous* (1937), *The Old Man and the Sea* (1958), and *Judgment at Nuremberg* (1961).

Trader Vic, see *Bergeron, Victor.*

Trails, the major transcontinental routes developed from the U.S. frontier in the 1840s to California were the Oregon Trail, with its southward extension from Fort Hall (Idaho), which became the California Trail, and its various cut-offs, of which the most notorious was that promoted by Lansford Hastings; the Old Spanish Trail, which dated back to the crossing of Escalante (1776) but was first developed for trade in 1829; the Sonora Trail, blazed by Anza (1774, 1775–76); and the Mormon Battalion Trail from Santa Fe to San Diego.♦ The major land route within California was El Camino Reál,♦ created to link the missions. Modern trails in California include the John Muir Trail through the High Sierra, created between 1915 and 1931, part of the Pacific Crest Trail, extending from Mexico to Canada, with 1,600 miles through deserts and mountains in the state, one-third completed between 1968 and 1977.

Transamerica Corporation, see *Giannini, A. P.*

Transamerica Pyramid, San Francisco office building designed by William Pereira for the headquarters of the great holding company. Constructed (1972) on the site of the old Montgomery Block and the Bank Exchange saloon, it tapers upward 48 stories, adding a distinctive form to the city's downtown skyline.

Transcontinental railroad, see *Big Four* and *Central Pacific.*

Transportation, in the earliest days was mainly by ship, since there were no good land routes from Mexico or overland from the U.S., and although a south-north road, the Camino Reál, linked the missions, communication between the pueblos was mainly by coastal vessels. By the time of the gold rush, many newcomers sailed around the Horn or crossed the Isthmus of Panama. They came also in large numbers via covered wagons over the California Trail. Communication was soon improved by the use of clipper ships, overland stages and other stagecoach lines, and the Pony Express.

The modern period of transportation began with the completion of the Central Pacific link with the Union Pacific, creating a transcontinental railroad (1869). In succeeding years, other railroads opened new routes within the state and to the rest of the U.S., as lines were laid by the Northwestern Pacific, Santa Fe, Southern Pacific, Union Pacific, and Western Pacific.

A State Bureau was founded (*c.* 1895) to improve roads for wagons, and early in the 20th century it began to develop highways for automobiles. To assist further the nearly 100,000 vehicles on the roads about 1910, an Automobile Club of Southern California, the forerunner of the California State Automobile Association, was founded. As roads were augmented and greatly improved, decade after decade, until the first freeway was built in 1940, the state came more and more to rely upon the automobile and to develop a car culture. Elaborate bus systems with large and comfortable vehicles drew more and more passengers from the railroads. Ever larger and more numerous trucks of diverse sorts, some equipped with refrigeration, others devised to tow special double-decked carriers of many automobiles, provided increasing competition to freight trains.

By the 1970s more than 2,000,000 trucks were traveling the state's highways. But passenger cars remain the major form of automotive transportation, with some 11,000,000 owned by the approximately 20,000,000 people in the state. Some regions of California depend upon the automobile for all their transportation, and even in the largest city, Los Angeles, and its environs, the commonplace use of private cars has long since ended the monopoly of Henry E. Huntington's great network of the Pacific Electric Railway, just as the building of bridges across San Francisco Bay ended the long heyday of the ferries.

Commercial airlines for passengers and freight are only about a half-century old, but various kinds of aircraft, from jumbo jets to small helicopters, serve the state through numerous airports designed for intrastate, national, and international flights. Indicative of the volume of traffic is the fact that 5,100,000 passengers traveled between Los Angeles and San Francisco in one year (1970–71).

Competition from automobiles and airplanes has led to modernization and diversification of railroad apparatus, particularly for freight, with the creation of such equipment as the piggyback freight cars built to pick up truck trailers and rack cars constructed to carry automobiles in ingeniously engineered spaces. Ships have also been developed to carry greater cargoes more rapidly by such devices as direct loading with cranes of goods prepacked in containers and loading of materials on barges carried aboard the big vessels. The barges are landed independently in harbors while the mother ship sails on to its next port. Huge transoceanic supertankers for oil have also augmented the shipment of foreign petroleum directly to ports with pipelines.

The great and constantly increasing demands for improved transportation to meet the needs of an ever-growing state population have led not only to the devising of new systems like that of BART for the San Francisco Bay area but to the creation (1972) of the California Department of Transportation, which links previously separate state offices and makes plans for new schemes and future programs. (*See also individual entries.*)

Trans-Sierra Intermontane Region, see *Desert*.

Transverse Ranges, sometimes called the Los Angeles Ranges or Southern California Mts., are also confused with the Coast Range, which are north-south mountains, whereas these are east-west oriented. From west to east they are the Santa Ynez, Topatopa, Santa Susana, Santa Monica, San Gabriel, and San Bernardino mountains. Thus they run from Gaviota Pass to San Gorgonio Pass, more than 240 miles, behind the cities of Santa Barbara, Ventura, Santa Paula, Los Angeles, Pasadena, and San Bernardino. All land routes from north and east into southern California come through or around the Transverse Ranges, major passes including Gaviota, Cajon, and Tejon, with San Gorgonio at their southeastern end. The highest are San Gorgonio (11,502 ft.), San Bernardino (10,624 ft.), and San Antonio, or "Old Baldy" (10,064 ft.). Mt. Wilson, with its famous observatory, is in the San Gabriel Mts. The Channel Islands are an extension of the Transverse Ranges into the ocean. (*See also individual entries.*)

Trapping, see *Fur trapping*.

TRASK, J[OHN] B[OARDMAN] (1824–79), Massachusetts-born doctor, moved to California (1850) and soon joined the Mexican Boundary survey. He then became the first State Geologist of California and published reports on the state's geology and topographical maps (1853–55). He was a founder of the California Academy of Sciences.

Travel Town, a transportation museum located in Griffith Park, Los Angeles.

Travis Air Force Base, major headquarters for trans-pacific cargo and troop handling. With it is associated a large medical center. Located near Fairfield (Solano County), north of San Rafael, it was named for Brigadier General Robert F. Travis, killed there in an accident (1950).

Treasure Island, flat man-made island in San Francisco Bay just north of Yerba Buena Island, to which it is linked by a causeway. Created for the Golden Gate International Exposition♦ (1939), it was intended to be San Francisco's airport, but it was recognized as being too small. It then became a U.S. Navy station and headquarters of its Western Sea Frontier.

Treasurer, elected at the same time and for the same term as the governor, is responsible for the sale and redemption of state bonds and the investment of state funds.

Trees of Mystery, tourist attraction north of Klamath in Del Norte County, consists of a park of redwood trees, some of which are very large and have exotic shapes, like those of animals.

Trinidad Head, promontory in the bay of the same name in northern Humboldt County. A granite memorial cross replaces the wooden one, erected June 11, 1775, the Trinity Sunday for which its name was chosen by Capt. Heceta and Lt. Francisco de la Bodéga y Cuadro♦ on their exploration of the coast. It was once the site of a whaling station, and the nearby town of Trinidad was a center for the Trinity County gold mines.

Trinity Alps, see *Klamath Mountains.*

Trinity County, one of the original 27 counties (1850), derives its name from Trinidad Head,♦ discovered by Capt. Heceta and Lt. Bodéga y Cuadro (1775). Trinity is bounded on the north by Siskiyou County, on the east by Shasta and Tehama counties, on the south by Mendocino County, and on the west by Humboldt County. Over three-quarters of the county's area lies within Trinity National Forest, which itself contains the Trinity Alps Wilderness Area and parts of Shasta and Six Rivers National Forest. Jedediah Smith ventured through the rough Klamath Mts. area in 1828. Pierson B. Reading♦ came in 1848 on explorations that led him to call the major river Trinity because he mistakenly assumed it emptied into Trinidad Bay. Reading also discovered gold, which

brought many more pioneers via the Trinity Trail and the Hyampom Trail that leads through the settlement of Hayfork. The major community founded during the gold rush was Weaverville,♦ which has always been the county seat, but it is not nearly as large as it was during the early mining days. As part of the Central Valley Project, Trinity Dam impounds water from the river of that name to create Lewiston Lake and the larger Clair Engle Lake in the northeastern part of the county. In the southwestern part of the county is Ruth Dam, which creates the reservoir of that name on the Mad River. The county's major economic resources come from lumbering, wood products, and livestock, along with tourists attracted by camping, hiking, fishing, hunting, and skiing. In 1970 the county had a population of 7,615, which, with an area of 2,042,688 acres, gave it 2.4 persons per sq. mi.

Trinity River, called Hoopah by the Klamath Indians and given its present name (1845) on the mistaken assumption that it flowed into Trinidad Bay, actually branches from the Klamath River about 25 miles east of the coast and 25 miles north of Eureka. It runs south about 25 miles to split into the South Fork, which continues about 70 miles southeast, while the Trinity itself travels eastward to the Central Valley Project dam bearing its name and the resultant Clair Engle Lake, which is also fed by another part of the river to the north that forms the East Fork.

Trinity Trail, route blazed by Jedediah Smith♦ (1828) through the upper Sacramento Valley and up the coast to southern Oregon. It was traveled by Hudson's Bay Co. trappers and later by miners en route to the gold mines in Trinity County.

Trout, game fish of the salmon family of many types, four of which are native to the state. They are: (1) *cutthroat,* with ruddy markings under its gills and large black spots on its body; the *Lahontan* type living in the Truckee, Walker, and Carson rivers and drainages, as well as in Lake Tahoe; and the *coast* type found in coastal streams. (2) The *rainbow,* with iridescent markings, the most common type, varieties being found throughout California's lakes and streams. (3) The *golden,* noted for the shades of yellow and red on its underside and for its round black spots, native to the upper Kern River only but stocked throughout Sierra lakes and streams and selected (1947) as the symbolic state fish. And (4) the *Dolly Varden,* with olive-green back shading to a white underside and pinkish-yellow spots that resemble the cloth pattern for which it was named, found only in the McCloud River.

Three types have been introduced to the state: (1) the *eastern brook,* distinguished by reddish-brown fins tipped with white, the most common lake trout; (2) the *lake,* or *Mackinaw,* a large, dark gray fish from the Great Lakes, now the main type in Lake Tahoe and Donner Lake; and (3) the *brown,* with a dark brown or green back shading down to golden brown and a light underside, a native of Scotland, found in many California lakes and streams.

The *steelhead* is midway between a salmon and a trout but is considered a variety of *rainbow trout,* although much larger, reaching 20 pounds. *Steelhead* come from the ocean in summer and fall to ascend the Klamath, Eel, and Smith rivers and smaller streams for spawning in fresh headwaters. The state stocks about 20,500,000 trout annually, but pollution, logging activities, and highway and dam construction reduce their numbers drastically, and even though they may not be fished commercially, sportsmen find them ever fewer.

Truckee River, rises in the Sierra, flows into the south end of Lake Tahoe, out near Tahoe City, then northeast through Reno, to end its course of less than 100 miles in Nevada's Pyramid Lake. It was named by the party of Elisha Stevens for the Indian who directed them to it (1844). He was a member of the Paiute tribe and a grandfather of Sarah Winnemucca.

Truck gardening, the large-scale production of fresh vegetables and fruit for marketing, has long been an important part of California agriculture. In the early days, during the gold rush, vegetable growers were almost entirely limited to local sales, and they gardened on land close to the cities for whose markets the products were cultivated. By the late 1870s, the produce began to be sold over a wider area as railroads permitted fast and distant distribution. Simultaneously, production increased as cheap Chinese labor became available after work was finished on the transcontinental railroad. The Chinese were able to provide economically the intensive work required for most truck crops.

Among these major crops were beans and onions, produced in large quantities in the Delta, which early turned from subsistence farming because of its proximity to San Francisco as a market and the Bay as an outlet for shipping. The earliest refrigerator cars were introduced in the late 1870s, and in 1890 Edwin T. Earl♦ combined a refrigerator and ventilator railroad freight car to ship fruit across the continent. By 1890, fresh tomatoes from California were being shipped east, and the combination of this market and the increased population of the state brought about between 1899 and 1909 a doubling of the acreage devoted to growing vegetables. By 1919 California had 217,000 acres planted in truck crops and was the leading state in the growing of miscellaneous vegetables.

Changing dietary habits also affected production, so that lettuce, little eaten before 1910, came to be a major crop of the Salinas and Imperial valleys. California also became the chief producer of artichokes, asparagus, cantaloupes, carrots, cauliflower, celery, lima beans, onions, strawberries, and tomatoes (the largest vegetable crop), among other increasingly popular products of truck farms. The major agricultural centers became Imperial, Los Angeles, Sacramento, and San Joaquin counties, joined later by Monterey County, and, more recently, by Fresno County.

Other important truck-farming regions include the coastal areas of Santa Cruz and San Mateo counties, which grow 90% of the nation's Brussels sprouts, the Coachella and Pajaro valleys, the Inland Valleys of the Los Angeles region, Santa Clara Valley, and Orange County. In 1975 California led the nation in growing fresh market produce, accounting for about 43% of the country's most commonly consumed vegetables and melons.

TRUMAN, Ben[jamin] C[ummings] (1835–1916), born in Rhode Island, had a career as a journalist and worked on the staff of President Andrew Johnson before being sent as a special Post Office agent (1866–69) to California, where he founded many new post offices and reestablished the Butterfield mail route. He later reentered journalism as a correspondent for *The New York Times* and the *San Francisco Bulletin,* then as editor of the *Los Angeles Evening Express,* and finally as owner of the *Los Angeles Star* (1873–77). He next became a press agent for the Southern Pacific (1879–90), editing for it *The Wave,*♦ which had been a public relations journal for the Del Monte Hotel. His book-length writings include *Semi-Tropical California* (1874); the *Life, Adventures, and Capture of Tiburcio Vasquez* (1874); *The Field of Honor* (1884), a history of dueling; and *Occidental Sketches* (1881).

TRUMBO, Dalton (1905–77), Colorado-born author, whose best-known work was the melodramatic antiwar novel, *Johnny Got His Gun* (1939). He was a major writer of film scripts, but was blacklisted as one of the Hollywood Ten,♦ after which he often wrote scenarios under pseudonyms, for one of which he won an Academy Award, though he could not accept it.

Tübatulabal, Indians of the Kern River area whose territory extended halfway between the forks of that river and the present Bakersfield. Kroeber estimated that there were 1,000 Tübatulabal in pre-contact times, but the census of 1910 lists only 150. In their funeral rites, a designated person, called the Anangat, performed the mourning ceremony and the deceased was represented by an image, as among the Maidu, Yokut, and Luiseño.

Tujunga, town incorporated into Los Angeles, northeast of Burbank near the valley and creek of the same name on the edge of the San Gabriel Valley's mountains. Its name may mean "mountain range" in Gabrieleño. The area was the site of a disastrous forest fire in 1975 and a severe flood in 1978.

Tulare, small city in western Tulare County, lying in an agricultural area, grew up as a division center for the Southern Pacific Railroad. Frank Norris called it "Bonneville" in *The Octopus*. In 1970 it had a population of 16,235.

Tulare County, formed (1852) from the southern part of Mariposa County and the northern part of Los Angeles County, was named for the tule marshlands of the lower San Joaquin Valley on its western side. Visalia has been the county seat since 1853. Fresno County lies on its north and west, and other contiguous counties (once partly in Tulare) are Kings on the west, Kern on the south, and Inyo on the east. Garcés and Moraga were early travelers through the area, and the Tulare Trail up the valley was pioneered by Jedediah Smith, Kit Carson, Joseph Walker, and Frémont, and later followed in part by the Butterfield Overland Stages. On the east the county is mountainous, almost entirely composed of Kings Canyon and Sequoia National parks and Sequoia National Forest. The last includes the world's largest sequoia, the General Sherman, once owned by the utopian Marxist colony, Kaweah Co-operative Commonwealth.♦ Mt. Whitney lies on the eastern border, partly in Inyo County.

Initially the county's economy was based on cattle and sheep ranching, to which some gold mining and lumbering were added. It then became the site of major wheat ranching on lands served by the Southern Pacific, and to which it laid claim, culminating in the Mussel Slough tragedy.♦ Part of that land now forms Kings County. Later Tulare became a center for citrus fruit growing and packing around Porterville, and olive raising and packing around Lindsay. Other important crops have been grapes (particularly Thompson seedless), sugar beets, walnuts, alfalfa, and other fruits and vegetables, while livestock ranching, poultry raising, and dairying are also important. From 1909 to 1918 an important town was Allensworth,♦ a community created by and for blacks. In 1970 the county population was 188,322. With an area of 3,100,096 acres, it had 39 persons per sq. mi.

Tule, term for cattail, bullrush, and similar reeds, derived from an Aztec word, used commonly in California from the era of Spanish settlement. Indians (e.g. the Modoc) used the reeds to make raft-like boats. They also ate its potato-like root, as did Chinese settlers. The reeds were used by the Spanish to support roof tiles in mission construction. Since they grow in marshland, places of this sort often bear such names as Tule Slough and Tule Lake (the Siskiyou County site of the Modoc War). Stockton was originally called Tuleburg. Tulare County takes its name from a derivative of the word. (Tularemia, a disease transmitted by infected rabbits and squirrels, is so called only because it was first identified in Tulare County.) Heavy fog♦ in marshy country is often called tule fog.

TULLY, RICHARD WALTON (1877–1945), born in Nevada City, graduated from the University of California, and became a popular playwright with such works as *Rose of the Rancho* (1906), written with David Belasco.

Tuna, ocean fish whose species, found off the California shore south of Point Concepcion, include *albacore, bluefin,* and *bonito.* Although fished for sport, the main catch is commercial and has been since about 1900. The catch, some 280,000,000 pounds annually since the late 1960s, is taken by large purse-seine ships that stay at sea for some time to get their huge hauls. California supplies most of the tuna for national consumption, and the greatest part of it is canned.

Tungsten, hard white metallic element also called wolfram, found in the minerals scheelite and wolframite, is used for electric light filaments and as an element incorporated in steel alloys. The largest U.S. mine is on the upper slopes of Mt. Morgan (13,729 ft.), 20 miles northwest of Bishop (Inyo County). Another major source is at the ghost town of Atolia in the Mojave Desert.

TUNNEY, JOHN [VARICK] (1934–   ), born in New York City, son of Gene Tunney, heavyweight boxing champion of the world (1926–28), after graduation from Yale and a law practice in New York, was admitted to the California bar (1963). After serving three terms in Congress as a Representative from Riverside, he was elected to a term in the U.S. Senate (1971–77).

Tuolumne County, one of the original 27 counties (1850), has always had Sonora♦ as its seat. Calaveras, Alpine, and Mono counties lie on its north. Mono also lies on its east, and Madera and Mariposa counties on its south. Across the boundary of the Stanislaus River on the west lies Calaveras County, and below it Stanislaus County. Most of Tuolumne County beyond its southwestern section lies in the Stanislaus National Forest, across which runs the Sierra Nevada. The northern part of Yosemite National Park lies in the county's eastern segment.

The county name derives from that of an Indian tribe, either Miwok or Yokut, which was visited by the first white explorer, Gabriel Moraga (1806). Later voyagers through this area were transcontinental travelers like John Bidwell's Party (1841) and those who went during the gold rush. Many took the route through Sonora Pass (9,628 feet in elevation), in the northeast corner of the county, but other routes of entry include Conness Pass and the now much used Tioga Pass♦ (9,941 feet in elevation), near which Mt. Dana (named for James Dwight Dana) rises to a height of 13,050 feet. In this eastern part of the county lies the spectacular Grand Canyon of the Tuolumne, where the Tuolumne River♦ drops 5,000 feet from Tuolumne Meadows down to Hetch Hetchy Reservoir.♦ To the west and north, outside Yosemite, lie numerous mountain lakes in the National Forest, including such resort areas as Twain-Harte, Long Barn, Strawberry, and Pine Crest along Dodge Ridge. Farther north and west on the county line lies the South Grove of the Calaveras Big Trees State Park.♦

The major mining activity occurred near or at Table Mt., a huge basalt mesa stretching some 30 miles along the Stanislaus River. Close to the northern end lies Columbia,♦ best preserved and most

restored of the southern mining towns. Near it is Sonora, the town in whose very streets rich diggings were uncovered. Four miles farther south is Jamestown, called Jimtown by Prentice Mulford and other residents. Close to both is Tuttletown. Beside its Jackass Hill was the cabin (now reconstructed) of the Gillis brothers, with whom Mark Twain spent five months during the winter of 1864–65. Farther down the Tuolumne River are the mining towns of Chinese Camp, site of a huge tong war (1856); Jacksonville, where the soil not only yielded gold but was used for the county's first orchard; and Big Oak Flat,♦ first mined and settled by James Savage.♦ On the Stanislaus River border lies the Melones Water Project,♦ and in the southwesternmost corner of Tuolumne County lies New Don Pedro Reservoir, another of the county's many developments for water and power.

Cattle ranching, lumbering, poultry raising, and field crops, in addition to tourism, are the mainstays of the economy. In 1970 the population was 188,322, which, with an area of 3,100,096 acres, gave the county 39.1 persons per sq. mi.

Tuolumne River, flows from Yosemite about 120 miles into the San Joaquin River northwest of Modesto. It runs through the spectacular Grand Canyon of the Tuolumne, whose western end is Hetch Hetchy,♦ and passes by Tuolumne Meadows campground (9,000 feet in elevation). The lower river was the site of gold-rush mining. The name was given by Gabriel Moraga (1806) after a Miwok or Yokut tribe that lived on the Stanislaus River.

Turkeys, see *Poultry.*

Turks in California, were always a very small part of the population. Some were brought in the 1850s to serve as drivers and keepers of camels♦ used as pack animals. From a different social and financial sphere came the most prominent (albeit distant) descendent of a Turk in California: James Ben Ali Haggin.♦

Turlock, see *Stanislaus County.*

Turtle, reptile having fresh water and marine types, both found in California. Of the former, the most common is the *western pond turtle,* found throughout the state west of the Cascade Range and Sierra Nevada except in the desert. The *desert tortoise*♦ is the official state reptile. The *spring softshell,* very aquatic, lives in the lower Colorado River and irrigation ditches, feeding on frogs and fish. The *snapping turtle, pond slider,* and *Texas tortoise* have been accidentally introduced into the state. Sea turtles include the *green, loggerhead,* and *leatherback,* the last by far the largest, living on marine animals and weighing up to 1,000 pounds.

TWAIN, MARK, see *Mark Twain.*

Twenty-mule teams, see *Borax.*

Twentynine Palms, San Bernardino County town, near which are located an Indian reservation and a large marine corps base used for artillery, bomb, and missile testing on its isolated Mojave Desert site. The town is now a resort community.

Twin Peaks, rising over 900 feet above central San Francisco at the head of Market St. These hills were once romantically called Los Pechos de la Chola ("The Breasts of the Indian Girl"). Although the city established a small park there (1915), much of the rest of the peaks has been covered with cheap, crowded, identical houses.

Two Years Before the Mast, personal narrative by Richard Henry Dana, Jr.,♦ published anonymously in 1840. Presented in the form of an extended diary, it was based on a succinct journal kept on the voyage. However, the final text was actually written after Dana's return, thus allowing the realistic details to be remembered, but from a distance, so as to depict "the life of a common sailor at sea as it really is,—the light and the dark together."

The work opens with Dana's change from his conventional patrician New England life as a Harvard student to his life as an ordinary seaman setting sail on the brig *Pilgrim* (Aug. 14, 1834) from Boston around Cape Horn to California, then a remote Mexican province. In a vivid but controlled style, presenting experiences with precise detail, Dana describes the routine as well as dramatic events, such as the drowning of a crew member during the 150-day voyage. In California waters (Jan. 13, 1835–May 8, 1836) the hard life continued aboard ship, climaxed by the flogging of two of Dana's shipmates by the dictatorial Capt. Thompson, but with relief afforded by visits to ports and pueblos.

Knowing Spanish, Dana was able to get a good sense of California life, which was thoroughly treated in his book. He admired the grace of the people, as in his description of the dancing of Don Juan Bandini at the marriage of Alfred Robinson to a de la Guerra daughter, but he also took a contemptuous Yankee view of the Latin's idleness and love of ease and luxury. Enjoyable months were spent ashore at a house curing hides and in association with such persons as Hope, a Kanaka "noble savage" who idolized Dana. However, he also underwent a good deal of drudgery collecting the hides, as well as making one daring, difficult, and successful effort to dislodge hides from a cleft in the high cliff over which they had been tossed, a feat recalled in the name Dana Point, given to the site near Laguna Beach.

After such experiences Dana was a changed man, and when he returned (May 8–Sept. 20, 1836) on the ship *Alert,* to which he had transferred, he discovered that the long voyage outward, the life in a new environment, and the stormy rounding of Cape Horn had assumed a significance of symbolic change, so that upon reaching Boston again "the emotions which I had so long anticipated feeling I did not find, and in their place was a state of very nearly entire apathy." In 1859 Dana wrote an appendix, "Twenty Four Years After," describing his nostalgic return visit that year as a distinguished lawyer, author, and pioneer. By that time California was greatly changed, and Americanized.

U

UCLA, initials used to designate the Los Angeles campus of the University of California,♦ located in the western part of the city near Beverly Hills. An outgrowth of the Los Angeles State Normal School (founded 1881), it became the "Southern Branch" of the University (1919) and achieved the status of a full-fledged institution (1927) parallel to the older Berkeley, from which it inherited a rich academic tradition. It established its own identity and distinction rapidly, and in 1929 it moved to its present campus in Westwood.

Under the aegis of President Sproul it moved early and on broad fronts into graduate instruction, granting the Ph.D. in 1936. During the 1930s and 40s it founded numerous professional schools, including a branch of the statewide College of Agriculture, the beginnings of a School of Business Administration, a College of Applied (later Fine) Arts, and law and medical schools. In 1935 it acquired the important rare book collection and building privately created by William Andrews Clark, and under Lawrence Clark Powell's administration of the University Library (1944–61) a fine, large library was formed with remarkable speed.

By 1960 it had become the peer of the Berkeley campus in stipulated enrollment (27,500) and diversity of programs and was widely esteemed for its high academic quality. By the 1960s UCLA was known for fielding national championship teams in both major and minor sports.

UGARTE, JUAN DE (1660–1730), faculty member of the Jesuit college of Mexico City who initially proposed the creation of the Pious Fund.♦ Later a missionary in Baja California, he taught the Indians to farm and to help him construct the area's first California-built ship, *El Triunfo de la Cruz* (1719), used for exploration and to reach sites for new missions.

Ukiah, seat of Mendocino County, located in a valley of the same name, perhaps derived from Pomo words for "deep valley." Orchards, vineyards, and lumbering are important to the area. The International Geodetic Association was established there (1898); it is an International Latitude Observatory, one of five in the world, all located on 39° 8' north latitude. In 1970 the city had a population of 10,095.

ULLOA, FRANCISCO DE (d. 1540?), Spanish soldier who accompanied Cortés in the conquest of Mexico and by whom he was sent (1539), against the orders of Viceroy Mendoza, to explore the Gulf of California♦ in hope of finding the legendary Seven Cities of Cíbola. His fleet of three ships sailed from Acapulco up the west coast to the head of the gulf, which indicated that Baja California was a peninsula, not an island. Then, as the first white man to round its tip, he sailed up its outer coast and discovered the island of Cedros before turning back. He never saw the shores of Alta California.

UNAMUNO, PEDRO DE, see *Manila galleons.*

Union Labor party, see *Ruef, Abe.*

Union Pacific Railroad, chartered (1862) for a line between Omaha and Sacramento. Its construction was begun (1865) under a corporation, the Crédit Mobilier, whose manipulation of funds and bribing of legislators created a national scandal. The line was speedily built westward to get as much government funding and as large land grants as possible, meeting its eastward-moving competitor, the Central Pacific,♦ at Promontory Point,♦ Utah (May 10, 1869), where the Gold Spike♦ was driven to connect the two tracks. Under Jay Gould and others it expanded its system and absorbed other lines, including the Oregon Short Line, with steamer connections to San Francisco. Mismanaged and bankrupt, the Union Pacific was bought by Edward H. Harriman (1897), whose reorganization included a line from Ogden to Los Angeles (1906), and a merger (1900–1913) with the Southern Pacific, dissolved by the federal government as a violation of the Sherman Anti-Trust Act.

Union party, a fusion of Republicans and Union Democrats (the Democratic party element formerly led by David Broderick) that existed during the Civil War, pledged to preservation of the Union.

It was headed by Senator John Conness; other major figures included Frederick Low and Cornelius Cole.

Union Square, landscaped block of downtown San Francisco, bounded by Powell, Post, Stockton, and Geary streets, the last named for Mayor John W. Geary, who gave the park's land to the city. Maiden Lane lies east of the square's center. In the middle of the formally planted park rises the 97-foot granite shaft topped by a bronze statue of Victory, sculpted by Robert I. Aitken to commemorate Admiral Dewey's victory at Manila (1898). A 4-level garage was constructed under the square in 1942.

United Farm Workers, see *Chavez, Cesar.*

United Nations, founded by the United Nations Conference on International Organization, which met in the San Francisco Opera House (April 25–June 26, 1945) and whose charter was signed there by 50 nations.

United States and Spanish California, see *Americans in the Spanish and Mexican periods.*

Universal City, located in North Hollywood, is the site of the oldtime Universal Studios, once the world's largest motion-picture production facility. Now used for films and television, it is also a great tourist attraction in which a tram tour takes visitors to see famous sets, entertainment by stunt actors, and a zoo for children.

University of California, state university, chartered (1868) and opened in Oakland (1869), having absorbed a College of California. It moved to the present Berkeley location in 1873 and graduated its first class (12 men) that year. Initially plagued by financial, administrative, and policy problems, not until 1895 did it enroll 1,000 students, 100 of them graduates. Nevertheless, it early attracted private gifts: an observatory on Mt. Hamilton from James Lick (1888); the forerunner of its medical school in San Francisco from Dr. H. H. Toland (1873); funds from the state's first chief justice, Judge Hastings, to establish the law school that bears his name; various benefactions from Phoebe Apperson Hearst,♦ including a physical plan for the Berkeley campus, an anthropology collection, and a building for mining; and a chair in classics, the Campanile, and the symbolic structural entry gate from the widow of an early trustee, Peder

Sather. The three latter structures were built by the University's notable architect, John Galen Howard.

Initially the great faculties were in agriculture (Ernest W. Hilgard), mining and geology (Joseph LeConte and Andrew C. Lawson), and engineering (Joseph N. ["Young Joe"] LeConte), as befitted the state's economy. But before long, important professors established other notable departments, e.g. George Davidson (mathematics and astronomy), Henry Morse Stephens (history), Herbert E. Bolton (history and director of The Bancroft Library♦), Charles Mill Gayley (English), A. L. Kroeber and R. H. Lowie (anthropology), J. C. Merriam (paleontology), Gilbert N. Lewis (chemistry), and Bernard Maybeck and J. G. Howard (architecture).

The University's energetic expansion and distinguished scholarship were stimulated by Benjamin Ide Wheeler, a classical philologist from Cornell who became the eighth president (1899–1919). During his administration, summer sessions were created to train teachers, great buildings were constructed, an increasingly distinguished faculty was augmented, the student body was enlarged to 7,000 (about half of them women) and 800 graduate students, a University Extension was created for general adult education, and the foundations of other campuses were started with the University Farm School at Davis, the Citrus Experiment Station at Riverside, the Scripps Institution for Biological Research at La Jolla, the Foundation for Medical Research in San Francisco, and the general Southern Branch in Los Angeles.

Further expansion of these and other parts of the University and augmented academic distinction occurred during the administration of Robert Gordon Sproul♦ (1930–58). Among the greatest contributions of his era were the development of co-equal campuses at Davis♦ in Yolo County♦ (est. 1905), Santa Barbara (est. 1944), and Riverside (est. 1954), and the effort to bring UCLA♦ to parity with Berkeley.

Berkeley continued to grow in academic distinction (its departments were rated second only to Harvard), particularly in the sciences. Its achievements in research were dramatized by the building of the world's first cyclotron, an invention of E. O. Lawrence,♦ the first of a number of faculty members to win the Nobel Prize, and by the manufacture of the original atomic bomb at the University's Los Alamos Laboratory in New Mexico. Sproul's last years were darkened by a bitter Loyalty Oath Controversy.♦

Berkeley Chancellor Clark Kerr♦ followed

Sproul as president (1958–67). To cope with the expanding population of the state and the University, he devised a Master Plan for what he called a multiversity that added still more campuses—at San Diego (1959), Santa Cruz (1961), and Irvine (1965). Kerr also raised the level of all campuses and led in the shaping of an overall program for the state's higher education♦ by assigning specific roles to each element of the tripartite system of junior colleges, state colleges (later including state universities), and the University, which was given special responsibility for graduate studies. Kerr's dynamic administration was ended by the student unrest related to the Free Speech Movement♦ that began at Berkeley (1964). It led eventually to Kerr's ouster by a split Board of Regents, whose majority was in accord with the conservative views of newly inaugurated Gov. Reagan, under whose administration the University was curbed financially and treated unsympathetically. Despite continuing stringent budgets, the University retained a great reputation as a leader in higher education.

University of San Francisco, private, Jesuit, coeducational institution, founded (1855) by Father Anthony Maraschi with support of the city's Italian community. Its original name, St. Ignatius College, was preserved until 1930, and its enrollment was restricted to men until 1964. The 21-acre urban campus has colleges of Liberal Arts; Science; Business Administration; Schools of Nursing and Law; and the Gleeson Library, which includes a good rare-book collection. The Sutro Library♦ is also located there, although it is a part of the State Library. In the 1970s the University had over 400 faculty members and some 6,000 students.

University of Southern California, nondenominational private coeducational institution founded (1880) by the Methodist Episcopal Church at its present downtown Los Angeles site, then a rural area. During the region's population boom (coincidental with the university's first decade) it ex-

panded rapidly and tried to establish branches elsewhere in southern California, but it had to retrench in the 1890s. Under the presidency of Rufus Bernhard von KleinSmidt (1921–46) it became truly nondenominational in faculty and student body and expanded its curricula, including schools of Education, Engineering, Medicine, and Library Service. It already had schools of law and of dentistry and an oceanographic institute established by G. Allan Hancock.♦ Under the impetus of Professor Rockwell D. Hunt♦ it began to grant the Ph.D. in 1924. Its sense of involvement with its region has led to a reputation as a community-service institution. It has the largest enrollment of any private university in the state, with a registration in 1970 that was over 20,000, taught by a faculty of nearly 2,000. The symbol of the university is a Trojan warrior, and its well-known football teams are called Trojans.

University of the Pacific, coeducational nondenominational institution founded by the Methodist Church (1851) at San Jose. In 1951 it moved to Stockton and in 1961 changed its name from College to University, at the same time establishing the first of its residential colleges, each specializing in a field of learning.

Uranium, radioactive element produced in modest amounts from deposits found mostly in the Sierra Nevada, Mojave Desert, and Great Basin. Although known in the first area as early as 1893, it was not marketed until 1954, when the need for nuclear power began to be developed.

USC, initials used to designate the University of Southern California.♦

Utilities, see *Electricity.*

Utopian Communities, see *Fountain Grove; Harris, Thomas Lake; Holy City; Kaweah, Llano del Rio; Point Loma;* and *Sienkiewicz, Henryk.* Also see *Cults.*

V

Vacaville, small city in Solano County,♦ named for the Vaca family. It is the center for fruit growing (early cherries) and processing. A state prison facility is located there. Edwin Markham lived and farmed there as a boy, as did Carleton Parker and Willis Jepson.

VACHELL, HORACE ANNESLEY (1861–1955), English-born rancher and author, educated at Harrow and Sandhurst, moved to California (1881), settling near San Luis Obispo. He not only ranched and sold real estate (helping to develop Paso Robles), but also introduced polo to California and considered his adopted land a sportsman's paradise. On it he commented more realistically in his novels, *Drama in Sunshine* (1898), a story of land speculation; *The Procession of Life* (1899); and *Bunch Grass* (1912), short stories about southern California changing from ranching to real estate subdivision. He returned to England in 1898, but continued to write fiction as well as autobiographical and descriptive works about California, such as *Distant Fields* (1937).

VALENTINO, RUDOLPH (1895–1926) [stage name of Rodolfo Guglielmi], Italian-born actor, came to the U.S. (1913), where after working at odd jobs he got a bit part in a motion picture which led to his casting in *The Four Horsemen of the Apocalypse* (1921). That film brought him stardom and idolization as the quintessentially romantic Latin lover of great sex appeal. Other films include *The Sheik* (1921), *Blood and Sand* (1922), *Monsieur Beaucaire* (1923), and *The Son of the Sheik* (1926). His sudden death caused an hysterical outburst of grief, encouraged by his studio, that led to melodramatic mourning at his huge funeral in New York and burial in Hollywood.

Vallecito Mountains, range in the midpart of the Anza-Borrego State Park.♦

VALLEJO, a leading California family founded by Ignacio Vicente Ferrer Vallejo (1748–1832), a native of Jalisco, Mexico, who went to California as a soldier with the expedition of Rivera y Moncada♦ (1774). He served at seven of Serra's eight missions and was granted a large *rancho* near the present Watsonville (1824). His house there came to be called the Casa Materna because it was the first, or mother, of all the Vallejo properties and dwellings. It was also known as the Glass House because of its many windows. He married María Antonio Lugo, and their thirteen children included daughters who married into the Alvarado and Soberanes families and Rosalia, who wed Jacob Leese. His sons included José de Jesus Vallejo (1798–1882), grantee of a vast *rancho* in the present Alameda County; Mariano Vallejo,♦ the military leader and great landowner on whose properties were established the towns of Vallejo and Benicia; José Manuel Salvador Vallejo (1813–76), whose wife María de la Luz Carrillo, was a sister of Mariano Vallejo's wife and aided Mariano in ranching and military enterprises and was taken prisoner with him at the outset of the Bear Flag Revolt; and Juan Antonio Vallejo (1816–57).

VALLEJO, MARIANO GUADALUPE (1808–90), leading member of his generation of the Vallejo family, the second in California, began his military career as a 15-year-old cadet at the Monterey garrison. At age 21 he became commander of the detachment that put down the uprising of Indians of Mission San José under Estanislao;♦ the following year he supported Padrés in his opposition to the policies and administration of Gov. Victoria.♦ In 1832 he married Francisca Benicia Carrillo (1815–91), whose sister, María de la Luz, wed Vallejo's brother José Manuel, allying two important families of *Californios*. Mariano and his wife had 16 children. Under Gov. Figueroa he was put in command of the northern frontier of California as a precaution against Russian encroachment and Indian troubles, as well as being named administrator of the Solano mission during the period of secularization. In these capacities and in this removed region, the General created a feudal barony, with his Casa Grande facing the plaza of the new pueblo of Sonoma that he founded. There he introduced vineyards and made the region's first wine.

In time, his estates included Rancho Soscal in present Solano County (on which the towns of

Vallejo♦ and Benicia♦ were later laid out during the era of American rule), and a large *rancho* at Petaluma, where he built his adobe home. After the death of Figueroa (1835), Vallejo supported his nephew Alvarado♦ in proclaiming a briefly independent state of California (1836). Although at first named military commander, Vallejo fell out with his nephew over the administration of mission properties, and having deported Alvarado's agent, Hartnell, he was left to live his own independent life in his part of California. Into this area Americans began more and more to infiltrate, and he countenanced them and the likelihood of U.S. annexation, considering them better than the divided and disorganized local governments. Nevertheless, at the outbreak of the Bear Flag Revolt he and his brother Salvador were jailed in Sutter's Fort for two months. Upon release, he worked to have California become part of the U.S. and was elected to the Constitutional Convention and to the new state's first Senate. In this capacity, he tried to make Benicia the capital. His last years were spent as a patriarchal figure on the Sonoma County *rancho* where he built a Victorian frame house called Lachryma Montis,♦ in which he lived after his Casa Grande burned down (1867).

Vallejo, city founded (1850) by Mariano Vallejo on his *rancho* where the Napa River flows into San Pablo Bay. The state legislature accepted the General's offer to create a capital there, but after one week (Jan. 5–12, 1852) they found the facilities insufficient and moved to Sacramento, returning (Jan. 3–Feb. 4, 1853) for a second and final try before going on to Benicia. Nevertheless, the town flourished because of the founding (1853), at nearby Mare Island, of a U.S. Navy shipyard. In time Vallejo became a railroad terminus and a shipping port for wheat, as well as the site of a maritime academy. In 1970 the population was 66,733.

Valley of the Moon, see *Sonoma Valley.*

Valley of the Moon, The, novel by Jack London, published in 1913, is based partly on the author's own experiences as a laborer in Oakland and later in the art colony of Carmel. It finds a solution to economic problems not in socialism, but in a Jeffersonian return to the land.

VAN BROCKLIN, NORMAN (1926–), South Dakota-born football player reared in Walnut Creek. After playing quarterback for the University of Oregon he joined the Los Angeles Rams (1949–57)

where he teamed successfully with Bob Waterfield♦ and made records in passing and punting. He later played with and coached other professional teams.

VANCE, ROBERT H. (fl. 1849–76), photographer who moved from New York to California (1849–51), where he made some 300 daguerreotypes of the mining country. He established a photographic studio in San Francisco (1852–64) and at the end of his career sold it to W. H. Rulofson and his partner, Bradley. His scenic views have been praised by Ansel Adams for their "clarity of line and edge, the simple arrangement of mass, the beauty of richness of tonal values."

VANCOUVER, GEORGE (1758–98), English naval captain sent (1791) to undertake an exploratory voyage around the world that led him to chart the west coast of North America. During his visit to San Francisco Bay (Nov. 1792), he was well received by Argüello and Hermenegildo Sal♦ and became the first foreigner to visit inland sites (Santa Clara) in a viewing of missions that took him to Monterey and San Diego. He returned twice in 1793 (May, Oct.–Nov.) to New Albion, as he consistently called California, emphasizing its English discovery by Drake, and in Nov.–Dec. 1794 came back to Monterey for a last visit. His fine maps and good account of the Spanish settlements, mission program, and commercial prospects appeared in his work, *A Voyage of Discovery* . . . (London, 3 vols., 1798).

Vandenberg Air Force Base, military installation of nearly 100,000 acres near Lompoc, created to test intercontinental ballistic missiles and to launch satellites. It was named (1958) for Gen. H. S. Vandenberg, Chief of Staff, U.S. Air Force (1948–53).

VAN DYKE, JOHN C[HARLES] (1856–1932), professor of the history of art at Rutgers College in his native New Jersey and author of numerous books in the field, first went to California (1897) to visit his brother, Theodore S. Van Dyke,♦ long a newspaperman in Los Angeles and San Diego and the author of *Southern California.* John C. was fascinated by the desert and in numerous trips observed its light, colors, and shapes with eyes that had already appreciated Monet and the Impressionists. The result was *The Desert, Further Studies in Natural Appearances* (1901), a sequel to his *Nature for Its Own Sake* (1898), and the progenitor of the work of Mary Austin, J. Smeaton Chase, George Wharton James, and others.

VAN DYKE, THEODORE S[TRONG] (1840–1923), member of a distinguished New Jersey family and brother of John C.,♦ moved to California for his health (1875), for which reason he lived outdoors as much as possible while writing for Los Angeles and San Diego newspapers. His several books include the enthusiastic *Southern California* (1886); *Millionaires of a Day* (1890), a satirical novel about the real estate boom of the 80s; and two works on San Diego, whose titles described it variously as a place of advantages and America's Italy.

VAN ERP, DIRK (1860–1933), Dutch-born craftsman, came to the U.S. (1886), and while working as a marine coppersmith at Mare Island began to create the art metalwork (1900) that led him to found a shop in San Francisco for the tableware, lamps, vases, and other works he designed. His craft and business were continued by his son of the same name.

VAN NESS, JAMES (1807–72), born in Vermont (the son of a governor), after graduation from Yale and a legal career in Virginia and Georgia, moved to San Francisco (1849). There he was elected mayor (1855–56) and confirmed the land ordinance bearing his name that he had sponsored as an alderman. It provided for a survey of the city west of Larkin St. to Divisadero (the Western Addition) and southwest of Ninth St. to grant land to persons already in possession of it, to divide the area into blocks and lots, and to reserve sites for schools, hospitals, and other public purposes, including the open area that forms Golden Gate Park. Van Ness Ave. was named for him. He moved to San Luis Obispo (1871) and from there was elected to the state Senate.

VAN NUYS, ISAAC N[EWTON] (1835–1912), moved to California (1865) from New York State for his health and there became a major rancher in San Diego County and the San Fernando Valley. With his father-in-law, Isaac Lankershim, he was a leading grower of wheat. The San Fernando Valley city of Van Nuys was named for him in the year of his death.

Van Nuys, city in the central San Fernando Valley of Los Angeles County, is a mixed residential and industrial settlement. Busch Gardens♦ is a tourist attraction associated with a local brewery. The city was named for Isaac Van Nuys,♦ and in 1970 it had a population of 149,000.

VAN SLOUN, FRANK (1879–1938), Minnesota-born painter, after a decade in New York associated with realists who formed part of the Ash Can school of art, moved to San Francisco (1911). There he continued his frank use of lower- and middle-class life for genre subjects but also painted murals, some in association with Maynard Dixon.

Vara, Spanish measurement approximating a British yard, equal to 33 inches, used in descriptions of land in early California.

VARIAN, RUSSELL (1898–1959), Washington-born scientist, after graduation from Stanford (1925), with his brother Sigurd (1901–61) invented and developed the klystron tube, which is essential for radar and television reception.

VÁSQUEZ, TIBURCIO (1835–75), notorious stagecoach robber and horse and cattle thief, who headed a gang that operated in his native Monterey County but also elsewhere in the state. He was captured in Los Angeles (1874) and executed for murder. An account of his activities, *Life, Adventures and Capture* (1874), was written by Ben C. Truman.

Vegetables, an important part of California's agriculture, the state's varying climate, terrain, and soil allowing the growth of every species. Many varieties were introduced by the fathers during the early years of the missions, but large-scale cultivation of crops began only after the gold rush. This increased substantially after the transcontinental railroad was completed and refrigerator cars were introduced (1877), permitting large exports to eastern markets. Beans, onions, potatoes, asparagus, and lettuce were among the first vegetables to be shipped east in quantities. Development of food processing and canning also substantially affected the greater growing of vegetables.

California currently leads the nation in the raising of vegetables, in 1970 producing 38% of the 27 principal fresh market vegetables consumed in the U.S. Tomatoes are the state's most valuable crop, but California also leads the country in production of artichokes, asparagus, avocados, broccoli, Brussels sprouts, carrots, cauliflower, celery, lettuce, lima beans, spinach, and squash. Irrigation and migratory labor have made California suitable for large-scale growing. Particularly important areas include the Sacramento River Delta, for asparagus, beans, onions, potatoes, and tomatoes; the Great Central Valley, for asparagus, cantaloupe, tomatoes, and white potatoes; Santa Clara Valley, for corn, cucumbers, and tomatoes; San Mateo and Santa Cruz counties, for over 90% of the nation's Brussels sprouts; Salinas Valley, for a great variety of crops, including artichokes, beans, broccoli, carrots, cauliflower, celery, lettuce, onions, sugar beets, and tomatoes; and the Oxnard Plain, for a variety of crops, including significant quantities of lima beans.

Other parts of southern California, including Orange, Riverside, and San Bernardino counties, are large growers of various vegetables; Coachella Valley produces large amounts of asparagus, sweet corn, and carrots; Imperial Valley raises great lettuce crops; and San Diego county is a great grower of tomatoes and avocados, the latter a vegetable that began to find a market only after World War I and that is grown almost exclusively in southern California. *(See also individual entries.)*

VENEGAS, MIGUEL (1680–1764), Spanish missionary in Mexico whose writings relate to California history. Missionary work in Baja California under Salvatierra◆ was treated in *El Apostol Mariano representado en la vida del V.F. Juan María de Salvatierra* (Mexico, 1754). An argument to extend to Alta California the successful missionary activity in Baja California, Sonora, and Sinaloa was made in *Noticia de la California, y de su Conquista Temporal, y Espiritual* (Madrid, 3 vols., 1757), also a major source on Vizcaíno. It was translated as *A Natural and Civil History of California* (London, 1759). A good deal of the writing is now thought to have been done by Father Andrés Burriel. None of it actually treats Alta California.

Venice, founded (1904) on ocean tidal flats west of Los Angeles (which absorbed it in 1925) by Abbott Kinney,◆ a wealthy promoter who conceived a pseudo-Italian city along the canals he dredged, enlightened by the chautauqua culture that he sponsored. In time his conception disappeared, along with his gondoliers, and only his Coney Island-type amusement park survived to differentiate that beach-resort and oil-drilling residential area from other southern California communities also located on Santa Monica Bay.

Ventana Wild Area, wilderness region of the northern Los Padres National Forest, founded in 1931. One of California's most serious forest fires consumed some 100,000 acres there in 1977.

Ventura, seat of the county of that name, grew up in the 1860s and 70s. It bears an abbreviation of the name of the neighboring mission, San Buenaventura. The site of a Chumash settlement, it was probably the landing place of Cabrillo (1542) and later the camping place of Portolá and Crespí (1769) and Anza (1774). The city developed as a port for the surrounding agricultural area and still has food-processing plants, but in the 1920s it profited from the nearby discovery of oil and now has a refinery. In 1970 the population was 55,797.

Ventura County, organized (1872) from part of Santa Barbara County to include both mainland territory and the Anacapa◆ and San Nicolás◆ islands. The name is a late-19th-century abbreviation of the original name, San Buenaventura, bestowed on the last mission to be founded by Serra (1782). The county is bounded by the ocean on the south and west. Santa Barbara County is also on the west, Kern County is on the north, and Los Angeles County is on the east.

This site, inhabited by Chumash Indians, was first visited by a white man when Cabrillo landed (1542), probably at the present city of Ventura, and was impressed by the natives, who built canoes caulked with asphalt. The next white visitors were Portolá and Crespí (1769) and Anza (1774 and 1776). The Indians for whom Serra founded the mission lived in small thatched houses to which the name *casitas* was given, now a placename for a lake, a pass, and springs north of the city of Ventura.

The county's coastline begins in the north at Rincón Point, where the forces of Juan Bautista Alvarado,◆ under Castro, defeated those of the rival governor, Cárlos Carrillo, under the Picos (1838). Less than halfway along the shore lies Ventura,◆ the county seat, followed by Oxnard,◆ the county's other major city, and its military installations at Port Hueneme◆ and Point Mugu. Behind them, in the mountains along the Ventura Freeway, lie Camarillo and Thousand Oaks, residential communities, the former with a State Hospital and with the Doheny Library of rare books at St. John's Seminary. Farther north along the Santa Clara River lie Saticoy; Santa Paula,◆ an agricultural and oil center; Sespe Village;◆ Fillmore; and Bardsdale, which is named for oil developer Thomas R. Bard. Close to the Los Angeles County line in the southeast and behind the Santa Monica Mts. lie the Simi Hills, Simi Valley, and the city of that name. The northern part of the county consists of rugged country in the San Rafael Mts., most of it within Los Padres National Forest, including the lower area of Cuyama Valley, and the Topatopa

Mts., which bound part of the Sespe Condor Sanctuary. Toward their Los Angeles County border lies Lake Piru, and toward the Santa Barbara County border lies the Ojai Valley and the sequestered town of Ojai,◆ initially called Nordhoff after Charles Nordhoff, whose name is still memorialized in a nearby range and peak.

The county's economy rests on its petroleum production, but it remains a major grower of citrus fruit, celery, tomatoes, strawberries, lettuce, avocados, and other fruits and vegetables, as well as of cut flowers and field crops. It is also a poultry center and a growing manufacturing area. Population, confined almost entirely to the coastal area and the inland valleys, almost doubled in the 1960s. In 1970 it stood at 378,497, which, with an area of 1,192,576 acres, gave it 203.1 persons per sq. mi.

VENTURI, KEN[NETH] (1931–   ), San Francisco-born golf star, a professional since 1956. In his first 15 years he won 13 major tournaments, including the U.S. Open (1964).

VERDUGO, prominent early California family whose founder was Mariano de la Luz Verdugo (1746–1822), a soldier on the Sacred Expedition. The Rancho San Rafael granted to José María Verdugo (1784, 1798) comprised 36,000 acres stretching from Mission San Fernando to Arroyo Seco, including the sites of present Glendale and Verdugo City, as well as Verdugo Canyon, Mts., and Wash.

Vermillion Sea, see *California, Gulf of.*

Vertigo, film produced and directed by Alfred Hitchcock (1958) with a San Francisco setting, treats a man's involvement with two women who closely resemble one another and whose lives are interrelated.

Viceroy, chief representative of the Spanish monarchy for New Spain at the capital of Mexico, with supreme responsibility for both military and civil government. The first viceroy was Antonio de Mendoza (1492?–1552), who, during his term (1535–50), dispatched the expeditions of Alarcón (1540) and Cabrillo (1542) to California and that of Coronado to New Mexico (1540–42). In 1550 he was appointed to the comparable viceroyalty established at Lima. Another early viceroy who directly affected California was Gaspar de Zúñiga y Acevedo, Conde de Monterrey (1560–1606), during

whose term of office (1595–1603) Cermeño (1595) and Vizcaíno (1602–3) were sent to California. The harbor of Monterey was named after him. A later viceroy, Marqués Francisco de Croix, worked with *Visitador-General* José de Gálvez◆ to dispatch the Sacred Expedition◆ (1769), which finally colonized California. Viceroy Antonio María Bucareli y Ursúa (1771–79) sponsored the program of Anza to create a land route to California, as well as sending Ayala, Heceta, and Bodéga y Cuadro to explore by sea.

VICTOR, FRANCES AURETTA FULLER (1826–1902), moved to San Francisco (1863), where she continued the literary career which she, like her sister, Metta Victoria Fuller Victor (1831–85), had begun as a popular writer and dime novelist in New York and the Midwest. In California she contributed to the *Golden Era* and *Overland Monthly.* From 1878 to 1890 she was on the staff of H. H. Bancroft, who published several of her works under his own name; her two-volume history of Oregon; one on Washington, Idaho, and Montana; and one on Nevada, Colorado, and Wyoming; as well as large parts of her texts on British Columbia, the Northwest Coast, and California. She lived in Oregon (1864–78 and 1890–1902), and during her earlier residence there she wrote her best-known book, *The River of the West* (1870), a biography of the mountain man Joe Meek.

VICTORIA, MANUEL (*fl.* 1830–33), 4th Mexican governor of California (Jan. 31–Dec. 6, 1831), was a military officer of Baja California when he was appointed by the conservative pro-clerical faction then in control of the Mexican government. José María Padrés, adjutant inspector of troops in California, had been appointed to the governorship of California by the preceding, more liberal Mexican administration and, although not formally installed, had received an order from his predecessor, Echeandía, to secularize the missions. However, Victoria overruled that decree, banished Padrés and others, and established a harsh, high-handed, and repressive regime. Echeandía, Bandini, Abel Stearns, Pío Pico, and others revolted against him, and he was wounded at the ensuing battle of Cahuenga Pass◆ (Dec. 4, 1831). He then gave up office and fled to Mexico, where he disappeared from history as silently as he had entered it.

Vigilance Committees, arose in California during the gold rush to act speedily on crimes. Properly titled Committee of Vigilance, the first that came into being in San Francisco (1851) was an outgrowth of an extra-legal trial to punish a robbery by the Sydney Ducks♦ and to stop other crimes, including arson, which had become common and daring and had gone unpunished by a weak city government. The Committee's leader was William T. Coleman;♦ other important figures among the original 103 signators were Samuel Brannan,♦ J. D. Stevenson,♦ and Selim Woodworth.♦ In June they apprehended a Sydney Duck and hanged him at Portsmouth Plaza. Opponents of this law by lynching♦ included David Broderick, Hall McAllister, and Gov. McDougal. Accused criminals were later given trials in the Committee's own courts, but two unconvicted prisoners were seized from the city jail and immediately hanged. In all, the committee hanged 4 men, whipped 1, sentenced 28 to deportation, handed 15 to the police for trials, and released 41. After 100 days this first committee dwindled away (Sept. 1851), having reached a membership of over 600 and inspired the creation of other vigilance organizations in the mining towns. The most notorious related event was the lynching of a Mexican woman named Juanita at Downieville (July 1851).

Another Vigilance Committee came into being in San Francisco in 1856, following the murder of Gen. William H. Richardson by Charles Cora♦ and of James King of William by James Casey.♦ The leader of the new committee was again Coleman, and its headquarters was Fort Gunnybags.♦ On May 18, 2,500 armed vigilantes seized Cora and Casey from the unresisting sheriffs, took them from jail, tried them hastily, and publicly hanged them four days later. Following a fight in which the vigilantes seized arms from the state militia, the Committee held a parade of 6,000 followers and then disbanded, turning that fall to the ballot box, to reform the government they considered corrupt. Vigilante action was common in mining towns, too, as an expression of lynch law.♦

VIGNES, JEAN LOUIS [JUAN LUIS] (*c.*1779–1862), moved to California (*c.*1831) from his native Bordeaux with grape cuttings, using his training as a cooper and grape grower to establish a vineyard, El Aliso, on the site of the present Union Station in downtown Los Angeles. He created fine wines and *aguardiente,* was probably the first orchardist to grow oranges in Los Angeles (1834), cultivated English walnuts, and became a wealthy social and business leader. He was joined in his wine business by his nephews, Jean Vignes and Pierre Sansevain, the latter marrying into the Suñol family and becoming a prominent Californian.

VINES, [HENRY] ELLSWORTH (1911–), Los Angeles-born tennis player, won the U.S. singles championship (1931 and 1932) and the English title at Wimbledon (1932). He was the youngest player (age 19) to be the U.S. champion. After he became a professional (1933), he was the leader of his class for five years, beating Tilden, and continued to be known for his fast serve. Still later he became a professional golfer.

Vineyards, established in California by the early fathers so that of the thirteen missions founded by 1798, ten grew grapes and made wine for sacramental and personal use. The major vineyards were in southern California, and by the 1820s Mission San Gabriel was producing 400 barrels of wine a year. However, all these vineyards declined severely after secularization (1834). Commercial growing of wine grapes, begun by Joseph Chapman in Los Angeles, was greatly improved by Jean Louis Vignes in the 1830s. The gold rush led to the establishment of many vineyards around the San Francisco Bay area for table grapes and wine and to a boom in southern California: acreage tripled in the 1850s. The state's vines increased from 1,000,000 in 1855 to 8,000,000 by 1860, and to 26,500,000 by 1870, when the varieties of grapes grown in Sonoma and Napa valleys and elsewhere had been enormously extended and improved by Haraszthy and others.

All vineyards were seriously threatened in the 1870s and 80s by phylloxera, a plant louse, which killed the imported root stock. Paradoxically, the severe loss brought benefits, too, eliminating poor vines, leading growers to concentrate on improved and immune American stock and to take greater care with their crops. The remaining, more sophisticated vineyardists increased their cultivation, so that by the late 1880s they had about 130,000,000 vines. They also began to produce great quantities of raisins in the dry, hot San Joaquin Valley. The value of the state's wine production rose from $600,000 in 1880 to almost $4,000,000 in 1900, when raisin making had also grown so much that 43% of all grapes were dried.

In the 1970s grape growing for winemaking increased enormously in acreage and dollar value as the state's wineries produced 85% of the wine made in the U.S. Most of it originated in the vineyards of Napa, Sonoma, Livermore, Santa Clara, and San Joaquin valleys, with some important exceptions, such as the areas near Monterey and Cucamonga. Among the leading long-established vineyards are those founded by the Beringer brothers, the Christian Brothers, the Gallo brothers, the Italian-Swiss Colony, Charles Krug, Louis Martini, Paul Masson and Charles LeFranc, the Mondavi family, Capt. Niebaum, Louis Petri, Jacob Schram, and the Wente brothers. (*See also individual entries.*)

VIOGET, JEAN JACQUES (1799–1855), Swiss-born soldier who served in Napoleon's army and later was a French engineer. He went to San Francisco (1837) as master of his own ship to trade with the *Californios*. He settled there and, as a skilled artist, was engaged to survey Yerba Buena by its first *alcalde,* Francisco De Haro♦ (1839). He also mapped Nueva Helvetia for Sutter. Later he made other sailing voyages, on one of which he was charged with escorting Micheltorena♦ back to Mexico (1845). His last years were spent in San Jose.

Virginia City, see *Comstock Lode.*

Visalia, seat and largest city of Tulare County, founded (1852) by Nathaniel Vise, a frontiersman from Kentucky, where a town of the same name honored members of his family. At one time the California city was the home of many Confederate sympathizers, and a pro-slavery newspaper was issued there by Lovick P. Hall.♦ Later it was a center for ranchers and others who opposed the Southern Pacific, like John Sontag.♦ It is now a center for the county's farm, orchard, and dairy products. In 1970 it had a population of 27,268.

VISCHER, EDWARD (1808–78), German trader in Mexico and South America, moved to California (1841?) to investigate trade with the missions. It was then that he began his extensive sketching of California life, particularly around the missions. He continued to do so after his return in the gold rush, when he also made many photographs, as, perhaps, the first photographer in California.

Visitador-general, title of an officer appointed by the monarch of Spain to conduct a formal inspection of a province, and thus oversee a viceroy♦ and even act upon his findings. The most significant *visitador-general* who had to do with California was José de Gálvez,♦ who was the instigating force, during the viceroyalty of the Marqués de Croix, for the dispatch of the Sacred Expedition♦ (1769) and the resultant missions and colonization of California. *Visitador-general* was also a title given to a lesser sort of inspector, a friar appointed to examine an apostolic college and its members.

VIZCAÍNO, SEBASTIÁN (*c.*1548–*c.*1629), after service in the Spanish invasion of Portugal (1580), went to Mexico (1583), voyaged to Manila (1586–89) as a merchant, and returned to Mexico before exploring the California coast (1602–3) under the auspices of the viceroy. With two small ships and a launch, he went north from Acapulco to find a good harbor for the Manila galleons.♦ His anchorages included San Diego Bay, Santa Catalina, and Monterey (which he praised extravagantly and named for the viceroy), although he missed San Francisco Bay. To those places, previously visited by Cabrillo, he gave the names they have retained. He sailed as far north as Cape Mendocino and made influential maps and descriptions of the coastline. His findings were invalidated by Antonio de la Ascensión, a friar on his expedition, whose contention that California was an island was picked up by another Franciscan, Juan Torquemada, in his *Monarquía Indiana* (1613) and widely popularized. Later (1611–17), as the King's envoy, Vizcaíno explored and mapped Japan's coast, and, still later, he fought Dutch attempts to disrupt the Manila galleons' trade.

VIZETELLY, HENRY (1820–94), English author who wrote, under the pseudonym of J. Terwhitt Brooks, *Four Months Among the Goldfinders in California* (1849), an early work on life in the mines. It was presented as personal experience and so accepted until discovered to be a mixture of fiction and secondhand reports.

VOLLMER, AUGUST (1876–1955), moved from his native New Orleans to Berkeley in the 1890s and there became the city's first chief of police (1905). During his long and distinguished career, he developed nationally recognized standards of departmental organization and new methods of criminal detection.

VON LANGSDORFF, see *Langsdorff, Georg Heinrich von.*

VON PERBANDT, CARL (1832–1911), German-born artist, resident in San Francisco and the northern California redwood country most of the time between 1875 and 1903, when he returned to his native land. While in California he painted landscapes of the woods and coast in a style akin to that of the Barbizon school.

VON SALTZA, [SUSAN] CHRIS[TINE] (1945–   ), swimming champion born in Saratoga. Between

1955 and 1960 she set 22 U.S. records, tied one, and established two world records (200-meter backstroke and 400-meter freestyle). She won five gold medals in the Pan American games (1959) and three gold medals and one silver medal in the Olympic Games (1960).

Vow Boys, name given to Stanford University football team (1933–35) because the players, in their freshman year (1932), vowed never to lose a game to the University of Southern California. They not only kept their pledge but were the first college team to appear in three consecutive Rose Bowl games, losing the first two to Columbia and Alabama but winning the last over Southern Methodist University.

VROMAN, A[DAM] C[LARK] (1856–1916), reared in Illinois by his Dutch family, moved to Pasadena, where he opened a bookstore (1894), his lifelong business. The next year he made the first of eight trips to the Southwest to photograph its Indians and their pueblos. He gained fame for his prints and for his equally sensitive documentary pictures of the ruined California missions and other vestiges of Spanish and Mexican culture.

W

WAGNER, HARR (1857–1930), Pennsylvania-born editor of the *Golden Era*♦ (1881–90) and publisher of the works of Joaquin Miller, whose biography he wrote (1929).

WAGNER, HENRY R[AUP] (1862–1957), born in Philadelphia, educated at Yale, after a career as a lawyer and manager of mines, retired to California (1917) to become a leading bibliophile and an authority on diverse aspects of western bibliography, cartography, and history. His books include *The Plains and the Rockies* (1920; later editions amplified by Charles L. Camp), *The Cartography of the Northwest Coast of America to the Year 1800* (1937), and *Sir Francis Drake's Voyage Around the World* (1926). The California Historical Society established an annual award in his name for authors in his field.

Wailaki, see *Athabascan.*

Wakamatsu Colony, first organized group (26 persons) to come from Japan to the U.S. (1869), settled at Gold Hill (El Dorado County). Composed of persons who had backed the losing side in Japan's civil war of 1868, the group was led by John Henry Schnell, a Dutchman who had married the daughter of a samurai of the Wakamatsu clan. They brought mulberry trees, grape cuttings, and other plants, hoping to establish silk and tea plantations, but failed. They disbanded within two years.

WAKEMAN, EDGAR (1818–75), Connecticut-born merchant marine captain, known for his command of vessels to the Pacific Coast and steamers between California ports. His adventures led to a friendship with Mark Twain. Other experiences, including service with the Vigilantes, are recorded in his *The Log of an Ancient Mariner* (1878).

WALDORF, PAPPY (LYNN O. WALDORF) (1902–   ), football coach of the University of California, Berkeley (1947–56). His team there won 67 games, lost 32, had four ties and played at the Rose Bowl (unsuccessfully) four times.

WALKER, FRANKLIN (1901–   ), Michigan-born scholar of California culture and literature, long a professor at Mills College. His works include *Frank Norris* (1932), a biography; *San Francisco's Literary Frontier* (1939); *A Literary History of Southern California* (1950); *The Seacoast of Bohemia* (1966), about the early art colony of Carmel; and editions of works by Prentice Mulford, Mary Austin, and other California writers.

WALKER, JAMES (1818–89), English-born artist, reared in New York, joined the U.S. forces in the Mexican War. He later painted large historical canvases, such as "The Battle of Chapultepec," for the U.S. Capitol, and then moved to California in the 1870s. There he produced many oil paintings depicting the fast-vanishing Mexican ways of life.

WALKER, JOSEPH REDDEFORD (1798–1876), born in Tennessee, became a frontiersman in Missouri before reconnoitering the Far West under Capt. Benjamin Bonneville,♦ who was ostensibly engaged in the fur trade but was probably gathering military intelligence about Mexican lands and adjacent territory. Walker's detachment of Bonneville's company were the first white men to make a westward crossing of the central Sierra (1833) and perhaps the first to see Yosemite, as recorded by one of their members, Zenas Leonard.♦ Walker returned east through the Tehachapi Mts. pass in the northeast part of present Kern County which is named for him. He later led an expedition with Chiles (1843) and was a guide on Frémont's second and third expeditions (1844, 45–46). He continued exploration of the Southwest until settling down in Contra Costa County, where he spent the last decade of his life.

WALKER, WILLIAM (1824–60), Tennessee-born adventurer, received his M.D. from the University of Pennsylvania when only 19, traveled a year in Europe, was admitted to the bar in New Orleans, and tried his hand at journalism before moving to California (1850). He was a newspaperman briefly in San Francisco and then in Marysville, where he expanded his fields to law and politics of a lurid sort.

He next decided to colonize part of neighboring Mexico, and upon landing with followers in La Paz

(1853), proclaimed Lower California an independent republic under his presidency, to which he annexed the state of Sonora by means of a paper proclamation. After the U.S. government blocked shipment of his supplies from San Francisco, he and his starving followers retreated to the U,S,, where they were tried in San Francisco and acquitted of violating neutrality laws.

With fewer than 60 followers, Walker in 1855 took part in a revolution in Nicaragua, and with the support of an American transit company of the region made himself both commander-in-chief of the army and president (1856). The self-proclaimed "gray-eyed man of destiny" planned to create one Central American empire whose agriculture would be developed by African slaves, but his seizure of the transit company's ships and other Nicaraguan property led Cornelius Vanderbilt, a major stockholder, to move military forces of other Central American nations to besiege him. He surrendered (1857), returned to the U.S., went back to Nicaragua, was arrested by the U.S. Navy and remanded to his native land, and finally planned another invasion of Nicaragua from Honduras (1860). There the British seized him and turned him over to local authorities, by whom he was court-martialed and shot.

Walker Pass, see *Walker, Joseph Reddeford,* and *Tehachapi Mountains.*

Walnuts, see *Nuts.*

WALTER, BRUNO (1876–1962), one of the major conductors of this century, left his native Germany (1933) and his later post in Vienna (1938) when forced out by the Nazis because he was Jewish. From 1939 to his death he lived in the U.S., mainly in Hollywood, where he frequently conducted at the Hollywood Bowl and led the Los Angeles Philharmonic Orchestra.

WALTON, BILL (WILLIAM THEODORE WALTON) (1952–), basketball player, born in La Mesa (San Diego County). At UCLA he was All-American center (1972–74), and in the first two years was College Player of the Year and led UCLA to NCAA championships and records of 30–0. A vehement opponent of the Vietnam War, he boycotted the Olympic Games in 1972. Later he was alleged to have sheltered Patricia Hearst while she was a fugitive.

WANDESFORDE, J[UAN] B[UCKINGHAM] (1817–1902), English-born artist who studied with the

water colorist John Varley, moved to New York, and then (1862) went to San Francisco, where he remained for the rest of his life. There he was noted for his landscapes, portraits, and still lifes; as a founder of the San Francisco Art Association; and as a teacher of R. G. Holdredge.

Wappo, Indian tribe whose area centered on the Napa Valley. Perhaps 4,600 dwelt in that region before the days of white conquest; in 1976 only one survived. They apparently participated in the Kuksu cult♦ and shared other relations with their neighbors, the Pomo, Miwok, and Patwin tribes.

WARBURTON, COTTON [IRVINE] (1912–), San Diego-born football player, quarterback on the University of Southern California team (1932–33). He later won an Oscar for film editing.

WARD, SAMUEL (1814–84), social and cultural leader of New York City, after losing his fortune, moved to California (1849) to try to retrieve it in the gold rush. His reminiscent articles, issued in *Porter's Spirit of the Times* (1861), were collected as *Sam Ward in the Gold Rush* (1949). He was later a lobbyist in Washington, D.C., for big business.

WARD, THOMAS MYERS DECATUR (1823–94), a bishop of the African Methodist Episcopal Church (1868 ff.), during his residence in San Francisco (1854–72) was also a civil rights leader.

WARFIELD, DAVID (1866–1951), San Francisco-born actor, after a career as an entertainer in his home city and in New York (where he moved in 1890), met David Belasco.♦ They entered into an association (1901–24) of unparalleled success as an actor and manager-producer team. Their productions were so popular that only five sufficed for almost a quarter of a century: Charles Klein's *The Auctioneer* and *The Music Master,* Belasco's *A Grand Army Man* and *The Return of Peter Grimm,* and Shakespeare's *The Merchant of Venice.* Warfield's favorite role was that of a crotchety, eccentric old man. In 1904 he joined with Marcus Loew in creating a New York penny arcade which developed into a motion picture theater and entertainment empire.

WARMERDAM, CORNELIUS A. (1915–), champion pole vaulter, born in Coalinga, was not only the first man to vault over 15 feet (1940), but did so 43 times before anybody else equaled his feat. He set a record of 15′ 7½″ (1942) that lasted for 15 years. While establishing those records, he was a high school teacher in Tuolumne City and Piedmont. In 1942 he won the Sullivan Award as the outstanding U.S. amateur athlete.

WARNER, JACK L. (1892–), Canadian-born film producer, with his brothers Harry, Albert, and Sam, established a motion picture studio in Hollywood (1919) that achieved great success when it created the first talking picture, Al Jolson's *The Jazz Singer* (1927). The firm continued with various successful films, including *My Fair Lady* and *Camelot,* made in the 1960s.

WARNER, JONATHAN TRUMBULL [also known as JUAN JOSÉ and JOHN J.] (1807–95), Connecticut-born trapper and trader, moved to California (1831) to hunt. He became a naturalized Mexican citizen, a trader, and a large landholder at Warner's Ranch, northeast of San Diego. He served Larkin as a confidential agent and supported the Americans in the conquest of California. He was co-author of *An Historical Sketch of Los Angeles County* (1876), about the area in which he was a pioneer.

WARNER, POP (GLENN SCOBEY WARNER) (1871–1954), New York-born football coach, reared in Texas. After graduation from Cornell (1894), on whose team he had played, he became football coach at Georgia, Cornell, Carlisle (where he taught Jim Thorpe), Pittsburgh, Stanford (1924–32), Temple, and San Jose State (1939). He helped change the game from a contest of strength into one of skill and strategy. The Rose Bowl victory (1932) of his Stanford team over Knute Rockne's Notre Dame team was a high point of his career.

Warner Mountains, in Modoc County on the northeastern corner of the state, about 90 miles long and 8 to 20 miles wide, with peaks rising to 10,000 feet, is in a wilderness area. The range was named for a pioneer, Capt. William H. Warner, who was killed by Indians (1849). The route through the mountains is Fandango Pass.◆

Warner's Ranch, see *Warner, Jonathan Trumbull.*

WARREN, EARL (1891–1974), after graduation from the University of California and its law school, and army enlistment in World War I, became district attorney of Alameda County and attorney general of the state, fighting graft and rackets but also supporting Roosevelt's executive order excluding American-born and other Japanese from the coastal area in 1942. His image as an independent, almost nonpartisan public servant won him the governorship in 1943 for the first of an unprecedented three terms. He began by cutting taxes, then worked for better medical care and unemployment insurance, better highways, improved mediation of labor disputes, and a water use and conservation program. Without a political machine, he worked with various citizens groups and advisory bodies and created a substantial civil service staff. He was clearly a Republican—he had run for the vice presidency under Gov. Dewey of New York in 1948—but gave the general impression of being above party. Shortly after he decided to give up the governorship, President Eisenhower named him Chief Justice of the U.S. Supreme Court. In that post (1953–69) he shaped the Court into a liberal body. Its most historic decision (1954), a unanimous one, found segregation into "separate and equal" schools to be unconstitutional, urged desegregation of schools with "all deliberate speed," and affected the status of minorities in numerous related matters. In 1964 he headed a presidential commission on the assassination of President Kennedy which found only one person responsible for the killing.

WARREN, JAMES LLOYD LAFAYETTE (1805–96), Massachusetts merchant, moved to California (1849) and established a general provisioning business in San Francisco. To counter scurvy in the mining camps, he sold fruit trees and vegetable seeds, advertising the value of fresh produce by creating in Sacramento a Great Agricultural Fair (1852), the forerunner of the annual State Fair (1854 ff.).

Warriors, see *Golden State Warriors.*

Washerwoman's Lagoon, once a small fresh-water lake on San Francisco, bounded, approximately, by Lombard, Filbert, Franklin, and Octavia streets, was called Laguna Pequeña by the Spanish, of whom Anza was the first to see it (1776). It served the Americans (1848 ff.) as a place to do laundry until a flume brought fresh water into the city from a more distant point (1858). It was later filled in and built over.

WASHINGTON, KENNY (KENNETH WASHINGTON) (1918–71), star halfback at the University of California, Los Angeles, and leading baseball player (1937–39). He joined the Los Angeles Rams (1946–48), helping to open professional football to black athletes, just as Jackie Robinson,♦ his UCLA team-mate, opened professional baseball to them.

Washo, Indians of the Hokan linguistic family, whose territory centered on Lake Tahoe and covered the drainage of the Truckee and Carson rivers. The Washo had sporadic conflicts with the Paiutes. They were excellent basket makers. Their prehistoric population of 1,500 was reduced to 800 according to the census of 1910. The tribe's name is also spelled Washoe, as in the Nevada county of that name.

Wasp, The, weekly San Francisco journal of social commentary and vitriolic colored cartoons (1868–1928), which in its dwindling days merged with the S.F. *News-Letter* to become the *Wasp News-Letter* (1928–41). Its greatest period was under the editorship of Ambrose Bierce (1881–86), who wrote much of the text and lashed out at political corruption, particularly in local government or related to the Big Four; at revolutionary social views, including those of organized labor and of Denis Kearney; and at Chinese immigration.

Water, the state's greatest natural resource, has also been its most controversial because of its imbalance in the state. The lightly populated, most northerly area has about 70% of the stream flow, while 77% to 80% of demand is in the more arid agricultural and heavily populated urban areas of southern California.

Initially, competition for water was localized and different in nature, as hydraulic miners dumped debris in the Yuba, Bear, American, and Feather rivers, causing floods and miring the lands of protesting farmers. Conflict later grew among farmers as the state adopted (1850) the English common law of riparian rights, allowing landowners on riverbanks to use the water and denying it to others, until the Wright Act (1887) permitted the formation of irrigation districts, which led to the creation of municipal and county water-conservation and flood-control districts. Farm land receiving irrigation♦ rose from 4.7% in 1889 to 14.4% in 1919, much of it engineered by George Chaffey,♦ who conceived the requirement that each settler of a given area had to buy water company stock with his land. Chaffey was also instrumental in introducing irrigation into the Imperial Valley.

Conflict between urban water needs and the views of land conservationists at the turn of the century grew particularly bitter in the fight over the flooding of Hetch Hetchy♦ Valley in the Yosemite

Valley area to supply San Francisco with water. Los Angeles also had great difficulties in getting enough water as it fought to secure an aqueduct to carry Owens River water 250 miles to the city. The project was carried out by the city engineer, William Mulholland,♦ despite the fact that it was several times dynamited by farmers who had been left with insufficient water and despite the collapse of its St. Francis Dam (1928), which flooded Santa Paula and killed 400 people. Not until 1941 was a suitable reservoir finished.

When the Owens River project was found to be insufficient, Los Angeles and other cities created a Metropolitan Water District of Southern California (1928) to build an aqueduct from the Colorado River. Though Arizona opposed it, the project was undertaken. Hoover Dam (for a time during Franklin Roosevelt's administration called Boulder Dam) was built on the Nevada-Arizona border for hydroelectric power, flood control, and irrigation from the Colorado River, which it taps above Yuma, and runs via the All-American Canal♦ to supply water to the Imperial Valley (1943) and Coachella Valley (1948). The resultant Lake Mead is named for the irrigation expert, Elwood Mead.♦

Lake Havasu,♦ created by Parker Dam on the Colorado River, carries water through an aqueduct to Riverside County. Another water-supply program is the Central Valley Project,♦ first proposed by Robert B. Marshall♦ (1919) and finally initiated in 1935. It uses Sacramento and San Joaquin river waters to supply the San Joaquin Valley. This is done by three major dams: Shasta Dam, impounding water from the Sacramento, McCloud, and Pit rivers in Shasta Lake;♦ the nearby Keswick Dam; and the Friant Dam, holding water of the San Joaquin River to be carried by the Madera Canal to the northwest and by the Friant-Kern Canal♦ for the Bakersfield area. The Delta-Mendota Canal♦ brings Sacramento River water to the Fresno area to replace that from the San Joaquin. In addition, there is a great complex of other dams, reservoirs, canals, pumping stations, and power plants.

An even more ambitious system is the state's California Water Plan, proposed by the California Water Resources Board in 1957 after a ten-year study. The largest water program ever undertaken in the U.S., its purpose is to deliver 4,230,000 acre-feet of water (an acre-foot is almost 326,000 gallons) annually to central and southern California regions for domestic, industrial, and agricultural purposes, as well as to provide flood control, generate electric power, and create recreation areas. The project, begun in the 1960s, is a long-term undertaking of vast magnitude and expense which requires hundreds of new reservoirs (the largest is Lake Oroville), pumping plants to lift water nearly 2,000 feet over the Tehachapi Mts., tunnels, and a vast aqueduct system. From the huge Feather River project the flow of water is regulated into the Delta and then through the Tracy pumping plant into the California Aqueduct.◆ The Aqueduct runs 500 miles down the west side of the San Joaquin Valley, providing irrigation there as well as carrying water into southern California. Meanwhile, the federal government has contrived its own New Melones Water Project◆ to impound and redirect water from the Stanislaus River.

Water ouzel, thrush-like bird of the dipper family, about seven or eight inches long, colored slate-gray with some brown on the head. It lives along mountain streams, in which it finds plants and larvae to eat. John Muir studied the bird in the Kings Canyon National Park area, where David Starr Jordan later named Ouzel Basin and Ouzel Creek.

WATERFIELD, BOB (ROBERT WATERFIELD) (1920–), football player born in New York but reared in Van Nuys. At the University of California, Los Angeles, he was the star quarterback and was named All-American. He played professional football with the Rams (Cleveland, 1945; Los Angeles, 1946–52), was named All Pro and Most Valuable Player in the NFL in his rookie year, and later led the league in passing, punting, and field goals. He coached the Rams from 1960 to 1962.

WATERMAN, ROBERT WHITNEY (1826–91), 17th governor of the state (1887–91), first moved to California in the gold rush of 1850, then returned to the state from Illinois in 1873, at which time he made a fortune in silver mining near Barstow.◆ In 1887 he was elected as a Republican lieutenant governor, though Washington Bartlett, a Democrat, was elected governor, the first time in the state's history that such a split occurred. Waterman became governor when Bartlett died after holding office only a few months.

WATKINS, CARLETON E[MMONS] (1829–1916), moved from New York in the gold rush, becoming a leading photographer of California, whose photos of sweeping landscapes, made from glass plates, were particularly admired. His subjects included Yosemite, the decaying missions, the Comstock Lode, and other parts of the Far West as they

appeared between the 1850s and 1906. In the latter year, his studio and the accumulation of his life's work were lost in the San Francisco earthquake and fire, so shocking him that in time he had to be committed to the insane asylum at Napa, where he died.

Watsonville, market and processing center in Santa Cruz County for the fruits (particularly apples and strawberries) and vegetables grown in Pajaro Valley. It was named for a town founder (1852). In 1970 it had a population of 14,569.

WATTERS, LU, see *Yerba Buena Jazz Band.*

Watts, district of Los Angeles, southwest of the downtown area, populated mainly by blacks and Mexican Americans. It became notorious as the site of violent riots (Aug. 11–16, 1965) in which 34 people were killed, over 1,000 injured, and $40,000,000 in damage done to property. Poor housing, unemployment, friction with police, a sense of second-class citizenship, long-standing grievances against whites, and attendant frustrations and tensions erupted when a white policeman arrested a black man for drunken driving. An angry crowd gathered and soon turned into a mob whose furious action grew more and more intense as more and more blacks were arrested and manhandled by armed police (mostly white), while roving bands of blacks set automobiles ablaze, occasional snipers opened fire, and shops that belonged to the hated whites were looted and burned. Law-abiding residents and black and white civil rights leaders could not control the violence, which only subsided after the National Guard moved in. Gov. Pat Brown quickly appointed an investigatory commission headed by John A. McCone, which issued a report that recommended more jobs, better housing, improved schools, and other remedies. Watts has a happier distinction of being the site of the towers built by Simon Rodia◆ to thank the U.S. for affording immigrants a good way of life. It is also the birthplace of Eldridge Cleaver.

WAUGH, EVELYN (1903–66), English author, popular for his witty and sophisticated satirical novels conveying the atmosphere of upper-class British life of the time, such as *Decline and Fall* (1928) and *Vile Bodies* (1930). He went on to create more serious fiction, such as *Brideshead Revisited* (1945), animated by his Catholic faith, but his residence in Hollywood to write film scripts led him back to satire. *The Loved One* (1948) is a farcical and macabre novel about southern California's ways of life and death and the spuriously sanctimonious funeral business of cemeteries like Forest Lawn.♦

Wave, The, San Francisco weekly journal (1890–1900), in its first months edited from Monterey by Ben C. Truman.♦ It was financed by the Southern Pacific to promote its elegant new Del Monte Hotel, for which reason it bore (until 1895) the subtitle, "A Weekly for Those in the Swim." As a San Francisco publication of broader interests, it treated diverse city matters in a sprightly style, emphasizing politics, drama and book reviews, original fiction and poetry, and society news, and used many photographs. A colorful local journal, its tone was set by its lively, liberal editor, John O'Hara Cosgrave, who had as assistant editors, and, therefore, as writers of most of the text, Frank Norris (1896–97), Gelett Burgess (1897–99), and Will Irwin (1899–1900). Collections of some contributions of Norris and Burgess were published in 1931 and 1968, respectively.

Wawona, part of the Yosemite National Park, was settled by Galen Clark♦ (1857), the discoverer of the Mariposa Grove, who lived at what he called Clark's Station until his death at age 96 (1910). The Washburn brothers, who established a popular hotel there (1875), gave it the Indian name, meaning "big tree." Thomas Hill♦ had a studio there.

WAYNE, JOHN (1907–), Iowa-born film star, reared in California, whose great successes since 1939 (a decade after he began his career) have been based on depicting one kind of character: the independent, strong man of the West. He formed his own producing company and also directed films. He is further known for his conservative political activities on behalf of Richard Nixon, Ronald Reagan, and other Republicans. A John Wayne Theatre displaying his memorabilia is located at Knott's Berry Farm.

Weaverville, seat of Trinity County, named (1850) for an early prospector of the gold mines in the region. During the gold rush the town had a large Chinese population which engaged in a devastating tong war (1854). The Chinese are commemorated in the state's oldest Chinese temple, Joss House State Historic Park. The town's population in 1970 was 1,489.

WEBB, CHARLES HENRY (1834–1905), born in New York State, had an adventurous youth on a whaler in the South Seas and the Arctic, then became a bohemian journalist in New York City and a *New York Times* correspondent from Civil War battlefields before moving to California (1863) as the newspaper's representative. In San Francisco he became literary editor of the *Evening Bulletin,* and a columnist and staff member of *The Golden Era.* He was known for his humorous social criticism, written under the pseudonyms Inigo and John Paul. He founded and edited *The Californian*♦ (1864–66) with Bret Harte and Mark Twain as major contributors, but including, among other writers, Charles Warren Stoddard, Ina Coolbrith, Ambrose Bierce, and Henry George. He also wrote a locally produced play, *Our Friend from Victoria* (1865), and was a correspondent for the Sacramento *Union.* Attacks on him for his satirical view of state history and leaders and his losses in mining investments probably caused him to leave California (1866). His subsequent life in New York as a journalist, Wall St. broker, and inventor of an adding machine was also marked by publications in the vein of western humor: *Liffith Lank* (1866) and *St. Twel'mo* (1866), parodies of Charles Reade's *Griffith Gaunt* and Miss Evans' *St. Elmo,* respectively; *John Paul's Book* (1874); and *Parodies: Prose and Verse* (1876).

WEBER, CHARLES M[ARIA] (1814–81), German-born emigrant to California (1841) with the Bartleson-Bidwell Party,♦ settled at San Jose, where he opened a store and flour mill and pioneered in manufacturing shoes. After naturalization (1844) he obtained a 50,000-acre land grant on which he raised cattle, mined gold, and, on the site called Tuleburg, later created a business center for the southern mines, naming it Stockton. He led the defense of San Jose during the uprising against Micheltorena (1845) and led a cavalry company to the aid of U.S. forces in the same region during the Mexican War. He later donated much of his Stockton land to the city and county formed there.

WEBER, FRANCIS J. (1933–), Franciscan priest whose historical studies include *A Bibliography of California Bibliographies, Missions and Missionaries of Baja California* (1968), a biography of Bishop Alemany, and articles on California's Catholic heritage. He is the archivist of the Archdiocese of Los Angeles.

WEDEMEYER, HERMAN (1924–), Hawaiian-born football player, was a star back on the team of St. Mary's University (1943, 45–46).

WEILL, RAPHAEL (1835–1920), moved to San Francisco (1853) from his native France, entered the dry goods business, and by the 1860s was a partner in the White House, which he developed into a leading department store. He was a member of the Vigilance Committee of 1856, a leader of the local French colony, a major member of the Jewish community, and a bon vivant whose culinary achievements included the creation of a chicken dish bearing his name.

WEINSTOCK, HARRIS (1854–1922), born in London, moved to New York and then to California (1869), where he and his half-brother, David Lubin,♦ began the business bearing their names that became a major Sacramento department store. He also held posts on state and federal commissions and was a founder of agricultural cooperative marketing associations as well as a supporter of the Progressive party.

WEISSMULLER, JOHNNY (1904–   ), California-born champion in swimming competitions,♦ who had a motion picture career as Tarzan. He was the first to act the role (1932–48) in talking films, for which he created a famous yodeling call.

WELCH, THADDEUS (1844–1919), landscape artist, born in Indiana, moved from Oregon to California (1866) and worked as a farm laborer and newspaper printer. After studying in Europe, he returned to establish a reputation for his canvases of Marin County and other bucolic scenes as well as for his portraits.

WELLER, JOHN B. (1812–78), had a career as a lawyer and Congressman (1839–45) for his native Ohio and in the army during the Mexican War before being appointed by President Taylor as a commissioner to settle the Mexican boundary under the Treaty of Guadalupe Hidalgo. Upon arriving in California (1850), he resigned that post to enter politics. Regarded as a pro-slavery Democrat, he was elected U.S. Senator (1851–57) to succeed Frémont and was later the 5th governor of the state (1858–60). He advocated that California, rather than siding with the North or South, should found on the shores of the Pacific "a mighty republic which may in the end prove the greatest of all." He was later made Minister to Mexico (1860–61) and then moved to New Orleans.

WELLES, ORSON (1915–   ), went to Hollywood (1939) to produce films after having had a successful career including stage productions of *Macbeth* with an all-black cast and *Julius Caesar* in modern dress, as well as a sensational 1938 radio broadcast of H. G. Wells' *The War of the Worlds* that appeared to be a real news broadcast. His first film, *Citizen Kane* (1941), critically acclaimed for the producer's acting and photographic techniques, was a remarkable interpretation of the life of William Randolph Hearst. His later career included other films he produced and directed and acted in, often considered uneven but marked by ingenuity in experimentation.

Wells Fargo, banking and express firm founded in New York and San Francisco as Wells, Fargo Express Co. (1852) by agents of two eastern expressmen, Henry Wells and William G. Fargo. It promptly opened a fast freight and passenger line of Concord coaches from San Francisco to Marysville and Sacramento, which was soon extended to other towns, where the firm also established offices or agents for banking. In the next decade, the express service was extended across the Sierra and became a transcontinental line by purchasing Ben Holladay's overland stages♦ in 1866, having previously held a contract for transportation and mail delivery from Salt Lake City to California. The firm briefly ran a local pony express♦ for the mining country (1852), operated the Salt Lake City-Sacramento part of the transcontinental operation (April–Oct. 1861), and had its own line between Virginia City and Sacramento (1862–65). The express business was separated in 1905, the year the banking business was merged with the Nevada Bank, founded (1875) by Fair, Flood, Mackay, and O'Brien, the Bonanza Kings.♦ It was then put under the presidency of I. W. Hellman, founder of the Union Trust Co. (1893), also merged with the enlarged bank. The bank's headquarters on California St. in San Francisco contains a History Room.

Welsh in California, first appeared with the brief and mistaken occupation by Commodore Thomas ap Catesby Jones,♦ who seized Monterey for the U.S. in 1842. More normal and longer-lasting settlement occurred during the gold rush, which attracted Welsh coal miners, many of whom turned to digging coal in Contra Costa County and quarrying granite in Placer and Tulare counties in the 1860s. Eisteddfods (ceremonial and competitive festivals) were held in Camptonville, Yuba County (1860), and San Francisco (1870). Prominent Welshmen include Albert Williams, organizer of the first

Presbyterian Church in San Francisco; Eleazar Thomas, Methodist minister and peace commissioner to the Modocs,♦ by whom he was killed; William Downie, founder of Downieville; and author Idwal Jones.

WENTE, ERNEST A. (1890–) and HERMAN L. (1892–1961), established the Wente Brothers winery (1934) in the Livermore Valley as an outgrowth of the business begun (1883) by their father, Carl H. Wente. They had operated it since 1918. A third brother, Carl F. Wente (1899–1971), was president of the Bank of America (1952–54).

WENZEL, HERMANN (1830–84), German-born clockmaker, moved to San Francisco in the 1850s. There he invented and manufactured a so-called air clock, a master or centrally located timepiece of his own devising, from which air impulses were transmitted through pneumatic pipes to subsidiary clocks. The secondary clocks were regulated by it, thus ensuring uniform time in public buildings such as schools, which needed many clocks.

WERFEL, FRANZ (1890–1945), prominent Austrian novelist, dramatist, and poet, fled to France from his native land when it was occupied by the Nazis, and after the fall of France made his way to the U.S., living in Los Angeles from 1940 until his death. During that period he published *The Song of Bernadette* (1942), a novel about the saint which was made into a popular film, and *Between Heaven and Earth* (1946) and *Star of the Unborn* (1946), which were issued posthumously.

WEST, JERRY (1938–), West Virginia-born basketball player, after graduation from his state's university (1960), where he had been an All-American star, played for the Los Angeles Lakers (1960–74), of which he became coach (1976). He was noted for his scoring, defensive game, and ability to shoot under pressure.

WEST, JESSAMYN (1907–), Indiana-born author, graduate of Whittier College and long a resident of California, best known for her first book, *The Friendly Persuasion* (1945), sensitive fictional sketches of Quaker life in her native state during the 19th century. Other works include *Cress Delahanty* (1953), a fictional account of an adolescent girl's life on a California ranch and in town; *South of the Angels* (1960), a novel about real estate development near Los Angeles at the beginning of the 20th century; and *To See the Dream*

(1957), about her experiences with the filming of her first work.

WEST, MAE (1892–), Brooklyn-born actress, began her stage career as a child, moved on to vaudeville and to great Broadway success in witty, *risqué* plays, including *Sex* (1926) and *Diamond Lil* (1928). The latter was also a popular starring vehicle in the Hollywood career she began in 1932, in which she presented herself as an easygoing, tough, sexually suggestive, hearty woman.

WEST, NATHANAEL (1903–40), pseudonym of Nathan Wallenstein Weinstein, New York author who in the 1930s began to publish brief novels whose fantasy exposed and satirized human corruption and the failure of the American dream. Late in the decade he went to Hollywood to write motion picture scripts. That background led to his major novel, *The Day of the Locust*♦ (1939), a surrealistic satire of the pathological condition of the movie capital and its residents.

West Coast Jazz, a development (1949) made by former members of the band of Stan Kenton♦ who played at the Lighthouse in Hermosa Beach, run by bassist Howard Rumsey, and were known for their "cool" restrained sound, tight arrangements, and unusual instruments. Recordings by Miles Davis (1949–50) featuring rich musical voicings and intricate arrangements were another major influence, as was saxophonist Gerry Mulligan,♦ who left Miles Davis to form his own pianoless quartet (1952). Many other leading figures of the movement played with one or more of these groups. In San Francisco Dave Brubeck♦ and his group played along similar lines, but there was little contact between the musicians of the two cities. West Coast Jazz, part of the "cool" jazz of the 1950s, had a close affinity with the Beat movement♦ in San Francisco during the same period.

Western Addition of San Francisco, see *Van Ness, James.*

Western History Association, organization founded (1961) "to promote the study of the American West in all its varied aspects" by professional historians and amateur scholars alike. It holds annual meetings and publishes *The American West*♦ and the more scholarly *Western Historical Quarterly* (1970–).

Western Pacific Railroad, name used by the Central Pacific Railroad♦ for a subsidiary line between

Sacramento and Oakland (opened 1869), later absorbed into the Southern Pacific. The important line of that name was the one built (1905–09) from Oakland through Feather River Canyon and Beckwourth Pass in the Sierra to Salt Lake City, to provide the first serious northern Californian competition to the Southern Pacific. High construction costs and lack of feeder lines to create traffic forced the company into receivership (1911), but reorganization and the acquisition of other lines for branches to Stockton, Turlock, San Jose, Sacramento, Chico, and Reno put it on a firm basis, and it later built a link to the Great Northern Railway (1926).

Westlands, popular name for the west side of the San Joaquin Valley. A desert area until the 1920s, it has been developed as prime farming land for cotton, alfalfa, barley, and tomatoes through water from deep wells and the San Luis Canal of the Central Valley Project.

WESTON, Brett (1911–), son of Edward Weston and also a distinguished photographer, some of whose pictures, emphasizing patterns in nature and in man-made objects, were collected in *Voyage of the Eye* (1975).

WESTON, Edward (1886–1958), born in Illinois, moved to California (1906) as a surveyor but soon became a photographer, located first in Glendale and later in Carmel. He was famous for his sharp-eyed, sensitive view of natural forms and the western scene. Some of his prints appeared in *California and the West* (1940), with commentary by his wife, Charis, the daughter of Harry Leon Wilson, and with his own philosophic views in his *Daybooks* (1961, 1966) on Mexico and California, respectively.

Westways, monthly magazine published by the Automobile Club of Southern California (1909–), called *Touring Topics* during its first 25 years. It emphasizes regional history and culture, and its many noted writers have included Idwal Jones, Phil Townsend Hanna, Carey McWilliams, Lawrence Clark Powell, and W. W. Robinson.

Westwood Village, residential and shopping community created when the University of California, Los Angeles, moved to its present campus (1929). In its hill area are located many elegant estates. Another Westwood, located in Lassen County, was the site of a pitched battle (1938) between

the CIO union members and the company union members of the Red River Lumber Co.

Wetbacks, pejorative term for Mexican nationals who illegally enter the U.S., so-called because many of them supposedly waded across the Rio Grande. As many as 500,000 were thought to have crossed (and often recrossed) the border annually just after World War II, generally to work as migratory laborers in the southwestern states and California. They are to be distinguished from *braceros,*◆ whose entry and work have been legally arranged by an American employer.

Whaling, an important activity in California for almost the first three-quarters of the 19th century, not only because gray whales and humpbacks annually migrated through the coastal waters but because California afforded a good area for trade, supplies, and repairs on long voyages that took ships to the Arctic and far out into the Pacific. Major ports, including Sausalito on San Francisco Bay, were visited by whaling vessels. Stations for offshore hunting in small boats were also established from Crescent City to Point Loma on San Diego Bay, with an important one at Monterey. The former sites were for ships mainly from New England; the latter were for local companies, the Monterey one run by Portuguese. The business began to fall off in the 1870s because hunting had made whales scarce, and whale oil had begun to be replaced by petroleum for lubrication and illumination. In 1976 the legislature named the gray whale the state's official marine mammal.

What Cheer House, San Francisco temperance hotel for men only, built (1852) on Leidesdorff and Sacramento streets, and famous for more than a decade for the reasonable cost of its rooms and food, and for its museum of natural history objects and Indian artifacts and 3,000-volume library. The name was derived from a common English greeting. The owner, R. B. Woodward, had a lavish home of his own made into a public park, Woodward's Gardens.◆

What Makes Sammy Run?, novel by Budd Schulberg,◆ published in 1941, portraying Sammy Glick, a tough, mean opportunist who claws his way to the top of the motion picture production world. The book is a satire on Hollywood.

WHEAT, Carl I[rving] (1892–1966), lawyer, bibliophile, cartographer, and historian of the West, active in regional book-collecting and historical societies and a leader in revivifying E Clampus Vitus.♦ His publications include an edition of the Shirley Letters, articles on Death Valley pioneers, and *Mapping the Trans-Mississippi West* (5 vols., 1957–63).

Wheat, first grown and mowed in a primitive style at some missions (31,000 bushels were produced in 1831, according to Alexander Forbes, and 4,000 *fanegas* just at Bodega in 1838, according to Faxon Atherton). The grain was not very widely cultivated during the early gold rush period, when flour♦ was imported, although 112,000 bushels were produced in San Joaquin and Tuolumne counties in 1852. The wide flat lands and soft soils of the San Joaquin and Sacramento valleys made them important producing areas for the state, which in 1868 harvested 20,000,000 bushels. California was the nation's major wheat-growing state in the 1870s, and by 1889 was sending some of its 40,000,000 bushels annually all over the world. Helping to achieve that output were developments in plows and harvesters, and the invention of the tractor by Benjamin Holt.♦ The great days of vast wheat production are dramatically depicted in Frank Norris' *The Octopus*. Because of their control, two men have been called the "Wheat King": James Glenn,♦ the grower, and Isaac Friedlander,♦ the shipper. Competition from the midwestern U.S., Russia, and Canada, and the possibility that irrigation allowed for raising other more profitable crops in California, led to a great drop in wheat growing during the last decade of the 19th century. Today it is a negligible crop.

Wheat King, see *Glenn, James* and *Friedlander, Isaac*.

Wheatland Riot, occurred on August 13, 1913, on the Yuba County hops ranch of Ralph Durst, the state's largest employer of migratory labor, who had widely advertised more jobs than were available, attracting great numbers of potential workers, to whom he offered low pay and bad housing. The opposition of Richard "Blackie" Ford, an I.W.W. organizer, led to a personal encounter with Durst. This confrontation occasioned the calling of the sheriff and his deputies, one of whom fired a shot in the air that started a riot in which the sheriff, the district attorney, and two workers were killed and many persons injured. As a result, Gov. Hiram Johnson not only sent in the National Guard but created a Commission on Immigration

and Housing to investigate the conditions of migratory farm laborers. The results were presented in an important report written by Carleton Parker. Another outcome was the organization of Kelley's Army.♦ The nearby town of Wheatland, on the county's southern border, once had a black mayor, Edward P. Duplex♦ (1888).

WHEELER, BENJAMIN IDE (1854–1927), after an academic career of teaching classics, German, and comparative philology at Brown, Harvard, and Cornell, was invited to become president of the University of California. His administration (1899–1919) was noted for raising the level of the institution and promoting dynamic growth. He worked not only effectively but also independently without consulting the faculty, until late in his career a "revolt" led to his ceding many powers to the Academic Senate.

Whilkut, Indians of the Athabascan family who had close ties to the Hupa♦ and the Chilula.♦ Their aboriginal population of 500 was reduced to 50 by the time of the 1910 census. They used bark slabs rather than planks in building houses, showing a central California, rather than a Yurok, influence. The Whilkut lived in the drainage area of the Mad River.♦

Whiskeytown-Shasta-Trinity National Recreation Area, National Park and forest lands comprising 100,000 acres in three segments. The first two are in Shasta County, west and north of Redding, respectively, while the third is nearby, on the eastern border of Trinity County. The major features are four man-made lakes created by damming the Trinity and Sacramento rivers: Whiskeytown, Shasta, Clair Engle, and Lewiston lakes.

WHITAKER, HERMAN (1867–1919), English-born journalist, novelist, and Socialist leader, long resident in California, where he was a friend of Jack London and Joaquin Miller. His daughter married Xavier Martinez.

WHITE, ELLEN GOULD [HARMON] (1827–1915), Maine-born religious leader, after disappointment with the Millerite movement (it had predicted the bodily appearance of Christ in the U.S. about 1843), had her own visions of His Advent. She advocated a special observance of the Sabbath that became a base of the Seventh-Day Adventist Church, formed by her and her husband, James Springer White (1821–81). Their church movement came to attract many followers, first in New York and then in Michigan, where they lived, and finally in California, where she resided first at Healdsburg (1881–85) and then at St. Helena (1903–15) after her husband's death. She wrote many texts for her denomination and promoted the founding of educational institutions, of which the most famous is the university, which emphasizes medicine, located at Loma Linda.♦

WHITE, STEPHEN MALLORY (1853–1901), San Francisco-born lawyer who practiced in Los Angeles, where he also became prominent in Democratic party politics. He was elected to the U.S. Senate (1893–99), where he championed the creation of a harbor for Los Angeles at San Pedro. Although he was the state's 21st U.S. Senator, he was the first to be born in California.

WHITE, STEWART EDWARD (1873–1946), Michigan-born author, summered in Santa Barbara as a child and lived there or in Burlingame after 1903. His youthful experiences in the upper Midwest among rivermen, miners, and lumberjacks provided both settings and subjects for his early novels of rugged outdoor life, including *The Claim Jumpers* (1901), *The Blazed Trail* (1902), and *The Rules of the Game* (1910). His *Story of California* (1927) is a trilogy of novels: *Gold* (1913), about the gold rush; *The Gray Dawn* (1915), about the Vigilante era of San Francisco; and *The Rose Dawn* (1920), about the southern California land boom of the 1880s. Another trilogy, *The Long Rifle* (1932), *Ranchero* (1933), and *Folded Hills* (1934), deals with a frontiersman's settling in early California and the life of his descendants. These, with a novelette, *Stampede* (1942), were gathered in *The Saga of Andy Burnett*. His many other books include short stories, collected in *Arizona Nights* (1907), and personal narratives of experiences in the Sierra: *The Mountains* (1904), *The Pass* (1906), and *The Cabin* (1911). In his last years he wrote books of personal philosophy revealing his belief in the occult.

White Mountain, third highest peak in the state (14,246 ft.), in the Inyo National Forest, northeast of Bishop, on whose summit is located a University of California station for high-altitude studies. In the White Mt. Range, to which it belongs, is located the Bristlecone Pine Forest.♦

White Wolf Fault, see *Earthquakes.*

WHITFIELD, JAMES MONROE (1822–71), member of a prominent family of free blacks in New Hampshire, moved to California in the early 1860s and resided in San Francisco after 1866. He was known for his poetry.

WHITFIELD, MAL[VIN G.] (1925–), Los Angeles-born middle-distance track star. In 1948 and again in 1952, he won the 800-meter race in the Olympic Games. In 1953 he established indoor world records for 500 yards, 500 meters, and 600 yards, and the outdoor record for 880 yards. In 1954 he became the first black to win the Sullivan Award as the outstanding U.S. amateur athlete of the year.

WHITNEY [CHARLOTTE] ANITA (1867–1955), native Californian of distinguished American lineage and niece of U.S. Supreme Court Justice Stephen J. Field. After graduation from Wellesley and settlement work on New York's Lower East Side, she returned home to become the first juvenile probation officer of Alameda County. She became an active pacifist, a defender of Mooney♦ and Billings,♦ a supporter of the I.W.W., a member of the Socialist party and, later, of the American Communist party, although she was in favor of democratic, peaceful change. Under the state's Criminal Syndicalism Act, she was convicted (1920) of belonging to a party advocating unlawful violence to accomplish political change. Fremont Older persuaded John Francis Neylan to handle her appeal. The year her conviction was upheld by the U.S. Supreme Court (1927), she was pardoned by Gov. C. C. Young, who declared that this philanthropist should not be made a martyr.

WHITNEY, JOSIAH DWIGHT (1819–96), scientist born in Massachusetts, after graduation from Yale and study in Europe, became a mining geologist and the author of *Metallic Wealth of the United States* (1854). He was appointed state geologist of California (1860) and made an extensive survey of the land, aided by William H. Brewer,♦ Clarence King,♦ Lorenzo Yates,♦ and other assistants. *Geology,* I (1865) was a preliminary report, but work ended in 1868 because of failure to get sufficient state funding. Whitney continued in office until 1874 and later published further studies, including *The Auriferous Gravels of the Sierra Nevada of California* (1880), issued by Harvard University, where he headed the School of Mines. He was a distinguished scholar but was once led astray: he declared that the so-called Calaveras Skull♦ was genuine. Mt. Whitney was named in his honor.

Whitney, Mount, see *Mount Whitney.*

Whittier, suburb of Los Angeles, lying on its east, founded by Quakers (1881) and named for the poet, was originally a center for citrus, avocado, and walnut ranches. It is now best known as Richard Nixon's home town, and for Whittier College,♦ which he attended. Another site is the State Park containing the home of Pío Pico. In 1970 the population was 72,863.

Whittier College, coeducational liberal arts institution (founded 1891), located in the town of the same name. Since 1901 it has been nondenominational. Alumni include Richard M. Nixon, Dorothy Baker, and Jessamyn West. In 1970 it enrolled fewer than 2,500 students.

WICKSON, EDWARD J[AMES] (1846–1923), New York-born horticulturist, moved to San Francisco (1875), where he worked on the staff of the *Pacific Rural Press* for the rest of his life. From 1879 on he was also a member of the faculty of the University of California and was widely known for such popular books as *The California Fruits and How To Grow Them* (1889), *The California Vegetables* (1897), and *Rural California* (1923).

WIDNEY, JOSEPH P[OMEROY] (1841–1938), Ohio-born doctor and educator, moved to San Francisco (1862), where he attended Toland Medical College. He then went to Los Angeles, where he became the city's first health officer; joined his brother (Judge Robert M. Widney) in founding the University of Southern California, of which he became the second president; and, as a civic leader, worked to develop San Pedro as the city's harbor.

WIERZBICKI, FELIX PAUL (1815–60), born in Poland, came to the U.S. (1834), entered California with Stevenson's Regiment,♦ and after the Mexican War continued his practice in San Francisco as a physician and surgeon. He wrote *California As It Is, And As It May Be* (1849), on the state's past, present, and potentialities. The first English language book printed in California, it was published by Washington Bartlett.

WIGGIN, KATE DOUGLAS (1856–1923), Philadelphia-born educator, moved to Santa Barbara (1873) and in Los Angeles was trained by Emma Marwedel♦ in the teaching of children. She established California's first free kindergarten in San Fran-

cisco (1878). To raise money for it, she wrote *The Birds' Christmas Carol* (1887), about an ethereal child. Moving to New York (1884) and then to New England, she later wrote even more popular fiction, *Rebecca of Sunnybrook Farm* (1903) and *Mother Carey's Chickens* (1911). While in San Francisco she influenced Sarah Cooper.♦

WILBUR, RAY LYMAN (1875–1949), Iowa-born doctor and educator, graduated from Stanford University (1896), and was its president (1916–43). He took a leave (1929–33), and while Hoover's Secretary of the Interior he named Hoover Dam.

Wildcat, also called lynx and bobcat, smaller than the mountain lion, being less than three feet long, with gray-brown fur, is found throughout California, except in open country and populous regions, and hardly at all in the southeastern part of the state, where the paler *desert wildcat* flourishes. Both feed on quail, squirrels, rabbits, and even deer. Their former frequency is indicated by over 50 place-names in the state incorporating the word "wildcat."

Wilderness Areas, primitive portions of National Forests♦ generally containing at least 5,000 acres. The areas and the forests within which they are located are Agua Tibia (Cleveland), Caribou Peak (Lassen), Cucamonga (San Bernardino), Desolation (Eldorado), Dome Land (Sequoia), Emigrant (Stanislaus), Golden Trout (Sierra), Hoover (Inyo and Toiyabe), John Muir (Inyo and Sierra), Marble Mountain (Klamath), Middle Eel–Yolla Bolly (Mendocino, Shasta, Trinity), Minarets (Sierra and Inyo), Mokelumne (Eldorado and Stanislaus), San Gabriel (Angeles), San Gorgonio (San Bernardino), San Jacinto (San Bernardino), San Rafael (Los Padres), Santa Lucia (Los Padres), South Warner (Modoc), Thousand Lakes (Lassen), Ventana (Los Padres). Additionally, Emigrant Basin (Stanislaus), High Sierra (Sequoia and Sierra), and Salmon–Trinity Alps (Klamath, Shasta, and Trinity) are Primitive Areas under consideration for acceptance as Wilderness Areas.

Wildflowers, once far more common and more widely distributed through the state before increased urbanization, industrialization, and agriculture overran the land, still consist of several hundred flourishing species. The best known are the coastal wildflowers, including the *California* or *golden poppy, matilija, castilleja* or *Indian paintbrush, lupine, ceanothus,* and *azalea,* as well as *iris* and *primrose.* Desert wildflowers include *penstemon, primrose, verbena,* and many flowering *cacti.* Mountain wildflowers generally bloom only in summer, as do *fireweed* and *Washington lily,* but also include *snowplant,* whose red flower is seen in snow patches. Indians used wildflowers for medication, hairdressing, fibers, food, and dyes. Some seeming wildflowers were originally domesticated plants, such as *mustard* and *Queen Anne's lace* (or *wild carrot*), a biennial herb. A large Poppy Preserve is located in Antelope Valley. *(See also individual entries.)*

Wildlife Refuges, areas under federal ownership and administration, totaling about a quarter of a million acres, preserved as refuges for wild creatures and as areas which permit people to undertake nature study. The 17 are Clear Lake (Modoc County), Colusa (Colusa County), Delevan (Colusa County), Graylodge (Butte County), Havasu (San Bernardino County), Humboldt Bay (Humboldt County), Kern (Kern County), Merced (Merced County), Modoc (Modoc County), Pixley (Tulare County), Sacramento (Glenn County), Salton Sea (Imperial County), San Francisco Bay, San Luis (Merced County), San Pablo Bay, Sutter (Sutter County), and Tule Lake (Siskiyou County).

Wild One, The, see *Hollister.*

WILKES, CHARLES (1798–1877), naval officer who commanded six ships on a major exploratory and scientific expedition covering South Pacific islands, Antarctica, and the northwest coast of North America (1838–42). He sailed into San Francisco Bay (1841) and also sent to it an overland detachment from Astoria via the Willamette and Sacramento rivers. His reports appeared as *Narration of the United States Exploring Expedition* (5 vols. and atlas, 1844), *Western America* (1849), and many scientific and cartographic monographs, totaling 28 works with data on and references to California based on information from his several exploring parties.

WILLEY, SAMUEL HOPKINS (1821–1914), after graduation from Dartmouth (1848), went to Monterey on behalf of the American Missionary Society (1849), became the army chaplain there, opened a school in Colton Hall, and founded what was probably California's first public library. He was a Presbyterian pastor in San Francisco (1850–62) and had Congregational churches in Santa Cruz (1870–80) and Benicia (1880–90). An organizer

of the College of California (1855), he was its acting president for a time before it became the University of California. He wrote several books about the history of his adopted state and its organizations with which he was associated.

WILLIAMS, ABRAM PEASE (1832–1911), miner and then a businessman in California, to which he moved from his native Maine (1858). A prominent Republican, he was chosen to fill the vacancy in the U.S. Senate left by the death of John F. Miller (1886–87).

WILLIAMS, [EG]BERT [AUSTIN] (1874–1922), black vaudeville comedian, born in the West Indies and reared in Riverside, began his career in San Francisco (*c.*1895). There he lived for a time, but his later success was continued on the New York stage.

WILLIAMS, ISAAC (1799–1856), fur trader who moved to Los Angeles (1832) with Ewing Young,♦ settled there, was naturalized, and married a daughter of Antonio María Lugo. In 1841 his father-in-law gave him the great Rancho Santa Ana del Chino (Riverside County), on which he cultivated orchards, vineyards, cattle, and sheep. He also made it a hospitable stop for travelers arriving by southern trails; later it was a Butterfield stage station. In 1846 it was seized by Americans who surrendered to a siege by *Californios,* to whom the owner was known not as Isaac, but Julián.

WILLIAMS, PAUL REVERE (1896–   ), Los Angeles-born architect, designed and built many structures in his native city, including office buildings and stores, as well as homes of film stars, known for their high style. He won the Spingarn Medal (1953), given to distinguished blacks by the National Association for the Advancement of Colored People.

WILLIAMS, TED (THEODORE SAMUEL WILLIAMS) (1918–   ), San Diego-born baseball player, was an outfielder for his home town's Padres (1936–37) and the Boston Red Sox (1939–60). He led the American League in batting six times and led it twice (1942, 47) in home runs and runs batted in, thereby winning the Triple Crown. Selected as his league's Most Valuable Player (1946, 49), he was also elected to the Baseball Hall of Fame (1966). He was later manager of the Washington Senators (1969–72).

WILLIAMS, VIRGIL (1830–86), artist born in Maine, studied in Rome and was brought to San

Francisco (1862) to provide copies of Italian old masters for the gallery of Woodward's Gardens.♦ He put that hackwork behind him and became known for his landscapes and genre scenes. He was the director of the San Francisco Art Institute♦ and, as a friend of his onetime student, Mrs. Robert Louis Stevenson and her husband, advised them to spend their honeymoon near St. Helena, the site of his ranch and scene of many of his paintings.

Willow, tree or shrub belonging to the genus *Salix.* Of the 31 species found in California the six most common are: the *yellow, red,* and *black willows,* which reach about 45 feet; the *arroyo,* which grows eight to 20 feet high; and the *Nuttall* and *velvet* (also called the *Sitka* or *silky willow*), which are generally shrubs of up to eight feet but sometimes grow to trees 25 feet high. Since they live where running water is found, early travelers often used them as place-name markers, leading to more than 200 Willow Creeks and over 100 each of such variants as Willow Springs and Willow Slough in California.

Willows, seat of Glenn County, named for the trees along its creek. The surrounding area is known for its rice, sheep, and lumber. The 10,000-acre Sacramento National Wildlife Refuge is just to the south. In 1970 the population was 4,085.

WILLS, HELEN (1906–), born and reared in East Bay, generally recognized as the greatest woman tennis player of her era, whose record of victories in the U.S., England, and France still stood unparalleled 40 years later. She won the U.S. woman's singles championship (1923–25, 27–29, 31, 35) and the comparable British title (1927–29, 32–33, 35, 38). Her great rival was her fellow Berkeleyan, Helen Jacobs.♦ Helen Wills was the model for Diego Rivera's symbolic portrait of California in his mural in the Stock Exchange Club of San Francisco.

WILLS, MAURY (MAURICE MORNING WILLS) (1932–), baseball player, was a shortstop with the Los Angeles Dodgers (1959–66, 1969–72). He was the first player to steal more than 100 bases in a single season, thereby being voted Associated Press Athlete of the Year (1962).

WILMERDING, JILLIS CLUTE (1833–94), moved to California (1849) from New York State and after a successful business career bequeathed $400,000 to the Regents of the University of California to establish a school of industrial arts to teach trades to boys. In 1915 the San Francisco school (est. 1900) became affiliated with the similar but more professionally academic one founded by the will of James Lick.♦ It cooperated with a school named for Miranda W. Lux, who provided funds for industrial education for girls. Lick-Wilmerding was separated from the university (1961), but had long since become a college preparatory academic institution.

Wilmington, see *Banning, Phineas,* and *San Pedro.*

WILSHIRE, H. GAYLORD (1861–1927), born in Ohio of a wealthy family, moved to California (1884), where he made and lost fortunes in orange and walnut growing, gold mining, a patent electric belt for therapeutic purposes, and real estate development. During the boom of the 1880s he not only made a subdivision in Fullerton but created a tract in what was then west Los Angeles, through which ran the great broad boulevard he named for himself. When those ventures failed, he became a Socialist, issued *Wilshire's Journal* to support the cause, and ran for Congress (1890). For a time he lived in England (1891–95) as an associate of the Fabians, but he returned to his southern California home.

WILSON, ADRIAN (1923–), Michigan-born book designer and printer, began his career in San Francisco (1947) by printing handsome and imaginative programs and announcements for a theater in which his wife, Joyce Lancaster, acted. That led to his writing and producing *Printing for Theater* (1957). While designing books for large publishers and printing fine limited editions, he has also written *The Design of Books* (1967) and, with his wife, *The Making of the Nuremberg Chronicle* (1976).

WILSON, BENJAMIN D[AVIS] (1811–78), Tennessee-born pioneer of U.S. interests in California, arrived in Los Angeles (1841) with the overland party of William Workman♦ after a career as fur trapper and Indian trader in the Santa Fe area. His great California landholdings began with the purchase, from Juan Bandini, of the Jurupa Rancho (including the present site of Riverside) and his marriage to a member of the Yorba family, whose properties included Santa Ana Rancho. He was a conciliatory figure during the American conquest, attempted to make southern California a separate state, was elected mayor of Los Angeles (1851), and was President Fillmore's Indian agent for the southern part of California, establishing many of its reservations. He extended his ranches by buying old Mission San Gabriel lands, coming to own properties that are now San Bernardino, San Pedro, Westwood, Pasadena, Alhambra, and San Gabriel. He worked with Phineas Banning to develop a harbor at Wilmington, and cultivated citrus fruits, walnuts, and vineyards for his winemaking, as well as raising sheep on land that he later subdivided into orchards and town lots. He was also a leader in attracting the railroad to the region and in developing San Pedro, as well as in drilling for oil, although the last venture was unsuccessful. Mt. Wilson is named for him. He was commonly known as Don Benito Wilson. Gen. George S. Patton was one of his grandchildren.

WILSON, DON BENITO, see *Wilson, Benjamin D.*

WILSON, HARRY LEON (1867–1929), Illinois-born author of humorous fiction, after a successful career collaborating with Booth Tarkington on comic plays, moved to Carmel (1910). In California he wrote his most successful novels: *Ruggles of Red Gap* (1915), depicting a British valet employed in a Far Western cattle town, and *Merton of the Movies* (1922), a lightly satirical story about a movie-struck young clerk who achieves stardom as a comic because by his over-acting he burlesques serious roles.

WILSON, J[ACKSON] STITT (1868–1942), Canadian-born Methodist minister, moved to Berkeley (1901), where as a Socialist he was elected mayor (1911–12). He advocated woman suffrage, temperance, prison reform, and a Henry George kind of tax system. He also ran for governor (1910) and for Congress (1912). In the congressional race he polled 40% of the vote to Joseph Knowland's 54%.

Wilson, Mount, see *Mount Wilson.*

Wimmer nugget, small lump of gold thought to be the one discovered by James W. Marshall (Jan. 24, 1848) in the tail race of Sutter's mill at Coloma. Its name derives from that of Peter L. Wimmer, Marshall's assistant in supervising the Indians who had dug the race. Wimmer's wife tested the metal by boiling it with home-made soap to assure that it would emerge untarnished. The nugget has long belonged to The Bancroft Library.

Winchester Mystery House, in the San Jose area, north of Campbell, was a private home built by the widowed Sarah L. Winchester, heiress of the Win-

chester Repeating Arms Co. A spiritualist, she believed she would die if the house were ever completed, so she kept a staff of carpenters at work on additions to the rambling, disorganized wooden structure between 1880 and her death in 1922.

Wine, production began in California when the mission fathers established vineyards♦ and from their grapes♦ made a sweet fermented juice for sacramental and personal use. During the 1820s, Mission San Gabriel was making 400 barrels of wine a year, but secularization (1833) led to a great decline there and at other missions. Commercial wine growing centered on Los Angeles, whose major producer, beginning in the 1830s, was a former Bordeaux vintner, Jean Louis Vignes.♦ The gold rush brought a demand for wine in the new cities and mining camps, so that winemaking throughout the state, particularly in Napa and other valleys around San Francisco, grew tremendously.

By 1860 California was among the three largest wine-producing states, and soon became the leader. Quality was greatly improved by the influx of Europeans, particularly Agoston Haraszthy,♦ who not only imported zinfandel and tokay stock from his native Hungary but also introduced hundreds of other grape varieties in the 1860s.

In the 1870s and 80s the roots of many grape vines were ruined by phylloxera, a plant louse. However, that devastation also had beneficial results, in that speculators in poor grapes and quick winemaking were driven out of business and the remaining producers had to take greater care with their vines and the resultant wines. The state legislature also attempted to improve the quality of wines by establishing a State Board of Viticulture (1880–95), which worked for favorable tax and tariff laws.

Although Prohibition (1919–34) ended wine production, grape production continued for table use, for raisins, and for the 200 gallons of wine that the law permitted to be made by each family in the U.S. With the repeal of Prohibition, winemaking was resumed not only in the old wineries of Napa,♦ Sonoma,♦ Livermore,♦ and Santa Clara♦ valleys but in many new ones there and elsewhere. They now produce a great variety of wines: table (or still); sparkling; and sherry and port, which are wines fortified with brandy. By the 1970s wineries varied from small, personal businesses to huge industries with vast storage tanks resembling those used for oil. More than 250 California wineries produce 85% of the wine made in the U.S., the leading ones having important vineyards of their own.

Winnedumah, an 80-foot-high granite monolith, on the pinnacle of the White Mts. east of Independence (Inyo County), often known as Piute Monument. One legend is that Winnedumah, a medicine man, was transformed into this great rock while calling for spiritual help during a battle. His brother Tinemaha is commemorated in the names of a nearby Owens Valley mountain and creek.

WINNEMUCAH, SARAH (c.1844–91), name given to Thoc-me-tony (''Shellflower''), the granddaughter of the Nevada chief of the Paiutes, called Truckee by Elisha Stevens,♦ whose party he guided across the Sierra in 1844. At her grandfather's urging she was educated at St. Mary's convent in San Jose, becoming not only a nominal Catholic while still holding to her native beliefs but also an accomplished linguist. After suffering brutal treatment by agents on an Indian reservation at Pyramid Lake (Nevada), she lectured in San Francisco and elsewhere on the lot of the Indians. As an interpreter she also aided army officers, whose handling of Indian reservations she found far better than that of civilian agents, and her husbands (both white), Lt. Edward Bartlett and Lambert Hopkins, were both army men. She wrote *Life Among the Piutes* (1883), and on land in Lovelock, Nevada, donated by Leland Stanford, she conducted a school for Paiute children.

Winning of Barbara Worth, The, novel by Harold Bell Wright♦ published in 1911. Set in the Imperial Valley, where the author lived, its plot deals with a beautiful young orphan girl, happy in the desert environment where she had been found as a child, and her wooing by a cultivated New York engineer, but as important as the story is the thesis that westerners have noble values while most easterners are sharp money grubbers as they both face nature to reclaim its wilderness for social good.

Wintun, Indians whose territory covered the west side of the Sacramento Valley north to the Pit and McCloud rivers, lying to the west and north of the lands of the Yana.♦ Prehistorically they may have numbered about 12,000 but they were reduced to about 1,000 by 1920. Despite their limited population, they had various cultures, since their territory was so extensive and adjoined that of so many other Indians, including the Pomo, Hupa, Miwok, and Yana. Thus the southeastern Wintun believed,

like the Pomo, in the transfer of shamanistic ability, while many of their mythological tales resemble those of the Maidu, such as that which attributes the origin of the earth to the turtle. The Wintun's Kuksu cult, spread to their neighbors, was a secret male society that performed ritual dances in a temescal.♦ The cultural variety of the Wintun is indicated by the fact that their language can be divided into the Wintu of the north; the Nomlaki in the central area; and the Patwin♦ in the south, down to the lower reaches of the Sacramento River.

Wiyot, Indians resident on the lower Mad and Eel rivers and at Humboldt Bay. They were related to the Algonquin, like their neighbors, the Yurok, whose culture they absorbed. Kroeber estimated that their population was about 1,000 in 1770, but, partly as the result of a great massacre at Eureka♦ (1860), their number was reduced to 100 by 1910.

Wolf, wild animal of the dog family similar in size and appearance to a large collie, has been very rare in California. Its region was probably the same as that of the coyote,♦ with which some early travelers probably confused it. The true wolf has probably been exterminated in the state.

WOLFE, TOM, (THOMAS KENNERLY WOLFE, JR. (1931–), Virginia-born journalist, known for his studies of alternative lifestyles in contemporary American culture, frequently finds the subjects for his jet-set sociology among such Californians as surfers and the Hell's Angels. His baroque prose style is evident also in his titles, including *The Kandy-Kolored Tangerine-Flake Streamline Baby* (1965) and *Radical Chic and Mau-Mauing the Flak Catchers* (1971). *The Electric Kool-Aid Acid Test* (1968) deals with the peripatetic Merry Pranksters of Ken Kesey.♦

Wolfman Jack, name used by Robert Smith (1938–), a disc jockey who first broadcast from Mexican radio stations close to the California border and later from Los Angeles. Known for his singing and other accompaniments to the jazz records he played and for his other antics, he became so popular that by 1973 his program was syndicated over 1,500 stations. He played himself in the film *American Graffiti*♦ (1973).

Wolframite, see *Tungsten.*

WOLFSKILL, WILLIAM (1798–1866), Kentucky-born fur trapper and trader in the southwest, entered Los Angeles (1831) via the Old Spanish Trail to seek furs. Settling there, he built a schooner to trap sea otter on the coastal islands. In 1841 he planted a commercial orange grove and became the largest grower in southern California. Though a rancher, he also established vineyards for wine, grew English walnuts, and helped to introduce eucalyptus to California. His brothers, John Reed (1805?–97), Milton, Mathus, and Sarchel, followed him to California and raised fruit and cattle on Rancho Río de los Putos in Solano and Yolo counties.

Wonder Team, term coined by "Brick" [Clinton R.] Morse, *San Francisco Chronicle* sports writer, for the University of California football team of 1920, and applied to two succeeding years of the original team and to the University's teams through 1925. In its three-year span the original team won 27 games, tied one, scored 1,220 points to its opponents' 81, made 173 touchdowns, 149 conversions, seven field goals, and six safeties. In the entire five-year span, the teams remained undefeated except for two losses toward the end of the 1925 season.

WOOD, CHARLES ERSKINE SCOTT (1852–1944), born in Pennsylvania, after a military career including a post at West Point (from which he had been graduated, 1874), service in various Indian campaigns (one of which was against Chief Joseph of the Nez Percé), and exploration of the Yukon and Alaska, resigned his commission to study law at Columbia University. He practiced law for both corporations and civil liberties causes in Portland (1884–1919) before moving to Saratoga (1929) with his wife, the poet Sara Bard Field,♦ and devoting himself to literature and liberal social causes. His books include *The Poet in the Desert* (1915), a poetic dialogue between Truth and a Poet concerning humanitarian ideals and social injustice; *Poems from the Ranges* (1929); *Heavenly Discourse* (1927), 40 witty dialogues written during World War I for *The Masses* satirizing the inhumanity of war and economic and social injustice in conversations that take place in Heaven among God, Jesus, Satan, various angels, and such visitors as Rabelais, Voltaire, Tom Paine, Mark Twain, Thomas Jefferson, and Billy Sunday; and a sequel, *Earthly Discourse* (1937).

WOODEN, JOHN [ROBERT] (1910–   ), Indiana-born basketball player and coach, was a three-time All-American guard at Purdue and a coach

in his native state before going to UCLA (1948) as its coach. He never had a losing year, and from 1964 through 1975 his teams won 10 out of 12 possible NCAA championships, a remarkable record, since no other coach has won more than three NCAA titles in his career. Between 1971 and 1974 his teams had 88 consecutive wins, and four times (1964, 67, 72, 73) they had perfect seasons of 30 wins and no losses.

Woodland, seat of Yolo County. Its early importance is suggested by two architectural monuments: the Opera House (1895) and the mansion of the Gable family (1885). Long an irrigation center for the surrounding farmlands of the Sacramento Valley, the city also has a large sugar beet refinery. In 1970 the population was 20,667.

Woodward's Gardens, originally the private San Francisco home (at Mission and Fourteenth streets), of Robert B. Woodward (1824–79), owner of the What Cheer House.♦ In 1866 he opened to the public its extensive gardens, lakes for boating, zoo, aquarium, and an art gallery with copies of old masters by Virgil Williams.♦ It was a popular amusement area (closed 1883) long remembered by visitors, including such youngsters as Robert Frost, the New England poet, who lived in San Francisco as a boy and later wrote a poem about the place.

Wool, see *Sheep*.

WORCESTER, JOSEPH (1836–1913), Boston-born minister of a Swedenborgian church in San Francisco (1876–1913) whose designs of his simple shingled homes in Piedmont and on Russian Hill influenced the area's professional architects in creating a Bay Region style. With A. Page Brown he designed his Church of the New Jerusalem, partly inspired by California's missions.

WORES, THEODORE (1858–1939), San Francisco artist who studied with Virgil Williams and in Germany. He is known for his romantic California landscapes as well as paintings of Chinatown and of foreign lands, particularly Japan.

WORK, JOHN (1792–1861), Irish-born member of the Hudson's Bay Co. and leader of its brigade of fur trappers which explored California (1832–33). His expedition took him along the Pit, Sacramento, and Russian rivers down as far as the Stanislaus and was described in his diary, printed as *Fur Brigade to the Bonaventura* (1945).

Workingmen's party of California, founded in San Francisco (1877) during an economic depression. It worked for employment of whites and against the cheaper Chinese labor, which had been brought to California to build the then-completed railroad, and opposed the economic power of bankers, railroad owners, large landholders, and their political representatives of major parties. The flamboyant speeches of the party's president, Denis Kearney,♦ attracted both great support and great opposition. For a time the party had an effect because its delegates to the state's Constitutional Convention (1878), together with some Grangers, could create a majority. The party also elected a San Francisco mayor, Isaac Kalloch,♦ 11 state Senators, and 16 Assemblymen, as well as most of the state Supreme Court, but it lacked organization and by 1880 had dwindled away, with Kearney returning to his own business.

WORKMAN, WILLIAM (1800–76), English-born trader in Taos, where he became a naturalized Mexican (known as Don Julián) and married a Mexican woman. Threatened by an uprising against Americans, he and John Rowland, another converted trader, led a party to Los Angeles (1841) which included William Gordon and William Knight, pioneers of Yolo County;♦ and Juan Manuel Vaca, a pioneer of Solano County;♦ as well as his future son-in-law, Francis P. F. Temple; and Benjamin D. Wilson.♦ In Los Angeles he was given a huge land grant and built a large adobe as headquarters for his ranching activities. Under the influence of Temple, he constructed a major office building, the Temple Block (1866–70), housing a bank they founded and named for themselves. When Ralston's Bank of California collapsed, it brought down Workman's, too, and Workman killed himself. His nephew, William Henry Workman (1839–1918), was mayor of Los Angeles (1887–88), and the Workman and Temple families have continued to be prominent there.

WORKS, JOHN DOWNEY (1847–1928), born in Indiana, where he practiced law and was a state representative before moving to California (1883). He became a superior court judge in San Diego County, a state Supreme Court Justice, a leading Los Angeles lawyer, and was elected to the U.S. Senate (1911–17) as a Republican.

World Series, championship finals of major league baseball, played between the winner of the American League and the winner of the National League,

has several times been won by California teams. The Los Angeles Dodgers (National League) won in 1959, 1963, and 1965. The Oakland Athletics (American League) won in 1972, 1973, and 1974. Losing competitors include the Los Angeles Dodgers (1966, 1974, and 1977) and the San Francisco Giants of the National League (1962). The first all-California World Series occurred when Oakland defeated Los Angeles four games to one in 1974. The Los Angeles Dodgers lost against the New York Yankees in 1977.

WOZENCRAFT, OLIVER MEREDITH (1814–87), Louisiana-born doctor, moved to California (1849), was a member of the first Constitutional Convention, and in 1850 became one of three U.S. commissioners empowered to negotiate treaties with the Indians and to establish reservations, but their sweeping recommendations were turned down by the U.S. Senate. He next proposed to use lower Colorado River water to irrigate the then arid area which became the Imperial Valley. His conception was eventually brought into being by George Chaffey.♦

WRIGHT, FRANK LLOYD (1869–1959), Wisconsin-born architect, recognized as one of the innovative leaders of his profession in the 20th century, built 25 structures in California. Between 1917 and 1923 he constructed five houses in the Los Angeles area, four of them featuring a patterned design with double walls of precast concrete blocks tied together by steel rods, of which the most famous example was Mrs. G. M. Millard's La Miniatura (1923) in Pasadena. The fifth building was Aline Barnsdall's Hollyhock House (1917), whose poured concrete design suggests a Mayan temple. It is now part of Barnsdall Park.♦ Other buildings include the former V. C. Morris gift shop (1948) in San Francisco, anticipating in small scale the spiral ramp of New York's Guggenheim Museum; Honeycomb House (1936), on the Stanford campus, built for Professor Paul R. Hanna and now the official residence of the provost; and the Marin County Civic Center (1957) on the outskirts of San Rafael. His son, Lloyd Wright, was the architect of the Wayfarers' Chapel (Swedenborgian) on the Palos Verde Peninsula (1949), featuring symbolic triangular and circular forms, and of the Hollywood Bowl.

WRIGHT, HAROLD BELL (1872–1944), born in upstate New York, after work as a painter and decorator and service as a pastor of the Disciples of

Christ sect's Christian Church in the Midwest and at Redlands (1907–8), retired to Redlands to become an author. His enormously popular fiction, often set in the open spaces of the Southwest and emphasizing the rugged individualist of unusually wholesome morality, includes *The Calling of Dan Matthews* (1909) and *When a Man's a Man* (1916). His most widely read work was *The Winning of Barbara Worth* (1911), set in the Imperial Valley, where he lived; it deals with the issues of irrigation and the conflict between the noble values he attributed to westerners and the practices of eastern financiers.

WRIGHT, MICKEY (MARY KATHRYN WRIGHT) (1935–), San Diego-born golfer, began her professional career in 1954. She won the U.S. open championship (1958, 59, 61, 63) and the Ladies' Professional Golf Association Championship (1958, 59, 61, 64). She is known for her powerful drive.

WRIGHT, WILLARD HUNTINGTON (1889–1939), like his brother, the artist Stanton MacDonald-Wright, was born in Virginia and reared in southern California. He was an editor of *Smart Set* and wrote books on modern art but became best known for his detective novels featuring the sleuth Philo Vance, which he wrote under the pseudonym of S. S. Van Dine.

Wright Act, state legislation (1887) sponsored by C. C. Wright, a Senator from Modesto, which altered the old English common law doctrine of riparian rights, permitting riverland owners to unrestricted stream use, and substituted for it the right of groups of farmers to create irrigation districts that can divert river water to dry lands for flood control and water conservation. Various refinements to the act were made by later amendments.

WURSTER, WILLIAM [WILSON] (1895–1973), Stockton-born architect, educated at the University of California, Berkeley, to which he returned as dean, first of architecture and then of environmental design, after an academic career at Yale and M.I.T. He is known for his simple homes employing modifications of Monterey colonial, American colonial, and Regency styles with both brick and board and batten. His larger structures include the Golden Gateway Redevelopment Project and Ghirardelli Square in San Francisco, and Cowell College at the University of California's Santa Cruz campus. His wife, Catherine Bauer Wurster (1905–64), a leader in housing and city planning, was also on the Berkeley faculty.

X

XÁNTUS, JÁNOS (1825–94), Hungarian naturalist, came to the U.S. (1851–64), where his diverse activities and wide-ranging travels took him to Fort Tejón as a member of the U.S. Army's Topographical Corps (1857–59). There he collected specimens of flora and fauna, mainly birds and mammals. He next made a biological exploration of Baja California for the U.S. government. He reported his voyages and experiences, with much romancing and plagiarism, in letters to Hungarian journals that were collected in two books (1857, 1860), translated and published in the U.S. as *Letters from North America* (1975) and *Travels in Southern California* (1976), respectively.

Y

Yachting, sailing a boat for sport and pleasure rather than for transportation, began early in the American period. An article in the *Alta California* in 1852 describes an outing on San Francisco Bay by an excursion group called the Pioneer Yacht Club. However, a permanent organization did not come into being until 1869, when the San Francisco Yacht Club was founded and held its first regatta with six boats. Even at that date the club was probably the fifteenth to be founded in the nation, since the first had been established in Detroit in 1839. Other Bay Area clubs soon followed with the founding of the Pacific Yacht Club (1877) and Corinthian Yacht Club (1886), leading to formation of the Pacific Inter-Club Yacht Association of Northern California (1896). The harbor created for the Panama-Pacific International Exposition in San Francisco (1915) was further developed for the St. Francis Yacht Club. The first big yacht on the Bay was the *Casco,* a 94-foot schooner owned by Dr. Samuel Merritt,♦ who chartered it to Robert Louis Stevenson for a cruise to the South Seas (1888). Since that date, large pleasure boats, including power craft, have become common. Yacht clubs were also established early in southern California in Los Angeles (South Coast Yacht Club), Santa Barbara, Catalina, and Newport Beach. They have developed greatly and proliferated widely, encouraged by the good weather and outdoor-oriented life of the area. The modern era of ocean yacht racing was begun in 1906 with the first annual transpacific competition from Los Angeles to Honolulu.

Yahi, see *Yana* and *Ishi.*

Yana, Indians of the Hokan family, whose territory extended from the region of Mt. Lassen north to the Pit River. They were divided into dialect groups: Gar'i, Gata'i, and Yahi. They probably numbered some 15,000 in the period before the American settlement of California, which in time led to their being entirely wiped out, through disease, malnutrition, guerrilla warfare, and one great massacre (1864), except for one surviving Yahi named Ishi,♦ who was discovered by whites in 1911, living in isolation as the last remnant of a Stone Age culture.

Yang-Na, Indian village once located on the site of downtown Los Angeles, in present Elysian Park.

YATES, LORENZO [GORDIN] (1837–1909), English-born naturalist, moved to Wisconsin (1853) and then to California as a member of the geological survey team of Josiah D. Whitney♦ in the 1860s. He settled in Santa Barbara, where he assembled the state's greatest private natural history collection (shells, fossils, plants, etc.) and Indian relics. He wrote many works related to those subjects.

YAW, ELLEN BEACH, see *Covina.*

YELLAND, RAYMOND DABB (1848–1900), English-born artist, reared in the U.S., moved to California (1873) to become an instructor at Mills College (1873–77), then at the California School of Design, where he succeeded Virgil Williams as director (1888), and at the University of California, although he also resided abroad temporarily. He was close to Tavernier and Rix, and, like Rix, depicted all aspects of the California landscape and coast and was known for the atmospheric light of his scenes.

Yellow Bird, pseudonym of John R. Ridge.♦

Yellow Peril, pejorative term applied to Oriental nations and their people. Although opposition to these groups was common among 19th-century Americans, it was particularly acute on the Pacific Coast and specifically in California, which had not only the major ports in contact with the Orient but also the greatest immigration from it. Chinese♦ were attracted in great numbers during the gold rush, and because of their appearance, culture, and language, they were isolated in ghetto-like Chinatowns and allowed only the poorest or hardest jobs. Great numbers of Chinese were brought in to help build the transcontinental railroad. When it was finished, they became available on the labor market to work at low pay, leading to cries that "The Chinese must go" in the harangues of Denis Kearney.♦ Laws restricting immigration and denying the Chinese citizenship were passed in the 1880s. Later large-scale American farmers brought in Japanese to get cheap labor, and the fear of Orientals was turned on the Japanese,♦ particularly as their nation developed naval power and was considered a military threat. As a result, exclusion acts were passed in the 1920s. Antipathy flared again at the time of the bombing of Pearl Harbor (Dec. 7, 1941) and the outbreak of World War II, leading to the evacuation of all Japanese (foreigners and citizens alike) from the California coast and their internment in relocation centers.

Yerba Buena, the American settlement on San Francisco Bay, far from the presidio and Mission San Francisco de Asís of Mexican background, became the forerunner of San Francisco, as it was officially renamed by Washington A. Bartlett♦ (Jan. 1847). Yerba Buena, meaning ''good herb'' in Spanish, because of the wild mint near its cove, was established as early as 1792. The settlement was begun by William A. Richardson♦ when he moved his family into a habitation there (1835) on the site of the present Grant Ave. between Clay and Washington streets. The bay islands called Yerba Buena and Alcatraz by Ayala (1775) had their names accidentally reversed in 1826 by Capt. F. W. Beechey, whose nomenclature has become permanent, even though the present Yerba Buena Island was long called Goat Island (1895–1931). It is now linked to the man-made (1939) Treasure Island.

Yerba Buena Jazz Band, The, San Francisco group (1940–50) organized by trumpeter Lu Watters, a native of Santa Cruz. They played in the contrapuntal, improvisational style of the 1920s, affecting the revival of New Orleans jazz on the West Coast. Two of its members later formed their own bands: trombonist Melvin E. (Turk) Murphy founded one at his Earthquake McGoon's in San Francisco, and the ragtime pianist, Wally Rose, had another in that city.

Yew, evergreen tree or shrub with red berries, of which only the *western* or *Pacific* is native. It grows 30 to 50 feet high in the Klamath Mts., the north central Coast Range, the Sierra Nevada, Santa Cruz Mts., Marble Mountain area, and on Mt. St. Helena. Maidu, Yuki, and Yurok Indians used the wood to make bows.

Yokut, Indians of the Penutian language family, resident on the floor of the San Joaquin Valley. Their territory was bounded on the east by the Sierra Nevada, on the west by the Fresno River, and on the south by Tehachapi Pass. Their aboriginal population was 15,000 to 20,000. The Yokuts practiced tribal political organization, consisting of an integration of a consciously shared name, a designated territory, and a common dialect. Because their lands were so accesible to the whites, they were extensively recruited by the mission fathers. By the time of the 1910 census, there were only 530 Yokuts remaining. Like the Miwok,♦ they observed exogamic totemic moieties, which, however, among the Yokuts descended through the father's line. They also practiced a variation of the toloache or jimson weed cult.♦

Yolla Bolley Mountains, south of the Trinity Range, part of the Klamath Mts.,♦ derive their name from the Wintu, ''Yo-la Bo-li,'' said to mean ''high snow-covered peak.'' Other place-names of the area incorporate Bally and Bully, variants of the word for ''peak.''

Yolo County, one of the original 27 counties (1850), is bounded on the north by Colusa and a bit of Lake County; on the east, across the Sacramento River, by Sutter and Sacramento counties; on the south, across Putah Creek,♦ by Solano County; and on the west by Napa and Lake counties. This land of the Suisun and other Wintun Indians was not explored by whites until Luís Argüello traversed it in his search for mission sites (1821). He was followed by fur trappers, including Jedediah Smith (1828), Hudson's Bay Co. expeditions, and Ewing Young (1830). Settlement began in the 1840s with the pioneer William Gordon,♦ whose ranch on Cache Creek was the site of the county's first wheat farming. In 1843 William Knight, also a settler with the Workman Party, founded Knights Landing, and later, in Stanislaus County, Knights Ferry.

The region of Cache Creek was also where the first alfalfa was grown in California (during the 1850s). Still another first may be attributed to Yolo County, since the Pacific Coast's first salmon cannery was founded (1864) on the Sacramento River to pack the great catches of fish from the river. The county's economic base still depends on the river, as it includes shipping through the port of the city of Sacramento (itself on the neighboring county's side) as well as cultivation of the rich soil of the southern part of the Sacramento Valley. Its major field crops today are sugar beets, alfalfa, rice, sorghum grain, barley, corn, wheat, and safflower, but the crop more valuable than any one of these is tomatoes. Almonds and fruit are also important agricultural products, as is the rearing of livestock.

The towns are the sites for the packing, canning, and freezing of food. They are generally small, including Woodland,♦ the county seat since 1862. However, Broderick and West Sacramento are important suburbs of the state capital, which lies just across the river. Davis, the outgrowth in the 1860s of a farm owned by a man of that name, has become a major settlement because of the University of California campus located there. It began as an experimental University Farm (1905), grew to be a branch of Berkeley's College of Agriculture (1922), then became a general campus of the University (1959), and soon thereafter offered graduate studies in diverse fields, including law. In 1970 the county had a population of 91,788, which, with an area of 657,984 acres, totaled 89.3 per sq. mi.

YORBA, prominent early California family founded by a Catalonian, José Antonio (1743–1825), who entered with the Sacred Expedition and settled in San Diego on a vast *rancho* near Santa Ana. His descendants married into other leading old California families. One of his sons, Tomás (1787–1845), married Vicenta Sepúlveda, who, after his death, wed Ramón Carrillo. Another son, Teodocio (1805–63), was associated with Pío and Andrés Pico in ranching on part of the present Irvine Ranch near Santa Ana. Still another son, Bernardo, married into the Alvarado family, and a daughter, Bernarda, married Leonardo Cota. On Bernardo's old *rancho* is located Yorba Linda, whose name, merging that of the family and the nearby settlement of Olinda, was given (1913) to the township where Richard M. Nixon was born. Bernardo's daughter Ramona married Benjamin D. Wilson♦ (1844).

YORTY, Sam[uel William] (1909–), Nebraska-born political figure, moved to Los Angeles (1927), where he studied law and was admitted to the bar. He was elected to the state Assembly and as a Democrat to Congress (1951–55). He was later a flamboyant mayor of Los Angeles (1961–73).

Yosemite Valley, aboriginal home of Indians named Awani, was probably first seen by whites with the Joseph R. Walker♦ (1833–34) party. W. P. Abrams and U. N. Reamer, gold rush pioneers, were the first to enter the valley (1849). When the Mariposa Battalion scoured the valley (1851) to remove to a reservation some obstinate Indians, Lafayette H. Bunnell,♦ a member of the state-authorized but volunteer militia, proposed the name "Yosem-

ity," which he understood to be that of the tribe of dispossessed Indians and which probably means "grizzly bear." The present spelling was first employed in 1852 but in the early days was often written "Yo-Semite." Tourist interest began when Thomas Ayres, with an exploring party led by J. M. Hutchings,♦ drew realistic drawings of the area. A hotel was built there as early as 1859. The valley was made a State Park in 1864. A National Park surrounded it in 1890, and the present 1,189 sq. mi. of Yosemite National Park, in Tuolumne, Mariposa, and Madera counties, was created in 1905, when the state ceded the valley and the Mariposa Grove♦ to the federal government. The scenic grandeur of the 7-mile-long valley, from which rise sheer walls of 3,000 to 4,800 feet, has annually attracted increasing thousands of tourists. They come to see such spectacular sites as Bridalveil Fall, Yosemite Falls, Inspiration Point, El Portal, Glacier Point, Half Dome, and Mirror Lake. Within the park but some 20 miles northwest of the main valley was the smaller Hetch Hetchy Valley,♦ the subject of a long dispute before it was flooded to create a source for San Francisco's water supply. Accommodations in the valley include the luxury Hotel Ahwahnee and Camp Curry,♦ a more rustic resort.

YOUNG, Clement Calhoun (1869–1947), 26th governor of the state (1927–31), brought from New Hampshire to California as a child. He spent a long career teaching English at Lowell High School in San Francisco, but in 1906 he went into the real estate business and then entered politics. He was lieutenant governor for eight years before his election as a Republican to the governorship. His administration was noted for efficient administrative organization and planning.

YOUNG, Ewing (*fl.* 1829–41), Tennessee-born fur trapper and mountain man, first entered California via Cajón Pass (1829) with a large party, including Kit Carson, in search of beaver. He returned to the Los Angeles area to hunt sea otter (1832), this time accompanied by Isaac Williams.♦ He improved the Old Spanish Trail♦ between New Mexico and California and later the trail to Oregon, where he settled in 1836.

YOUNGER, Maud (1870–1936), San Francisco-born suffragist who, although she came from a wealthy pioneer family, dedicated her life to improving the lot of women and of laborers. She became president of the local waitresses' union, worked and spoke for the state's woman suffrage amendment, participated in a strike of garment workers, and was generally militant on behalf of women and labor.

YOUNT, GEORGE CALVERT (1794–1865), North Carolina-born trapper, entered California with Wolfskill (1831), hunted sea otter in the Channel Islands, worked for M. G. Vallejo, was naturalized and given the name Jorge Concepción, and settled in the Napa Valley on the large grant in the Yountville area named for him.

Yreka, seat of Siskiyou County, came into being as a gold-mining camp (1851) and was given its Indian name (perhaps meaning "north mountain" or named after Mt. Shasta) when the county was established (1852). In 1970 it had a population of 5,394.

Yuba City, seat of Sutter County, named for the river (so called by Gen. Sutter), which there joins the Feather River. It was laid out by Samuel Brannan and others as a gold rush development (1849). It is a marketing center for the surrounding agricultural area and has fruit-packing plants for its nearby peach orchards. Beale Air Force Base and the Sutter National Wildlife Refuge are close by. J. J. Montgomery, the pioneer of gliding, was born there. In 1970 the population was 13,986. Directly across the river lies Marysville, in Yuba County.

Yuba County, one of the original 27 counties (1850), is bounded on the west by the Feather River, across which lies Sutter County; on the north by Butte County and the southern tip of Plumas County; on the east by Sierra and Nevada counties, with the Yuba River as part of that boundary; and on the south by the Bear River, across which lie Placer and Sutter counties. The county derives its name from the river that bisects it, which was discovered by Jedediah Smith (1828) and named by John A. Sutter (c. 1842). This region of the Maidu was also known to Hudson's Bay Co. trappers and to those who were traveling the last leg of the California Trail.

The first white settlement was made when Sutter expanded his territories into the area (1841) and leased part of the lands to Theodore Cordua, a Prussian emigrant, who called his settlement New Mecklenburg (1842). Its center was at the site of Marysville, to which he added a seven-league grant of his own (1844). Marysville,♦ which has always

been the county seat, was named for a settler who was a member of the Donner Party. Its site at the confluence of the Feather and Yuba rivers made it a great supply port and trade center for the many mining towns that sprang up along the rivers and creeks of the foothills and up north into the mountains of the Sierra Nevada during the gold rush.

Hydraulic mining in the late 1850s and the following decades washed away many of these mushroom communities and so clogged the Yuba River with debris that levees had to be built to protect neighboring land. That form of mining was succeeded by dredging, which proved profitable for another hundred years.

The county's economy later came to be based on agriculture, and the bad working conditions of migratory hop pickers led to the tragic Wheatland Riot♦ (1913). In more recent times the main crops have been rice, peaches, prunes, and other fruits, as well as nuts. Lumbering and livestock and poultry raising are also important. The county has major reservoirs for hydroelectric uses, flood control, and irrigation. Near Marysville is Beale Air Force Base.♦ In 1970 the county had a population of 44,736, which, with an area of 409,408 acres, gave it 70 persons per sq. mi.

Yuba Pass, see *Sierra County.*

Yuba River, discovered by Jedediah Smith (1828) but given its present name by Sutter for the Maidu village at the confluence of the Yuba and Feather rivers, about 25 miles east of Yuba city in Sutter County. It then splits into a South Fork running 40 miles east and the North Yuba and Middle Yuba. A well-traveled route through the Sierra went between the Middle and South forks, and there was much mining along all the river, up into its northernmost reaches by Downieville in Sierra County.

Yucca Valley, desert settlement of San Bernardino County, east of its National Forest and north of Joshua Tree National Monument. Yucca is another name for the Joshua tree,♦ and is also found as a place-name for several sites in Sequoia National Park. At Yucca Valley is Desert Christ Park, with huge cement sculptures depicting the life of Christ.

Yugoslavs, first arrived in California during the gold rush from the lands that have since become Yugoslavia, but as late as 1880 there were fewer than 1,500 in the state, located mainly in or near San Francisco. In the 20th century Yugoslavs engaged in sardine fishing around San Pedro, lumbering near Fort Bragg, the restaurant business in San Francisco and Oakland, and construction and steel work elsewhere. Despite post-World War II increases, in 1950 the population totaled only 34,000. The best known of all is Henry Suzzalo (originally Zucalo; 1875–1933), born in San Jose of emigrant parents, educated at Stanford, and president of the University of Washington and the Carnegie Foundation.

Yuha Desert, like the Buttes, Basin, and Well of the same name, is located south of the Salton Sea in Imperial County, just above the Mexican border.

Yuki, Indians residing mainly in the northern part of present Mendocino County on the Eel River, were settled in village communities. The eight or nine geographic divisions had different dialects. Americans gave them their name, a word meaning "stranger" in the language of the Wintun. Kroeber estimates that there were once 2,000 Yuki; the 1910 census showed only 95. Their culture was simpler than that of the Indians to the south, but their mythology was typical of other Indians in north central California, and they belonged to the Athabascan tribes.◆

Yuma, Indians who lived at the junction of the Colorado and Gila rivers on the present border between California, Arizona, and Mexico. They farmed, growing corn, beans, and pumpkins, and entered into trade. Their prehistoric population of 2,500 was reduced to 834, according to the 1910 census. Since 1884 they have been located on a reservation in Bard Valley. They practiced the anniversary mourning ceremony and the girls' adolescent initiation rite, but lacked a boys' initiation, perhaps because they were ignorant of the toloache cult. Above all, like the neighboring and similar

Mohave Indians, they thought of their land as a nation and prized mortal combat to protect their country, particularly against the Pima, Papago, and Maricopa of Arizona. They also defended it fiercely on July 17, 1781, when they attacked Capt. Rivera y Moncada◆ and Father Garcés,◆ then en route via the Sonora Trail to California with men, women, and children as colonists. The Yumas massacred all the men, took many women and children into slavery, and destroyed two missions—Purísima Concepción and San Pedro y San Pablo—established near the Colorado River crossing as way stations to California. The Indians, infuriated by mistreatment by Spanish soldiers and settlers and by Rivera's troops marching through their cornfields and pumpkin patches, thus ended the use of that route to California, essentially cutting off communication by land between Mexico and California.

Yurok, Indians resident on the Klamath River and along the coast, where they had over 50 settlements with houses built of split planks. They probably had a population close to 2,500 in 1850, which was reduced to 668 by the time of the 1910 census. They were independent politically as well as socially, held private property for hunting and fishing, built small personal fortunes of shell money, and enslaved fellow tribesmen indebted to them. Their main foods were acorns and salmon. They built canoes; wove baskets; and made wooden implements, elk-horn utensils, and wood flutes. They were remotely related to the Algonquin family. (Upriver from the Yurok lived the slightly smaller tribe of Karok, identical to the Yurok in all ways except for speaking a different language.) The Yurok also traded with and had a culture similar to that of the Hupa; for example, they performed ritualistic dances to celebrate major events of the year, such as the catching of the first salmon, as part of a "world renewal" cult. A collection of *Yurok Myths,* collected by Alfred Kroeber, was published posthumously (1976).

Z

Zabrieskie Point, site within Death Valley National Monument (Inyo County), named for Christian B. Zabrieskie, onetime head of the Pacific Coast Borax Co. The location, near Furnace Creek, is famous for providing the title of a film by Antonioni (1970) which made a bitter attack on contemporary materialistic values in the U.S.

Zaca, Lake, like the creek and peak of the same name, is located in the San Rafael Mts. of Santa Barbara County, not far from Solvang. The word is said to be Chumash, meaning "peaceful place."

Zacatecas, see *San Fernando College.*

ZAMORANO, Agustin Juan Vicente (1798–1842), born in St. Augustine, Florida, where his father, a Castilian, was an official of the Spanish province of East Florida. The son, later reared in Mexico, served in the army as a cadet and then as a military engineer. He went to California (1825) where José María Echeandía, having been named governor of California, appointed him his secretary. Zamorano continued in that office under the next governor, Manuel Victoria, and served him also as commandant of the presidio at the capital, Monterey. When Victoria was overthrown, Zamorano, as the senior officer, maintained the government in the north while Echeandía returned to power as the chief officer for the south, each serving as regional de facto governor from Jan. 1832 to Jan. 1833, when Figueroa came into office. Zamorano returned to his former posts under Figueroa and Gutiérrez until the revolt of Alvarado (1836). He was later military commander of Baja California (1839–40) and died upon his return to California to serve in Micheltorena's new government.

Zamorano is best known as the first printer of California. From 1826 until 1829 he created letterheads from woodblocks and during 1830–31 he used type, but all imprints were made by pounding proofs without a press. In 1834 he obtained a Ramage wooden press and type from Boston and soon issued a broadside advertisement. From then until he left California in 1836 he issued eleven broadsides, six books—the first was the region's

Reglamento Provincial (1834), the largest was Figueroa's *Manifiesto a la Republica Mejicana* of 1835 in 188 pages—and six miscellaneous works in addition to letterheads.

Zamorano Club, Los Angeles society of bibliophiles founded in 1928. It issues a journal, *Hoja Volante,* keepsakes, and an occasional book for its members. It is similar to the Roxburghe Club of San Francisco, with which it holds a biennial joint meeting. In 1945 it published *The Zamorano 80, A Selection of Distingusihed California Books.*

Zanja, water ditch for irrigation, built by Indian labor under Spanish and Mexican direction. Major examples include one at Olvera St., Los Angeles, and another at San Bernardino.

ZANUCK, Darryl F. (1902–), Nebraska-born film producer, went to Hollywood as a scenario writer and rose to form Twentieth Century Pictures in 1933. The films for which he was responsible include those of Shirley Temple, *The Grapes of Wrath* (1940), and *The Longest Day* (1962).

ZAPPA, Frank (1940–), Baltimore-born rock musician,♦ reared in the Mojave Desert area east of Los Angeles near Lancaster. He formed a band, Mothers of Invention (1964), whose very loud music was only part of its distinctive stage activities, which also included social satire, invective against the prevailing culture of California and the U.S., and grotesque comedy. His *Freak Out* (1966) was the first album to treat all the records as one long piece of rock music. In the 1970s he created a new band and even merged his music with classic forms in a concert with Zubin Mehta.♦

Zebra Case, crime wave of random murders in which 25 white persons were killed or wounded on San Francisco streets from Oct. 20, 1973, through April 16, 1974, by black assailants. Called Zebra after the radio channel police used in the manhunt, the case led to the arrest, trial, which took 376 days (1975–76), and conviction of four killers said to be part of a "Death Angels" cult, supposedly an outgrowth of the religious group of Black Muslims (The Nation of Islam).

ZELLERBACH, prominent San Francisco family, founded by Anthony Zellerbach, (1832–1911), who, with his brother Mark, emigrated to the U.S. from Germany and then to California during the gold rush. After unsuccessful business and banking ventures in the mining country, Anthony moved to San Francisco (1868), where he became wealthy in the paper business. Among his grandsons were J[ames] D. Zellerbach (1892–1963), president of the family firm for which Skidmore, Owings & Merrill built a handsome headquarters (1960), and U.S. Ambassador to Italy (1957–61) and Harold L. Zellerbach (1894–1978), a patron of the arts in San Francisco.

Zodiac, name employed by an unknown but confessed murderer in notes sent to newspapers in order to taunt police on their inability to capture him. The notes also describe his numerous killings, including those of a high school boy and his girlfriend in Vallejo (Dec. 20, 1969) and a taxicab driver in San Francisco (Oct. 11, 1969). According to one message, he murdered a total of 37 persons between 1969 and 1974.

Zoos, in California date back to the display in San Francisco during the 1850s of a grizzly bear and other wild animals captured by James Capen Adams♦ and to the zoological and aquarium exhibits annexed to Woodward's Gardens♦ (1866). In the last decade of the 19th century, the *San Francisco Examiner,* as a circulation stunt, captured a great grizzly bear, named it Monarch, and displayed it.

Modern public zoos came into being in the 20th century in several cities. The one in San Diego, now by far the greatest in the state, was an outgrowth of that city's Panama-California Exposition (1915), and since 1922 has been housed at its Balboa Park site. On its 125 acres some 5,500 animals of 1,600 species roam open areas behind moats and low walls. In 1973 the zoo opened to a San Diego Wild Animal Park as a preserve and exhibition area in San Pasqual Valley, where some 2,000 animals roam a relatively free 1,800-acre preserve, viewed by visitors from a monorail or a hiking trail.

San Francisco did not get a zoo of consequence until 1922, when a Zoological Gardens was established on 60 acres. It was generally called Fleishhacker Zoo after a former president of the Park Commission, Herbert Fleishhacker, who was a donor of some of its first animals and of the adjacent huge swimming pool. A related facility, in nearby Golden Gate Park, is the Steinhart Aquarium, administered by the California Academy of Sciences.

Oakland had a zoo early in the 20th century, initially on the shores of Lake Merritt, but in the 1950s it was modernized, expanded, and relocated in Knowland State Park. Los Angeles also got its first zoo in the early part of this century, located in Eastlake Park, but the modern facility is in Griffith Park and was greatly expanded and modernized beginning in 1964. Other zoos are located in Sacramento, Merced, and Fresno's Roeding Park. During the heyday of William Randolph Hearst's estate, San Simeon, he maintained what was said to be the world's largest private zoo, and its zebras still run loose there. A variant of a private zoo, but run for profit, is Lion Country Safari,♦ a tourist attraction near San Juan Capistrano. Analagous commercial displays of wildlife are to be found in the several attractions featuring ocean creatures: Marineland near San Pedro; Sea World at San Diego; and Marine World/Africa U.S.A. near Redwood City, the last combining an oceanarium and a live African game exhibit.

Zorro, Spanish word for "fox" or "cunning fellow," used as the name of a Robin Hood kind of highwayman during the Mexican era of California in the picaresque romance *The Mark of Zorro* (1920) by Johnston McCulley. The story was further popularized by a motion picture starring Douglas Fairbanks, Sr., and by a television serial.

ZUKOR, ADOLPH (1873–1976), Hungarian-born film producer, came to the U.S. (1889) and by 1903 owned a penny arcade with Marcus Loew. They then went on to buy a regular theater for vaudeville and motion pictures. This he developed into a chain of theaters. To supply them, he established Famous Players Film Corp. (1912), a producing company in Hollywood. His stars came to include Mary Pickford, William S. Hart, Rudolph Valentino, and Clara Bow; Cecil B. De Mille was a major director.

Chronological Index

1778—Alexander Forbes (c.1778–1864)

1779—De Neve issues *Reglamento*, first laws for California; site of Santa Clara log mission moved; Jean Louis Vignes (c.1779–1862)

1780—Non-Indian population, c.600; Mission San Diego rebuilt after Indian attack

1781—Los Angeles founded

1782—Mission San Buenaventura founded; Santa Barbara presidio established; Pedro Fages, governor (1782–91)

1783—Mission San Diego quadrangle completed; Cárlos Antonio Carrillo (1783–1852)

1784—Serra dies; Palóu named head of Alta California missions; Luís Antonio Argüello (1784–1830)

1785—Lasuén named head of Alta California missions (1785–1803); García Diego y Moreno (1785–1846)

1786—Mission Santa Barbara founded; La Pérouse visits Monterey

1787—Mission La Purísima Concepción founded; Palóu's Life of Serra; La Pérouse, *Voyage* . . .

1788—Construction of Mission La Purísima Concepción begun

1789—Palóu dies

1790—Costansó journal published in English; William A. Gale (1790?–1841)

1791—Missions Santa Cruz and Soledad founded; Roméu, governor (1791–92); Mission Dolores dedicated; Malaspina visits Monterey; Concepción Argüello (1791–1857)

1792—Arrillaga, governor (1792–94); Vancouver's first visit to California; José Figueroa (1792–1835)

1793—Missions San Carlos (Carmel) and Santa Cruz begun; Vancouver returns to California

1794—Borica, governor (1794–1800); Castillo de San Joaquín fort built in San Francisco; Royal Presidio Chapel (Monterey) built; Vancouver's final visit to California; George Yount (1794–1865)

1795—Mission Santa Cruz quadrangle completed

1796—Ebenezer Dorr's *Otter* first U.S. vessel to anchor in California; John Gilroy (1796–1869); William B. Ide (1796–1852); James Lick (1796–1876)

1797—Missions San José, San Juan Bautista, San Miguel, and San Fernando founded; Branciforte founded; Walter Colton (1797–1851)

1798—Mission San Luis Rey founded; Vancouver, *A Voyage of Discovery;* James P. Beckwourth (1798–c.1867); W. E. P. Hartnell (1798–1854); Abel Stearns (1798–1871); John Temple (1798–1866); Joseph Reddeford Walker (1798–1876); William Wolfskill (1798–1866); Augustín Zamorano (1798–1842)

1799—Henry Delano Fitch (1799–1849); John Marsh (1799–1856); Jean Jacques Vioget (1799–1855)

1800—Arrillaga, governor (1800–14); population of Los Angeles c.140; Juan Bautista Alvarado (1800–82); Juan Bandini (1800–59); Peter Lassen (1800–59); William Workman (1800–76)

1801—First de la Guerra settles in Santa Barbara; Pío Pico (1801–94)

1802—Alonzo Delano (1802?–74); Thomas O. Larkin (1802–58); Nathan Spear (1802–49)

1803—Tapis named head of California missions; Mission San Diego destroyed by earthquake; Shaler and Cleveland land in San Diego illegally; John A. Sutter (1803–80)

1804—California divided into Alta California and Baja California; Arrillaga first governor of Alta California only; Mission Santa Inés founded; J. Goldsborough Bruff (1804–89)

1805—Mission San Gabriel completed; Gabriel Moraga begins explorations; John Bigler (1805–71); Edwin Bryant (1805–69); William M. Gwin (1805–85)

1806—Missions San Juan Capistrano and San Fernando completed; Boscana's missionary career (1806–31); Moraga names Merced River; Rezanov visits San Francisco; Alfred Robinson (1806–95)

1807—Rezanov visits San Francisco Bay; Langsdorff makes drawings of the Bay Area; Peter Burnett (1807–95); James Van Ness (1807–72); Jonathan Trumbull Warner (1807–95)

1808—Shaler's "Journal," first extended account of California published in U.S.; Mariano Guadalupe Vallejo (1808–90)

1809—Mission San José de Guadalupe completed; Russians settle Bodega Bay; Richard Brydges Beechey (1809–95); Kit Carson (1809–68); Jacob Leese (1809–92)

1810—José Castro (1810?–60); James Marshall (1810–85)

1811—Kuskov begins Russian settlement; Edward Dickinson Baker (1811–61); Benjamin D. Wilson (1811–78)

1812—Missions Santa Barbara, La Purísima Concepción, San Buenaventura, and San Juan Capistrano destroyed by earthquake; Mission San Juan Bautista dedicated; Fort Ross established; John B. Weller (1812–78)

1813—Final Mission San Diego built; Mission San Antonio de Padua completed; John C. Frémont (1813–90); Mark Hopkins (1813–78); José Vallejo (1813–76)

1814—John Gilroy becomes California's first non-Hispanic settler; Argüello, governor (1814–15); José Sadoc Alemany (1814–88)

1815—Mission San Luis Rey dedicated; San Antonio de Pala *asistencia* established; de Solá, governor (1815–22); Faxon Dean Atherton (1815–77)

1816—Kotzebue expedition; Thomas Doak, first U.S. citizen to settle permanently in California; Samuel Marsden Brookes (1816–92); Stephen J. Field (1816–99); Henry W. Halleck (1816–72)

1817—Mission San Rafael founded; Mission Santa Inés dedicated; Domingo Ghirardelli (1817–94)

1818—Mission San Miguel completed; Mission San Rafael built; Santa Ysabel *asistencia* built; Bouchard's raids; Lola Montez (1818–61); C. C. Nahl (1818–78)

1819—Francisco Arce (1819–78); John Bidwell (1819–1900); Samuel Brannan (1819–89); Louise Amelia Knapp Smith, "Dame Shirley" (1819–1906)

1820—Non-Indian population, *c.*3,270; population of Los Angeles, *c.* 650; David C. Broderick (1820–59); George Hearst (1820–91)

1821—Mexico achieves independence from Spain; J. Ross Browne (1821–75); James Ben Ali Haggin (1821–1914); Collis P. Huntington (1821–1900); William Sharon (1821–85)

1822—Iturbide proclaimed Emperor of Mexico (1822–23) and thus of California; Argüello, governor (1822–25); W. E. P. Hartnell goes to California; Charles Crocker (1822–88); William Heath Davis (1822–1909); Peter Donahue (1822–85); Alvinza Hayward (1822–1904); James King of William (1822–56)

1823—Mission San Francisco Solano (Sonoma) founded; George Derby (1823–61)

1824—William T. Coleman (1824–93); Jessie Frémont (1824–1902); Hugh J. Glenn (1824–82); Thomas Starr King (1824–64); James McClatchey (1824–83); Leland Stanford (1824–93)

1825—Final Mission Santa Clara completed; Echeandía, governor (1825–31); Durán named head of California missions (1825–27; 1831–33); George Davidson (1825–1911); Henry H. Haight (1825–78)

1826—Zamorano prints wood blocks without a press; Beechey explores San Francisco Bay aboard *Blossom*; James C. Flood (1826–89); William C. Ralston (1826–75)

1827—Duhaut-Cilly visits California; Pattie visits California; Jedediah Smith, first white man to cross the Sierra Nevada

1828—Jedediah Smith discovers Yuba River; "Lucky" Baldwin (1828–1909); William Henry Brewer (1828–1910); Jane Lathrop Stanford (1828–1905)

1829—Revolt of Joaquín Solís; Thomas Hill (1829–1908); Lester A. Pelton (1829–1910); Carleton Watkins (1829–1916)

1830—Phineas Banning (1830–85); Horace Bell (1830–1918); Eadweard Muybridge (1830–1904); Adolph Sutro (1830–98)

1831—Victoria, governor (Jan. 31–Dec. 6, 1831); battle at Cahuenga Pass; Echeandía, governor (1831–33); James G. Fair (1831–94); John W. Mackay (1831–1902)

1832—Pío Pico, governor (Jan.–Feb.); Zamorano, de facto governor in north (Feb. 1832–Jan. 1833); Hubert Howe Bancroft (1832–1918); Edward Bosqui (1832–1917); David D. Colton (1832–78)

1833—Figueroa, governor (1833–35); Joseph Walker and Zenas Leonard lead first white men westward through the Sierra Nevada

1834—Híjar and Padres colonizing plan; Figueroa proclamation to secularize the missions; Zamorano acquires first printing press in California; Prentice Mulford (1834–91)

1835—José Castro, governor (Oct. 1835–Jan. 1836); Figueroa, *Manifiesto;* Dana arrives in California; William A. Richardson settles in Yerba Buena; Isaac Van Nuys (1835–1912)

1836—Gutiérrez, governor (Jan. 2–May 1); Mariano Chico, governor (May 1–July 30); Gutiérrez, governor (July 30–Dec. 7); Alvarado, governor (1836–42); "Free and sovereign state" of California declared by *diputación* and Alvarado; Belcher leads naval expedition into California; Dana leaves California; John Marsh arrives in Los Angeles; Bret Harte (1836–1902)

1837—Carlos Antonio Carrillo appointed governor but unable to assume office; La Place visits California

1838—First child (Rosalia Leese) born in San Francisco; John Muir (1838–1914)

1839—Sutter arrives in California; Vioget surveys San Francisco; Forbes, *California; Narrative of Zenas Leonard*; Henry George (1839–97); William Keith (1839–1911)

1840—Non-Indian population, *c.*6,000; Mission San Francisco Solano (Sonoma) built as a parish chapel; Dana, *Two Years Before the Mast*

1841—Bartleson-Bidwell Party to California; Wilkes Expedition; Fort Ross sold to Sutter; Leidesdorff arrives in San Francisco; Ina Coolbrith (1841–1928); Edward Rowland Sill (1841–87); Joaquin Miller (1841?–1913)

1842—Micheltorena, governor (1842–45); gold discovered in Placerita Canyon; ap Catesby Jones seizes Monterey (Oct. 20–21); Allen Allensworth (1842–1914); Ambrose Bierce (1842–1914?); Phoebe Apperson Hearst (1842–1919)

1843—Lillie Hitchcock Coit (1843–1929); Charles Warren Stoddard (1843–1909)

1844—Larkin appointed U.S. consul; Stevens-Murphy Party to California; Frémont discovers Lake Tahoe; Duflot de Mofras, *Exploration*; Robert Dollar (1844–1932); Thaddeus Welch (1844–1919)

1845—Non-Indian population, *c.*7,000; Alvarado and Castro defeat Micheltorena at Cahuenga Pass; Frémont crosses Sierra into California; Marshall arrives in California; Pío Pico, governor (1845–46); Lansford Hastings, *Guide*

1846—Flores, governor (Oct. 31, 1846–Jan. 11, 1847); Bear Flag Republic (June 10–July 9); Battle of Olompali (June 24); California involved in Mexican War (July 7, 1846–Jan. 13, 1847); Sloat, military governor (July 7–29); U.S. flag raised in Yerba Buena and Sonoma (July 9); Stockton, military governor (July 29–Jan. 19, 1847); Brannan and his Mormon colonists arrive in Yerba Buena (July 31); Stockton and Frémont seize Los Angeles (Aug. 13); Stockton appoints Frémont military commander of California (Sept. 2); ride of Juan Flaco Brown (Sept. 24–28); Battle of San Pasqual (Dec. 6); Pauma Massacre (Dec.); Golden Gate named by Frémont; Washington A. Bartlett, first American *alcalde* of San Francisco; *Californian* founded

(Aug. 15); Donner Party; Robinson, *Life in California*

1847—Cahuenga Capitulation Treaty (Jan. 13); Mormon Batallion arrives (Jan.); Yerba Buena renamed San Francisco (Jan.); military governors: Frémont (Jan. 19–March 1), Kearny (March 1–May 31), Mason (May 31–Feb. 28, 1849); Benicia founded; *California Star*; Lotta Crabtree (1847–1924); Denis Kearney (1847–1907)

1848—Guadalupe Hidalgo Treaty; Marshall discovers gold (Jan. 24); Bryant, *What I Saw in California*; Frémont, *Geographical Memoir*

1849—Persifor Smith, military governor (Feb. 28–April 12); Bennet Riley, military governor (April 12–Dec. 20); Peter Burnett, first civil governor (Dec. 20, 1849–Jan. 9, 1851); Constitutional Convention (Sept.–Nov.); state government activated prior to admission to Union (1850); San Jose made capital; Wierzbicki, *California As It Is, And As It May Be,* first English language book printed in California; Colton, *Three Years in California; Alta California*; Luther Burbank (1849–1926)

1850—Population: State, 92,597 (estimate, excluding lost returns from San Francisco, Contra Costa, and Santa Clara counties); Los Angeles, 1,610; San Francisco, 24,000 (est.); original 27 counties formed; State Library founded; Society of California Pioneers founded; Mariposa Battalion discovers Yosemite; Bayard Taylor, *Eldorado*; Henry E. Huntington (1850–1927)

1851—Capital moved to Vallejo; Nevada and Placer counties founded; Klamath County (1851–76); Vigilance Committee; Garrá Revolt; John McDougal, governor (Jan. 9, 1851–Jan. 8, 1852); Santa Clara University founded; University of the Pacific founded; *Los Angeles Star* (1851–79); *Sacramento Union* (1851–   ); *San Jose Mercury* (1851–   )

1852—State population approximately 255,000; Sierra, Siskiyou, and Tulare counties founded; Pautah County founded; John Bigler, governor (1852–56); Wells Fargo founded; *Golden Era* (1852–93); Dumas, *A Gil Blas in California*; Edwin Markham (1852–1940)

1853—Benicia becomes state capital; Alameda, Humboldt, and San Bernardino counties founded; California Academy of Sciences founded; San Quentin prison opened; Montgomery Block built; Hollister drives sheep across continent to California; William Walker seizes La Paz; David Belasco (1853–1931)

1854—Sacramento made state capital; Amador, Butte, Plumas, and Stanislaus counties founded; sequoias discovered; Fort Tejón founded; State Fair instituted; California Stage Co. founded; Delano, *Across the Plains and Among the Diggings*; Ridge, *Joaquín Murieta*; "Shirley Letters" in *Pioneer*

1855—Merced County founded; Territory of Nataqua created; Modoc battle at Castle Crag; Mechanics Institute founded; St. Ignatius College (later University of San Francisco) founded; St. Mary's College founded; *Annals of San Francisco*; Derby, *Phoenixiana*; Helper, *Land of Gold*; Marryat, *Mountains and Molehills*; *El Clamor Público* (1855–59); Josiah Royce (1855–1916)

1856—San Mateo and Tehama counties founded; J. N. Johnson, governor (1856–58); James King of William murdered; second Vigilance Committee of San Francisco; Casey and Cora hanged; Borax discovered; Farnham, *California, In-doors and Out*; *Hutchings' California Magazine* (1856–61); Marriott's *News Letter* (1856–1941); Edward L. Doheny (1856–1935)

1857—Del Norte County founded; Broderick elected U.S. Senator; Anaheim founded; Camels imported by E. F. Beale; Tejón Pass earthquake; Fort Point constructed; State Normal School system founded; Judah projects transcontinental railroad; Borthwick, *Three Years in California*; *Sacramento Bee* (1857–   ); Gertrude Atherton (1857–1948); Kate Olivia Sessions (1857–1940)

1858—Weller, governor (1858–60); Archy Lee case; Butterfield founds stagecoach line; Spring Valley Water Co. founded; Davidson, *Directory of the Pacific Coast*; C. K. McClatchey (1858–1936); Milicent Shinn (1858–1940)

1859—Comstock Lode discovered; Bodie founded; Terry kills Broderick in duel; H. H. Bancroft's library begun; Dana revisits California; William Keith settles in California; Morrisey loses state boxing championship to Heenan; Charles Fletcher Lummis (1859–1928)

1860—Population: State, 379,994; Los Angeles, 4,385; San Francisco, 56,802; Latham, governor (Jan. 9–14, 1860); Downey, governor (1860–62); Pony Express; Josiah D. Whitney appointed state geologist; Harte, "M'liss"; A. Page Brown (1860–96); Douglas Tilden (1860–1935)

1861—Lake and Mono counties founded; James Bouchard begins evangelical career; Fort Point completed; James D. Phelan (1861–1930)

1862—Leland Stanford, governor (1862–63); first state normal school founded in San Francisco; direct telegraph between San Francisco and New York;

Haraszthy, *Grape Culture*; Bernard Maybeck (1862–1957); Charles Rollo Peters (1862–1928)

1863—Low, governor (1863–67); Central Pacific Railroad begins construction; Sagebrush War; blacks first allowed to testify in court against whites; Clemens first signs himself "Mark Twain"; first Cliff House opened; *San Francisco Examiner* founded; Dwinelle, *Colonial History of San Francisco*; William Randolph Hearst (1863–1951)

1864—Alpine and Lassen counties founded; State Parks system created; Mark Twain in California (1864–66); John Galen Howard (1864–1931); Franklin K. Lane (1864–1921); Abe Ruef (1864–1936)

1865—Sagebrush War; Southern Pacific Railroad founded; Mark Twain, "Celebrated Jumping Frog of Calaveras County"; Derby, *Squibob Papers*; Harte, *Outcroppings*; *San Francisco Chronicle* founded; *Elevator* (1865–89); Willis Polk (1865–1924)

1866—Inyo and Kern counties founded; Berkeley founded; Pacific School of Religion founded; Albert M. Bender (1866–1941); Gelett Burgess (1866–1951); James J. Corbett (1866–1933); Hiram Johnson (1866–1945); Lincoln Steffens (1866–1936); David Warfield (1866–1951)

1867—Anti-Chinese demonstrations in San Francisco; first steamer sails from San Francisco to Alaska; Haight, governor (1867–71); Anita Whitney (1867–1955)

1868—Hayward earthquake; Bakersfield founded; University of California founded; *Overland Monthly* founded; *San Diego Union* (1868–   ); *The Wasp* founded; John Muir goes to California; Mary Austin (1868–1934); Lloyd Osbourne (1868–1947)

1869—Central Pacific Railroad meets Union Pacific tracks at Promontory Point, Utah; Marriott flies his Avitor; Emperor Norton commands bridges to be built across San Francisco Bay; Harte, "Outcasts of Poker Flat"; James Rolph (1869–1934); George Sterling (1869–1926)

1870—Population: State, 560,247; Los Angeles, 5,728; San Francisco, 149,473; Golden Gate Park founded; Harte, *Luck of Roaring Camp and Other Sketches* and "Plain Language from Truthful James"; Herbert E. Bolton (1870–1953); A. P. Giannini (1870–1949); Frank Norris (1870–1902)

1871—Booth, governor (1871–75); mob attacks and murders of Chinese in Los Angeles; California Historical Society founded; San Francisco Art Institute founded; Porter Garnett (1871–1951); John Henry Nash (1871–1947)

1872—Ventura County founded; Owens Valley earthquake; Great Diamond Hoax; Modoc War (1872–73); Asians and American Indians first allowed to testify in court against whites; Bohemian Club founded; King, *Mountaineering in the Sierra Nevada*; Mark Twain, *Roughing It*; Julia Morgan (1872–1957)

1873—University of California moves to Berkeley campus; first San Francisco cable car; Miller, *Life Amongst the Modocs*; Blanche Bates (1873–1941); John E. Borein (1873–1945)

1874—Modoc and San Benito counties founded; *Oakland Tribune* founded; Tiburcio Vásquez captured; Charlotta A. Bass (1874–1969); Raymond Duncan (1874–1966); Herbert Hoover (1874–1964)

1875—Pacheco, governor (Feb. 27–Dec. 9); Irwin, governor (1875–80); Native Sons of the Golden West founded; Palace Hotel (San Francisco) opened; Fountain Grove colony founded; Edgar Rice Burroughs (1875–1950); Maynard Dixon (1875–1946); James J. Jeffries (1875–1953); John Hudson Thomas (1875–1945)

1876—Dan De Quille, *The Big Bonanza*; Alfred L. Kroeber (1876–1960); Jack London (1876–1916)

1877—Denis Kearney campaign: "The Chinese must go!"

1878—Hastings College of Law founded; Muybridge, *The Horse in Motion*; Isadora Duncan (1878–1927); Herman Scheffauer (1878–1927); Upton Sinclair (1878–1968)

1879—Second Constitutional Convention; University of Southern California founded; Robert Louis Stevenson visits California; tennis introduced to California; Edward A. Dickson (1879–1956)

1880—Population: State, 864,694; Los Angeles, 11,183; San Francisco, 233,959; Perkins, governor (1880–83); Mussel Slough battle; borax discovered in Death Valley; George, *Progress and Poverty*; Ernest Bloch (1880–1959); Peter B. Kyne (1880–1957)

1881—State Normal School founded in Los Angeles, forerunner of UCLA; *Los Angeles Times* founded; Bell, *Reminiscences of a Ranger*; H. H. Jackson, *A Century of Dishonor*; Charles Caldwell Dobie (1881–1943)

1882—Loganberry created; John Dolbeer invents donkey engine; Oscar Wilde visits San Francisco; Henry J. Kaiser (1882–1967)

1883—Stoneman, governor (1883–87); Historical Society of Southern California founded; J. J. Montgomery

flies glider; Thomes, *On Land and Sea*; Douglas Fairbanks, Sr. (1883–1939); Imogen Cunningham (1883–1976)

1884—Leland Stanford, Jr., dies; *Modesto Bee* (1884–   ); H. H. Jackson, *Ramona*

1885—Kaweah colony founded; Santa Fe Railroad reaches Los Angeles; T. H. Hittell, *History of California* (1885–87); Shinn, *Mining Camps*; George S. Patton (1885–1945)

1886—George Hearst, U.S. Senator (1886–91); Bancroft, *History of California* (1886–90); Royce, *California*

1887—Bartlett, governor (Jan. 8–Sept. 12); Waterman, governor (1887–91); Wright Act; Hearst begins journalism career; Pomona College founded; California Club founded; May Sutton Bundy (1887–1975); Robinson Jeffers (1887–1962)

1888—First black mayor elected (Edward P. Duplex of Wheatland); Lick Observatory founded; Occidental College founded

1889—Orange County founded; Kipling visits California; Davis, *Sixty Years in California*; Mulford, *Prentice Mulford's Story*; Charlie Chaplin (1889–1977)

1890—Population: State, 1,213,398; Los Angeles, 50,395; San Francisco, 298,997; Yosemite and Sequoia National Parks founded; Tournament of Roses established; David S. Terry shot dead; *The Wave* founded; Beniamino Bufano (1890?–1970); Hazel Hotchkiss (1890–1974)

1891—Glenn County founded; Markham, governor (1891–95); Stanford University opened; Throop Institute, predecessor of California Institute of Technology, founded; Whittier College founded; state's first golf course opened; Sidney Howard (1891–1939); Robert Gordon Sproul (1891–1975); Earl Warren (1891–1974)

1892—Angeles National Forest, first in state, established; Sierra Club founded; first "Big Game"; Corbett knocks out Sullivan for world's heavyweight boxing championship; Bierce, *Tales of Soldiers and Civilians*; Donald Douglas (1892–   ); Frederick Faust (1892–1944)

1893—Kings, Madera, and Riverside counties founded; Stephen M. White, first native Californian to become a U.S. Senator; Hopkins Marine Laboratory; Greene Brothers begin architectural practice in Pasadena; Burlingame Country Club founded; Bierce, *Can Such Things Be?*

1894—Midwinter Exposition in San Francisco; *Land of Sunshine* founded; Manly, *Death Valley in '49*; Muir, *Mountains of California*

1895—Budd, governor (1895–99); *The Lark* (1895–97); Busby Berkeley (1895–1976); George R. Stewart (1895–   ); William W. Wurster (1895–1973)

1896—Sutro Baths opened in San Francisco; Fernald, *The Cat and the Cherub*; Lawrence Tibbett (1896–1960)

1897—Long Beach incorporated; Lummis founds The Landmarks Club

1898—Ferry Building (San Francisco) opens; *Sunset* founded

1899—Gage, governor (1899–1903); Jeffries, heavyweight boxing champion (1899–1905); Atherton, *A Daughter of the Vine*; Markham, "Man with the Hoe"; Norris, *McTeague*

1900—Population: State, 1,485,053; Los Angeles, 102,479; San Francisco, 342,782; Automobile Club of Southern California founded; Family Club founded; Burgess, *Goops*; Stephen D. Bechtel (1900–   ); Charles F. Richter (1900–   )

1901—Pacific Electric Railway incorporated; Angel's Flight constructed; Norris, *The Octopus*; Harry Bridges (1901–   ); Walt Disney (1901–66); Harry Partch (1901–   ); Franklin Walker (1901–   )

1902—Eugene Schmitz, mayor of San Francisco (1902–07); Atherton, *The Splendid, Idle Forties*; Ansel Adams (1902–   ); Thomas D. Church (1902–   ); John Steinbeck (1902–68)

1903—Pardee, governor (1903–07); *golden poppy* named official state flower; Los Angeles adopts initiative, referendum, and recall; Commonwealth Club founded; Pacific Coast League (baseball) founded; *Los Angeles Examiner* founded; *San Francisco News* (1903–65); Austin, *The Land of Little Rain*; London, *The Call of the Wild*; Sterling, *The Testimony of the Suns*

1904—Venice founded; Giannini founds Italian Bank of California; London, *The Sea-Wolf*; Ralph J. Bunche (1904–71); Bing Crosby (1904–77)

1905—Salton Sea flood (1905–07); Yosemite Valley added to National Park; UC establishes Davis campus; Bancroft Library sold to University of California; California Fruit Growers Exchange founded; Pacific Gas and Electric Co. founded; Julia Morgan opens office; Dipsea race inaugurated; Howard Hughes (1905–76); Edmund G. Brown, Sr. (1905–   )

1906—San Francisco earthquake and fire; Beverly Hills founded; first motion picture studio in Los Angeles; first Los Angeles-Honolulu transpacific yacht race; Lawrence Clark Powell (1906–   ); Helen Wills (1906–   )

1907—Imperial County founded; Gillett, governor (1907–11); Lincoln-Roosevelt League founded; California State Automobile Association founded; California College of Arts and Crafts founded; Dorothy Baker (1907–68)

1908—Cleveland National Forest created; Abe Ruef sentenced to jail; Helen Jacobs (1908–   ); William Saroyan (1908–   )

1909—Allensworth founded; Southern California Edison Co. established; Redlands University founded; London, *Martin Eden; Touring Topics* (later *Westways*) founded

1910—Population: State, 2,377,549; Los Angeles, 319,198; San Francisco, 416,912; first junior college founded; *Los Angeles Times* bombed by McNamara brothers; Carrie Jacobs Bond, "A Perfect Day"

1911—Johnson, governor (1911–17); State Flag adopted; state adopts initiative, referendum, and recall; Devil's Postpile National Monument established; Hollywood's first film studio; Ishi discovered by whites; Bierce, *Devil's Dictionary*; Wright, *The Winning of Barbara Worth*; Clair Engle (1911–65); Clark Kerr (1911–   ); David Park (1911–60); Ronald Reagan (1911–   )

1912—Book Club of California founded; McGroarty, *The Mission Play*, produced; David Brower (1912–   ); William Everson (1912–   ); David Packard (1912–   ); Glen Seaborg (1912–   )

1913—Wheatland Riot; Sutro Library given to the state; Chase, *California Coast Trails*; London, *The Valley of the Moon*; James Broughton (1913–   ); William R. Hewlett (1913–   ); Alice Marble (1913–   ); Richard M. Nixon (1913–   )

1914—Jeffers settles in Carmel; Lummis opens Southwest Museum; Kelley's Army; Cowan, *Bibliography of California*; Norris, *Vandover and the Brute*; Joe DiMaggio (1914–   ); Budd Schulberg (1914–   )

1915—Panama-Pacific International Exposition; Panama-California Exposition; first transcontinental telephone call, San Francisco to New York; Ina Coolbrith named Poet Laureate; Robert Motherwell (1915–   )

1916—Lassen Volcanic National Park founded; de Young Museum founded; Preparedness Day Parade bombing in San Francisco; John Henry Nash founds his own press; Elmer Bischoff (1916–   ); Donald Budge (1916–   ); Herb Caen (1916–   );

Lawrence Halprin (1916–); Yehudi Menuhin (1916–)

1917—Stephens, governor (1917–23); Hiram Johnson, U.S. Senator (1917–45); San Francisco Conservatory of Music founded; Forest Lawn Memorial Park begun; Thomas Bradley (1917–); Wilson Riles (1917–)

1918—Save-the-Redwoods League founded; Aimee Semple McPherson settles in Los Angeles

1919—California Farm Bureau Federation formed; Criminal Syndicalism Act; UCLA established as Southern Branch of University; Hoover Institution founded; W. R. Hearst begins to build San Simeon; Pauline Betz (1919–); Pauline Kael (1919–); Jackie Robinson (1919–72)

1920—Population: State, 3,426,861; Los Angeles, 576,673; San Francisco, 506,676; California Institute of Technology adopts that name; Grabhorn Press founded; UC football Wonder Teams (1920–22); Ray Bradbury (1920–); Lawrence Ferlinghetti (1920–); Ruggiero Rici (1920–); Wayne Thiebaud (1920–)

1921—Oil discovered at Signal Hill; Simon Rodia's Watts Towers begun; "California, Here I Come" introduced; Henry J. Kaiser settles in Oakland

1922—Hollywood Bowl opened; *Fresno Bee* (1922–); Wilson, *Merton of the Movies*; Richard Diebenkorn (1922–); Jack Kerouac (1922–69); Charles Schulz (1922–)

1923—Richardson, governor (1923–27); Hetch Hetchy dam completed; Berkeley fire; Elk Hills Petroleum Reserve leased to private oil producers; San Francisco Opera Association founded; President Harding dies in San Francisco; Sam Francis (1923–)

1924—California Palace of the Legion of Honor founded; Miss California contest inaugurated; first airmail flight San Francisco to New York; Howard, *They Knew What They Wanted*; Jeffers, *Tamar*; Evan Connell (1924–); Mel Patton (1924–)

1925—Lava Beds National Monument established; Santa Barbara earthquake; East-West annual football game inaugurated; Claremont Graduate School founded

1926—Scripps College founded; Mission Santa Clara burned down; Sterling, *Robinson Jeffers*; Allen Ginsberg (1926–); Marilyn Monroe (1926–62)

1927—Young, governor (1927–31); Philo T. Farnsworth transmits first television picture; Los Angeles Open golf tournament founded; Dumbarton Bridge opened; Jeffers, *Women at Point Sur*; Sinclair, *Oil!*; Cesar Chavez (1927–)

1928—Hoover elected President of the U.S.; St. Francis Dam collapses; Kettleman Hills oil discovery; daily passenger flights between San Francisco and Los Angeles; Jeffers, *Cawdor*; Shirley Temple (1928–)

1929—Highway Patrol organized; E. O. Lawrence invents cyclotron; California Maritime Academy founded; Academy of Motion Pictures Arts and Sciences first award; Henry Meade Bland named Poet Laureate

1930—Population: State, 5,677,251; Los Angeles, 1,238,048; San Francisco, 634,394; St. Ignatius College renamed University of San Francisco; Robert Gordon Sproul, president of UC (1930–58); Bob Mathias (1930–); Gary Snyder (1930–)

1931—Rolph, governor (1931–34); High Sierra Wilderness Area established; E Clampus Vitus revived; Goat Island renamed Yerba Buena; Plantin Press founded; Steffens, *Autobiography*

1932—Olympic Games in Los Angeles; San Francisco Opera House opened; Jeffers, *Thurso's Landing*; Steinbeck, *Pastures of Heaven*

1933—Long Beach earthquake; Townsend Plan; Moffett Field opened; Coit Tower (San Francisco) erected; *Westways* founded; McGroarty, Poet Laureate (1933–44); Lawton Kennedy founds his press

1934—Merriam, governor (1934–39); San Francisco General Strike; Upton Sinclair's EPIC campaign for governorship; East Bay Regional Parks established; Clark Library added to UCLA; California Republican Assembly founded; Rafer Johnson (1934–); N. Scott Momaday (1934–)

1935—Transpacific airmail inaugurated from San Francisco; Steinbeck, *Tortilla Flat*; Richard Brautigan (1935–); Eldridge Cleaver (1935–)

1936—San Francisco–Oakland Bay Bridge opened; Cow Palace constructed; passenger flights begun between San Francisco and Honolulu; Steinbeck, *In Dubious Battle*; Stewart, *Ordeal by Hunger*

1937—Golden Gate Bridge opened; Pepperdine University founded; *Santa Barbara News-Press* (1937–); Steinbeck, *Of Mice and Men*

1938—Ham 'n Eggs plan; Lake Havasu created; Hollywood Park racetrack opened; Edmund G. Brown, Jr. (1938–)

1939—Olson, governor (1939–43); Treasure Island (San Francisco Bay) created for Golden Gate International Exposition; Olson pardons Tom Mooney; Maritime Museum (San Francisco); Steinbeck, *Grapes of Wrath*; West, *The Day of the Locust*

1940—Population: State, 6,907,387; Los Angeles, 1,504,277; San Francisco, 634,536; Kings Canyon National Park founded; first freeway (Pasadena) completed; Saroyan, *My Name Is Aram*

1941—U.S. enters World War II; Hoover Tower opened to house Hoover Institution; Orson Welles, *Citizen Kane*; Stewart, *Storm*

1942—Japanese submarine shells oil field near Goleta; Japanese relocation centers created; Camp Pendleton founded; Sleepy Lagoon murder

1943—Warren, governor (1943–53); All-American Canal completed; Billy Jean King (1943–)

1944—UC establishes Santa Barbara campus

1945—United Nations founded in San Francisco; Steinbeck, *Cannery Row*

1946—Nixon elected to Congress; Stanford Research Institute founded; McWilliams, *Southern California Country*

1947—Hollywood Ten; Steinbeck, *The Wayward Bus*

1948—All-American Canal extended to Coachella Valley; Squaw Valley resort opened

1949—Loyalty Oath instituted for UC faculty and staff; Stewart, *Earth Abides*

1950—Population: State, 10,586,223; Los Angeles, 1,970,358; San Francisco, 775,357; Levering Act passed; Dominican College founded; Mark Spitz (1950–)

1951—"I Love You, California" named official state song; University of the Pacific moves to Stockton; Pro Bowl founded

1952—Bakersfield earthquake; Steinbeck, *East of Eden*

1953—Knight, governor (1953–59); Earl Warren, Chief Justice of U.S. (1953–69); grizzly bear named official state animal; redwood named official state tree; California Democratic Council founded

1954—UC established Riverside campus; Center for Study of Democratic Institutions founded

1955—Disneyland opened; Harvey Mudd College founded

1956—City of Fremont founded; Beat movement

1957—Kerouac, *On the Road*

1958—San Francisco Giants and Los Angeles Dodgers bring major league baseball to state; Vandenberg Air Force Base established; Clark Kerr, president of UC (1958–67)

1959—Edmund G. Brown, Sr., governor (1959–67); UC establishes campus at San Diego

1960—Population: State, 15,717,204; Los Angeles, 2,479,015; San Francisco, 740,316; Winter Olympic Games at Squaw Valley; Los Angeles Dodgers, first California team to win a World Series; Master Plan for Higher Education; Candlestick Park opened; Avery Brundage collection of Oriental art given to San Francisco

1961—UC establishes campus at Santa Cruz

1962—California surpasses New York to become most populous state; Steinbeck wins Nobel Prize; San Francisco Giants win National League Pennant; Graduate Theological Union founded; Cultural Heritage Board established; Kerouac, *Big Sur*; Kesey, *One Flew Over the Cuckoo's Nest*

1963—Rumford Act; Pitzer College founded; Alcatraz prison closed; Kerr, *The Uses of the University*

1964—Free Speech Movement at University of California, Berkeley; *bracero* program ended; Music Center (Los Angeles) opened; Pierre Salinger appointed U.S. Senator

1965—Watts Riots; San Francisco Bay Conservation and Development Commission established; U.C. establishes campus at Irvine; Los Angeles County Museum of Art buildings opened; *Berkeley Barb* (1965–)

1966—Chavez forms United Farm Workers Organizing Committee; Black Panther party founded

1967—Reagan, governor (1967–73); Levering Act declared unconstitutional; Linear Accelerator opened at Stanford University; *Queen Mary* docked at Long Beach; *Rolling Stone* founded

1968—Redwood National Park founded; San Onofre Nuclear Generating Station opened

1969—Manson murders; People's Park attack; "I Left My Heart in San Francisco" made official city song

1970—Population: State, 19,953,134; Los Angeles, 2,809,813; San Francisco, 715,674; Indians occupy Alcatraz

1971—San Fernando Valley earthquake; Fort Point becomes National Park; Stegner, *Angle of Repose*

1972—Golden Gate National Recreational Area established; BART opened; Fine Arts Museums of San Francisco created by merger

1973—Postsecondary Education Commission established; Zebra murders in San Francisco

1974—Symbionese Liberation Army kidnaps Patricia Hearst; Oakland Athletics defeat Los Angeles Dodgers in first all-California World Series

1975—Edmund G. Brown, Jr., governor (1975–); Tujunga Forest fire

1976—Gray whale named as official state marine mammal; Gov. Brown runs for Democratic nomination and former Gov. Reagan for Republican nomination for President, both unsuccessfully

1977—Year-end population estimated as exceeding 22,000,000; second year of very low rainfall causes drought that requires widespread water rationing; severe Santa Barbara fire; death penalty restored by legislature; Bakke case appealed to U.S. Supreme Court

1978—Floods and landslides in Los Angeles area; floods in Tulare and Kern counties; avalanche in Mono County; Redwood National Park greatly enlarged; Constitutional amendment limiting property taxes